Praise for *Public Enemies*

"Massively researched, ludicrously entertaining."
—*Time*

"[A] colorful new history of the early days of the Federal Bureau of Investigation. . . . [Burrough] has written a book that brims with vivid portraiture . . . Excellent true crime." —*The New York Times Book Review*

"*Public Enemies* [is] Bryan Burrough's spellbinding new account of America's first War on Crime . . . a model of narrative journalism and an often gripping read." —*BusinessWeek*

"In the telling Mr. Burrough displays a genius for historical reconstruction and an attention to detail so vivid that the reader can almost smell Bonnie and Clyde, neither of whom showed much inclination to bathe during their months sleeping in cars or open fields when they were on the run."
—*The New York Times*

"Burrough's narrative is fast-paced, his prose captivating. Drawing upon several hundred thousand FBI documents, Burrough has conducted important new research. He re-creates in vivid detail the criminals' whereabouts, characteristics, and ignominious rise to Depression-era fame. . . . By shining a spotlight on the FBI's birth . . . Burrough has altered our view of the early 1930s." —*Chicago Tribune*

"It is superb—readable, thorough and critical."
—*The Denver Post*

"Fascinating . . . A rich and colorful cast of characters parades through the pages. . . . It is a wild and amazing story, and Burrough tells it with great gusto. Truth is often not only stranger than fiction but also a lot more interesting. Burrough's research is careful and extraordinarily thorough. . . . *Public Enemies* is a significant book, and a very readable one. It is easy to toss around terms like 'definitive,' but this book deserves it. It is hard to imagine a more careful, complete and entrancing book on this subject, and on this era. Readers will not be disappointed."
—*The Washington Post*

"[An] excellent new history [of] this country's greatest crime wave . . . [Burrough] brings a historian's touch to the material, exploding myths on every page. . . . *Public Enemies* is knockout nonfiction entertainment as well as serious history." —*The New York Sun*

"It is quite superb . . . with masses of new information."
—*Chicago Sun-Times*

W9-BAQ-609

PENGUIN BOOKS

PUBLIC ENEMIES

Bryan Burrough is a special correspondent at *Vanity Fair* and the author of numerous bestselling books, including *Barbarians at the Gate: The Fall of RJR Nabisco* (with John Helyar), *Public Enemies: America's Greatest Crime Wave and the Birth of the FBI, 1933–34,* and *The Big Rich: The Rise and Fall of the Greatest Texas Oil Fortunes.* A former reporter for *The Wall Street Journal,* he is a three-time winner of the Gerald Loeb Award for Excellence in Financial Journalism. He lives in Summit, New Jersey, with his wife Marla and their two sons.

AMERICA'S

GREATEST

CRIME WAVE

and the

BIRTH *of*

the FBI,

1933-34

PUBLIC ENEMIES

BRYAN BURROUGH

PENGUIN BOOKS

PENGUIN BOOKS

Published by the Penguin Group
Penguin Group (USA) Inc., 375 Hudson Street, New York, New York 10014, U.S.A.
Penguin Group (Canada), 90 Eglinton Avenue East, Suite 700, Toronto,
Ontario, Canada M4P 2Y3 (a division of Pearson Penguin Canada Inc.)
Penguin Books Ltd, 80 Strand, London WC2R 0RL, England
Penguin Ireland, 25 St Stephen's Green, Dublin 2, Ireland (a division of Penguin Books Ltd)
Penguin Group (Australia), 250 Camberwell Road, Camberwell,
Victoria 3124, Australia (a division of Pearson Australia Group Pty Ltd)
Penguin Books India Pvt Ltd, 11 Community Centre, Panchsheel Park, New Delhi – 110 017, India
Penguin Group (NZ), 67 Apollo Drive, Rosedale, North Shore 0632,
New Zealand (a division of Pearson New Zealand Ltd)
Penguin Books (South Africa) (Pty) Ltd, 24 Sturdee Avenue,
Rosebank, Johannesburg 2196, South Africa

Penguin Books Ltd, Registered Offices:
80 Strand, London WC2R 0RL, England

First published in the United States of America by The Penguin Press,
a member of Penguin Group (USA) Inc. 2004
Published in Penguin Books 2005
This edition published in Penguin Books 2009

3   5   7   9   10   8   6   4

Photograph Credits
AP/Wide World Photos: Insert pages 1, 2, 3 (top and bottom right), 6 (bottom),
7 (top), 8 (bottom), 9 (top), 10, 11, 12 (top and bottom), 16 (bottom).
Mansell/Time Life Pictures/Getty Images: Insert page 3 (bottom left).
Bowersock Collection, Kansas City Museum/Union Station, Kansas City, Missouri:
Insert pages 4 (top), 14 (top).
© Bettmann/Corbis: Insert pages 4 (bottom), 6 (top), 9 (bottom), 13, 15.
Texas/Dallas History and Archives Division, Dallas Public Library: Insert page 5 (top and bottom).
New York Daily News: Insert page 7 (bottom right).
Minneapolis Historical society: Insert page 8 (top).
Federal Bureau of Investigation: Insert pages 7 (bottom left), 14 (bottom), 16 (top).

THE LIBRARY OF CONGRESS HAS CATALOGED THE HARDCOVER EDITION AS FOLLOWS:
Burrough, Bryan, 1961–
Public enemies : America's greatest crime wave and the birth of the FBI, 1933–34 /
Bryan Burrough.
p.   cm.
Includes bibliographical references and index.
ISBN 1-59420-021-1 (hc.)
ISBN 978-0-14-311586-1 (pbk.)
1. Crime—United States—History—20th century.   2. Criminals—United States—History—20th century.
3. United States. Federal Bureau of Investigation—History.   I. Title.
HV6783.B85   2004
364.973'09'043—dc22   2004044315

Printed in the United States of America
Designed by Michelle McMillian

For Marla, Griffin, and Dane
"The Unit"

CONTENTS

AUTHOR'S NOTE

Never before have I enjoyed researching and writing anything as much as I did the book you hold in your hands. If you derive half the pleasure from reading it as I did from creating it, I will be thrilled.

This is a book I always suspected I would attempt someday. The first stories I can remember hearing as a boy, the stories that made me want to become a writer, were tales my grandfather told of Bonnie and Clyde. As a young deputy in northwest Arkansas, John Vernon Burrough manned road-blocks set up to apprehend the couple. In his later years he was mayor of Alma, Arkansas, a town where Clyde Barrow was blamed for the murder of one of his predecessors. My grandfather's stories sounded like tales out of the Wild West; I could hardly grasp the fact that these events had occurred barely forty years earlier. I grew up in the 1970s, and the formative events of my youth were the Vietnam War, Watergate, and the Iranian hostage crisis. I couldn't believe America had changed that much in a single lifetime.

Later, I learned that Clyde Barrow had murdered the great-uncle of one of my boyhood friends in my hometown of Temple, Texas, and my interest grew. Stricken with insomnia late one night in 1997, I found myself watching a cable-television documentary on Ma Barker. I wondered whether the Barker Gang had been in operation before or after Bonnie and Clyde. I walked upstairs to my office and hopped on the Internet, ran a search, and was surprised to find that both gangs had been at large in the years 1933 and 1934. My curiosity aroused, I checked John Dillinger: 1933 and 1934. Pretty Boy Floyd, Baby Face Nelson, Machine Gun Kelly: all 1933 or 1934. This was my introduction to the War on Crime.

I picked up John Toland's 1963 book, *Dillinger Days,* a biography that deals glancingly with Dillinger's criminal contemporaries. I searched for a comprehensive history of the FBI's fight against Dillinger and his peers, and I was surprised to find there wasn't one. Any number of books had been published on the individual outlaws themselves, but, to my mind, no one had tackled the whole story. Then I learned that the FBI files on all these cases had been released only in the late 1980s. That's when I decided to write this book.

This, then, is the first comprehensive narrative history of the FBI's War on Crime, which lasted from 1933 to 1936, a period that saw the rise and fall of six major criminal factions: those of John Dillinger, Baby Face Nelson, Pretty Boy Floyd, the Barker-Karpis Gang, Machine Gun Kelly, and Bonnie and Clyde. It is a big, sprawling story, with gunfights and investigations in dozens of American cities involving literally hundreds of major and minor players, including an army of FBI agents, sheriffs, and policemen. On the following pages you'll find a cast of characters to help you keep everyone straight.

Complexity is one reason authors have tended to focus their books on a single public enemy. Yet these six story lines truly comprise a single narrative, the unifying element being the involvement of the FBI. The Bureau told a sanitized version of the War on Crime story in several books, beginning with the lurid *Ten Thousand Public Enemies* in 1935 and culminating with Don Whitehead's *The FBI Story* in 1956. These books are, at best, incomplete; at worst, misleading. They were the stories J. Edgar Hoover wanted told, not the ones that actually happened.

For years the principal obstacle to an objective narrative was the FBI's penchant for secrecy; Hoover was unwilling to share information with anyone interested in telling the whole truth. This helps explain why, as large as these criminals loom in American legend, there are surprisingly few credible books about them. For twenty-five years the stories of the Depression-era outlaws remained the province of newspaper reporters and pulp writers, many of whom weren't above concocting dramatic scenes and imaginative dialogue. Not till the late 1950s, with the popularity of *The Untouchables* television show, did serious authors begin to approach the subject of the War on Crime. Dillinger and Floyd have since attracted multiple biographers. Bonnie and Clyde, buoyed by the popularity of the 1967 movie, have garnered a half-dozen books. The first biography of Machine Gun Kelly didn't appear until 2003.

By far the best of these books is *Dillinger Days.* Writing thirty years after the events told, Toland was able to interview a number of participants, including several former FBI agents. While he accepts an FBI canard or two—most notably the myth of Ma Barker's criminal genius—his remains the book by which all others must be measured. What makes a fresh look at the War on Crime possible is the release of the FBI's files. Prodded by local historians, such as Robert Unger in Kansas City and Paul Maccabee in St. Paul, the Bureau has now made public all its files on Dillinger, Floyd, Nelson, the Barker Gang, Machine Gun Kelly, and the Kansas City Massacre. Taken together, they comprise nearly one million pages of daily reports, telegrams, and correspondence, as well as hundreds of statements taken from witnesses and participants, everyone from Dillinger's sister to Nelson's tailor.

As one might expect, the files are a trove of new information. There are dozens of never-before-seen statements from the criminals and their gun molls, an unpublished autobiographical essay from Kathryn Kelly, disclosure of the bribes that freed Dock Barker from prison, as well as confirmation of an overlooked Dillinger robbery two months before his death. For all this, the FBI files shed the most penetrating light on the FBI itself. They vividly chronicle the Bureau's evolution from an overmatched band of amateurish agents without firearms or law-enforcement experience into the professional crime-fighting machine of lore—a story Hoover was never eager to have told. In the early months of the War on Crime, we see Hoover's men botching stakeouts, losing suspects, forgetting orders, and repeatedly arresting the wrong men—their mistakes would be comical if not for the price paid by the innocent. But deep amid the thicket of reports and correspondence, many of them festooned with Hoover's tart, handwritten comments, one can literally see the FBI grow up. The agents learn how to use guns, establish professional methods, and recruit informants. Above all, this is a book about how the FBI became the FBI.

The files allowed me to pursue one of my central aims: to reclaim the War on Crime for the lawmen who fought it. Men like Charles Winstead and Clarence Hurt, the two agents who killed Dillinger, have long remained anonymous, even as movies are made about the murderers they hunted. The FBI wanted it that way. Critics say this was because Hoover wanted the glory for himself, which may be true. But keeping agents anonymous also fueled Hoover's institutional aims, fostered teamwork, and allowed agents to slip into undercover assignments. For the first time, the FBI files allow us to understand which agents did what, and who screwed up when. By and large, it is not a pretty story; one can understand why Hoover wanted the files kept secret.

Over the course of four years of research, I was able to augment the stories from FBI files with much new information uncovered in the last forty years. A manuscript discovered in 1989 by two intrepid Dillinger buffs, William Helmer and Thomas Smusyn, shines new light on Dillinger's final weeks. Another valuable resource was two thousand pages of unpublished interview transcripts that Alvin Karpis of the Barker Gang gave before his death. Several FBI agents also wrote unpublished manuscripts I was able to review. I've listed all my sources of information in notes at the back of the book.

Please keep one thing in mind as you read: This book was not "imagined," as with some recent popular histories. It was reported. The conversations and dialogue in this book are taken verbatim from FBI reports, the Karpis transcripts, contemporary news articles, and the memories of participants. If you're wondering how I learned something, check the source notes. If I don't know something, I'll tell you. If there's a mystery I can't clear up—and there are a few—I'll make that clear. Any errors are mine and mine alone. I hope you enjoy it.

Bryan Burrough
Summit, New Jersey
December 2003

CAST OF CHARACTERS

Federal Bureau of Investigation

John Edgar Hoover,
Director

Harold "Pop" Nathan,
Assistant Director

Hugh Clegg,
Assistant Director

Samuel P. Cowley,
Inspector

Melvin Purvis,
Special Agent in
Charge, Chicago

William Rorer,
Inspector

Gus T. "Buster" Jones,
Special Agent in
Charge, San Antonio

James "Doc" White,
Special Agent

Herman "Ed" Hollis,
Special Agent

John Madala,
Special Agent

James Metcalfe,
Special Agent

Earl Connelley,
Special Agent in
Charge, Cincinnati

Also: Special Agents Charles Winstead, Clarence Hurt, Jerry Campbell, Tom McDade, Ray Suran, Ed Guinane. Doris Rogers, secretary.

The St. Paul Yeggs

Harvey Bailey

Frank "Jelly" Nash

Verne Miller

George Barnes, a.k.a.
"Machine Gun Kelly"

Also: Vi Mathias, Frances Nash, Kathryn Kelly.

Pretty Boy Floyd

Charles Arthur
"Pretty Boy" Floyd

Adam Richetti

The Barrow Gang

Clyde Barrow

Bonnie Parker

Buck Barrow

W. D. Jones

Henry Methvin

Raymond Hamilton

The Posse: Frank Hamer, Manny Gault, Bob Alcorn, Ted Hinton, Henderson Jordan, Prentiss Oakley.

The Barker–Karpis Gang

Fred Barker

Alvin Karpis, a.k.a. "Ray"

Arthur "Dock" Barker

Kate "Ma" Barker

Fred Goetz, a.k.a. "Shotgun George Ziegler"

Bryan Bolton

Volney Davis

Harry Sawyer

Harry Campbell

Delores Delaney

Also: Paula Harmon, Wynona Burdette, William Weaver, Charles Fitzgerald, Willie Harrison.

The Baby Face Nelson Gang

Lester Gillis, a.k.a. "Baby Face Nelson"

Helen Gillis

John Paul Chase

Fatso Negri

Also: Clarence Lieder, Jack Perkins, Jimmy Murray.

The Dillinger Gang

John Dillinger

Billie Frechette

Harry "Pete" Pierpont

Mary Kinder

John "Red" Hamilton

Charles Makley

Russell Clark

Opal Long, a.k.a. "Bernice Clark"

Pat Cherrington

Tommy Carroll

Louis Piquett

Homer Van Meter

Also: Arthur O'Leary, investigator; Jimmy Probasco, safe house owner; Polly Hamilton; and Ana Sage.

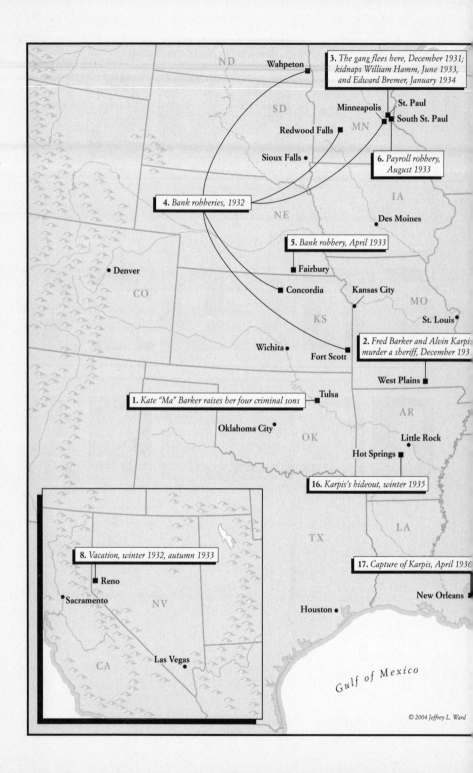

ND

Wahpeton ■

3. *The gang flees here, December 1931;*
kidnaps William Hamm, June 1933,
and Edward Bremer, January 1934

SD

Minneapolis   St. Paul
                ■
Redwood Falls ■   MN   South St. Paul

Sioux Falls ●

6. *Payroll robbery,*
August 1933

IA

4. *Bank robberies, 1932*

NE

Des Moines ●

5. *Bank robbery, April 1933*

● Denver

■ Fairbury

CO

■ Concordia   Kansas City
                ●

KS   MO

St. Louis ■

2. *Fred Barker and Alvin Karpis*
murder a sheriff, December 193.

Wichita ●

Fort Scott ■

West Plains ■

1. *Kate "Ma" Barker raises her four criminal sons*   Tulsa ■

Oklahoma City ●

AR

Little Rock ●

OK

Hot Springs ■

16. *Karpis's hideout, winter 1935*

LA

TX

8. *Vacation, winter 1932, autumn 1933*

17. *Capture of Karpis, April 1936*

■ Reno

Sacramento ●

NV

New Orleans ■

Houston ●

Las Vegas ●

CA

Gulf of Mexico

© 2004 Jeffrey L. Ward

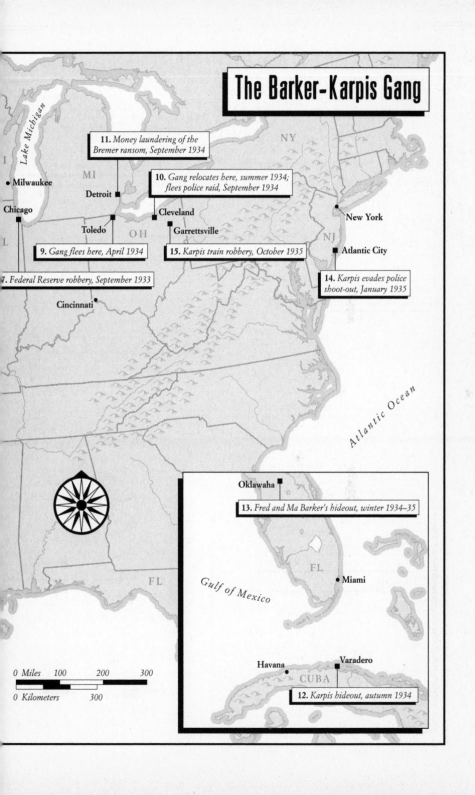

The Barker-Karpis Gang

11. *Money laundering of the Bremer ransom, September 1934*

10. *Gang relocates here, summer 1934; flees police raid, September 1934*

Lake Michigan

NY

MI

• Milwaukee

Detroit ■

Cleveland •

Chicago

Toledo

O H

Garrettsville

New York •

NJ

Atlantic City ■

9. *Gang flees here, April 1934*

15. *Karpis train robbery, October 1935*

7. *Federal Reserve robbery, September 1933*

14. *Karpis evades police shoot-out, January 1935*

Cincinnati •

Atlantic Ocean

Oklawaha ■

13. *Fred and Ma Barker's hideout, winter 1934–35*

FL

FL

• Miami

Gulf of Mexico

Havana •

Varadero ■

CUBA

12. *Karpis hideout, autumn 1934*

0 Miles 100 200 300

0 Kilometers 300

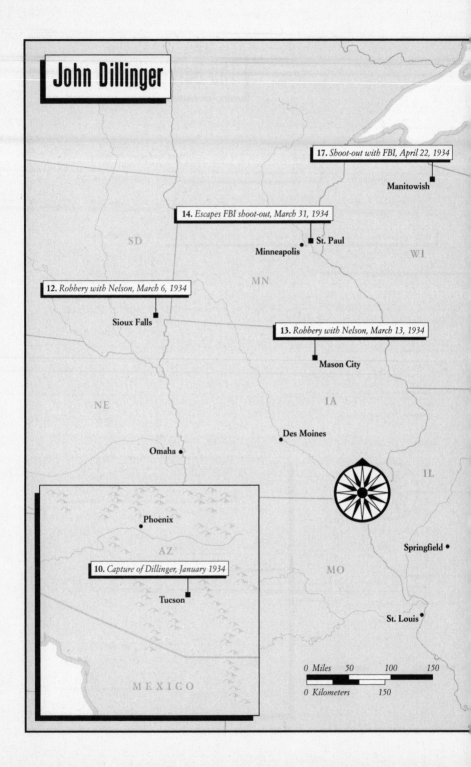

John Dillinger

17. *Shoot-out with FBI, April 22, 1934*

Manitowish

14. *Escapes FBI shoot-out, March 31, 1934*

SD

St. Paul

Minneapolis

WI

MN

12. *Robbery with Nelson, March 6, 1934*

Sioux Falls

13. *Robbery with Nelson, March 13, 1934*

Mason City

NE

IA

Des Moines

Omaha

IL

Springfield

Phoenix

AZ

MO

10. *Capture of Dillinger, January 1934*

Tucson

St. Louis

0 Miles   50   100   150

0 Kilometers   150

MEXICO

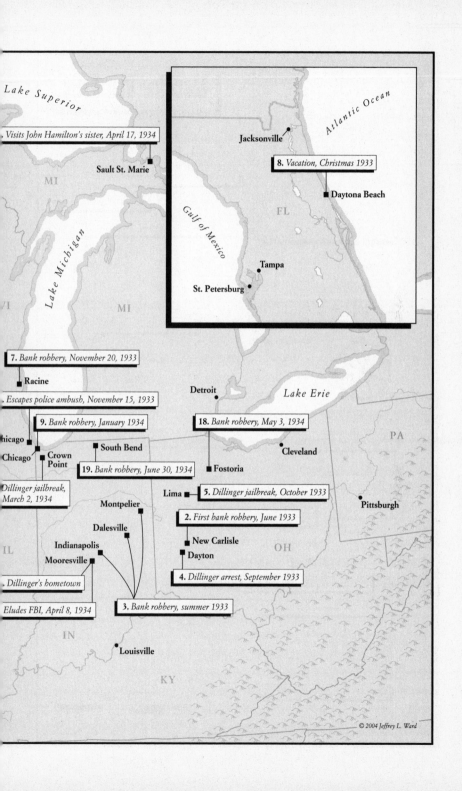

Lake Superior

Visits John Hamilton's sister, April 17, 1934

Sault St. Marie

MI

Lake Michigan

Atlantic Ocean

Jacksonville

8. *Vacation, Christmas 1933*

Daytona Beach

FL

Gulf of Mexico

Tampa

St. Petersburg

7. *Bank robbery, November 20, 1933*

Racine

Detroit

Lake Erie

Escapes police ambush, November 15, 1933

9. *Bank robbery, January 1934*

18. *Bank robbery, May 3, 1934*

PA

hicago

Chicago   **Crown Point**   **South Bend**

Cleveland

19. *Bank robbery, June 30, 1934*

Fostoria

Dillinger jailbreak, March 2, 1934

Lima   **5.** *Dillinger jailbreak, October 1933*

Pittsburgh

Montpelier

2. *First bank robbery, June 1933*

Dalesville

New Carlisle

Indianapolis

OH

Dayton

Mooresville

4. *Dillinger arrest, September 1933*

Dillinger's hometown

IL

Eludes FBI, April 8, 1934

3. *Bank robbery, summer 1933*

IN

Louisville

KY

© 2004 Jeffrey L. Ward

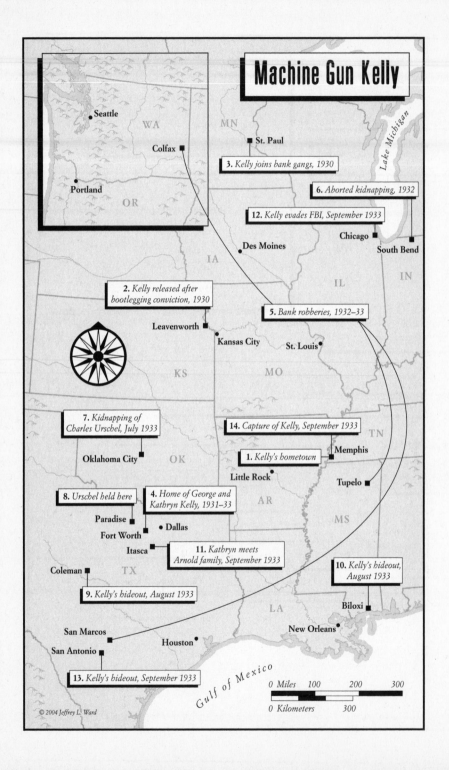

Machine Gun Kelly

Seattle

WA

MN

St. Paul

Colfax

3. *Kelly joins bank gangs, 1930*

6. *Aborted kidnapping, 1932*

Portland

OR

12. *Kelly evades FBI, September 1933*

Lake Michigan

Chicago

South Bend

Des Moines

IA

IL

IN

2. *Kelly released after bootlegging conviction, 1930*

Leavenworth

Kansas City

St. Louis

5. *Bank robberies, 1932–33*

KS

MO

7. *Kidnapping of Charles Urschel, July 1933*

14. *Capture of Kelly, September 1933*

TN

Memphis

1. *Kelly's hometown*

Oklahoma City

OK

Little Rock

Tupelo

8. *Urschel held here*

4. *Home of George and Kathryn Kelly, 1931–33*

AR

Paradise

Fort Worth

Dallas

MS

Itasca

11. *Kathryn meets Arnold family, September 1933*

10. *Kelly's hideout, August 1933*

Coleman

TX

9. *Kelly's hideout, August 1933*

Biloxi

LA

New Orleans

San Marcos

San Antonio

Houston

13. *Kelly's hideout, September 1933*

Gulf of Mexico

0 Miles 100 200 300

0 Kilometers 300

© 2004 Jeffrey L. Ward

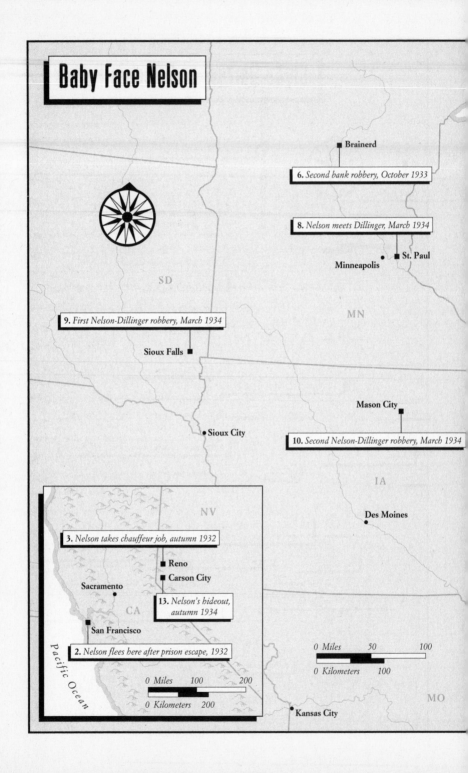

Baby Face Nelson

■ Brainerd

6. *Second bank robbery, October 1933*

8. *Nelson meets Dillinger, March 1934*

Minneapolis ● ■ St. Paul

SD

MN

9. *First Nelson-Dillinger robbery, March 1934*

Sioux Falls ■

Mason City ■

10. *Second Nelson-Dillinger robbery, March 1934*

● Sioux City

IA

Des Moines ●

NV

3. *Nelson takes chauffeur job, autumn 1932*

■ Reno
■ Carson City

Sacramento ●

13. *Nelson's hideout, autumn 1934*

CA

■
San Francisco

2. *Nelson flees here after prison escape, 1932*

Pacific Ocean

0 Miles 100 200
0 Kilometers 200

0 Miles 50 100
0 Kilometers 100

MO

● Kansas City

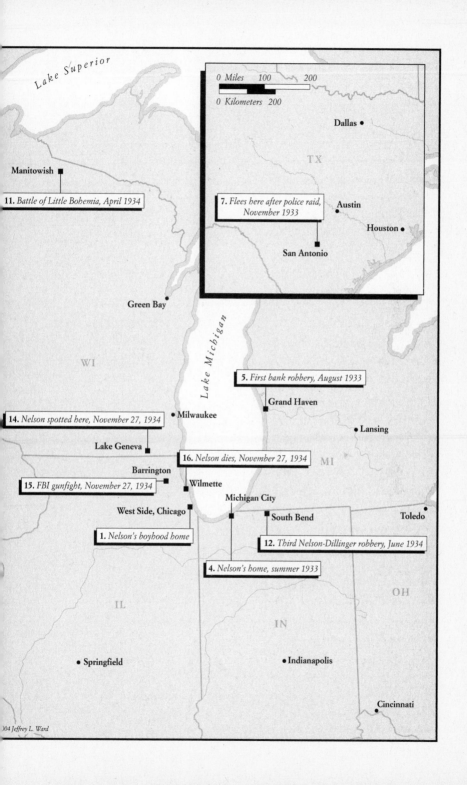

Lake Superior

Manitowish

11. *Battle of Little Bohemia, April 1934*

0 *Miles*   100   200

0 *Kilometers*   200

Dallas •

TX

7. *Flees here after police raid,*
November 1933

Austin •

Houston •

San Antonio •

Green Bay •

Lake Michigan

WI

5. *First bank robbery, August 1933*

Grand Haven •

14. *Nelson spotted here, November 27, 1934*   • Milwaukee

• Lansing

Lake Geneva •

16. *Nelson dies, November 27, 1934*   MI

Barrington •

15. *FBI gunfight, November 27, 1934*   Wilmette •

Michigan City

West Side, Chicago •   • South Bend   Toledo •

1. *Nelson's boyhood home*

12. *Third Nelson-Dillinger robbery, June 1934*

4. *Nelson's home, summer 1933*

OH

IL

IN

• Springfield

• Indianapolis

Cincinnati •

PUBLIC ENEMIES

PROLOGUE

Torremolinos, Spain
August 26, 1979

In a tourist town on the white-sun Spanish coast, an old man was passing his last years, an American grandfather with a snowy white crewcut and a glint in his turquoise eyes. At seventy he was still lean and alert, with high, slanting cheekbones, a sharp chin, and those clear-frame eyeglasses that made him look like a minor-league academic. He spent much of his time holed up in his cluttered garage apartment, watching the BBC on a flickering black-and-white television, surrounded by bottles of Jack Daniel's and pills and his memories. If you met him down on the beach, he came across as a gentle soul with a soft laugh. Almost certainly he was the most pleasant murderer you'd ever want to meet.

It was sad, but only a little. He'd had his fun. When he'd first come to Spain a decade before, he still knew how to have a good time. There was that frowsy old divorcée from Chicago he used to see. They would go tooling around the coast in her sports car and chug tequilla and down their pills and get into these awful screaming fights.

She was gone now. So were the writers, and the documentary makers, the ones who came to hear about the old days; that crew from Canada was the worst, posing him in front of roadsters and surrounding him with actors in fedoras holding fake tommy guns. He'd done it for the money, and for his ego, which had always been considerable. Now, well, now he drank. Out in the cafés, after a few beers, when the sun began to sink down the coast, he would tell stories. The names he dropped meant little to the Spaniards. The Brits and the odd American, they thought he was nuts—an old lush mumbling in his beer.

When he said he'd been a gangster, they smiled. *Sure you were, Pops.* When he said he'd been Public Enemy Number One—right after John Dillinger, "Pretty Boy" Floyd, and his old protégé Baby Face Nelson— people turned away and rolled their eyes. When he said he and his confederates had single-handedly "created" J. Edgar Hoover and the modern FBI, well, then he would get bitter, and people would get up and move to another table. He was obviously a kook. How could you believe anyone who claimed he was the only man in history to have met Charles Manson, Al Capone, and Bonnie and Clyde?

Few in Torremolinos knew it was all true. In those last years at Terminal Island in the '60s, he'd taught Manson to play the steel guitar. He'd been at Alcatraz for twenty-one damp winters before that, leaving for Leavenworth a few years before they closed the place in 1963. In fact, he was the longest-serving prisoner in the history of The Rock. He'd known the Birdman and that gasbag Machine Gun Kelly, and he'd seen Capone collapse into one of his syphilitic seizures, flopping around on the cafeteria floor like a striped bass on a cutting board.

In his day he'd been famous. Not "fifteen minutes" famous, but *famous* famous, *New York Times*–page one–above the fold famous. Back before Neil Armstrong, before the Beatles, before *American Bandstand,* before the war, when Hitler was still a worrisome nut in a bad mustache and FDR was learning to find the White House bathrooms, he was the country's best-known yeggman. Folks today, they didn't even know what a yegg was. Dillinger, he liked to say, he was the best of yeggs. Pretty Boy Floyd was a good yegg. Bonnie and Clyde wanted to be.

And today? Today he and all his peers were cartoon characters, caricatures in one bad gangster movie after another. You could see them on the late show doing all sorts of made-up stuff—Warren Beatty as some stammering latent-homosexual Clyde Barrow, Faye Dunaway as a beautiful Bonnie Parker (now *that* was a stretch), Richard Dreyfuss as a chattering asshole Baby Face Nelson (okay, they got *that* right), Shelley Winters as a machine gun–toting Ma Barker, a young Robert De Niro as one of her sons.

To him they were all ridiculous Hollywood fantasies, fictional concoctions in an artificial world.

At that point the old man would just shake his head. As he sprawled on his couch at nights, sipping his Jack Daniel's and popping his pills, what galled him was that it had all been *real*. It had all *happened*. Not in some fantasy world, not in the movies, but right there in the middle of the United States—in Chicago, in St. Paul, in Dallas, in Cleveland. The truth of it all seemed lost now, forgotten as totally as he was. Dillinger, Floyd, Nelson, Bonnie and Clyde, Ma Barker: He had known them all. He was the last one left alive. He had even outlived Hoover himself.

Hoover.

Fucking Hoover.

He leaned over and reached for a bottle of his pills.

1

A PRELUDE TO WAR

Spring 1933

Washington, D.C.
Saturday, March 4, 1933

It was a morning as bleak as the times. Gray clouds sagged low over the city, nudged along by a north wind and gusts of rain. A hundred thousand people stood outside the Capitol, waiting. The mood in the crowd was hushed, anxious. A few pointed to the rooftops. "What are those things that look like little cages?" someone asked.

"Machine guns," said a woman.[1]

The sense of crisis was underscored by the nervous young soldiers who stood by on street corners, fingering their rifles. "The atmosphere," wrote Arthur Krock in the *New York Times,* "was comparable to that which might be found in a beleaguered capital in wartime."

The analogy was apt. It did feel like war. People were shell-shocked. The country they had known—the fat and happy America of the Jazz Age, of speakeasies and fun and sloe gin fizzes—had vanished, destroyed as utterly as if wiped out by an enemy's bombs. Women who once spent their evenings dancing the Charleston now shuffled forward in breadlines, grimy and hopeless. Fathers who sank their savings in the stock market now sat in gutters, begging for change.

A bugle called. Everywhere, heads turned. The president-elect, appearing unsteady, stepped up the maroon-carpeted ramp to the lectern. The chief justice, Charles Evan Hughes, read the oath of office.

When he was finished, Franklin Delano Roosevelt stepped to the lectern and gripped it tightly. His face was grim. "Let me assert my firm belief that the only thing we have to fear is fear itself," he intoned, "nameless, unreasoning, unjustified terror which paralyzes needed efforts to convert retreat into advance." Roosevelt looked out over the crowd. "This Nation asks for action, and action now," he continued. "We must move as a trained and loyal army willing to sacrifice for the good of a common discipline . . . I shall ask the Congress for the one remaining instrument to meet the crisis—broad executive power to wage a war against the emergency, as great as the power that would be given to me if we were in fact invaded by a foreign foe."

Afterward, when the president disappeared back inside the Capitol, few in the crowd felt reassured. Mention of war left many frightened. There was talk of martial law, anarchy, dictatorship. Few understood what kind of war the president intended. Anything seemed possible.

What no one could know that morning was that one theater of the metaphoric war Roosevelt invoked would in fact involve guns and blood and death on American soil. It would be fought across a great swath of the country's midsection, beginning at a railroad station in Kansas City before engulfing the streets of Chicago, pine-shrouded lodges in northern Wisconsin, dust-bowl farms in weary Oklahoma, and battle sites scattered from Atlantic City to Dallas, St. Paul to Florida. It would be fought not by soldiers but by another branch of the federal government, an obscure arm of the Justice Department, headed by an equally obscure bureaucrat named John Edgar Hoover, who in a span of twenty short months would rise from nowhere to hunt down a series of criminals whose exploits were to become a national soap opera, and then a legend.

When one looks back across a chasm of seventy years, through a prism of pulp fiction and bad gangster movies, there is a tendency to view the events of 1933–34 as mythic, as folkloric. To the generations of Americans raised since World War II, the identities of criminals such as Charles "Pretty Boy" Floyd, Baby Face Nelson, "Ma" Barker, John Dillinger, and Clyde Barrow are no more real than are Luke Skywalker or Indiana Jones. After decades spent in the washing machine of popular culture, their stories have been bled of all reality, to an extent that few Americans today know who these people actually were, much less that they all rose to national prominence *at the same time.*

They were real. A wastrel Dallas thief turned multiple murderer, Clyde Barrow was born in 1909, the same year as Barry Goldwater and Ethel Merman. Had he lived, he would have been sixty-five years old when Richard Nixon resigned the presidency in 1974, an aging coupon-clipper, maybe, spending evenings in a Barcalounger chuckling at Archie Bunker. Baby Face Nelson's widow died only in 1987, after years of watching her grandchildren drum their fingers to MTV. After spending twenty-five years in prison, Machine Gun Kelly's widow died in Tulsa in 1985. There remain people alive today who crouched behind teller cages as Dillinger robbed their neighborhood bank, who watched as Bonnie and Clyde shot innocent sheriffs, who tossed baseballs with Baby Face Nelson. Kelly and Floyd gave birth to children who still tell their parents' stories.

They were the bogeymen for the children who have become known as The Greatest Generation. In the spring of 1933, when men like John Dillinger were ascending the national stage, a twenty-two-year-old named Ronald Reagan was broadcasting college baseball games on WHO radio in Des Moines, twenty-year-old Richard Nixon was acting in plays at Whittier College in Southern California, while a pair of third graders, James Earl Carter in Plains, Georgia, and George Herbert Walker Bush in Greenwich, Connecticut, were learning multiplication tables. At high school dances in Hoboken, New Jersey, girls were swooning to a seventeen-year-old crooner named Francis Sinatra. At a house on Judson Avenue in Evanston, Illinois, a hyperactive nine-year-old named Marlon Brando was learning to box.

Yet as these and other members of that generation pass from the scene, it is difficult to imagine a time when name-brand outlaws stalked twentieth-century America. In a world of pocket telephones, Internet shopping, and laser-guided bombs, the notion of marauding gangs of bank robbers wreaking havoc across the country is almost too outlandish to grasp, a story one might hear of the Wild West. But it wasn't the Wild West. It was America in 1933, eight years before Pearl Harbor, twelve years before Hiroshima, twenty-three years before Elvis, thirty-six before Woodstock. For all the surface contrasts—there was no Internet, no television, no infrared cameras or satellite imagery—America in 1933 wasn't all that different from America today. Long-distance telephone calls were routine. So was air travel; both cops and robbers could and sometimes did fly to their jobs. The most influential publications included the *New York Times* and *Time* magazine.

Men and women dressed much as they do today; the only marked difference was a preference for hats—men in sharp fedoras and jaunty straw boaters, society women in frilly lace things, ordinary girls in Gilligan hats pulled low over their bangs. Hollywood dominated mainstream culture; popular films that spring were Boris Karloff's *Frankenstein,* Johnny Weismuller's first *Tarzan,* and *Dr. Jekyll and Mr. Hyde. Mutiny on the Bounty* topped bestseller lists. Radio was up and running, but barely half the country's homes had a set.

What distinguished those early months of 1933 was that so many Americans had no money to enjoy any of this. The stock market crash of 1929 had degenerated into an economic depression. Hundreds of thousands of men lost their jobs. On reflection, that spring would be seen as a low point. Muddy shantytowns spread along the Potomac River, beneath Riverside Drive in New York, and in Chicago, Boston, and San Francisco. Thousands of families, including a legion of dirty children, lived nomadic lives in railroad cars rumbling across the Midwest, lurching from town to town in search of a better life that was nowhere to be found. In Washington there were marches, some of them violent, scenes of tanks and soldiers pushing back desperate men hungering for jobs. People were angry. They blamed the government. They blamed the banks.

As Roosevelt delivered his inaugural address that drizzly March morning, a group of government bureaucrats in dark suits listened around a radio in a third-floor office at the corner of Vermont and K Streets in downtown Washington. What they did was little known to anyone outside their families. Their supervisor was a squat, beady-eyed man, thirty-eight years old, with a flattened nose and loose bags under his eyes. His resemblance to a bulldog was much remarked upon. That morning J. Edgar Hoover was preoccupied with keeping his job.

Today, going on four decades after his death in 1972, it's difficult to remember a time when Hoover was not the monolithic figure whose secret files cowed American presidents, who underwrote Senator Joseph McCarthy's star chamber, who hounded national figures as varied as Martin Luther King, Jr., Alger Hiss, and the Rosenbergs. For four decades Hoover dominated American law enforcement as no person before or since, single-handedly creating the country's first national police force. His legacy is as complex as the man himself. Before Hoover, American law enforcement was a decentralized polyglot of county sheriffs and urban police departments too often crippled by corruption. By and large, it was Hoover who brought the level of efficiency, professionalism, and centralized control the nation knows to this day. But his accomplishments will forever be sullied by the abuses of power—rampant illegal wiretapping, break-ins, and harassment of civil rights groups—of his later years.

Hoover's power did not evolve slowly. It erupted during the Great Crime Wave of 1933–34. He entered this period an anonymous federal functionary, his bureau struggling to shake past scandals. In twenty months he emerged a national hero, a household name lauded in films, books, and comic strips. In six hundred days, the modern FBI was born. This book is the story of how it happened.

That morning, Hoover was director of the Justice Department's Bureau of Investigation. Not the Federal Bureau of Investigation; it wouldn't get that name for another two years.* He had been in office nine years, since 1924, but he had enemies, lots of them, and Roosevelt's men made it clear that he would probably be replaced. The final decision was to be made by the new attorney general, a confirmed Hoover-hater named Thomas Walsh. That Thursday, two days before Roosevelt's address, Walsh, a seventy-two-year-old senator from Montana, had boarded a train from Miami to Washington with his new bride, a Cuban debutante. Friday morning Mrs. Walsh awakened aboard the train in North Carolina and found her husband dead; whispers in the capital suggested the elderly senator had expired following an athletic bout of sex.

For Hoover the reprieve was temporary. After all he had achieved in the last nine years, it was galling to him that mere politicians held his fate; if not for him, the Bureau of Investigation might have been eliminated years before. It was an odd little outfit, "a bureaucratic bastard," one critic called it, responsible for investigating a grab bag of federal offenses, including sedition, interstate auto theft, breakouts from federal prisons, and crime on Indian reservations. One writer termed it "an odd-job detective agency with fuzzy lines of authority and responsibility." Hoover's agents did not possess arrest powers; if they wanted to mount a raid, they were obliged to bring

---

* For simplicity's sake, it will be referred to as "FBI" throughout this book.

along local policemen. Nor did they carry guns. This was a policy, not a law; Hoover's model was Scotland Yard. His men were investigators, not policemen. "Fact finders" was the word his aides used.

The Bureau had a sordid history. Created in 1908 to investigate antitrust cases, it had devolved over the ensuing fifteen years into a nest of nepotism and corruption. By the early 1920s, its agents, scattered across fifty domestic offices, were hired mostly as favors to politicians. Its most notorious employee, a con man named Gaston Means, earned his money blackmailing congressmen, selling liquor licenses to bootleggers, and auctioning presidential pardons. In the wake of a mid-1920s Congressional investigation, the Bureau acquired the nickname "The Department of Easy Virtue."

The day he was promoted to clean up the Bureau in 1924, Hoover was a stoic twenty-nine-year-old government attorney who still lived with his adoring mother in the house where he was raised, a two-story stucco building at 413 Seward Square in Washington's Capitol Hill neighborhood. He was a boyhood stutterer who overcame his disability by teaching himself to speak rapidly, in staccato bursts so fast that more than one stenographer was unable to keep up. Neat, intense, and disciplined, Hoover grew up surrounded by civil servants in the bosom of the Washington bureaucracy. There was little question that he would follow his father, a deskman at the U.S. Coast and Geodetic Survey, into government work. Hoover went to night school at George Washington University, where he joined the Kappa Alpha fraternity. Working days as a clerk at the Library of Congress, he received his bachelor of law degree in 1916 and his master's a year later, the same year that he passed the District of Columbia bar.

In July 1917 he took a job as a clerk at Justice. Many of the department's up-and-coming young lawyers were gone, enlisted in the war effort, and Hoover, sharply dressed and a demon for detail, stood out, earning two promotions in his first six months. He went to work in the alien-registration section and moved up quickly; by 1919, at the age of twenty-four, he was named head of the General Intelligence Division, a newly created bureau charged with prosecuting labor radicals, anarchists, and Communists. He earned high marks—and his first interview in the *New York Times*—as a driving force behind the department's January 1920 raids on Communists in thirty-three cities, which led to the arrest of more than three thousand people. He lobbied for and received his new job as assistant director of the Bureau of Investigation in August 1921.

A Senate probe of the Bureau in 1924 led to the resignations and indictments of the BI chief and the attorney general. The new attorney general, Harlan Fiske Stone, was at a loss about what to do with the Bureau. He scribbled down notes of its problems: "filled with men with bad records . . . many convicted of crimes . . . organization lawless . . . agents engaged in many practices which are brutal and tyrannical in the extreme."[2] Stone had no idea who could reform such an outfit. A friend suggested Hoover. He was young, but he was honest and industrious. Stone asked around, liked what he heard, and on May 10, 1924, summoned Hoover to his office and handed him interim leadership of the Bureau.

Hoover's first priority was transforming his force of field agents (which numbered 339 in 1929). His vision was precise: he wanted young, energetic white men between twenty-five and thirty-five, with law degrees, clean, neat, well spoken, bright, and from solid families—men like himself. He got them. In a matter of weeks Hoover cleared out the deadwood, stopped patronage hiring, and instituted a meritocracy. Applicants were screened on "general intelligence," "conduct during interview," and "Personal Appearance," either "neat," "flashy," "poor," or "untidy."

Hoover ruled by absolute fiat. His men lived in fear of him. Inspection teams appeared at field offices with no notice, writing up agents who were even one minute tardy for work. Hoover tolerated no sloth, sloppiness, or deviation from the new rules that came pouring into every field office, each commanded by a special agent in charge, known as a SAC. (There were twenty-five in 1929.) The tiniest infraction could cost a man his job; when a Denver SAC offered a visitor a drink, he was fired.

"I want the public to look upon the Bureau of Investigation and the Department of Justice as a group of gentlemen," Hoover told an audience in 1926. "And if the men here engaged can't conduct themselves in office as such, I will dismiss them."

Those who survived, and those Hoover hired, were a homogenous lot. Many were Southern. More than a few came from Hoover's alma mater, George Washington, especially its Kappa Alpha chapter. Hoover's wizened number two man, Harold "Pop" Nathan, a BI administrator since 1917, was a KA; for years he was also the Bureau's only Jew. Visiting agents sometimes stayed at the Kappa house. It was there that Hugh Clegg, a courtly young Mississippi attorney who would rise to become an FBI assistant director, was hired. Like all new men, Clegg was rotated through a series of field offices in his first few months. It was in the field that many of the new hires first encountered the hostility of police departments, who viewed

Hoover's men as unarmed, inept dilettantes intent on seizing their territory. They mocked them as "Deejays" or "College Boys."

The cops were onto something. In Hoover's new Bureau, appearance, loyalty, and hard work were prized above law-enforcement experience. Few of his new hires had any, as Hoover was uncomfortably aware; the saying within the Bureau was that Hoover liked his men "young and grateful." While publicly mandating that all agents have law degrees, Hoover quietly retained some nonlawyers as well, mostly veteran Southwestern lawmen. These "Cowboys" were a breed apart. They chewed tobacco and drank and spit, infractions Hoover ignored. The Cowboys knew how to run investigations, and that's what they did. In violation of Bureau regulations, several carried guns: in Washington, John Keith wore matched Colt .45s; in Dallas, Charles Winstead used a .357 Magnum; in Chicago, the former Texas Ranger James C. "Doc" White favored a bone-handled Colt, accenting it with a knife hidden in his boot. The two agents assigned to run key cases in Hoover's early years were veteran Cowboys: Gus T. Jones, the San Antonio SAC, and Doc White's older brother, an ex-Ranger named Thomas White, the Oklahoma City SAC.

Hoover's reorganization transformed the Bureau. Unproductive field offices were closed. Bureaucracy was streamlined. A chain of command was drawn. Paperwork was standardized. After six months the Bureau was on its way to becoming the very model of a modern, efficient government organization. The "interim" was removed from Hoover's title. Once the Bureau was retooled, the challenge became finding something for its agents to do. In Hoover's first six years his men spearheaded a corruption investigation at the federal prison in Atlanta and a probe of murders and oil-rights thievery on Indian lands in Oklahoma. They were minor cases, all run by the Cowboys; Tom White handled the Atlanta and Oklahoma investigations. When White was named warden at Leavenworth in 1927, Hoover summoned Gus Jones to supervise a vain attempt to capture a set of high-profile escapees.

On all these cases Hoover's men did the legwork but stepped aside when it was time to make arrests, sometimes to the snickers of police. "I can remember [calling] policemen when a wanted fugitive is at such-and-such place," Hugh Clegg recalled. "The policeman will tell me, 'Well, you guard the back and I'll go in the front. You don't have a gun, so I'll go in.' I've stood at the back door of a house, had [only a] brickbat in my hand, hoping that [the fugitive] would not come out that way . . . If he'd come out shooting, I had no defense at all, no weapons, no offensive weapons, and you're just at his mercy."[3]

Hoover's role was strictly administrative. He seldom left Washington, where he worked from an office decorated with fine Chinese antiques. In the spring of 1933, while billing himself as the nation's leading law-enforcement expert, Hoover himself had never made an arrest, much less fired a gun in anger. The SACs ran the investigations, Hoover peering over their shoulders, firing off memos at anything he disliked. He and Pop Nathan could be scathing in their appraisals. Privately both knew they had few competent men. "I believe that the trouble with many of our offices is that our Agents in Charge are somewhat foggy mentally," Nathan wrote in a memo to Hoover in June 1932. "Or at any rate they function slowly along mental lines."[4]

Like any good civil servant, Hoover made certain the public knew how well he was doing. He gave speeches and occasional newspaper interviews, emphasizing the Bureau's integrity and its devotion to what he called "scientific policing," based on fingerprints and evidentiary analysis. Not all the press was receptive. A 1933 article in *Collier's* characterized the Bureau as Hoover's "personal and political machine. More inaccessible than presidents, he [keeps] his agents in fear and awe by firing and shifting them at whim; no other government agency had such a turnover of personnel." It was the *Collier's* article that first hinted at Hoover's Achilles' heel, the rumors of his sexual orientation. "In appearance Mr. Hoover looks utterly unlike the story-book sleuth," it noted. "He dresses fastidiously, with Eleanor blue as the favored color for the matched shades of tie, handkerchief and socks . . . He is short, fat, businesslike, and walks with mincing step."

After eight years of pursuing minor crimes, Hoover's first opportunity to perform on the national stage came in June 1932, with the passage of the Lindbergh Law, three months after the kidnapping (and subsequent murder) of Charles Lindbergh's infant son in Hopewell, New Jersey. The new law made kidnapping a federal crime but only where the kidnapper or his victim had crossed a state border. The Lindbergh kidnapping spawned a rash of copycat crimes throughout 1932, but to Hoover's frustration, none of the kidnappings fell in his domain.

But as word spread in the underworld of massive ransoms to be had, kidnappings flourished. The year 1933 brought twenty-seven major cases, more than twice the number reported in any previous year, so many that the *New York Times* began charting them in a periodic column. Beginning with the kidnapping of the millionaire Charles Boetscher II in Denver that February, FBI agents stormed into a half-dozen high-profile cases, for the first time finding themselves involved in solving crimes the public actually cared about.

As Roosevelt took office that spring, kidnapping stories thronged front pages across the country. Coming on the heels of the surge in crime during the 1920s symbolized by Al Capone, these reports added fuel to the debate over the need for a federal police force. On one side were reformers who charged that municipal police were too often corrupt and ineffective, and unable to deal with increasingly mobile criminals who crossed state lines like cracks in a sidewalk. On the other side were powerful city governments, jealous of their turf, backed by congressmen who viewed federal policing as the first step toward an American Gestapo. Antifederalism still ran strong in America. There remained, especially in the South and Midwest, an undercurrent of deep mistrust toward Washington, feelings that grew as citizens came to blame politicians for the Depression. The debate intensified with Roosevelt's election. His advisers were pushing hard for a strong central government that could revive the economy by taking control of many areas managed by state and municipal governments, including law enforcement.

During the first hundred days of the Roosevelt administration, a period that famously saw dozens of pieces of New Deal legislation stream through Congress, the leading voice for a federal police force was a Roosevelt adviser named Louis Howe. The attorney general chosen to replace Thomas Walsh, a Connecticut attorney named Homer S. Cummings, was, perhaps unsurprisingly, possessed of similar views. That spring Howe and Cummings began discussing how best to reform the Justice Department and what role, if any, it might play in federal policing.

For Hoover, Roosevelt's election was an all-or-nothing proposition. Of the few pundits who took notice, most believed Hoover would be fired. Had Senator Walsh lived, he almost certainly would have been. But if he could somehow persuade the White House of his value, Hoover could see there was a chance—a remote one, to be sure—that his little bureau might serve as the centerpiece of a federal police force. A number of his government competitors had the same idea, most notably Elmer Irey, the head of the Internal Revenue Service's aggressive investigative arm, which could boast of its 1931 toppling of Capone.

That spring, Hoover launched a vigorous lobbying campaign to keep his job and to position himself for something more. SACs were ordered to arrange letters of support from prominent politicians. Hoover's old boss Harlan Fiske Stone, now a Supreme Court justice, wrote Justice Felix Frankfurter, who contacted Roosevelt. Still, anti-Hoover sentiment remained widespread. One Roosevelt adviser later wrote there was "tremendous pressure on Roosevelt by various city politicians to replace Hoover with this or that police chief whom they believed would be more amenable to them for patronage."[5]

All that spring Hoover's future hung in the balance. Only a cynic would have pointed out the obvious. What Hoover needed was a tangible achievement, something to grab headlines, a case that would thrust him into the public spotlight and underscore the Bureau's transformation. He was about to get it, but from a group of criminals over whose activities the FBI had absolutely no jurisdiction: bank robbers.

The first recorded U.S. bank robbery, actually a nighttime burglary, came in 1831, when a man named Edward Smith snuck into a Wall Street bank and made off with $245,000. He was caught and sentenced to a five-year term in Sing Sing. Smith's brainstorm led to an early advance in U.S. bank security—the advent of safes—in 1834. Until the Civil War, armed robberies of banks were all but unknown. During the war, Confederate raiders robbed several Northern banks, but the first recorded bank robbery by a civilian came on December 15, 1863, when an irate man named Edward Green wandered into a bank in Malden, Massachusetts, shot a banker in the head, and, as an afterthought, scooped up $5,000. For his place in history Green earned an 1866 date with a noose.

The first organized bank robbery in peacetime, an 1866 raid in Liberty, Missouri, was carried out by a ragtag band of out-of-work Confederate irregulars led by the brothers Frank and Jesse James. The James Gang's string of robberies over the next fifteen years was glamorized by the press, bringing bank robbery to the attention of a number of Western imitators, including the Dalton Brothers, Bill Doolin, and the Hole-in-the-Wall Gang of Butch Cassidy and the Sundance Kid. With the migration of Cassidy's core group to South America in 1901 and the shrinking of the Western frontier, bank robbing faded from popular consciousness. Banks continued to be robbed, but no outlaw achieved national notoriety, and while statistics are unreliable, the number of armed robberies probably fell during the years before World War I.

Nor did they soar after the war. Until the mid-1920s, most ambitious thieves preferred nocturnal bank burglaries. A case in point was the Newton Gang, a band of four Texas brothers who hit dozens of Midwestern banks between 1919 and 1924. Their tactics were those of burglars across the nation; they broke into banks at night, used a nitroglycerine explosion to "pop" safe doors, and were generally gone before a sheriff could mobilize pursuit. This strategy worked until banks reacted in the mid-1920s by introducing reinforced safes and alarms. The Newtons and their peers were forced to initiate daylight robberies. Their biggest strike, the $2 million robbery of a mail train in Roundout, Illinois, outside Chicago, was the decade's largest.

When the federal government suddenly found itself engaged in open warfare with groups of heavily armed bank robbers in 1934, many asked why. The common answer was the Depression. It was true, as far as it went: many bank robbers were desperate, unemployed men. But blaming the Great Crime Wave of 1933–34 on the Depression ignores the fact that the years between 1925 and 1932 amounted to a golden age for American bank robbers, known in the press as "yeggmen," or "yeggs." Robberies along what came to be known as the "crime corridor," from Texas to Minnesota, soared. Between 1920 and 1929, the Travelers Insurance Company reported that property crimes—from bank robberies to drugstore stickups—jumped from 17 to 965 a year in its Dallas office; 30 to 300 in Gary, Indiana; 9 to 836 in Saginaw, Michigan.[6] The violence that catapulted men like John Dillinger to prominence in 1934 wasn't the *beginning* of a crime wave; it was the end of one.

The spread of bank robberies was the result of technology outstripping the legal system. Faster, more powerful weapons, especially the 800-bullet-per-minute Thompson submachine gun introduced after World War I, allowed yeggs to outgun all but the best-armed urban policemen. But the greatest impetus was the automobile, especially new models with reliable, powerful V-8 engines. While a county sheriff was still hand-cranking his old Model A, a modern yegg could speed away untouched. A Frenchman may have been the first to use a car to escape a bank robbery, in 1915; one of the first Americans to try it was an aging Oklahoma yegg, Henry Starr, who used a Nash to rob a bank in Harrison, Arkansas, in 1921. The practice caught on.

"Seventy-five percent of all crimes now are perpetrated with the aid of the automobile," one crime writer noted in 1924. "Automobiles and good roads have done much to increase certain types of banditry. We now have a definitely established type called an automobile bandit who operates exclusively in motor vehicles, whether it is to perpetrate a holdup on a bank or merely to stick up pedestrians and rob homes."[7]

Lawmen were powerless to chase the new auto bandits across state lines, making border areas, especially the notorious tristate region of Missouri, Oklahoma, and Kansas, magnets for crime. The federal government was of no help: bank robbery wasn't yet a federal crime. Coordination between police departments was spotty; only a few states had introduced statewide police, and those that had had seldom possessed the resources to break a major case. In their place, vigilante committees sprang up across the Midwest. Not that it mattered: if a yegg fled a bank robbery without getting shot, there was little chance he would ever be caught.

All of which made bank robbery a tempting vocation to a Midwestern populace that faced more temptations than ever. During the 1920s, mass-produced goods such as dresses, washing machines, and radios became widely available. Yet with the drought and the resulting downturn in the Midwestern farm economy, fewer citizens could afford the goods that lay out of reach behind department-store windows. A single bank robbery could change a dirt farmer's life. At a time when the average household income in states like Oklahoma and Missouri hovered below $500 a year, bank robbers could make off with $10,000 for a morning's work.

The Newton Brothers typified the mistake-prone amateurs who ushered in the motorized age; they were arrested in the wake of their Roundout, Illinois, job. The criminal credited with introducing a new level of professionalism to bank robbery was Herman K. Lamm, a German émigré known as "The Baron." Born in 1880, Lamm is a quasimythic figure; some claim he began his career with the Hole-in-the-Wall Gang. What is known is that around 1917, while in a Utah prison, he developed a rigorous system for robbing banks. Lamm pioneered the "casing" of banks, the observation of bank guards, alarms, and tellers; a bank was known as a "jug," and an expert caser of banks was known as a "jug marker." Each member of Lamm's gang was assigned a role in the robbery: the lookout, the getaway driver, the lobby man, the vault man.

Most important, Lamm is credited with devising the first detailed getaway maps, or "gits." Once he targeted a bank, Lamm mapped the nearby

back roads, known as "cat roads," to a tenth of a mile, listing each land-
mark and using a stopwatch to time distances. Any teenager with a birdgun
could rob a bank; it was getting away that posed a challenge. Lamm's detailed gits, clipped to the dashboard of a car, took the guesswork out of the
getaway. His gang was credited with dozens of robberies during the 1920s,
until Lamm was shot and killed near Clinton, Indiana, in 1930. By then his
system had been widely imitated. Two of his men would teach it to an Indiana prison inmate named John Dillinger.

Baron Lamm's peers included three older men who would influence
many of the yeggs who rose to prominence in 1933 and 1934. One was Eddie Bentz, a nomadic Seattle-born bank robber and book lover who fancied
himself an intellectual. Bentz, who mentored both Machine Gun Kelly and
Baby Face Nelson, traveled with a chestful of the classics and in his spare time
could sometimes be found leafing through a copy of *The Pilgrim's Progress.*

Another notable Jazz Age yegg was Harvey Bailey, a onetime bootlegger
so gentlemanly he termed the female hostages he loaded into his getaway
cars "hostesses." Bailey masterminded the most celebrated raid of the
1920s, the robbery of cash-laden messengers outside the Denver Mint in
1922. He was so successful he retired for a time, opening a chain of gas stations and car washes on Chicago's South Side, until he lost almost everything in the 1929 stock market crash. Resurrecting his career from a base in
St. Paul, Bailey mentored a number of young bank men who congregated
at the city's notorious Green Lantern tavern, including Machine Gun Kelly,
Alvin Karpis, and the Barker brothers. Arrested on a Kansas City golf
course in 1932, he led a massive prison breakout on May 31, 1933, and
went back to robbing banks.

The last of the great Jazz Age yeggs was the man whose smuggled guns
freed Bailey from prison, his friend Frank "Jelly" Nash. Nash, a stout figure with a comic toupee who began his career robbing trains on horseback
in his native Oklahoma, was a Leavenworth escapee who also worked out
of St. Paul, robbing banks with Bailey and the Barker Gang.

All three of these men—Eddie Bentz, Harvey Bailey, and Frank Nash—
were destined to play roles in the Great Crime Wave of 1933–34. It was
Nash who accidentally triggered the war with J. Edgar Hoover's FBI. He
did it not with a bank robbery or a high-profile kidnapping, but with the
simple desire for a quiet Arkansas vacation.

2

A MASSACRE BY PERSONS UNKNOWN

June 8 to June 15, 1933

From a newsman's point of view, the month of June opened quietly. In Washington, senators debated the Roosevelt administration's industrial recovery bill. Each morning brought a worrisome new headline from Germany; on Tuesday, June 6, it was the ouster of Otto Klemperer, a Jew, as conductor of the Berlin State Opera under the "non-Aryan" section of the Civil Service act. In India, Mahatma Gandhi was fasting to protest mistreatment of the "untouchables" caste. All that week readers of the *New York Times* followed daily updates of Texas pilot James Mattern's attempt to break the around-the-world speed record; at the moment, he was hopscotching across Siberia. In Chicago, a dust storm blew in off the plains, toppling trees, downing power lines, and sending thousands at the newly opened World's Fair scurrying for shelter.

On Thursday evening, June 8, 1933, an Oklahoma schoolteacher named Joe Hudiberg finished a poker game in the kitchen of his white frame house outside the town of Cromwell. Hudiberg walked into the warm evening air and stretched. As his friends stepped to their cars, he ambled down to his garage and padlocked the doors.

Locked inside the garage was Hudiberg's prized black Pontiac—and Pretty Boy Floyd, who had come to steal it. In the darkness, Floyd cursed. This was the way his luck had been going for months now. Charley Floyd—

no one but the newspapers called him "Pretty Boy"—was twenty-nine years old that summer evening. He was only five-feet-eight; his shoulders and upper arms were thick and powerful, his face moony and flat. He resembled a young Babe Ruth. Floyd's eyes were gray and he kept his hair slicked back with a thin part down the left side. Up close you could smell his hair tonic, a whiff of lilac.

Of all the criminals who rose to prominence in 1933 and 1934, Floyd was the only one who was already famous, at least in Oklahoma, where he was a hero to legions of disaffected dust bowlers. Everyone knew his story. The son of upstanding parents, he had been a restive farm boy in his hometown of Akins, working on harvest crews and the occasional burglary, until he robbed a Kroger store in St. Louis in 1925, for which he drew a five-year sentence in a Missouri prison. Paroled in 1930, Floyd moved to Kansas City and tried to go straight but was constantly rousted by police, an experience that left him with a deep sense of victimization. Teaming up with some prison pals, he relocated to Ohio but was arrested after robbing a bank. He jumped out a window on the train ride to prison and fled to Oklahoma.

In the fall of 1931, Floyd began robbing country banks in his home state in earnest, earning his first mentions in Oklahoma newspapers. But it was a crime in which he took no part that catapulted him onto the front pages. On January 2, 1932, two ex-convicts ambushed and killed six peace officers in a shoot-out near Springfield, Missouri, in what remains the largest such massacre in American history. An Associated Press dispatch carried speculation that Floyd was involved, and Oklahoma newspapers leaned heavily on the local angle.

It was the spark that fired the Floyd legend. Floyd, wrote the *Muskogee Daily Phoenix,* now "steps into the rank of real 'bad hombres' with the questionable honor of [killing] 11 men, all officers, to his credit. The exploits of Billy the Kid . . . pale before the cool, monotonous killings of the fair haired 'Pretty Boy' Floyd, who has introduced the submachine gun and the armored vest to the Oklahoma bad men." The notion of a modern-day Billy the Kid was too appealing for the newspapers to ignore. In January 1932 alone Floyd was identified as robbing banks in three separate towns, only one of which he probably robbed. It didn't matter. The *Daily Oklahoman* called for mobilization of the National Guard; on January 14 insurance rates on rural Oklahoma banks were doubled, a move blamed directly on Floyd. Governor William "Alfalfa Bill" Murray announced a $1,000 reward for his capture.

It was a classic case of media hysteria, of hype that would shape reality that would in turn create a legend. Every morning that winter brought a story of Floyd's exploits, a bank robbed, a supposed sighting, speculation where he might strike next. Lawmen combed eastern Oklahoma in a futile manhunt. Floyd understood the situation and made a crude bid for public support. In a letter to the governor, he demanded that the reward be withdrawn. "I have robbed no one but the monied men," Floyd wrote, a claim guaranteed to find favor in rural Oklahoma. Floyd thus cannily positioned himself as an attacker of only "monied" interests, making the governor their defender. In doing so he created a socioeconomic debate he was guaranteed to win.

Floyd's fame grew after he survived a pair of wild shoot-outs with police in the streets of Tulsa. When Governor Murray appointed a special investigator named Erv Kelley to track him down, Floyd shot Kelley dead in a midnight firefight. But by late 1932, Floyd was growing weary of life on the run. Hiding with relatives, he attempted to "retire" by supervising a ragtag group of bank robbers led by a grimy alcoholic named Adam Richetti. But Richetti's gang proved hapless, and by the spring of 1933, Floyd had withdrawn from bank robbing altogether, preferring to spend his days baking pies in his cousins' kitchens. Only when several of his relatives were arrested did Floyd decide to leave Oklahoma for a time. He had arrived at Joe Hudiberg's farmhouse that Thursday night looking for a car.

As Hudiberg walked toward his house after locking the garage, he heard a noise behind him. Something was bumping against the garage doors. As Hudiberg turned to investigate, his black Pontiac came crashing through the wooden doors. Dumbfounded, he watched as the car roared through his yard and shot onto the road. Hudiberg's friends ran to their cars and mounted a fruitless pursuit. Far ahead of them, Pretty Boy Floyd turned north, toward Kansas City.

Two mornings after Floyd burst out of an Oklahoma schoolteacher's garage, a man named Horace Grisso walked through the streets of New Carlisle, Ohio, north of Dayton. Grisso, the bookkeeper at the New Carlisle National Bank, stopped when he got to the bank's front door and took out his keys and opened it. His footsteps echoed on the marble floor as he crossed to the teller cages. The moment he stepped behind the cages, three men wearing handkerchiefs across their faces rose before him. "All right, buddy, open the safe," ordered the trio's twenty-nine-year-old leader, who that morning was robbing his first bank.

His name was John Dillinger, and he had been released from the Indiana State Pen barely three weeks before. Like Floyd, Dillinger was a nobody from nowhere, one more ex-con tossed out into the Depression to make ends meet. He was a small, slender man, five-feet-seven, with close-cropped brown hair, an easygoing wiseacre with a lopsided grin who had served nine long years for the drunken mugging of a grocer in his hometown outside Indianapolis. He had promised his father, a stoic farmer, that he would go straight, but, in fact, he had a secret plan. Dillinger's only friends were those he made in prison, and that morning he was trying to raise enough money to break them out.

Horace Grisso reached for the drawer where the bank's combination book lay. Dillinger grabbed his hand, then allowed him to slowly open the drawer. Stepping to the safe door, Grisso fumbled with the lock, unable to open it. He was nervous. "Let me drill 'em," Dillinger's teenage partner, William Shaw, said. "He's stalling."

Dillinger put up his hand. "Take your time," he told Grisso.

Just then the front door opened. Dillinger leaped to it and intercepted the bank's clerk as she entered. "I don't want to hurt you," Dillinger told her, directing her to lie on the floor. Dillinger grabbed a smock off of a chair and politely laid it beneath her, then wrapped wire around her hands and feet. By then Grisso had opened the safe, and Shaw and the third man, a teenager named Paul "Lefty" Parker, began lifting out bags of cash. Dillinger remained by the front door, corralling two more employees who entered. "You hadn't ought to come in the bank so early," he said with a grin.

Within minutes Dillinger and his accomplices were back in their car, speeding toward Indiana. They counted the money and found it totaled $10,600, not a bad haul. But Dillinger wasn't satisfied. That night he and Shaw pulled up outside a Haag's Drugstore in Indianapolis. Inside, Shaw headed toward the main cash register while Dillinger took the smaller one at the soda fountain. He stuck his gun at the three employees. When they stared into his face, he said, "Look the other way!" The employees turned their gazes toward Shaw. "Don't look at me!" Shaw shouted. The employees turned back to Dillinger. "I said don't look at me!" Dillinger repeated.

A moment later the two men, cash from the registers in hand, backed out onto the sidewalk, only to find that Lefty Parker had parallel-parked the car at the curb, snugly wedged between two other parked cars. As Dillinger simmered, Parker bumped the cars in front and behind several times before wheeling out and making their getaway. Dillinger had to explain to young Parker how to park a getaway car.

Still, the night wasn't over. A half hour later Dillinger showed Parker where to pull up in front of a City Foods supermarket. Robbing the store had been Shaw's idea. What he neglected to tell Dillinger was that he had robbed it once before. The minute the two men entered the store, guns drawn, the manager hung his head.

"Here they are again," he said. Dillinger gave Shaw a look. "You guys have started the company collecting [our cash]," the manager said. "And the collector just left."

There was no money in the registers. Dillinger stalked out of the store. Shaw tarried a moment to scoop up several boxes of cigarettes. The moment Dillinger slipped into the car beside him, Parker gunned the car forward, leaving Shaw behind in the store.

"Stop! Stop!" Dillinger shouted as Parker drove up the block.

Parker hit the brake and drove in reverse toward the store as Shaw, breathing heavily, ran up the street to meet them before jumping in. Parker was so rattled he ran the next stop sign. "If you can't drive," Dillinger said, "let the kid have the wheel!" The men drove on, aiming for Dillinger's father's farmhouse.

So began the criminal career of the man who would within months transform the FBI.

Near Wellington, Texas
Saturday, June 10

That same Saturday night, as Dillinger returned to his father's farmhouse, Clyde Barrow and his girlfriend Bonnie Parker were driving through the Texas Panhandle, heading to a meeting with Clyde's brother Buck at a bridge on the Oklahoma border. With them was Clyde's gofer, a pimply Dallas teenager named W. D. Jones. At first glance all three appeared to be children. Clyde, baby-faced and five-feet-seven, was twenty-three that evening. Bonnie was an inch under five feet, maybe ninety pounds, with yellow hair and baby-blue eyes. She was twenty-one.

Seventy years after their deaths, no Depression-era criminals loom larger in America's consciousness than Bonnie and Clyde—thanks to the 1967 film *Bonnie and Clyde,* which portrayed Clyde as a sexually ambivalent man-child struggling to cope with a beautiful, fiery Bonnie. While entertaining, the cinematic Bonnie and Clyde were a screenwriter's creation, a celluloid paean to 1960s-era themes of youth rebellion and antiauthoritarianism. The movie characters had little in common with their real-life counterparts, lazy drifters who murdered nearly a dozen innocent men during and between holdups.

The real Clyde Barrow and Bonnie Parker were neither rebels nor philosophers. Vain and insecure, Clyde was a preening Dallas burglar who, a friend claimed, had been repeatedly raped in prison and would do anything to avoid going back. Bonnie was a bored waitress, a drama queen with a failed marriage who viewed Clyde as a ticket out of her humdrum existence. Crime was a kind of game to them; you can see it in the photographs they took of each other, play-acting with big guns and fat cigars. Contemporaries showed them little but contempt. One called them "just a couple of cheap filling station and car thieves," and he was right; at a time when veteran yeggs reaped $50,000 from a single bank robbery, Bonnie and Clyde's biggest payday was barely $3,800. They robbed far more gas stations and drugstores than banks.

They came from Dallas. Both the Barrow family, subsistence farmers from south of the city, and Bonnie's mother, a West Texas widow, had joined the rising tide of rural families moving into Southwestern cities in the early 1920s. The Barrows were so poor they lived for a time beneath a viaduct. In time Clyde's father started a scrap metal business and built a house in a poor, unincorporated area known as the Bog, just across the Trinity River from downtown. Subject to flooding, crisscrossed by railroads, its air and water polluted by cement plants and foundries, the Bog was a dusty latticework of bleak houses and lean-tos, unpaved roads and littered yards.

Dropping out of school at sixteen, Clyde became a teenage burglar, joining his older brother Ivan, known as Buck, sneaking into stores at night. The boys were a study in contrasts. Where Buck was a lethargic, monosyllabic figure who talked little and drank lots, Clyde was small, peppy, and bright, a fast talker with rosy cheeks who loved guns and played the guitar and the saxophone. In later years Dallas lawmen would remember stopping the brothers for stealing scrap metal, no doubt to help their father. According to Clyde's sister Nell, their first arrests came after they stole a flock of turkeys from an East Texas farm; stopped by police in a truck full of hot poultry, Buck drew a few days in jail and Clyde was released.

For a time Clyde tried a series of menial jobs: messenger boy, movie usher, mirror factory worker. None lasted. By eighteen he evidenced the first signs of a powerful ego, a sense that he was entitled to something better than life in the Bog. In a telling stab at reinvention, he changed his middle name from Chestnut to Champion, hoping that "Clyde Champion Barrow" might elevate him to the status that he believed he deserved. It didn't: he was still a two-bit burglar. He spent 1928 and 1929 ransacking stores throughout North Texas with Buck, until Buck was captured one night after a foot chase in the town of Denton.

Clyde met Bonnie Parker one night in January 1930, when he showed up at a west Dallas home where she was babysitting. A temperamental girl with a histrionic bent, Bonnie married a teenage layabout and had fallen into a depression following the breakup of their marriage. She was an avid reader of detective and movie magazines, and her diary entries portray a young woman desperate to break out of a routine of waitressing and babysitting. "Blue as usual," she wrote one night in 1928. "Not a darn thing to do. Don't know a darn thing." And the day after that: "Haven't been anywhere this week. Why don't something happen?"[1]

The attraction between Bonnie and Clyde was immediate, but the romance was short-lived. Several nights later Dallas police arrested Clyde for burglary. When the charges fell through, he was transferred to Waco to face another set of charges. Bonnie, who was obsessed with Clyde and his exciting adventures with the law, moved into a cousin's home in Waco. When another inmate told Clyde he had a gun at his home, Clyde persuaded Bonnie to smuggle it into the jail. Clyde and two other men used the pistol a few days later to make their escape. They lit out north, crossing Oklahoma into Missouri and driving on into Indiana, stealing cars and burglarizing stores. Police finally caught up with them in Middletown, Ohio, taking Clyde into custody following a car chase. He was returned to Waco, where a judge gave him a fourteen-year sentence in the brutal state prison at Huntsville.

He served barely two years. After bombarding Clyde with teary letters for months, Bonnie finally began dating other men, but when Clyde was released in February 1932, they were immediately reunited. Clyde avoided crime for a time, taking a construction job in Massachusetts that his sister arranged. But, complaining of loneliness, he soon returned to the Bog and began hanging around the service station his father had opened on its main thoroughfare, Eagle Ford Road. Within days he was rousted by Fort Worth police, arrested, then released. He returned home incensed. "Mama, I'm never gonna work again," Clyde told his mother. "And I'll never [be arrested] again, either. I'm not ever going back to that [prison] hell hole. I'll die first. I swear it, they're gonna have to kill me."[2]

The arrest appears to have deepened Clyde's sense of persecution and victimization. Crime was the only avenue open to him, he rationalized; police had given him no choice. He and several partners returned to burglarizing stores. As she did throughout Clyde's career, Bonnie took no part in these crimes, though occasionally she sat in the getaway car. On one such excursion in the town of Kaufman, Texas, Clyde was surprised by a night watchman and forced to flee; when their getaway car stalled on a muddy road, he and Bonnie stole a mule and set off cross-country. Cornered by a posse the next morning, Bonnie was arrested. Clyde got away. Bonnie languished in jail for three months before being released in July 1932. Clyde's crimes grew more violent in her absence. He murdered a storekeeper in Hillsboro, Texas, and, after Bonnie was freed, killed a sheriff in Oklahoma.

The moment Bonnie and Clyde became "Bonnie and Clyde" came on a Saturday evening, August 6, 1932, when Clyde's partner, Raymond Hamilton, spirited Bonnie away from her mother's side to Clyde's side, where she remained for the rest of her life. The couple commenced a routine they would follow for two years, disappearing for a few weeks, sometimes months, then slipping back to Dallas for clandestine family reunions. These rendezvous, at out-of-the-way roadsides near Dallas, followed a pattern. Clyde and Bonnie announced their return by tossing a bottle onto a family member's porch, sometimes with a note inside. Word passed among family members in code; for the Barrows, the mention of "cooking red beans" meant a meeting was at hand. The families drove to the meeting point at dusk, spread blankets on the grass, and listened as Bonnie and Clyde rambled on about their latest adventures.

Their wanderings had no aim or focus. Clyde simply drove from state to state, robbing a gas station or drugstore or sometimes a bank when they ran low on cash. It makes their story a jerky, alinear narrative, a string of scattered episodes with no discernible arc. But that's the way they lived, ricocheting across an area loosely defined by Minnesota, Mississippi, Colorado, and New Mexico, rarely staying in one place long. Unlike Dillinger and Pretty Boy Floyd, Clyde and Bonnie made no effort to establish a permanent base until the last weeks of their lives; for months the closest they came to a home was an abandoned barn outside the Dallas suburb of Grand Prairie. As their notoriety grew, they would resort to living out of their car, which was littered with guns, license plates, and food wrappers. They gave up bathing and normal hygiene. Their clothes were dirty. They smelled.

Clyde clearly aspired to be a bank robber, but his first attempts were humiliating. On November 30, 1932, he and a partner entered the bank at Orinogo, Missouri, north of Joplin. A gunfight ensued, during which Clyde's partner managed to scoop up some loose bills. He and Clyde scrambled to the getaway car and avoided a desultory pursuit. The take came to $80.* All that winter Bonnie and Clyde continued their murderous travels, killing a man in Temple, Texas, who tried to stop them from stealing his car on Christmas Day, murdering a Dallas detective who surprised Clyde one night in the Bog, taking a motorcycle cop hostage in Springfield, Missouri, when he stopped Clyde for speeding. Their notoriety, however, was limited to Dallas, where their crimes were front-page news. Outside Texas they remained all but unknown.

In March 1933 Clyde's brother Buck was paroled from prison and, accompanied by Buck's wife, Blanche, the brothers reunited in Joplin, where they rented a garage apartment and set to burglarizing jewelry stores. On April 13 a group of Joplin lawmen arrived at the apartment, responding to a call from a suspicious neighbor. Clyde and Buck surprised them, murdering two officers before speeding away untouched. The Joplin killings thrust the "Barrow Gang" onto front pages outside Texas for the first time. The discovery of Bonnie's poetry and photos of Bonnie and Clyde posing with guns and cigars made Bonnie a public figure, though her real fame would be posthumous.

Two weeks later the two couples, accompanied by the teenage W. D. Jones, drove through the northern Louisiana town of Ruston, looking for a bank to rob. When W.D. stole a car, its owner, a local undertaker, and his girlfriend gave chase, forcing Clyde to take them hostage. After an all-day drive (which later served as a memorable scene in the 1967 movie), Clyde let the couple go. In the confusion, the homesick W.D. disappeared. Clyde and Bonnie finally found him on a Dallas roadside on Friday, June 9. That night the three drove to the Panhandle, heading toward a rendezvous with Buck and Blanche Barrow.

---

* Nell Barrow said Clyde had later attempted to rob another Missouri bank by himself but failed. The bank had been closed for weeks.

. . .

That Saturday night, Clyde was driving east on Texas Highway 203, a dirt grade rarely maintained by state construction crews. Six miles east of the hamlet of Quail, the bridge over the Salt Fork of the Red River had been destroyed. In the darkness Clyde passed the fallen danger sign at over seventy miles an hour. He didn't see the ravine until it was too late. With no warning at all, the big Ford was suddenly airborne. It soared down the slope, rolled twice, and crashed into the sandy soil beside the shrunken river. For a moment, everything was still. Steam rose from the ruined car. Gasoline began to seep into the sand. Clyde, thrown from the wreck but unhurt, was the first to come to his senses. He pulled himself to his feet and smelled the gasoline. He realized the car could explode.

Just then two farmers, Steve Pritchard and Lonzo Cartwright, scuttled down the slope. They had seen the wreck from Pritchard's porch above the river. Together they pulled W.D. from the backseat, groggy but unhurt. Pritchard noticed the guns and glanced at Cartwright, wondering what they had gotten themselves into. Bonnie, unconscious, was stuck in the front seat, her leg trapped by the crushed car door.

Suddenly, with an audible whoosh, the gasoline caught fire. Flames leaped all around the car and began to lap at Bonnie's legs. She woke and began screaming. Together Clyde and the two farmers tried to pry her from the seat while W.D. gathered the guns and tossed handfuls of sand onto the fire. As they worked the flames grew higher, engulfing Bonnie's legs, then licking at her head and shoulders. Her stockings began melting into her legs. Panicking, she screamed for Clyde to kill her. Clyde, ignoring the flames, wrapped his arms around Bonnie and, with the farmers' help, finally managed to pull her free.

Her legs were badly burned. Clyde carried her up the slope to Pritchard's ramshackle farmhouse, where his parents and Cartwright's wife, Gladys, stood watching. Inside, Clyde laid Bonnie on a bed as the elderly Mrs. Pritchard inspected the burns. Bonnie's entire leg, from ankle to hip, had been burned black, exposing the bone in several places. Her face and arms were blistered. "She needs a doctor," Mrs. Pritchard said, quickly applying a salve to Bonnie's wounds.

"No," Clyde and Bonnie said in unison. "We can't afford that," Clyde went on. "Try and do what you can."

Clyde stepped out onto the front porch and conferred with W.D., then ran back down to the car to retrieve their guns. The Pritchards milled about nervously, unsure what to do. Lonzo Cartwright didn't know who these people were, but he was certain they were outlaws of some kind. When W.D. wasn't looking, Cartwright slipped out the backdoor and ran across the fields toward a neighbor's house, intending to call the police. "Where'd the other guy go?" W.D. asked after a moment.

"I don't know," Pritchard said. "He's probably out back."

Just then Clyde hurried up to the house, carrying a canvas bag full of guns. He, too, noticed Cartwright's absence. "I could kick your butt for letting that guy leave," he snapped at W.D. "Now keep an eye on these people." W.D. pointed the shotgun at the Pritchards while Clyde knelt beside Bonnie and smoothed her hair. "Honey, I don't know what to do about moving you," he said.

"I can travel," Bonnie murmured. "It'll hurt for sure. But we can't stay here."

A few minutes later, headlights flashed through the woods in front of the house. "Everybody get on the floor," Clyde ordered. He and W.D. skipped outside and disappeared into the bushes.

A car drove up to the house. Into the night air stepped the Collingsworth County Sheriff, George Corry. With him was Tom Hardy, the Wellington town marshal. Lonzo Cartwright had driven to the jail and told them of the scene at the house. The two lawmen figured they had a trio of drunken teenagers to deal with.

Clyde stepped from behind the bushes, his Browning automatic rifle trained on the two lawmen. "Raise your hands," he shouted. He and W.D. disarmed the two men and used their handcuffs to bind them together. As they did, W.D. noticed a movement inside the house. Glancing through a kitchen window, he saw Gladys Cartwright, her four-month-old son on her hip, reaching for the backdoor. Thinking she was trying to escape, he fired his shotgun, hitting her in the hand.

As her family rushed to apply bandages to the wound—Mrs. Cartwright's thumb would later be amputated—W.D. stalked back to the car. "Let's get out of here," he said. He glanced over at an old car in the weeds and proceeded to shoot out all four of its tires. Clyde walked into the farmhouse and returned to the patrol car with Bonnie in his arms. He carefully laid her on the backseat. He and W.D. shoved the officers in beside her and without another word drove off.

They drove through the Texas darkness in silence, the only sounds Bonnie's moans from the backseat. Clyde glanced in the rearview mirror and was pleased to see the marshal, Tom Hardy, stroking her hair, trying to comfort her. After a while she seemed to stabilize. Clyde lightened up and began talking. "Did you coppers ever hear much about the two Barrow brothers?" he asked at one point.

"No, I can't say that I have," Hardy answered, not wanting to anger Clyde. "We have no record of them in the office," Corry added.

"Don't you mugs ever read the papers?" Bonnie whispered.

At a bridge six miles west of the town of Sayre, Clyde stopped and honked the horn. "Everybody out of the car," W.D. ordered. The officers lined up against a bridge rail. Clyde covered the men while W.D. walked to the far end of the bridge and talked to someone in a car parked in the shadows. By and by he returned with the lethargic Buck Barrow at his side. "When do we get going?" Buck asked.

"What we gonna do with these coppers?" W.D. asked.

Clyde thought a moment. "Let's march 'em down the river a piece and tie 'em up." Buck and Clyde herded the two lawmen down toward the river. At the water's edge Clyde ordered them to stop.

"What would you do if we turned you loose?" he asked.

Hardy said they would head straight home. He tried to look brave. He would not beg for his life.

"Yeah, I know," Clyde said, his voice heavy and tired. "You'd run your legs off getting to a phone."

"What're you gonna do with 'em?" Buck asked. "Want 'em tended to?" He raised his rifle.

Clyde pondered the two men. "You get a bunch of wire off that fence," he told Buck, motioning toward a string of barbed wire. "Yeah, they've been pretty decent cops. But I've said I'd never take a cop for a ride and let him live to squeal his head off."

Buck brought the barbed wire, and together they tied the men to a tree. They stood before the two lawmen a minute, then started back up the slope. After a moment Buck stopped and turned, his rifle pointed at Hardy. There was a long moment of silence.

"Come on," Clyde finally said. "Let's get going."

They let the men live.

Clyde's elusiveness always owed more to his skill with cars than with guns; he thought nothing of driving a thousand miles in a day, if that's what it took to outdistance the law. That night he drove the length of Oklahoma, reaching Arkansas around dawn. Bonnie deteriorated, pitching and moaning in her sleep. Just after sunrise they pulled up at the Twin Cities Tourist Camp in Fort Smith. After Blanche registered, Clyde carried Bonnie to a bed. She whimpered for her mother. Clyde drove into town alone and found a doctor named Walter Eberle. He told Eberle that his wife had been injured by an exploding oil stove, and the doctor followed Clyde back to the motel. "This woman needs to be hospitalized," Eberle said after dressing Bonnie's burns.

At wit's end, Clyde drove back to Dallas to get Bonnie's sister Billie. He reached the Parker home early that evening. Both Mrs. Parker and Mrs. Barrow offered to come to Fort Smith, but Clyde waited instead for Billie, who was at the movies. Clyde paced the Parkers' living room anxiously, at one point breaking into tears. He hadn't slept in two days, and the strain was showing. Finally Billie returned and after packing some clothes, left with Clyde.

Ted Hinton, a deputy sheriff who knew Clyde, was on night patrol when he spotted the car heading east. He hesitated because he didn't recognize Billie. By the time he turned to follow, Clyde was gone. Driving fast through the East Texas night, he and Billie reached Fort Smith at dawn to find Bonnie on the verge of death.

Minneapolis, Minnesota
Thursday, June 15
12:45 P.M.

Five days later, as Clyde hovered over Bonnie's deathbed in Arkansas, the familiar smell of fresh hops and barley hung thick outside Hamm's Brewery, which rose from the streets of Minneapolis like some medieval European castle. Festooned with flags, its eight-story brick facade had been constructed in the 1840s by a German immigrant named Theodore Hamm. The family's Tudor mansion loomed on a steep hill above.

On the street outside the brewery, a twenty-four-year-old man in a chauffeur's cap sat in a black Ford sedan, watching the scene with expressionless eyes. His name was Alvin Karpis, though everyone called him by his alias, "Ray." Cold, aloof, a ringer for Boris Karloff, Karpis had a frosty demeanor, which earned him the nickname "Old Creepy." He was the brains behind the unsung villains of Depression-era crime, the Barker

Gang, or as Karpis liked to call it, the Barker-Karpis Gang. His partners, the diminutive brothers Fred and Arthur "Dock" Barker, were from Tulsa. Fred was twenty-nine, five-feet-four, lean, feral, and menacing, with three gold teeth and greasy black hair cut high above his ears. His older brother Dock was a borderline moron with three facial moles, an unreliable drunk just six months out of the Oklahoma state prison.

When it was over, J. Edgar Hoover would label the Barkers the "brainiest and most dangerous" gang of the War on Crime. During their lives, however, they received a fraction of the publicity afforded the likes of John Dillinger. Yet the scale and ambition of the Barker-Karpis Gang's crimes dwarfed those of their peers, and their ability to strike alliances with Northern crime syndicates—no small achievement for what was essentially a pack of murderous hillbillies—would make them the most difficult of the FBI's public enemies to defeat.

Seventy years after their heyday, all that remains of the gang's legacy is the FBI-sponsored myth of Kate "Ma" Barker, Fred and Dock's sixty-something mother, who in a blaze of posthumous notoriety was portrayed as the murderous, machine gun–wielding brains of the gang. "The most vicious, dangerous, and resourceful criminal brain this country has produced in many years belonged to a person called 'Mother Barker,'" Hoover wrote in 1938. "In her sixty years or so this woman reared a spawn of hell . . . To her [her sons] looked for guidance, for daring, resourcefulness. They obeyed her implicitly."

It is a characterization advanced by otherwise credible books, notably John Toland's 1963 *Dillinger Days,* as well as by B-movies like Roger Corman's *Bloody Mama.* Yet there is no evidence whatsoever to support the myth of Ma Barker's criminal genius. According to FBI files and those few who lived to tell of her, Ma Barker wasn't even a criminal, let alone a mastermind. There's no evidence she ever robbed a bank or fired a gun. She was never arrested. Hoover's portrayal of her as "the most feared woman in American crime" is baseless. During her life, Ma Barker was unknown; no one outside the gang knew who she was.

Short and plump, with stringy black hair she styled into comical piles of curls on special occasions, Arizona Donnie Barker was a frowsy hillbilly woman whose only interest, aside from doing jigsaw puzzles and listening to *Amos 'n' Andy,* was the welfare of her sons. She knew of their crimes and lived on their ill-gotten income, but the idea that she was the leader of the gang was "the most ridiculous story in the annals of crime," Karpis once said. One of the gang's mentors, the Jazz Age yegg Harvey Bailey, scoffed at the idea that Ma planned their exploits. "The old woman couldn't plan breakfast," Bailey once said.

Ma Barker was born in Ash Grove, Missouri, outside Springfield, probably in 1873. By the time she and her husband moved to Tulsa around 1910, they had four sons, all of whom would become criminals. The eldest, Herman, was a stickup man who wandered the West robbing stores before shooting himself in the head after police cornered him in a vacant lot in Wichita, Kansas, in 1927. The second son, Lloyd, had his career in crime cut short by a twenty-five-year sentence in Leavenworth for robbing a mail truck in 1921. Raised in Tulsa, their younger brothers, Fred and Dock, fell in with a rowdy group of teenage burglars and car thieves known as the Central Park Gang, several of whom would join the Barker-Karpis Gang fifteen years later. In later years the FBI characterized the Central Park Gang as a "school" of crime taught by Ma Barker. There's no evidence to back up this assertion. Ma's role, such as it was, was to hector policemen and prosecutors who detained her boys.

They kept her busy. A car thief turned cat burglar, Dock drew a life sentence in an Oklahoma penitentiary after shooting a night watchman in 1922. Freddie, meanwhile, was arrested for burglary in Kansas and thrown into a reformatory. There he met Karpis, the son of Lithuanian immigrants, who had grown up in the streets of Wichita before graduating to a life of petty crime. In the spring of 1931, the two were released separately, and Karpis went to Tulsa to find Freddie. He never forgot his first encounter with Ma Barker, at her shack in a trash-strewn lot beside a set of railroad tracks.

"As I approached, I saw this little dumpy old woman standing on a box, wearing a pair of bib overalls over a man's sweater," Karpis remembered years later. She was trying to fix a window screen. He introduced himself and she invited him inside. Karpis was appalled. There was no electricity, no running water. In the backyard was an outhouse. Flies buzzed everywhere. Ma volunteered to send a telegram to Fred in Joplin, and in the ensuing days she and Karpis became friends. In time she all but adopted him. Fred said she preferred Karpis to her own sons. "You don't get on her nerves the way I do," her son said.[3]

Barker and Karpis began pulling nighttime burglaries around Tulsa. Before long both were arrested. Karpis was released, but Barker was detained and forced to escape. Fleeing the authorities, they took Ma and her boyfriend, an old drunk named Albert Dunlop, to southern Missouri, where they robbed their first bank and used the proceeds to buy Ma a farm. All went well until the week before Christmas, 1931, when the sheriff in the town of West Plains approached them at a gas station for questioning. Karpis panicked and shot the sheriff dead.

They fled one step ahead of a posse, grabbing Ma and racing to the home of a Barker family friend, a worldly confidence man named Herbert "Deafy" Farmer, who operated a kind of safe house for outlaws from across the region at his farm five miles south of Joplin. It was Farmer who suggested that Karpis and Barker take refuge in St. Paul, Minnesota, whose corrupt police force had transformed the quiet river city into the crime capital of the Midwest. And so a few days after Christmas, the two aspiring bank men walked into St. Paul's Green Lantern tavern—and entered the major leagues of Midwestern crime.

The Green Lantern, run by a roly-poly Orthodox Jew named Harry Sawyer, was St. Paul's criminal headquarters, a clubhouse that drew every major bank man in the Midwest. The Jazz Age yeggs Harvey Bailey and Frank Nash were regulars, as were vacationing gunmen from Chicago and scores of wannabes, including George Barnes, later known as Machine Gun Kelly. Karpis was dazzled. He and Freddie moved Ma and Albert Dunlop into a house on the south side and went to work guarding cigarette shipments and pulling burglaries. In March 1932 they were invited on their first major bank job, in downtown Minneapolis.

Just days afterward, their landlady's son saw their pictures in a detective magazine. The corrupt detectives who took the call delayed long enough for everyone to get away, but Karpis and Barker blamed the drunken Albert Dunlop for their exposure, dragged him to a lake outside town, and shot him dead. Relocating to Kansas City, they robbed a bank that June in Fort Scott, Kansas, alongside Harvey Bailey. When Bailey was subsequently arrested, they struck out on their own, robbing a series of banks across the Upper Midwest. By autumn Fred had enough money to bribe his brother Dock and one of Dock's Tulsa friends, Volney Davis, out of prison.* Dock and Davis became the gang's newest members.

---

* Crime historians have long speculated that bribery was behind Dock Barker's release. According to FBI files, it was. In 1934 an FBI agent interviewed Jack Glynn, a private detective in Leavenworth, Kansas. A local fixer who specialized in securing paroles for federal prisoners, Glynn admitted he had been approached by Freddie's friend Jess Doyle, who wanted to know how much it would cost to get Dock

Drawing from the most desperate of the St. Paul yeggs, the Barker-Karpis Gang had few qualms about gunplay. In a robbery that December, they machine-gunned two Minneapolis cops; when they stopped to change cars during the getaway, a bystander glanced at Fred Barker a moment too long and Fred shot him dead. After a winter vacation in Reno, where Karpis befriended a gangland chauffeur named Jimmy Burnell, whom he would later introduce around St. Paul, the gang robbed a Nebraska bank in a hail of gunfire. One gang member was killed, and Karpis began thinking of safer ways to make money. It made him open to the idea of the kidnapping that Harry Sawyer brought to him that spring.

As Karpis watched, William Hamm, the brewery's thirty-eight-year-old chairman, stepped out a backdoor into the noon sun. Turning left, he began walking up the hill toward the mansion for lunch. Across the way, Dock Barker raised his arm, giving the signal. As Hamm stepped onto the sidewalk, another gang member, Charley Fitzgerald, wearing a homburg and a dark suit, walked up to him and offered his right hand.

"You are Mr. Hamm, are you not?" he asked.

"Yes," Hamm said, shaking the stranger's hand. Suddenly Fitzgerald tightened his grip, put his left hand onto Hamm's elbow, and guided him toward the curb. At that point Dock ran up, taking Hamm's other elbow. "What is it you want?" Hamm asked, confused.

Just then Karpis pulled the Hudson up to the curb, and Hamm was shoved into the backseat. Dock Barker followed, slipped a pillowcase over Hamm's head, and pushed him down onto the floorboards.

"I don't like to do this," Fitzgerald said to Hamm. "But I'm going to have to ask you to get down on the floor because I don't want you to see where you're going. I hope you don't mind."

They drove east. Thirty miles outside of St. Paul, the car pulled along-

---

Barker out of prison. They met at Leavenworth's National Hotel. Glynn said it would cost between $150 and $300 to get Barker out of prison. Doyle gave him $200 and told him to try. Glynn visited Barker in prison, and on the way out asked a guard the best way to "spring" him. The guard suggested he contact a state senator named Pres Lester. Lester was an old Okie pol; as the senator for McAlester's district, he had tremendous pull at the prison.

According to Glynn, Lester said $200 would get Barker paroled. Glynn deposited the money in a McAlester bank, payable to Lester. It worked so well Glynn tried it again a month later to free Dock Barker's old friend Volney Davis. With a bribe paid to Pres Lester, Davis too was furloughed.

side a Chevrolet. Inside sat Freddie and a smooth Chicago gangster named "Shotgun George Ziegler" (whose real name was Fred Goetz), who had been brought in with his partner Bryan Bolton to help on the job.* Ziegler shoved a typewritten ransom note into Hamm's hands. "I guess you know what this is all about," he said. "Sign these papers and sign them quick."

Hamm, on his knees, did as he was told. "Who do you want as a contact man?" Ziegler asked.

Hamm named William Dunn, the brewery's vice president of sales.

Karpis suppressed a smile. It was exactly what they wanted him to say. Billy Dunn was a bagman for the St. Paul mob, a friend of Harry Sawyer's, and a man the gang members knew they could count on.

At 2:40 that afternoon, Billy Dunn was sitting in his office at the brewery when his phone rang.

"Is this W. W. Dunn?" a voice asked. It was Karpis.

"Yes, sir."

"I want to talk to you and I don't want you to say anything until I get all through. We have Mr. Hamm. We want you to get one hundred thousand dollars in twenties, tens, and fives."

---

* Seldom did the worlds of syndicate hit men and rural bank robbers like the Barkers cross, but in Ziegler they did. A rarity among Capone's gunmen, Ziegler moonlighted as a bank robber, driving out from Chicago to hit banks in rural Illinois and Wisconsin. His claim to fame, however, was the St. Valentine's Day Massacre of 1929, in which he was believed to have been one of the gangsters dressed as policemen who machine-gunned seven associates of gang boss Bugs Moran in a North Side garage. The identities of the shooters have never been proven, but the FBI and Ziegler's friends believed the story.

No one knew how Ziegler entered Capone's orbit. He had been a varsity football player at the University of Illinois and served as a second lieutenant during World War I. But in 1925, while working as a lifeguard on a Chicago beach, he had been arrested for attempting to rape a seven-year-old girl. He jumped bail and soon surfaced as a creative hit man for the Capone mob. Among Ziegler's inventions, it was said, was a time bomb with leather straps that could be tied to a kidnapping victim; it did wonders for extorting money from the target. Ziegler was known for his unfailing courtesy to strangers. "His character was one of infinite contradictions," one FBI agent wrote. "Well mannered, always polite, he was capable of generous kindness and conscienceless cruelty."

Ziegler's partner, Bryan Bolton, was a weak link, and everyone except Ziegler knew it. At forty Bolton had worked as a carpenter, a car salesman and a golf pro before emerging as a driver for another of the St. Valentine's shooters, "Killer" Fred Burke. Bolton too, the FBI later learned, played a role in the massacre. It was Bolton, two sources told the Bureau, who as a lookout that day in 1929 had given Capone's gunmen the premature go-ahead to begin shooting, a mistake that allowed Bugs Moran himself to escape. Irate, Capone was said to have ordered Bolton's execution, a fate he avoided only after Ziegler's intervention. Bolton's loyalty to Ziegler was unquestioned.

Dunn would later say he thought someone was playing a joke on him. "Hey, hey, what the hell is going on here?" he said.

"Now shut up and listen to what I have to say," Karpis went on. He gave Dunn instructions on how the ransom should be delivered. "If you tell a soul about this," Karpis said, "it'll be just too bad for Hamm—and you."

Dunn started to ask how he could raise $100,000, but before he could spit out the thought, the line went dead. He phoned Hamm's office and the family mansion; Hamm was nowhere to be found. Dunn began calling Hamm's brothers. Around five they met Dunn at the mansion to break the news to their elderly mother. Mrs. Hamm insisted on bringing in the police. A meeting was arranged at the Lowry Hotel. There Dunn briefed St. Paul's police chief, Thomas Dahill, an honest man who was frustrated by the corruption on his force.

Dahill contacted the head of the local FBI office, Werner Hanni, who sent a man to Dunn's home at 1916 Summit Avenue to install a recording device on his telephone in preparation for the kidnappers' next call. Two members of the St. Paul Police Department's new kidnap squad were summoned as well. One was Tom Brown, a former St. Paul chief of police whom the gang was paying for inside information.*

As the police and FBI gathered at Dunn's home, William Hamm was driven across Wisconsin into northern Illinois. Karpis did the driving; Fred Barker and Shotgun George Ziegler stayed behind to deal with the ransom negotiations. Around midnight Karpis pulled up beside a two-story house in the northwest Chicago suburb of Bensonville. It was owned by the local postmaster, a friend of Ziegler's. They guided Hamm into a bedroom whose window had been boarded shut. Karpis gave him some magazines and a beer, and left him alone. Hamm sat, stared, and waited.

---

* For decades St. Paul historians have debated what role, if any, six-foot-three-inch, 280-pound "Big Tom" Brown played in the Hamm kidnapping. There were always rumors, but not until FBI files were opened in the late 1980s would the extent of his involvement become clear. According to FBI files, the forty-four-year-old Brown agreed to keep the gang fully updated on what police were doing. In return he was to receive a full quarter of the $100,000 ransom, a cut three times larger than any of the actual kidnappers. The files even raise the possibility that it was Brown who initiated the scheme.

Midnight

Billy Dunn was waiting in his home when the phone rang. "Well, Dunn, you're following instructions very well so far," a voice said. "Now, I have given you time to recover from the shock of the telephone call this afternoon and you must realize that the call was not a joke as you thought. All you've got to do is follow instructions."

Dunn was struck by the caller's tone; it intimated that he knew precisely what Dunn had been doing all day and didn't appear upset that the police had been brought in. Dunn phoned Tom Brown, who had run home for a late dinner. Around two, as Brown returned, he saw a taxi cruising by, throwing a spotlight on the quiet homes, obviously looking for an address. Brown walked up to the taxi, and the cabbie gave him a note for Dunn. He said a man—later identified as Shotgun George Ziegler—had handed it to him outside of a downtown garage. *You know your boyfriend is out of circulation,* the note read. *You are to pay off $100,000 in the manner explained to you this afternoon . . . If you fail to comply with our demands, you will never see Hamm Jr. again.*

Brown took the note inside to Dunn. Everything was on schedule.

Near Boliver, Missouri
Friday, June 16
Dawn

The next morning, Pretty Boy Floyd and his sidekick Adam Richetti said good-bye to their family and friends and headed to Kansas City. At dawn, they were driving north on Highway 16, a rough road heading out of Springfield, Missouri, when the Pontiac they had stolen from Joe Hudiberg's garage coughed, sputtered, and died. Irritated, Floyd flagged down a passing farmer, who agreed to tow them into nearby Boliver, where, as it happened, Richetti's brother Joe worked as a mechanic. The two men piled into the farmer's truck and thanked him for his trouble.

The drowsy town was still slumbering that morning when the farmer's truck pulled into the driveway of the Bitzer Chevrolet dealership about ten minutes past seven. Floyd gave the old man a few bills and watched as a group of mechanics pushed the Pontiac into the garage. There was nothing to do but wait, so Floyd paced the garage as Joe Richetti opened the hood. Adam unscrewed a Mason jar of moonshine and began drinking. Floyd eyed him with disgust. He had repeatedly warned Richetti to watch his drinking. It made him sloppy.

Before long a group of car salesmen, freshly scrubbed in saddle shoes and khaki suits, gathered to admire Floyd's big new Pontiac. No one appeared to recognize Floyd. Around eleven, as Joe Richetti continued working on the car, Ernest Bitzer, the dealership's owner, wandered in, sat on a bench beside Floyd, and shook his hand. "That car looks as if it could go pretty fast," Bitzer remarked.

"It'll hit eighty-five," said Floyd.

It took Bitzer a moment, but this was a face he had seen in the newspapers—and then he realized who his customer was. Before Bitzer could do anything, another man entered the garage. "Looks like it's been traveling pretty fast," said the man, motioning toward the Pontiac. Floyd looked up at the stranger. It was the new county sheriff, Jack Killingsworth. A former Bitzer salesman in his sixth month as Polk County Sheriff, Killingsworth often dropped by his old dealership for coffee. That morning he was wearing neither uniform, badge, nor gun. As Killingsworth's eyes fixed on Floyd's face, he recognized him from the Wanted posters in his office.

But Adam Richetti recognized Killingsworth, too, from trips to Boliver to visit his brother. He stepped to the Pontiac, opened the backdoor, and grabbed a submachine gun hidden under a blanket. He whipped out the gun and trained it on Killingsworth. "That's the law!" Richetti barked to Floyd. To the half-dozen salesmen and mechanics milling about in the garage, Richetti shouted, "Line up against the wall! If you try to get away, we will kill you!"

Joe Richetti stepped in front of Killingsworth as his brother turned the machine gun toward the sheriff. "If you're going to shoot the sheriff, you'll have to shoot me first," he said.

Adam, who had now been swilling moonshine for three hours, appeared confused. "All right, get him out of here, then," he said, motioning to the sheriff. Killingsworth walked toward the garage door, Richetti poking the machine gun in his back. Killingsworth reached the door, opened it, and then felt the cold touch of a pistol against his temple. "Take one more step and I'll kill you," said Floyd.

Inexplicably, Richetti began cursing at the sheriff, urging him out the door. Floyd cut him off. "That liquor is getting the best of you," he snapped. Floyd maneuvered the sheriff inside, where he joined the employees against the garage wall. Floyd apologized. "This is life and death for us. We had to do [this]."

Floyd had to move fast before the situation spun out of control. While Richetti covered the hostages, he stuck his head out of the garage door. There were no signs of additional lawmen or alarm. Stepping back inside, Floyd covered the hostages while Richetti stepped to his brother Joe's new Chevrolet sedan. Inside, Floyd motioned for Killingsworth to come with him.

"Why take me?" the sheriff asked.

"You know all the roads and can keep me off the highways," Floyd said.

The two outlaws, assuming a posse would soon be on their tails, loaded their guns into the Chevrolet. Floyd and Killingsworth slipped into the backseat while Richetti slid behind the wheel. As they drove off, Floyd hollered out the window to Richetti's brother: "You can have my car, Joe!"

Richetti steered the sedan west, streaking out of town. "You know the roads," he yelled at Killingsworth. "Get us out of here!"

"Where do you want to go?" the sheriff asked.

"Kansas City."

Hot Springs, Arkansas
11:30 A.M.

That same Friday morning, as Pretty Boy Floyd raced toward Kansas City, two agents of the Bureau of Investigation cruised the downtown streets of Hot Springs, Arkansas, looking for a fugitive. The Roman-nosed agent behind the wheel was Joe Lackey; beside him sat a white-haired, grandfatherly Cowboy named Frank Smith, a former Dallas police officer. They had driven from their office in Oklahoma City to check a tip that the old yegg Frank Nash was in town. The information was dead-on: though close to Karpis and the Barkers, Nash had chosen an Arkansas vacation over a role in the Hamm kidnapping.

In the summer of 1933, Hot Springs was a corrupt resort town famed for the red carpet it rolled out for vacationing gangsters who came from across the country to enjoy its mineral baths and freewheeling casinos: Al Capone and a long line of New York crime lords were among its infamous guests. The town's main thoroughfare, Central Avenue, cut between two wooded hills. On one side stretched seven ornate bathhouses. On the other were a line of pool halls and taverns that ended at two casinos, the Belvedere and the Southern Club. Brothels and cabarets dotted the surrounding houses. It was all illegal, but everyone, from the governor of

Arkansas on down, looked the other way. The mayor and the local police ran it all like a corporation, taking their cut from every whore, blackjack dealer, and pool shark.

Agent Lackey slowed the car when he spotted Otto Reed on the sidewalk across from the White Front Cigar Store. The two men had brought Reed, police chief in the Oklahoma town of McAlester, because he had followed Nash's career and knew him on sight. Reed leaned down to talk as Lackey pulled to the curb. "That's Nash," Reed said, motioning toward a man standing inside the White Front's door.

"I'm not so sure, Otto," Smith said. "That fella's got a mustache and he's got a full head of hair. Nash is bald."

"He's heavier than the description," Lackey said.

"That's Nash," Reed repeated. "I know him too well."

They decided to take Nash themselves. Reed climbed into the car and Lackey made a U-turn, drawing up to the White Front. The store sold cigars and 3.2 beer up front; in back was a poolroom. Run by a gambler named Dick Galatas, the White Front was a hangout for visiting gangsters. All three men checked their pistols, then stepped out onto the sidewalk. Though carrying guns violated FBI regulations, the Bureau had a "look away" policy for certain veteran agents.

First through the door, Agent Lackey stepped to the counter and asked to buy a cigar. There was no sign of Nash. The others followed. A dozen customers were clustered around a set of café tables; more men appeared to be in back, by the pool tables. Lackey noticed a double-barreled shotgun leaning against a wall. Otto Reed saw it, too.

Just then Nash stepped out of the poolroom, holding a glass of beer. He walked toward the front door as if to leave. Lackey and Smith drew their guns and took a step toward Nash. Reed produced a pistol and pointed it toward the other customers. Everyone froze.

"Frank Nash," Smith announced. "Stick up your hands."

No one identified themselves as FBI; no one said anything about an arrest. Nash didn't recognize Reed; he thought he was being murdered. "Don't shoot," he yelped. He was frisked, then hustled out to the waiting car. Outside, Reed shoved Nash into the front seat then ducked in behind him. Agent Lackey slid behind the wheel and drove east out of town, toward the road to Little Rock.

After a moment, Agent Smith leaned forward, told Nash to raise his hands, and snapped on a pair of handcuffs. He then tugged lightly at Nash's toupee. It came off. "Take it easy with the hairpiece," Nash protested. "It set me back a hundred bucks."

Smith reached for Nash's mustache, but the prisoner raised his hands. "It's mine," he said.

The White Front's owner, Dick Galatas, was inside the café when Nash was taken. The moment the lawmen left, he was on the phone to Herbert "Dutch" Akers, the town's corrupt chief of detectives. Galatas said a Chicago businessman named George Miller had just been kidnapped by three men in a black sedan. "Stop 'em! Now!" he hollered. Akers, who knew Miller's real identity, began phoning nearby police departments.*

Akers's calls produced fast results. Twenty miles east of Hot Springs, at the town of Benton, the FBI agents rounded a turn and were stunned to see a group of armed men lined up across the highway. Agent Lackey had no choice but to stop. A man stepped forward and introduced himself as the local sheriff. He explained he was looking for the kidnappers of a "Mr. Miller," out of Hot Springs. The agents flashed their identification cards and explained who their prisoner was. After a few tense moments, the sheriff waved them on.

Word of the encounter was passed on to Dutch Akers, who relayed it to Galatas. It was a measure of institutionalized corruption's arrogance in America circa 1933 that Galatas, rather than giving up, redoubled his efforts to retrieve Nash from the men he now knew were federal agents. Leaving the White Front, he drove to the Oak Park tourist camp to break the news to Nash's wife, Frances. She grew hysterical, but Galatas told her not to worry; he would take care of everything. Galatas drove Frances and her daughter to the home of a friend. There both Frances and Galatas began working the phones. One of their first calls went to a gangland hangout called the O.P. Inn in Chicago. A bartender promised to make calls on Nash's behalf.

Nash and his captors, meanwhile, sped to Little Rock, covering the fifty-five miles in fifty-eight minutes by Lackey's watch. Another police car pulled them over. Two officers approached the car, and Lackey flashed his

* Akers was to play a recurring role in the War on Crime. Though the identity of the informant who tipped the FBI to Nash's appearance in Hot Springs has never been disclosed, the Bureau's files strongly indicate that it was Akers who later claimed the $500 reward on Nash.

ID and explained who they were. The officers escorted the coupe to the far side of the city, where the two cars parted at the roadside.

"Where ya headed?" one of the lawmen asked.

"Joplin," said Lackey.

Lackey headed northwest up Highway 64. "I sure hope we get out of this state alive," Nash said a bit later.

"You and me both," said Lackey.

News of Nash's sighting in Little Rock, as well as the agents' plans to head to Joplin, was relayed to Hot Springs, and thus to Galatas. He dialed a Joplin number. The phone rang at the home of Deafy Farmer, the hulking confidence man who eighteen months earlier had sent Alvin Karpis and Fred Barker to St. Paul. Galatas spoke to Farmer for a minute, then hung up and turned to Frances. "This is all going to be taken care of," he said. "You can meet Frank in Joplin."

Two hundred miles north of Hot Springs, amid the browning fields of western Missouri, a very different pursuit continued through that same hot Friday afternoon. Police from across the state, alerted by Floyd's kidnapping of Sheriff Jack Killingsworth, had scrambled in pursuit, soon aided by dozens of local sheriffs and policemen.

Floyd was steering northwest for Kansas City, speeding up Highway 83, then zigzagging across dirt roads into Hickory County. Thirty-five miles out of Boliver, he had taken over the driving from Richetti, whose moonshine swigging made Floyd nervous. To the sheriff's surprise, Floyd was downright chatty. For his part, Killingsworth did his best to help the two outlaws. He was acutely aware of the shoot-out that would ensue if they were caught, and he wanted no part of it: he'd noticed the automatic pistol Floyd had in his lap.

Floyd stayed cool as they headed into Henry County, about halfway to Kansas City. At a country store they stopped for candy bars and sodas, and Floyd asked the woman behind the counter whether she had heard any news of the kidnapping down in Boliver. She said a group of officers had just passed by, saying they figured Floyd was making for the Oklahoma border. Floyd smiled.

At midmorning, police were alerted that Floyd's car had roared through the towns of Wheatland and Quincy. Finally, outside the village of Brownington, Floyd spotted a state patrol car in his rearview mirror. Richetti grabbed the submachine gun. Floyd took the safety off his pistol and calmly told the sheriff, "Wave 'em back."

Killingsworth took off his panama hat and waved it furiously out the window. It worked; before long the car disappeared. They had been spotted, though, and Floyd was taking no chances. Two miles west of Deepwater, he slowed the car and began looking for a replacement. Within minutes a Pontiac zoomed past. "That looks like a likely car," Floyd said. He hit the accelerator and gave chase, and they waved the other car to a stop.

The Pontiac's driver, a Baptist deacon named Walter L. Griffith, appeared confused as Floyd opened the driver's door and barked, "Move over!" Griffith did as he was told; Richetti and Killingsworth slid into the backseat. In seconds Floyd had the big car rolling north. He told Griffith not to worry. "You seem like pretty good fellas. I believe I'll let you get out of this."

At one point an airplane glided over the highway in front of them. Floyd hunched forward and watched it. Around six o'clock he coasted off the road east of Ottawa, Kansas, and brought the Pontiac to a stop in a ravine. They would wait till it was dark to drive into Kansas City.

Frank Nash and his three captors stopped for a bite to eat in Conway, Arkansas. At a pay phone, Agent Joe Lackey called his boss, Ralph Colvin, at the FBI's Oklahoma City office. Colvin was thrilled that Nash had been arrested, but he didn't like the sound of two agents being tracked across rural Arkansas by gun-toting posses. He told Lackey to forget driving to Joplin and to head to Fort Smith instead, where they could catch an overnight train to Leavenworth. Colvin checked train schedules. There was a train leaving Fort Smith at 8:30 that night. It arrived in Kansas City at 7:00 A.M. before going on to Leavenworth. He called Kansas City to arrange an escort.

Meanwhile, in Hot Springs, Dick Galatas took Frances Nash and her daughter to the airport, where he arranged for a plane to fly them to Joplin. When Frances said she was too frightened to fly, Galatas climbed in after her to calm her nerves. At 5:45 the plane touched down in Joplin. By nightfall they were at Deafy Farmer's house south of town.

"It's a hell of a life being dogged around, and having to hide all the time," Floyd was saying. In the secluded Kansas ravine, he sat on the grass, talking to Sheriff Killingsworth, who leaned back, his head resting on a rock. Walter Griffith sat in his Pontiac, as if guarding it, while Richetti snored lightly in the backseat.

The more he talked, the more depressed Floyd appeared. "There's no turning back for me now," he said at one point. "Too many policemen want me. I haven't got a chance except to fight it out. I don't aim to let anybody take me alive."

Killingsworth gave him a look. "They'll get me," Floyd said. "Sooner or later, I'll go down full of lead. That's the way it will end. I might not have to been this way, you know, but for the damned police. I might be going straight, be living with a family and working for a living. I finally decided, you're determined I'm a tough guy, a bank robber, that's what I'll be. They have themselves to thank."

Killingsworth, hoping to gain Floyd's sympathy, mentioned his own family, his wife and young son. A cloud fell over Floyd's face.

"You shouldn't kick about one day," he said. "How would you like to be hunted night and day, day and night? How would you like to sleep every night with this thing across your knees?" He fingered the submachine gun lying beside him on the grass. "I have a son, too. Maybe you think I wouldn't like to see him. When you get home, you can have your son with you every day and sit and talk with him. All I ever get to do is see mine once in a long while. Then all I can do is stand off and look at him for a minute."

At nightfall they drove into Kansas City without event. Around ten Floyd pulled to a stop in the packinghouse district. Floyd left the car and made a phone call, then drove to a spot near the corner of Ninth and Hickory. Another car soon coasted up. Killingsworth watched as Floyd and Richetti transferred their guns and a footlocker into the second car. After a minute Floyd got back in the Pontiac and ordered his two captives out onto the sidewalk.

"Wait five minutes and then walk down and get the car," Floyd said, motioning toward a spot where he intended to leave the Pontiac. "Drive on home and don't call anyone, 'cause you'll be watched." As he drove off, Floyd told Killingsworth to take a set of golf clubs he had left in the trunk. "Something to remember me by," Floyd said.

"I won't need anything to remember you by," said the sheriff.

Fort Smith, Arkansas
8:30 P.M.

The train to Kansas City was ten minutes late, and the three lawmen—
Frank Smith, Joe Lackey, and Otto Reed—were nervous. They stood on
the platform, peering down the track, glancing at the exits. Nash stood by
in handcuffs. Suddenly a man approached Lackey. Everyone relaxed when
he introduced himself as an Associated Press reporter, in the station by
chance. The reporter motioned to Nash: Who was the prisoner?

For the rest of his life, Joe Lackey swore he never answered the reporter's
questions. But someone did. A half hour after the three men and their prisoner boarded the train for Kansas City, the reporter's dispatch crossed the AP
wire: *Frank Nash, one of the last surviving members of the notorious Al Spencer
Gang of bank and train robbers that operated a decade ago, was recaptured today at Hot Springs, Arkansas, by three Department of Justice agents—who "kidnapped" him on the streets of the resort city.* The six-paragraph flash described
the kidnapping, the escape, and, amazingly, the agents' intention to take the
night train to Kansas City. It went out to dozens of AP offices, including the
one in Hot Springs, where Dick Galatas had friends.

Oblivious to the AP story, Nash and the three lawmen traveled to
Kansas City in Drawing Room A, Car 11, Nash handcuffed to the upper
berth. They were scheduled to arrive at Kansas City's Union Station at 7:00
the next morning.

In a hotel room barely two miles from where Frank Nash was stepping onto
the train to Kansas City, Bonnie Parker was emerging from her delirium. It
had taken six full days, her family would recall, for Bonnie even to recognize her sister Billie, who remained at her side, wiping her brow, changing
her bandages. Clyde, too, stayed at her bedside all that week, never leaving
for more than minutes.

They were in a bind. They couldn't stay in Fort Smith much longer.
Clyde searched his mind for a safe place Bonnie could convalesce. Dallas
was too risky. What they needed was a friend of importance, someone who
knew how to hide. The more he thought about it, the more he was certain
only one person fit the bill. As soon as Bonnie could travel, Clyde decided,
he would go in search of Pretty Boy Floyd.

Joplin, Missouri
10:09 P.M.

The phone rang at Deafy Farmer's house. It was Hot Springs, for Galatas. Galatas took it, listened, then hung up. There was a change in plans. "They're taking Frank by train to Kansas City," he said.

Frances Nash searched her mind for someone who could rescue her husband. She had only one hope, her husband's best friend, Verne Miller. A onetime South Dakota sheriff who turned to crime after an embezzlement conviction, Miller was a rarity among Midwestern yeggs, a successful bank robber who moonlighted as a hit man for the Chicago and New York syndicates; his marksmanship was so accurate it was said he could write his name with a Thompson. A loner, cool and Nordic, Miller robbed banks alongside Harvey Bailey and the Barkers. At the moment, he was living in Kansas City with his girlfriend.

At 10:17 Frances Nash reached Miller at his house on Edgevale Road. Miller already knew Nash had been arrested; a bootlegger friend, Frank "Fritz" Mulloy, had tracked Miller down on the golf course, relaying the message left in Chicago. "What shall I do?" Frances asked Miller. "What shall I do?"

Miller assured Frances he would take care of everything, then hung up. Two hours later, the phone rang at the Farmer house.

"Let me answer it," Frances said. "I know it must be for me."

"This is Verne," Miller said. "I'm down at the station." Kansas City's Union Station.

Frances broke down again, sobbing into the phone.

"Don't take it so hard," Miller told her. "You'll see your Jelly again."

"What shall I do?" Frances sniffled. "Where can I get in touch with you? I can't go home. I have no place to go."

They talked for a minute or two more. Miller knew he couldn't handle the rescue alone. From the station he telephoned the Green Lantern in St. Paul looking for the Barkers, not knowing they were busy with the Hamm kidnapping. He was running out of time.

Joe Lackey, the Roman-nosed FBI agent, hung out the door as the train eased down Track 12 into Union Station. He had been awake for forty-eight hours and his nerves were on edge. Everyone knew what kind of town Kansas City was, rough and corrupt, a magnet for bank robbers, pimps, and confidence men from Chicago to the West Coast. Everything that mattered, from the police to the polls, was controlled by the political boss Thomas J. Pendergast, whose take from gambling, prostitution, and narcotics approached $30 million a year. (One cog in the sprawling Pendergast machine was a forty-nine-year-old county judge named Harry Truman, who would be elected to the U.S. Senate the following year.)

The train was scheduled for a one-hour layover before heading to Leavenworth, but the agents agreed that the risk of staying in Kansas City, even for an hour, was too great. Instead the Oklahoma City office had devised a plan with the Kansas City SAC, Reed Vetterli, a baby-faced twenty-nine-year-old Mormon. Vetterli assembled a squad of lawmen to drive Nash the thirty miles to Leavenworth.

Ahead on the platform, Lackey spied Vetterli, in a dark suit, standing with three men. When the train coasted to a stop, Lackey hopped off and Vetterli made the introductions. Agent Ray Caffrey was thirty years old, an earnest, plain Nebraska native who wore his brown hair parted down the middle. The other two men on the platform, older, seedy, and disheveled, were Kansas City policemen, snaggletoothed Frank Hermanson and Bill "Red" Grooms. Hermanson and Grooms had brought the department's armor-plated "hot car."

Lackey briefed the officers, then returned to the train to get Nash. A few moments later, the three lawmen emerged from the train, pushing their prisoner before them. Nash wore an open-necked white shirt and had a handkerchief thrown over his handcuffed hands. The plan was to drive Nash straight to Leavenworth, escorted by the hot car; with any luck, they would all be back by lunchtime.

There was little chitchat. Together the seven lawmen formed a wedge around Nash and herded him up the platform. Quickly they ascended the stairs into the cavernous expanse of Union Station, already filling with early-morning travelers. Agent Caffrey walked in back, his .38-caliber pistol jammed into Nash's ribs. All across the station, heads turned as the strange phalanx strode across the dramatic open space toward the front archway and the parking lot beyond. Lottie West, a Traveler's Aid Society worker, was standing in front of the Fred Harvey Restaurant, chatting with the manager, when the eight men marched by. "That must be Pretty Boy Floyd," Mrs. West remarked, motioning toward the prisoner. The morning papers carried the news that Floyd had arrived in town the night before; it was all anyone was talking about.

The group strode across the plaza to Agent Caffrey's two-door Chevrolet in the first row of cars. The parking lot was already coming to life, taxis swerving to the curb, a trio of nuns milling about. Caffrey unlocked the passenger door, and Joe Lackey slid in back, followed by Chief Reed. "Get up front," Lackey told Nash. "We'll ride like we did out of Hot Springs. That way we can all watch you."

Nash climbed into the front seat. Frank Smith joined Reed and Lackey in back. The cops, Grooms and Hermanson, stood facing each other by the right front tire, waiting. Reed Vetterli stood beside the car, poised to slide in beside Nash. Ray Caffrey squeezed past the two cops and stepped around the front of the car, making for the driver's door.

Suddenly, from in front of the car, someone yelled, "Up! Up! Get your hands up!"

All seven lawmen turned. A split second later there was a gunshot.

"Let 'em have it!" a voice shouted.

A fusillade of machine-gun bullets raked the car. The two police officers, Red Grooms and Frank Hermanson, jerked like marionettes, splashes of blood erupting across their chests and faces; both men were dead before they hit the ground. In the front seat Frank Nash's head exploded. Behind him Otto Reed's head burst as well.

In front of the car, Ray Caffrey was blown against the hood and crumpled to the pavement in a heap. A bullet grazed Reed Vetterli's right arm, and he fell beside the car. An instant later he sprang to his feet and ran back toward the station, a spray of bullets kicking up dust behind him. In the backseat Lackey raised his shotgun, but three bullets hit him and he dropped it; still alive, he fell forward and played dead, as did Frank Smith beside him. Both men had their heads between their knees when the shooting stopped. They heard the sound of footsteps approaching.

"Everyone's dead in here," a voice outside the car said.

It would be called the Kansas City Massacre. At the time, it was the second-deadliest murder of law-enforcement officers in American history, and it shocked the nation. Coming less than forty-eight hours after the kidnapping of William Hamm, it generated a shock wave felt all the way to Franklin Roosevelt's desk in the Oval Office.

The War on Crime had begun.

3

THE COLLEGE BOYS TAKE THE FIELD

June 17 to July 22, 1933

Kansas City
Saturday, June 17
7:20 A.M.

"That one's alive! He's alive!"

The haze of gunsmoke still hung over the Union Station parking lot as the first bystanders ran up to the FBI car. Ray Caffrey's fallen body lay sprawled on the pavement next to the front fender, his eyes still open, his jaw working silently; he would be dead within minutes. Six feet away the two Kansas City detectives lay dead in a spreading pool of blood, Red Grooms's head nestled against Frank Hermanson's chest. Inside the car, Frank Nash was slumped in the driver's seat, mouth open, head back, rivulets of blood running down his neck and reddening his chest. In the backseat Otto Reed's body looked worse.

First to reach the car after the gunmen fled was Mike Fanning, a policeman who had been on duty at the station and had fired shots at the fleeing sedan. He had no idea what was going on. He yanked open a car door, trained his pistol on the men inside, and yelled for them to get out.

"Don't shoot, I'm a federal officer," said Frank Smith, raising his hands. There were tears in his eyes as he glanced at his old friend Otto Reed. To his left Joe Lackey moaned in pain. He'd been hit three times in the back. "Steady now, steady," Smith said, turning to Lackey. "You'll make it all right." The Kansas City SAC, Reed Vetterli, ran up, helped pull Lackey from the seat, and laid him on the pavement. Smith cradled the wounded agent's head in his arms. "I'll be all right," Lackey whispered. "Look after the others."

A crowd was gathering—businessmen in straw boaters, taxi drivers in flat caps, a farmer or two in denim overalls. Several slipped in the spreading pool of blood. A woman screamed. A wire-service reporter tiptoed through the scene, staining her white shoes red. Ambulances were on the scene within minutes, and Lackey was taken to Research Hospital; he would recover and return to duty within weeks. Vetterli, bleeding lightly from his arm wound, rushed to the FBI offices in the Federal Reserve Bank Building. He picked up the phone, called Washington, and was put through to the director.

"It was a massacre, Mr. Hoover," Vetterli said. "Ray Caffrey is dead. Joe Lackey may not pull through. Two Kansas City detectives and the chief of police from McAlester, Oklahoma, were killed. So was Frank Nash." Vetterli listened a moment. "Well, I lost a good summer coat and a shirt . . . No, I didn't go to the hospital . . . Yes, sir, I'll go to a doctor at once." An agent was dispatched to Ray Caffrey's apartment to break the news to his wife.

The remaining agents descended on the Union Station parking lot to interview witnesses. Crowds milled about through the morning, and there was no shortage of people who thought they had seen the assassins. Still, the stories that filled the agents' notebooks were a jumble. The shooters used one car; no, two. There were two gunmen, or maybe three. Someone else saw five. The assassins were tall and thin, or short and fat, maybe swarthy, maybe not. It was a frustrating beginning to what would quickly become an exasperating investigation.

The FBI did receive one break that morning. Down in Joplin, Dick Galatas had already returned to Hot Springs, but the remaining conspirators—Frances Nash, Deafy Farmer and his wife—panicked when they heard news of the massacre on the radio. Frances was dumbstruck. "I can't believe it. I can't believe it," she kept saying.

The trio did the only thing they could: they ran. By two o'clock all three had disappeared—but not without being noticed. A local woman heard something suspicious over the telephone line—a party line—and reported it to Joplin police, who raided the Farmer home at noon.* They found only a caretaker but telephoned Kansas City nevertheless. Two FBI men jumped in a car and drove to Joplin the next morning, in case someone returned.

By lunchtime, barely five hours after the last gunshot at Union Station, Hoover was mulling who to place in charge of what was clearly the most important investigation in Bureau history.† Reed Vetterli's men were fresh-faced College Boys; while eager, none was fit to lead a major investigation. Hoover needed the kind of agent he had so few of, a professional investigator with maturity, diplomacy, and street smarts. Ray Caffrey was the third Bureau man ever killed. Hoover decided to bring in the man who had handled the case of the first. He picked up the phone and dialed San Antonio. He was bringing in Gus Jones.‡

Jones, the San Antonio SAC since 1921, was the prototype of the dozen or so no-bullshit Cowboys Hoover employed to tutor his College Boys and work major cases. At fifty-one Jones was a creature of the old Texas frontier, stout and moonfaced, with thinning blond hair, wire-frame spectacles, and a fondness for ten-gallon hats. Born in San Angelo in 1882, he came from a family of West Texas lawmen; his father had been killed in a late-nineteenth-century skirmish with Indians. As the El Paso SAC during the World War, Jones spent much of his time trying to head off arms shipments

---

* The raid was conducted by Joplin's chief of detectives, Ed Portley, who would later write a series of magazine articles about his pursuit of Bonnie and Clyde in the wake of the murders they committed in Joplin that spring.

† No one dwelled on the fact that the Bureau had no jurisdiction whatsoever to investigate the massacre. Even though one of its own men had been murdered, it was not yet a federal crime to kill a federal agent. Such a law would not be passed until the following spring.

‡ Jones achieved prominence inside the Bureau with his role in the case of the first FBI agent murdered in the line of duty, Ed Shanahan. Shanahan was a tall, slender I agent in Chicago who one evening in October 1925 stepped up to a car blocking his path in a downtown garage and tapped at the driver's window. Unfortunately for Shanahan, the driver turned out to be a car thief named Martin Durkin. When Shanahan produced his Bureau identification card and asked him to move his car, Durkin brandished a pistol and shot him through the chest.

   Hoover declared Durkin's apprehension the Bureau's top priority, and in the ensuing three months, with agents across the country working nights and weekends, Durkin was tracked to New York, then to Los Angeles and San Diego. From California Durkin and his wife drove east across Arizona and New Mexico until a deputy sheriff in Pecos, Texas, spotted a pistol on his front seat. Durkin drove off, but not before the sheriff called the Bureau office in El Paso. A search was launched, and Durkin's car was found abandoned nearby, at the height of a January blizzard. It was Jones who discovered Durkin had boarded a train to Chicago. Agents arrested him outside of St. Louis.

to Pancho Villa and other Mexican revolutionaries. Transferred to San Antonio, he became one of Hoover's best men.

After talking with Hoover, Jones boarded a flight out of San Antonio and arrived at the Kansas City airport at 2:30 Sunday morning, seventeen hours after the massacre. Downtown, he went into conference with Vetterli and his men, and at 10:00 took two of them to meet with the Kansas City Police Department's new chief, Eugene Reppert. Reppert, a pawn of the Pendergast machine, was already working to deflect responsibility for the massacre, telling reporters that the Nash arrest had been an FBI operation.

"This is some mess you've gotten us into," Reppert told Jones.[1] Jones emphasized that the Bureau was willing to aid the police investigation any way it could, but Reppert said he had no intention of investigating the massacre. "This is a government case and not a police matter," he said. Afterward Jones said it was the most amazing thing he had ever heard a police chief say; two of his men were dead and he wasn't investigating. The FBI could only wonder why.

The Bureau was on its own. No one said it aloud, but there were some among Hoover's men who doubted they could carry off the complex investigation they now faced. The FBI had never attempted anything like it before. Gus Jones wondered what weaponless agents would do if confronted by the well-armed massacre assassins. When Hoover sent a wire demanding that he use every resource to apprehend the gunmen, Jones cabled back: "With what? Peashooters?" Suddenly, the FBI's unofficial ban on guns was lifted. In Washington one of Hoover's top men, Clyde Tolson, secured two machine guns to send to Kansas City.

Returning to the FBI office, Jones convened a meeting to go over leads. Some agents thought the massacre was a gangland hit directed at Frank Nash. Jones thought it more likely that it was a rescue attempt gone awry. Several suspects had already jumped to the fore. Their two best theories, in fact, were already being debated in the Kansas City newspapers. One posited that Pretty Boy Floyd was behind the killings. After his release, Sheriff Killingsworth had given several interviews, and stories about Floyd's arrival in Kansas City were everywhere. The problem was, of the dozens of witnesses, only one, the Traveler's Aid lady, Lottie West, identified Floyd. In fact, Mrs. West said she had seen Floyd sitting at her desk when she arrived for work. Though her story was prominently reported, none of the agents took it seriously.

The stronger theory rested on rumors that Nash had arranged the escape of Harvey Bailey and ten other convicts from the Kansas State Penitentiary on May 31. Jones theorized that Bailey's group had attempted to rescue Nash and for some reason ended up killing him. This theory gained momentum when several eyewitnesses identified photographs of Bailey as one of the assassins. The best was a businessman named Samuel Link. Link said he had stepped out of his car that morning next to a Reo sedan just as a man he recognized as Bailey emerged from the Reo, knocking off Link's hat. Link said he watched as Bailey and another man fired on the FBI car. Best of all, Link said he had been a deputy sheriff in Kansas City in 1926 and had once seen Bailey on the street. He pointed to a photo of one of Bailey's co-escapees, a murderous Oklahoma yegg named Wilbur Underhill—the papers called him "The Tri-State Terror"—and identified him as the other assassin.

The best witnesses should have been the three agents who survived the shooting: Vetterli, Lackey, and Frank Smith. Their stories were disappointing. From his hospital bed, Lackey said he had seen two of the shooters but couldn't identify them; the car windows were too dirty for a clear view. Smith had seen one man he couldn't identify, then ducked his head when the shooting began. Only Vetterli made a concrete identification of a man he said he saw wielding a submachine gun: "Big" Bob Brady, an Oklahoma bank robber who had escaped with Bailey. By Sunday night Jones had focused the Bureau's efforts on finding Bailey and the other escapees. Wanted posters were drawn up.

By Sunday night, thirty-six hours after the shootings, their best lead was a series of suspicious phone calls the Oklahoma City office traced from Hot Springs to Deafy Farmer's house south of Joplin. This suggested that someone from Hot Springs had called on Farmer to rescue Nash; now agents needed to learn who Farmer had telephoned in Kansas City. Phone records were in St. Louis. Amazingly, Reed Vetterli decided to write the phone company a letter instead of just telephoning. It would take four days for the records to arrive, during which time Verne Miller and everyone else involved in the massacre conspiracy got away.

That Saturday night, fifteen hours after the Kansas City Massacre, William Hamm's intermediary, Billy Dunn, left St. Paul in a Ford coupe whose doors had been removed. It had been Shotgun George Ziegler's idea to order the doors taken off; this way, no one could be hiding inside to ambush them. On the floorboard beside Dunn was a satchel containing $100,000 in cash.

Dunn's late-night drive followed three notes from Hamm's kidnappers.

The first had been delivered to a pharmacy near Dunn's home: *You're so god damed* [sic] *smart that you'll wind up getting both of you guys killed. Furthermore we demand that you personally deliver the money so that if there is any doble* [sic] *crossing we will have the pleasure of hitting you in the head.*

Saturday morning a second note was left in the car of a brewery worker. It gave instructions on how to deliver the ransom and warned Dunn to come alone: *You brought the coppers into this, now you get rid of the assholes.* The St. Paul SAC, Werner Hanni, debated whether to set a trap for the kidnappers when the ransom was delivered. The corrupt detective Tom Brown alerted the Barkers. A third ransom note was delivered to Dunn that afternoon: *If you are through with the bullshit and balyhoo* [sic], *we'll give you your chance. First of all,* get away from the coppers.

Just after ten o'clock that night, Dunn drove north on Highway 61. He passed the town of White Bear Lake and continued north in the darkness. Just before Pine City, about halfway to Duluth, a car roared past at a speed of over seventy miles per hour. A second car followed. Dunn slowed and watched as the two cars pulled to the side of the road. They let him pass, then pulled out and passed him again. After a few minutes, Dunn saw headlights ahead of him in the darkness. They flashed five times. It was the signal. He stopped the car and threw out the money.

Dunn drove on to Duluth, where he had been told Hamm would be waiting at the New Duluth Hotel. He wasn't there. Soon Dunn was joined by the kidnappers' secret liaison, Tom Brown, and another detective. They sat all night, waiting. Hamm never showed.

Fred Barker and George Ziegler returned to the Bensonville safe house the next morning and threw the satchel on the kitchen table. "You better round up some Hamm's beer," Ziegler announced. "I got a feeling that it'll be my favorite for a long time to come."

The next morning at dawn, after an all-night drive back to Minnesota, Karpis left William Hamm blindfolded in a field outside the town of Wyoming. After a few minutes, Hamm took off his blindfold and trudged to a farmhouse, where he telephoned his mother in Minneapolis. By noon he was back at his mansion, standing dazed before a crowd of reporters.

Several members of the gang also returned to the Twin Cities that morning, and if not for the intervention of Tom Brown, the Barkers' careers would have ended that day. At the house Fred Barker was renting on Vernon Street, neighbors had noticed his strange habits and the arrival and departures of all sorts of large cars at all hours, and had taken to joking that the home's occupants were gangsters, maybe even the Hamm kidnappers. As the gang piled out of its Buick that morning, one neighbor joked, "There goes the ransom money."

Not everyone was joking. One young man was suspicious enough to phone in a tip to an editor at the *St. Paul Pioneer Press.* The editor phoned the police who, to the Barkers' good fortune, turned the matter over to Tom Brown. Brown slipped out of his office and phoned a friend, who alerted the Barkers. All that evening neighbors watched as the gang scurried through the house, slamming doors and tossing suitcases into their cars. When two officers arrived to check out the house the next morning, they found it empty.

By that Monday, as the Barkers scrambled to escape St. Paul, the rest of the gang had already decamped to apartments in Chicago. There they read in amazement newspaper stories of the Kansas City Massacre. Everyone affiliated with the gang realized Verne Miller must have done it to rescue his best friend, Frank Nash.

In the suburb of Maywood, Dock Barker's friend Volney Davis paced his second-floor apartment all that morning. "That shooting is sure going to turn the heat on," he told his girlfriend, Edna "Rabbits" Murray. Davis and Murray were still debating what to do around noon when they heard a car horn blaring. Murray stepped to the window. To her horror, she looked down on the blond head of Verne Miller.

"Is Curly there?" Miller asked.

"Yes," Murray said.

Davis stepped to the window. "Come downstairs for a minute," Miller hollered.

Murray watched as Davis walked downstairs, drove Miller's car into a garage across the street, then handed Miller the keys to his own car. Afterward Miller came upstairs, plopping down on a divan. "I'm all in," he said. "Had a tough time getting out of Kansas City. Got any iodine?" He had a small wound on one finger. As Murray swabbed it with iodine, Miller's discourse grew fatalistic. "I'm the hottest man in the country," he said. "I know I'll hang for this. I talked to Nash's wife the night before it happened and told her I would do all I could for Jelly. She'll put the finger on me."[2]

The next day, Miller returned with his girlfriend, Vi Mathias. They stayed in the Davis apartment for three days, then vanished.

• • •

With ten seconds of machine-gun fire and the deaths of five men, the Kansas City Massacre forever changed the American legal landscape. It put the FBI on a wartime footing that in coming months would transform it into the country's first federal police force. It probably saved Hoover's job; six weeks later, he was formally reappointed as the Bureau's director. Most important, it led to the public declaration of an ambitious federal War on Crime that in time would thrust Hoover's men into their first confrontations with real criminals.

None of this happened overnight. Contrary to myth, there was no morning-after press conference in which Hoover declared war on gangsters. He took calls from reporters in his office, but his answers were limited to the massacre itself. "We will never stop until we get our men," he told the *Kansas City Star* hours after the shootings, "if it takes ages to accomplish it. There will be no letup in this case."

In fact, the driving force behind the broader War on Crime was not Hoover but his new boss, the attorney general Homer Cummings, who had spent the spring studying the feasibility of some kind of federal drive on organized crime. The massacre gave the administration the pretext it needed to sell this idea to the public. On June 29, twelve days after the massacre, Cummings announced a series of measures that composed the new War on Crime: the hiring of a special prosecutor, Joseph Keenan; a legislative package that would, among other things, make it a federal crime to kill a federal agent; and the formation of "special squads" inside the Bureau to tackle major cases. Cummings suggested he would study the formation of a federal police force, built around the Bureau, augmented by agents from the soon-to-be disbanded Prohibition Bureau. The *New York Times* carried the story on Page 1.

"Racketeering has got to a point when the government as such must take a hand and try to stamp out this underworld army," Cummings told reporters, in the first of a series of interviews and speeches he was to give that summer. "We are now engaged in a war," he told the Daughters of the American Revolution in August, "that threatens the safety of our country—a war with the organized forces of crime."

Public reaction to this new "war" was by turns encouraging and doubtful. "Defiance of law," the *Washington Post* editorialized the same day, "has seldom been more flagrantly manifested than it was at Kansas City Saturday." But government officials had called for wars against gangsters before, and many doubted whether the FBI or any other agency could make a difference. "Department of Justice officials are marvelous at finding and arresting counterfeiters," one columnist wrote. "Perhaps they will do as well with highway murderers."

The call for a War on Crime wasn't without self-interest; Cummings badly wanted a way to focus and grow his shrinking Justice Department. Nor did it create any immediate groundswell of support for federal policing; that was yet to come. In fact, national interest surrounding the FBI's new headline cases—the Kansas City Massacre and the Hamm kidnapping— paled before that of, say, the Lindbergh kidnapping; intensive coverage was limited to Midwestern newspapers.

But Cummings's call dovetailed with the desires of New Dealers in Roosevelt's cabinet, who picked up the attorney general's cries and placed them in the context of the government's fight to overcome the Depression. By that autumn the War on Crime would become a centerpiece of Roosevelt's push to centralize many facets of American government. It would be a focal point of his State of the Union Address in January. Thus a little-known bureau of the Justice Department became a cutting edge of Roosevelt's New Deal policies. If Hoover and his neophyte agents could defeat "name brand" gangsters, it would be immediate and tangible evidence of the New Deal's worth.

It was with these issues in mind that resources were shoveled toward Hoover in the days after the massacre. Dozens of new agents were hired and hustled into training classes. Guns were purchased and for the first time the men were shown how to use them—sort of. The FBI's firearms-training program was initially a hit-and-miss affair. Agents in New York trained at one agent's farm, shooting at pumpkins and soda bottles, while the Cincinnati office prevailed on local police to teach its men. In Chicago the SAC simply handed out pistols and said, "Here they are, boys. Learn how to shoot 'em."[3] "We had one .32 caliber pistol in the Kansas City office," one agent remembered. "That was it. I was told one time to get the gun and some bullets and come to a particular office. When I got there, I found out the bullets wouldn't even fit the gun."[4]

This was the state of the army of raw young agents Hoover commanded in his mission to give the White House victories in its two lead cases in the War on Crime. The two investigations quickly became intertwined. On Thursday, June 22, five days after the massacre, Agent Gus Jones received a call from the St. Paul office. Agents there had searched the house Fred Barker had rented, suspecting it was linked to the Hamm kidnapping. They had no idea who lived there, but fingerprints taken from beer bottles at the house turned out to be Frank Nash's. Hoover's men scratched their heads: Was Nash somehow mixed up in the Hamm kidnapping?*

The same morning, the Kansas City office finally received Deafy Farmer's telephone records. What they discovered changed the course of the investigation: A series of calls had been placed to an address, 6612 Edgevale, in Kansas City. Agents found the house empty. Agent Dwight Brantley, accompanied by the landlord and a Kansas City policeman, supervised the search.† In a desk drawer they found a pile of papers, mostly telephone and electric bills made out to the Vincent Moore family. In the cellar Brantley discovered empty beer bottles, as well as a two-gallon milk can filled with roofing nails.

An FBI fingerprint expert arrived to dust the house, and within hours the identification was made: Vincent Moore was in fact Verne Miller, as several agents familiar with Frank Nash had begun to suspect. A week later, on July 6, the Kansas City newspapers broke the story, naming Miller and two local hoodlums as the massacre gunmen. For the FBI, Miller became the most wanted man in the country.

Within days agents began to reel in people. Deafy Farmer and his wife were arrested on July 7 when they inexplicably returned to Joplin. Agents tracked Frances Nash to a relative's home in Illinois and took her into custody. After several days of questioning, all three broke down and told everything: the flight from Hot Springs, the phone calls to Miller. But none could answer the questions the FBI needed answered most: Where was Miller now? And who were his partners?

Gus Jones put together a list of likely gunmen. It included Pretty Boy Floyd, Bonnie and Clyde, Alvin Karpis, and the Barker brothers. But Jones remained convinced Miller's confederates were the men Nash had broken out of the Kansas prison: Harvey Bailey, the Oklahoma bandit Wilbur Underhill, and their fellow escapees. Bailey knew it, too, and went to extraordinary lengths to proclaim his innocence. One morning Jones opened a letter and was stunned to see it was from Bailey and his comrades. The let-

---

* Nash had visited the Barkers in St. Paul a week before the kidnapping, a fact the Bureau would not learn for months.
† A native of North Carolina, Dwight Brantley served in the FBI from 1924 to 1950. In 1957 he was named Kansas City's police commissioner. He died in 1967 at the age of sixty-eight.

ter claimed that Bailey and the others could not have carried out the massacre for the simple reason that they had robbed a bank at Black Rock, Arkansas, that same morning. *We the undersigned are the perpetrators of the robbery,* Bailey wrote. He affixed a collection of the gang's fingerprints to bolster their case.

Seated in the FBI's Kansas City office, Jones was still studying the letter on Thursday morning, July 20, when word came of a massive firefight on the edge of town the night before.

It was Bonnie and Clyde.

Platte City, Missouri
Tuesday, July 18

That night around ten o'clock the Barrow Gang cruised into a tourist court just north of Kansas City, outside the town of Platte City, Missouri. They had fled Fort Smith three weeks earlier after Buck and W.D. got into a wild shoot-out following a grocery store robbery in Fayetteville, Arkansas. After a vain attempt to find Pretty Boy Floyd—they did manage to find his brother Bradley—they had spent much of the time holed up in a motel at Great Bend, Kansas. Their only crime of note had been a raid on a National Guard armory at Enid, Oklahoma, where they made off with five Browning automatic rifles, a half-dozen Colt .45 automatics, and ten thousand bullets. There were so many guns in the backseat, Clyde joked, it was hard to find a place to sit.

By most accounts, the gang had left Great Bend the day before, July 17, camping that night in a field in southern Kansas. On Tuesday morning a farmer found bloody bandages at their abandoned campground and phoned the Kansas State Police. Knowing of Bonnie's injuries, the police broadcast a multistate alert, urging sheriffs to be on the watch for unusual purchases of medical supplies. That night, after robbing three filling stations at Fort Dodge, Clyde passed the outskirts of Kansas City and arrived at a highway junction in Platte City. The two red-brick cabins the gang checked into stood alone behind a bar, the Red Crown Tavern. Blanche and Buck went in for lunch the next day but left when they spotted the local sheriff, a man named Holt Coffey. That afternoon Blanche drove into town and bought hypodermic syringes and atropine sulfate from a druggist. The druggist thought her purchase odd and telephoned Sheriff Coffey, who remembered the police alert.

The druggist told Sheriff Coffey that Blanche had mentioned that she was staying at the Red Crown tourist court, and with a quick call Sheriff Coffey confirmed that two couples were staying there. Alerted by state-police circulars, he was convinced he was dealing with the Barrow Gang. The sheriff contacted the Missouri Highway Patrol, which sent reinforcements from Kansas City, including an armored car. They decided to strike that night: By evening Sheriff Coffey had gathered thirteen deputies and troopers for the raid. Convening at the Red Crown at midnight, the group had Thompson submachine guns, metal shields, tear gas, and riot guns.

Around one A.M. they moved in, taking positions in front of the two darkened cabins, which were linked by a small garage. Two state troopers climbed to the top of the tavern and trained their guns on the cabin doors. The armored car quietly coasted to a stop in front of the cabins themselves, blocking any exit from the garage. When the car was in position, Sheriff Coffey crept toward the cabin on the left, the one occupied by Buck and Blanche. He banged on the door.

"Yes?" Blanche answered. She was washing some of Bonnie's things in a sink. "Who is it?"

"I need to talk to the boys," Sheriff Coffey answered.

"Just a minute," Blanche said. "Let us get dressed."

Clyde was lying in bed beside Bonnie in the adjoining cabin when he heard the exchange. He rose and grabbed his Browning. "That's the law," he whispered to W.D. "Get the car started."

W.D. slipped into the garage as Clyde stepped to the front door. Opening it a few inches, he saw the armored car blocking their escape. He ran to join W.D. in the garage and jumped up on the rear fender of their Ford, peeking through a high window in the door. There, barely ten feet away, standing on the front porch of the leftmost cabin, stood Sheriff Coffey. Clyde raised his Browning and fired through the window. A bullet grazed the sheriff's neck and he fell, then gathered himself and ran for the tavern.

All the officers opened fire, their bullets chewing up the cabins' brick facades and shattering windows. Clyde dashed back through his cabin like a madman, firing the Browning through the windows. Everywhere officers scattered; inside the tavern, a crowd of the curious dived beneath the tables. Reloading, Clyde stepped to the front door, kicked it open, and fired an entire clip into the armored car, the bullets pinging up and down its sides. One struck the driver, a deputy named George Highfill, in the knees.

A second hit the horn, which began blaring steadily. Highfill panicked and threw the armored car into reverse, backing away from the garage.

As bullets whizzed through the cabins, Buck and Blanche found themselves trapped; there was no entrance to the garage from their cabin. They decided to run for it. Hoisting a mattress in front of them, they walked out their front door and began to step toward the garage.[5] The mattress was too bulky, however, and they dropped it. Buck had taken only a step or two when he stumbled, his automatic rifle firing wildly as he fell; a .45 caliber bullet struck him flush in the left temple, boring a hole through his skull and exiting out his forehead. Blanche screamed for Clyde to open the garage door as she helped Buck to his feet; he was alive.

Braving the hail of bullets, Clyde opened the doors and helped the couple inside. They shoved Buck into the Ford, where he joined Bonnie, who had limped in unaided. Clyde jumped into the car and backed out of the garage into the storm of gunfire. A bullet fragment struck Blanche in the forehead; a glass shard struck her in the left eye.

"Oh my God!" she screamed. "I'm blinded!"

Standing on the running board, W.D. opened up with one of the Brownings as Clyde ran the gauntlet of gunfire, bullets hitting the car from all directions. The Ford barreled through the yard, vaulting over a ditch before hitting the highway. Behind it, the deputies and highway patrolmen raced for telephones to arrange pursuit. Three had suffered minor bullet wounds. As the gang drove north, Blanche begged Clyde to stop the car to minister to Buck, who was dying. "No," Clyde said. "We ain't stoppin'. Shut up about it."

After a whirlwind trip to the World's Fair, John Dillinger had returned to Indianapolis on July 7, intent on quickening the pace of his crime spree. For the first time he explained his plans for a prison breakout to his teenage partner William Shaw. Together the two men bought Dillinger his first car, a maroon 1928 Chevrolet sports coupe. Dillinger didn't know how to drive, so Shaw taught him.

Impatient for a major score, Dillinger began casing a downtown bank Shaw had mentioned, the Massachusetts Avenue State Bank. While he did, Shaw disappeared. A few days later, Dillinger received a message Shaw had decamped to Muncie, fifty miles east, after learning police were looking for him in connection with a robbery pulled while Dillinger was still in prison.

Dillinger drove to Muncie on Friday, July 14, and found Shaw and a group of friends lying around an apartment on South Council Street. The apartment's other occupant was a hard-drinking ex-con named Harry Copeland, a dim bulb Dillinger would use on a number of later bank jobs. That afternoon they took Copeland and drove ten miles west to the farm town of Dalesville, whose bank Dillinger had scouted; they agreed to rob it on Monday.

For some reason, probably because they were low on cash, they decided to rob a Muncie roadhouse, the Bide-a-Wee Tavern, that same night. A few minutes after midnight, Dillinger and a partner walked in, guns drawn, handkerchiefs over their faces, and within minutes backed out of the bar with about $70. On the way out the front door, Dillinger encountered a couple coming in. With a grin he pinched the woman's bottom; when her male friend objected, Dillinger slugged him.[6]

Robbing the tavern turned out to be a mistake. The next morning, a Saturday, Dillinger and Copeland had just left the boardinghouse to move Dillinger's car into the rear garage when they heard someone yell, "Hands up!" It was a pair of Muncie detectives, backed by two patrolmen, who had guns trained on Shaw and the others in an alley behind the house. The detectives, following up on the previous night's robbery, had easily traced Copeland's car, a green sedan with yellow-wire wheels.[7] Dillinger encountered the officers as he turned his new Chevrolet into the alley. Without a word he threw the car into reverse and backed away. The policemen never saw him. Shaw and the others were taken to the Muncie jail, where they named their accomplice as "Dan Dillinger," a name that meant nothing to detectives.*

Dillinger, shrugging off the arrests of his confederates, went forward with plans to rob the bank in nearby Dalesville. A twenty-two-year-old teller, Margaret Good, was alone in the bank when Dillinger, wearing gray summer slacks and a straw boater, strolled in at 12:45. He asked for the bank president. When Miss Good said he wasn't in, Dillinger smiled and

---

* Under questioning William Shaw admitted participating in several Indianapolis robberies. He received a sentence of ten years in a state reformatory for the Bide-a-Wee robbery. Twenty-five years later, Shaw became the principal source for writers researching Dillinger's early months as a bank robber. He gave extensive interviews to John Toland, Dillinger historian Joseph Pinkston, and a writer named Allanna Nash. In and out of various Midwestern prisons for all but seventeen months of his next forty-four years, Shaw burned to death in a Chicago hotel in 1977 after falling asleep holding a lit cigarette. His body lay unclaimed for a week.

slid a pistol through the teller cage. "Well, this is a stickup," he said. "Get me the money, honey."[8]

Miss Good, who had been robbed twice in the preceding two years, pointed at the open vault and raised her hands. As Harry Copeland stood by, cradling a pistol, Dillinger leaped over a low railing leading to the vault area. Copeland corralled a trio of customers who arrived as Dillinger scooped up an estimated $3,500 in cash and a grouping of diamond rings inside the vault. When he was finished, Dillinger led Miss Good and the customers into the vault, shut the door, and strolled out to the getaway car, a green Chevrolet sedan. The two men were in and out of the bank in less than ten minutes.[9]

It was a smooth and easy job, and he had done it on his own. Dillinger's confidence was growing.

After a month, the pursuit of William Hamm's kidnappers had gone nowhere. Agents in St. Paul had interviewed any number of underworld characters but hadn't yet uncovered any clue that the job had been masterminded by Alvin Karpis and the Barker brothers, who had settled into lakeside cottages around Chicago for the summer. Ma Barker remained in her Chicago apartment, immersed in her jigsaw puzzles.

Then, on Wednesday, July 19, a call came into the FBI's Chicago office. A secretary passed it to the SAC, a boyish twenty-nine-year-old South Carolinian named Melvin Purvis who was destined to become a pivotal figure in the War on Crime. Unhappy as an attorney in his hometown, Purvis had enrolled at the Bureau in 1926 and swiftly moved up the ranks. At five-feet-seven, with delicate facial bones and a high, reedy voice, he could pass for a teenager. He was Hoover's favorite SAC. Their correspondence strikes a far more familiar tone than the director's letters to other agents. Hoover's notes began "Dear Mel" and were signed "J.E.H." or "Jayee." Purvis addressed Hoover as "Mr. Hoover" until Hoover admonished him to "stop using *mister*." One of Hoover's favorite themes was Purvis's attractiveness to women. At one point, he told Purvis that should he come to Washington for a costume ball, an FBI secretary would escort him "in a cellophane gown." Hoover ribbed Purvis that a newspaper's description of him made him sound suited for Hollywood: "I don't see how the movies could miss a 'slender, blond-haired, brown-eyed gentleman.' All power to the Clark Gable of the service."[10]

"We all suspected Melvin was Hoover's favorite—we thought he was Daddy's boy early on," Purvis's secretary Doris Rogers remembers. "He obviously was someone Hoover thought was very polished, a kind of ornament, but very bright and ready for the job."*

What set Purvis apart from the deskrows of stolid young agents in their dark suits and shiny black shoes was an air of Southern privilege. Confident to the point of cockiness, he had an ego, a sense of style and entitlement, and he wasn't afraid to show it. He wore sharply cut double-breasted suits, puff handkerchiefs, and straw boaters. Where other bachelor agents lived six to an apartment and rode the El to work, Purvis arrived in Chicago with his own horse, which he stabled in Lincoln Park and rode on weekends. He brought a manservant, a black man named President, who chauffeured Purvis through the streets in a sparkling Pierce Arrow, "an old-fashioned but real name-droppy car," Doris Rogers remembers, "the kind of car that turned heads. That's the way Melvin was. He was seen as very South Carolina."†

That Wednesday, Purvis had been the Chicago SAC for eight months, and as his behavior would show, he hadn't yet mastered the arcane politics of gangland Chicago. On the phone was the chief investigator of the state prosecutor's office, a former Chicago cop named Dan "Tubbo" Gilbert. Purvis was working with Gilbert to crack the strange kidnapping of a syndicate con man named Jake "The Barber" Factor. Many in Chicago thought the kidnapping a sham, an effort by Factor to evade extradition to face criminal charges in Great Britain. Purvis believed it was genuine. It was his first major kidnapping case.

That morning Tubbo Gilbert broke the news that the Factor and Hamm kidnappings had suddenly become intertwined. Two weeks earlier, Gilbert had announced to the press that Jake Factor had probably been kidnapped by an Irish gangster named Roger Touhy, whose suburban bootlegging and gambling empire was an old rival of Al Capone's. With Capone in a federal prison after his conviction on tax evasion charges, Touhy was locked in a struggle with Capone's successor, Frank Nitti, to take control of several large Chicago unions.

---

* Purvis's son Alston, now a professor at Boston University, speculates that Hoover's infatuation with his father was romantic in nature. If so, it was unrequited. Purvis was a dedicated lady's man who would later marry.

† Another sign of Purvis's Southern heritage: he called black people "darkies."

Now Gilbert claimed he had evidence that Touhy had kidnapped Hamm, too. Better yet, Gilbert told Purvis, he had just learned that Touhy and three of his gangmates were in custody after a fender bender that morning in Elkhorn, Wisconsin. There are no records of the conversations between Gilbert and Purvis, but by late that afternoon Gilbert had Purvis believing Touhy was responsible for the Hamm kidnapping, too. Purvis made no independent investigation of Touhy. As far as he was concerned, Gilbert's word was enough for the Bureau.

Friday morning Gilbert and a pair of Purvis's men arrived in Elkhorn, and afterward the prisoners were ferried to Chicago, where they were fingerprinted by an FBI man. Touhy was led into Purvis's office. Purvis told him he was being held for the Hamm kidnapping. "What do you mean a ham, Mr. Purvis? A ham sandwich?" Touhy cracked. "Or did I kidnap a ham steak?"

The next day, William Hamm and several eyewitnesses to his kidnapping were brought to Chicago to identify Hamm's kidnappers. Looking through a one-way mirror, Hamm wasn't at all sure they were his kidnappers and said so to reporters. But one eyewitness, a cab driver named Leo J. Allison, was, and that was all Purvis needed. He emerged from his office to tell reporters that the Bureau had assembled "an ironclad case against Touhy" for the Hamm kidnapping.

"We have positive identification of all four of the prisoners," Purvis said. "The government men worked carefully and thoroughly on this case, and we are sure of ourselves."[11] In Washington, Hoover was thrilled. "[T]his is a splendid piece of work, which was consummated only by the untiring and resourceful efforts of the entire Chicago staff," he wrote Purvis.[12]

It was nothing of the sort. In fact, Purvis was fooled into arresting the wrong men by a corrupt investigator in league with the Chicago Syndicate, a fact that would be confirmed twenty years later by a federal court. Roger Touhy would ultimately be convicted of the false kidnapping of Jake Factor; only after two decades in prison was he able to convince a judge he had been framed. In 1954 Judge John Barnes, in an opinion that led to Touhy's release, noted that the Illinois state prosecutor's office, which he found to be dominated by Tubbo Gilbert, had never brought charges against a single member of the syndicate. Judge Barnes found "sinister motives [by] Captain Gilbert and the politico-criminal syndicate for wanting to remove [Touhy] permanently from the scene." With Purvis as his unwitting ally, the judge found, Gilbert and the FBI "worked in concert to convict Touhy of *something.*"[13]

"That Touhy was indicted at all in the Hamm matter," the judge concluded, "is something for which the Department of Justice should answer." Of course, it never did. Within days several prosecutors involved in the case expressed doubts about its strength, but for the moment no one cared. That Saturday Hoover and his College Boys could rejoice: one of the two major fronts in their new War on Crime had been conquered. No one realized that night would bring a third.

Oklahoma City
Saturday, July 22
11:15 P.M.

Two miles west of the Oklahoma Capitol, in a beige-brick mansion topped by a burgundy Mission-style roof, two couples were sitting in wicker chairs around a card table in their sunroom, playing bridge. The man of the house, a stolid forty-three-year-old oilman named Charles F. Urschel, sat across from his wife, Berenice. He wore linen slacks and a tie and had comb marks in his oiled hair. His wife, one of the wealthiest women in the Southwest, was the widow of famed wildcatter Tom Slick, who before his death had run the world's largest independent oil company. Charles Urschel had been Slick's partner and was now an executor of his estate, estimated to be worth $50 million before Wall Street's collapse. When Urschel's wife died, it was only natural he should marry Berenice. The couple's partners were Walter Jarrett, a roundish, balding oilman, and his wife.

The bridge game was winding down when suddenly there was a noise in the darkness outside. Urschel turned in his chair. "It's me, Betty," came a voice. Jarrett rose and unlatched the screen door. In walked sixteen-year-old Betty Slick, Mrs. Urschel's daughter. Betty, who had been visiting friends, said a few words and disappeared upstairs.

Mrs. Jarrett glanced at her watch. "It's almost eleven-thirty," she said. "Time we were going home, Walter."

Jarrett pushed his chair back. "I suppose so," he said.

"No, wait," Berenice said, placing her hand on Jarrett's wrist. "One more rubber."[14]

The first floor of the Urschel mansion was aglow with yellow light when the big Chevrolet coasted to a stop beside the house about eleven-thirty.

The driver, Albert Bates, a pug-faced jack-of-all-crimes with a foot-long rap sheet, gripped the steering wheel so tightly that his knuckles whitened. The stout, handsome man sitting beside him noticed. "Okay, Al, calm down," he said. "It's gonna be a piece of cake."

The handsome man, who wore a snap-brim Panama hat, was five-feet-nine, about 180 pounds, with a fraternity man's fleshy apple cheeks, bedroom eyes, and a Thompson submachine gun. He and Bates stepped from the car. The night was still, the expensive neighborhood quiet.

"Okay," said the handsome man. They walked up the driveway toward a vine-covered garage. Ahead, on the sunporch behind the house, they could see the two couples at the card table. As they peered through the darkness, Bates couldn't tell who was who. "Jesus!" he whispered. "Which one's Urschel?"

The handsome man couldn't tell, either.

"Come on," he said, and walked toward the porch.[15]

Berenice Urschel drew the card from her hand, lifted it gingerly above the table, then stopped. Her brow furrowed.

"What is it?" Urschel asked.

"I thought I heard something," she said. "Someone moved outside."

Urschel considered the screen door, then peered into the darkness beyond. They'd all heard the car drive up; probably just the neighbors, they decided. They finished the hand, dealt another, and began to bid. Berenice had just uttered the words "two hearts," when the screen door opened. Everyone turned. Two men stepped inside, both holding guns. Berenice let out a little yell and threw up her hands.

"Stop that! Keep quiet or we'll blow your heads off," said the handsome man. "Now which one's Urschel?" When no one answered, he repeated the question. Still no one spoke. The hint of a smile crossed the man's face. "All right," he said, "we'll take both of you then." He pointed his submachine gun at the two men.

Urschel and Jarrett slowly rose. "Hurry," the handsome man said. The two complied, stepping outside. The gunman lingered at the door. "Don't move now," he told the women. "And keep away from that phone."

A minute later Berenice heard a car start and drive away. Both women sprang to their feet. "Hurry!" Berenice said. "Up the stairs!" They ran up the staircase, locking the bedroom door at the top behind them. Berenice grabbed the first telephone she saw, dialed the police, and told them what had happened. Then she remembered an article on kidnapping in a recent issue of *Time* magazine. She and her husband had discussed it just that afternoon. It was on her dressing table. She flipped to the article and dialed the hotline number it mentioned.

A woman's voice came on the line.

"National 7-1-1-7," she said.

"I need to report a kidnapping!" Berenice said.

A few moments later a man's voice came on the line.

"National 7-1-1-7," he said.

"This is Mrs. Charles F. Urschel in Oklahoma City. I wish to report a kidnapping."

"This is J. Edgar Hoover, Mrs. Urschel," Hoover said. "Give me every detail you can."[16]

4

THE BAYING OF THE HOUNDS

July 22 to August 25, 1933

Oklahoma City
July 22, 1933

"I couldn't get a look at their features, but they both seemed dark and had full round faces," Berenice Urschel was saying. "They appeared to be foreigners."

It was 1:00 A.M., ninety minutes after her husband's abduction, and Mrs. Urschel was back at her bridge table, reciting every detail she could remember for the Oklahoma City SAC, Ralph Colvin.

"I want you to be assured," Colvin intoned, "that our first thought will be your husband's safe return. Every highway within a hundred miles of Oklahoma City will be watched." What they needed now, Colvin continued, was for her and Mrs. Jarrett to come to police headquarters to look at mug shots. "I'll go at once," Mrs. Urschel said, standing. "Wait until I get my coat."

The phone rang. She reached for it. Colvin stopped her. "Is there an extension?" he asked.

"Yes, in the hall."

It was Walter Jarrett, calling from police headquarters. He had been released outside of the city after the kidnappers searched his wallet and found he wasn't Urschel. "They took Charlie," he said. "He's not hurt. They say they'll get in touch with you. I found a pickup and rushed to police headquarters."

Downtown, Mrs. Urschel and the Jarretts sorted through mug books; a few photos looked vaguely familiar. Footprints outside the sunporch were inconsequential. There were no fingerprints on the screen door. By daylight Jarrett and a group of FBI agents managed to retrace the kidnappers' route northeast out of the city about ten miles, but there the trail was lost. "This kidnapping has the look of a job carefully planned by highly trained professionals," Colvin told Mrs. Urschel. "They are not local men or they would've known your husband by sight. It should reassure you to know that they are professionals, because there's less chance of your husband being harmed."

After daylight Hoover telephoned Kansas City and ordered Gus Jones to Oklahoma City to take charge of the case. Colvin met him at the airport. On the drive to the mansion, they discussed possible suspects. Colvin was already suspicious of Walter Jarrett and one or two of Urschel's employees. If it wasn't an inside job, they agreed, their best suspects were probably Harvey Bailey and the gang of escapees who had fled the Kansas pen that May.

At the mansion, Jones gave Mrs. Urschel a fatherly lecture on what to expect. They would wait for the kidnappers to contact them. They would deliver the ransom. Her husband would be returned. "The moment Mr. Urschel is released," Jones said, "we go to work."

It was the FBI's good fortune that Charles Urschel had been kidnapped by the man who was probably the most inept of Depression-era criminals, the handsome George F. Barnes, better known as Machine Gun Kelly. Seventy years after the crime that made him famous, the most impressive thing about Kelly remains his nickname. He was never the menacing figure his moniker suggests. He was glib, a dreamer and a joker, the kind of man who said things like "Working hard or hardly working?" It's unlikely he would have risen to prominence if not for his wife, Kathryn, a sly blonde whom J. Edgar Hoover would repeatedly demonize in press accounts.

Though his talents were few, Kelly's career trajectory was unique; he was the only major criminal of 1933–34 who came from an upper-middle-class background and had attended college. Born in Chicago in 1900, Kelly moved with his family to Memphis when he was two. His father was a successful insurance agent. Kelly grew up in an affluent neighborhood, attended Sacred Heart Catholic Church, and earned money throwing a paper route and caddying. At Central High School he was called a "jellybean"— a sharp dresser and skirt-chaser, who enjoyed throwing around money.

When his mother died and his father took up with another woman, Kelly began getting into trouble. After dropping out of high school, he became a bootlegger, reselling shipments of whiskey he bought in Missouri and Kentucky. He made a stab at college, a single semester at Mississippi A&M, but dropped out; his father disowned him. An ambitious young man who longed for finer things, Kelly soon eloped with Geneva Ramsey, a Memphis millionaire's daughter. He went to work for his father-in-law's construction company and fathered two, but his life began to crumble after Geneva's father was killed in an accident.

His mother-in-law bought him a parking garage and a dairy farm to run, but Kelly preferred bootlegging. In 1924, when he was twenty-four, he was arrested, and the judge sentenced him to six months in a work camp. Geneva left him. Despondent, he attempted suicide, swallowing a bottle of bichloride of mercury, but succeeded only in making himself sick. Rather than face jail, Kelly fled to Kansas City, where he soon embezzled enough money as a supermarket clerk to buy a truck.

He used it to transport whiskey as far afield as New Mexico, where he was briefly imprisoned in 1927. When he was arrested selling liquor on an Indian reservation, a federal judge threw the book at him, sentencing him to five years in Leavenworth. It was in prison that Kelly fell in with a group of St. Paul yeggs, at one point lending help on an escape attempt orchestrated by Frank Nash. After his 1930 parole, he headed for Minnesota, where he was quickly accepted at the Green Lantern tavern and began tagging along on bank jobs.

That September, Kelly married Kathryn Thorne, an Oklahoma-born party girl whose second husband—Kelly was her third—died under mysterious circumstances. Kathryn was a haughty self-indulgent alcoholic whose daughter was being raised by Kathryn's mother. Of all the women the FBI pursued in 1933 and 1934, she was to gall Hoover like no other. "Kathryn Thorne Kelly was one of the most coldly deliberate criminals of my experience," Hoover wrote in his 1936 book, *Persons in Hiding.* To Hoover, Kathryn was Kelly's Svengali, "man-crazy," "clothes-crazy," a "cunning, shrewd criminal-actress" who created, marketed, and dominated her husband. "If ever there was a henpecked husband," Hoover wrote, "it was George [Machine Gun] Kelly."[1]

As compelling as this portrait sounds, there is no evidence in FBI files that Kathryn was anything more than her husband's knowing accomplice. She could do little to improve his criminal skills. Kelly was a lousy bank robber, so nervous he sometimes vomited before bank jobs, and was eventually shunned by Harvey Bailey, Verne Miller, and other St. Paul yeggs. He was no better at kidnapping. In January 1932, Kelly and a partner kidnapped an Indiana businessman named Howard Woolverton; Kathryn had picked his name out of a phone book. Kelly was forced to release Woolverton when his family was unable to raise the ransom.

Between forays to Chicago and St. Paul in search of partners, Kelly lived at Kathryn's home on East Mulkey Street in Fort Worth, Texas, where the couple quickly attracted the attention of police. The good-natured Kelly befriended a cop or two, at one point even helping police apprehend a neighborhood burglar. But he longed to be a bank robber. According to Hoover, Kathryn acted as a kind of press agent for her husband, boasting of Kelly's exploits in an effort to get him work. This may have been true; Kathryn did like to brag about Kelly, especially when she drank. Eventually Kelly hooked up with the Jazz Age yegg Eddie Bentz, and with Bentz and a crook named Albert Bates robbed banks in Washington, Texas, and Mississippi during 1932.

In time Kathryn's boasting caught the ear of a canny Fort Worth detective named Ed Weatherford, who led Kathryn to believe he was corrupt. When Verne Miller was identified in the massacre case in July 1933, Weatherford recognized the name as one of the bank men Kathryn bragged of knowing. He contacted the FBI. The Dallas SAC, Frank Blake, passed the tip to Kansas City, the first time Kelly came to the Bureau's attention.* "[Fort Worth] tells me that Kelly is most proficient with a machine gun," Blake wrote, "it being said he can write his name with the bullets discharged from such a gun."[2]

Overnight, Kelly became a suspect in the massacre case; in Kansas City, agents wrote Leavenworth asking for his record. Blake, meanwhile, drove to Fort Worth one afternoon and watched the East Mulkey Street house for several hours, jotting down the license number of a Cadillac in the driveway. On July 13, Agent Charles Winstead was sent to reconnoiter a scraggly ranch outside Paradise, Texas, north of Fort Worth, where Kathryn's mother lived with a cantankerous old rancher named Robert "Boss" Shan-

---

* Born in 1883, Frank Blake attended Vanderbilt University, where upon graduation he briefly coached the football team. After five years as a rancher, he joined the Bureau in 1919, moving up through the ranks to become the Dallas SAC in 1930. Small and wiry, with a soft Texas drawl, Blake served in the FBI until a heart attack forced his retirement in 1942. He died at his home in suburban Dallas in 1948.

non. Winstead found it, arranged with the postmaster for a cover on in-coming mail, and returned to Dallas.[3] With nothing linking Kelly to the massacre case, the FBI lost interest.

It was to the Shannon Ranch that the Kellys brought the blindfolded Charles Urschel nine days later. In return for a cut of the ransom money, Boss Shannon and his son Armon agreed to watch Urschel while Kelly han-dled ransom negotiations. Kathryn, meanwhile, took her daughter Pauline to Fort Worth. That Sunday morning, July 23, she invited Ed Weatherford to her house; if anyone was watching them, Kathryn suspected, he would warn her. Weatherford found Kathryn on her front steps in a chatty mood; she said she was just back from St. Louis.

It was a short talk. Walking down the driveway, Weatherford glanced at Kathryn's car. He noticed an Oklahoma paper on the front seat, the head-lines blaring the Urschel kidnapping, and red dirt caked on the wheels. Okla-homa was red-dirt country, Weatherford reflected as he drove off. Back at his home, Weatherford studied the *Fort Worth Star Telegram*'s stories on the Urschel kidnapping. The more he read, the more convinced he became that the Kellys were behind it. The next morning he again telephoned the FBI office in Dallas, which passed the tip to Gus Jones in Oklahoma City.[4] Jones ignored it.

Dexter, Iowa
Sunday, July 23

That Sunday, as Gus Jones assumed command at the Urschel home in Okla-homa City, a man named Henry Nye took a walk near his farm outside of Dexter, Iowa, a town twenty miles west of Des Moines. Walking down a country lane, he approached an open field where ten years earlier there had been an amusement park called Dexfield Park. These days the twenty-acre field, bordered by tall maples, heavy underbrush, and a coil of the Middle Raccoon River, functioned mostly as a lovers' lane. Through the trees, Nye spotted a 1933 Ford. There were people beside it. At first he thought they were campers. Then he spotted a shirt thrown on the ground. It was caked in what appeared to be blood. Nye hurried to his house and telephoned the town night watchman.

Clyde had found the field three days earlier, on Thursday, the afternoon after fleeing the shoot-out at Platte City. Their campsite, a collection of blankets and seat cushions scattered on the grass, resembled a field hospital. Somehow Buck was still alive. His head bandaged, he lay on the ground semiconscious, nearing death. Blanche was blinded in one eye. Bonnie could barely walk. Clyde couldn't risk a motel, much less a doctor. Their car had been so riddled with bullets that even the most myopic sheriff would notice. W.D. had slathered mud across the damage, then stolen a car in the town of Perry.

Clyde used the car that Friday to drive into Dexter. He bought five chicken dinners and a block of ice at Blohm's Meat Market, gauze and alcohol at Pohle's Pharmacy, and shirts and shoes at a clothing store. He repeated his errands the next day. That Sunday morning, they woke to find Buck still alive. No one could see how. Occasionally Blanche would press her hands against the wound in his temple in an effort to keep his brains from oozing out. He didn't have long.

By Sunday afternoon, word of the bloodied campers at Dexfield Park was relayed to the sheriff in the town of Adel. He had read of the Platte City shoot-out and immediately thought of the Barrow Gang. The sheriff drove to Dexter and questioned the merchants who had sold items to Clyde. Their descriptions of the man matched those on the Wanted posters in his office. He called the state police in Des Moines, asking for help. A pair of officers arrived at nightfall. By then word had spread of the approaching raid. Farmers began arriving in beat-up pickups, birdguns on their hips, looking for action. By nightfall dozens of people lined the dirt roads leading to Dexfield Park. It was an oddly festive atmosphere. Some boys brought dates. More than a few brought bottles. In the darkness around forty men with guns began moving into the woods, waiting for daylight.

Dexter, Iowa
Monday, July 24

A heavy dew lay across the field. Clyde woke a few minutes after five to find Blanche already up, still attired in the tight riding breeches and sunglasses she had worn since fleeing Platte City. W.D. was roasting frankfurters over the fire. Clyde sat beside Bonnie on a seat cushion. He was ready to leave. He and W.D. had serviced the car and cleaned the guns the night before.

"Where are we going?" asked Bonnie, still in her nightgown.

"*We* aren't going anywhere," Clyde said. "I'm taking Buck home to Mother's." They had promised Cumie Barrow that should anything happen to one of them, the wounded brother would be brought home.

"You aren't going without me," Bonnie whispered. "And why should you drive all that way to take Buck back? You know he's dying, honey. He'll be dead by night."

"I'm taking him back *because* he's dying," Clyde said.[5]

As they talked Clyde glanced up and saw movement in the trees: men were approaching, maybe a half-dozen. Clyde grabbed his favorite Browning, aimed it over the men's heads, and began firing, trying to scare them off. But if he thought they were farmers out for a morning walk, he immediately realized his mistake. His shots were answered by a rolling fusillade of gunshots from the surrounding trees; within moments the campsite was engulfed by a swarm of flying bullets. W.D. was standing at the campfire, a skillet still in his hands, when a buckshot pellet struck him in the chest and knocked him down. As Clyde returned fire, he yelled for everyone to get into the car they had stolen in Perry.

As Clyde sprayed the trees with bullets, W.D. stumbled into the car, but he was unable to get the engine started. Shooting the Browning from his hip, Clyde scrambled to W.D.'s side, shoving him in the backseat. Bonnie limped in to join them, and a moment later Blanche half-carried the semiconscious Buck in as well. The moment they were inside, Clyde threw the car into reverse, heading for the field's only exit, a narrow dirt path leading to the paved road that ran along the west side of the clearing. Bullets smashed into the car, shattering the windows. Clyde saw a half-dozen men with guns blocking his exit. Reversing course, he drove back toward the center of the field, crashing through bushes and underbrush. A bullet struck him in the shoulder, and he lost control of the car and ran over a tree stump.

W.D. leaped out and tried to shove the car off the stump. It was no use. "Everybody outta the car!" Clyde hollered. "Pile out—for God's sake, pile out!"

Clyde ran for the Platte City car, but by the time he reached it the black Ford was a wreck; sixty-four bullets had ripped up the tires, blown out the windows and cracked the engine block. Clyde scanned the trees for an escape route. Beyond the camp, a hundred yards to the north, rose some scrubby trees beside the river; there seemed to be no gunfire emanating from that quarter. Clyde lit out for the river. The others did their best to follow. As they ran, a bullet struck W.D. a glancing blow to the forehead. He fell, then scrambled forward. Bonnie took two shotgun pellets in the stomach and fell hard in the grass. W.D. grabbed her and together the two made it to a ravine leading down to the river's edge. Before they reached it, Buck fell. Blanche screamed. Clyde hurried to his brother's side. "Take Blanche and run for it," Buck rasped. "I'm done for."[6] Clyde ignored him, dragging Buck into the thick underbrush beside the river.

Miraculously, Clyde seemed to have chosen an escape route unblocked by possemen. Down in the riverside thicket, no one was shooting at them. Heading for the paved road with thoughts of stealing a car, they thrashed west along the river for several minutes until they came to a rise. Buck collapsed. "Take Blanche," he whispered to Clyde. "I can't make it." Clyde peered down the river. In the distance he could just make out a bridge. "I'm going after a car," he said. "Hide here. They'll never find you in these thickets."[7]

As the others crawled beneath some bushes, Clyde climbed the little hill and trotted through the trees toward the bridge. As he emerged from the woods, he saw two deputies standing on the road beside it, one of them leaning against the concrete archway that marked the entrance to the old amusement park. The deputies saw Clyde first, raised their guns, and fired. Clyde ducked behind a tree.

"Hey, don't shoot!" he hollered. "I'm a state man!"[8]

When the deputies lowered their guns, Clyde stepped out and fired. The deputies fired back, one of their bullets knocking the Browning from his hands. Clyde grabbed a pistol from his waistband and retreated into the thicket. A minute later he reached the others. "You okay?" he asked Bonnie. She nodded, hugging him.

"They've got the bridge blocked," Clyde said to W.D. "Can you help Bonnie cross the river? We'll have to swim for it." Abandoning Buck and Blanche to their fates, the trio slid into the shallow river and swam the twenty yards across, Bonnie holding on to W.D.'s neck. On the far side, Clyde looked up through the trees and saw a farmhouse. Leaving Bonnie and W.D. sitting by the river, he made for it.

The first indication of trouble eighteen-year-old Marvelle Feller had as he walked out to feed his father's cattle was his German shepherd, who began growling and baring its teeth. Suddenly the dog raced toward the Feller family's cornfield. A moment later Feller saw a man emerge from the cornstalks, his tattered shirt streaked with mud and blood. Standing behind a barbed-wire fence, Clyde brandished his pistol.

"Call that dog off," he yelled, "or I'll kill him."

Feller ran to the dog and grabbed its collar. Feller's father and a hired hand came out to see what the commotion was about. "Y'all get down here!" Clyde yelled, pointing the pistol. They obliged.

Clyde placed his fingers to his lips and let out a loud wolf-whistle. Moments later W.D. and Bonnie appeared behind him. W.D., wiping blood from his eyes, was bleeding from several flesh wounds. The front of Bonnie's nightgown was red with blood.

"Help me get her over the fence," Clyde ordered the elder Feller, who stepped forward and lifted Bonnie over the barbed wire.

Just then Mrs. Feller and her daughter ran out of the farmhouse. "They've got a bunch of outlaws cornered in the park," she started to say, and then she lost the words. "We ain't gonna hurt you folks," Clyde said. "We just need a car."

The Fellers had three cars; unfortunately, two sat up on blocks. Clyde waved his gun at a Plymouth in the garage. "Okay," he said. "Back it out." The Fellers placed Bonnie in the backseat. Marvelle had to show Clyde how to start the car. With the teenager's help, Clyde drove to the road outside and headed north, away from Dexfield Park.

An hour later the possemen combing the woods around Dexfield Park found Buck and Blanche in the thicket and took them into custody. Buck was taken to King's Daughters Hospital in the town of Perry. His mother and other family members soon arrived. He lasted almost a week before dying the following Saturday afternoon, July 29. He was taken back to Dallas and buried. Blanche was thrown into jail. Bonnie and Clyde, meanwhile, eluded roadblocks and vanished. Bonnie later told her mother that they stole a car in Polk City, Iowa, and headed west toward Denver. It would be a long time before they were seen again.

All that week, as posses fanned out across Iowa in search of Bonnie and Clyde, reporters and photographers swarmed the streets around the Urschel mansion in Oklahoma City. The kidnapping was the biggest national crime story since the Lindbergh case a year before, capturing the public's attention in a way William Hamm's brief weekend detention had not. The mansion, the millions, the interruption of a simple bridge game—it was irresistible to the nation's press.

On Wednesday morning, July 26, two days after Bonnie and Clyde escaped from Dexfield Park, a Tulsa oilman named John Catlett was standing in the bathroom of his home, shaving. One of his servants walked into the adjoining bedroom with a manila envelope; a Western Union messenger had brought it to the front door. "Put it down," Catlett said, and continued shaving. When he was finished, Catlett rinsed his face, walked over to the envelope, and opened it. Out tumbled three of Charles Urschel's business cards. Inside Catlett found three typewritten letters. One was from Urschel, asking him to take the other two to his wife. Catlett jammed the letters into his coat pocket, trotted to his car, and drove to Oklahoma City.

Berenice Urschel cried as she read her husband's letters. A typewritten note from the kidnappers demanded a ransom of $200,000 for Urschel's return. The letter included the text of a bogus classified advertisement for the sale of a ranch that was to be placed in the *Daily Oklahoman* each day for a week. When the kidnappers saw the ad, they would make contact once more. One of Urschel's friends, a tall, sinewy oilman named E. E. Kirkpatrick, placed the ad that night.

The next day, a letter from the kidnappers arrived at the newspaper. It instructed Kirkpatrick to take the 10:10 P.M. train to Kansas City that Saturday night. At some point along the way, he would see a signal fire. When a second fire came into view, he was to toss a Gladstone bag containing the ransom money from the train. If anything went wrong, he was to proceed to the Muehlebach Hotel in Kansas City to await further instructions.*

Reading the letter in her drawing room, Mrs. Urschel paused as she considered the ransom demand: $200,000. "That's a lot of money," an FBI man said. "Yes, but we'll have to spend it," she replied. "Charlie's life is at stake. There's no other way."

As the ransom negotiations advanced, Ed Weatherford, the Fort Worth detective, continued pestering the FBI's Dallas office to investigate the Kellys. Had the Dallas agents made anything more than nominal efforts to do so, they might have broken the case. As it was, they came close. On

---

* As Depression-era ransom notes go, this one was commendably free of melodramatic threats. It included only one: *Remember this—if any trickery is attempted you will find the remains of Urschel and instead of joy there will be double grief—for some-one* [sic] *very near and dear to the Urschel family is under constant surveillance and will likewise suffer for your error.*

July 24, two days after the kidnapping, Weatherford and Dallas agent Dwight McCormack arranged for a tap on Kathryn's phone at East Mulkey Street.* The tap was a low priority, however: it was manned not by an FBI agent but by a Southwestern Bell supervisor, who was told to call if she heard anything suspicious.

Weatherford, meanwhile, watched the house. Kathryn had disappeared. He was certain she was at the Shannon Ranch. Weatherford begged the Dallas office to tap the ranch's phone, but it was a party line, and agents said it was unlikely the Kellys would discuss anything incriminating on it. Another opportunity was missed when the FBI failed to secure a photo of Kelly. The Fort Worth police had a single image of Kelly, taken voluntarily in December 1930, and agents asked for it in order to show Mrs. Urschel. Had she identified Kelly's photo, the case might have come to a swift conclusion. But the photo had been lost.

"[Weatherford] states that the last time he saw the photograph it was on [another officer's] desk," an agent wrote. "[He] advised Agent that possibly one of the boys picked it up and forgot to return it."9 The disappearance of this photo cost the FBI weeks.

At 8:00 that Saturday night, E. E. Kirkpatrick hunched in the bushes behind the Urschel mansion with four other family friends and a deputy sheriff. Berenice Urschel appeared at an upstairs window and flashed a floodlight. At the signal a car rolled into the driveway. From the car stepped an Oklahoma City banker. He trotted to the shrubs and handed Kirkpatrick a tan Gladstone bag carrying $200,000 in cash.

Two hours later Kirkpatrick and the Tulsa oilman John Catlett boarded the "Sooner" Katy-Limited train bound for Kansas City. The two men made their way to the rear of the train, pulling up stools by the backdoor. They carried matching Gladstone bags, one with the cash, the other stuffed with newspapers; if anyone attempted to rob them, they planned to hand over the decoy bag.

There was a delay when the conductor added two cars to the train to accommodate a group of World's Fair excursionists.

"Think this will foul up their plan, Kirk?" Catlett asked.

* Born in Illinois in 1905, Dwight L. McCormack served in the FBI from 1929 to 1944. In later years he served as a juvenile court judge in Dallas. He died there in 1959.

"I wish I knew," Kirkpatrick said.

Finally, whistles blew, and the train chugged out of the station, heading northeast toward the Kansas border. As it picked up speed, the dwindling dust-bowl towns of northern Oklahoma slid by in the night. Witcher. Arcadia. Luther. Fallis. Tryon. Kirkpatrick was nervous, but Catlett seemed without a care, discussing fishing lures and turkey hunting. At each town Kirkpatrick stepped out into the night air, lighting a cigarette beneath the platform light. Both men agreed the most likely place for the drop was the wild Osage Hills. Kirkpatrick allowed himself to ruminate on all the outlaws who had crisscrossed these train tracks in years past—the Daltons, the James Brothers, the Doolins, Al Spencer, Frank Nash. Some things never changed.

Hours ticked by. The train passed Bartlesville, then Dewey, then crossed into Kansas. No fires were seen. As they approached Kansas City, dawn broke. Kirkpatrick was distraught. Either they had bungled the drop or the whole thing had been a hoax. In Kansas City the two men trudged off the train and checked into the Muehlebach Hotel, as the kidnappers had ordered. Not long after, a bellboy brought Fitzpatrick a telegram. It read: UNAVOIDABLE INCIDENT KEPT ME FROM SEEING YOU LAST NIGHT. WILL COMMUNICATE ABOUT 6:00 O'CLOCK. E.W. MOORE.[10]

Exactly why Kelly missed the drop was never explained. According to one story, he flooded the engine of his car.[11]

All that Sunday, Kirkpatrick and Catlett waited in their hotel room and listened to the dulcet tones of a lobby pianist playing Mendelssohn's "Spring Song," Rubenstein's "Melody in F," and Schubert's "Serenade." Finally, at 5:40, the phone rang. "This is Moore," a man's voice said. "Did you get my wire?" When Kirkpatrick said he had, the voice told him to proceed to the LaSalle Hotel on Linwood Boulevard—alone. He would be met outside. They agreed to meet at 6:20.

Kirkpatrick had a Colt automatic jammed in his belt when the taxi let him out at the LaSalle. The Gladstone bag in hand, he walked a few yards and lit a cigarette. After a moment he saw a barrel-chested figure striding toward him on the sidewalk. The man wore a pressed summer suit, a panama hat, and a cinched knot in his tie.

It was Kelly. "I'll take that grip," Kelly said.

Kirkpatrick studied the man, trying to memorize every detail.

"Hurry up," Kelly said.

"How do I know you're the right party?"

"Hell, you know damned well I am."

"Two hundred thousand dollars is a lot of money," Kirkpatrick said. "What assurance have we that you'll do what you promise?"

"Don't argue with me," Kelly said. "The boys are waiting."

"Wait. Tell me definitely what I can tell Mrs. Urschel."

"Urschel will be home within twelve hours." Then the man stepped forward, grabbed the Gladstone bag, and walked off into traffic.

Back at the hotel, Kirkpatrick telephoned Mrs. Urschel. "I closed the deal for that farm," he said. "It will require about twelve hours for the lawyers to examine the abstracts, then title will pass."

"Thanks," Berenice said and hung up.[12]

It rained hard all that Monday in Oklahoma City. Berenice spent the day pacing the drawing room, waiting. When Kirkpatrick returned from Kansas City, Gus Jones drove him to the FBI office to review mug shots. Weatherford saw no one he recognized.

"What do you think? Will they release him?" Kirkpatrick asked as they returned to the mansion.

Jones shook his head. "It's a poor bet," he said. "If they feel he can identify the hideout, he doesn't stand a chance. They told you he'd be home within twelve hours. He isn't. Their letter said they were gonna hold him until all the money had been examined and exchanged. Now that's something that could take weeks. The longer they hold him the more dangerous it becomes."

"Then you don't think he'll make it back?" Kirkpatrick asked.

"I won't say that," said Jones. "But I will say that if he's not back by sunup tomorrow, he won't be back."

When night fell, tensions rose in the Urschel mansion. The only moment of levity came after one of the lawyers saw a mouse. He retrieved a mousetrap from the kitchen and slipped it under a divan, then forgot about it. Later that night, as the rain drummed outside, a loud pop sounded. Mrs. Urschel jumped to her feet, frightened.

"What was that?" she asked. The lawyer smiled. "Just the mouse being caught, Berenice," he said.

And then, around eleven, the backdoor opened and Charles Urschel walked in. He was unshaven. His eyes blinked. Mrs. Urschel ran to him and fell into his arms. He had been dropped off in the suburb of Norman an hour earlier and had taken a taxi home.

Gus Jones was called and arrived at 11:00. Urschel said he was too tired to talk. Jones insisted. Urschel said he couldn't identify the kidnappers and didn't know where he had been taken. Jones took him by the arm and told him it was okay. Then he led him into the study, closed the door, and began to ask questions.

With Gus Jones transferred to the Urschel case, the Kansas City Massacre investigation began to drift. No one in custody had shed any light on Verne Miller's whereabouts or who his partners were. The Hot Springs bookie Dick Galatas had vanished, as had Pretty Boy Floyd, though most agents discounted his involvement. Harvey Bailey and the other Kansas escapees were loose in Oklahoma, robbing banks at will, but the Bureau had mounted no credible efforts to apprehend them.

Then on July 31, the day Urschel was released, came a rocket from New York: agents there had found Verne Miller's girlfriend, Vi Mathias. She was living under the alias "Vivian Allen" in a luxurious apartment on Central Park West. The initial report of the New York SAC, Frank X. Fay, identified her host as thirty-six-year-old "Louis or Philip Buckwalt (also known as Bucholtz, Buchouse or Buchalter)" and added: "Preliminary investigation with respect to him has disclosed that even though he resides in luxury, he is somewhat of a notorious character."[13] It is a measure of the FBI's meager knowledge of the American underworld in 1933 that Fay had little sense of who this man was.

Vi Mathias's host is better known to history as Louis "Lepke" Buchalter. A founding member of the New York syndicate along with Meyer Lansky and Charles "Lucky" Luciano, Buchalter had just been named head of its syndicate's enforcement arm, Murder, Inc., which he ran alongside his traditional narcotics and labor-union rackets. How Buchalter came to meet Verne Miller will never be known for certain, but the FBI later picked up reports that Buchalter had hired Miller on several occasions to murder rival mobsters. However they met, Buchalter knew Miller well enough to hide his girlfriend.

New York agents had been closing in on Vi Mathias since July 19, when the St. Paul office, which was intercepting her parents' mail, called to say her daughter Betty had received a box of saltwater taffy sent from Atlantic City. A New York agent tracked down the store where the taffy was bought and retrieved a sales receipt. Handwriting on the receipt was confirmed as Mathias's, but the trail ended there.

Then on July 22, the day Charles Urschel was kidnapped, came word that Betty had received a second package, this one a pen-and-pencil set, mailed from a novelty store in Lake Placid, New York. New York agents were at the store within hours. They discovered that two well-dressed women had purchased the gift a week earlier. One of the women was described as thirty-eight years old, "very stout, very broad shoulders and heavy chest, very dark throughout, dark hair, dark complexion, looked Jewish and wore a yellow sweater ensemble and a very large green pin." This was Buchalter's wife, Betty. The second woman, a slim "straw blonde" wearing heavy makeup, was decked out in a blue silk ensemble and a white tam. A salesman identified her from a photo as Vi Mathias.

Agents spread across the Lake Placid area, checking every hotel, resort, and Western Union office. They found nothing concrete, but on a tip that a woman who resembled Mathias had told a salesperson she was heading to Montreal, agents expanded their search into Canada. Finally, on the night of July 27, a hotel detective in Montreal told agents a woman who resembled Mathias had checked out of the Mt. Royal Hotel hours before. Identifying the photos of Mathias and Betty Buchalter, he said the two women had been driving with two men, one a Columbia Pictures executive, the other the owner of an Adirondack tourist camp. The next day, agents located the camp owner, who described how the two couples had toured Montreal nightclubs and upstate New York hotels for a week, drinking heavily and having a wild time. Mathias had fallen hard for the Columbia executive. Neither of the women seemed bothered by the absence of their respective life partners.

The camp owner volunteered that the women were now at the New Sherwood Hotel in Burlington, Vermont. Two agents were dispatched from Manhattan, and at 11:00 the next morning, Sunday, July 30, they watched as Mathias, wearing a low-cut green dress, drove a black Lincoln away from the hotel. Beside her sat the buxom Betty Buchalter. The two agents followed the Lincoln across the New York line, where it turned south. All went smoothly until the two cars passed through the town of Troy, New York, where the FBI car got a flat tire. Mathias and Buchalter continued south, disappearing into a warm Sunday afternoon.

Losing Vi Mathias was the kind of blunder the FBI made often in 1933 as Hoover's men learned the ins and outs of professional law enforcement. Still, they recovered nicely. By then, thanks to an inspection of hotel registries, the New York office knew where Mrs. Buchalter lived, in Apartment 17J at the Majestic Apartments on Central Park West.* A team of agents was put on twenty-four-hour surveillance, and the next night, July 31, Mrs. Buchalter was spotted leaving the building alone. The agents followed her for a few blocks but let her go. They had already placed a tap on the Buchalters' phone and secured an informant inside the building, apparently a bellman. If Mathias was still in New York, the agents bet she would return.[14]

Three days later, the informant at the Majestic alerted the New York office that the Buchalters were preparing to leave for a vacation and had sent a grouping of trunks to Pennsylvania Station. A pair of agents reached the station just as a party of seven, including people identified as Mr. and Mrs. L. Buchalter and Miss V. Allen, boarded a train for Vermont. The agents scrambled onto the train, which reached Vermont that night. But inexplicably, by the time the two agents disembarked, they found the Buchalters' party had already driven off.

This time Hoover's men caught a break. Agents from the New York office had been canvassing hotels in Atlantic City for weeks, chasing unconfirmed reports that Verne Miller was hiding in the area. The next evening, Friday, August 4, the assistant manager of the Ritz Carlton in Atlantic City telephoned to say the Buchalters and their son, accompanied by a Miss Vivian Allen, had just checked in to the hotel.

By midnight five agents had gathered at the Ritz Carlton. The Buchalters and "Miss Allen" were staying in Rooms 1519 and 1520, overlooking the ocean. When questioned, the hotel's assistant manager told agents the party had reserved beach chairs for the weekend. The next morning several agents donned bathing suits and took seats on the beach behind the Buchalter party, which consisted of Buchalter and his wife, a young boy, and three other men "of Jewish extraction." There was a second woman with them, but she wasn't a blonde; in their report the agents described her

---

* One year later the Majestic would figure prominently in the Lindbergh kidnapping case, when a German-born carpenter named Bruno Richard Hauptmann said he couldn't possibly have kidnapped the Lindbergh baby because he had been working at the Majestic.

as having "henna colored hair which she wore in a Greta Garbo fashion." It was Mathias, her hair newly dyed.

Monday morning around eleven, after an uneventful weekend, the Buchalters checked out. Along with Mathias they stepped into a black Lincoln sedan outside the hotel. As the Lincoln pulled away, the New York agents were behind it, two agents driving in a Packard, another agent following in a chauffeur-driven limousine. They trailed the Buchalters north, toward Manhattan. When the FBI car overheated, only the chauffeured limo remained behind the Buchalters' Lincoln as it headed into downtown Newark and stopped at the Robert Trent Hotel. A bellman unloaded several bags. The Buchalter family, Mathias, and an unidentified man stepped out of the car and walked inside.

After a few minutes the Buchalters emerged from the hotel and stepped into the Lincoln. There was no sign of Mathias. The agent inside the limousine had to make a split-second decision: follow the Lincoln, or follow Mathias. Assuming Mathias had checked in to the hotel, he chose the Lincoln, trailing it just far enough to be certain it was heading for the Holland Tunnel into Manhattan. At that point, the agent told his chauffeur to return to the Robert Trent. Reaching the hotel, he hurried inside to make sure Mathias had checked in. To his horror, she hadn't. According to the assistant manager, she had loitered inside the lobby for twenty minutes, then left.

A half-dozen agents descended on the hotel and questioned bellmen, taxi drivers, and anyone else they could find. It was no use. Vi Mathias had vanished, and this time the FBI couldn't find her.

Behind closed doors at the Urschel mansion, Gus Jones slowly drew from Charles Urschel every memory he could retrieve of his captors. Jones's manner was soothing. Though Urschel insisted he had nothing to offer— he had been blindfolded—Jones asked him to proceed on the premise that when one sense is removed, remaining senses grow more acute. As the hours wore on, Urschel realized that Jones was right.

He remembered passing through an intense rainstorm about an hour after leaving Oklahoma City. He recalled stopping at a filling station where an attendant had made a remark about "broom corn," a crop grown mostly in southern Oklahoma. He remembered the car crossing a long wooden bridge. Jones thought he knew the bridge. It crossed the Red River near Ardmore. It meant Urschel had been taken to Texas.

He was taken to a farm, he was certain. Roosters crowed. He could hear pigs squealing. He had been given water to drink in a battered tin cup. Well water, he guessed. He could hear the well's pulley squeak. The water tasted strongly of minerals. When his blindfold loosened after several days, he was able to snatch glimpses of the shack where he was held. Jones made a sketch. Urschel nodded. It was close.

Jones pushed for more. An airplane passed overhead twice each day, Urschel remembered, in the mornings around nine and the afternoons at five or six. Jones's interest grew. Airline schedules could be checked. Finally, Urschel remembered a terrific rainstorm the Saturday night before his release. He had asked his guard—a young man, he thought, not one of the kidnappers—whether it was a tornado. "No," the man had replied. "But they have a lot of those down in Oklahoma."

Jones smiled. "That was a plant," he said. "You weren't north of Oklahoma, you were south of it." He leaned forward. "Now I want you to think hard, Mr. Urschel. This may be the most important question of all the ones I've asked you here today, so take your time before you answer it. Did you hear the airplane the night of that windstorm?"

Urschel closed his eyes, then shook his head. "No," he said. "I'm sure I didn't."

Jones smiled. "For a man who was blindfolded and chained," he said, "I'd say you saw one helluva lot."[15]

Jones's debriefing of Charles Urschel became famous within the Bureau, and for years afterward, while rarely crediting Jones by name, Hoover cited his work as a shining example of the FBI's "scientific" approach to crime solving. In fact, as canny as Jones's deductions proved, they proved unnecessary. As Jones launched a furious effort to find a North Texas farm that matched Urschel's description, the Fort Worth detective, Ed Weatherford, had persuaded agents in Dallas that the Kellys were the kidnappers.

The morning after Urschel's release, Weatherford coaxed a Dallas agent named Kelly Deaderick out to the town of Paradise, where they interviewed the woman who ran the town switchboard.* She reported that

---

* Kelly D. Deaderick, a World War I veteran born in Jonesboro, Tennessee, served in the FBI from 1927 to 1951. In later years he was a prosecutor in Yakima, Washington. He died there in 1970 at the age of seventy-one.

Kathryn Kelly, whom she knew well, had been at the Shannon Ranch with her mother all week. Everyone in town was suspicious of the Kellys and their flashy cars and the twenty-dollar bills they threw around like confetti, she said. The man at the telegraph office said much the same thing. He said Kathryn boasted that her husband was a bank robber.

Agent Deaderick returned to Dallas convinced they were onto something. He called and briefed Gus Jones. But Jones continued to ignore the Kellys; he had secured a plane from Phillips Petroleum and was busy flying agents across North Texas, trying to find the farm Urschel described. Despite all Weatherford had learned, an FBI case summary prepared August 5 made no mention of the Kellys. The Dallas office's frustration peaked two days later when its number two, Dwight McCormack, wrote a report summarizing the evidence. In place of a title for his memo, McCormack put an argument: "Investigation of activities of George Kelly and gang at Fort Worth and Paradise, Texas, indicates strong possibility they were involved in Urschel kidnapping."

Still, Jones didn't listen. He continued peppering the Dallas office with requests for airline schedules and weather reports all across Oklahoma and North Texas. FBI legend, and Jones's own version of events, holds that it was only after a rigorous analysis of this data that the Paradise area was identified as the kidnappers' probable hideout. In fact, what was happening was something more subtle: each time Jones asked for data, the Dallas office checked conditions at Paradise and pointed out how they fit Urschel's descriptions. The clincher came late on Wednesday, August 9, when Dallas forwarded data on rain patterns at Paradise. They fit Urschel's memory exactly.

At last, Jones saw the light and ordered the Dallas office to reconnoiter the Shannon Ranch. Early the next morning, Thursday, August 10, Ed Weatherford drove an FBI agent named Ed Dowd to the town of Decatur, five miles from Paradise, where they interviewed an officer at Boss Shannon's bank. Dowd became convinced of the officer's honesty and decided to take a risk. He explained that Shannon might be mixed up in the Urschel kidnapping. The bank man called in his credit investigator, and Dowd laid out a map Urschel had drawn of a small shack. The investigator said he knew just such a shack on Shannon's property.

A plan was devised. The bank officer drew up a meaningless document for Shannon to sign. The credit investigator said he would take Dowd to the ranch and ask Shannon to sign the document; Dowd could masquerade as a bank examiner. Dowd slid into the man's Ford coupe and was taken along bumpy dirt roads to the Shannon Ranch, where they found Boss Shannon's son Armon standing outside his shack. While the credit investigator talked with Armon, Dowd asked for a drink of water. Armon helped him draw it from the well. Dowd noticed that the well's pulley squeaked. The water had a mineral taste. Armon's wife emerged from the shack and offered everyone a plate of freshly cut watermelon. After a moment Dowd rose and wandered inside the house. It matched Urschel's description exactly. Afterward, Dowd raced back to Dallas and reported his findings to Gus Jones in Oklahoma City.

Jones decided to raid the Shannon farm the next day, Friday, August 11. When Urschel demanded to come, Jones reluctantly consented. Everyone rendezvoused Friday afternoon in Denton, north of Dallas. There were fourteen men in all: Jones and three Dallas agents, four detectives from Fort Worth led by Ed Weatherford, four Dallas cops, plus Urschel and an Oklahoma City detective. By the time they reached Decatur, the light was fading. Jones stopped the caravan and gathered the men around him.

"Boys, we've got about twenty-six miles to go over slow roads," Jones said. "We might reach the place before dark, but even if we did I doubt we'd be able to finish the job before it got black." He dropped to one knee and drew a map of the Shannon Ranch in the dirt. "This is the way the place is laid out," Jones said. "There is only one road into it, and that's as plain as the devil. We can't creep up on the place because it's so flat you can see an ant a mile off. The only way to get in there is to just bang straight in, and for that we need daylight . . . I've done enough shooting in my time not to want to go barging into a strange place where the odds are all on the other side. My judgment is to back off, go down to Fort Worth and get a little sleep, then hit this place right at sunrise."[16]

In Oklahoma City that night the SAC, Ralph Colvin, was so confident of success he cabled Hoover, WE CAN'T GO WRONG. EXPECT IMPORTANT DEVELOPMENTS BY NOON SATURDAY.[17] In Fort Worth, Jones and his men ate dinner and grabbed a few hours of sleep at the Blackstone Hotel. At 4:00 A.M. they reconvened in the hotel's parking lot and drove to the town of Rhome, seventeen miles from Decatur, where they waited for ninety minutes to be joined by a local sheriff. When the sheriff hadn't arrived by six, Jones decided to proceed without him.

On radio station WBAP the new day began with a song by Cecil Gill, the Yodeling Country Boy. As the eastern horizon reddened, the three-car caravan sped north along dirt roads toward Paradise, clouds of dust billowing in its wake. The Shannon house was dark when the lead car skidded to a stop in front. Jones leaped out carrying a submachine gun, with Charles Urschel behind him; amazingly, the agents allowed Urschel to carry a sawed-off shotgun. They ran around the side of the house, where they encountered Boss Shannon pulling on his suspenders.

"What do you think you're doing here?" Shannon demanded.

"That's the old man who guarded me!" Urschel blurted out.

As agents trained their guns on Shannon, Jones glimpsed something odd in the rear yard: a makeshift cot atop two sawhorses. Someone was sleeping on the cot. Jones ran toward the figure, machine gun ready. As he approached, he saw it was a man, sleeping in his underwear. A pair of pants and a white shirt lay at the foot of the cot, alongside a Winchester rifle and a Colt .45 pistol. The man wasn't moving. Jones crept up and looked down on the face. He recognized the features—the wavy hair, the concrete jawline—and quietly cursed in surprise.

Jones brought the tommy gun's barrel down inches from the man's face until the tip brushed against his nose. The sleeping man's nose twitched. His eyelashes fluttered, and suddenly Jones was staring into the blinking brown eyes of the man who had mentored Verne Miller, Machine Gun Kelly, Alvin Karpis, and the Barker brothers, the man who had emerged as the primary suspect in the massacre case. It was Harvey Bailey. For several seconds, as they peered at each other in the dim light of dawn, neither spoke. Bailey's eyes took in the submachine gun, now pointed at his chest. His Colt lay on the ground, inches from his right hand. A Dallas agent, Charles Winstead, was standing to one side.

"Go ahead!" Winstead snapped. "Reach for it!"

Bailey didn't move.

"Get up, Harvey," Jones finally said. "Who's here with you?"

Bailey said nothing.

"Harvey," Jones went on, "if a head bobs up anywhere around here, or a shot is fired, I promise I'll cut you in two with this machine gun."

"I'm here alone," Bailey said. "You have me." Slowly he sat up and stretched. A weak smile crossed his face. "Hell," he said. "A fella's gotta sleep sometimes."[18]

Agents poured into the Shannon house and its outbuildings, handcuffing the Shannon family. Kathryn's mother, Ora Shannon, was fierce in her denials of wrongdoing. "Don't you tell 'em nothing!" she snapped at her husband. It was no use. Gus Jones took the Shannons' son Armon for what he called "a fatherly talk," and the young man soon broke down and told him everything. It was the Kellys, he said—the Kellys and Albert Bates. And they were all long gone.

Harvey Bailey and the Shannons were taken to the Dallas jail, where Boss Shannon soon joined his son in a full confession. Hoping to catch the Kellys unaware, Jones managed to keep a lid on the story for almost seventy-two hours, but Monday night the news broke in the *Dallas Times-Herald,* and by the next morning it was all over the country. Most papers heralded Bailey as the mastermind behind the kidnapping, as well as the Kansas City Massacre. In fact, Bailey had nothing to do with the Urschel case. He had simply dropped by the Shannon Ranch, as he had done once or twice before at Kelly's behest, because he needed a place to sleep.* It was a lucky arrest, but the FBI's luck was overflowing that weekend. Saturday afternoon, just hours after the Shannon raid, police arrested Albert Bates in a downtown Denver parking lot.† Bates, however, gave no useful information on the Kellys, or on the whereabouts of his share of the ransom money.

Thanks to Ed Weatherford, the hunt for the Kellys got off to a fast start. For two weeks an agent had been noting return addresses on the Shannons' incoming mail—addresses that only now did the FBI begin running down. Two letters had come from Kathryn, one sent from St. Paul on August 4 and a second mailed from Madison, Wisconsin, three days later, bearing a return address of General Delivery, Indianapolis. An agent was assigned to watch the Indianapolis post office, while a bulletin describing the Kellys' car was dispatched nationwide.

The first scent of the Kellys' trail came in Cleveland, where on Sunday, August 13, agents inquired about a bill found at the Shannon Ranch from a Cleveland Cadillac agency. A salesman told agents the Kellys had visited him just three days earlier, on August 10, to pay off the balance on the Cadillac they were driving and to inquire about purchasing a new one. But

---

* Two other Lansing escapees, "Big" Bob Brady and Ed Davis, had arrived at the Shannon Ranch the previous night with Bailey but had left after dinner. Had FBI agents staged their raid the previous night, as planned, they might have faced a major shoot-out.

† For years afterward, Hoover allowed writers chronicling the Urschel case to report that the FBI had apprehended Bates. In fact, as case files make clear, Bates was arrested following an exhaustive investigation by an unlikely source, the American Express Company. Company investigators had been after Bates since he passed traveler's checks stolen in the Tupelo, Mississippi, robbery in 1932. In the end, his arrest was pure luck. According to an FBI report, an American Express operative was riding a train to Denver from Omaha that Friday, August 11, when he saw Bates aboard the train. The AmEx man alerted Denver police, who made the arrest.

they left before buying a new car, saying they were driving to Chicago. Agents in Chicago and Cleveland descended on garages and airline offices in both cities.

The hunt for Machine Gun Kelly had begun.

Years later Kelly told his son of the wondrous few days he and Kathryn enjoyed following delivery of the ransom money. He said they had fled across the Mexican border to Chihuahua, where they spent ten days lying in bed and drinking tequila. Kelly described how he had learned of Bailey's arrest on the radio in his Mexican hotel room.

Kelly's story, like so many he told, was pure fantasy, probably concocted to impress his son. In fact, after releasing Urschel outside of Oklahoma City on July 31, the Kellys drove north to St. Paul, where they rented an apartment and began looking up underworld contacts to launder the ransom money. Harry Sawyer's partner, a casino owner named Jack Peifer, took $7,000 of it, charging Kelly 20 percent. Peifer, in turn, parceled out the money to a half-dozen runners to exchange the cash through area banks. Kelly took the proceeds and bought Kathryn a fur coat and jewelry, paying $1,150 for a bracelet of 234 tiny diamonds and $850 for a ring set with eight round diamonds.

From St. Paul the Kellys drove to Cleveland, where they were staying when they heard the news that the FBI had arrested several of Peifer's confederates. They bought a Cadillac and drove it to Chicago, and then on to Des Moines. They were hiding at the Fort Des Moines Hotel when news broke of the arrests at the Shannon Ranch. Kathryn was enraged that her mother was now in custody and swore she would do anything to free her. From that point on, in fact, Kathryn seemed far more concerned about her mother's welfare than her husband's.

Determined to find a lawyer to represent her mother, Kathryn and Kelly drove south to West Texas, where Kathryn had relatives in the town of Coleman. On August 16, they arrived at a tumbledown ranch owned by Kathryn's forty-three-year-old uncle, Cass Coleman. Kathryn got out of the car, lugging two leather cases containing the ransom. With her uncle's help, they transferred the remaining money to a water jug and a bucket, then buried it beside a willow tree behind Coleman's barn.

The next morning Kelly slept late while Kathryn drove to the town of Brownwood to buy a car. She returned that afternoon with a beat-up Chevy sedan. The next morning she left it with Kelly, and then left Kelly with her uncle, saying she was driving to Dallas to hire an attorney for her mother and would return in a few days. Cass Coleman, less than thrilled to find himself alone with a wanted man, deposited Kelly at another ranch, outside the neighboring town of Santa Ana, where a sixty-year-old farmer named Will Casey agreed to let Kelly stay in a vacant house on his property. Coleman brought Kelly bedsheets and cooking utensils, then sat back to await Kathryn's return.

It was then that the FBI arrived in town. Dallas agents had discovered that Kathryn had family in Coleman and fanned out across the area, seeking to question them. It took only a day for word of their arrival to reach Kelly. Just before noon on August 23, he drove up to Coleman's farmhouse. He ran inside and told Coleman, "I need a piece of paper."

"What's wrong with you?" Coleman asked. Kelly explained. When Coleman handed him a piece of paper, Kelly wrote something down, slipped it into an envelope, and sealed it.

"Give that to Kathryn," he said, "and tell her 'Mississippi.'"

Kelly hopped back in the car and drove off, heading east. When Kathryn arrived back at the farm several nights later, she read Kelly's note and cursed. "He's a damned fool," she told her uncle before driving off in search of her wayward husband.

Throughout those blazing-hot late-summer days, as the nation's attention remained riveted by the hunt for Machine Gun Kelly, John Dillinger kept busy on his own little-noticed crime spree, ricocheting between dozens of towns in Indiana, Ohio, and northern Kentucky, casing banks between side trips to visit the World's Fair and a girlfriend or two. He kept on the move, though at some point he appears to have rented two apartments, in East Chicago and Gary, to use as hideouts.

Dillinger remained unknown to the public, but his robberies had attracted the notice of a detective named Matt Leach, who worked for the fledgling Indiana State Police. Leach, whose obsessive pursuit of Dillinger would become an Indiana legend, was a Serbian immigrant who arrived in western Pennsylvania in 1907 at the age of thirteen.* Three years later the

* According to an excellent 1992 article in *Serb World USA* magazine, Leach's real name was Matija Licanin. His family came from the Serbian town of Kordun.

family moved to Indiana when Leach's father took a job in a Gary steel mill, and Leach worked in the mills before joining the U.S. Army in 1915. After serving with John J. Pershing's expedition against Pancho Villa and on the Western Front during World War I, he returned to Gary and became a policeman, moving up through the ranks to head the department's vice division. As a local cop Leach was active in the American Legion, and when its national chairman, Paul McNutt, was elected governor of Indiana in 1932, Leach was named first captain of the state police force McNutt formed. Only the superintendent of police, Al Feeney, ranked above him.

Much like the FBI, the Indiana State Police was ill equipped to fight crime. In 1933 its forty-one members (including clerks) were, like Leach and Feeney, political appointees, charged with cruising state highways on motorcycles and a handful of old cars with no two-way radios; before Dillinger, their biggest headaches consisted of directing World's Fair traffic and apprehending a band of chicken thieves.[19] But Leach, gaunt and serious, was game for bigger things. He read books on psychology and prided himself on being an astute analyst of criminal types. Unfortunately, what most people noticed about him was his stutter, which became more pronounced at times of stress.

When newspaper articles described an unidentified bank robber as having leaped over a railing to rob the bank in Dalesville, Leach was intrigued. This yegg had a flamboyant streak, which suggested to Leach that he might move on to bigger and better targets. On a hunch, Leach drove to Muncie to interview Dillinger's teenage partner, William Shaw, who was in the jail. Shaw named Dillinger. Leach checked with Dillinger's parole officer, who reported that he had disappeared.

Two weeks after the Dalesville job, on Friday afternoon, August 4, farmers spotted a dark blue Chrysler sedan cruising past the green cornfields outside the eastern Indiana farm town of Montpelier. At precisely 2:40 P.M. the car stopped in front of the First National Bank on Main Street, which had been robbed just three years earlier. Dillinger, wearing a straw boater, walked inside, drew a revolver, and smiled. "This is a stickup," he announced, chewing a piece of gum.

As his partner Harry Copeland forced three employees onto the floor, Dillinger leaped a low railing and asked the bank manager, Merle Tewksbury, how much money the bank had on hand. As Dillinger scooped cash off the counters, Copeland corralled a pair of arriving customers, also forcing them to the floor. At one point a teller reached for an alarm. "What are you trying to do, set off that alarm?" Dillinger demanded, still chewing his gum.

"I would if I could," the woman snapped.

It was a perfect robbery. After herding the employees and customers into the vault, Dillinger and Copeland stepped back onto the sidewalk ten minutes after entering the bank, carrying $10,110 in cash and coins in a single sack; they had left behind exactly forty cents. "Looks like the bank's being held up again," an old man standing on Main Street remarked as they emerged.

Dillinger turned and smiled. "I'm not surprised," he said, before ducking into the Chrysler and driving off.[20]

Neither was Matt Leach. The rail-leaping stunt convinced Leach that Dillinger was behind the Montpelier robbery, and he redoubled his efforts to bring him in, putting the homes of Dillinger's father and sister under surveillance. A few days later, Leach received unexpected assistance from a private detective named Forrest Huntington, who worked for the Montpelier bank's insurance company. At the Muncie jail, Huntington grilled William Shaw for names of anyone Dillinger might contact. Shaw produced the name of an ex-con in Lebanon, Kentucky, and from the Kentucky man Huntington wrangled the address of an apartment Dillinger was using in East Chicago, Indiana.*

On Monday, August 14, Leach and a squad of state police raided the East Chicago apartment and arrested three ex-cons. One claimed Dillinger had been staying off and on at East Chicago's Inland Hotel. A few days later the snitch volunteered he had heard that Dillinger had relocated to an apartment in Gary. Leach raided that apartment, but Dillinger had moved on, taking an apartment in Chicago.

By late August, the manhunt was gaining momentum. More insurance investigators joined the chase, and on August 25 one of them, a divisional manager for the Pinkerton Agency in Cincinnati, passed a tip to the Dayton Police Department that Dillinger was dating the sister of a state prison inmate named Jenkins. A phone call to Michigan City produced the name of Mary Longnaker. Two Dayton detectives swung by Longnaker's rooming house on West First Street and, ushered in by the landlady, searched her room. They found a letter from Dillinger.

The landlady volunteered that this Mr. Dillinger wrote regular letters to

---

* Dillinger cased and may have robbed at least one bank in northern Kentucky. He was suspected but never charged with the August 11 robbery of a bank in Gravel Switch, Kentucky.

her tenant Miss Longnaker; she volunteered to telephone the detectives the next time one arrived. A few days later she proved as good as her word: a new letter had arrived. In it, Dillinger promised to visit soon. Excited, the detectives prevailed on the landlady to rent them a room, and she agreed. A few days later they moved in and sat in wait for Dillinger.

5

THE KID JIMMY

August 18 to September 25, 1933

The house Alvin Karpis rented for the summer lay on a secluded thread of dirt road that snaked along the southern shore of Lake Michigan east of Michigan City, Indiana. In the woods behind the dunes lay scores of bungalows, many the summer homes of wealthy Chicagoans. Karpis rented his from a Cicero politician connected to the Syndicate. Located on a rise above the lake, the house was a striking Spanish mansionette, with white stucco walls and a red-tile roof. The sunken dining room featured a brass chandelier and a Steinway piano.*

Most days Karpis and his teenage girlfriend Delores Delaney lazed on the beach or barbecued with friends, chief among them the old yegg Ed Bentz, who had parted with Machine Gun Kelly before the Urschel kidnapping. For amusement they watched Bentz teach the fine art of robbing banks to another neighbor, a small, blond twenty-four-year-old from the rough Polish neighborhoods around Chicago's Humboldt park. It was the same kid who until that spring had been a gangland chauffeur in Reno, and whom Karpis had introduced around St. Paul. Everyone called him Jimmy—Jimmy Burnell, Jimmy Burke, Jimmy Williams, whatever alias he was using at the time. His real name was Lester Joseph Gillis.

History would know him as Baby Face Nelson.

---

* The home still stands, at 2000 Golden Gate Drive, in Long Beach, Indiana.

• • •

Seven decades after he entered American public life, Baby Face Nelson re-mains the least known of the Great Crime Wave's major figures. Overshad-owed by Dillinger, his eventual partner, Nelson and his background were long cloaked in mystery; for years what little information detective maga-zines gathered was riddled with myths and half-truths. Writing in 1963 John Toland introduced Nelson simply as "a young man the [Dillinger] gang . . . met in an underworld tavern."

In fact, by the time he joined forces with Dillinger in 1934, Nelson was an up-and-coming gang leader in his own right, his exploits notable for both their geographic diversity—he was equally at home in San Francisco, Reno, and Chicago—and their gratuitous violence. He was a figure of con-tradiction: a family man who traveled with his wife and sometimes their two small children, he was to earn—and wholeheartedly deserve—a repu-tation as the most violent of the Depression-era outlaws, a manic multiple murderer who drew disdain even as Dillinger and Pretty Boy Floyd at-tained the status of folk heroes. At his worst, Nelson was a caricature of the public enemy, a callous, wild-eyed machine-gunner who actually laughed as he sprayed bullets toward women and children in at least two of his robberies. Nelson's behavior was so clichéd that it was as if he were acting out scenes from a gangster movie, perhaps Jimmy Cagney's 1931 hit *Public Enemy.*

Gillis, or Nelson as he will be referred to hereinafter, was tiny, just over five-feet-four, which begins to explain the boulder-size chip on his shoulder. He was born on December 6, 1908, the seventh and last child of Belgian immigrants, Joseph and Mary Gillis. His father, described as a brooding man who drank heavily, worked in a tannery. The Gillises were upstanding people, with no history of problems with the law. The high hopes they had for their blond little boy would be dashed again and again. From an early age, Nelson was headstrong and insecure, the kind of boy who picked fights with teenagers a head taller. By the time he was eleven he was running with a gang of teenage toughs, leaping over soda counters to yank money from cash registers and stealing cars. Among his friends was a kid named Jack Perkins, who would be at his side in 1934. In time, Nelson's truancy became so chronic he landed at a school for wayward boys.

On July 4, 1921, when Nelson was twelve, he found a pistol in the car of a friend's father. Thinking he might scare some children playing in an alley, Nelson fired the gun over their heads. A ricochet lodged in one boy's jaw.

The police arrested Nelson. It was his first encounter with the law; it also began his obsession with guns. Even at the height of his pursuit by the FBI, Nelson rarely missed an issue of *Field & Stream,* with its articles on the latest weaponry. A juvenile court, ignoring Nelson's pleas that the shooting was an accident, sentenced him to twelve to fifteen months in a state reformatory.

He served a year. Back at home, Nelson was free to pursue his second obsession—automobiles. As an adult, Nelson was a car nut; between robberies, he could often be found hanging around a garage, talking with mechanics. As a thirteen-year-old the only way he could drive was to steal a car, and he did—often. The police arrested him again, and this time, in October 1922, he was packed off to the Illinois State School for Boys in St. Charles. Eighteen months later he was paroled. This time he managed to remain free five months. Caught in a stolen car, he was sent back to St. Charles in September 1924.

By the time Nelson was paroled the following summer, his father was dead. Joseph Gillis had quit his job to buy a restaurant that was now failing, and he had grown despondent. He was found dead, his head beside a kitchen gas jet. Low on money, Mary Gillis was forced to take in boarders, and Nelson tried to help out, taking a job as a mechanic at a Chrysler dealership. Three months later the cops caught him in another stolen car. Back to the reformatory he went. Nine months later he earned a parole, and went back to work at the dealership.

In early 1927 he was laid off. Nelson was eighteen now, a skinny blond brimming with nervous energy. He joined a couple of pals stealing tires, until police caught them one night inside a car dealership. He got off with a year's probation and managed to wangle a job in the garage at Commonwealth Edison. It was while working at Commonwealth Edison that Nelson fell in love. Her name was Helen Wawrzyniak, a surname her family Anglicized to Warwick. She was a neighborhood girl, a mousy fifteen-year-old who worked after school as a clerk in the toy department at Goldblatt's on Western Avenue. When she got pregnant, they married, signing papers at the Porter County Courthouse in Valparaiso, Indiana, on October 30, 1928. The following April Helen gave birth to a son they named Ronald, who was followed two years later by a daughter, Darlene. The family moved in with Nelson's mother.

In 1928 Nelson went to work at a Standard Oil station that was a hangout for neighborhood toughs. Two doors north was an auto-parts store run by a man named George Vande Houten, and Vande Houten's twenty-eight-year-old son, Albert, began organizing the kids hanging around the station into roving crews of tire thieves known as "strippers." Nelson joined up. He and his pals roamed the streets of Chicago, stealing tires they resold to the Vande Houtens and others. In this way Nelson met scores of crooks. One gave Nelson work as a driver hauling bootleg whiskey all across the Chicago suburbs and as far afield as Iowa. For the first time Nelson came to know the back roads and taverns of towns like Summit, Cicero, and Wheaton.* It was during this period that Nelson took up weekend stock-car racing at tracks outside of Chicago. One of his mechanics, a Polish kid named Clarence Lieder, would be at his side in later years.

With a wife and children to support, Nelson began looking for ways to make more money. He fell in with a group of burglars, including a thief named Harry Lewis; together they conspired to move up in the world. The year 1930 was when Nelson went from petty thief to armed robber. He has long been credited with two jewelry robberies and two bank jobs in 1930; FBI files indicate these incidents amounted to but a fraction of the crimes he committed in a yearlong rampage.[1]

It began at a brick mansion on Lake Shore Drive early on the evening of January 6, a month after Nelson's twenty-first birthday. Five men, led by Nelson, pushed their way into the home of a magazine executive named Charles M. Richter, then rounded up and used adhesive tape to bind Richter's family. After cutting phone lines, they ransacked all twenty-two rooms of the house, returning downstairs with jewelry valued at about $25,000.[2] Two weeks later Nelson's gang struck again, posing as decorators to gain entrance to the suburban home of an attorney. After binding two maids with adhesive tape, the gang made off with $5,000 in jewelry.[3] A Chicago newspaper christened them "the tape bandits."

Two months later Nelson's gang served as guest stars in a soap opera that Chicago society had been following for months. Their victim, Lottie Brenner Von Beulow, was the widow of a wealthy manufacturer who had married a mysterious German count during a Mexican vacation. When the count turned out to be an imposter, Mrs. Brenner filed for divorce. The case was heading for trial on the evening of March 31 when Nelson and two

---

* It was probably through the garage owner that Nelson made his first contacts in Roger Touhy's gang. According to Touhy's 1959 biography, Nelson worked briefly as a "torpedo" in the labor struggles between the Touhy and Capone outfits; the assignments did not last long, but Nelson's association with the Touhys would cause him trouble in later years.

partners, posing as census takers, appeared at the front door of Mrs. Brenner's brick mansion at 5539 Sheridan Road. Buzzed upstairs, they pulled pistols and swiftly bound and gagged Mrs. Brenner, her sister, and four servants. They searched Mrs. Brenner's bedroom and found $50,000 in jewelry. But before the gang could flee, their work was interrupted by the arrival of "Count" Von Beulow, who also was bound, gagged, and robbed; added to their take were $95 and two watches.[4]

The Nelson gang's crimes grew steadily more ambitious. On April 21, Nelson robbed his first bank, making off with $4,000. Then on May 16, a Chicago jeweler named Walter Lynne Akers returned to his suburban Danville home to find four men with pistols waiting inside. Addressing Mr. and Mrs. Akers by their first names, gang members threw a blanket over his wife and two-year-old son. "I guess you know what we are here for," one told Akers. "We have come for the keys to the store and the combination to the safe, and if we get them without trouble none of you will be harmed." Akers turned over the information, and two of the robbers left for the store, the other two guarding the family. After the robbers ransacked the store, stealing jewelry valued at $25,000, they returned to the Akers home and forced the family into its car.

On the drive into Chicago, the gang's leader, apparently Nelson, noticed that the infant was shivering. "We wouldn't hurt that kid for the world," Nelson said. "I've got two of my own." The gang unloaded the Akers family on Mannheim Road and drove away, telling Akers, "Well, Lynne, we hate to impose on you this way, but this is as far as we can take you." The family returned home without incident.

The first signs of trouble came after one of Nelson's partner's girlfriends was arrested and told police about his little gang's exploits. Arrest warrants were issued, forcing Nelson to adopt the alias "George Nelson" more or less full-time. The warrants didn't stop him from working, however. On October 3, Nelson led the robbery of the Itasca State Bank outside of Chicago; the gang made off with almost $4,600. Afterward a teller identified Nelson.

Three nights later, Nelson pulled off his most brazen robbery to date, the sidewalk mugging of the wife of Chicago's mayor, William "Big Bill" Thompson. On the evening of October 6, Mary Walker Thompson was returning to her Sheridan Road apartment building from an evening at the theater when two men accosted her on the sidewalk, thrusting pistols against her chest and side; a third robber slugged her bodyguard and put a gun to his stomach.

(The origin of Nelson's nickname, "Baby Face," has never been confirmed, but it almost certainly arose from Mrs. Thompson's description of the young robber who poked his gun to her chest and snapped, "Throw 'em up!" According to an October 8, 1930, article in the *Chicago Herald,* Mrs. Thompson said of her attacker: "He had a baby face. He was good looking, hardly more than a boy, had dark hair and was wearing a gray topcoat and a brown felt hat, turned down brim."[5])

Nelson shoved Mrs. Thompson into the lobby and demanded she hand over a six-carat blue-diamond ring, a bracelet lined with 40 diamonds, and a brooch set with 140 small stones; the three pieces were later valued at $18,000. When Nelson ran for their car, Mrs. Thompson fainted.

Not until years later would FBI agents, after debriefing Nelson's former partners, link him to a pair of bloody unsolved crimes in late November 1930. According to Stanton J. Randall, a member of the Nelson gang interviewed by the FBI in 1934, Nelson was the leader of a group of eight men who entered a roadhouse on Archer Avenue in suburban Summit in the early-morning hours of Sunday, November 23. Mary Brining, a twenty-two-year-old University of Illinois student, was singing "The Kiss Waltz" to a roomful of dancers in a smoky back room when the men burst in the front door, shotguns and pistols drawn. The gang's leader, later described by newspapers as an "unmasked youth of about 18"—presumably Nelson—pushed the bartender and another man into the back room, where Nelson stood in the middle of the dance floor shouting, "Everyone up! Face the walls!"

As his men began to rob the patrons, Nelson shoved the tavern's owner against a wall. Nelson then yelled for a gang member to turn up the lights, but in the confusion the gang member apparently hit the wrong switch: the room went completely dark. Just then, the owner's dog, a Great Dane, attacked Nelson, biting him in the leg. Nelson fired at the dog. Other gang members panicked and began firing wildly in the darkness. A railroad detective named James Mikus emerged from the bathroom and began firing at the robbers.

Chaos ensued. In less than a minute three young women were dead or dying, including the singer, Mary Brining; three others were badly wounded. "Let's get outta here!" Nelson shouted, and the gang ran out the front door. Mikus, though wounded, limped to his car and gave chase, but lost Nelson's gang in traffic.

Three nights later Nelson's gang burst into a tavern on Waukegan Road in the northern suburbs. Only three men were in the bar: the owner, Frank Engel; a waiter; and one of Engel's friends, a twenty-seven-year-old stock-broker from a prominent North Shore family named Edwin R. Thompson, who had stopped by for a late dinner after visiting his sick wife in the hospital. When Nelson ordered the trio to raise their hands, Thompson made the mistake of smiling nervously. "Don't smile, you!" Nelson snarled, then raised his shotgun and fired a single blast into Thompson's chest. Thompson fell dead. "Guess we ain't tough, eh?" Nelson said as he stood over Thompson's body. He turned to Engel, who stood, stunned. "Now open that safe!" Nelson shouted. Engel did as he was told, handing Nelson the $125 inside. "Come on, let's go!" Nelson shouted, and it was over.

Police finally arrested most of the gang in February 1931. Nelson was arrested at an apartment in Cicero. In the single article the *Chicago Tribune* devoted to his arrest, he was identified as George "Baby Face" Nelson, the first time his new nickname made it into print.[6] Convicted of one robbery, Nelson drew a sentence of one year to life in the state prison at Joliet.

In February 1932, Nelson was taken in handcuffs to the town of Wheaton, just west of Chicago, where in a quick trial he drew a second sentence of one year to life. Late on a Wednesday afternoon, February 17, a prison guard named R. N. Martin led Nelson to the train back to Chicago. Reaching Chicago an hour later, they transferred to the southbound train. At Joliet, Martin pushed Nelson into a yellow cab for the short ride to the prison. Just as the cab approached the prison on Collins Street, Nelson produced a pistol; apparently someone had slipped it to him on the train. "If you move I will kill you," he told Martin. "Now unlock the handcuffs."

Nelson put the pistol against the cab driver's temple and said, "You continue on to Chicago and do exactly as I tell you." In the suburb of Summit, Nelson ordered the driver to pull to the side of the road beside a cemetery. He forced Martin and the driver out of the car and took Martin's wallet.[7] Nelson knew he could no longer remain in Chicago. He reached out to old friends in Roger Touhy's gang, which is how he found himself several weeks later on a train to Reno, Nevada, holding in his pocket the phone number of a man the Touhys had said could take care of him: William Graham, the gambler who, with his partner, James McKay, all but controlled the city of Reno.

Nelson stepped off the train in Reno in March 1932. Using the alias

"Jimmy Johnson," he phoned Graham and told him who he was. After several weeks Graham sent Nelson on to San Francisco, where he arranged for him to work for a Sausalito bootlegger. Nelson worked as a guard on liquor shipments for six months. He and other men would meet ships in secluded coves in Marin County, watch as the crates were unloaded, then ride the trucks into San Francisco. On these missions he made two friends, a handsome simpleton named Johnny Chase and a roly-poly Italian named Joseph "Fatso" Negri. At the height of Nelson's notoriety in 1934, the two men would be his most trusted associates.

In the fall of 1932 Nelson left the Bay Area. According to Negri, his departure came after Negri saw Nelson's photograph in a detective magazine. Nelson fled back to Reno, where he sought refuge with Bill Graham. Graham hired Nelson as his driver. It was in Reno that winter that Nelson met the vacationing Alvin Karpis. Karpis told Nelson vivid stories of the Barker Gang's yearlong bank-robbing spree across the Upper Midwest and volunteered to introduce him to the right people if he returned east. Nelson slipped back into Chicago that spring, taking a room at the Inland Hotel in East Chicago in May. As fate would have it, it was the same hotel John Dillinger frequented that summer; the two future partners had several mutual acquaintances and may have met, though there is no confirmation of this. Nelson began hanging out with Karpis at Louis Cernocky's Crystal Room in the northwest suburb of Fox River Grove, hoping the gang would invite him on a robbery.

But Karpis, after hearing of Nelson's temper from friends in Reno, had second thoughts. Instead of asking him to join the Barker Gang, Karpis introduced him to Ed Bentz, the Jazz Age yegg, who agreed to teach Nelson the ins and outs of robbing banks.* A few days later, Nelson, along with his wife and his mother, Mary, moved into a bungalow next to Bentz's on the Indiana lakeshore, just across the road from Karpis's stucco mansionette. As Bentz recalled twenty years later, he and Nelson walked into the dunes to talk. "I know you're hooked up with the best troupe in the country and that it's impossible for an outsider to get in," Nelson said. "I'm not asking you to try and get me in the troupe. What I want is some experience."

"In what line?" Bentz asked, teasing.

Nelson laughed. "You know damn well—in your line, of course."

---

* In a 1953 article for *Argosy* mgazine, Bentz recalls being introduced to Nelson by an Indiana tavern owner. While possible, he was more likely to have befriended Nelson with the endorsement of a fellow yegg like Karpis.

"You mean bank—"

"Absolutely," Nelson said.

"You can't do that alone," Bentz said. "You have to organize a troupe first. You have to buy equipment, a car and what not. It would take at least three thousand for you to start properly."

"Supposing we left out the car. I can get that in Chicago. How much for equipment?"

"You shouldn't try to rob a bank with a stolen car," Bentz said. "You should buy it like any businessman would. But that's your business. You can use a hot car but it increases the danger."

"I know that," Nelson said, "but I'll take my chances."

"All right, then about a thousand will do for your other essentials. But your troupe—where are you gonna recruit them?"

Nelson mentioned he had friends in St. Paul. "How about 'gits'?" Bentz asked, mentioning yeggman slang for a getaway map. "Can any one of you run a safe git?"

"No, none of us know a darn thing about roads."

Bentz sighed. "Here you are proposing to go out with a four-man inexperienced troupe, to rob a bank, and none of you know the operation. It just isn't done—unless you want to get killed."

"Wait a minute," Nelson said. "I was just telling how I stood. I want your help. I figured that you could help us get started. Get us a mark, plan the getaway and select what equipment we'd need. I don't mean for you to go on the actual robbery—just line it up for us. We'll give you an even split."

Bentz agreed.

With a target selected, on June 8 Nelson drove to St. Paul, where he recruited three yeggs to join his new gang. When one was late arriving on the Indiana lakeshore, Bentz suggested he be replaced with two parolees from the Michigan City prison he had met at an underworld hangout in Indiana Harbor.* "They're as bad as you fellows," Bentz said with a grin. "No experience."

"Who are they?" Nelson asked.

---

* The establishment was Art's Army Store at 3318 Michigan Avenue, a retailer of military clothing whose back room was a gathering spot for local hoodlums. Bentz and Nelson were known to have frequented the store in June 1933, as were John Dillinger and Homer Van Meter. Nelson and Dillinger may have met there.

"One is Homer Van Meter," Bentz said. "Went to stir for eight years for shooting at a policeman in South Bend. The other's name is Dillinger."

No, Nelson said, no strangers.[8]

Grand Haven, Michigan
Friday, August 18, 1933

As FBI agents fanned out across the Southwest in search of Machine Gun Kelly, they assembled a list of Kelly's known associates. Topping the list was his bank-robbing partner, Eddie Bentz. On August 18, as the names and addresses of Bentz's brothers and sisters spit out of FBI Teletype machines across the country, Bentz was standing in a grove of trees outside of Grand Haven, Michigan, a resort town on Lake Michigan. Standing beside him was his new protégé, the former Lester Gillis. This was the day Baby Face Nelson would stage his first real bank robbery. "Now if you fellows will crowd around here I'll explain where each man should go," Bentz announced. He went over each man's role. Nelson was to lead the gang inside the bank.

Something was bothering Nelson. "Bentz," he interrupted, "I'm afraid we'll miss the big money by you staying outside."

"What the hell do you mean?" Bentz asked.

"Well, it requires experience to have those people open those safes."

"You got me up here against my better judgment," Bentz said. "I agreed to take the street and drive; now you expect me to go inside? Who's to take the street?"

Nelson nodded toward their driver, a Touhy man named Monahan. "Freddie here could drive and take care of the street."

"Impossible!" Bentz blurted. "You propose to put an inexperienced man on the street? He doesn't know the first thing about cleaning a street.* I wouldn't agree to it—not in this town."

"Will you go in if we leave two men outside?" Nelson asked.

Bentz fumed. "All right," he finally said. "But now we'll take one machine gun in with us. You take it in."

"Okay with me," Nelson said.

Then Bentz took out his diagrams, and they went over everything one last time.

---

* "Cleaning a street" refers to the job of keeping armed citizens and law officers away from a robbery in progress.

. . .

A cool breeze was blowing off Lake Michigan as Bentz and Nelson strode into the Peoples Savings Bank a few minutes before its three o'clock closing time. Nelson, carrying a picnic basket, walked down to the last teller cage, slid a twenty-dollar bill beneath the grillwork, and asked for two dollars in nickels. He was nervous. When the teller slid him the nickels, Nelson asked for another two dollars in dimes. Beside him, Bentz snickered. Nelson and the teller exchanged glances. Nelson awkwardly whipped the Thompson out of the picnic basket and yelled, "Hands up!" The teller pressed a silent alarm.

Two other gang members entered the lobby as Bentz ordered the bank employees and two customers to lie on the floor. Nelson covered them as the others yanked down window shades. Their driver pulled up in an alley behind the bank. As the others rifled the teller cages, Bentz ordered the cashier to open the vault. Bentz stepped in and began shoveling packages of bonds into laundry sacks.

The alarm rang at a furniture store across the street. The store owner, Edward Kinkema, who doubled as Grand Haven's mortician, grabbed a shotgun and ran into the street. Spying the getaway car in the alley, Kinkema raised his gun, and the getaway driver drove off. Kinkema began yelling that the bank was being robbed.

Inside the bank, Nelson turned his head. "Hurry, we got a rank!" he yelled. A policeman. Bentz peeked through the window and saw people running up and down the streets. "Don't shoot unless they start shooting first," he ordered.

Nelson was first out the door, pushing the cashier in front of him. Across the street Kinkema saw him and fired. Nelson ducked, then fired in return, bullets from his submachine gun shattering several car windows. Bentz came out next, one arm around the waist of a teller. The others followed, herding hostages before them.

Then they noticed the getaway car was gone. "Our car—where the hell is it?" someone yelled.

For a moment Bentz was too stunned to speak. Then, spying Kinkema crouched behind a car across the street, he raised his pistol and shot out more car windows. Kinkema ran back into his store. Other gang members fired bursts up and down the street, sending townspeople fleeing for cover. Bentz and Nelson gathered the hostages into a scrum and walked the group down the street, away from the bank. When he reached an intersection,

Bentz jogged into the oncoming traffic, waving his pistol, and forced a Chevrolet to stop. The woman driving the car refused to get out until Bentz shoved his gun in her face. Nelson and the others leaped inside—all except a gang member named Earl Doyle, who was tackled by a bank manager and arrested. Nelson demanded that Bentz circle back for Doyle, but Bentz was stopping for no one.

They were in trouble. The "git" was in the getaway car, forcing Bentz to drive the escape route from memory. Worse, the commandeered Chevy had barely a gallon of gas. Eight miles south of Grand Haven they spotted a car parked at the side of the road. They ordered the two women inside to get out and took the car, but two of its tires soon went flat. The gang commandeered yet another car, this one driven by four college students. They didn't reach Long Beach until dawn.

They pulled up near a local riding academy and counted the take. It was miserable, barely $3,500, or roughly $600 a man. The next morning, Bentz moved out of his Long Beach bungalow. He'd had enough of Baby Face Nelson and his little gang of amateurs. He would never see Nelson or any of the others again. Back at his beach house, meanwhile, Nelson crossed the road to tell Alvin Karpis about his first real bank robbery. But Karpis was gone. He had a job of his own to handle.*

St. Paul, Minnesota
August 30, 8:30 A.M.

"Have you checked out that medicine kit and everything's all right?" Freddie Barker asked.

"Yeah," said Karpis. "We've got everything in there."

The mood in the living room was tense. Everyone was there: Freddie and Dock Barker, Alvin Karpis, Bill Weaver, old Chuck Fitzgerald. Everything was set: the guns were oiled, the ammo checked. No one was eager for this job but they needed the money. Karpis had flown out to Reno and passed the Hamm ransom at a cost of 7.5 percent, but even in 1933, $95,000 cut fourteen ways didn't last forever.†

---

* Fred Barker and his girlfriend Paula Harmon had spent the summer at a rented house in Long Lake, Illinois.

† According to a gang member who was debriefed by the FBI in 1935, the largest share of the Hamm ransom, $25,000, had gone to the corrupt detective Tom Brown. Jack Peifer received $10,000. The six men

"We've got the booze," Karpis went on, "in case we have to wash out any holes anybody gets put in them, and I've got the morphine and all those little vials with them. I got quarter-grain and half-grain vials there. Plenty of bandages and everything."

Barker forced a laugh. "You know," he said, "it just might be that we're going to need some of that stuff on all of us today."

The five men rose and walked out to the cars.

South St. Paul
9:30 A.M.

Every Wednesday morning the Minneapolis Federal Reserve shipped the payroll for the Swift & Co. meatpacking plant to the railway depot in South St. Paul. There two messengers picked up the heavy bags of cash and, escorted by two police officers, walked around the corner to the South St. Paul post office, where they picked up more cash.

That morning when the train coasted to a stop at 9:19, Karpis and the Barkers were waiting. The two young messengers, Joe Hamilton, twenty-one, and Herbert Cheyne, twenty, took the bags, exited the station, and turned up an alley along with the two uniformed officers assigned to escort them that morning: Leo Pavlak, a rookie patrolman and father of two, and John Yeaman, a father of three. Standing at the head of the alley, inside a café on North Concord Street, Dock Barker's friend Bill Weaver watched them approach.* Nervous, he had already downed a beer. In his right hand he carried a shotgun wrapped in newspaper.

Weaver watched as Officer Yeaman slipped into his squad car in the alley in front of him. From watching the policemen work the last two weeks, the gang knew Yeaman would sit in the car and wait for the others to come out of the post office next door. Weaver was assigned to make certain Officer Yeaman stayed put. Meanwhile, Officer Pavlak accompanied the mes-

---

who actually carried out the kidnapping—Karpis, the Barker brothers, Shotgun George Ziegler, Charles Fitzgerald, and Bryan Bolton—each received $7,800. The gang also gave its old friend Deafy Farmer $2,500 to cover legal expenses for his defense in the Kansas City Massacre case.

* Weaver, an Arkansas-born prison pal of Dock Barker's, had been with Karpis and the Barkers since their first bank robbery in southern Missouri in early 1931. He had a rap sheet dating to 1918 and had been paroled for murdering an Oklahoma policeman. Weaver would work alongside Karpis and Barker for the rest of their careers.

sengers around the corner into the post office, where a few moments later they reemerged in front of the building.

Just then a black sedan pulled up in front of the post office. Karpis was behind the wheel. Dock Barker, dressed in denim overalls, jumped out and trained a sawed-off shotgun on Officer Pavlak. Chuck Fitzgerald, wearing a gray suit, followed, a pistol in his hand. "Stick 'em up!" Barker yelled.

Pavlak froze, then slowly raised his hands above his head. Fitzgerald bent forward and took his gun.

"Throw down those bags!" Barker commanded. The two men did as they were told. Fred Barker slipped out of the car and positioned himself in the street, circling warily, a submachine gun in his hands.

Around the corner, Officer Yeaman finished his break and began to back the car up the alley toward Concord Street. Standing beside the car, Bill Weaver threw the newspaper off his shotgun, raised it, and fired through the driver's window. The blast struck Yeaman in the head, knocking his cap off; he slumped in his seat, badly wounded.

Startled by the shots, Dock Barker thought the gang was under attack. He raised his shotgun into Officer Pavlak's face, shouted, "You dirty rat son-of-a-bitch!" and fired. The blast all but decapitated Pavlak; he died instantly. Fred Barker began firing as well. Spotting Yeaman's squad car, he opened fire, hitting the wounded officer in the head and chest. Fred then wheeled in a circle, shooting into storefronts all around him. Everywhere passersby dived for cover. The two messengers hit the ground, then scrambled beneath a parked truck.

Behind the wheel of the getaway car, Karpis also thought they were under attack. In fact, no policeman had fired a single round. Suddenly Fitzgerald fell, struck by a ricochet. "I'm hit!" he yelled. Both Barker brothers thought Fitzgerald had been hit by fire coming from inside the post office. Dock pulled two .45 caliber pistols from his overalls and joined Freddie as he fired on the building's brick facade. Windows shattered. Women screamed.

After a minute the Barkers stopped firing, picked up the money bags, and turned toward the car. "Goddamnit, don't leave me here!" cried Fitzgerald. He lay on the sidewalk. The Barkers threw the money bags in the car and returned for Fitzgerald, lifting him into the backseat. Bill Weaver ran up and jumped in the car, and Karpis stomped the accelerator. The car shot forward, swerving to avoid a streetcar. With Freddie shouting out directions from the git, Karpis turned up a hill and within minutes was into the countryside.[9]

"Fuck! Fuck!" Fitzgerald cursed from the backseat. Blood was streaming down his legs.

"Where ya hit?" Freddie asked. "It looks like you're hit in the leg."

"In the hip!" Fitzgerald said. Stopping at the first gasoline cache, they jabbed Fitzgerald with a shot of morphine and washed his wound with alcohol. Karpis headed toward Chicago. They gave Fitzgerald two more shots of morphine on the way, but by the time they crossed the Illinois line he was thrashing in pain. Karpis drove past downtown, left the highway, and coasted to a stop in the driveway of a friend's home in Calumet City, a gritty suburb on the Indiana border.

After finding a doctor for Fitzgerald, Karpis drove back to his lake house. At the house he and Delores Delaney sat around the kitchen table talking until it got late. He told her he had been on a business trip to New York; she knew enough not to ask questions. At one point, Delores said, "Well, I got something to tell you."

Karpis braced himself. "What is it?" he asked.

"I'm pregnant."

"You're what?"

"Yeah, I'm pregnant."

"Well, how in the hell did this happen?"

"You're grown up," Delaney said. "How in the hell do you think it happened?"

"You should have been a little more careful," Karpis said. Immediately he saw it was the wrong thing to say. He bent over and kissed her. "Well, it's okay," he said quietly. "We'll figure out what to do. I'm sure you don't want a baby right now, do you?"

Delaney sulked.

"I tell you what," Karpis said. "I'm going to have you go to St. Paul and visit your sister and I'll make arrangements for an abortion. You want to do that?"

After a moment she nodded.

Karpis adopted a cheerful, encouraging tone. "While we're at this," he went on, "why don't you go ahead and have your tonsils taken out at the same time? You get everything done at once." Nels Mortenson, a prominent St. Paul doctor they knew, could do it.

"All right?" Karpis asked.

"Yeah," she said. "All right."

The next day, Karpis swung by Freddie Barker's South Side apartment. "George Ziegler wants to see you," Barker said.

Karpis found Ziegler at a Cicero tavern. "What's going on, George?" Karpis asked.

"Well, I don't exactly want to see you," Ziegler said. "But there's some fellows in the outfit downtown, they want to ask you some questions." The outfit. The Syndicate. Karpis was immediately on guard. "What have you been up to, anyway?" Ziegler asked. He meant: *What have you done to anger the Mob?*

"I don't know what the hell you're talking about."

"Well, they're getting a little skeptical of you. They was asking me if you might be tied with the Touhy outfit or anything." Frank Nitti's Chicago Syndicate remained at war with the suburban Touhys.

"Well, you know I'm not," Karpis said.

"Yeah, I told them that you wouldn't have nothing to do with, but . . . ." Ziegler's voice trailed off. "Anyway, go on downtown, over to the Motion Picture Operators Union. There's some guys waiting to see you there."

As Karpis drove downtown, he tried to relax: if Nitti wanted him dead, he would already be dead. At the union office he found three Syndicate men waiting for him in a back room. Two Karpis knew: Willie "Three-Fingered" White and Klondike O'Donnell. A third man, Phil Deandre, pulled up a chair and asked Karpis whether he was involved with the Touhys. "Hell, you know I'm not," Karpis said.

O'Donnell smiled. "We know," he said. But Baby Face Nelson was another matter. Nelson had old ties to the Touhys, and for some reason Nitti wanted Nelson dead. "We found out these guys are out there by you, and well, we're gonna wipe 'em out," Deandre said. "What we want you to do is move out 'cause there's gonna be a lot of heat out there, and we don't want you getting caught in it."

Karpis promised he would move immediately. He rose, and Deandre admonished him not to warn Nelson. He patted Karpis on the shoulder. "You're all right," he said. "It's just too bad that you went to stealing and got hot. You should have come and worked for us guys. We need guys like you."

Karpis's mind raced. He had to move fast. He drove back to Long Beach and made reservations for Delores Delaney's flight to St. Paul. The next night, with Delaney safely in St. Paul, Karpis crossed the road to Nelson's bungalow. "You want to come out to the car with me for a minute?" Karpis asked Nelson.

The two men walked into the evening air. To the north, Lake Michigan was blacker than the night. "Have you got any of these Touhy guys out here?" Karpis asked.

"What the hell are you talking about?" Nelson said.

"Listen. If you have any of them here or whether you haven't is beside the point. You guys get the hell out of here right away."

"What the hell? Are you telling us what to do?"

Karpis explained the situation with Nitti. "I'm sticking my chin right out there for a real bad left hook if something goes wrong with this," he told Nelson. "I'm not supposed to talk to you guys about this but I'm not going to see you guys get slaughtered out here when you shouldn't be, because you haven't done anything except steal. So I'm leaving, and I'm telling you guys if you don't leave, once I've left, both of these houses are liable to get blown clear out in the lake."

Nelson thought a moment. "We'll be gone by midnight." He suggested they relay messages through Louis Cernocky in Fox River Grove. Karpis said it wouldn't be safe, since Frank Nash's wife, who knew Cernocky's place, was in FBI custody. Karpis then left, cleaned out the lake house, and drove to a new apartment he had rented, at the South Shore Country Club building in Chicago.

A few days later Ziegler dropped by with a disquieting message: Frank Nitti himself wanted to see him, right away. Karpis swallowed hard. The meeting was set at a downtown bar. Karpis arrived early. The bar was empty except for a bartender, who eyed him nervously. When Nitti, along with Three-Fingered Willie White, walked in, his greeting was chilly. They took seats in a back room. There was a long silence.

"I'm gonna tell you something, Ray," White began, using Karpis's alias. "I vouched for you with the outfit. Now we got some questions we want to ask you."

"Well, go ahead," Karpis said. "What are they?"

"Well," White said, "the first one is, did you say anything to those fellas living in them two houses over there? And the second is, can you tell us why they were gone right after we talked to you?"

Karpis had already decided what to say. "I'm gonna tell you the truth," he began. "I talked to them, and Nelson assured me that there was no rackets guys around there with them, especially none from the Touhy outfit, and that they were strictly bank robbers, and I decided I'd tell them and get the hell out of there because there was going to be trouble out there. I'm the guy. I'm the reason they're not out there no more."

Another silence. Nitti stared. "Well, didn't you tell us you wouldn't?" White asked.

"I did," Karpis said, "but I changed my mind on the thing."

Nitti spoke. "I suppose you have a gun on you," he said.

"Forty-five," Karpis said.

Nitti told Karpis to wait outside. Karpis took a seat at the bar. A minute went by, then two. Karpis stared at the clock. Five minutes later, the door to the back room opened. "Come on in, Ray," White said. Karpis took a seat. He looked in Nitti's eyes. "We're gonna give you a pass on this 'cause we know you're not a racket guy," he said. "We know Freddie, none of the guys like Frank Nash, Harvey Bailey, or any of you guys, are. There's only one guy among you that was mixed up in the rackets, and you know as well as I know who that is, that son of a bitch Verne Miller."

"I didn't know you guys were hot at him," Karpis said.

"Everybody's hot at that bastard," Nitti replied.

With a final warning never to get mixed up in syndicate business again, Karpis was allowed to leave. He drove home in silence. Delaney was there. She had returned from St. Paul, where she had endured a tonsillectomy and an abortion, then spent five days in a Chicago hospital when the tonsillectomy incisions ruptured. In bed Karpis reached for her. She made a face. "You know, we're not going to be able to do anything tonight," Delores said.

"What's the matter?"

"The doctor says no, not for thirty days after that operation."

"Jesus Christ," Karpis said.

They lay in the darkness in each other's arms, until Delores fell asleep. Karpis wasn't much for cuddling, but as he watched her there in the dim light, he felt a sense of contentment. Dawn came quickly.

The next day, Karpis drove by to thank George Ziegler, who asked him to take a drive.

"What are you guys going to do now?" Ziegler asked.

"What do you mean?"

"To make money. You guys haven't been doing anything, have you?"

Karpis didn't mention the St. Paul robbery, from which they had excluded Ziegler. "Why?" Karpis asked. "What have you got in mind? You don't need any money right now, do you?"

"Hell yes," Ziegler said. "I've blown what I had on the wheat market. The damn thing took a turn for the bad and here I am, I'm gonna have to make some money."

"What do you want to do, another kidnapping?"

"No," said Ziegler. "I got a hell of a good thing."

Then Shotgun George Ziegler explained: he wanted to hit the Federal Reserve Bank of Chicago. It sat in the heart of the financial district, adjacent to the Bankers Building, nineteen floors below the Chicago offices of the FBI.

It was a muggy, damp Labor Day on the Potomac. In the Bureau offices at Vermont and Constitution, Hoover and his men remained focused on Machine Gun Kelly. They had traced the Kellys to Des Moines, but there the trail went cold. Agents were nosing around Kathryn's old haunts in West Texas and had secured the cooperation of her father, who had allowed agents to search the East Mulkey Street house. But all efforts to determine Kelly's actual identity had turned up nothing. To the agents who pursued him, Machine Gun Kelly was just a name.

While Hoover's men scoured the country, the Kellys themselves were in disarray. This was like no other crime they had committed before. This time there were national headlines, and federal agents, from a bureau they had barely heard of, hounding them across state borders, night and day. After fleeing West Texas one step ahead of FBI agents, Kelly drove to Biloxi, Mississippi, checking into the Avilez Hotel on Thursday night, August 24. Three days later he moved to the Avon Hotel on West Beach Boulevard, registering as "J.L. Baker."

Never the brightest soul, Kelly made the mistake of cashing a handful of American Express Travelers Cheques, and a clerk identified him. Agents from New Orleans scrambled to Biloxi, where word of their arrival leaked to a newspaper. Kelly was standing on a Biloxi street corner on Monday, August 28, when he heard a newsboy cry, "Machine Gun Kelly in town!" He panicked, ran to the bus station, and bought a ticket to Memphis. He had abandoned his luggage, including his clothes and a loaded .45 caliber pistol, at his hotel.

As inexperienced as its agents were, the FBI had learned to watch a fugitive's old haunts: had Hoover known anything of Kelly's past, agents might have been waiting for him in Memphis. But they weren't. Later that day, at a pay phone outside the Memphis bus station, Kelly called his former brother-in-law, an up-and-coming attorney named Langford Ramsey. Ramsey, at the time the youngest lawyer to have passed the Tennessee bar, had no idea the George Barnes he had known eight years earlier was now Machine Gun Kelly, the nation's most wanted man. Ramsey arranged for him to bunk at the home of a friend, a crippled attendant at a downtown parking garage.

Kathryn, meanwhile, after driving across Texas and Louisiana, arrived in Biloxi to find Kelly gone. Kathryn was beside herself. She was certain Kelly had run off with a woman he knew in Biloxi. Not knowing what else to do, she drove back to Texas, reaching a point south of Temple, where on Saturday night, September 2, she drove up to the house of her longtime maid, Junie.* Inside, Kathryn slathered her face in cold cream and began to curse her husband. "I don't know where George is," she said, "but I'm trying to get in touch with the s.o.b. to get him to surrender so they'll release me and my mother from that indictment."[10]

The next day Kathryn bought a red wig and checked into Waco's Hilton Hotel, where she spent the day brooding about her mother's coming trial. She needed to know whether Sam Sayers, the Fort Worth attorney she had hired to represent her mother, had made any progress on her proposal to turn in Kelly. The next morning, Kathryn telephoned Sayers in Fort Worth. "Hello, this is your girlfriend," Kathryn said.

"Which girlfriend?" Sayers asked.

"Your best girl—the one with the Pekinese dogs. I must see you right away." She told him where to meet her in Waco.

"I can't talk to you now," Sayers said. "You know better than to call me on this phone." He hung up.† At wit's end, Kathryn jumped back in her pickup and drove north toward Fort Worth, unsure how to contact Sayers safely. Just past Hillsboro, at the town of Itasca, she spotted a family of three forlorn hitchhikers outside a filling station. She pulled up beside them. She had an idea.

"Y'all want a ride?" Kathryn asked.

---

* The name is a pseudonym; the maid's actual name is blacked out in FBI files.
† This brief conversation, reported verbatim in an October 3, 1933, FBI memo, is curious. It suggests the FBI tapped Sayers's phone, though approval for such a tap is mentioned nowhere in FBI files. The FBI memo further indicates that Sayers went to Waco in search of Kathryn that day but failed to locate her.

The hitchhikers were Depression refugees, an itinerant Oklahoma farmer named Luther Arnold; his wife, Flossie Mae; and their twelve-year-old daughter, Geralene. They had been thrown off an uncle's farm outside Ardmore following a bank foreclosure and had been hitchhiking across Texas ever since, living off odd jobs and handouts.* They eagerly accepted the ride from the red-haired woman in the blue gingham dress.

"What are y'all doing?" Kathryn asked after a bit.

"Just hiking," Arnold said. "I'm looking for anything that will feed three hungry people."

Kathryn oozed sympathy. She said she might be able to help. They drove on to the town of Cleburne, where they stopped at a tourist camp for the night. Kathryn paid for everything. The next morning she took Flossie Mae and Geralene into town and bought them housedresses. When they returned to the tourist camp, Kathryn took Luther Arnold aside.

"I like you people, and would like to fix it so you could make a little money," she said. "Can I trust you?"

"Absolutely," Arnold said.

"What would you people think if I told you who I am?"

"Go ahead," Arnold said. "You can trust us."

"I'm Kathryn Kelly—no doubt you've read about me in the papers," she said. "Mr. Arnold, I am going to place a big trust in you." She handed him $50 and told him to take the bus to Fort Worth, contact her attorney, Sam Sayers, and find out whether he had struck a deal with government prosecutors.

Arnold agreed. When he reached the lawyer's office, Sayers said there had been no progress on any deal. When Arnold returned to Cleburne that night, Kathryn began to think. Sayers was a Texas attorney who wouldn't know the Oklahoma environs where her mother was to be tried. She asked Arnold if he knew an Oklahoma attorney she could hire, and Arnold said he did, a lawyer in Enid. The next morning Kathryn dropped Arnold outside Fort Worth with $300 and a note instructing Sayers to give him a car she had left with him. Arnold was to proceed to Enid, hire the attorney for her mother, then drive south to San Antonio, where Kathryn said she would leave instructions for him at the post office's General Delivery window.

This time things didn't go as planned. When Arnold phoned Sayers, the

* Luther Arnold's sadsack story about the Oklahoma farm was true, but he pointedly failed to mention his two arrests for passing bad checks in Los Angeles.

lawyer wasn't in. Arnold wasn't disappointed. In fact, he was growing happier by the minute. After a month of tramping across Texas, begging for food and shaving in gas station bathrooms, he was free in a big city, his pockets full of cash. Outside the bus station Arnold asked a Yellow Cab driver where a man could buy a drink. The driver took him to a bar, where Arnold ordered a beer. Afterward Arnold felt even better. He asked the barkeep where he could obtain some female companionship. The barkeep stepped to a telephone, called a number, and in no time a girl showed up. She said her name was Mae.

Arnold and Mae got along so well he bought an entire case of beer. He took it with him back to Mae's apartment, where the two made themselves at home. After a while Arnold was feeling so good he asked Mae if she had any friends. Before long a girl named Hilda arrived.* Together Arnold and his two new lady friends and their case of beer enjoyed a long evening.

The next morning Luther Arnold succeeded in reaching Sam Sayers, who drove out to meet him with Kathryn's Chevrolet. Arnold took the car, loading his two lady friends into the rumble seat, and drove to Enid, where he hired the lawyer for Kathryn's mother. Arnold and the girls drove on to Oklahoma City and registered at the city's nicest hotel, the Skirvin, where they began a loud party.[11] By the next morning several attorneys Kathryn had hired also arrived at the Skirvin.

It was then, on Saturday, September 9, that Gus Jones received a tip that the attorneys were meeting with an emissary of Kathryn Kelly's at the Skirvin. Luther Arnold was placed under surveillance. Apparently there was some debate whether the hard-drinking Arnold was really mixed up in the Kellys' affairs. The quality of surveillance that weekend reflected this ambivalence. On Monday morning, September 11, agents noticed something that made their stomachs drop: Luther Arnold was gone. Arnold's two lady friends remained, but Jones realized the FBI's best chance at finding the Kellys had simply walked out the door.

While Hoover's men closed in on Machine Gun Kelly, John Dillinger received the disappointing news that a set of guns he had thrown over the wall at Michigan City had been found and turned over to the warden. He

---

* Both "Mae" and "Hilda" are pseudonyms; the women's actual names are blacked out in FBI reports.

realized he would need to try again, and for that he needed more money. At noon on Wednesday, September 6, Dillinger and his partner Harry Copeland strolled into the lobby of the State Bank of Massachusetts Avenue in downtown Indianapolis. Without a word, Dillinger, his trademark straw boater tilted jauntily to one side, scrambled atop a seven-foot-high teller cage and trained a pistol on the bank's assistant manager, Lloyd Reinhart. "This is a stickup," he said.

Reinhart, deep in conversation on a telephone, kept his head down and ignored the comment, thinking someone was joking.

"Get away from that damn telephone!" Dillinger snapped.

Reinhart looked up into the barrel of Dillinger's gun and realized this was no joke. Reinhart and another cashier raised their hands, and Dillinger hopped down and began shoving cash from the counters into a white sack. Behind him, Copeland, fidgeting with the handkerchief across his face, kept glancing outside.

"Hurry up!" Copeland urged more than once. Within minutes Dillinger and Copeland scurried from the bank into a waiting getaway car. Later, when they counted the take, it came to more than $24,000—at the time the second costliest bank robbery in state history.

To this day, no one is sure how Dillinger slipped the second batch of guns into the Michigan City prison. One of the inmate plotters later told authorities that the guns were smuggled in a box of thread sent to the prison's shirt factory. According to another version, Dillinger once again tossed the guns over a prison wall. Whatever happened, the guns finally made it into the hands of Dillinger's friends.

His mission accomplished, Dillinger was ready for a few days off. He hopped into his new car, a fast Essex Terraplane, and headed to Dayton, to see the girl he had been courting all summer, Mary Longnaker, whose apartment was still being watched by two police officers.

After parting with Luther Arnold, Kathryn Kelly drove Arnold's wife, Flossie Mae, and their daughter, Geralene, back to her uncle's ranch in West Texas. It was a risky move: FBI agents had been canvassing the area for weeks. But it was the only place Kathryn knew to look for her wayward husband. When she drove up, Cass Coleman told her he hadn't seen Kelly in two weeks. Kathryn lingered barely thirty minutes, just long enough to load some cots into the pickup and scribble out a note for Kelly. She told Coleman to write her care of General Delivery, San Antonio, the moment Kelly appeared.

Four nights later, on Saturday, September 9, Kelly finally arrived, having spent ten days lying around Memphis, draining bottles of gin. Worried that Cass Coleman's ranch was under surveillance, he walked unannounced into a neighbor's kitchen, startling the neighbor's wife. His hair alone would have frightened most people. Kelly had dyed it a bright yellow; with the additional ten pounds or so he had gained while a fugitive, he looked like a bloated canary. The neighbor woman, who had heard rumors of Kelly's real identity, drove straight to Cass Coleman's and angrily demanded that he take Kelly away. Instead, Coleman sent a telegram to Kathryn: MOTHER BETTER.

Kathryn received the telegram two days later. She took Flossie Mae Arnold to the San Antonio post office and sent her in to get it. "Mother started to open the telegram at first," Geralene Arnold said later, "but she waited till she got back to the car where Kathryn was, and Kathryn just jerked it right out of her hand and told her it wasn't hers." After reading the telegram, Kathryn took Geralene and drove to Coleman's ranch. She left Flossie Mae behind.

After three weeks apart, the Kellys' reunion that evening was hardly a warm, fuzzy moment. As Geralene recalled, "[Kathryn] went up to [Kelly] and said, 'I don't know whether to kill you or kiss you.'"[12] Cass Coleman later told the FBI: "As soon as she got there Kathryn told George he was a damned fool, and should have had better sense than to go off to Mississippi where she couldn't get in touch with him, as he knew she needed money, and that he had just gone down there chasing after [some] woman. He said he was just trying to take care of himself until he could get in touch with her. Kathryn called him a damned liar, and he called her another damned liar."

The squabbling Kellys climbed into Kathryn's pickup and drove back to San Antonio, where Kathryn had rented a five-room furnished bungalow. Flossie Mae and little Geralene listened as the Kellys debated their next move. Kelly wanted to head east, to Chicago or New York, where he felt they could hide for months. But Kathryn insisted on doing something to free her mother. She told Kelly he should surrender to the FBI in return for a deal that would enable her mother to go free. To Kathryn's surprise, Kelly agreed.

"Go ahead and make your dicker and when you get it made, let me know," Kelly said. "I'm willing to go, but you know I can't go to them and do any dickering [myself]."[13]

The next day, Tuesday, September 12, Luther Arnold arrived in San Antonio, brimming with details of his trip to Oklahoma City and completely oblivious to how close he had come to being arrested. Kathryn gave him more money to pay her mother's attorneys. The next day Arnold returned north, stopping en route in Fort Worth, where he tarried for a night of barhopping. When he finished he was so drunk he hired a young man to drive him on to Oklahoma City. Arnold had barely stepped into the Skirvin hotel the following afternoon, Wednesday, September 14, when Gus Jones's men arrested him.

By now the FBI men were losing patience. According to one internal report, agents employed "vigorous but appropriate" methods to persuade Arnold to talk (this term would later emerge as Bureau shorthand for roughing up a subject). Arnold broke quickly.[14] Gus Jones telephoned San Antonio. Within hours agents there led a squad of San Antonio police to the Kellys' bungalow. Bursting through the front door, they found only a flustered Flossie Mae Arnold. The Kellys had left the day before, she said, heading back to Cass Coleman's ranch. Flossie Mae was frightened. The Kellys had taken her daughter, Geralene, with them.

The Dallas office had several agents in West Texas that night, and all converged on Coleman in search of the Kellys. One agent was already in town when the Kellys, with Geralene in tow, arrived just hours before the San Antonio raid. For the moment, the couple's luck held. One of Cass Coleman's neighbors, Clarence Durham, returned home from work that day to find the Kellys lying on a bed on his front porch. Durham demanded that they leave immediately.

The moment the Kellys drove off, Durham headed to the sheriff's office and told him everything.[15] By the next day, every sheriff's office in West Texas was on high alert. Sightings of the Kellys came in from Abilene, San Angelo, and a series of towns leading toward Wichita Falls, which suggested they were making for Oklahoma. Highway Patrol officers were placed on the Red River bridges, but they were too late. The Kellys crossed into Oklahoma early that day, speeding north.

Hungry and tired, they reached Chicago on Sunday, September 17. In search of a new and untraceable car, Kelly stopped at a pay phone and tried in vain to reach a Cicero garage owner; at that very moment, the man was completing a special armor-plated car for the Federal Reserve raid Alvin

Karpis and the Barkers planned. The Kellys drove downtown, rented an apartment, and, after unpacking their luggage, trudged out to a diner to eat.

Over dinner, Kelly grew nervous when a pair of diners seemed to stare at him. Afterward, fearing they had been spotted, he and Kathryn took Geralene and drove downtown streets for an hour before returning to the apartment. Kathryn sent Geralene inside to pack and retrieve their luggage, then let Kelly out at the Piccadilly Theatre, where he disappeared inside to watch a movie and wait. If they had been spotted, it wasn't by the FBI. By evening's end, they had successfully rented a new furnished apartment on Chicago's North Side.[16] They told the landlady they were in town to visit the World's Fair.

The next day, Monday, September 18, the kidnapping trial of Albert Bates, Harvey Bailey, and the Shannons began in Oklahoma City. The trial was front-page news in Chicago. Kathryn read the newspapers in a fury, stomping around the apartment, swearing revenge on Urschel and the government prosecutor, Joseph Keenan. At some point, she wrote a letter to Keenan. Postmarked Chicago, it arrived in Oklahoma City the next day. *The entire Urschel family and friends, and all of you will be exterminated soon,* Kathryn wrote. *There is no way I can prevent it. I will gladly put George Kelly on the spot for you if you will save my mother, who is innocent of any wrong doing* [sic].

The next day, a second letter, this time signed by Kelly, arrived at the Urschel mansion. "Ignorant Charles," it began.

Just a few lines to let you know that I am getting my plans laid to destroy your so-called mansion, and you and your family immediately after this trial. And young fellow I guess you've begun to realize your serious mistake . . . You are living on borrowed time now . . . I have friends in Oklahoma City that know every move you make, and you are still too dumb to figure out the finger man there. If my brain was no larger than yours, the government would have had me long ago, as it is I am drinking good beer and will yet see you and your family like I should have left you at first—stone-dead . . . Adios, smart one. Your worst enemy, Geo. R. Kelly . . . See you in hell.

The Kellys' letters dropped like bombs in the Oklahoma City courtroom, which was packed with the nation's press. The Bureau's number two man, Harold "Pop" Nathan, who had arrived to oversee the trial, sent agents to trace the letters, but to no avail. But not all the Kellys' letters proved untraceable. Before leaving Texas, Kathryn had mailed a note to

Flossie Mae Arnold, directing her to check into an Oklahoma City boardinghouse to wait for further instructions. This letter was intercepted by FBI agents in San Antonio and forwarded to Pop Nathan in Oklahoma City.

Nathan had Flossie Mae brought to Oklahoma, reunited with her husband, Luther, and installed in the boardinghouse to await word from Kathryn. On Thursday, September 21, it finally came, a letter, saying the Kellys could be reached via Special Delivery mail at a bar on Chicago's South Side, the Michigan Tavern, at 1150 South Michigan Avenue. *I am taking care of the baby honey,* Kathryn wrote, alluding to Geralene. *She's never out of my Sight* [sic], *and Be careful to take care of my clothes for they are all I have so don't lose them.*

The FBI closed in. Nathan telephoned the Chicago office and briefed Melvin Purvis. All Purvis had to do was to stake out the Michigan Tavern. When the Kellys arrived, they could be arrested. Purvis listened and promised to take care of it. And then he did something extraordinary: he forgot about it. Weeks later, when Hoover realized the blunder and demanded an explanation, Purvis was unable to come up with one. "I recall that upon receipt of this information I omitted making a memorandum, which was possibly due to the fact that at that time there were so many important developments . . ." he wrote Hoover.[17]

The next morning, as luck would have it, Kelly was preparing to leave Chicago. Between angry letters he had spent much of his time wandering the streets of the North Side, stopping at pay phones to make calls in search of anyone who would help him. He reached a member of Frank Nitti's mob, who told Kelly he was "too hot," adding that "he would not be seen talking to [the Kellys] for $10,000." Finally, Kelly arranged to buy a car through an intermediary, Abe Kaplan, who ran the Michigan Tavern. Leaving his old car on the street, Kelly took Kathryn and Geralene, piled their bags into a taxi, and headed to the bar.

Inside, they settled into a rear booth. Kaplan arrived after fifteen minutes, plunking down a whiskey bottle. He started to speak, then hesitated, glancing at Geralene. "She's a nice little girl," Kelly said, taking out a roll of bills. "She's all right."

By coincidence, at a bit after nine, just when the Kellys were en route to the Michigan Tavern, Melvin Purvis suddenly remembered Pop Nathan's call. But instead of dispatching his men to the tavern itself, Purvis sent two agents to the downtown post office to find the postman who delivered the tavern's mail. After being told that the postman was walking his route, the agents drove to the tavern's neighborhood, arriving around quarter past ten, while the Kellys were sitting in their booth. The agents found the postman, who said he knew nothing about any Special Delivery letters sent to or from the Michigan Tavern. Rather than check the tavern itself, the agents returned to the Bankers Building.[18]

As they did, the Kellys emerged from the tavern. They took a taxi to a Cicero garage and picked up their new car. By noon they were gone. Not until an hour later did Purvis realize his mistake. At 2:00 he sent men to stake out the Michigan Tavern and kept them there through the weekend. Weeks afterward, when Hoover realized what had happened, he scrawled on a memo: "This was a miserable piece of work."

Dayton, Ohio
Friday, September 22
1:05 A.M. (Eastern Time)

Just hours before the Kellys' narrow escape from the FBI in Chicago, John Dillinger arrived back in Dayton, hoping to rekindle his romance with Mary Longnaker. As it happened, that very afternoon the two detectives watching Longnaker's boardinghouse had given up the surveillance and returned to their desks.

Longnaker's landlady telephoned police when Dillinger showed up.

"He's here," she told the night sergeant, W. J. Aldredge.

"Who's here?" Aldredge asked.

"John Dillinger, you dumb flatfoot!"

Within an hour police had the boardinghouse surrounded. Sergeant Aldredge and the two detectives, Russell Pfauhl and Charlie Gross, met the landlady at the backdoor. Dillinger, she whispered, was upstairs, in Longnaker's room. Pfauhl, cradling a shotgun, and Gross, armed with a submachine gun, crept up the carpeted stairs. At the top, they knocked on Longnaker's door. A moment later Longnaker opened it. Detective Gross stepped into the room, followed by Pfauhl. Dillinger, wearing an undershirt and gray suit pants, was standing in the living room, holding a sheaf of photographs he had taken at the World's Fair.

"Stick 'em up, John," Gross said. "We're police officers."

Dillinger slowly raised his hands, the photos fluttering to the floor. For a split second his hands wavered.

"Don't, John," Pfauhl said, leveling the submachine gun. "I'll kill you."[19]

Downtown Chicago
12:15 A.M. (Central Time)

A little after·midnight, at almost the same moment Dayton detectives arrested Dillinger and escorted him in handcuffs to the city jail, Alvin Karpis and the Barker brothers sat in a darkened Hudson sedan on Jackson Street in Chicago's financial district. The car sat in the shadow of the Bankers Building, nineteen floors below Melvin Purvis's window, but Karpis's attention was drawn to the Federal Reserve Building, a block ahead through the gloom. As he watched, two men emerged onto the sidewalk, one of them wheeling a hand truck stacked with bulging sacks. Two armed guards followed them.

"Okay," someone said.

Karpis eased the Hudson ahead as he pushed a button on the dashboard. From behind the car a dense cloud of black smoke poured, forming a smokescreen intended to block oncoming traffic; Karpis had ordered the smoke machine installed because he was worried about the heavy flow of tourists driving west from the World's Fair at the lakefront. Karpis had also had bulletproof glass installed in the driver's side window and the entire car lined in armor plate.

A moment later, the Hudson pulled to the curb beside the Federal Reserve couriers and their guards. Fred Barker and George Ziegler, handkerchiefs drawn over their faces, leaped out and trained submachine guns on the messengers, who handed over the five bulky bags on their dolly. The two were back in the car in less than a minute. Karpis pulled away, following the git he had drawn; Ziegler's sidekick, the tall, tubercular Bryan Bolton, sat beside him with a Thompson on his lap. Two blocks west he swerved right on Franklin, sped north two blocks, then veered left onto Adams, heading west. The Hudson shot down Adams and soared across the Chicago River bridge.

At Halsted, Karpis turned north—straight into an oncoming Ford coupe. The two cars collided violently, sending the gang's Hudson crashing into a telephone pole at the northwest corner of the intersection. As it happened, two uniformed Chicago policemen were standing on the southwest corner, walking toward their beats. One, Maurice Fitzgerald, forty-six, ran across Halsted to the wrecked Ford coupe, where inside several women could be heard screaming.

The second policeman, Miles Cunningham, a thirty-five-year-old father of two, stepped toward the Hudson. Dock Barker, a .38 in his right hand, emerged from the car, whose front end was caved in. "Cops!" he yelled. Bryan Bolton raised his submachine gun and fired a burst directly into Officer Cunningham, who crumpled, dead. Dock cried out; one of Bolton's ricochets struck his right pinky finger, knocking the diamond out of a new ring. As Karpis and the others piled out of the Hudson and commandeered a passerby's car, Bolton turned and began firing at Officer Fitzgerald, who took cover behind a traffic sign.

Furiously the gang began transferring items into the commandeered car. As they drove south, Karpis noticed the gas tank was nearly empty. At Ashland Avenue they jumped out and stopped a second car, once again ordering its occupants out and transferring the bags and the guns. They drove in silence to a garage on the southwest side, shut the doors behind them, and emptied out the five money bags. It was then they learned that they had just stolen fifty pounds of mail.

The Barkers were furious. "Who the hell set this thing up?" Dock snapped, studying his bleeding finger. Ziegler looked sheepish as Dock turned on Bolton. "For Christ sake, you might have shot my whole hand off!" Fred Barker stepped in. "These things'll happen," he said. "There's no need of arguing about this. The big thing is, did anybody leave their damn fingerprints in that damn Hudson? That's more important than anything right now."

The shoot-out in the heart of downtown Chicago was front-page news across the country. The next morning, at his South Side apartment, Karpis spread the Chicago papers across his kitchen table. Around ten Fred joined him. At first glance they were stunned by headlines of the massive manhunt launched by police and the FBI: 10,000 HUNT FOR POLICE KILLER GANG, blared the *Chicago American*. On closer reading Karpis realized things weren't so bad. Detectives had found several guns in the abandoned Hudson, but apparently no fingerprints. The police, in fact, were saying they believed the robbers to be some combination of Machine Gun Kelly, Verne Miller, and Pretty Boy Floyd.

"I don't know what the hell to tell you," Karpis said. "This thing is going to turn out real bad, or it may turn out good, but I'll tell you one thing right now. You go get your mother outta that building, don't wait a goddamn minute. There's too many people knowing now where you live and your mother lives."

Fred made a face. He didn't relish the idea of confronting his mother. "If you want, I'll go with you," Karpis said. "I know how you are. You'll want to put it off."

They found Ma a new apartment on South Shore Drive and arranged to have it furnished. That afternoon, as police raided underworld joints across the city, Karpis and Fred stood in a furniture-rental store, pointing out pieces they wanted for Ma's new place. Afterward they moved her in. Only then did Ma realize Fred wouldn't be living with her. For the first time since leaving Oklahoma, she would be alone. To Karpis, she suddenly looked very old and very small.

Later Karpis and Barker walked down to their cars. Fred was clearly irritated at Ziegler for botching the Federal Reserve job.

"Tell that son of a bitch maybe he can find another caper as good as the one that we just went on," he said.

"Hell, you can't blame the guy," Karpis said. "I'm sure he didn't go on it for kicks. He thought we were going to get money the same as I did. In fact, I already had planned on going to Australia if we had got anything like what we were supposed to have got."

Barker looked at him. "Australia?" he said.

"Hell yeah," Karpis said. "You don't think if I'd have got a lot of money that I wouldn't get the hell out of this country? This country's going to be pretty hot. That damn thing in Kansas City where Verne killed all them cops and Frank Nash? This thing is going to wind up being the worst thing that ever happened to guys like us. In another year or so, the government will probably be taking over the banks to stop bank robbery, so you'd better just figure now that we ain't got too much damn longer to make a lot of money and get away."[20]

Barker made a face; he hated when Karpis got big-picture on him. But he was right. The police were drawing closer. That weekend Chicago detectives traced the gang's getaway car to the mob mechanic who had serviced Machine Gun Kelly. The mechanic's detention, in turn, led to the arrest of a syndicate money launderer named Gus Winkler, a man both Kelly and Karpis had done business with. Both were handed over to the FBI. Monday morning Melvin Purvis stepped in front of reporters and announced—inexplicably—that the bullets that killed Officer Cunningham had been fired from the same gun used in the Kansas City Massacre. He speculated that a pair of octagonal glasses Gus Winkler wore might be connected to a pair of glasses Kelly was known to wear.

"There is a possibility that Kelly and Winkler are associated together," Purvis intoned, "and that they may have had the same idea about octagon glasses, which are used by the extremely sedate type of person. Or they may even have interchanged glasses."[21]

Once again others were being blamed for the Barker Gang's crimes. But it was the heat that police were bringing to bear on the Syndicate that worried Karpis most. Chastened by his meeting with Frank Nitti, he reflected that it might be time the gang left Chicago.

That Friday night, as Karpis prepared for an urgent vacation, Machine Gun Kelly arrived in Memphis with Kathryn and twelve-year-old Geralene Arnold after a daylong drive from Chicago. Kelly headed straight to the garage attendant's bungalow on East Raynor Street where he had hidden before; the attendant, a small man whose left side was paralyzed, waved the Kellys in without a question.

The next day, Kelly called at the home of his former brother-in-law, Langford Ramsey, and enjoyed a reunion with his two young sons, Bruce and George, Jr. Years later Bruce Barnes remembered his father that day as a smiling, yellow-haired man wearing a charcoal gray suit, a shoulder holster, and pistol. He said he was an FBI agent on a secret mission and gave the boys $20 apiece he peeled from a fat roll of bills.

Kelly and Kathryn began drinking gin with Lang Ramsey that afternoon and continued well into the evening. At some point, Kelly revealed to Ramsey that he was Machine Gun Kelly. For years afterward Ramsey would claim that he thought Kelly was joking. Whatever he believed, Lang Ramsey agreed to do his former brother-in-law a favor, a big one. The Kellys were running low on money; they needed the cash they had buried on Kathryn's uncle's ranch in West Texas, but were afraid to retrieve it themselves. Ramsey agreed to get it for them.

The next morning at dawn Ramsey drove west. Beside him on the front seat sat the homesick Geralene Arnold, whom Kathryn had strong-armed into guiding Ramsey to her uncle's spread. While the Kellys remained at the house on East Raynor Street, Ramsey steered across Arkansas and into Texas, passing Dallas and then Fort Worth. The eastern horizon was reddening when he coasted to a stop at Cass Coleman's front gate around five Monday morning. Coleman saw them arrive and stepped into the yard.

"I came after—" Ramsey started to say.

Coleman cut him off. "I know what you came after," he said. Since last seeing the Kellys, Coleman had been questioned by FBI agents and mistakenly assumed he was under surveillance; the Dallas office wanted to watch him, but it simply didn't have enough agents.

"Well, I'm contact man for George and Kathryn Kelly," Ramsey said. "My name is—"

"I don't care anything about your name," Coleman said. He told Ramsey he wanted nothing further to do with the Kellys.

"Will it be safe for me to take her furs with me?" Ramsey asked.

"No, it won't be safe for you to take anything or bring anything," Coleman said. "You'll be arrested before you get [a hundred yards]. This place is covered with laws . . ."

"I'm not hot," Ramsey said.

"You will be before you get far," Coleman said. "They will tail you out of here."[22]

Ramsey left, badly shaken. He drove north to the town of Gainesville, stopping at noon at the Western Union office, where he sent a telegram to Kelly: HAD SEVERAL TOUGH BREAKS . . . , it read. DEAL FELL THROUGH. TRIED TO GET LATER APPOINTMENT. BEST PROSPECT WAS AFRAID. IMPOSSIBLE. CHANGED HIS MIND. DON'T WANT TO BRING HOME A SAD TALE. CAN GO ON IF ADVISABLE. WIRE INSTRUCTIONS HERE.

By that point Geralene was begging to rejoin her parents. On the drive to Gainesville, Ramsey dropped her off at the train station in Fort Worth and bought her a ticket to Oklahoma City, where her parents remained under the FBI's care. It was a fateful decision. No sooner had Geralene left Ramsey than she sent a telegram to her father. It read: MEET ME ROCK ISLAND STATION TEN FIFTEEN TONIGHT. GERRY.

The Arnolds were waiting for Geralene when she arrived in Oklahoma City that night. So was the FBI. The little girl told Pop Nathan everything she knew. The Kellys, she said, were staying at a home on East Raynor Street in Memphis.

This time Hoover was determined the Kellys would not escape. Briefed by Pop Nathan, he phoned William Rorer, the thirty-one-year-old SAC in Birmingham, Alabama, and ordered him to Memphis to raid the East Raynor Street home by first light. It was already past midnight in Alabama, and Rorer, a lean, handsome World War I veteran who had joined the Bureau in 1929, realized he could never drive to Memphis by dawn.

An airplane was his only hope. He phoned and woke the man who ran

Birmingham's sole air-charter service, but the man insisted he wasn't allowed to fly at night. He told Rorer to try the National Guard, which had planes at Birmingham's Roberts Field. After several more calls Rorer tracked down a National Guard colonel in Montgomery. The colonel said he was pleased to help but had no authority. Rorer called the colonel's superior, a National Guard general at Fort McPherson, Georgia, and "after considerable persuasion" managed to arrange a plane for the flight to Memphis.[23]

Rorer and another agent boarded an army plane at Birmingham's Roberts Field at 3:20 A.M. and touched down at the Memphis airport two hours later, at 5:30. There they were met by the Bureau's resident agent at Memphis and a half-dozen policemen he had rounded up. The group drove to the foot of East Raynor Street, where uniformed cops were already waiting. East Raynor was a quiet street lined with matching brick bungalows, just off busy Speedway Avenue on the city's south side. The house at 1408, six houses up from Speedway, was dark. Rorer wasted no time with unnecessary reconnaissance. In the predawn darkness he sent two Memphis detectives creeping up either side of the house. Then he and a detective named William Raney drew their guns and stepped onto the front porch.

No sound came from inside the house. Rorer tried the screen door. It opened. Glancing at Detective Raney, he tried the front door itself. It too opened. Quietly Rorer stepped into the house. In the dim light he could see he was in a cluttered living room. On a divan lay a copy of *Master Detective* magazine; it was opened to an article entitled "My Blood Curdling Ride with Death." Detective Raney stepped in behind Rorer. To their right was an open bedroom door. On a bed lay two men in their underwear, asleep. Neither, they could see, was Kelly.

Rorer crept down a hallway toward the back of the house, where he could see a screened-in porch; the floor was strewn with empty bottles of Old Log Cabin bourbon. To his right he saw a second bedroom door. Stepping to it, he looked inside and saw a woman in green silk pajamas asleep on a bed. It was Kathryn. Detective Raney, meanwhile, stepped into the front bedroom where the two sleeping men lay. As he did, Kelly, having heard footfalls, stepped from the rear bedroom through a hallway toward the front bedroom. Detective Raney saw his shadow on the wall. He raised his shotgun. A moment later Kelly stepped into the room and came face-to-face with Raney's two loaded barrels.

Kelly, wearing only underwear, his bright yellow hair rumpled by sleep, was holding his .45.

_____

"Drop that gun," Raney said.

"I been waiting all night for you," Kelly said with a smile.

"Well," said Raney, "here we are."

Kelly slowly placed his pistol on a sewing machine, then raised his hands. It was over.* Within minutes the other lawmen poured into the house, handcuffing Kelly, the garage attendant, and the second sleeping man, an unsuspecting friend. Before handcuffing Kathryn, Rorer gave her fifteen minutes to get dressed. She emerged wearing a smart black dress with monkey-fur epaulets and orange buttons and walked curtly to the waiting cars. She told one of the agents she was waiting for a young man to return from Texas with her furs and her Pekinese dogs and asked him to please make sure these things were taken care of.

Kelly went quietly. At police headquarters he was taken to a sergeant's desk. "What's your name?" the sergeant asked.

"George R. Kelly."

"What's your age and where do you live?"

"I am thirty-seven years of age and I live everywhere."

By noon, as word spread of the arrests, more than three hundred people crowded in and around the jail to catch a glimpse of the Kellys. Policemen were forced into the street to direct traffic. Thrown into a cell, Kelly brightened as he renewed acquaintances with a dozen Memphis policemen he knew from high school or previous arrests. "Bill! Hey! Gari!" he shouted as officers filed by to see him. Before long Kelly was joshing with everyone. "Lend me that machine gun, will ya?" he asked one FBI agent. To Rorer he quipped: "You ought to start a hamburger stand outside the jail and make some money with this crowd."

Held in another part of the jail, Kathryn wasted no time betraying Kelly. "I'm not guilty and I can prove it," she told the reporters who clustered around her cell. "And afterward I'll be rid of him and that bunch." Kathryn portrayed herself as an innocent wife who lived in fear of her murderous husband. "I was going back to Oklahoma City tomorrow to give myself up," she insisted. "Kelly told me he would kill me if I did, but I was going anyway."

_____

* Afterward Kelly would claim he had stayed up all night, watching for the possibility of a raid. Given the half-dozen gin bottles in his bedroom, and the ten more empty bottles of Old Log Cabin bourbon on the back porch, that's unlikely. Whether he slept or not, Kelly had risen early, waiting for the newspaper's delivery. Around seven he heard a thump on the front porch, the sound of the paper being delivered. He walked out and grabbed it, then returned inside, failing to relock the front door.

But if Kathryn thought she could talk her way free, she was sadly mistaken. She and Kelly were taken aboard an army airplane the following week to Oklahoma City, where in October they stood trial. Like Albert Bates, Harvey Bailey, and the Shannons, both received life sentences.* Kathryn ended up at the federal women's prison in Milan, Michigan, where for several years she acted as an FBI informant in an effort to reduce her sentence. Kelly, Bates, and Bailey were all shipped to Leavenworth, and then, when it opened the following year, to Alcatraz.

Machine Gun Kelly was the first nationally known fugitive the FBI had ever captured, and his arrest marked a turning point in the Bureau's history. It furthered the notion that there existed a realm of larger-than-life supervillains loose in the land, popularized the idea that the nation was actually at war with these criminals, and catapulted the Bureau into the public consciousness as the nation's proxy in that war. The Kansas City Massacre, by contrast, though front-page news across the country, had never seized the public's imagination in the same way.

The story of Kelly's arrest would become one of Hoover's favorites, one he told and retold for forty years. According to Hoover's version of events, as advanced in numerous FBI-approved books, magazine articles, and B-movies, Kelly had pleaded with arresting agents, "Don't shoot, G-men!" It was the first time FBI agents had heard the term. When agents asked what he meant, Kelly explained that G-man was short for "Government man." This story, debunked as early as a 1946 article in *Harper's,* is almost certainly untrue. Hundreds of articles written in the weeks afterward make no mention of it. Years later Kelly himself told his son he'd never used the term. It first surfaced in a series of FBI-sponsored feature stories the journalist Rex Collier wrote nine months later, in July 1934, prompting some to suggest the term "G-man" sprang not from the mouth of Machine Gun Kelly but from the fertile minds of Hoover's publicity men.

Research for this book, however, indicates that the term actually *did* originate with Kelly's arrest, though it didn't happen quite the way Hoover told it. In a single, long-forgotten telephone interview Agent Rorer gave to a *Chicago American* reporter hours after Kelly's capture, Rorer said it was Kathryn who uttered the historic words. As Rorer told the *American*

---

* All those involved in harboring Kelly, including Lang Ramsey, drew brief prison sentences.

reporter, at the moment she was arrested, "Kelly's wife cried like a baby. She put her arms around [Kelly] and said: 'Honey, I guess it's all up for us. The 'g' men won't ever give us a break. I've been living in dread of this.'"[24]

And so a nickname was born.

Dayton, Ohio

That Tuesday morning, as steel bars clanged shut behind the Kellys in Memphis, John Dillinger sat in a cell of his own in Dayton, Ohio. For four days sheriffs and deputies from across eastern Indiana and western Ohio had paraded through the jail, showing Dillinger to more than a dozen people who had witnessed bank robberies that summer. He was identified as a participant in robberies at New Carlisle and Bluffton, Ohio, and Indianapolis and Dalesville, Indiana. The Indiana detective Matt Leach had been the first to arrive, just hours after Dillinger's arrest Friday morning. He interviewed Dillinger in his cell, asking about several different bank robberies. All he got for his effort was a grin. "What are you talking about?" Dillinger asked.

That Tuesday, however, there was only one topic of conversation at the jail, and it wasn't bank robberies. The news was splattered all over the papers. The night before, ten convicts, including all of Dillinger's old pals, had escaped from the Indiana State Prison at Michigan City. Matt Leach was convinced they were coming for Dillinger.

6

THE STREETS OF CHICAGO

October 12 to November 20, 1933

Of all the criminals of our present era whose activities have been brought so
forcibly to the eye of the public, there is probably no one whose career so graphi-
cally illustrates the inadequacies of our systems as does that of John Dillinger.
—MELVIN PURVIS

Lima, Ohio
Thursday, October 12

John Dillinger sat at a table in a jail bullpen, playing pinochle with three
other prisoners. Armed officers had brought him to Lima, a crossroads
town in northwestern Ohio, to stand trial for an unremarkable robbery he
pulled in nearby Bluffton that August. It wasn't an imposing jail, just a
stone-block wing at the rear of Sheriff Jess Sarber's house on the town square;
the Allen County Courthouse loomed across an alley. Sheriff Sarber was a
roundish, kindly sort, a former used-car salesman who turned to law enforcement when the Depression forced him out of business. His wife was a fine
cook, serving the prisoners meals of pork chops, ribs, and mashed potatoes.

This wasn't how Dillinger thought it would end. He hadn't robbed
banks long enough for Pretty Boy Floyd's brand of fatalism to set in. In
fact, Dillinger remained almost relentlessly cheerful. It was what people remembered for years afterward—the courtesy, the easy wink, the whiff of
manly joie de vivre. The times he grew depressed were usually when he

thought about his family. He was thirty years old, but he still valued the approval of his father and sister. If he was going to be an outlaw, he wanted to be the type of outlaw people admired. He wanted to support his family during hard times. Above all, as the son of a remote man who never paid much attention to him, Dillinger craved respect.

Unlike Baby Face Nelson and other Depression-era criminals, Dillinger was not a product of poverty or neglect. He was born in a middle-class Indianapolis neighborhood on June 22, 1903, the son of a drab, stoic grocer, John Wilson Dillinger, and his wife, Mollie, who died following a seizure when John was four. The Dillingers were well off. John Dillinger, Sr., owned his own store, ferried bags of groceries around their neighborhood, and put away enough money to invest in real estate, buying four houses. By all accounts the elder Dillinger worked long hours and showed little interest in his son. In his father's absence, Dillinger, like Clyde Barrow, was raised by his older sister. Audrey Dillinger, a red-haired girl thirteen years older than John, married in 1906, but she and her husband lived with her father for several years, until the elder Dillinger remarried in 1912.

Like Machine Gun Kelly, Dillinger resented his new stepmother, a feeling that appears to have deepened as she and his father began having children of their own. These emotions manifested themselves in a streak of adolescent rebelliousness, though on reflection, his friends and teachers saw nothing that caused real concern. At Public School 38, Dillinger was a boisterous, joshing kid but a dreadful student. His D's and F's sparked increasingly angry arguments with his father.

By the sixth grade, Dillinger was the nominal head of a group of rowdy boys who called themselves the Dirty Dozen Gang. Their idea of mischief was snatching watermelons from a farmer's field or stealing buckets of coal they sold to neighbors. At one point, Dillinger was arrested for a coal theft but got off with a lecture from the judge. His father was less forgiving. According to John Toland, who interviewed several of Dillinger's boyhood friends in the early 1960s, the elder Dillinger chained his son to his grocery wagon for a time in an effort to rein him in. A firm hand only stoked Dillinger's rebelliousness. One friend told Toland that Dillinger embarked on a series of petty crimes as a teenager, stealing whiskey and terrorizing another boy with a buzz saw. None led to more trouble with the law.[1]

At sixteen Dillinger quit school and worked various jobs around Indianapolis. A year later, in March 1920, his family moved to a farm outside Mooresville, fifteen miles southwest of the city. They soon moved to a larger spread, sixty acres on Highway 267, north of town. Mooresville was a sleepy little burg, and it bored the teenage Dillinger to tears. Avoiding farmwork, he spent his days hunting squirrels or handling second base on a sandlot baseball team, his nights shooting billiards at the Idle Hour poolroom or similar haunts in Martinsville, fifteen miles south. Like Pretty Boy Floyd, he met and befriended older men at the pool halls, hard men he strove to emulate.

Dillinger spent several years passing time in his hometown, throwing dice, shooting pool, hunting, living off his father's hard work and the occasional odd job. In 1923 he turned twenty, and he hadn't the slightest idea what to do with his life. Like Floyd, Dillinger considered joining the armed forces. Dillinger, however, actually signed up, with the navy. When his basic training ended on October 4, 1923, he was assigned the job of fireman third class on the U.S.S. *Utah,* a battleship anchored in Boston Harbor. Like Clyde Barrow, Dillinger grew homesick in Massachusetts. Three weeks after joining the *Utah,* he briefly went AWOL. He was courtmartialed, given ten days solitary, and docked pay. Once out of the brig, he went AWOL again; after a second court-martial, Dillinger fled for good. He was listed as a deserter. For the first time, a price was put on his head: $50.

By the following spring he was back in Mooresville, telling his family he had received a medical discharge due to hay fever. Dillinger then decided to give marriage a try, wedding a sixteen-year-old named Beryl Hovious. They lived at her family's farm for a time, then took an apartment in Martinsville, but domestic life did nothing to settle Dillinger. He had no job, no focus, and no future. He went back to his old routines, hanging around pool halls.

The night that changed Dillinger's life forever came on a Saturday—September 6, 1924. He had gone out drinking with one of his pool hall pals, a thirty-one-year-old ex-con named Ed Singleton. Fueled by stupidity and alcohol, they decided to mug an elderly Mooresville grocer named Frank Morgan, a friend of Dillinger's family; Dillinger had been told Morgan carried cash home after work. Morgan was walking home that night when Dillinger stepped out of an alley by the Mooresville Christian Church and struck him over the head with a large bolt wrapped in a handkerchief. When Morgan fell and began shouting for help, Dillinger pulled a pistol. It went off. Dillinger ran. Singleton, waiting in a car nearby, drove off, abandoning him.

On Monday a deputy sheriff drove out to the Dillinger farmhouse and arrested him. A prosecutor suggested the judge might be lenient if Dillinger pled guilty and apologized. Dillinger went along, not even bothering to hire a lawyer. It was a fatal misjudgment. Judge Joseph W. Williams decided to make an example of him, sentencing Dillinger to a jaw-dropping sentence of ten to twenty years in a state reformatory. The Dillingers were floored, the more so when Ed Singleton hired a lawyer, wangled a new judge, and, despite Dillinger's testimony against him, received a sentence of two to fourteen years; Singleton ultimately served two. "When we got the word," Audrey recalled, "my dad just about keeled over. It liked to kill him. I think he died of a broken heart. And when John got that sentence, it just seemed like he went from bad to worse."[2]

In late 1924 Dillinger arrived at Indiana's Pendleton Reformatory a bitter young man. In his first weeks at Pendleton, Dillinger tried twice to escape. Once he was caught hiding in a trash pile. Another time, while being transported to Mooresville to testify against Singleton, he lit out down an alley and was recaptured within minutes.

Dillinger's career would be defined by a series of close friendships. Two of the most influential he made at Pendleton. One was Harry "Pete" Pierpont, a strikingly handsome hard case with piercing gray eyes doing ten to twenty-one years for a bank robbery in Kokomo, Indiana.* Another was Homer Van Meter, a tall, gangly runaway from Fort Wayne, Indiana, who was to be Dillinger's longest-running associate. A loner and a bit of a flake, Van Meter had a harder childhood than Dillinger, running away to Chicago in the sixth grade. He worked as a bellboy until convicted of stealing a car at seventeen. Paroled a year later, he was free for two months before he and a pal were arrested for robbing passengers on a train in Toledo. "This fellow is a criminal of the most dangerous type," a Pendleton official wrote. "Moral sense is perverted and he has no intention of following anything but a life of crime . . . He is a murderer at heart, and if society is to be safeguarded, his type must be confined throughout their natural lives."

His friendships with Pierpont and Van Meter hardened Dillinger. When

---

* Pierpont was the kind of inmate who seemed at war with the world. His problems began at nineteen, when he tried to steal a car; when the owner intervened, Pierpont drew a gun and fired at him four times, missing. He drew a term in a reformatory, until his mother told the superintendent he had been mentally unstable since he'd been hit on the head with a baseball bat as a boy. He was released to a hospital for the insane, then paroled, then sent to Pendleton for the Kokomo robbery. Pierpont cursed the guards, launched innumerable escape attempts, and drew the respect of other inmates as a result. The superintendent wrote his mother's lawyer that he was "a mustang and must be curbed."

the two were transferred to the state prison at Michigan City, Dillinger asked to be transferred, too. On July 15, 1929, he got his wish. He was twenty-six. The transfer introduced Dillinger to a wide new world of crime. In Pendleton the inmates had been kids—stickup artists and car thieves. At Michigan City the men were older, their crimes more serious. There were raw-boned bank men out of Texas and Oklahoma, smooth syndicate murderers, and gray-haired confidence men.

If not a model prisoner, Dillinger managed to pass three years with few problems. He drew various punishments, including two stretches in solitary, for stealing a watermelon, for hiding a straight razor in his cell, and, once, for being caught in bed with another inmate; like Alvin Karpis, Dillinger may have dabbled in homosexuality behind bars. At Michigan City, Dillinger grew up. By and large, he was easygoing and nonconfrontational. He made friends easily.

His friend Pete Pierpont was forever trying to escape, hiding in garbage cans and the like. In mid-1932, Pierpont began talking about a different kind of escape, a mass breakout using weapons. The inmate who appears to have influenced Pierpont's thinking was Charles Makley, a forty-three-year-old bootlegger–turned–bank man serving fifteen years following a 1928 arrest in Hammond. Squat and roundish, with an anvil-like jaw and twinkling eyes, Makley counseled patience and planning.

As they studied the feasibility of a large-scale escape, Pierpont and Makley were joined by two other bank men: Russell Clark, a handsome, garrulous Detroit yegg doing twenty years for a 1927 bank job, and John "Red" Hamilton, an absentminded thirty-four-year-old from northern Michigan doing twenty-five years. Hamilton, who had lost two fingers on his right hand in a childhood sledding accident, would be at Dillinger's side for much of his career. For several months these four men debated the best way to break out. In the end, all their planning had one glaring deficiency: the guns. They couldn't escape without them, yet there was no easy way to get them inside. What they needed, they could see, was someone on the outside.

It was then, probably in late 1932, that they thought of Dillinger. He was perfect. Dillinger spent all these years peppering the parole board with letters, and his release finally appeared imminent. Pierpont took Dillinger aside and offered him a proposition. Thirty years later, prison officials said they believed Pierpont had filled Dillinger's ears with stories of the riches bank robbers could reap, how they wore silk suits, stayed at the finest hotels, and bedded the most expensive whores. If Dillinger could help his group escape, Pierpont promised, he could become a member of their gang, perhaps as the driver. In all likelihood, Dillinger didn't need much convincing. He could read the newspapers; every morning brought a new story of some Midwestern bank knocked off by an enterprising band of yeggs—seven different banks by the Barker-Karpis Gang alone. Everyone said it was easy money.

Whether he did it out of loyalty, ambition, or simply because he had no other goal in life, Dillinger agreed to help. According to lore, Pierpont then gave Dillinger two lists. One was of banks Pierpont and Makley thought he could rob; they may have tutored him on the best ways to "crack a jug," the best times of day to strike, how to handle customers, how to get a safe opened. The second list ticked off a series of potential partners he could trust. If Dillinger could rob a few banks, Pierpont and Makley reasoned, he could raise enough money to have guns smuggled into the prison. Though the story is plausible, there is nothing in prison or FBI files to substantiate any of this.

In late April, the Dillinger family, along with John's sentencing judge and the grocer he mugged nine years earlier, petitioned the board for a parole. They argued that Dillinger was needed on the family farm. Two of the three board members agreed; a third abstained. On May 10, Governor Paul McNutt approved Dillinger's parole. He was a free man.

Once on the outside, as we have seen, Dillinger wasted no time fulfilling his promise to Pierpont. He waited three months before attempting to smuggle the guns into Michigan City, apparently going ahead only after Pierpont's parole was denied. The escape, thanks to Dillinger's smuggled guns, went off without a hitch. And now, in a crushing irony, Dillinger was back behind bars while his friends were free. Without a miracle, he would remain there the next twenty years.

That Thursday, October 12, was just another night in the Lima lockup. After a dinner of pork chops and mashed potatoes, Dillinger joined the pinochle game. Down the hallway, Sheriff Sarber sagged into his desk chair and opened the *Lima News*; the banner headline on the front page gave an update of Machine Gun Kelly's trial in Oklahoma. Sheriff Sarber's wife, Lucy, sat across from him, working a crossword puzzle. Around six their deputy, Wilbur Sharp, came in, loosened his gun belt, and threw it on a spare desk, then plopped onto a davenport. The Sarber's dog Brownie nuzzled him. Sharp scratched its ears.

At 6:25 the jail's outside door opened and three men in suits stepped in. Mrs. Sarber, buried in her puzzle, didn't bother to look up. "Whaddya need?" Sheriff Sarber asked the first man, who wore a dark gray suit, an overcoat, and a light-felt fedora.

"We're from Michigan City," said the first man. "We want to see John Dillinger."

"Let me see your credentials," Sheriff Sarber said.

"Here's our credentials," said the first man. His piercing gray eyes were probably the last thing Jess Sarber saw before the man raised a pistol and fired straight into his chest.

The mass escape from Michigan City the night of September 26 was front-page news across the country. A hard rain had fallen as Pierpont, Makley, and eight other inmates, using the three .45 caliber pistols Dillinger had smuggled into the prison, took a group of guards hostage, then used them to parade into the administration building; guards on the wall, seeing the prisoners apparently escorted by the day captain, were not suspicious. Four of the inmates took a visiting sheriff hostage and forced him into his car. As they drove off, Pierpont took the other five inmates and sprinted to a Standard Oil station across the street, where they commandeered a car of their own.

That night, eluding roadblocks the Indiana State Police threw up across the state, Pierpont's group, which included Charles Makley, Russell Clark, John Hamilton, a con named Ed Shouse, and Dillinger's onetime cellmate Jim Jenkins, arrived safely at the Indianapolis apartment of Pierpont's old girlfriend, Mary Kinder. They were lucky; three of the other four escapees ended up dead or recaptured within days. The next night, after one of Kinder's girlfriends ran out to buy them clothes, Dillinger's partner Harry Copeland arrived at the apartment and said he had arranged a hideout, at a rented house in Hamilton, Ohio, north of Cincinnati.

From the moment Mary Kinder told them Dillinger had been arrested, there was never any question that Pierpont's band wouldn't try to free him. Their preparations weren't without incident, however. After stealing a car for the drive to Hamilton, the six escapees were spotted by police outside Indianapolis; in a chase, Jim Jenkins somehow fell out an open car door. Fleeing on foot, he was spotted, shot, and killed by a group of vigilantes in the town of Bean Blossom. The remaining five escapees reached Hamilton that night.

There they began laying plans for Dillinger's rescue. For food, cigarettes, and gasoline they needed money, and for that they decided to rob a bank. On Tuesday afternoon, October 3, a week after their escape, the gang filed into the First National Bank in Charles Makley's hometown of St. Mary's, Ohio, just south of where Dillinger was being held in Lima. The raid went smoothly, with no gunplay, and that night they returned to Hamilton $11,000 richer. The money was too new to spend, and Mary Kinder spent several days baking and ironing the bills to make them appear worn.[3]

Once the money was safe to pass, they began reconnoitering Lima. Despite Matt Leach's hunch that they might attempt a rescue, Pierpont could see no additional guards around the jail. They decided to move in the next day, Columbus Day, Thursday, October 12.

Sheriff Sarber was mortally wounded. Blood spilled from the ragged hole in his chest as he tried to rise from the floor. Pierpont stood over him, screaming, "Give us the keys to the cells!" When Sarber didn't answer, Makley leaned over and bashed him in the head with his gun butt. The gun accidentally went off, startling everyone. Pierpont pointed his gun at Sarber. "Give us the keys," he repeated.

"Don't hurt him no more!" Mrs. Sarber pleaded as she scrambled to her husband's side. She grabbed the keys from a drawer and handed them to Pierpont, who stepped to the barred door of the cell block. When one of the inmates peeked his head around a corner, Pierpont raised his pistol and fired a shot into the bullpen area. "Get back, you motherfuckers!" Pierpont yelled. "We only want John!"

Dillinger ducked into his cell, grabbed his coat and hat, and jogged through the cell-block door. Sheriff Sarber was lying in a pool of blood. Dillinger looked down at the dying sheriff but said nothing as he hustled outside. "Oh men, why did you have to do this to me," the sheriff moaned. He turned to his wife, who hovered above him. "Mother, I believe I am going to have to leave you."

Ninety minutes later, Jess Sarber died at a local hospital. Sirens echoed through the streets of Lima all that evening, as police and vigilantes spilled from their homes to man roadblocks. Dillinger, meanwhile, sped south with the gang, arriving at the rented house in Hamilton that night. At that point, Dillinger faced a crossroads. He could have left the gang and fled to parts unknown. Instead, he decided to stick with his friends and become a full-time bank robber.

To rob a bank, they needed weapons—not just pistols, but Thompson submachine guns and bulletproof vests. That Saturday night in Auburn, a town just across the Indiana line, an officer named Fred Krueger had just sat down at the police station's front desk to eat a bag of popcorn when two men in suits walked in. Both had two pistols in their hands. "You might as well sit still," one said. "We don't want to kill anyone unless we have to. Have you got any guns?"

"Yes," Krueger said as he slid his hand toward his pistol.

"Oh no," the man with the gun said politely. "I'll get it."[4]

Both Krueger and the desk officer were disarmed and locked in a cell. Taking the key to the gun cabinet, the intruders lugged a small arsenal out to their waiting car: a Thompson submachine gun, a .38 caliber Smith & Wesson pistol, a .401 Winchester rifle, a 44-40 Winchester sixteen-shot rifle, a .45 caliber Colt pistol, a Luger, several hundred rounds of ammunition, and three bulletproof vests.

From Auburn the gang headed to Chicago, betting they could lose themselves in the city.* They spent the next several days renting apartments. By October 20, four days after the Auburn raid, the gang was back on the road, in search of more guns and ammunition. That Friday night, three men walked into the city hall in Peru, Indiana, an hour north of Indianapolis, and leveled guns at the desk officers.

"I haven't plugged anyone for a week," one of the men, later identified as Pierpont, said, "and I would just as soon puncture one of you cops as not."[5] Pierpont covered the officers while his two confederates, one of them Dillinger, broke into the gun cabinet, emptied the contents onto a blanket, then lugged it all out to their car. The evening's take came to six bulletproof vests, two sawed-off-shotguns, two Winchester rifles, and a half-dozen .38 caliber pistols. As they left, they stripped the officers of their guns and badges.

Only then did Pierpont and Dillinger feel strong enough to take a bank. They decided on the Central National Bank in Greencastle, Indiana, west of Indianapolis, the home of DePauw University. That Saturday was Homecoming, and Makley argued that the banks would be bursting with cash. At 2:45 that Monday afternoon, a black Studebaker eased along Jackson

---

* An unidentified Michigan City inmate later told the FBI that the gang initially hid at a Syndicate-operated hangout called the Steuben Club. According to this source, Dillinger was greeted personally at the club by Frank Nitti, who gave the gang free run of a gun room nicknamed "The Arsenal." This would seem unlikely, especially given the gang's subsequent armaments raid in Peru, Indiana, several days later.

Street in downtown Greencastle and parked in front of the bank. Five men emerged: Dillinger, Pierpont, Makley, John Hamilton, and either Harry Copeland or Russell Clark. All wore overcoats, guns tucked inside. Walking into the bank, Pierpont stepped to a teller's window and asked to change a twenty-dollar bill. The teller suggested he go to another window. Pierpont pulled his tommy gun.

Dillinger, pistol in hand, vaulted a railing and trained his guns on the tellers, herding them into the vault. Later, the bank employees and their customers would all say they were struck by how calm and methodical the robbers were. The gang cleared the cash from drawers and counters into muslin sacks so quietly that no one at the sheriff's office across the street realized a robbery was in progress.

When they were finished they threw the heavy muslin bags over their shoulders like a band of evil Santas and walked out to the Studebaker. In moments they were gone, easily evading pursuit. From Greencastle the gang sped to Chicago, where they counted the money; it came to almost $75,000, roughly $15,000 a man. All told, it had been an eventful two weeks. Now it was time to have some fun.[6]

The Dillinger Gang returned to Chicago just after the Barker Gang left to escape the dragnet spreading in the wake of the Federal Reserve fiasco. Leaving in ones and twos, the men drove across the Great Plains all the way to Reno. Karpis and Delores Delaney were the first to arrive, on September 27, after overnight stops in Council Bluffs, Iowa, and Rawlings, Wyoming. In Reno, Karpis parked outside the Bank Club, gave Delaney $20 to play the slots, then went in back to meet with the city's crime boss, Bill Graham. After backslapping hellos, Graham's partner, Jim McKay, took Karpis aside. "You remember that kid we had out here, that Jimmy?" McKay asked. He meant Baby Face Nelson.

"Yeah," said Karpis. He described how he had introduced Nelson around St. Paul and Chicago.

"That damn kid, he's dangerous," McKay said. "He's gonna wind up real bad. I hope to Christ you guys ain't got him with you, do you? He's not coming back out here, is he?"

Karpis smiled. "He's just a wild kid, Jim."

"That's the problem," McKay said. "The guy'll shoot in a minute. I was with him one time over in California up by Lake Tahoe and one of them

State Patrol cars stopped us, to check our lights, and he damn near killed the guy. He was almost ready to shoot."

The others trickled in over the following days, Dock Barker arriving with the gang's newest member, a drunken boyhood friend named Harry Campbell. Ma was left in Chicago. She had sullenly accepted the decision, barely glancing up from her jigsaw puzzle when Karpis went to bid farewell. In Reno the days drifted into weeks. Karpis and Delaney took weekends at a dude ranch, shooting jackrabbits, taking hikes, turning in early. The others lolled in the casinos and took in movies.

At one point Karpis drove Delaney to San Francisco. They dropped Dock Barker, whose wounded finger had become infected, at a Vallejo, California, hospital run by an underworld character named Tobe Williams, a onetime safecracker whose doctors operated on gangsters from around the country. In San Francisco they looked in on a group of bootleggers Bill Graham had mentioned, who turned out to be Baby Face Nelson's old gang. They met a bartender who claimed to know people in Hollywood, and afterward it was all Delaney talked about.

"Do you think if we took him down to Hollywood he could introduce us to some of the movie stars?" she asked.

Delaney's pleading continued after they returned to Reno, and Karpis finally agreed to take her to Los Angeles. Promising to return in a week, they cruised south to a sleepy desert town named Las Vegas, where they looked in on a pair of Harry Sawyer's friends who were running a desultory little casino; Karpis thought Vegas was the end of the world. After a few days they headed west to Los Angeles, found a hotel downtown, then struck off into Beverly Hills, hoping to spot a movie star. Karpis drove up and down the palm-lined avenues, looking for a recognizable face. It was no use. Delaney was crestfallen.

"How in the hell would you know these people, everyone running around with sunglasses on?" she groused. "I mean, the only way you'd know someone is a movie star is if some people would all crowd around them and start asking for autographs."

They drove up into the Hollywood hills, trying to find Clark Gable's house. Once or twice Karpis got lost, and after a while he noticed a patrol car behind him. "Let's get the hell out of here," he mumbled. "We're gonna get stopped if we don't."

Spooked, Karpis checked out of the hotel and drove straight back to Reno, taking the direct route, across Death Valley. Rejoining the gang, they fell back into its routines, hanging around the casinos, playing keno, talking about Hawaiian vacations they would never take, debating whether to rob a bank outside of San Francisco. The only excitement came when the new man, Harry Campbell, shoved a pistol into his pocket and it went off, nearly blowing off his testicles. Everyone agreed it was time to head back to Chicago.[7]

Leaves were beginning to fall across the Midwest, and the mystery of the Kansas City Massacre was no closer to being solved. On September 13, Missouri prosecutors had indicted a dozen figures in the case, but it was a half-hearted gesture, a compromise between federal lawyers who wanted murder indictments and local prosecutors who found scant evidence for any case at all. The known conspirators—Deafy Farmer and company—were charged along with a half-dozen possible assassins—Pretty Boy Floyd, Harvey Bailey and Bailey's gang—but only for obstruction of justice. The Bureau's theory remained that Verne Miller had carried out the massacre with Bailey and the Kansas escapees; Bailey, of course, strenuously denied any involvement as he was packed off to Leavenworth following his conviction in the Urschel kidnapping.

Hoover's men couldn't shake Bailey's alibi. After three months, they hadn't uncovered any evidence placing him or his men at Union Station. Their best witness, Samuel Link, who placed Bailey at the scene, had been discredited after a friend told agents that "Link makes very wild statements at times and claims that he was with Teddy Roosevelt in South America and has personally met all the crown heads of Europe."[8] Worse, bullets from Bailey's guns didn't match those at the scene. Almost every time a Midwestern bank was robbed, bullets were sent to a Kansas City lab. It checked rounds fired by Bonnie and Clyde at Platte City, by Baby Face Nelson at Grand Haven, but found no matches.

With the case against Bailey's gang tenuous at best, agents focused on finding the remaining conspirators. Dick Galatas, the Hot Springs gambler, had vanished. Members of Bailey's gang were robbing banks all across Oklahoma; one, Big Bob Brady, was shot and captured in New Mexico in early October, but one of the massacre survivors, Reed Vetterli, returned dejected from his hospital room, unable to identify him. Most important, there were still no leads on Verne Miller or his girlfriend, Vi Mathias. In

St. Paul, Chicago, and Kansas City, agents returned to the files to check leads pushed aside that summer.

Three weeks later, the break came in Chicago. Agents there remembered a months-old tip that a nightclub waitress named Bobbie Moore was Vi Mathias's best friend. Melvin Purvis had placed Moore under surveillance for a time that summer but had dropped her once agents began chasing Mathias all over the East Coast. Inexplicably, it took weeks before anyone suggested they recheck Bobbie Moore. Her last known address was the Sherone Apartments on Sheridan Road. When the building's manager was summoned to the FBI office on Friday, October 26, she identified not only Moore's photograph but that of Vi Mathias as well. Verne Miller's girlfriend, or a woman who looked strikingly like her, had moved into the building in late August.

In late 1933, the FBI was still only a shadow of the professional crime-fighting organization it was to become. The capture of Machine Gun Kelly was anomalous. Hoover's College Boys were long on energy but short on experience, and it showed: suspects like Vi Mathias were found, then lost; tantalizing leads went ignored in file cabinets; most of the men were still learning how to use a pistol.

In retrospect, Melvin Purvis's Chicago office was worse than most. So far that year, as we have seen, Purvis and his men had solved their first two kidnappings—the William Hamm and Jake Factor cases—and in both it would turn out they had arrested innocent men. In his first attempt to capture a major criminal, Machine Gun Kelly, Purvis had "forgotten" the assignment.* The office that would eventually become the War on Crime's epicenter occupied the entire nineteenth floor of the Bankers Building in Chicago's financial district. The entrance was at the end of a hallway lined with chairs; these were usually occupied by reporters from the wire services

---

* In the lone major operation where his men had been prepared to fire their weapons, things had gone even worse. It happened in August, when the syndicate-connected con man Jake Factor reported someone was trying to extort him. A meeting was arranged with the extortionists at a 22nd Street park, and Purvis, commanding an army of two hundred Chicago cops and FBI agents—the largest such strike force in memory, the *Chicago American* reported—prepared to move in when they appeared. When the extortionists arrived, the police moved. In the confusion, their quarry managed to get away. The *American* dubbed it "a huge fiasco."

and the six Chicago newspapers. The reporters passed the hours reading, smoking cigarettes, and pestering Purvis's twenty-four-year-old secretary, Doris Rogers.* Purvis had brought Rogers from his previous posting, in Birmingham, Alabama. She was his gatekeeper; no one passed through the swinging gate beside her desk without her say. Purvis's office door opened behind her.

"Melvin's office had no glamour at all," she recalls. "A standard SAC desk, wooden. No pictures or memorabilia. This was not a nest, not some guy's hangout, with his baby's pictures. It was very restricted and disciplined."

Beside Purvis's office was the door to the nineteenth floor's inner sanctum, the file room. Nowhere was Hoover's passion for order more apparent than a Bureau file room. Seven carbon copies were made of every memo, Teletype, and telegram; a single typographical error was grounds for disciplinary action. The files were housed in government-issue gray-metal cabinets. Agents were not allowed in the file room. Only the clerk, Helen Dunkel, or her assistant had access. When an agent wanted a file, he asked one of them.

There was a single spartan conference room, usually used for interrogations. Out to Doris Rogers's left stretched the pool, sometimes called the bullpen, a vast room lined with nearly one hundred identical wooden desks where the agents sat. Each desktop was the same, just a black telephone and a blotter; personal memorabilia or family pictures were not allowed. Desktops were left spotless at the end of each day; any work was expected to be returned to the file room or taken home. Agents did not type their own reports. They were dictated to the two stenographers, twin sisters surnamed Barber. Only Purvis ate at his desk; crumbs or stains were grounds for disciplinary action. Most of the forty or so agents grabbed sandwiches at a lunch counter in the lobby, which featured a thirty-five-cent special. "I remember Melvin saying, 'I'll be so goddamn glad when I get to someplace where they don't call a ham sandwich a gentleman's lunch,'" Rogers recalls.

On the surface, the agents were as similar as their desks: dark suits, black socks, shiny black shoes, crisp parts in their oiled hair. They signed in on entry and exit; if an agent was even one minute late for work, Purvis had to explain why to Washington. Two tardies risked a suspension. Many of

---

* Seventy years later, Doris Rogers (now, in 2004, Doris Lockerman) is the only denizen of the nineteenth floor who remains alive, an alert, gregarious ninety-four-year-old living in Atlanta.

the men, like Purvis and his number two that autumn, a kindly Arkansan named Douglas O. Smith, were Southerners with state-college degrees.* A few were married; most shared apartments.

Seven decades later, few of the men she worked with have left lasting impressions on Doris Rogers. One who did was the office boy, an energetic Polish kid from the South Side named Johnny Madala who was forever pestering Purvis to let him do something official. "Johnny was my favorite: laughing, smiling, helpful, unprepossessing, unassuming," Rogers remembers. "Everyone loved Johnny Madala."

In an unusual twist, both Madala and Doris Rogers were to be pulled into the hunt for Verne Miller. Purvis was out of town the day the tentative identification of Vi Mathias was made. Madala volunteered to watch her. Posing as a traveling auditor, he moved into her apartment building that weekend. His unit, 211, was tucked into an alcove sixty feet down a carpeted hallway from Mathias's. The only view of her door was through a shuttered ventilator grate in his kitchenette.

Three days after moving in, Madala got his first glimpse of their suspect on the street below. She was five-feet-six, slender, and blonde, with a mole on her left cheek. It was Mathias. That afternoon Madala watched as a stream of children began filing into Mathias's apartment. It took him a few minutes to realize that she was having a Halloween party. Then, at 4:30, Madala heard a commotion in the hallway outside. He stepped to the ventilation shutter and saw Bobbie Moore running down the corridor, hollering for Mathias, who stepped out of her apartment.

"He's here, Vi, he's here!" Moore enthused.

Standing at her apartment door, Mathias grew excited. "Where is he, Bobbie?" she asked. "Quick, tell me where is he?"

"He's downstairs," Moore said. "I told him you had a lot of children in your apartment and that you would be downstairs just as soon as you could get rid of your kids."

"Tell him I'll be down in a few minutes," Vi said, disappearing back into her apartment.

---

* Purvis brought Smith, known as "D.O.," to Chicago from Oklahoma City to be his number two, or ASAC. A popular mentor to many young agents during his distinguished FBI career, Smith had been married the week before the Sherone Apartments stakeout; he had been introduced to his wife by Frank Smith, the agent who survived the Kansas City Massacre. A native of Fort Smith, Arkansas, D. O. Smith served in the FBI from 1928 to 1958. In later years he taught in the Fort Smith schools. He died in January 1977 at the age of seventy-nine.

Just then Madala saw a man round the corner from the elevators and enter the hallway. He had a sandy mustache and wore horned-rim glasses. Bobbie Moore ran to the man, threw her arms around him, and kissed him. Together they turned and walked back toward the elevators. Madala slid away from the ventilator opening.

It looked like Miller. Madala called the Bankers Building and briefed a senior agent, Ed Guinane. At 6:15, Guinane arrived to take charge of the situation. He arrayed groupings of agents and Chicago cops around the building. A half-dozen others clustered in Madala's apartment. To make sure it really was Miller, Guinane brought along Doris Rogers, who had grown up in Huron, South Dakota, and seen Miller when he was a deputy sheriff there. Guinane positioned her at the ventilation shutter. When and if she saw Miller leave Mathias's apartment, an agent alongside her was to make a chopping motion with his hand, the signal for the squad to rush into the hallway. Guinane told the men outside to watch his window. If Miller appeared, he would flap a jacket in the window as a signal.

An hour passed. A tap had been placed on Mathias's phone, and at 7:30 an agent heard her call Bobbie Moore downstairs.

"Miss Moore?" Mathias asked.

"Speaking."

"Verne wants you to put the Auburn [the car] away," Mathias said, then hung up. It appeared Miller and Mathias were staying in for the night.

The call prompted a sharp debate among the agents assembled in Apartment 211. John Madala urged Guinane to immediately storm Mathias's apartment. Guinane said no. They had to be certain it was Miller.

November 1

Dawn broke. On the streets outside, a new rotation of agents and policemen replaced the men who had kept watch through the chill night. In Apartment 211 agents took turns grabbing naps in the bedroom. At midmorning, when there was still no sign of Miller, Agent Edward Notesteen arrived from St. Paul.* He, too, had known Miller in South Dakota. Guinane posted him in the kitchenette, taking shifts with Doris Rogers.

---

* Edward N. Notesteen, a graduate of the University of Minnesota Law School, served in the FBI from 1930 to 1956. He died in San Diego in 1970 at the age of seventy-one.

Hours passed. By noon no one had seen the suspects. At midafternoon Guinane called the Bankers Building to ask what to do. A call was placed to Hoover in Washington; Hoover ordered them to stay put until Miller was firmly identified. The afternoon stretched on. Finally, at 8:15 that night, Mathias called Bobbie Moore and asked her to bring a car around to the building's side entrance.

Inside Apartment 211, the tension level rose sharply. Agent Notesteen, who had been napping and was clad only in socks and shorts, returned to his position in the kitchenette. A half-dozen agents and Chicago cops stood nervously at the apartment door, waiting to pounce. Outside, two agents in a parked car watched Bobbie Moore retrieve an Auburn car from a parking garage and pull up beside the Sherone's side entrance. She began honking its horn.

Just then a man and a woman stepped out of Mathias's apartment. Agent Notesteen and Doris Rogers saw them. The woman, in green silk pajamas, was Mathias. The man had a snap-brimmed fedora pulled low over his forehead.

"That's Miller," Rogers whispered. "I know that's Miller."

"You can't tell from this distance," Notesteen said.

The couple strode briskly down the hall. There were three overhead lights in the hallway. As Miller passed beneath the first, Notesteen still couldn't make out his face.

"That's Miller!" Mrs. Rogers urged. "It's Miller!"

The man was heading straight for Notesteen's hiding place behind the ventilation shutter. As he passed beneath the second light, Notesteen still wasn't certain. "It's him!" Miss Rogers blurted.

At the door, agents stood ready. Johnny Madala, the office boy, opened the door a few inches.

"It's Miller!" Madala mouthed. *"It's Miller!"*

Just then the man passed beneath the third light, not twelve feet in front of Notesteen. In an instant Notesteen glimpsed the familiar face, the strong jaw, the flattened cheekbones.

It was Verne Miller.

Notesteen gave the signal, making the chopping motion with his hand. But Agent Guinane had stepped into the living room and didn't see it. At that instant Miller paused, sensing something. Suddenly he broke into a run, darting around the corner toward the elevators.

Agent Notesteen yelled, "It's him! It's him!"

"There he is!" Madala shouted, flinging open the apartment door. There was a split-second logjam as everyone scrambled into the hallway. First through the door was a beefy Chicago police sergeant, Frank Freemuth, followed by a group of agents. They raced toward the corner, intending to confront Miller at the elevators. But as the group turned the corner, they encountered a rude surprise.

Miller was gone.

"The staircase!" someone yelled.

Sergeant Freemuth rammed through the stairway door. Bounding down the stairs, he burst into the lobby, where he spotted a man in a brown suit standing at the front desk.

"What's your name?" Freemuth demanded.

An agent jammed his pistol into the man's ribs. When the man turned, everyone could see it wasn't Miller.

"He's gone out to the car!" someone shouted.

Outside, Agents Allen Lockerman and Julius Rice were watching Bobbie Moore when they noticed the man in the fedora emerge from the side entrance.* The man trotted toward the car, hands sunk into the pockets of his trench coat. "That looks like the man," Lockerman said.

But, both agents thought, it couldn't be Miller. There had been no signal from Guinane upstairs, no coat or shirt flapped in the apartment window; in the excitement Guinane had forgotten to give the signal. Just then, as the man stepped into the door of Bobbie Moore's Auburn, several officers and agents tumbled out the side entrance.

As Miller slammed the car door, the big Auburn surged forward down Galt Street, heading east toward the lakefront. An agent named Lew Nichols ran alongside it, still uncertain the man in the passenger seat was really Verne Miller. "Stop that car!" he hollered.

Miller turned in his seat, a pistol in his hand, and fired two shots at Nichols, missing. Nichols fell to one knee and fired. Agent Lockerman sprang from his car and began firing as well. Everywhere, up and down the sidewalks, people dived for cover. As the car surged down Galt, a state

---

* Allen Lockerman married Purvis's secretary, Doris Rogers. He retired from the FBI in the mid-1930s and went on to a career as a successful attorney in Atlanta.

Julius H. Rice was in the third year of a distinguished forty-one-year FBI career. In later years Rice emerged as a favorite of Hoover's; they called each other by their first names. Born in 1904, Rice was another George Washington graduate, joining the Bureau in 1931. He was based in Portland, Oregon, from 1946 until his retirement in 1972. He died there in 1975, at the age of seventy.

trooper fired two bursts from his tommy gun. The Auburn's rear window exploded. Bobbie Moore screamed but kept control of the car, swinging the steering wheel left, squealing north onto Sheridan Road. The agents ran after it, but it was already gone.[9]

Agent Guinane hustled to a drugstore to call downtown. A citywide alert for Miller's car was broadcast, and twenty minutes later the Auburn was found abandoned in a cul-de-sac several blocks north of the Sherone. Eyewitnesses said a man had run from the car and leaped a fence into the backyard of an apartment building on Clarendon Avenue. (In a bizarre co-incidence, this was the very building where John Dillinger was then living.) There were seven bullet holes in the car and traces of blood. All that night Chicago police raided underworld haunts and checked local hospitals, but there was no sign of Miller. Vi Mathias was taken into custody. Bobbie Moore surrendered a few days later. Both women told the FBI absolutely nothing.*

In the wake of the Dillinger gang's raids at Peru, Auburn, and Greencastle, the state of Indiana descended into something approaching wartime hysteria. Criminals and escaped convicts were nothing new, but the Midwest had never seen anything like this, heavily armed desperadoes in automobiles raiding a state's armories and banks at will. It was the kind of news people were accustomed to reading from Texas or Oklahoma, not Indiana. Scrambling to mount a defense, Governor Paul McNutt stationed seven hundred National Guardsmen at armories across the state. Guard officials announced they were prepared to deploy tanks, airplanes, and poison gas to fight the gang. Jumpy guardsmen threw up roadblocks across the state, so many that Matt Leach's boss was obliged to warn Halloween partygoers against doing anything that might cause them to be confused with Dillinger. The Indiana American Legion volunteered to have thirty thousand of its members deputized to patrol the highways.

---

* The FBI's subsequent review of Miller's escape, written by Assistant Director Vincent W. Hughes, was scathing. Hughes found that "the plan to take Miller was far from perfect and the execution of the plan even more to be criticized." Among the "vital errors" Hughes cited: The lack of a single supervising agent and the absence of cars in position to give pursuit. Hughes suggested that Miller's apartment should have been raided, a rare if indirect criticism of Hoover, who had ordered the agents to hold off. Miller's escape underscored the FBI's lack of experience in fundamental law-enforcement techniques.

"Convict gang running wild," the editor of the *Indianapolis News* telegraphed his paper's owners in Washington. "Can you have Homer Cummings offer federal aid to Indiana[?] One sheriff dead, one kidnapped, two police stations robbed of arms, bank raided."[10] The attorney general passed the request to Hoover, whose reaction was cool. Even if he had jurisdiction, which was unclear, Hoover knew the Bureau's limitations, and he preferred cases he could win; a manhunt like this, requiring a vast commitment of resources toward an uncertain outcome, was a clear loser. "I told [the attorney general's assistant] we had offered assistance with reference to fingerprint matters," Hoover wrote in a memo-to-file, "but in so far as helping to catch them is concerned, we were not [going to]."[11]*

In the Bureau's absence, responsibility for apprehending the gang fell to Matt Leach and the year-old Indiana State Police. They quickly became a laughingstock. The *Indianapolis News* ran a cartoon featuring an armed gunman chasing a group of troopers around the state; the caption read, HAPPY HUNTING GROUND. Leach pleaded for more weaponry, and Governor McNutt obliged, handing over $10,000 for bulletproof vests, machine guns, and ten new squad cars. To use them, however, Leach first had to find Dillinger. Without the first clue where the gang would strike next, he attempted to drive a psychological wedge between the gang's members. A magnet for reporters, Leach gathered a group of Indianapolis journalists and asked for help.

"The real rascal we have to deal with is Pierpont," Leach said. "He's a super egotist. We'll offend him deliberately and start jealousy in the gang. We'll name it the Dillinger Gang. That will cook Pierpont. He'll blow his top. After a lot of people have been killed and banks robbed, we'll wind it up and Pierpont will get the works."[12]

It was a harebrained ruse, one that drew chuckles from Pierpont and Dillinger as they settled into their new quarters and read the papers. The happiest days of Dillinger's life, in fact, were probably those first weeks in Chicago, when his profile was low enough that he could still live in the open. He had money, he had reliable partners, and for the first time since leaving prison, he had a girlfriend.

Her name was Evelyn Frechette, but everyone called her "Billie." Five-

* FBI agents in Chicago, Detroit, and Cincinnati actually did do some poking around on the Dillinger case that autumn, writing a half-dozen reports and attending a conference or two. But, by and large, the Bureau ignored the case, just as Hoover wished.

foot-two and 120 pounds, with jet-black hair she wore in a bob, the twenty-six-year-old Frechette had tranquil brown eyes and high cheekbones she covered with Max Factor pancake powder to mask acne scars. Like most of the women who found their way into the beds of criminals like Dillinger, she was a refugee from hard times, forced from poor rural upbringings to an uncertain life in the big city.

Frechette was half American Indian, raised on the Menominee Reservation in Wisconsin, the daughter of French Canadian half-breeds. She graduated from a Catholic-run Indian school in 1924 and eventually drifted to Chicago. By early 1932, she was a quiet young woman with a taste for cheap whiskey working as a hatcheck girl in a Chicago nightclub with her best friend, a zaftig thirty-year-old chorus-line dancer named Patricia Cherrington. Brassy and melodramatic, the redheaded Cherrington fancied herself a bed-hopping party girl; she, too, was a refugee, a Texas-raised high school dropout at thirteen, a bride at fifteen, a divorced mother by her early twenties. She and Frechette worked in a series of nudie nightclubs and were drawn to the scarred men who frequented them. In June 1932 they were arrested with their boyfriends, a pair of stickup men named Welton Spark and Arthur Cherrington. The women were released. Spark and Cherrington were remanded to Leavenworth for mugging a mailman. On the eve of their departure, the women impulsively married them.

In the summer of 1933, Frechette and Cherrington, never to be reunited with their husbands, were drifting through life, dating the wrong men, living in fetid hotels. A gallbladder infection had ended Cherrington's dancing days, and she was rooming with her younger sister Opal Long, a chunky redhead with thick eyeglasses and a derriere so bounteous she earned the nickname "Mack Truck." No one knows precisely how the three women were drawn into Dillinger's orbit. Much later, Frechette insisted she met Dillinger in a nightclub that November. In fact, it's likely she met him earlier, probably in August, when Dillinger first took an apartment in Chicago. It was then that his partner, Harry Copeland, met Cherrington, who at a cabaret one night introduced Dillinger to Frechette as "Jack Harris."

Billie would claim she never forgot Dillinger's first words. He was standing beside her at the table, looking down with that lopsided grin. "Hey Baby," he said. "Where have you been all my life?" They danced. Dillinger was polite, which was enough for Frechette. If she needed further motivation, it came from the large roll of bills in his pocket. "I didn't ask any questions," she wrote months later. "Why should I? From the very first night I met him there was nobody else in my life, and I didn't want anybody else. He treated me like a lady."[13]

In Chicago, Dillinger and Pete Pierpont decided to live together with Frechette and Mary Kinder, renting a four-room apartment at 4310 Clarendon Avenue on the North Side. The bellman would recall that the two couples' luggage was extremely heavy. Most mornings everyone slept late, rolling out of bed at ten or eleven. Dillinger kept the guns in a locked closet and handled the cleaning chores, wrapping a towel around his waist as he scrubbed the dishes and ran a dust mop over the floors. Hands on hips, Billie and Mary would watch in awe; Dillinger explained that cleaning was a habit he learned in prison. They had a phone but never bothered to hook it up. Delivery boys rang the bell at all hours, arms brimming with covered dishes from neighborhood restaurants and the downstairs delicatessen. When they came, Dillinger hid.

Most afternoons the two couples went out driving, stopping at shops up and down State Street to buy new clothes. Dillinger bought several new blue suits and a brown one, and admonished the others not to buy anything too flashy, although he did spend $149 to buy Billie a new winter coat. Like generations of striving farm boys before him, Dillinger was a bit of a clothes horse, keeping his suits pressed and his hats blocked; Mary Kinder was impressed that he changed his underwear every day. When they weren't shopping, the four could usually be found at a dentist's office on Washington Avenue, enduring a numbing series of cappings and fillings. By Kinder's count, at least one of them sat in a dentist chair every day for two weeks.

Nights were for fun. Their first stop was usually a movie theater. Dillinger, who had entered prison before the advent of talking pictures, was a movie fanatic, pushing the group to go three and four nights a week; soon they had seen every picture on the North Side. Afterward they would hit a restaurant and then a nightclub, usually the College Inn or the Terrace Garden. All refrained from hard liquor, mostly drinking beer, and Dillinger drank less than the others. He couldn't really dance but reluctantly allowed Billie to show him a step or two. Pierpont laughed from their table, absolutely refusing to step on the dance floor. Sitting beside him, Kinder watched how kind Billie was with Dillinger. Both had lived such scarred and disappointing lives. She could see they were falling in love.

They saw surprisingly little of the others—Russell Clark and Charles Makley and John Hamilton—but when the boys were tired they would have everyone over to play poker, the men chomping on handfuls of peanuts and exchanging war stories about their years behind bars.[14] For a bunch of murderous ex-cons, they were an amiable lot, with few disagreements between them. "They were all friends," Opal Long was to recall. "They were like a lot of old graduates getting together, only their school was prison and the things they had to talk about were not football games and parties, but the way they 'snitched' on jail keepers and the weeks they spent in 'the black hole' on bread and water. Those were the things that kept them together at a time when they would have been a lot safer to split up and go their own ways. They stuck together because they were afraid of strangers."[15]

The one exception was Dillinger's obvious dislike of the gang's sixth member, Ed Shouse, a slick character Dillinger thought was trying to seduce Billie. The others noticed the sarcastic comments Dillinger aimed Shouse's way, but it was the discovery that Shouse wanted to rob a bank on his own that led to his exile. Mary Kinder overheard him trying to get John Hamilton to join him. "You ain't gonna do a damn thing," Mary snapped. "This has always been a friendly bunch and you ain't gonna take no two or three and go rob a bank."[16]

The other members of the gang voted to banish Shouse that same night, and the next morning, when he arrived at Dillinger's apartment, they each threw a roll of bills on the couch before him. "There's your money," Dillinger spat. "Now get your ass out."[17]

The gang was wary of making new contacts in Chicago—Dillinger, like Alvin Karpis, was worried that police might bring heat on the Syndicate and anger Frank Nitti. The few people they did see tended to belong to an extensive network of Indiana State Prison alumni that flourished in the city. The ex-cons bunked in crowded apartments, dirty flophouses, or with girlfriends, and were always up for a quick buck. It was through this motley group, well monitored by the Chicago police, that word of Dillinger's presence in the city filtered back to the growing pack of lawmen and private eyes who were hunting him.

Into this network one of the insurance investigators, Forrest Huntington, managed to insert a paid snitch, a former Michigan City acquaintance of Dillinger's named Art McGinnis. In Chicago, McGinnis spread the word he was working as a fence eager to buy stolen bonds; Dillinger and Pierpont already had a middleman trying to move bonds from the Greencastle and St. Mary's banks. Each week McGinnis passed a trove of rumors to Huntington, few of which could be verified. There were stories that Dillinger was trying to buy mortars at an army depot, casing banks in Indianapolis, looking to rob the Federal Reserve. Matt Leach squabbled with Huntington over McGinnis, whom he sought to control. Huntington balked. He considered Leach publicity-hungry and blamed him for the bungled attempts to capture Dillinger that August.

"I have tried to work with Captain Leach and confided information to him two months ago that, had it been handled properly, would have resulted in the arrest of John Dillinger," Huntington wrote his superiors. "[But] Leach, by his indiscreet methods of sensationalizing criminal information to the press, by his domineering attitude toward city and county officers and by other irrational and erratic acts, has antagonized the majority of police officials of the state and they will not cooperate with him."[18]

Huntington's supervision of McGinnis was further complicated by the Chicago police, who placed the informant under surveillance as part of its own attempts to find Dillinger. Huntington was obliged to sit down with Lieutenant John Howe, head of the Chicago Police Department's Secret Squad, and strike a deal: if Howe's men ignored McGinnis, they could handle any arrests he might arrange. Huntington pressed McGinnis to arrange a face-to-face meeting where Dillinger could be captured.

On Monday morning, November 13, McGinnis called Huntington in a state of excitement. Dillinger had just been at McGinnis's apartment, McGinnis said, looking to pass eight $1,000 Liberty Loan bonds. They had agreed to meet in a downtown parking lot that afternoon. But there was a catch. McGinnis wanted rewards he had been promised for capturing *all* the gang members, not just Dillinger, and he refused to reveal the parking lot's address until Huntington promised the Chicago police would *not* arrest Dillinger that day. Huntington telephoned Sergeant Howe, who checked with his superiors, who told him to use his best judgment. Howe told Huntington they would just watch. No arrests.

And so Huntington and Sergeant Howe found themselves in a Loop cafeteria that afternoon when a car driven by a man who looked very much like John Dillinger plucked McGinnis off a nearby corner. Three hours later McGinnis phoned. He had driven around Chicago all afternoon with Dillinger and had dozens of stories to relate. Almost offhandedly, he mentioned that Dillinger was suffering a case of barber's itch, an inflammation of hair follicles.* McGinnis had arranged for him to visit a doctor named Charles Eye, who worked from offices around the corner from McGinnis's apartment, on Keeler Avenue just below Irving Park Boulevard. Once again McGinnis insisted Huntington refrain from anything that would lead to Dillinger's arrest.

Two of Matt Leach's men were visiting Sergeant Howe's office when Huntington arrived to relay the news. They immediately phoned Leach in Indianapolis, who within minutes initiated an angry series of phone calls with Howe and Huntington. Leach demanded that Dillinger be taken that night: they might never have a second chance. But Huntington, like his snitch, was eager to capture the whole gang, and Sergeant Howe backed his play. The two men reluctantly acceded to Leach's demands to bring his two men along that night.

At 7:15, Howe, Huntington, and Leach's men sat in a darkened car and watched as Dillinger arrived at Dr. Eye's office in an Essex Terraplane sedan. A man and a woman, probably Pete Pierpont and Mary Kinder, remained in the car while Dillinger ran inside. Fifteen minutes later he came out and drove off. The officers let him go.

The next morning a cold front blew in, driving temperatures down to 15 degrees. When McGinnis checked in with Huntington, he told him that Dillinger had a follow-up appointment at Dr. Eye's office that night. McGinnis urged that this time officers trail Dillinger to wherever he was living, where no doubt they could find the whole gang. By late afternoon, Sergeant Howe was again refereeing a vigorous debate over what to do. Huntington agreed with his informant: he wanted Dillinger followed. Leach, who had driven up from Indianapolis, wanted him captured, or dead. The day was ultimately carried by an officer who walked into Howe's office that day from Lima, Ohio. He argued that Dillinger should be taken out to avenge the death of Sheriff Sarber.

By seven that night three squads of Chicago police had gathered on a side street two blocks from Dr. Eye's office. Leach was there, stamping his feet to stay warm, as were Huntington and Howe. Because Dillinger was wanted in Indiana, the squads had been placed under Leach's supervision. A little after seven, Huntington and a Chicago cop crept forward to watch

---

* According to some stories it was a ringworm infection.

Dr. Eye's office. At 7:25 Dillinger drove up in the Essex. Billie sat beside him. As the two men watched, Dillinger hustled into the building, leaving Billie in the car.

Huntington trotted back to where the others were waiting and briefed them. Everything was set. The men piled into four cars and cruised to their positions. Three of the cars eased to the curb on Keller, a quiet street, facing Dillinger's car. A fourth car, driven by a Chicago detective named Howard Harder, parked across Irving Park Boulevard, fifty yards behind the waiting Essex. They had Dillinger in a box. Leach had taken aside one of his men, Art Keller, and told him he had no interest in capturing Dillinger alive. He wanted Keller to shoot him. (It is a measure of how far civil rights have advanced in the intervening seventy years that both men enthusiastically related this story for years afterward.)

Minutes ticked by. Men shivered inside the unheated squad cars. Everyone saw Dillinger when he emerged onto the sidewalk, steam curling from his mouth. Dillinger glanced at the parked cars. Several, he noticed, were pointed the wrong way. He opened the driver's-side car door, slid behind the wheel, and told Billie to hang on. Before anyone could react, Dillinger threw the Essex into reverse, tires squealing as he backed the car directly into the thick of Irving Park Boulevard traffic.

Across the street, Detective Harder hollered for his driver to ram Dillinger's car, but in his haste the car's engine flooded. Dillinger threw the Essex into first and it shot forward, heading east on Irving Park, narrowly avoiding an onrushing car. Behind Dillinger only one of his pursuers, a car driven by a Chicago detective named John Artery, managed to give chase. Sitting beside Artery was Art Keller, the officer with orders to kill Dillinger. Artery pushed the accelerator to the floor and in seconds the officers' car pulled abreast of Dillinger's fleeing Essex. "Get down!" Dillinger shouted to Billie, who scrunched into the floorboards.

Keller leaned out a window and opened fire, emptying a .38 and then a shotgun into Dillinger's car. Dillinger screeched right onto Elston Avenue. Keller's car stayed with him. In the years to come those involved would inflate the ensuing chase to a multimile, half-hour marathon. In fact, the chase was relatively short, lasting maybe a mile. Keller leaned out the window, repeatedly firing into the Essex, but no one was hit. At one point, Dillinger swung a sharp right off Elston, then swerved into a dead-end street. Behind him Detective Artery didn't react in time. He raced by the street even as Dillinger reversed the Essex, rocketed in the opposite direction, and made his escape. "That bird sure can drive," Keller breathed.

Dillinger and Billie abandoned the bullet-riddled Essex on the North Side and took a cab to Russell Clark's apartment, where the gang was holding an impromptu party, dancing to the tunes on a radio. Mary Kinder heard someone pounding on the door, opened it, and was surprised when Dillinger and Billie tumbled in. Dillinger was convinced it was a syndicate assassination attempt; not till the next morning's papers were they certain their pursuers had been police.

Front-page stories of the shoot-out introduced Dillinger to thousands of Chicagoans. The *Tribune,* writing that Dillinger's "prowess in crime has been compared to the James boys and Harvey Bailey,"[19] passed on a breathless account of how police had traded shots with a machine gunner firing from an "unseen portal" within Dillinger's car. In fact, Dillinger had never fired a shot; he was too busy driving. Several of the city's six papers drew comparisons to Verne Miller's escape sixteen days before.

While everyone had an idea who had betrayed them, Dillinger and Pierpont were certain it was Art McGinnis. They wasted no time clearing out of the Clarendon Avenue apartment, moving across town to Russell Clark's. The Chicago police were right behind them; detectives raided the Clarendon flat the next day. Coincidentally, Dillinger's old partner, Harry Copeland, whose heavy drinking made him a liability, was arrested the following night, after he had the stellar idea of pulling a gun on a woman with whom he was arguing outside a North Side bar. In his absence Pat Cherrington began sleeping with John Hamilton. Her sister Opal Long was already occupying Russell Clark's bed.

Dillinger did not let police pressure disrupt his schedule. Gang members had been trying to pass stolen bonds through a fence in Milwaukee and had spotted an attractive bank en route, the American Bank and Trust Company, in the small lakeside city of Racine. That weekend, the gang rented an apartment in Milwaukee and cruised Racine's downtown streets, studying the bank and scoping out escape routes. The money was beginning to run low, and Dillinger was brimming with expensive dreams, from buying and learning to fly an airplane to taking a long Florida vacation. They planned to hit the bank on Monday.

7

AMBUSHES

November 20 to December 31, 1933

Racine, Wisconsin
Monday, November 20
2:30 P.M.

The numbing cold front had moved on, but as the five gang members cruised toward the American Bank and Trust Company, a cool wind was still blowing off Lake Michigan behind the bank. Russell Clark did the driving, dropping the others on downtown corners before parking in a lot behind the bank.* It was a mistake: the bank didn't have a back door. Worse, the gang either didn't notice or didn't care that the Racine Police Department was only three blocks away.

Pete Pierpont, wearing a gray overcoat and matching fedora, was first into the lobby. He unfurled a Red Cross poster and without a word taped it up in the bank's front window, obscuring the view of the teller cages from the outside. Dillinger, Makley, and Hamilton walked in a moment later. At the cages the head teller, Harold Graham, was counting a stack of bills. He had just pulled a NEXT WINDOW, PLEASE sign in front of his window when he heard someone say, "Stick 'em up!"

---

* The gang's exact lineup at Racine has long been in dispute. Witnesses uniformly counted five robbers that day. A man named Leslie Homer later confessed and was convicted of taking part. If so, that means one of the others, probably Russell Clark, did not come along.

Graham kept his head lowered and ignored the order, thinking someone was joking.

"Stick 'em up!" Makley repeated.

Graham still didn't look up. "Next window, please," he said, with what one imagines was a touch of attitude.

Without a word, Makley raised his pistol and shot him. The bullet went through Graham's right arm and lodged in his hip. He fell backward, stunned and bleeding. Somehow Graham kept his senses enough to press the alarm button. Outside, the alarm began ringing loudly, echoing up and down Main Street. Dillinger turned his head. Out on the sidewalks, passersby did the same. Two more alarms rang at police headquarters. Dillinger and Pierpont strode past the teller cages, ordering the eight or nine employees there to lie on the floor. Dillinger frog-marched the bank's president, Grover Weyland, to open the vault, then hustled inside and began shoveling stacks of bills into a sack. Pierpont kept an eye on the front door. Among the frightened tellers and customers who watched him that day, all described the handsome, forceful Pierpont as the clear leader of the robbers.

At police headquarters, officers weren't exactly scrambling to join the action. The bank had suffered a series of false alarms, and Officer Chester Boyard figured this was one more. He grabbed two men, strolled to a squad car, and drove to the bank. A few minutes later, Boyard was first out of the car in front of the bank. The moment he entered the lobby, he heard a voice yell, "Stick 'em up." Before he could react, one of the robbers—later identified as Russell Clark—leveled a submachine gun at him and took his pistol. Sergeant Wilbur Hansen was next through the door, his submachine gun pointed toward the floor. From the back of the bank Pierpont shouted, "Get that cop with the machine gun!"[1]

Makley, who was covering the lobby, turned and fired. A bullet grazed Officer Hansen's right hand and scorched a flesh wound in his side. He pitched forward, stunned. A woman fainted, slithering to the floor like a shrugged-off overcoat. A vase of flowers crashed down. Makley stepped over and tried to wrench Officer Boyard's pistol from its holster. It wouldn't come free. He took a moment to unbutton the holster and take the gun. Outside, the third officer ran for help.

Gunsmoke was rising inside the lobby. Outside, a crowd was beginning to form. The manager of Goldberg's Shoe Store, four doors north of the bank, jogged down to investigate. Officer Boyard made eye contact through the front door and vigorously shook his head. The man then stepped onto a window ledge and peered into the bank. Makley saw him and fired a burst from a submachine gun, sending the man scrambling for cover and glass crashing out into Main Street.

Dillinger was finishing inside the vault. He glanced out a back window. It was a long drop to the parking lot below. "We'll have to shoot our way out the front!" he yelled. He waved his gun at Grover Weyland and three woman tellers hiding under a counter, beckoning them to come forward. When Weyland tarried, Pierpont slapped him, sending his eyeglasses skidding across the floor. Weyland glared. "If you didn't have that gun in your hand, you wouldn't have that much guts," he said.[2]

At that point another policeman walked into the lobby. "Come right in and join us," Dillinger quipped.

"What the hell's going on?" the man asked.

Officer Boyard shook his head and the man went quiet.[3]

Each of the five robbers selected a hostage or two, and together they headed out the front door. So many people had gathered on the sidewalk, however, that the gang literally had to push their way through the inquisitive crowd. A number of onlookers, noticing Officer Boyard, assumed he had taken the gang members hostage and crowded forward to get a look. "Get back! Get back!" people yelled.

As the crowd began to part, two detectives burst around a corner twenty yards away.

"Mack!" Pierpont cried.

Makley turned and fired a burst from his submachine gun. The detectives took cover in the Wylie Hat Shop.

The crowd lingered on the sidewalk even as the scrum of gang members and their hostages inched east toward the lakefront and their waiting car. Several hostages melted into the crowd. At least one passerby found himself briefly taken hostage. It was chaos. As the gang reached the parking lot, Pierpont again spied the two detectives peering down an alley to the south. "There's that fellow with the gun again," Pierpont snapped to Makley. "Get him!"

Makley loosed a volley down the alley, and the detectives dived into the rear entrance of the Liberal Clothing store, showers of dust and asphalt erupting at their heels. When they reached the car, Dillinger slid behind the wheel. "C'mon, Mr. President, you're going with us," Pierpont said to Weyland. He turned to a teller named Anna Patzke and said, "And you in the red dress." The two hostages took positions on the running board beside Dillinger. Officer Boyard stood opposite them.

Dillinger sped away, the car whizzing past two running police officers. Weyland waved his arms as they passed, indicating they should not shoot. With Hamilton reading the git, Dillinger drove west across town, running two red lights before sagging into a traffic jam. They told Boyard to beat it and pulled the two remaining hostages inside the car, not wanting to attract attention.

The traffic jam cleared after a moment, and within minutes they were driving on dirt roads into the yellowing fields of the Wisconsin countryside. They stopped to change license plates, then again to fill up at a gasoline cache they had left. When Mrs. Patzke said she was cold, Pierpont lent her his coat. He gave Weyland his hat. Tensions ebbed. Dillinger's mood, in fact, turned buoyant. They kept to the cat roads, passing several farms. At one point they passed an old man on a tractor. "Hi, Joe," Dillinger hollered with a wave.

Finally they pulled into a glade and tied the hostages to a tree. Pierpont plucked his hat off the bank president's head, and with that they were off.

The gang was back in Milwaukee by day's end. Mary Kinder was waiting when they walked in, Dillinger kidding Pierpont about lending Mrs. Patzke his new coat. The take came to roughly $5,000 each.

By nightfall, as posses spread across southern Wisconsin in a vain attempt to track the robbers, reporters and police from Milwaukee to Indianapolis descended on Racine. One of Matt Leach's men was there, and the Dillinger Gang's responsibility was quickly confirmed. Asked what Dillinger was like, Grover Weyland told reporters the gang had been "genial." At one point, he said, one of the robbers in the getaway car—later identified as Makley—had cursed, and Dillinger had told him to cut it out, because of the presence of a lady in the car.

This kind of small courtesy was becoming a Dillinger hallmark. Like most of his peers, Dillinger was an avid reader of his own press clippings, and one suspects this penchant for niceties had less to do with good manners than with an increasing awareness of his own public image. Dillinger knew how the public tended to celebrate daring bank robbers, and he craved its adulation. He got it. Just as Pretty Boy Floyd had aroused populist sentiment in dust-bowl Oklahoma, Dillinger was quickly perceived by many Midwesterners as a force of retribution against moneyed interests who had plunged the nation into a depression. Letters of support began popping up in Indiana newspapers.

"Why should the law have wanted John Dillinger for bank robbery?" read one. "He wasn't any worse than bankers and politicians who took the poor people's money. Dillinger did not rob poor people. He robbed those who became rich by robbing the poor. I am for Johnnie."

And this was only the beginning.

By mid-November there had been no confirmed sighting of Bonnie and Clyde for three months, not since they were seen fleeing the bloody shoot-out at Dexfield Park, Iowa, on July 24. No one knows where they hid, but anecdotal evidence suggests they spent several weeks with cousins of Clyde's who lived on farms deep in the East Texas pines. Distant Barrow relatives, several of whom were interviewed by a band of schoolchildren for a class project decades later, remembered an incident during this period in which Bonnie attempted to learn how to fire a pistol and nearly shot off one of her toes.

Wherever Bonnie and Clyde were hiding, only two men were actively pursuing them. A Dallas FBI agent, Charles Winstead, poked around where he could, but the pull of other cases kept him from the chase full-time. In the FBI's absence the manhunt, such as it was, fell to the Dallas county sheriff, Smoot Schmid, who handed the case to a veteran investigator named Bob Alcorn. That fall Alcorn began working with a young deputy named Ted Hinton; both had met Bonnie during her waitressing days in downtown Dallas, and both knew Clyde and his old west Dallas haunts.

By October Alcorn and Hinton were reasonably certain Bonnie and Clyde were hiding somewhere in the countryside outside of Dallas. Worried they would be seen, the two law-enforcement agents refrained from systematic surveillance of the Barrow and Parker families. Instead they worked their sources, panning for tips on Clyde's whereabouts, and spent endless days and nights cruising county roads around the city, parking on hillsides and staring at traffic; on one occasion they thought they saw Clyde's Ford and gave chase, but the V-8 in question outran their squad car. Realizing they needed a more powerful vehicle, Hinton prevailed upon the Ben Griffin Motor Company to loan him a fast new Cord sedan: if anything could catch Clyde Barrow, the salesman promised, it was the Cord.

Late one night, on a hillside overlooking Duncanville, Hinton was sitting behind the wheel of the Cord, watching cars pass; there were reports that members of the Barrow family had been seen in the area. Suddenly Alcorn pointed at a passing Ford and barked, "That's him!" Hinton shoved the car into first. "Get going!" Alcorn snapped. Rolling onto the blacktop, Hinton shoved the car into second gear, but he shoved too hard. The linkage ripped; the car sagged and died.

The deputies returned the Cord and leased a powerful Cadillac limousine. Driving one night on Loop 12 in far east Dallas, Hinton thought he saw Clyde in a passing Ford. Hinton floored the accelerator, but the Ford was too fast. Within minutes it outdistanced them and disappeared into the night. Back went the limousine. At this point, the two frustrated deputies were ready to try anything. Looking for something that might stop Clyde, they prevailed upon an excavating company to lend them a massive gravel-moving truck. The idea was to trap Clyde. Alcorn would sit in a squad car on a stretch of road where Clyde had been seen. When Alcorn saw him pass, he would flash a signal to Hinton in the gravel truck. Hinton would then drive into the road, blocking it or smashing into the side of Clyde's Ford.

It almost worked. Sheriff Schmid was along one evening when they spotted Clyde driving with Bonnie. When Schmid flashed the signal, Hinton edged the truck onto the road. But other cars materialized around him. Rather than take the chance of injuring passersby, Hinton stopped. He could follow the car only with his gaze as it drove out of sight.*

Outside Dallas, Texas
Wednesday, November 22

After two months working their sources, Alcorn and Hinton finally hit pay dirt just before Thanksgiving. The tip came to Hinton. A dairy farmer who lived near the town of Sowers, fourteen miles northwest of Dallas, called to say he had seen Clyde parked on a section of State Highway 15 beside his farm.† He described how Clyde blinked his headlights, a sign for a car carrying the Barrow and Parker families to pull up alongside. The tip sounded good, and it apparently wasn't the only one Hinton received.

---

* There's a chance Ted Hinton's car stories, especially the gravel truck episode, were apocryphal. He told them in a 1978 book, *Ambush,* published shortly after his death.

† Today the site lies just outside the Dallas–Fort Worth Airport.

Though he never divulged his source, someone—apparently close to the Barrow family—told Hinton there was a meeting that Wednesday night.

An animated discussion ensued when Alcorn and Hinton broke the news to Sheriff Schmid. The deputies insisted on ambushing Clyde. He had sworn never to be taken alive, they said; there was no way to bring him in—except dead. But Schmid, intoxicated by the idea of photographers snapping his picture alongside a handcuffed Clyde Barrow, insisted on attempting to capture him. It was an argument the deputies couldn't win. They thought Schmid wanted to be the next governor.

As the sun set that evening, two nights after Dillinger's robbery at Racine, the three lawmen and another deputy parked their cars a half-mile from the purported meeting site, then hiked back and took positions in a ditch about seventy-five feet from the spot where the farmer claimed to have seen Clyde. About half past six, as darkness set in, a car approached. It pulled up on the road and stopped. In the gloaming, the officers could just make out the Barrow and Parker families.

At 6:45, as the four lawmen watched from the weeds, they heard the sound of a V-8 engine approaching from the north. A moment later a Ford hove into view. Clyde was driving. Later he would say he had a bad feeling that night. He started to drive on past, but when he was roughly seventy-five feet from the officers' hiding place, Sheriff Schmid suddenly popped up out of the ditch. "Halt!" he shouted.

The sheriff had initiated his plan; now Hinton and Alcorn carried out theirs, opening fire on the oncoming Ford. The bullets pounded into the driver's-side door, Hinton's submachine gun doing much of the damage. As Clyde struggled to control the car, three of the Ford's tires burst. The windshield and windows shattered. Bullets tore into the steering wheel, shearing off chunks of it in Clyde's hands. Strips of the interior dangled from the ceiling over his head.

Clyde floored the accelerator, and the wounded car wobbled forward down the gravel road, crested a hill, and passed from sight. The car containing the Barrow and Parker families drove off, leaving Schmid and his deputies alone, powerless to give chase. "It's my fault, boys," Schmid said after a moment. "I should have listened to you fellas."

Clyde knew he couldn't get far driving on three flat tires. Four miles south he spied an oncoming Ford coupe and swerved in front of it, forcing the car into a ditch. Clyde leaped from the car, a shotgun in his hand, and yelled at the Ford's driver, "Get out of there!"

Neither the driver, Thomas R. James, nor his friend Paul Reich replied. Clyde placed the shotgun against the glass of the driver's-side window, tilted it upward, and pulled the trigger; the resulting blast blew a hole in the Ford's roof. James and Reich tumbled out the far side, glass cuts on their faces. They stood by the car, hands above their heads. Bonnie ran to the Ford and got in. But Clyde couldn't find the ignition switch. "Where's the key?" he demanded.

"You're so smart," James snapped. "Find it yourself." A moment later Clyde did, and he drove the coupe off into the Texas night.

All that autumn Hoover fended off attempts from Midwestern lawmen and editors to draw the FBI into pursuing the Dillinger and Barrow gangs. His position only hardened in mid-November when the Bureau was dealt devastating blows on back-to-back days in the War on Crime's two major cases, the Hamm kidnapping and the Kansas City Massacre.

The Hamm trial began in St. Paul on November 17. The case against the Chicago mob boss Roger Touhy and his gangmates was weak, and prosecutors knew it. Almost all the eyewitnesses were unsure of their identifications, and the defendants' alibis proved unbreakable. Hamm himself, who remained shaken by his experience, couldn't identify any of his kidnappers and seemed reluctant to testify. Pop Nathan told an aide he was "disgusted with Hamm's attitude" and "was suspicious of the entire matter, believing that Hamm had been dealing with the gangster element in distributing his beer."[4] The federal prosecutor, Joe Keenan, closed the door to Hoover's office before bluntly telling the director, "We have no case."[5] And they didn't. After a weeklong trial, Touhy and his codefendants were acquitted of all charges.* Editorialists decried the verdict, saying it would only encourage kidnappers. Hoover was apoplectic.

News in the massacre case went from bad to worse. Verne Miller had vanished, though in the wake of his Halloween escape, agents had learned much about his travels. A search of the car Miller abandoned in Chicago turned up a pair of riding breeches sold by a shop at the luxurious Greenbrier Hotel in White Sulphur Springs, West Virginia. A check of hotel records indicated Miller had registered on August 13 as a doctor from Maplewood, New Jersey, then moved on to the Greystone Inn in Roaring

---

* Touhy would be convicted the following February of the Jake Factor kidnapping.

Gap, North Carolina. His golfing partners complained to agents that Miller was a poor sport, quitting one game at the Greenbrier after a bad shot.

Miller had posed as a traveling optician, as indicated by a bag of eyeglasses, frames, lenses, and business cards found in his car. These items led agents to the Mason Optical Service in Newark, New Jersey, whose owner told agents he'd supplied the equipment to a man named Irwin Silvers. Newark police recognized Dr. Silvers as the brother of a gangster named Al Silvers, a member of the Longy Zwillman Mob that dominated the New Jersey underworld. Agents brought in Irwin Silvers on November 15; the doctor admitted buying the equipment for his brother but denied knowing Verne Miller. "This bird certainly is a liar," Hoover scrawled on a memo the next morning.

Arrest orders were issued for Al Silvers, and the good news came fast: Silvers was found the next day in Connecticut. The bad news was, he was dead. Silvers's nude body had been found in a field near the town of Somers, with a clothesline wrapped around his neck, his face a bloody mess, apparently thanks to a hammer. The next day an informant for the New York City police reported that Silvers had been killed by Zwillman's gang for giving Miller unauthorized aid, thus bringing heat onto the gang's operations. Seventy years later, the killing remains unsolved.

In fact, the FBI had been hearing rumors for months that the underworld wanted the Miller manhunt, with its attendant raids and political pressure, to end quickly. Now it appeared the Bureau was in a race with underworld bosses to get Miller. If the syndicate got to Miller first, Hoover realized, the massacre case might never be solved. Which is why, on the afternoon of November 28, eight days after Silvers's body was discovered, four FBI men found themselves sitting in a midtown Manhattan lawyer's office, interviewing Lepke Buchalter.

What the agents expected from the suave head of Murder, Inc., isn't clear. In the event, Buchalter proved a quiescent witness. He freely admitted knowing Miller, telling agents of a 1932 Thanksgiving dinner with the Millers and Frank Nashes, playing golf with Miller in Hot Springs that winter, even about squiring Vi Mathias that summer. "No one will have anything to do with Miller now," Buchalter said, according to an FBI summary of the meeting.[6] "[But] if Miller shows up in New York, you will know about it." When the agents pressed, asking if Miller might be "bumped off" within the next thirty days, Buchalter "gave a knowing smile and said he didn't know about that but would have to make some inquiries around town."

The next evening, Wednesday, November 29, the FBI got its answer. A man named Vernon W. Northrop was driving home from work when he spotted something in a vacant lot on the outskirts of Detroit. It was a man's naked body, lying in a drainage ditch, trussed up with rope and in a fetal position. Police were called. When they examined the body, they found a man about five-feet-seven, 150 pounds, with his hair and mustache dyed red. He had been killed by eight or nine blows to his forehead, apparently with a clawhammer. Tied around his neck, so tight that it had crushed his Adam's apple, was another clothesline, the last twenty feet of which trailed off into the lonely lot.

It was Miller. Though his murder was never solved, everyone realized that Lepke had won the race. Hoover was beside himself. "Be absolutely certain it is Verne Miller," he scrawled on one memo. "Do not merely accept the word of the police."[7]

But the police were right. Miller was dead, and with him went any hope of a quick solution to the massacre case. Once again agents returned to their files, poring over old leads and reinterviewing people. No one the FBI arrested had anything useful to say. There remained only two suspects at large, Pretty Boy Floyd and one of the men who had escaped prison alongside Harvey Bailey, the wild-eyed Oklahoma outlaw Wilbur Underhill. Hoover's men were combing the eastern half of Oklahoma in search of both men, but so far had nothing.

In the wake of Miller's death, the massacre investigation began to spiral off in bizarre new directions. The next morning Ted Conroy, the new Kansas City SAC, wrote a letter to Hoover. Based on interviews his agents had been doing at the Kansas State Penitentiary, Conroy wrote, he had "vitally important" information on the identity of Miller's partners in the massacre. According to Conroy's theory, they were none other than Fred and Dock Barker.[8]

It was progress, of a sort. The FBI was looking for the right suspects, but for the wrong crime.

In late November, the Barker Gang returned from their Nevada vacations invigorated and ready to work. Once settled into a new set of Chicago apartments, Fred and Karpis drove up to St. Paul, where one night in early December the Green Lantern's Harry Sawyer had them out to his farm. There was much to catch up on. The Touhy trial had just concluded, and they all had a good laugh at the FBI's expense. They spent the better part of an hour speculating about who had killed Verne Miller.

Finally Karpis asked Sawyer if he had any jobs in mind for them. He did. To Karpis's surprise, it was another kidnapping, of another Twin Cities millionaire, Edward Bremer, the thirty-seven-year-old son of Adolph Bremer, one of President Roosevelt's principal financial backers. The Bremers owned the Schmidt brewery. Karpis thought Sawyer had lost his mind. "Do you realize how much heat there would be?" he asked.

"What do you mean, heat?" Sawyer said. "You know I'm connected here. Hell, you guys won't have any trouble getting that money. Just like that Hamm thing. You guys didn't have any trouble doing that or getting the money."

"This is going to be a hell of a lot different thing," Karpis said. "You know as well as I do how much money that guy put up for Roosevelt's goddamn campaign. I was told he put up three hundred fifty thousand dollars and could have been the ambassador to Germany."

Sawyer laughed. "Well, I don't know how much he put up, but he could have been ambassador, that's right."

"This ain't gonna be like the Hamm thing," Karpis said. "This is going to be a hot son of a bitch. How much money you think you ought to get for the guy? I wouldn't want to do it for less than half a million dollars if I did it."

"Hell," said Sawyer, "you ain't gonna get that kind of money from nobody. Let's be reasonable about this thing."

"How much?"

"Well, you could get two hundred thousand dollars without any trouble."

"Don't hand me any crap about trouble," Karpis said. "'Cause that's all you're going to get out of this goddamn thing."

Sawyer turned to Barker, who hadn't said a word. "What do you think about it, Freddie?"

"Two hundred thousand dollars sounds real good to me."

Barker turned to Karpis. "What the hell is all this talk about heat? That's all we've had anyway since 1931 is heat."

"Okay, Freddie," said Karpis. "But I'm telling you now, if we do this thing, this ain't gonna be like anything else we ever did." He'd go along if they wanted, Karpis said. "But I'd hell of a lot rather rob a bank any day. I'd rather do anything than kidnap this guy. If we're gonna kidnap somebody, let's kidnap somebody besides this guy here. Let's go to some other town, too." They talked about working in Chicago or Indiana, but neither seemed promising: the Dillinger Gang had brought swarms of police into both areas. Sawyer argued that St. Paul was the perfect venue: corrupt cops, good men to work with, and no Dillinger. By daybreak they reached a compromise: if Shotgun George Ziegler favored the job, Karpis said he would go along.

He and Fred continued debating the merits of kidnapping Bremer on the drive back to Chicago. Karpis had a million reasons not to. Among other things, he pointed out how easily the FBI had traced Machine Gun Kelly's ransom money. "God, all you do is worry," Fred said. It was true. Karpis had realized the stress he was under only when his girlfriend mentioned how much weight he had lost. He had promised to eat a pint of ice cream each day to put it back on.

"We'd better start making some money," Karpis said, "and start figuring on getting the hell out of this country because things are going to get real bad. You can read the papers, you can see for yourself what Hoover's saying, what the attorney general is saying. They want all them laws passed, and they're going to get a lot more of them FBI guys . . . So whatever we're going to do to make money, we'd better make it by next summer and get the hell out of here or we're both going to get killed or get caught."

Barker said nothing. "Which brings me to your mother," Karpis said. "Now I've brought it up two or three times to you about you're going to have to do something with her. We're going to have to quit living with her. You know that, don't you?" Barker got defensive, as he always did when Karpis brought up Ma. "I got that apartment, didn't I?" Barker said, alluding to a new flat he had rented for Ma.

"Yeah, but hell, you ain't staying there. You're staying home." Even on the nights when he went out with his girlfriend, a drunken harpy named Paula Harmon, Barker was sneaking home to sleep at his mother's. He let the matter drop. It was impossible to talk to Fred about Ma. She was a meddler, always complaining about their girlfriends, and if Fred wasn't careful, she would get them killed. If the FBI found them, how nimble in flight would a sixty-year-old woman be? "Come on," Barker said when they reached Chicago, "let's go on over with my mother. She gets kind of lonesome. She keeps wondering why you don't come over more often."*

The next day Karpis found Ma immersed in her jigsaw puzzles. She worked on them for hours each day, and whenever Karpis came by, she dragged him into sorting the pieces at her side. As Karpis sat down beside

---

* These conversations are taken from the Karpis transcripts.

Ma, Fred staggered out of his bedroom. He had obviously been up late. "I was over at Paula's last night," he said in a low voice.

"What did your mother say?" Karpis asked. "Anything about coming home late?" Fred was more frightened of his mother than of the police.

A few days later Karpis dropped by George Ziegler's apartment and briefed him on the Bremer job. "I think it's a pretty good score myself," Ziegler said. "Yeah, I'd go on the damn thing."

On the other hand, Ziegler went on, there was something else they could do. A kidnapping in Chicago.

"Who?" Karpis asked.

"It's one of the syndicate guys."

Karpis's heart flip-flopped. "The Syndicate?"

"Hell yeah. What's wrong with that?"

Karpis didn't mention his encounter with Frank Nitti.

"Did you ever hear of a guy named Dennis Cooney?" Ziegler asked.

"Ain't he in charge of all the hookers, all the whores and whorehouses?"

"Yeah, that's the guy. His wife has got three hundred thousand dollars put away in a safe deposit box. He'd be a cinch to snatch." At Ziegler's behest, Karpis spent the next two weeks shadowing Dennis Cooney, studying the best way to kidnap him. Sitting outside of Cooney's home one night, he found himself wondering which would be worse, being hunted by J. Edgar Hoover or Frank Nitti. Ultimately Ziegler made the decision for him. Late one night they drove out into the country. Ziegler was silent much of the way. Finally he said, "They had me downtown today."

"Who?"

"You know who I work for."

Karpis glanced at him. "Yeah."

"They asked me if I had heard any rumor about Dennis Cooney being kidnapped."

As Ziegler told the story, the syndicate bosses had asked him to investigate the rumor and, if true, track down and kill the would-be kidnappers. Ziegler couldn't figure out where the rumor had started. Whoever was responsible, the Cooney job was clearly off. "Well," Ziegler said, "we can go on up to St. Paul and that guy up there."

And so it was decided. Against Karpis's better instincts, they would stage another kidnapping in St. Paul. Karpis knew it was the wrong thing to do, but he made himself a promise: if they carried out this one last score, he would leave the gang.

San Francisco
Late December

Garish neon lights, red, blue, and yellow, glowed in the damp fog that crept in off of San Francisco Bay. A half mile from the waterfront, on a narrow block of Pacific Street crammed with taverns and tinsel halls, Christmas revelers staggered from bar to bar, laughing and backslapping. From the doorway of a joint named Spider Kelly's came a blast of fresh jazz. Out on the sidewalk a roly-poly Italian man waved in the tourists. It was Fatso Negri, Baby Face Nelson's old rum-running friend. Negri felt a tug at his elbow. He turned, annoyed, and his jaw dropped. There, a cap shoved down on his forehead, was Nelson himself.

"Why . . . Jimmy Burnell!" Negri exclaimed, using Nelson's old alias. "Where'd you pop from?"

Nelson grinned. "Oh, I just blew in from the east," he said. "Say, you're getting fatter by the day." He turned to a girl standing at his side. "This is my wife, Helen," he said.

"Glad to know you," Negri said, extending his hand.

They went in and Nelson briefed Negri on his new gang and its exploits. After scrambling away from his Indiana lake house a step ahead of Frank Nitti's enforcers in September, Nelson had relocated to St. Paul. The August robbery with Eddie Bentz in Grand Haven, Michigan, had convinced Nelson he was ready to lead his own gang, and he easily recruited from the Green Lantern's pool of talent. One recruit was Homer Van Meter, the string-bean loner who had befriended Dillinger in prison.* Another was Tommy Carroll, who had joined the Grand Haven bank job that August. A handsome, five-foot-ten-inch tough guy with a flattened nose, Carroll was a drinker, a flirt, and a lady's man who loved the St. Paul nightclubs; he had a wife, a steady girlfriend, and was already romancing a new girl named Jean Delaney, the older sister of Alvin Karpis's teenage lover Delores Delaney.

The trio's first target had been the First National Bank in Brainerd, two hours north of St. Paul. In October, after hiring two local thugs as muscle, Nelson and his men moved into cabins at the Sebago Resort, thirteen miles north of Brainerd. They spent ten days cruising the streets of Brainerd, fil-

---

* After his parole, Van Meter lingered around East Chicago. He met Nelson in Indiana Harbor, and FBI files indicate he bunked with both Dillinger and Nelson for periods that summer. Eager to flee Indiana, where he felt police knew him, Van Meter followed Nelson to St. Paul and signed on for anything he planned.

ing in and out of the bank on ruse errands, learning the names of every employee they could. Nelson even hired a guide to show him around, ostensibly to scout real estate.[9] The night before they struck, Nelson cut the bank's phone lines.

On Monday, October 23, they made their move. When a janitor arrived to enter a basement door at 5:55 A.M., he felt a pistol in his back. One of the robbers told him to open the door. The janitor said he had no key. "Like hell you don't," the robber snapped. "You've been opening the door for the last ten days."

When the janitor opened the door, Carroll waved his hand and two men with submachine guns hustled up. One was Nelson. The three men took up positions in the lobby, while Van Meter, dressed in hunting clothes and carrying a submachine gun in a bushel basket, stood outside. As employees arrived for work, they were ordered to lie on the floor. Nelson grabbed one, a seventeen-year-old clerk named Zane Smith, struck him in the jaw, and dragged him into a side room. He asked Smith how much money was in the vault. When Smith pled ignorance, Nelson threatened to put burning cigarettes in his ear "to get better answers."

A cashier finally opened the vault. After ransacking it and emptying the cash drawers, the gang herded the hostages into the men's room, threatening to shoot the first one who stuck his head out. Nelson was the last to leave, backing out the front door. As he stepped onto the sidewalk, he raised his submachine gun and shot out the glass in the front door. Bystanders saw him shoot the gun into the sidewalk next, bullets ricocheting wildly. As the gang jumped into a car and drove off, Nelson stuck his gun out a window and fired indiscriminately, peppering the YMCA with bullets.[10] No one was hurt.

It was a good haul, $32,000, more than $6,000 a man. Everyone returned to St. Paul, where they were living three weeks later when police raided Carroll's apartment. Though Carroll escaped after a struggle, Nelson ordered everyone out of town. Leaving his baby girl with his mother in Chicago, he took Helen and his four-year-old son, Ronald, and drove south to San Antonio, where they registered at the Johnson Courts Tourist Camp on South Presa Street on November 22.* The other gang members arrived

---

* Nelson had visited the Texas city twice already that summer to buy guns from a gunsmith named Heinie Leibman. Eddie Bentz had introduced them.

soon thereafter, and everyone settled in for an extended vacation. Nelson spent much of his time hanging around a neighborhood garage and in the basement workshop of a downtown gunsmith. The others lolled around whorehouses and bars.

The trouble began two weeks later, when the madam of the whorehouse that Carroll and a gang member named Chuck Fisher were frequenting saw a submachine gun in their car. On December 9 she called a local detective, saying she suspected they were "high-powered Northern gangsters." The detective passed the tip to the San Antonio SAC, Gus Jones. No one realized who the two men were; even if they had, the name "Baby Face Nelson" meant nothing to anyone. The manager of Fisher's apartment building was a friend, so Jones drove over and looked over the room. He found nothing out of the ordinary.

Two days later, on Monday afternoon, December 11, the madam called the San Antonio police with a second tip. One of the gangsters was coming to her house to take a girl horseback riding. Two detectives, H. C. Perrin and Al Hartman, were sitting in a car outside of the whorehouse when a taxi pulled up and Tommy Carroll stepped out and jogged up to the door. A moment later Carroll and the girl returned to the taxi. As the cab eased away from the curb, the detectives followed.

Carroll glanced in the rearview mirror and spotted the tail. Driving down East Commerce Street in the middle of downtown, a half mile from the Alamo, Carroll ordered the driver to stop the car. He jumped out and ran around a corner into an alley. Detective Perrin, armed with a sawed-off shotgun, and Hartman, with his service revolver, leaped from their car onto the sidewalk and raced after him.[11]

The alley was a dead end. As Perrin ran toward it, Carroll stepped out and shot. His first bullet struck the detective between the eyes; he fell in a heap. His next shots shattered Detective Hartman's right wrist and elbow. Carroll ran off down the street, shoved his gun at the driver of a pickup truck, jumped inside, and was gone. By that night the Nelson gang was gone, too. The only member who didn't escape was Chuck Fisher, captured by Gus Jones at his apartment.*

---

* Chuck Fisher gave the San Antonio police nothing. "All I got out of him you could put in your eye and not get hurt," the city's police commissioner told reporters. Fisher was sent to Leavenworth on an outstanding robbery warrant, where he told the FBI nothing, too. Not for four more months would anyone realize Nelson had been in San Antonio.

The gang scattered. Van Meter and Carroll returned to St. Paul, while the Nelsons drove west, crossing New Mexico and then Utah before reaching San Francisco a few days before Christmas. It was then that Nelson found Fatso Negri outside the bar on Pacific Street. Over the course of several days, Nelson laid out his plans to a Midwestern bank-robbing blitz the following spring. Negri signed on.

The Dillinger Gang's good times ended suddenly on December 14 when a Chicago police detective was sent to investigate a tip that one of the gang's Auburns was being serviced at a Broadway garage. John Hamilton appeared at the garage that afternoon. Approached by Detective William Shanley, Hamilton panicked, drew his gun, and fired, killing Shanley. Hamilton ran into the street and escaped. The killing of Detective Shanley was front-page news, and two days later it led the Chicago Police Department to form a special forty-man Dillinger squad.

Dillinger decided it was time to take the Florida vacation he had been thinking about. The gang left in a four-car convoy. Dillinger was the first to arrive at Daytona Beach, on December 19, and he and Billie Frechette quickly rented a sprawling two-story beach house with enough rooms for everyone. They spent the next week strolling the beach and fishing, happy to be away from Chicago; it was the first time most of the gang had ever been to an ocean beach. After a few days everyone piled into the cars and took a two-day trip to Miami, where they took in the dog races and a nightclub or two.

A few days after Christmas, having returned to Daytona, Billie decided to leave to visit her family in Wisconsin for the holidays. There have long been reports that her decision followed a fight with Dillinger—thirty years later Mary Kinder claimed Dillinger had blackened one of her eyes—but there is no evidence to back this up. Dillinger stayed behind, saying he would see her after New Year's.

Shawnee, Oklahoma
Saturday, December 30
1:45 A.M.

Of all the skills Hoover's men were attempting to master that winter, the strategies and tactics of gunplay were by far the most difficult. Marksmanship courses were under way at most offices, but soda bottles and paper targets didn't return fire. Capturing armed fugitives was a skill the men of the FBI would learn only after funerals.

After the debacle of Verne Miller's escape at Halloween, the Bureau's next test of fire came in a cold rain in Shawnee, a small town east of Oklahoma City. That night Ralph Colvin, the Oklahoma City SAC, and a squad of FBI agents and policemen crept through a heavy fog toward the back of a clapboard house where an informant said the outlaw Wilbur Underhill was hiding. Colvin had been nipping at Underhill's heels for weeks. Unlike Pretty Boy Floyd, who had vanished, Underhill had been spotted robbing banks all across the state. He represented the FBI's best chance to break the Kansas City Massacre case.

As Colvin approached the back of the house, a dog began to bark. At Colvin's side was an Oklahoma City detective named Clarence Hurt; Colvin liked Hurt, and would lure him to the FBI within months. The two men hustled through the muddy backyard toward a bedroom window. The blinds were up. Inside, standing in his long underwear, they saw a man. It was Wilbur Underhill. A woman was sitting on a bed beside him.

"Stick 'em up, Wilbur!" Hurt shouted. "It's the law!"

Underhill froze. He started to raise his arms, then whirled toward the window. Hurt fired a tear-gas canister; it crashed through the window and struck Underhill flush in the chest before falling to the floorboards, hissing. Colvin braced his submachine gun and fired three bursts. Glass shattered. Underhill fell.

At the sound of shots, the lawmen in front of the house cut loose with a barrage of automatic shotguns, pistols, and submachine guns. The house shook as bullets tore through its wood frame. Colvin and Hurt ducked, then retreated. Officers behind them began firing. Windows shattered. A cloud of tear gas rose and began to fill the house.

Suddenly Underhill emerged from the front door, clad only in his socks and underwear. A trio of agents fired, a rookie named Tyler M. Birch emptying his shotgun.* Underhill twisted, hit, then leaped off the front porch. He slipped in the muddy front yard and fell. Bullets whizzed everywhere as

---

* Born in Falls Church, Virginia, in 1901, Tyler M. Birch joined the Bureau just two months before the Underhill shooting. He resigned from the FBI in 1938, fought in World War II and the Korean War, and died in December 1981 at the age of eighty.

he rose, then fell again, then rose and staggered into a neighboring yard. Inexplicably, the FBI men kept their guns trained on the house. Underhill disappeared into the fog.

When the firing stopped, there was movement inside the house. Colvin hollered for everyone inside to come out. One of Underhill's partners crawled out the front door, blinded by gas and bleeding from wounds in his elbow and shoulder. A woman followed him out, screaming, bleeding from two bullet wounds in the stomach. A few minutes later Detective Hurt coaxed Underhill's wife to come out as well.

Once the three were packed into an ambulance, lawmen fanned out across the town, shining flashlights down alleys and beneath houses in search of Underhill. He was wounded and couldn't get far. Colvin telephoned the state prison at McAlester, a hundred miles east, and asked for bloodhounds. By sunrise there was still no sign of him.

Then, a little before seven, Shawnee police took a call from the owner of a secondhand furniture store, who said Underhill was in his store on Main Street. Eight Shawnee cops and sheriff's deputies scrambled to the store. They found Underhill lying in bed in a back room. The sheets were reddened with blood. Underhill himself was a mess. As the officers stood over him, he offered no resistance. A bullet had hit him in the forehead, torn a groove across his hairline, and sheared off his left ear. His abdomen was pockmarked with bullets, including one that exploded through his back.

"I guess you've got me," Underhill croaked.

Stanley Rogers, the Oklahoma City sheriff, stepped forward. "You're in a pretty bad way, Underhill," Rogers said.

"Yeah, I'm shot to hell," Underhill said. "They hit me five times. I counted them as they hit me."

Underhill was taken to a hospital, where he lapsed in and out of delirium all that day. Agents clustered at his bedside, attempting to question him about the massacre. It was Frank Smith, the old Cowboy who had survived the shooting, who got Underhill to talk. "[Underhill] thought he was dying and under such conditions positively asserted to Agent Frank Smith that neither he nor Harvey Bailey had anything to do with the Kansas City massacre," an agent wrote Hoover. "This statement, made under such conditions, is believed to be true."

The next day, Underhill was taken to the prison hospital in McAlester, where he died on January 7. For Hoover, there was no choice but to accept his deathbed denials. After six months the Bureau's efforts to solve the Kansas City Massacre had come to a dead end.

The year was over, the new federal "War on Crime" almost six months old. In retrospect, as eventful as it was, 1933 served only as a prelude, a kind of extended training session, for the FBI and the nation. Despite the efforts of Attorney General Homer Cummings to make crime a national issue, to this point it remained a regional phenomenon; while newspapers in Chicago and Kansas City ran blazing front-page headlines over stories of Verne Miller's Halloween escape, for instance, the news merited barely eight paragraphs on an inside page of the *New York Times*.

What was missing was a set of national criminals for Hoover's national police to fight on a national stage. The year 1934 would produce five such groups. Each would emerge into public view as easily recognized, media-friendly icons: the family of kidnappers, the fugitive lovers, the charismatic escape artist, the psychotic killer, the misunderstood country boy. For each of these groups the holiday season was a moment to relax before the approaching storm.

No one is certain what Bonnie and Clyde did; according to Clyde's sister Nell, they probably spent Christmas alone at the abandoned house in Grand Prairie. In the Oklahoma hills, Pretty Boy Floyd's family wondered what he was doing; no one ever found out. Baby Face Nelson spent the holidays in the Bay Area. In her Chicago apartment, the cranky Ma Barker surprised the gang by holding a Christmas dinner. Everyone exchanged presents, swapping handbags and perfume and shiny shaving kits.

All evening Ma was a woman transformed, smiling and laughing and paying attention to the gang's girlfriends. "Now you come over any time you want!" she told Delores Delaney at evening's end. "Why don't we go downtown and go shopping together?" As they drove home, Delaney and Karpis tried to fathom the change in Ma's demeanor.

"What the hell got into her?" Karpis asked.

"That old lady," Delaney said. "She's lonesome."

In Daytona Beach the Dillinger Gang threw a rousing party. It was the only time members of the gang ever recalled seeing Dillinger drunk. As the last minutes of 1933 ticked away, he stepped out onto a balcony with Mary Kinder, swinging his submachine gun. He motioned toward the moon. "Think I can hit it?" he asked. As the clock struck midnight and church-bells pealed across the town, Dillinger pointed his gun into the air and fired a deafening volley of bullets out over the Atlantic.

As scattered as they were that night, in San Francisco and Chicago and Florida, virtually all the members of all the gangs had at least one thing in common: it was the last New Year's Eve celebration of their lives.

8

"AN ATTACK ON ALL WE HOLD DEAR"

January 2 to January 28, 1934

In the opening days of 1934, the Dillinger Gang, Bonnie and Clyde, and the Barkers all began to mobilize for major operations. Karpis and the Barkers got to work first, driving from Chicago to St. Paul on January 2 and converging on an apartment Fred Barker had rented. They had seven men for the kidnapping of Edward Bremer: Karpis, the Barker brothers, Shotgun George Ziegler, Dock's old friends Bill Weaver and Volney Davis, and the new man from Tulsa, Harry Campbell.

All that week Karpis and Fred Barker tailed Bremer. The obvious time to take him was in the morning when the young bank president dropped his nine-year-old daughter off at the Summit School on Goodrich Avenue. He would be alone, and the streets near the school were quiet. Ever the worrier, Karpis fretted about the cars they would use. St. Paul was frigid in January. The temperature plunged to ten below zero each night. They purchased two new Buicks, and Karpis had them outfitted with radios, extra-strength heaters, and frost shields. The last thing they needed was a getaway car seizing up in the subzero cold.

Each night, Karpis and Barker gathered the gang to review the day's progress in Bill Weaver's second-floor apartment at the Kensington, a brick apartment building on Portland Avenue. Their planning was in the final stages on Friday, January 12, when the two returned to Weaver's apartment after nightfall. They parked beside the building, then stopped. Down an alley, they watched as a man hopped onto a box to peer into a window in the building next door. When the man saw them, he dropped to the ground and disappeared around a corner.

Karpis and Barker exchanged glances: it looked like a cop, probably checking the wrong building. "This is bad," Dock Barker agreed when they briefed the group upstairs. "I'm gonna walk out and see what's going on." Dock returned after several minutes. "I see a guy standing on the corner down there," he said, "and it don't look right, him standing on the corner without an overcoat in this kind of weather." They debated what to do. Finally Karpis said he would check with Harry Sawyer at the Green Lantern. If they were under surveillance, Sawyer could call his police contacts and find out. ·

They decided to leave the building in pairs. Dock went out first, to reconnoiter. He returned a few minutes later, worried. "There's a goddamn car with two policemen parked in the alley," Dock said.

"Oh Christ, this is bad," said Karpis.

They decided to send Dock down to retrieve the cars and park them in front. When he returned this time, he said the policemen had ignored them. They appeared to be watching the adjacent building. "Let's go," someone said. Outside everyone hustled into the waiting cars. There were no cops in sight. They drove to Fred's apartment without incident. But Fred wasn't satisfied. He had to know if the plan was blown, and he couldn't wait for Sawyer; if they were being watched, they could all be in Chicago by sunrise. Fred decided to return to Weaver's building.

"Well if we do this," Karpis said, "you'd better take some equipment over there. Don't just go with a pistol."

Barker stepped to the closet and brought out a submachine gun with two 50-shot drums. He and Karpis returned outside, where they slipped into Dock's Chevy. Fred drove, Karpis beside him, the tommy across his lap. By the time they reached Weaver's building, it was past midnight. "Should I go down the alley?" Barker asked.

"Yeah, go on down the alley," Karpis said.

They eased down the alley, deep in shadow. The patrol car was gone. Reaching the far end, they turned into the street. The neighborhood was chockablock with brick apartment buildings, the streets lined with darkened cars. As they turned the corner, a set of headlights flashed behind them, a parked car coming to life. As Barker watched in the rearview, the car pulled out.

Karpis turned in his seat.

"They're following us," he said.

"Yeah," Barker said. "I can see."

They turned a corner, then another, driving slowly. The car stayed with them. Karpis peered backward, trying to make out the car's occupants. There were two. In silhouette Karpis could just make out the driver's peaked hat: a patrolman in uniform. "Them guys look like cops all right," Karpis said. "What the hell are we gonna do?"

"Only one thing we can do," Barker said. "That's stop 'em."

They eased around another corner, threading their way through the lines of parked cars in the narrow streets.

"How do you want to do it?" Karpis asked.

"I'm gonna pull around a corner real fast and stop, and you jump out with that machine gun and if they come around, start shooting."

Butterflies danced in Karpis's stomach as they approached the next corner. They surged around it and stopped. Karpis stepped out into the frigid night air, holding the submachine gun. Barker jumped out the other door, pointing his .45. When the car behind them turned the corner, both men opened fire. The night exploded: Karpis fired from the hip, emptying the entire fifty-shot drum into the car. Barker fired the pistol. The car shook as bullets ripped into it. When they had emptied their guns, both men peered at the car. They couldn't see anyone sitting upright. They jumped back in their Chevy and drove off. Back at Fred's apartment they turned on the radio, waiting for the news. They sat up all night waiting, listening. Not till dawn, when Dock ran out to fetch a newspaper, did they discover they had just machine-gunned a uniformed Northwest Airlines employee.

The man in the car turned out be a radio operator named Roy McCord, and he was following Barker and Karpis because he thought they were peeping toms. When McCord returned home from work that evening, his wife had told him of a prowler, presumably the man Karpis and Barker had seen earlier. McCord, still dressed in his aviator's uniform and peaked cap, left his apartment with a friend to check out the report, spotted Barker's car, and ended up in a hospital with three bullet wounds. He survived. The other man was unhurt.

All that day the gang debated whether to abort the Bremer job. In the end, they decided to put it off two days, till Wednesday, January 17. In the interim, both Dillinger and Bonnie and Clyde struck.

East Chicago, Indiana
Monday, January 15

After three weeks in the Florida sun, Dillinger headed back to the Midwest with John Hamilton. The others planned to extend their vacation by driving cross-country to Tucson, Arizona. Dillinger said he wanted to pick up Billie Frechette; he promised to meet the others in Tucson. While in Chicago, he would try to cash bonds the gang had been unable to pass. Hamilton hoped to reunite with Pat Cherrington.

According to Cherrington, who later told her story to the FBI, Dillinger and Hamilton left Florida on Sunday, January 14. Hamilton sent her a telegram that afternoon from Savannah, asking her to meet him in a Chicago hotel.[1] Driving through the night, Dillinger reached Chicago the next morning. That same day, probably low on cash and unable to move the stolen bonds, he decided to rob a bank. It was an impetuous decision. Some would credit it to Dillinger's growing belief in his own invulnerability, others to restlessness, a yearning to return to the limelight; he hadn't robbed a bank in two months.

Whatever the case, that day Dillinger performed like a hungry actor on a brightly lit stage. The bank he selected was in East Chicago, the corrupt mill town where he had spent time the previous summer. There is evidence Dillinger knew certain members of the East Chicago police department, and some have suggested his decision to hit the First National Bank that day was a prearranged affair. If so, somebody forgot to tell the rest of the East Chicago police.

At 2:45 Dillinger and Hamilton stepped out of a car double-parked outside the bank. They left a driver in the car; his identity has never been established. Inside the marble lobby, Dillinger pulled a submachine gun out of what several eyewitnesses thought was a trombone case. "This is a stickup!" he shouted, startling the dozen or so customers in the bank. "Put up your hands everybody!"

A bank vice president named Walter Spencer pressed a silent-alarm button beneath his desk; a block away, it rang at police headquarters. As the customers raised their hands and lined up against a wall, one forgot his cash on a counter. "You go ahead and take your money," Dillinger said. "We don't want your money. Just the bank's."[2]

Hamilton stood by, apparently unsure what to do.

"Come on," Dillinger told him. "Get the dough."[3]

Hamilton hustled behind the teller cages and began clearing stacks of cash off the counters into a leather satchel. Just then a police officer named Hobart Wilgus appeared at the front door, apparently unaware of the robbery in progress.

Dillinger saw him. "Cop outside," he said to Hamilton, who hesitated. "Take your time," Dillinger admonished. "We're in no hurry." When Wilgus entered, Dillinger stepped forward and disarmed him. He emptied the cartridges from the officer's gun and tossed it back to him. He noticed Wilgus eyeing his submachine gun. "Oh, don't be afraid of this," Dillinger said. "I'm not even sure it'll shoot."

As Hamilton worked the cages, Dillinger saw men in suits hurry toward the bank: plainclothes detectives, answering the alarm. Hamilton saw them, too. Dillinger, playing to his audience, seemed eager to display his insouciance. "Don't let those coppers worry you," he told Hamilton. "Take your time and be sure you get all the dough. We'll take care of them birds on the outside when we get there."

A few moments later Hamilton was finished. Dillinger waved his submachine gun at Walter Spencer, the vice president. "Come on out here with me, Mr. President," he said. Spencer asked if he could grab his coat. Dillinger shook his head. "You're not going very far," he said. He then grabbed Officer Wilgus by the arm. "You go first," Dillinger said. "They might as well shoot you as me. We love you guys anyway."[4]

As he had at Racine two months before, Dillinger shoved the hostages ahead of him as a human shield. This time, however, he wasn't facing a curious crowd. Arrayed outside, behind parked cars and in storefronts on both sides of the front door, were seven East Chicago policemen. As he edged onto the sidewalk, Dillinger hunched behind Officer Wilgus; Hamilton kept an arm around Walter Spencer.

For a long moment, as the four-man scrum scuttled across the sidewalk toward the waiting getaway car, no one spoke. Dillinger locked eyes with at least one of the officers, several of whom stood no more than twenty feet away. They were just steps away from the car, and for a fleeting second it appeared Dillinger could brazen it out. Then one of the officers, a forty-three-year-old detective named Patrick O'Malley, shouted, "Wilgus!" Officer Wilgus turned, giving O'Malley a clear shot at Dillinger. O'Malley fired his pistol four times, at least one of the bullets striking Dillinger's bulletproof vest.

Dillinger appeared stunned. For the first time in his career, he appeared to lose his temper. "Get over!" he snapped to Wilgus, shoving him aside. "I'll get that son of a bitch."[5] He raised his submachine gun and fired a burst directly into Detective O'Malley. The policeman, a father of three little girls, fell dead on the sidewalk, eight bullet holes across his chest.

As O'Malley crumpled, the six remaining officers opened fire. The sidewalk erupted in gunshots. Dillinger and Hamilton dashed for the getaway car, jumping between a line of parked cars. Hamilton didn't make it. He was struck by several bullets, one passing through his bulletproof vest, and fell to the ground. Dillinger stopped and helped him into the car, grabbing the money satchel as well. Miraculously the two managed to dive into the car's open door without further injury. As bullets pounded the getaway car, the driver careened off down Chicago Avenue, eluding police pursuit. In minutes they were gone.

Eyewitnesses made the identification, and the evening newspapers made it official: John Dillinger, the man who many in Indiana cheered for fighting greedy bankers, was now a murderer. For the rest of his life the killing clearly weighed on Dillinger's mind. He would repeatedly deny shooting Detective O'Malley, to lawyers, lawmen, and friends. More than once, he volunteered this to complete strangers. His denials probably had less to do with the prospect of a murder conviction than with his own sense of self and his public image. At the heart of his appeal, Dillinger knew, was his joshing Robin Hood spirit, the sense people had that he was a regular guy making the best of hard times. Dillinger didn't want to be the bad guy. He wanted to be someone people like his sister Audrey and her family could cheer.

After murdering Detective O'Malley, Dillinger drove the badly wounded Hamilton to the hotel where Pat Cherrington was staying. Together they spent most of the evening locating a doctor to treat Hamilton's wounds. One bullet had hit him in the stomach, at least one more in the left shoulder. For the next few weeks Hamilton remained in a Chicago apartment with Cherrington nursing him back to health.

Dillinger, meanwhile, after splitting the $20,000 in proceeds with Hamilton, picked up Billie. They stayed in Chicago just long enough to visit a divorce attorney; as soon as Billie could end her marriage, she and Dillinger planned to wed. Afterward they drove south to St. Louis, where Dillinger wanted to visit a large auto show. There they bought a new V-8 Ford, checked into a downtown hotel, and spent an evening dancing in its roof garden. Then they struck out west on Route 66, looking forward to a vacation in the Arizona sunshine.

East Texas, near Huntsville
Tuesday, January 16
Dawn

The morning after Dillinger's East Chicago raid, a black Ford coupe bumped along rutted dirt roads through pine woods lining the Trinity River bottoms in a remote corner of East Texas. A thick fog rose from the river, making driving difficult. Behind the wheel sat Clyde Barrow, Bonnie beside him. In back sat a cadaverous forty-eight-year-old heroin addict named Jimmy Mullins. The car crossed a thin wooden bridge and came to a stop. Clyde got out, tucking a Browning automatic rifle beneath his arm. Mullins did the same. Leaving Bonnie in the car, they walked into the woods, disappearing into the mist.

For six months Bonnie and Clyde had been alone, living out of their car on handouts from family and friends. Now that Bonnie's leg had healed, Clyde wanted to get back to work. For that he needed a partner. Yet the couple's notoriety had grown to the point where Clyde was unable to approach anyone he didn't know. The only man he felt he could trust, his old partner Raymond Hamilton, was now being held at the Eastham Prison Farm. That morning Clyde planned to bust him out.

It wasn't Clyde's idea; it was Hamilton's. In early January, Hamilton had promised $1,000 to the unreliable Mullins, an eight-time loser about to be paroled, if he would find Clyde and arrange with him to smuggle guns into the prison farm. After his release, Mullins headed to Dallas and found Raymond's brother Floyd. Floyd Hamilton was part of Bonnie and Clyde's support network, ferrying food and other items to the couple every few nights outside the city. He took Mullins to see Clyde, at a roadside clearing outside Irving, ten miles west of Dallas.

Mullins recognized Clyde from prison. Bonnie's appearance surprised him. She was dirty and appeared to weigh no more than eighty pounds. Her leg remained bandaged. She limped. Sitting in his car in the darkness,

Clyde listened to Mullins's plan. The appeal of working alongside Raymond Hamilton was strong; with Hamilton as his partner he could be a bank robber instead of a beggar. But Clyde didn't trust Mullins. The Hamilton brothers wanted the guns smuggled in Sunday night. Fearing a trap, Clyde said they would do it Saturday night. He told Floyd Hamilton to stay with Mullins every minute until they left.

The next evening, after buying a pistol at a pawnshop, Hamilton and Mullins met Bonnie and Clyde on a highway east of Dallas. At sunset they drove south toward Madisonville, then turned onto the cat roads, hoping to find one that would lead them to the spot where the guns were to be planted. Around one-thirty A.M., they came to the edge of the prison farm. Mullins took the pistol, two clips of ammunition and one of Clyde's .45s, wrapped them in an inner tube, and crept toward the prison buildings. About a hundred yards from Hamilton's dormitory, Mullins slid the package beneath a culvert.

They were back in Dallas by dawn. Sunday was visitors' day at Eastham, and Floyd Hamilton drove down to tell Raymond the guns were in place. Clyde and Bonnie, meanwhile, returned to the edges of the prison farm. It took several hours, but they found the field where Hamilton's work group was clearing brush that week. They took several more hours mapping their escape. It was raining and the roads were muddy. Twice they were forced to cut through fields, closing gates behind them.

The escape was set for that Tuesday morning. At dawn, after leaving Bonnie in the car, Clyde and Mullins pushed through underbrush to the edge of the field, squatted behind a bush and waited. An hour later they were still waiting. If Hamilton's escape was delayed, they had promised to be in place three straight mornings. They were about to leave when out of the fog they heard two shotgun blasts.

Clyde strained to hear. Two shotgun blasts was the guards' signal for help. A minute passed, then two. Worried, they headed back to the car. Suddenly they heard voices approaching through the mists. "Get something else!" someone yelled. It was Raymond Hamilton.

"What?" Clyde hollered.

He didn't understand. Assuming Hamilton was being pursued by guards, Clyde raised his Browning and fired into the treetops. Mullins did the same. When the guns were empty, they handed them to Bonnie to reload. A moment later, four men emerged from the fog: Hamilton, a convicted murderer named Joe Palmer, and two prisoners who had run after them. All were breathing hard after running almost a mile.

"Nobody but Raymond and Palmer can get in the car," Mullins announced. "Everybody else go back."

"Shut your damn mouth, Mullins," Clyde snapped. "This is my car. I'm handling this. Three of you can ride back there." He motioned to the trunk. "Guess four of us can ride up here."

Within an hour roadblocks were being thrown up across the area. Sticking to the cat roads, Clyde drove north and west through the towns of Centerville, Jewett, Teague, Wortham, and Mexia before reaching Hillsboro, thirty miles north of Waco. At a gas station an old man approached the car. "Did you folks hear what Clyde Barrow pulled this morning?" he asked Clyde. The man rattled on for several minutes before Clyde had to ask him to please pump their gas.

From Hillsboro, Clyde, worried that his old haunts in Dallas would be watched, drove the group south, to Houston. They made it back to Dallas three nights later, on January 20, meeting their families outside the city. There was much to tell—and much to plan. For the first time in seven months, Clyde Barrow had the makings of a gang.

The man who headed the Texas prison system, Lee Simmons, was a lean, curt fifty-year-old, a member of the same generation of no-nonsense Lone Star lawmen as his FBI friend Gus Jones. He was at the state prison in Huntsville, forty miles south of Eastham, when he received a call about the raid at nine that morning. By ten he was at the farm. Two guards had been wounded in the escape, one of them, Major M. H. Crowson, seriously. The shooting had all been done by the fleeing inmates, but Simmons knew Clyde Barrow had done this. His instinct was confirmed the next day when one of the opportunistic escapees was recaptured.

That night, after a day spent briefing reporters and orchestrating roadblocks, Simmons visited Major Crowson at the Huntsville hospital. He'd taken a bullet through the stomach and wasn't expected to live. "Mr. Simmons, don't think hard of me," Crowson whispered. "I know I didn't carry out your instructions. I'm sorry."

"Don't bother about it," Simmons said. "Those fellows had their day. We'll have ours. I promise you I won't let them get away with it." Crowson died the next day, and Lee Simmons swore an oath. No matter what it took, he would have Clyde Barrow brought in, dead or alive. He stewed on the matter for several days. The more he thought about it, the more he was certain he knew the man who could do it.

St. Paul, Minnesota
Wednesday, January 17

The morning after Clyde Barrow's Eastham raid, the temperature hung near zero in St. Paul as Edward Bremer drove away from his mansion on North Mississippi River Boulevard, his daughter beside him in his black Lincoln sedan. A slender man of great wealth, Bremer had been born into the Twin Cities' first family. His father, Adolph, had married the daughter of a German brewer named Jacob Schmidt in 1896 and had taken over management of the Jacob Schmidt Brewing Company after his father-in-law's death. A friend and financial supporter of President Roosevelt, Adolph Bremer had weathered Prohibition by producing soft drinks and "near beer," and by diversifying into financial investments. Edward ran the family's largest bank, the Commercial State Bank at Washington and Sixth.

But the Bremers were not the Chamber of Commerce men they appeared, as the FBI would learn. Their interests, like William Hamm's, were intertwined with those of St. Paul's underworld. The family brewery supplied "near beer" to many of St. Paul's gangland gathering places, including Harry Sawyer's tavern. In fact, according to an affidavit Sawyer's wife, Gladys, later gave the FBI, the Bremers secretly sold *real* beer to Sawyer's tavern from 1926 to 1932, which Sawyer bootlegged throughout Minnesota. Gladys Sawyer said the relationship went one step further; she claimed the Bremers actually *owned* the Green Lantern.

What the Bremers did to anger the underworld is unknown, but they did something. Edward Bremer's bank handled Harry Sawyer's finances as well as those of other St. Paul bootleggers, and according to FBI reports, Bremer had helped Sawyer fence stolen bonds, including, it was alleged, bonds Harvey Bailey stole from the Denver Mint in 1922. No doubt the dispute between Sawyer and Edward Bremer was financial. But Bremer's thorny personality may also have been a factor. As an FBI memo noted, "Bremer is very much disliked not only by his family but generally; he has an uncontrollable [*sic*] temper, is very selfish and inconsiderate and has few friends."

That frosty morning, after years of living in his father's shadow, Edward Bremer was about to become famous. A minute after dropping his daughter at her school, he pulled up to a stop sign at the corner of Goodrich and Lexington Parkway. As he did, Shotgun George Ziegler pulled his car into the intersection, blocking Bremer's way. Karpis stopped a second car behind Bremer's, boxing him in.

Dock Barker and Volney Davis jumped out. Dock opened Bremer's door and pointed his pistol at the young heir. "Don't move or I'll kill you."

Bremer panicked. He tried to throw the car into gear but Dock cracked him across the forehead with the pistol. Bremer attempted to escape out the passenger door, but Davis opened it first and joined Dock in hammering Bremer with his pistol. Bremer kicked open the door but Davis slammed it shut on his knee. The struggle took only a moment, but by the time Bremer surrendered, blood was streaming from a gash in his scalp. Karpis watched the tussle and fretted. "If a squad car pulls up," he mumbled, "we're going to have a hell of a lot of trouble here."

Finally Dock managed to shove Bremer down onto the front floorboard. Davis attempted to start the car, but nothing happened.

"No monkey business, start the car," Dock ordered Bremer.

Wiping the blood from his eyes, Bremer leaned up and pushed a button to start the car. As the car eased forward, Dock pushed a pair of goggles over Bremer's head, its eyes taped so Bremer couldn't see. No one had noticed the kidnapping; there was no pursuit. The little procession drove several miles into the countryside and pulled over to the side of the road. As he had done with Hamm, George Ziegler thrust two ransom notes forward for Bremer to sign. The young heir complained he was in great pain from the gash on his head and a wrenched knee. Karpis told him it was his own fault for struggling. "Well," Bremer said, "I got excited."

While Karpis took Bremer and drove south toward Chicago, Ziegler and Fred Barker took the ransom notes into St. Paul. Two hours after the kidnapping, Walter W. Magee, a contractor and a close friend of the Bremer family, took a phone call from a man who called himself "McKee." "Hello," McKee said. "We've snatched your friend Ed Bremer. We want two hundred grand."

"McKee" said Bremer's car would be found beneath a water tower on Edgecumbe Road. He said Magee would find a note with instructions beneath a staircase outside his office, then hung up. Magee walked outside and found the note. It read:

You are hereby **declared** in on a very **desperate** undertaking. Don't try to cross us. Your future and B's are the important issue. Follow these instructions to the letter. Police have never helped in such a spot and wont this time either. **You** better take care of the **payoff first** and **let them** do the **detecting later.** Because the police usually butt in your friend isn't none too comfortable now so don't delay the payment.

We demand $200,000.

Payment must be made in **5 and 10 dolar bills—no new money— no consegutive numbers—large variety of issues.**

Place the money in **two large suit box catons** big enough to hold the full amount and tie with heavy cord.

No contact will be made until you notify us that you are ready to pay as we direct.

You place an ad in the Minneapolis Tribune as soon as you have the money ready. Under personal colum (We are ready Alice)

You will then receive your **final instructions.** Be prepared **to leave at a minutes notice** to make the payoff.

Dont attempt to stall or outsmart us. Dont try to bargain. Don't plead poverty we know how much they have in their banks. Don't try to communecate with us we'll do the directing.

Threats arent necessary—**you just do your part**—we **guarantee** to do ours.

Magee phoned Bremer's office, thinking it might be a prank. He wasn't there. Magee then called the brewery and left a message for Adolph Bremer to meet him at the Ryan Hotel. The St. Paul police chief was notified, and at 11:05 he phoned Werner Hanni, the St. Paul SAC. Hanni walked straight to the hotel and found the Bremers talking with the chief, who had brought along the head of the kidnap squad, Tom Brown, who remained in league with the Barkers. Brown's presence meant the gang would know every move the police made.

The meeting was businesslike; Adolph Bremer was not the kind of man who panicked easily. He took Walter Magee to look for his son's car, and they found it after a half-hour's search. The front seat was streaked with blood, and Magee told Bremer not to approach. Magee had the car taken to a car wash, where the blood was removed—along with any fingerprints the gang might have left. Other members of the family, meanwhile, arranged for the "Alice" advertisement to run in the *Tribune.*

Night had fallen when Karpis drove up to the safe house in Bensenville, the same house where William Hamm had been kept seven months before. One of Ziegler's pals was waiting in the kitchen. They guided Bremer into a bedroom and sat him facing a boarded window.

They guarded him in shifts. Around eleven Karpis stuck his head in the kitchen, where Ziegler's friend, Harold Alderton, was listening to the radio. "Heard anything yet?" Karpis asked.

"Oh Christ, yeah," Alderton said. "This thing is going to be hot as hell."

"What do you mean?"

"They think this guy's dead. They found his car and it's full of blood, and according to the radio, they think he's been killed."

"Oh for Christ's sake," Karpis said. "This is going to be real bad."

St. Paul, Minnesota
Saturday, January 20

For two days members of the Bremer family paced Adolph Bremer's stone mansion across from the Schmidt Brewery, waiting anxiously for news from the kidnappers. The "Alice" ad had run Thursday morning; there had been no response. News of the kidnapping had leaked to the newspapers, and Thursday night Bremer had given a statement to reporters, promising the kidnappers that his family had no plans to cooperate in any police investigations. "We want to get Eddie back home safe," he said. FBI agents were posted at both Bremer homes.

Werner Hanni, the St. Paul SAC, tapped eighteen separate phone lines at the brewery and the Bremer homes. Hanni was so busy, in fact, he forgot to keep headquarters updated despite Hoover's repeated admonishments. "It appears that it is necessary for me to rely upon the press for information concerning important cases being investigated by the Division under my supervision," Hoover wrote Hanni after reading in the Washington *Post* of the blood found in Bremer's car. "With such explicit, definite and repeated instructions it is difficult for me to understand why you neglected, in a case of such significance as the present one, to fully advise me." Hoover's anger, stoked by pressure from the White House, grew through the weekend when Hanni failed to forward some paperwork. "Phone and tell him I want these at once and to stop quibbling and procrastinating," Hoover scrawled on one memo.

The family was deluged with phone calls and letters, many of them supportive, others from cranks. A postcard received that Friday stated that Edward Bremer had been killed and buried near the town of Anoka, Minnesota. Then, around six Saturday morning, H. T. Nippert, the Bremer family doctor, was in bed at his St. Paul home when he heard a crash downstairs. Thinking it was a fallen dish, he went back to sleep. An hour later, while he was shaving, his phone rang. "Go to the vestibule," said a voice. "See what you can find."

Downstairs Nippert discovered a bottle that had been thrown through his plate-glass front door. Beneath the door was an envelope containing three letters. One, written by Edward Bremer, directed him to take the other two to Adolph Bremer. Dr. Nippert drove to the Bremer mansion and disappeared with Bremer into the library. Neither man said a word to the FBI agent standing in the foyer, Edward Notesteen. Notesteen asked what was going on. He was told Adolph Bremer had suffered a mild heart attack. But ninety minutes later, when the elder Bremer emerged from the library, he seemed in perfect health.

Notesteen noticed an air of anxiety that seemed somehow different from concern for a son's safety. During several quiet talks with family members, he learned that what worried Adolph Bremer most was the amount of the ransom. Because of flagging investments, he was cash-poor at the moment; if forced to pay the entire $200,000, one family member confided, the Bremers might lose the brewery. Weeks later the FBI would learn that Adolph Bremer suspected the kidnapping had been arranged by the chairman of another St. Paul bank in an effort to cripple and take over Edward Bremer's First Commercial Bank.

The ransom payment was uppermost in Adolph Bremer's mind Saturday afternoon when he paid a visit to Minnesota governor Floyd Olson. That morning's note directed the family to place four blue NRA eagle stickers in Walter Magee's office windows when the ransom was ready to be paid. Bremer was candid with Olson about his finances, and the governor suggested displaying half a sticker, as a message to the kidnappers that the family sought to negotiate the ransom amount. Late that afternoon Magee posted the half-stickers.

The next day, Sunday, the FBI's second-in-command, Pop Nathan, met with Adolph Bremer and his financial advisers, a pair of New York bankers. Bremer asked Nathan whether he felt the kidnappers would accept only $50,000, which one of the bankers declared was an "outside figure." Nathan, who still knew nothing of the notes delivered by Dr. Nippert, said negotiations hadn't led to reduced ransoms in other cases. He emphasized that the Bureau would remain in the background until the ransom was paid, but that once Bremer was released, it would expect the family's full cooperation.

Monday morning another letter arrived at the Bremer mansion. It had been left outside the office of a local coal company executive.

> If you can wait O.K. with us. Your people shot a lot of curves trying to get somebody killed then the copper's will be heroes but Eddie will be the marteer. The copper's think that's great but Eddie don't.
>
> Were done taking the draws and you can go fuck yourself now. From now on **you** make the contact. **Better not try it** till you **pull off every coppers, newspaper and radio station.** From now on you get the **silent treatment** until you rech us someway **yourself.** Better not wait **too** long.

The note left Adolph Bremer confused. Contact the kidnappers? How? He was incensed at the St. Paul police. Too many details were leaking to the newspapers, which angered his son's captors, and he suspected someone in the department. He decided it was time to come clean with the FBI. He sent for Pop Nathan. When Nathan arrived at the mansion at three, Bremer took him into his mahogany-paneled library and briefed him on the notes from the kidnappers. Bremer handed all the notes to Nathan, who wrapped them in cellophane, took them to the Bureau's downtown office, and air-mailed them to Washington.

A half hour later, Nathan was handed a copy of the afternoon *St. Paul Daily News;* he was stunned to see that the lead article contained full details of the ransom notes. Nathan phoned the police chief, Dahill, and told him to meet him at his hotel room. Somewhere there was a leak, and a bad one, Nathan said. Dahill said he had no doubt who it was: Detective Tom Brown. And then Dahill went one step further. "It is my belief," he told Nathan, "that Tom Brown 'cased' both the Hamm and the Bremer kidnappings."[6]

At the safe house outside Chicago, tensions were rising. Unlike the stoic William Hamm, Ed Bremer was a complainer: he was cold, his head hurt, his knee hurt. It made Karpis tired. All day Bremer sat in front of a boarded window, the taped goggles over his eyes. The Hamm job had lasted four days, and Karpis couldn't fathom why things were dragging on. At one point he asked Bremer.

"Well, I'd have to know how much money you're asking for first," Bremer said.

"I ain't having anything to do with that," Karpis said. "It shouldn't be too much trouble getting the money, don't you think?"

"It depends on how much."

"Goddamn, your family's the richest in the Northwest, what do you mean, 'depends on how much'? How much money is in that bank?"

"Sometimes we have twenty-five or thirty thousand dollars in there," Bremer said. "That's at the peak of the business month."

"Supposing we were to turn you loose," Karpis said. "Would you go in and get this money and bring it back for us?"

Bremer got excited when Karpis talked this way. He suggested several schemes to raise money; at one point, to Karpis's dismay, he named a wealthy St. Paul railroad executive he felt could be kidnapped. In an effort to bond with his captors, Bremer was candid about his own dealings with the underworld. He talked openly about how he had fenced Harvey Bailey's stolen bonds. At one point, he asked Karpis whether he knew Harry Sawyer or his partner, Jack Peifer. Karpis said no.

"Well," Bremer said, "they run the town and if you find out who they are, then you'll find out who I am. You just ask them about me and how many times I've handled hot bonds for them. I'm a good guy. If you guys had come to me first instead of kidnapping me, you'd have made more money by kidnapping somebody else that I told you about."

"Well, let's wait and see first if we get that $25,000 you're talking about," Karpis said. "Maybe we'll get forty."

Bremer became glum. "I don't think they can pay that much."

One night Freddie and George Ziegler arrived unannounced from St. Paul. They were tired and frustrated. They had seen the eagle stickers split in two, and concluded that the Bremers wanted to pay only half the ransom. "I don't know what the hell to tell you," Ziegler said. "That town is so hot, every time we try to get a note to them people, the G beats us to it. Every time we try to phone and tell them where there's a note, the G's listening in. They just don't want to make the payoff, they don't want anything. Did you hear what Roosevelt had to say?"

"The president?" Karpis asked.

In a radio address, Roosevelt had termed the Bremer kidnapping "an attack on all we hold dear." "Yeah," Ziegler said, "he brought it up about Bremer being a friend of his and that he would see to it that this crime wasn't going to go unpunished. This is the hottest goddamn thing since the Lindbergh kidnapping."

"Well, what do you think about them paying the money, or turning him loose without any money?"

"No, no, no," Ziegler said. "We'd never be any hotter than we are right now, whether we get the money or not. Don't tell them other guys I said this, but we're gonna be in big trouble after this is over with. This might even turn out worse if we have to kill the guy."

As the days passed, Karpis grew steadily more depressed. At best he was a babysitter with a machine gun. At worst he would be an assassin. This, he thought, was not why he became a thief.

Tucson, Arizona, a sun-baked desert city of thirty thousand people, was about as far from the Dillinger Gang's Midwestern roots as they were likely to get. After the long drive from St. Louis, Dillinger arrived that Sunday a changed man, the hubris he had displayed in East Chicago knocked from his personality as if by a punch. The shoot-out on the sidewalk that day taught him a lesson, to take fewer chances, to live more quietly; there would be no more nights machine-gunning the moon.

Dillinger and Billie found the others already enjoying the city's tequila-fueled nightclubs and whorehouses.* Russell Clark was staying with Charles Makley at the city's premier place of lodging, the Congress Hotel. Makley had hooked up with a torch singer, and everyone was having a grand time. Dillinger and Billie checked into a tourist court on South Sixth Street, registering as "Mr. and Mrs. Frank Sullivan" of Green Bay, Wisconsin. A few hours later Pete Pierpont and Mary Kinder drove in as well, after several days visiting family around Albuquerque.

To the men of the Dillinger gang, whose lives to that point had been confined to Midwestern farms and jail cells, Tucson seemed like another planet. Men wore cowboy hats and boots. Mariachi music floated through the evening air. There were mountains and cacti and rattlesnakes; downtown, there were hitching posts on the sidewalks. It was like visiting the set of a Western; Chicago seemed a world away.

It was intoxicating, and it made them careless. On his first afternoon

---

* Dillinger's cross-country drive may not have been uneventful. According to FBI files, he received a traffic ticket in Albuquerque.

driving the streets, Pierpont inexplicably stopped to chat with a pair of policemen. He introduced himself as a Florida vacationer, then pointed out a car and told the officers he thought he was being followed. One of the cops chatted with Pierpont while the other followed the strange car. Pierpont proudly showed him his new Buick's appointments, the speedometer, the power steering. They talked about the desert weather, getting so friendly Pierpont volunteered the name of the place he was staying. When the second officer returned he said the other car was harmless. With a wave and a thank-you, Pierpont drove off. All in all, it was a perfectly idiotic thing to do.

Days they spent sightseeing, nights in the clubs. Things went smoothly until Tuesday morning around six, when a leaky oil furnace in the Congress Hotel's basement caught fire. Flames leaped up the elevator shaft, and the building was soon wreathed in smoke. Firefighters arrived within minutes, and one, William Benedict, was puzzled to see two men propping a ladder against a third-floor window. It was Makley and Clark, who explained they were trying to retrieve their luggage. Once the fire was under control, Benedict went upstairs to Room 329, kicked down the door, and brought out a heavy fabric box. Unbeknownst to Benedict, it contained Makley and Clark's submachine guns. Makley thanked him profusely and tipped him two dollars.

Three days passed. On Friday morning, January 25, the fireman who had helped Makley and Clark, William Benedict, was leafing through an issue of *True Detective* magazine when there, staring up at him from the page, was the "Mr. Davies" whose luggage he had rescued from Room 329. When a deputy sheriff drove by, Benedict hollered and showed him the magazine. By lunchtime Benedict's story was making the rounds at police headquarters. It struck a chord with a patrolman named Harry Lesly, who had heard a strange story from a pair of tourists that same morning. The night before the hotel fire, the tourists said, they had shared a few drinks at a nightclub with a man who introduced himself as Art Long. Mr. Long, actually Russell Clark, had a few too many tequilas, and was soon telling the pair how easy it was to weather the Depression if a person could use a submachine gun. The two noticed that the men in Mr. Long's party appeared to be wearing shoulder holsters.

The two stories sent detectives thumbing through Wanted posters. "Mr. Davies," it turned out, perfectly matched a photo of Charles Makley. A patrolman telephoned the Hotel Congress and learned that Mr. Davies's luggage had been taken to a rented bungalow on East Second Street. By 1:30

that afternoon three Tucson policemen were sitting in a squad car watching the house. Not long after they arrived, Makley walked out to his Studebaker with his torch-singer girlfriend. As he pulled away from the curb, the squad car slid out behind him.

The three policemen followed the car into downtown Tucson, where it parked outside the Grabe Electric Company. The cops walked inside, found Makley standing at a counter, and told him he was under arrest. Makley protested, saying he was a vacationing Florida businessman. An officer told him he could explain the mix-up downtown.

At the station, Makley was led into Chief C. A. Wollard's office.

"What's your name?" Wollard asked.

"J. C. Davies," Makley said. "Come up to my house. I can clear this up in a minute. All of my papers are there."

The chief, eyeing Makley's mug shot, said he needed to fingerprint him. Makley objected.

"Well, Makley," Wollard said, "we're gonna fingerprint you whether you like it or not." He was thrown in a cell.

One down, three to go. The chief called in three of his best men, Sergeants Frank Eyman and Dallas Ford and a detective named Chet Sherman. Somewhere in Tucson, Wollard suspected, the rest of the Dillinger Gang was hiding. Making sure the three studied photographs of the other gang members, he told them to keep Makley's Second Street bungalow under surveillance. Maybe someone would show.

The three officers were soon parked outside Makley's bungalow. They had been watching the house for a little over an hour when they began to grow impatient. The least they could do, they agreed, was check whether anyone was inside. They came up with an easy ruse. Detective Sherman got out of the car and walked toward the house, taking a letter from his jacket pocket. On the porch, he rang the bell. A woman opened the door. It was Russell Clark's girlfriend, Opal Long.

"Yes?" she asked.

Thrusting the letter forward, Sherman said he had a delivery. When she reached for the letter, Sherman threw his shoulder against the door and stepped inside. There he came face-to-face with Russell Clark. Sherman drew his service revolver and ordered Clark to raise his hands. Instead Clark lunged for the gun, grabbing it by the barrel. The two men wrestled for the pistol, whirling in circles through the living room and into a bedroom. Outside, spying the commotion, Detectives Eyman and Ford broke into a run, bounding up the front steps. Opal Long saw them coming and slammed the door, just as Ford thrust his hand forward; the door shut on his finger, breaking a bone.

Sergeant Ford kicked the door open, knocked Long aside, and burst into the bedroom to find Clark and Sherman grappling on a bed. Clark was reaching for a pillow when Ford brained him with his pistol. Sergeant Eyman grabbed Clark's shoulder and pulled him off the bed. In moments they had him in handcuffs. Beneath the pillow they found a .38. A further search turned up two Thompson submachine guns, an automatic rifle, two pistols, two bulletproof vests, and $4,526.68 in cash. The three officers bundled Clark and Long into a car and took them downtown. No one thought to remain at the house.

Two down, two to go. Downtown, Chief Wollard canvassed his men. Dillinger and Pierpont had to be out there; if they learned of the arrests before the police located them, they could melt into the desert within minutes. The chief's instincts were dead-on. As he spoke, Pierpont arrived at Makley's bungalow. Walking up the steps, he noticed drops of what appeared to be blood on the porch. He jogged to his car, drove back to his tourist cabin, and told Mary Kinder to start packing.

As the couple packed, a patrolman walked into Chief Wollard's office and mentioned the friendly Florida tourist he had encountered a few days earlier. The description matched Pierpont. The chief dispatched Sergeant Eyman and two patrolmen to check out the tourist camp where the "Florida tourist" had said he was staying. Just as the three men drove up, they spotted Pierpont driving off in his new Buick. The three lawmen followed the car for several blocks, discussing how to proceed. They decided to stage a routine traffic stop; maybe they could take Pierpont unprepared. Honking their horn, Sergeant Eyman waved for Pierpont to pull over. He complied. The sergeant stepped out.

"How do you do," Eyman announced. "May I please see your driver's license?"

Pierpont handed over the license—a fake—and Eyman looked it over. He handed it back and apologized, pointing out that Pierpont didn't have a visitor's inspection sticker on his car, as the law required. It was no trouble to get one, Eyman went on. If Pierpont could just drive down to the police station, he could have a sticker within minutes. Outnumbered, Pierpont had to agree. "I'll even ride down with you," Eyman volunteered, sliding into the backseat.

Pierpont adjusted his rearview mirror to keep an eye on Eyman as he drove downtown. Eyman kept up a stream of happy chatter as they went, going on about Tucson's beautiful weather. Pierpont nodded a lot and smiled. Mary Kinder sat frozen. Slowly Sergeant Eyman drew his gun and slid it between his legs, out of sight. He took out a pack of cigarettes and offered one to Pierpont. He declined.

At the station, Sergeant Eyman led Pierpont and Kinder down a flight of stairs to Chief Wollard's office. The guns collected from Makley and Clark lay spread across the chief's desk, and the second Pierpont entered the ruse was blown. Instinctively he reached for the gun in his shoulder holster. But Eyman was too fast. He drew his gun and said, "Drop it!" Pierpont went for his gun anyway. Eyman and two other officers tackled him, and the group fell to the floor in a heap.

"Drop that gun!" Eyman shouted. "Or I'll kill you!"

Pierpont went slack. An officer vigorously twisted his arm while the others searched him. "You're treating me pretty rough, aren't you?" Pierpont said, forcing a smile.

"What do you want us to do? Kiss you?" Eyman said.

Three down, one to go. John Dillinger was somewhere in Tucson; the police were sure of it. Night was approaching. With no clues to work on, officers kept watch on the Makley bungalow and the Sixth Street motor court. A squat Irish detective named James Herron and two uniformed policemen drew up to the bungalow. The sun was just beginning to set as they parked out front. The two officers slipped into the house through the back door. Detective Herron circled back to move his car, thinking it might scare Dillinger off should he appear.

Just then a shiny new Hudson sedan rounded the corner and parked in front of the house. Herron shrank behind a bush as a man in a brown suit got out and approached the front porch, leaving a woman sitting in the front seat. Herron stepped from behind the bush just as the man lifted his foot to climb the steps. As he did the man paused, looking down at the bloodstains. He whirled, as if to run to his car—and came face-to-face with Detective Herron.

Dillinger and Herron stood five feet apart on the front lawn. It was a moment out of the Wild West. Herron drew first, a pistol appearing in his right hand. "Put up your hands!" he ordered.

Dillinger stared. Herron stepped forward and jammed his pistol into his ribs. "Up with those hands or I'll bore you!" he snapped.

Dillinger slowly raised his hands.

"What's this all about?" he asked.

Just then the two officers materialized on the front porch.

"Cover the car!" Herron said.

As the two officers hustled past, Herron grabbed Dillinger by the coat and shoved him forward. It was then that Dillinger realized he could not fake his way free. He went for the gun in his shoulder holster. Herron jabbed his pistol deeply into his back and one of the officers poked a riot gun in his face. Dillinger gave up.

Game, set, match, Tucson police.

The arrests in Tucson were front-page news across the country. The next day crowds of the curious swarmed the Pima County Jail, where the four gang members and their girlfriends were kept under guard. Chief Wollard's office was inundated with telegrams and phone messages. Out at the airport, every arriving plane disgorged a stream of reporters and photographers from Chicago, New York, and other cities. Every time a cop left the jail, he ran a gauntlet of flashing cameras.

At 10:00 that morning, all seven of the prisoners were led in shackles into a packed courtroom to be arraigned. Dillinger glumly slumped in a chair. "Stand up," the judge ordered.

"I ain't Dillinger," Dillinger mumbled. A bailiff yanked him to his feet. The gang members were ordered held on $100,000 bail each. Flashbulbs popped madly as the prisoners were led out of the courtroom. Billie smiled at Dillinger, who smiled back. He leaned over and kissed her.

That afternoon a steady procession of reporters, politicians, and policemen filed by the gang's jail cells, ogling the infamous gangsters from the distant Midwest as if they were monkeys in a zoo. Dillinger warmed to the attention, finally admitting his identity and playing his favorite role of gregarious, big-time bank robber.

"I'm an expert in my business," he told a group of scribbling reporters hovering at his cell. "I can play tag with the police any time. They just dodge around on old trails like fox hounds that don't know what's going on. And the dumbest ones in the world are the Chicago kind. Right now none of these smart-aleck coppers have got a bit of evidence that I killed anybody or robbed any bank."

The others took their cue from Dillinger, smiling and mugging for the cameras. Pete Pierpont actually traded wisecracks with the governor of Arizona. "These cops out here ain't like the ones in Indiana," Pierpont joked. "They pull too fast for us."

The giddy mood ebbed when the reporters left. By Sunday morning, when delegations of prosecutors from Ohio, Wisconsin, and Indiana arrived in Tucson to argue for extraditions, the gang members were in no mood for chitchat. At the sight of Matt Leach, who had briefly jailed his mother that fall, Pierpont flew into a rage.

"I should have killed you when I had the chance, you dirty son of a bitch!" he shouted. "You put my mother in jail . . . If I ever get out of this the first thing I'm gonna do is kill you, you rat!"

Leach regarded Pierpont for a moment, then turned to a reporter. "There's a man who really loves his mother," he said. When he reached Dillinger's cell, Leach extended his hand through the bars.

Dillinger hesitated, then shook it.

"Well, we meet again, John," Leach said. He took a step back and studied Dillinger a moment, then complimented him on the mustache he had grown. Leach asked if he was ready to return to Indiana.

"I'm in no hurry," Dillinger said. "I haven't a thing to do when I get there."[7]

Once again, it appeared Dillinger's career was over. In fact, it had barely begun.

9

A STAR IS BORN

January 30 to March 2, 1934

The plane carrying Dillinger touched down at Chicago's Midway Airport at 6:10 on a dark and snowy Tuesday evening, January 30. It had been a long flight, the outlaw's first. His departure from Tucson followed a spirited two-day struggle between lawyers from Wisconsin, Indiana, and Ohio, each making the case to prosecute the gang first. In the end, Arizona's governor ordered Dillinger to Indiana to stand trial for Detective O'Malley's murder in East Chicago; if convicted, he faced the electric chair. Pierpont, Makley, Clark, and Mary Kinder were sent to Ohio to answer for Sheriff Sarber's murder; Kinder was later released. Billie Frechette and Opal Long went free. They took a bus to Chicago.

Dillinger hadn't gone quietly. After a circuslike day that Monday in which crowds of onlookers were allowed into the jail to see him, deputies had to drag him from his cell. "They're not taking you to Indiana!" Pierpont shouted. "They're putting you on the spot, boy!" Dillinger wrestled as his wrists were handcuffed. "You're shanghaiing me!" he barked. "They can't take me east without a hearing!"

In Chicago, Dillinger descended the airplane stairs into a throng of photographers and eighty-five members of the Chicago Police Department—"a reception such as had never been accorded a criminal in Chicago," noted the *Chicago Tribune*. As flashbulbs popped and reporters strained to get a glimpse, two officers shoved Dillinger into the back of a car.[1]

The Chicago police, many outfitted with submachine guns and bullet-proof vests, took no chances. Thirteen cars and a dozen motorcyclists, sirens blaring, made up the caravan that wound its way out of the airport into city streets lined with the curious. Across the border into northwest Indiana, the procession headed for the town of Crown Point, the seat of Lake County, where Dillinger was to be tried. A crowd of reporters and photographers was waiting outside the Lake County Jail when Dillinger arrived at 7:40 P.M.

Inside, Dillinger was led into Sheriff Lillian Holley's office. Mrs. Holley had become sheriff upon the murder of the previous sheriff, her husband; her inexperience would soon become an issue. Thirty reporters followed, jamming inside as they yelled questions.

"Are you glad to see Indiana again?" someone asked.

"About as glad as Indiana is to see me," Dillinger said, chewing a wad of gum. He seemed utterly unfazed by the crowd.

"You're credited with having smuggled the guns into the Indiana State Penitentiary just before the big outbreak of September 26," a reporter said.

Dillinger grinned. "I'm not denying it," he said.

"How did you get them in?" a reporter yelled.

A smile creased Dillinger's face.

"You're too inquisitive," he said.

Reporters traded glances. This was something new, a headline-making criminal with charm, a bank robber who could crack wise on his way to the electric chair. A Lake County prosecutor, Robert Estill, who had accompanied Dillinger from Arizona and experienced firsthand his disarming friendliness, was standing beside him. A photographer yelled for Estill to put his arm around Dillinger; forgetting himself for one fateful moment, Estill did. As flashbulbs popped, Dillinger propped his elbow on the prosecutor's shoulder. The resulting photograph was widely reproduced around the country. It outraged many people, including J. Edgar Hoover, who publicly condemned Estill for fraternizing with a man he was scheduled to prosecute.

Sensing a friendly crowd, Dillinger freely unspooled his life story. "I was just an unfortunate boy," Dillinger said. "Back in Mooresville, the old hometown, I got drunk ten years ago and held up a grocery. I got $550 and then I got caught . . . In the prison I met a lot of good fellas. I wanted to help them out. There's no denying that I helped fix up the break at Michigan City last September, when ten men got away. Why not? I stick to my friends and they stick to me."

One could sense the reporters' excitement as Dillinger spoke. "How long does it take you to go through a bank?" someone asked. Dillinger chuckled. "One minute and forty seconds flat," he said.

The unhurried way he chewed his gum, the easy quips, the lopsided grin, the poise, the obvious charisma—it all made a powerful impression on a group of reporters accustomed to tight-faced syndicate gangsters. But then John Dillinger, more than any other Depression-era criminal, had star quality. "He had none of the look of the conventional killer—none of the advertised earmarks of the crook," a starstruck *Chicago Daily News* reporter wrote the next day. "Given a little more time and a wider circle of acquaintances, one can see that he might presently become the central figure of a nationwide campaign, largely female, to prevent his frying in the electric chair for the murder of Policeman Patrick O'Malley." The *Daily News* went on:

John Dillinger stood there in his shirt sleeves, his soft collar open at the throat, as informally as if he had been talking over crop reports with a visitor to his father's farm, the farm from which he came many years ago in Mooresville, Ind. His diction was amazing—better in many instances than that of his interviewers—his poise no less so.

His hands, freed of manacles for the first time in many hours, hung at his sides. His weight rested as prescribed in the military formula upon the balls of his feet. His chin jutted forward, the muscles of his face working as he chewed his gum between strong jaws.

It was difficult to realize that here was one of the most ruthless killers of a period that has produced plenty of them. There was no hint of hardness about him save for the set of his mouth—no evidence save in the alert presence of armed policemen that he had spent his formative years in a penitentiary. He had none of the sneer, the blatant toughness of the criminal . . . The whole business seemed to be a joke to him . . .

One versed in the ways of gunmen, looking at him for the first time, can hardly realize that in a very few days, a month or two at the outside, this cheery, affable young man will probably be a corpse, and a very good one. For, though the finger is definitely on Mr. Dillinger, he rates in the eyes of calloused observers as the most amazing specimen of his kind ever seen outside of a wildly imaginative moving picture.

For a national press that uniformly painted criminals as "rats" and "cold-blooded killers," this and similar reviews were unprecedented. It was

a turning point in Dillinger's career, the moment he molted the skin of a re-
gionally notorious yegg and emerged as a true national figure, an accessible,
amiable, down-to-earth fellow, someone Northern audiences, unaccustomed to identifying with criminals, would soon find themselves rooting
for. No less an organ than the *New York Times* took note of the spectacle,
noting that Dillinger's appearance came off "as a modern version of the return of the Prodigal son."

The half hour Dillinger spent joshing with reporters in the Crown Point
jail set the tone for all the press coverage of his coming exploits: Dillinger
the accidental yegg, the misunderstood farm boy, the loyal friend who had
robbed banks only to help his pals. Dillinger seemed to understand how
well he was doing that night and cannily played it for sympathy. "I am not
a bad fellow, ladies and gentlemen," he said as deputies finally led him
away. "I was just an unfortunate boy who started wrong." The *Tribune*
noted the next morning, "something like a tear glistened in one eye as [the]
interviewers left." It was the performance of a lifetime.

For seven days the Bremer family paced the hallways of the family mansion,
waiting for word from the kidnappers. By Saturday, February 3, they were
desperate. Several feared Edward was dead.

That morning the FBI's Pop Nathan received a summons to the Lowry
Hotel suite of Adolph Bremer's New York bankers. The two bankers told
Nathan the family was preparing to make one final appeal to the kidnappers. The catalyst was not just a concern for Edward's life, but pressure
from the newspapers. Several reporters told of disquieting rumors that
might find their way into print. One rumor was that Edward Bremer's bank
was failing; it was suggested that he faked the kidnapping to extort money
from his father to save it. Another concerned a supposed swindle of a man
named Wunderlich, who had for some reason blamed Edward Bremer for
his losses and kidnapped him.

The two bankers showed Nathan a letter Adolph Bremer planned to
read to the press. Nathan objected only to a line that promised that the
family wouldn't cooperate with the FBI. "I told them that the Division
would never tolerate any such situation," Nathan wrote Hoover.[2] The bankers ignored him.

Sunday afternoon Adolph Bremer walked out his front door and handed
the statement to reporters. In it he candidly warned the kidnappers not to

attempt to contact the family directly, since their phones were tapped. Instead he suggested they try some new intermediary; the Bremer family would then deliver the ransom.

"[I]f the following suggestions are carried out I will have no interest in any activity after my son is returned," Bremer said. "If I have not heard from Edward within three days and three nights, I shall understand that you do not wish to deal with me and I will feel I am released from any obligations as contained in this note."

In Washington, Adolph Bremer's appeal enraged Hoover. At the safe house in the Chicago suburb of Bensenville, it cheered the gang. Fred Barker ordered Edward Bremer to write two more notes to his father and a pair of intermediaries he had suggested. "If we get the money this time, good," Barker told Karpis afterward. "If we don't we'd better forget it and that guy's had it."

The next evening, Monday, February 5, the game was renewed. Around seven-thirty Lillian Dickman, a cashier at Edward Bremer's bank, was sitting in her parents' home on Cortland Street in St. Paul when she heard a knock at her backdoor. On the doorstep was a man.

"Are you Lillian Dickman?" he asked.

"Yes," she said.

He handed her two envelopes. Dickman hurried to Adolph Bremer's mansion and handed them to him. In one was another handwritten appeal from Edward for his father to pay the ransom.* "Now please do just as the boys instruct you to & don't waste any time. The sooner the better," Bremer wrote. "Pa I'm relying on you this is most unbearable. Its just a living hell. I'm trying the best that's in me to fight it through so I can see you . . . again."

---

* Bremer's note to Dickman read,

Dear Lil: As my old standby I am calling on you to do something for me that it seems no-one else can do. I must get the enclosed letter to my father—unopened—& I know if I intrust it in your case it will be done. I suppose you know that my father has made a special appeal to everybody police & government officers included to lay off for three days so that he can make his own arrangements to get me back. Now the next thing is—is to get the instructions to him—& your old pal will not fail me I know . . .

  Please girl hurry—but don't loose your head—I know you wont & I'm sure you'll do just as I ask you to do. We always did understand each other.

  It's a living hell here & the time I've been here seems like ages. Please do your part & I'm assured I'll be home soon. Please hurry & be careful

As always
ED

There was also a typewritten letter from the kidnappers. It promised they would make one last attempt to receive the ransom. Instructions were to follow. An hour after the notes were passed to Adolph Bremer, one of his bankers knocked on Pop Nathan's door at the St. Paul Hotel. To avoid reporters, the two men sneaked down a fire escape to a suite where Bremer was waiting. He needed Nathan's word that the FBI wouldn't interfere in delivery of the ransom. Nathan said it wouldn't. For the moment, the Bremers were on their own.

Crown Point, Indiana
Monday, February 5
2:00 P.M.

Dillinger shuffled into the courtroom, his hands and feet in shackles, a grin on his face. The Lake County Criminal Courts Building was lined with forty deputies for his initial hearing. The newspapers were carrying reports of rumors that John Hamilton, the only gang member still at large, would stage a raid to rescue Dillinger, and deputies searched everyone who entered the courtroom. Hundreds crowded the hallways, straining to get a look at the prisoner.

Dillinger, wearing a blue shirt and the vest of his blue serge suit, listened quietly as a one-armed attorney his father had hired, Joseph Ryan, argued for more time to prepare his case. Ryan spoke in a low voice, so low many struggled to hear him. From Dillinger's body language, he seemed unimpressed with his representation. Judge William Murray listened and gave Ryan four days. Dillinger would be arraigned on Friday, February 9.

Among the spectators that afternoon was a white-haired forty-nine-year-old Chicago attorney named Louis Piquett. Piquett was a caricature of the gangland mouthpiece, a melodramatic, arm-waving former bartender who worked his way through Democratic circles to become Chicago's chief prosecutor in the early 1920s until his indictment on corruption charges in 1923, charges that were later dropped. In Piquett's private practice, his clients were the scum of syndicate Chicago, abortionists, bootleggers, and killers; in his spare time, Piquett engaged in a variety of minor stock market swindles. Like a host of Chicago criminal-defense attorneys, he saw Dillinger as a ticket to fame, and he had managed to have one of his cards slipped to him the week before. When Dillinger sent word he would meet him, the two met twice inside the jail. They were perfunctory conversations, both men feeling each other out, and ended when Dillinger's father hired Joe Ryan.

After the hearing Monday afternoon, the head jailer, Lewis Baker, took Piquett aside: Dillinger wanted to see him. They met in a cell at the jail. Worried their conversation might be overheard, Piquett loudly tapped a coin throughout their talk. Gone was the cocky front Dillinger had erected for reporters. Here was a man worried about the electric chair. "Mr. Piquett," Dillinger said, "I can't have that fellow Ryan. My God, he's going to send me to the hot seat! He all but convicted me just in asking for a continuance."

"Ryan's all right," Piquett said.

"I want you to represent me. How about it?"

"I'll be frank with you," Piquett said. "It's going to cost you money."

"All right."

Dillinger said he could raise the lawyer's fee, and Piquett agreed to represent him.[3] Piquett quickly became, in every way imaginable, the most important person in John Dillinger's life. Publicly, he became Dillinger's principal defender, the flamboyant leader of the burgeoning John Dillinger admiration society. But it was behind closed doors that Piquett was to serve Dillinger most ably, doing everything from ferrying secret messages to fielding book offers. Dillinger's relationship with Piquett, and with Piquett's investigator, an easygoing mook named Arthur O'Leary, became the foundation upon which the outlaw's future exploits would be built. In time the two became his secret partners, his enablers, fixers who handled his every need.*

For now, Piquett returned to his Chicago office and got to work preparing for Dillinger's trial. It was to be the high point of his legal career; it would bring him untold fame and fortune. And it would never happen.

---

* The role Piquett and O'Leary played in Dillinger's story was not fully understood until the 1990 discovery of an unpublished manuscript written by a Chicago advertising man and would-be novelist named Russell Girardin. The manuscript's unveiling was a story in itself. In late 1934, Girardin secured the cooperation of both Piquett and O'Leary for a book he hoped to write about Dillinger. They told him everything, supplying dates and affidavits to back up their assertions, but Girardin was never able to publish more than a series of truncated magazine articles. His manuscript lay forgotten on a shelf in his Chicago home for five decades until, at the age of eighty-nine, he was tracked down by two Dillinger enthusiasts, William Helmer and Joseph Pinkston. The Girardin manuscript sheds a swath of new light on Dillinger's story; many of its key points can be confirmed in newly released FBI documents.

St. Paul, Minnesota
4:30 P.M.

Father Deere, a Catholic priest who lived outside St. Paul, answered a knock on his door at 4:30 that afternoon. A man with sunken eyes and a pasty complexion stood on his doorstep.

"Are you Father Deere?" he asked.

"Yes."

"Can you get to St. Paul by six o'clock?"

"Yes."

The man thrust an envelope into the priest's hands, then walked out to a waiting brown sedan and was driven off. Father Deere, an acquaintance of the Bremer family, saw that the envelope was addressed to Adolph Bremer. He returned inside and picked up the phone.

By 6:00 the envelope was in Adolph Bremer's hands. It contained detailed instructions for delivery of the ransom. The money, $200,000 in small bills whose serial numbers the FBI had recorded, had been loaded into two suit boxes. A little after seven the boxes were loaded into Walter Magee's car at the brewery. Worried about being robbed, Magee drove through backstreets to the spot on University Avenue where, as the kidnappers' note promised, he found a parked Chevrolet coupe. Shell Oil signs were bolted to the front doors, giving it the appearance of a company car. Magee slid behind the wheel of the Chevrolet. He noticed that the windows had been clouded with some kind of chemical that made it difficult for him to see out.

In the left-door pocket Magee found the keys and a typewritten note. Following its instructions, he drove to the town of Farmington, twenty miles south of St. Paul, where he pulled up to the bus station. The bus to Rochester left at 9:15. Magee fell in behind it. He followed the bus through the towns of Cannon Falls and Zumbrota, pulling over when the bus stopped to disgorge passengers. Then, four miles south of Zumbrota, Magee saw the four red lights on a hill above the highway. He hit the brakes. Three hundred feet farther, just as the instructions promised, there was a dirt road. Magee turned into it.

Magee inched down the darkened road. About a half mile later, a car materialized behind him and flashed its headlights five times. Magee got out, walked around to the passenger door, took out the two suit boxes, and placed them on the road. Then he got back in the car and drove forward, eventually reaching the small town of Mazeppa.

Wednesday, February 7

Fred Barker was wearing a huge smile when he reached the safe house outside of Chicago the next morning. "We got it!" Barker shouted as they lugged the suit boxes into the kitchen.

"How much did you get?" Karpis asked.

"We got the whole thing," Barker said. "Two hundred thousand dollars."

It fell to Karpis to return Bremer. They forced him to shave and gave him a new suit of clothes to wear. Karpis explained to Bremer that he had read an article that outlined how the FBI could retrieve fingerprints from clothing, and he wanted to ensure Bremer returned with nothing they had handled. They burned his old clothes, even his underwear. Bremer asked for his garters back, but Karpis refused.

At nightfall they threw a handkerchief over Bremer's head and led him to the Buick they had parked in the alley. Karpis drove, Dock Barker beside him in the front seat, Bremer pushed down on the rear floorboards. In central Wisconsin they found a gasoline cache Fred Barker had laid. Karpis held the funnel while Dock poured the contents of the first can into the Buick's tank. In the darkness his hand slipped and the ice-cold gas splashed inside his glove. "Jesus Christ, don't you know you got me half froze?" Karpis said, shaking his hand.

"Well, I got it on my gloves, too," Dock said.

Dock took one of his gloves off while he poured the second can. "Goddamn, you ought to keep your gloves on," Karpis said.

"I got gasoline in one of 'em."

"That don't make no difference, goddamnit, you might leave some prints or something."

"Well, nobody'll find the cans anyway. Even if they did, they wouldn't know we used 'em." Karpis was too cold to argue.

They drove through the night to Rochester, Minnesota, pulling up behind a downtown building about eight o'clock. Dock pushed some bills into Bremer's fist, guided him out of the car, and told him to count to fifteen before taking off his blindfold. Shivering, Bremer began to count. "We haven't left," he heard a voice say. "Start again."

On the drive back to Chicago, Dock was almost giddy. "I guess you're going to take Delores now with your end of the money and go to Florida, ain't you?" Dock kidded Karpis, who remained glum.

"You know something, Dock?" Karpis replied. "We're a long way from spending any of that money."

St. Paul, Minnesota
Thursday, February 8

The last of the well-wishers left the Bremer mansion around midnight. In the darkness Adolph Bremer walked across the street to the brewery to do some work. Agent S. L. Fortenberry was sitting on the side porch when he heard a tapping sound at the outside door. Fortenberry opened it, and Edward Bremer staggered inside, ashen and shaking.

Agent Fortenberry ran across the street and retrieved Adolph Bremer from the brewery. Back at the mansion, there were hugs and smiles and tears. Agent Fortenberry asked "for the privilege" of calling Pop Nathan to break the news. Edward insisted he couldn't. He had promised the kidnappers nothing would appear in the morning papers. Both Bremers prevailed upon Fortenberry to wait until dawn to notify the Bureau. Reluctantly he agreed. Edward Bremer downed two fast glasses of beer before the words came spilling out. When he finished, Agent Fortenberry asked if he could identify any of his captors. "I know it sounds unreasonable," Bremer said, "but they kept me for twenty-two days and I never got a look at one of them."

Bremer repeatedly told his father "they could not have anything to do with prosecution," as Agent Fortenberry later reported in a memo. The kidnappers had threatened his wife and child. Finally, around three, sleepy and exhausted, Edward Bremer went to bed. The moment he disappeared upstairs, Fortenberry went for the phone.

Friday morning Nathan telephoned Edward Bremer's doctor, who agreed that Bremer could be interviewed, but only for a half hour, at 2:00. After notifying Washington, Nathan headed to Adolph Bremer's mansion, where he found a family meeting under way in the kitchen. Adolph Bremer asked Nathan what he thought about Edward's insistence that he couldn't identify the kidnappers. Nathan termed it "bunk and worthless from a standpoint of investigative aid." Adolph urged Nathan to "go easy" on his son. He was fragile. He would be better in a few days. Nathan said he didn't have a few days. Every day they lost, the evidence was growing colder.

At two Nathan saw Edward Bremer. He found him frightened and deeply ambivalent about cooperating with authorities. "The police are okay," Bremer said, "but I have no use for federal agents." Nathan asked what he meant; Bremer waved him off, saying he was just joking. Now it was Nathan's turn to get irritated. He told Bremer it was obvious he wasn't telling everything he knew. Bremer bridled. He insisted he couldn't identify any of his captors, saying he "didn't see a darned soul." Afterward Nathan returned downtown, incensed. He was convinced Edward Bremer was hiding something.

That Friday morning, while Pop Nathan grappled with Edward Bremer, Louis Piquett took center stage at Dillinger's arraignment in Crown Point. It was another packed courtroom, the walls lined with deputies holding submachine guns, reporters scribbling, flashbulbs popping. In the crowd were two of the Arizona cops who arrested Dillinger. Both said they were mulling movie and vaudeville offers, but were holding out for more money.[4]

The moment Judge Murray quieted the crowd, Piquett was on his feet. "Your Honor!" Piquett thundered. "Are we to have a hearing in accord with the spirit of the laws of this state and of this nation, or are we to witness merely a mockery of the name of justice? Is the state to be permitted to continue inciting an atmosphere of prejudice and hatred? The very air reeks with the bloody rancor of intolerant malice. The clanging of shackles brings to our minds the dungeons of the czars, not the flag-bedecked liberty of an American courtroom. I request the court to direct that those shackles be removed."

It was vintage Piquett, melodramatic and bellicose. The prosecutor, Robert Estill, was no match. "This is a very dangerous man, Your Honor," he said.

"Remove the handcuffs from the prisoner," Judge Murray said.

Piquett was just warming up. "Thank you," he said. "May I also point out that this is a civil court, and not a military court-martial. Could anything be more prejudiced than machine guns pressed into the defendant's back, and an army of guards cluttering up the room? May the court direct that all guns be removed from the courtroom?"

Sheriff Holley's nephew, a deputy named Carroll Holley, rose. "I'm responsible for the safe-guarding of the prisoner," he said.

"Who are you?" Piquett demanded. "Are you a lawyer? What right have you to address this court?"

Judge Murray ordered the guns removed. Piquett then launched into an argument for more time, saying he would need four months to prepare Dillinger's defense. Estill said it should only take ten days. "To go on trial in ten days would be a legal lynching of this poor lad!" Piquett shouted. "There is a law against lynching in this state!"

"There is a law against murder, too," Estill shot back.

"Then why don't you observe it?" Piquett asked. "Why don't you [just] stand Dillinger against a wall and shoot him down? There's no need to throw away the state's money on this kind of mockery . . . Your Honor, even Christ had a fairer trial than this!"

Estill was about to shout something back when Judge Murray told both attorneys to calm down. Piquett apologized to the court and motioned to Estill. "Bob and I respect each other," he said.

"He'll be putting his arm around you soon," Murray quipped. Laughter rippled through the courtroom. After more desultory argument, the judge gave Piquett a month: Dillinger's trial would begin on March 12. Estill pouted. "Your Honor," he said, "why don't you let Mr. Piquett take Dillinger home with him, and bring him back on the day of the trial? You've given him everything else he has asked for."

Dillinger sat through it all wearing his trademark grin. As the handcuffs were reapplied for his return to the jail, he leaned over to Piquett and whispered, "Atta boy, counsel."[5]

The agent Hoover selected to supervise the Bremer case was William Rorer, the handsome World War I veteran who had arrested Machine Gun Kelly. Rorer, now promoted to inspector, arrived in St. Paul on Saturday, February 10, the day after Dillinger's hearing. After reading over reports that day, he interviewed Bremer at his home on Sunday.

They got off to a bad start. The two men repaired to the sunporch, where Rorer emphasized it would be necessary for Bremer to tell him everything he knew. Again Bremer bridled, saying he had already told Pop Nathan everything. Rorer said it was obvious he hadn't. "Who said I haven't told the truth?" Bremer demanded.[6] In that case, he went on, he wouldn't say anything at all. Rorer reminded him of the duty he owed the government and the American people.

"To hell with duty," Bremer said.

The meeting broke up when the young bank president stormed from the room in tears. In Washington, Hoover had no sympathy for Bremer. He was ready to take dramatic action. For several days he had considered issuing a statement criticizing Bremer for failing to cooperate with the Bureau. Nathan asked him to hold off, but Hoover sent a draft to Cummings anyway. Beginning with a lecture on a victim's duty to help capture his kidnappers, it noted that "in spite of the cooperation of the Special Agents of this Department's Bureau of Investigation in restraining their activities to permit the safe return of Mr. Bremer, his cooperation has not yet been of a type that should be expected . . . Neither temerity, nor fear, nor indifference will excuse the lack of full, wholesome, wholehearted effort and cooperation."

Monday morning, when Bremer arrived at the Bureau's office for further questioning, Rorer read him the statement. It had a dramatic impact. Suddenly Bremer began remembering things. That morning, and in interviews every day that week, his memory sprang vividly to life. The kidnappers let him smoke Chesterfields, he said; no, there was no state stamp on the box. He remembered the wallpaper in the room where he had been held, and the red flower design on the serving dishes. He said he had been driven about eight hours away.

Bremer's change in attitude coincided with the discovery of a trove of evidence. The afternoon after his release, agents had taken Walter Magee and retraced the route he had taken to deliver the ransom money. On Highway 55 south of Zumbrota, Magee pointed out the rise where he had seen the red lights. Scrambling up the grassy embankment, agents found three heavy brass lamps and a swinging lantern; all were then wrapped in cellophane and sent to Washington for analysis.

Agent Sam McKee, meanwhile, drove to Portage, Wisconsin, where the sheriff was holding what he considered a suspicious set of gasoline cans. There were four five-gallon jugs and a funnel. The sheriff took McKee out to see a farmer named Reuben Grossman, who had found them. Grossman said he had first seen the cans the night Bremer was released, lying on the side of a dirt road just off Route 16. The next morning they were still there, so he picked them up and returned them to his garage. It crossed his mind they might be connected to the Bremer case, Grossman said, so he called the sheriff. McKee took the cans and the funnel and sent them to Washington. Within days they had the word. A single fingerprint had been identified, on one of the gas cans.

It belonged to Dock Barker.

Kansas City, Missouri
Monday, February 12

While the FBI scrambled to learn about the Barkers, the Kansas City Massacre investigation was going nowhere. Hoover harangued the Kansas City and Oklahoma City offices to keep him informed of their efforts. "I have been particularly embarrassed by your failure to keep this office advised concerning developments in the Floyd case," Hoover wrote to the new Oklahoma City SAC, Dwight Brantley. "I receive more information from private parties in New York City concerning the handling of this matter in Oklahoma than I do from you."*

Two agents were still working the case full-time, and their contrasting theories led to friction. A new man, A. E. "Gyp" Farland, was debriefing inmates at Leavenworth who knew the Barkers. He argued in a January 29 memo to Hoover that the Bureau "has been wrong as to the identity of those who assisted Verne Miller in the Kansas City Massacre." Farland argued that Fred Barker and Alvin Karpis were almost certainly Miller's partners. Other agents disagreed.

Hoover read the memo in anger. Farland's theory looked half-baked, and it underscored the meandering nature of the investigation. Hugh Clegg followed up. "I telephoned Acting Agent in Charge M. C. Spear at Kansas City," Clegg wrote Hoover that afternoon, "and told him [you] were very much displeased with the reported lack of vigor in this investigation of the Kansas City Massacre case; that it appeared that they had let this case fall by the wayside and it was being handled intermittently by any one of a number of agents and it was not being pursued vigorously toward a logical conclusion."

Spear briefed Clegg on the office's contrasting theories of the case. "I informed Spear that the various theories they might develop had no bearing on

---

* Hoover's New York friends may be an allusion to his friend Walter Winchell.

the case," Clegg told Hoover, "that it was not the policy of agents of the division to get into disputes over theories; that we were seeking the facts, whatever they might be, and that he should not tolerate any friction in the office."

Hoover erupted. "This must stop *at once,*" he scrawled on Clegg's memo. "See that a sharp letter is sent K.C. re such bickering. It must stop *at once.*"

At Hoover's instruction, a single new agent, Harold Anderson, was ordered to review the massacre file from top to bottom.* The files themselves, which filled two four-drawer cabinets, were a mess. It took ten days for Anderson to get them organized. But what he discovered when he did was startling. In one drawer he found a sheaf of fingerprint photos taken from Verne Miller's house. The prints, lifted from beer bottles in Miller's basement, had been checked against those on file in the Kansas City office but had never been forwarded to Washington, which kept a national file of fingerprints. It was a blunder, and Anderson realized there would be hell to pay.

That Monday morning the fingerprints were forwarded to Washington for examination. Hoover's wrath was immediate; he demanded to know why the prints had languished in the files for seven months. "It appears," a Kansas City agent wrote Hoover, "that in the excitement in connection with this investigation at that time shortly after the massacre happened, [the fingerprint file] was overlooked."

Anderson's search of the files generated a dozen new leads. He went to work even as the FBI laboratory, already busy on the Bremer case, began analyzing the beer bottles for fingerprints.

That same Monday, Louis Piquett returned to Crown Point. Rumors persisted that John Hamilton was preparing to raid the jail to free his partner. Sheriff Holley had asked that Dillinger be moved to the prison at Michigan City. Dillinger pleaded with Piquett to block the move. "Quit worrying," Piquett said. "You're not going to Michigan City."

In Judge William Murray's chambers, Piquett listened as Sheriff Holley argued that the prison was the only place they could guarantee Dillinger could not escape. Piquett easily short-circuited her request with a sly bit of

---

* Born and raised in Oregon, Harold E. Anderson served in the FBI from 1927 to 1943. He later served as an investigator for the National Board of Fire Underwriters and the State Gaming Control Board in Nevada. He died in Las Vegas at the age of seventy-five in 1975.

flattery. "I think that's a very nice jail you have here," he said to Mrs. Holley. "What makes you think there's anything wrong with it?"

"There isn't anything wrong with it," Mrs. Holley said. "It's the strongest jail in Indiana."

"That's what I thought," Piquett said. "But of course, I don't want to embarrass Mrs. Holley. I appreciate that she's a woman, and if she's afraid of an escape—"

"I'm not afraid of an escape," the sheriff said. "I can take care of John Dillinger or any other prisoner."

That pretty much did it, but just to make sure, Piquett said he would file for a change of venue if Dillinger were transferred. Judge Murray clearly didn't mind the press attention he was receiving as Dillinger's judge, and it was all he needed to hear. He ruled that the prisoner would remain in Crown Point.

Piquett returned to the jail three days later, on Thursday, February 15. For the first time he brought his investigator, Art O'Leary. Piquett was planning to send O'Leary to Florida to establish their alibi; Dillinger was claiming he had still been in Daytona Beach when eyewitnesses put him at the East Chicago bank robbery.

"Wait a minute," Dillinger said as they rose to leave. "I'm gonna give you a note for Billie."

Piquett and O'Leary looked at the folded note on the drive back to Chicago. Dillinger had drawn a floor plan of the Crown Point jail and a suggestion to Hamilton as to how he could break him out. The note instructed Hamilton to dynamite a corner of the jail, then use blowtorches to cut through the steel walls into the cell block where Dillinger would be waiting.[7] O'Leary let out a low whistle. It was the first hint they had that Dillinger had no intention of standing trial. The note frightened both men. It was a ridiculous scheme, one that would no doubt get everyone involved killed. Nevertheless, after some debate, Piquett passed it to Frechette, who got it to John Hamilton.

Hamilton, however, was in no shape to help anyone; he was still recuperating from the bullet wounds he had suffered in East Chicago a month before. He had been holed up in a Chicago apartment ever since, tended to by Pat Cherrington. In desperation he contacted the one yegg he thought he could trust, their old friend Homer Van Meter. Van Meter was in St. Paul, where as fate would have it, he had just reunited with that most unstable of Depression-era outlaws, Baby Face Nelson.

. . .

In the wake of the Eastham raid, Clyde Barrow had a new gang for the first time in seven months, and from all appearances he was determined it would be his ticket into the criminal elite: finally, he would become a bank robber. It's possible banks intimidated Clyde. Even when he worked with partners in the past, he had kept to jewelry stores and gas stations. But if Clyde now viewed himself as a Dillinger-like figure commanding a band of seasoned yeggmen, he was deluding himself, as soon became apparent. The problem was his new partner, Raymond Hamilton. The cocky, needling Hamilton had an ego to rival Clyde's, and he wasn't taking a backseat to anyone.

What little is known of those first weeks after the Eastham raid comes mostly from Joe Palmer, one of the convicts who escaped alongside Hamilton. Recaptured in Paducah, Kentucky, in August 1934, Palmer narrated a patchy version of events before dying in the electric chair. According to Palmer, a thin, jug-eared murderer who suffered from bleeding ulcers and various chronic stomach problems, he and three other prisoners stayed with Bonnie and Clyde after the raid: Raymond Hamilton; a double murderer named Hilton Bybee; and an acne-scarred twenty-one-year-old Louisiana kid named Henry Methvin.

After forming in Dallas, this five-person group drove east to Louisiana to visit Henry Methvin's parents in a remote section of Bienville Parish, east of Shreveport. In Shreveport they bought clothes and guns. Afterward they headed north, intending to rob a bank in Iowa, which soon became Clyde's favorite hunting ground. Tensions within the group broke to the surface after they robbed the bank at Rembrandt, in the northwest corner of Iowa, on January 25, eight days after the Eastham raid. It was an uneventful in-and-out affair; the take came to $3,800. According to Palmer, he was too sick to take part, and stayed behind in the getaway car with Bonnie. Still, Clyde insisted Palmer receive an equal share. Hamilton objected, but Clyde won the argument. It wouldn't be their last: a clear rift was developing between Hamilton and the others. Perhaps sensing the explosive situation, Hilton Bybee left the gang after the Rembrandt robbery; he was arrested five days later in Amarillo.*

---

* Few books on Bonnie and Clyde include the Rembrandt robbery, perhaps because its only mention comes in the handwritten notes Lee Simmons took of Joe Palmer's debriefing. The notes are included verbatim in Simmons's 1957 memoir, *Assignment Huntsville.* Contemporary news accounts report the bank's robbery on January 25.

The bickering continued as the gang returned south through Missouri a few days later. They had almost reached Joplin when Palmer and Hamilton began arguing in the backseat. According to Palmer, he called Hamilton a "punk blabbermouth braggart." Afterward, Hamilton simmered as Palmer threw a blanket over his head and fell asleep on the rear floorboard. According to Palmer, Clyde, who was driving, saw Hamilton take out his pistol, as if to shoot Palmer. Clyde reached back and slapped Hamilton in the face, losing control of the car in the process. They careened into a ditch, damaging the car's left wheel.* Palmer thanked Clyde for saving his life but wanted nothing more to do with Hamilton. He prevailed upon Clyde to leave him at Joplin's Conner Hotel. Clyde promised to return in several weeks.[8]

If the gang left Missouri, it soon returned, because on February 12 Bonnie and Clyde were involved in a gunfight there. According to the next day's *Springfield Press,* it began that morning when a Springfield woman spotted a man stealing her car from a driveway on East Walnut Street. An alert was broadcast, and a little before noon the stolen car was spotted passing through Galena, south of Springfield, then again in Reeds Spring, west of Branson.

Clyde was lost. Outside Reeds Spring, he picked up a hitchhiker, a forty-year-old farmer named Joe Gunn, pointed a pistol at him, and ordered him to guide them to Berryville, across the state line in Arkansas. Gunn climbed into the backseat beside Hamilton and Henry Methvin, who were perched atop a pile of automatic rifles and thousands of bullets. Gunn had been in the car barely five minutes when Clyde spotted a roadblock ahead. It was the Reeds Spring city marshal. Clyde turned onto a dirt road, found it was a dead end, and returned toward the roadblock. "We've gotta let 'em have it, boys," Clyde said, stopping the car.[9]

Clyde snatched up an automatic rifle, jumped onto the road, and, along with Hamilton and Methvin, opened fire on the roadblock. As they did, another police car appeared behind them. Inside were two Springfield deputies. Hamilton wheeled and fired behind him. Clyde emptied his automatic rifle at the roadblock twice. Each time, Gunn noticed, he handed

---

* Some authors, including E. J. Milner in *The Lives and Times of Bonnie & Clyde* (Southern Illinois University Press, 1996), have put this incident several weeks later. However, according to Simmons's notes, Palmer clearly said it occurred "about the 1st of February," putting it immediately after the Rembrandt robbery. Milner does not mention the Rembrandt robbery.

the rifle to Bonnie to reload. The gang's firepower was overwhelming, and within minutes both sets of lawmen withdrew to call for reinforcements. Bonnie, Gunn recalled, appeared "delighted." Hamilton hopped into the backseat wearing a wide smile. "I sho' tried to kill that fucker back of the car," he said.

The gang headed across the Arkansas border, eventually stopping eight miles south of Berryville. According to Gunn, who was let out of the car, Clyde leaned over, tweaked Bonnie's nose, and said, "There's no use carrying this dead weight, baby." Gunn trudged back north to give his account to the Springfield newspaper that afternoon.

From Arkansas, Clyde drove the group to Dallas, where he and Hamilton began studying several banks in the area. On Monday night, February 19, believing they needed still more firepower, they burglarized a National Guard Armory at Ranger, Texas, west of Fort Worth, carting out armloads of Browning automatic rifles, Colt .45s, and thousands of bullets. They ferried it all back into Dallas.

It was during this period, between February 12 and early March, that Bonnie and Clyde experienced one of the stranger episodes of their careers. Hamilton was lonely, and in Dallas he managed to reunite with a heavily made-up piece of trouble named Mary O'Dare, the nineteen-year-old wife of a jailed friend.* It was the first time another woman had joined the gang since Blanche Barrow, and while Bonnie had tolerated Blanche, she loathed Mary O'Dare. Almost everyone connected to the gang did. By all accounts O'Dare was immature, a sarcastic, gossipy girl who couldn't understand why Bonnie and Clyde preferred sleeping in the car and bathing in ice-cold creeks to staying in a nice hotel. Raymond Hamilton's brother Floyd termed O'Dare a "gold digger" and a "prostitute" who wore enough makeup to "grow a crop."[10] Behind her back, Clyde and Bonnie called her "The Washerwoman."

O'Dare was with the gang when Clyde and Hamilton agreed on a bank to take, the R. P. Henry and Sons Bank in the town of Lancaster, twenty-five miles south of Dallas. On Tuesday morning, February 27, after leaving the women in their Ford north of the city, the two men took Henry Methvin and drove to Lancaster, stepping onto the sidewalk by the bank's side en-

---

* O'Dare's husband was Gene O'Dare, the man who had been arrested with Hamilton at a Michigan ice-skating rink in late 1932.

trance a few minutes before noon. Clyde's behavior that day suggests his ambition to become a first-tier bank man. Gone were the wrinkled, dusty suits he usually wore. That day he wore a smart checkered overcoat and a matching Stetson. Hamilton wore a tailored overcoat of his own. They left Methvin in the car.

There were five people in the lobby when Clyde walked in, pulled out the sawed-off shotgun from beneath his coat, and said, "Everybody on the floor." An elderly man named Brooks didn't understand.

"What?" he asked. "What are we doing?"

A WPA laborer named Ollie Worley, who had just cashed a paycheck for $27.00, said, "We have to get on the floor."

Brooks remained standing.

"Say, old man," Clyde said. "You'd better get down."

"Please," a bank executive said.

It took another minute of prodding for the elderly man to take his place on the floor. As he did, Hamilton walked behind the teller cages, scooping cash into a sack. He led a teller into the vault, grabbing bricks of cash from the shelves, then emerged, ready to leave. At that point, a funny thing happened. While Hamilton was inside the vault, Clyde had snatched the $27.00 from Ollie Worley's hand. As they left, he turned to Worley. "You worked like hell for this, didn't you?" Clyde asked, motioning to the money in his hand.

"Yes sir," Worley said. "Digging ditches . . ."

"Here," Clyde said, thrusting the money at Worley. "We don't want your money. We just want the bank's."[11]

Among the dozens of eyewitness accounts of Clyde's behavior, this exchange is unique. If Worley's memory is to be believed—he related the story to the Dallas historian John Neal Phillips in 1984—it is perhaps the only time Clyde ever expressed anything approaching an altruistic impulse toward one of his victims.* Moreover, Clyde's choice of language is telling: the words he spoke to Worley were precisely the same words newspapers reported Dillinger using six weeks earlier when robbing the First National Bank of East Chicago. The incident, along with his tailored clothing and uncharacteristically polite behavior that day, suggests that Clyde was adopt-

---

* Worley's 1984 version differs from the story he told newspapers fifty years earlier. The day of the robbery, he told Dallas reporters he thought it was Hamilton who had returned his money, which he said was $3.00, not $27.00.

ing Dillinger as a role model, that at the very least he was aware of Dillinger's exploits and was attempting to emulate his successes. It's not a reach to suggest that Clyde craved the adulation Dillinger enjoyed and was altering his behavior in hopes of attracting something similar.

But any dreams Clyde had that he and Hamilton could forge a criminal enterprise to rival Dillinger's were dashed that same day. Speeding out of Lancaster, they picked up the girls and headed north toward Oklahoma. Clyde drove; Hamilton and O'Dare sat in the backseat with Henry Methvin. At one point, Hamilton began to divide their take, which totaled about $4,000, into three parts.

Suddenly Mary O'Dare said, "What about me?"

"You get nothing," Clyde barked.

As Clyde later told the story to his family, he watched Hamilton closely in the rearview mirror as he divided the money. He claimed he saw Hamilton slide a wad of bills into O'Dare's hand. At this point, he stopped the car, confronted Hamilton, and searched him, finding an extra $600. It is certainly a dramatic anecdote, perhaps too much so to be believed. But whatever occurred that day, it marked the end of the Barrow-Hamilton partnership. Some versions of the story state that Bonnie and Clyde separated from Hamilton and O'Dare right there, on the highway.

This is unlikely. In a story Bonnie told her mother, she suggested that the final break came several days later, during a nightmarish trip the gang took north into the Midwest. They drove as far as Indiana, where the men bought sharp new suits, hats, and overcoats, the girls purchased dresses, and everyone attended a movie or two; it's tempting to suggest Clyde was drawn to Indiana because it was Dillinger's territory, but the gang's precise itinerary is unknown.

All during the trip O'Dare bickered with everyone, even the monosyllabic Methvin. As Bonnie told it, the final straw came after a furious argument she had not with O'Dare, but with Clyde. Bonnie didn't explain the argument, but it was bad enough she stomped off in tears, swearing she was "going home to mama." Afterward, Bonnie said, O'Dare tried to sympathize with her.

"I wouldn't put up with him," O'Dare said. "I'd fix him."

"I'm going home," Bonnie said. "I simply hate him."

"I'd fix him before I left," O'Dare said.

"I'm going to," Bonnie said. "You wait and see."

"I'd poison him," O'Dare said.

The suggestion startled Bonnie. "Poison him?" she said. "Poison Clyde?"

"Well, just dope him then," O'Dare said. "Then, while he's out, you can take his roll and beat it. Boy, think of the good time you could have on that money."

"If I hadn't been so mad at Clyde," Bonnie told her mother, "I believe I'd have slapped her. But that finished me up with [O'Dare]. I told Clyde and he told Raymond that if [she] stuck around, it was all off. They split up right there and we came back to Texas with Henry."[12]

Given Bonnie's penchant for melodrama, Mary O'Dare may or may not have suggested poisoning Clyde; whatever she did was bad enough that, according to Joe Palmer, Bonnie, Clyde, and Methvin later discussed killing her. The dissolution of the gang marked the last time Clyde ever worked with Raymond Hamilton.

Afterward, the two couples returned separately to the Dallas area. Hamilton teamed up with his brother to rob a string of Texas banks. Clyde had enough money for the moment and consented when Henry Methvin, now falling into W. D. Jones's old role as Clyde's gofer, asked to visit his parents in Louisiana. One afternoon in early March, deep in the pines east of Shreveport, Clyde drove them down a rutted dirt road to the shack of Methvin's parents, Iverson and Ava Methvin. "Ivy" Methvin was a grubby drunk in overalls; Ava didn't talk much.

Even so, there was something about the area that appealed to Clyde. Over the course of several lazy days at the Methvin place, he and Bonnie took long walks into the pines. The area was impossibly isolated, with few paved roads, no large towns to speak of, and no police in sight. Few of the back-country shacks had running water or indoor plumbing, much less radios or telephones. Clyde told Bonnie he liked the feel of the area. There was a lake nearby with largemouth bass. Both Bonnie and Clyde were exhausted. Neither had slept in a bed since the shoot-out at Platte City eight months before. At some point, Clyde suggested that maybe they could find a shack of their own nearby. They could fix it up, use it as a vacation spot. Bonnie liked the idea of a little house in the woods, just the two of them. It seemed perfect.

It wasn't perfect. What Bonnie and Clyde didn't know, as they explored the woods of northern Louisiana, was that for the first time in two years they had attracted a professional pursuer, and he was already driving the Louisiana back roads looking for them.

He had been hired by Lee Simmons, the man who headed the Texas prison system. Simmons wanted revenge for the raid on his work camp, and if the FBI and the Dallas County Sheriff were too uninterested or inept to bring in Bonnie and Clyde, he was determined to do it himself. On February 1, fourteen days after the Eastham jailbreak, Simmons visited the governor's mansion in Austin and explained his idea to the governor, Mildred "Ma" Ferguson. Beside the governor sat her husband, the former governor Jim Ferguson, whose impeachment on corruption charges two years earlier had led to his wife's decision to run for office on the slogan "Two Governors for the Price of One." Simmons told the Fergusons he wanted to hire someone to eradicate Clyde Barrow. When the governor asked who he had in mind, Simmons said, "Frank Hamer."

He didn't need to say much more. Everyone in Texas knew of Frank Hamer. Hamer was a Lone Star legend, a cantankerous forty-nine-year-old former Ranger who had spent much of his law-enforcement career chasing cattle rustlers and exchanging gunfire with Mexican bandits on the Rio Grande. A big man, six-foot-two, just over two hundred pounds, Hamer was seen as the walking embodiment of the "One Riot, One Ranger" ethos, a stereotypically quiet loner who bridled at authority, shot first, and asked questions later. Long a darling of the Texas press, he was the kind of celebrity lawman who befriended movie stars, in Hamer's case the silent-film actor Tom Mix. He was also a friend and contemporary of several current and former FBI men, including the San Antonio SAC Gus Jones. After a series of minor controversies, including the dismissal of one case for an illegal search, Hamer left the Rangers in November 1932. Any number of reasons were given for his departure, but the Rangers had become increasingly politicized and ineffective, and Hamer was no fan of Ma Ferguson and her corrupt husband. He had reluctantly taken a security job with a Houston-based oil company.

Sitting in the governor's office, Simmons was surprised to learn that whatever bad blood existed between Hamer and the governor, the Fergusons would not object to his hiring. "Frank is all right with us," Mrs. Ferguson said. "We don't hold anything against him."[13] Leaving the mansion with a sheaf of written authorizations in his briefcase, Simmons drove to Hamer's Austin home and explained his proposal. Hamer would work alone, in secret. No one but Simmons and the governor would know what he was doing. Hamer's sole objective would be to bring in Bonnie and Clyde, dead or alive. No politics, no bureaucracy, no one looking over his shoulder. "How long do you think it will take to do the job?" Hamer asked.

"That's something no man could guess," Simmons said. "It might be six months; it might be longer. Probably it will take you thirty days to get your feet on the ground before you start to work. No matter how long it takes, I will back you to the limit."

"Well, if that's the way you feel about it, I'll take the job," Hamer said.

Simmons made only one suggestion. "Captain," he said, "it is foolish for me to try to tell you anything; but in my judgment, the thing for you to do is put them on the spot, know you are right—and then shoot everybody in sight."

Hamer didn't respond to the suggestion, but it stuck in his mind. The next day he got to work. Little is known of his first weeks on Bonnie and Clyde's trail. For the rest of his life, he never described his pursuit in detail. In the only lengthy interview he ever gave on the subject, with the Texas Ranger historian Walter Prescott Webb, Hamer spoke in general of how he studied both Bonnie and Clyde:

> I interviewed many people who knew him and studied numerous pictures of him and [Bonnie]. I knew the size, height, and all the marks of identification of both Clyde and Bonnie. But this was not enough. An officer must know the mental habits of the outlaw, how he thinks, and how he will act in different situations. When I began to understand Clyde Barrow's mind, I felt that I was making progress . . . Before the chase ended, I not only knew the general appearance and mental habits of the pair, but I also had learned the kind of whiskey they drank, what they ate, and the color, size, and texture of their clothes.

On February 10, two days before Bonnie and Clyde's shoot-out at Reeds Spring, Missouri, Hamer climbed into his black V-8 Ford and headed to Dallas. There he debriefed W. D. Jones, who had been captured that November, and also Jimmy Mullins, who had been arrested and interrogated by the Dallas authorities and the FBI. Hamer also made the first of several visits to the Dallas FBI office, where he talked with the agent assigned to the case, Charles Winstead. Bonnie and Clyde were low priorities for the Bureau, but Winstead had been cruising East Texas for several months chasing tips on the pair. He believed he had found one of their cars outside the town of Gilmer, east of Dallas. On another occasion he and a sheriff had discovered a suitcase full of clothes that relatives had left for them in a creek bed near Athens.[14]

The FBI declined to get more deeply involved, but Hamer had more luck with Smoot Schmid, the Dallas County sheriff. Schmid agreed that his two deputies, Bob Alcorn and Ted Hinton, would work with Hamer. The three men had several long talks, plotting strategy, then drove east together. An examination of Clyde's wanderings showed his affinity for the triangle of country between Dallas, Joplin, and Shreveport, and after his initial research Hamer began contacting law-enforcement friends there, especially in East Texas, where Clyde had family.

He first struck their trail at Texarkana. From there he followed signs of the pair to the western Louisiana town of Logansport, then north to Keatchie, where they had purchased gasoline, then on to Shreveport, where Clyde bought pants, underwear, gloves, and an automatic shotgun. Hamer found one of their camps on the Wichita River, near Wichita Falls, Texas, where he traced a sales receipt to a store in Dallas where Bonnie bought a dress.

"But the trail always led back to Louisiana," Hamer told Walter Prescott Webb. It was there, on February 17, after only a week of travel, that Hamer claimed, "I located their hideout." This may have been wishful thinking, or even braggadocio; Hamer's ego was sizable. He gives no detail of the supposed hideout, only to say that it was in a parish where he could not trust the sheriff. "And so it was arranged to have Barrow's hideout moved into a parish where the officers were more reliable." How this could have been arranged Hamer doesn't say. But, he goes on, "in a comparatively short time the hideout was established in Bienville Parish at a place well known to me."

Bienville Parish was the home of Henry Methvin's parents. Hamer said he cruised the dirt roads there for several days before reaching out to the local sheriff, a tall, laconic man named Henderson Jordan. As it happened, their timing was perfect. Jordan had just been approached by a neighbor who brought a message from the Methvin family. If a deal could be struck for Henry Methvin's pardon, Ivy and Ava Methvin were prepared to betray Bonnie and Clyde.

• • •

Baby Face Nelson's three-man gang reassembled in St. Paul in the last week of February. Spring meant the opening of bank season. The cat roads would soon be passable, and Nelson sat down with Harry Sawyer's favorite jug marker, a red-haired ex-con named Eddie Green, to map a plan of attack. It was Green who had identified the string of banks the Barkers had robbed in 1932 and early 1933. For the spring of 1934, Green had targeted three banks for the Nelson Gang, one in Sioux Falls, South Dakota, and two in Iowa, at Mason City and Newton. The problem was manpower. Everyone agreed they needed more than three men. But with the arrests of Harvey Bailey and so many others, the pool of experienced yeggs in St. Paul was dwindling; no one was eager to hire strangers.

A solution came with the strange phone call from John Hamilton asking if Nelson's gang might be able to free Dillinger from the Crown Point jail. By all accounts, Nelson was intrigued by the idea. Hamilton had suggested they smuggle Dillinger a gun. Nelson didn't know how. But he knew someone who did. Alvin Karpis had once told him of having smuggled a gun to Harvey Bailey in a Kansas jail; the gun was discovered, but at least they managed to get it inside. Using Harry Sawyer as an intermediary, Nelson sent word to Karpis in Chicago.

Karpis drove up from Chicago with Dock Barker for the meeting, a little irritated that Nelson wouldn't explain what it was about. When darkness fell they drove out to the river cliffs, pulled up to Jack Peifer's elegant restaurant-casino, The Hollyhocks Club, and left their car with the valet. In an upstairs office they found the Nelson Gang.

"So," Karpis asked, "what do you guys want?"

"You can go ahead and explain to him if you want," Nelson said to Van Meter.

"You go ahead, Jimmy," Van Meter said.

Nelson smiled. "Hey, you remember when you guys robbed that bank in Fort Scott, Kansas?"

"Yeah, I remember it," Karpis said. "What about it?"

"Well, you remember Bailey was in jail there, and when he got took, they shook his cell down and they found a .45 automatic in the mattress? You probably were the one that got that gun brought in there to him, wasn't you?"

"Yeah, as a matter of fact," Karpis said. He explained how he had planned an escape, but had given up in the face of tight security.

"How did you go about getting that gun in there and why wasn't Bailey able to use the damn thing?" Nelson asked.

Karpis explained that Bailey was watched too closely. "Why do you ask? What's going on?"

Nelson glanced at Van Meter. "Well, look," he said, "you know we got a guy, a pretty good lawyer in Chicago, and he's got a real good connection over in Indiana and they can get a gun brought in to Dillinger. But he wanted to know what we were going to do and how we were going to do it, and they wanted five thousand dollars to do the damn thing. We were thinking maybe we could just do this ourselves."

Karpis sighed. "You mean to say you had me come all the way up here to talk about this goddamn thing?" Nelson apologized. Attempting to placate Karpis, he asked whether anyone in the Barker Gang would join them in the robberies they planned. Karpis begged off; he liked Nelson, but considered him too unstable to work with. "Well, we'd like some guys that could go on that damn thing," Nelson said.

He turned to Barker.

"Can you go on it, Dock?"

"Yeah, I could," Dock said. "Why? How many guys do you need?"

"Two," Nelson said.

"What do you think about Bill Weaver?" Barker asked Karpis.

"Hell yeah, he'd go on it," Karpis said.

"When are you guys gonna go?" Dock asked.

"Well first," Nelson said, "we think we can get Dillinger out of there and hell, we got all the arrangements made in Chicago that if he beats that jail, we'll have him up in St. Paul inside ten hours, and we'd go ahead and take this damn bank in South Dakota."

"It's liable to get pretty hot here," Karpis said. Everyone knew the FBI was flooding agents into St. Paul for the Bremer case. Van Meter spoke up. "We thought so too, but hell, I go down around the Green Lantern there, at Sawyer's joint, and nobody bothers me."

Afterward they walked out into the chilly night air. "You know, if I'd have listened to you," Nelson told Karpis, "I wouldn't be mixed up in this damn thing."

Karpis laughed. "It seemed to me like you told me once in Reno that if you could get ten thousand dollars, you was going back out to Reno. What happened? You got more than that on your first caper."

"Yeah," Nelson said with a grin, "but when I got that I wanted twenty. And when I got twenty, I wanted forty. You know how these damn things are."*

Back in Chicago the next day, Karpis mentioned the brewing rescue attempt to Fred Barker. "Geez, I hope they have better luck than we had with Bailey," Barker said.

"I don't know," said Karpis. "I've got a feeling that Dillinger'll get killed there in that jail. I don't think he's gonna make it, but they're goddamn sure gonna try."

---

* The sole source for this discussion is the Karpis transcripts, and his chronology is clearly confused. Karpis puts the meeting in late March. In all likelihood it occurred in late February.

10

DILLINGER AND NELSON

March 3 to March 29, 1934

Crown Point, Indiana
Saturday, March 3

A hard rain pelted the streets of Crown Point that morning, sluicing down the gutters on Joliet Street behind the jail. It was a chilling dawn, raw and gusty, low gray clouds skidding south off Lake Michigan. Sam Cahoon, a sixty-four-year-old janitor, trotted through the dim light into the jail a few minutes after eight. He shook the rain from his overcoat and waved hello to a guard. His first duty was to clean the criminal cell block, where Dillinger was held. Cahoon passed through the receiving room and trudged up the seventy-two-foot corridor that ran the length of the jail, ending at the barred door to the cell block.

After gathering his mops, Cahoon hollered for a guard named Win Bryant to let the prisoners out of their cells so he could clean. Together the two men opened a metal box on the corridor wall and threw the lever that opened the cells, allowing Dillinger and his fourteen fellow prisoners to roam the corridor behind the barred cell-block door. A few minutes later, after doing some other chores, Cahoon returned, and, with Bryant looking on, pulled the lever to open the barred door, letting in two trustees, who carried a box of toilet paper, soap, and Dutch cleanser.

Cahoon had just stepped into the cell block when Dillinger sprang forward and thrust what appeared to be a gun into his stomach. He turned Cahoon around and faced Bryant, poking the gun into Cahoon's back. "Come on, Sam, we're going places," Dillinger said. "You're gonna be good, aren't you?"

Cahoon, flummoxed, said something like "I'm always good."

A hulking black prisoner, Herbert Youngblood, materialized at Dillinger's side, holding a toilet plunger menacingly over his head; he was the only inmate Dillinger had been able to lure into helping him. "You got a gun?" Youngblood asked Bryant. The guard shook his head no. It was jail policy; no one carried guns near the cell block.

Dillinger motioned toward an open cell. "Come on, boys," he said. "Get in there." Bryant and the two trustees filed in. When Dillinger shut the door, Cahoon stepped toward the cell. "No, I got use for you," Dillinger said. "You're gonna get me outta here."

Dillinger pushed the janitor outside the cell block. Seventy feet down the concrete corridor the warden and a group of guards were sipping their morning coffees in the warden's office at the front of the jail. It was the only way out. A flight of four steps bisected the corridor, dividing the old jail from the new addition. It put Dillinger just above the group's line of sight.

"How many doors between me and the outside?" Dillinger asked.

Cahoon thought a moment, then said, "Four."

Dillinger knew he didn't have long, maybe minutes, before someone wandered back to the cell block. Quickly he fired questions at Cahoon, demanding the locations of guards, doors, and guns. He produced a pencil and drew a diagram of the jail on a shelf. Cahoon nodded. It was close. Then Dillinger, his gun still in Cahoon's back, led Youngblood slowly along the corridor, stopping at the head of the steps. Squatting to peer down the hallway, they saw a man cross between rooms. "Who's that?" Dillinger demanded. His voice was low, cool.

"Ernest Blunk," Cahoon said. Blunk was a thirty-two-year-old deputy sheriff. "Call him back here," Dillinger commanded.

Cahoon hollered: "Blunk! Come here a minute."

When Blunk approached, he looked up the steps and saw Dillinger.

"Get up here, you son of a bitch, or I'll kill you," Dillinger said. Blunk froze. He saw a flash of the gun in Dillinger's hand. "I've got it on you," Dillinger said. "You haven't got a chance."

Dillinger led Blunk back to the cell block and shoved him into the cell with the others. The moment Dillinger stepped away, Blunk asked Win Bryant if he had seen the gun. Bryant said it looked like a .45. "They'll kill the son of a bitch now," Blunk said.

Dillinger herded Cahoon back to the top of the steps, where he ordered him to call for the jailer, Lew Baker. But Cahoon had had enough. "I'll be goddamned if I'll help you get outta here," he said. "I'm not going any farther. Shoot and be god damned."

Youngblood stepped forward and raised the toilet plunger, as if to strike the elderly Cahoon.

"None of that," Dillinger said. "I'll handle this."

Dillinger shoved Cahoon back toward the cell block.

"Contrary to what people say," Dillinger said as they walked, "I'm no killer. But I'm gonna get outta here."

"They'll kill you before you get halfway down the hallway."

"Watch me," Dillinger said.

In the cell block Dillinger thrust Cahoon into the cell and ordered Ernest Blunk to come out. He shoved Blunk down toward the steps. "I'm gonna make this today," Dillinger said.

"You can't," Blunk said. "They'll kill you."

"I have everything to gain and nothing to lose," Dillinger said. "You can either be a dead hero or a live coward."

Blunk said he wouldn't help him escape.

"You have a wife and baby that you love dearly and would like to see again, haven't you?" Dillinger said.

Blunk gave in. "All right," he said.

"How many guards are in the office?" Dillinger asked.

"I don't know."

"Don't lie to me, you son of a bitch, or I'll kill you."

"I said I don't know." Dillinger told him to lower his voice. He took a moment to think. "Well," Dillinger said, shoving Blunk forward, "let's see what we can see."

They reached the top of the steps. Dillinger told Blunk to call for Warden Baker. Blunk hesitated. Dillinger jabbed the gun into his back. "Oh, Lew?" Blunk hollered.

"Just a minute!" Baker shouted back. The warden was still in his office with the guards. A moment later, he stuck his head out into the hallway. "Come on back!" Blunk said.

Baker walked all the way back to the cell block, where he could now see Blunk standing. The moment he entered, Baker felt a gun thrust into his back. Dillinger grabbed a fistful of the warden's shirt and shoved him into the cell with the others. "Get in there and you won't get hurt," Dillinger said, shutting the door behind him.

One by one, Dillinger used Blunk to lure the four guards in Warden Baker's office back to the cell block, where they were each surprised and pushed into the cell with the others. One, Kenneth "Butch" Houk, reached for Dillinger's gun, but Dillinger overpowered him and shoved him in the cell. When the last of the four was locked away, Dillinger ran down to the office and grabbed the warden's two submachine guns. He took one and handed the other to Youngblood. Armed and ready to make his break for freedom, Dillinger couldn't resist one last bit of showboating. Trotting back to the cell block, he took out the gun he had been using. Warden Baker and the guards stared in amazement. The gun was made of wood. It was a fake.

"This is how tough your little jail is," Dillinger announced with a grin. "I did it all with this little wooden pistol." He tapped the "gun" on the cell bars to make his point.

Dillinger turned to Warden Baker.

"Where are the cars kept?" he asked.

"In the garage. In back."

"Where are the keys?"

"In the cars."

The only entrance Dillinger knew to the garage was outside, meaning he would have to creep along the jail's outer wall to get to the cars. From Sam Cahoon's description Dillinger knew that a door led outside from the kitchen, which could be reached through the warden's office. Now armed with the two submachine guns, Dillinger and Youngblood guided Ernest Blunk down to the warden's office and to the kitchen door. Dillinger glanced at Youngblood. Youngblood nodded. He was ready.

Dillinger shoved Blunk through the kitchen door, surprising two guards and the jail's chef, William Zieger. Zieger, a combative sort, took one look at Dillinger and his submachine gun and said, "I'll take that thing away from you and shove it up your ass."

Blunk blanched. "My God, Bill!" he said. "He means business!"

Zieger surrendered. Blunk stepped forward, and, on Dillinger's orders, took one of the guards' pistols and laid it on a table. Dillinger grabbed it. He then opened a closet, took out a raincoat and hat, and walked out the kitchen door into the rain. Behind him came a curious procession, Youngblood training his gun on Blunk, then the chef and the two guards, followed by three more prisoners who wanted to escape. None of the last six men had a gun trained on them.

Dillinger trotted down the side of the red-brick jail until he reached a side door to its garage at the rear. A trustee named John Hudak was hunched over the engine of a 1927 Nash—Sheriff Holley's car—when he felt something hard shoved into his back. He turned to see Dillinger. "Get in and drive," Dillinger said.

"I, I don't have the keys," Hudak stammered.

"Where are they?" Dillinger asked.

"In the warden's office, I think."

Dillinger shoved Blunk toward the car and asked him to check for the keys. Blunk looked inside and said, "No keys."

"That son of a bitch Baker, he lied to me," Dillinger said. "I ought to kill him."

For a moment Dillinger pondered his next move. He needed the car keys. Leaving Youngblood to guard the crowd in the garage, Dillinger led Blunk and Hudak back outside to the kitchen door. Inside, they surprised a National Guardsman and three other men. Blunk took their guns and Dillinger locked them in the receiving room. Hudak, meanwhile, was unable to find the sheriff's car keys. "I gotta steal a car," Dillinger said to Blunk. "Where's the nearest garage?"

By the time Dillinger stalked back outside toward the jail's garage, Warden Baker and the other hostages had freed themselves from the cells upstairs. Still locked inside the cell block, Baker went to a secret peephole that led into a closet in his residence. He banged on the wall. A moment later his wife's eyeball appeared at the peephole.

"Irene," he said. "Has the car left the garage?"

She didn't understand.

"Call for help," Baker said. "John Dillinger is out!"

Mrs. Baker wasn't sure what to do. She picked up the phone, but for some reason the line was dead. She opened a window, spied a passing postman, and shouted "My God! John Dillinger is out!" The postman just stared. At wit's end, Mrs. Baker hurried out of the apartment and down a flight of interior stairs to the garage. Bursting inside, she found Ernest Blunk standing with a man she didn't recognize.

"John Dillinger is out!" she exclaimed.

The man stepped toward her. Suddenly she noticed the submachine gun in his hand, the two pistols jammed into his belt, and the two other pistols in his front pockets.

"Oh, no," she said. "You're not Dillinger."

Dillinger smiled and took her by the arm. "Mrs. Baker," Blunk said, "you do as he tells you and no one will get hurt."

Dillinger locked the whole crowd, now numbering more than ten people, in a side room and got ready to leave. Shoving Blunk in front of them, they walked out the side door and circled behind the jail and the Criminal Courts Building. Dillinger's luck held. There were no guardsmen or deputies in back that morning.

Next to the Criminal Courts Building stood a squat brick building, the Main Street Garage. The three men jogged through the rain to its back entrance. Inside, they walked through the garage toward the front. Two mechanics saw them, shrugged, and went back to work.

"I need a car," Dillinger told Blunk.

"There's lots of cars," Blunk said. "Take what you want."

They walked up to a thirty-year-old mechanic named Edwin Saager, who was hunched over an engine.

"What's the fastest car in the garage?" Dillinger asked.

Saager noticed the submachine gun hanging at Dillinger's side. He thought he was a deputy. "The V-8 Ford," he said, returning his attention to the engine. Dillinger raised the gun and said, "Get going." Saager was looking at the engine. He didn't seem to hear.

"Get going," Dillinger repeated.

Saager turned and saw the gun pointed at him.

"He means business," Blunk said. Finally Saager realized this was no deputy. Dillinger led the two men to the V-8 Ford, which was also owned by Sheriff Holley. "You want me to drive?" Saager asked.

"No, Mr. Blunk will do the driving," Dillinger said. "You get in the backseat." Youngblood slid in beside him. Dillinger sat in the front seat, the submachine gun across his lap.

"Someone open the doors!" Dillinger shouted. A mechanic pressed the air-compressor button and one of the garage's two rear doors opened. Blunk drove the Ford out of the garage onto Joliet Street, then headed west through city streets in the rain. Dillinger told him to keep his speed down. Crossing the town square, Blunk narrowly avoided a collision with another car; Dillinger told him if they had a wreck, he would be the first to die. At the edge of town, Dillinger said to keep heading west, keeping to dirt roads. A few minutes later they crossed the state line into Illinois. As he had at Racine four months earlier, Dillinger turned buoyant as they entered the countryside. He began singing, warbling a rendition of "The Last Roundup," repeating the phrase "Get along, little dogies, get along."

The singing stopped when the Ford slid off the muddy road into a ditch. After ten minutes Youngblood and Saager managed to push it back onto the road. Saager then took a half hour putting chains on the car. As they continued driving west, Dillinger turned chatty. Blunk asked if he planned to rescue Pierpont and the others in Ohio.

"They'd do the same for me," Dillinger said.

Outside the town of Peotone, Dillinger began looking for telephone wires. When he didn't see any, he had Blunk stop the car and get out. He pulled a wad of bills from his pocket, peeling off four singles. He offered them to Blunk, who shook his head. Dillinger offered the money to Saager, and Saager took it.

"It's no use for me to tell you fellas not to get in touch with the police, 'cause I know you will," Dillinger said.

"Put yourself in our positions and you would do the same as we'll do," Blunk said.

"I could make you shut up now if I wanted to," Dillinger said, brandishing the Thompson gun.

"I don't think you would kill a man without giving him a chance," Blunk said.

Dillinger grinned, slid behind the wheel of the Ford, and drove off. Blunk and Saager stood in the mud, watching Dillinger disappear toward Chicago.[1] By noon he would be the most wanted man in the country.

Lou Piquett and his investigator, Art O'Leary, arrived at the lawyer's office that morning, waiting for news. Billie Frechette showed up around eight. Piquett's gofer, an ex-con named Meyer Bogue, drifted in later. They were sitting around at 9:30, already drinking gin, when Piquett's nephew telephoned to say he had just heard of Dillinger's escape on the radio.[2] "Seems that everything worked out," Piquett announced as he put down the phone. "I think I'll call Warden Baker."

Piquett dialed Crown Point. "Hello! Mr. Baker? This is Lou Piquett, in Chicago."

"Yes hello, Lou," Baker said.

"What truth is there in the radio report that my client just broke jail?"

"That's right. He just left us."

"Anybody killed or hurt?"

"No, nobody was hurt."

"That's good, I'm glad to hear that," Piquett said. "Say, he didn't leave a forwarding address, did he?"

When Piquett put down the phone he said, "By golly it's true! He got away!"

Billie let out a little yell and thrust her face into her hands. "Poor Johnnie!" she said. "Oh my God, they'll kill him!"

"Quit your squawking," Piquett said playfully. "They'll probably never get another look at his coattails."

The gin flowed freely for the next few hours as the four celebrated. Bogue ran out and grabbed newspaper extras that were already appearing, and they read them between drinks. Outside, police were swarming into the streets, taking positions at the main entryways to the city from the south. Piquett realized his office would be watched. He thought of a former secretary, a woman named Esther Anderson, who lived on Wellington Avenue, on the North Side. He sent Billie over, then followed in a taxi. O'Leary stayed behind, waiting for Dillinger's call. It came around three. Dillinger's only words were, "Where will I go?"

"Go to 434 Wellington Avenue," O'Leary said. "Piquett will be waiting."

Piquett was leaning against the Wellington Avenue building, hat tucked down, hands stuffed in his pockets, when Dillinger drove up.

"Hi ya, counsel," he said with a wave.

Piquett stepped to the car. Herbert Youngblood was lying flat on the backseat, the two tommy guns clutched in his hands. "Is this the place I'm gonna stay?" Dillinger asked, eyeing the building.

"No," Piquett said, "I just want to bring you up here for a few minutes so we can talk."

The two men walked into the lobby, where Billie leaped into Dillinger's embrace. Upstairs, Esther Anderson took one look at Dillinger and told them to get out. Dillinger returned downstairs to the car, Billie attached to his side. Piquett came down a minute later.

"Billie says we can go over to her sister's place on Halsted," Dillinger said. "Come over there this evening about half past seven. And I need some money. Let me have whatever you've got with you."

Piquett fished in his pocket and handed Dillinger a roll of bills, about three hundred dollars.

"Thanks, counsel," Dillinger said. "I'll see you soon."

On the way to the apartment, Dillinger put Youngblood on a streetcar, handed him $100, and thanked him.* He and Billie drove to her sister's place, a second-floor flat at 3512 North Halsted. That night Piquett visited and listened as Dillinger, snuggling with Billie on a davenport, told them what had happened at Crown Point.

"Say, Dillinger," Piquett said at one point. "When am I gonna see some money? I haven't had a dollar yet, you know?"

A cloud passed over Dillinger's face. "What? Didn't [that lawyer my father hired] give you anything? He took my dad's last five hundred dollars. You tell him to cough up those five C's, or I'm coming down and take care of him."

The next day Dillinger stayed in the apartment, speaking at one point with John Hamilton, who briefed him on the arrangements with the Nelson gang. Everything was set. That night Nelson's partner Tommy Carroll drove up in front of the building in a green Ford. Dillinger and Billie came out a side entrance, carrying suitcases as they ducked into the backseat. Under their coats both carried submachine guns.

They headed northwest out of the city, toward St. Paul and Dillinger's rendezvous with his new partner, Baby Face Nelson.†

---

* Youngblood was killed in a police shoot-out in Michigan two weeks later.

† Seventy years later, the questions that swirled in the wake of Dillinger's spectacular escape from Crown Point's "escape-proof" jail still prompt debate among historians of American crime. Two loom largest: Did Dillinger really use a wooden gun, as he claimed? And what, if any, help did he receive from allies in and out of the jail?

As for the gun, many still refuse to believe Dillinger was able to escape using only a wooden replica. Ernest Blunk and others would later insist Dillinger had used a real pistol. Some writers, including John Toland, agree; Toland posited that Dillinger had used a wooden gun *and* a real gun. But FBI files make clear Dillinger, at least initially, had only the wooden gun. Agents took statements from everyone involved that morning, and several, including Warden Baker, saw it up close. Some, including Sam Cahoon, insisted Dillinger had whittled the gun himself from shelving in his cell. In fact, as the Girardin manuscript makes clear, the wooden gun was smuggled in from outside. Art O'Leary did it. After reading of a Wisconsin man who had escaped a local jail using a toy gun, O'Leary asked a Chicago gunsmith to whittle him one.

The second and far thornier question surrounds what, if any, help Dillinger received from allies in Crown Point. Ernest Blunk and Sam Cahoon were later indicted for helping Dillinger; both were acquitted after perfunctory trials. Afterward, an assistant state attorney general named Edward Barce was tasked with investigating the escape. Eight months later, in November 1934, Barce produced a secret report for Governor Paul McNutt, a copy of which survives in FBI files. On its face, the Barce report was a bombshell. In it, Barce alleged that Art O'Leary held two meetings with Warden Lew Baker, one at a barbecue stand on the outskirts of Crown Point, and handed Baker $1,800 to help Dillinger escape. Barce quoted employees of the barbecue stand and a Crown Point tavern, who claimed that Piquett boasted

. . .

While Indiana politicians and prosecutors squabbled over responsibility for his escape, Dillinger arrived in Minnesota that Sunday night, thirty-six hours after fleeing Crown Point, and tossed his things into Apartment 106 at the Santa Monica Apartments on South Girard Avenue in Minneapolis. The jug marker Eddie Green had rented the flat for him under the name "Mr. and Mrs. Olson." Billie handed the janitor a fifty-dollar deposit, and they wired the shades closed.

No record exists of Dillinger's first meeting with Nelson's gang the next day. The two gang leaders probably knew each other; there are unconfirmed accounts they met in East Chicago the previous June, and there had been talk of teaming up for a train robbery that autumn. Certainly they knew each other by reputation. Dillinger was grateful for Nelson's acceptance after his escape; for weeks afterward he remarked to people what a huge favor Nelson had done for him.

As for Nelson, working with Dillinger meant instant respect, and prestige, things Nelson craved; this, after all, was a twenty-four-year-old who just twelve months before had been a gangland chauffeur. Now he would "command" the nation's most wanted bank robber. Dillinger gracefully accepted a secondary role in Nelson's gang, but it was a distinction that would be entirely lost on the press. When the two were eventually linked the newspapers dubbed them "The Second Dillinger Gang," a view that angered Nelson. Before long his envy would curdle into jealousy.

It is unclear whether Dillinger realized he was joining forces with a psychopath. The night Dillinger arrived in the Twin Cities, Nelson was driving through Minneapolis with his gofer Johnnie Chase when the two cut in front of a car driven by a thirty-five-year-old paint salesman named Ted Kidder, who was returning from a birthday party with his wife and her mother.

---

that Dillinger had promised him $50,000 if he could arrange his freedom. Barce even uncovered a series of letters O'Leary had supposedly written to a corrupt East Chicago politician to further the conspiracy.

It was stirring stuff, but almost certainly untrue. The Barce report had a single glaring flaw. Its sole source of information was Meyer Bogue, the slender con man who had briefly functioned as Piquett's gofer; not long after the Crown Point escape, Bogue went to work for Barce at $15 a day. FBI agents later interviewed every person mentioned in the Barce-Bogue conspiracy, as well as the supposed eyewitnesses. All denied every salient point Barce made. None of those named were ever indicted, much less prosecuted.

If there was a conspiracy, it was a small one, perhaps a single man, the man who smuggled Dillinger the wooden gun. O'Leary or Piquett could have done it. They later told Russell Girardin that the gun had, in fact, been smuggled into the jail by Ernest Blunk, who they insisted had taken a bribe to do so. The truth is lost to history.

"Damn it, they can't do that to me," Kidder said as Nelson's car veered in front of him.

Irritated, Kidder sped up and cut back in front of Nelson's Hudson. This enraged Nelson. He pulled alongside Kidder's car and attempted to force it into the curb. Kidder pulled ahead, but Nelson stayed directly behind him as they neared the salesman's home in the St. Louis Park section of Minneapolis. Not wanting to lead the angry driver to his house, Kidder headed toward a drugstore to call the police. Reaching the store, he had just leaped out of his car when Nelson drove up and shouted something. A moment later three shots rang out. Two struck Kidder in the midsection, and he fell, dying.

His wife, Bernice, ran to his side.

"You've killed him!" she screamed.

"Keep your damn mouth shut," Nelson snapped, "or I'll let you have it, too."[3] He backed up the car and drove off.*

This was John Dillinger's new partner.

Sioux Falls, South Dakota
Tuesday, March 6

The temperature hung at the freezing point as the green Packard sedan pulled up in front of the Security National Bank & Trust Company a few minutes before ten. Six men in dark overcoats stepped out into the street, glancing about, wisps of steam rising from their lips. Stern, unsmiling, and unshaven, wearing fedoras tugged low over their foreheads, they were a rough-looking bunch. A bank stenographer saw them through a window. "There's a bunch of holdup men," she joked to a clerk. "I don't like the look of this," the clerk said.

Just three days after his escape from Crown Point, Dillinger was about to rob a bank. One of the men remained by the car as Tommy Carroll took a position on the sidewalk by the front door, a submachine gun beneath his coat. Dillinger led Nelson and the others inside. Nelson threw open his

---

* In a 1941 series of articles for *True Detective Adventures,* Nelson's friend Fatso Negri quoted Nelson's version of the Kidder murder. "[W]e happened to cut in ahead of another car," Nelson said. "The driver, one of those fresh guys, cut right back in front of us. He stopped the car, got out, and came back toward us and said to me: 'What the hell do you mean? Get out of that car and I'll slap your face for you.' He had taken a step or two toward us when I leveled on him and hit him. Then we had to tear out of that place."

overcoat and drew his Thompson gun. "This is a holdup!" he shouted. "Everyone on the floor!"

A clerk pressed a button, and as the dozen or so employees and customers inside the bank lay on the floor or backed against the walls, the alarm began ringing loudly outside the bank. At the sound of the alarm, Nelson flinched. Dillinger, by now accustomed to working to the sound of an alarm, strode coolly behind the teller cages and, with Van Meter, began clearing stacks of cash off the counter. The alarm enraged Nelson. In contrast to his partners, who remained calm, he began pacing the lobby nervously, sticking his submachine gun at people.

"I'd like to know who set that alarm off!" Nelson shouted. "Who did it? Who?"

As Dillinger and Van Meter shoved the bank president toward the vault door, Nelson seemed to be working himself into a frenzy. He pointed his gun at one frightened employee after other.

"If you want to get killed, just make some move!" he announced. "If you want to get killed, just make some move!"

Within minutes policemen began to arrive. A traffic cop, Homer Powers, was the first to run up. Tommy Carroll met him with his submachine gun, and within moments Powers was standing on the sidewalk, hands above his head. The police chief, M. W. Parsons, and a detective arrived next. They were disarmed and joined Powers on the sidewalk. A crowd of townspeople began gathering, drawn by the alarm and the spectacle of three policemen standing with their arms raised.

In the lobby, Nelson was working himself into a lather. Just then a motorcycle cop named Hale Keith pulled up beside the bank. Spotting him through a window, Nelson leaped a low railing, scrambling atop a loan officer's desk, and let loose a deafening burst of gunfire through a plate-glass window. Women screamed as Keith fell, struck by four bullets. "I got one! I got one!" Nelson cried.

As Dillinger and Van Meter finished in the vault, the crowd outside was still growing. People were hanging out of second-story windows, watching Tommy Carroll pace up and down in the street, his gun trained on the policemen he had taken hostage. A sheriff and several deputies headed onto rooftops, hoping to pick off one of the robbers as they tried to escape. Inside, Dillinger and Van Meter were finishing up. Just as the first Dillinger Gang had done at Racine, they grabbed a bank manager and four tellers and herded them out onto the sidewalk to the car. As they left, Nelson shot out the bank's front window.

Scattered gunshots rang out as the gang loaded the bank manager, Leo Olson, and the tellers onto the Packard's running boards. The car had just begun to move when a patrolman fired a shot into its radiator. Steam began to rise from the hood. The car stopped, and the hostages jumped off. One of the women began to run.

"Come back here!" one of the robbers shouted. A minute later, the hostages back on the running boards, the Packard again moved forward slowly through city streets, south toward the frozen prairie at the edge of town. Once they hit Route 77, the main road south, Dillinger reminded the others to toss roofing nails behind them. With the Packard's engine coughing and sputtering, he could see it was only a matter of time before a posse caught up with them.

A few miles later the Packard began to falter, and everyone jumped out, hailed an oncoming Dodge, and sent the frightened owner scurrying out into the fields. They shoved the hostages out onto the highway and began transferring a set of gas cans to the new car.

Just then Sheriff Melvin L. Sells, in pursuit with three men in a squad car, spotted the cars parked on the highway. Sells stopped a hundred yards back, not wanting to jeopardize the hostages. One of the robbers, probably Nelson, fired a volley their way. The officers saw Dillinger grab Nelson and pull him into the car.

The gang sped off south. Years later Sheriff Sells insisted he chased the speeding bandits for two hours, giving up only after he lost them somewhere in Iowa. In fact, the next morning's newspaper reported that the sheriff and two other cars turned back the moment the robbers opened fire. The gang's fleeing car was last seen in southwestern Minnesota, heading toward St. Paul, but the local sheriffs who gave chase were unable to catch up to it.[4]

"Was it Dillinger?" a headline in the *Daily Argus-Leader* of Sioux Falls asked that evening. Several eyewitnesses, including the bank president, insisted it was. Almost no one believed them, including the FBI. The idea that Dillinger could strike three states away from Crown Point only three days after his escape was considered outlandish. A St. Paul agent arrived in Sioux Falls the next day, but the Bureau investigation went little further.

The gang returned to its apartments in the Twin Cities to count the haul. It came to roughly $46,000, nearly $8,000 a man. What Dillinger thought of

Nelson's crazed display is unknown, but the day's events were a clear indication of the two gang leaders' philosophical differences. Whatever he thought, Dillinger needed Nelson's gang. For the first time, he had bills to pay, to Piquett, and to attorneys representing Pete Pierpont, Charles Makley, and his other former gangmates, whose trial for the murder of Sheriff Jess Sarber opened that week in Lima, Ohio. He needed more money, and fast.

The hunt for John Dillinger would become the most important case in FBI history. More than any other single event, it would validate the Roosevelt administration's push for a national law-enforcement authority and enshrine the Bureau as an American institution. Conventional wisdom holds that Hoover eagerly joined the manhunt. In fact, as FBI files make clear, Hoover viewed the Dillinger case as a potential quagmire and long resisted being drawn into it.

The previous fall, when the governor of Indiana made direct pleas for the FBI's help following the death of Sheriff Sarber, Hoover had ignored them. When the attorney general asked him to review the situation, Hoover notified the Chicago, Detroit, and Cincinnati offices to render "all available assistance," but that help had been limited to a smattering of interviews. Melvin Purvis and other SACs attended a conference or two with local officials, but only to monitor the situation. Hoover showed little interest in anything more.

Nor was Hoover any more eager to chase Dillinger in the hours after his escape from Crown Point. The massacre and Bremer investigations were still unresolved, and drew the daily attention of dozens of agents, fourteen on Bremer in Chicago alone. Purvis drove down to Crown Point to survey the situation that Saturday, but reporters' calls to the Bureau produced only shrugs. "[Newsmen] inquired as to why we did not know more about [the escape]," an aide memoed Hoover, "and I informed them that Dillinger was not a federal prisoner."[5]

But when Dillinger's escape dominated national newspaper headlines Monday morning, Hoover telephoned Purvis. He did not immediately order Purvis onto the case. Instead, FBI memoranda indicate he attempted to gauge the Bureau's chances of success if it joined the manhunt. Specifically, Hoover asked Purvis what information his informants could furnish that might lead to Dillinger's arrest. Purvis's reply was sobering, as Hoover noted the next day.

"In talking with you last evening," Hoover wrote Purvis, "I gathered that you had practically no underworld informants or connections with which your office could contact in the event of an emergency arising . . . I am somewhat concerned."[6]*

And with good reason. Purvis not only had no informants in place, he was unsure how to proceed with any information he might gather. In fact, his questions to FBI headquarters suggest an investigator badly out of his depth. Purvis thought he might want to tap some telephones, but he was unclear as to the legality of wiretaps in Illinois. He twice called Sam Cowley, the agent who served as the Bureau's investigative chief, and asked whether he needed to bring Chicago police along to launch a raid. By law he did, Cowley reminded him. Hoover sarcastically suggested Purvis needed a police escort to buoy his confidence. "He must have some brass buttons along," Hoover scrawled on a memo that Wednesday, "otherwise he would feel lost."[7]

Stung by Hoover's criticism, Purvis hired a confidential informant—a source he had used before, at five dollars a day—and mounted a raid with Chicago police that Tuesday night. They stormed the apartment of a woman named Anne Baker, whom the informant erroneously charged with harboring Dillinger after his escape. The raid was a debacle. No one named Baker was home. Not till the next morning did Purvis learn that he had raided the wrong address.

The onslaught of headlines forced Hoover's hand. On Wednesday morning, March 7, the day after the Sioux Falls robbery, he sent a wire to all FBI offices, directing SACs to "give preferred and immediate attention"

---

* In later years, Hoover became notorious for inserting into FBI files memoranda that tended to absolve himself of blame in controversial matters. The morning after speaking to Purvis, he wrote a memo to Pop Nathan that appears to be an early example of this:

Last evening I had occasion to call Mr. Purvis at Chicago to inquire of him what steps had been taken in the Chicago office toward bringing about the apprehension of Dillinger, and much to my surprise the Chicago office has done practically nothing in this matter . . . I am also somewhat concerned that the supervising officials at the Seat of Government did not take immediate steps to instruct our field offices as soon as Dillinger escaped, to put forth every effort to bring about his apprehension, notwithstanding the fact that Dillinger at that time was not known to have violated a Federal Statute. The reason I am surprised . . . is because when Dillinger made his previous escape, this Division did take steps to endeavor to bring about his apprehension, so consequently, there was no reason why we should not take similar steps when he made his recent escape.

This was remarkably disingenuous. The FBI had done next to nothing to pursue Dillinger that fall. No SAC would dare initiate a major new case without Hoover's approval, and Hoover hadn't given any. If the FBI was tardy in its pursuit of Dillinger that week, Hoover had only himself to blame.

to the Dillinger case. The rationale for the FBI's entry into the case was ostensibly that Dillinger had stolen a car during his escape and driven it into
Illinois, a violation of the federal Dyer Act. It was the thinnest of fig leaves.
The fact was, Hoover was forced into the Dillinger case by his own ambitions: if the FBI wasn't hunting the nation's most wanted man, what good
was it?

With no evidence that Dillinger had left the Chicago area, the impact of
Hoover's directive fell heavily on the overmatched Purvis. Unsure where to
begin, Purvis sought guidance from John Stege of the Chicago Police Department's Dillinger Squad. But Stege, as Purvis wrote Hoover, "has not
been particularly anxious to furnish any information concerning any of his
activities to anyone, including other police."[8]

Purvis thus started from scratch, pulling five agents off the Bremer case
to hunt Dillinger. It's difficult to say whether the miserable quality of this
group's work in the ensuing weeks was due to the Bureau's ambivalence or
Purvis's ineptitude. Agents descended on the Crown Point jail, taking statements from everyone involved in the escape, and visited the prison at
Michigan City, where Dillinger's onetime gangmate Ed Shouse gave them
Billie Frechette's name. For ten days, as Dillinger sightings poured in from
cities as far afield as Los Angeles and Seattle, Purvis and his men probed
the backgrounds of Frechette and various relatives of Dillinger's jailed
partners. They found precisely nothing.

Dillinger would dominate headlines around the country for weeks to come.
With no sign of the man himself, crowds of reporters descended on Lima,
Ohio, to attend the trials of his former partners Pete Pierpont, Charles
Makley, and Russell Clark. One line of speculation ran through every story:
would Dillinger ride to their rescue?

Ohio officials were ready if he did. Lima was an armed camp. Governor
George White called out the National Guard, and guardsmen patrolled the
town's streets day and night. Their commander, a bellicose artilleryman
named Harold Bush, surrounded the Allen County Courthouse with sand
bags and a trio of machine-gun nests. After a rumor spread that Dillinger
intended to kidnap Governor White, two squads of guardsmen took up
positions outside the governor's mansion.

The three trials themselves were cursory affairs. Ed Shouse was brought
under guard from Indiana, and his terse recitation of events leading to

Sheriff Sarber's murder was all the ammunition the juries needed. In three consecutive trials spanning two weeks, Pierpont was convicted, then Makley, then Russell Clark. Pierpont and Makley received death sentences. Clark got life. Dillinger never showed.

Mason City, Iowa
Tuesday, March 13

Wet clots of snow were blowing diagonally across the yellow fields of northern Iowa as two cars came to a stop at a sandpit just beyond the southern edge of town. A harsh wind tore at the flaps of the men's overcoats as Homer Van Meter and Eddie Green stepped out of one of the cars, a navy Buick. The rest of the gang—Dillinger, Baby Face Nelson, John Hamilton, and Tommy Carroll—emerged from the second. They huddled together in a ragged circle, talking.

Green and Van Meter had spent the weekend in Mason City studying the layout of the First National Bank, staying in a room at the YMCA. They briefed the others, who had driven down from St. Paul. Everyone knew this was a high-risk job. Years of robberies had turned many Midwestern banks into small fortresses, and the Mason City bank, located on the town's main square, was Iowa's Fort Knox. A guard sat in a steel cage behind bulletproof glass on the second floor of the lobby, fifteen feet above the front door. He was armed with tear gas and a rifle. But the payoff, Green emphasized, was huge. He estimated the vault held a quarter million dollars. If everything went according to plan, they wouldn't have to work again for months.

A few minutes after two o'clock, the circle broke. They transferred the guns into the Buick and headed into town. Tommy Carroll drove. As he headed up Pennsylvania Avenue, a local couple, Mr. and Mrs. W. E. Barr, fell in behind the car. "Isn't that peculiar?" Mrs. Barr remarked, motioning at the Buick. "They have the rear window [knocked] out."

"It's probably hot," said Mr. Barr, eyeing the carload of well-dressed men. "There's an awful lot of them. It looks like a car full of pallbearers."[9]

A minute later, a freelance cameraman named H. C. Kunkleman watched as the Buick pulled to a stop beside the First National Bank's towering seven-story red-brick facade. Standing beside a tripod in the square, Kunkleman watched, curious, as five of the six men inside stepped from the car. One of them noticed Kunkleman's camera. "Hey you," the man snapped.

"If there's any shooting to be done, we'll do it. Get that thing outta here."
Kunkleman, startled, stopped filming.*

Carroll remained in the car, cradling a rifle. Nelson, wearing a charcoal
cap, black leather gloves, and a camel-hair overcoat, trotted up the sidewalk beside the bank, taking a position at the head of its rear alley. Dillinger, wearing a gray fedora, matching overcoat, and a striped muffler,
lingered outside the front door as the others—Van Meter, Hamilton, and
Eddie Green—hustled inside the bank.

The two-story lobby was filled with customers, about two dozen of
them, standing in short lines in front of the teller cages; the trio's first challenge was to get their attention. This was achieved in short order when one
of the men raised a submachine gun and fired a deafening volley into the
ceiling. Bits of plaster fell like rain as all three men began yelling, "Hands
up! Hands up! Everybody on the floor!" The effect was akin to three wild-
eyed berserkers storming a prayer meeting. Forty years later it was the
sheer manic intensity of the gang's orders that stuck in the mind of the
guard perched above them in the steel cage, Tom Walters. "I swear they
were all doped up or something," he remembered in a 1973 interview.
"Their faces were purple and their eyes were blazing. They never stopped
screaming. I had never seen anything like it."[10]

Tellers looked up, startled. A few employees ducked into closets and beneath desks. "Down! Down!" Eddie Green screamed. "Everybody on the
floor!" One of the adrenalized robbers, apparently Van Meter, strode
toward the bank's president, Willis Bagley, who sat at his desk near the
front door, talking to a customer. Bagley, dumbfounded to see a man stalking toward him carrying a Thompson submachine gun, had the presence of
mind to duck into his office and slam the door.

Van Meter thrust his submachine gun forward, preventing the door
from closing. Bagley threw his weight into the door as Van Meter, after a
moment of struggle, pulled the gun free. Stepping back, he fired a burst of
bullets through the door. Women screamed. Bagley, a bullet creasing his

---

* To this day, local historians have no idea who Kunkleman was or why he was filming that day. His
footage of the robbery's prelude and aftermath was later developed and shown in a Mason City theater. It
then disappeared. For decades local historians tried in vain to locate Kunkleman or his fabled film. It was
finally found in the hands of a Mason City camera-store owner in 1996.

chest, dived for cover as Van Meter gave up and began storming through the lobby, ordering everyone onto the floor.

As he did, Tom Walters, the thirty-three-year-old guard sitting on a chair in the steel cage above the front door, recovered from his initial shock and jammed an eight-inch canister into his tear-gas gun. He aimed it through a gun slit in the bulletproof glass and fired at Eddie Green, directly below him. The canister struck Green in the back and fell to the floor amid a tangle of prone customers. A man on the floor kicked the spewing canister away. It skidded toward another man, who kicked it back. "It was funny," a teller named Emmett Ryan recalled in 1982. "But it wasn't funny at the time."[11]

Standing in the middle of the lobby, a dense cloud of tear gas rising around him, Green swore and glanced up at Walters, who was struggling to clear his gas gun. The gun was jammed and nothing he could do would clear it. Green collared a bank executive named R. L. Stephenson, thrust him forward as a shield, and opened fire on Walters. The bulletproof glass cracked and splintered, and a bullet ricocheted through the gun slit, searing a bloody line across the guard's chin and right ear. Furious, Green demanded to know how he could access the cage. "Get that son of a bitch with the tear gas!" Green yelled at Hamilton, who was already scooping money off the counters.

Hamilton looked up and saw Walters crouching on his chair, struggling with the tear-gas gun even as he grabbed a Winchester rifle. For several moments they engaged in a face-off: Hamilton could see it was no use firing at bulletproof glass, and Walters couldn't fire his gun without endangering the innocent. "Hamilton called me every obscenity in the book, and dared me to shoot," Walters recalled. "But I couldn't because I would've plugged half the people in the lobby."

Billowing clouds of tear gas were filling the lobby, and more was coming. From a position on the mezzanine, a bank officer named Tom Barclay grabbed a tear-gas candle and tossed it into the lobby. Gas had reached the second floor when the switchboard operator, Margaret Johnson, ran to the railing. Falling to her knees, she crawled to a window and opened it. Looking down, she spied a small man in a camel-hair overcoat standing in the alley. "Hey you!" Johnson called. "Don't you know the bank is being robbed? Get some help!"

The man turned. It was Nelson. "Are you telling me, lady?"

By now, everyone inside the bank was coughing. The gas was so thick it was difficult to see. As Green and Van Meter prowled the aisles, ordering people onto the floor, Hamilton turned his attention from the bank guard to the assistant cashier, a slender fifty-nine-year-old named Harry Fisher. Hamilton, a white cloth bag filled with money from the teller cages in one hand, pressed a pistol into Fisher's back and shoved him toward the vault. Though frightened, Fisher was uncomfortably aware that more than $200,000 in cash sat in the vault.

"All the way back [to the vault], I kept wondering how I could keep from giving him all that money," Fisher remembered in an interview in 1942.[12] "I must have walked too slowly to suit him for he gave me a boot in the tailbone to hurry me along."

When they reached the barred door leading to the vault, Fisher got an idea. Fishing a key from his pocket, he opened the door, then shoved a bag of pennies against it as a doorstop. When Hamilton snatched up the bag, the door shut behind him, just as Fisher had intended to do himself. There was now a barred door between the two men: Hamilton kept his gun trained on Fisher through it. Fisher then stepped to the vault door, which was unlocked. Hamilton didn't know that, however, and Fisher spun the combination, locking it. Wiping tears from his eyes, Fisher turned to Hamilton and said, "I don't know whether I can see to work the combination."[13]

"You'd better open it goddamn quick," Hamilton snapped.

Fisher took his time opening the vault as Hamilton wiped tears from his face. Finally swinging the giant door back onto its hinges, he stepped back to the barred door where Hamilton stood. "Now this door is locked," Fisher lied, nodding toward the door separating the two men, "and I can't open it."

Hamilton told him to shove the money through the bars. Determined to proceed as slowly as possible, Fisher walked into the vault, grabbed an armload of bags containing one-dollar bills, and plodded back to the barred door, sliding them one by one into Hamilton's arms. When he was done, he plodded back into the vault and grabbed more bags of ones. "If you don't hurry up," Hamilton said, "I'm gonna shoot you."

As Harry Fisher cannily slowed the robbery to a crawl, a huge crowd was gathering outside the bank. People streamed from stores and homes all around the town square, drawn by the sound of gunfire. For a few minutes it was a congenial affair, some of the people actually laughing and giggling. A few, spying H. C. Kunkleman's tripod-mounted camera, thought some kind of movie was being shot. "Hey, there, Hank!" someone yelled, spotting a friend in the crowd.[14]

Dillinger was standing on the sidewalk by the front door, smiling faintly as he kept the crowd at bay, when Van Meter pushed ten hostages out to join him. The two lined the group in front of the bank, a row of human shields. Dillinger then ducked back into the bank to see what was taking so much time. "Gimme three more minutes!" Hamilton hollered.

Dillinger corralled another group of six or seven people and herded them toward the front door. After East Chicago, he was taking no chances. "Stand close to me," Lydia Crosby, a bank stenographer, heard him say. "Come up, get around me." Outside, Dillinger lined up these people with the others. More than fifteen bank employees and customers were now standing on the sidewalk in front of the bank, hands held above their heads. Van Meter strode into a shoe store and forced a half-dozen shoppers out onto the sidewalk to join them.

Then, from their right, came gunshots. It was Nelson, loosing a volley at a reporter from the *Mason City Globe Gazette* who had heard the shots; the reporter dived into the Yelland and Hanes Book Store. A moment later a large Hudson sedan drove by. Nelson yelled, "Get back!" then shot at it, too, the bullets striking the radiator; the car stopped with a loud squeal of brakes, reversed direction, and sped back into the town square, narrowly missing bystanders. A little girl in the crowd began crying hysterically.

Nelson swung his gun in a menacing circle, watching for police. As he did, several eyewitnesses said, he began laughing. He fired a burst at a row of parked cars, then another at the second story of a hardware store. Several bystanders thought he must be deranged. Just then a man named R. L. James, secretary to the Mason City school board, strolled up the sidewalk beside the bank, unaware of the robbery in progress. "Stop right there!" Nelson yelled, but James, who was hard of hearing, kept walking. Nelson fired, hitting James in the leg. He fell bleeding to the sidewalk. Nelson trotted up to him, snatched up a portfolio James was carrying, and searched it.

"I thought you were a cop, you son of a bitch," Nelson said.

"I'm not a cop," James moaned.

Dillinger took a few steps down the sidewalk, toward Nelson. Spotting the wounded James, he said, "Did you have to do that?"[15]

"I thought he was a cop!" Nelson snapped.

As Dillinger stepped back behind the wall of hostages, an elderly judge named John C. Shipley was peering down from a third-floor window directly above him. In Shipley's hand was an old revolver he had fished from a desk drawer. Drawing a bead on Dillinger, he pulled the trigger. The bullet struck Dillinger a glancing blow in the right shoulder. Dillinger whirled, staring upward, then raised a pistol and fired several times at the windowsill. Shipley ducked down, unharmed.

As he turned back toward the hostages, Dillinger spied a city patrolman darting through the town square. The officer, James Buchanan, dived behind a large boulder used as a Civil War monument. Dillinger raised his gun and fired, the bullet ricocheting off the boulder. "Come out from behind there and fight like a man!" Dillinger shouted.

"Get away from that crowd and I will!" Buchanan shouted back. He peered around the boulder but held his fire.

Dillinger could see that the situation was getting out of hand. Van Meter stepped back into the lobby, waving away the tear gas, and yelled to Hamilton, "We're leaving!"

"Give us three more minutes!" Hamilton yelled back. In the vault, Harry Fisher's pace had gone from slow to glacial. "Gimme the big bills!" Hamilton snapped at Fisher, who ignored him, carefully bringing out one bag of singles after another.

"We're going!" Van Meter hollered again.

"Just gimme another minute!" Hamilton replied. He was torn. "It's hell to leave all that money," Fisher heard him say.[16] The bags in Hamilton's hand contained about $52,000. There was another $200,000 in the vault. Hamilton decided he couldn't wait. A moment later he turned from the vault door, grabbed a bank employee, and pushed him toward the front. In a minute all six gang members were on the sidewalk outside, surrounded by about twenty-five hostages. Each man shoved a knot of people toward the Buick. They were in a foul mood. When Eddie Green spied a jeweler staring from behind a parked car, he snarled, "Pull in that damn turtleneck! I'll cut your head off!" He fired a single shot as the jeweler ducked behind the car.

Just then Judge Shipley raised his head to peer out his third-floor window, directly above the gang. Spying Hamilton with the money sack, he fired one final shot. The bullet struck Hamilton in the right shoulder. Hamilton lurched forward, stumbling into the getaway car. The wound was not serious, nor was Dillinger's.

Five hostages were shoved onto the running boards, two more onto the front fender and several more on the rear fender. "Get up there, you bald-headed son of a bitch, or I'll drop you," one of the robbers, apparently Nelson, snapped as an assistant cashier named Ralph Wiley hopped onto the back fender. Several women were shoved into the backseat. In minutes the car windows were jammed with arms and legs. As Tommy Carroll inched the car from the curb, witnesses counted anywhere from twenty to twenty-six people inside and outside the car.

The car crept along at about fifteen miles an hour as it zigzagged through city streets toward the edge of town. At one point, as they passed the Kirk Apartments, a woman named Minnie Piehm hollered, "Let me out! This is where I live." Amazingly, the car stopped and Miss Piehm trotted off. An assistant cashier was about to follow when one of the gang said, "Get back here, you."

The situation wasn't funny to the hostages who remained clinging to the car's fenders and running boards. "Stop looking at me or I'll kill you," one of the gang members said several times. The Buick's slow pace gave the police chief, E. J. Patton, time to catch up; his was one of two squad cars that managed to pursue the gang. Patton followed at a safe distance as the Buick turned south onto Highway 18 and picked up speed. At one point, as the fleeing car crested a rise, Nelson said to Carroll, "Wait till they come over the hill and then I'll pop them off." Sitting in the front seat, Nelson took a rifle and fired several wild shots at Chief Patton's car.

Just beyond the city limits, the Buick stopped. Nelson hopped off, fired a shot or two at Chief Patton's car, which also stopped, then began tossing out handfuls of roofing tacks. Dillinger watched as several bounced under the Buick. In a serene voice, he said, "You're getting tacks under our own car."[17]

When Nelson jumped back into the car, Carroll once again headed south, driving at about thirty miles an hour. It was still snowing, and several of the hostages outside the car were freezing. One of the tellers, Emmet Ryan, gave a woman his jacket. For some reason, this angered Dillinger, who fired him a cold stare. "The coldest eyes you ever saw," Ryan remembered years later. "Cold eyes and white skin."

Ryan again irked Dillinger when the car turned onto a dirt road to release several hostages. Ryan began to leave. Then, realizing how cold another hostage was without a coat, he suggested the other man leave instead. "Who the hell is running this show?" Dillinger asked.

Chief Patton was still behind them. He pulled to the roadside when the car stopped. Nelson fired three shots from his rifle, hitting the squad car but missing Patton. "You phone the law!" Nelson shouted at one of the departing hostages. "Tell 'em if they don't stop following us we're gonna kill everyone in the car!"

They proceeded that way for forty-five minutes or so, eventually finding their way back to the sand pit and their second car. Most of the hostages were left there, but two accompanied the gang on the drive north; they were released only when Chief Patton turned back to Mason City. When they were certain they had gotten away cleanly, the gang stopped and bandaged Dillinger's and Hamilton's shoulder wounds.

They were back in St. Paul by nightfall. Tired and bleeding, the gang headed for Harry Sawyer's Green Lantern tavern. Sawyer wasn't there, but his bartender said he knew what to do. That night a doctor named Nels Mortensen was awakened by the sound of someone ringing the bell at his home on Fairmount Avenue in St. Paul. Thin, gray-haired, and locally prominent, the fifty-year-old Mortensen was president of the state board of health; a friend of Harry Sawyer's, he had treated Fred Barker for syphilis and performed the tonsillectomy on Alvin Karpis's girlfriend. Downstairs, he parted the curtains. Two cars were at the curb. Opening the door, he found a group of men he didn't recognize.

The bartender explained that two of the men had just been injured in a gunfight downtown. Mortensen said he didn't have his medical bag, but let the men inside anyway. Standing in his foyer, Mortensen tore off Hamilton's bandages and examined the wound; it wasn't serious. Dillinger almost fainted when he stripped off his shirt. He stumbled into a chair, and Mortensen got him a glass of water. Dillinger's wound was deeper but no more serious. Mortensen said the men could visit his office the next morning if they needed further treatment. As they left, the doctor caught a glimpse of a submachine gun beneath Van Meter's coat. He returned to bed without telling anyone of the incident.[18]

A month later, when FBI agents learned of it, Hoover decided to make an example of Dr. Mortensen. He received a prison sentence of one year. When Dr. Mortensen died in 1971 at the age of eighty-seven, he was still insisting he had no idea his patient had been John Dillinger.

After seeing Mortensen, the gang divided the money. A rare glimpse at the delicate nature of intragang relations comes from the FBI's debriefing of Pat Cherrington, who fell into federal hands later that spring. According to Cherrington, Nelson "was very much disliked by all members of the mob . . . [T]hey had a continuous fear when they were around him, and particularly subsequent to a bank robbery; that the usual procedure after a bank robbery, at which time they would all meet to divide the loot, was that they would invariably have Nelson sit in the middle of the room, although he was not aware that they were arranging things in that way, and allow him to count off each one's share; that all the hoodlums would get around the room as that each one would be facing Nelson, as they expect at any time . . . that Nelson would shoot them and take the entire amount."[19]

After dividing the money, the gang began to scatter. Van Meter and his girlfriend Mickey Conforti settled into their apartment on Girard Avenue in St. Paul. Dillinger and Billie had already moved into a new set of rooms on South Lexington Avenue; they had been obliged to vacate their Minneapolis flat after Hamilton's gun accidentally went off: Dillinger didn't want to take the chance they had been noticed. In the new apartment Hamilton slept on the couch with Cherrington.

For the moment, Hamilton and Cherrington had the place to themselves, for Dillinger had business to attend to. On the Wednesday morning after his midnight visit to Dr. Mortensen, he took Billie and drove to Chicago. Art O'Leary was in Piquett's office when the phone rang. "Be in front of your office, on the Wacker Drive side," a voice said. "I'll pick you up in about fifteen minutes."[20]

It was a short meeting. O'Leary listened as Dillinger talked and drove. He wanted Piquett to help Billie arrange a divorce so they could be married. O'Leary promised to relay the message. Piquett could only roll his eyes. For the trouble of representing America's most-wanted man, he had yet to receive a cent. That night and the next, Dillinger and Billie bunked in a basement room at Louis Cernocky's Crystal Ball Room in Fox River Grove. They had another quick meeting with O'Leary Sunday afternoon, in which O'Leary had the pleasant task of explaining to Dillinger that Piquett wasn't a divorce attorney. If Billie wanted a divorce attorney, O'Leary said, she should find one herself.

The next morning Dillinger dropped off a package of money for O'Leary. It contained $2,300, including a thousand each for Piquett and Pete Pierpont's parents. He then drove Billie to the airport, where she boarded a flight to Indianapolis to see Dillinger's father. In Mooresville, Billie gave the elder Dillinger several bundles of cash and the wooden gun Dillinger had used to escape from Crown Point.[21] Billie also passed on a note Dillinger had written his sister Audrey. It read:

Dear Sis:
    I thought I would write you a few lines and let you know I am still perculating [sic]. Don't worry about me honey, for that wont help any, and besides I having a lot of fun. I am sending Emmett [Audrey's

husband] my wooden gun and I want him to always keep it. I see that
Deputy Blunk says I had a real forty five that's just a lot of hooey to
cover up because they don't like to admit that I locked eight deputys
and a dozen trustys up with my wooden gun before I got my hands on
the two machine guns and you should have seen their faces Ha! Ha!
Ha! Pulling that off was worth ten years of my life Ha! Ha! I will be
around to see all of you when the roads are better, it is so hot around
Indiana now that I would have trouble getting through so I am sending my wife Billie . . . Now honey if any of you need any thing I wont
forgive you if you don't let me know. I got shot a week ago but I am
all right now just a little sore I bane one tough sweed Ha! Ha! . . .
Lots of love from Johnnie.[22]

While Billie spent that Friday at the Dillinger home in Indiana, Dillinger
drove east to visit Pete Pierpont's parents in Ohio, where he sat on the front
porch and made sure the family had received the money he had sent for his
partner's defense. Afterward he returned to Chicago, where he reunited
with Billie. Amazingly, the FBI still hadn't put the Dillinger or Pierpont
homes under surveillance.

While Dillinger crisscrossed Illinois, Indiana, and Ohio, Baby Face Nelson headed west to Reno, where within days his homicidal tendencies em-
broiled him in a mystery it would take the FBI years to solve. Reno's two
crime bosses, Bill Graham and Jim McKay, were in the midst of fighting a
federal mail-fraud case involving their support for a gang of con men that
flourished in the city. Somehow the two had learned that the government's
star witness against them was to be Roy Fritsch, the controller of a Reno
bank Graham and McKay owned.

On Thursday, March 22, a week after the Mason City robbery, Fritsch
disappeared after parking his car near his home. An eyewitness later told
the FBI he had seen two men hit Fritsch over the head and drag him to a
waiting car. The crime has officially never been solved. But according to informants who spoke to the FBI in later years, the culprits were Nelson and
his friend John Chase. According to FBI files, Nelson murdered Fritsch and
dumped his corpse down a mineshaft. Fritsch's body has never been found.

Just as it struggled to come to grips with its most ambitious manhunt to
date, the FBI discovered something that was to open an entirely new front

of the War on Crime. In February the Kansas City office had belatedly forwarded to Washington seventeen latent fingerprints taken from Verne
Miller's home after the Kansas City Massacre. It took weeks for technicians
to compare the prints against those of dozens of suspects. But on March 14,
the day after Dillinger's Mason City robbery, they made a jaw-dropping discovery: a print taken from a beer bottle in Miller's basement matched that
of Adam Richetti, Pretty Boy Floyd's moonshine-swilling sidekick. The
conclusion was inescapable: despite widespread doubts about their involvement, Richetti and Floyd really were Miller's partners in the massacre.

The news triggered a series of thunderbolt memos from Hoover to the
Kansas City office, demanding to know how the prints had been overlooked and who was responsible. More important, it prompted a sweeping
reassessment of the massacre investigation to date. The supposed involvement of the Barkers was forgotten. The FBI made no public announcement
of its discovery, but agents involved in the case now focused all their efforts
on finding Floyd and Richetti.

There was just one problem: there hadn't been a reliable sighting of the
two in six months. From all appearances, Floyd had fallen off the face of
the earth. An army of over a thousand Oklahoma lawmen and National
Guardsmen had swept the Cookson Hills in February, but found no sign of
him. The Bureau's own search for Floyd had been desultory; unless he was
involved in the massacre, Floyd was not a federal fugitive. Agents in Kansas
City and Oklahoma City collected tips as they came, but did little digging
on their own. Kansas City didn't identify Floyd's longtime girlfriend Juanita
Baird till February.

All that changed on March 14. Suddenly Floyd catapulted into the front
ranks of FBI fugitives, joining Dillinger and the Barkers. Responsibility for
finding him fell heavily on the Oklahoma City office, whose agents were already straining under the weight of thirty-one separate major cases, including the hunts for the Barkers and Bonnie and Clyde. Hoover dispatched
Pop Nathan to Oklahoma to assess the situation, and Nathan's report was
bleak. The SAC, Dwight Brantley, was working till midnight most evenings,
yet Nathan found dozens of new leads on the Barkers and Bonnie and
Clyde piling up in the files, untouched. Brantley complained he didn't have
enough men.

Nathan thought the problem was quality, not quantity. Only two of the
ten agents in Oklahoma City, he told Hoover, were sufficiently "competent" to handle a major case. The best, Frank Smith, the old Cowboy who

had survived the massacre, was assigned to pursue Floyd full-time, and he began making the rounds of Oklahoma sheriffs and snitches, dredging up what tips he could. But Nathan could see the writing on the wall. If a posse of a thousand men couldn't find Pretty Boy Floyd, the chances that the FBI's young and inexperienced agents—already burdened with searches for Dillinger, the Barkers, and many others—would succeed were close to zero.

Chicago, Illinois
The Irving Hotel, Room 234*

Fred Barker sat at the table in his pajamas. Dr. Joseph Moran, his eyes rheumy and bloodshot, leaned over and grasped his fingers, a scalpel already in his hand.

"You ready?" Moran asked.

Beside them Karpis looked on, transfixed. They had come to Dr. Moran's office after dinner, carrying overnight bags with underwear and fresh shirts. The doctor was a sad-eyed drunk who coughed a lot and had a pulsing red vein in his nose. Moran had fought in World War I and trained at the Tufts medical school in Boston, then had done a brief stretch in Joliet for performing illegal abortions. On his parole in late 1931 he had gone to work for a Touhy-controlled union in Cicero, and had performed successful surgeries on several of Roger Touhy's men. When Capone interests took control of the union the following spring, Moran had gone into private practice.

The ever cautious Karpis, asking around for someone who could alter their fingerprints, had heard about him in an underground tavern.† When they arrived that evening, Moran wrapped rubber bands around the first joint of each of Barker's fingers. Then he mixed a batch of a purplish antiseptic liquid and swabbed it on his fingertips. When Barker's fingers went numb, Moran injected each one with cocaine.

Barker took a deep breath. "I'm ready," he said.

Moran leaned over and slowly began whittling the meat off the end of one of Barker's fingers. Karpis couldn't believe it; it was exactly like sharpening a pencil. Thanks to the rubber bands there was little blood, but as the

---

* The precise date of Barker's and Karpis's surgeries has never been definitely established. The best guess is March 10, give or take a day.
† The bar was called the Green Lantern, named after but unrelated to Harry Sawyer's place in St. Paul.

skin sliced away, Karpis could see even the doctor growing pale. Freckles on Moran's forehead pulsed. He was sweating.

When Moran finished carving the fingers on Barker's right hand, he excused himself and stepped into a back room. "How you feeling?" he asked when he returned a moment later. "You want a drink?" It was obvious the doctor did. "Yeah, I'd take a drink," Barker said. "I'd take about anything I could get right now."

Moran handed Barker a bottle of whiskey and he drank deeply, lifting the bottle with his left hand. It took another ten minutes for Moran to carve the ends off the fingertips on Barker's left hand. When he was done he applied large cotton swabs to both hands and wrapped them in bandages. "I'm gonna give you a shot of morphine," Moran said, "because you're gonna start hurtin' in a few hours."

The doctor led Barker into an adjoining room and laid him on a bed. In minutes Barker was asleep. "Come on," Moran said to Karpis. "I'm gonna work on you now."

Karpis sat at the doctor's table.

"What the hell is it you're going to do?" he asked.

"Well, your face is kind of lopsided," Moran said. "I'm going to straighten it up." He described the series of incisions he planned to make around the temples and how he would use them to pull the skin of Karpis's face taut. Karpis had no idea what he was talking about. "You just be damn sure you know what you're doing," he said.

Moran gave Karpis a shot of morphine. In minutes Karpis felt as if he were floating in a happy sky; he didn't care what the doctor did next. Moran then administered several small shots of cocaine around the edges of Karpis's face and began making the incisions. Karpis felt so good he barely paid attention.

"Are you ready for your hands?" he asked after a bit.

"Yeah," Karpis mumbled.

Afterward Moran and his assistant tucked Karpis into a bed in another room. He awoke the next morning in incredible pain. The assistant showed him how to prop up his hands so that the blood would run out of his fingers and ease the throbbing.

"How's Freddie?" Karpis asked.

"Oh, he woke up in the middle of the night," the assistant said. "He was hurting like hell. I gave him a real stiff shot of morphine. Hell, he'll be out another few hours."

For three days Barker and Karpis drifted in and out of consciousness. In waking hours Karpis read the newspapers. On Thursday, March 15, he saw an article that stunned him: the Barker gang had been named the FBI's primary suspects in the Bremer kidnapping. Karpis read how the Bureau had identified Dock Barker through fingerprints found on the gas cans in Wisconsin. He cursed. "We'd better plan on getting the hell out of Chicago," he told Fred.

Barker was falling asleep. "I don't know what to do," he mumbled. "When I wake up, I'll talk. I want to sleep now."

Karpis sat up in a chair and watched Barker sleep until he, too, finally dozed off. Sometime before dawn Barker woke him.

"Where do you think we ought to go?" Barker asked.

"Well, what do you mean by 'we' now? Just who is we?"

"Well," said Barker, "Ma and me and you."

"No, not Ma," Karpis said. "She ain't going with us, Freddie. I've told you this before. She's gonna get you killed. Mark my words."

Barker made a face. "Well maybe you're right. Maybe we'd better make her stay here. You think she'll stay?"

"She'll have no choice."

"How are we gonna do this?"

"You want me to talk to her?" Karpis asked.

"You think you can do it?"

"You're damn right I can do it."

They moved into a Winthrop Avenue boardinghouse to recuperate; both men remained swathed in bandages and didn't want to be seen at their apartments. It gave Karpis an excuse to put off confronting Ma. He dreaded it. He procrastinated several days until they received a second dose of startling news: Shotgun George Ziegler was dead. It happened in Cicero. Ziegler was walking out of a bar when a car drove by and someone fired a shotgun, nearly blowing his head off. For the first time in months, Karpis was frightened. It was clearly a Syndicate hit. Did Frank Nitti want them dead?*

Dock Barker came by the next morning. Ziegler's death, they agreed, meant Chicago was no longer safe; if they had somehow roused the Syndicate's ire, every minute counted. Dock suggested they move to Toledo. A friend knew people there. Karpis and Fred agreed; it sounded as good as

---

* Ziegler's murder was never solved.

anywhere else. The next day Dock drove to Ohio and rented an apartment. When he returned Karpis faced the moment he had been dreading for days: telling Ma.

He made Dock go with him. Freddie was too scared.

"Jesus Christ!" Ma exclaimed the moment they entered her apartment. "Were you with George Ziegler?"

"No, why?" Karpis asked. His face was still bandaged.

"Well, look at your face. What the hell happened to you?"

"Oh, I had a, a car wreck."

"Where's Freddie?" Ma demanded. "What's wrong with Freddie? Why ain't he here?" She insisted that Freddie be brought to her.

"Well, he was in the wreck too," Karpis said. "And he got hurt a little worse than I did, and they've got him where he's real safe." Ma got angry. "He couldn't be no safer than he would be here!"

Karpis tried to give it to her easy. He didn't mention that they were moving, not at first. He said they wouldn't be visiting her any longer, not much anyway. Ma grew hysterical. For an hour she railed. She and Freddie were going to Florida, she insisted. And if they didn't, well, she was going back to Oklahoma. Karpis let her vent. Dock looked on the whole time, never saying a word. "Now, are you finished?" Karpis finally asked. "We're moving, and I ain't gonna tell you where the hell we're going. We'll keep in touch. You got plenty of money."

"What the hell good is money if I gotta be by myself?" Ma asked. It took another hour of arguing before Ma gave in, beaten. "All right," she said sadly. "If you boys will come and visit me when you're in Chicago. But that don't mean it'll be like this forever. This summer we'll get a cottage on a lake. How'll that be?"

Karpis promised a summer cottage, even as he realized it would never happen. He would have said anything to get Ma Barker to shut up. The next day they all drove to Toledo. Ma stayed behind. It was the last anyone would hear of most of the Barker Gang for a long time.

By the time Karpis and the Barkers fled Chicago, the FBI's pursuit was losing steam. Unlike the Dillinger Gang, which shed talkative confederates like dandruff, the Barkers seemed like clannish urban hillbillies, opaque and unknowable. A month after identifying them as Edward Bremer's kidnappers, the FBI hadn't found a single reliable source of information on the gang. Agents had prison snitches and old wanted posters from Oklahoma and Missouri, but little more.

It took weeks to compile lists of the Barker Gang's relatives and prison contacts. Brothers and sisters of several gang members and their girlfriends were put under surveillance, as were Karpis's parents in Chicago. Letters poured in to FBI offices from people who said they thought they knew or had seen members of the gang. Only one, a Texas prison inmate named Henry Hull, offered solid information. A prison pal of Dock Barker's, Hull had once visited Barker in Nevada. FBI agents descended on Reno and identified every apartment, grocery, dry cleaner, and gambling house the gang had visited during its two stays there. They collected phone records and assorted arcana—from a tailor they learned Fred Barker had a 13½-inch neck—but none of it led anywhere. The most recent sighting of the gang was six months old.

For his part, Hoover was obsessed with identifying the house where Bremer had been kept. Thousands of hours were spent searching for a town in Wisconsin or Illinois that matched the descriptions Bremer had given. More than a hundred were surveyed. Police and mailmen were interviewed in each one, but none seemed to match Bremer's memory. One of Purvis's men, Ralph Brown, actually checked the correct town, Bensonville, but failed to recognize it.*

If anything, progress in the Dillinger case was even slower. By the end of March, Purvis and his men had spent four weeks on the case, yet had failed to unearth a single lead on the gang's whereabouts, nor any hint they were behind the robberies at Sioux Falls and Mason City. As the Crown Point publicity died down, in fact, the Bureau's investigation lost what little momentum it had. In hindsight Purvis's choices seem inexplicable. He didn't bother placing the Dillinger farm in Mooresville under surveillance; had he done so, agents might have been waiting for Billie when she visited on March 19.

---

* The most vigorous questioning the FBI did wasn't of anyone associated with the Barkers: it was of FBI agents themselves. When news of Dock Barker's identification leaked to the St. Paul newspapers, Hoover exploded. He demanded to know the source of the leak, firing off a cascade of angry memos at the two most likely sources, the offices in Minneapolis and Oklahoma City. Pop Nathan interrogated several Oklahoma agents who appeared to have mentioned the fingerprints to local lawmen, who had then mentioned them to a Minnesota reporter doing research on the Barkers. The likely leaker was an agent named Herman Hollis, a former SAC in Detroit; Hollis denied it. The investigation dragged on for weeks, until Nathan admitted they would probably never find the source.

The one solid lead the Bureau managed to generate was appropriated from Matt Leach's men, who had discovered Russell Clark's girlfriend, Opal Long, living with her mother in Detroit. The Detroit office forced the Indiana police to withdraw and took over their surveillance in hopes Long might contact Dillinger. Even this minor lead Purvis managed to squander. On Thursday, March 29, agents in Detroit followed Long to the downtown train station, where she boarded a train to Chicago. When she arrived in Chicago, Purvis had his men tail her to the Commonwealth Hotel, where Hoover approved a tap on her phone. Long, however, realized she was being followed.

That night she climbed into a taxi, peering through its rear window at a pair of agents following her. The cab took what Purvis described as "a zigzag course" through downtown streets, easily eluding the FBI men. Weeks later agents learned that Long had gone straight from Chicago to St. Paul, where she joined Dillinger.

By the end of March, Hoover was growing impatient. Irked by newspaper coverage of Dillinger raids police were making in Chicago, the director sent Purvis a sharply worded letter. "The Division has never been informed by your office of the details concerning this raid or of the information leading up to it," Hoover wrote Purvis. "The Division is inclined to wonder concerning the intimate acquaintance on the part of your office with the actual developments in the Chicago district relative to the search for Dillinger."[23]

But there were no developments. After a month of searching, neither Purvis nor any other FBI agent had the first clue where Dillinger was. And then a funny thing happened. Dillinger found them.

11

CRESCENDO

March 30 to April 10, 1934

As the FBI's half-hearted manhunt continued, Dillinger rested and let his wound heal in his new set of rooms at the Lincoln Court Apartments, a compact, thirty-two-unit building on busy South Lexington Avenue, in the heart of St. Paul's toniest neighborhood. Conditions were cramped with John Hamilton and Pat Cherrington sleeping in the living room. At least Nelson was gone, disappearing on one of his jaunts out west. Van Meter came and went like a ghost, his eyes always scanning the cars outside for a government license plate.

There was a theater down the street, and several nights Dillinger took Billie to the movies. One evening they watched a newsreel interview of Dillinger's father. "John isn't a bad boy," the old man said. "They ought to give him a chance. He just robbed some banks." Dillinger smiled. It was probably the nicest thing his father ever said about him. On Friday night, March 31, at the end of his second week in St. Paul, Dillinger took Billie to see *Fashions of 1933,* a review of the latest designer work from New York and Paris. That night Opal Long arrived from Chicago, having ditched her FBI tail there. She assured Dillinger she hadn't been followed. He went to bed Friday night happy. The weekend loomed. Maybe they would take a ride in the country.

Snow lay thick on the streets of St. Paul that Friday afternoon when a woman named Daisy Coffey walked up the white-marble stairway of the

Federal Courts Building and entered the FBI's offices in Room 203. The SAC, Werner Hanni, and his men were focused on the Bremer case, but Hanni stepped away long enough to take her statement. Mrs. Coffey, who said she managed the Lincoln Court Apartments on South Lexington Avenue, told Hanni she was suspicious of the couple renting Apartment 303. Her new tenants, "Mr. and Mrs. Carl P. Hellman," had frequent guests, always used the building's rear door and kept their blinds lowered till 10:30 each morning. Hanni was unimpressed. "She says that she just has a feeling that there is something mysterious and questionable" about the Hellmans, he wrote in a memo.

After Mrs. Coffey left, Hanni handed her statement to a pair of young agents, Rosser L. "Rusty" Nalls and Rufus Coulter.* Later that day the two drove uptown and showed Mrs. Coffey photographs of the only men the St. Paul office was interested in, Karpis and the Barkers. Mrs. Coffey couldn't identify any of them. But she had taken down Mr. Hellman's license plate number. Returning downtown, Agent Nalls ran a check and found the car registered to a Carl Hellman in North St. Paul. But when he called the post office for Mr. Hellman's address, he found there was none. The name appeared to be fictitious.

The Lincoln Court was a three-story red-brick building; out back was a paved alley with a residential neighborhood beyond. That night Nalls and Coulter cruised through the alley and parked on a side street. They could see that the blinds in Apartment 303 were lowered. It seemed a normal thing to do; otherwise anyone could see right in. In the space beneath the shades they could see a man and a woman moving around inside the apartment. After three hours they returned downtown and reported they had seen nothing out of the ordinary.

Nonetheless, they returned the next morning at 9:00 to question the occupants of Apartment 303. Inspector William Rorer, who remained in St. Paul supervising the Bremer case, decided they needed a police escort. Agent Coulter volunteered to find a patrolman while Nalls drove ahead to

---

* Rosser Nalls was born in Washington, D.C., joined the Bureau in 1929, and served in many offices before his retirement in 1956. He died in 1983 at the age of eighty-two.

Rufus C. Coulter was born in Tennessee and orphaned at an early age. Without graduating from elementary school, he attended night classes and managed to obtain a law degree from the University of Arkansas. Coulter served in the FBI from 1929 to 1945 and worked for many years afterward for Motorola. He died in 1975 at the age of seventy-two.

establish surveillance. Nalls reached the building just before ten and parked beside it. A few minutes later he watched as two women left the back entrance. They walked to a parked car, talked to a man inside, and then drove off. As a matter of routine, Nalls wrote down their descriptions. Not till later would anyone realize he had seen Opal Long, Pat Cherrington, and John Hamilton. They were heading out for breakfast and grocery shopping. Nalls didn't recognize them.

At 10:15 Nalls saw Agent Coulter and a policeman drive up and disappear inside the building. A minute or two later Nalls watched as a thin man drove up in a green Ford sedan, got out, and walked inside. Agent Nalls was still sitting in his car a few minutes later, watching the front entrance, when he saw Agent Coulter running toward him across the building's snowy front yard, holding his pistol. Coulter turned and exchanged gunshots with the thin man who was chasing him.

Agent Coulter and a sixty-five-year-old St. Paul detective named Henry Cummings had stood before the door of Apartment 303, waiting for someone to answer their knock. After a long minute, the door opened a few inches. A woman peeked out over a chain. Detective Cummings identified himself and asked to speak with Carl.

Billie forgot Dillinger's alias.

"Carl?" she said. "Carl who?"

"Carl Hellman."

Billie gathered her senses. "He's just left and won't be back till this afternoon," she said. "Come back then."

"Are you Mrs. Hellman?" Cummings asked.

Billie nodded.

"We'll talk to you then," he said.

"I'm not dressed," Billie said. "Come back this afternoon."

"We'll wait until you dress," Coulter said.

Billie said it would take a second. She closed the door. Coulter heard a second latch close inside.

Dillinger was still in bed when Billie ran toward him.

"It's the cops!" she said. "What should I do?"

Dillinger jumped out of bed and began dressing. "Keep your shirt on," he said, "and get some things into the large bag."

As Billie tossed clothes into their bag, Dillinger opened a dresser drawer and lifted out the parts of his submachine gun. Then he walked toward the door. Outside, Coulter and Detective Cummings waited in the hallway. Coulter didn't like this. "We'll have to call for some help," Coulter whispered. "You can go call or I will."

"Who do you want?" Cummings asked. "Your department or ours?"

"I want to get our department," Coulter said.[1]

Coulter trotted downstairs to the manager's office to phone the office. When he returned upstairs, Cummings was still standing in the hallway. Together they waited, nine more minutes by Coulter's estimate.

It was then that Homer Van Meter, having parked his green Ford outside, appeared at the head of the third floor's rear stairwell. He sensed trouble the moment he saw the two outside Dillinger's door. His head lowered, Van Meter walked right up to the two lawmen, shouldered past them, and stepped to the head of the front stairwell. Then he stopped. "Is your name Johnson?" he asked Coulter.

"No," Coulter said.

As Van Meter headed down the front stairwell, Coulter stepped forward and said, "What's your name?"

Van Meter turned and stopped on a landing. "I'm a soap salesman," he said.

"Where are your samples?" Coulter asked.

"Down in my car."

Coulter asked if he had any identification.

"No. But I have down in my car."

Van Meter disappeared down the stairs. After a moment, Coulter decided to follow him. He walked down to the lobby and peered outside. The "soap salesman" was gone. Coulter had just turned to walk back upstairs when he saw Van Meter crouched in the shadows of the basement stairs, a pistol in his hand.

"You want this, asshole?" Van Meter asked. "Here it is!"

As Van Meter raised his gun to fire, Coulter leaped backward, crashing through the front door. He turned and ran across the snowy yard, and Van Meter gave chase, firing wildly, his shots throwing up little explosions of dirty snow. In the calm of a St. Paul Saturday morning the gunshots sounded unreal—*pop, pop, pop*—like firecrackers. As Coulter raced across the snow, he pulled his pistol, wheeled, and returned fire. Van Meter ran back into the building.

Up in Apartment 303, Billie begged Dillinger not to start a gunfight. But the minute he heard shots, Dillinger raised his submachine gun and fired a burst through the door. He opened the door a few inches, stuck the Thompson gun's muzzle outside and began firing down the hallway. Detective Cummings flattened himself into an alcove as bullets whizzed by his chin. The moment Dillinger stopped shooting, Cummings ran down the front stairs. Inside the apartment, Billie came out of the bedroom and found Dillinger smiling. Thin shafts of sunlight stabbed into the room through the holes he had blasted in the door.[2]

"Keep your shirt on," Dillinger repeated when Billie begged him not to fire again. "You're coming with me. Snap that suitcase together and follow along." Dillinger stepped to the door and fired another burst of bullets down the hallway. Billie followed, lugging his heavy suitcase with two hands; there were more guns inside.

Outside, chaos had engulfed the neighborhood. Cars were stopped, and people were leaning out of windows. Recognizing Coulter's assailant as the man from the green Ford, Agent Nalls pointed out his car, and Coulter promptly shot out one of its tires. Nalls ran toward a drugstore to telephone for reinforcements.

Neither agent thought about the building's rear entrance. It was from this door that Billie and Dillinger emerged; Van Meter sprinted out the same door a minute later. Dillinger, in a light-gray suit and no tie, walked casually down the alley, carrying the Thompson gun close to his right leg. He handed Billie the car keys and took the suitcase, watching over his shoulder as he walked.[3] Billie hurried ahead to the garage where they stored their black Hudson and backed the car out. Dillinger threw the suitcase into the backseat and got in. Billie stomped the accelerator, and the Hudson roared down the alley. "Slow down! Slow down!" Dillinger ordered. "You'll attract attention."

None of the FBI agents and St. Paul police who descended on the neighborhood had any idea who was doing the shooting. One agent telephoned Washington to say the suspects didn't match the descriptions of anyone in the Barker Gang. Not until two hours later, when agents finally stormed Apartment 303, did the FBI realize who it had found. Inside, amid an arsenal of pistols and submachine guns and drawerfuls of men's suits and ladies undergarments, they found three photos. One showed a baby boy, another a teenager. The third was a Navy sailor with a crewcut and a familiar crooked grin. It was Dillinger. Fingerprints taken from a Listerine bottle confirmed it. And from the drops of blood agents found in the hallway outside, they guessed he had been hit.

. . .

In the getaway car blood reddened Dillinger's pant leg. He had been hit by a ricochet, one of his own bullets. It struck high on his left calf, a "through and through" just below his knee. As sirens sounded over St. Paul, Dillinger told Billie to head to the apartment of Eddie Green, the red-headed jug marker. He needed a doctor.

Green directed them to an office building in downtown Minneapolis, and a doctor named Clayton May. May was a forty-six-year-old general practitioner whose practice included fifty-dollar abortions and treating the venereal diseases rampant in St. Paul's underworld. When Green said he had a friend injured in the explosion of an illegal still, May followed him outside. Dillinger was sitting in the backseat with Billie. They drove to an apartment complex on the south side, where the doctor treated his shadier clients. Billie threw an arm around Dillinger and helped him limp into a first-floor apartment.

Dr. May later insisted that Dillinger had threatened his life, but in fact the roll of cash the outlaw was carrying was all the persuasion Dr. May needed. The wound wasn't serious. They bandaged it and applied a mercury solution to clean it. Dr. May told Dillinger to rest; he would need several days to heal. He gave him a tetanus shot and left. In time Dillinger drifted to sleep.

Outside Dallas, Texas
Easter Sunday, April 1
3:30 P.M.

As the FBI scrambled to find Dillinger that morning, Bonnie Parker sat stroking a white rabbit beside a car parked north of the Dallas city limits, on an unpaved stretch of road overlooking Texas State Highway 114. The rabbit was a gift for her mother. Clyde was stretched out across the backseat, trying to take a nap. Henry Methvin was pacing. After an extended visit with Methvin's family in Louisiana, they had picked up the ulcer-plagued Joe Palmer in Joplin and sent Palmer into Dallas to alert their families to their arrival.

At about three-thirty, Bonnie glanced up and saw a trio of motorcycle policemen passing north on the highway below them. They were state troopers. As Bonnie watched, two of the men, spotting the Ford parked alone on the hillside, slowed, then turned around, heading toward the entrance to the dirt road where Bonnie and Clyde waited.

According to the version of events Clyde told his family, Bonnie walked back to the car and roused him. He stepped out with a sawed-off shotgun. Methvin was already standing by the car, cradling a Browning automatic rifle. As Clyde told the story, he said to Methvin, "Let's take 'em."[4] Clyde claimed he meant to take the officers hostage, just as he had a half-dozen times before.

Methvin misunderstood. The two patrolmen, E. B. Wheeler, twenty-six, and a twenty-two-year-old rookie named H. D. Murphy, who was on his first day of duty, were just coasting up to the parked Ford, their sidearms still holstered, when Methvin raised his rifle and fired a burst of bullets directly into Wheeler's chest, killing him. Murphy stopped his motorcycle and began to grab for a sawed-off shotgun. When Clyde saw him go for the gun, he fired three shots, killing Murphy as well. A passing motorist watched as the three then leaped into the Ford and drove off.

The Dallas County sheriff, Smoot Schmid, immediately announced that Clyde had done the killing. "He's not a man," Schmid said. "He's an animal." Governor Ferguson announced $500 rewards for the arrest of Clyde and his unidentified co-assassin.

Frank Hamer arrived in Dallas the next morning.

As initial reports of the St. Paul gunfight crossed his desk that Sunday, Hoover was apoplectic. Nothing about this made sense: Why had two men conducted a raid, and why was one of them a member of the notoriously corrupt St. Paul police? Why were his men armed with pistols instead of machine guns? Why wasn't he told of the raid beforehand? And why, above all, had his men let Dillinger get away?* In a phone call with Purvis, Hoover condemned the St. Paul office for "their atrocious bungling of the raid yesterday." From now on, Hoover said, all information on Dillinger—

* There remained widespread confusion among Hoover's men exactly when and how they were to include local police on FBI raids. According to a memo Hoover wrote to file, when he asked Inspector William Rorer that Sunday why he had requested help from St. Paul police, Rorer said "he had been proceeding on the assumption that to take a suspect into custody it was necessary to have a police officer along." Hoover replied "that this assumption is entirely wrong," that there were only two instances where local police could join an FBI raid: when the FBI needed extra men or extra equipment. Rorer apparently also complained that not all his men knew how to use submachine guns. "If the agents cannot handle the equipment," Hoover said, "they should be instructed immediately in the use of it."

no matter how trivial—was to be relayed to headquarters. And, as Hoover repeated to agents in St. Paul, police were never to join FBI raids again, unless agents "were short of equipment, like machine guns or gas guns."[5]

The St. Paul shoot-out had a galvanizing effect on Hoover. From the tone of his memoranda, he seemed amazed that Dillinger had the temerity to actually fire on his men. Then and there, Hoover decided to make Dillinger's apprehension the Bureau's highest priority. That Tuesday he ordered all offices to give Dillinger precedence "over all other pending cases." New agents poured into St. Paul. Cots were arranged in the FBI office and at the post office, where the men grabbed catnaps between calls.

Monday night they got their first break. The Lincoln Park's manager, Mrs. Coffey, telephoned the St. Paul office with a tip. Her husband had found the address of one of Dillinger's visitors, the man who had exchanged shots with Agent Coulter; he rented an apartment at 2214 Marshall Avenue. Agents had the building surrounded within an hour. By daylight there was no sign of Dillinger or any other suspects, but the manager identified a man who matched the description of Coulter's assailant. He lived in Apartment 106. The unit had been rented two weeks earlier by another man, who gave his name as D. Stevens. The manager hadn't seen either man for days.

The apartment's windows were closed; from the outside it looked vacant. Betting their suspect was too smart to return, agents had the manager unlock the apartment at 7:30. Inside they found what was clearly a bank robber's lair: a Thompson submachine gun stock, a two-foot dynamite fuse, road maps and airline schedules, license plates, three notebooks filled with getaway maps, and bullets—lots and lots of bullets. After dusting for fingerprints and collecting stray receipts and laundry tags, everyone but two junior agents returned downtown.

A few hours later, just before noon, the two agents were pacing the apartment, submachine guns in their hands, when they heard a key enter the front latch. The agents leaped to the door just as a startled "negress"— as an FBI report termed her—stepped into the apartment and found herself facing the muzzle of a Thompson gun. She said her name was Lucy Jackson. She was a maid. She said her sister had asked her to clean the apartment. The sister, whose name was Leona Goodman, was sitting in a car outside. The two agents brought her in.

The story Leona Goodman told the FBI would prove as important as any the Bureau heard all year. She said she worked for a man she knew as "Mr. Stevens"; as agents were to learn later, "Mr. Stevens" had arranged for

Mrs. Goodman to clean the homes of a series of major criminals, from Van Meter to Frank Nash to Harry Sawyer. Just that morning, Mrs. Goodman said, Mr. Stevens had visited her home, handed her a key, and asked her to clean out this apartment. She was feeling sickly, so she had asked her sister to do it. She had promised to pack some clothes into a tan suitcase and bring it to her house. Mr. Stevens had promised to come for the bag later that day.

The agents took Mrs. Goodman downtown, where the tan suitcase was emptied and refilled with stacks of Wanted posters. Inspector Rorer approached Ed Notesteen, the agent who had manned the infamous kitchenette viewing post during Verne Miller's Halloween escape in Chicago, and told him to take Mrs. Goodman, the bag, and two agents back to Mrs. Goodman's home to await the arrival of the mysterious "Mr. Stevens." As he left, Notesteen asked Inspector Rorer what to do if he appeared. According to Agent Notesteen's memorandum on the day's events, Rorer's reply struck him as unusual: "Shoot him."

By early afternoon, Notesteen and the other two agents had taken up positions in Mrs. Goodman's faded clapboard house, located on a quiet street in a black neighborhood. From the tone of his memos, it's clear that Notesteen wasn't comfortable with the setting or his orders. Agent George Gross, who sat in a window with a submachine gun across his lap, noticed several suspicious cars driving by.* Notesteen called Inspector Rorer and asked for reinforcements; a little later he was relieved to see several agents driving nearby streets. While on the phone, Notesteen pointedly asked Rorer to restate his orders. It all depended on Mrs. Goodman's identification of "Mr. Stevens," Rorer said. "If she says that's the man," he said, "kill him."[6]

As the afternoon wore on, Notesteen paced from room to room. This wasn't right. They didn't have the first clue who "Mr. Stevens" was. He could be a real estate agent. He could be anyone. And Notesteen had orders to shoot him on sight. Notesteen repeatedly asked Mrs. Goodman, who sat in the kitchen, whether she could be certain if she saw Mr. Stevens. "I'll know him," she assured him.

Three hours passed. Then, about five-thirty, Agent Gross saw a green Terraplane sedan coasting to a stop outside. "There's a car," he said. "It's stopping across the street."

---

* George Gross was a St. Louis native who served in the FBI between 1930 and 1935. In later years he was an attorney. He died in 1958.

A man in an overcoat jumped out of the car and in three or four long strides was at the kitchen door. Mrs. Goodman saw him coming. She opened the door, shoved the suitcase outside, and slammed the door in her visitor's face without a word.

As the door closed, Agent Notesteen scrambled into the kitchen. "Is that the man?" he asked.

"Yes," Mrs. Goodman. "That's the man who came by this morning, and that's the man from the apartment."

"Let him have it!" Notesteen shouted to Agent Gross.

There was a burst of machine-gun fire and the sound of shattering glass. A moment later, Notesteen stepped to the window. Lying on the sidewalk outside was a man with a suitcase. To Notesteen's surprise, a woman was leaning over his fallen body, sobbing. "Are you positive that was the right man?" Notesteen asked Mrs. Goodman, who had begun crying hysterically. "Oh yes," she managed to say. "It was."

Notesteen telephoned Inspector Rorer and told him what happened. Then he ran outside, where he saw agents jogging toward the fallen man, who had been shot in the head and appeared to be dead or dying. No one knew who the wounded man was. The crying woman wouldn't say. It wasn't Dillinger, they could see that. A driver's license identified him as Clarence Leo Coulter. It was a fake. The next day the FBI would identify him as Eddie Green. The crying woman was his wife, Beth.

Both knew where Dillinger was hiding.

Eddie Green was still alive when attendants wheeled him into St. Paul's Ancker Hospital. In fact, he was raving. Lapsing in and out of consciousness, thrashing and babbling incoherently, Green was tucked into a hospital bed. A bullet had entered the back of his head through the brim of his fedora, traced a half-circle around his skull, and come to rest above his right eye. Doctors said he couldn't live long. A pair of agents took positions by his bed, jotting down everything he said.

All night Green hollered for someone named Jim, who agents later learned was one of his brothers. He asked for a Fred, then a George and a Lucy, then asked: "Honey, back the car to the door." As daylight approached, the agents began peppering Green with questions about Dillinger. Much of what he said was unintelligible. At one point, agents heard him say, "I've got the keys, he wants them."

"Whose keys are those?" an agent asked.

"John's."

"John who?"

"Dillinger."

Green made no meaningful responses when agents pressed where Dillinger could be found. At one point, however, he mentioned a doctor he had paid. Agents asked if anyone had been shot at the Lincoln Court Apartments. Green said "Jack . . . In the leg." They pressed for the doctor's address and Green said, "Wabasha Street."

Where on Wabasha Street? "980, I guess." The agents checked; there was no 980 Wabasha Street.

When the sun rose Green remained alive. In fact, he was stabilizing. But his pronouncements remained gibberish. By nightfall on Wednesday, April 4, Green was still talking. A new set of agents arrived. In an effort to focus Green's rambling soliloquies, they decided to question him while posing as doctors and gang members. To their surprise, their tragicomic masquerade began to work. At one point, Agent Roy Noonan, posing as a doctor, asked Green if he knew the man who drove the green Ford and fired on Agent Coulter.*

"Doc, you sure are a nosey fella," Green said. "Give me a shot so I can sleep."

"I will if you tell me who drove the green Ford," Noonan said.

"You know as well as I do."

"No, I don't know."

"What do you want to know that for?"

"Well, I just want to know. Did Jack drive it?"

"Yes."

"Jack who?"

"You know without asking me."

"No, I don't know. Who was he?"

"Dillinger," Green said. "Doc, will you give me that shot?"

And so it went. Bit by bit, agents coaxed more information from the dying man. A breakthrough came around eleven that night when an agent tricked Green into naming an address in Minneapolis where he said

---

* Roy T. Noonan, a Minnesota native nicknamed "Stub," was a popular FBI agent from 1928 until his retirement in 1954. From 1955 to 1967 he served as superintendent of the Minnesota Bureau of Criminal Apprehension. He died in 1981.

Dillinger was hiding: 635 Park Avenue. Down at the FBI office, adrenaline surged through the ranks. Agents scrambled to Park Avenue, but found no 635. An agent at Green's bedside telephoned a few minutes later. Green was now saying the correct address was 1835 Park Avenue, Apartment 4. This address they found. It was a two-story rooming house in a run-down area where, FBI agents would later learn, a doctor named Clayton May kept a hideaway office to perform abortions.

The FBI's assistant director, Hugh Clegg, who had arrived from Washington that day to supervise the hunt for Dillinger, ordered every available man to surround 1835 Park Avenue. By midnight they had every exit covered. The building was quiet. The only light came from a single apartment downstairs. An agent knocked on its door, saying he was looking for someone who had just moved into the building. A man said everyone there had been living there at least six months. They were working people and most had children. To the FBI men, it looked like a dead end. Assistant Director Clegg returned downtown, leaving a group of agents to watch the building. With daylight a new group arrived. They watched the building's occupants come and go. None looked familiar. There was no activity they could see in Apartment 4.

Finally, late that afternoon, Clegg decided to raid Apartment 4. After positioning men around the building, he and a trio of agents armed with submachine guns crept to the door and knocked. As Clegg described the raid, "[We] knocked on the door and a man about 45 to 50 years of age came to the door; upon opening the door machine guns were punched right in his stomach and he was ordered to 'stick 'em up'; he did not stick 'em up, but seemed to be amused. His wife, a small woman, was quite excited and wanted to shoot [the agents]. No shooting was done. There was a little girl in the place."[7]

It was the wrong apartment. Not for several days would agents learn that Dillinger's hideaway was downstairs. It didn't matter. Dillinger had left the building at 6:00 the previous night, about five hours before the delirious Eddie Green revealed where he was hiding.

Frank Hamer arrived in Dallas that Monday with Manny Gault, a highway patrolman who was being assigned to the case. Clyde's trail was already cold, but Hamer had a hunch, and the next day he took the Dallas deputies Bob Alcorn and Ted Hinton and pursued it.

From what he had deduced, Hamer could see that Clyde tended to head north whenever there was trouble in Dallas. Tuesday morning the lawmen headed up Highway 77 to Sherman and began showing photos of Bonnie and Clyde to gas station attendants. By Wednesday afternoon they had reached the busy Oklahoma county seat of Durant, where they became mired in noontime congestion. The two cars were stopped in traffic when, according to Ted Hinton, Alcorn noticed a car coming toward them. To their amazement, it was Bonnie and Clyde.

"Here they come!" Alcorn yelped.

Clyde's car passed directly beside them. Hinton drew his gun, but Alcorn shook his head. They were too hemmed in by traffic: they were under orders not to start any firefight where civilians could be shot. As Hinton watched Clyde's car disappear, he pulled over and flagged down Hamer. Together the two cars managed to extricate themselves from traffic and sped off in pursuit, but by then Clyde was gone.[8]

On Thursday afternoon, April 5, Alcorn and Hinton checked in with their office and learned that Bonnie had been sighted in a Texarkana drugstore. The four lawmen raced southeast, reaching Texarkana around dusk. There they learned that Clyde had been sighted at a lunch stand five miles north of town. By the time they reached the lunch stand the couple had been seen driving across the Index Toll Bridge ten miles north without paying the toll. The bridge led into southeastern Oklahoma.

Clyde drove through the night in a pounding rain, heading past Tulsa into the state's far northeast corner. After midnight he turned off Route 66 outside the town of Commerce, cruised down a dirt road a quarter mile and parked for the night. It was a remote spot, located between two industrial mines, ten minutes from both the Kansas and Missouri borders. Bonnie and Clyde curled up with blankets in the front seat and fell asleep. Henry Methvin slept in the back.[9]

The next morning they woke to find that their parking spot had become a mud hole. Clyde got up first, stepped out into the road, and stretched. A cattle buyer named J. W. Cox drove by and saw him. Clyde waved. A half hour later Cox returned down the road, noticed Clyde still there, and, thinking he needed a tow, jotted down the Ford's license plate number. He drove into Commerce and found the police chief, a lean thirty-seven-year-old named Percy Boyd, at the barbershop. Thinking the parked car might be a crew of rowdy drunks—he'd had several such calls in recent weeks—Boyd asked the town constable, a soft-spoken sixty-year-old named Cal Campbell, to drive out with him and take a look.

The two officers pulled up in front of Clyde's car a few minutes after nine. Bonnie and Methvin were still asleep, but Clyde saw them coming, jumped behind the wheel of the Ford, and slammed it into reverse. Boyd and Campbell had just stepped out of their car when the Ford spun its wheels backward down the muddy road. Boyd began to run after it, but it outdistanced him. Clyde got only a hundred yards when the car slid into a ditch, its rear wheels sinking in the mud.

Boyd and Campbell were running back toward their car when Clyde leaped from the Ford, a Browning automatic rifle in his hands. "Look out, Percy!" Campbell yelled as Clyde opened fire. His first bullets whizzed over the lawmen's heads; he may have been trying to frighten them off. Boyd and Campbell drew pistols and returned fire. Clyde hunched down and fired back at them. One of his bullets struck Boyd a glancing blow to the head, and he fell, dazed. Back in the car, Methvin awoke and grabbed a rifle. He scrambled out the passenger-side door, took aim at Campbell, and fired. One of his bullets hit Campbell square in the chest, tearing a bloody hole in his midsection. Campbell dropped to his knees, rose for a moment, then fell backward, dead.

"Bring 'em up," Clyde said to Methvin.

Methvin walked toward the fallen Boyd, who was moaning in the mud. "Get up and come with me," Methvin said.

Boyd rose, his hands in the air, and walked toward the Ford, Methvin behind him, covering him with the rifle. Together the three men tried to push the Ford out of the muddy ditch. It was no use. Clyde took his rifle, stood in the road, and began flagging down passing vehicles. He forced several drivers to help extricate his car.

"Boys," he said at one point, covering the men with his rifle, "one good man has already been killed, and if you don't obey orders, others are liable to be." After ten minutes nearly a dozen men were pushing and pulling the Ford in the mud, but the car remained mired until Clyde stopped a truck and forced the driver to attach a chain to the Ford's bumper. In a minute, the Ford was free. Clyde motioned for Chief Boyd to get in the back. He was going with them.

They drove north, eluding pursuit, and crossed into Kansas. Clyde struck up a conversation with the wounded Boyd, stopping at one point to bandage the chief's head wound. At nightfall they stopped at a store in Fort Scott. Methvin hustled inside, emerging a few minutes later with four plates of food and an evening newspaper that blared headlines of the shoot-out. "I'm sorry about shooting the old man," Clyde said quietly. After that he fell silent.

Just north of Fort Scott they let Boyd out on the roadside. Clyde handed Boyd a ten-dollar bill and shook his hand. "Take this for the bus and be sure to see a doctor," he said.

"Bonnie," Boyd said. "What do you want me to tell the press?"

Bonnie thought a moment. She had long been irked by the repeated tendency of Southwestern newspapers to reprint the infamous photo taken at Joplin the previous year of her posing with a cigar.

"Tell them I don't smoke cigars."

Dillinger had left St. Paul just hours before the FBI surrounded his hideaway. The bullet wound in his left leg bandaged, he drove Billie south into Iowa, then east across Illinois and on into central Indiana. A few hours after agents raided the apartment building at 1835 Park Avenue, Dillinger coasted to a stop in a field behind his father's farm outside of Mooresville. It was a little after midnight on Friday, April 6, just hours before Bonnie and Clyde took Percy Boyd hostage in Oklahoma.

Amazingly, the FBI still had not placed the Dillinger farm under surveillance. The Cincinnati SAC, Earl Connelley, whose territory covered central Indiana, hadn't joined the hunt for Dillinger until Hoover's directive earlier that week. One of the Bureau's best investigators, Connelley was an intense World War I veteran with a pencil mustache who had joined the Bureau in 1920 and worked at Hoover's side during the 1920 raids. He had been a SAC since 1927, and after running offices in Seattle, St. Louis, and New York, had taken over Cincinnati the previous year. Already Connelley's men had fanned out across Ohio and Kentucky, checking dozens of leads. But he didn't have enough agents to maintain stakeouts. He had asked for more.

The first inkling twenty-year-old Hubert Dillinger had of his half-brother's return came when he walked into his father's house Friday morning. Dillinger leaped from behind a door, pointed a finger at him, and said, "Stick 'em up!" There were hugs and smiles; both Hubert and his father were happy to see him. Dillinger introduced Billie as his new wife, "Anne," and seemed at pains to persuade them they were married; he repeated it several times. Dillinger had parked his Hudson in a barn out back, and after breakfast Hubert went out and helped him remove the tires, clean them, and paint them black.[10]

When darkness fell Dillinger announced that he and Hubert were going on a quick trip. They would be back by daylight, Dillinger assured Billie. Sliding into the Hudson, Hubert drove them east across Indiana into Ohio. On the way Dillinger described in detail his escapes from Crown Point and St. Paul. When Hubert asked if he was surprised at Herbert Youngblood's behavior at Crown Point, Dillinger sighed and said, "You know how a nigger is."[11]

Around midnight they reached the farm of Pete Pierpont's parents outside the town of Liepsic. Hubert stayed in the car while Dillinger ran in and gave the Pierponts some money to cover legal fees. They stayed barely fifteen minutes. On the drive back to Mooresville, Dillinger fell asleep. About three that morning, as they passed Noblesville, east of Indianapolis, so did Hubert. The Hudson sideswiped a pickup truck carrying a load of horseradish, careened off the highway and smashed through a wire fence, coming to rest in a small woods. The car was a wreck, but neither Dillinger was hurt. The horseradish truck was demolished. Its driver, a man named Joe Manning, limped over to Dillinger's car in time to see Dillinger remove the front and rear license plates; Hubert waved Manning off, saying they were okay.

Dillinger removed his submachine gun from the car and wrapped it in a blanket, then took Hubert and struck out across the fields. They walked about three miles, until they reached a road. At that point Dillinger told Hubert to hitchhike to Indianapolis, fetch another car, and come back for him. He pointed to a haystack and said he would hide inside it until Hubert's return.

By the time a state patrol car arrived at the wreck site, both Dillingers were long gone. But a submachine gun clip was found in their car. The officers, their suspicions aroused, phoned Matt Leach when they returned to their posts later that morning. As it happened, two FBI agents were in Leach's office. They all drove out to inspect the wreckage. The car's engine number was relayed to Cincinnati, which checked it with St. Paul. To the surprise of almost everyone in the FBI, who assumed Dillinger was still in Minnesota, the number matched that of a car "Carl Hellman" had purchased two weeks before.[12] Leach ordered roadblocks thrown up all across Central Indiana.

Suddenly the FBI's focus swiveled to Indianapolis. Earl Connelley set up his headquarters at the Spink Arms Hotel. He asked Hoover for ten more men, and all that weekend agents arrived at the Indianapolis airport, trickling into Connelley's headquarters in ones and twos. For the first time FBI agents began studying Dillinger's family in earnest. By Saturday afternoon Connelley and his men had identified the homes of John Dillinger, Sr., Dillinger's sister Audrey Hancock, and the Indianapolis filling station where Hubert worked. Until he could arrange watchposts, Connelley established a regular circuit that agents could drive to watch them all.

While FBI men poured into Indiana that Saturday, Hubert returned to the farm with Dillinger, who had spent several nervous hours inside an itchy haystack. If he was worried the FBI knew he was back in Indiana, Dillinger gave no sign. He lay down on the living room couch to rest his wounded leg, the submachine gun resting beneath his blanket. What he needed was a new car. Around ten he gave Hubert some money and sent him into Indianapolis with Billie to get one. They bought a new Ford for $722 and stored it in a Mooresville garage.

Mooresville, Indiana
Sunday, April 8

Dillinger was lying on the living room couch, laughing aloud while reading of his exploits in a pile of newspapers his father had saved, when family members began to arrive that morning after church. His beloved sister Audrey, who had raised him, was the first to arrive, along with her husband, Emmett, their teenage daughters, a plate of fried chicken, and three coconut-cream pies, her brother's favorite. Dillinger walked outside when they came up the driveway, trading kisses with all the women. A little later two of Audrey's sons, Norman and Fred Hancock, drove up as well.

Though the Dillingers were not by nature demonstrative, it was a warm reunion, with quick hugs and arms slung across shoulders. There was sadness, too, an unspoken acknowledgment that this might be the last time any of them saw "Johnnie." To Audrey's relief, her brother seemed unchanged by life on the run. He had the same easy smile, and was always ready with a quip. Everyone watched Billie closely. She was quiet. Audrey thought she had a hard face. There seemed to be a scar beneath her pancake makeup. Again, Dillinger said they were married.

With children in the room, they didn't talk about Dillinger's exploits at first. They clung to mundane details: a cousin's trip to Texas in search of work, Hubert's job at the gas station. While the adults caught up, Dillinger's favorite niece, eighteen-year-old Mary Hancock, gave him a manicure; when she bumped his leg, she saw him wince. At one point Audrey's husband, Emmett, took Dillinger aside and asked him what had happened at Crown Point.

"Big boy, lemme tell you something," Dillinger said. "If you don't know anything, you can't tell anything, can you?"

"No."

"Let that be a lesson to you," Dillinger said. He was more forthcoming when Audrey took him aside. He described the Crown Point escape in detail, sketching her a map, then burning it with a match.

They ate the chicken while sitting on the ground outside the backdoor. It was a gorgeous spring day, with a high sun and few clouds. Afterward everyone walked across the fields into the woods. Dillinger held hands with his niece, Mary. "You believe what's in the papers if you want to," Dillinger told her, "but take it from me, I haven't killed anyone and I never will." He smiled. "Take about half a grain of salt, believe half of what's left, and you've got it made."

After a while they walked back up to the house and Dillinger posed for snapshots, clowning around with the submachine gun and the wooden gun from Crown Point. When a plane appeared overhead—the FBI later determined it was a stunt flyer—Dillinger returned inside the house. It was the first time the others saw him worried. The spell, the illusion of a carefree Sunday picnic, was broken.

Back inside, Dillinger seemed on edge. He kept stepping to the window to watch the plane. Hubert and Fred Hancock took the children outside to fly a kite. A little later, around three, Mary Hancock walked into the living room and said, "There's a car out there with a couple of fellows and it looks suspicious." With the mysterious plane still flying overhead and the cars streaming by outside, Dillinger announced that it was time to leave. He asked Hubert to take Fred Hancock and retrieve the Ford they bought the day before.

3:00 P.M.

As Dillinger relaxed with his family, a stream of cars passed by the farm on the two-lane blacktop of Route 267. Many were curiosity seekers, Sunday drivers from Indianapolis craning their necks to catch a glimpse of the infamous Dillinger homestead.

According to FBI memoranda, one of these cars was manned by a pair of young agents. J. L. Geraghty and T. J. Donegan had just arrived in Indiana. Donegan had come from Cincinnati the night before. He had been given a whirlwind tour of the area at 2:00 A.M., but in the darkness his mind had registered little. He was working on barely two hours' sleep and trying his best not to get lost. His partner, Geraghty, was even more out of his element; he had arrived in Mooresville from the streets of New York just that morning.

As they cruised past the Dillinger farm around three, the two agents noted three cars in the driveway: two sedans and a Chevy coupe that matched the description of Hubert's car. This was good; their orders were to find Hubert and keep an eye on him. Two miles past the farm, they turned and headed back. When they passed a second time they glimpsed a number of children and two men outside the house.

Farther down the road Donegan and Geraghty turned around once more, trying in vain to find a spot to watch the driveway's entrance. When the FBI agents passed the Dillinger farm a third time, they noticed Hubert's car was gone. They set off to find it. Cruising through Mooresville they spotted the car, driving toward them, back toward the Dillinger farm. A black Ford cruised just ahead of it. A few blocks later, the agents turned and headed back toward the farm, taking their time to avoid arousing suspicion.

Hubert saw the agents' car and assumed its occupants were FBI men. He returned to the farm, left the Lincoln, and told Dillinger they were being followed. He and Fred Hancock then drove off in Hubert's Chevy, promising Dillinger they would see him later that night. By the time Donegan and Geraghty passed the farmhouse a fourth time, the two young men were already gone. When the agents saw Hubert's car was missing again, they grew worried. They drove faster, hoping to overtake Hubert farther down Route 267. They proceeded as far as the town of Plainfield before giving up. Thinking Hubert might have turned off on a side road, they returned up the road toward the Dillinger farm.

By that point Dillinger had hatched a plan to evade anyone watching the farm. He had hoped to leave after nightfall, but between the airplane and the FBI agents, he needed to move fast. He arranged for everyone to leave in a three-car caravan. Audrey and her husband drove out first, turning left toward Mooresville. John Dillinger, Sr., drove the next car, turning right.

Billie climbed behind the wheel of the third and final car, the new Lincoln, along with the two teenage girls. Dillinger slid down onto the rear floorboard, pulled a blanket over his head, and clutched his machine gun.

No one saw them leave. Billie turned right and drove a short ways toward Plainfield. When Dillinger thought it was safe, he told her to stop the car. Just as she did the two FBI agents, Donegan and Geraghty, approached from the south. They saw the shiny new Lincoln parked on the roadside and recognized it as the car they had seen earlier.

As they neared the Lincoln, the two agents saw three women and a man inside. Just as they passed, the man stepped out of the passenger door. He began to walk around the rear of the car. Both agents got a good look at him. He was about thirty-five, they guessed, not quite six feet tall, and well built, wearing a gray summer suit and a matching hat. It was Dillinger.

They didn't recognize him.

Later, they would swear to their superiors it couldn't have been him. But it was. Dillinger turned and watched over his left shoulder as they drove away. After a roadside meeting with friends that night, he and Billie headed for Chicago.

The following week, local newspapers confirmed rumors of Dillinger's weekend visit. The story made national headlines. Confronted by reporters, Audrey spoke freely of their warm reunion. There was speculation FBI agents had been in the area, but the Bureau never said a word. Only now, after the release of FBI case files, is the extent of the Bureau's foul-up clear: two FBI agents drove right by Dillinger on a bright spring day, and never even knew it was him.

Chicago, Illinois
Monday, April 9

The next morning, Dillinger and Billie slept late. Lying in bed they talked about the future. Dillinger was in a warm mood. He spoke about finding a quiet place, maybe somewhere in the country, where they could settle down, live like normal people. Billie said she would like that. Dillinger said he was thinking about cosmetic surgery on his face. Doctors nowadays could make a man almost unrecognizable, he said.

When they finally reached Chicago around noon, Dillinger telephoned Piquett's investigator, Art O'Leary. He trusted O'Leary, who was to become his primary contact in coming weeks. They met at 3:00 at the corner of Sacramento and Augusta, then drove neighboring streets as Dillinger described what had happened at St. Paul and Mooresville. "By the way," Dillinger asked at one point, "doesn't Piquett know a doctor who does plastic surgery work?" He pronounced the lawyer's name "Pikwatt," as he sometimes did.

"Why?"

"I'd like to have him work on me. I want to live like other people. Billie and I would like to be married and settle down somewhere."[13]

O'Leary promised to ask Piquett about a doctor. Afterward Dillinger drove downtown to the U Tavern on State Street, where Billie walked in and talked to one of Opal Long's old boyfriends, a man named Larry Strong. She needed a place to stay. Strong said he would try to find something, and they agreed to meet at a bar called the Tumble Inn at eight. What Billie didn't know was that Strong had already been questioned by the FBI. When she left, he—or someone he talked to—walked to a phone and telephoned Melvin Purvis.*

The Tumble Inn
8:00 P.M.

Purvis pushed through the front door of the dim, dingy tavern a few minutes past eight. He had dressed down for the occasion. Larry Strong was sitting at the bar, half-drunk, talking to a middle-age bartender. The only other people in the room were an elderly man and a boy. Purvis took a seat at the bar, making small talk with Strong and the bartender. Neither man recognized him. A few minutes later a musician wobbled in, and Strong asked him to play something on the piano. There was no piano. It was that kind of place.

Outside, a dozen agents lurked in the streets. About eight-thirty Dillinger slid his Ford down Austin Street and pulled to the curb beside the tavern. Standing down the block, Agent James J. Metcalfe saw the car pull up. A small, quiet man, born in Germany and raised in Texas, Metcalfe was one of the few members of the group of agents who would come to be known as the Dillinger Squad who would achieve prominence after his FBI

---

* An FBI memo explicitly states Larry Strong was not its informant that day. Either the memo was drafted in an effort to obscure Strong's identity or Strong talked to someone else, perhaps his brother, who then notified the FBI.

career. He wrote poetry, and after leaving the Bureau he embarked on a career as a journalist and then a syndicated poet, his sentimental verse published in newspapers across the country.

Unfortunately, Metcalfe was a far better poet than FBI agent. Studying
the car in the gathering darkness, he couldn't see the features of the man
behind the wheel. When he saw a woman step from the car, he realized he
needed to get a better look. As Billie disappeared into the Tumble Inn,
Metcalfe strolled down the sidewalk past the parked car. Dillinger sat behind the wheel, a Thompson gun in his lap. Metcalfe passed no more than
five feet from him.

Inside, Purvis saw Billie when she walked in. She stepped to the bar,
standing between him and the drunken Larry Strong. Purvis offered her a
stool. She shook her head no, ordered a beer, and leaned toward Strong to
talk. Purvis strained to hear the whispered conversation but he couldn't. After a minute he stepped outside, saw one of his men and nodded. Agent
Ralph Brown, pulling a submachine gun from beneath his coat, hustled inside, followed by the other agents. In seconds Billie and Strong were arrested.

Amazingly, no one said anything about the man in the car outside. Instead, for reasons he failed to mention in subsequent reports, Purvis took
two agents and searched the tavern's basement. Only after returning upstairs did it dawn on Purvis to ask how Billie had arrived. In a car, someone
said. Several agents dashed outside, but for the second time in twenty-four
hours, Dillinger was gone.

When Billie was arraigned several days later, she openly mocked the FBI
to reporters, saying that Dillinger had been inside the Tumble Inn when she
was arrested. "I have no comment to make on such a ridiculous statement,"
Purvis replied. Dillinger hadn't been in the bar, of course, but Purvis belatedly realized that he *had* been the man in the car. His agents' memoranda
on the topic were small masterpieces of apologia. Two said they had seen
the man and were certain it wasn't Dillinger. Agent Metcalfe, who had
walked within inches of the car, said he hadn't gotten a clear look inside
"due to the fact that the car stood beside a curb of unusual height, so it
would have been necessary to stoop very low in order to look into the car
from the sidewalk."[14]

Art O'Leary was at his apartment that night when the phone rang. It
was Dillinger. "The G's just picked up Billie," he said.

"How did it happen?"

"I was sitting in my car right around the corner. There were too many of them for me to take her away. It was that rat Larry Strong. Where's Mr. Piquett? Is he still in Washington?"

"Yes," O'Leary said.

"Well, phone him right away, and tell him to try and get a writ to get Billie out."[15]

Frechette was taken in handcuffs to the Bankers Building, where agents pushed her onto a chair beneath a bright light in the conference room. All that night and into the next day they pelted her with questions. Frechette would say nothing about Dillinger. She begged them to let her sleep, but the agents refused. At one point, Purvis's secretary, Doris Rogers, took her a sandwich and was appalled. Seventy years later Rogers still remembers what she did next. "After I left," she recalls, "I came back and I told Melvin, 'This is inhumane.'"

"What do you think we should do?" Purvis asked.

"Let her sleep."

"Where?"

"I'll take her to the ladies' room."

With Purvis's consent, Rogers returned to the conference room and invited Frechette to the ladies' room.

"I can't," Frechette said. "They won't let me."

"Come on," Rogers said.

There was a leather sofa in the ladies' room. Rogers poured Frechette a glass of water and told her to lie down. She fell asleep. An hour later Rogers woke her up. Frechette begged not to be returned to the conference room. She said she would tell Rogers everything. But Rogers had no choice. Frechette went back under the hot lights.

"These women were such pities," Rogers remembers. "Everybody was broke, and they were running with these men because they couldn't get a meal. They all had a baby or two, and they were treated like dirt. I tell you, the Depression was a terrible time in America."

As FBI agents fanned out across central Indiana in pursuit of Dillinger, Assistant Director Hugh Clegg pulled up a chair in the Bureau's St. Paul office and began to talk to Eddie Green's wife, Beth. Newspapers in the Twin Cities were already alive with rumors of the mysterious red-headed woman the FBI had captured, but to Clegg's consternation, Beth Green wasn't saying a thing. Not at first, anyway.

They made an interesting pair. Clegg was thirty-five but seemed older, a pudgy, compact attorney from rural Mississippi who was near the beginning of a long, distinguished FBI career. He was trained as an agent, but his skills were those of a bureaucrat; Hoover circulated Clegg's inspection reports throughout the Bureau as models. Clegg was the very model of the yes-men who came to surround Hoover in later years. He worshiped Hoover, calling him "my hero"; Hoover, in turn, prized Clegg for his unwavering loyalty and his easy Southern way with the Washington elite. He had been promoted to assistant director after Hoover received glowing letters from the vice president, whom Clegg had escorted on a West Coast trip the previous year.

Forty-five years later, Clegg would remember Beth Green as the only criminal he ever liked. The two had several long talks, but Green remained reluctant to discuss Dillinger. Then on Tuesday, April 10, Eddie Green lapsed into a final coma; he died the following afternoon, seven days after he was shot. When she heard the news, Beth Green began telling Clegg everything she knew.* The names and places gushed out of her. It was from Green that the FBI first learned the names of Dillinger's gang: Van Meter, Tommy Carroll, a man known as "Red"—she identified John Hamilton— and a vicious little twenty-four-year-old named George "Baby Face" Nelson, who Green said was "just a kid."

But Beth Green's knowledge wasn't limited to Dillinger. Eddie Green did business with the Barkers, and his wife knew everyone in that gang as well. She quickly filled the sizable gaps in the FBI's knowledge of its struc-

---

* As portrayed in FBI files, the death of Eddie Green amounted to an execution. The official rationale behind the shooting, as explained to reporters, was that Green was shot after making "a menacing gesture." In their reports, every agent present used that same phrase, "menacing gesture." Some added that Green wheeled around as if to shoot, or stuck his hand in a pocket as if to pull a gun. There was no gun. Hugh Clegg's report even quoted the reluctant Agent Notesteen as seeing the "menacing gesture." But Notesteen's own report pointedly says he could not see Green. Notesteen clearly states he ordered the shooting on the strength of Mrs. Goodman's identification alone. The key words had been uttered by Inspector Rorer hours before: "Kill him."

Inspector Rorer's order was probably the all-too-human product of overwhelming public pressure and the Bureau's vengeful mindset, spiced by sleep deprivation, nerves, and inexperience. Even so, senior FBI officials were keenly aware of their vulnerability on the Green killing. When a reporter named Tommy Thompson persuaded the local coroner's office to investigate, the Bureau moved swiftly to defend itself. If anyone asked, Clegg told Hoover, he would refuse to name the agent who shot Green, or any witnesses; they would be subpoenaed, Clegg said, which would be "undesirable." Thompson, meanwhile, had taken loans from underworld figures, Clegg said: "If necessary, [we] could bring pressure to bear to prevent any adverse publicity on his part." In the end, the FBI needn't have worried; the coroner ruled the killing justified.

ture. She identified every gang member and his girlfriend, including Karpis's teenage paramour Delores Delaney, whom Green described as "a poor dumb little thing." For the first time agents learned of Harry Sawyer's role in St. Paul's criminal web, and his role as Bremer's "finger man." Green described Louie Cernocky's place outside Chicago as a rendezvous point for both gangs.

At least initially, Beth Green's encyclopedic knowledge did the Bureau little good, in part because Hoover didn't have enough men to chase down all the leads. The Bureau's resources were stretched to the breaking point, as Pop Nathan pointed out in a call to Hoover that week. Hoover had no choice but to put his trust in Melvin Purvis.

"Well, son, keep a stiff upper lip and get Dillinger for me," Hoover told Purvis in a handwritten note, "and the world is yours."

12

DEATH IN THE NORTH WOODS

April 10 to April 23, 1934

Dillinger was devastated by Billie Frechette's arrest. In the days afterward, he searched his mind for a way to rescue her. She was too heavily guarded at the Bankers Building, he could see, but the papers said she would soon be transferred to St. Paul to face harboring charges. He decided to attempt a rescue en route. It would be a firefight, and for that he wanted bulletproof vests.

The night Billie was arrested, Dillinger walked through the backdoor of Louis Cernocky's tavern in Fox River Grove. Cernocky grilled him a steak and handed him a bottle of whiskey, which Dillinger took to a basement bedroom. The gang had agreed to relay messages via Cernocky, and the next day the Nelsons, who had reunited with Tommy Carroll and his girlfriend in St. Paul, arrived. By the next evening, Wednesday, April 11, Van Meter and Hamilton showed up, too, with Pat Cherrington in tow.* None of the men were wild about Dillinger's idea of rescuing Billie, but Van Meter knew where they could find vests.

---

* Following the shoot-out in St. Paul, the trio had hidden out at Harry Sawyer's farm, then driven to Tennessee, where they took rooms in a tourist court outside Nashville. One morning Van Meter and Hamilton returned from a shopping excursion in a terrific hurry. As Cherrington later related the story to the FBI, Van Meter said he and Hamilton had been parked outside a Nashville drugstore, drinking Coca-Colas, when they spied two teenage loiterers they suspected were about to rob the store. Lingering to watch, Van Meter said, they were suddenly approached by a uniformed patrolman who asked their names. Ac-

At 1:15 that Friday morning, a fifty-four-year-old police officer named Judd Pittenger was standing on a corner in downtown Warsaw, Indiana, thirty miles west of Fort Wayne. Warsaw was a sleepy town, and Pittenger, as its night patrolman, walked a sleepy beat: the odd prowler or vandal was the only break in his normal predawn routine. But when Pittenger turned at the sound of footsteps, he found two men in raincoats pointing submachine guns at him. He would later say he recognized one as Dillinger; the other was Van Meter.

"We want your vests," Dillinger said, "and we mean business."

Pittenger grabbed the barrel of Dillinger's gun and struggled with him a moment, until Van Meter jammed a tommy gun into Pittenger's back.

"Leave loose," Dillinger said. "We don't want to kill you."

Van Meter snatched Pittenger's pistol from its holster and whacked him twice over the head with it.

"Don't hit me any more," Pittenger yelped.

"Don't hit him," Dillinger said.

Dillinger ordered Pittenger to take them to the police station. They wanted access to the department's weapons closet.

"I don't have the key," Pittenger said.

"Who has the key?" Dillinger asked.

"I don't know," Pittenger said.

"Don't be a fool," Dillinger said. "We don't wanna be forced to kill you."

"I don't want you to kill me," Pittenger said. "I have a couple of kids at home."

"That's the reason we don't want to kill you," Dillinger said.

With a sigh, Pittenger reached into his pocket and handed over the key. They marched him to the deserted police station and up a set of stairs to the weapons closet. While Van Meter covered Pittenger, Dillinger took out three bulletproof vests and two pistols.[1]

Within hours Matt Leach had roadblocks thrown up all over northern Indiana. Vigilantes sprang from their beds to man them. All the efforts were in vain. By daylight Dillinger was safely back in Chicago, where the

---

cording to Van Meter's story, he produced a submachine gun, barking, "Here's your credentials." The officer stumbled and fled.

The FBI would later find articles of clothing belonging to Van Meter and Hamilton that contained tags from a Nashville men's store, apparently confirming Cherrington's story.

evening papers carried the news that Billie would be transferred to St. Paul
at any moment.*

Locked away in the FBI's nineteenth-floor conference room, bathed in hot
lights and interrogated around the clock for two long days, Billie gave
Purvis nothing, and he was happy to send her to St. Paul for trial. In Indianapolis, Earl Connelley was having no better luck with Dillinger's relatives. He rounded up and browbeat Hubert Dillinger and several of the
cousins, but none seemed to know where Dillinger was hiding. One, Fred
Hancock, helpfully suggested they check Arizona.

What they needed, Purvis saw, were better informants. The ones they
had were offering plenty of tips; unfortunately, almost all were worthless.
The Detroit SAC, Bill Larson, spent that week working one talkative snitch
in Muncie. Purvis sent men to Muncie, Fort Wayne, Elkhorn, and South
Bend checking the man's stories; none panned out. An informant Earl Connelley had hired, the onetime insurance-company snitch Art Maginnis, had
been sent to hang around the Dillinger filling station, but his leads were no
better. By the time Dillinger raided the Warsaw station Friday morning,
Maginnis had Connelley on a fruitless stakeout in Louisville, Kentucky.
Purvis talked to Washington and suggested they post a $5,000 reward for
information leading to Dillinger's capture. Hoover vetoed the idea.

The Warsaw raid suggested to Purvis that Dillinger was still close; without Billie, the chances he would take another Florida or Arizona vacation
seemed slim. That weekend Purvis drove to South Bend and then to
Muncie checking more dead-end tips. By the following Monday, April 16,
Hoover was growing impatient. They were charging off into the countryside without a plan, without discipline. What they needed, Hoover saw,
was an orderly system for analyzing leads. That Wednesday, Hoover told
Purvis to quit running around Indiana and stay in Chicago. Connelley and
the other SACs were to clear all leads through Purvis and telephone him at

---

* It's possible Dillinger returned to Chicago via Louisville, Kentucky. That Saturday, the day after the
Warsaw raid, a Louisville doctor claimed he had been approached by a man asking for help with a
wounded leg; he identified photographs of Dillinger as the man. Earl Connelley, who was already investigating a tip Dillinger was in the area, established a surveillance of the doctor's office, but when the tip surfaced in the Louisville newspapers, he abandoned it. The story of Dillinger's visit to Louisville was later
lent some credence by Pat Cherrington, who told the FBI she and Hamilton met Dillinger at an unidentified Kentucky "resort" that Saturday, April 14. If Dillinger did visit Louisville, he was back in Chicago
by that afternoon, when he met with Art O'Leary.

least once a day. The very next morning they got the word that Dillinger had been seen in Sault St. Marie.

While Purvis, Connelley, and their men scrambled across Indiana and northern Kentucky in search of him, Dillinger remained in Chicago. A light rain was falling that Saturday, the day after the Warsaw raid, when Art O'Leary went to meet him at the corner of Belden and Campbell Avenues. When O'Leary saw Dillinger standing across the street, he tipped his hat to signal that he hadn't been followed. When Dillinger did the same, O'Leary crossed the street and got into his car. Dillinger climbed behind the wheel, his hat tugged so low it obscured his face. Two men O'Leary didn't recognize were sitting in the back, and for a split-second he feared he had stepped into a trap.

"Johnnie, is it you?" he asked.

"Of course it's me."

"Take off your hat."

Dillinger laughed as he doffed his wet hat and introduced O'Leary to John Hamilton. O'Leary shook his hand, noticing the missing fingers. Dillinger made no effort to introduce Van Meter. It was a fast meeting. Dillinger wanted O'Leary to tell him how Billie would be taken to St. Paul. He said he would call on Monday for details.[2] No one thought Dillinger's idea of rescuing Billie was sound; both Van Meter and Hamilton had tried to talk him out of it. Least enthusiastic by far were O'Leary and Louis Piquett. The two men agreed between themselves that they would make no effort to ascertain details of Billie's trip to St. Paul.

O'Leary was nervous when he met Dillinger at 4:00 Monday afternoon at the corner of North and Kedzie Avenues. (Dillinger had left a cryptic phone message, "32 west and 16 north," and O'Leary had figured it out.) Pat Cherrington climbed into the backseat to let O'Leary in front; Hamilton sat with her, a submachine gun in his lap under a blanket. When Dillinger expressed his disappointment that O'Leary had come empty-handed, O'Leary urged him to have faith in the courts.

"Will Mr. Piquett go to St. Paul and help defend her?" Dillinger asked.

"I'll have to speak with him, but I'm sure that he will."

"That's fine, Art; give him this five hundred dollars." Dillinger produced a roll of bills. "By the way, did you hear anything more about the doctor who does the plastic surgery?"

"Yes," O'Leary said. "Lou says his name is Dr. Ralph Robiend."

"Did you find out what he charges?"

"It'll cost you five thousand dollars."

"Five grand? Don't you think that's pretty high?"

"Not when you consider how dangerous it is," O'Leary said. "Hell, don't you realize you're the hottest person in the whole United States?"[3]

Dillinger reluctantly accepted the fact that Billie was out of his reach; the FBI soon ferried her to St. Paul, where Piquett arrived to help defend her. Alone now, robbed of the woman he wanted to marry, Dillinger fell into a deepening funk. His mood would only have darkened had he known the FBI, acting on an anonymous tip, was already looking for Dr. Ralph Robiend.

If Dillinger was heartsick, John Hamilton's mood was even bleaker. With each passing day he grew more fatalistic. He kept saying he would die soon. On several occasions he mentioned how badly he wanted to see his sister in his hometown of Sault St. Marie before he died. Dillinger tried to dissuade him, but the more Hamilton stewed, the more he wanted to go. Dillinger had gotten to say good-bye to his family: why couldn't he? With a sigh Dillinger agreed to go along.

On Tuesday, April 17, Dillinger strapped on one of the new bulletproof vests, jammed a pistol into his shoulder holster, and climbed into his Ford V-8. That morning, his eyes scanning side roads for speed traps, he followed Hamilton's car out of Chicago into Indiana. As the two cars drove north into Michigan, Dillinger spent the day alone with his thoughts. Beside him, where Billie had nestled, lay a pair of binoculars and a Thermos filled with cold water; in the backseat a row of guns sat in their cases.

At nightfall, the two cars stopped for gas at a station outside Sault St. Marie, at Michigan's northern tip. As the attendant filled his tank, Dillinger stood in his overcoat in a light rain, his gray fedora pulled down over his forehead, watching the man's every move. He didn't want to be here; this was stupid.

"You're a long way from home," the attendant said, noticing the Minnesota plates. "What line of business you in?"

"Clothing salesman," Dillinger said.*

---

* When questioned later by FBI agents, the attendant said he thought he recognized Dillinger but refrained from calling the local sheriff because he felt it couldn't be true.

When night fell they drove into town. At 8:30 Hamilton's thirty-nine-year-old sister, Anna Steve, answered a knock at the kitchen door of her frame house at the top of a steep hill on 14th Street. It was Pat Cherrington. "Are you Mrs. Steve?" she asked, and Mrs. Steve nodded. "Now don't be afraid, don't say a word," Cherrington said. "I've got a surprise. There's someone here who wants to see you."

A moment later Hamilton materialized from the darkness, carrying a machine gun wrapped in a blanket. Dillinger was right behind him, holding a rifle. At the sight of her brother, whom she hadn't seen in seven years, Mrs. Steve began to cry. Hamilton held her and said they couldn't stay long. Wiping away her tears, Mrs. Steve said she wanted to go out and buy steaks to celebrate, but Dillinger shook his head and urged her to cook what she had in the house. Shooing her three children upstairs, Mrs. Steve prepared a dinner of bacon, eggs, and toast, and ate it with the trio at the kitchen table as they reminisced about Hamilton's childhood. Afterward both men shaved. Mrs. Steve took out a pair of clippers and gave the men quick haircuts.[4]

For the first time in weeks Hamilton seemed happy. He was home; it was all he had left. Around ten, the kitchen door swung open, startling both men, who grabbed their guns off the table. But it was only Mrs. Steve's eighteen-year-old son, Charles Campbell. Dillinger lowered his gun. "Charles, this is Johnnie," Hamilton said. He didn't have to say more.

Everyone adjourned to a sitting room, where young Campbell watched the two men closely. Hamilton made a clicking sound when he breathed, the result of his earlier wounds. Dillinger, still walking with a limp, remained on edge. He sat by a window saying little, reading a newspaper between peeks outside. After a bit, Hamilton sent his nephew to fetch one of his boyhood friends, a man named Paul Parquette, who came over and was stunned to find himself face-to-face with the country's most-wanted man. It was an awkward moment, a parody of a reunion; no one knew what to say, so Hamilton showed his old pal how his machine gun worked. This was far too chummy for Dillinger, who rose around eleven and announced it was time to leave. Hamilton begged for just one night to sleep in his sister's house. But Dillinger said it wasn't safe. The FBI was out there somewhere, he said, watching.*

---

* They weren't. Even though the FBI now knew the identities of Hamilton and Van Meter, Purvis had made no effort to place their families under surveillance.

As they gathered their guns, Mrs. Steve began to cry. Not knowing what to say, she handed her brother a jar of venison to take. Hamilton held her for a long moment and softly kissed her cheek. "Bye," Hamilton said. "I hope we see you again."

They wouldn't. The last time Anna Steve saw her brother, he was walking down the muddy hill away from her house; Hamilton left his car behind for her as a gift. At the bottom he slid into Dillinger's car and drove to the town of St. Ignace, only to find they had missed the last ferry across Lake Michigan. Dillinger found a hotel where they could stay the night, and Cherrington signed them in.[5]

Purvis's men were alerted by one of Mrs. Steve's neighbors, but by the time they reached Sault St. Marie the next day, Dillinger was gone. The agents, accompanied by local deputies, raided the Steve home and led Hamilton's sister and her son away in handcuffs. In Washington, Hoover had no sympathy for their plight; he wanted a message sent to anyone who would harbor dangerous criminals. For Mrs. Steve, the price for a bacon-and-eggs dinner, two haircuts, and a three-hour reunion with her brother was three months in a federal women's prison.

While Purvis's men questioned Anna Steve that Friday, Dillinger returned to Chicago and found refuge at a place that should no longer have been safe: Louie Cernocky's Crystal Ballroom in Fox River Grove. A week earlier, Beth Green had told the FBI all about Cernocky's tavern, how it served as a rest area for both the Barker and Dillinger Gangs; she described a visit there by Dillinger just weeks before.

The Bureau, in fact, had been sniffing around Cernocky since the previous summer, when Frank Nash's widow told them of Nash's fondness for the place. Cernocky's name popped up repeatedly in the Bremer investigation; Hoover, in fact, had approved a tap on his phones in March. FBI men had interviewed Cernocky's neighbors, and a squad of agents searching for the Bremer safe house had driven by the tavern just that weekend. Amid the blizzard of tips his men followed that week, however, Purvis never found time to place it under surveillance.

Had he done so, Purvis would have greeted a sight from his dreams, the gathering on Thursday, April 19, and Friday, April 20, of the entire Dillinger Gang. It was the first time the men had assembled in one group since scattering in St. Paul three weeks before; for some reason, Nelson brought along Harry Sawyer's bartender, Pat Reilly. Everyone agreed they needed a spot to regroup, to kick back and decide their next move in safety. The weekend loomed; they needed a getaway. Maybe it would improve Dillinger's mood. Cernocky said he knew just the place, a country inn in far northern Wisconsin run by an old friend who could be trusted. No one, Cernocky assured Nelson, would look for them there. Cernocky scribbled out an introductory note, sealed it in a white envelope, and handed it to Nelson.

By that point there were clear signs of tension among the gang members, much of it emanating from Nelson. There is very little concrete information about the gang members' feelings toward one another. Many of those involved would die within the year, and the FBI didn't much care how they got along; what little is known comes from asides Pat Cherrington and a handful of others would make months later.

From these comments, it appears Nelson's problem with Dillinger was equal parts envy and resentment. Nelson felt, with considerable justification, that it was he who had sheltered Dillinger after Crown Point, who invited him along on the Sioux Falls and Mason City raids, who arranged for Cernocky to act as their host. And what did he get for his trouble? Not acclaim: all the newspapers could write about was Dillinger—Dillinger, Dillinger, Dillinger. Nelson considered this the Baby Face Nelson Gang. But to the public he remained unknown.

But envy was only part of it. Both Nelson and his wife Helen felt Dillinger was reckless; Mrs. Steve's arrest made the papers that Friday, and the Nelsons feared it was only a matter of time before Dillinger brought the FBI down on all of them. It was a high price to pay for doing a man a favor, and Nelson resented it. For his part, Dillinger viewed Nelson as unstable. The only time he spent with him was planning and carrying out robberies. As Cherrington told the FBI months later, "all [the gang] knew Nelson as a vicious character and one who loved blood, and had a great desire to kill anyone who got in his path; . . . none of [them] desired Nelson's company but it was often necessary to have him in on a job when they had one to perform."[6]

For the moment, at least, everyone got along. Cernocky roused the gang early Friday morning, served them breakfast and pushed them out the door around seven. Their timing was fortuitous; a few hours later a group of Chicago cops, unaware of Cernocky's role as a way station on Dillinger's underground railroad, dropped by for lunch. The gang drove north through Wisconsin in four cars. Dillinger's group left first, followed by Van Meter's. The Nelsons and Carroll brought up the rear.

The trip was uneventful until Nelson passed east of Madison. Driving north on Highway 51 he ran a red light. A car slammed broadside into his driver's-side door, caving in the Ford's left side. Everyone involved was lucky. Nelson and his wife were shaken but unhurt, as was the driver of the second car, owned by a local cannery. Better yet, Nelson kept his temper; no one got shot. Best of all, Tommy Carroll was behind him and stood by to help. Worried that police would appear, Nelson got his car started and enticed the other driver to follow him to a garage. There Nelson shoved $83 into the man's hand and drove off. With Carroll following, Nelson managed to reach the next town north, Portage—where Dock Barker had left his fingerprints on a gas can two months earlier—and left the Ford at a garage. When the manager walked inside for a pencil and paper, he discovered that the polite young man in the brown suede jacket had vanished.[7]

Van Meter was the first to reach their destination, an isolated area of interconnected lakes and thick pine forests; it was around one o'clock. Just before the village of Manitowish he turned left off the potholed oil-and-gravel Route 51 and drove beneath an imposing cement arch with white letters announcing the little lodge's name: Little Bohemia.

The pine woods around Manitowish were settled by loggers in the late 1800s, but when logging began to wane in the 1920s, the locals, many of them second-generation French-Canadian and Scandinavian immigrants, turned their attention to tourism. Tiny resorts, no more than clusters of rustic cabins, sprang up as early as 1908, drawing people from as far south as Chicago who came in the summers to fish the sparkling blue lakes, swim off the rocky beaches, and hunt. In the spring of 1934 Manitowish was the kind of inbred backwoods village where everyone knew everyone, everyone married someone's sister and every little lake had at least one illegal still working overtime.

The first family of the Manitowish area was the LaPortes. The elder daughter, Ruth, married a Milwaukee printer named Henry Voss, who began building tourist cabins in 1912. In 1928 the Vosses completed the area's premier resort, the grand Birchwood Lodge on Route 51, which boasted a modern kitchen, a lavish dining room overlooking Spider Lake and a roar-

ing fire in its great lobby hearth. There were three LaPorte boys: Lloyd, a
fishing guide; lean, stoic George, who ran the grocery store; and the black
sheep, Louis, a bootlegger who kept two stills running on Grants Lake all
through the Depression.[8]

The younger daughter, Nan, transported her brother's moonshine down-
state, selling it to speakeasies there. In Racine, Nan met Emil Wanatka, a
squat, gregarious Austro-Hungarian restaurateur. The two married and
moved to Chicago, where they ran a rough little bar, a favorite of underworld figures, called Little Bohemia. In 1926 the Wanatkas returned to
Manitowish and Emil bought land on Star Lake, just up from Birchwood
Lodge, for a lodge of his own, a new Little Bohemia, completed in 1931.
More a roadhouse than a lodge, the new Little Bohemia was little more
than a two-story log cabin with a barroom, kitchen, and dance floor downstairs, a row of bedrooms above, and a cottage beside the back porch. It lay
out of sight of the road, two hundred yards down a tunnel of towering
pines from Route 51. Wanatka borrowed heavily to build it, forcing him to
keep it open all winter. He ran dinner specials to lure the locals and kept his
fingers crossed.

Working in the barroom that Friday afternoon, Wanatka was surprised
when Van Meter entered and hailed him by name, explaining that he had a
party of ten en route to Duluth and needed a place to stay. Wanatka said
that was fine, and served the trio a pork-chop lunch while Mickey Conforti's little bulldog, Rex, lapped at a saucer of milk. Van Meter spent the
afternoon pacing the grounds, making his mental getaway map. The lodge
was remote and empty. It would do fine.

Around five Nelson and Tommy Carroll drove up. Dillinger arrived a
little later. Six men and four women now, they were the lodge's only guests.
At first Wanatka was thrilled. But he wasn't stupid. He saw how Nelson
ripped up the introductory note from Cernocky after letting him read it.[9]
The lodge's sixteen-year-old waiter, George Baczo, carried the gang's luggage and noticed that the bags seemed extremely heavy.

"There must be lead in this one," he joked to Wanatka. "What are these
guys, hardware salesmen?" Wanatka nodded. He knew these kinds of men
from Chicago. With luck they wouldn't stay long. Wanatka's wife, Nan,
sensed it, too. Everyone was given rooms upstairs except for Nelson and
Carroll, who unpacked their bags in the cottage. Nelson was irked that
Dillinger got a better room. "Well, who in the hell does he think he is?"
Nelson snapped. "We'll put *him* in the cottage."[10]

Nan Wanatka served the gang steaks for dinner. "You play cards?" Tommy Carroll asked Wanatka once the dishes were cleared.

"Pinochle," Wanatka said.

"How about poker?"

They played in the barroom, seven-card stud, Wanatka, Carroll, Dillinger, Nelson, and Hamilton. On the third or fourth hand the pot grew to $34, no small amount during the Depression. The last two in were Wanatka, showing a six and a king, and Dillinger, a king and an eight. When the bidding ended Wanatka reached for his winnings.

"Wait a minute," Dillinger said. "Whaddya got?"

"I got kings and sixes."

"Too bad, Emil. I got kings and eights."

As Dillinger raked in the pot, his coat opened and Wanatka glimpsed the holstered pistol he was wearing. As he dealt the next hand the innkeeper peered at Nelson, sitting to his left, and the other players. All had similar bulges in their coats. After the hand Dillinger asked, "Where's the washroom?"

Wanatka told him, then stepped into the kitchen. This was worse than he thought. Six men with guns in a remote lodge on a late-winter weekend: the first thing he thought of was Dillinger. In the kitchen he found a *Chicago Tribune.* On the front page was a photo of Dillinger. It was him. Wanatka's heart raced. He returned to the table but found he had lost his appetite for cards. He studied the men. They appeared to be split into two groups. The cool one, Johnnie, seemed closest to the one with the missing fingers, Red. The chatty kid, Jimmy, was with the pug-nosed Tom. The quiet skinny one, Wayne, was the loner.

At one point Nan's sister Ruth brought her daughter over from Birchwood Lodge to chat. Dillinger asked Wanatka who they were, then bought them drinks. Ruth's daughter asked why the nice man had hair a different color from his eyebrows.[11] The women shushed her.

Around ten Wanatka, urgently wanting to quit the game, began to fake yawn. He rose to say he was turning in,[12] walked upstairs with his two collies, Shadow and Prince, and readied for bed. In a minute Nan was beside him, pestering him with questions: Who were they? Bank robbers? What should they do? Wanatka took a deep breath. "I think the one with the dyed-red hair," he said, "is Dillinger."

They lay in bed, staring at the ceiling. Eventually Emil nodded off, but Nan lay awake, listening. Every time one of the dogs yipped, every time a door opened during the night, she froze. She heard someone—a man, she thought—pacing the corridor.

The next morning Emil was first to awake, padding downstairs to let the dogs out at six. Tommy Carroll was already in the barroom, stretching. "Good morning, Emil," he said. "Boy did I sleep. How about breakfast?"[13]

Wanatka said he'd have something ready when everyone got up. Carroll went upstairs to wake the others, and before long all the gang came shuffling down the stairs, yawning, the women in their robes. They ate in the kitchen. When they were finishing up, Wanatka said to Dillinger, "Johnnie, could I talk to you?"

The two men walked into the lodge office, where Wanatka shut the door. "Emil, what's wrong?" Dillinger said.

Wanatka couldn't stand it any longer. He had to know.

"You're John Dillinger," Wanatka said.

Dillinger's expression remained unchanged.

"You're not afraid, are you?" he said.

"No," Wanatka lied. "But everything I have to my name, including my family, is right here, and every policeman in America is looking for you. If I can help it, there isn't gonna be any shooting match." Dillinger placed a hand on Wanatka's shoulder. "Emil, all we want is to eat and rest for a few days," he said. "We'll pay you well and get out. There won't be no trouble."[14]

Afterward the mood at Little Bohemia took a sharp turn; Dillinger presumably told other gang members Wanatka knew who they were. From that point on, Dillinger or Nelson kept a watch on the lodge phone and made an effort to overhear any conversations; whenever a car entered the drive, Dillinger asked Wanatka who it was. After breakfast Dillinger sent Pat Reilly on a run to St. Paul. They were low on ammunition, and Van Meter wanted some cash Harry Sawyer was keeping for him. Pat Cherrington volunteered to go as well. They left around eight, promising to return the next day.[15]

When they left, Dillinger got out a .22 rifle, and he and Van Meter and Nelson took target practice, shooting at a can on a snowbank a hundred yards away. Dillinger asked Wanatka to take a few shots as well. For years afterward Wanatka would brag that only he and Van Meter could hit the target. Van Meter grabbed a submachine gun, and everyone shot that, too. A little later the Wanatkas' eight-year-son, Emil, Jr., brought out his baseball mitt. Dillinger and Nelson played catch with the boy until he quit, complaining that Nelson threw too hard.

This was too much for Nan Wanatka. She didn't want her son around these kinds of men: who knew what they could do? Worse, the morning paper carried the news of Anna Steve's arrest by the FBI: they could all end up in jail. After lunch Nan announced she was sending Emil, Jr., to a birthday party. Dillinger gave the kid a quarter for ice cream, but as father and son readied to leave, he decided to send Van Meter along, just in case. By nightfall, in fact, Dillinger had gang members watching all the Wanatkas. When Nan ran into town to buy groceries, she was certain she saw Baby Face Nelson watching her from the parking lot.

Saturday evening passed quietly, but by Sunday morning Nan had had enough. She had taken her sister aside and talked about calling the authorities. That morning she wrote a note to her brother-in-law, Henry Voss, and slipped it into a pack of cigarettes. "Henry," it read, "You can go to Rhinelander and call as planned. Not one word to anyone about it. Tell them to line up the highways. There will be more here tomorrow and don't let anyone know where you are going or why. We want to be protected by them as best as they can. Tell them that."[16]

Around ten Dillinger handed Wanatka $500 in cash and told him the gang would be leaving the next morning, Monday. A little later Lloyd La-Porte, the fishing guide, appeared in the barroom. Nan noticed Dillinger and Nelson to one side, listening. "Gee," LaPorte said, "I left my cigarettes at home. You got a pack, Nan?" Nan handed her brother the pack with the note in it. He strolled back to his car and drove to Birchwood Lodge, where Henry Voss read the note. The telephone was a party line, and neither man trusted it. They headed south, toward the town of Rhinelander, where they planned to call the FBI.

Purvis was reading papers in his Chicago apartment around one, enjoying a rare day off, when his manservant, President, brought him the phone. It was the U.S. Marshal's office in Chicago, relaying an urgent message from someone named Henry Voss in northern Wisconsin. Purvis dialed the number he was given and found himself talking to Voss. "The man you want most is up here," Voss said, cryptically.

"You mean Dillinger?"

Voss wouldn't say. Purvis pressed, thinking he might be a kook, but finally Voss admitted it: yes, he said, Dillinger and four other men were holed up at the Little Bohemia Lodge at Manitowish. Purvis asked where the nearest airport was. Here in Rhinelander, Voss said, fifty miles south of the lodge. Purvis told Voss to meet him there at six. For identification he was to wear a handkerchief around his neck.

Purvis dialed Washington and briefed Hoover, who agreed that the call sounded authentic. Hoover ordered Purvis to round up every available agent and head immediately to Rhinelander. Purvis phoned St. Paul and relayed Hoover's orders to Hugh Clegg, who set about doing the same. Both offices erupted into scenes of barely controlled chaos; the atmosphere was martial, kinetic, aviators scrambling madly for the runway. Phone calls ricocheted between agents grabbing catnaps at their homes; several leaped into cars half-dressed, tires squealing as they headed for the office. Purvis arrived at the office buttoning his shirt and tightening his tie. In both cities men unlocked their weapons lockers and hauled out every piece of heavy equipment they had, including machine guns and tear-gas guns.

In St. Paul, Clegg arranged a thirty-five-cent-per-mile charter from Northwest Airways. He would take Inspector Rorer and three agents and fly north; Werner Hanni and three others, who admitted their fear of flying, threw the tear-gas guns into a car and drove. In Chicago, Purvis chartered two planes and chose eleven men to fill them. Rhinelander was a three-hour flight. It took an hour just to get everyone to Municipal Airport. As they piled into the planes, Purvis noticed the pilot had only a road map to guide them. He crossed his fingers.

As that Sunday afternoon wore on, the men of the Dillinger Gang began to grow restless. Everyone sensed it; something wasn't right. There were too many people coming and going, too many people who had seen them. That night there would be dozens more: Wanatka was having one of his dollar-a-plate dinners. Dillinger had the cars stowed out of sight in the lodge's garage. At one point Van Meter asked Wanatka if he knew a place to which they could move, somewhere more private. A local man came into the barroom after lunch, planted himself at a stool, and began to drink; once or twice he tried to collar Hamilton to drink with him.

This was too much for Dillinger. Around four he told Wanatka there had been a change in plans. The group would be leaving that night, as soon as Pat Reilly returned from St. Paul. He asked Wanatka to serve them an early dinner, steaks with garlic.

Nan Wanatka was nervously preparing the meal when her sister Ruth appeared at the kitchen door. She started to say that her husband had driven to Rhinelander to call the FBI when Nan shushed her. "We bought so much meat for the weekend," Nan said, glancing toward the barroom where the gang was eating. "Won't you take some?" She motioned for her sister to join her in the meat locker. "They're leaving as soon as Reilly gets back!" she hissed.[17]

When her sister left, Nan stepped through the kitchen door and poured herself another drink from the bar. Her husband was stunned. "Nan, are you drinking?" he asked. She started to respond when her eyes met Nelson's. Nan swallowed. Emil tried to smile. Nelson said nothing, but he could tell they were up to something. Nan turned and returned to the kitchen. Nelson started after her, then apparently thought better of it, taking a seat by his wife instead.

Nan had just walked into the kitchen when she saw Pat Reilly drive up to the lodge; beside him in the car sat Pat Cherrington. Dillinger and the others, busy with their steaks, didn't see them. Reilly seemed unsure what to do. There were no cars in the driveway—Dillinger had hidden them in the garage—and Reilly was worried that the gang had fled. As Nan Wanatka watched, he turned and drove away.[18]

Hugh Clegg's five-man party reached Rhinelander first; its plane touched down a few minutes past five. On the runway Clegg was met by George La-Porte and Henry Voss. A crowd was forming, attracted by the airplane, so Clegg drew the two men into a glade beside the runway. Clegg produced photos of all the Dillinger Gang's members. The only one Voss could identify was flat-nosed Tommy Carroll. But they were mobsters, he was sure of that.

Voss drew a rough sketch of Little Bohemia, its outbuildings and grounds. There was no way to escape across the lake behind the lodge, he emphasized to Clegg; there was no boat, and the water remained partially frozen. There was only a thin gravelly beach between the lodge and the lake. The Wanatkas had even formulated an attack plan. The gang appeared ready to depart the next morning. The family and staff would hide in the cellar at 4:00 A.M., just before daybreak. It was then that the FBI had to attack. Clegg was impressed with Voss's enthusiasm.

First they needed cars. Voss drove Clegg into Rhinelander to a Ford dealership, where Clegg spoke to the manager. He explained that they were federal agents and needed to rent three cars. The manager said he had no license to rent cars, and only had one old coupe to spare anyway. He asked Clegg if he was raiding bootleggers in the area, because if he was, he could forget the whole thing; if word got around he was helping such a raid, the man said, half his business would disappear. When Clegg said he wasn't after bootleggers, the manager asked if he was after Dillinger. Clegg said they needed the cars, and fast. The manager said it would take an hour or two.

As they talked, Clegg saw a plane coming in low over the trees: Purvis had arrived. They met at the airport. Purvis was a little shaken by a rough landing—his plane had actually spun around twice on touchdown—but they were ready to go. It was a fifty-mile drive to Little Bohemia but they had plenty of time, which they needed. While they waited for the cars, Purvis decided to send Agent Ray Suran ahead with Henry Voss to Manitowish to reconnoiter. Suran jumped in Voss's car and headed north, but on the outskirts of Rhinelander they ran into Voss's wife, Ruth, who had come to alert them: Dillinger was leaving tonight, she said, after dinner. They had to move fast.

This changed everything. They returned to the airport. Purvis turned to see Henry Voss running toward him, yelling, "Mr. Purvis! Mr. Purvis!" When Voss explained the change in Dillinger's plans, Purvis and Clegg decided to move immediately. By then the cars were ready, and Purvis persuaded a seventeen-year-old boy to lend them his coupe, giving them five in all. At 7:15 the FBI caravan headed toward Little Bohemia.

As the lights of Rhinelander winked out behind them, the roads turned bad. They were unpaved, muddy from the spring thaw and riddled with potholes. The FBI cars bumped and slid north until one, then another, careened into a ditch. There was no time to push them out. Quickly the eight agents in these cars grabbed their guns and climbed onto the running boards of the remaining three. As temperatures dropped into the thirties, numbing their hands and faces, they struggled to hold on. Purvis kept an eye on his wristwatch. It was going to be close.

The FBI cars rumbled into the driveway of Henry Voss's sprawling Birchwood Lodge, a mile down Route 51 from Little Bohemia, just before nine. Inside, Voss discovered Nan Wanatka and her daughter; they had sneaked out in anticipation of the raid. She said Dillinger was still at the lodge, or had been a half hour earlier, and urged Clegg to move fast; the gang was leaving any minute. Clegg decided to head to Little Bohemia and devise a plan of attack once they surveyed the ground. He told the men to extinguish their cigarettes and check their guns.

Minutes later the FBI caravan, headlights off, inched through the darkness up Route 51, passing several well-lit homes, until it reached the mouth of Little Bohemia's two-hundred-yard driveway. The confidence level among the men could not have been high. No one dwelled on the fact the FBI had never attempted a raid of this scale, that agents hadn't been trained for massed gunfights, that few in the raiding party had ever fired a gun in anger. Everyone knew the FBI's abysmal record in gunfights. Three times in the preceding six months agents had managed to engage armed outlaws: The fiasco leading to Verne Miller's escape in Chicago at Halloween; Dillinger's escape in St. Paul; and the ambush of Wilbur Underhill. Only the latter produced an arrest, and only after Underhill had escaped from a house the FBI had surrounded. Nor, as the cars swung into the driveway, did anyone need to be reminded it was the fourth time in twenty-three days agents had been within a baseball's toss of Dillinger without capturing him.

It was pitch dark as the three cars turned up the muddy driveway into the tunnel of tall pines. There was no moon. The only sound was the wind, whistling through the branches above. Patches of snow and dirty ice lay amid fallen leaves and underbrush. Ahead, the back porch of Little Bohemia was bathed in the light of a single bulb. It glinted off the rear fenders of a row of parked cars. For several moments Purvis, riding in the second car, thought conditions were perfect. If Dillinger was still in the lodge, they had achieved complete surprise. While still well back in the trees, Clegg stopped the lead car and stepped out into the driveway. Purvis stopped behind him.

Then, just as agents opened their car doors, dogs began barking. No one had mentioned anything about dogs. As he stepped into the driveway, Purvis glanced at the lodge and saw four or five men appear on the porch. As he watched, three of the men hustled into a Chevrolet coupe. His heart sank. This was the worst way a raid could begin: dogs barking, an alarm raised, gang members hustling for a getaway car.

In the years since that frigid night in Wisconsin, those involved have gone to great lengths to explain their actions. John Toland, who interviewed several agents who were at Little Bohemia, wrote in 1963 that Clegg "mapped out an attack" that afternoon at Rhinelander. In fact, as FBI files make clear, there was never any plan other than a vague idea that the inn would be surrounded. Inspector Rorer told Hoover afterward that they "had been unable to make plans because of the lack of time, but expected to do so upon their arrival."[19]* Worse, though Assistant Director Clegg was the senior agent on the ground that night, there was considerable confusion who was in charge. At various times Clegg, Purvis, and Inspector Rorer all issued orders.[20]

As the men on Little Bohemia's porch scrambled into a Chevrolet coupe, Inspector Rorer, whose capture of Machine Gun Kelly gave him a certain authority, snapped at Purvis: "Hurry! Hurry!" Hoping to encircle the lodge, Purvis told him to take two men and head into the woods on the left. Clegg told other men to head into the trees at their right. As they spoke the Chevrolet's headlights flashed on. Music could be heard, eerily wafting through the chill night air. The car began to back up toward them. Suddenly the driver threw it into forward and made a sharp U-turn, the Chevrolet's headlights swinging around toward where Clegg and Purvis stood frozen in the driveway.

There was no time to concoct a plan; there was barely time to think. Instinctively—no one seems to have shouted an order—Clegg and Purvis, along with an agent named Carter Baum, jogged toward the car, guns drawn. As the car veered toward them, Purvis and Clegg yelled, "Police! Stop! Federal agents!" Other agents—scrambling into the black woods—joined the chorus of shouts: "Stop the car! Federal agents!" The car surged forward. Two men appeared on the inn's porch and began yelling; in the din no one could hear their words.

The car wouldn't stop; as Purvis and Clegg moved up the driveway, it was heading straight for them. "Fire!" both Purvis and Clegg shouted. Shots rang out all across the clearing. Purvis's submachine gun jammed, but Agent Baum raked the car with his own tommy gun. Glass shattered; tires exploded. The car sagged to a stop.

Just then a shadowy figure darted out of a cottage from the right side corner of the inn. The figure fired a pistol at Purvis—bullets struck the

---

* Other agents confirmed this. "We had no particular orders as to where we would be," Agent William Ryan said in his debriefing. Agent Arthur McLawhon: "The only orders that I received from the time we left Rhinelander to the time of arrival was to drive the automobile." Agent Ken McIntire: "The situation arose so quickly that it was almost impossible for orders to be given, every man doing as he thought best." Agent Sam Hardy: "Mr. Purvis and Mr. Clegg seemed to be directing the party, but this Agent did not know just what actual plan was to be used on arrival at the Little Bohemia Resort."

ground at his feet—then disappeared into the woods at the right. In the confusion no one gave chase.

All this occurred in barely ten seconds, by the later estimate of Inspector Rorer. As the firing began, Rorer and two agents, T. G. Melvin and Lew Nichols, fast-walked into the trees toward the left side of the lodge. As they walked, Rorer told the two agents to keep space between them. Just as he spoke Rorer rounded the side of the lodge, where he glimpsed the shadow of a man preparing to jump from a second-floor window.

"Police! Stop!" Rorer yelled, then fired.

A burst of machine-gun fire answered from the window. Bullets zinged through the trees. In the light of the muzzle flash Rorer could see two men at the window. Agent Melvin fired three blasts from his shotgun. A moment later Rorer looked up; the men at the window were gone. He was certain they had been forced back inside the lodge.

Back in the driveway the firing had stopped. Purvis and Clegg began shouting for the men inside the damaged Chevrolet to come out with their hands up. The driver's door opened. "Hold your fire!" someone yelled. Before anyone could react a man jumped out of the car and sprinted into the woods on the right, where a half-dozen FBI men were running toward the lake. Several had already passed behind the lodge's wood-frame garage and stumbled into a barbed-wire fence, from which they were attempting to extricate themselves in the darkness.

Agent Harold H. Reinecke was right behind these men, running toward the lake, when the man fleeing the car nearly crashed into him. "Halt!" Reinecke yelled. But the man turned and ran. "Halt!" Reinecke yelled again. When the man kept running, Reinecke raised his shotgun and fired twice, missing. As the man disappeared into the darkness, he fired one more blast, missing once more.

As Agent Reinecke chased the unidentified man in the woods, a second man emerged from the car, slowly, swaying, and slumped to the ground, obviously wounded. "Hands up!" Clegg shouted.

"Identify yourself!" Purvis shouted.

The man on the ground groaned.

"John," he said.

"Hands up! Hands up!"

Purvis and Clegg shouted at the fallen man to come toward them. He ignored them. It was dark; at a distance of fifty feet, Purvis couldn't see the man's features clearly. He called for Agent Sam Hardy to run back and bring the third FBI car up the driveway, so they could shine headlights on the man. Hardy scrambled back to the car, but the keys were missing. The driver, Agent Arthur McLawhon, was out in the woods on the right. Hardy shouted for him to bring the keys. Precious minutes were lost until McLawhon finally appeared and handed over the keys. Hardy drove the car up the driveway.

When the headlights reached him everyone could see the fallen "John" wasn't Dillinger. He was elderly, heavyset. Purvis shouted for him to come forward and surrender. The man seemed to oblige, rising to his feet. But then he staggered backward, fell heavily on his rump, took a flask out of his pocket, and took a deep swig. Purvis yelled for everyone to hold their fire.

The lodge was still. FBI men had taken up stations in the woods to the left and right, where they could see the beach at the back of the inn. Word was relayed from both positions: no one had gotten through. The elderly man stood, staggered onto the porch, and disappeared into the lodge. As Purvis and Clegg watched, unsure what to do, they could see the man inside, weaving past the windows.

Purvis was still trying to decide his next move when the headlights of a car swung into the driveway behind them. It drove right up behind the parked FBI cars. The two agents standing with Purvis, Carter Baum and Sam Hardy, called for the driver to identify himself. Suddenly the car leaped backward, rocketing down the driveway toward Highway 51. Baum opened fire with his submachine gun. Purvis ran after the car, firing at the tires and hitting the radiator. The car sped out of the driveway and disappeared into the darkness.

Purvis realized they were in a precarious position. Agents were spraying bullets at anything that moved, not having any idea who they were shooting at. Worried that one of his own men might be shot, Purvis called out for every agent on the grounds to shout out his identity and his position. As he did, Agent Hardy ran up. He said he could still see the headlights of the retreating car moving slowly out on the road behind them. Purvis told Hardy and two other agents to creep back through the woods to try and take it by surprise.

The three agents reached the end of Little Bohemia's driveway at about the same time as the car. Again they called for the occupants to get out and identify themselves. Again the car sped away. All three men opened fire.

There was a loud pop, a tire exploding. As the car disappeared down the highway, this time for good, they heard it running on one rim. There was no way to stop the car. In the rush to reach the lodge, no one had thought to arrange roadblocks. The local sheriff had no idea the FBI was even in his jurisdiction.

Back in the driveway, Inspector Rorer materialized from the left and discussed with Purvis and Clegg what to do. They had now fired on at least five different cars and people, and no one had a clue who a single one of their targets actually was. And now there was a sixth. By this point everyone could see a man sitting in the wounded Chevrolet coupe, its motor still running. Music could be heard; the car radio. Purvis called to the man in the car. He wasn't moving.

Rorer was elected to reconnoiter the car. As Purvis covered him, Rorer dropped to his hands and knees and crawled to the Chevrolet. In the front seat he found a young man, his head drooped forward, his right chest and shoulder covered with blood. Rorer felt for a pulse; there was none. He reached over and switched off the radio and the motor, then slipped his hand into the man's coat pocket and took his wallet. He returned to where Clegg and Purvis were standing and reported, as he later put it, "that the man was young and dead."

Rorer opened the dead man's wallet and lifted out his driver's license. It was then that the three FBI supervisors learned that the man they had just killed was a thirty-five-year-old worker at a nearby federal work camp named Eugene Boisneau.

They waited. Other than the wounded "John," whom they could still see staggering inside the lodge, there was no sign of life in the building. Even though they had apparently killed an innocent man, Purvis tried to put it from his mind. Dillinger and his gang were trapped inside the lodge; eventually they would have to make a break for it. For the moment, Purvis and Clegg decided against storming the place. There weren't enough bullet-proof vests, and they had no tear-gas guns at all. Purvis had inexplicably failed to bring Chicago's. Clegg's were being brought by Werner Hanni and the other St. Paul agents, who were still en route. The minutes ticked by. All around the lodge, agents hunched behind trees, blowing on their hands for warmth.

An hour passed. Then, around eleven o'clock, a new set of headlights appeared in the driveway. It was an ambulance from the federal work camp, Camp Mercer. Purvis was surprised. No one had called for it. The camp doctor, a man named S. X. Roberts, stepped out of the ambulance and told Purvis he had received a call that a worker named John Morris had been wounded. Purvis realized Morris must be the "John" who had retreated into the lodge. This was getting worse by the minute.

When the ambulance drove up, another man emerged from the woods. His name was John Hoffman; he was a gas station attendant. Hoffman had been the third man in the Chevrolet coupe, the one Agent Reinecke had shot at in the woods. He had a gunshot wound in his right arm and glass cuts all over his face. Together Hoffman and Dr. Roberts called for John Morris to come out of the lodge. A moment later he did so. To Purvis's surprise, Morris was followed by three men, who walked out with their hands up. It was Emil Wanatka, his bartender, and the busboy. Wanatka said Dillinger and his men were still inside the lodge, hiding in an upstairs bedroom on the left side of the building.

Word passed through the agents in the trees: they had the Dillinger Gang trapped. That was the good news. In whispers the bad news passed from man to man, that someone, apparently a civilian, had been killed in the Chevrolet. No one took the news harder than Carter Baum, the handsome twenty-nine-year-old who had fired the fatal shots. Baum was sitting in one of the FBI cars, brooding and trying to keep warm. An agent named Ken McIntire sat with him. "I think there's a man in that car," McIntire said at one point, "and I think he is dead."

"Certainly he is," Baum said. "I killed him." McIntire tried to assuage Baum's guilt. Several agents had fired at the car, McIntire said. It was dark. He couldn't be certain he had killed the man. He should forget about it. But Baum couldn't forget. He had killed an innocent man. Touching the submachine gun in his lap, Baum said, "I can never shoot this gun again."[21]

Outside, Purvis and Clegg continued debating whether to storm the lodge. Again they decided to wait for Werner Hanni and the tear-gas equipment: with the building surrounded, Dillinger wasn't going anywhere. Purvis collared Agent Jay Newman and told him to take one of the FBI cars and drive to Birchwood Lodge, phone the Rhinelander airport, and leave a message for Hanni to hurry forward the moment he arrived. Newman, a Mormon laypreacher, noticed Carter Baum's plight and asked to take him along. Maybe they could talk. Purvis agreed.

Newman drove Baum to Birchwood Lodge, where he phoned an agent left at Rhinelander and relayed the message. When Newman finished his call, the operator told him he had just heard something about a Packard being stolen in town, in Manitowish. Newman, worried that a member of Dillinger's gang might be escaping, took Agent Baum and drove back past Little Bohemia and on into the town, where they spotted a constable named Carl C. Christiansen. Christiansen jumped in the car and accompanied them back to Birchwood Lodge, hoping to assemble a posse.

On their return, the three were greeted with a second piece of news. The switchboard operator, a man named Alvin Koerner, who lived between the two lodges, had just phoned, saying there was a suspicious car parked outside his house. Newman decided to investigate. Returning to his car, Newman drove, with Baum beside him and Christiansen at the window. It only took a minute to reach Koerner's gravel driveway, where they saw the car parked on Route 51.

"Have your guns ready," Newman said.

As they approached the car, they could see it was empty. Agent Baum jotted down the license number. They turned into the gravel lane leading to Koerner's house. It was lined by a white picket fence. There was a Ford parked in front. When his headlights swept the car, Newman could see it was filled with people. He pulled up behind it and rolled down his window. "I'm looking for Mr. Koerner," Newman said.

No answer. Suspicion flickered in Newman's eyes.

"Who's in that car?" he asked.

A small young man in a brown suede jacket jumped out of the car's passenger's-side door and stepped to Newman's open window.

"I know you bastards are wearing bulletproof vests," the man barked, "so I'll give it to you high and low."

Baby Face Nelson raised his gun and opened fire.

Not until it was far too late did Purvis and Clegg realize that every assumption they had made that evening was horribly wrong. While the two men remained rooted in the driveway at Little Bohemia, studying the lodge for a glimpse of the gang they believed trapped inside, Dillinger was already gone, and moving fast. So were Van Meter, Hamilton, Carroll, and Nelson. Each had made his escape in the opening minutes of a debacle that would haunt the Bureau for years to come.

As the FBI pieced it together afterward, this is what happened. When the three Bureau cars first entered Little Bohemia's driveway, all the gang members except Nelson had been upstairs packing. Nelson was out in the cabin beside the lodge's porch. The only guests left in the barroom were John Hoffman, a twenty-eight-year-old gas station attendant, and two of his friends from the work camp, a fifty-nine-year-old cook named John Morris and thirty-five-year-old Eugene Boisneau. The three had just put on their coats and stepped onto the porch when the FBI cars pulled up.

The bartender and the busboy followed them out to wave good-bye. The Chevrolet was Hoffman's, and when he turned the ignition, the radio came on. No one saw the FBI cars out in the darkened drive. Hoffman started the car and headed up the driveway, still unable to see the agents, who began shouting for him to stop. Hoffman couldn't hear them over the car radio. In fact, none of the three men in the car knew what was happening until bullets crashed through the windshield. On the porch behind them, the bartender and the busboy began shouting, "Stop! They're our customers!" In the din of gunfire, no one heard them.

At the sound of gunshots, Dillinger and the men upstairs grabbed their weapons, opened a second-story rear window, and prepared to jump. As they did, Inspector Rorer and his men rounded the left side of the lodge, saw them, and opened fire. Dillinger fired a burst from his Thompson gun in return. The critical mistake of the evening was Rorer's. He believed his shots had driven the gang members inside. They hadn't. When Rorer and his men ducked to avoid the return fire from the roof, Dillinger, Van Meter, Hamilton, and Carroll each jumped from the second-story window onto a ten-foot mound of frozen snow behind the lodge. By the time Rorer looked back, they were gone.

When Rorer glanced toward the lake, he saw no one escaping. But what Rorer couldn't see was that an eight-foot incline divided the beach from the backyard; Henry Voss hadn't included this feature on the map he sketched for the agents that afternoon. Dillinger and his men sprinted down a set of wooden steps to the beach, turned right, and ran along the lake, their escape hidden from sight by the incline. Over on the right, Nelson sprang from the cabin, fired at Purvis, and darted into the woods. By the time FBI agents fought their way through a barbed-wire fence, he too was gone, melting into the darkness.

The car that entered the lodge's driveway after the initial shooting was driven by the gang's gofer, Pat Reilly, returning to the lodge with Pat Cherrington. Cherrington had just opened the car door when she heard a voice yell, "Halt!" She replied, "Go to hell," jumped back into the car, and told Reilly to step on it. When he reached the highway, Reilly lingered a minute, unsure what to do. When shots rang out, he lost control of the car, running it over a tree stump.

Fighting to get the car off the stump, he threw two pistols into Cherrington's lap and told her to start shooting. She told him to go to hell. When the car was freed they passed the lodge a second time, drawing gunshots that struck their tire; the car door swung open and Cherrington fell out, fracturing her left shoulder. Later that night, after replacing their punctured tire at a filling station, the two hapless fugitives drove their car into a mud hole. Stuck, they sat in a field drinking whiskey, becoming drunk.[22] Not till the next day, after a series of further misadventures, did the two reach St. Paul.

Dillinger and the others, meanwhile, thrashed through the pines, looking for a house with a car they could steal. In the darkness Tommy Carroll became separated. In the end it was Carroll who had the easiest time of it; he made his way to Manitowish, stole a Packard, and drove toward St. Paul. Dillinger, Van Meter, and Hamilton emerged from the woods a quarter mile north of Little Bohemia; had the FBI established roadblocks or patrolled Route 51 they might have been spotted. As it was, Van Meter was free to step out onto the road and attempt to flag down a passing car; the car, driven by Nan Wanatka's brother, George LaPorte, was following the ambulance to the lodge and didn't stop.

Across the road, Dillinger spotted Mitchell's Rest Lake Resort, a wood-frame house with several cabins behind. Inside, its seventy-year-old owner, Edward J. Mitchell, was trying to explain something to his German handyman. His wife was lying on a couch, sick with the flu, when they heard a knock at the door. It was Hamilton, who after asking for a glass of water, casually walked across the living room and yanked the phone from the wall. The Mitchells had heard the rumors about gangsters at Little Bohemia. They'd heard the shots, too.

"You couldn't be Dillinger, could you?" Mrs. Mitchell asked.

Dillinger grinned. "You couldn't have guessed better," he said. He noticed the terrified look at Edward Mitchell's face. "Now don't worry, old man," he said, "I'd never harm a hair on your head."

"My wife is just getting over the flu," Mitchell said.

Dillinger took a moment to drape a blanket across the old woman. "Here you are, mother," he said.[23]

All he needed, Dillinger said, was a car. Mitchell said he had a Model T, but it had been sitting on blocks all winter. Van Meter walked outside and saw a Model A truck, but it wouldn't start. He asked Mitchell who owned a green Ford coupe parked next to it. Mitchell said it was his carpenter's. He lived in one of the cabins. The carpenter, Robert L. Johnson, had been asleep when he was awakened by a knock on his door. He dressed, grabbed a flashlight, and shuffled in his slippers to the door, where he found Dillinger, Van Meter, and Hamilton hovering outside. Dillinger said they needed a doctor for Mrs. Mitchell. The .45 in his hand suggested the matter was more urgent than that. Johnson led them to his car.

Baby Face Nelson had the worst of it. Cut off from the rest of the gang, he ran the other way, south along the lakeshore, stumbling through underbrush for a half hour until he saw the lights of a cabin a half mile beyond Little Bohemia. Inside was another elderly couple, Mr. and Mrs. George W. Lange. Nelson didn't bother knocking; he walked right in, pistol in hand. "Now don't get excited," he told the Langes. "I won't harm you, but this is a matter of life and death."

Nelson sagged onto a couch, stuck his pistol inside his coat, and began petting the Langes' dog, which began barking. After resting a few minutes, he pointed his gun at the frightened couple and said he wanted Lange to drive him in his car, a 1932 Chevrolet coach. Mrs. Lange began to cry. Nelson needed her to calm down, but as always the human touch that came so easily to Dillinger eluded him. "Come on now, shut up" was the best he could come up with.

The Langes put on their coats and got in the car, Mr. Lange driving with Nelson beside him. The headlights wouldn't come on. Nelson told him to drive anyway. Lange edged out onto Route 51 and turned right, toward the Birchwood Lodge a half mile down the road. The car had only gone a few hundred yards when it stalled.

Nelson was in a precarious position; any minute he expected a carload of FBI men to drive by. To his left he saw a house ablaze in light. "Who lives there?" he asked Lange.[24]

"Alvin Koerner," Lange said.

Koerner was the switchboard operator. At that moment he was sitting with his wife in his living room, petrified, having heard the gunfire at Little Bohemia followed by the panicked call from the wounded John Morris. His maid and two children were asleep in a back room. Peeking out his window, Koerner saw the Langes' car before he saw them, and hurriedly telephoned Birchwood Lodge to report it.

Nelson shoved his pistol into George Lange's back and marched the couple up the muddy lane to Koerner's front door. Koerner, not seeing Nelson behind them, let the trio in. Nelson announced he wanted the Koerners to drive him to the town of Woodruff. Koerner, groping for an excuse, said he couldn't; he had children to care for. Nelson trained his gun on him and said it didn't matter.

The two men were still arguing when a car drove up.

"Who's that car belong to?" Nelson demanded.

"Don't know," said Koerner.

It was George LaPorte and a friend named Carl J. Christiansen (no relation to the constable), who after declining to pick up the hitchhiking Van Meter had stopped by Little Bohemia, where Emil Wanatka and his two employees jumped in the car. Wanatka's group needed coats and had decided to come to Koerner's to get some. Leaving Christiansen in the car, the men walked into the house. Nelson let them in. "Hello, Jimmy," the bartender said. The two men had gotten along well that weekend; Nelson was a great tipper. "Never mind the bullshit," Nelson said, producing the pistol. "Just line up against the wall."

Wanatka reached for Nelson's gun. "Put that gun down, Jimmy," he said. "These people are friends of mine."

Nelson stepped back.

"Who's in that car out there?" he asked Wanatka.

"Nobody," Wanatka said, forgetting that Christiansen was still in the backseat.

"Are there any G-men in that car?"

"No."

"Now I'm getting out of here," Nelson said, motioning to Wanatka and Koerner, "and you two are going with me."

Nelson jabbed the gun toward the two men and they walked outside. Mrs. Koerner began to cry. Nelson ordered Wanatka to drive; he sat beside him in the front seat, keeping the pistol pointed at his side. Koerner got into the backseat beside Carl Christiansen.

"Jimmy," Wanatka said, "I have no keys for this car."

Just then a car drove up behind them. At the wheel was Agent Jay Newman.

Adrenaline surged through Nelson as he leveled his gun inches from Agent Newman's face.

"I'll kill you!" he snarled. "Get out of that car!"

Newman leaned back in his seat, hoping Carter Baum, who had a sub-machine gun in his lap, or the constable, Carl Christiansen, might take a shot. When neither man moved, Newman slid his hand inside his coat and reached for his pistol.

"Don't reach for that gun!" Nelson said. "I'll kill you! Now get out of the car!"

Newman stopped. Beside him Baum, the agent stricken by guilt over shooting an innocent man, ducked his head behind Newman's shoulder, as if to hide; he made no move for his gun. Christiansen ducked his head behind Baum. Slowly Newman opened the door and stepped into the driveway. Newman's foot had just touched the ground when Nelson fired. His first bullet struck Newman in the head, a glancing wound just above his right eye; he fell facedown in the mud, dazed but alive.

Nelson turned and fired into the car, at Agent Baum and Christiansen. Both men tumbled out the passenger door, Baum landing atop Christiansen. Baum stood to run but Nelson shot first. Three slugs tore into Baum's neck. He toppled over the white fence, landing on his face, a sick gurgling sound coming from his throat. Christiansen stumbled forward, into the headlights. Nelson turned on him. Two bullets struck Christiansen in the hip, knocking him off his feet. As he fell into a ditch Nelson kept firing, hitting him three more times.

At the sound of shots Emil Wanatka ran. Nelson was crazed; he shot at everything that moved. Wanatka dived into a snowbank, bullets kicking up gravel behind him. Alvin Koerner made it back to the house and locked the door.

When he ran out of moving targets, Nelson jumped into the FBI car, threw it into reverse, and stomped the accelerator, the Ford's tires circling so violently they sprayed bits of gravel against the side of Koerner's house. Just as Nelson backed down the lane, Agent Newman came to his senses. Finding his gun in his hand, he raised it and fired, emptying it at the Ford. It did no good: Nelson disappeared down Route 51.

Newman stood. He was woozy; the bullet had grazed his forehead. Blood gushed down his face and into his eyes. He wobbled to the parked car and saw LaPorte's friend, Carl J. Christiansen, cowering in the backseat. "Come out with your hands up!" Newman ordered.

"Please don't shoot me," Christiansen begged. "I'm a resident."

Newman heard a moan and saw the fallen bodies. He shoved Christiansen toward Koerner's front door; even in his dazed state, he could see they needed immediate medical attention. Christiansen banged on the door, shouting, "Alvin! Open up!," but Koerner wouldn't answer. The two men circled to the back of the house, where they could see people in the kitchen. Newman banged on the window, slapping his badge against the glass. No one moved. After yelling for another minute or two, Newman said, "I'm going to Voss's and you're going with me."

"The hell I am," Christiansen said. "I'm staying here."

"Goddamn you," Newman said, pressing the pistol into Christiansen's side. "You're going with me."

They climbed into the car and headed out onto the road.

Moments after Nelson escaped from the Koerners' home, the car carrying Werner Hanni and three other agents from St. Paul sped north along Highway 51 toward the Birchwood Lodge. As they neared the lodges, Hanni saw a black Ford approaching on the two-lane road. He dimmed his lights and peered at the car, thinking it might be FBI men.

Suddenly a spotlight flashed from the oncoming car and momentarily blinded Hanni as the two cars passed each other. Several of the agents craned their heads to see whether the car would stop. A minute later Hanni pulled into the drive at Birchwood Lodge to see whether the car would return; it didn't. Later that night Hanni realized the car with the spotlight had been driven by Baby Face Nelson.

As Hanni and his men stood at the roadside, another car drove up. Two deputy sheriffs got out; they had been called about some kind of shooting. A minute later a third car drove up. "Are you officers?" someone from the car shouted.

"This is Hanni," Hanni said.

A man bleeding from a head wound stepped out of the car. "This is Newman. Where's the nearest doctor?"

. . .

Purvis still crouched in the driveway at Little Bohemia, studying the lodge for signs of a gang that was no longer inside. The first inkling he had of his woes came when Emil Wanatka hustled up out of the woods. He had run all the way from Koerner's, and was so winded he couldn't raise his hands when an agent ordered him to. "All your men are dead," Wanatka finally managed to say. "At Koerner's."

Purvis looked at him skeptically. He asked Wanatka for his name and address. When Wanatka couldn't spell Manitowish, Purvis got snippy with him. "Who'd you come here for?" Wanatka shot back. "Me or Dillinger?" Purvis told a pair of agents to drive to the Koerner home and check out Wanatka's story.

Werner Hanni's men reached the Koerner house first, a half hour after the shooting. They found the wounded constable, Carl C. Christiansen, sitting up, leaning against the picket fence. An agent named Thomas Dodd took Christiansen's flashlight and after a minute found Carter Baum lying facedown in a pool of blood, dead.* No one had come out of the house to check on them; they were all too scared.

As the wounded were ferried to hospitals, Purvis and Clegg remained at Little Bohemia, convinced despite all the evidence that at least some of the gang remained inside the lodge. An hour passed. After midnight they grew so cold they opened the garage and took positions inside. The rest of the agents remained out in the woods, freezing, until the eastern sky began to redden around four. At that point Clegg was told the local sheriff and a group of deputies were down the road and wanted to join them. He called them up. The locals wanted to storm the lodge, but Clegg insisted they fire in gas grenades first.

Even that didn't go smoothly. There was only a single gas gun, and despite all their efforts, the agents couldn't get it to fire a grenade through the inn's window screens; the grenades hit the screens and fell to the ground, hissing. A group of five agents stood behind the garage debating what to

---

* Thomas J. Dodd was a Connecticut lawyer who served as an FBI agent from 1933 to 1935 before embarking on a career in politics. After World War II he was the chief U.S. prosecutor at the Nuremberg trials of German military leaders. In 1958 he was elected to the first of two terms in the U.S. Senate; his son is the current Connecticut senator Christopher Dodd. Thomas Dodd died in 1971.

do. It was decided that the only way to get a grenade inside the inn was for someone to run up and throw one through the door. If Dillinger was still inside the lodge—and everyone believed he was—it was likely to be a deadly errand. An agent named John T. McLaughlin volunteered to do it. "I am the only single man here," McLaughlin explained. "It was the bravest act that I saw during those days and to me, John McLaughlin has always been a hero," another agent, Robert G. Gillespie wrote years later.*

A little after four o'clock McLaughlin ran forward and lobbed gas grenades into the lodge. One or two of the deputies fired guns as well, until Clegg told them to stop. As the first curls of gas rose inside the house, a woman's voice yelled out from inside: "We'll come out if you'll stop firing."

"Come out and bring everyone with you, with your hands up," Purvis shouted. A moment later the gang's women—Jean Delaney, Helen Gillis, and Mickey Conforti, hugging her bulldog pup—appeared on the porch. Agents rushed into the lodge but found no one inside. On the beach behind the building they discovered footprints leading into the woods. For the first time the enormity of the debacle hit Purvis. As the women were led off he stood and stared, dumbfounded, running the events of the night through his mind, as he would again and again for the rest of his life. Two men were dead, and Dillinger was gone.

---

* Born and raised in New Hampshire, John T. McLaughlin served in the FBI from 1926 to 1941. He was a prominent Reno, Nevada, attorney until his death in 1975.

  Born in 1903 in Alabama and raised in Mississippi, Robert G. Gillespie served less than a year in the FBI. Afterward he practiced law in Jackson, Mississippi, and served as Chief Justice of the Mississippi Supreme Court from 1954 to 1977.

13

"AND IT'S DEATH FOR BONNIE AND CLYDE"

April 23 to May 23, 1934

Monday, April 23

It was beginning to snow as the agents trickled into Birchwood Lodge for breakfast that morning. Purvis couldn't bring himself to eat. In his darkest dreams he'd never conceived of a moment as nightmarish as this: Dillinger was gone, one of his men was dead, and they had killed a civilian. Purvis felt personally responsible.

On the drive to the airport Purvis thought of tendering his resignation. Out on the runway, waiting for the plane back to Chicago, he overheard a group of men cursing him by name for bungling what the press was already calling "The Battle of Little Bohemia." It got worse when Purvis returned to the Bankers Building that afternoon. A petition had begun circulating in Wisconsin calling for his resignation. URGE PURVIS OUSTER, blared the *Chicago American*'s evening headline. DEMAND PURVIS QUIT IN DILLINGER FIASCO.

By noon Little Bohemia was a national scandal. In Washington, Hoover stepped before a crowd of reporters and tried to explain what had happened; for the moment, he wasn't so sure himself. Testifying before a House committee that afternoon, Homer Cummings pleaded for armored cars and airplanes. "If we had had an armored car up there in Wisconsin," he said, "our men could have driven up to the house where Dillinger was. The terrible tragedy then would not have happened."

Cummings's pleas were drowned out in the din of scathing commentary, much of it fueled by the Bureau's go-it-alone policies. Wisconsin politicians, echoing complaints from the Chicago police and Matt Leach's Indiana State Police, criticized the Bureau for failing to work with local authorities. "There has been a pathetic lack of cooperation between federal, state, and local authorities," snapped Senator Royal Copeland, chairman of the Senate Racket Investigating Committee. The special prosecutor, Joe Keenan, shot back: "I don't know where or when we will get [Dillinger], but we will get him. And you can say for me that I hope we get him under such circumstances that the government won't have to stand the expense of a trial."

For the first time, the Bureau found itself the target of withering press attacks. In fact, it was the first many Americans had ever heard of the Bureau of Investigation or J. Edgar Hoover or Melvin Purvis; several newspapers ran articles explaining who they were. More than one suggested Hoover would be forced to resign. COMIC OPERA COPS, the *Milwaukee Sentinal* called them. "The government authorities . . . have made [the Dillinger manhunt] a farce-comedy—except that it has turned to tragedy in killing innocent bystanders rather than the hunted desperado," the *Chicago Times* editorialized. In his syndicated column, Will Rogers joined the jeering section. "Well, they had Dillinger surrounded," Rogers quipped, "and were all ready to shoot him when he came out. But another bunch of folks came out ahead; so they shot them instead. Dillinger is going to get in accidentally with some innocent bystanders some time, then he will got shot."[1]

Back on the nineteenth floor, Purvis tried to avoid the reporters, but it was impossible; they thronged the hallway beyond Doris Rogers's desk. Simply walking to the elevator meant running a gauntlet. When they managed to corner him Monday night, Purvis tried to put a positive spin on things. "We've got more evidence to work on than we ever had before in hunting Dillinger," he said. "We'll have him before long. His trail is getting broader every minute."

Doris Rogers was struck by how beaten the agents appeared as they returned to their desks that day. They seemed shell-shocked, but it was more than that; it was the first time, Rogers realized, that many of the younger men understood they could actually get killed. Their thrilling postgraduate job was no longer a game. For the moment, none of the men could bring themselves to talk about what had happened. No one wanted to talk about Jay Newman, who lay in a Wisconsin hospital bed, nor about Carter Baum, an office favorite. Baum's body was returned to Washington, where it was buried in Rock Creek Cemetery.

"I am in a rather depressed mood," Cummings told reporters after the private service. "In any event, this will serve to accentuate the seriousness of the problem which confronts the people of this nation. As I have said before, those who had expected that the campaign against organized crime would be easily won were those who did not realize the situation. As things move along, there inevitably will be disappointments, setbacks, and sorrows. We have had a setback. We have been touched by sorrow. That is the part which makes all of us the more determined to go on. We will go on. This campaign against predatory crime will be finished."[2]

Internally, Hoover's reaction to Little Bohemia was curiously muted. The man who fired off blistering memos to agents a minute late for work had almost no criticism for Clegg and Purvis. Too many senior men were involved—men Hoover had hired—to identify a scapegoat. Of all the internal reports generated in the following two weeks, the sole note of disfavor came in a memo Hoover wrote three nights after the raid, summarizing a talk with Purvis. In an out-of-character bit of understatement, Hoover wrote he told Purvis "that I wanted less raiding and more confidential informants."[3]

The more Hoover learned, the more ringing his defense of his men. In a memo to the attorney general, Hoover wrote, "I do not believe . . . the facts which have been presented me to date [justify] any criticism leveled at the Agents for the action which they took in this matter. They were approaching a known gangsters' hide-out, and they saw three men leaving this hide-out. These three were called upon to halt, but instead of doing so, they entered an automobile and proceeded to drive away, and consequently, the Agents fired." In the same memo, Hoover went out of his way to defend Purvis, pointing out that Hugh Clegg, as Assistant Director, "was in charge of the detail at all times."[4]

He would not be so sanguine for long.

As Hoover spent that Monday trying to fathom what had gone wrong, the five men of the Dillinger Gang struggled to reach safe havens. None had an easy time of it. By daylight police had thrown up roadblocks all across Wisconsin and Minnesota. Hundreds of flannel-clad lumberjacks and vigilantes poured from their homes, grabbed up shotguns, and piled into cars, scouring the back roads in search of the gang. First to reach safety was Tommy Carroll. His car bogged down on a muddy logging road; striking out on foot, he managed to hitchhike back to St. Paul.

Dillinger, meanwhile, accompanied by Van Meter and Hamilton, drove their stolen Ford coupe south, dropping the car's owner outside the village of Park Falls, Wisconsin, around nine A.M. Then they, too, headed for St. Paul. Sticking to country roads, they dodged the posses and crossed into Minnesota without incident. Figuring the city's northern approaches would be guarded, Dillinger circled south.

There, at 10:30, the trio approached the bridge over the Mississippi River at Hastings, twenty miles below St. Paul. A policeman named Fred McArdle, accompanied by three deputy sheriffs, was parked at the bridge's southern end, checking license numbers against an FBI bulletin in his lap. As Dillinger approached the bridge, McArdle was startled to recognize the plate. He pulled out to give chase, but just as he did, a cattle truck edged in front of him. By the time McArdle's car reached the far side, Dillinger was gone.

McArdle and the three deputies pressed northward, toward St. Paul, hoping to catch up; they had no radio, and thus no way to alert anyone that Dillinger was heading into the city. Ten miles north of the bridge, McArdle spotted the Ford, which was driving at barely forty miles an hour in an effort to avoid attention. One of the deputies fired at its rear tires, missing. The Ford surged forward. Dillinger bashed out the rear window and opened fire.

For several minutes a wild running gunfight ensued at more than eighty miles per hour. As the two cars hurtled toward South St. Paul, a bullet struck John Hamilton in the lower back, and he slumped down in the front seat, badly wounded. Rounding a sharp curve, Van Meter spun to the right, veering onto a dirt path called Cemetery Road. Momentarily losing sight of the car, Officer McArdle drove past. By the time he noticed the Ford was no longer in front of him, it was gone.

Van Meter found a secluded spot and pulled over. Hamilton was bleeding heavily and needed a doctor. First, Dillinger realized, they needed a new car. They cruised the dirt roads south of the city for an hour without spotting one. Finally, around noon, Van Meter parked on the side of a gravel road three miles south of South St. Paul. At 12:45 a Ford approached. It was driven by Roy Francis, a district manager for the Northern States Power Company. Francis was on his lunch hour, taking his wife and their infant son for a drive to help the baby sleep. Ahead, Francis saw a man standing in the road.

It was Van Meter. He was holding a pistol. "I'm sorry to trouble you," he said as Francis stopped his car, "but I've got to have your machine." Francis stepped out and began to raise his hands. "Keep your hands down," Van Meter said, "we won't shoot you."

Mrs. Francis, carrying her baby, got out of the car as Dillinger helped Hamilton into the backseat. As he did, Van Meter was apparently struck by a pang of envy. "What do you do?" he asked Francis.

"I work at the power company," Francis said.

"You're lucky to have a nice job and family," Van Meter said.

Before leaving, Dillinger patted the baby on the head. "Don't worry," he said, "we like kids." After a few minutes, Van Meter and Dillinger drove both cars away. The Francis family walked two miles to a service station and called for help.

Hamilton was in excruciating pain as they hid the stolen coupe on a side road and transferred the guns to the Francis car. The shooting meant St. Paul would soon be crawling with FBI agents. Dillinger decided to head to Chicago, with a dying man in the backseat.

Lac Du Flambeau Indian Reservation, Wisconsin
2:00 P.M.

Outside a tarpaper shack deep in the north woods, a fifteen-year-old girl named Dorothy Schroeder was pinning up clothes to dry when she saw the man tromping through the brush toward her. His green fedora, tie, brown suede jacket, and gray slacks marked him as a stranger.

"Where is Woodruff from here?" the man called out as he approached. The man was clearly lost. Dorothy went and got her mother. The man was standing in the yard when Mrs. Schroeder walked out.

"Can I buy a cup of coffee?" Baby Face Nelson asked.

The FBI car Nelson had stolen had thrown a rod that morning, barely an hour's drive west of Little Bohemia. Rather than raise suspicion by hailing a ride, Nelson had struck off across country. He'd walked twenty miles into the woods before he stumbled onto the shack.

In the kitchen Mrs. Schroeder handed him a cup of coffee and a slice of buttered bread; he thrust three dollar bills at her over her objections. Nelson was sipping the coffee a few minutes later when Mrs. Schroeder's aunt and uncle, Ole "Ollie" Catfish and his wife, Maggie, walked up. Catfish, a weathered sixty-seven-year-old Chippewa who spoke broken English, used the shack to tap maple trees. He and his wife had walked the seven miles from their home outside the town of Lac Du Flambeau. Nelson explained that he was a game warden and would need to stay with them two or three days. Catfish didn't object. That night Nelson slept in the Catfishes' bedroom, on a bed beside the elderly couple. Chicago was a long way off. He had no idea how he would get there.

While the nation remained transfixed by the unfolding story of the FBI's pursuit of Dillinger, the Barker-Karpis Gang's days of relative anonymity were drawing to a close. While most of its members hid in Toledo, Dock Barker had remained behind in Chicago with his old Tulsa pal, Volney Davis. Both men chafed at the gang's inability to launder the Bremer ransom; fences in Reno and St. Paul had declined to take it, saying it was simply too hot.

In early April, running low on money, Dock drove to Toledo to sit down with Karpis and his brother Fred. He had been talking with Dr. Moran, the drunken abortionist who performed their cosmetic surgeries. Moran insisted he could launder the Bremer ransom, and Dock wanted to try it. Against their better judgment, Karpis and Fred agreed.

Dr. Moran was almost giddy when Dock Barker came to his office in the Irving Park Hotel on April 15 and handed him $10,000 wrapped in a newspaper; the gang agreed to pay 6.25 percent for every dollar he exchanged at local banks. Moran gathered a motley assortment of his underworld clients, including one of Dock's Oklahoma pals, a gonorrhea case named Russell Gibson, also known as Slim Gray; a neuralgia case, an old prison pal of Moran's named Izzy Berg; and a diabetes case, an aging former state legislator named "Boss" John McLaughlin. McLaughlin brought in more men, including his chauffeur, his seventeen-year-old son Jack, and a thirty-four-year-old bookie runner named William Vidler.

While his assistant Jimmy Wilson tended their patients, Moran closeted himself in Room 210 above his office in the hotel. He spread the money on the bed. At one point, Wilson, unaware of the scheme, knocked on the door. Moran, who was drunk, opened it, a bottle of beer in his hand. Wilson peered inside. He saw Boss McLaughlin, Izzy Berg, and Russell Gibson standing over the bed, counting the largest stack of money he had ever seen. He watched as McLaughlin put a brick of bills into a briefcase. "How much more do you want?" Wilson heard Berg ask.

"What's going on?" Wilson asked.

"Don't get nose trouble," Moran slurred.

"Close that door," McLaughlin snapped.[5]

They moved the first $10,000 quickly, and when they were finished Dock Barker came by and picked up the laundered cash.

"Any problems?" Dock asked.

"Nope," Gibson replied.

"Good," Dock said. "We have a lot more."

It took a few days to move the next $20,000. Boss McLaughlin and his friends did the leg work, while Moran drank himself into a stupor. Everything went swimmingly until Monday, April 23, the day after Little Bohemia. That morning, as FBI agents waved the last wisps of tear gas from Emil Wanatka's barroom, a Chicago bank teller discovered he had been passed a bill whose serial number was listed on the FBI's Bremer-ransom circular. A supervisor called the FBI. The very next day, as Purvis's men scrambled to trace the bill, Dock Barker got the call that Dillinger wanted to meet.

That Tuesday morning, as police and vigilantes combed Minnesota and Wisconsin in search of him, Dillinger limped back into the Chicago suburbs. It was as desperate a moment as he had faced since escaping from Crown Point. In the backseat John Hamilton lay dying; his blood was all over the inside of the car. They had bought bandages and medicine in Dubuque, Iowa, but if Hamilton was to have any chance to live, they needed a doctor. They had stolen a set of license plates, but Dillinger knew he couldn't drive the streets of Chicago long with a bleeding man in the backseat before someone noticed.

The doctor Dillinger attempted to find that day was none other than Joseph Moran, who at that moment was closeted in his hotel room laundering the Bremer ransom.* Failing to find him, Dillinger drove to the Hi-

---

* How Dillinger knew of Moran has never been explained; it's possible he heard Moran's name from Baby Face Nelson, who had debriefed Alvin Karpis about his surgery. Several accounts claim Dillinger visited Moran that Tuesday, and that Moran turned him away. This is unlikely; none of Dr. Moran's laundering

Ho Inn, a Cicero nightclub operated by a pair of syndicate men, brothers named Bobby and Joie O'Brien. The O'Briens apparently wanted nothing to do with him. They sent Dillinger away, promising to find Dr. Moran and bring him to a rendezvous that night.

Dillinger's visit set off a flurry of phone calls. The O'Brien brothers telephoned Elmer Farmer, the man who owned the Bremer safe house, who they believed could find Moran. In turn, Farmer called Dock Barker, who tried to reach Moran but couldn't. Meanwhile Joie O'Brien drove to suburban Aurora, thirty miles west of downtown Chicago, and retrieved Volney Davis, who had been living in an Aurora apartment for several weeks. Everyone gathered that night in a parking lot behind the Seafood Inn, a restaurant in suburban Elmhurst.[6]

It was the first time Dillinger met members of the Barker Gang, but there was little time for pleasantries. They lifted Hamilton out of the car and put him in the back of Volney Davis's Buick. Dillinger and Van Meter then followed Davis back to his apartment in Aurora. Davis sent his girlfriend, Edna Murray, to stay with friends, and Hamilton was carried in and placed on a bed. He didn't have long, they could see. Gangrene had set in. Not even a doctor could help Hamilton now.

Members of the two gangs tended to the dying man all that night and the next day, doing their best to ease his pain. Hamilton lasted two more days, finally dying around three on Thursday afternoon, April 26. At dusk, Dock Barker and Volney Davis drove to a quarry six miles south of Aurora and dug a grave. After dark they loaded Hamilton's body into a car, drove him to the quarry, and laid him in the ground. Davis had purchased several cans of lye to destroy his features. Dillinger bent over the dead man and in a low voice said, "Red, old pal, I hate to do this, but I know you'd do the same for me."[7] And then he poured the lye over Hamilton's head. Barker and Van Meter filled in the grave, and Davis found a roll of barbed wire to place over it as a marker.*

When they returned, Davis's apartment was a mess, so Davis called

---

confederates, several of whom would later be grilled by the FBI, mentioned such an episode. In fact, later statements from members of the Barker Gang suggest Dillinger tried to find Dr. Moran but couldn't.

* Curiously, there is no suggestion that Dillinger attempted to contact Louis Piquett or Art O'Leary upon returning to Chicago. In later conversations with the two men, in fact, Dillinger repeatedly lied about this period. He said he and Van Meter had hidden for a time in an abandoned mine in Wisconsin and later buried Hamilton in dunes near Lake Michigan. He never mentioned the Barkers, just as he never mentioned others who would give him aid in the coming weeks.

Edna Murray to come clean it. Murray nearly fainted when she arrived. White disinfectant powder covered the bedroom floor. Bloody sheets sat in a heap, waiting to be burned. The sink was piled high with dishes, medicines, and reddened bandages. Murray opened a closet door and yelped when the grave-digging shovel fell out. Over everything there hung the stench of gangrene and death.[8]

The last thing on Purvis's mind that week was the Bremer case, even though a dozen agents were still working it full time. On Hoover's orders, the exasperating search for the house where Bremer had been held was continuing, taking up hundreds of man-hours. Even as half the Chicago office hunted Dillinger, the other half stayed on the road, revisiting every town between Joliet and central Wisconsin in search of the right combination of trains, church bells, and factory whistles Bremer had heard while in custody. The agents churned out hundreds of reports but had found nothing. Some griped that it was a useless exercise. In St. Paul, Hugh Clegg had actually floated the idea of hiring Boy Scouts to canvas their hometowns.

Circulars listing the serial numbers of every bill in the Bremer ransom had been mailed to banks across the country. That Monday morning, as Purvis and his men trudged back to their desks from Little Bohemia, an officer at the Uptown State Bank on Wilson Avenue discovered that a customer had passed one of his tellers $900 of the Bremer ransom. The customer had disappeared, but that afternoon agents descended on every bank in the area, checking for signs of other bills. By nightfall they managed to find Bremer money at the Main State Bank on Milwaukee Avenue and several other institutions.

For two days agents continued canvassing North Side banks. Then, that Thursday morning, April 26, the day John Hamilton died, a call came in from the City National Bank and Trust Company on LaSalle Street, a few blocks from the Bankers Building. More Bremer money had been passed, and when agents interviewed the teller who had taken the bills, he said his customer had mentioned that he worked at a bookie joint in the neighborhood. Two agents walked the teller to the bookmaking establishment, on the second floor of an office building at 226 South Welles Street. The teller pointed out his customer. It was William Vidler, Boss McLaughlin's friend. Agents handcuffed Vidler and took him to the Bankers Building, where he was searched. In his pocket they found $2,200 of the Bremer ransom.

Vidler talked. Friday morning at 10:30, Pop Nathan led a squad of agents to Boss McLaughlin's apartment building on West Jackson Boulevard, leading the old pol and his son away in handcuffs.* That night, as headlines in the evening papers carried news of the arrests, agents began interrogating the McLaughlins at the Cook County Jail, hoping they would lead them to the Barker Gang. No one had any inkling that the same trail could lead them to Dillinger.

Lac Du Flambeau Indian Reservation, Wisconsin
Friday, April 27

That same morning, as Pop Nathan took Boss McLaughlin into custody in Chicago, Ole Catfish rose from his bed, leaving Baby Face Nelson asleep. For three days everything had gone smoothly at the little shack. The women cooked Nelson meals, and he passed the days mostly in silence, watching the woods. Around noon that Friday a trapper tromped up and talked with Catfish; Nelson hid in the kitchen, watching. Afterward he demanded to know who the man was. All afternoon Nelson grew increasingly nervous. At 6:00 he told Catfish it was time to leave and demanded the old Indian lead him to the next town.

Catfish protested that he was sick. Nelson produced his gun and said, "Start walking." They headed down an old railroad bed, Ole's wife, Maggie, behind them, until Nelson waved her back. Into the woods they trekked, the gloom deepening around them. Catfish complained that his heart was weak, and they stopped several times to rest. Night fell. A full moon, as bright as a spotlight, rose over them.

Around nine, after walking six miles, they spotted a fire. Three fishermen Catfish knew were clustered around it. Nelson walked up to the fire and warmed his hands. A few minutes later a car parked about fifty yards away. "Come on, let's go over and see who those fellows are," Nelson told Catfish. Two Indians were standing beside a 1928 Chevrolet sedan. An-

---

* Agents questioned McLaughlin all that day at his apartment, but he would say nothing. While they talked, McLaughlin's wife sat in a front window, smoking. At one point, agents saw her throw something out the window. Mrs. McLaughlin insisted it was just a cigarette butt. But when agents went outside to retrieve the thrown item, they found the McLaughlin's son, Jimmy, standing on the sidewalk, reading a note his mother had tossed to him. It read in part: "Government men here since 10:00 A.M. . . . Don't come in. Beat it. You will be held prisoner." Taken into custody, the boy led agents to his locker at the Board of Trade, where they found a roll of Bremer money tucked into a hat.

other car, a Plymouth, drove up just as Nelson approached. Inside were two locals heading out for a night of fishing. As the men stood, swapping small talk, Nelson walked over to the Plymouth and studied it. "Is that yours?" Nelson asked its driver.

One of the men gave Nelson a dark look. He asked on what authority Nelson was fishing on the reservation. Nelson whipped out his gun. "This is my authority," he said. "You line up with those Indians over there." Nelson yanked the distributor cable out of the old Chevy, disabling it. He told Catfish to get in the Plymouth. Catfish doubled over, as if in great pain. "Me sick," he said.

Nelson poked the pistol in the old Chippewa's ribs and told him to get in the car. Nelson slid behind the wheel, then yanked a hatchet hanging by a cord from Catfish's neck. "Don't want you killin' me while I'm driving," Nelson said.

Catfish guided Nelson to an intersection with State Highway 70, at which point Nelson let him out of the car and drove off, heading south. Driving the length of Wisconsin, he pulled up the next morning at Louis Cernocky's tavern at Fox River Grove. Cernocky welcomed him inside and fixed him something to eat. Nelson's luck held. Despite the tips from Beth Green, despite the fact that Emil Wanatka had told the FBI it was Cernocky who sent the Dillinger gang to Little Bohemia, despite wiretaps and numerous interviews with Cernocky's neighbors, Purvis had failed to put the tavern under surveillance.

While Nelson made his way toward Chicago that Friday, Dillinger sat hunched over the radio in Volney Davis's apartment in Aurora, shuttling between the radio and police bands. Edna Murray watched him carefully. Dillinger's charm was lost on her. She thought he had a killer's eyes, and his lopsided grin struck her as a smirk. He ignored her and spoke rarely, usually to curse.[9] Much of his anger was directed at Louis Cernocky, who Dillinger believed had led the FBI to Little Bohemia; he and Dock Barker agreed it must have been Cernocky who had betrayed Frank Nash, triggering the Kansas City Massacre. Dillinger and Van Meter kept their steel vests on, submachine guns across their laps. They were tired and tense and dirty. Hamilton's death had hit both men hard, especially Dillinger. No one wanted to die like that.

There was a rare moment of humor when they heard a news flash about

Nelson's stay with Ole Catfish. "Well, Baby Face isn't hungry," Van Meter said. "He has plenty of catfish with him."

But the real jolt came with the Friday evening papers. Boss McLaughlin's arrest was front-page news. This was bad. McLaughlin knew Davis lived in Aurora. Dock Barker explained the situation to Dillinger. If McLaughlin talked, the FBI could be on their doorstep within hours. Dillinger caucused with Van Meter. They couldn't leave without a new car. For the moment, they decided to stay. If the FBI came, Dillinger said, they would be ready.

As night fell, everyone took positions in the living room. It was a first-floor apartment; they could step through each of the three large windows onto the sidewalk. Dock Barker took a Thompson gun and stationed himself by one window, Van Meter a second, Dillinger the third. Volney Davis lingered outside in the streets, watching.

An hour went by, then two. Edna Murray was sitting in the bedroom worrying when suddenly Davis burst through the front door. "Dock, I think we got it!" he hissed at Barker. "They're here! A car pulled up on Fourth Street and parked and two men got out and walked up the street. There's another car on Fox Street. Three men got out of that!"

Davis ran to a closet, yanked out a suitcase, and threw it in the middle of the living-room floor. "Rabbit, you get out of here—get in my car," Davis told Murray. "Let's all get ready!"

Dock Barker's voice was even. "Rabbit, you stay right where you are," he said. "You don't leave this apartment. If fireworks start, you get behind me and this tommy and I'll take you out of here."

Suddenly Barker uttered an oath and swung his submachine gun toward a pair of men who had appeared across the street. One lit a cigarette. Barker thought it was a signal for FBI men to attack. He raised the gun to fire.

Dillinger's voice was a harsh whisper. "Don't do that, Dock!" he snapped. "Wait till we're sure we're right. Then we'll give it to 'em!" The room went quiet. Murray could hear herself breathe. The two men in Barker's gun sights walked on, disappearing around a corner. Barker lowered his gun. The moment passed. It wasn't the FBI.

They remained like that, poised with guns at the windows, until later that night, when Dock's pal Russell Gibson pulled up in front. He came to the door and was surprised to find himself staring into the barrel of Dillinger's Thompson gun. Inside, Gibson told them everything was okay:

McLaughlin wasn't talking. How long that would last he didn't know. He urged everyone to leave as soon as possible.[10]

Dillinger talked it over with Van Meter. They decided to stay another night.

At the Cook County Jail, Purvis's men questioned Boss McLaughlin until dawn. Only after they threatened to bring charges against his son did the wily old pol decide to talk. He said he had been approached three weeks earlier by a con man he knew who had introduced him to two men named "Smith" and "Jones." McLaughlin insisted he never found out more about the pair, nor met any members of the Barker Gang. But he did say Smith and Jones were working out of the Irving Park Hotel and seemed to be from Toledo. It was the first hint the FBI fielded that the Barkers were in Toledo, but in the uproar over Dillinger, Purvis never found time to pursue it. In a subsequent search of Dr. Moran's phone records, there were several calls to Toledo, but Purvis's men wouldn't get around to checking them for months.

They were swamped. Purvis was grappling with a deluge of new information that flowed to the FBI in the wake of Little Bohemia. New leads, most of them worthless, poured into the office. Dillinger was dead, Dillinger was in California, Dillinger was in Canada. By now reporters had created a permanent encampment in the hallway in front of Doris Rogers's desk; Purvis couldn't go to the bathroom without one of them shouting questions. Worse, every sheriff in Indiana was certain Dillinger was hiding in his jurisdiction, and each one cried out to be debriefed. Every day that week, while Dillinger sat watching John Hamilton die in Aurora, Purvis dispatched agents to a new town to check out a new tip: On Wednesday it was East Chicago, Thursday Muncie, Friday Fort Wayne, Saturday South Bend. None of it led anywhere.

The three Dillinger women captured at Little Bohemia, ferried to a jail in Madison, Wisconsin, were all but useless. Facing charges of conspiracy and harboring a fugitive, they gave fake names and fake stories and initially resisted all efforts to question them. After a few days Jean Delaney and Mickey Conforti finally talked, but they said little the agents could use. Conforti gave her correct name but said she had no idea her boyfriend "Wayne Huttner" was really Homer Van Meter. Agents found Conforti's invalid mother in a Chicago-area sanatorium and fired questions at her as she drooled. Just the fact the women were in FBI custody was a cause for mockery. Coming on the heels of Billie Frechette's capture, wiseacres cracked that the Bureau may not always get its man, but it always got his women.

What Purvis had was cars. They found the ones Nelson and Tommy Carroll used to escape, both abandoned on dirt roads deep in the north woods. They found the car Nelson had wrecked on the way to Little Bohemia. They ran checks on the two cars Dillinger had left in Little Bohemia's garage. None of it led anywhere.

Purvis had high hopes they would find something useful in the sixteen pieces of luggage the gang abandoned. But other than an enormous collection of guns and license plates, the bags proved only that the gang members were pedestrian dressers. There were black suits and green ties and blue silk bathrobes, scraps of Mickey Conforti's poetry, an overdue novel from the St. Paul library. The best lead was a business card found in Nelson's bag for a priest named Philip Coughlin, an old family friend whom agents tracked down in the Chicago suburb of Wilmette. Coughlin cooperated, filling the Bureau's growing file on Nelson.* Purvis put Nelson's mother and sister under surveillance.

That Saturday night, as Boss McLaughlin's questioning continued, Volney Davis drove into Chicago and stole a car for Dillinger. The next day Dillinger and Van Meter thanked Dock Barker for his help and, after leaving their bloodied car on the North Side, drove to East Chicago, where after two days they managed to reunite with Tommy Carroll.

The next evening, Wednesday, May 2, the three men pulled up behind a frame house in Fort Wayne. The house was owned by Audrey G. Russ, a construction worker who knew the Van Meter family. Startled by the appearance of the country's most-wanted man on his doorstep, Russ agreed to let them stay the night. His wife and eleven-year-old daughter looked on, amazed, as Dillinger lugged in four submachine guns, several bulletproof vests, and a bundle of two dozen license plates.

---

* The Bureau had begun investigating Nelson in the wake of the Mason City, Iowa, robbery in March, when a bank employee had identified his photograph. Purvis had no idea at the time that Dillinger had been present at Mason City as well, and it wasn't until Little Bohemia that the Bureau belatedly realized the two were working together.

According to an FBI report, Dillinger was in a voluble mood as he sat in the Russ's kitchen, regaling the frightened family with details of his escapes from Crown Point and Little Bohemia. "Dillinger stated that they'd never take him alive and that before he went he would take several with him; the inference being that he would manage to kill a few officers before he could be taken," the report says. "Dillinger also stated that he was sore about the fact that the newspapers thought that he had bought his way out of the Crown Point jail, stating that the credit for the best trick he had ever pulled was taken away from him. He also stated that he had rounded up ten trustees and seven deputy sheriffs before he managed to get his hands on a real gun."

Dillinger laughed at the police who were hunting him, calling them "a lot of clucks." It was the "Feds" he said he feared; they could go anywhere, he said, spend anything, even rent airplanes. As he talked he rubbed his leg, the one wounded in St. Paul. He'd aggravated it in a fender bender a couple of days before, he said, when Tommy Carroll lost control of their car and smashed into a tree.[11]

The next morning Dillinger and Van Meter asked for steaks for breakfast. They were hungry; they had a big day ahead. For the first time in two months, they had a bank to rob.

By that Monday, April 30, though he had missed his chance to capture Dillinger in Aurora, Purvis felt he was making progress. After the debriefing of Boss McLaughlin, agents dispatched to the Irving Park Hotel identified the mysterious "Smith and Jones" as Russell Gibson and Izzy Berg; a doorman said the two had been working on something with Dr. Moran the last few weeks. Unfortunately, Moran and his pals had disappeared the previous Friday, the day the papers carried news of McLaughlin's arrest. Agents fanned out across Chicago, interviewing anyone who knew Moran in hopes of finding his wastrel bunch.*

---

* As they did, Purvis managed to locate the first of the Little Bohemia refugees. It was Pat Cherrington. After fleeing Little Bohemia, Cherrington and Harry Sawyer's bartender, Pat Reilly, had returned to St. Paul, where after a week in hiding Cherrington boarded a train to Chicago, sending a telegram to her sister-in-law to meet her at the station. The FBI, who had the sister-in-law under surveillance, intercepted the telegram that Monday; agents boarded Cherrington's train at a stop in Janesville, Wisconsin, and followed her to Chicago and then to Detroit. After a monthlong stakeout that produced no leads on Dillinger or anyone else, Cherrington would finally be arrested in late May. She drew a one-year sentence in a federal women's prison.

In Indiana, meanwhile, Earl Connelley increased pressure on Dillinger's family. His men had been questioning Hubert Dillinger and other relatives for weeks. The outlaw's nephew Norman Hancock proved the most pliable. That day Connelley persuaded Hancock to drive to help John Dillinger, Sr., build a fence. If Dillinger was hiding at his father's farmhouse, Connelley told Hancock to take out his handkerchief and wipe his face. Two dozen Indianapolis cops stood by to move if the signal was given. Connelley and a half-dozen agents were stationed in haystacks and outbuildings when Hancock drove up and disappeared inside the house. At 2:10 he and the elder Dillinger appeared on the porch. Hancock took out his handkerchief and twice wiped his face.

As Hancock and Mr. Dillinger trudged down the road to build the fence, a squadron of FBI cars screeched to a halt beside them. Agents leaped out and surrounded the two men, taking them aside for questioning. Hancock appeared dazed. Once they were out of earshot, he told Connelley it was a mistake. Dillinger wasn't at the house. That morning Mr. Dillinger had received an anonymous letter from someone in Minnesota, saying Dillinger was safe there. He had given the signal, Hancock insisted, only to tell the FBI about the letter.[12]

Connelley fumed. The agents climbed back in their cars; the Indianapolis police retreated. By the following day Matt Leach was complaining to reporters that Connelley's ham-handed raid had ruined any chances of capturing Dillinger in the state of Indiana. Ill will between the FBI and the state police was growing by the hour.

Two days later, on Wednesday, May 2, the car Dillinger had stolen outside St. Paul was found on a North Side street. From the dried blood on the backseat, Purvis could see one of the gang members had been wounded. The evening headlines screamed the news that Dillinger was back in the city, probably recovering from gunshot wounds. Purvis wasn't so sure. He thought the car might be a plant to dupe agents into concentrating their search in Chicago. For once Purvis was right.

Fostoria, Ohio
Thursday, May 3

Sipping coffee from a pair of Thermos jugs, Dillinger, Van Meter, and Tommy Carroll drove east to Toledo, where they stole another car. They were almost out of money. Van Meter said he knew a bank.

People in Fostoria, a rail hub forty miles south of Toledo, considered the town's banks robbery-proof; so many slow-moving trains crisscrossed the area that police believed they would dissuade any robbers from putting together a getaway map. But Van Meter knew the town from boyhood vacations. He and Dillinger didn't spend much time canvassing the First National Bank or drawing gits. They just needed money.

At 2:50, as the bank was preparing for its 3:00 close, two men walked in with submachine guns hidden beneath overcoats over their arms. The lobby, though almost empty of customers, presented an immediate challenge; there was a mezzanine above, and two side entrances, one opening directly into the O. C. Harding Jewelry Store, the other leading into a drugstore. While Tommy Carroll waited outside with the car, Van Meter laid his overcoat across a railing and pointed his Thompson at the teller cages. "Stick 'em up!" he shouted.

There was no joy to Dillinger that day, no smiles or courtesies anyone would remember; his days of leaping over teller cages were a vague memory now. His movements were grim and mechanical. As the employees raised their arms, Dillinger stepped through a swinging door and began clearing piles of cash off the counters into sacks. Van Meter gathered the tellers and a few other employees together in a group. Two women began to cry. "Don't kill me," one begged Van Meter.

"You be quiet," Van Meter said, "and I won't."[13]

Neither Dillinger nor Van Meter noticed a teller named Frances Hillyard slip out a door. Hillyard ran to find the police chief, a man named Frank Culp. As Culp ran toward the bank, he got an idea: if he could just get up to the mezzanine, he could take the high ground and drive the robbers away. Bursting into the lobby, he found the mezzanine elevator was on the second floor. Van Meter fired his submachine gun; a single bullet ripped into Culp's chest and burst a lung. Culp staggered backward into the jewelry store and hollered for more men.[14]

When Tommy Carroll heard gunfire, he stepped out of the getaway car and began firing wildly. His bullets shattered windows up and down the street, sending citizens ducking for cover. The slow and the unlucky got hit, one man in the leg, another in the foot. Inside the bank, Dillinger hustled to clear the remaining cash off the counters; the bank's president later estimated he made off with more than $17,000. "It's too hot out there," a customer overheard Van Meter say. "Let's go through the drugstore."

They grabbed two employees, a man and a woman, shoving them through the drugstore. Outside, the two were loaded onto the running boards; as the car roared off down Tifflin Street, Van Meter kept a tight grip on the woman's hand. They sped west out of town, tossing roofing nails in their wake. Outside town they let the hostages go.*

Back in Fort Wayne, meanwhile, Van Meter's old friend Audrey Russ was paralyzed with fear that Dillinger would return to his home. He approached his boss at the Western Gas Construction Company, told him everything and asked what to do. His boss had once met the FBI's resident agent at South Bend, W. J. Devereaux. That Thursday, as Dillinger was busy in Fostoria, he telephoned Devereaux and, withholding his name, described in general terms what had happened. Devereaux thought he recognized the man's voice. Afterward he phoned Chicago, briefed Purvis, and asked if he should follow up. For the moment Purvis told him to do nothing.

It was an order he would soon come to regret.

Inside the FBI, it took two weeks for the simmering frustrations born at Little Bohemia to come to a boil. While recriminations might be expected in other agencies, the Bureau had no history of internal dissension; throughout the high-pressure manhunts of 1934, the squabbling that ensued in the wake of Little Bohemia was unique.

The unlikely squeaky wheel turned out to be the St. Paul SAC, the mild-tempered Werner Hanni. Hanni had clearly not enjoyed having his office commandeered by Inspector Rorer and Hugh Clegg, and his annoyance turned to outrage in the days after the raid. The final straw had been his encounter on a darkened country road with the fleeing Baby Face Nelson, which had left him deeply shaken. Hanni's anger came to light when Clegg, sorting through papers on a desk, found a memo from Hanni he had never seen. It was a lightning bolt, addressed but apparently never sent to Hoover. It read in part:

[There] does not appear to exist any good reason whatsoever for Dillinger and his accomplices making a getaway. It was quite evident

* Despite eyewitnesses who positively identified Van Meter, historians have traditionally dismissed Fostoria as just another of the many unconfirmed robberies credited to Dillinger. Town residents long insisted it was Dillinger that day, though as the local historian Paul Krupp wrote in 1981, "[T]here is no sound evidence that Dillinger himself came to town." In fact, FBI files confirm it was Dillinger: the license plates of the Fostoria getaway car matched those of a car he would use in his next robbery, in June.

that the raid was fully staged with a lack of organization, and lack of knowledge and judgment cannot be concealed. The writer himself and those accompanying him to Bohemia proved to be tripped into a regular death trap. No preparation appeared to have been made, in spite of the fact that a chart of the locality had been furnished prior to proceeding there. Had it not been for the fortunate good treatment accorded the motorist who flashed a spotlight right into the writer's face, four more agents would, undoubtedly, not be here today.

Hanni had a bad word for almost everyone. He criticized Inspector Rorer for failing to help lift Carter Baum's dead body; Rorer, he said, had complained of a "kink in his back." Nor did he limit his broadsides to the events at Little Bohemia. He criticized Hugh Clegg, though not by name, for hindering the earlier pursuit of Dillinger by pestering his men with questions about Eddie Green's death.

If, on the evening of April 3, when every man at the St. Paul office, including the writer, were working their heads off, those in charge of these investigations had undertaken leadership and steps with a view of pursuing an intelligent investigation on red hot leads, instead of questioning the agents, keeping them from working, to determine whether or not the shooting of Green was justified, information could have been obtained that would have made the capture of Dillinger possible.

Everyone involved wrote sharply worded memos disagreeing with Hanni. As Hoover studied these memos, he received a far more worrisome bit of news. The Justice Department prosecutor, Joe Keenan, told him he had heard a reliable story that the agents at Little Bohemia had mutinied against Purvis and Clegg, and actually locked them inside a shed while Dillinger got away. Hoover pressed Keenan for the source of the story, and Keenan named a former agent named Thomas Cullen. Agents interviewed Cullen and confirmed he was the source.

Hoover handed the whole mess to Pop Nathan, directing him to "make a very thorough and vigorous inquiry."[15] Perhaps unsurprisingly, Nathan's report, finished three weeks later, defended the Bureau's actions and excoriated poor Hanni. Hanni's allegations "would appear to indicate a disordered and possibly hysterical state of mind," Nathan wrote Hoover, terming them "manifestly absurd."[16] Hanni was quietly shoved out of St. Paul and relocated to Omaha.

It was the last time any agent would criticize the Bureau for a very long while.

Little Bohemia persuaded Dillinger that for the moment there was no place safe for him to hide. After he and Van Meter spent a few nights huddled in a leaky shack outside East Chicago, Baby Face Nelson came to their rescue.* On Monday, May 7, four days after the Fostoria robbery, Nelson arranged to purchase a red panel truck, a Ford Model A, the kind grocery stores used for deliveries, with an enclosed rear, windows in back, and a sliding door on the side. Dillinger intended to use the truck as a portable hideout and did; they threw a double mattress in back where they slept. The next few days he and Van Meter stayed on the move, driving the truck along the Indiana back roads as they planned their next step. More than anything, Dillinger wanted the cosmetic surgery he had been pestering Louis Piquett about for weeks.

Late on the night of Wednesday, May 9, running low on food, Dillinger and Van Meter pulled up behind Audrey Russ's house in Fort Wayne. Had Purvis pursued the tip Russ's boss gave him a week earlier, FBI agents might have been there to greet them. As it was, Russ climbed out of bed and let Dillinger inside while his wife prepared a meal. Both Dillinger and Van Meter appeared exhausted. They wore denim overalls, work shirts and battered caps. Mrs. Russ noticed Dillinger's leg was still bothering him; he staggered when ascending the stairs, clutching the leg. Neither man said much, and after eating they left.

The next morning Audrey Russ went to his boss again. Together they

---

* Though he avoided lingering in the city itself—he still feared Frank Nitti's wrath—Nelson had a network of Chicago contacts Dillinger didn't. He needed them. After stumbling into Louis Cernocky's bar after his flight from Little Bohemia, Nelson had reached out to one of them, a veteran fence named Jimmy Murray, who owned a South Chicago roadhouse called the Rain-Bo Inn. Murray was the man who had masterminded the Newton Brothers's famed train robbery at Roundout, Illinois, in 1924; after a stretch in the Atlanta federal prison, he had returned to Chicago and resumed business. The FBI would later establish that Murray had handled stolen bonds for both the Nelson and Dillinger gangs that autumn. After Little Bohemia, Murray allowed Nelson to stay in a cottage he owned in Wauconda, northwest of the city, where Nelson would spend most of the month of May. There he eventually reunited with Carroll and his California gofer, Johnny Chase.

telephoned the FBI, this time revealing their names, and told of Dillinger's second visit. It was the FBI's best lead since Little Bohemia. Though short of men, Purvis decided to station three agents at the Russ home. When Dillinger returned, they would be ready.*

Indianapolis, Indiana
Thursday, May 10

It was another lazy spring afternoon at the Dillinger filling station on LaSalle Street. Outside, a little boy on a bicycle traced circles in the dirt. Dillinger's cousin, Fred Hancock, was waiting on a customer at 3:45 when he noticed the stranger standing by a kerosene drum in one corner of the yard. Hancock didn't recognize the man, who was unshaven and wore overalls, a sleeveless jacket, and rimless eyeglasses. When the customer left, the stranger stepped over to the station window and rapped on the glass. Hancock looked the man in the eyes and was startled: it was Dillinger. In a parked car across the street, an FBI man named Whitson saw the stranger, too.

Dillinger handed the package to Hancock. In it were four smaller packages containing $1,200 in small bills: $300 for his father, $300 for Hancock's mother Audrey, and $100 each for Hancock and Hubert Dillinger. Tell my father, Dillinger told Hancock, that if anything happens to me, he should give some of the money to Billie. Then Dillinger left.

Agent Whitson watched as the stranger crossed LaSalle Street and walked toward Washington Street. Glimpsing a deep cleft in the man's chin, Whitson got out of his car and decided to follow him. The man walked quickly, reaching the corner of Washington Street about thirty yards in front of Whitson. Whitson trotted up to the intersection and turned the corner—nothing. The man was gone. Whitson walked up and down the street, peering into parked cars. Nothing. After a bit he walked back to his car, wrote up the incident in his notebook, and dismissed it from his mind. The man was probably a bum.†

---

* Purvis missed another opportunity by failing to broadcast an alert on the red panel truck Dillinger was driving. The Russes gave the Bureau a complete description of the vehicle, everything but the license number.

† FBI agents wouldn't learn the stranger's actual identity until several months later, when Hancock told a reporter of the incident.

. . .

Dillinger's legend was growing. By mid-May, though there had been no confirmed sighting of him since Little Bohemia three weeks before, most American newspapers were carrying daily stories of the manhunt, the Chicago papers three and four a day. Seemingly every Dillinger sighting, no matter how nonsensical, was grounds for a new article.

"Mr. Dillinger," a *Chicago Tribune* columnist noted at the height of the hysteria, "was seen yesterday looking over the new spring gloves in a State Street store in Chicago; negotiating for a twelve-cylinder car in Springfield, Illinois; buying a half-dozen sassy cravats in Omaha, Nebraska; bargaining for a suburban bungalow at his home town of Mooresville, Indiana, and shaking hands with old friends; drinking a glass of soda water in a drugstore in Charleston, South Carolina; and strolling down Broadway swinging a Malacca cane in New York. He also bought a fishing rod in a sporting-goods store in Montreal and gave a dinner at a hotel in Yucatán, Mexico. But, anyhow, Mr. Dillinger seems to have kept very carefully out of London, Berlin, Rome, Moscow, and Vienna. Or at least if he did go to those places yesterday he was traveling [incognito]."[17] *Time* magazine noted, "If John [Killer] Dillinger has really been at all the places he was reported to have been in the last month, he must leap along the central plains like a demented Indian's ghost."[18]

Much of the press treated the manhunt as a rollicking adventure story. In its May 7 issue, *Time* portrayed it as a board game set in a Midwestern "Dillinger Land"; GAME STARTS HERE, read the notation above Crown Point. The *Time* spread went out of its way to categorize Dillinger as an all-American anti-hero. "Great Desperadoes from little urchins grow," it read. "When John Dillinger was 10 he, like Tom Sawyer, was a poor country boy. Sometimes he may have dreamed of being another Abe Lincoln or Jesse James . . . [but not] that he would achieve a great unwritten odyssey: Through the Midwest with a Machine Gun."

The tone of this and other articles suggested that Dillinger was a harmless Roadrunner pursued by a hapless federal Wile E. Coyote. Not surprisingly, children ate it up. When a Boy Scout named Richard Neff visited the Indiana governor's office, a reporter asked what he thought of Dillinger. "Personally," the boy said, "I'm for him." When he glimpsed the governor's look of amazement, the boy stammered, "Err . . . I mean, I'm always for the underdog."[19]

That underdog quality, underscored by the widely published photos and interviews at Crown Point, struck a chord in a country in which many felt slighted by the government. In Chicago and New York moviegoers applauded when Dillinger's face appeared in newsreels. *Detective* magazine polled theater owners and found Dillinger was drawing more applause than Roosevelt or Charles Lindbergh. "In point of popularity," its editor wrote, "they ranked in that order, Dillinger first, President Roosevelt second, and Colonel Lindbergh third, thereby actually making this notorious thief, thug, and cold-blooded murderer the outstanding national hero of the hour!"

As his fame grew, Dillinger's name was inevitably drawn into political debate. He was already a favorite in the London tabloids, and in Germany a Nazi newspaper used him to argue in favor of sterilizing criminals everywhere. In Washington, Attorney General Homer Cummings employed Dillinger's name to urge passage of a half-dozen anticrime measures, including one that made it a federal crime to kill a federal agent, a law Hoover had been seeking for years. The measures passed the House of Representatives on May 5 even as several Republican senators continued criticizing the FBI. The pressure on the Roosevelt administration was growing. "Looks like if the Democrats don't get Dillinger [they] may lose this fall's election," Will Rogers wrote.

The President himself got involved. Without mentioning Dillinger by name, Roosevelt urged radio listeners to cooperate with the authorities to wipe out gangsterism. "Law enforcement and gangster extermination," he said, "cannot be made completely effective while a substantial part of the public looks with tolerance upon known criminals, or applauds efforts to romanticize crime."

Every day brought new Dillinger sightings, almost all of them spurious. On May 4, after Louis Piquett made a joshing comment to a reporter, there was a flurry of articles that Dillinger was heading for England; Canadian, British, and American authorities searched dozens of transatlantic ships in vain. Every morning Purvis's men shuttled out to a new town to check a new sighting; every night they returned to the nineteenth floor, exhausted and depressed. Two agents looked into the Fostoria robbery, but returned unpersuaded it was Dillinger's work; not for two more months would the FBI confirm it was. One of the stranger reports agents repeatedly checked was that Dillinger was receiving coded messages from a pirate radio station. Despite dozens of similar tips, the FBI was never able to find such a station.

Purvis's best hope remained the stakeout at the Audrey Russ home in Fort Wayne. For the agents who pulled rotating assignments there, it was a nightmare. The problem was Mrs. Russ, who possessed, as one agent put it, "a mean and avaricious disposition." In one memo, Agent John T. McLaughlin described her as "demented." At various times Mrs. Russ accused agents of spitting on her floors, scratching her grand piano, and shooting out a window. The agents paid her $2.50 a day rent until Mrs. Russ demanded and received three dollars. "[H]er whole desire seemed [to be] to secure as much money from the agents as possible, and furnish them the least amount of food," Agent McLaughlin complained. As the days wore on with no sign of Van Meter or Dillinger, the agents began to suspect Mrs. Russ had concocted the story of Dillinger's visits in order to lure wealthy government boarders.[20]

In Mooresville, Earl Connelley's men kept the Dillinger farmhouse under round-the-clock surveillance, but no one thought Dillinger would return there now. In desperation Purvis sent agents to interview anyone who had ever known Dillinger, including William Shaw, his teenage partner from the previous summer, and Mary Longnaker, the Dayton woman he romanced. Other agents began rounding up Baby Face Nelson's boyhood pals and some of Tommy Carroll's old girlfriends. None had anything useful to offer. For the moment Purvis had nothing. Nothing at all.

For two weeks Dillinger and Van Meter remained in their portable hideaway, the red truck. When they needed a bath, or just got tired of the truck, they ducked into a tourist camp. At one point they spent several nights in a cottage outside Crown Point. They were still living in the truck when Dillinger reestablished contact with Art O'Leary on May 19. O'Leary drove to a tavern on the outskirts of Chicago and waited until Dillinger drove up after nightfall. He followed the truck until it eased to the side of the road at a remote site.

Dillinger was sick. By O'Leary's estimate, his temperature was 104. O'Leary hopped into the truck and they idly drove the back roads, Dillinger driving and talking, while Van Meter remained in the back, peering out the windows with his machine gun. Dillinger's mood had grown bleak. He needed a doctor but was afraid to visit anyone he didn't know. He asked about Billie Frechette, whose harboring trial was under way in St. Paul, and about the cosmetic surgery he still wanted Piquett to arrange.

When they returned to O'Leary's car, he asked him to return the next evening with medicine and cough syrup.

The next night O'Leary brought Dillinger his cough syrup and a pint of whiskey. Both Dillinger's health and his mood were improved, and his spirits lifted further when O'Leary handed him a note from Frechette, who remained in a St. Paul jail cell. In it, O'Leary recalled, Billie beseeched Dillinger not to attempt her rescue. She would only be killed. She promised to do her time in prison and meet him afterward. Dillinger appeared moved. He handed O'Leary a letter for Billie, plus $600 in cash for Piquett. Afterward O'Leary opened and read Dillinger's note. In it Dillinger expressed his love for Billie, offered again to rescue her and asked to die in her arms.[21]

While the nation thrilled to stories of Dillinger's exploits, another, far less public pursuit was under way in the Southwest. Inexorably, Frank Hamer was closing in on Bonnie and Clyde.

The two manhunts were a study in contrasts. Newspapers from Chicago to London treated Dillinger as an international phenomenon, bringing in psychologists and sociologists to render opinions on his significance, but northern journalists all but ignored Bonnie and Clyde. Though they remained front-page news in Dallas, the couple's crimes typically rated no more than five or six paragraphs in the New York and Chicago papers. Sunday features on Dillinger in places like Pittsburgh and Buffalo carried sidebars introducing readers to Clyde or Pretty Boy Floyd; both were treated as minor-league outlaws, gas-station bandits doing battle with hick sheriffs. Bonnie was seldom mentioned at all; her fame would be largely posthumous. No one, not even their fellow public enemies, gave Bonnie and Clyde respect.

The papers reflected law-enforcement priorities. Hoover allowed an agent or two to track sightings of Bonnie and Clyde, but never treated the case seriously. While the FBI mobilized every office in pursuit of Dillinger, Bonnie and Clyde merited a posse of four men.*

Both hunters and prey stayed on the move. After murdering three law-enforcement officers in a span of five days in early April, Clyde, Bonnie,

---

*While the number of FBI agents on the Dillinger case fluctuated, about thirty-eight were devoted full time that spring, twenty-two in Chicago, sixteen in Indiana under Earl Connelley.

and Henry Methvin had fled north into Kansas, then circled back to Texas to see their families. They dropped Methvin in Wichita Falls and sent him ahead to arrange the rendezvous. On the train into Dallas, Methvin rode with a pair of Texas Rangers who couldn't stop talking about Bonnie and Clyde. Downtown, he walked to the Sanger Hotel to find Clyde's sister Nell, who worked in a shop there; it was the same hotel where Hamer stayed when in Dallas. Unable to locate Nell, Methvin went to the Parkers' house, gathered up family members, and drove to the meeting point east of Dallas, near the town of Mount Pleasant.

That night, lying on blankets by their cars in an isolated meadow, the Barrow and Parker families made their strongest arguments yet to persuade Clyde and Bonnie to leave the country. If you won't surrender, Mrs. Parker begged, go to Mexico. Run for the border. Clyde turned their arguments against them. If they went to Mexico, he said, they would never see their families again. "Seeing you folks is all the pleasure Bonnie and I have left in life now," he said. "Besides each other, it's all we've got to live for. Whenever we get so we can't visit our people, we might as well die and be done with it. We're staying close to home, and we're coming in as long as we're alive."

Clyde then unveiled his plan. They had been visiting the Methvins over in Louisiana, he said. They had seen a house they could buy. Bonnie wanted to fix it up, mend the roof, maybe put up lace curtains. Once they were settled, all the families could come to Louisiana and visit them. Mrs. Parker just shook her head. Everyone knew how this would end. After a while all the serious talk grew tiresome. Clyde spent much of the evening leafing through clippings and cartoons from the Dallas papers, laughing.

From Dallas they returned north. Running low on money, Clyde drove to his favorite Iowa hunting grounds in search of a bank. On Monday, April 16, Clyde and Henry Methvin robbed the First National Bank in Stuart, Iowa, just five miles west of Dexter, the town where Buck Barrow had been killed the previous July. From Iowa Clyde drove south, picking up Joe Palmer in Joplin, where Palmer had returned after becoming separated from the others after the Easter Sunday shoot-out. From Joplin they drove south to Louisiana, where Bonnie and Clyde hoped to vacation at the Methvins' home. Ivy Methvin, who was now talking regularly with Sheriff Henderson Jordan, had other ideas. Deathly afraid of Clyde, he suggested a better place for them to stay.

It was during this visit, at the Methvins' urging, that Clyde and Bonnie began bunking in the house they had mentioned to their parents, an abandoned home ten miles south of the town of Gibsland. Locals called it the John Cole house, after its last owner, who died of tuberculosis there with his wife and two daughters four years earlier. It was a four-room, unpainted wooden house at the end of a dirt road in the pines, two rooms on each side of an open-air hallway. There were a few pieces of furniture and a tin roof, but water dribbled in when it rained. It was such a wreck the Cole family left it vacant, but for Bonnie and Clyde it was their first home, and it seemed like heaven.

How they came to claim the house isn't clear. Clyde told his family he rented or purchased the house from the Cole family. A local historian, Carroll Rich, maintains that Clyde and Bonnie moved in without the family's knowledge. Years later, John Cole's son, Otis, told Rich that he visited the house when a friend told him squatters had moved in. Otis Cole said he walked up to the house one afternoon and found Ivy Methvin sitting on the front porch, drunk. Cole could see two other people moving around inside. When Methvin asked him where he could find some more bootleg whiskey, Cole said, "I don't fool with that stuff," and hurried off. He asked no more questions.[22]

Soon, however, word spread that the "squatters" were none other than Bonnie and Clyde. Carroll Rich, a Bienville Parish native, paints an evocative picture of how the stories filtered through the pines; there was nothing romantic about Bonnie and Clyde in these tales, nothing free or rebellious or heartwarming. They were murderers, modern-day bogeymen whose approach could mean only death.

As Rich recalled:

Country children shivered to hear old folks speculate on who had come to the piney woods, and at night when families sat rocking on front porches, they looked across a cornfield . . . and wondered whose yellow carlights were moving under the trees. Sometimes when cousins came to spend Friday night, as many as five children slept in one bed, the older children telling Bonnie and Clyde stories late into the night, stories of policemen shot in the face, of fat sheriffs tied up and bleeding, crying for mercy, tales designed to make the younger ones whimper with fright and weariness and finally fall into uneasy sleep.[23]

If Clyde realized that people knew he was in the area, he showed no signs of worry. In those days Bienville Parish seemed mired in the nineteenth century. The country people scraped by on dusty farms or driving rickety logging trucks. For most there were no phones, no indoor plumbing, no movie theaters, and no newspapers; many couldn't read. On those moist spring evenings in 1934, stories of Bonnie and Clyde spread like the morning fog that crept in from the swamps.

People whispered that they had been seen at the crossroads store at Sailes, stopping to buy cheese and crackers and a cold Coca-Cola. There was the man in sunglasses who parked his big Pontiac outside area farms, asking to buy a chicken to fry; it was Clyde, they had no doubt. A sharecropper swore he saw Clyde and Bonnie on a quilt spread on pine needles beneath the trees, their naked bodies moving rhythmically. Maybe these tales were concocted, maybe not. For the moment no one said a thing to the law. No one wanted to be murdered in their beds.

Bonnie and Clyde's springtime idyll did not last long. Their money was running low, and by Friday, April 27, they were back on the road.* After stopping in Memphis, Clyde drove north, cutting across Arkansas and Missouri and driving into Kansas. On Sunday afternoon, April 29, they reached Topeka, where they cruised neighborhood streets in search of a car that struck Clyde's fancy. They found it at 2107 Gable Street, a spanking new cordova-tan Ford V-8 Deluxe, sitting in a driveway. They stole it and headed toward northwestern Iowa, where they drove through greening fields looking for a bank to take. On May 3, Clyde led Methvin and Joe Palmer into the bank at Everly, Iowa, while Bonnie waited in the car. It was a disappointing haul, about $700.

Afterward, on May 4 or 5, they dropped Palmer off in Wichita and drove to Joplin, where Clyde scribbled a letter to his mother, telling her he was heading back to Louisiana. But if Clyde thought he could put off seeing the families for a few weeks, Bonnie had other ideas. She begged him to take her to Dallas to see her mother. On Sunday, May 6, they drove past the Barrow filling station and tossed out a bottle; inside were instructions to

* That morning in Memphis, Clyde mailed a letter to the Dallas sheriff, Smoot Schmid. It was about Raymond Hamilton. Hamilton had been captured that Wednesday following the robbery of a bank in Lewisville, north of Dallas. Carted back to the Dallas County Jail, he freely sparred with reporters, answering questions about his break with Bonnie and Clyde. Though he stopped short of criticizing Clyde, the interviews angered Clyde nonetheless, as had a letter Hamilton had written to his lawyer denying involvement in the killing of Constable Cal Campbell; the lawyer had given it to reporters. The reply Clyde mailed from Memphis mentioned both the Lancaster robbery and the subsequent argument over division of the loot, excoriated Mary O'Dare and, oddly, accused Hamilton of being "too yellow to fight" during the Reeds Spring shoot-out in February.

meet them four miles east of Dallas that night. It was a warm night, with a soft breeze, and Bonnie sat outside with her mother on a blanket talking for two hours. They looked through pictures Bonnie had brought: Clyde and Palmer in jaunty spring suits, arms around Bonnie; Clyde looking tough, a rifle across his knees.

"Mama," Bonnie suddenly said, "when they kill us, don't let them take me to an undertaking parlor, will you? Bring me home."

Mrs. Parker seized Bonnie's wrist. "Don't Bonnie," she said. "For God's sake."

Bonnie smiled. "Now, Mama, don't get upset," she said. "Why shouldn't we talk it over? It's coming. You know it. I know it. All of Texas knows it. So don't let them keep me at the undertakers. Bring me home when I die. It's been so long since I was home. I want to lie in the front room with you . . . sitting beside me. A long, cool, peaceful night together before I leave you. That will be nice and restful."

She put her finger on a photo of Clyde holding her. "I like this one," she said. "And another thing, Mama. When they kill us, don't ever say anything ugly about Clyde. Please promise me that, too."

Before leaving Bonnie gave her mother a new poem, hugged her, and promised to return in two weeks. Then she slid into the Ford beside Clyde and they drove east, and vanished. There would be no sign of them for two weeks, no confirmed bank robberies, no letters, no word of their whereabouts, then or now. They seem to have driven through Arkansas, Mississippi, and Tennessee, but even that is conjecture.

What is known is that on Monday evening, May 21, Clyde drove them back to their ramshackle new home in Bienville Parish, the tan Ford bumping along the rutted back roads deep into the towering pines. Everyone was happy to be back, especially Henry Methvin; he kept saying how much he wanted to see his parents. They were all dirty and exhausted, sick of bathing in streams and sleeping in the car; Bonnie said she hadn't slept in a real bed since the shoot-out at Dexfield Park the previous summer. Now they had a home, such as it was, and Clyde was eager to spread out and rest, maybe do some fishing and hunting.

He would never get the chance. Frank Hamer was waiting.

Of all the American legends that arose from the War on Crime, few are burdened with as many conflicting viewpoints as the story of the trap Frank

Hamer laid for Bonnie and Clyde. When it was over, Hamer would give his own version of events. In 1979, in a book published two years after his death, the Dallas deputy Ted Hinton would give a contradictory account; and each of the half-dozen or so books published on Bonnie and Clyde over the last forty years has devised its own story of those fateful days in the Louisiana backwoods; no two are the same. Many believe Henry Methvin betrayed Bonnie and Clyde. Others say this was a canard concocted later to keep the younger Methvin out of jail.

In the end, for all the myths and half-truths that swirl around the events of those humid Louisiana days, the facts are surprisingly clear. They can be found in a set of musty court papers from Methvin's 1936 trial for the murder of Constable Cal Campbell, and in newly discovered FBI documents and statements from members of Hamer's posse. Taken together, these papers suggest that the key figure in the plot was not Hamer. It was the Bienville Parish sheriff, Henderson Jordan.

Jordan was a prototypical backwoods sheriff, an easygoing, sun-burned fellow in a fawn-colored Stetson. Afterward he rarely spoke of what had happened, and never gave a detailed public interview on his role in the affair. But in 1958, shortly before his death, he consented to discuss it with his nephew, a history professor named Glenn Jordan. In this interview, Jordan traced the genesis of Bonnie and Clyde's demise to early March, after their first visit to the Methvins' shack. Whether it was Henry Methvin or his father who initiated the idea, the two men were of one mind on the proposal the elder Methvin took to one of their neighbors, a man named John Joyner: if the state of Texas would pardon the younger Methvin for his crimes, the Methvin family would betray Bonnie and Clyde. Ivy Methvin sent Joyner to make the proposal to Sheriff Jordan in Arcadia, fifty miles east of Shreveport.

As Sheriff Jordan told the story, he knew Henry Methvin had been in some kind of trouble in Texas. But he initially had no idea that he was traveling with Bonnie and Clyde:*

In the early spring of 1934, I got word that Ivy Methvin, who lived down in the southern part of the parish, wanted to talk with me. I was also told that we had to meet Methvin in private and that no one was to know that I was meeting with him. I did not know what Methvin wanted to see me

---

* This suggests that Sheriff Jordan had no contact with Frank Hamer before early March. Some versions suggest Hamer spoke with Jordan as early as February.

about. I did know that he had a son, Henry, who had been in trouble with the law in Texas and a couple of other places . . . It took several days to set up a meeting. I attempted to do what Methvin asked and keep the meeting quiet. Finally, and I think that it was early March, Prentiss Oakley, my chief deputy and friend, and I met with Methvin.

At a roadside clearing late one night, Ivy Methvin told the sheriff that his son had escaped from prison with the help of Bonnie and Clyde and was now traveling with them. As Methvin described it, the trio had begun visiting his home in February, about two weeks after the prison break, and had dropped by a time or two afterward. They arrived without notice, stayed several days, and then disappeared. Ivy Methvin was deathly afraid of Clyde. He was certain he would get his son killed.

As Jordan remembered the conversation:

I suggested that Henry simply give himself up. He would have to answer for his crimes in Texas and would serve time in jail but he would be alive. Methvin would not listen to that. He said that if Henry surrendered to the law, Bonnie and Clyde would kill him and his wife. Methvin said that the only way for all of the Methvin family to be safe was for Bonnie and Clyde to be dead. He said that if he agreed to help the law captured [*sic*] Bonnie and Clyde if some agreement could be made that would help his son. He said that if he agreed to help the law with Bonnie and Clyde, his son should not have to return to jail. Methvin said that his help should wipe his son's slate clean.

Jordan told Methvin he had no power to make such a deal, but would think about who might. Jordan spent several days mulling Methvin's offer before telephoning the FBI office in New Orleans, where he was passed to an agent named Lester Kendale. The two men had several conversations, and at some point the FBI man suggested they meet with Hamer. According to testimony at Methvin's 1936 trial, the meeting occurred at an isolated roadside clearing in Bienville Parish.* In attendance were Sheriff Jordan, Agent Kendale, Hamer, the Dallas deputy Bob Alcorn, and Methvin's intermediary, John Joyner.

---

* In testimony during Henry Methvin's 1936 murder trial, John Joyner said this meeting occurred near the town of Castor in Bienville Parish.

As Sheriff Jordan remembered the meeting:

> Hamer agreed that a deal could be offered to the Methvin family . . .
> While Hamer did not promise that all charges against Methvin would
> be dropped by the state of Texas, he came real close to saying that. Be-
> fore the meeting was over, I came to realize that was the offer that I
> was to make to Methvin. If he would help capture Bonnie and Clyde,
> Henry would not have to go back to prison.

Hamer carried Methvin's proposal to Lee Simmons in Dallas. Simmons
took it to the Texas governor's mansion, where Ma Ferguson approved it in
principle. She wrote a letter explicitly stating that if Henry Methvin would
help apprehend Bonnie and Clyde, he would be pardoned of all crimes in
Texas. Simmons gave the letter to Hamer.

This process took a week or more, during which Sheriff Jordan relayed
updates to Ivy Methvin. "[A]ll of our meetings were held late at night on
country roads back in the woods," Jordan recalled. "When I got back to
Methvin, I told him we had a deal." Methvin, in turn, gave Jordan worrisome news. Since seeing him last, Bonnie and Clyde had again visited the
Methvin home, and it was then Methvin had persuaded the couple to use
the John Cole house.

In his own retelling, Frank Hamer makes no mention of Sheriff Jordan
or Ivy Methvin. Hamer told the Texas Ranger historian Walter Prescott
Webb that he managed to locate Bonnie and Clyde's hideout in Bienville
Parish. He gives no details, but he can only be referring to the John Cole
house. As Hamer recalled:

> On several occasions I went alone to this secret place. It was my hope
> to take [Clyde] and Bonnie alive; this I could do only by finding them
> asleep. It would have been simple to tap each one on the head, kick
> their weapons out of reach, and handcuff them before they knew
> what it was all about . . . There was always plenty of sign in the camp—
> stubs of Bonnie's Camels (Clyde smoked Bull Durham), lettuce leaves
> for their white rabbit, pieces of sandwiches, and a button off Clyde's
> coat. I found where they had made their bed.*

---

* Sometime in late April or early May, Hamer claimed, he came close to capturing Bonnie and Clyde at
the John Cole house. "The end would have come [then]," Hamer remembered, "had not some local and

Hamer and Jordan debated whether to storm the John Cole house the next time Bonnie and Clyde returned to Bienville Parish. According to Jordan, Ivy Methvin argued against doing so, saying they would only succeed in getting lawmen killed. As Henderson recalled:

> I was beginning to get concerned about Methvin because he was literally scared to death. He was so scared of Bonnie and Clyde, but he was also scared to be with us in capturing them. He kept saying that we did not know what we were doing . . . He said that they had no concern at all for human life. If we tried to capture them, they would just kill all of us.

Sheriff Jordan listened as Methvin suggested places for an ambush. Methvin said Clyde kept a mailbox at Shreveport. They had their laundry done in Bossier City. There was only a single dirt road between the John Cole house and the nearest town, Gibsland, Methvin said. Maybe they could surprise them along the road. After each of their meetings, Jordan telephoned Hamer, who was chasing leads across Texas.

Weeks dragged by with no sign of Clyde or Bonnie. By mid-May, with no confirmed sighting of the couple for over a month, Hamer decided to camp out in Shreveport and wait for their return to Bienville Parish. He wanted the FBI involved. On May 11 he stopped at the Dallas office and asked the SAC, Frank Blake, to give him Charles Winstead.[24] Blake declined. Hamer also had no luck trying to lure the New Orleans agent, Lester Kendale, to Shreveport.

And so, late on Saturday night, May 19, Hamer and his three Texans checked into Shreveport's Inn Hotel alone, ready to wait for news of Bonnie and Clyde's return. Sunday morning, after a breakfast of ham, eggs, and grits, they spread out in the rooms and played poker. Sheriff Jordan came by with his deputy, Prentiss Oakley, and they went over plans for the ambush should the outlaws appear.

Nothing about Hamer's trap is as confusing as accounts of those next two days. Years later, the participants could not even agree whether the ambush party itself lay in wait for one day or two. A close reading of court

---

federal officers made a drag on Ruston, Louisiana, and when Clyde heard of it, he quit the country and I had to wait for him to return."

documents, however, makes clear that the final chapter of Bonnie and Clyde's two-year crime spree began on Monday night, May 21, two days after Hamer's posse arrived in Shreveport.

That evening Bonnie, Clyde, and Henry Methvin arrived back in Bienville Parish. Before bedding down at the John Cole house, Methvin asked to see his parents. Clyde pulled up to the Methvin shack after nightfall. He and Bonnie stayed in the car, while Henry talked in low tones with his mother. Henry asked if they had made arrangements with the sheriff. His mother said they had. Henry said Clyde would probably head into Shreveport the next morning to get sandwiches. He would make his move then. Henry told her to alert the sheriff and make sure the ambush was arranged. Ava Methvin said they would try.[25]

The next morning, Tuesday, May 22, Clyde drove them into Shreveport. He parked the tan Ford in front of the Majestic Café. Methvin ran in for sandwiches and soft drinks, sitting at the counter while a waitress prepared the order to go. As he waited, Clyde noticed a police car coming toward them. Leaving Methvin behind, Clyde jammed his foot onto the accelerator, the sound of his squealing tires causing heads to turn. Methvin realized he had been abandoned. It was the break he had been looking for. Slowly he eased out of the café, leaving the sandwich order unfilled. Looking both ways, careful to make sure Clyde was really gone, he walked out onto the sidewalk and made his escape. On the edge of town he caught a ride and by mid-afternoon was safely at his brother's home back in Bienville Parish.[26]

Henry Methvin had held up his end of the bargain, but his parents were tardy holding up theirs. Not wanting to be seen with Sheriff Jordan, Ivy Methvin waited till that morning to find his intermediary, John Joyner, and send him to Arcadia with the news that Bonnie and Clyde had returned. In his testimony at Henry Methvin's 1936 trial, Joyner said he was unable to locate Sheriff Jordan till after nightfall that Tuesday, May 22. Meantime, Bonnie and Clyde swung by the Methvin shack in search of Henry, startling the Methvins. When they left, the elder Methvin went in search of Jordan, too.

By the time Sheriff Jordan telephoned Frank Hamer in Shreveport, Hamer's posse already knew Bonnie and Clyde had returned. According to Ted Hinton, he had telephoned the Shreveport police chief, thinking he would introduce the chief to Hamer as a courtesy. The chief surprised Hinton by telling him two of his officers believed they had seen Clyde outside

J. Edgar Hoover: The director ruled by absolute fiat, suspending agents who arrived even one minute late for work. While extolling the benefits of "scientific crime-solving," he privately admitted he had few competent men.

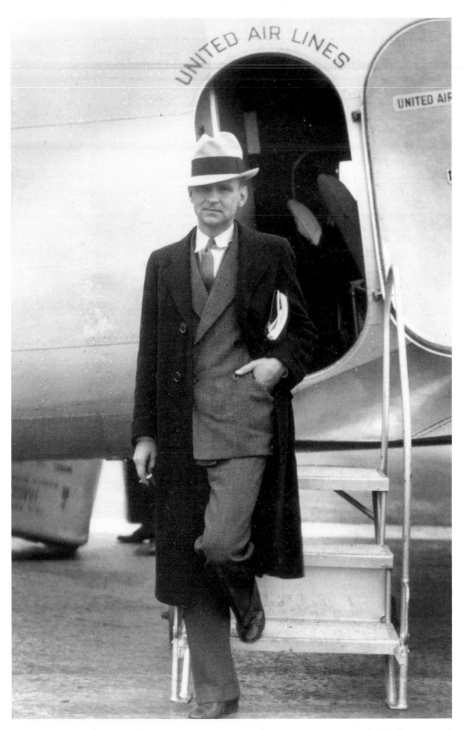

Melvin Purvis: The most famous operative in FBI history, Hoover's "Little Mel" appeared badly out of his depth during the Dillinger manhunt. No agent ever flew so high or fell so far.

(Above) Hoover confers with Purvis and a Justice Department attorney, and *(below left)* sets his sights. *(Below right)* Earl Connelley, the taciturn agent who headed the Indiana theater of the Dillinger campaign.

(*Above*) The aftermath of the Kansas City Massacre: Five seconds of machine-gun fire that created the modern FBI. (*Below*) Samuel P. Cowley, homely and deskbound, the unlikely star of the third act of Hoover's War on Crime.

Clyde Barrow and
Bonnie Parker:
Murderous children
who longed for the
big time, Bonnie and
Clyde have garnered
an artistic and cultural
relevance in death
they never found or
deserved in life.

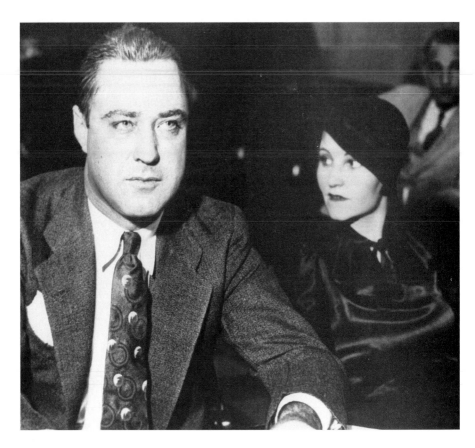

Machine Gun Kelly and his wife, Kathryn *(above)*: The garrulous Kelly and his overbearing wife were startled to find themselves hounded by a federal agency no one had ever heard of. Pretty Boy Floyd *(right)*: An Oklahoma antihero who ceaselessly whined about his own victimization, by 1933 Floyd was so fatigued by life as a fugitive that he wanted little more than to hide in his family's kitchen, baking pies.

Dock Barker: A borderline moron dominated by his younger brother Fred, he earned his parole thanks to bribes paid to an Oklahoma politician.

(Left) Ma Barker: A cranky old hillbilly consumed with jigsaw puzzles, she was posthumously enshrined by the FBI as the mastermind of the Barker-Karpis gang, a canard Hoover concocted to explain her death at the Bureau's hands. *(Right)* Alvin Karpis: The brains of the Barker gang, he was probably the smartest Depression-era criminal.

(*Above*) Edward Bremer, the prickly St. Paul heir kidnapped by the Barkers. (*Below*) The suburban Chicago house where Edward Bremer was held when he was kidnapped by the Barkers.

John Dillinger, under arrest at Crown Point, Indiana: Reporters accustomed to hard-eyed Chicago gangsters found the wisecracking Indiana farmboy something new and altogether fresh, an easygoing murderer with a lopsided grin and a gleam in his eye. Their adulatory reviews created a sympathetic criminal whom Northern audiences could root for, setting the stage for a melodramatic manhunt that consumed the nation for four months.

Pete Pierpont, Dillinger's first partner, was the acknowledged leader of their escaped-inmate gang, but Dillinger's easy charm and penchant for niceties eluded him.

Dillinger with his Indiana prosecutor, Robert Estill: The photo that enraged Hoover.

The Little Bohemia women: Helen Gillis, Jean Delaney, and Mickey Conforti were delivered into Hoover's hands, but the Chicago office's bungling allowed them to rejoin the Dillinger gang.

(Above) The driveway at Little Bohemia: The shoot-out and Dillinger's subsequent escape was a turning point in the War on Crime. *(Below)* Dillinger's Judas, Ana Sage.

The Biograph Theater.

(Above) Bonnie Parker in death. *(Below)* Dillinger in death.

Crowds surround Homer Van Meter's fallen body.

The Florida lake house where FBI agents confronted Fred and Ma Barker. *(Below)* Alvin Karpis, after his capture.

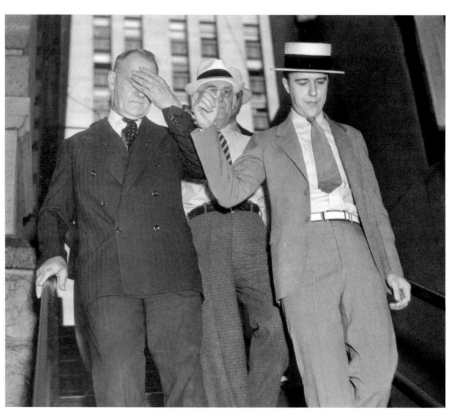

the Majestic Café that morning.* When the chief mentioned that a young man had fled the café shortly after, leaving his order behind, Hinton glanced at Bob Alcorn. "Henry Methvin," Alcorn said.

They drove to the Majestic, found the waitress who had taken Methvin's order, and spread several photographs before her. "See anybody in there who looks like the man who wouldn't wait for his sandwiches?" Hinton asked. The waitress pointed at a photo of Methvin.

"That's him," she said. "Same eyes, same pimply face. There's no mistake."[27]

Not till that night did Sheriff Jordan, alerted by John Joyner, reach Hamer. It was time to set the ambush. They agreed to meet in Gibsland. Before leaving, Hamer dialed Lee Simmons in Austin and left a cryptic message: "The old hen is about ready to hatch. I think the chickens will come off tomorrow."

According to Sheriff Jordan, the ambush party rendezvoused in Gibsland a little after midnight. There were seven of them: Jordan and his deputy, Prentiss Oakley, Hamer and Manny Gault, Bob Alcorn and Ted Hinton, and Ivy Methvin. They grabbed sandwiches, checked their guns, and drove down darkened dirt roads to the spot Jordan and Hamer had chosen. It was nothing more than a brush-covered embankment on the roadside, wreathed by mossy oaks and evergreens. Its only advantage was the view it gave of the road between Gibsland and the John Cole house. Standing back in the brush, they could see a good half mile in either direction. Hamer was satisfied. They pulled the cars back into the trees. In the darkness they constructed an impromptu blind of sticks and stray bushes and sat back to wait. If Clyde and Bonnie were coming to or from the John Cole house, they had to pass this point.

The hours passed slowly. "One of the longest nights I ever spent," Jordan recalled. The men took turns dozing in the cars, two at a time. Those awake slapped at chiggers and mosquitoes. Ivy Methvin drove home and reappeared in his rattletrap truck just before dawn. He begged them to call the whole thing off. "He said we would all be killed," Jordan recalled. "It was warm and the mosquitoes like to eaten us alive. Besides being concerned about the next morning, we had to listen to Methvin who was con-

---

* Forty years later, Ted Hinton put this discussion on Sunday, May 20, leading many researchers to believe Methvin separated from Bonnie and Clyde on Saturday, May 19; in fact, if Hinton did talk with the Shreveport police about the sighting of Clyde, it must have been Tuesday afternoon, May 22. In his 1936 testimony, Methvin clearly stated the incident at the Majestic Café occurred that Tuesday morning.

stantly talking about the fact that we were all about to be killed. Finally I told him [to] shut up."*

Methvin's irritating pleas only highlighted the debate over what to do if Bonnie and Clyde appeared. Jordan insisted they give the pair a chance to surrender. Hamer wouldn't hear it. "Hamer and I had argued about that for days," Jordan recalled twenty-five years later. "I wanted to step out in the road and demand their surrender, but Hamer said that if I did, I was a dead man." Jordan didn't care. As dawn broke, he was still determined to give the outlaws one last chance.

The sun rose. Hamer had been dwelling on how they could bring Clyde to a stop; they couldn't easily shoot him if he whizzed by at fifty miles an hour. He told Methvin to park his truck in the road. They took off the left-front tire and placed the truck on a jack. If Clyde did drive by, Hamer wagered, he would stop to help out.

Seven o'clock came, then eight. A logging truck and a car or two passed. "After each car passed, Methvin would run over to us and beg us to call the whole thing off," Jordan remembered. "Each time, I would patiently listen to him and then firmly send him back to his place on the road beside his truck. At one point I told him that if he did not get back to his truck and do what he was told to do, Bonnie and Clyde would not get the chance to kill him because I would."

By nine they were debating whether to pack it in. Someone said give it another half hour. For a few minutes they went back to slapping mosquitoes and flicking at tics. Then, at 9:15, came the high-pitched whine of a car. It was approaching from the east at high speed. Everyone peered down the road. They saw it as it crested a rise: a tan Ford. Each of the men squinted at the car as it approached down the incline. "This is him," Hinton whispered. "This is it. It's Clyde."

Bob Alcorn waited another moment till he could make out the driver's face.

"It's him, boys," he said.

No one knows where Bonnie and Clyde spent their last night together. It almost certainly wasn't the John Cole house, given their approach that morn-

---

* Ted Hinton claimed Methvin grew so bothersome he was briefly handcuffed to a tree.

ing from Gibsland. At 8:00 A.M. Clyde pulled up in front of Canfield's Café, where he and Bonnie ate a light breakfast of donuts and coffee. Bonnie wore the same red dress she had been seen wearing off and on for days, Clyde a blue silk suit and a tie. They ordered sandwiches to go, and as they returned to the car to drive to the John Cole house, Bonnie began to eat hers. Clyde kicked off his shoes and placed his sunglasses on the dashboard.[28]

Eight miles south of Gibsland, they crested a rise and spotted Ivy Methvin standing beside his truck, which was jacked up in the road. Bonnie put her sandwich down, and placed it on the magazine spread across her lap. Beneath the magazine was a Colt .45. Clyde took his foot off the accelerator and let the Ford coast to a stop beside Methvin's truck. Clyde turned his head to the right, toward Methvin and his truck, away from the six guns that were aimed directly at his head.

"Hey," Clyde said to Methvin.

Just then Methvin doubled over as if in pain and stepped away. Twenty feet to Clyde's left, hidden in the brush, Sheriff Jordan was just about to put down his gun and yell something—halt, surrender—he wasn't sure what. Just then Clyde took his foot off the brake for a moment, and the Ford began to ease forward.

The moment the car moved, Jordan's deputy, Prentiss Oakley, fired. In a split second each of the five other posse members fired. Bonnie screamed "like a panther," Jordan remembered. The first bullets tore into Clyde's head and shoulders. His foot left the brake and the car began to roll forward. But the shooting didn't stop. On and on it went, a never-ending barrage, bullet after bullet, more than 150 in all, tearing into the car and their bodies as the Ford rolled forward. The car came to a stop against the embankment thirty yards down the road.

And then, silence. Hinton ran up to the driver's-side door. Inside was a scene he would never forget—"like a slaughterhouse," he would recall. Clyde lay back against the seat, his hair matted in blood. Hinton tried to open the door but there was no room; the car was wedged against the embankment. He scrambled over the hood and opened the passenger's-side door. Bonnie fell out into his arms. She seemed so tiny, still soft and warm. He caught a whiff of her perfume. Her right hand had been shot off. She was covered with blood. He laid her back on the front seat and grabbed a pistol from beside Clyde. It was cold to his touch.[29] Neither Clyde nor Bonnie had gotten off a shot.

Ivy Methvin ran up. There was a blanket in the backseat. Something was under it. "You've killed my boy!" Methvin snapped. Sheriff Jordan leaned into the backseat and pulled back the blanket. Beneath it was a row of guns. "We haven't killed your boy, Mr. Methvin," he said.

The county coroner was called. By the time he arrived, word had spread of the deaths, and a long line of dusty cars and logging trucks thronged the gravel road as dozens of the curious ogled the death car and Bonnie's and Clyde's bullet-riddled bodies. As Ted Hinton passed through the crowd, filming the scene with a movie camera he had brought, Sheriff Jordan had to restrain a man who produced a pair of scissors and was attempting to cut off one of Clyde's ears. He was unable to stop someone else from shearing off locks of Bonnie's hair.

Soon a wrecker arrived, towing away the death car. By lunchtime the bodies had arrived at Conger's Furniture Store in Arcadia, which doubled as the parish funeral parlor. A crowd, later estimated at sixteen thousand people, thronged the streets, struggling for glimpses of the fallen outlaws. When they loaded Clyde's body onto a stretcher, someone cried out, "He was nothing but a little bitty fart!"

The next day family members arrived and carted the corpses back to Dallas for burial. Enormous crowds greeted Bonnie and Clyde on their return. Bonnie's body was put on display at the McCamy-Campbell Funeral Home, and in a single day twenty thousand people passed in to stare at her. Amid crowds of newspapermen and photographers, she was buried in the Fishtrap Cemetery. Clyde was laid to rest beside his brother Buck in the Western Heights Cemetery, a mile away. At the funeral home beforehand, a drunk weaved in to view his body, dropped a cigarette butt on the carpet, ground it in, and said, "I'm glad he's dead."

In death Bonnie and Clyde proved far more newsworthy than in life. The story of their killings was splashed across the front pages of dozens of Northern newspapers, including the *New York Times,* the first and last time the couple would rate such coverage. That their profiles should rise so precipitously was a byproduct of the ongoing hysteria over Dillinger: the idea that there were other Dillinger-like desperadoes at work across the country's midsection was an idea that appealed to editors eager to spot a trend. Within days, however, the story would ebb, in part because Frank Hamer, Sheriff Jordan, and other posse members refused to discuss the ambush in detail.

For the next thirty years Bonnie and Clyde would remain dimly remembered, the province of detective magazines and pulp writers, until a pair of

Hollywood screenwriters read of their exploits in John Toland's 1963 *Dillinger Days* and created the 1967 movie that led to their rediscovery. Art has now done for Bonnie Parker and Clyde Barrow something they could never achieve in life: it has taken a shark-eyed multiple murderer and his deluded girlfriend and transformed them into sympathetic characters, imbuing them with a cuddly likability they did not possess, and a cultural significance they do not deserve.

14

NEW FACES

May 24 to June 30, 1934

We sure did run down a lot of bum leads and embarrass
ourselves and innocent people a lot of times.
—SPECIAL AGENT JOHN WELLES

The morning after Bonnie and Clyde were killed, Dillinger was still wandering the back roads of northwest Indiana in his red panel truck. He and Van Meter had been living in the truck three weeks now, and Dillinger knew they couldn't do it much longer. The last time he had seen Art O'Leary, O'Leary said Louis Piquett had a cosmetic surgeon standing by who could render Dillinger's face unrecognizable. As soon as he got the word, Dillinger was prepared to go under the knife.

That night, a little after eleven, two detectives from the East Chicago Police Department, Martin O'Brien and Lloyd Mulvihill, left their station house to check a Dillinger sighting. The two had investigated the East Chicago bank robbery that January and had been working the Dillinger case off and on ever since. Barely a half hour after they left their posts, the two detectives were found dead in their car on a lonely road outside town. They had been shot multiple times in the head and neck, apparently by a machine gun.

Dillinger later told O'Leary what happened. He said the two detectives had spotted the red truck, pulled alongside, and ordered Dillinger to pull over. Van Meter machine-gunned them from the passenger seat, raking the two men with his bullets as they sat in the car.

From Dillinger's later remarks, it appears the killings were linked to protection money Dillinger was paying members of the East Chicago Police Department; the only cop Dillinger mentioned by name was a detective named Martin Zarkovich. Dillinger claimed at one point that the two detectives had been attempting to "shake him down" for more money. Another time he suggested the two were honest men who had become suspicious of Zarkovich's relationship with Dillinger. Zarkovich, Dillinger said, had dispatched the two to find the red truck knowing they would be killed.

"Those two police should never have been bumped off," O'Leary quoted Dillinger saying. "They were just trying to do their job and there's nothing wrong with that. Their trouble was that they were getting to know too much and Zark was getting antsy. They were sent off to shake down a couple of suspicious characters who were driving around in a red truck. I think Van felt bad about it, too, but there was nothing else that he could do, and Zark knew what was going to happen."[1] Whether or not Martin Zarkovich played a role in the murders, it wasn't to be his last appearance in the Dillinger drama.

The next morning the Chicago papers carried speculation that Dillinger was responsible. At the Bankers Building, Purvis studied the reports and decided to ignore them; when one of Hoover's aides called and asked why, Purvis explained that "it would be practically impossible to determine the identity of those doing the killing in that there were no eyewitnesses except those who were killed."[2]

Despite the FBI's lack of interest, the May 24 killings appear to have convinced Dillinger that his nomadic life was no longer safe. That same night he and Van Meter drove into Chicago, where they reestablished contact with Baby Face Nelson and Tommy Carroll. Both were living in a cottage in Wauconda, northwest of Chicago, taking some meals at Louis Cernocky's tavern in Fox River Grove. Nelson had spent much of May plotting ways to free his wife, Helen, who remained in custody in Madison, Wisconsin; he arranged for a lawyer instead.

Other than Piquett and O'Leary, Dillinger had no one he could trust in Chicago. But Nelson did. That night, after stowing the red truck in a friend's garage, Nelson drove Dillinger and Van Meter to the Rain-Bo Inn, where he persuaded an old friend, a fence named Jimmy Murray, to shelter them in an attic room. Murray consented, but soon had second thoughts. The next night, Murray told Nelson things weren't working out. Dillinger had broken his promise to stay hidden and, to Murray's dismay, had come downstairs and circulated among his patrons, several of whom remarked how much he resembled John Dillinger.

Everyone involved—Nelson, Murray, and Piquett, who was drawn into the situation—realized they needed a place for Dillinger to hide. As it happened, Murray and Piquett had a mutual friend in Jimmy Probasco, a grimy little Italian who worked the fringes of Chicago's underworld, fencing stolen goods and selling liquor.* The sixty-seven-year-old Probasco had his eye on a tavern he wanted to buy but needed money. On Sunday, May 27, Probasco got house guests.

Chicago, Illinois
Sunday, May 27

Jimmy Probasco's weatherbeaten frame house stood beside a Shell station at 2509 Crawford Avenue, in an industrial area of Chicago's North Side. It had a sickly green hedge in front and a board fence that extended around the back, where Probasco kept his two temperamental police dogs, King and Queen. From what the neighbors could hear, his favorite pastime appeared to be cursing at the dogs. The house had two stories. Probasco rented out the top floor.

Piquett and O'Leary were standing outside the Shell station at midnight when Dillinger appeared with Van Meter. Probasco was startled when he opened his front door and found Piquett and two strangers on his doorstep; in the interest of secrecy, no one had told him they were coming. "Jimmy, this is my famous client, John Dillinger," Piquett said. "Have you got someplace we can all sit down and talk?"[3]

Dillinger and Van Meter stepped inside. There was a living room and two bedrooms, one in front, the other in back. Probasco shook their hands and led them into the kitchen. He was nervous.

"So this is it," Dillinger said, looking around. "Have you worked out the price, Mr. Piquett?"

Piquett said $50 a day.

"Don't you think that's high?" Dillinger asked.

"Well, you're pretty hot, you know," Probasco said, "but I want you to be satisfied. What do you think is fair?"

"How about thirty-five a day?" Dillinger asked.

---

* James J. Probasco was no stranger to Chicago police. Since 1921 he had two arrests for possession of stolen goods but had never been convicted. Over the years he had dabbled in everything from prize fighting to a veterinary business.

Agreed. Dillinger asked Piquett about the doctors. Everything was set. They would come to Probasco's house the next night to perform the surgery. Dillinger took out his wallet and counted out $3,000. "You'll get the rest after the operation," he said.

Just then a stout woman with dark hair entered the kitchen. Dillinger looked annoyed. "Who's the woman?" he asked. She was Probasco's live-in girlfriend, Piquett explained, a nurse who worked during the days. When Probasco promised she was a great cook, Dillinger said she could stay.[4] Afterward, Probasco showed Dillinger the front bedroom, pointing out the fold-out couch where the outlaws could bed down. Dillinger said it was fine. And then he went to sleep.

Monday, May 28

Art O'Leary brought the two doctors to Probasco's house the following night. They edged into the front bedroom and looked around; Probasco had laid out a cot for the surgery. The man who was to lay his scalpel on Dillinger's face was a tall, thin German named Wilhelm Loeser, who went by the alias "Ralph Robiend." Loeser was already known to the FBI; the Bureau's Oklahoma City office, looking for the doctor in an unrelated case, had alerted Chicago to watch for him that spring. The fifty-eight-year-old Loeser, a self-important type who had immigrated to America at the age of twelve, had studied medicine at the University of Kansas and Northwestern University. In the mid-1920s, he made his living selling illegal drugs out of his Chicago pharmacy; arrested and sentenced to a three-year term in Leavenworth in 1931, he obtained parole and promptly skipped it, fleeing to Mexico when it appeared he might be rearrested. Piquett was his attorney. When Loeser slipped back into Chicago as "Ralph Robiend" in early 1934, Piquett hired him to perform cosmetic surgery on a con man named William Elmer Meade.

Loeser's assistant that night was a jittery thirty-two-year-old alcoholic named Harold Cassidy. He was Art O'Leary's cousin. Seven years out of the University of Illinois medical school, the cash-strapped Cassidy had an ex-wife who was forever pestering him for alimony; Piquett was his lawyer, too. In his North Side office, located above one of Al Capone's old speakeasies, Cassidy performed illegal abortions and anything else to make money. He had assisted Loeser in the earlier surgery and was to receive $600 for his work on Dillinger.

Standing in Jimmy Probasco's front bedroom, Dillinger told Loeser what he wanted from the surgery; Loeser said he foresaw no difficulties. "Do you want a general or a local anesthetic?" he asked Dillinger.

"A general would put me completely out, wouldn't it?" Dillinger asked.

"Yes, it would."

"Are you going to be here, Art?" Dillinger asked O'Leary.

"I'll stay if you want me, Johnnie," O'Leary said.

"I want you to stay."

Loeser asked what Dillinger had eaten that day. Only a grapefruit and some toast for breakfast, Dillinger said. It wasn't true. Dillinger, in fact, had a full meal just an hour earlier, but he was anxious to get started. While Loeser washed his hands in a bathroom, Dillinger stripped off his shirt and lay on the cot. After assembling his things, Cassidy leaned over him, placed a towel over his face, and began dripping ether onto it.

"You there, Art?" Dillinger asked.

"I'm right with you, Johnnie," O'Leary said.

After a minute or two Dillinger was still semiconscious. Frustrated, Cassidy emptied an entire can of ether onto the towel. Suddenly, he noticed a change in Dillinger's complexion. He seemed to be turning blue. His breathing stopped. Cassidy panicked, backing up against the wall. "What is it?" O'Leary asked.

"He's not breathing!" Cassidy yelped.

Dillinger's food intake was causing a reaction to the anesthesia. Loeser darted into the room and furiously began pumping Dillinger's chest. Behind him Probasco appeared in the doorway, a panic-stricken look on his face. "My God he's dead!" he shouted. "Oh my God!"

As O'Leary opened a window to vent the ether fumes, Loeser continued pumping Dillinger's chest. Finally, after a few more tense minutes, he began breathing. O'Leary and Probasco exchanged sighs of relief. They had no doubt what Van Meter and Nelson would do to them had Dillinger died; no one would believe they hadn't betrayed him.

Once Dillinger was stabilized, Loeser leaned over his face and began. It was slow going. Dillinger vomited several times during the surgery and bled heavily, staining the cot. Loeser cleaned away the vomit and blood and pressed on. He first removed three facial moles. He then gave Dillinger a facelift, making slits beneath each of the outlaw's ears, then pulling back the skin to eliminate wrinkles. With skin from the cheek incisions, he filled Dillinger's chin dimple. Then he sutured the wounds and bandaged them.

When he was finished, Dillinger looked like a bloody mummy. In an hour he came to.

He was very groggy. O'Leary explained that he had almost died. Dillinger managed a tiny laugh. "It might just as well have been now as some other time," he said.

Dillinger remained in the small bedroom, recuperating, for two days. On Thursday, May 31, Cassidy visited and took off the bandages. Dillinger stared at himself in a mirror. The telltale chin dimple was gone, as were the moles. He smiled. He looked like a new man.

All that May Hoover brooded on the disastrous course the War on Crime had taken. Little Bohemia had made the Bureau a national laughingstock. Dillinger had vanished. So had the Barkers. The mystery of the Kansas City Massacre remained unsolved, and there hadn't been a reliable sighting of Pretty Boy Floyd in months. The Bureau received—and deserved—no credit for the killings of Bonnie and Clyde. Frank Hamer gave an interview saying he would hunt down Dillinger if the FBI asked. Hoover's position was obvious: over my dead body.

Little Bohemia made several things clear to Hoover. More than anything it demonstrated how unprepared his men were for gunfights. Despite months of crash training, the College Boys remained hopeless with guns and utterly lost in anything approaching a combat situation. Hoover was determined that the next time the FBI shot it out with Dillinger, they would be ready. That meant one thing: bringing in the Cowboys. Hoover had Pop Nathan canvas the Southwestern bureaus in search of men with firearms skills. Several fit the bill, and that May they began trickling into Chicago.

Among the first to arrive was thirty-eight-year-old Charles Winstead, the craggy Texan who had chased Machine Gun Kelly and Bonnie and Clyde, and had taken part in the capture of Harvey Bailey. Winstead arrived on May 12, flying up from Love Field in Dallas. Arriving on the nineteenth floor, Winstead renewed acquaintances with another old Texan, the onetime Ranger J. C. "Doc" White, a wisecracking younger brother of Tom White, Hoover's best man during the 1920s. At fifty-five, Doc White became the eldest member of the Dillinger Squad and a mentor to many younger agents.

Not all the new men arriving in Chicago were Texans. One of the best was thirty-one-year-old Herman Hollis, the resident agent in Tulsa, who has been nosing around the Barker Gang's old Eastern Oklahoma haunts for months. Hollis, known as "Ed," was the rare College Boy who could handle a gun; a long-nosed lawyer from Des Moines, he earned a sharpshooter's medal with the Thompson submachine gun. Energetic and hardworking, Hollis was rated as one of the FBI's top investigators.

But Hollis had issues. He had been the Detroit SAC until performance reviews questioned his administrative abilities. He was forever pestering the Bureau to transfer him to California or Arizona; his wife, Genevieve, had "a nervous condition" that doctors said would improve in a warmer climate. A lady's man, chatty with the stenographers, Hollis was also vain. "He possibly takes an unusual amount of pride in the neatness of his attire," Hugh Clegg noted in one memo, "particularly when passing mirrors."[5]

But Hollis was a capable investigator, good with a gun, and Hoover didn't have enough men like him. In fact, when Pop Nathan drew up a roster of agents "particularly qualified . . . for work of a dangerous character," Hollis was one of only eleven names on the list. In desperation Hoover cast his eyes to Southwest police departments. From Dallas he hired the chief of detectives, R. L. "Bob" Jones. From Waco he brought a detective named Buck Buchanan. From Oklahoma City, Hoover lured two members of the department's pistol team, a thirty-year-old detective named Jerry Campbell and the night police chief, Clarence Hurt, thirty-nine, who had taken part in the Underhill shoot-out; both men were destined for long FBI careers. Hurt's earlier application to the Bureau had been turned down, Pop Nathan noting he "sees nothing in applicant to indicate the possession of any particularly constructive imagination." But Hurt was good with a gun, and that was enough.

These men were to form the heart of a new and improved Dillinger Squad. The new hires were sent to Washington for a month of training. The day they finished, Clarence Hurt wrote a friend that he and his partner Jerry Campbell were the only men in the class who weren't lawyers.[6] That was the point; all the new men understood they were brought in not to capture the likes of Dillinger, but in all likelihood to kill them. "They hired me as a hired gun, no question about it; they were getting too many accountants and lawyers killed," D. A. "Jelly" Bryce, an Oklahoma City detective hired later that year, told friends, according to Bryce biographer Ron Owens.

But importing gunmen alone wouldn't find Dillinger, Hoover realized.

The problem was leadership. The problem was Purvis. In later years Purvis's fall from Hoover's favor would be attributed to jealousy. Hoover, a generation of writers concluded, couldn't abide the attention his subordinate drew from the nation's press as he pursued Dillinger. While this may have been true, the roots of Purvis's demise lay less in his thirst for publicity than in his own yearlong series of blunders. Arresting the wrong suspects in the Hamm kidnapping and "forgetting" orders to capture Machine Gun Kelly were bad enough. Hoover stuck with his beloved "Little Mel" through it all, even defending his performance at Little Bohemia. But there was no denying Purvis's ineptitude in the Dillinger hunt. Suspects were found then lost. His informants were hopeless. He raided the wrong apartments. He built no bridges to the Chicago police while annoying other departments. He'd had his car stolen from in front of his house.

Hoover's doubts were mounting when Purvis was handed the best bait the Bureau had been served in months. On May 26 a federal judge in Wisconsin granted the Little Bohemia women—Helen Gillis, Jean Delaney, and Mickey Conforti—probation. Before being released, the three women were questioned at the Bankers Building. Purvis assigned a half-dozen men to shadow them. Conforti went to her foster parents' home, while Gillis and Delaney went to the apartment of Nelson's sister, Juliette Fitzsimmons, on South Marshfield Avenue. All three women settled into quiet routines. They knew they were being watched.

Purvis searched for a way to make his agents less noticeable. There was a gas station across from the Fitzsimmons home, and he pressed the owner to let an agent work there. On Tuesday, May 29, three days after Helen's release, Purvis called on the man, and was stunned when he mentioned he had seen Nelson visiting his wife the day before. Nelson had circled the block four times, apparently looking for surveillance, then walked right up to the building and gone inside.[7]

This was too much for Hoover. He fired off an ominously worded letter to Purvis. "I am becoming quite concerned over some of these developments in the Chicago district," Hoover wrote Purvis. "We have had too many instances where surveillances have not been properly conducted, and where persons under surveillance have been able to avoid the same . . . I cannot continue to tolerate action of investigators that permits leads to remain uncovered, or at least improperly covered. It is imperative that you exercise the proper supervision over the handling of this case."[8]

Purvis's position deteriorated further that same day when a Chicago newspaper reported that Eddie Green's widow had arrived in the city and was talking with the FBI. When a Hoover aide questioned Purvis about the leak, Purvis said the reporter had probably "concocted" it. "It's strange they should concoct the truth," Hoover scrawled on a memo.[9] Hoover had just sent a terse wire to Purvis requesting an explanation when a rash of articles the next morning quoted Purvis saying he thought Dillinger was dead. Once again Hoover demanded an explanation. Once again Purvis insisted it was all a product of reporters' imaginations. "I would not have made such a statement to the effect that John Dillinger is dead because, primarily, I do not believe that he is dead," Purvis wrote Hoover.[10]

For Hoover the turning point came the next night, Thursday, May 31, the same day Dillinger had his facial bandages removed across town. The agents watching Helen Gillis were staying in an apartment across the street. Purvis had put Ed Hollis in charge. It was a problematic stakeout from the outset, as "[Helen] is quite aware that she is being followed at all times," Purvis wrote Hoover. Still, he assured him, "This matter is receiving my closest attention."[11]

What was needed, Purvis decided, was someone who could gain Helen's trust. His choice for the assignment was a poor one, a Michigan City parolee named George Nelson. A convicted swindler, Nelson claimed he had known Dillinger in prison; he further claimed Baby Face Nelson had "stolen" his name. Purvis agreed to pay Nelson $20 a day. That Thursday night he dispatched him to the building on Marshfield Avenue.

From their position across the street, Hollis and the other agents watched as George Nelson drove up. As he did, Helen and Jean Delaney emerged from the building. Nelson approached the women, saying he was a messenger sent by Dillinger and Baby Face Nelson. Neither woman knew him, however, and both would later say they assumed he was an FBI plant. Helen and Delaney then walked around a corner, where Helen disappeared into a movie theater. Nelson followed.

Rather than tail the women themselves, Hollis and his men decided to wait, assuming they would return shortly. When there was no sign of them after fifteen minutes, the agents scrambled down to the street and jogged around the corner. There they saw Nelson sitting in his car. To their surprise, Nelson recognized them and came over to talk. He said Helen was in the theater and assured them he had the situation in hand. He didn't. Hol-

lis and his men returned to their apartment and waited for the women to return. At dawn they were still waiting.[12]*

The women were gone. Purvis passed the bad news to Hoover in a
phone call Saturday morning, June 2. Later that day Hoover took aside one
of his top aides, an agent named Sam Cowley. It was time to make some
changes, he said. Cowley, who had spent the last year riding a desk at FBI
headquarters, was being sent to Chicago to assume command of the Dillinger case.

Samuel P. Cowley, who would emerge as the unlikely star in the third act of
Hoover's War on Crime, was everything Melvin Purvis was not: sad-eyed,
quiet, stern, jowly, clerkish, the very face of the faceless Washington bureaucrat. Cowley came from a prominent Mormon family in Utah. His
father, Mathias, was one of the international church's twelve governing
apostles until forced to resign in 1903, when Cowley was four. The problem
was Mathias's devotion to polygamy, which the church had outlawed.
Growing up, young Sam Cowley belonged to one of four separate families
Mathias created with four separate wives.

After graduating from high school in 1916, Cowley served as a Mormon
missionary in Hawaii; he spoke fluent Hawaiian. Returning home in 1920
he attended Utah Agricultural College, played on the football team, and in
the summers worked as a salesman peddling knit goods across Nebraska
and the Dakotas. He wanted to be a lawyer, but at the time Utah had no law
school. He was accepted instead at Hoover's alma mater, George Washington University, in 1925.

On graduating in 1929, Cowley wanted to practice law in Utah, but
couldn't find a job. As a stopgap he applied to the FBI, telling his family he
would return west when the economy improved. He was accepted as a special agent. He was twenty-nine. In the next three years Cowley was shuffled
through FBI offices in Detroit, Chicago, Butte, Salt Lake City, and finally
Los Angeles, where he met and married a Utah girl, Lavon Chipman. He
was a solid, industrious investigator, nothing special, distinguishing himself

* News of Helen Gillis's disappearance did not surface in the Chicago papers for three weeks. When it
did, on June 22, Ed Tamm called Sam Cowley and told him to deny the story.

mostly in clerical duties; he peppered Washington with suggestions to improve the Bureau's filing system.

Impressed, Hoover transferred him to headquarters in October 1932, putting him on the new kidnap desk. At five-feet-nine and 170 pounds, with an oatmeal complexion and baggy suits, Cowley was often underestimated. "This employee is frankly rather umimpressive in certain personal characteristics, which is accentuated by his thoughtlessness or carelessness in the selection of his tailor," a reviewing officer wrote of Cowley in early 1934. Still, the reviewer went on, he "has acquired considerable poise and self-confidence . . . This employee has a habit of consistently doing things right."

Bland but hardworking, Cowley was at his desk early in the morning, late at night, Sundays and holidays. He was a memo-writing machine, capable of condensing a towering stack of files into a single crisp page; he was so deskbound, in fact, he never bothered to qualify on the Bureau's new pistol range. Vincent Hughes, the director of investigations, noticed Cowley's appetite for work and made him his assistant in late 1933. This drew Cowley into the thick of the War on Crime. He spent hours each day on the phone with the field offices, relaying their tips, leads, needs, and concerns to Hoover.

His work was so impressive that when Hughes dropped dead in January 1934—overwork, some said—Cowley inherited his job. His workload mushroomed, to the detriment of his young family. When his wife gave birth to their second son that March, Cowley couldn't make it to the hospital; he was so busy, in fact, he couldn't find time to name the boy. Lavon joked that if he didn't come up with a name soon she would name the child "Junior."[13] By May, as Hoover was souring on Purvis, Cowley had emerged as one of the director's most trusted aides; hundreds of calls from SACs in the Bremer and Dillinger cases passed through his typewriter on the way to the director's desk.

No announcement about Cowley's appointment to supervise Purvis was made, publicly or privately, which would lead to years of confusion over Cowley's role; in the months to come, newspaper accounts would repeatedly refer to him as "Purvis's chief assistant." At least initially, Purvis was told that Cowley's assignment to Chicago was a kind of inspection tour, a chance for Hoover's main aide to assess the organization Purvis had built to apprehend Dillinger.

But the truth was obvious to everyone the moment Cowley arrived in Chicago. "No one said anything, but we all knew," Doris Rogers remembers. "It was on the office grapevine, you know, just whispering and glances. 'Cowley is coming.' You just nodded. We knew what that meant. You knew it without being told."

Cowley wasted no time taking charge. After a morning flight from Washington on Sunday, June 3, he was at the Bankers Building by noon. When he reached the nineteenth floor Purvis wasn't there, so he busied himself debriefing the agents responsible for losing Helen Gillis. It was shoddy work, and Cowley said so. When Purvis arrived he tried to defend his men, but Cowley decreed the surveillance a failure. Of the fourteen agents assigned to the Dillinger case, four were watching Nelson's sister's home. Cowley immediately designated three for reassignment.

From all appearances, Purvis accepted his demotion without comment. But from the tone of their memoranda it's clear there was little warmth between the two; in his 1936 book, *American Agent,* Purvis tellingly fails to mention either Cowley or his own demotion.* "You could see the strain on their faces," Doris Rogers recalls. "I felt sorry for Cowley. He was just doing his job. He was as ill at ease as Purvis. When you looked at Cowley, and you looked at Purvis, we all knew the fix was in. There was a sense Melvin had been betrayed. We all felt betrayed, defeated. You could see it by the way [Purvis] walked, by the way he wore his hat. A little hunched, a little bit shoulders. We all felt under siege. The enemy was moving in. The friends we had [in Washington] had all turned to enemies."

On the nineteenth floor, morale sagged. It wasn't just that Purvis's men were exhausted, that their loyalty to Washington was shaken. The nature of their jobs had changed. Few sought a career in law enforcement. For most the FBI was to be a temporary job, a postcollege adventure, something to do till the Depression ended and real jobs beckoned. They hadn't signed up to be killed. Doris Rogers was dating several of the agents, and many confided their doubts to her.

"When the feeling came that Purvis was being undermined, every agent in the office would have resigned if he could," she remembers. "It wasn't just loyalty to Melvin. By that time the agents were all tired, worn out. They wished they were home jerking sodas in a drugstore. They would have done anything to get out. They were being thrown into situations where they

---

* It is not clear from FBI files how or when Purvis learned of his demotion. The files contain a single mention of a trip Purvis made to Washington that week; presumably it was then that Hoover explained the changes to him.

could get killed. None of them asked for that. It wouldn't get them a Medal of Honor. It would only get them dead. They knew that. This was not their goal in life. The sense was, 'What are we doing in this dreadful job?'"

Tension hung thick that Sunday afternoon as Cowley and Purvis drove to Fort Wayne to assess Purvis's second major surveillance, at the Audrey Russ home. It, too, had degenerated into a fiasco. The three agents had actually moved from the Russ home to a hotel twelve miles away because the combative Mrs. Russ was expecting houseguests; she had graciously consented to telephone if Dillinger appeared. After an all-night debriefing, Cowley ordered the agents back to Chicago. He and Purvis returned to the Bankers Building at 5:15 A.M.[14]

Cowley, whose capacity for work appeared boundless, spent Monday reviewing the rest of Purvis's apparatus, quizzing him on the efficacy of informants and getting up to speed on the Bremer case, on which six agents were working full-time. That night he drove to Indianapolis, where the next morning he toured the Mooresville area with Earl Connelley; Connelley had sixteen agents on the ground around Indianapolis, watching the Dillinger farmhouse and other family homes, two more men in Dayton and another in Columbus, Ohio. Cowley was skeptical Connelley's stakeouts could accomplish anything. "[Cowley] remarked that they have had the covers there for a month or six weeks," Hoover wrote in a memo that night, "and it is hardly believable that it is not known, and it is likewise hardly believable that [Dillinger is] going to contact [them] when they know this."[15]

Still, Cowley told Hoover he could see no changes worth making. Hoover liked what he heard. For the first time in weeks, he seemed pleased. Two days later he phoned Cowley and, as he wrote in a memo, "advised that I was of the opinion that the [new] situation at Chicago would work out all right, and that I had told Mr. Purvis that until we complete the Dillinger investigation I wanted Mr. Cowley to take complete charge."[16]

While Cowley assumed command, Purvis's run of bad luck continued. Pete Pierpont's old girlfriend, Mary Kinder, had gotten engaged, and Connelley had befriended her fiancé; the boy told him Kinder expected to meet Dillinger soon. That Tuesday, Purvis drove down to the town of Mishawaka, where agents had trailed Kinder to a shack where Pierpont's parents were opening a barbecue stand. Purvis and his men watched the building until midnight when, to their dismay, a convoy of eight police cars drove up. Out spilled a dozen cops in bulletproof vests; rifles raised, they demanded to know who Purvis was. Sheepishly Purvis explained, apologizing for his failure to notify authorities he was in the area. Afterward he trudged to a phone to once again break bad news to Washington. "Mr. Purvis stated that of course the matter is 'shot' from our point of view," an aide wrote Hoover, "and I approved his suggestion that it be turned over to the police to cover. I told him to caution the police, however, to give the matter no publicity."[17]

On the Sunday Sam Cowley arrived in Chicago, Van Meter followed Dillinger into the brave new world of cosmetic surgery. He paid $5,000 for it. Once again Dr. Loeser came to Probasco's house to perform the procedure, with Harold Cassidy assisting. This time everything went smoothly. Loeser slit open Van Meter's nose, flattening a bump and removing tissue from the bulb. After cutting down the size of Van Meter's upper lip, Loeser used acid to remove the "Hope" tattoo on his right forearm. Apparently, no one viewed this as a bad omen.

Two mornings later Loeser returned and used a hydrochloric acid solution to remove both Van Meter's and Dillinger's fingerprints. Dillinger endured the treatment in silence, grimacing, beads of sweat appearing on his forehead. Van Meter cursed loudly, dancing around the room, flapping his hands in an effort to fight the pain. Afterward Baby Face Nelson dropped by, plopping on a living room couch to smirk at his partners' faces. "So you two decided to go out and buy yourselves a pair of new mugs," he cracked. "Maybe you needed them."

"At least I'll be able to go out on the street and get around now," Dillinger said.[18]

At one point, Piquett dropped by and told Dillinger he needed cash to pay attorneys who had helped represent Billie Frechette at her trial in St. Paul; as expected, she had drawn a yearlong sentence in a federal women's prison. Dillinger sent O'Leary to his father for the money. On Wednesday night, June 6, O'Leary checked into the Claypool Hotel in Indianapolis. The next morning he found Hubert Dillinger at his filling station. Hubert cocked his head in the direction of Art McGinnis, the FBI informant who had been loitering around the station for over a month. "Be careful what you say," Hubert said.

"What's that rat doing here?" O'Leary asked.

"I want him around where I can keep an eye on him."

"I have a note from Johnnie for your dad," O'Leary said.[19]

Telling McGinnis that O'Leary was an FBI agent who wanted to see his father, Hubert drove him out to the Dillinger farmhouse in Mooresville. John Dillinger, Sr., met them at the roadside. O'Leary handed him the note. It read in part:

Dad:

I got here all right and find I still have some friends that won't sell me out. Would like to have stayed longer at the house. I enjoyed seeing your [sic] and the girls so much. I have been over lots of country but home always looks good to me . . . This sure keeps a fellow moving. I will be leaving soon and you will not need worry any more. Tell the girls hello. Hope everybody is well.

JOHNNIE[20]

"How is Johnnie?" Mr. Dillinger asked.

"He's fine, Mr. Dillinger," O'Leary said.

The elder Dillinger walked out to his barn. After a moment he returned with a package wrapped in newspaper. Inside, O'Leary found $3,000; it was the money Dillinger had given his father after the Fostoria robbery. "If you see Johnnie when you get back," Hubert told O'Leary, "mention to him that Art McGinnis is at the filling station with me."[21] O'Leary promised he would.

There is no indication in FBI files that agents watching the Dillinger home noted O'Leary's visit; if they had, they might have followed him back to Jimmy Probasco's house in Chicago that night. Art McGinnis, however, had his suspicions. The next day, Earl Connelley called Washington to report "that some private individual endeavoring to locate Dillinger has represented himself as a Government Officer, in contacting John Dillinger's half-brother, Hubert. Mr. Connelley states that he has an informant advising that an unknown person took Hubert away for several hours yesterday and talked to him."[22] The FBI never learned the person's identity; presumably, this was O'Leary.

When he returned to Chicago that night, O'Leary found Dillinger at Probasco's house, pacing from room to room in a foul mood. They had heard the news on the radio, he said. It was Tommy Carroll.

Waterloo, Iowa
Thursday, June 7

Carroll and his girlfriend Jean Delaney had taken a trip through Iowa, intending to end up at Delaney's parents' home in St. Paul. After spending the night outside Cedar Rapids, they were cruising through the town of Waterloo when they had car trouble and stopped at a filling station to have the car serviced. Afterward, about lunchtime, a Waterloo police detective named Emil Steffen took a call from the station's mechanic, who said he had just worked on a bronze Hudson and had seen a rifle and a collection of license plates beneath a floor mat. He said the driver looked like a "tough customer."

Detective Steffen grabbed another officer, P. E. Walker, and went cruising the streets of Waterloo, looking for the car. They couldn't find it, and after an hour or so returned to the police station downtown. There, parked across the street, they saw the car. They pulled up beside it and waited. After a bit they saw a young man and a pretty blonde approach the car. As the detectives watched, Carroll opened the passenger door of the Hudson, allowing Delaney to slide in. Then he walked around to the driver's-side door.

The detectives stepped out of their car. "Hey!" Officer Walker said. "Just a minute there. Who are you?"

"Who are you?" Carroll said.

"Police officers," Walker said.

Carroll took a step backward and reached beneath his coat. Thinking he was going for a gun, Walker charged. Just as Carroll drew his pistol, Walker swung his fist and smashed him in the nose. Carroll fell onto his rear, by the curb. In an instant he was up, the gun in his right hand. He ran onto the sidewalk. Detective Steffen drew his revolver and fired. From a distance of about fifteen feet, his bullet struck Carroll beneath the left armpit. Delaney screamed.

Dropping his gun, Carroll stumbled away from the sidewalk, into an alley. Detective Steffen set his feet and fired three times; two of the bullets struck home. Carroll fell on his side in the alley.

Steffen ran up. Standing over the fallen man, he demanded to know his name. "Tommy Carroll," he rasped. Carroll refused to answer any more questions. "I got seven hundred dollars on me," he said. "Be sure the little girl gets it. She doesn't know what it's all about."

They placed Jean Delaney under arrest and took Carroll to the hospital.

Two agents from the St. Paul office made it to the hospital that afternoon. Doctors said Carroll didn't have long. The agents stood over his hospital bed and fired questions at him for forty-five minutes, but it was no use. Tommy Carroll died at 6:55 that evening.[23]

Closeted at Jimmy Probasco's house, Dillinger and Van Meter had sharply different reactions to their friend's passing. Van Meter swore he would never die like that, gunned down in some filthy alley, and the rest of his career he did his best to stay out of public view.

Not Dillinger. Once his wrappings were removed, he wanted nothing more than to taste life. The day after Carroll's death, Friday, June 8, Dillinger decided to attend a Chicago Cubs baseball game at Wrigley Field. Piquett went with him, and later said he saw John Stege of the Chicago police's Dillinger Squad there as well. "Fuzz,"[24] Piquett whispered to Dillinger outside the ballpark. "Big fuzz."

If Dillinger worried about being seen, he rarely showed it. By all accounts, he appeared intoxicated by his ability to circulate among the crowds without being recognized. Later, some would attribute this to his "new face," others to his burgeoning ego. By that weekend Dillinger was feeling well enough to visit a Chicago nightclub, and he may have visited a whorehouse. By the following Monday, June 11, he had met a pretty waitress named Polly Hamilton and was thinking of seeing more of her.* "That reminds me of Marie," Van Meter remarked, mentioning his former girlfriend, Mickey Conforti, whom he hadn't seen since abandoning her at Little Bohemia two months earlier.[25]

By Wednesday morning, June 13, Van Meter was feeling chipper enough to go in search of his old flame. He rose early, put on his best dark suit and white shoes, then added his latest bit of disguise, a set of delicate pince-nez eyeglasses, attached by a long black ribbon to his vest. Thus attired, he walked outside and slid behind the wheel of his maroon Ford sedan. Reuniting with Mickey Conforti, he knew, was a calculated risk. The FBI had been watching her for weeks.

---

* On June 11 Dillinger accompanied Hamilton to the Chicago medical examiner's downtown office, where she received injections and filled out papers necessary for a new waitressing job. That visit, and three others to the same office, were disclosed by the *Chicago Daily Times* after Dillinger's death.

. . .

The death of Tommy Carroll gave Hoover's men their first new batch of clues in weeks. None came from Jean Delaney; the morning after Carroll's death, agents questioned her till 4:15 A.M., but she said little of use. Even the persuasive Hugh Clegg got nothing out of her. She was sentenced to a year and a day and shipped to the federal women's prison in West Virginia.

The clues were in Carroll's luggage, a black leather Gladstone bag. Two of the dead man's dress shirts were still in wrappers from a laundry in suburban Niles Center.* When the owner was shown a photo of Carroll, she identified him as one of her customers; he'd only been in a few times. Shown photos of other Dillinger and Barker Gang members, she identified Baby Face Nelson as Carroll's friend, "Mr. Cody," a "nice young man" who had been bringing in his laundry since early May. Once, she remembered, when he arrived to pick up a load of shirts that wasn't yet ready, he snapped his fingers and remarked that he had driven fifty miles to pick it up.

Despite some progress, Cowley still had a lot to learn. His worst mistake was taking his men off Mickey Conforti. Conforti knew she was being watched; Cowley thought it a waste of time to keep her under surveillance when she was unlikely to contact Van Meter. He was wrong. On the night of June 14 his office received a call from Conforti's foster mother. Conforti had disappeared.

Cowley could kick himself. Van Meter had simply approached one of Conforti's girlfriends, sending her to Conforti's house with the message he wanted to reunite. She had thrown some things in an overnight bag, met him on a corner, and vanished. Two weeks to the day after Purvis had let Baby Face Nelson retrieve his wife—the debacle that prompted Cowley's reassignment—Cowley had done the same thing. The last known link to the Dillinger Gang had slipped from his hands.

Losing Mickey Conforti was bad enough. But Cowley's most inexplicable oversight in those sultry days of June was his failure to put a tail on Louis Piquett. Cowley's men had investigated Piquett's background, dredging up

---

* Now the suburb of Skokie, Illinois.

bits of dirt on his involvement in various stock swindles. They had interviewed his former secretary Esther Anderson, the woman who turned Dillinger away after his Crown Point escape; Anderson wasn't asked about that day's events and she didn't volunteer anything. Through it all, Piquett was allowed to roam free.*

As a result, Piquett and Art O'Leary were able to continue tending to Dillinger's needs right under the FBI's noses. The two visited Probasco's house every few days. Piquett was brimming with schemes to cash in on Dillinger's notoriety. He offered a reporter for the *Chicago American* an interview with Dillinger for $50,000; the paper declined. Piquett and the paper also discussed the possibility of the *American* handling Dillinger's surrender. Dillinger was game for anything short of surrender, even an autobiography; Piquett said he would bring in a tape recorder so Dillinger could record his memories.

Dillinger was most excited by the idea of a movie. Piquett proposed that they purchase cameras and recording equipment and have Dillinger and Van Meter filmed lecturing on the evils of crime.

"I'll give out a message to the youth of America!" Van Meter enthused.

"No, that's not the idea, Van," Dillinger said. "We just want to tell them that crime does not pay."

"Well," Van Meter said, "you tell them that crime does not pay, and I'll give my talk to the youth of America."[26]

When he wasn't discussing these and other pipe dreams, Dillinger spent much of his time in Probasco's living room reading newspapers. Van Meter, who wasn't a reader, spent hours hunched over the police band of Probasco's radio, avidly relaying items he heard to Dillinger. They chuckled over the stream of bogus sightings the FBI and Chicago police were forced to pursue. There were reports Dillinger had been seen in Kentucky, in Wisconsin, even hiding in the Ozark Mountains with Pretty Boy Floyd. For the most part, Dillinger just laughed. He only lost his temper when the radio carried the spurious news that the attorney general had issued orders that he be shot on sight.

When O'Leary came by the house that night, Dillinger handed him a slip of paper. On it he had scribbled the home addresses of Melvin Purvis and Agent Harold Reinecke, who had earned Dillinger's ire after news-

---

* The Bureau had made a stab at tailing Piquett on May 19 but had given up the surveillance after barely two days. Apparently it took too many men.

paper reports that he had browbeat Billie Frechette while she was in FBI custody. "I want you to check up on these addresses and see that they're right," Dillinger said. O'Leary went to Piquett. Harboring was one thing, murder another. Piquett confronted Dillinger the next day. "Just what are you planning to do, Johnnie?" he asked.

"They're out to kill me, aren't they?" Dillinger said. "Why should I sit around and wait for it? We're going to be parked outside their houses one of these nights and get them before they get us."

"Don't you realize what a stunt like this would mean?" Piquett said. "They'd call out the army and place the town under martial law, and hang me from a lamppost."

Piquett won the argument, but in it lay the seeds of a rift between the two men. It widened when Dillinger and Van Meter playfully warned Piquett they were planning to rob "all the banks" in his Wisconsin hometown. Piquett didn't get the joke. Losing his temper, he swore—as he did over the idea of assassinating Purvis—that if Dillinger went forward, "you and I will be through."[27]

Nor was Piquett too excited about Dillinger's forays into the streets of Chicago. He was going out almost every night now, days as well. He took in another Cubs game or two, revisited the World's Fair, and apparently began regular trips to a North Side whorehouse. No one seemed to notice him. Dillinger further disguised his appearance by dying his hair black, growing a mustache, and buying a pair of gold-rim wire spectacles. After the dark weeks spent in the red panel truck, his confidence was growing. Van Meter, who had rented Mickey Conforti a room on the South Side, thought Dillinger was nuts for cavorting so openly and said so. "You're going to get it one of these days, running around so much," he chided.[28]

The subject arose again on June 23, when Homer Cummings announced a new $15,000 in rewards for Dillinger's capture. Nelson warranted only $7,500. "Looks like my price is going up," Dillinger joked to Van Meter. "Watch Jimmy burn when he finds the government put a cheaper price tag on him than on me. And you, Van, you don't rate at all."

"Nuts to you," Van Meter said. "You just better watch out that someone doesn't cash in on that reward."

At the Bankers Building, Cowley had agents on half a dozen stakeouts. He asked Washington for more men and got them. Eight agents had been added to the Dillinger Squad that month, bringing the total in Chicago to twenty-two. Still, by Wednesday, June 27, Cowley was no closer to catching Dillinger than when he arrived three weeks before. That day he held a strategy conference at the Bankers Building. Earl Connelley drove up from Indianapolis, Hugh Clegg came down from St. Paul, and a headquarters supervisor named Ed Tamm flew out from Washington.

They debated every lead and reassessed every stakeout. In Indiana, Connelley's agents were watching a dozen places, while Connelley himself was keeping in regular touch with the informant Art McGinnis. Tamm argued they should increase the pressure on the Dillinger family. Clegg's agents were launching raids all around the Twin Cities; that same day they had their first success, picking up Harry Sawyer's bartender, Pat Reilly, who had been at Little Bohemia. Reilly prompted a flurry of news articles by stating he thought Dillinger was dead. Reporters flocked out to Mooresville to see John Dillinger, Sr., who assured them his son was still very much alive.

Cowley's most promising stakeout was back at the Audrey Russ home in Fort Wayne; the Russes were insisting that Van Meter would return any day. Reversing himself, Cowley stationed four men there around the clock, including two of his best new marksmen, the Cowboys Charles Winstead and Clarence Hurt, who passed the days dodging the wrath of the combative Mrs. Russ.[29] For the moment, Cowley was satisfied. They had agents working half the towns between Indianapolis and Chicago. Unfortunately, none were in the northern Indiana city of South Bend, which is where Dillinger struck that Saturday.

Dillinger's robbery of the Merchants National Bank in South Bend was probably the most chaotic and confusing episode of his career. Among the few things known for sure is that the planning took place at a remote schoolhouse in Nelson's territory, the northwest Chicago suburbs.* Several nights that June, Van Meter and Dillinger drove out to the school to meet Nelson, who was usually accompanied by his growing band of acolytes, now including his California pal Johnny Chase; the rotund Bay Area bouncer Fatso Negri; his childhood friend, the racketeer Jack Perkins; and a

* The schoolhouse, which no longer exists, stood two miles north of the intersection of State Highways 53 and 62 (now Algonquin Road), in the town of Arlington Heights.

Chicago mechanic Nelson knew from his racing days named Clarey Lieder.* Only Negri was to give accounts of these meetings, and his versions changed over the years.†

To this day, no one is certain exactly who took part in the South Bend robbery. Eyewitnesses variously counted four, five, or six robbers; most versions put the number at five. Dillinger, Van Meter, and Nelson were confirmed participants. Jack Perkins was later tried and acquitted of joining them. It's possible, if unlikely, that the fourth and fifth robbers that day were Johnny Chase and Fatso Negri.

The most intriguing theory about the other robbers' identities has long centered on Pretty Boy Floyd and his sidekick Adam Richetti, whose disappearance had been so complete the FBI had not fielded a confirmed sighting of the pair in a year. One eyewitness firmly identified Floyd as the dark-complexioned "fat man" who worked alongside Dillinger in South Bend that day. Floyd's involvement was suggested months later by Fatso Negri, who told the FBI he overheard gang members say they would be working with a "big-name Southwestern outlaw." If it was Floyd, it's conceivable he contacted Dillinger via Richetti, who served time in Indiana's Pendleton Reformatory. It's also possible Negri concocted the story to cover his own involvement.

Whoever accompanied Dillinger that day, it's clear that tensions were rising between members of the gang. As usual, Nelson was the irritant. He thought Dillinger and Van Meter were living far too openly, and he repeatedly said so. This led to an angry confrontation at the schoolhouse one night between Nelson and Van Meter, after Nelson discovered Van Meter had reunited with Mickey Conforti, whom Nelson deemed untrustworthy. As Negri put it:

> Jimmie [Nelson] got into an argument with Van Meter, something about his living with a girl and he said the girl is no good and Van Me-

---

* It was Lieder who stowed Dillinger's red panel truck in his garage that May. At the same time, he sold Van Meter his new maroon Ford.
† Negri was thoroughly debriefed by the FBI after his capture in December 1934. He gave the Bureau only fragmentary accounts of the South Bend planning meetings. In 1941 Negri co-authored a series of lurid articles on Baby Face Nelson's career in *Master Detective* magazine. In these articles, he elaborated considerably. Unfortunately, many of these details, including a tale of a Dillinger visit and aborted raid on Nevada's Hoover Dam, are clearly figments of his imagination. The author has accepted Negri's accounts only where they parallel what he told the FBI in 1934 and 1935.

ter said the girl is good, and Johnnie [Chase] said [to me], "Let's take a walk," and I take a walk because I expected [shooting] any minute. And so they settled it and after awhile Johnnie was telling me, he says that Van Meter promised Jimmie that he was going to hit his girl—bump her off . . . The argument got so hot that I could pretty near hear everything . . . [Van Meter] promised Jimmie that he was going to hit that girl and that if he didn't, I think Jimmy will kill him . . . I thought there was going to be an awful shooting scrap there.[30]

The anecdote illustrates Nelson's renowned volatility and the lengths Dillinger and Van Meter would go to humor him; there's no suggestion Van Meter ever seriously considered killing Marie Conforti. It was in this emotional climate that the gang debated its next target. According to Negri, they studied several banks in Illinois and Indiana before eventually choosing the bank in South Bend. Van Meter had reconnoitered it that week, wearing his pince-nez. On Friday night, June 29, the gang made final plans at a meeting at the schoolhouse, checking their guns and bulletproof vests. They would need them.

South Bend, Indiana
Saturday, June 30

It was a hot, bright summer morning when the gang's car pulled up just past the intersection of Wayne and Michigan Streets in the heart of downtown South Bend at 11:30 A.M. Trolleys rattled up and down Michigan Avenue. The sidewalks were thronged with shoppers. Out in the intersection a twenty-nine-year-old policeman named Howard Wagner was directing traffic. An amateur boxer named Alex Slaby had just parked his car on Wayne Street when a brown Hudson pulled alongside him, double-parking. Slaby watched as four men jumped out. One looked familiar. He wore overalls, a straw boater, and a handkerchief over his right hand. As Slaby stared, trying to place him, Dillinger drew back the handkerchief and thrust a pistol toward him. "You better scram," Dillinger said.

Slaby watched, stunned, as Dillinger and two of the others disappeared around the corner, toward the Merchants Bank. With a start, he realized the bank was about to be robbed. Slaby got out of his car, studying the waiting Hudson, whose engine was idling, and began to reach for the keys, which dangled in the ignition.

"What are you doing?" a voice said. Slaby turned and saw a young blond-haired man in front of the car, a machine gun barely hidden beneath his suit coat. It was Nelson. "Nothing," Slaby said. He walked off unmolested, heading to a pay phone to summon police.

Around the corner, Van Meter pulled out a rifle and stationed himself at the bank's front door while Dillinger and the unidentified "fat man" entered the bank. Dillinger wasted no time with niceties that day. Two dozen customers were in the lobby, lining up in front of the teller cages. Dillinger whipped out a Thompson submachine gun and shouted, "This is a holdup!"

Instinctively, most of the customers raised their hands and backed away, lining the walls and inching toward a rear wall. A bank vice president hid below his desk. A group of nine or ten people scampered into a conference room and locked the door. Ignoring them all, Dillinger stalked through a waist-high swinging door and began clearing stacks of cash off the counters. Suddenly another robber—probably the "fat man"—raised his submachine gun and fired a deafening volley into the ceiling. As bits of plaster rained into the lobby, he turned and grinned. Women screamed.

At the sound of gunshots, people on the sidewalks turned their heads. It sounded like firecrackers. Out in the intersection, Officer Wagner heard it, too. He strode toward the bank, his traffic whistle dangling from one hand. Van Meter saw him coming. He raised his rifle and fired. His bullet hit Wagner flush in the chest. The policeman staggered backward, slumping to the pavement even as he grabbed at his holstered pistol. He would be dead in half an hour.

Panic broke out. Everywhere, people were running and screaming. A few doors down Wayne Street, a jeweler named Harry Berg emerged onto the sidewalk carrying a pistol. Spying Nelson holding a submachine gun on the corner, he opened fire. His first bullet hit Nelson square in the chest; Nelson's career might have ended there if not for the bulletproof vest he wore. Stunned, Nelson turned and fired a burst that sent Berg scurrying back into his store. Most of his bullets raked a parked car, shattering the windshield and wounding the man inside. Another man was struck in the stomach by a ricochet. He staggered into the jewelry store and collapsed, badly wounded.

Nelson swung the gun menacingly as people ran for cover. Just then a seventeen-year-old boy named Joseph Pawlowski ran across the intersection and leaped onto Nelson's back. The two grappled for a moment before

Nelson swung his gun butt into Pawlowski's temple, stunning him. The teenager fell to the sidewalk, then ran off.

Alone and vulnerable outside the bank, Van Meter stepped into the Nisley Shoes store and ordered a half-dozen people out onto the sidewalk, where he lined them up before him as a human shield. Three traffic cops, hearing the shots, hustled up Wayne Street and saw the group, their hands in the air. Van Meter fired, sending the cops running for cover behind parked cars.

Just then Dillinger and his unidentified partner emerged from the bank, carrying cloth sacks containing more than $28,000 in cash. With them were three hostages, including the bank president, Delos Cohen. From across the intersection the patrolmen opened fire. Cohen fell, hit in the ankle. Another hostage, a cashier, was hit in the leg.

"I'm shot!" he yelped.

"Keep going," Dillinger said, shoving him forward.

As Dillinger, Van Meter, and the fat man herded the hostages toward the getaway car, a furious gun battle broke out. Shielded by parked cars, the three patrolmen fired again and again. Standing beside the waiting Hudson, Nelson swung his submachine gun, firing wildly, bullets striking store windows and the State Theatre's marquee.

Suddenly Van Meter fell. Dillinger turned and saw blood gushing from his head. Abandoning the two hostages, he grabbed Van Meter beneath the armpits and dragged him into the Hudson. The car was riddled with bullets, and more struck it as it sped away.[31] A half-dozen policemen claimed to have chased the car as it fled west out of South Bend. It was later found abandoned outside the town of Gibsland.

Van Meter was bleeding badly when the gang returned to their rendezvous point at the white schoolhouse that afternoon. Fatso Negri was called, and when he arrived he found Van Meter lying on the ground, covered with blood. As Negri later described the scene to the FBI, "Van Meter is lying down, he is in agony and I think he is dying." Negri wanted to get a doctor, but Nelson said no. Someone suggested they "yaffle," or kidnap, a doctor. Dillinger and Nelson got into a heated argument. Eventually, Dillinger decided to take Van Meter back to Jimmy Probasco's. They could get a doctor there.

Dillinger drove the bleeding Van Meter back into Chicago, pulling up behind Probasco's house after nightfall. Probasco tried to reach the anesthetist, Harold Cassidy, but couldn't. In the doctor's absence, Probasco bandaged Van Meter's wound. The next evening O'Leary and Piquett came by. They found Probasco stalking the apartment, cursing. "Where's that damn Cassidy?" Probasco said. "I called him a dozen times yesterday to come over, and the son of a bitch never showed up. If we had to rely on him, Van Meter would be dead now. It's just lucky I happen to be a pretty good doctor. Here, show them your head."

Van Meter was sitting on a couch, recovering nicely. "I saved your life, didn't I?" Probasco asked him. "Why, I was up all night picking hairs out of that wound."

A little later Cassidy arrived. As Probasco and Van Meter cursed him, he cleaned the wound and rebandaged it. Dillinger regaled the group with the story of the wild shoot-out, dwelling on the story of the Jewish jeweler who had brazenly fired on Nelson. "You know, Johnnie," Van Meter said at one point. "We'll have to go back to South Bend in the next few days and take care of that little Jew."

"Sure we will, Van," Dillinger said, laughing. "Sure we will."

15

THE WOMAN IN ORANGE

July 1 to July 27, 1934

By the weekend of the South Bend robbery, Dillinger had already made up his mind to leave Jimmy Probasco's house. Probasco was a quarrelsome drunk, and Dillinger worried he might let something slip. According to one source, he and Van Meter overheard a telephone conversation in which Probasco had a heated argument with someone, telling him at one point, "I don't care if you bring the cops. Go ahead and see what happens when they get here." Dillinger was not amused. The final straw came on Wednesday, July 4, when he and Van Meter returned to the house and found Piquett and Probasco drinking heavily. Once the two left, the two outlaws packed their things, threw them in Van Meter's car, and never came back.[1]

That same day, July 4, Dillinger moved into an apartment at 2420 North Halsted Street, in a German-immigrant neighborhood on the North Side.* Three other people lived in the apartment, two of them women, and in their shadowy relationships—with each other, with Dillinger, and with an Indiana police detective—lay the seeds of Dillinger's demise. One of the women was Dillinger's new girlfriend Polly Hamilton, a twenty-six-year-old divorcée who waitressed at the S&S Café on Wilson Avenue. The other was Ana Sage, a squat forty-two-year-old Romanian immigrant whose principal

---

* Dillinger knew the neighborhood: the address was one block from the apartment of Billie Frechette's sister, where he had taken refuge the night of his Crown Point escape.

means of support since arriving in America in 1908 had been running a series of brothels.

Precisely how Dillinger came to know Hamilton and Sage has never been explained. For decades the accepted version of events, as advanced by Hamilton in a newspaper article after Dillinger's death, was that she met Dillinger at a Chicago nightclub called the Barrel of Fun, where he introduced himself as a Chicago Board of Trade clerk named Jimmy Lawrence. In fact, it's far more likely that Dillinger met Hamilton through the dowdy Ana Sage, who for years had been a prominent member of the northwest Indiana underworld, a milieu Dillinger knew well. They had at least two mutual friends.

The madame who would go down in criminal lore as "the woman in red" was born Ana Campanas in 1892, in the village of Komlos, Romania, outside the Black Sea port of Costanza. At seventeen she married a man named Mike Chiolek. They emigrated to Chicago, had a son named Steve, and separated in 1917, when Ana was twenty-five. Abandoned with an eight-year-old son, she moved into the Romanian-immigrant community in Indiana Harbor, the lakeside warren of row houses and tumbledown bars that was East Chicago's toughest neighborhood. There she worked as a prostitute and a waitress, eventually landing at the Harbor Bay Inn, where the menu included prostitutes for two dollars a tumble.

When her boss drew a six-month sentence for running afoul of state liquor laws, Ana ran the place herself. She was good at it. Five-feet-seven and a stout 165 pounds, with a thick Eastern European accent, Ana was an imposing presence. With intermittent help from her boss, she turned the inn into Indiana Harbor's preeminent den of inequity. She kept order by cozying up to East Chicago policemen. By all accounts her closest benefactor was a flamboyant, and flamboyantly corrupt, detective named Martin Zarkovich—the same Martin Zarkovich to whom, Dillinger hinted, he had paid protection money.

Zarkovich was a legend in the Harbor. "A fastidious, immaculate peacock," as a latter-day Indiana columnist termed him, Zarkovich cruised the streets of East Chicago in a felt fedora and suits so sharp he earned the nickname "The Sheik."[2] A loyal soldier in a police force whose primary duty was keeping the peace in East Chicago's gambling halls and whorehouses—he was named chief of detectives in 1926—Zarkovich was indicted for corruption three times during the 1920s and was convicted once, of violating Prohibition laws, in 1929. Half of East Chicago's power structure was convicted in the same case, so it was no surprise when "Zark" returned to the force; if anything, his conviction cemented his ties to the Lake County power structure. By the early 1930s, in fact, Zarkovich knew everyone who mattered in northwest Indiana politics and many who didn't, from William Murray, Dillinger's trial judge at Crown Point, to Louis Piquett's investigator, Art O'Leary. O'Leary had known Zarkovich for years.

Ana Campanas came to know Martin Zarkovich in her earliest days in East Chicago. According to Mrs. Zarkovich's divorce papers, filed in 1920, she apparently knew the detective a bit too well; Mrs. Zarkovich named Ana in her complaint, charging she had "overly friendly" relations with her husband. Zarkovich remained Ana's protector after she opened her first brothel in neighboring Gary in 1921. By 1923 she was doing so well she rented an entire hotel, the forty-six-room Kostur. It was by all accounts a riotous place, hosting so many gun- and knife-fights that police dubbed it "The Bucket of Blood." Ana, doing business as "Katie Brown," became known as "Kostur House Katie."

Zarkovich's ties to the Lake County establishment helped Ana weather a half-dozen prostitution arrests. She was convicted on two occasions, but both were pardoned by the Indiana governor. Her luck finally ran out in 1932 when, after yet another conviction, the new reform governor, Paul McNutt, refused her request for a pardon. The "Bucket of Blood" closed down and Ana, ominously, was referred to federal immigration authorities for deportation.

Defeated, she withdrew to Chicago, where she had been commuting since at least 1928, following her marriage to a fellow Romanian immigrant named Alexander Suciu, who Anglicized his last name to Sage. Now Ana Sage, she had enough money saved to buy an apartment building in Chicago's Uptown section, which may or may not have functioned as a brothel. When the Sages separated in 1933, the building was sold, and Ana, after shuffling through a series of apartments, washed up in the one on North Halsted in late June 1934, a part-time madame whose long-running deportation proceedings weighed on her mind.

One of her friends was Polly Hamilton, a girl from North Dakota who had moved to Gary during the 1920s, marrying and divorcing a local cop while working for Sage in some capacity at the Kostur Hotel. Hamilton's role at Sage's apartment on North Halsted is similarly unclear. Virtually every account of the Dillinger affair describes her as a waitress. But more than once, FBI records refer to Hamilton as a prostitute, suggesting that

Sage was using her apartment as a call house, and Hamilton was moon-lighting as a whore; Dillinger, in fact, may have met her while procuring her services. Sage later admitted to the FBI she let prostitutes use the spare rooms of her various apartments, and had done so as late as that June. FBI documents suggest Hamilton kept a separate residence in a Chicago hotel, but from at least July 1 on, she lived with Ana Sage. The apartment's third occupant was Sage's twenty-three-year-old unemployed son, Steve.

How did Dillinger come to meet Ana Sage? Though there is no concrete evidence to back it up, the most plausible explanation is that they were in-troduced by Martin Zarkovich, who knew both Sage and Dillinger's inter-mediary, Art O'Leary. There is considerable evidence Zarkovich knew Dillinger as well. In interviews after Dillinger's death, Zarkovich portrayed himself as a gallant detective obsessed with bringing Dillinger to justice for the murder of his friend, Patrick O'Malley, during the East Chicago bank robbery that January. Zarkovich said he had taken time off his job to pur-sue Dillinger single-handedly.

That may be. But for months *someone* had been lending aid to Dillinger in East Chicago, securing the shack where he stayed briefly that May, among other things. Dillinger hinted to Art O'Leary that it was Zarkovich, calling him "Zark." As we have seen, without explicitly stating that Zar-kovich had helped him, Dillinger told O'Leary that Zarkovich had been re-sponsible for the May 24 murders of the two East Chicago detectives.* Yet as intriguing as the links between Dillinger and Zarkovich appear, there is no irrefutable evidence that Zarkovich was the outlaw's contact in East Chicago, or that he arranged for Dillinger to stay in Ana Sage's apartment. The FBI, the one entity that could have discerned the truth, never tried. For reasons that will soon be clear, the Bureau had no interest in investi-gating Zarkovich.

What is certain is that by late June, Dillinger was spending a lot of time with Ana Sage's girlfriend, Polly Hamilton, who would later insist, despite considerable evidence to the contrary, that she never knew that her new

---

* A number of latter-day Dillinger enthusiasts have theorized that in this role Zarkovich aided Dillinger at several key moments in his career, providing the shack that May and suggesting the robbery of the East Chicago bank in January. It's even been speculated it was Zarkovich who smuggled the wooden gun to Dillinger at Crown Point. The notion is not altogether far-fetched; FBI records indicate Zarkovich visited Dillinger at the jail. After Dillinger's escape Zarkovich did become deeply involved in the escape investi-gation, a fact some found curious. "I never could understand why Zarkovich was so active in the grand jury investigation," Judge William Murray told the *Chicago Tribune* later that summer. "He practically wore a path between the grand jury room and [the prosecutor's] office."

boyfriend "Jimmy Lawrence" was the country's most-wanted man. Dillinger fell hard for Hamilton, the first woman to take his mind off Billie Frechette. In those warm days of early July, theirs was an endless whirl of Cubs games, amusement parks, and movies by day, dinners and dance clubs by night. Dillinger was polite and flush with cash, though Hamilton thought it strange he always wore the same light-gray suit; Dillinger explained he simply wore the same clothes until he grew tired of them, then threw them out. When she asked about the fresh scars on his face, he said he had been in an automobile accident.

They took taxis everywhere. At Riverview Park, where Dillinger insisted they ride the same roller-coasters again and again, he would scream on the downslopes and kiss her on the curves; he was so adept at the shooting galleries, other customers lined up to watch him. At the Grand Terrace and French Casino nightclubs they were usually among the first on the dance floor; Dillinger liked dancing the carioca, and would ask the orchestra leaders to play him one. When his favorite songs were played—"All I Do Is Dream of You" or "For All We Know"—he would lean in close and sing lightly in Hamilton's ear. He didn't drink much, a gin fizz or two, and every night before retiring, he insisted they stop for a hot dog. Dillinger called Hamilton "Contessa" or "Countess" and on her birthday bought her an amethyst ring. She gave him a gold ring with an inscription inside—WITH ALL MY LOVE, POLLY—and a watch with her picture tucked in the back.

On Sunday, July 1, when Sage moved into the apartment on North Halsted, Hamilton moved in, too. Three days later Dillinger joined them. Sage gave him two keys, to his room and to a closet, where he stowed his guns and a bulletproof vest; Dillinger wrapped the keys in a rubber band and carried them in his pocket.* The day Dillinger moved in, Hamilton telephoned her boss at the S&S Café and said she had been in a car accident and wouldn't be in for several days; in fact, she took the next three weeks off, spending every available hour with Dillinger.

At the apartment, Dillinger proved an amiable tenant. He was just an Indiana farm boy, he told the two women, who took to making his favorite farm fare, baking-powder biscuits with chicken gravy, steak, strawberries, and, occasionally, frog legs. After dinner, just as he had with Billie, Dillinger

---

* It's likely Dillinger met Hamilton the weekend of June 9–10, during the first days after having his facial bandages removed.

would strap on an apron and help with the dishes. In off hours he played cards, usually pinochle, with Sage and her son, Steve. Several times he and Hamilton double-dated with Steve and his girlfriend, taking in the movies *Viva Villa,* with Wallace Beery, at the Grenada, and *You're Telling Me* with W. C. Fields, at the Marbro. Steve Choliak thought "Jimmy" was a swell guy.

For the first time in months, Dillinger seemed to relax. He liked the neighborhood around Sage's apartment. He bought a new white shirt at the Ward Mitchell store, placed a few bets with the bookie who worked around the corner in a loft above the Biograph Theatre, and had his hair trimmed at the Biograph Barber Shop. Much later, the *Chicago Daily News* would report he felt safe enough to visit Chicago's detective bureau four separate times. Hamilton was applying for a new waitressing job, and her prospective employer required she obtain a medical certification. The medical examiner was in the same building as the detective bureau; four times Dillinger waited for Hamilton outside the examiner's thirteenth-floor office, while two floors below, the Chicago police busied themselves looking for him.

As he settled into his new routines, Dillinger remained in touch with O'Leary and Van Meter. On Tuesday night, July 10, the two bank robbers took their girlfriends on a double date to the World's Fair, wandering through the crowds at the lakeside. Two nights later Dillinger met O'Leary, and the two drove south, into the suburbs, where they found Van Meter at a barbecue stand. The two talked for a half hour in Van Meter's car, then returned to O'Leary's. O'Leary listened as Van Meter began complaining about Nelson. Apparently the two were having a disagreement over the disposition of some bonds.

"I had it out with Jimmy," Van Meter said. "I told him I wasn't going to pay him any twenty-five hundred dollars. I never did care a hell of a lot for that guy anyway."

"He was always complaining about you, too," Dillinger said.

"We had it pretty heavy there for a while," Van Meter said. "I thought we were going to draw guns on each other."

"Forget it, Van," Dillinger said. "We're through with Nelson, anyway. He's outta the gang."

"I suppose that's good," Van Meter said. As he left, he told Dillinger, "Don't forget about the 'soup.'"

As they drove back into Chicago, Dillinger told O'Leary about their next job. It was to be a train robbery. In fact, it had been proposed by Nelson's pal Jimmy Murray, who ten years earlier had masterminded the Newton Brothers' Roundout robbery. Murray was claiming that this train too would be carrying millions.

"It'll be one of the biggest jobs in the world," Dillinger enthused. "Just me and Van. We're not cutting anybody else in on this. We've got it spotted, we've been watching it for weeks, we know all its stops. We need the 'soup'"—nitroglycerin—"to blow the door of the mail car. We know how much money it will be carrying, and it's plenty. We'll have enough to last us the rest of our lives, and right after it's over we're lamming it out of the country."

Van Meter's tightfistedness forced Dillinger to take yet another meeting with O'Leary two days later, on Saturday, July 14. Their surgical assistant, Harold Cassidy, was pestering Van Meter to be paid for tending him after the South Bend robbery. Dillinger, O'Leary, and Cassidy met that afternoon in a park at the corner of Kedzie and North avenues. Dillinger slid Cassidy $500, saying it was from Van Meter. In all likelihood it wasn't. It was just Dillinger's way of defusing a bad situation; the last thing he needed was someone feeling unsatisfied.

Dillinger spent Sunday with Polly Hamilton. At one point, while she and a girlfriend went bicycle riding, Dillinger spent several hours watching Steve Chiolek play softball. When she returned, Hamilton found Dillinger buying bottles of beer for both teams. He seemed without a care in the world. By nightfall they were back at the North Halsted apartment. The next morning they woke to find the newspapers reporting a vicious gunfight northwest of the city. It was Nelson.

Monday, July 16
2:00 A.M.

That night Nelson held a meeting of "his" gang on a wooded side road deep in the northwest suburbs. Johnny Chase and Fatso Negri arrived first, followed by Jack Perkins. They parked their black Fords, turned off the headlights, and got out to talk. Helen sat in Nelson's car, reading a magazine by flashlight.

The men were deep in conversation around two o'clock when a pair of state troopers, Fred McAllister and Gilbert Cross, passed by the entrance to the road, heading home after long days on duty. McAllister spotted the three darkened cars back in the woods and decided to investigate. He turned into the dirt lane, stopped, and got out. Four men were standing in a ditch beside the cars.

"What's the trouble here?" McAllister asked.

"No trouble at all," a voice answered.

Then there came a burst of gunfire, almost certainly from Nelson's submachine gun. McAllister was struck in the right shoulder and fell, but most of the bullets raked the squad car, hitting Officer Cross six times. He managed to open a door and roll into the ditch. The two troopers lay bleeding as the men leaped into the cars and drove off. McAllister, after emptying his pistol at the fleeing cars, was able to drive them to a hospital. Both he and Cross survived.[3]

The shootings were front-page news in Chicago the next day, and all the articles speculated that Dillinger was involved. Agent Arthur McLawhon was dispatched to the Des Plaines hospital to interview one of the wounded troopers. He showed him photographs of Helen Gillis and Marie Conforti, but he could identify neither. The trooper assured McLawhon the shootings were the work of a band of bootleggers tending a 2,000-gallon illegal still that troopers found inside a barn about 250 yards from the site of the shooting. After talking to several other officers, McLawhon wrote Sam Cowley that "they were quite positive that the Dillinger Gang were not involved in any way."[4]

And so it went. Cowley was spending much of his time on Nelson. Agents picked up his mechanic friend, Clarey Lieder, but released him when Lieder said he hadn't seen Nelson in years. The FBI's most intriguing new lead surfaced on Monday, July 9. Several days earlier the Bureau had secured an informant inside Louis Piquett's office; the informant's name is blacked out in FBI files.* Whoever it was, he or she suggested agents follow Piquett that day. When they did, they saw Piquett engage in a street-corner argument with an unidentified man. When the two parted, the agents followed the stranger, trailing him to a two-story house in Oak Park. The next day a check with the landlord revealed that the man was the mysterious "Ralph Robiend"—Wilhelm Loeser, Dillinger's surgeon. An agent rented an apartment next door to Loeser's building and settled in to watch him.[5]

---

* The informant may have been Piquett's gofer, Meyer Bogue. It might also have been Piquett's secretary.

. . .

In hindsight, Homer Van Meter was right: Dillinger *was* a fool to be living so openly. By that third week of July, a dozen different people knew of his stays with Jimmy Probasco or Ana Sage, and Dillinger's carefree new life-style constituted a bet that not one of them would be tempted by the $15,000 reward for turning him in. Given the realities of the Depression, it was a bet he could only lose. During the week of July 16, while Dillinger continued cavorting with Polly Hamilton and studying the train robbery, there were hints of no fewer than three separate conspiracies to betray him.

According to FBI records, the first involved Wilhelm Loeser. Loeser feared he would be returned to prison if his surgery on Dillinger became known. But he was too weak a man to turn himself in. Instead, in an appar-ent effort to cushion the blow should he be arrested, he sent two anonymous letters to the FBI. The first, mailed earlier that summer, detailed work Pi-quett had paid him to do in an unrelated case; there is no suggestion in FBI files this tip was acted upon. A second letter described the work Loeser did on Dillinger. Loeser, however, did not mail this letter until Monday, July 23, at which point it would have no bearing on Dillinger's fate.

Art O'Leary became aware of a second, more worrisome, potential be-trayal that Tuesday, July 17, when he swung by Probasco's house to pick up a rifle and a radio Dillinger had left there. After swearing him to secrecy, Probasco told him that Piquett had come to him with a proposal to turn in Dillinger. Further, Probasco insisted that Piquett proposed to have *O'Leary* murdered, thus eliminating the only man who could contradict whatever tangled yarn they concocted for the FBI.[6]

O'Leary left Probasco's home badly shaken. That evening at six he kept a meeting with Dillinger in the park at Kedzie and North. Dillinger was sit-ting on a large white rock when O'Leary drove up. He rose and walked to the car, sliding into the front seat.

"Hello, Art," he said. "Have you seen Probasco?"

"I was up there this afternoon."

"Did he tell you about Piquett?"

So Dillinger knew.

"Yes," O'Leary said. "But I don't believe any of that bunk."

"Well," Dillinger said. "I believe it."

"Oh, don't pay any attention to Probasco. You know he's drunk practi-cally all the time. He doesn't know what he's talking about."

"Well . . . ," Dillinger said, "Van Meter has also been warning me against him. He said he's been talking surrender too much."

Dillinger stared off into the distance for several moments. "Art, I want you to get out of town," he finally said. "Take your family and go on up to the north woods or some place."

"What do you think you're going to do?"

"I'm going up to Piquett's office and leave him my card."

"You're crazy, Johnnie," O'Leary said. "You can't get away with anything like that. Anyway, Lou isn't going to double-cross you. He isn't that kind [of person]."

"I'm telling you to get out of town for a week," Dillinger said, "and then I'll get in touch with you. How soon can you go?"

"I can leave tonight, I suppose."

"That's fine," Dillinger said. "How are you fixed for money?"

"I've got enough."

Dillinger flipped open his billfold. He handed O'Leary $500.

"That'll take care of you for a while."

And then Dillinger got out of the car and disappeared into the park. Afterward O'Leary drove back to his house, gathered his family, and drove to northern Wisconsin. Later he claimed Dillinger had telephoned Piquett in his absence. According to O'Leary, Dillinger told Piquett he wanted to discuss a surrender. The two men set a date, Monday, July 23, to discuss it.[7] It was a meeting Dillinger would never make. There was a third conspiracy afoot, and this one was real.

Saturday, July 21

It was another hectic Saturday on the nineteenth floor of the Bankers Building. Cowley and a group of agents were busy running down tips the old yegg Eddie Bentz's brother had given them on Dillinger; none led anywhere. Matt Leach, meanwhile, had dredged up an informant who said Dillinger was in Culver, Indiana, preparing to rob a bank there. Reporters picked up on it and were pelting everyone with calls.

Purvis was in his office a few minutes after four o'clock when a call came in from Captain Timothy O'Neil of the East Chicago police. Purvis knew O'Neil, but not well. The sergeant said he and one of his men, a detective named Martin Zarkovich, had "real" information on Dillinger's whereabouts. He wanted to meet right away.

Purvis met them outside the Bankers Building a little after six. Together the three men drove to the Great Northern Hotel, taking the elevator up to Room 712, where Cowley was staying. In Cowley's room, Zarkovich did most of the talking. He said he had an informant, a woman he had known for years, whose girlfriend was dating Dillinger. The three were going to a movie on the North Side the next night, Sunday. The informant was prepared to tell the FBI which theater they would be attending. The Bureau, Zarkovich said, could handle it from there. All O'Neil and Zarkovich wanted, they said, was the $15,000 reward.

Before he cut any deals, Cowley said he wanted to meet the informant. Zarkovich said it had already been arranged; Sage had agreed to meet them that night. A bit later the four men left the room and walked downstairs. Outside, Purvis and Zarkovich got into one car, Cowley and O'Neil into a second. With Zarkovich leading they drove into the North Side, and a half hour later parked across from the Children's Memorial Hospital at 707 West Fullerton Street.

It was a sweltering night, the temperature in the low nineties; Chicago was in the midst of a record-setting heat wave. Out at the lake beaches, hundreds of people were still thronged, trying to catch a breeze. On the stoops and corners of the North Side, mothers fanned themselves with newspapers and children begged for ice cream. At about nine-thirty, as the four men sat in their cars waiting, Ana Sage appeared on the sidewalk beside them. She walked past, surveying the situation. After a minute she returned and got into Purvis's car. They drove east, toward the lake, eventually pulling up in a secluded spot overlooking the water. Cowley remained in O'Neil's car behind them.

Sage demanded Purvis show proof he was an FBI agent. Purvis took out his badge. Satisfied, Sage said she was prepared to tell everything she knew. She wanted only one thing: to stay in America. She asked if the FBI could make her deportation proceedings go away. Purvis said he had limited authority in such matters, but promised that if Sage helped apprehend Dillinger, he would do everything he could to help her.

It was enough for Sage. The following week she repeated the story she told Purvis for an FBI stenographer. At the very least she dissembled; she said only that Dillinger visited her apartment to see Hamilton, denying he actually lived there. "He did stay at my house while Polly was ill as a result of an automobile wreck about two weeks, and then only stayed there till about daylight, five or six o'clock in the morning," Sage said in her statement.[8]

According to Sage, who would always deny arranging to hide Dillinger, she first met him when Polly Hamilton brought him to her apartment in June, introducing him as Jimmy Lawrence.* "He kept his head down but I looked at him and got a glimpse of his profile and immediately recognized him as Dillinger," Sage said. "I told him immediately that his name might be Jimmy Lawrence, but he was John Dillinger. I made the remark in front of Polly and I called Polly out in the bathroom and told her that her boy-friend was John Dillinger. I told Polly that I was going to make that man, meaning Jimmy Lawrence, admit that he was Dillinger or he could leave."

This account is unlikely on its face, and it contradicts everything Polly Hamilton later said about her unknowing courtship with Dillinger; in all likelihood both Sage and Hamilton were lying. In any event, Sage said she then returned to her living room and confronted Dillinger again. Again, she said, he denied he was Dillinger.

"I told him to wait a minute," Sage went on, "and I went out in the other room and got several pictures which appeared in the newspapers and showed them to him and told him then that if he was John Dillinger he would have a gun on him and if he had no gun he was not Dillinger. He did have a gun in his pocket."

According to Sage, the matter was left unresolved. It was not until the next night, she claimed, that Dillinger admitted to Hamilton who he really was. As Sage told it, Hamilton didn't care if he was Dillinger or not; she loved him. Sage didn't. She told Purvis she began thinking of ways to alert the police. If so, it took her several weeks to summon the courage. From all available evidence, it was not until July 13 or 14 that she made an effort to betray Dillinger. What Sage didn't tell Purvis was that on July 12 she had received a letter from the U.S. immigration service. In it she was informed that her appeals to remain in America had been denied. A warrant was is-sued for her deportation. Almost certainly it was this letter that spurred Sage's betrayal.[9]

At first, Sage said, she was unsure how to proceed. Initially she was in-clined to approach her immigration attorney. She said she arranged a meet-ing, then backed out, unsure whether she could trust him. It was then, she claimed, she thought of Martin Zarkovich. "I called Martin Zarkovich and talked to him in a casual conversation and told him I wanted to talk to him

---

* This actually occurred at an apartment Sage had rented at 2838 North Clark Street.

sometime about something," Sage said. Zarkovich promised to telephone on Sunday, July 15, the day Dillinger watched Sage's son playing softball.

According to Sage, and this too contradicts Polly Hamilton's statements, she kept Hamilton informed of her talks with Zarkovich. "I told Polly that Martin was coming to see me and Polly said not to tell John," Sage said. "[She said] to tell Martin anything to keep him from coming to the house, and to meet him somewhere else."

In any event, it didn't matter; according to Sage, Zarkovich didn't call that Sunday. Two nights later, on Tuesday, July 17, the evening he told Art O'Leary to take a vacation, Dillinger left Chicago. According to Sage, Dillinger said he was driving to Wisconsin on business and would return in two or three days. The next morning, Wednesday, July 18, Sage again telephoned Zarkovich. He said he would visit her apartment the next day, Thursday, and did, arriving at 3:00. According to Sage's account, it was only then that she explained that Hamilton was dating Dillinger, who was scheduled to return the next day. "I told him that I would call him on Saturday and let him know definitely if John Dillinger had returned to Chicago and if he hadn't, if Polly had heard from him and knew where he was located," Sage said.

Friday morning Dillinger returned from his trip. In all likelihood he had been off with Van Meter, studying details of his train robbery; that same day, in fact, the two outlaws swung by Jimmy Murray's Rain-Bo Inn, where they found Fatso Negri and told him to arrange a meeting with Nelson the next night. According to Sage, Dillinger spent the rest of the day playing cards with Hamilton. The next morning, Saturday, he went with Hamilton, Steve Chiolek, and two girls to the beach. The moment he left, Sage said, she telephoned Zarkovich and gave him the go-ahead to bring in the FBI.

Sitting in Purvis's car, Ana Sage said she expected to attend a movie the following evening with Dillinger and Hamilton. They would probably go to the Marbro Theatre, on West Madison Street. As soon as she knew for certain, Sage said, she would telephone the FBI; Purvis gave her his private number, Andover 2330. Sage said she would wear an orange dress to help the agents spot her on the street.

It took only a few days for the FBI to poke substantial holes in Ana Sage's story. If Purvis, sitting in the car beside the lake, had any doubts, he kept them to himself. All he wanted was Dillinger, and Ana Sage was handing him to them on a plate.

• • •

The night Ana Sage cut her deal with Purvis, Dillinger drove out to the northwest suburbs to discuss the train robbery with Nelson; if he really was planning to exclude Nelson, he hadn't told him. Nelson was enthusiastic about the job, and would remain so the rest of his life. As before, only Fatso Negri would ever give details of the meeting, and those were scant. Negri said he arrived late to find Nelson, Dillinger, and Jimmy Murray waiting impatiently for Van Meter. Nelson was cursing. At one point, as they stood waiting for Van Meter, it was mentioned that Negri wanted to return to California.

Nelson said it was fine with him. But Dillinger objected. "He knows too much," Dillinger said, smiling as he turned to Negri. "Why not stay here and play ball? We'll make a lot of money. Then you can go home and go about your business, and no one will find you. You'll have some real dough in your pockets. I heard Johnny say your folks are poor. You can smother them in money when we're finished. You can do that, can't you, Fats?"

"Sure," Negri said, "I can stay."

When another hour passed with no sign of Van Meter, they decided to call it a night. As they left, Nelson's last words to Dillinger were a suggestion that he find Van Meter and "kick his skinny ass." They agreed to meet again two nights later, on Monday.[10]

Sunday, July 22

It was another steamy summer day. By late morning the temperature had reached the nineties and was inching toward one hundred degrees. Cowley and Purvis arrived on the nineteenth floor early. They telephoned most of the squad, telling them to stay in touch; something might break. After a bit the East Chicago cops, Zarkovich and O'Neil, showed up, along with two of their colleagues. Cowley and O'Neil went over their plans for the evening. O'Neil repeatedly told Cowley he didn't think they had enough men to capture Dillinger; Cowley was planning a group of about fifteen. "Captain O'Neal [*sic*] was all for calling in the Chicago police," an aide wrote Hoover the next morning, "but [Cowley] put his foot down . . . O'Neal told Cowley if it was a blunder, he could just forget about them; in other words, if they failed it was [the FBI's fault] and if successful, then O'Neal would get the credit."[11]

Cowley had decided against watching Ana Sage's apartment or otherwise monitoring her; presumably he didn't want to risk the chance of Dillinger recognizing a surveillance and fleeing. For the moment this was Sage's show, and the FBI did nothing to interfere. All they could do was wait. The night before, after meeting Sage, Cowley had taken an agent and visited the Marbro Theatre, scribbling notes on entries and exits. Afterward Cowley had telephoned Hoover, who said he wanted Dillinger taken alive if possible.

Around two o'clock, Cowley and Purvis began calling the men and ordering them to come into the office by three. The agents came in ones and twos, sweat stains in their jackets. No speeches were made, no orders were given. But soon word spread among the men fanning themselves with newspapers out in the bullpen. They had a new informant, and this one might be real. Wilting in the heat, the men checked their guns, and waited.

Dillinger was a careful dresser, especially around Polly Hamilton. That morning he pulled on a fresh pair of white Hanes briefs, size 34, then slid into a pair of lightweight gray slacks, black socks, red Paris garters, and white buckskin Nunn Bush shoes. He buttoned on a white kenilworth broadcloth shirt and twisted on a red-print tie, then put the keys to Sage's apartment in his front-right pocket along with a La Corona–Belvedere cigar and a money clip.

Dillinger probably spent the day with Hamilton, who wasn't feeling well, playing pinochle at Sage's apartment. That was what he was doing around five o'clock, when Sage began preparing dinner. They were having one of Dillinger's favorites, fried chicken. As she began work in the kitchen, Sage announced she didn't have any butter. She said she would run down to the store to get some. She slid out the apartment door, walked downstairs, and made her way to a pay phone.

Purvis took the call. Everything was going as planned, Sage said; she pointedly failed to mention that Dillinger was at her apartment as they spoke. After dinner they planned to see a movie. They would probably leave around eight. "I'll call when I know something definite," Sage said. She hung up the phone and hurried back to her apartment.

At the Bankers Building, Purvis and Cowley paced. By 6:00 Sage had not called. By 6:30, they had still heard nothing. By 7:00 Purvis was growing nervous. This was cutting things close. Then, a few minutes after seven, his phone rang. It was Sage.

"He's here," she said. "We'll be leaving in a short while. I still don't know if we're going to the Biograph or Marbro." She hung up before he could ask any questions.

Purvis was startled. No one had said anything about the Biograph. It was on North Lincoln Avenue, a narrow street just around the corner from Sage's apartment. Immediately, Cowley sent two agents to reconnoiter the theater. This was not good. Cowley and Purvis discussed what to do. In the end, they had no choice. Both theaters would need to be covered, and quickly.

At 7:15 Cowley summoned the men into Purvis's office; about two dozen crammed into the room.[12] Cowley introduced Zarkovich, who did the talking. He said Dillinger would be attending a movie at either the Marbro or Biograph theater that night. Due to cosmetic surgery, Zarkovich said, Dillinger's appearance was somewhat different than the photos printed on FBI Wanted posters. His face was rounder. He had removed the identifying moles. The telltale cleft in his chin was gone. He had dyed his hair jet black, Zarkovich said, and grown a full mustache. According to their informant, he would be wearing a gray checkered suit, white shoes, and straw hat. Without naming them, Zarkovich then described the two women who would be accompanying Dillinger. The older one, he said, was "heavily built," about 160 pounds. She would be wearing a bright orange skirt.*

When Zarkovich was finished, Purvis stepped forward. He wore a single-breasted blue jacket, white slacks, and a straw boater.

"Gentlemen," he said, "you all know the character of John Dillinger. If he appears at either of the picture shows and we locate him and he effects his escape, it will be a disgrace to our Bureau. It may be that Dillinger will be at the picture show with his woman companions without arms—yet, he may appear there armed and with other members of his gang. There of course will be an undetermined element of danger in endeavoring to apprehend Dillinger. It is the desire that he be taken alive, if possible, and without injury to any agent of the Bureau. Yet, gentlemen, this is the opportunity we have all been awaiting, and he must be taken. Do not unnecessarily endanger your own lives and if Dillinger offers any resistance each man will be for himself and it will be up to each of you to do whatever you think necessary to protect yourself in taking Dillinger."

---

* Not, as legend has it, a red dress.

They went over the plan in the event Dillinger appeared. Five men were selected to make up the party that would physically apprehend him. Purvis was to lead this group. His two best gunmen, Charles Winstead and Clarence Hurt, would assist. Two East Chicago cops, Glen Stretch and Peter Sopsic, would complete the group. Purvis said he would stand outside the box office—at whichever theater Dillinger appeared—and keep watch. When Dillinger appeared, he would give the signal to move in by lighting a cigar. If Dillinger should elude these five men, Purvis said, the rest of the agents should do as they saw fit.

"What type of guns shall we take?" someone asked.

"Your pistols only," Purvis said.

When the meeting broke up, Purvis took Agent Ralph Brown and drove to the Biograph. Cowley stayed behind to coordinate; Purvis promised to phone every five minutes. Zarkovich and Agent Winstead were sent to the Marbro. Sage's inability to pinpoint a theater meant they wouldn't be able to assemble in force until after Dillinger appeared—*if* he appeared. They would have to take him when the movie let out.

Purvis and Brown pulled up in front of the Biograph at 7:37. Brown stood by the car while Purvis walked up to the box office. The movie that night was *Manhattan Melodrama,* a gangster film starring Clark Gable and William Powell. The next showing was at 8:30. Purvis returned to the car and slid in next to Brown.

It was hot. Sitting in the car, shifting nervously in his seat, Purvis yearned to swing his gaze up and down the street, but was afraid he might be noticed; instead he willed himself to sit still, scanning those passing beside him on the sidewalk.[13] By 8:15 people had already begun filing into the theater. Every five minutes, Brown jogged to a bar down the street and used a pay phone to check in with Cowley.

If Sage had done as she promised and left her apartment at eight, Dillinger would appear at any moment. Five minutes went by, then ten, then fifteen. There was no sign of Dillinger. Across town at the Marbro, Winstead and Zarkovich stood uneasily in front of the theater, waiting, watching. In Washington, Hoover sat in the library of his home, fielding updates every few minutes from Cowley. Between calls, Cowley paced. Out in the bullpen, agents checked and rechecked their weapons. No one had much to say.

Something was wrong. Purvis could feel it. By 8:25 he was beginning to feel the whole weekend had been wasted: another sweaty night, another deluded informant, another long week ahead. This was stupid. They never should have trusted the East Chicago police.

Then, at 8:36, Purvis glanced to his side and saw two women and a man walk by on the sidewalk. To his amazement, he realized that it was Ana Sage, a girl who had to be Polly Hamilton—and John Dillinger. Sage was wearing the orange skirt and tilted white hat, just as Zarkovich said she would. Dillinger wore a straw boater. Ralph Brown saw them, too. The moment the three passed, Brown got out of the car and trotted off to call Cowley. As he did, Dillinger walked up to the ticket booth and slid the girl behind the glass several bills. Stunned that he was finally laying eyes on the man he had sought so long, Purvis studied Dillinger in profile, the gray slacks, the clean white shirt, the dark glasses. He wore no jacket; that was good. It meant he had one gun at most. And he was alone. No Nelson, no Van Meter.

It was happening. As Purvis watched from the car twenty feet away, Dillinger bought his tickets and guided the women into the theater. Inside it was crowded, but Dillinger found two seats in the third row; Sage took a seat alone in the back. Dillinger snuggled up to Hamilton and in a stage whisper asked for a kiss; she obliged. Later she would say Dillinger was unusually amorous that evening.

Outside, Purvis stepped from the car, walked to the ticket booth, and purchased a ticket of his own. He shuffled in with the crowd. Inside the theater, Purvis scanned the seats. The place was jammed. If he could find three seats behind Dillinger's, he thought, maybe they could grab him during the show. Purvis walked down one aisle, then another. He couldn't see more than a handful of empty seats. He couldn't see Dillinger. They would have to take him when he left.

Purvis returned to the car. Brown said Cowley's men were on their way. The two agents began to get nervous. What if Dillinger left before the others arrived? What if he sensed something awry and left early? They would have to take him themselves. Purvis studied his watch. He got out and talked to the girl selling tickets. She said the movie lasted ninety-four minutes. With newsreels and trailers, it would let out in two hours and four minutes. If he stayed for the entire movie, Dillinger should exit the theater around 10:35.

Purvis grew more anxious as the minutes ticked by. Not for another twenty minutes did Purvis spy the first agents taking positions on the street around him. He and Brown exchanged relieved glances. When Cowley arrived, he and Purvis spoke in low tones, discussing how to position the men. They put the two East Chicago cops, Stretch and Sopsic, on the sidewalk north of the theater entrance. When Charles Winstead arrived from the Marbro, he and Clarence Hurt took positions on the south side, the direction Dillinger would take if he returned to Sage's apartment. Cowley fanned the other men in pairs up and down the street. The Biograph had two side exits and one in the rear. The side exits opened into an alley that could be used as a shortcut to Sage's apartment. Cowley put four men in the alley.

By 9:30 everyone was in place. Standing in a doorway beside the box office with Agents Winstead and Hurt, Purvis bit the end off his cigar and chewed it. His throat was parched, but he couldn't go for a drink of water. When he stood in one place, he realized his knees were trembling. Ten o'clock came and went. No one left the theater.

Tension rose as the end of the movie neared. All along the street agents shifted their weight, keeping their eyes down, trying to look inconspicuous. It didn't work. Suddenly, at 10:20, two sedans pulled into the alley beside the theater. Several men jumped out, guns in their hands. One of the men leveled a sawed-off shotgun.

"Police!" one of the men yelled. "Put up your hands!"

One of the agents, E. J. Conroy, flipped out his badge. Each of the three other FBI men did the same. "Federal agents," Conroy said. Conroy explained they were on a stakeout. When one of the cops asked who they were after, Conroy refused to say. One of the officers explained they were responding to a report of suspicious men hanging around the theater. The cop asked if they could help. Conroy said no and asked the cops to leave. Grudgingly, they piled back into their squad cars and drove off.

Ten minutes passed: 10:30. The movie would be letting out any moment. Just then another car drove up in front of the theater. Two men got out. One stepped across the street and approached Agent Jerry Campbell, while the other accosted the two East Chicago cops, Stretch and Sopsic. They turned out to be plainclothes Chicago detectives, responding to the same call.* Campbell and the East Chicago men tried to shoo them off, but they were suspicious and insisted on lingering.

The two detectives were still asking questions five minutes later when

---

* The call had come from inside the Biograph, where the manager believed the mysterious men lurking outside were about to rob the theater.

the first people began filing out of the theater. Purvis tensed. Leaving Hurt
and Winstead in the doorway, he stepped to the box office, into the path of
the exiting patrons. The cigar in his mouth was shaking. More people came
out, forming a crowd on the sidewalk around him. Purvis noted the women
and children. He tried to remain calm.

Then, at 10:40, there he was: Dillinger, shuffling out with the crowd,
Polly Hamilton holding his left arm, Ana Sage inching forward on her left.
Purvis strained to look nonchalant. Dillinger was barely five feet from him;
with one step, he could reach out and touch his arm. Purvis glanced at
Dillinger and for the briefest moment their eyes met. For a fleeting second
Purvis thought he had been recognized.

But Dillinger dropped his eyes and moved forward. As he did, Purvis
took out a matchbook, struck a match, and lit the cigar. Dillinger stepped
to his left, guiding the women south, the way they had come, toward Hurt
and Winstead. In the doorway twenty feet down the sidewalk, both agents
saw the signal. Hurt whispered to Winstead, "That's Dillinger, with the
straw hat and the glasses."

Directly across the street, Jerry Campbell saw Dillinger at the same
time. "There they go," he said to another agent. Both men edged south
down the sidewalk, moving parallel to Dillinger.

Of all the agents outside of the Biograph that night, only a handful reacted to Purvis's signal. According to FBI memos, in fact, no more than a
half-dozen agents saw it. He was too far away and surrounded by too many
people. Cowley, standing further down the block, did not see Purvis light
the cigar. Nor did the two East Chicago cops, standing barely twenty feet
north of Purvis; as Purvis watched, amazed, they continued talking with
the curious Chicago detectives. Across the street, Martin Zarkovich recognized Dillinger himself. He began walking toward the East Chicago cops,
hoping to rouse them.

Purvis was unsure what to do. He took a step or two to follow Dillinger.
Then he took out a second match and once again applied it to the cigar,
hoping to draw the attention of more agents. He couldn't tell whether Winstead, Hurt, or anyone else knew what was happening. In frustration he
mouthed the words, "Damn it! Come on!"

Ten feet down the sidewalk, Dillinger and the two women were inching
forward in a knot of six or seven people. As the crowd loosened and Dillinger lengthened his stride, Purvis walked after them. As he did, Dillinger
and the women strode past the doorway where Winstead and Hurt stood.

When the trio passed, Hurt stepped behind them, crossing the sidewalk, and turned to follow. Agent Ed Hollis, who stood in the gutter beside the FBI car, was right beside him. Dillinger glanced to his right, at Hollis. Winstead took a step forward. Dillinger half-turned and looked straight into Winstead's face.

He knew it then. Standing across the street, a rookie agent named Jack Welles noticed that Dillinger "appeared to realize that he was trapped; there was a tense look on his face." For years afterward the agents on the sidewalk would remember those next few seconds as if in slow motion. Turning forward, Dillinger appeared to lean into a crouch. At the same time, he slid his hand into his pants pocket, reaching for his .38. Behind him, Winstead pulled his .45. Hurt and Hollis drew their guns as well.

Dillinger broke from the women and took a step or two forward, as if to run for the alley that opened ten feet in front of him. He never had a chance. No one yelled "Halt" or "Stop" or identified themselves as FBI agents.* It happened in a split second: The moment he saw Dillinger reach for his gun, Winstead fired his .45 three times; the sudden retort startled bystanders all around. Hurt fired twice, Hollis once. Four bullets struck Dillinger. Two grazed him. A third struck him in the side. But a fourth bullet hit Dillinger in the back of the neck, smashing a vertebra, severing his spinal cord and tearing through his brain before exiting through his right eye.†

Dillinger pitched forward, bumped into a woman in front of him, then

---

* In his 1936 book, *American Agent*, Purvis claimed he yelled, "Stick 'em up, Johnny, we have you surrounded." In numerous newspaper interviews and memos he authored on that night, this is the only time Purvis made such a claim. It is not substantiated by any other interviews or memos authored by any other agent present that night. It's tempting to suggest Purvis concocted the claim to offset occasional sentiment that the FBI's killing of Dillinger amounted to an assassination.

† For decades, no one in the FBI would confirm which agent fired the bullets that killed Dillinger. Inside the Bureau, however, there was little doubt. "Upon my inquiry," Hoover wrote in a memo the next day, July 23, "Mr. Purvis stated there is no question but that Mr. Winstead fired the fatal shots . . . Mr. Purvis said that nobody knows it was Winstead who actually killed Dillinger." In fact, Winstead, Purvis, and other agents made a pact among themselves never to disclose who fired the fatal bullets.

Not until 1970 did Winstead break his silence. In an interview with the FBI agents' alumni newsletter, *The Grapevine,* he said, "I knew right away it was Dillinger . . . Polly knew something was up. She grabbed Dillinger by the shirt. He whirled around and reached for his right front pocket. He started running sideways toward the alley. When a guy like Dillinger reaches for his pocket, you don't ask questions. Or read a warrant from the U.S. attorney. Clarence and I fired about the same time. The first shot hit him. He started spinning like a top. When the shooting started he was about six feet from the alley. After Dillinger whirled around he fell face down in the entrance to the alley. He never did get to the alley. I was the first to reach him. I leaned down. He mumbled some words that I couldn't understand. That was the end. Mel Purvis took a .380 automatic out of his hand. It was loaded and he had an extra clip of bullets in his pocket."

staggered a step or two before falling face first to the pavement at the entrance to the alley. Winstead was the first to reach him. Purvis hustled up and grabbed the pistol from Dillinger's hand. The rookie, Jack Welles, ran up in time to see Dillinger's lips moving.[14] Someone said, "Don't move," but Dillinger lay still. He was dead.

Pandemonium erupted. Women ran screaming. A Chicago woman named Etta Natalsky was hopping about, shouting, "I'm shot!" She had been hit in the leg by a ricochet, as had a housemaid named Theresa Paulus, who was struck in the knee; she lay beside the alley, blood staining her dress. Neither woman was hurt seriously. When they realized the shooting had stopped, a number of people stepped forward to stare at the body. A circle formed, men craning their necks to get a glimpse. A dozen FBI agents ran up, urging the crowd to move back.

Within moments the name began surging through the crowd: *Dillinger. They got Dillinger.* An ambulance was called. Two cars of police rolled up, responding to a call of shots fired, and their occupants pushed back the crowd. Attendants arrived and lifted the body into an ambulance and took it to Alexian Brothers Hospital, where it was laid on the front lawn until a coroner came out and pronounced Dillinger dead. The body was then taken to the Cook County Morgue.*

A mystery that bedeviled Dillinger enthusiasts for years was the disposition of $1,200 in cash Dillinger carried at the time he was shot. Agent Dan Sullivan found the money. According to a story that Sullivan told the FBI alumni newsletter in 1978, he was one of two agents who accompanied Dillinger's body to the morgue. When the ambulance arrived a crowd formed, and at one point two men identifying themselves as Chicago detectives stepped forward. As Sullivan recalled, "One of them asked if that was really Dillinger in the wagon and when I said it was, he asked if they could climb inside and look at the body. They came out a minute later and left. When we got inside the morgue and they started stripping the body, they found something like fifty-seven cents on him. I sat there bug-eyed."†

---

* Dillinger's autopsy report was misplaced after his death. It was eventually found in 1984, in a paper sack at the Cook County Medical Examiner. Interestingly, it said the autopsy found evidence that Dillinger had suffered from "rheumatic heart disease."

† Born in 1906, Daniel P. Sullivan joined the FBI after graduating from Georgetown University Law School in 1932. After leaving the Bureau in 1942, he became executive director of the Crime Commission of Greater Miami for thirty years.

The actual figure was $7.70—a five-dollar bill, two singles, and seventy cents in change.

When word of the shooting hit the radio, hundreds of Chicagoans descended on the Biograph. Crowds thronged the alley's entrance until nearly dawn. All that remained to be seen was a pool of Dillinger's blood. Even that didn't last long, as dozens of men and women pressed their handkerchiefs into it, taking home gruesome souvenirs to show their families. The bloodlust wasn't limited to the crowds. The next morning a man showed up at the Bankers Building to offer Purvis cash for the shirt he had worn; it contained a drop of Dillinger's blood.

Late that night a reporter brought news of his son's death to John Dillinger, Sr. He collapsed into a chair at his farmhouse. "Is it really true?" he asked. "Are you sure there is no mistake?" Told there wasn't, the elder Dillinger said, "Well, John is dead. At last it has happened—the thing I have prayed and prayed would not happen. I want the body brought back here. I'm so sick I can hardly talk."[15]

In Washington, reporters confronted Hoover as he hurried into his office. He deflected entreaties to boast, emphasizing the Bureau's hunt for Van Meter and Nelson. "This does not mean the end of the Dillinger case," he said. "Anyone who ever gave any of the Dillinger mob any aid, comfort, or assistance will be vigorously prosecuted."[16]

Attorney General Homer Cummings, tracked down at Washington's Union Station, where he was boarding a cross-country train toward a Hawaiian vacation, put Dillinger's death in the broadest context, making clear it was a product of New Deal–style federalist thinking. "This marks the end of the trail for John Dillinger, but it is not the end of the trail for the Department of Justice," he said. "For us this is but one more episode in the carefully planned campaign against organized crime which we have been conducting for more than a year." Without any hint of irony—given the lack of cooperation between the FBI and Chicago police—he added, "What has happened is an illustration of the success that can be accomplished by concentrated effort and fullest coordination between federal and local authorities. To bring about this sort of friendly and helpful cooperation is one of the cardinal points in our movement to suppress crime."

The next morning Dillinger's death was front-page news around the world, dominating headlines in New York, London, Moscow, and Berlin. The European papers played up the lack of warning Dillinger was given before being shot in the back. In Germany a Nazi newspaper used this as ammunition for a broadside against America. "Is a cop calling a man by his first name before shooting him down a sufficient trial?" an editorialist wrote. "Does a country in which this happens still deserve the name of a country of law and order?"[17]

American newspapers had no such doubts. Much of their coverage focused on Purvis, who while reading congratulatory telegrams gave interviews and posed for photographers in his office all day Monday. The caption beneath his picture in the *Chicago Daily Times* that evening— HE GOT HIS MAN—was typical. The *New York Evening Journal* printed a series of Dillinger photos arrayed like scenes from a movie, calling it "Underworld Melodrama—in Three Scenes—(A U.S. Production directed by Melvin Purvis)." *Time* printed a photo of Purvis shaking hands with Homer Cummings captioned, MELVIN PURVIS AND FRIEND. While Sam Cowley, whom the *Tribune* continued to identify as "Purvis's chief assistant," shunned the press, Purvis gave interviews in which his ego was vividly on display. Talking to a *Daily Times* reporter, he referred to the FBI's as-yet-unnamed snitch as "my informant" and embellished the story of lighting his cigar.

"There was no response from my men," Purvis said. "I'll confess I was under a strain and extremely uncomfortable when Dillinger saw my signal and gave me a dirty look . . . Once I spotted him I knew him at once, because of those killer's eyes of his."[18]

This was not the way Hoover wanted FBI agents to behave, as Purvis would soon learn. There was much work still to be done, in fact, and Cowley excluded Purvis from almost all of it. Monday night, while Cowley grappled with an array of pressing issues, Purvis was sent to the railroad station to pose for photographs with Homer Cummings. The following evening he flew to Washington, where he posed for more photos with Hoover; Cowley apologized, saying he was too busy to go. Hoover announced both Purvis and Cowley were given raises. For the moment, it appeared Purvis had been freed from the director's doghouse.

"The shooting and killing of John Dillinger by the Agents of your office under your admirable direction and planning are but another indication of your ability and capacity as a leader and an executive," Hoover wrote Purvis the morning after the shooting. "[I]t again confirms the faith and confidence which I have always had in you . . . This would not have been accomplished had it not been for your unlimited and never-ending persistence, effective planning and intelligence . . ."[19]

The attention lavished on Purvis did not sit well with the East Chicago police. Zarkovich gave several interviews, trying hard to direct credit to the East Chicago police. Like Purvis, he freely embellished his story, telling reporters he had seen Dillinger attending movies at the Biograph several times. He also claimed the East Chicago police had Van Meter and Nelson under surveillance. It was no use. The press had annointed Purvis "the man who got Dillinger," and nothing the East Chicago police said changed anyone's minds. Later that week, Captain O'Neil told reporters he made a "big mistake" agreeing to let Purvis handle the initial publicity.

"This story that Purvis has put out about his office being tipped off Sunday afternoon about Dillinger planning to attend the show at the Biograph is all bunk," O'Neil groused. "We merely played a strong hunch that Dillinger would show up at the theater Sunday night and turned that information over to Purvis to act on."[20]

While Purvis basked in glory, Cowley mopped up. On Monday, after testifying at the coroner's inquest—where he refused to identify the agents who shot Dillinger—he was forced to deal with a frantic Ana Sage, who was convinced Dillinger's gang would hunt her down. The moment Dillinger was shot, she and Hamilton had run from the scene. Two days later, a boy swimming in Lake Michigan found a submachine gun, a pistol, and a bulletproof vest in shallow water off a pier near Lincoln Park. They were Dillinger's; the Thompson was identified as one of the guns stolen from the Warsaw, Indiana, police department. Though it was never proven, the Chicago police told reporters they suspected Sage had run back to her flat and cleared it of Dillinger's things, tossing the guns and the vest into the lake. Afterward Hamilton hid at a girlfriend's. Sage locked herself inside her apartment.

By Monday afternoon, rumors began to swirl about the mysterious "woman in red" who betrayed Dillinger. Purvis and Zarkovich refused to comment, but the outlines of the conspiracy leaked anyway. DILLINGER DOOMED BY GIRL IN RED, read the *Chicago Daily Times* banner headline Monday evening. At her apartment, Sage panicked. Zarkovich drove her to the Bankers Building, where Sam Cowley found her "most hysterical." In tears she begged him to hide her. Cowley said he would do whatever she wanted, then sent her home. The next morning he talked with Hoover. "[Cowley] thinks that if we don't pick her up the newspapers will most likely find out who she is and cause a lot of publicity," Hoover wrote in a memo that morning. "I asked Mr. Cowley if they could get her and hold her inncommunicado [*sic*]. He thought they could, and I instructed him to take this action."

That same morning Cowley telephoned Sage and asked to meet her at the Stevens Hotel. There he instructed her to go home, pack her things, leave town, and let him know where she was going. Returning to her apartment, Sage was throwing clothes in a suitcase when her doorbell rang. Through the peephole she saw men outside. Frightened, she phoned Purvis, who said he would send an agent over. The men turned out to be Chicago police detectives. They took Sage in for questioning.

At the Sheffield precinct house, Captain Thomas Duffy fired questions at Sage for several hours. Amazingly, he allowed a group of newspaper reporters to listen in. Sage proved a skilled liar, denying just about everything. Again and again, she insisted she was just on her way to the movies when FBI agents had burst out of nowhere and killed her girlfriend's date. When Cowley learned Sage was in custody, he headed to the precinct house. Both Cowley and Sage acted as if they didn't know each other. Cowley asked Detective Duffy if he was filing charges against Sage. Duffy said he only wanted to question her. Cowley left, telling Duffy to notify him when he was finished. Later, Cowley told Hoover he felt the police had detained Sage on the urging of friends at the *Chicago Daily News,* who wanted her story.

That night, when the evening newspapers identified Sage as "the woman in red," Cowley telephoned the precinct to find Sage still there. Detective Duffy said he intended to hold Sage till the next day. "No you're not," Cowley said.[21] He telephoned Chicago's police commissioner, persuaded him to release Sage into the FBI's custody, then dispatched two agents to remove her from the precinct house. Reporters followed them as they drove Sage to the Bankers Building, where they bombarded Cowley with questions. He firmly denied Sage was responsible for "fingering" Dillinger.

Behind closed doors, Cowley told Sage to call Polly Hamilton, whom the Bureau had been unable to locate. By 2:00 A.M. both women were secreted safely on the nineteenth floor. They were questioned all night. Hamilton steadfastly denied ever knowing "Jimmy Lawrence" was Dillinger, though this flatly contradicted Sage. Still, Cowley accepted her story. "He is positive she knows no more than the informant," Hoover wrote in a memo after talking to Cowley the next day. "Mr. Cowley believes that she is telling the truth."[22]

They decided to get both women out of Chicago. Wednesday morning, three days after the shooting, Cowley had a pair of agents drive Sage back to her apartment. Inside they encountered a crowd of reporters, ushered in by the helpful Chicago police. After Sage packed a suitcase, tossing a few choice epithets at reporters as she did, agents drove her and Hamilton to Detroit. They spent the next several days in a hotel.

While Cowley dealt with the women, his men began rounding up those who had helped Dillinger. The first was Wilhelm Loeser. Once the FBI confirmed that Dillinger had undergone cosmetic surgery, Cowley had no doubt who had performed it. Agents arrived on Loeser's doorstep Tuesday morning. When no one answered the bell, a half-dozen men broke down the side door. Barging up the stairs, they heard a man's voice ask, "Who's there?" A moment later Loeser, shirtless, appeared on the landing. He was taken to the Bankers Building.

Downtown, Loeser told them everything. Charles Winstead led a raid on Jimmy Probasco's house the next evening. By midnight Probasco was locked inside a conference room at the Bankers Building. When they searched Probasco's house, agents found what was later described as a suicide note. Cowley ordered Probasco watched all that night. At 9:00 Thursday morning, a twenty-five-year-old rookie agent named Max Chaffetz took Probasco to be fingerprinted, then returned Probasco to the conference room. A few minutes later Chaffetz returned to find the room empty. A chair was propped beneath the window. Chaffetz stepped to the window and looked down. There, in the alley nineteen floors below, lay the splattered remains of Jimmy Probasco.* "Mr. Cowley [called and] stated that Probasco had just jumped out of a window at the Chicago office, which is on the 19th floor," Hoover wrote in a memo that morning at 10:30. "I remarked that this was extreme carelessness."[23]

Probasco's demise led to rumors that he had been pushed from the window, or perhaps fallen while being dangled by interrogating agents. A crestfallen Cowley recommended to Hoover that both he and Chaffetz be suspended for two weeks. Hoover chose to suspend only Chaffetz. Given that Boss McLaughlin, who had passed the Bremer ransom money, had complained to reporters that agents had dangled him from a nineteenth-

---

* In later years FBI agents gossiped that the ill-fated Probasco had struck a fire escape during his long fall, beheading him.

floor window, both Cowley and Hoover were concerned about bad publicity. For the most part the Chicago press ignored the story.

Louis Piquett, Art O'Leary, and Harold Cassidy were all rounded up in the following weeks. By that point, Cowley was deeply involved in the pursuits of Baby Face Nelson, Homer Van Meter, Pretty Boy Floyd, and the Barker Gang. The Dillinger case, however, was not quite closed.

As the FBI's own reports make clear, the story of Dillinger's betrayal told by Ana Sage and Polly Hamilton, though accepted by two generations of historians, made as little sense in 1934 as it does today. The two women told completely contradictory stories, and it was only a matter of time before someone questioned their veracity.

That Friday, July 27, someone did. It was Matt Leach. Leach came to the Bankers Building and met with Cowley behind closed doors. There was already tension between the FBI and the Indiana State Police, and the ill will only grew after this meeting.

Leach told Cowley he had an informant who said that Martin Zarkovich had sheltered Dillinger in East Chicago for at least two months, that Zarkovich had arranged the May 24 murders of two East Chicago detectives to cover this up, and that he had conspired to have the FBI kill Dillinger so that he could steal Dillinger's money. Leach said a "serious investigation" was warranted, and suggested the FBI conduct it. Cowley was skeptical. He said the Bureau was investigating the possibility Hamilton and Sage had harbored Dillinger, but noted that since Zarkovich had participated in his killing, there was no way a court would convict him of harboring. If Zarkovich had arranged to have the detectives murdered, he went on, that was a state crime, over which the FBI had no jurisdiction.

When Leach left, unsatisfied, Cowley telephoned Hoover. "Mr. Cowley stated he believes this is a frame-up," Hoover wrote in a memo that day. "I stated I am of the same opinion; that I believe they are jealous because they didn't get him themselves . . ."[24]

The FBI had no intention of investigating Hamilton and Sage, much less Zarkovich; the mysterious trio had become the Bureau's de facto allies, and Hoover's attitude appears to have been that anything that reflected badly on them, reflected badly on the Bureau. In the weeks after Dillinger's death, FBI agents took a single signed statement from Sage and none at all from Hamilton or Zarkovich. Two agents did interview Hamilton in Detroit on August 2, and from her evasive answers they believed she was hiding something.

"[I]t may clearly be seen that [her] information is very sketchy, and is in direct conflict with information furnished by Mrs. Anna [*sic*] Sage," the two agents wrote Cowley afterward. "In this regard, it is the conviction of both agents that no information will be developed that Dillinger ever resided at the residence of Mrs. Sage, as she has cautioned Polly against furnishing any information concerning this matter, and she, Mrs. Sage, is very careful that no opportunity is had to question Polly out of her presence."[25]

That was the last questioning of Hamilton the FBI ever did. Both she and Sage were released after their stay in Detroit. Hamilton vanished, hiding out with her parents in South Dakota. On Cowley's urging, Sage fled to Los Angeles, where in October Cowley visited her and handed over her share of the Dillinger reward money, $5,000.

Rather than delve further into the conspiracy that Matt Leach alleged, the Bureau began asking questions about Leach himself. Earl Connelley nosed for dirt around Indianapolis, and in mid-August notified Cowley that Leach had been paying "considerable attention" to a lady—not his wife—who was staying at the Spink Arms hotel.[26]

Leach was not intimidated. "We want to get to the bottom of this whole mess," he told the *Chicago Tribune.*[27] He never would.

They buried John Dillinger in the sprawling Crown Hill Cemetery in Indianapolis, amid a sudden summer rainstorm and a symphony of heavenly thunderclaps. His father had brought the body back from Chicago, the hearse trailed by a line of cars packed with reporters. A crowd of five thousand people pressed against a high stone fence beside the gravesight. John Dillinger, Sr., stood by solemnly as his son's coffin was lowered into the ground. The rain that ran in rivulets down his face looked like tears. Later that day he returned to his empty farmhouse. The reporters returned to their offices. The show was over.

16

THE SCRAMBLE

July 23 to September 12, 1934

Baby Face Nelson refused to panic, but he needed to get out of Chicago. The night after Dillinger's death he met his friend Jack Perkins in a North Side restaurant and asked him to come west with him and bring his wife and three-year-old son, Jackie. The group would look less suspicious with a child along, Nelson explained, and he couldn't bring his own; he assumed the FBI was watching them. Perkins agreed.

Two days later, Nelson's little band left Chicago in two cars, driving west across Iowa. Sleeping at out-of-the-way tourist camps, they reached Reno two nights later. Skirting the city, Nelson drove to the Cal-Neva Lodge, rousting a gambler friend, Tex Hall. Nelson wanted a place to hide. "Can't do it, Jimmy," Hall said. "You're too hot."

Irritated, Nelson moved on, looking for refuge in his old Bay Area haunts. The two cars crossed into California separately on the theory that two cars with Illinois plates might arouse suspicion at the border agricultural checkpoint. The next morning everyone rendezvoused at a sprawling country inn, the Parente Hotel, in the wine-country town of El Verano outside Sonoma. The inn was owned by Louis Parente, a cousin of the bootlegger who had employed Nelson in Sausalito. Nelson wasn't sure whether to trust Parente, but Negri, whose familiarity with the northern California underworld now made him Nelson's de facto guide, assured him Parente was "all right."

Parente was outside the hotel that morning when Nelson drove up, wearing white flannel slacks and a straw boater. "Hello, Louis," Nelson said. "How's the chance to get rooms in the hotel?" Parente just stared. "Don't you remember me?" Nelson asked. "I used to work for your cousin." Parente pointed Nelson to the front desk, where Nelson muttered that Parente had given him "the cold shoulder." The manager, Gus Zappas, assigned Nelson rooms on the first floor.

"Don't you remember me?" Nelson asked Zappas.

"You're Jimmy," Zappas said.

"Haven't I changed a lot?" Nelson asked.

"Not very much," Zappas said.

After lunch Nelson sent Perkins to the post office to see whether their wanted posters were displayed; to his relief, they weren't. He sent Negri into San Francisco to fetch his old bootlegging foreman, Soap Mareno. Mareno reluctantly agreed to drive up to El Verano, arriving around midnight. During a walk around the darkened hotel grounds, Nelson asked whether Mareno could arrange a hideout for the gang, preferably an isolated ranch. After an hour Mareno returned to San Francisco, leaving Nelson bitterly disappointed. "Can you believe that?" he told Negri. "Soap won't do a thing for me."

Any hopes Nelson had of hiding at the inn were dashed the next day after lunch. As they were leaving the dining room, someone yelled, "Hey, Fatso!" Negri turned and saw David Dillon, an officer with the San Francisco Police, eating with his wife. Negri stepped over to chat. "Who was that?" Nelson demanded when Negri returned. Negri explained that Dillon was a friend; he wouldn't say anything. Nelson was irate. He walked straight to the front desk and checked out.[1]

Nelson lingered in the wine country while trying to coax a hiding place out of old friends. The next night, after dinner in the town of Agua Caliente, he had the first of two meetings with Louis "Bones" Tambini, a bootlegger up from San Francisco; Tambini also said Nelson was "too hot" to hide. That night the Nelsons camped in a field, while Negri went to a hotel in Napa. Homesick, he walked to a pool hall and called his mother.

The next morning, Negri mentioned the call and Nelson became irate. "Haven't I told you never to use a telephone or write to anyone that you know?" he demanded. Nelson told Negri to go home to his mother and watch the *Chicago Tribune* classifieds; if they needed him, they would place an ad containing the word "Nondo."

His old haunts closed to him, Nelson stayed on the move, flitting between tourist camps in towns all across Northern California, in Caspar, Scotia, Eureka, Weaverville, and Sacramento, before heading south, staying in motels outside Salinas and Stockton.[2] Nelson saw that too many sets of eyes were seeing them at too many places; they needed a spot to settle down, even if it meant camping.

That's what it meant. Crossing into Nevada the morning of August 9, Nelson's band pulled up beside the Fallon Mercantile Store in Fallon, Nevada, east of Reno. Nelson stayed in the car while Perkins and the others shopped. They bought a $5.95 Coleman camping stove, a $5.95 Coleman lantern, an $18 Range Tent, camping utensils, groceries, and a Winchester rifle. Perkins paid for everything from a fat roll of one-dollar bills then, politely declining the owner's offer to help, used a hand truck to wheel the gear out to the cars, where he piled it onto a trailer they had bought in Reno.[3]

The following day Nelson found their new home, the Mount Grant Lodge, fourteen miles south of Hawthorne, Nevada, on the shores of Lake Walker. It was little more than a sprinkling of cabins, but it had running water and electricity, and for the first few days that was all Nelson felt they needed. The problem was Johnny Chase. He was the only single man in the group, and he was, for lack of a better word, lovesick. He pined for his girlfriend, a San Francisco newsstand clerk named Sally Backman, and nagged Nelson to let her join them in the desert. Everyone was against it. Nelson didn't trust new faces and said so, loudly.

Chase would not be dissuaded. One night he drove into San Francisco and arranged to see Backman. Negri picked her up at her newsstand by the Sausalito Ferry and drove her to a beach where Chase was waiting. They stayed that night in a hotel on Mission Street. In the quiet of their room, Chase explained he was traveling with someone who was "hot"; if Backman came with him, he couldn't guarantee her safety. She asked for time to think about it. Chase returned to the desert. Two weeks passed.

The longer they remained in Nevada, the more Chase missed Backman. Finally, tired of his friend's carping, Nelson relented. On Thursday, August 16, Chase got in his car and drove to San Francisco to get his girl. It was the worst decision Baby Face Nelson ever made.

On Wednesday, August 15, Ed Guinane, the San Francisco SAC, took a call from an Oakland detective who said he had a tip on Nelson. Guinane drove across the bay to hear it.* The detective's wife was Louis Parente's niece. The previous night Parente told the detective that Nelson had been at his inn three weeks before.

The next morning, Guinane convened a conference of FBI agents and detectives from the Oakland and San Francisco police departments. After briefings the group proceeded to the El Verano Inn to interview Louis Parente. Parente and his manager told them everything they knew. They identified Fatso Negri—the first time the FBI learned of him—and described Chase and the Perkins family. They also described Nelson's Hudson, though they hadn't noted the license plate number.

By Friday afternoon, Ed Guinane was dictating a memo to Hoover, laying out details of Nelson's stay in Napa County. The Teletype crossed Hoover's desk the next morning. "Take up with Cowley & I suggest he send by plane 4 or 5 agents familiar with Nelson to San Francisco," Hoover scrawled on it. Five men from the Dillinger Squad boarded a flight to San Francisco that night.†

Working with the San Francisco and Sausalito police, the new men quickly hit pay dirt. An informant reported that Chase had a girlfriend named Sally Backman. She had disappeared.[4]

On Saturday, August 18, the day the new FBI agents arrived in San Francisco, Chase drove up to the cabins on Walker Lake with Fatso Negri and Sally Backman. The desert heat was approaching one hundred degrees as Chase introduced Backman to everyone, giving only first names: Jack and Grace and their little boy, Jackie, and Helen, a quiet girl in a gingham house dress. Backman took an immediate dislike to the slender, cocky blond Chase introduced as "Jimmy," and Nelson made no effort to hide his distaste for her: he made snide comments about how everyone should work hard to ensure that Backman was "comfortable." The lodge's owner, John Benedict, noticed the friction between the two. He found Nelson "surly" but liked the others. When Benedict remarked that Backman seemed ill at ease, Chase told him she was a "city girl" unaccustomed to desert camping.[5]

The gang occupied three cabins, the Nelsons in one, the Perkins family

---

* It was the same Ed Guinane who had supervised the Halloween stakeout of Verne Miller in Chicago.
† This trip, and others like it, spawned a new nickname for the Dillinger Squad, "The Flying Squad." In time it would become known simply as the Special Squad.

in another, Chase and Backman in the third. Negri slept on a cot in the open air. They were the camp's only guests. Days they spent in idle pursuits. The women swam. Nelson slept for long periods. Sometimes he and Chase fished, though they rarely caught anything. Nelson, typically attired in faded tan corduroys and a wrinkled open-necked white shirt, liked to shoot rabbits and squirrels with his .22 rifle.

Most mornings Negri drove into Fallon or Hawthorne to buy food and newspapers. Nelson avidly scanned the papers or sometimes a copy of *Field & Stream;* he liked the articles on guns. Some evenings everyone but Nelson would drive into Hawthorne for dinner at a restaurant called the Oasis; Helen would bring Nelson back a tray of food. She usually found him sitting in the Hudson listening to news on the car radio. When they ate at camp, Helen handled the cooking and cleaning, consulting handmade recipe cards she carried in a little box.

Backman didn't help and didn't offer to, which raised tensions within the group. When she and Chase were alone, she constantly asked when they would leave. Chase said soon; they were "waiting for news." Backman wasn't dumb. She demanded to know who "Jimmy" really was. After a day or two of pestering, Chase told her the truth. Backman was startled. She began to nag Chase to leave the group.

Nelson was preparing to head back east. One morning the men took the Hudson into Reno to have it overhauled. Another day Nelson took the trailer into Hawthorne to have a tail light fixed; the last thing he needed was for a patrolman to pull him over. Then, on Thursday night, August 23, Nelson was slouched in the Hudson's front seat, listening to the radio, when he heard the news. It was Van Meter.

The night Dillinger was killed, Homer Van Meter took his girlfriend Mickey Conforti and drove to St. Paul, where he hoped to find shelter with Harry Sawyer at the Green Lantern or his partner Jack Peifer at the Hollyhocks Club. But Sawyer had disappeared that spring, and Peifer wanted nothing to do with the FBI agents on Van Meter's trail. In desperation Van Meter rented a room at a tourist camp outside the town of Walker, Minnesota. Nights he drove into St. Paul, trying to find someone who could hide him someplace safer.

For the next month, Van Meter and Conforti shuttled among tourist cabins in the pines north of St. Paul. The FBI suspected they might be in the area, but could find no one with hard information. "About 75 percent of the gangsters and mobsters of the underworld have scuttled out [of town], had their telephones disconnected and have moved," Cowley wrote Hoover at one point. "[E]verybody is on the hideout, knowing that they would be brought in for questioning."

Just who betrayed Van Meter will never be known. According to a story an informant told the FBI five years later, it was probably Jack Peifer. On Thursday morning, August 23, according to this story, Van Meter visited the Hollyhocks, where he met with Peifer, who may or may not have been holding several thousand dollars of cash for him, just as he was still holding money for Fred Barker and Alvin Karpis. The informant told the FBI Peifer waited until Van Meter left before telephoning his old friend Tom Brown, the corrupt detective who had worked with the Barker Gang on the Hamm and Bremer kidnappings. Brown had fallen under intense suspicion in St. Paul and presumably welcomed the idea of bringing in a noted yegg to burnish his image.

At 5:00 that afternoon, a car dropped Van Meter off a car dealership near downtown St. Paul. He wore a blue suit with a matching tie, white oxfords, and a straw boater; apparently he was expecting to meet someone. When he walked out of the dealership's front door at 5:12, he was confronted instead by Tom Brown, Police Chief Frank Cullen, two detectives, and their guns.

"Stick 'em up!" one of the officers yelled. Van Meter pulled a pistol from his waistband and sprinted across University Avenue, firing two shots over his shoulder; his straw boater teetered on his head and he grabbed it off, holding it in his hand as he ran. Brown and his men fired several shots and then, noticing a woman in their line of fire, ran after him. Dodging oncoming cars, Van Meter dashed down Marion Street, then ducked left into an alley.

It was a dead end. Van Meter stopped and turned to find the officers behind him. The first blast from Brown's sawed-off shotgun knocked Van Meter two feet in the air, slamming his body into the brick wall of a garage. He struggled to stand, but all four men opened fire, riddling his body with fifty bullets. Homer Van Meter, who always said he didn't want to die in some filthy alley, did just that.

When the news reached Washington an hour later, Hoover was incensed. "The Director is very upset over the fact that that thing could take place in St. Paul without our knowing about it," a St. Paul agent noted the next day. No one mentioned the obvious: the local police were excluding the FBI just as it had famously excluded the Chicago police from Dillinger's death. "I think our St. Paul office has shown utter lack of aggressiveness," Hoover scribbled on a memo.

Picked up several days later, Mickey Conforti told the FBI Van Meter had been carrying $6,000. The St. Paul police reported finding only $923. If Tom Brown took Van Meter's $5,077, there was an eerie symmetry at work: when Alvin Karpis and the Barker brothers read of Brown's involvement the next day, they unanimously decided to keep his $5,000 share of the Bremer ransom. The next day Homer Van Meter's body was taken to his hometown of Fort Wayne, Indiana. No one but an undertaker and a handful of reporters awaited its arrival. He was buried without event in Fort Wayne's Lindenwood Cemetery.

The morning after Van Meter's death, Baby Face Nelson sent Fatso Negri into town for newspapers. Like the Barkers, Nelson was stunned to read of Tom Brown's involvement. "The son of a bitch," Nelson said. "He's the fella that we paid a thousand dollars."[6]

Nelson announced they were leaving for Chicago. They packed the trailer with five-gallon cans of gasoline and oil; Nelson wanted to travel without stopping at service stations. They left a pile of cleaned trout for the cabins' owners, then drove across Nevada to Colorado and on into Kansas. Nelson allowed the group to sleep in auto camps, but was careful never to approach one before eleven at night.

Negri and the Perkins family rode in Negri's Plymouth, while Johnny Chase and Sally Backman sat in the backseat of Nelson's car. Packed into the tight confines of the Hudson, the simmering tensions between Backman and Nelson burst into the open. Nelson was a wild driver, the Hudson fishtailing across the dirt roads, and Backman asked him to slow down. He ignored her, starting in with comments about her "being scared" and asking if she was "comfortable." In time Nelson became even more aggressive, telling Chase in front of Backman that he should leave her, that she would tire of him in six months and go home.

According to a story Negri told a detective magazine in 1941, the ill will between Nelson and Backman came to a head at a roadside stop somewhere in Nebraska. Helen had made lunch on their camp stove and was cleaning up when Nelson snapped at Backman, "Why don't you get in there and help cook and clean up?"

"You go straight to hell!" Backman said. Negri described what he called "an electric shock" that passed through the rest of the group when they realized someone had openly challenged Nelson, something no one else, not even Dillinger, had ever done.

According to Negri, Nelson stared at Backman, then walked off. They drove that afternoon in silence, stopping after nightfall outside another Nebraska town. Everyone but Nelson decided to drive in to a restaurant; according to Negri, Nelson asked him to stay behind. When they were alone, Nelson said, "I'm going to hit Sally."[7]

Negri was struck by Nelson's choice of words. "It was the deadliest word Nelson could use against Sally," he recalled seven years later. "There was something about that word 'hit' when Nelson used it that struck me as the worst word any human being could utter against another. It was as cold as he was."

"What for?" Negri asked.

"She knows too much. I'm afraid of her . . . She looks queer to me." Nelson studied Negri's reaction.

"Jimmy, this is an awful tough spot," Negri said. "You know, Johnny would object. He's nuts about her." The gang, Negri suggested, would split apart. Chase knew too much to be an enemy.

Nelson thought a moment. "Well, if I hit her, I'll hit Johnny too," he said.

Negri was flabbergasted. "Jimmy, you wouldn't kill a swell guy like Johnny over a girl, would you?" he asked. "She and Johnny are going together now, but that won't last long. You and Johnny have been together a long time. He's the loyalest guy on earth. You can't find another [like him]." Negri went on, repeating himself for emphasis.

"Well," Nelson said, "I'll talk to Johnny about it."

When the others returned later that night, it was clear Chase had told Backman to make amends. She took Nelson a tray of food. "Here, Jimmy, is some swell food for you," she said.

Without a word Nelson kicked the tray out of her hand. Food and dishes fell to the ground. Chase stepped forward, startled.

"What's the argument?" he asked.

"I don't want nothing off that bum," Nelson said, meaning Backman.

"I don't talk to your wife that way," Chase said.

According to Negri, who was known to inflate his stories, Chase and Nelson each drew guns. Nobody moved. Finally Helen reached a hand toward Nelson, as if to mediate. "Get away from here," Nelson snapped.

"We'll settle this." For several long moments the two men stood facing each other, guns drawn. And then it passed. They lowered their guns, walked off into the darkness, and talked. The next day Backman and Chase rode across Iowa in Negri's car.

That night, Wednesday, August 29, the group crossed the Mississippi River, stopping at East Burlington, Illinois; the Perkins family was anxious to get home and drove on to Chicago, taking Negri with them. For the next three days Nelson wandered Chicago's western suburbs, stopping at road-houses to look up old friends, gauging the "heat" and sending out feelers to trusted contacts.

On Sunday afternoon, September 2, a hard rain was falling when Nelson pulled up in front of Hobart Hermanson's tavern in Lake Geneva, Wisconsin; Nelson had spent several weeks that spring living in a cottage at Hermanson's Lake Como Lodge, and wanted to do so again that autumn. Chase ran inside, returning a minute later to say they could probably find Hermanson or his handyman, Eddie Duffy, at Hermanson's home outside town. They drove through the rain to Hermanson's house. Duffy was home and welcomed them. Helen walked to the icebox and took out enough chicken for everyone. Nelson seemed relieved.

The tension between Nelson and Sally Backman remained, however, and Backman finally told Chase she couldn't take it anymore. If he stayed with Nelson, she was going back to San Francisco. Chase talked it over with Nelson, and the two couples decided to split up. That night, Tuesday, September 4, Nelson dropped Chase and Backman on a corner in Elgin, Illinois. For three days the two young lovers slept till noon; at night they took the train into Chicago to dance. On the fourth day Nelson dropped by, handed Chase $3,500 in cash, and told how to reach him via a coded classified advertisement in the Reno paper. Chase promised Backman he would never work with Nelson again.

Despite the hysteria over Dillinger that summer, the Bureau continued its efforts to solve the mystery of the Kansas City Massacre. In March the be-lated identification of Adam Richetti's fingerprint on a beer bottle found in Verne Miller's basement had redirected the hunt for answers toward Pretty Boy Floyd. Sightings came in from every corner of the country: Montana, New Mexico, Miami, New York, New Orleans. Floyd's estranged wife,

Ruby, was touring off and on with a vaudeville show, *Crime Doesn't Pay.* Agents bugged her hotel rooms but could find no evidence she was in touch with her husband.

Then, on May 16, Dwight Brantley, the Oklahoma City SAC, took a phone call from a seventy-six-year-old attorney in Pawhuska, Oklahoma, named A. W. Comstock. Comstock told Brantley he had been contacted by Floyd, who had asked him to negotiate a surrender. He said Floyd was broke and badly wounded, having been shot in the back by parties unknown. Comstock sought two assurances, that Floyd would not be killed and that he would receive medical treatment.[8] The Bureau agreed. Hoover called and arranged to have prison hospitals at Leavenworth, Kansas, and Springfield, Missouri, ready to accept Floyd's surrender.[9]

Talks with Comstock went on for one week, then two, as he sought information about reward monies and state charges Floyd faced in Ohio. Hoover grew impatient. "[T]his matter must be pressed, and pressed vigorously," Hoover wrote Cowley on May 31. "This matter has now dragged along for several weeks, and we don't seem to be any nearer toward the getting hold of Floyd than we were when the original negotiations were entered into."[10] Brantley stayed in contact with Comstock for two more weeks but eventually came to believe the attorney's only contact had been Ruby Floyd, not her husband. Comstock "impresses me as being silly, inane and bordering on senility," Brantley wrote Hoover on June 15. "[I]t is my best judgment that it is a waste of time, effort and money to deal with him further."[11]

An ensuing set of negotiations, this time with a flamboyant Texas minister named J. Frank Norris, at first seemed a little more promising. Norris, pastor of the First Baptist Church in Fort Worth, was a fire-breathing radio preacher with a past—tried and acquitted of murder at one point, accused of burning his own church at another. Ruby Floyd was one of his listeners, and on Father's Day, June 17, she arranged to have her son, Jackie, baptized at his church. The ceremony was broadcast before an audience of five thousand on Norris's radio show; a four-minute film of the baptism was incorporated into Ruby's vaudeville show, which was booked at Fort Worth's Palace Theatre. Agents shadowed Ruby and her entourage throughout her ten-day stay in Fort Worth.

Afterward Norris telephoned the Dallas SAC, Frank Blake, and offered to negotiate Floyd's surrender. Hoover, skeptical after the Comstock episode, took a hard line. "I told Mr. Blake I felt we would have to take the attitude that we will agree not to kill Floyd" if he surrenders, Hoover wrote in a memo June 23. "I suggested, in this connection, that [Blake] make it clear that orders are out to kill Floyd on sight, and if he doesn't surrender in short time, he will no doubt be killed by our men."[12] The same day, Hoover ordered Pop Nathan to concentrate exclusively on Floyd's capture. "I think the time has come . . . when we should definitely concentrate upon the handling of this case," Hoover wrote Nathan, adding in a separate memo, "we are going to kill him if we catch him."[13]

Ruby's run at the Palace Theatre ended on June 27 and she returned to Oklahoma. But the Reverend Norris would not give up. He pleaded with Pop Nathan to let him take an agent to Oklahoma to meet with Floyd's mother. To the surprise of almost everyone at the Bureau, Norris was as good as his word, and on July 10 an agent accompanied the reverend to a meeting with Mrs. Floyd and Pretty Boy's siblings. The scene devolved into a gripe session, with his family insisting Floyd had been hounded by police into a life of crime. Still, it represented the first time in nearly a year of investigation the Bureau was able to assemble the names and addresses of Floyd's immediate relatives.

They were getting nowhere. Though agents combed the towns of eastern Oklahoma and northern Arkansas for months, there hadn't been a confirmed sighting of Floyd since the previous summer. By July, four months after identifying Richetti's fingerprint and a year after the massacre itself, the Bureau had a tentative theory of the case—that Floyd and Richetti had somehow teamed with Verne Miller—but other than a single fingerprint, they had no evidence to back it up. They talked to dozens of informants who claimed to know Miller or Floyd, but none produced anything suggesting the two outlaws knew each other.

The mystery of the massacre began to unravel only on July 10, when the Kansas City Mob boss Johnny Lazia was shot down as he stepped from his car outside the Park Central Hotel. The killing initially meant nothing to the FBI, which had no jurisdiction. Not until August 6, when a Kansas City newspaper reported that a hospitalized gangster named Jack Griffin had been one of Lazia's assassins, did the Bureau stir. The Kansas City office had been looking for Griffin, suspecting—inaccurately—that he was a member of the Barker Gang. For the moment the Bureau had no clue that Griffin might be linked to the massacre.

Two agents visited Griffin in the hospital. He was suffering from multiple gunshot wounds, the result of a botched attempt on his life. He refused to answer questions, but suggested the agents return a few days later, when he might have something to say. The agents waited seventeen days. When they returned to interview Griffin on August 23, he had disappeared. No one seemed to know where he had gone. For the moment, no one really cared. Griffin was just another yegg.

Then one of the bullets used to kill Lazia, sent for tests to a Kansas City ballistics laboratory, was found to match bullets fired at the massacre. With a start, the Kansas City office realized Jack Griffin might hold the key to the massacre case. The new SAC, Bruce Nathan, shared the news with Kansas City's chief of detectives, Thomas Higgins. It was then, on August 24, six weeks after Lazia's assassination, that Higgins told the Bureau what everyone in the Kansas City underworld already knew: Griffin and three of his pals had killed Lazia in a gambling dispute. Lazia's men had been hunting them ever since. If the FBI thought Griffin and his men could solve the massacre case, they needed to find them before the Mob did.

Once again, the Bureau found itself in a race with the syndicate. Belatedly, the Kansas City office mobilized. They first tried to find Griffin. A little digging turned up the disquieting fact that he had been discharged from the hospital into the care of a notorious Kansas City detective named Jeff Rayan. Rayan was considered to be a mob enforcer; Griffin hadn't been seen since. All three of Griffin's partners, a St. Louis racketeer named Al O'Brien, a Kansas City nightclub owner named Nugent LaPlumma, and a skinny drug addict named Michael LaCapra, known as "Jimmy Needles," had disappeared.

All that week the Kansas City office tracked leads on the four men. On Friday morning, August 31, they managed to pull in Griffin's girlfriend. Agents had just begun to interview her when the *Kansas City Journal Post* hit the streets. The newspaper reported that "Jimmy Needles" LaCapra was in custody in Wichita, Kansas, along with three Kansas City gangsters who had tried to kill him.

Two Kansas City agents, Harold Anderson and Walter Trainor, reached Wichita that night. A desk sergeant briefed them. LaCapra had been hiding in his hometown of Argonia, twenty miles southwest of Wichita. The night before, he had been out driving when a black Ford pulled alongside; three men inside opened up with submachine guns. LaCapra ducked, uninjured, and the Ford sped off. LaCapra scrambled to the Wichita police station for safety even as the men who tried to kill him had a traffic accident and were arrested by the Kansas State Highway Patrol. All four men were now sitting in cells.

Anderson and Trainor first tried to talk to LaCapra's would-be assassins, whose bruised faces gave vivid testament to the interrogation techniques of Kansas lawmen. "Each of these men sat mute throughout the interviews and all they would say was they had just been out for a little friendly ride," Trainor wrote in his report. "It was evident from the appearance of the three . . . that they had undergone physical punishment, probably at the hands of the Kansas Highway Patrol."[14]

Jimmy Needles was another matter. A jittery, emaciated career criminal in his early forties, LaCapra was ecstatic to see the two FBI men approaching his cell. The words came spilling out of him, so fast the two agents at first couldn't keep his stories straight. "The statements of LaCapra were, of course, very jumbled and rambling and he appeared to be under a very great nervous strain, although he did not appear to be out of his mind in any manner," Trainor noted in his report. "He asked the Agents to give him protection, stating that he might be killed at any minute by the mob . . . He said that he knows he has but a short time to live but that any help the Government may be able to give him would be reciprocated by him."[15]

And then he said the words the FBI had waited to hear for more than a year: *The massacre. Verne Miller. Pretty Boy Floyd. Johnny Lazia.* He could tell them the whole story.

Cleveland, Ohio
September 3

Alvin Karpis lay on the warm roof of his Ford, watching the heavens. It was a glorious late-summer day, cotton clouds floating in a turquoise sky. Delores Delaney lay beside him. He could hear her breathing. She was pregnant, almost four months along and starting to show. Above them, the Cleveland Air Show was nearing its climax. Airplanes dived and spun. All around, hundreds of couples sat out on blankets, faces turned upward, watching.

It had been five months since the Barker Gang fled Chicago in the wake of George Ziegler's murder, five blissfully quiet months without a hint the FBI knew where they were. Karpis had a new job and new friends. He hadn't committed a notable crime since washing his hands of Ed Bremer in

February; he hadn't robbed a bank in seventeen months. The gang had all but fallen apart. He had done everything he could to distance himself from the others. They were dumb and they drank and they took chances. He and Delores lived a quiet life, in bed most nights by eleven. They could almost relax.

Tensions inside the gang had risen after the move to Toledo. They kept low profiles; a local vice lord, Joe Roscoe, looked after them. Within weeks the money ran low. They still had $150,000 of the ransom money and covered their expenses passing bits of it in Chicago supermarkets. But after the drunken Dr. Moran's money-laundering operation was uncovered, they could find no one to move the bulk of it. Dock Barker ran out to Reno, but friends there refused to get involved. All the Dillinger publicity had changed the public mood. Now even the gang's old contacts shunned them. Karpis dwelled on the Syndicate. Dillingermania had brought unwanted heat on its operations, and Karpis wondered whether Frank Nitti wanted them dead.

So they had sat and waited and worried, passing the days drinking beer, fishing on Lake Erie, riding roller-coasters at the Willow Bay Amusement Park, and requesting their favorite songs at Toledo's premier underworld hangout, the Casino Club. They were all regulars at the club, Karpis and the Barkers sitting in a corner booth, nursing their drinks, old Charlie Fitzgerald cursing the waitresses when they watered his bourbon. An errand boy they brought from Chicago, a onetime golf pro named Willie Harrison, kept everyone entertained, mock-directing the band. One night a singer, a Scottish crooner who performed in a kilt, didn't take to direction, so Harrison slugged him, igniting a brawl that ended only when Fred Barker coolly placed a pistol to Harrison's temple. Freddie didn't like scenes. They drew attention.

The odd donnybrook aside, it was boring. They had little to do but drink. Fred's girl, Paula Harmon, gulped whiskey all day every day, and she was a nasty drunk. Another gang member, Harry Campbell, bought his nineteen-year-old girlfriend Wynona Burdette an ill-tempered Pekinese. One day Karpis and Freddie were sitting in Barker's apartment when they heard gunfire. "Did you hear what I heard?" Karpis asked.

"Yeah," said Barker. "That's a machine gun."

A few moments later they heard running steps in the stairwell outside. The bell rang. Someone began kicking the door. Karpis darted into the bedroom, grabbed a submachine gun, and stood to one side of the door.

He motioned to Freddie to jerk the door open. Campbell tumbled into the apartment, a bloody towel wrapped around his arm. "What the hell happened?" Karpis demanded. "Is someone after you?"

"No, no," Campbell said. He was in obvious pain. "That goddamn dog. He went in the neighbors' yard and I sneaked up behind to grab him. He wouldn't come when I called him and that son of a bitch spun around and got me right on the arm. He bit me two or three times."

Karpis laughed. They unwrapped the towel and found deep, bloody teeth marks up and down Campbell's arm. "I got to get some kind of shots for this," he said.

"I'll get hold of Joe Roscoe and find out if he's got a doctor who can take care of this," said Karpis.

Just then Dock Barker walked in. "Well, hell, that Doc Moran, he wants to come here and get away from Chicago," Barker said. "Why the hell don't we have him give the shots to Campbell? I'll go to Chicago and get him and bring him up here."

A few days later Dock returned with Moran, his assistant and their pal Ollie Berg, all eager to flee Chicago. The trio stayed in a hotel and spent their days drinking. Karpis began to get edgy. "I don't think I'm gonna stay around here," he told Fred in May. "There's too many people and there's too much drinking going on."

Karpis's concerns coincided with a job offer from a pair of new friends, a squat mobster named Shimmy Patton and his partner, a thin blond named Art Heberbrand. The two were opening a swank new casino called the Harvard Club in the Cleveland suburb of Newberg Heights and, worried about threats from a rival syndicate, they asked Karpis if he would handle security. Looking for anything to fill his days, and eager to distance himself from the rest of the gang, Karpis accepted. Fred sulked when he wasn't asked as well. Within days Karpis packed up and moved with Delores to a brick bungalow near the Cleveland airport. It was a quiet neighborhood, green squares of lawn, children in the streets. Delores got busy buying furniture. Karpis liked it.

The casino job was a breeze. Most evenings Karpis threw on his new tuxedo, drove over to the club, and drifted among the gamblers, checking the dice, watching for trouble, and tossing out the occasional drunk. After midnight he propped himself against a wall and watched the accountants count the cash. It was good money, and in idle moments Karpis allowed himself to imagine his life if he had found such a job early on, before he set to robbing banks. He made a list of the rival syndicates' addresses and each of their children, then sent it to an intermediary with a blunt message: if the Harvard Club was harassed in any way, their houses would be burned down and their children roughed up. There was no trouble after that.

He drove down to Toledo every few days to talk with Fred. The situation there was deteriorating fast. The drunken Dr. Moran had performed fingerprint-removal "surgery" on Dock Barker and was now demanding a share of the ransom money as payment. He was spending evenings at a Toledo brothel, and its madame, Edith Barry, took Dock aside one night and told him Moran had been bragging about the surgeries. "Everything in general is getting bad with this guy," Dock told Karpis. "I don't know what the hell to do." Actually, they did. A few nights later Fred and Dock forcibly removed Moran from the Casino Club, shot him in the face, and buried him in an unmarked grave in Michigan. The FBI would continue to hunt Moran for months and only reluctantly accepted the fact of his death. His body has never been found.

Moran's demise did little to assuage Karpis's concerns. Despite all his efforts, the others stuck to him like tar. Restless in Toledo, they followed him to Cleveland one by one. Freddie and Paula Harmon took a bungalow on West 171st Street. Harry Campbell rented an apartment on Franklyn Boulevard. Even Harry Sawyer and his wife, Gladys, came, taking over Fred Barker's spare bedroom. The Sawyers had fled St. Paul one step ahead of the FBI that spring, and had been shuffling between Nevada tourist camps ever since. To Karpis's dismay, they brought their five-year-old adopted daughter, Francine, with them. Karpis so detested their presence he moved to a new house on West 140th Street. He told only Fred his new address, and he forbade Delores from seeing the gang's other women. They were trouble.

Matters came to a head when Volney Davis arrived from Chicago and began demanding his cut of the ransom. The money was an increasingly sore subject. Dock had kept it for a while, but eventually they decided to stow it at Bill Weaver's lakeside cottage. It fit into two Gladstone bags, and Karpis gave it all to Weaver, but warned him never to leave it in the house unattended. Weaver wasn't the brightest soul, however, and the next time they visited the cottage they discovered the house unlocked and empty. They found Weaver walking on the beach and roundly cursed him. After that Fred and Karpis took the money and buried it in the soft dirt beneath Karpis's garage.

By mid-summer only Ma Barker remained in Chicago, lost in her jigsaw puzzles. Karpis drove over to visit her one weekend and found she was doing surprisingly well. He and Dock took her to see a movie. To their horror, the film was preceded by a newsreel warning moviegoers to be on the lookout for Dillinger, Nelson, Pretty Boy Floyd, Karpis, and the Barkers. Karpis scrunched low in his seat as their pictures flashed on the screen. "One of these men may be sitting next to you," the announcer said. Karpis pulled his hat low over his forehead. Afterward he made the rounds of Cicero taverns, trying to deduce whether the Syndicate was after them. An old friend told him to beat it. Karpis got the message. He quickly returned to Cleveland.

Weeks crept by. Fred and Karpis talked about taking an Ohio bank, but until the money ran out there was no rush. Delores got pregnant and asked Karpis whether she should get another abortion; he didn't have the heart to put her through it again, so he would soon be a father. Then one night in July, Karpis showed up for work at the casino and Art Heberbrand took him aside. "An hour from now, there's going to be a couple of guys coming in, we want you to talk to 'em," he said. Karpis asked if they expected trouble. "No, no, no trouble," he said. They waited in the office until darkness fell, and Heberbrand rose from his chair. "Let's walk out to the parking lot," he said.

Karpis followed. Outside he sat on a car's running board and wondered what all the mystery was about. Finally one of Heberbrand's men materialized and said, "They're here, boys."

"Come on," Heberbrand said.

Karpis followed him toward a Ford sedan. Inside were two men. Karpis immediately recognized the driver. He couldn't believe it: it was Pretty Boy Floyd. Beside him sat Adam Richetti. Heberbrand made the introductions. The four men took seats in a shack at the back of the parking lot. Floyd was morose. "Chances are we'll both get killed or get caught in the end," he said. "But I'm hoping that we both get killed rather than get caught." Karpis nodded. He knew the feeling.

Floyd hemmed and hawed a few minutes before coming around to the purpose of his visit. He wanted to take a bank with the Barker Gang. As he put it, "Us guys would like to make some money if you guys got anything that you'd like to take that you need more guys on."

Karpis thought about a Cleveland bank Fred had been casing. "Well, we might have something in a few weeks, but I'm not too certain about it," he said. "But you know how these things are. It may be good, it may be bad. If you guys are willing to go on it and we need someone, how'll we get ahold of you?" Floyd pointedly declined to reveal where he was hiding. "You can get hold of me through these guys here, they know how to get ahold of me," he said. Afterward Karpis watched Floyd drive off. "I wish to Christ you hadn't even let them guys know we're around here," he told Heberbrand.

"Hell, I thought all you guys stick together."

"Don't believe everything you read," Karpis said. "We could have been with Dillinger, we could have been with this guy or that guy, but we didn't want no part of 'em. These guys, they seem to get jumped up every week or so. Just any day now I expect to see where Dillinger's been hopped up and maybe even killed. It won't be long. These guys, I don't know, they just seem to draw the heat wherever they go."

Karpis never saw Floyd again, and a few nights later he emerged from a movie to hear newspaper vendors calling out news of Dillinger's death in Chicago.* Karpis considered it an assassination. It could just as easily have been him; just a few nights earlier, he and Delores had seen *Manhattan Melodrama,* the same movie Dillinger watched before his death. A month after that came news of Van Meter's death in St. Paul. Karpis read of Tom Brown's involvement and guessed that Van Meter had been betrayed. This was bad. Chicago and Reno were already closed to them. And now St. Paul. "You and I can expect that same goddamn thing from now on," he told Fred. "No one wants us around."

The more he stewed, the more antsy Karpis grew. He had been in one place too long. It was time to make a clean break from the rest of the gang. First they had to dispose of the remaining ransom money, about $100,000. In August they finally found someone to move it, a wealthy Detroit hoodlum named Cash McDonald. McDonald said he could fence it through gambling friends in Havana, who would disperse the money via banks in Mexico and Venezuela.

Karpis and Fred Barker received a rude surprise when they went to dig

---

* Karpis's new friends weren't limited to criminals. He would later claim to have dined with Joseph Keenan, the Justice Department attorney who prosecuted Machine Gun Kelly and Roger Touhy. In interviews recorded years later, Karpis said the introduction was made by one of Keenan's high school classmates, a Cleveland detective named Frank Noonan. Karpis claimed that he masqueraded as a gambler and that Keenan had no idea who he really was. During their dinner Keenan boasted of "putting Harvey Bailey away" even though everyone in the FBI knew he wasn't guilty of the Urschel kidnapping. The story is impossible to confirm, and although Karpis would seem too smart to take such a risk, there is circumstantial evidence to back it up. The FBI would later investigate Noonan for harboring Karpis. And according to FBI files, Keenan was in Cleveland during the week of July 20, 1934.

up the money. Water had seeped into the Gladstone bags. The bills were sopping wet. The day McDonald was to arrive for his trip to Cuba, the two spent several furious hours scattering wet bills around Karpis's bungalow, erecting fans to dry it out. McDonald wasn't happy when they gave him $100,000 in damp bills, but he took it. They sent Harry Sawyer and Willie Harrison along to keep an eye on him. McDonald promised he would return via Miami in several days.

As he lay on the roof of his car that afternoon, watching the planes overhead, Karpis had already decided to leave Cleveland when McDonald returned with the laundered cash. Sitting in the warm sun, his mind wandering, he became transfixed by a biplane flown by a German fighter ace from the Great War. It was odd to see a German pilot here in Ohio, a onetime American enemy now allowed to fly freely in the skies over a Midwestern city; just sixteen years before, the man had tried to kill American fliers, and they had tried to kill him. Now here he was, as free as the proverbial bird.

The German plane flitted about like a mosquito, zooming low over the trees, then climbing straight up toward the sun. At one point another plane came in so low Karpis sat up to follow. As he watched, the plane plunged directly into the ground. The pilot was killed instantly. Black smoke curled into the sky. Karpis stared. For reasons he didn't entirely understand, he was overwhelmed with sadness.

Homer Van Meter's death marked a turning point for the FBI. The Dillinger Gang was finished. As far as Hoover was concerned, what remained of the War on Crime was strictly a mopping-up operation. More than once, he said there was no place left for the "rats" to hide, and in large part he was right. One benefit of Dillingermania was the publicity given the other Public Enemies; their mug shots now scowled regularly from the pages of newspapers from Miami to Seattle.

Hoover had supreme confidence in Sam Cowley. On September 6 the Director formalized Cowley's position as the Bureau's wartime field general, handing him unrestricted power to hunt down Baby Face Nelson, Pretty Boy Floyd, Karpis, and the Barkers; he could go anywhere, mobilize any agent, assume command of any office. "I would like to have these three cases concluded within the next thirty or forty-five days if possible," Hoover wrote Cowley on September 5.[16]

Cowley's elevation came at Melvin Purvis's expense. Since the Dillinger shooting, Purvis had fallen deeper and deeper into Hoover's disfavor. Twice Hoover had fired off terse letters when he was unable to reach Purvis by phone. The smallest things set Hoover off; he sent Purvis one letter demanding to know why a delivery of Chicago newspaper articles had been delayed. For the most part, Purvis was removed from all investigative work. As his secretary, Doris Rogers, looked on with sympathy, he spent his days filling out personnel reports, interviewing job applicants, and shining his shoes.

Cowley knew Hoover was underestimating the difficulty of apprehending Nelson, Floyd, and the Barkers. He made the Barkers his new priority, switching a dozen agents from the Dillinger case and putting them to work on the Barkers. Unfortunately, there weren't many leads to chase. Working at his desk in the Bankers Building late into the night, Cowley cranked out several thick reports listing every member of the gang, their girlfriends, family members, and relatives. He had precious little information on the gang's inner workings, however. The Barkers seemed far more secretive than Dillinger. They made no contact with their families, as the FBI learned during several frustrating months watching Dock and Fred's father, George Barker, putter around his Missouri service station. There were no girlfriends to interview; six months after debriefing Beth Green, she remained the only person who had given the FBI any firsthand insight into the gang.

A second had dropped into Cowley's lap on August 18, when agents arrested a woman named Helen Ferguson at her Chicago apartment. Ferguson had dated a minor member of the gang who had been killed during a robbery in Nebraska; she gave agents chapter and verse on the gang. Unfortunately, she hadn't seen any of the Barkers for more than a year. After a week of interrogation Cowley released her, but told her to stay in touch. She might prove useful down the line.

The clue that finally led the Bureau to Toledo had been moldering in the Chicago file room for four months. It was contained in a list of phone calls made from Dr. Moran's office. In the heat of the Dillinger hunt, agents simply hadn't enough time to track down all the numbers. Not until Dillinger's death did the Detroit office discover that Moran had phoned a Toledo gambler named Ted Angus, owner of the Barker's favorite nightspot, the Casino Club. On Tuesday night, September 4, the Detroit SAC, William Larson, took a risk and telephoned Angus at his club. Larson identified himself as a friend of "Dock's" and said it was urgent he reach Dock Barker. "Well, you know Dock is a pretty hard man to get in touch with," Angus replied.

Yes, Larson went on, Dock was hard to find, but it was urgent he know of some things developing in Chicago. "Where can I call you tomorrow?" Angus asked. Larson said he was at a pay phone and couldn't be reached. He promised to call again the following night.

Larson put down the phone convinced that Angus knew where the Barkers were. Now he needed someone inside, someone who could gain Angus's confidence. He telephoned Chicago and told one of Cowley's men to send Helen Ferguson to Detroit as soon as possible.

Cleveland, Ohio
Wednesday, September 5

The morning after Larson's ruse call to Toledo, a man walked into Cleveland police headquarters and asked if he could see a photograph of Baby Face Nelson. He thought he might know where Nelson was living. The man was taken to the Bureau of Identification, shown the picture and shook his head, saying it wasn't the man he had seen. He asked to see other Wanted posters but was told the department didn't keep such a file. Well, the man said, he was positive there was a fellow living at 4419 West 172nd Street in Cleveland who was a wanted criminal. Then he left. No one got his name.

A few hours later, at a bungalow at 4419 West 171st Street, three women were preparing for an afternoon on the town. Life as a fugitive was ponderous, and Paula Harmon, Gladys Sawyer, and Wynona Burdette had taken to coping the best way they knew. They drank. That afternoon, the three women put on their finest clothes and jewels and, along with Sawyer's adopted daughter, Francine, drove downtown to the Cleveland Hotel, where they took seats in the hotel bar, the Bronze Room.

By five o'clock all three women were thoroughly and loudly drunk. When the manager asked them to leave, Harmon told him to go to hell. The manager called a house detective, who confronted the women and, as Harmon loudly cursed him, escorted them to the lobby, where Gladys Sawyer vomited impressively on the marble floor. The police were called. At 5:30 a policewoman named Mildred Wilcox arrived and told the women they were under arrest for disturbing the peace. Harmon took off a diamond bracelet and offered it to Wilcox if she would leave them alone.

Wilcox declined the offer. The women went quietly—at first. Gladys Sawyer was so drunk they had to cart her out in a wheelchair. It was when they were being led to a waiting patrol car that the trio realized they were in trouble. Cursing and shouting, Sawyer swung at Officer Wilcox, hitting her beneath the right eye. Wilcox charged the three women and all four fell in a heap on the sidewalk, Harmon and Burdette cursing and kicking Wilcox in the ribs. The policewoman yelled for help. Two beat cops heard her cries. Harmon was trying to run off when they arrived. Together the three policemen dragged the struggling, cursing trio into a squad car. Little Francine came along, too.

The two male cops jumped onto the running board as they headed downtown. As they drove, Harmon opened a window and attempted to dump out the contents of her purse. The officers stopped the car and retrieved the things she dropped. At the Women's Bureau of the Cleveland Jail, all three women gave false names and refused to answer any questions. Thrown into cells, Harmon screamed and cursed, demanding that someone call Shimmy Patton, the Harvard Club's boss. Gladys Sawyer sat and cried, worrying about Francine. Wynona Burdette stood in a corner, brooding. "Keep a stiff upper lip," Burdette hollered to Gladys at one point. "Don't say nothing."[17]

About 11 P.M.

Karpis sat down on the bed, his Thompson submachine gun on the side table, as Delores slid beneath the covers. Suddenly there was a loud knock at the front door. Karpis sprang to attention; no one but Freddie knew his new address. He put on his shoes and trousers and grabbed the Thompson. "You go to the door and if it's anybody at all that we don't know, just let them come on in," he whispered to Delores. "I'll take care of the rest of it."

Delaney threw a coat over her nightgown, walked into the living room, and opened the door. Karpis heard Freddie's voice. Freddie, Dock, and Harry Campbell walked in.

"What the hell's going on?" Karpis asked.

"Go ahead get your clothes on," Freddie said. "Things are real bad." Karpis and Delores finished dressing, then sat in the living room. Freddie told them what had happened. He wasn't worried about the women. "But they're questioning that little girl and she's gonna tell them everything," Freddie said. "They've probably sent for the FBI."

They hadn't. The Cleveland Police Department, in fact, had no idea who the three drunken women hauled into headquarters that evening actually were. Harmon gave her name as "Mrs. Earl J. Matterson," Burdette as "Wynona Walcott." Only Gladys Sawyer inexplicably gave her real name. She even gave her address in St. Paul. None of it meant anything to the desk clerk who checked them into jail that night.

But the policewoman, Mildred Wilcox, suspected something was amiss. The jewelry, the screaming fight, the attempted bribe—she could tell the women were hiding something. She and a detective sat little Francine in a chair and gently questioned her.

What did her daddy do for a living? they asked.

"He runs a joint," Francine said. In St. Paul.

And her daddy's friends? "They never work and they have lots of money." How did her mommy get to the Cleveland Hotel? "In the Packard," Francine said. She mentioned the name of the garage where they had parked. "Do the men ride around in the Packard, too?" one of the detectives asked. "Oh, no!" Francine answered. "They go out in the little car they get in just outside town. They put blue license plates on it first." And could she remember the license plate number?

"No, sir," said Francine. "I am only a little girl and I can't count higher than thirteen."[18]

When another detective mentioned the man who thought he had seen Baby Face Nelson, his superiors smelled something big. Escorted by Francine, detectives descended on the garage she had mentioned and found the Packard. In it they discovered a .38 caliber pistol and a slip of paper with two addresses written on it. One was 4419 West 171st Street. It was one block away from the address of the supposed Nelson sighting. At 4:00 A.M. a squad car under the direction of Detective Lieutenant Kirk Gloeckner was sent to raid the house on West 171st Street.

Thursday, September 6

Midnight came and went as the gang clustered in Karpis's living room, debating how long their homes would be safe. There was talk of leaving town immediately, but that made no sense. At the very least, they needed their guns. Between them the four men had a single machine gun and the pistols they carried. Freddie wanted his clothes.

They drove to Freddie's house on West 171st Street, cruising by without seeing police. Freddie ran inside. He returned with several Gladstone bags filled with his guns. From there they drove to Harry Campbell's flat, thinking they could retrieve another machine gun. From the street they saw three men inside.* Karpis cursed. The machine gun was the one they had used in the South St. Paul robbery. If it was identified, there would be no doubt who they were. They returned to Karpis's bungalow to debate their next move.

The squad car commanded by Lieutenant Gloeckner pulled up outside 4419 West 171st Street a little after four. Officers pounded on the door. No one answered. The cops forced their way in. Inside, Gloeckner and his men found papers indicating the occupants were Mr. and Mrs. Earl Matterson, Gladys Sawyer, and one other man. But what drew Gloeckner's attention were the contents of a bedroom drawer. In it he found a notebook. The pages were covered with penciled notations. It was a route map between two locations. The FBI would later identify it as a getaway map.†

Beside the notebook Gloeckner found a rolled-up piece of paper that turned out to be the fingerprint portion of a torn-up Wanted poster. On the back was a notation that "Fred Barker" was wanted for murder; later that day, a clerk at the police headquarters would identify the fingerprint as Fred Barker's. Gloeckner's boss, Captain Frank Story, realized the Barker Gang must be hiding in Cleveland. After the sun rose he hurriedly canvassed other detectives for any stories of suspicious new faces in town. One detective told him of a man his sister-in-law had mentioned. He lived on a bungalow on 140th Street. On a hunch, Story had the woman review photographs of the Barker Gang. Immediately she chose a picture of Alvin Karpis. Story dispatched a car to the 140th Street bungalow.[19]

As police closed in, the four gang members remained at Karpis's bungalow in the hours before dawn, debating their next move. "The best damn thing we can do now is somebody leave and get into Toledo and get an apartment," Karpis said. "First thing in the morning we're gonna duck in some place till we decide what to do, but you can bet we're gonna have to get the hell out of here."

Dock and Campbell took one car and left for Toledo, promising to meet them by the Casino Club later that day. Karpis called his boss, Shimmy Patton, and asked him to check the women's situation. Then he and Freddie

---

* If Karpis's memory is correct, it's unclear who these men were. The Cleveland police would not locate Campbell's apartment for several days.

† The list was the gang's git from the South St. Paul payroll robbery. It showed detailed driving instructions from St. Paul to Davenport, Iowa.

switched off the lights and sat in the dark, waiting. Delores actually managed to go to sleep. At dawn Karpis was pacing in a back room when Delores materialized and said there was a car out front. Karpis peeked out the blinds. It was a Ford coupe. He recognized the men inside as Patton and Art Heberbrand. Karpis went out to the car, glancing down the street as he walked.

"You guys are gonna have to get out of here in the next half hour," Patton warned. Patton had called a friend on the force. He said the women hadn't talked. But little Francine had said plenty. One call to St. Paul would be enough. FBI men would arrive within hours.

"Just get the hell on out of town," Heberbrand said. "In a few weeks, if you want, come on back and we'll let you know how things stand around here."

"How do things look now?" Karpis asked.

"Well, down the street a little ways from here, there's a police car with two guys in it. But you don't worry about them, they're not gonna bother you. They just want to make sure you're out of that house before they call in to get a raiding party."

In minutes Karpis and others were on the road to Toledo. Around ten they rendezvoused with Dock and Campbell, who had already rented an apartment that Karpis quickly saw would not be suitable. It was a rundown room in a bad part of town. Karpis's philosophy had always been to rent in the best areas of a city. Wealthy neighbors didn't gossip like poor ones, he had found. "This ain't gonna cut it," Karpis said. "If we last here till night, we'll be doing good."

"What do you think we should do?" Freddie asked.

"What I think we should do is you and Dock go ahead to Chicago, get your mother out of that apartment, put her in a hotel, a nice hotel, for a week or so, or maybe not even that long. But get her out of there. Me and Campbell and Delores will get there this evening."

What worried Karpis most was the prospect of Cash McDonald returning to Cleveland from Havana with the laundered ransom money and walking into a police trap. "We can just kiss all that money good-bye if that happens," he said. Somehow McDonald had to be alerted. They split up the guns. The Barkers took a suitcase with two Thompsons. Karpis kept his favorite Thompson gun. Freddie and Dock left immediately for Chicago. Karpis followed that night, meeting them at Ma's apartment. They had already moved her into a hotel. Ma was on the verge of panic. For the first time she seemed to fully understand their plight. "What's gonna happen now?" Ma asked. To Karpis she seemed small and weak. All the fight had gone out of her.

Karpis couldn't get his mind off Cash McDonald. They had to warn him not to return to Cleveland. Then he had an idea. They would leave a message with the manager at McDonald's Miami hotel, the El Commodoro, in hopes that he would return there after leaving Havana. They would tell McDonald to go straight to Detroit. Willie Harrison could come to Chicago when everything was set. Karpis walked over to a pay phone on 79th Street and made the call. After a few minutes he returned.

"They were in Havana, he's expecting them back any minute," Karpis told Freddie. "I explained to him that they were not to go to Cleveland, things had developed there that made it inadvisable for them to return there." He left instructions for Harrison to meet them in Chicago when everything was set. Then they sat back and waited.

Cleveland, Ohio
Friday, September 7

The FBI didn't learn of the Cleveland raids until Friday morning, when the news broke in the newspapers.* By then police had firm identifications on all the gang members and had raided Karpis's bungalow, finding nothing but dirty clothes strewn throughout. Sam Cowley flew to Ohio the next morning to interrogate the three women, who remained in a Cleveland jail. At first they gave bogus stories of having met each other in a nightclub. Paula Harmon threw a series of screaming fits, thrashing and biting at deputies who tried to control her. At one point, she actually defecated on an agent's shoe.

But by Sunday, when the three women allowed themselves to be taken to Chicago, the fight was going out of them. All three gave long, detailed narratives of their months with the Barker Gang. A few days later Harmon

---

* On Thursday afternoon, twenty-four hours after the women's arrest, Captain Story did telephone the resident agent in Cleveland. He described the arrest and speculated that it might be linked to the "kidnappings in St. Paul." But according to an FBI report, Captain Story did not mention the possibility that Karpis or the Barkers were hiding in Cleveland. The FBI did nothing until seeing newspaper stories the next morning.

even took agents on a driving tour of northern Illinois in a vain attempt to locate the house where Ed Bremer had been kept.

Karpis and the Barkers, meanwhile, had vanished. Cowley's last hope of picking up their trail was their informant Helen Ferguson, but he told Hoover he had little confidence she could renew contact with the gang after so long. An agent took Ferguson to Toledo, where she visited the Casino Club and left a message for the Barkers. She was told to stand by; Ferguson took a hotel room, as did her FBI minder. Two days passed. On Sunday, September 9, the agent was called away. He told Ferguson to stay in touch. It looked like a washout. Cowley forgot about her.

For three days Karpis and the Barkers paced Ma's apartment in Chicago, waiting for word that the money had been exchanged in Havana. Tuesday morning, Dock said to Karpis, "You want to take a look at something?" Karpis stepped to the window and glanced down. Outside, Willie Harrison was standing on the corner, a newspaper under his arm.

Freddie trotted downstairs to get him, and relief swept the group when Harrison walked into the apartment. Everything was fine, he said. The money had been exchanged in Havana. McDonald was waiting with the clean money in Detroit. Karpis and Freddie left immediately. They had only one stop to make, at the Casino Club in Toledo. They had received a message that Helen Ferguson needed to meet.

They should have been driving into an FBI trap. But by the time Ferguson was summoned to the Casino Club that night, she hadn't talked with an FBI agent in two days. Inside, Bert Angus told her to sit and wait. According to a statement Ferguson later gave the FBI, she was then "contacted" by Fred Barker. Apparently it was a quick conversation. Ferguson asked for money. Barker said he didn't have any. She asked to see him again. Barker told her to meet him in three nights, in front of the Sears store on East 79th Street in Chicago. Then Barker walked out to the car where Karpis waited and drove off. There wasn't an FBI agent within fifty miles.[20]

As Helen Ferguson scurried back to her hotel to telephone her missing FBI handlers, Karpis and Barker left Toledo and drove through the night to Cash McDonald's house in the Detroit suburb of Grosse Pointe. McDonald was waiting with Harry Sawyer. The money, almost $66,000, was on a table; McDonald had taken a 15 percent cut. McDonald insisted that Karpis count it, and he did. "Are you sure now that this money is going to show up as you said, in Caracas and Mexico City?" Karpis asked McDonald.

"Yes, there's no question about that," McDonald said.

"I just wanted to know . . ."

"Why?" McDonald asked. "You figuring on going down to Cuba to live?"

"I don't know where I'm going to go," Karpis lied.

"Where you gonna go, Ray?" Sawyer asked.

"I really don't know. What do you want to know for?"

"Well, just in case you wanted to get hold of me or I wanted to get hold of you."

"You know something, Harry?" Karpis said. "You'd better not be planning on getting ahold of anybody. If I were you, I'd try to figure out where the hell to go to get out from under this heat. This thing is going to be real bad, and you might as well face it. You can forget every connection you had, everything. If you want to stay here, you're going to have to stay away from everybody."

They slept that night at McDonald's. The next morning, they said their good-byes and drove back to Chicago. Karpis and Freddie looked up George Ziegler's old sidekick, Bryan Bolton, gave him Ziegler's share of the money, and told him to get it to his widow. Afterward they returned to Ma's apartment. "I'm leaving tonight," Karpis announced. "I'm not staying in this goddamn town no longer." Karpis refused to say where he was heading. Dock volunteered that he and Campbell planned to return to Toledo; maybe they could learn something about the women's situation. They left. When they were alone, Karpis told Freddie he was heading for Miami. He pointedly failed to mention where he was going from there.

"How can I get ahold of you?" Freddie said.

Karpis suggested they relay messages through the Miami hotel, the El Commodoro. The manager could be trusted. "But I don't want nobody else to know where I'm going," Karpis said. They drove on to Ma's hotel, where Karpis told Delores to pack up. She didn't understand. It was almost midnight. "We're not coming back here," he said. "We're leaving tonight."

"Well, am I going to see you again soon?" Ma asked.

"I don't know," Karpis said. "But right now I'm taking Delores with me and we're going down to Florida. Now if you come down there, well and good, I'd like to see you and Freddie, but I couldn't care less whether I see any of the rest of them or not."

Karpis shook Ma's hand, then returned to her apartment, where he had left his Ford. He threw in a briefcase with his .45s and clips. Willie Harrison was there, and Karpis agreed to give him a lift to his wife's house in Gary. After that, it was every man for himself.

Chicago, Illinois
Friday, September 14

That night Helen Ferguson stood on the corner by the Sears store, frightened and alone. Cowley had decided against watching or following her, apparently fearing it would tip the Barkers off or even place Ferguson's life in danger. Once again, she was on her own.*

At 10:00 a Chevrolet sedan approached at a high rate of speed, stopping suddenly in front of Ferguson. She stepped into the front seat and the car drove off. Cowley's men didn't hear another word from Ferguson for twenty-six hours, when she called the Chicago office. She had made contact, she said, but not with Fred Barker. For twenty-four hours she had driven nonstop through the streets of Chicago with Dock Barker and his friend Russell Gibson. As Ferguson told it, Gibson had driven while Dock Barker sat behind her, cradling a machine gun. The two men claimed Freddie had gone to Kansas City but were careful to reveal little else. At one point, Dock pointedly asked Ferguson about a rumor that she had been picked up by the government. She denied it.

Cowley wasn't sure how much of Ferguson's story to believe. She said she had a follow-up rendezvous the following week. When the appointed night came, Ferguson again stood outside the Sears store. This time no one showed up. It was the end of Helen Ferguson's useful service to the Bureau. A month later Cowley approved her request to take half-ownership in a Toledo whorehouse.

As September gave way to October, the FBI was no closer to catching Karpis and the Barkers than it had been a month before.

---

* There is no indication Cowley even assigned agents to observe Ferguson at the Sears store, a decision that would at least allow agents to note the license plate number of any car that picked her up. It's unclear whether his failure to do so was a lack of confidence in Ferguson or a fear for her safety.

17

A FIELD IN OHIO AND A HIGHWAY IN ILLINOIS

September 18 to November 27, 1934

"Fuck you."

—PRETTY BOY FLOYD TO SPECIAL AGENT SAM McKEE

The story of the Kansas City Massacre as told by Michael "Jimmy Needles" LaCapra was everything Hoover could have wanted. Pacing a Wichita, Kansas, jail cell in the predawn hours of September 1, LaCapra told agents he had learned details of the massacre from his brother-in-law, one of the mob boss Johnny Lazia's henchmen.

What happened, LaCapra said, was this:

Late on the night of June 16, 1933, barely two hours after learning FBI agents were bringing Frank Nash to Kansas City the next morning, Verne Miller had driven to Union Station. The FBI knew this much was true; they had traced calls Miller made from a pay phone outside the station around midnight. But surveying the ground for the rescue was only one reason Miller drove to the station, LaCapra explained. The other was to see Johnny Lazia, who held court at the station's Harvey Restaurant. According to LaCapra, Miller asked Lazia for men to help him rescue Nash. Lazia demurred, saying he didn't want the heat that would bring.

Instead, LaCapra said, Lazia had mentioned someone else, a man who had arrived in Kansas City with his partner that same evening: Pretty Boy

Floyd. Floyd was staying that night at the Sexton Hotel, where one of Lazia's men ran a gambling parlor. According to LaCapra, Lazia had taken Miller to meet Floyd; short of money, Floyd agreed to help out, apparently after Miller emphasized that there would be no gunplay involved. LaCapra wasn't certain whether a third man—a "little wop"—might have participated in the massacre. The agents assumed the "little wop" was Adam Richetti.

It was Floyd, LaCapra said, who had shouted "Hands up!" the next morning outside the station, a command that was greeted with a gunshot from the lawmen's car. In the ensuing gunfire Floyd was wounded in the left shoulder, presumably by a ricochet. Afterward Floyd fled to a safe house, where a doctor had treated his wound. Miller, meanwhile, had returned to see Lazia and apologized for the heat the massacre would bring. Afterward Miller fled. Once his wound was bandaged, Floyd was smuggled out of the city by several of Lazia's men.

LaCapra's story was perfect. It explained almost everything: how Miller and Floyd, strangers to one another, could have teamed up, and why Adam Richetti would have stayed at Verne Miller's home, leaving behind his fingerprint on a beer bottle. As far as Hoover was concerned, there was just one problem. A secondhand story told by a frightened junkie would do little to sway a jury. What they needed was confirmation, and there was only one person in custody who could furnish that: Verne Miller's girlfriend, Vi Mathias.

Mathias had been languishing in the federal women's prison in Milan, Michigan, since the previous November. She was to be paroled on Tuesday, September 18, a fact the Chicago office noted several days before her release. For months Kathryn Kelly had been trying to pry information out of Mathias, but to no avail. Now, with her impending release, Sam Cowley proposed a bold, if extralegal plan. Mathias should be released onto the steps of the prison with no guard present, Cowley suggested, and at a time when no buses or taxis were available. No one would be allowed to meet her.

Because Mathias would be isolated and alone, Cowley wrote headquarters, "there will be no attorneys or any other person present at the time she is released, and . . . she [can be] taken by Agents of the Division and held incommunicado in some apartment where she can be thoroughly questioned concerning the massacre case." In effect, she was to be kidnapped. Given enough time, Cowley was confident he could break Vi Mathias. "Mr. Cowley pointed out that the success obtained at the Chicago office in questioning the women has been the result of holding them indefinitely and breaking down their mental resistance and obtaining from them, piece by piece, the story of their activities," an aide wrote Hoover.[1]

Cowley's plan was approved. When Mathias was released that Tuesday evening, three Chicago agents took her into custody. They drove to Detroit, where they had rented an apartment for the interrogation. The agents started in on her immediately. But Vi Mathias, while alone and unsure of her legal status, was a tough woman. She admitted knowing the Barkers and a dozen other criminals, but as the week wore on she refused to answer questions about the Kansas City Massacre.

New Orleans, Louisiana
Saturday, September 22

For fifteen months Dick Galatas, the Hot Springs bookie who had taken Frank Nash's wife Frances to Joplin on the eve of the massacre, had proven as elusive as Pretty Boy Floyd. Theorizing that Galatas was the true mastermind behind the killings, Hoover's men had tracked down tips on his whereabouts from St. Louis, where he had gambling friends, to Los Angeles, where he owned some land outside the city. They had questioned and shadowed his relatives, an aunt and uncle in upstate New York, a brother in Chicago, still other family members in California. At one point, in an effort to eavesdrop on his college-age stepson, they had inserted an undercover agent into a University of Alabama fraternity house. For their efforts they had absolutely nothing to show. Galatas and his wife, Elizabeth, had vanished.

That Saturday morning, David Magee, the New Orleans SAC, took a call from the New Orleans U.S. Attorney, Rene Viosca. Viosca asked him to come to his office in the Federal Building; he had a citizen with a tip that Galatas was hiding in the city. At Viosca's office, Magee was introduced to a man whom FBI files identify only as Confidential Informant Number One. The man said he had seen a photograph of Galatas in the September 15 issue of *Liberty Magazine,* which advertised a $1,000 reward for information leading to his arrest. Galatas, the man said, was a dead ringer for Edwin W. Lee, the southeastern distributor for a paint company, Liquid Celophane Corporation. Lee's office was in the Stern Building downtown. He stayed there until 2:00 most Saturdays.*

---

* New Orleans newspapers would later identify the informant as a job-seeker who had answered a help-wanted ad "Lee" placed in the *New Orleans Times-Picayune.*

Agent Magee telephoned Washington and asked whether they should place Lee under surveillance. No, he was told. If Lee was really Galatas, they should arrest him immediately. At 1:00 Magee took two men and drove to the Stern Building, just across Canal Street from the French Quarter. Leaving one man in the car, Magee and a second agent proceeded to Room 503, the offices of Liquid Celophane. Three salesmen shouldered by Magee as he entered; they were heading out to lunch. A woman greeted them. Magee recognized her as Elizabeth Galatas. Without identifying himself, he asked for Mr. Lee. The woman showed him into an adjoining office. A man was hunched on the floor painting a sample board. He glanced up at the agents, then turned back to his painting.

"Are you Richard Tallman Galatas?" one of the agents asked. They drew their guns.

Galatas looked up. He gave the agents a long, appraising glance. "I knew this was coming," he said. "But I never in the world would have surrendered." Then he turned and continued painting.

Dick Galatas and his wife were taken to the Bureau office, then, on orders from Washington, held incommunicado in Agent Magee's apartment. Like Vi Mathias, no court or attorney was notified of their detention. Hoover broke the news to Cowley. "I stated [to Cowley] that I intend to have Galatas held by our Division until we are able to obtain some information," Hoover wrote an aide. "[W]e know he is the key man and he may clear up many doubts in our minds and may confirm some of the information already in our possession."[2] In a call to Dwight Brantley, the Oklahoma City SAC, Hoover said, "[I]n my estimation, this is the solution of the Kansas City Massacre case."[3]

By the time of his arrest, Galatas was a broken man. Handcuffed to a chair at Agent Magee's apartment, he answered questions in a listless monotone, freely admitting his role in the massacre conspiracy. At one point, when asked why he did it, Galatas sighed.

"Because I was crazy," he said.[4]

He had been running ever since. St. Louis. Reno. Sacramento. Los Angeles. Finally, New Orleans. Galatas swore he had no idea who Verne Miller's partners were. What he told the agents instead, though no one in the FBI especially cared, was the genesis of the events that led to the massacre, and thus indirectly to Hoover's War on Crime.

It started after he purchased the White Front Cigar Store that spring, Galatas said. He took bets in the back, and it was common knowledge that he kept the proceeds at his home. For that reason, Galatas said, he was in constant fear of being kidnapped. That May two muscular men from Chicago paid him a visit and asked if he would help persuade city officials to let them distribute Blue Ribbon Beer in the town. Galatas demurred; he didn't like the pair's looks. A couple of nights later the men returned and strongly suggested Galatas accompany them to the Eastman Hotel. Galatas went along, but became frightened when he saw the men were carrying guns. When they stepped into the hotel elevator Galatas slipped out just as the doors closed, ran back to the White Front and hid. He thought the men wanted to kidnap him.

A day or two later one of the Chicago men appeared at the White Front. With him was Frank Nash, whom Galatas had met but barely knew. Galatas suspected Nash was the brains behind his would-be kidnappers. Frightened, he briefed his friend Dutch Akers, the Hot Springs chief of detectives, and suggested they find a way to turn Nash into federal authorities. It was Akers, Galatas assumed, who had called the FBI.* Once Nash was arrested, Galatas explained, he feared "the mob" would suspect him of having set Nash up. He went out of his way to help Frances Nash, Galatas insisted, in order to avoid any such suspicion.[5]

An interesting tale, but it got the FBI no closer to Pretty Boy Floyd. Hoover ordered in reinforcements. On Monday, September 24, Agent R. G. Harvey in New York was dispatched to New Orleans. One of Hoover's assistants, Ed Tamm, told Harvey to "go to work" on Galatas, because "he is yellow and, of course, there is a way to deal with people like that."[6] Tamm made it clear to Harvey that he would need to get rough with Galatas. "What we want," Tamm told Hoover on September 24, "is a good vigorous physical interview."[7] To assist Harvey, Tamm called the St. Louis office and said "we need a substantially built agent in New Orleans for a few days."[8]

Agent Harvey arrived in New Orleans on Tuesday; that night he and two other agents went to work on Dick Galatas. "Subject Galatas was brought to the office after dark and was kept there until shortly before daylight," Harvey wrote Hoover the next morning. "The interrogation was continuous and vigorous."[9]

---

* The informant who turned in Frank Nash is identified in FBI files as "Informant A." Several memos carry indications that Informant A was a policeman. In all likelihood, the informant was Akers.

In a motion his lawyer filed two months later to suppress Galatas's statements, Galatas laid out what a "vigorous physical interview" with the FBI entailed. In daylight hours he was kept manacled to a chair in Agent Magee's apartment. He was given little or no food. He was not allowed to lie down, much less sleep. At night he was taken to the Bureau office. First he was given warnings: "You are going to tell us what we want to know . . . You haven't any rights and you are not going to have counsel until we finish with you . . . We are going to get the story one way or another." Then came the threats. "I ought to kill you now . . . You could easily be found dead on the street and all we would have to say is you tried to run."

Several days later, after he was flown to Chicago and chained inside the Bureau's nineteenth-floor offices, Galatas said the threats became more vivid: "I'll use the necessary tactics to get what I want . . . If you are found dead in the streets, the same as others were found, no one would ever make inquiries and they will think gangsters killed you." At one point, Galatas was escorted to an open window. "You are a long way up," an agent told him, "and you won't bounce when you hit bottom." Finally, Galatas said, the threats turned to beatings. Agents struck him in the face with their fists until he bled. His hair was pulled. He was beaten at the base of his neck until unconscious. He was beaten with rubber hoses and kicked in the ribs. Finally an agent standing outside the door entered and said, "That's enough."

No one paid much attention to Galatas's claims when they were eventually aired at his trial. But Galatas was telling the truth. According to Melvin Purvis's secretary, Doris Rogers, agents in the Chicago office were rarely physical with prisoners during the early months of the War on Crime. But as the pressure on them increased during mid-1934, Rogers says, the agents began beating certain prisoners in the nineteenth-floor conference room. "They had heard about the 'third degree' and tried to use it without knowing how," she wrote in a 1935 article for the *Chicago Tribune*. "Their attempts were stupid and useless. They picked the wrong men to hit and got little information for their pain. These instances were isolated and few. The older and wiser heads in the organization quickly brought the men who had tried it, victims of misdirected enthusiasm, back into line."[10]

What the FBI got for its "vigorous physical interview" was a stream of increasingly detailed statements from both Galatas and his wife—none of which shed any light on what role Pretty Boy Floyd played in the massacre. In Detroit, meanwhile, Vi Mathias's reaction to the FBI's tactics proved far different. After eleven days closeted in an apartment where she was berated by a revolving roster of agents, she was brought to Chicago on September 30 to give a statement. In it, she confirmed virtually every detail of the story "Jimmy Needles" LaCapra had told the FBI. She identified photos of Floyd and Richetti as men Miller had brought to their house after the massacre. She said Floyd had some sort of wound in his left shoulder, and had left with Richetti within hours of arriving. She said she never saw either man again.

It was all Hoover needed. On October 10 he stepped before a crowd of reporters and announced the capture of Dick Galatas. He also revealed the Bureau's theory of the case, naming Verne Miller, Pretty Boy Floyd, and Adam Richetti as the massacre assassins. The next day the headlines were large and bold in Oklahoma, Kansas, and Missouri, where Floyd was well known, smaller in Eastern cities, where Floyd was typically introduced to readers as "a Southwestern outlaw." It is an indication of Floyd's posthumous notoriety; during his day he was hardly a household name. His fame paled before Dillinger's.

In a nondescript boarding house in a poor section of Buffalo, New York, a man known locally as George Sanders read the stories with a frown. Neighbors had noticed Mr. Sanders pacing his room for much of the previous year. Putting down the newspaper, the man turned to his girlfriend and sighed. "You wanna go home?" said Pretty Boy Floyd.

While the FBI turned up the heat on Floyd, Baby Face Nelson was camped in the Nevada desert, passing his days tinkering with cars and taking potshots at jackrabbits. After parting with John Chase outside Chicago, Nelson had taken his wife, Helen, and Fatso Negri and driven back to Reno. For a week they crisscrossed Nevada, searching for a tourist camp where they could hide. Nothing appealed to Nelson; the nicer places had too many people, the more isolated ones didn't have electricity or running water. One day Nelson's Hudson hit a bump going about eighty, damaging the car, so on the evening of September 21 they crept into Reno in search of a mechanic they knew named Frank Cochran.

They slid the Hudson into the garage behind Cochran's home and transferred the guns and luggage into an aging Buick sedan he lent them; Cochran even installed a siren in the car at Nelson's request. Nelson's group returned to its nomadic existence, cruising the back roads of Nevada as far south as Las Vegas. Sleeping in the open, they returned to Reno a week later. Searching for Nelson's Hudson, they drove downtown and spotted it parked outside a movie theater. Nelson was apoplectic; the FBI might spot the car. When Cochran emerged from the theater, they returned to his house and switched their things back to the Hudson, paying Cochran $250 before driving off.

Finally, on October 1, Nelson found a place to live, a tourist camp at Wally Hot Springs, Nevada, fifteen miles south of Carson City. Helen rented a two-room cottage; she and Nelson slept in one room, Negri the other. Every morning Nelson sent Negri into town to fetch food and newspapers. They were looking for John Chase's message in the personals section of the *Reno Evening Gazette.* On Thursday, October 11, Nelson saw the ad. Chase had returned. The FBI knew it, too.

All that September, Ed Guinane, the San Francisco SAC, built an intricate superstructure atop Nelson's contacts in California. There were taps in place on the phones of Fatso Negri's mother and Johnny Chase's brothers, and extensions at Tobe Williams's gangland hospital in Vallejo.* Wanted posters were distributed up and down the California-Nevada border. Guinane felt certain Nelson was still in the area. He had been seen in Vallejo on September 26, by a man who had sold him a car the year before, and in a Reno tavern on September 29.

Guinane's best lead was Johnny Chase's missing girlfriend, Sally Backman. Agents had searched her apartment and questioned her family; everyone said it was unlike her to simply disappear. At some point, Guinane wagered, she would return to Sausalito. He was right. The Bureau's first major break came on Saturday, October 6, when Manuel Menotti, Sausalito's police chief, spotted Backman on the street. He took her into custody and called Guinane, who hurried to begin debriefing her that afternoon.

It was slow going. For days Backman refused to say anything about her travels with Nelson. Then Guinane decided to use her love for Chase against her. If Chase stayed with Nelson, Guinane said, he would almost certainly be killed. Chase's only chance to live, he insisted, was to leave Nel-

---

* An agent actually walked into the hospital and saw Chuck Fitzgerald, the Barker Gang member who was recovering from a gunshot wound, on October 11. He failed to recognize him.

son. Backman asked for a promise that FBI agents wouldn't kill Chase when he was arrested. Guinane said they would do everything they could to bring Chase in unharmed.

It worked. By Monday, October 8, Backman was installed in a room at the Shaw Hotel in San Francisco, pouring out her story. After parting with Nelson outside Chicago, she said, Chase had taken her to New York City, where they checked into the St. Andrews Hotel at the corner of Broadway and 72nd Street as "Mr. and Mrs. John Madison." For three weeks they melted into the crowds of Manhattan, two young lovers spending their days ogling Radio City Music Hall and the new Empire State Building. Their only scare came a few days after arriving when Chase walked into a barbershop and a man yelled, "Johnny Chase!"

It turned out to be an old bootlegging pal of Chase's named Arthur "Fat" Pratt, who had left the Bay Area to join his family's jewelry business in Helena, Montana. Pratt and his girlfriend, who were also on vacation, joined Chase and Backman for a trip to Coney Island, a few dinners, and a Mae West movie, *Belle of the Nineties.*

In quiet moments Backman begged Chase to leave Nelson permanently, and Chase seemed to be swayed. A simple man, he talked of buying a gas station somewhere and settling down, and Backman believed him. They couldn't stay in New York forever. In bed at night, they discussed whether it was safe for Backman to return to Sausalito. Chase told her the FBI would pick her up for questioning. She promised she wouldn't talk. He told her how to reach him, via a personal ad in the *San Francisco Examiner.** Once she returned to Sausalito and got her things in order, Chase promised, she could return to him and they would go straight. On September 30, Chase put her on a bus to the Newark airport. Back in San Francisco, she flitted between friends' apartments for five days before Chief Menotti arrested her.

Backman's story represented a trove of new leads. In New York, agents descended on the St. Andrews Hotel, where they identified a car Chase had purchased as an Airflow DeSoto sedan. Teletypes listing the car's license plate number were sent to FBI offices and police stations across the West. Just as promising was the discovery that Chase had mailed a parcel to an Arthur Pratt in Helena, Montana. This information was relayed to the

---

* Her ad was to read, *Mother received radio. Communicate with me.*

FBI's Butte office on Tuesday, October 9, which called the sheriff's department in Helena and asked it to check hotels for a man using the name "John Madison." Hours later came word from Helena: Chase, aka Madison, had left the city just that morning.

After picking up a package of money he had mailed to Pratt for safe-keeping, Chase drove south to Nevada, reaching Reno that afternoon, just as the FBI learned he had been in Montana. Chase left his car at Frank Cochran's garage on Virginia Avenue, asked for some minor repairs, then walked downtown and checked into the El Cortez Hotel, again using the name "John Madison." The FBI was right behind him. Reno police found Chase's car at Cochran's garage the next day, Wednesday, October 10. That night, Agent Guinane and a group of agents arrived in Reno. The next morning they interviewed Cochran, who said a man had brought the car into his garage for repairs on Tuesday. "I don't know him," Cochran lied. "I presume he is a tourist."

Guinane set a trap. "I'm going to need several armed men in the garage," he told Cochran. "Chase will be back for the machine and we will grab him." Guinane had brought along the Sausalito police chief, Manuel Menotti, who had known Chase for years. "Your duty, Chief," Guinane told Menotti, "is to walk up to Chase when he comes into the garage. You talk to him and I believe you can get him away from Nelson. We'll make Chase put the finger on Nelson."

Though the agents didn't know it, their plan was stillborn. That morning, even as Guinane arrayed his agents around the garage, Chase walked out of his hotel to stretch his legs. He decided to stroll by Cochran's garage to check on his car. A block from the garage, Chase noticed two men in suits, talking. He suspected they were plainclothes policemen or FBI agents. Slowing to eavesdrop, he heard the words "federal agents" and "car."[11]

Keeping his head, Chase walked to the offices of the *Reno Evening Gazette,* where he placed an ad in the personals section. The next day Nelson saw it. That night he took Helen and Fatso Negri and drove by Frank Cochran's house to find Chase. Cochran's car was in the driveway, a pre-arranged signal that Cochran was "hot." Helen pleaded with Nelson to leave. Instead Nelson drove out into the desert and stopped the car. "C'mon, let's put on our vests," he told Negri. Negri protested: hadn't he seen the car in the driveway?

"To hell with the signal," Nelson snapped. "You put on that bulletproof vest and go up to the front door."

They drove back into Reno and Nelson parked down the street from Cochran's house. Approaching the house was a risk Nelson was fully prepared for Negri to take. "Go ring that front door bell and ask Frank where Johnny is," he repeated.

Negri was afraid. "Jimmy, it's slaughter for me to go across this street and ring that bell," Negri said. "The G-men are there, and they'd just riddle me. I can't do [it]."

"Go ahead," Nelson urged. "I'll stay here, and if I see anybody, I'll let 'em have it. I'll have good aim from here."

Negri was sweating now. "I know, Jimmy, but that's murder for me," he said. "They've probably got us spotted now. Have a heart, Jimmy. I wouldn't do [this] to you."

Nelson wouldn't be deterred. "Go ahead, Fatso; it's all right," he said. "I can plug 'em first."

"Well, let's both go," Negri said.

Nelson lost his temper. "No! Go ahead!" he said. "I'll protect you."

Negri got out of the car, trotted to Cochran's front porch and rang the bell. Cochran opened the door, but only a few inches. "Get away from here," he hissed. "Didn't I tell you what that car meant? Get away from this door."

"Where is Johnny Chase?" Negri asked.

"He's walking down the highway," Cochran said before closing the door. "Get away from here!"[12]

Negri hustled back to the car without incident; the FBI, which had no idea Cochran was secretly helping Nelson, wasn't watching the house. Nelson drove out toward the town of Sparks, looking for Chase. After a while a red sedan passed them; inside was Cochran, along with Chase. Nelson yelled, "Follow us," and led Cochran into the desert.

They parked in the sagebrush. Jackrabbits scampered about in the cool evening air. Cochran told Nelson about the FBI trap at his garage. "To hell with them G-men!" Nelson snapped. "I'm going back to the garage and fill them with lead. I'll get Johnny's car for him!"

Cochran pleaded with Nelson not to do anything rash. "I know how to handle one of these tommies," Nelson said. "I won't splatter up your garage too much!" Chase interceded, saying they had nothing to gain from killing FBI men. Nelson calmed down when Cochran promised to furnish him the license plate numbers of FBI cars. If he couldn't shoot the agents in Cochran's garage, he would get them someplace else.

On the drive back to Wally Hot Springs, Chase told Nelson all about his trip to New York. "The heat's everywhere," he said. "It's in New York, Chicago, San Francisco, Reno, and all spots in between. In New York I contacted some of the boys in various rackets, and they all gave me the cold shoulder, in a polite way, but firmly."

"Aw, those yellow racketeers back East," Nelson snapped. "The G-men can't bluff us. All we need right now is a little time for one or two more good jobs, like the Milwaukee train. And then we can beat it over to Europe and take it easy." Negri recognized the familiar refrain: One more job, always one more job, and then retirement.

All that night Nelson, Chase, and Negri kept watch in shifts, anticipating an FBI raid that never came. As they stood out in the desert night, cradling their submachine guns, Sam Cowley arrived at the Reno airport, having just handed the $5,000 Dillinger reward to Ana Sage in Los Angeles the day before. All that next day, Friday, October 12, Cowley joined agents staking out Frank Cochran's garage. Cowley was discouraged by Cochran's failure to identify the photographs of either Chase or Nelson. In a phone call to Washington that afternoon, he reported "the situation does not look any too hopeful."[13]

That night Cochran met Nelson in the desert outside Reno. He handed over the license plate numbers of several FBI cars and even furnished Nelson the address of the apartment house where several agents were staying. Nelson was all for driving into town and murdering every FBI agent he could find, but Chase calmed him down.

Neither Baby Face Nelson nor Sam Cowley ever learned how close they came to facing off that day. Cowley left Reno the next morning for Salt Lake City before moving on to Montana, where agents were questioning Chase's friend, Arthur Pratt. No one knew it at the time, but the day Cowley would finally confront Nelson was coming, and sooner than anyone expected.

October 20

When night fell, Pretty Boy Floyd, Adam Richetti, and their long-suffering girlfriends, sisters named Juanita and Beulah Baird, left Buffalo. In darkness they drove through Pennsylvania and crossed into Ohio, then turned south. Richetti had relatives in Dillonvale, across from Wheeling, West Virginia, and they may have been heading there. Floyd drove past Youngstown and around three A.M. reached the Ohio River at East Liverpool, where he turned onto Highway 7, the two-lane blacktop that ran along the west side of the Ohio. Rain was falling as fog rolled off the river, and just before the city limits of Wellsville, four miles below East Liverpool, Floyd lost control of the car on the wet pavement and skidded into a telephone pole.

Steam rose from the hood as Floyd stepped out to inspect the damage. Irked, he looked up and down the road. An abandoned brickyard stretched into the gloom to their right. Moonlight sparkled on the river to their left; a mile across the water they could make out the lights of West Virginia. They managed to get the car back on the road, but Floyd saw they wouldn't make it far without repairs. He told the Baird sisters to drive into Wellsville and find a mechanic. The girls coaxed the car south, disappearing toward the dwindling river town.

Frost lay silver on the grass as Floyd and Richetti took some blankets and their guns and hiked up a wooded hill to await the girls' return. From their position above the brickyard Floyd could see up and down Highway 7 and across a set of railroad tracks to the river below. A few dozen yards behind them, at the top of the hill, sat a row of darkened houses, several no more than shacks. It was cold, and they gathered some leaves and twigs, started a fire, and sat back to wait.

Hours passed. At dawn lights began flickering in the homes above them. By eight there was still no sign of the women. Around ten a man named Joe Fryman emerged from his hilltop home to check his riverside vegetable garden. He was standing near the highway with his son-in-law when his eye caught a flash of white on the hill below. He said they should investigate. Halfway down the hill Fryman stumbled onto Floyd and Richetti, sitting on their blankets. At first he thought they were tramps; a glance at their clothing—Floyd was wearing a navy suit with no tie—suggested otherwise. "We're out taking pictures," Floyd said. "We had a couple of girls and got lost. We're waiting for them."

Suspicious, Fryman climbed the hill to his home, where he found a neighbor named Lon Israel. "It looks kind of fishy to me," Israel agreed. Israel walked to a store and phoned the chief of Wellsville's two-man police force, a pugnacious little fellow named John H. Fultz. That Thursday a bank had been robbed in Tiltonsville, an hour's drive south, and it occurred to Fultz the two strangers might be connected. Before leaving he deputized two local men, William Erwin and Grover Potts, and asked them to come along. A few minutes later the three arrived on the hilltop. None wore a uniform. Only Fultz had a gun, a .38. "Do you know where these people are located?" Fultz asked.

"I don't know exactly but I can tell you about the location, pretty near," Israel said.

Israel led the group down a muddy path. About twenty-five feet down the hill, just as they rounded a clump of bushes, Floyd materialized before them. "What do you want?" Floyd demanded. Without waiting for an answer, he pulled out a pistol and leveled it at Fultz.

"Stick 'em up!" Floyd said.

Fultz tried to pass himself off as a worker on his way to the brickyard. "I won't stick 'em up," Fultz said.

"I said put 'em up," Floyd said.

"I won't put 'em up," Fultz said. "I'm going down to the brickyard and I don't see why I should put my hands up."

Fultz took a step forward. "Don't come another inch, fellow, or I will pump you," Floyd said.

"You wouldn't shoot a working man," Fultz said. Floyd stepped forward and stuck his pistol into the chief's stomach. Fultz brazenly pushed past him, followed by Lon Israel and the two deputies. Floyd let them walk by, then descended the path after them, his gun still aimed at Fultz. "Now don't run or I will shoot you," he said.

"There's nobody going to run," Fultz said.

They descended another hundred feet down the dirt path. They bickered all the way to the point where Fultz came upon Richetti, still lying on his blanket. "Hello, buddy, how are you?" Fultz asked. "You seem to be taking it pretty easy."

"Yeah," Richetti said.

Floyd had had enough. "Don't let him kid you," Floyd said. "Shoot him! He's an officer!"

Richetti dutifully produced his .45, aimed at Fultz, and pulled the trigger. The gun misfired. Fultz pulled his .38, turned back toward Floyd, and snarled, "You big yellow son of a bitch." He fired at Floyd, missing, then turned and fired toward Richetti. In the confusion the other men scattered into the trees. Fultz stopped to reload his gun. When he was finished, Floyd was nowhere to be seen. Fultz spied Richetti running through the woods. He ran after him.

Richetti raced through the trees across the hillside, leapt a fence, and made for the back of a house. Fultz reached its yard just as Richetti reached the backdoor. Fultz fired once, the bullet striking the house about two feet from Richetti's shoulder.

"I give up!" Richetti shouted.

While Chief Fultz handcuffed Richetti, Floyd stepped out of the trees and pulled a Thompson gun from beneath their blankets. Meanwhile, Lon Israel and the two deputies hustled up the hill, where Israel grabbed shotguns from his house. The three men had just stepped back into Israel's yard when, to their left, they saw Floyd emerge from the woods. Floyd turned and fired a burst from his machine gun; then it jammed. One bullet struck Deputy Potts in the shoulder; he fell, wounded. Deputy Erwin got off one blast of his shotgun before diving for cover. Floyd dived into a ditch, then rose and ran across the hilltop into the trees on the far side, throwing his gun in the weeds.

The woods Floyd entered lay on the northern reaches of Appalachia. West of the river, the land bunched together in steep, rocky hills; the hollows between were creased with shallow brown creeks and pockmarked with tar-paper shacks and trash-strewn hillsides. On the far side of the hill, a thirty-one-year-old auto mechanic named Theodore Peterson and his brother William were standing outside their garage talking to a teenager, George McMillen, who had stopped to buy a vacuum tank for his Model T Ford. McMillen looked up and saw a mud-streaked man in a dusty blue suit scrambling down the hill into the Petersons' yard.

Floyd walked up and asked if he could pay any of them five dollars to drive him to Youngstown.

"Why?" one of the men asked.

Floyd explained he had been out hunting when his car broke down. "What part broke?" one of the Petersons asked. "Maybe we can fix it for you."

"The front axle," Floyd said. He put his foot on the axle of McMillen's Ford to show where the break had occurred. "I've got to get to Youngstown," Floyd went on. "I've got business to attend to up there. I'll give you ten dollars." He pulled a wad of ones out of his pocket to show he had the money.

Ted Peterson turned to Floyd and said, "We'll take you." He and Floyd got into Peterson's car. Peterson was backing out of the yard when his mother stuck her head out of the house.

"Where are you goin'?" she yelled.

"I'm takin' this man to Youngstown," Peterson shouted back.

"You can't take this man to Youngstown and get across the river at one o'clock," she shouted. It was 12:40; Peterson was due at another man's house in twenty minutes.

"Sorry, buddy," Peterson said.

"That's all right," Floyd said.

He turned to the teenager, George McMillen, and offered him the ten dollars. "Will you take me?" Floyd asked.

"I will," McMillen said, taking Floyd's money.

Once in McMillen's Ford, Floyd said to stick to the back roads.

"I suppose you know who I am," Floyd said at one point.

"Don't believe I do," McMillen said.

"My name's Floyd. Pretty Boy Floyd."

McMillen stared.

"The radios are flashing it all over the country, the papers are full of it," Floyd said.

"I don't know [anything about] it," McMillen said. "I'm just back from Cannon's Mill and haven't been readin' the papers except the funnies or to look through the paper for a job."

Five minutes later McMillen's car stalled. Above the road was a set of greenhouses owned by a florist named James H. Baum. Baum sold his flowers at his shop in Wellsville; his biggest customer was the local funeral home. He and a friend were stacking lumber when Floyd and McMillen walked up his driveway. "How about some gas?" Floyd asked, motioning down to the stalled Model T. "I'll pay you for it."

"I haven't any gas," Baum said.

Floyd eyed Baum's Nash sedan. "How about draining some out of your car?"

Baum shook his head. "Can't get it out," he said.

Floyd asked if Baum would take them to a gas station, and Baum agreed. McMillen went, too. Climbing into Baum's Nash, Floyd pulled his gun. "Now, Dad," he told Baum, "I want you to do just what I say."

He told Baum to drive north toward Youngstown, keeping to the back roads. They bumped along muddy dirt tracks for nearly two hours, eventually reaching the highway ten miles north. Just as they gained speed, they spied a roadblock. Two deputies had placed a railroad car across the road. A long line of automobiles was waiting to pass.

At the roadblock, Deputies George Hayes and Charley Patterson watched the Nash stop and turn around. It looked suspicious. "Let's go," Hayes told Patterson. The two men hopped into their car and tried to give chase, but were slowed by the snarl of stopped cars.

Ahead, in the Nash, Floyd peered through the back window. "Here comes someone," he said to Baum. "Step on it." The mouth of a hilly dirt road—so swaybacked locals called it "Roller Coast Road"—opened to the left, and Floyd told Baum to turn onto it. The Nash roared into the little road and sped east into the woods north of East Liverpool. The deputies followed. A half mile down Roller Coast Road, they began honking their horn. At that point, James Baum decided he had had enough and stopped the car. The deputies' car stopped about fifty yards behind it. From the backseat, Floyd rose and fired. His shot blew out the back window of the Nash, then struck the deputies' windshield. The deputies ducked as Floyd scrambled out of the car and ran into the woods.

By nightfall Columbiana County was in an uproar. Farmers in black armbands, signifying their status in the gathering posse, spilled into Wellsville, milling around the riverside jail complex. Inside, Chief Fultz tried to question Adam Richetti. Locked in a cell, Richetti gave his name as Richard Zamboni. He said his partner was a Toledo gambler; inexplicably George McMillen had told no one that the "gambler" had identified himself as Pretty Boy Floyd.

Sunday morning the manhunt for the missing "gambler" continued. An overnight rain had erased any footprints Floyd left. He had disappeared into the wildest area of Columbiana County, a dim maze of steep wooded hillsides that lined Little Beaver Creek. Around one o'clock Sunday afternoon, Ray B. Long, the sheriff in Steubenville, Ohio, arrived in Wellsville to join the posse. Shown into the jail, he recognized Richetti from a Wanted poster. "That's Adam Richetti," he told Fultz. "He's wanted in the Kansas City Massacre." He called Richetti by his name, and Richetti admitted who he was.

Sheriff Long said they had to call the FBI. Fultz objected; he was enjoying his moment in the sun and apparently didn't want to share it. Long called anyway. The switchboard at the FBI's Cincinnati office forwarded the message to the senior agent in the area, who just happened to be Melvin Purvis.

Purvis was in Cincinnati with a team of agents hunting the kidnapper of a Kentucky woman. It wasn't glamorous, but it beat writing memos, which was all Hoover wanted him to do. Their relationship had gone from cool to glacial. In one bizarre letter in mid-September, Hoover had hectored Purvis for refusing to speak clearly over the telephone. "I have had the phone checked here, and found that our phone is technically satisfactory," Hoover wrote. "It might also be desirable for you to speak in a little louder tone of voice."[14]*

That Sunday morning Purvis was in his hotel room when he received the call about Floyd. He telephoned Hoover in Washington, and the director grudgingly approved Purvis's plan to charter a plane to Wellsville and supervise the manhunt. By 2:00 Purvis and his men were aboard a plane floating over the brilliant autumn foliage of southern Ohio. Looking down on the trees, Purvis let his mind drift back to the flight that had taken him to Little Bohemia. No one used words like redemption around Purvis, but its scent hung unmistakably in the air.

At the Wellsville jail, Purvis immediately butted heads with Chief Fultz. It was dusk and the posses had dispersed, heading home for warm dinners; there had been no sighting of Floyd for more than twenty-four hours. Purvis said he wanted the entire area cordoned off. Fultz said it couldn't be done. To make matters worse, Fultz refused to release Richetti to the FBI. He said he had an "open and shut case" against Richetti for assault. Purvis telephoned Hoover and reported the situation was "impossible to control."[15]

Leaving the jail, Purvis drove to East Liverpool and set up his command post at the Travelers Hotel. By 3:00 Monday morning, almost twenty agents from Pittsburgh, Cleveland, and Cincinnati had assembled in his room. Purvis split them into five squads of three and four men apiece. He decided to send two squads to raid the homes of Richetti's relatives at Dillonvale, an hour's drive south. The other three squads were to patrol Highway 7 and its spidery network of adjoining roads north of East Liverpool. Floyd was believed to be wounded, and other agents were put to work checking hospitals, doctor's offices, and taxi companies. More than two hundred police and sheriff's deputies, arriving from across the state, manned roadblocks at bridges up and down the Ohio River Valley.

---

* On October 2 Hoover sent Purvis a telegram berating him for failing to report a man who had visited the Chicago office with a tip on the Lindbergh kidnapping. "I am instructing Mr. Cowley to take personal charge of this matter," Hoover wrote, "so that it will be given the proper attention."

1:00 P.M.

Early Monday afternoon, after two days with no news of Floyd, a reliable report came in. Three of Purvis's men were checking farms north of East Liverpool when they were waved down by a constable, who reported Floyd had just been seen at a farm north of Little Beaver Creek. A farmer's wife had fed him a sandwich and allowed him to wash up. The news was relayed to Purvis. Hoover telephoned just as he was leaving his room. The director told Purvis to depart at once.[16] If Floyd was to be captured, Hoover wanted to make sure it was by the FBI.

Purvis rendezvoused with his men on a dirt road seven miles north of East Liverpool. He was willing to bet Floyd was heading north, making for Youngstown. They split into two groups and began checking farmhouses and outbuildings. In one barn, Purvis was rooting around in the loft when he heard a noise below. Purvis drew his gun. He heard footsteps coming up the ladder and aimed his .45, ready to fire—and felt silly when one of his own men popped up. They were all nervous.

Around three o'clock, as they cruised dirt roads watching the adjoining fields, Purvis and his men met a car driven by the East Liverpool police chief and three of his men. They decided to join forces.

2:50 P.M.

As they did, Floyd emerged from the woods north of Little Beaver Creek. His white shirt was streaked with sweat, his suit sprinkled with thistles and pine needles. He had covered eight miles, due east, since fleeing the sheriff's deputies forty-eight hours earlier. Behind him the creek gurgled past a fallen-down gristmill and a set of long-abandoned canal locks, remnants of another century. The metaphor was lost on Floyd, who only wanted a warm meal and a ride out of Ohio. Ahead lay an isolated farmhouse. Beyond it, green fields.

Ellen Conkle, a widow who worked her fifty-acre farm with the help of in-laws, was cleaning her smokehouse when the stranger knocked on her backdoor. "Lady, I'm lost and I want something to eat," Floyd said. "Can you help me out with some food? I'll pay you."

Mrs. Conkle knew nothing of Pretty Boy Floyd or the manhunt. "I look like a wild man, don't I?" Floyd said. "I was hunting squirrels with my brother last night and I got lost. The more directions I got, the more confused I became. I don't know where I am now."

Mrs. Conkle knew no one hunted squirrels at night, certainly not in a business suit and black oxfords, and said so. A sheepish look crossed Floyd's face. "To be honest, I've been drinking," he said. "I guess I got lost." Mrs. Conkle, who for years afterward would be portrayed as a simple woman kindly helping a stranger, was not naive; in fact, she was frightened. As she told an investigating panel several days later, she was afraid what would happen if she denied the stranger food, so she agreed to make him something, hoping it would hurry him on his way. She asked what he would like. "Meat," said Floyd. "All I've been eating is apples, and some ginger cookies. I'm hungry for meat."

Floyd sat in a rocker on the back porch, reading the Sunday edition of the East Liverpool *Review,* while Mrs. Conkle walked to her smokehouse to fetch some spareribs, then disappeared into her kitchen. A few minutes later she returned with a plateful of ribs, fresh bread, and pudding. Floyd devoured it all, except for the pudding, then accepted the widow's offer of coffee and a slice of pumpkin pie. Afterward he pronounced the meal "fit for a king."

Floyd asked for a ride to Youngstown. Mrs. Conkle said she couldn't take him, but her brother-in-law Stewart Dyke and his wife were out in her field picking corn. When they returned, maybe they would take him. Floyd climbed into Dyke's Model A and waited. The keys were in the ignition, but he did not steal the car.

Around four o'clock Dyke and his wife walked up to the house. Floyd asked for a ride to Youngstown. He could pay. Dyke said he was too tired. "I'll take you to Clarkson, though," he said, where there was a bus to Youngstown. "Come on get in." Dyke said.

Floyd climbed back into the car, borrowed Mrs. Dyke's powder puff and began to apply it to his face, apparently in a feeble attempt to disguise himself. Dyke slid behind the wheel. As the car backed out of the yard, everyone waved good-bye to Mrs. Conkle.

Then Stewart Dyke saw the two cars coming up the road.

4:10 P.M.

The two cars eased around a wide curve and rolled up the rise toward the last farm on the Sprucevale Road, the Conkle place. One of the East Liverpool policemen, Glenn G. "Curly" Montgomery, saw Floyd first. "Stop!" Montgomery hollered. "That's him!"

Floyd spotted the lawmen a moment before they saw him. He ducked down and drew his pistol. "Drive behind that building!" he ordered Dyke. "They're looking for me." Dyke did as he was told, pulling his car behind a corn crib—a fifteen-foot-wide raised wooden shed used to store corn. Dyke reached over and unlocked the car door.

"Get out, you son of a bitch," he said. Floyd scrambled out of the car and behind the corn crib.

Officer Montgomery was the first man out of the East Liverpool patrol car as it entered the Conkles' yard. Purvis's car pulled up behind it, and the four agents scrambled out. "There he is!" one of the cops shouted. "Behind the corn crib!"

Everyone drew their guns. The corn crib was elevated about twelve inches off the ground; they could see Floyd's feet as he scurried from one side to the other, obviously unsure what to do. "Floyd, come to the road!" Purvis shouted. "If you don't we will shoot!"

Floyd left the shelter of the corn crib and darted across an open space, toward the Conkle's garage. "Look out, he's gonna run!" one of the policemen yelled.

"Halt!" Purvis shouted. Shouts of "Halt! Stop!" came from all directions. Floyd kept running. Behind the garage he raced into an open field. At the far end of the field, maybe two hundred yards away, was a stand of woods. Floyd ran for it, zigzagging across the open field.

"Let him have it!" Purvis shouted.

Gunshots rang out. The Bureau men had pistols and shotguns and a Thompson gun. Their bullets splintered Mrs. Conkle's apple tree; leaves and limbs rained down into the yard. Floyd kept running through the field, looking back over his right shoulder, then his left. More shots rang out. Several officers fired where they stood, others ran after Floyd into the field. As he neared the crest of a rise, Floyd's right arm flew up and he fell forward, landing heavily on his left side in the grass.

Three of the East Liverpool policemen were the first to reach him. As they did, Floyd swung his arm around to defend himself, his .45 caliber pistol poised to fire. Officer Chester Smith grabbed Floyd's wrist and wrenched the gun from his hand as a second officer fell onto Floyd and pinned him to the ground. Floyd reached for a second pistol in his waistband, but the third officer, Herman Roth, took it first.*

"Lay still! Lay still!" one of the men yelled as Floyd finally ceased struggling.

The East Liverpool police chief, Hugh McDermott, ran up.

"How bad are you hurt?" he asked.

"I'm done for," Floyd rasped. "You've hit me twice." He was right: A .45 slug had hit below the left shoulder blade and lodged in his chest. Another bullet had struck his right side and come to rest below his heart. His lungs, ribs, and heart had all been damaged.

"What's your name?" Officer Montgomery asked. By then Purvis and the other FBI men had run up.

"Murphy," Floyd said. "Where's Eddie?" He was using Richetti's alias.

"Eddie who?" Montgomery asked.

"Where's Eddie?"

"I don't know," Montgomery said.

"Oh hell," Floyd said.

"What's your name?" Montgomery asked again.

"Murphy!" Floyd said. He spat the word.

"Your name's Floyd!" Purvis said.

Floyd just stared.

"Is your name not Charles 'Pretty Boy' Floyd?" Purvis repeated.

Floyd's mouth twisted into a half smile.

"Yeah, I'm Floyd," he said.

Purvis trotted back to his car to call a doctor and notify Washington of Floyd's capture; there was no phone at the Conkle farm, so Purvis took an agent and drove back to a store in the town of Clarkson. When Purvis left, Agent Sam McKee hunched down beside Floyd and began questioning him. He asked if Floyd had been involved in the Union Station Massacre. "To hell with Union Station," Floyd said.

"You're dying," McKee said.

"I know I'm through," Floyd said. He was weakening fast.

---

* Purvis would later claim to have kicked the pistol out of Floyd's hand. He may have kicked it to one side after it was removed.

"Then do the decent thing and tell me what you know about the massacre at Union Station," McKee said.

Floyd said nothing.

"Is it not true that you, Adam Richetti, and Verne Miller did the shooting at Union Station?"

Floyd's eyes flashed. "I ain't tellin' you nothin', you son of a bitch," he said. A moment later Floyd seemed to lapse into a state of semiconsciousness. McKee gave up the questioning. Floyd's condition deteriorated quickly. In minutes he seemed to be near death.

"Who tipped you I was here?" he asked in a lucid moment. Several times he tried to rise. The East Liverpool men held him down. Floyd was fading fast. "Fuck you," he said at one point. At 4:25 he said, "I'm going," and died.*

Floyd's body was brought into the Sturgis Funeral Home in Wellsville, which was soon mobbed with reporters and curious townspeople. Much to Hoover's dismay, more reporters were drawn to Purvis than the body. He

---

* Pretty Boy Floyd's death was the most controversial of all the public enemies the FBI hunted down in 1934. Forty-five years later, in 1979, one of the East Liverpool policemen, Chester Smith, made international headlines with the charge that the FBI had murdered Floyd as he lay helpless in Mrs. Conkle's field. According to Smith, who first told this story to the *Akron Beacon-Journal* in 1974, Purvis had briefly questioned Floyd about the massacre. When Floyd refused to answer his questions, Smith claimed, Purvis ordered Agent Ed Hollis to "Fire into him," at which point Hollis fired a single shot into Floyd's chest, killing him.

It is a story that achieved wide currency; one otherwise credible author entitles his chapter on Floyd's death "The Assassination." This is entirely unfounded. Agent Hollis was not even at the Conkle farm that afternoon. According to the local coroner's report, there was no gunshot wound to the chest. Floyd had been hit twice, as he admitted to lawmen; neither bullet entered through his chest. No one present that day even hinted such a thing might have occurred.

So why, a number of writers have asked, would Chester Smith make up such a story? Smith's old friends sigh when the question is put to them. "I knew Chester; we were close," says Bob "Brassy" Beresford, a former Columbiana County sheriff. "We called him 'Cap.' Cap would tell different stories at different times. I heard a couple of different versions. That version [involving Agent Hollis] was a new version. I don't much think anyone around here took it seriously."

For all the stories Cap Smith told over the years, the one constant was his own crucial role in Floyd's death. He told the East Liverpool *Review* in 1969 that it was he, not Glenn Montgomery, who first spotted Floyd, he, not Montgomery, who was the first man out of the car that day. These assertions are contradicted by testimony given by other officers two days after the killing. Further, Smith claimed, it was his own shots that killed Floyd. This was demonstrably untrue, inasmuch as Smith admitted carrying a rifle and Floyd was killed by .45 caliber ammunition. Most tellingly, Smith in a 1969 interview said nothing about anyone murdering Floyd; that version cropped up only later. In the end, Smith's allegations must be dismissed as a canard generated by an elderly man embittered that others received the fame he felt he deserved.

was mobbed when he showed up at the funeral home, where Hoover reached him about five-thirty, an hour after the shooting. "Purvis advised that he had his picture taken, that he had been receiving inquiries from newspapers, whereupon I instructed him to tell the newspapers [all] statements would have to come from Washington," Hoover wrote in a memo. Purvis promised he would say nothing, saying "he did not want to face anything like he did before."[17]

All evening, even as friends and reporters phoned in congratulations, Purvis remained uppermost in Hoover's mind. Around nine Purvis and Sam Cowley, who had arrived from Chicago, telephoned Hoover to report that they expected to take custody of Richetti within an hour; when Purvis stepped away from the phone, Hoover told Cowley that he wanted Purvis out of Wellsville immediately. Purvis is "to leave tonight and the curtain pulled down on the publicity there," Hoover wrote an aide. He repeated himself for effect. "I again stated [to Cowley] that I wanted Mr. Purvis and the men to get out of there tonight because if they stay over, there will be a lot of motion pictures and the like," Hoover wrote.

But Purvis couldn't help himself. After three months in Hoover's doghouse he was once again a star, and when reporters asked what happened, he told them. The next morning's newspapers uniformly portrayed Purvis—"the man who got Dillinger"—as the FBI hero who had now brought down his second major public enemy. PURVIS' STORY OF U.S. TRAP, read the *Chicago American* headline. "Melvin Purvis, youthful attorney who turned sleuth, marked another notch on his gun [today]," wrote the *Chicago Tribune*. "[A] normally mild-mannered southerner, who 'sees red' when dealing with criminals, Purvis today became the most dangerous nemesis of the desperado [element]."

In Washington, Hoover fumed. He wanted accolades to flow to the Bureau, not Purvis; if any one man was responsible for bringing in Floyd and Dillinger, he felt, it was Sam Cowley, whom the newspapers continued to portray as Purvis's second-in-command. Two nights later a headquarters supervisor named Bob Newby reached Purvis at his home in Chicago and told him to stay away from the office; in fact, Newby told Purvis to tell no one he even was in the city. Purvis, who had taken a victory lap through official Washington after Dillinger's death, asked if he could come east; Newby said he saw no reason to. What remained of the relationship between Hoover and Purvis was damaged beyond repair.[18]

• • •

With Dillinger and Floyd dead, Sam Cowley focused on Baby Face Nelson. His files were thick with new intelligence: the work on Nelson outshone anything achieved during the Dillinger and Floyd manhunts. That the two earlier cases had been resolved at all was seen by cynics as dumb luck, the FBI capitalizing on an opportunistic snitch and a car wreck. Cowley was determined that Nelson's capture would be different. The Nelson files were an indication of how sharply the FBI's professionalism had risen in mere months; the Purvis-era embarrassments of Roger Touhy, Verne Miller, and Little Bohemia were fast receding into memory. War conditions honed many organizations into fighting shape, and the FBI was no exception.

Under Cowley's direction, agents had rounded up almost every contact from Nelson's early days, interviewed his partners in the 1930 crime spree, and staked out the homes of his and Helen's siblings. Several family members were quietly cooperating with the FBI, including Nelson's brother-in-law, Robert Fitzsimmons, whose wife had taken in the Nelsons' son Ronald. On October 9, Fitzsimmons had called to tell Cowley his family was leaving to visit relatives in Bremerton, Washington. It took a week for the family to drive cross-country. Two of Cowley's men followed the entire way.

Cowley's best hope of finding Nelson was still John Chase's girlfriend, Sally Backman, who remained in custody in San Francisco. Cowley was transfixed by a vague story she told of visiting a town in Wisconsin where Nelson said he planned to spend the winter. In San Francisco agents spent several days poring over maps with Backman, trying to identify the town, but it was no use. No matter how she tried, Backman couldn't seem to remember its name.

The day after Floyd was killed, Tuesday, October 23, Cowley had Backman flown to Chicago in hopes that a tour of northern Illinois and Wisconsin might refresh her memory. Charles Winstead took two agents and drove her. They headed northwest out of Chicago on Highway 12, inspecting the Illinois towns of Crystal Lake, Harvard, and Woodstock, then crossed into Wisconsin to examine Delavan and Walworth. At Elkhorn, where Roger Touhy had wrecked his car the year before, Backman thought she recognized a tavern. But when Winstead took her inside, there was a lunch counter where Backman remembered a bar.

Winstead, realizing this could take forever, dropped by to see a deputy sheriff he knew in Elkhorn. Winstead described the town Backman remembered. It had an inn, two small lakes, and an iron bridge. He also described a man named "Eddie" she recalled meeting. Luck was with them: without hesitation the deputy identified the resort town of Lake Geneva, where there was a character named Eddie Duffy who ran errands for the Lake Como Inn—an inn agents had inspected the previous summer after finding one of its pillow cases in Tommy Carroll's luggage.

Winstead took Backman and drove to Lake Geneva. She immediately recognized the town, pointing out a tavern where she had eaten breakfast, then leading Winstead to a lakeside cottage where they had visited the man named Eddie. As luck would have it, Backman spotted Eddie Duffy on the street an hour later. She was certain the slender twenty-six-year-old was the "Eddie" she had met before.

On Friday, November 2, after putting Backman on a return flight to San Francisco, Winstead returned to Lake Geneva and confronted Duffy in his room at the Gargoyle Hotel. Duffy, described in Winstead's subsequent report as "very nervous," claimed he knew nothing about Nelson. He admitted he knew John Chase, but only as a guest at the Lake Como Inn. He insisted the agents talk to the inn's owner, Hobart Hermanson. Duffy acted as Hermanson's errand boy, driving a beer truck.

Cowley approached Hermanson directly. On Sunday night, November 4, Hermanson voluntarily appeared at the Chicago office for questioning. Confronted with the possibility of an indictment for harboring Nelson, Hermanson admitted everything, confirming Nelson's visit to his home as well as the gangster's plans to return to Lake Geneva for the winter. The next day Cowley, along with Winstead and Agent Ed Hollis, drove to Lake Geneva to inspect Hermanson's home. Hermanson volunteered to let agents stay in a nearby cottage. Cowley chose Hermanson's house itself. By the end of the week Winstead and two agents were camped out in a second-floor bedroom. If Nelson returned to Lake Geneva for the winter, they would be waiting.

All that October, Nelson remained in a drafty cabin at Wally Hot Springs, Nevada. By early November he was getting antsy. The nights were growing cold, and there was no heat. Money was running low, and he was increasingly irritable. Nelson rarely left the camp. He knew FBI agents were combing Reno for him, but so far he had no indication they had expanded their search outside the city.* One night in the desert, the mechanic Frank Cochran mentioned he had seen an FBI car that day.

"It was all dirty and muddy," he said. "Looks like they been out visiting all the auto camps and traveling all the dirt roads in this part of the state."

Cochran's remark was the nudge Nelson needed to return east. They filled the back of the pickup with five-gallon cans of gasoline and covered them with a tarpaulin. In mid-November they left. Nelson drove the Hudson, Fatso Negri the truck. Outside Durango, Colorado, the Hudson's transmission gave out. They took it to a garage, where a mechanic said parts would have to be ordered. Nelson wanted to abandon the car, but Negri volunteered to stay and bring it to Chicago once it was repaired. Nelson agreed. He took Helen and Chase and drove east in the truck.

Nelson reached the Chicago suburbs several nights later. As always, his hometown held everything he needed and everything he feared. Nelson trusted no more than a handful of men in Chicago; everyone else was a potential stool pigeon. The FBI was only one of his worries. As far as he knew, the Syndicate still wanted him dead. He and Chase prowled the small towns on Chicago's outskirts, Nelson and Helen sleeping in their car every night, in pastures, behind service stations. They dropped Chase at a hotel each evening, in Morris or Elgin or Palestine, and picked him up the next morning. They drove all day every day, stopping in roadside taverns to make phone calls. Most nights they met Nelson's friend, the mechanic Clarey Lieder, outside the city. If Nelson had a plan other than a vague idea of eventually escaping to Europe, he told no one. In the short term, he needed men and money. He had mulled Jimmy Murray's train-robbery scheme for months, and Murray was among the first people Nelson saw upon his return.

Monday, November 26, Nelson and Chase braved a drive into the city, depositing Helen on a street corner on the North Side; she said she wanted to see a movie. Instead, without telling anyone, Helen wandered into their old neighborhood. She walked by the homes of her parents and siblings,

---

* Nelson never learned how close he had come to being discovered at Wally Hot Springs. On three separate occasions during his stay there, a sheriff from nearby Gardnerville had visited the camp, each time asking about a Hudson. They escaped notice only because the camp cook, Ethel Tyler, thought Nelson's car was a Plymouth.

hoping to see someone she knew. Helen was never the most complicated soul, and it's easy to imagine what she felt when she peered into the warm, well-lit homes of her family. As Helen wandered the streets, Nelson and Chase stole a sparkling black V-8 Ford from a dealership. Afterward they drove to a clearing outside Chicago to meet Clarey Lieder and Fatso Negri, who had arrived with Nelson's Hudson.

"Well boys, nearly all the gang's dead," Nelson said, "so the first thing we gotta do is organize a new gang. There are plenty of jobs for us to do, but we can't charge on anything until we get some more members. I want good reliable men, fellas like Ray Karpis."[19]

Nelson still wanted what he had from the start, to team up with Karpis and the Barkers. The problem was, he couldn't find them. Negri suggested they enroll Chicago gangsters. "Not in a million years!" Nelson said. "I know those rats. I grew up in Chicago. Do you think the G-men would have to hunt for months to run down a bunch of rats like those? No, every one of 'em would turn tail and surrender."

Later that evening Nelson picked up Helen on the North Side. That night they slept in their car, as always. Nelson needed his rest. The next day, Tuesday, he had people to see in Wisconsin, after which he hoped to drive into Chicago and talk to Jimmy Murray about the train robbery. With any luck, it would be an eventful day.

Lake Geneva, Wisconsin
Tuesday, November 27, 2 P.M.

Charles Winstead sat waiting in the upstairs bedroom of the Hermanson home, as he had done every day for three weeks. Cars came and went all day, many stopping on the way to the Lake Como Inn up the road. Agent Jim Metcalfe, the aspiring poet, was in the kitchen. They had sent a rookie named Colin McRae into town for groceries.

Around two, Winstead saw a big Ford V-8 coming up the road. "Get ready, here comes a car," he hollered downstairs to Metcalfe.

Metcalfe wasn't concerned: some days a dozen cars visited the Hermansons. He glanced out the window. The approaching car was caked with dust. It looked like the Hermansons' Ford; they had left on a trip the previous Saturday, and he assumed they were returning.

"Everything's okay," Metcalfe yelled. "It's Mrs. Hermanson."

Metcalfe stepped onto the front porch to see if Mrs. Hermanson needed help unloading the car. The midday sun was glowing on the Ford's windshield as it pulled into the yard; neither Metcalfe nor Winstead could see inside. Squinting, Metcalfe could just make out a woman sitting in the front seat. She was a kid, maybe twenty-one, wearing a dark coat with a fur collar.

From inside the car the driver asked if Hermanson was home.

"No," Metcalfe said, "he isn't here."

"Well is Eddie here?" the driver asked.

"No."

"Where is he?"

"He went downtown to do some shopping," Metcalfe said.

The driver thanked him and backed out toward the road. Upstairs, Winstead took his rifle and, though he couldn't make out a face, aimed it directly at the driver's head. As the Ford drove off, Metcalfe caught a glimpse of the man behind the wheel wearing sunglasses and a flat cap. "Who was that?" Winstead yelled.

Metcalfe didn't make the connection until the car had driven out of sight. "That's Baby Face Nelson," he breathed.

He leaped off the front porch and ran for the inn, where there was a telephone.

"Sure as hell that was a G-man, and we caught him with his pants down," Nelson said as they drove away. He caressed a .38 caliber pistol between the legs of his light-gray suit; he'd been prepared to kill Metcalfe. All his senses on alert, Nelson drove into Lake Geneva, hoping to find Eddie Duffy. Instead Nelson was the one seen, by Agent McRae, who spotted his car as he returned to the Hermanson house with groceries. McRae jotted down the plate number, Illinois 639578.

Nelson nervously cruised through Lake Geneva, then drove back south. He had the feeling the town was alive with government agents. He reached the highway and turned southeast toward the Chicago suburbs.[20]

Cowley took the phone call from Lake Geneva at 2:45. It was a poor moment for a crisis; most of his men were out of the office. Cowley called in two agents and told them to head for Lake Geneva at once, watching for Nelson's car. He then took a phone call from Agent Bill Ryan, who was manning a phone tap with a rookie named Tom McDade.* Cowley told Ryan and McDade to proceed to Lake Geneva as well.

Cowley thought a moment. If the driver in Lake Geneva really was Nelson, four men wouldn't be enough. He spotted Ed Hollis; they would go as well. On their way out, Cowley passed Purvis's office.

"Baby Face Nelson has just left Lake Geneva," Cowley said.

"Let's get going," Purvis said, rising from his desk.

"It won't be necessary," Cowley said. "Hollis and I are just going to cruise around and see if we can spot the car on the highway. When we get set, I'll phone you."[21] Purvis volunteered to call Washington. Cowley told him not to bother "as the information [is] rather vague." Purvis called anyway, briefing one of Hoover's aides.[22]

A half hour later, Agents Ryan and McDade were the first to reach Highway 12, parallel two-lane blacktops separated by a grassy median. They sped northwest toward the Wisconsin line, scanning approaching cars; Ryan had written down Nelson's license plate number, 639578, and pinned it to the sun visor. McDade was driving their Ford coupe as they shot through Fox River Grove, where Ryan told him to pull over so they could check Louis Cernocky's tavern. There was no sign of Nelson or his car, so they headed back toward Wisconsin.

Then, just as they left Fox River Grove, a black Ford raced past, heading southeast toward Chicago. Both agents peered at the plate.

"578!" they shouted in unison.

"Turn around!" Ryan snapped. He craned his neck to look at the passing Ford. "There's two men and a woman in it," he said; that met the description of the car in Lake Geneva. McDade eased into the median and completed a U-turn to follow the Ford.

Nelson watched the FBI car slow and turn. "What the hell is this?" he asked Chase, who was in the backseat, a Browning automatic rifle in his lap. "Let's see who those birds are."[23]

Nelson slowed the Ford, turned into the median and completed a U-turn of his own, pulling into the northbound lanes.

"They're turning around!" Ryan snapped at McDade.

* William C. "Bill" Ryan was the first of three brothers who served as FBI agents. His son was also an agent. A member of the Bureau basketball team that won the 1931–32 government-league championship, Bill Ryan had been at Little Bohemia and the Biograph. He served in the Bureau from 1932 to 1958. He died in 1967 at the age of sixty.

McDade and Ryan watched as Nelson's car turned and drove north, passing them. A minute later, Ryan saw the Ford again head into the median and complete a second U-turn, reentering the southbound lanes.

"They've turned around again!" Ryan said.

Now Nelson was following the FBI car. "Let's keep ahead of them," McDade said.

"No," said Ryan. "Let 'em come up and we can get a look at them." Ryan slid his .38 between his legs.

Nelson stayed a few hundred yards behind the FBI car, going about 40 miles an hour. Both drivers kept their eyes on the other car. Then, without warning, Nelson slammed his foot on the accelerator, and the big Ford shot forward. Agent Ryan watched it approach.

"They're right behind us!" he told McDade.

A moment later, Nelson pulled up beside the FBI car and honked his horn. "Pull over!" Nelson shouted.

McDade and Ryan glanced over and saw Chase pointing the automatic rifle at them. "We gotta get outta here!" Ryan shouted. McDade ducked, then hit the accelerator. The FBI car surged ahead.

"Let 'em have it!" Nelson shouted, pushing Helen down in the seat. Chase hesitated; he didn't know who was in the car.

Agent Ryan didn't wait. He aimed his pistol at Nelson's car and fired, squeezing off seven shots, the shells ejecting into McDade's face. Nelson, holding a pistol in one hand and driving with the other, fired back. Windows on both cars exploded. Chase still hesitated.

"What the hell are you gonna do, sit there?" Nelson screamed. "Can't you see they're shooting at us!"

As the FBI car pulled ahead, Chase began firing the automatic rifle; somehow his shots missed the FBI car. Ryan and McDade pulled ahead. Nelson couldn't catch up. "They must've hit the motor!" he said. "We're losing speed!"

Ahead, Agent McDade lost sight of Nelson's car behind him.

"Where are they?" he snapped.

"They're falling back!" Ryan said.

Just then Sam Cowley and Ed Hollis, heading northwest in a black Hudson sedan, drove past the gunfight in the southbound lanes. Hollis pulled a U-turn of his own. Ryan and McDade, meanwhile, scanned the traffic behind them for Nelson's car. Unable to spot it, McDade veered into a roadside field. Both agents jumped out, lay flat in the tall grass, and waited for Nelson to approach.

Nelson, whose car was fast losing speed, saw Cowley's car make the U-turn. In the rearview mirror he watched as the FBI car approached. "There's a Hudson," Nelson said. "It's gaining on us." Nelson tried to pick up speed, but it was no use; his engine was failing. Cowley and Hollis drew closer. Suddenly, just as they approached a roadside park in the town of Barrington, Nelson spun the steering wheel hard to the right and veered off the highway. He stopped on a dirt road beside the park and yelled for everyone to get out of the car. Helen scrambled into a ditch.

Agent Hollis didn't see Nelson's car until he was abreast of it. He slammed on the brakes, which screeched loudly, enough to draw the attention of customers at a Standard Oil station across the highway and a Shell station about 750 feet further down the blacktop. The FBI car skidded to a diagonal stop in the right lane, 150 feet past where Nelson and Chase stood beside their car, readying their guns.

Nelson stood on the running board and opened fire with an automatic rifle before Hollis and Cowley got out of their car. Gunshots slammed into the back of the Hudson. Chase laid a rifle across the hood of the Ford and began firing as well. Then Nelson's rifle jammed; he threw it to Chase, yelling for him to reload it. Nelson snatched up a Thompson and resumed firing.

Cowley leaped out of the FBI car, a submachine gun in his hands. A desk man his entire career, the squat, jowly Mormon was the last man Hoover would have wanted facing off with Nelson. Neither Cowley nor Hollis wore a bulletproof vest; Cowley complained they were too heavy. Nor had Cowley, despite the Bureau's pleas, bothered to qualify on the pistol range. Nonetheless, crouching beside his car, Cowley fired a burst at Nelson, who returned the fire. At least six of his bullets struck Nelson in the stomach and chest, shredding his intestines.

Nelson doubled over in pain but, with adrenaline coursing through his body, somehow continued firing at Cowley. Two rounds hit Cowley in the midsection. He sagged to the pavement, rolling into a ditch beside the car. One bullet had torn through Cowley's stomach, the other his chest. A bulletproof vest would likely have stopped both rounds.

Hollis jumped out the driver's-side door onto the highway and fired blasts from his sawed-off shotgun, a blizzard of pellets that struck Nelson up and down both legs. Nelson still would not fall. He staggered forward, now firing at Hollis, who retreated across the highway, seeking the slender cover of a telephone pole. After emptying the shotgun Hollis pulled his pistol and fired as he ran. A bullet from Nelson's submachine gun hit him flush in the forehead. Hollis crumpled to the pavement just as reached the telephone pole.

Nelson staggered toward Hollis, badly wounded. Onlookers at the two gas stations watched in amazement as Nelson lurched over to the fallen agent. Several witnesses later claimed that Nelson fired into Hollis as he lay on the ground; he didn't. Ignoring Cowley, who lay in the ditch, Nelson limped to the FBI Hudson and slid behind the wheel. He slipped it into reverse and managed to back it up to his car.

"Throw those guns in here, and let's get going!" he rasped to Chase. Chase did as he was told, grabbing up guns on the ground and tossing them into the Hudson. He started to get into the front seat when Nelson said, "You'll have to drive. I'm hurt." Chase circled around the car, opened the driver's door and pushed Nelson across the front seat. Blood was everywhere. "What'll we do about Helen?" Chase asked as he slid behind the wheel.

"We can't fool with her now," Nelson said. "We'll have to leave her."

Just then Chase spotted Helen running toward the car. She hopped into the backseat with the guns and Chase drove off.

The first onlooker to reach the scene was William P. Gallagher, an Illinois state patrolman who happened to be selling tickets for an American Legion benefit at the Shell station down the highway. Hearing the shots, Gallagher had taken a rifle from the station and fired at Nelson's fleeing car. As it drove away, Gallagher and another man, who had stopped his car upon seeing the gunfight, sprinted across the highway to Hollis. Hollis lay facedown beside the telephone pole, a gold badge pinned to his chest. The back of his head was blown off. Gallagher tried to speak to him. Hollis, who had minutes to live, managed only a heavy gasp. His eyes moved.

Gallagher then hustled over to Cowley, who lay in the ditch, his feet on the pavement, blood covering the right side of his face; there appeared to be a gunshot wound to the side of his eye. "Don't shoot, government officer," Cowley whispered. Gallagher leaned down.

"Was Hollis hurt?" Cowley asked.

Gallagher nodded.

"Look after him first," Cowley said. He told Gallagher to call the Chicago office, Randolph 6226, and report what had happened. He also asked Gallagher to reach his wife and tell her he had been called out of town and wouldn't make it home for dinner.

Traffic was backing up. A crowd was forming. Gallagher flagged down a car and loaded Hollis inside, directing the driver to Barrington Central Hospital. Hollis died en route; Gallagher lifted a rosary from the agent's pocket and called a priest.* A few minutes later an ambulance arrived and took Cowley to a hospital in the town of Elgin.

Agents Ryan and McDade were still lying in a field further down Highway 12. They knew nothing of what had transpired; when Ryan ran to a pay phone and called Purvis with the news at 4:15, he reported only his own actions. Five minutes later Purvis was on the phone briefing Hoover when the police chief in the nearby town of Stamford called with news that Hollis was dead and Cowley had been shot.

Purvis left immediately for the hospital in Elgin. He arrived as Cowley was being rolled into surgery. Cowley asked a doctor whether he was going to die. Then he saw Purvis. Whatever tensions remained between the two men vanished for a few moments. "Hello, Melvin, I am glad you are here," Cowley whispered.

"Rest quiet and you will be all right," Purvis said.

"Do you have doubt about that?" Cowley asked.

"No," Purvis said.

"I emptied my gun at them," Cowley said.

"Who were they?"

"Nelson and Chase."

Nelson was dying; even Helen could see it. He was bleeding from seventeen separate gunshot wounds. Five were in his stomach and side, two in his chest, and five in each of his legs where Hollis's shotgun had done the

---

* At the moment Hollis died, his wife, Genevieve, and their young son were waiting in the lobby of the Bankers Building, taking a moment from a downtown shopping trip to surprise him at the end of his workday. An agent saw her and called her upstairs, where Doris Rogers watched one of the agents break the news to her.

damage; the worst injury was a wound to the left of his navel where one of Cowley's .45 caliber slugs had struck and traveled sideways through his lower abdomen. Blood gushed from the wound, soaking Nelson's gray slacks and trickling onto the seat.

From Highway 12 Chase turned east onto Highway 22, a two-lane blacktop that wound through dense woods into Chicago's northern suburbs. They turned south when they hit Waukegan Road, where by one account they stopped at the Techny monastery. Nelson, who remained lucid throughout the drive, was looking for his old friend Father Coughlin. After driving south into the suburb of Wilmette, they found his sister's house at 1115 Mohawk. The house, which stills stands, was a large two-story brick home with a tree-ringed rear driveway.

According to Father Coughlin, he was sitting in his sister's home about four-forty-five when the back doorbell rang. A maid answered and called for him. It was Helen. She said "Jimmy" had been shot and needed help. Father Coughlin shrugged into his overcoat, threw on a hat, and followed her to the garage, where Chase had parked. Inside the garage Chase was supporting Nelson, who leaned against the car.

Coughlin said they couldn't stay; his sister was due home from her bridge game at any moment. "He's dying," Helen pled. "He's got to go someplace where he can lie down." Coughlin said he would take them someplace safe; they could follow him in his car. "You wouldn't fool with us, would you Father?" Chase asked.

Coughlin helped load Nelson into the front seat. Nelson could barely speak. He whispered in the priest's ear, "Hello."

Father Coughlin drove his car, and Chase followed. The priest later told agents he didn't know where he would go. It didn't matter. After following Coughlin for several minutes, Nelson suspected treachery. "Lose him; I think he's wrong," Nelson said. "Turn around and go the other way." When Father Coughlin lost sight of Nelson's car, he drove back to his sister's and called the FBI office at 6:15. Agents were at his home within the hour.

On Hoover's go-ahead, FBI agents began raiding all of Nelson's gangland contacts that night. Three hustled into Cernocky's roadhouse at Fox River Grove. Agent Ryan led two squads of Chicago police in raids on Clarey Lieder's garage and home, taking Lieder into custody. Two more agents, accompanied by four squads of Chicago police, stormed into Jimmie Murray's home, his parents' home, and the Rain-Bo Inn; there was no sign of Murray. They also raided the home of Nelson's sister on South

Marshfield Avenue. Another group of ten agents descended on Murray's cottage in the town of Wauconda. There was no sign of Nelson.

As the raids progressed that night, Cowley was wheeled out of surgery. Doctors said his condition "was, of course, serious, but that he had a chance to pull through if peritonitis did not set in," Hoover told Cowley's brother Joe.[24] In fact, Hoover confided to an aide, the doctors gave Cowley a 1-in-25 chance of making it through the night.[25]

Characteristically, even as Cowley lay dying, Hoover was preoccupied with publicity. It was Purvis—again. Hoover couldn't understand it; it was as if reporters were a drug Purvis couldn't kick. He had remained at the hospital and actually given an interview to a *Chicago American* reporter as they watched the unconscious Cowley in a hospital bed, his wife, Lavon, and her two little boys beside him.

"If it's the last thing I do, I'll get Baby Face Nelson—dead or alive," Purvis whispered to the reporter, Elgar Brown. "Nelson ought to know he hasn't a chance at eventual escape . . . We aren't particular whether we get him alive or dead."[26]

Hoover was beside himself. He cast about for anyone to rid him of Purvis. His deputies, Hugh Clegg and Pop Nathan, were delivering speeches in Pittsburgh and Tuscon, respectively, and Hoover ordered both to Chicago. Hoover wanted Purvis out of the hospital and away from any reporters; he told Clegg to "impress upon Mr. Purvis the necessity of staying away from the office and from any public place."[27] Clegg suggested that Purvis could work in a back room at the FBI office; Hoover refused even that. Within days word would leak to the *American* that Purvis "is incapacitated by overwork and is on sick leave . . . Insiders do not expect him to return to the command of the Chicago office."[28]

As the night wore on, Cowley's condition worsened. Just after midnight an agent overheard doctors say he wouldn't make it till dawn. An hour later Purvis, who had returned to the office, called Washington to report "Mr. Cowley is sinking fast and is not expected to live more than two hours." Purvis returned to the hospital. Cowley died at 2:17 A.M., November 28, the day before Thanksgiving. His wife, Lavon, collapsed in tears. Doctors gave her a sedative.

Five hours later, at 7:30, police in suburban Winnetka found the FBI car Nelson had stolen in a ditch. Then, as FBI agents descended on the area, an anonymous caller phoned the Sadowski Funeral Home in suburban Niles Center (now Skokie), telling the undertaker, Philip Sadowski, he could find a body beside a local cemetery.* Sadowski passed the tip on to Niles Center police, who passed it to the FBI. Just before noon, police found blood-soaked pants, a shirt, underwear, and socks in a ditch near the cemetery. A half hour later, in another ditch at the corner of Niles and Long Avenues, they found the bullet-riddled nude body of a man wrapped in a blanket. It was Nelson.

Chase had driven the dying Nelson through the streets of Wilmette, following his mumbled directions. About six-thirty they turned into an alley behind a house on Walnut Street and parked in a covered garage. The home was owned by a man named Ray Henderson, who appears to have been an acquaintance of the fence Jimmy Murray. Chase carried Nelson inside and laid him on a bed. Helen stripped off his clothes and wrapped a towel around his midsection in a vain attempt to staunch the blood. Nelson faded quickly, lapsing in and out of consciousness. His last minutes, like his final gunfight, resembled a scene from one of the gangster movies he loved.

"It's getting dark, Helen," he whispered at one point. "Say good-bye to mother." He recited the names of his brothers and sisters. When he asked her to bid farewell to their children, he began to cry. A few minutes later he said, "It's getting dark, Helen. I can't see you anymore." He died at 7:35 P.M.

The next morning Chase laid Nelson's body in the ditch, then fled. Helen, frightened and unsure what to do, took refuge with her family, where the FBI took her into custody two days later. She missed Nelson's funeral. He was laid to rest beside his father, in the suburban Chicago cemetery where his grave remains to this day.

The bloodiest day in the FBI's brief history was followed by two somber funerals. Herman "Ed" Hollis was buried in his native Des Moines, Sam Cowley in Salt Lake City. Cowley's body lay in state beneath the capitol rotunda while thousands filed by in silence.

Pop Nathan gave Cowley's eulogy. "We are bringing [Sam] back [to Utah] a national martyred hero," Nathan said. "The columns of the press are replete with his exploits, and men, women and children in all parts of the country know him now. He is famous, and justly so. And yet Sam Cowley was one of the simplest men I ever knew. He was greatly simple. He was simply great. His was the simplicity of the saints, seers and heroes of the

---

* The caller's identity was never confirmed. It may have been Nelson's sister; his wife, Helen; John Chase; or another family member.

ages, the simplicity of true worth, of true dignity, of true honor. We, of the Division, are very proud of him. As generations of new agents come into our service they will be told of the life and death of Sam Cowley. He will become a tradition. He will have attained earthly immortality."

Nathan was as good as his word. For decades to come, Hoover held up Cowley as the ultimate FBI man, quiet, hardworking, and dedicated. He remains the most senior agent ever killed in the line of duty.

18

THE LAST MAN STANDING

December 3, 1934, to January 20, 1935

Chicago, Illinois
Monday, December 3

That morning a somber group of FBI men began hauling files into a new set of offices in the New York Life Insurance Building, two blocks from the Bankers Building. The situation on the nineteenth floor had grown untenable. Reporters lingered around the clock, pestering Doris Rogers, straining to overhear phone calls and filing stories any time a handful of agents headed for the elevator at once. Before his death, Cowley had been agitating for a new "secret office" where he could finish the War on Crime free of scrutiny. After his funeral he got it.[1]

To replace Cowley, Hoover brought in Earl Connelley, the taciturn Cincinnati SAC who had overseen the Indiana theater of the Dillinger hunt. Connelley found morale in the old Dillinger Squad—now known as the Flying Squad—low. The men were on their last legs. Three were now dead. No one wanted to be next. A few agents were sending out feelers to hometown law firms, hoping for a new, safer job.

That morning Connelley convened a staff meeting to go over leads on the Barkers. Since the gang fled Cleveland in September, there had been no sign of them, but the Cleveland raids had shaken loose a torrent of information on the gang, much of it from the Barker women. Cowley left behind dozens of promising tips. They were close. Connelley could feel it. In late September they had missed capturing Ma Barker by only a week; agents had raided her apartment on South Shore Drive after learning her address from Shotgun George Ziegler's widow, who had suffered a nervous breakdown and washed up in a Chicago sanatorium.

Just before his death, Cowley's hottest tip had come in Miami, where on November 16 a car Karpis had registered under an alias in Ohio was suddenly reregistered in Florida. Cowley and three of his best men flew down to investigate. Together they found the car and quickly deduced that the man driving it was not Karpis. His name was Duke Randall. He was a gofer at the El Commodoro, a hotel Miami police characterized as "a joint for racketeers and undesirables." Cowley decided to keep Randall under surveillance. Three weeks later, two agents were still living in the hotel, waiting and watching.

Havana, Cuba

That same Monday, as Connelley and his men moved into their new offices, an agent named Loyde E. Kingman arrived in Havana.* In his pocket he carried photos of Willie Harrison, the Barker Gang gofer whose passion for horse racing had spurred Cowley to have his photo posted at every racetrack between New Orleans and Miami. That day Kingman showed Harrison's photo to officials of the International Racing Association, who agreed to circulate it at the Cuban tracks. The rest of the week Kingman planned to check the expatriate hangouts, Sloppy Joe's Bar, Donovan's Bar, the Eden Concert Night Club, the Habana-Madrid Jai Alai Fronton. At the end of the day, Kingman trudged to the Parkview Hotel and took his place in line at the front desk.

A man in front of him lingered, talking with the clerk.

"Excuse me sir," Kingman finally said. "Would you allow me to register?"

The man turned.

"No," said Alvin Karpis. "Not at all."[2]

Karpis had told no one, not even Fred Barker, of his plans to hide in Cuba. After dividing up the ransom money in Chicago that night in September, he had confided only that he could be reached through the El Commodoro in

---

* Born in 1894, Loyde E. Kingman served in the FBI from 1927 to 1953. A popular mentor to many agents, known as "King" inside the Bureau, Kingman died in 1978.

Miami. Karpis and the pregnant Delores Delaney had driven two hundred miles that first night, staying over in a drafty tourist camp in southern Indiana. They reached Birmingham, Alabama, the following evening. They hit the Atlantic Coast just as a tropical storm struck, the high winds jostling their Ford. Just past Fort Pierce the skies cleared. It was a warm night. Karpis allowed himself to relax. Delaney threw her head out the window, luxuriating in the tropical breezes, marveling at the palm trees. Karpis didn't see the squad car until its lights filled his rearview mirror. He was doing eighty-five.

Karpis pulled over. He watched a trooper in rain gear approach his car. "Are you in a big hurry?" the trooper asked.

"Well, not necessarily," Karpis said. "I'm trying to get down to Miami."

"You're going pretty fast."

Karpis said he didn't think Florida had a speed limit yet.

"Well," the trooper said. "If you're going too fast, we can get you on a charge of reckless driving. When you're going eighty-five, ninety miles an hour on a night like this, I'd say it's kind of reckless. But I can see you've got Illinois tags and you're coming down for a vacation, so I'm not going to spoil it for you."

"I'll drive a little slower," Karpis said. He let the man go.

The next morning Karpis and Delaney cruised into Miami and drove to the El Commodoro, where Karpis checked in and introduced himself to the manager, Joe Adams, who had friendly ties with the South Florida underworld. Karpis left his car with Adams, along with his machine gun and a pair of bulletproof vests, all of which Adams volunteered to dispose of. (It was Adams who lent the car to his gofer, Duke Randall.) At Adams's suggestion, Karpis and Delaney scampered through a rainstorm to the Burdine's department store, where they bought the silk shirts and bathing suits they would need in Cuba. At nightfall Adams sent champagne and New York strip steaks to their suite for dinner.

The next morning, Adams dropped Karpis and Delaney off at the train station. By noon that Saturday, September 15, the two were in Key West, shuffling through the queue waiting to board the S.S. *Cuba* for the six-hour cruise to Havana. Delaney was transfixed by a suntanned young man who dived for coins the tourists threw. In fact, she was thrilled at everything, the aquamarine sea and the palm trees and the piña coladas. She was seventeen and pregnant and in love with the world. Karpis looked at her and thought, *God it's great to be a criminal.*

. . .

Havana in September 1934 was a city barely twelve months removed from the revolution in which a thirty-two-year-old sergeant named Fulgencio Batista had seized control of the government. American tourists had flocked to Cuba's pristine beaches and sophisticated casinos during the 1920s, but the sporadic violence that littered the wake of Batista's coup scared many away. Havana's two casinos had begun a decline that wouldn't be reversed until a little-known operator named Meyer Lansky arrived in 1938 to institute professional controls.

In the harbor, Karpis and Delaney descended the gangplank and were at once overwhelmed by the chaos of the Havana docks. Porters clamored to carry the gringos' suitcases. Karpis had never seen such confusion. At the Parkview Hotel a bellhop took their bags. Karpis left a message for the owner, Nate Heller, a man Joe Adams said could be trusted. After washing up, Karpis went to scout the streets. He stopped at another place Adams had recommended, George's American Bar, and introduced himself to the owner, who gave him two rum-and-Cokes on the house and briefed him on police customs. Karpis, never much of a drinker, found his knees weak when he left the bar.

At his room he found a message from Nate Heller. They met downstairs. "I'm going to live here awhile and I don't think I care much for Havana," Karpis said. "I thought maybe you might point out some place up the coast that would be suitable for me. I want a quiet place and I want to be away from everybody, the police and everybody else."

Karpis watched for Heller's reaction, but Heller only smiled. "We've got a lot of people here that don't want to talk to the police," he said. "You know, we've had some trouble here."

"Yeah, I understand that."

"Batista's got control, but not like people think he has," Heller continued. "You'll hear shooting tonight. But don't get excited about it because he's only been in for a little while and things aren't very stable. If anyone tries to talk about politics with you, just don't get into a conversation with them. You understand?" Karpis nodded. Heller promised to find him a secluded beach house, and they agreed to meet the next day.

Afterward Karpis stood out on the sidewalk, soaking up the humid night air. "Excuse me," a voice said. Karpis turned and saw another tourist. "Do you know where a drugstore is?" the man asked.

A bellman overheard the question and pointed out a drugstore down the block. "Hell, I'll walk down there with you," Karpis volunteered. "I'll buy a deck of cards."

Inside, Karpis bought a box of Bicycle cards, then stepped onto the sidewalk with the other American. Karpis was going to say something about the weather when suddenly there was a deafening explosion. A block to his left the Prado was filling with smoke. A bomb had exploded. "Come on!" the tourist yelled, running toward the smoke.

"Hell no!" Karpis said. He ran for the hotel, worried that police would soon be on the scene. In the lobby the clerk suggested Karpis stay in his room. Snipers would be on the rooftops soon. "Jesus Christ," Karpis said, "I thought I was getting away from crime."

Karpis wasted no time getting out of Havana. Heller arranged for him to rent a six-room beach house down the coast outside the town of Veradero. It was as beautiful a spot as Karpis had ever seen. The sand was white as snow, the water alive with glints of blue and green. The house came with a fourteen-foot motorized skiff that Karpis used almost every day to fish in the Gulf of Mexico. He hired a maid and a houseboy and a Korean cook, none of whom could speak English. It was heaven.

A month passed. They did nothing but fish and walk the beach, collecting seashells. One evening at dusk, Karpis was sitting on his veranda when a pack of children approached to tell him there was a call for him at the town switchboard. It was Nate Heller with a message: Ma was on her way to Varadero for a visit; she had learned from Joe Adams where they were staying. Later that night Karpis was listening to *Amos 'n' Andy* on the radio when he realized he was late to pick her up. He drove to the bus stop and found a red-faced Ma involved in a manic tug-of-war with a Cuban boy who was intent on helping her with her baggage. When Karpis walked up, Ma turned her anger on him, yelling that he was late. Karpis laughed and handed the boy a peso.

For three days, Karpis took Ma beachcombing and fishing, a peaceful interlude marred only by an afternoon when Ma failed to catch a fish and accused Karpis of sabotaging her fishing line. Karpis just rolled his eyes; that was Ma. When it came time for her to leave, Karpis drove her to Havana and put her on the flight to Miami.

While in Havana, Karpis dropped by George's American Bar, where he was known as "Mr. Wagner." The proprietor's wife, whose hobby seemed to be drinking rum-and-Cokes from dawn to dusk, showed him a detective magazine. She opened it to a photograph of the Barker Gang.

"Why Mr. Wagner," she slurred. "If I didn't know you so well, I would swear this was you."

"It does look a little like me, doesn't it?" Karpis said.

She wouldn't let it go, prattling on about what an uncanny resemblance the photograph was. Karpis forced a chuckle and offered to buy the magazine from her for thirty-five cents. "No, no, no" the woman said. She wanted to show it to her friends. At this point, the owner stepped from behind the bar and angrily snatched up the magazine. "Take the thirty-five cents!" he snapped. He winked at Karpis.

When he returned to Varadero the next day, Karpis could see Delores was growing restless. "Why don't you go over to Miami for a few days?" he suggested.

"Would you let me?"

"Sure," Karpis said. "Check into the El Commodoro and maybe if you want, you can go up there where Freddie and his mother are. While you're over there, look around and maybe you'll find someplace maybe you'd like to live 'cause we may not stay here much longer." Karpis, too, was growing restless. Cuba was too violent for his tastes.

Delores spent a week in Miami and returned with a bulldog pup. She and Karpis fell back into an easy rhythm of eating, fishing, and sunbathing, until one night Karpis was listening to Lowell Thomas's newscast and heard that Pretty Boy Floyd was dead.

"Jesus Christ!" he snapped. "They're knocking everybody off!" He felt nothing. *Better him than me,* he thought.

Then, on a trip into Havana a few days later, he changed a one-thousand-dollar bill at a branch of the Royal Bank of Canada. Some of the bills he received in exchange, he noticed, were discolored. He checked the Federal Reserve numbers. They were from Minneapolis. He realized with a start that it was some of the Bremer kidnap money—money that was supposed to be in Caracas and Mexico City. Karpis felt double-crossed. This could mean FBI men streaming into Cuba.

He was still stewing a few weeks later when the radio carried news of Baby Face Nelson's death. After a few days he drove into Havana. He needed to gauge whether Cuba was still safe. At the Parkway Hotel he took a room and asked for Nate Heller. He tarried a moment, talking to the clerk. It was then the pleasant-looking American asked if he would step aside so he could register.

Karpis watched the young man closely. He could tell from his felt hat and his winter suit he was American. Karpis was immediately suspicious. He watched as the man filled out a registration card, giving his name as Kingman and an address in Jacksonville.

Karpis walked to the elevator. To his alarm, Kingman followed him. The door closed. They were alone. As the elevator rose, neither man said anything. Karpis got off at his floor. In his room he turned the episode over in his mind. After a moment he told himself to forget it. This was stupid; the man was probably a salesman.

That evening Karpis kept a dinner appointment at George's. Just as he sat down a car began honking outside. Karpis glanced out and saw it was Heller's Model A Ford. He excused himself and walked out to the car. Heller was excited. Kingman *was* an FBI man. He had been to see him, seeking an introduction to the Associated Press bureau chief. They'd had drinks. "Well, I see according to the radio and the newspapers, you've just about wiped out all the gangsters over there," Heller had told Kingman, as he related the conversation to Karpis.

No, Kingman said, they hadn't. "Here's the son of a bitch we really want," the FBI man said, placing a photograph on the table.

Heller looked at Karpis. "Who the hell do you think it was?"

"Who?" Karpis asked.

"You."

Afterward, Heller had taken the agent to see the AP man. The two had disappeared into a back room, leaving Heller outside. When the meeting was over Kingman emerged and, in Heller's presence, asked the reporter, "What time can I get a bus for down there?"

The reporter turned to Heller. "What time can he get a bus in the morning for Matanzas?"

Matanzas was the capital of Varadero province.

Karpis kept his head. He drove through the night to Varadero, arriving around three the next morning. He and Delaney left at dawn, telling the servants nothing. They drove straight to the Havana airport, where Karpis put Delaney on a flight to Miami.

As he had in Cleveland, Karpis stayed behind to assess the situation, promising to take the boat to Key West the next morning. That afternoon he spoke to Heller, who had debriefed the AP man. Agent Kingman had given the impression that a horde of FBI men were on their way to Havana, lured by reports of Bremer money circulating in Cuba.

The next morning Karpis showed up at the dock for the steamer to Key West. He studied the crowds. Finally he took a deep breath, ascended the gangplank, and found his stateroom. Minutes ticked by. He was sweating. Finally he felt the throb of the engines and heard whistles blowing. The boat was casting off. He was safe.[3]

The break came in Toledo. On Monday, December 3, the day the Flying Squad moved into its new offices in Chicago, a Detroit agent was sitting in the office of the Toledo district attorney, Frazier Reams, when Reams brought up something odd his brother had told him. Dr. Glen Reams was a Toledo surgeon. One of his patients said a woman he knew named Mildred Kuhlmann, a twenty-four-year-old from Liepsic, Ohio, had married Dock Barker that summer. After what one imagines was a jarring double take, the agent recognized it made sense; one of the Barker girls had mentioned that Dock dated someone named Mildred.

Eleven days later, on the morning of Friday, December 14, as agents scrambled to locate Mildred Kuhlmann, Frazier Reams called the Detroit SAC, Bill Larson, and asked to meet at Toledo's Commodore Perry Hotel. When Larson arrived, Reams told him Kuhlmann was in Chicago. She had just telephoned one of her girlfriends, a woman named Mrs. J. A. Ranlow. After swearing Mrs. Ranlow to secrecy, Kuhlmann had spoken of how thrilling it was living with the Barkers, how Dock had bought her a five-hundred-dollar mink coat, how she was driving around with an actual submachine gun between her legs. She invited Ranlow to come join the fun. Mrs. Ranlow had left on a train before dawn, but not before leaving a forwarding address: Room 3121 at Chicago's Hotel Morrison.

Larson called Earl Connelley in Chicago. Two agents, Sam McKee and the little poet Jim Metcalfe, walked up to the Hotel Morrison's front desk an hour later. There were no Kuhlmanns or Ranlows registered at the hotel. But in Room 3121 there was a Mrs. A. R. Esser. They checked her phone records. All the calls were to Toledo.

A half-dozen agents kept the lobby under surveillance all that day. At 7:15, the two women came downstairs and announced they were checking out. Connelley stood by, watching. The women returned upstairs and a half hour later emerged from the elevators, a bellman carrying their luggage. With them was a short, heavyset man wearing a derby hat. The agents took note; they hadn't seen him before.

Outside all three suspects filed into a Ford coupe. Agent Ray Suran followed in a Bureau car as the Ford swung out onto Lake Shore Drive and headed north, then turned left into a side street. The car stopped in front of one apartment building, then another, each time one of the women scurrying out to check something, as if looking for an address. The procession pulled onto Broadway and then to Melrose, where Suran's car got caught in traffic. In frustration he watched as the two women who were their best leads on the Barker Gang drove out of sight.

It took four days to find them again. Armed with its license plate number, agents tracked the car to a local dealership, where a salesman identified a photo of Dock Barker's friend Russell Gibson as the man who had bought the car. Meanwhile, a check of phone calls the women made from the Hotel Morrison led to the Hotel Commonwealth on Pine Grove Avenue. The room they called was occupied by a man named John Borcia, who the manager described as five-six, heavyset, and typically wearing a dark overcoat and derby hat. It matched the description of the man at the Morrison.

Hoover approved a tap on Borcia's phone. Agents traced one of his calls to a North Side apartment house where, four days later, they spotted Mildred Kuhlmann on the sidewalk, her arms full of Christmas packages. Two of Connelley's men tailed her into a neighborhood of luxury apartment buildings off Lake Shore Drive. As they watched, Kuhlmann disappeared into the Surf Lane Apartments. The next day agents found the name A.R. ESSER on Apartment G-1; it was the false name Kuhlmann had used at the Hotel Morrison. The manager said "Mrs. Esser" had rented her apartment two weeks earlier. For several days, he added, "Mr. Esser" had lived there, too, but he was now traveling. Downtown, Connelley was willing to bet "Mr. Esser" was Dock Barker.

Connelley arranged to rent a surveillance apartment at the Surf Lane and sat back to wait for "Mr. Esser" to return. Agents followed Kuhlmann through her routines, leaving her apartment most afternoons and returning after nightfall, always alone. One day they followed one of her visitors to a

building at 3912 Pine Grove Avenue. Connelley rented yet another surveillance flat, installed a set of agents, and sat back and waited for the Barkers.

The day Karpis boarded the steamer in Havana, December 5, the waves
were unusually high and he got seasick. At Key West he boarded a train for
Miami, where he found Delores waiting at the station as they planned.
With her, to his surprise, was the gang's gofer, Willie Harrison. Harrison
drove them into Miami and briefed Karpis on the gang's whereabouts.
Freddie and Ma were living in a house on Lake Weir in Central Florida.
Another gang member, Harry Campbell, had driven to Oklahoma and re-
united with his teenage girlfriend Wynona Burdette. They were at Lake
Weir, too. Karpis was suspicious. The last Karpis had heard of Burdette,
she was in FBI custody in Cleveland.*

In Miami they checked into the El Commodoro; as luck would have it,
agents watching the hotel had returned to Chicago the previous week. Delaney was in the eighth month of her pregnancy, and she asked Karpis if
she could give birth in Miami. Karpis said sure. The hotel's manager, Joe
Adams, hardly recognized Karpis his tan was so deep. Karpis asked about
a house to rent, and Adams said he knew a place, an old bootlegger's bungalow on 85th Street. Karpis told him to hold off. He needed to get a sense
of how hot he was in Miami before he decided to stay.

The next morning, Karpis went downstairs and found Adams in his office. He needed a car, so Adams dispatched Duke Randall to buy him a
Buick sedan. Adams also sent a telegram to Fred at Lake Weir, asking him
to come to Miami. The next morning Fred arrived at the hotel. He and
Karpis hadn't seen each other in almost three months. Barker told Karpis
all about the excellent fishing and deer hunting in central Florida. He said
Ma was dying to have Delaney come visit. "Well wait a minute," Karpis
said. "Is that Yona Burdette up there?"

Barker laughed. "Yeah, Campbell's got her there."

"How the hell did she get away from the FBI?" he asked. "And how
come your mother is letting her stay there with you and her?"

---

* Burdette, Gladys Sawyer, and Paula Harmon had all been released after giving detailed statements. The
Bureau inexplicably failed to keep them under regular surveillance, allowing Burdette and Sawyer to reunite with their men. Never the most stable of the Barker women, Paula Harmon had returned to Texas,
where her family had her committed to an asylum.

Again Barker laughed. "It's kind of a long story," he said. "You know when you left Chicago and went to Cuba, why, Campbell came down to Florida when my mother and I did and he was living with us. And he finally decided that he wanted to get Yona again. He decided he'd drive all the way to Oklahoma to get her."

They talked for hours. Barker asked if he might be interested in returning to Cleveland to rob an armored car. Karpis begged off. "By the way," Karpis said. "Where's Dock?"

"He's living in Chicago now," Barker said. "He's living with some guys around there, Rusty Gibson and some guys."

It went without saying that neither man wanted much to do with Dock Barker. He was an unreliable drunk. Karpis suggested they look at banks in Georgia and Alabama. The only reason nobody hit Southern banks, Karpis knew, was the notoriety of Southern prisons. There were plenty to rob. When Barker returned north, he took with him Karpis's promise that he would visit as soon as he got settled.

The next day, Karpis took Delaney to look at the house Joe Adams recommended on 85th Street. They liked it, and Karpis handed over $1,000 to rent it for the winter. Adams arranged a nurse who would double as a maid. They moved in a few days later and settled into their quiet routine, listening to the radio, turning in early. Delores's little bulldog took to doing battle with the coconuts that dropped like bombs onto their lawn. Karpis hated the falling coconuts. The dents they made in the perfect green grass offended his sense of order.

The following week Freddie and Ma appeared at the El Commodoro, and Karpis accepted their invitation to go deep-sea fishing. On the drive back, Freddie again suggested they make a run to Cleveland. This time Karpis agreed. Delores pouted at the news, reminding him that the baby could come any day, but the following Monday, Karpis followed the Barkers to central Florida anyway. He found Freddie and Ma's lake house outside the hamlet of Oklawaha, thirty miles south of Ocala. To his surprise, it lay just a stone's throw off the main road. It was a far more accessible site than he would have chosen; when they walked in the yard, Karpis noticed, they could be seen by anyone driving by.

The next morning they headed north. In Cleveland they received a hearty welcome from Karpis's old boss, Shimmy Patton, who briefed them on the FBI's investigations in the city. Cleveland, Karpis decided, was still far too hot for their return. He returned to Miami, relieved.

New Year's came and went quietly. Then, in the first week of January, Freddie drove up to Karpis's house. With him were Dock Barker and Russell Gibson. Irritated, Karpis took Freddie aside.

"What the hell are they doing down here?" he hissed.

Dock had wanted to pull a job in Cleveland, Freddie explained. But Shimmy Patton had insisted that Freddie and Karpis be brought in. No one wanted to do business with Dock by himself. Karpis sighed. There seemed no way to get rid of Freddie's brother.

A few days later Karpis returned to Lake Weir to discuss the Cleveland job with Freddie. Dock was packed and ready to drive back to Chicago when Karpis arrived. Everyone sat around the kitchen table planning how to get in touch once everything was set for the Cleveland job. Dock would send word, but he wanted to be certain he could remember how to find Freddie's lake house. He hunched over a road map. "Well hell, I know, I'll just circle it right here," Dock said, "and I'll know this is the town you want me to send the word to. I'll send it in a letter. Is that the way you want it?"

"Yeah," Freddie said, "just send a letter down here. Say anything in it, that my brother's sick or anything, we'll know they want us in Cleveland."

Dock stuffed the map into his suitcase.

Chicago, Illinois
Tuesday, January 8, 1935
11 A.M.

Earl Connelley stared out the window of the cramped second-floor apartment at 3920 Pine Grove Avenue, one of the two apartment buildings agents had been watching for a week. The night before, "Mr. Esser," the man they suspected was Dock Barker, had returned to the other building, the Surf Lane Apartments. Below, in the Pine Grove apartment, two couples were living. The agents suspected one of the men was Dock's pal Russell Gibson. The other, tall and thin, they couldn't place. An hour earlier they had seen one of the women take her brown Chow tinkling in the alley. A little after that they had seen the thin man on the back porch in his bathrobe.

Connelley studied the ground. The apartment had a single rear entrance, up a flight of wooden stairs from a scrubby backyard. Twenty feet behind the stairs a four-foot fence fronted the alley. Along the walls of the surrounding apartment buildings and garages, Connelley saw, he could station twenty agents. He was satisfied. If all four occupants were inside the apartment, they would raid the building at nightfall. After that they would hit the Surf Street address.

Downtown, Doris Rogers watched the men assemble for the raids. She was struck by the transformation they had undergone these last few months. The nervousness and unsteadiness she had seen in the Verne Miller and Dillinger raids were gone; in its place was a cool professionalism, men comfortable with their guns, jaws set, eyes confident. All that afternoon FBI agents filtered into the two surveillance apartments. Connelley would wait until all the occupants were inside. Then they would move in.

Surf Lane Apartments
6:30 P.M.

It was a mild January evening, the temperature in the upper thirties. Old snow, gray and gritty, clogged the gutters and lined the sidewalks. A dozen agents lingered at spots all around the building. Connelley had left orders to await the raid at 3920 Pine Grove unless the man they believed was Dock Barker attempted to leave.

Jerry Campbell, the marksman Hoover had hired from the Oklahoma City Police Department, was sitting in a car outside the Surf Lane with a rookie named Alexander Muzzey when they saw Mildred Kuhlmann and Dock Barker emerge into the apartment's courtyard and begin walking toward them. Campbell, a veteran police officer, reacted immediately. Tucking a Thompson gun beneath his overcoat, he stepped from the car. Muzzey got out, too. As the couple strolled out onto the sidewalk and turned west, away from Lake Michigan, the two agents fell in behind them, about twenty feet back.

"Are we gonna take them?" Muzzey whispered.

"Yeah," said Campbell.

They walked a few more feet. Barker glanced over his shoulder. Kuhlmann kept walking. When Barker turned around once again, Campbell took out his machine gun, Muzzey his pistol. They could see other agents converging all around.

"Stick 'em up!" Muzzey hollered. "We're federal agents!" Three agents in front of the couple drew their guns.

Barker froze. He made a whimpering noise. He began to raise his hands, then wheeled and stepped between two parked cars into the street. He had barely begun to run when he slipped on the ice, pitched forward and fell facedown in the muddy slush. The agents were on him within moments. Jerry Campbell dragged Barker to his feet while another agent applied the handcuffs. Other agents pinioned Kuhlmann.

Someone asked Barker his name.

"You know who I am," he spat.

As agents began to haul Barker toward their cars, he sighed. "This is a helluva time to be caught without a gun," he said.

3920 Pine Grove Avenue
11:00 P.M.

The night stretched on. The occupants of Apartment One North hadn't been seen since 6:45. Finally, at 11:00, agents saw a man stroll down the back alley. He slid into the darkness behind the apartment. A moment later the kitchen light clicked on. At the same time, agents saw the tall man and the two women walk up the front sidewalk and into the lobby. It was time.

Connelley, stationed with ten agents next door, walked out into the night air in front of the building. He strode to a waiting car and ordered the four agents inside to proceed to the back alley to reinforce the ten agents already there. He took a moment to arrange other men around the front of the building. When he was satisfied, Connelley took three agents into the lobby. There was no doorman; the apartment was up a flight of stairs and down a hallway. Standing in the lobby, Connelley pressed the call button for Apartment One North.

"Hello?" A woman's voice.

"Is Mr. Bolton in?" Connelley asked. It was the name on one of the suspect car's registrations. A pause. Then the woman said, "No, he'll be back at the end of the week." Connelley identified himself as an agent of the United States Department of Justice. "The building is completely surrounded," he said. "All of you come downstairs, one at a time, with your hands up, and no one will get hurt."

Connelley glanced at Agents Sam McKee and Ralph Brown, cradling Thompson submachine guns at the foot of the stairs. A third agent drew his service revolver. There was no response from the woman upstairs. Again Connelley pressed the call button. "All persons occupying the apartment come down immediately or the place will be gassed," he said.

Nothing. The agents traded glances. A minute ticked by. Then two.

"All persons occupying the apartment come down immediately," Connelley stated a third time. "Do not attempt to escape through the rear. The apartment building is completely surrounded, and anyone attempting to escape will be killed."

A moment later a woman shouted down the stairs, "We're coming down!" Clara Gibson, who was married to Russell Gibson, stepped down the stairs into the lobby, her brown Chow in her arms. Behind her came a woman the agents later learned was Willie Harrison's wife. Connelley ordered both women to lie on the lobby floor. A few moments later Shotgun George Ziegler's sidekick, tall, thin Bryan Bolton, walked down the stairs, hands in the air. He too lay on the lobby floor. Connelley demanded to know the first woman's name. "Clara Gibson," she said.

"Are there any others in the apartment?"

"My husband."

The words had scarcely escaped her lips when gunshots rang out behind the building. "Ooooooh!" Clara Gibson wailed. "They've shot my husband!"

A dozen agents were arrayed at the rear of the apartment, hiding behind fences and garages. Nearest to the backdoor were the old Cowboy Doc White and an agent named Al Barber. They crouched in the darkened alley, no more than twenty feet beyond the steps. The rookie agent Jack Welles peeked from behind a garage on the far side of the alley, forty feet from the kitchen window.* At 11:30 he heard a woman's voice, apparently talking to someone in the lobby.

As the woman spoke, Welles saw a second woman peek from behind the kitchen blinds. With his service revolver he drew a bead on her head. The woman disappeared behind the blind. A second later a man attempted to open the kitchen window. Welles put the man's head in his sights. The man gave up after several moments, then moved to a second window, beside the backdoor. He tried to raise it but failed.

The kitchen light went off, throwing the back porch into deep shadow.

---

* John R. Welles was the scion of a wealthy family who owned a mill in the northeast Pennsylvania village of Wyalusing. He was a George Washington Law graduate who resigned from the FBI in 1939 to join the family business. In later years Welles was active in the FBI agents' alumni association. He died in May 1981 at the age of eighty-three.

The agents waited several long moments. There was the sound of a door closing. Then came what one agent would later describe as "soft noises" on the back stairs. In the darkness Agents White and Barber saw the outline of a man step carefully down the outside stairs. When he reached the bottom, White saw the rifle in his hands.

"Stop!" White yelled.

The man raised his gun and fired. The bullet struck the fence in front of the two agents and ricocheted into a brick wall. White fired, six shots in all, and the man in the shadows fired again, and again. Agent Barber raised his gas gun and fired a shell into an apartment window. Tear gas hissed inside. The agents heard what sounded like a body hitting the pavement. A second later, another group of agents racing up the side of the building saw a man in silhouette, staggering into an adjacent vacant lot. "Halt!" someone yelled.

The man turned and fell. Agent John T. McLaughlin was the first to reach him. He was bleeding heavily from gunshot wounds in his head and chest. He was wearing a bulletproof vest, but not a good one; at least one bullet had blasted right through it.

"Are you Alvin Karpis?" McLaughlin demanded.

"No," the bleeding man mumbled. "Russell Gibson."

It was over. In minutes agents stormed the empty apartment. Gibson was loaded into a Bureau car and taken to the American Hospital on Irving Park Boulevard. Doctors in the emergency room summoned a surgeon. A bullet had entered Gibson's back and blown through his stomach. He didn't have long. Two agents peppered Gibson with questions. Did he know the Barkers? Karpis? Volney Davis? Gibson shook his head. The doctor told Gibson he was on the verge of death. He urged him to answer the agents' questions.

Just before dying at 1:40 A.M., Russell Gibson rasped his last recorded words: "Tell you nothing."[4]

By Wednesday morning, January 9, Dock Barker was locked away at the Bankers Building. Several newspapers, including the *Chicago Tribune,* carried unattributed comments from police castigating the FBI for failing to notify them of the raids. Hoover blew up. "Well if they cleaned up their own dirty mess and ran out of town this underworld mouthpiece, The Chicago Tribune, the Federal Govt wouldn't have to do so much work in

Chicago," he scrawled on a memo. "There must be a good reason why most criminals gravitate to Chicago."

But it was what the papers didn't say that excited Earl Connelley. While all carried news of the shoot-out at Pine Grove Avenue, none had learned of Dock Barker's capture. That gave Connelley's men an opportunity: maybe, just maybe, they could persuade Dock to divulge the rest of the gang's whereabouts before the others learned he was in custody. His capture wouldn't stay a secret long, Connelley suspected. That afternoon a reporter called to inquire about a rumor that another suspect was in custody. An agent named Mickey Ladd denied it. But from Connelley all the way up to Hoover, the FBI realized it was in a race against time. They gave Dock a code name, "Number Five," to ensure that no one would hear his name mentioned in the office. For the plan to work, however, Dock had to talk, and for the moment he wasn't.

"Mr. Nathan stated that Barker is a tough one and is not going to talk," an aide memoed Hoover Tuesday night. "They are going to work in shifts during the night."

By the next morning, Dock had still said nothing. As the hours wore on, Hoover grew convinced that Chicago wasn't working hard enough. One of his top men, Ed Tamm, told Connelley to use "vigorous physical efforts" to break Dock.[5] Just what those efforts were, the FBI never disclosed. But in later years one agent, Ray Suran, reportedly bragged that he had broken two telephone books over Dock's head. Whatever tactics agents employed, Barker still wouldn't talk.

Bryan Bolton was no Dock Barker. Connelley's men initially had no idea how much Bolton knew, dismissing him in one memo as a "minor member of the gang." Friday morning, after more than fifty hours in custody, Bolton suggested otherwise. If the Bureau would put him back "on the street," as he put it, he would tell them everything: who committed the Hamm and Bremer kidnappings, what became of the money and, best of all, where Freddie and Karpis were hiding.

Pop Nathan briefed Ed Tamm, who wrote Hoover that he "advised [Nathan] that we must consider the possibility that in making the complete statement about the case [Bolton] may implicate himself. Consequently we should be careful in making inducements to him, that no promises be made to him to hold him free of any of his own activities. Mr. Nathan advised that we have nothing against [Bolton] now, and I stated that you had suggested, in questioning him, we not show how little we know about the facts in the case."[6]

Connelley sat down with Bolton and made the proposal that policemen have made since the beginning of time. He could make no promises, Connelley said. But if Bolton produced information that helped the FBI, it would be taken into account at his sentencing.

Bolton talked. To Connelley's amazement, the man was a geyser of information. Bolton laid out every detail of the Hamm and Bremer kidnappings, naming every participant and identifying the location of the long-sought safe house in Bensenville. Best of all, Bolton said Fred Barker and Karpis were staying at a lake house in central Florida. He had visited in December, but couldn't remember how to get there. He said it was south of Ocala, a six-hour drive from Macon, Georgia. Nor could Bolton remember the name of the lake. But, he went on, it was locally famous as the home of a gigantic alligator named Big Joe. At one point, Freddie had towed a pig behind a motorboat in a vain attempt to catch him. That was all Bolton knew.

Then they found the map. Why it took three days to discover Dock Barker's map to his family's Florida hideout is a mystery. It wouldn't be the last time agents overlooked an important item during a search, a phenomenon that never failed to drive Hoover to apoplexy. When the map was handed to Connelley that Thursday, it had a ring drawn around the area of Lake Weir, twelve miles south of Ocala.

There were probably dozens of houses around the lake, Connelley could see, as well as several smaller lakes nearby. They had to narrow down the search area, and fast. It was only a matter of time before reporters figured out they had Dock Barker, and when that hit the papers, the Barkers would be gone.

Saturday, January 12, Connelley and three agents boarded a 1:00 P.M. charter flight that got them to Jacksonville by nightfall. Ten more agents, toting trunkloads of machine guns and rifles, took an overnight train and arrived Sunday morning. Everyone gathered at the Marion Hotel in Ocala. Connelley was in a touchy position. The area south of Ocala was sparsely populated, dotted with tiny towns where strangers would be noticed. He knew only that the Barkers were in the area. Already the arrival of fifteen men in dark suits was attracting notice.

Connelley moved gingerly. He sent agents to check the maternity ward at Munroe Hospital in Ocala to see if Delores Delaney had been there; she hadn't. Meantime they needed to find the lake with the alligator, Old Joe. Connelley dispatched two of the Cowboys, Jerry Campbell and Bob Jones, twenty miles east to check out Lake Bryant. Connelley took another agent to look at Lakes Weir and Bowers. Neither group came up with anything, and both felt they had been noticed. Connelley realized they needed help. Monday morning he contacted a deputy sheriff named Milton Dunning and described the story of Old Joe. Dunning said it sounded like Lake Warburg. But when he called a friend on the lake, he found Lake Warburg's Old Joe had died in 1925.

Connelley decided to forget about the alligator; every lake in Florida seemed to have an Old Joe. The more he mulled Dock Barker's map, the more he became convinced the Barkers must be hiding on Lake Weir; it lay at the center of the ring Dock had drawn. BELIEVE WE HAVE SPOT LOCATED, IT BEING LAKE SIX MILES LONG FOUR MILES WIDE WITH MANY HOUSES AND COTTAGES IN VICINITY, he telegraphed Hoover Monday night. EXPECT COVER FURTHER TOMORROW IN EFFORT TO LOCATE ACTUAL HOUSE.

In Washington, Hoover paced his office. Already rumors were flying in Chicago that Dock Barker had been arrested. They had days, maybe hours, before the story broke. Tuesday morning, as Connelley's men set out to study Lake Weir, a reporter from the *Chicago American* called the Bankers Building and was again passed to Mickey Ladd. "What can you tell me about Dock Barker?" the reporter asked.

Ladd denied Barker was in custody. But the reporter wouldn't give up. "Where are you holding Dock?" he asked in a second call. After the second call, Ladd called Washington. If they kept Barker in Chicago, Ladd warned, the story would get out.[7] Hoover ordered Barker moved to the Detroit office, which had a gun room with bars on the windows. Ladd promised to move him at nightfall.

As Chicago jousted with the inquisitive reporter that morning, Agent Bob Jones climbed into a motorboat with the deputy sheriff, Milton Dunning, and cruised the shoreline of Lake Weir. While the two inspected lakeside cottages, Connelley took a gamble on the postmaster in the village of Oklawaha, on the north bank of the lake. The postmaster couldn't identify photographs of Barker or Karpis. But when Connelley asked if any strangers had moved into the area, he mentioned a Mr. Blackburn, who was renting a nice lakefront house with a dock. He received several out-of-town newspapers. The postmaster suggested they approach Mr. Blackburn's neighbor, a man named Frank Barber, who had once worked as a guard at Leavenworth. Connelley drove to Barber's house and immediately received the confirmation they needed. Barber identified a photo of Fred Barker as his new neighbor Mr. Blackburn.

Connelley studied the Blackburn house through the trees. It lay on the south side of Route 41, the area's main road, and as he cruised past it at 11:00, he caught a glimpse of a small man and an aged woman in the yard. It was Fred Barker and his mother.

Back in Ocala, Connelley called and briefed Washington. The situation looked ideal. The house sat a hundred yards back from the road, maybe ten from the lakeshore. There were no natural obstructions around it, only what appeared to be a guesthouse, a garage, and some chicken coops. They could use these buildings as cover. Connelley was determined to avoid another Little Bohemia. He sat down with his men later that day, drew detailed maps of the Blackburn house, and outlined every man's position in the raiding party. Weapons were checked, then double-checked. They would move in before dawn.

Oklawaha, Florida
Tuesday, January 15

The inky tropical night still enveloped the hamlet of Oklawaha as the FBI cars slid to a stop and extinguished their headlights out on Highway 41. Fifteen agents stepped from the cars into a primeval scene of lush woods dominated by ancient oak trees dripping with Spanish moss. Deep in the shadows they could just make out a smattering of darkened houses and outbuildings. There was no movement, no light, no clue anyone knew they were coming.

The Barker house, a two-story white clapboard with green trim, sat a hundred yards off the road, facing south toward the lake. There was a screened-in porch facing the water in front, a long dock out to a boathouse, and two grassy lanes on either side of the house. Connelley positioned cars at the end of each lane. At 5:30 they moved in and surrounded the house. Connelley took five men and crept down the west side of the property, jogging through a grove of spindly orange trees to the lakefront; they took shelter behind a small guesthouse, which sat thirty paces from the front porch. It was a strangely intimate setting for a potential shoot-out; Connelley's position was so close to the porch he could underhand a softball and hit it.

A group of the Cowboys—Charles Winstead, Jerry Campbell, and two other marksmen—took positions behind the stone wall at the roadside, covering the back of the house. Two more agents trotted down the east side of the yard, hunching behind Frank Barber's home. The last two agents were placed on the highway to block traffic.

The sun was to rise at seven, and Connelley planned to wait until daylight to make his move. In the meantime they waited. Crouching behind a tree beside Connelley stood Agent Johnny Madala, the onetime office boy, fighting his nerves. This wasn't Dillinger or Floyd; they wouldn't be catching the Barkers by surprise. Inside the shadowy house were gang members no doubt armed with Thompson submachine guns. They couldn't get away, and they probably wouldn't surrender. His mind drifted to Sam Cowley and Ed Hollis.

Finally, when the first rays of dawn seeped over Lake Weir, Connelley emerged from behind the guesthouse and took two steps toward the front porch. "Fred Barker, come out!" he shouted. "We are Department of Justice agents, and we have the house surrounded."

Silence. Connelley repeated the command. If they came out with their hands raised, he announced, no one would get hurt.

Connelley stood in the yard. No sound came from the house. Minutes crept by. Another agent shouted for the Barkers to come out and surrender. A few men thought they saw furtive movements behind the window screens, but they couldn't be sure. The only sound was the lake water, lapping against the dock. In the orange grove, Agent Bob Jones took a block of concrete and laid his rifle across it.

After a period of time he later estimated to be fifteen minutes, Connelley repeated his challenge: "Fred Barker, come out with your hands up! We have the house surrounded." Once again, silence. Connelley glanced at Doc White, the smiling Cowboy who had shot Russell Gibson. White stood behind an oak tree to his left.

Five more minutes passed, and still there was no sign of life. Back in the trees, a few men wondered if the Barkers had already fled town; their car, a black Buick, was parked in the wood-frame garage beside the house, but that meant nothing. Connelley motioned to a pair of rookie agents, Alexander Muzzey and Tom McDade, to fire tear-gas guns. Both men raised their guns and fired, but the gas projectiles missed the windows, thumping against the side of the house and falling to the ground, where gas escaped and began filling the yard.

"Fred Barker! Kate Barker!" Connelley shouted once again. "Come out now with your hands in the air!"

Hiding behind a mossy oak to Connelley's side, Doc White thought he heard a woman's voice from inside the house.

"What are you gonna do?" the voice asked.

There was no answer he could hear. But a moment later the woman's voice rang clear across the yard: "All right, go ahead!"

Lying on the ground beside the guesthouse, Connelley glanced at White. Both interpreted this to mean the Barkers were coming out to surrender. Connelley shouted, "Come ahead! Fred, you come out first!"

Just then a machine gun fired from a second-story window. Bullets chopped the sandy grass all around where Connelley lay and whizzed through the limbs of the orange grove, tiny green leaves fluttering down everywhere. Connelley rolled behind the guesthouse as Doc White fired his .351 rifle. The morning exploded in gunfire. All around the yard agents opened up on the house. White crouched behind his oak tree as bullets struck all around him. He was pinned down.

Seeing White's predicament, Connelley rose and raced around the guesthouse, emerging on the far side, closer to the front porch. He raised his shotgun and fired, hoping to draw the fire from White. It worked. Machine-gun bullets chattered against the side of the guesthouse. Connelley dived for cover. So did White. Beside them three agents retreated into the trees.

For five minutes the gunfight raged. Shots seemed to be coming from all over the house, from bedroom windows at the north and south, and from the front door. And then, as suddenly as it began, the firing stopped. Connelley peered at the upstairs windows. He guessed the gang was conserving ammunition. He needed gas canisters. He sent an agent back to the cars to get more and ordered a second tear-gas attack. Again the canisters thudded against the window screens and fell to the ground. Gas drifted aimlessly into the trees.

By this time, there was a commotion behind Connelley, in the trees down at the lakefront. The woods were filling with teenage boys.

Within minutes of the first shots, many of Oklawaha's three hundred or so residents were peering out their windows and standing in their yards, asking what the sound was. By eight o'clock, crowds of people were milling out on the highway, barred from advancing by two agents. The more curious, many of them teenagers, crept into the woods, where they could make out the figures of FBI men firing at the house. A sixteen-year-old named Harry Scott watched in awe as shots ricocheted through branches above him. "The agents were firing all over the place because Fred was running all around from room to room," Scott remembered sixty-seven years later. "They must have thought they had the whole gang inside."

Across the grassy lane to the east of the Barker house, Mrs. A. F. Westberry was asleep when the shooting began. Bullets seared through the walls of her thin frame house, striking the headboard of her bed. Panic-stricken, she crawled to a window and saw men in dark suits firing at her neighbor's house. She had no idea who they were, but she was so close she could see flames spouting from gun barrels. Not wanting to see any more, Mrs. Westberry grabbed her daughter's hand and jumped out a window. Once to the ground the two women began running.

Fifty yards away, Agent Ralph Brown saw the women take off. He had no idea who they were. For all Brown knew it was Ma Barker making a getaway. He yelled "Stop! Halt! Federal officers!," but the women kept running. He began firing over the women's heads, stopping only when they reached another house.

The outside world, including Hoover, learned of the unfolding gunfight from an Associated Press reporter in Ocala, who received a call from a local hotel wondering what all the shooting was about. On a hunch, the reporter phoned the FBI's Jacksonville office at 10:45, where the SAC, Rudolph Alt, passed news of the gunfight to Washington.* Hoover, worried that Connelley might run out of ammunition, told Alt to charter a plane and take extra bullets to Oklawaha.

Back at the Barker house, intermittent gunfire continued for the next hour. It was an odd, stop-and-start affair. When shots seemed to come from one window, agents fired at it. They were never able to get a tear-gas canister inside. Around ten, firing from the house ebbed. By 10:30 it had gone silent. Connelley watched the windows. There was no way to know if the Barkers had run out of bullets or were waiting to ambush agents storming the house.

At one point Connelley turned to see a pair of agents bringing up Willie

* Rudolph A. "Rudy" Alt served in the Bureau from 1926 to 1952. He died in 1977 at the age of ninety-four.

Woodbury, the home's twenty-five-year-old caretaker. Woodbury and his wife had been asleep in the guesthouse when the first shots rang out, and had crawled under their bed as bullets flew through their windows. Eyeing the house, Connelley asked Woodbury if he would be willing to check inside. Woodbury looked petrified. Connelley assured him the Barkers wouldn't shoot him. If they were still alive, maybe he could talk them out. Reluctantly Woodbury agreed to try.

Woodbury scampered to the front porch and tried the screen door. It was locked. He ran back to where Connelley stood by the guesthouse. "That door's shut," Woodburry said. The gas was getting to him; he was beginning to cry. Someone handed him a pocketknife.

"Go back and cut the screen and kick it down," Connelley said.

Again Woodbury ran to the door. He cut the screen, shoved the door open, and, pressing a handkerchief over his mouth against the drifting tear gas, stepped across the porch to the front door. Inside, the house was still. Beer bottles were scattered around the dining room. "It's okay, Ma, it's me!" Woodbury announced. "They're makin' me do this!" There was no answer.

He saw blood on the stairs. In tears Woodbury crept up the staircase to the second floor. The house was silent. Upstairs, there were four bedrooms. He stepped to the door of the southeast bedroom, Ma's room, and looked inside. It was empty. The door to the southwest bedroom, where Fred usually slept, was ajar. Woodbury stepped to it.

Outside, Connelley and his men waited. There was a minute of silence, maybe two, then Woodbury's face appeared at a bedroom window. Tears were streaming down his face. It was a sight that would stay with several of the agents for years afterward.

"They both up here!" Woodbury shouted.

"What are they doing?" Connelley replied.

"They all dead!"[8]

Connelley led a group of agents into the house. They found Ma Barker dead on the bedroom floor, a single bullet hole in her forehead. Fred lay beside her. It was impossible to know how long they had been dead. There was no sign anyone else lived in the house. But a search uncovered an assortment of hotel bills, business cards, and receipts from the El Commodoro Hotel in Miami, the same hotel where Sam Cowley had found a man driving Karpis's car in November. Several receipts were made out to a "Mr. D. Wagner," an alias Karpis was known to use. The conclusion was inescapable: Karpis was in Miami. Connelley ordered Ralph Brown and three agents onto the first available flight south. They would hit the ground in Miami at 3:30.

When Hoover stepped before a Washington press conference that after-noon, he was in a delicate position. There was little chance the Bureau would be criticized for killing Fred Barker; he was a stone-cold killer who had fired on agents with a machine gun. Ma was another matter. Hoover had to explain to the nation's press just why his men had killed a grand-mother with no criminal record. Rather than wait for the question, he took the offensive, taking advantage of the fact that the Barker-Karpis Gang was the least known of the public enemies.

As reporters scribbled into their notebooks, Hoover announced that Ma, who none of the newspapers or their readers had ever heard of, was the "brains" of the gang. He said she had been found dead with a machine gun in her hand, which was flat-out untrue. To advance the idea that the elderly woman had been an active participant in the morning's gunfight, Hoover described a dramatic scene in which Earl Connelley approached the Ok-lawaha house and talked with Ma, who slammed shut the door and yelled to Fred, "Let 'em have it!" Needless to say, there is no evidence of any such incident in agents' reports of the gunfight.

History is written by the victors, they say, and there was no one alive who would come forward to dispute Hoover's fabricated story. Never mind that there was no indication whatsoever in Bureau files that Ma Barker had ever fired a gun, robbed a bank, or done anything more criminal than live off her sons' ill-gotten gains. According to Hoover, Ma Barker was "a crim-inal mastermind." Reporters ran with it.

As vivid a portrait as Hoover painted, their stories did not immediately produce anything like the public fascination with Dillinger. It took time for reporters to embroider the FBI myth. Not for six weeks would the notion of Ma Barker's criminal genius be explored in any detail, in a multipart fea-ture distributed by the King Features Syndicate. The FBI cooperated with the piece, which was headlined MA BARKER: DEADLY SPIDER WOMAN. "[T]he withered fingers of spidery, crafty Ma Barker," it read, "like satanic tenta-cles, controlled the skeins on which dangled the fate of desperadoes whose activities hit the headlines on an average of once a week."

"In many ways they were the smartest outlaws we've encountered," Hoover was quoted saying. "And Ma was the mind behind the operations.

She was so smart that we never got anything on her—although we knew plenty. We had to kill her to catch up with her."⁹

Hoover never deviated from that line. It became one of his favorite stories; he made the tale of Ma's "criminal genius" the centerpiece of his 1938 book, *Persons in Hiding,* which is chock-full of dramatically imagined scenes inside the Barker Gang. Hoover's demonization of Ma Barker, much like that of Kathryn Kelly, went beyond the need to defend the facts of her death. It neatly fit into themes he had been airing in interviews since the 1920s. The root causes of crime, he argued, were not poverty and economic disparity. Crime was the result of a widespread deterioration in family values, of parents who did not teach their children right from wrong. In time, Ma Barker became Hoover's favorite symbol of all that was wrong in American families. It was far more than she had ever been in life.

Ralph Brown's four-man detail arrived at the El Commodoro Hotel in Miami around five that afternoon. After checking in, one of the agents, who had stayed at the hotel two months before, motioned to a clerk he knew, L. E. Grey, to join him in his room. There they showed Grey a collection of Barker photos. Nervous, Grey identified photos of the Barkers as frequent guests. More important, he pointed to a picture of Harry Campbell as a man who had just checked in that Sunday, leaving the next morning. The agents emphasized that anything Grey could do to locate Campbell would be an enormous help to the government.

As the FBI descended on the El Commodoro that afternoon, Karpis and Campbell were wrapping up a long day of mackerel fishing off Everglades City. They tossed their rods into Karpis's Ford around five o'clock and reached the bungalow on 85th Street after dark. Delores Delaney and Wynona Burdette were waiting in their car a block away from the house. The moment Karpis pulled to the curb, Delaney ran to him. She was frantic.

"You should have come home sooner!" she said.

"Take it easy," Karpis said. "What's the matter?"

Delaney took several deep breaths. "The FBI shot up Freddie and Ma's place. Freddie's dead. Ma's dead."

Karpis was stunned. He made Delaney repeat everything she knew. He had to think fast. There was no time to grieve. He knew what this meant. They had to get out of Miami. Delaney's advanced pregnancy, however, meant they couldn't hide just anywhere. They would need a safe, clean place, and a doctor. He thought of going to Joe Adams at the El Commodoro but wisely judged it too risky.

That night at 11:30 Adam's errand boy, Duke Randall, was working his usual shift at a window at the Biscayne Kennel Club, a dog-racing track. A dark-haired girl he would later identify as Wynona Burdette appeared and asked him to join her in the parking lot. There Randall found Karpis waiting in a car. Karpis said he was heading north fast and needed a safe place to stay. Randall suggested a hotel he knew in Atlantic City, the Dan-mor. Karpis wrote it on a card. He told the girls to go with Randall. They could head north on a train the next morning. Karpis and Campbell would go that night. It was too risky for Delaney to ride with them. The FBI was everywhere.

As Karpis spoke, agents flooded into Miami. By midnight they had staked out the Pan American and Eastern Airlines terminals, and were checking every hospital and maternity ward in search of Delaney. But as they fanned out across the city, Karpis was already speeding up Dixie Highway, the lights of Miami growing dimmer behind him.

Atlantic City, New Jersey
Saturday, January 19

Just after midnight Karpis and Campbell drove up to the Dan-mor Hotel on Kentucky Avenue, three blocks from the boardwalk. They had driven all day, bypassing the major cities, and were dead tired. The night clerk, Daniel Young, noticed they smelled of liquor. Young assigned them to Room 403, just across from where Delores and Burdette waited in Room 400; the women had taken a train and arrived the previous day. Upstairs Karpis tipped the bellhop a quarter and told him to run out and buy them a pint of whiskey.

The next morning at 8:45 Karpis walked out into the streets. He wandered near the boardwalk for fifteen minutes, glancing around warily. Back in the lobby, he slipped the bellhop a twenty-dollar bill and asked him to fetch some shaving cream and Listerine. Karpis had arranged for a doctor to attend to Delaney, and at 11:30 Dr. Carl Surran, who happened to be the official surgeon of the Atlantic City Police Department, examined Delaney in a downstairs room. She was due any day.

Karpis invited the manager, William Morley, to his room, offered him a shot of rye, and inquired about renting a furnished home or apartment in the area; Morley promised to look into it. Around lunchtime Karpis, escorted by the hotel's handyman, walked up to Sloteroff's, a men's store on Arctic Avenue, and bought winter clothes, a black box-shouldered overcoat and two suits, a banker's gray single-breasted model and a double-breasted oxford, both of which needed to be altered. Karpis took the overcoat, arranged to pick up the suits at five, then went with the handyman to a veterinarian's office, where he waited while the vet explained why the handyman's dog had just died.

Outside, Karpis noticed a man and woman in their forties he had seen earlier. He thought he was being followed. All that afternoon Karpis, Campbell, and their girlfriends meandered through stores buying winter clothes, dresses, and slips for the women, and a second overcoat for Karpis, which he paid for with a bill he peeled from a roll of fifties. Campbell also thought they were being followed. Karpis arranged to have the car oiled. They would leave the next morning.

Miami, Florida
That afternoon

The maid thought it strange that her employers at the house on 85th Street, the Greens, had disappeared. Ever since the pregnant Mrs. Green had bolted from the house with her luggage Wednesday afternoon, she hadn't heard a word. The maid had stayed alone in the house two nights, then returned to her parents'. Saturday she found the house still empty. Unsure what to do, she phoned the landlady, Grace Thomas. Mrs. Thomas said she suspected the Greens wouldn't be coming back. In fact, she thought they might be connected to the shoot-out at Lake Weir. Mrs. Thomas picked up the phone and called the Miami Police Department.

On Saturday afternoon two detectives arrived to see Mrs. Thomas. They interviewed her, then spoke with the maid. The description of the Greens matched that of Alvin Karpis and Delores Delaney. Inside the rented house the detectives found dozens of papers left behind when the Greens left. Among the papers was a description of the black two-door Buick the Greens had purchased at the Ungar Buick Company. The detectives passed the information to the FBI's Miami office.

Just after nightfall the news was relayed to Earl Connelley, who had remained in Ocala, cleaning up loose ends. After checking with Washington, Connelley ordered a description of the car broadcast to police departments up and down the Eastern Seaboard.

Atlantic City
Sunday, January 20

At 2:30 that morning an urgent message spit out of the Teletype machine at the Atlantic City Police Department: INFORMATION WANTED BY FLORIDA POLICE ON A SERIOUS CRIMINAL CHARGE WHITE MAN FIVE FOOT TEN DARK COMPLEXION DARK HAIR DARK EYES VERY SLENDER BUILD ACCOMPANIED BY WOMAN WHO WILL BECOME MOTHER IN FEW DAYS DRIVING NINETEEN THIRTY FIVE BUICK SEDAN D5306 . . . HE IS ARMED WITH 45 CALIBRE AUTO-MATIC AND RIFLE REPORTED TO BE DANGEROUS USE EXTREME CAUTION IN APPREHENSION.

At 3:25 Officer Elias Saab was walking his beat near the Atlantic City boardwalk when he checked in from a phone box and was notified of the alert. He strolled into the Coast Garage on Kentucky Avenue and walked through, glancing at license numbers. To his amazement he found the Buick mentioned in the Teletype. He called his captain, who dispatched three detectives to the garage. The attendant told the men the car belonged to someone staying at the Dan-mor Hotel.

The detectives crossed the street to the Dan-mor and woke the manager, William Morley. Morley stonewalled. The police wouldn't explain why they wanted to question his new guests, and Morley later said he assumed the matter involved the pregnant girl who wasn't wearing a wedding ring. He didn't want to cause a commotion over such a trivial matter. But the police wouldn't leave. One took a bellboy to headquarters while the others con-tinued questioning Morley.

At dawn Morley's wife, Elizabeth, who an FBI report dryly noted "does not appear to be gifted with a pretentious amount of intelligence," stirred from her bed. She came downstairs to see her husband, discussed the situ-ation privately with him and decided to try to defuse the matter. Without telling the detectives, she walked up to Room 403 and tapped softly. Karpis came to the door, wearing only long underwear. She asked him to follow her. The two walked ten feet down to Room 404, a vacant room, and slipped inside.

"The law is downstairs," Mrs. Morley whispered, "looking for someone from Florida who has gotten a girl in trouble." If he was guilty, Mrs. Mor-ley went on, he should give himself up. Karpis's eyes widened. He went to hide under the bed, but Mrs. Morley objected. He opened a closet and found a suit he tried to put on, but Mrs. Morley again objected. She pushed him toward the door, which was ajar.

Just then the door opened. In stepped an Atlantic City cop. Karpis, caught unaware, allowed himself to be pulled into the hallway. "All right, put up your hands," the officer ordered. Karpis saw two more cops outside his room, where Campbell was sleeping. The cop pointed a pistol at Karpis and demanded to know his name.

Karpis, shivering in his long underwear, mumbled something inaudible. It took a moment to gather his thoughts. "What is all this?" he asked. He raised his voice, hoping Campbell would overhear. "Don't point those guns at me. I haven't done anything."

Mrs. Morley pointedly didn't tell the policemen Karpis was one of the men they wanted. Instead she stepped between them and announced she would be able to persuade "the men in 403" to surrender quietly. She stepped to the door of Room 403 and knocked. There was no answer. One of the policemen took out a key and began fiddling with the lock. "Come out of there," he ordered. "Come out with your hands up."

There was no answer. Karpis stepped forward and volunteered to try. "He's probably a little hung over," he said. "We had a party last night and he drank too much. Is that why you're here? Did we make too much noise?" The policemen said nothing. "Look, I'll go in there and get the guy out," Karpis continued. "He's probably still drunk. He doesn't realize that you guys are policemen. I'll get him."

Karpis stepped to the door. Just then it opened and he ducked inside, closing the door behind him. The detectives began pounding on and kicking the door, demanding that the men inside surrender. Mrs. Morley jumped forward to stop them, saying she didn't want the door broken. She took out a passkey and inserted it into the lock.

Just then the door was yanked open from inside. Campbell opened up with a .45. The first bullet sawed off the key in Mrs. Morley's hands, sending the ring of keys jangling to the floor. She dived for cover, as did the detectives. More bullets erupted from the doorway; one pierced the wall of Room 400 and struck Delores Delaney in the right leg. She screamed. The officers later claimed they emptied their guns in the resulting firefight, but only one policeman's bullet was subsequently found. In fact, the officers ran for their lives.

Karpis took Campbell and grabbed the women, quickly tied a strip of bedsheet around Delaney's bleeding leg, and raced down the rear staircase to a back alley. Delaney did her best to keep up. In the vestibule Karpis told the girls to wait while they retrieved the car. Barefoot and shivering, they did as they were told.

Karpis and Campbell circled around the side of the hotel, emerging across from the garage. They glanced to their right and saw policemen milling around the hotel entrance. The two men had just stepped off the sidewalk toward the garage when an attendant began shouting, "Hey! Hey! Here they are! Down here!"

Karpis and Campbell ran for the garage. Campbell stopped at the entrance, raised his pistol, and began firing toward the policemen, who scattered. Inside, Karpis searched in vain for his Buick. He couldn't find it. Instead he hopped into a pea green Pontiac, whose keys dangled from the ignition. Karpis gunned the engine and Campbell jumped into the backseat. Emerging onto Kentucky Avenue, they turned away from the hotel, trying to find the alley where the women were waiting.

Karpis hated this, hated driving through streets he didn't know and hadn't mapped. It was careless. The first street he turned into was a dead end at the boardwalk. He looked back and saw policemen running around the corner behind them. They were trapped. Karpis wheeled the car into a 180-degree turn and drove straight at the officers. "We'll run right through!" he told Campbell. "Get the gun ready!"

At that moment Karpis spied an alley. As the police opened fire, he swung the steering wheel to the right and the car skidded into the alley. The Pontiac shot down the narrow space between buildings. One exit was blocked by a mail truck. More shots echoed behind them. Karpis tried another exit and emerged onto a side street, then took several more random turns. To his surprise, he found himself in the alley where they had left the women. The women weren't there.

"Maybe the cops got 'em," Campbell said. In fact, the girls, cold and frightened, had returned to their rooms, where Delaney got back in bed and Burdette called her a doctor.

"They'll get us if we hang around here," Campbell said.

Karpis was torn. But not that torn. He mashed the accelerator, and the Pontiac shot forward. He never saw Delores Delaney again.

19

PAS DE DEUX

January 1935 Until . . .

I made Hoover's reputation as a fearless lawman. It's a reputation
he doesn't deserve . . . I made that son of a bitch.
—ALVIN KARPIS

Karpis steered the Pontiac toward the Atlantic City causeway, expecting to
find a roadblock. Instead he spotted a car full of police parked at the roadside. As they sped by, Campbell aimed the tommy gun. The cops either failed
to notice or lost their nerve; they ignored them. Once across the causeway
Karpis turned onto a dirt road, then bumped along a set of train tracks until
he found a glade where they waited, hungry and cold, till nightfall.

Rain was falling that night when they inched back onto the highway.
Spying no roadblocks, they drove west until they reached a gas station
at Camden. Karpis thought the attendant recognized them, but the man
handed them a road map and said nothing. As the rain changed to snow
they crossed into Pennsylvania, where they began looking for a new car.
Outside Quakerstown Karpis spotted a Plymouth sedan and began to
honk, waving for it to pull over. When the car, driven by a thirty-one-year-
old Philadelphia psychiatrist named Horace Hunsicker, coasted to a stop,
Karpis got out, pointed his machine gun at the doctor, and slid in back.
Campbell got in front and told Hunsicker to drive.

It snowed heavily as the startled Dr. Hunsicker guided the Plymouth west across Pennsylvania. They drove all night and the next day, keeping to slippery back roads, stopping only for gasoline; Hunsicker was too frightened to attempt an escape. Karpis and Campbell said little, keeping their comments to the roads. They crossed into Ohio on a dirt road and at 9:30 that night stopped in the town of Guilford Center, outside Akron, where they led Hunsicker into a vacant Grange Hall and used a pair of pajamas to tie him to a radiator. Hunsicker struggled free twenty minutes later and walked to a farmhouse. Within an hour an alert was broadcast for his stolen car.

The fugitives continued west, passing Toledo, then turned north into Michigan. Outside Monroe, south of Detroit, they stopped at a filling station, and Karpis called their old hangout, Toledo's Casino Club, where he spoke to a friend named Coolie Monroe. Monroe arrived with a cab driver about two-thirty the next morning. Karpis and Campbell, collars turned up, hats tugged low, tossed their guns into the backseat and abandoned their car, its headlights still on and its engine running; Karpis hoped police would guess he was heading for Canada. They drove to the Casino Club, but the owner, Bert Angus, waved them away. "You're too hot," he said.[1]

Eventually Karpis found their old protector, the vice boss Joe Roscoe, who arranged for them to stay in Edith Barry's whorehouse on the edge of downtown. The FBI was right behind. Police found the abandoned getaway car that morning at 5:30 and identified it four hours later. Even before the car was found, agents guessed Karpis was heading to his old haunts in Cleveland or Toledo. The Flying Squad was scattered between Chicago and Florida, and Connelley could spare only two men. The Cleveland and Detroit offices didn't have the manpower or the mission to physically search for Karpis, so they got to work establishing surveillance and phone taps on the Harvard Club in Cleveland, and in Toledo at the Casino Club and Joe Roscoe's home. Within days an informant confirmed that Karpis had returned to Toledo.

The Detroit SAC, William Larson, begged for more men. Hoover asked for more proof Karpis was in the area. Larson came up with only raw intelligence, nothing concrete. Still, on the night of February 1, Connelley arrived to lead a raid on a cottage owned by Bert Angus. There was no sign of Karpis. In the ensuing days the tone of FBI memoranda suggests Hoover's enthusiasm for pursuing Karpis had ebbed. After all, he was the last major figure of the War on Crime still at large. He had stumbled onto police in Atlantic City. It was only a matter of time, Hoover wagered, before it happened again.

Karpis, meanwhile, was safely hidden in an upstairs room at Edith

Barry's brothel. He had escaped the FBI's dragnet for now, but the world around him was changing, and Karpis knew it.

The killings of Fred and Ma Barker marked the end of the active phase of the War on Crime, and as such presented an opportunity for the nation to appraise what the FBI had wrought. After all it had achieved, one might presume Hoover and his "G-men" were acclaimed national treasures. At least initially, they weren't. What glory flowed to the FBI that winter flowed largely to one man, Melvin Purvis, whose tenuous position inside the Bureau was lost on the public; a magazine poll that winter named Purvis the seventh-most-respected person in the country.

If that galled Hoover, he wasn't yet in a position to change it. Historians make much of the FBI's vaunted public-relations apparatus, which at its height in the mid-1930s churned out a blizzard of Bureau-sponsored comic strips, newspaper articles, and books, but that winter it remained in its infancy. During the War on Crime, Hoover did surprisingly little public-relations work. The decision to publicly promote the FBI, in fact, had not been Hoover's; it was Homer Cummings's. In August 1933, at a time Cummings was attempting to publicize the War on Crime, he had met with the Washington columnist Drew Pearson, asking how best to broadcast his message. Pearson and others suggested playing up the FBI, and Cummings hired a Brooklyn newspaperman named Henry Suydam to do just that.

Suydam, in turn, brought in a flamboyant freelancer named Courtney Ryley Cooper, a specialist in pulp crime stories. In a series of sixteen articles in *American Magazine* beginning in late 1933, Cooper placed Hoover at the nexus of the War on Crime, describing him in one article as "the master detective who simply does not conform to any picture of the average crime chaser." Hoover liked Cooper's articles so much they began collaborating on a book. Cooper was given a desk at headquarters and widespread access to agents and their reports.

It wasn't Hoover or even Courtney Cooper, however, who created the G-man legend. It was Hollywood. Just days after the Barker killings, word reached Hoover that Warner Brothers was developing a script called *G-Men*. The studio billed it as "The First Great Story of the Men Who Waged America's War on Crime." Neither Hoover nor Homer Cummings was wild about the idea. Cummings actually issued a statement refuting the studio's claim that the film was an official record of the War on Crime. Inside the FBI, Hoover's men debated whether even to embrace the term "G-Man"; in the end, they did.*

Courtney Cooper's book on the War on Crime, *Ten Thousand Public Enemies,* was still weeks away from publication when *G-Men* was released that April with a massive publicity campaign. The movie, starring Jimmy Cagney as a young FBI agent battling a vicious band of kidnappers modeled on Dillinger, Floyd, and Nelson, was a smash. In just days it did what reality hadn't, enshrining Hoover as the symbolic head of the nation's crime-fighting forces. *G-Men* was so successful it spawned seven more FBI-themed movies by the end of the year, from *Public Hero Number One* to *Let 'em Have It.* Whatever qualms Hoover had about relinquishing his image-control efforts to Hollywood fell away. He sat for scores of interviews and even posed for photos with Pat O'Brian, the star of *Public Enemy's Wife.* The Bureau was inundated with fan mail. Overnight, Hoover and the FBI were crowned the nation's supreme symbols of justice and strength.

Ten Thousand Public Enemies, released that May, rode the crest of this wave onto bestseller lists. It told Hoover's version of the War on Crime as a single seamless narrative, promoting the FBI's clean-cut agents as the mirror image of the criminals they fought. All but forgotten in the hoopla was Hoover's boss Homer Cummings, who had launched the War on Crime. "After 1935," the historian Richard Gid Powers has noted, "the attorney general faded from the public's image of federal law enforcement. Hollywood had done something Hoover would not have dared, something that Cummings could not prevent—it had turned the top G-Man into a star and it had demoted the director's boss to an offscreen nonentity."[2]

At least Cummings still had his job, which was more than Purvis could say. Purvis resigned from the Bureau that June after months of harassment from Hoover and his aides. Feted as a national hero, Purvis wrote a book, *American Agent,* which was published in 1936. The book, a primer on the FBI and the War on Crime, tellingly made no mention of either Hoover or Cowley. In response Hoover declared Purvis persona non grata. He began

* Some argued against it, saying it unnecessarily glorified the Bureau. "I do not believe it would be wise for Bureau officials to attempt to protest against the appellation 'G-men,'" Pop Nathan wrote Hoover on May 21, 1935. "Neither do I think it would be wise for the Bureau to approve it. I believe it would be futile to attempt any campaign against this term. As a matter of fact, I can think of much worse terms that might be applied to us. In other words, if, as would appear probable, that is to be the verdict of destiny, I do not think we should struggle against it." As usual, Nathan carried the day.

amassing scurrilous gossip on him. In time Purvis's FBI file grew as thick as that of the criminals he had hunted.

The FBI's rise to prominence, coming as it did on the backs of public enemies, was generally greeted with favor by the press. Only a handful of liberal organs raised red flags. In a November 1934 article entitled "The American National Police: The Dangers of Federal Crime Control," *Harper's* magazine asked the question, "How many persons know that there is at this moment a national police force, or, if they know it, realize what this implies?" Citing the new criminal-enforcement powers Congress had bestowed on the federal government at the height of the Dillinger hysteria, *Harper's* opined, "Never had legislation been enacted which was more unnecessary or dangerous despite all the glowing propaganda in its favor."[3] The magazine worried about the potential for abuse. It was a concern that would not be shared by other leading voices for decades.

The pursuit of Alvin Karpis lagged that winter because the Bureau was stretched thin. Members of the Flying Squad were already furiously compiling evidence for the trial of Dock Barker and other gang members. Others were building files for the trial of Johnny Chase, who had been arrested in northern California a month after Baby Face Nelson's death, of Louis Piquett and of those who harbored Nelson in Reno. Still more men were needed to track down the remaining members of the Barker Gang.

It was a riotous roundup. On February 6, 1935, two weeks after Karpis's escape from Atlantic City, Volney Davis was arrested in St. Louis and packed onto a charter flight for Chicago. When the plane refueled in Yorktown, Illinois, Davis joined two agents drinking beer at a local bar. When one agent went to make a phone call, Davis smashed the other agent in the face with a beer mug, jumped out a window, and disappeared. The same day, Davis's girlfriend, Edna Murray, and another gang member were arrested after a running shoot-out in Kansas. Davis wasn't rearrested until June 1, in Chicago.*

Harry Sawyer was next. The FBI had concentrated its search for the mastermind of the Hamm and Bremer kidnappings in New York. They had put Sawyer's picture in Jewish newspapers, hoping someone of "that race" would turn him in, as an FBI memo put it. In the end, a motorcycle cop arrested Sawyer. He was captured in his car at the seawall in the Gulf Coast town of Pass Christian, Mississippi. He had been running a bar in a poor

* The arrest of Volney Davis was Melvin Purvis's last.

section of town. Police found his wife in a nearby tourist camp. Sawyer went without a fight, and was extradited to St. Paul for trial. Three months later the FBI tracked the Barker Gang's last member, Bill Weaver, to a farm in northern Florida. Weaver was arrested when he went to feed his chickens.

Those who survived the War on Crime were paraded through courtrooms all through 1935. In January the Kansas City Massacre conspirators—Deafy Farmer and company—were each convicted in a trial at Kansas City; all received light sentences. The same month twenty-three people, including members of both the Barrow and Parker families, were put on trial in Dallas for harboring Bonnie and Clyde; all but one were convicted and received prison sentences. Three months later Clyde's one-time partners Raymond Hamilton and Joe Palmer were executed. In March, Delores Delaney and Wynona Burdette received five-year sentences for harboring Alvin Karpis and Harry Campbell.

The Dillinger trials began in Chicago that same month. Johnny Chase received a life sentence for the murders of Sam Cowley and Ed Hollis. Helen Gillis received a one-year sentence for harboring her husband. That summer Louis Piquett received a two-year sentence for harboring; his investigator, Art O'Leary, received a suspended one-year sentence. Another set of trials, for those indicted for harboring Baby Face Nelson, were held in San Francisco. Everyone involved, including the mechanic Frank Cochrane, drew brief sentences. In two trials in St. Paul members of the Barker Gang were convicted of the Bremer kidnapping. Dock Barker, Harry Sawyer, Volney Davis, and Bill Weaver all drew life sentences and were sent to the new federal "super prison" on Alcatraz Island in San Francisco Bay.

In June, Pretty Boy Floyd's sidekick, Adam Richetti, went on trial for the Kansas City Massacre.* From an analysis of the FBI's own files, the proceedings were a travesty. Each of the agents who survived the massacre—Frank Smith, Reed Vetterli, and Joe Lackey—took the stand and identified Floyd and Verne Miller as the shooters; this despite the fact that all three agents had repeatedly told their superiors they could not identify any of them. Lackey went one step further, identifying Richetti himself. Richetti's attorneys put up a hapless defense. Richetti was convicted and sentenced to death, and died in the gas chamber at Jefferson City, Missouri, on October 7, 1938.

---

* Richetti was formally charged only with the killing of one of the two murdered Kansas City policemen, Frank Hermanson.

So who were Verne Miller's confederates that morning in Kansas City? Historians have debated their identities for seventy years. Many, including Floyd's biographer, Michael Wallis, have come to the conclusion that Floyd was not involved.* He almost certainly was. Research for this book identified three people who discussed the massacre with Floyd or Miller before their deaths; two of these witnesses gave detailed, nearly identical statements to the FBI—statements that, tellingly, were not introduced at Richetti's trial. Nor are they included in the FBI's massacre files. Instead, they are located in the Barker-Karpis files; the statements were given by Volney Davis and his girlfriend Edna Murray, who spoke with Miller two days after the massacre, when he visited their Chicago apartment. According to Davis and his girlfriend, who had no reason to implicate Pretty Boy Floyd, Miller said his partner that morning was in fact Floyd. According to Miller, Richetti wasn't with them. He had been too hungover to go.

In the only known occasion where Floyd told what happened at Union Station, he related an almost identical story. The source of this conversation is none other than Alvin Karpis, who discussed the massacre with Floyd when the Oklahoma outlaw visited him in Cleveland during the summer of 1934. According to unpublished interviews Karpis gave his biographer, Bill Trent, in 1970, Floyd admitted he had carried out the massacre. He did not mention whether Richetti was involved.

An era had passed. There would be no more of this sort of American outlaw for the simple reason that there was no more outdistancing the law; the FBI could go anywhere. Moreover, the harboring trials sent exactly the message Hoover intended; one by one, the yeggmen's havens were closing down. St. Paul's days as a crime center were passing; the Green Lantern had closed. In Chicago the Syndicate wanted nothing to do with the heat yeggs brought. Louie Cernocky was already gone, felled by a heart attack in September 1934. Miami, Reno, and Cleveland were shutting down.

No one felt the winds of change more acutely than Alvin Karpis. Pacing a Toledo whorehouse that winter, Karpis tried to make sense of the new world he faced. He thought about putting together any number of bank

---

* Kansas City journalism professor Robert Unger investigated the case for a decade; it was only after his prodding that the FBI released massacre case files. In his 1997 book, *The Union Station Massacre,* Unger reaches no conclusion about who was with Miller that morning but says it probably wasn't Floyd.

jobs, but finding partners was difficult. All the good yeggs were gone. He was lonely; he missed Freddie. He passed the days reading newspapers, *Reader's Digest, Time, Field & Stream, The Saturday Evening Post*. He read that Delores had given birth in a Philadelphia hospital. He was now the father of a son named Raymond. He read that his parents had taken the boy when Delores drew a five-year sentence in Milan, Michigan. She was put in a cell near Kathryn Kelly.

After a few weeks, Karpis stirred. The Toledo police were still launching periodic raids around the city. A friend from his Harvard Club days, a slender, stuttering blackjack dealer named Freddie Hunter, found him a new place to live, at the Youngstown home of a sheet-metal worker named Clayton Hall; Hall's house was so small that for a time Karpis was obliged to sleep with Hall's teenage son. In time his money ran low. Hunter suggested robbing a payroll shipment bound for Hall's employer, the Youngstown Steel & Tube Plant in Warren. Hunter couldn't go; Warren was his hometown, and he feared he would be recognized.

Karpis studied the job and felt he needed three men in total; with Harry Campbell, who had remained in Toledo, as his partner, he needed one more. Karpis and Campbell drove to Tulsa on a recruiting trip. They could find no one to join them; they were too hot. Karpis returned to Ohio and, at wit's end, hired one of Freddie Hunter's pals, a heroin addict named Joe Rich who lived with a whorehouse madame in Canton. Karpis joked that he would have hired the madame at that point.

On the afternoon of April 24, 1935, Karpis drew up to the train station at Warren. The mail truck was already parked, waiting for the train to arrive. Campbell and Joe Rich got out, guns beneath their overcoats. Karpis thought they looked too conspicuous on the empty platform. Apparently the station master thought so, too. He watched them intently. Campbell returned to the car, worried.

"Do you realize we're gonna have to kill a lot of people to take this payroll?" he asked. Karpis sighed and said everything would be fine. Suddenly a cat darted in front of the car.

"That was a black cat," Campbell said.

"Forget it," Karpis said. "The cat had white marks all over its chest."

"That cat was black as coal," Campbell said.

Karpis sighed: here they were, ready for their first job in over a year, and they were arguing about black cats. A whistle sounded; the train was coming. When it arrived, they watched the couriers load the payroll bags into the truck. As the truck pulled away from the curb, Karpis eased in front of it. He stayed abreast of the truck for several blocks, until it came to a stop at a railroad crossing. Campbell and Joe Rich jumped out of the car, .45s in their hands. The driver took one look at them and tossed his pistol into the street.

Campbell and Rich climbed into the cab, took the driver hostage, and followed Karpis to the outskirts of Warren, where they found their way to an abandoned shed they had rented. There was no pursuit; they had gotten away clean. In the truck Karpis found what he was looking for, a burlap sack packed with bricks of cash. They counted it on the floor of the shed, all $72,000. Joe Rich was so excited he took out a syringe, drained water from the radiator, boiled his morphine, and shot up. Within minutes he was telling Karpis they should rob the Cleveland Federal Reserve. They returned to Toledo safely, where Karpis's luck held; the next day two local hoods were arrested for the robbery.

Flush with cash, Karpis and Campbell loitered in Toledo the next month, posing as gamblers. Campbell, who was blessed with an uncluttered mind, paid $10 one night to have sex with an eighteen-year-old girl, proposed to her two days later, and married her a month after that, settling into a trailer behind her mother's house.* But Karpis was restless. With Campbell idled by domestic bliss, he hit the road with Freddie Hunter. They took a drive through New York State into New England, stopping at tourist camps as far north as Maine. In Saratoga Springs, Karpis thought a man recognized him, and he was right; news of the sighting made the local papers the next day, by which time Karpis had returned to Ohio. They drove on from there, passing through St. Louis and Tulsa, finding none of their old friends happy to see them.

In June they wandered into Hot Springs. Hunter knew the resort town from a visit in 1929, when he sought treatment there for gonorrhea. Karpis liked the feel of the place, and for good reason. Reform may have been sweeping other cities, but Hot Springs was operating exactly as it had in 1933. Six months later it would welcome another criminal vacationer, Charles "Lucky" Luciano, who would seek its shelter to avoid extradition to New York, where Thomas Dewey was hounding him.

It was somehow fitting that Karpis, the last survivor of the War on

---

* This made Campbell a bigamist, among other things. He had an estranged wife and daughter living in Texas. The FBI was watching them closely.

Crime, should end up where it all began. The White Front Cigar Store, where Frank Nash had been picked up, was still there, as were the casinos, the Belvedere and the Southern Club. Even Dick Galatas was still in town, awaiting an appeal of his sentence in the massacre case. Dutch Akers, the corrupt detective who had collected the $500 reward for betraying Nash, was still in office. Most evenings he could be found lounging around the town's newest whorehouse, the Hatterie, next to the towering Arlington Hotel, Al Capone's onetime hangout.

At the Hatterie, Akers enjoyed the favors of the brothel's madame, a plumpish, sharp-eyed thirty-two-year-old named Grace Goldstein. Goldstein's real name was Jewel Laverne Grayson; her family in Texas thought she owned a hat shop. Goldstein entertained the cops because it was smart business; they ran the town. But once Karpis began appearing, she later told the FBI, she "made a play for him." He wasn't much to look at, but the roll of cash in his front pocket was a Depression-era whore's dream. Freddie Hunter, meanwhile, fell hard for one of Goldstein's prostitutes, a teenage runaway from Oklahoma named Connie Morris.

In July, Karpis and Hunter took another long drive, lazing through Texas and along the Gulf Coast all the way to Florida. They returned to Hot Springs in August, renting cottages on Lake Hamilton outside town. Posing as gamblers named Fred Parker (Hunter) and Ed King (Karpis), they spent their days swimming and fishing, Karpis sitting at the lakeside for hours in khakis and a white T-shirt, casting for bass. Evenings they spent at the Hatterie or dining with their girls. In September Harry Campbell, tiring of life in his mother-in-law's backyard, arrived and was soon squiring one of Goldstein's girls. He was followed by another of Karpis's old Oklahoma pals, a McAlester parolee named Sam Coker.* At midmonth Hunter left for New York City, where he attended the heavyweight title fight between Joe Louis and Max Baer.

Among the other ninety thousand spectators that evening was J. Edgar Hoover. Their juxtaposition that night was symbolic: While Hoover was off winning accolades and attending prize fights, the hunt for Karpis lagged.

---

* Sam Coker was born in Nowata, Oklahoma, in 1895. Convicted of bank robbery in 1924, he drew a sentence in the McAlester penitentiary, where he became friends with Dock Barker and Volney Davis. Paroled in the spring of 1931, he took a message from Dock to his brother Fred in Tulsa and thereupon joined Fred and Karpis in their first burglaries after their release from prison. Coker was arrested with Barker and Karpis that June, and his parole was revoked. He was released a second time in September 1935, joining Karpis in Hot Springs; some sources suggest Karpis paid a bribe to secure his release.

There hadn't been a confirmed sighting of him since he had vanished in Toledo eight months before. The truth was, while the Oklahoma City office was still poking around Tulsa, no one was looking that hard. Earl Connelley admitted as much when he sat down with one of Hoover's aides, Ed Tamm, after the Barker and Richetti trials in August. Tamm tried to put a positive spin on it for the director.

"Mr. Connelley and I believe that the lack of concentrated activity upon known contacts of the Karpis mob for the past two months will have a beneficial effect in that it has allowed these contacts to 'cool off' to such a point where the members of the mob will be more careless" in contacting them, he memoed Hoover on August 1.[4] Connelley decided to assign four members of the Flying Squad to hunt Karpis full-time, concentrating the search on Toledo and Chicago. Picking up rumors that Karpis had been seen at Edith Barry's whorehouse, they rented a surveillance flat and installed wiretaps.

Meanwhile, Karpis was once again growing restless. In early September, he and his three-man gang checked out of the cabins at Lake Hamilton. After a two-day party at the Hatterie, they left Hot Springs, heading north. The day they departed, the corrupt detective Dutch Akers called in a group of reporters and announced his discovery that Karpis had been staying at Lake Hamilton. He telephoned the FBI's Little Rock office and furnished the gang's license plate numbers and aliases. The news made headlines around the country. It must have seemed a canny move. In one fell swoop Akers had not only covered himself, he had all but assured that Karpis would not return to Hot Springs and bring attention to Akers's enterprises.

To the FBI, Akers's announcement appeared to be just one more supposed sighting, the kind of Chinese fire drill agents had endured in spots as disparate as Grant's Pass (Oregon), Sarasota Springs, Atlantic City, Dallas, Houston, Chicago, New Orleans, and half the towns in Oklahoma and Missouri. An agent named B. L. Damron drove down from Little Rock and chatted with Akers, who emphasized he had never seen the suspects himself. Damron drove to the lake and searched the cabins. He found three bottles of gonorrhea medicine. The doctor's records listed the patient as Freddie Hunter. The name meant nothing to the FBI, and when no one at Dyer's Landing seemed able to identity photos of Karpis, Damron wrapped up the investigation.[5]

Because Karpis had been posing as a gambler from Ohio, the gang's aliases were sent to the Cleveland office, which checked them with police.

No one had ever heard of gamblers named Fred Parker or Ed King; unfortunately, agents neglected to ask for information on Freddie Hunter. Afterward, Hoover's men took the Hot Springs articles, threw them in a file and forgot about it.

Drinking, whoring, and bass fishing were pleasant pastimes, but they weren't why Karpis had become a criminal. In the balmy days of September, sitting out on the shore of Lake Hamilton in his khakis and white T-shirt, he found himself yearning to take a big score, something exciting, something to get his adrenaline up. He was bored. Hunter suggested a target, a mail train that ferried bags of cash from the Cleveland Federal Reserve to Youngstown to fill the payroll needs of eastern Ohio's sprawling steel mills. The idea of a train robbery appealed to Karpis's sense of history. Jesse James robbed trains. Butch Cassidy robbed trains. Now Alvin Karpis would rob a train.

They drove to Toledo, visiting Edith Barry's brothel just days after the FBI abandoned surveillance and phone taps on the house. After hearing rumors the FBI had been nosing around, they relocated to the steelworker Clayton Hall's home outside Youngstown. Karpis decided to hit the train at Garrettsville, north of the city. Fearing the FBI, he decided to bring train robbery into the modern age and escape by air. Hunter knew a pilot in Port Clinton named John Zetzer, who had flown bootlegging missions during Prohibition, ferrying Canadian whiskey into northern Ohio. Zetzer no longer had a plane, so Karpis bought him one, a red four-seat Stinson; it cost $1,700. Zetzer was just one of several new men Karpis brought in to handle aspects of the job. He had four for the robbery itself: Hunter, Harry Campbell, Sam Coker, and an aging yegg named Ben Grayson.* He also brought in a twenty-one-year-old Oklahoma kid named Milton Lett who was sweeping floors at the Harvard Club.

Preparations went smoothly until October 19, when Lett and Clayton Hall bought the getaway car at an Akron Ford dealership. The roll of cash they flashed attracted attention. Later that day Akron detectives arrested the two at a local hotel as "suspicious persons." They were released on bail, and Karpis decided against allowing the incident to derail his plans. He

---

* Grayson, whose real name was Bensen Groves, was born in 1880 in West Virginia. He had served two concurrent five-year sentences in Atlanta for post-office robberies.

should have; the brief detention of his new partners would come back to haunt him. Two weeks later, on November 2, Karpis gathered the men at Edith Barry's brothel to go over their assignments. There was a snag. Sam Coker had come down with gonorrheal rheumatism. Karpis called one of his oldest friends, a Tulsa fence named Burrhead Keady, and had him send up his bartender to substitute.*

Finally, on the morning of November 7, they were ready. At 2:00 that afternoon Karpis, driving a new Plymouth sedan, cruised into the station lot at Garrettsville. There were about sixty people milling about on the platform. The men took their positions. At 2:13 the train appeared, coasting to a stop just where Karpis knew it would. The engine exhaled. Stepping to the mail car, Karpis saw the new man, Ben Grayson, climb into the cab. Fred Hunter was standing in the parking lot, making sure no one left. The mail-car door opened, and Karpis whipped out his Thompson gun, startling a pair of clerks. Before he could say a word, they disappeared inside. Just then he was distracted by a commotion in the parking lot. He turned and saw Hunter chasing two men, taking his attention off a couple who were starting their car.

Karpis stalked to the car, opened the door and, as the terrified driver froze, grabbed the car keys and threw them across the parking lot. In a moment he was back to the mail car. The clerks were nowhere to be seen. He tossed in a stick of unlit dynamite. "I'm gonna heave another stick in there," he hollered, "and it'll be burning. You've got five, and I'm counting now. One, two . . ."

A moment later the clerks appeared, hands raised.

"You can't do this, man," one of them said.

Karpis set the Thompson gun to single-shot and aimed it over the clerks' heads. It jammed, but the clerks got the message. He jumped into the car and followed them to the mail bags. Karpis asked for the payroll to Warren. A clerk lifted one padlocked sack and handed it to him. When he asked for the Youngstown payroll, the clerk said it wasn't on the train. Karpis aimed his Thompson gun at the man's chest. Just then Harry Campbell climbed into the car. "Look out, Harry," Karpis said, "I'm gonna shoot this guy."

---

* The bartender, John Brock, was another McAlester alumnus, a prison pal of Volney Davis and Dock Barker. He had come to Ohio that spring for a time, intending to be the third man in the Warren payroll robbery. But he had second thoughts and returned to Tulsa.

The clerk, on the verge of tears, produced a ledger and pointed to it, trying to show Karpis the Youngstown payrolls weren't on the train. Irate, Karpis told him to snatch up several bags of registered mail instead. Then he ordered the clerks to load them into the back of the waiting Plymouth. It was all over in five minutes.

The getaway went smoothly. They followed Karpis's git to the Lake Erie town of Port Clinton, where they emptied the money bags in the pilot John Zetzer's garage. Karpis was disappointed. The take came to only $34,000; he was expecting five times that much. The next morning they were airborne by 10:30, but it was a short flight; the plane ran out of gas over southern Indiana, forcing them to land outside Evansville. Zetzer hitchhiked into town, bought forty-seven gallons of gasoline at a Standard Oil station, and they were soon airborne once more, only to run out of gas a second time, forcing a landing in a field in Missouri. Once again Zetzer was obliged to trek to a filling station. They slept in the plane that night, reaching Memphis the next morning. By noon the next day they were safely back in Hot Springs.

The FBI had no idea Karpis was behind the Garrettsville job. Karpis and Hunter picked up their girlfriends and drove into Texas, where they spent several days relaxing at the home of Goldstein's brother. They then took a drive along the Gulf Coast, fishing and sunbathing. After three weeks they returned to Hot Springs, where they shuttled from flat to flat, never staying in one place too long.

Karpis sent for Clayton Hall in January, handing him $1,100 to buy him a new car. Afterward, believing it was safe to arrange a more permanent home, Karpis rented a lake house. They passed the days fishing, the nights at the Hatterie. Fred Hunter was gone much of the time, driving through Florida and Texas with his girlfriend. In March, Karpis moved once more, renting a farmhouse south of Hot Springs. A genteel, two-story affair, with trellises flanking the front door, it stood on a wooded hill overlooking the Malvern Road. Karpis liked it. If the FBI staged a raid here, he decided, he would see them coming.

For the Bureau, the story of the Karpis manhunt is one of the least flattering chapters in the War on Crime. There was an air of lethargy and anticlimax about it from the start; none of the agents could get too excited about risking their lives in one last battle of a war they had already won, and it showed.

After ten months of work, following tips from Boston to Havana to Los

Angeles, at the moment Karpis robbed the Garrettsville train the FBI had no serious leads on his whereabouts. The Bureau had no jurisdiction for the Garrettsville robbery, and thus performed no investigation. But Garrettsville triggered the entry of another force into the manhunt, an intrepid squad of federal postal inspectors whose dogged pursuit of Karpis quickly eclipsed the FBI's search. Working from Youngstown, the inspectors needed only twenty-four hours to finger Karpis and Campbell for the Garrettsville robbery; eyewitnesses easily identified photos of both men.* Keeping this to the postal inspectors, the lead inspector, Sylvester J. Hettrick, reached out to the Kansas State Highway Patrol, which already had a detective named Joe Anderson pursuing rumors Karpis was involved in several Kansas robberies.

Anderson would have made a first-rate FBI agent. Within weeks, working his contacts in the Tulsa underworld, he had identified Sam Coker as a participant in the Garrettsville job; Coker had disappeared in the days before Karpis struck, stupidly telling friends he was heading east to participate in a mail robbery. At first Anderson and the postal inspectors freely cooperated with the FBI, passing on tips about Coker and others. When Connelley heard the rumor Karpis had robbed the Garrettsville train, he asked the Cleveland office to investigate; agents there simply chatted up the inspectors, who happily shared their leads. For the most part the FBI ignored them.

Through December and into January the inspectors' investigation gained momentum. They traced the car used in the robbery to Akron, where a salesman identified Milton Lett as its purchaser.† They soon identified the steelworker Clayton Hall, and then Freddie Hunter. Connelley ignored it all. From all appearances the FBI simply couldn't bring itself to believe a rival agency had mounted a more credible investigation than its own. Despite the obvious progress the inspectors were making, Connelley was dismissive.

"[T]he Post Office Inspectors have themselves all worked up to a heat, and think they are going to catch Karpis and Campbell in a short time," an aide wrote Hoover after a talk with Connelley. "Connelley said that he does

---

* The same band of inspectors had investigated the Warren robbery that April and had picked up rumors that Karpis had been involved.

† Connelley discounted rumors of Milton Lett's involvement because the FBI had already interviewed Lett and considered him a confidential informant.

not believe they have half as much as they would have you believe; that they have a few leads here and there, and when these are exhausted they will probably let us have the information."[6]

Instead the Bureau stepped up its surveillance of the Karpis and Campbell families. In Chicago agents had the Karpis family apartment thoroughly bugged, going so far as hiring a Lithuanian man to translate conversations between Karpis's parents. All they learned was how much his mother and father bickered over who was more responsible for their son's life of crime. In Tulsa they kept watch on Karpis's friend Burrhead Keady, even as rumors flew that the inspectors would arrest him. Connelley demanded regular updates on the inspectors' progress. "[W]e should protect our interests in this," he wrote the Oklahoma City office on February 17, "to see that nothing is done which will interfere with [our] investigation."[7]

The FBI learned of Keady's arrest only when the Cleveland *Plain Dealer* announced it on February 27. When agents demanded to know if the report was true, the senior inspector, Sylvester Hettrick, denied it. Arguments broke out between Hettrick's men and the Cleveland office; the inspectors, openly resentful of the adoring publicity lavished on the Bureau, finally stopped sharing leads with Hoover's men. Pop Nathan, who shared Connelley's contempt for the inspectors, ordered agents to ignore them and concentrate on breaking the case on their own. Two weeks later the inspectors picked up Keady's bartender.

Many of the same leads flowed to the Bureau, but Hoover's men repeatedly failed to follow them up. Joe Rich, the heroin addict who had robbed the Warren payroll with Karpis, washed up in a Canton, Ohio, jail, where he attempted to swap knowledge for freedom; FBI agents who debriefed Rich simply didn't believe his tale of robbing the Warren train with Karpis, terming it "quite a fanciful story." Nor were they all that interested in Clayton Hall. The FBI fielded tips on Hall's involvement with Karpis from at least three sources. Still, it wasn't until March 1, six weeks after hearing the first of these tips, that two agents drove out to Hall's home outside Youngstown. They watched it a few hours, then left. The idea that Karpis might be employing a sheet-metal worker was apparently too far-fetched for the agents to pursue. They left Clayton Hall for the inspectors.*

In Chicago, Connelley wearily took stock of their investigation. They

---

* On March 13, FBI agents arrested Ed Bentz in Brooklyn. The last of the great Jazz Age yeggmen, the

were getting nowhere, and he knew it. The only ones making any progress were the inspectors. As irksome as he found the task, Connelley needed to know what they knew. He couldn't simply ask; the two sides were now openly hostile to each other. Somehow Connelley had to force their hand. Thumbing through his papers, he came upon the Cleveland office's report of its visit to Clayton Hall's house. There were rumors the inspectors had been seen with Hall.

On Wednesday, March 25, Connelley telephoned the Cleveland SAC and asked him to find Hall. An agent named E. J. Wynn drove to Youngstown that day and discovered him at home. Hall conceded that he had known Freddie Hunter for years. He identified a photo of Karpis as Hunter's pal "Ed King," and admitted the two men had visited him as recently as January. It was the best lead the FBI had uncovered in more than a year. Agent Wynn gave Hall $5 and told him to be at the Bureau's Cleveland office for a debriefing the next day at 1:00.

Connelley hurried to Cleveland for the meeting. But at 1:00 Hall didn't show. When he hadn't appeared by nightfall, Connelley drove to Youngstown to look for him. His wife said he had left that morning. She thought he was going to the FBI. The next morning two more agents visited the Hall home. Mrs. Hall said her husband had come home late the previous night, but had left again that morning. Suspecting Hall was trying to avoid them, the two agents parked nearby and watched the house. A few minutes later a Ford drove by. One of the two men inside could be seen jotting down their license plate number. They were postal inspectors; the agents were sure of it. Irked, the agents drove to the Youngstown post office, where the inspectors were based. They saw the Ford parked outside. From an upstairs window, the inspectors saw them.

A little bit later, the phone rang in the Cleveland office. On the line was

---

man who had mentored Machine Gun Kelly and Baby Face Nelson, Bentz had cannily relocated to New England when the Bureau mounted its great hunts for Dillinger and other Midwestern outlaws. He had robbed several banks in Vermont and New Hampshire; agents tracked him down after finding one of his girlfriends. In time the bookish Eddie Bentz became Hoover's favorite bank robber. Devoting an entire chapter to Bentz in his 1938 book *Persons in Hiding,* Hoover termed him "a superman . . . known to thousands of honest persons as one of the most gracious men, generous attributes, enviable education, and impeccable morals."

Connelley spent hours debriefing the talkative old yegg. Bentz told a strange tale of meeting Karpis in Chicago in 1935 and of following him to an Indiana hideout at what he described as a yeggmen's "burial ground," where various bank robbers buried stolen bonds. Connelley spent a week trying to find the place before giving up.

Sylvester Hettrick, the lead postal inspector. He wanted to meet. Agent Wynn drove to the Youngstown post office and found himself in a room with eight irritated inspectors, their point man, Joe Anderson, and two members of the Ohio State Highway Patrol. Inspector Hettrick announced that they had detained Clayton Hall. After being threatened with prosecution for the Garrettsville robbery, Hall was now claiming he could produce Karpis. But he insisted he would divulge all details only if an FBI agent was in the room.

The next morning Connelley sat down in the Cleveland office with one of the inspectors, who reluctantly agreed to let him talk to Hall. Just before noon Connelley phoned Pop Nathan in Washington to break the news. Nathan was palpably unimpressed. His lack of enthusiasm was attributable to the humiliating fact that the Bureau was piggy-backing on the inspectors' work. "[I]f this goes through," Nathan told Hoover, "this incident is going to break into the newspapers."[8]

The next morning Connelley drove to Youngstown and spent several hours closeted with Hall. Afterward he called Washington to say the frightened steelworker had given them everything, including the location of the house Karpis was renting seven miles south of Hot Springs. Connelley was already arranging a charter flight to Arkansas. With luck, he said, he could be on the ground there by noon the next day. He was obliged to take a group of inspectors along, he admitted, "for the reason that the informant [Hall] is theirs, and it was only through their cooperation that we have the information at all."[9]

Connelley's group didn't arrive in Little Rock until 4:35 on Sunday afternoon, March 30.* A reporter caught wind of their arrival. G-MEN HERE ON MYSTERIOUS MISSION, read the next morning's headline in the Arkansas *Gazette*. Realizing he had only hours before that news broke, Connelley hurried to Hot Springs at nightfall and found the house Hall had told them of; it stood alone on a wooded hill overlooking the Malvern Road seven miles south of town. Lights blazed inside. Someone was there.

"Examined place designated by informant Clayton Hall and it checks in every way," Connelley notified Hoover in a coded telegram at 3:05 Sunday

---

* In Cleveland a wire-service reporter got wind of the flight and issued a dispatch saying a group of FBI agents were en route to Arkansas. The leak enraged Hoover, who ordered an investigation. In the meantime, reporters were told the agents were gathering in Arkansas for a conference.

morning. "House fully lighted and party apparently there . . . at about day-break will arrest party at place above indicated."[10]

Connelley had fourteen men for the raid, including Clarence Hurt, one of the agents who shot Dillinger; Rufus Coulter, who had traded gunfire with Homer Van Meter in St. Paul; and Loyde Kingman, who had shared an elevator with Karpis in Havana. In the predawn darkness they crept into positions around the house. In Washington, Hoover waited by the phone. He wanted Karpis, but just as important he wanted the FBI and not the postal inspectors to get credit for his capture; he had told Connelley to "spare no expense" to make certain he received the news first so that he could make the announcement. In Little Rock agents phoned Washington every fifteen minutes, just to say they hadn't heard anything.

By 8:00 Connelley's men were ready to move in. It was quiet; it appeared they had achieved total surprise. Connelley called for Karpis to come out with his hands up. There was no answer. With a wave of his hand Connelley signaled for the tear-gas guns. Canisters whistled through the air, crashing through windows into the house. As tentacles of gas began to waft through the shattered panes, Connelley again called for Karpis to surrender. He called again, and again, but there was no answer. When the FBI stormed the house, they found it empty.*

Karpis and Hunter had fled Hot Springs four days earlier, after learning of the inspectors' presence in town. It was a stupid thing: one of the inspectors had approached a taxi driver who was sweet on Fred Hunter's girlfriend, Connie Morris, and the man had gotten drunk and lectured Morris that agents were prepared to arrest her. Grace Goldstein warned the men. They were gone within minutes, leaving behind their clothes. After the raid agents marveled at how much weight Karpis had lost. The pants they discovered had a twenty-six-inch waistline.

Karpis drove west into Texas. He dropped a suitcase containing his machine guns at the home of Goldstein's brother, then headed to Corpus Christi, where he met Hunter and Morris and took rooms in a tourist camp.

---

* Not for several weeks would FBI agents learn who had been in the house the night before. It was Grace Goldstein, removing her things in anticipation of a raid. With her was the Hot Springs police chief, Joe Wakelin. According to FBI files, while Connelley was watching the house that night, Wakelin and Goldstein were having sex inside.

They spent several days fishing in the gulf, until Karpis picked up a newspaper and read of the Hot Springs raid. Hunter bought a new car, and when he walked into a police station to register it, he overheard a police scanner broadcasting details of the red coupe Karpis was driving. Karpis abandoned the car and drove to Mississippi, where on April 2, he rented a pair of rooms outside Biloxi. A week later they moved into New Orleans. Karpis rented an apartment on St. Charles Avenue. Hunter and Morris took rooms in a building on Canal Street.

The FBI was one step behind. Connie Morris was naïve enough to mail a letter to her mother from Corpus Christi. Agents were on the Texas coast within hours, but Karpis was gone. Connelley, meanwhile, had Grace Goldstein picked up. She confirmed that Karpis had visited the Hatterie, but said little else. Connelley, unaware how well she actually knew Karpis, released her and returned to Ohio. He didn't think her important enough to place under surveillance.

Karpis was gone, but agents lingered in Hot Springs. Everyone they contacted pointed them to Grace Goldstein. In Youngstown, Clayton Hall said he thought he could get her to confide in him. Connelley approved the plan, and on Tuesday, April 10, Hall arrived in Hot Springs, escorted by Agent John Madala. The two checked into the Majestic Hotel, and at 2:00 Hall telephoned the Hatterie. He was told Goldstein had left town, and wasn't expected back for two weeks. News of Goldstein's disappearance triggered a frantic scramble to find her; agents now assumed she had run off with Karpis. When Clayton Hall said Karpis had once mentioned visiting Goldstein's family in East Texas, agents poured into the area trying to locate them.

It was notable that Washington politics had seldom interfered with the War on Crime. The day of Goldstein's disappearance produced a moment when it did. That morning Hoover walked into a Senate hearing room to seek a doubling of the FBI's budget. He was expecting trouble. All the hoopla over the War on Crime—the fawning press, the movies, the radio serials—was generating a backlash against the Bureau, especially among supporters of other law-enforcement arms. The budget subcommittee's chairman, a Tennessee senator named Kenneth McKellar, was an old Hoover enemy, his animus dating to Hoover's refusal to hire a pair of Tennessee men the senator had endorsed. When McKellar complained, Hoover had promptly fired three Tennessee agents.[11]

That morning Hoover made his case with an array of statistics, charts, and graphs, pointing out that the FBI had all but eliminated kidnapping as a national threat. When he finished, McKellar attacked.

"Is any money directly or indirectly spent for advertising?" he asked.

"There is not," Hoover said. "We are not permitted in any way to engage in advertising."

"Do you take part, for instance, in the making of any moving pictures?"

"That is one thing that the Bureau has very strongly objected to. You have seen several of the G-men pictures, I believe." Hoover had in fact objected to some of the movies, but only because he wanted the FBI, not Hollywood, to produce them and reap the profits.

"I have," McKellar said. "They virtually advertised the Bureau, because your picture was shown in conjunction with them frequently . . . I think they have hurt the Department [of Justice] by advertising your methods."

McKellar was just getting warmed up. He pressed Hoover whether any writers or publicists were on the FBI payroll. Another senator asked why the Bureau didn't cooperate more with local police. Hoover insisted it did, when they weren't corrupt.

"It seems to me that your department is just running wild, Mr. Hoover," McKellar said. "I just think that, Mr. Hoover, with all the money in your hands you are just extravagant."

"Will you let me make a statement?" Hoover interjected.

"I think that is the statement," McKellar said.

They proceeded to quibble over how many cases the FBI had solved. "How many people have been killed by your department since you have been allowed to use guns?" McKellar asked.

"I think there have been eight desperadoes killed by our agents and we have had four agents in our service killed by them."

"In other words the net effect of turning guns over to your department has been the killing of eight desperadoes and four G-men."

Now clearly seeking to embarrass Hoover, McKellar pressed for his qualifications to run the Bureau. Hoover pointed out he had been with the Department of Justice nineteen years.

"I mean crime school," McKellar said.

"I learned first-hand," Hoover said.

"Did you ever make an arrest?"

"No sir; I have made investigations."

"How many arrests have you made, and who were they?"

Hoover mentioned several cases he had handled as a Justice Department prosecutor. "Did you make the arrests?" McKellar asked.

"The arrests were made by . . . officers under my supervision."

"I am talking about the actual arrests," McKellar said. "You never arrested them, actually?"[12]

Afterward, Hoover returned to his office, as angry as he had been in his life. It was galling that after everything the Bureau had achieved—Dillinger, Kelly, Floyd, Nelson, the Barkers—he was still subject to petty politics. He got on the phone with Earl Connelley. His message to Connelley was clear: he wanted Alvin Karpis arrested, he wanted it done immediately, and he wanted to do it himself.

By the time FBI agents realized Grace Goldstein was missing she was already in New Orleans, strolling through Audubon Park at Karpis's side; he had slipped into Hot Springs unnoticed and picked her up himself. After reuniting with Freddie Hunter and Connie Morris, they took a vacation, stopping in Biloxi before heading to Florida. Along the way Morris got sick; she had a bad case of syphilis. The couples returned to New Orleans and Morris began treatments. Karpis ferried Goldstein back to Hot Springs. The FBI was waiting for her.

By now the town was teeming with both postal inspectors and FBI men, each group determined to reap the credit for capturing Public Enemy #1. Hoover's desire to personally arrest Karpis only increased the pressure on his agents. Agent John Madala kept out of sight, babysitting Clayton Hall at a tourist camp. The moment Goldstein returned, Hall was certain he could get her to divulge Karpis's whereabouts. The FBI men spent as much time watching the inspectors as they did the Hatterie. Connelley had assigned Frank Smith, the old Cowboy who had survived the Kansas City Massacre, to work alongside the inspectors and their point man, Joe Anderson; Agent Smith's sole duty, an aide wrote Hoover, was "to keep an eye on [Anderson] and find out what he is doing and why at all times."[13]

Finally, on Friday, April 24, one of the Hatterie whores told an agent that Goldstein was expected back any day. Hoover's men were beside themselves. Somehow they had to eject the inspectors from Hot Springs. That day the Little Rock SAC, Chapmon Fletcher, "instructed Agent Smith to use his best efforts to get [the inspectors] out of Hot Springs using any excuse that he might think best in order."[14] Somehow Smith pulled it off. That afternoon, via a ruse undisclosed in FBI files, all the inspectors were pulled out of Hot Springs.

And just in time. The next day, Saturday, April 25, Goldstein returned to the Hatterie. But before FBI agents could move in, she was picked up by Detective Dutch Akers and the Hot Springs police chief Joe Wakelin, who spent three hours haranguing her to turn over Karpis; the two corrupt cops promised Goldstein she could split the $12,000 reward with them if she did. That night, after Goldstein returned to the Hatterie, John Madala sent in Clayton Hall. For once an informant was as good as his word; Hall and the unsuspecting Goldstein talked for hours. At 4:00 A.M. agents saw Hall emerge from the brothel and walk to the Southern Grill restaurant. Hall was jubilant: Goldstein had told him everything. She said Karpis and Hunter were now renting apartments in New Orleans, where Connie Morris was taking syphilis treatments. The only thing she failed to mention was Karpis's address.

Connelley needed that address. He left Ohio that afternoon, after telling John Madala to send Hall back to the Hatterie that night. Hall talked with Goldstein again that evening, but was unable to learn the address. Connelley couldn't wait another night. Monday morning he boarded a train for New Orleans. They would find Karpis themselves.

Everyone involved realized they were close. In Washington, Hoover was already busy lining up a national audience for his moment on the stage. On Monday, April 27, the morning Connelley arrived in New Orleans, Hoover met with executives from the NBC radio network. NBC was proposing to broadcast two separate programs on Karpis's capture, both of which would highlight the director's personal involvement.[15] Hoover's memo to Clyde Tolson afterward was entitled "Proposed broadcast of the capture of Alvin Karpis."

There was just one hang-up: the FBI still wasn't sure where in New Orleans Karpis was hiding. Connelley told Hoover he planned to check every doctor in the city until he found the one treating Connie Morris. Their only hope of a faster conclusion was Grace Goldstein. Agents arrested her on the street in Hot Springs Monday afternoon. Whisked away to Little Rock, she was subjected to intense questioning. For the moment, Goldstein refused to reveal Karpis's address.

The next day, as Connelley's men began canvassing doctor's offices in New Orleans, Goldstein continued to hold out. She said she didn't want to end up a pariah like Ana Sage. The FBI's leverage was her family. Agents had tracked her siblings to their homes in Texas. They made clear to Goldstein that they could be indicted for harboring Karpis. It worked. The next day, Wednesday, April 29, Goldstein agreed to a deal: If the FBI promised not to prosecute her family, she would hand over Karpis's address—but only to Connelley himself.

That night agents drove Goldstein to Jackson, Mississippi, and checked her into a motel. Connelley hurried up from New Orleans and debriefed Goldstein for three hours, winding up at 3:00 A.M. As it turned out, she didn't know Karpis's address. But she knew Freddie Hunter's, and she said Karpis ate most of his meals there. By daylight agents in New Orleans had Hunter's apartment building under surveillance. It was right on Canal Street, on the busy corner with Jefferson Davis Parkway. Two of the Bureau's most reliable shooters, Clarence Hurt and Jerry Campbell, flew down to join the raiding party.

Now all they needed was Hoover. A charter flight, a DC-3, was arranged via Trans World Airlines; Hoover and Tolson arrived in New Orleans that evening at 9:30, taking rooms at the Roosevelt Hotel. Connelley told Hoover there would probably be no raid until morning. He had two men in a vacant house across from Hunter's apartment building, but there had been no sign of Hunter or Karpis.

By daylight the next morning, Friday, May 1, the situation remained unchanged. In his hotel room, Hoover paced. Then, at 9:45, from his position in the vacant house, a rookie agent named Raymond Tollett spotted a red Essex Terraplane coast to a stop in front of Hunter's apartment. A man got out. Tollett lifted his binoculars to study his face. It was Karpis. He entered the building, then emerged with another man. Both got into cars. When they drove off, Tollett trotted to a drugstore to telephone Connelley.

Karpis had been in Mississippi several days, studying a pair of possible jobs, a construction-company payroll and a train score in the town of Iuka. He had returned just that morning, dropping his things in his apartment on St. Charles Avenue before swinging by to pick up Hunter. They headed to a deserted street near Lake Pontchartrain, where Karpis transferred his guns to Hunter's car. Then they dropped Karpis's car at a garage to be serviced. While they waited, they drove idly around the city. Hunter was nervous. He had seen strangers around his building. At one point, Hunter thought a maroon coupe was following them. Worried, they drove back to the apartment.

In the vacant house across the street, Connelley watched them pull up. Everything was in place. Leaving two men behind, he headed downtown to the FBI office. Hoover was waiting. Connelley gathered the raiding party and drew a diagram of the neighborhood on a blackboard. He had fourteen men. Two would remain in the vacant house. Two groups would guard the rear of Hunter's building. When they were certain both Hunter and Karpis were still inside the apartment, the raiding party itself—Connelley, Hoover, Dwight Brantley, and the Cowboys Clarence Hurt and Buck Buchanan—would go in the front door.

At 4:30, as Connelley finalized his plans, Connie Morris asked Karpis and Hunter to run to the grocery to buy strawberries for dinner. Karpis and Hunter exchanged glances. As Karpis stood by the window cradling a submachine gun, Hunter stepped onto the sidewalk, testing the air. He walked to the car; everything seemed fine. Karpis put the gun down and followed. At the grocery Karpis remained in the car. He watched as a DeSoto sedan pulled behind him. Hunter came out a minute later and said he had seen the DeSoto the day before. Karpis said they were imagining things. They had to calm down.

They returned to the apartment. It was a muggy day; the temperature had risen to eighty-seven degrees. In the kitchen Morris had changed into a white halter top and shorts. Karpis tried to relax but couldn't. He walked to a drugstore—the same one the FBI agents were using—and bought a pack of Chesterfields and a *Reader's Digest.* He walked back to the apartment, studying every man on the street. Karpis willed himself to relax, and in time he did. His car was to be ready at 5:00, and a few minutes after that he stood, announcing it was time to pick it up. He put on his straw boater. It was too hot to wear his suit jacket, so he slid his pistol beneath a sofa cushion.

As Karpis rose to leave, the five-man raiding party was sitting in two parked cars across the intersection of Canal and Jefferson Davis. Connelley and Clarence Hurt were in the lead car, Hoover and the others behind them.[16] A few minutes after five, word was relayed that the other groups were in position. The two cars slid away from the curb and began to cross the intersection. Their plan was to park beyond the building and return on foot. Just then, Karpis and Hunter emerged onto the sidewalk and stepped toward their waiting Plymouth. Karpis slid behind the wheel, rolled down the window, and popped the lock for Hunter. Connelley saw them and re-acted immediately; he swerved his car in front of the Plymouth and jammed on the brakes to block it. In the second car Hoover saw a boy on a bicycle veer between him and Karpis.[17] The boy was just moving past when Con-nelley and Hurt leaped from the car, guns drawn.

What happened next is in dispute. According to Hoover's version of events, recounted in dozens of articles and books in subsequent years, he jumped from the second car and rushed to the driver's-side door while Connelley took the passenger door. Before Karpis could reach for a rifle on the backseat, Hoover said he grabbed Karpis by the collar.

"Stammering, stuttering, shaking as though he had palsy," a reporter briefed by Hoover wrote the next day, "the man upon whom was bestowed the title of public enemy number one folded up like the yellow rat he is." Karpis offered no resistance, raising his hands as he stepped from the car. "Put the cuffs on him, boys," Hoover said.[18]

Hoover's story of the arrest, as told to reporters the next day, was flat wrong in several details. He said, for instance, that Connie Morris had been in the car when Karpis was arrested. "We nabbed the three after they had entered their car," Hoover told the Associated Press. "Hunter and the woman stepped from the car with their hands over their heads."[19]

One possible explanation for Hoover's confusion was raised in 1971, when Karpis published his autobiography. According to Karpis, at the mo-ment he was arrested, Hoover was nowhere to be seen. He didn't reach for a rifle on the backseat, he claimed, because the coupe had no backseat. An agent from the blocking car, apparently Connelley, jumped out and aimed a gun at him. "All right, Karpis," Connelley barked, "just keep your hands on that steering wheel."[20] It was only after he surrendered, Karpis claimed, that one of the agents began yelling, "Chief, we got him!" It was then, Karpis said, that Hoover emerged from behind the apartment building and helped arrest him.

"The story of Hoover the Hero is false," Karpis wrote. "He didn't lead the attack on me. He waited until he was told the coast was clear. Then he came out to reap the glory." Hoover's reaction to the allegation was to be expected. On a 1971 memo summarizing Karpis's book, the last of the hun-dreds of comments he scribbled in the margins of reports on the War on Crime's major figures, Hoover wrote, "Karpis or/and his coauthor must be on dope."

FBI files, perhaps unsurprisingly, suggest Hoover's version is closer to the truth. Both Connelley's report on the arrest and an aide's memo detailing a conversation with Hoover the next morning make clear that Hoover was in the raiding party, not behind the apartment building. But neither source—nor any other report in the massive Barker-Karpis file—says anything about Hoover approaching Karpis's car, much less grabbing him by the collar.* According to FBI files, Connelley and Clarence Hurt made the arrest, with Hoover arriving almost simultaneously in the second car. In the end it made little difference. The next day's front-page headline in the *New York Times* read: KARPIS CAPTURED IN NEW ORLEANS BY HOOVER HIMSELF.†

However it happened, Karpis and Hunter gave up with no resistance. Within minutes a crowd began to form. All around people hung out of apartment windows, trying to see what the commotion was about. None of the agents had a pair of handcuffs handy, so one took off his tie and wrapped it around Karpis's wrists. They loaded Karpis into a Bureau car and headed to the FBI office downtown. Clarence Hurt was driving, and he got lost. "Does anyone know where the Post Office Building is?" Hurt asked at one point.

"I can tell you," Karpis said.

"How do you know where it is?" asked Clyde Tolson, who sat in the backseat with Hoover.

"We were thinking of robbing it," Karpis said.[21]

In the end, it took a circuitous twenty minutes to bring Karpis into a holding cell at the Post Office Building. It was a triumphant moment for Hoover. The odd Congressional critic aside, the Karpis arrest cemented Hoover's position as a national hero, celebrated in newsreels, movies, and comic books. The spotlight shone only on him, not on the disgraced Melvin Purvis or the all-but-forgotten Homer Cummings, and certainly not on the dozens of anonymous FBI agents who had risked and in some cases given their lives ending the careers of John Dillinger, Pretty Boy Floyd, Baby Face Nelson, Machine Gun Kelly, Fred Barker, and Alvin Karpis. The FBI was

* FBI files do back up Hoover's assertion about the rifle in the backseat. An inventory of items seized from Karpis's car lists two .45 caliber pistols, two shoulder holsters, a hunting knife, a tackle box, and a .22 caliber Remington rifle.
† The key role played by postal inspectors in Karpis's capture was never revealed.

now America's preeminent national police force, the Bureau of Hoover's dreams, a department whose unchallenged resources would make Hoover a power in American government for the next four decades. Three years after it began with the deaths of five men in a Kansas City parking lot, the War on Crime was over.*

---

* Harry Campbell and Sam Coker were arrested the following week in Toledo. Checking Coker's records for his hospitalization the previous fall, agents learned he had dated a Toledo nurse. The nurse, who was unaware of his identity, led agents to both Coker and Campbell. Hoover went on that raid as well.

EPILOGUE

In the years since the War on Crime, critics have questioned almost everything about it: Was it necessary? Was it real? Were rural bank robbers the public menace the FBI said they were? A number of historians have argued that the War on Crime was little more than a public-relations ploy, a federal giant stomping out criminal insects, a dovetailing of Hoover's ambition with the needs of the Roosevelt administration's New Deal policies. This line of thinking suggests that the events of 1933–34 were all sound and fury, signifying nothing.

It's certainly true it wasn't much of a "war." In the narrowest sense, the War on Crime constituted only four groupings of criminal cases: Machine Gun Kelly's kidnapping of Charles Urschel, the Barker-Karpis kidnappings of Edward Bremer and William Hamm, the Dillinger manhunt, and the Kansas City massacre; there were no broader drives on the Chicago syndicate or Italian mafias, no war on counterfeiting or other crimes. Nor can one argue that the public enemies of 1933–34 could have been extinguished only by the federal government; Frank Hamer's work suggests otherwise. Bank robbery was a problem in 1933, but one that didn't require federal intervention.

Still, it's baseless to argue that the War on Crime was some kind of ploy. Though he reaped its benefits, Hoover didn't create the war. It sprang from real events. Its immediate cause was the Kansas City Massacre; few would question the FBI's decision to pursue the killers of its own men, never mind that it technically had no jurisdiction. The underlying cause was the Lindbergh Law, which made it the FBI's job to track down kidnappers. For the Bureau, the only "elective" segment of the War on Crime was the decision to pursue Dillinger. Here Hoover was indeed hemmed in by his own ambitions. But Hoover didn't "create" Dillinger, as some have argued; Dillinger was already a national figure when the FBI entered the case. He was precisely the type of interstate criminal a national police force should attempt to apprehend.

No one involved in the War on Crime believed it would end criminality or capture every major criminal. It didn't. More than anything, the War on Crime was a war on the *idea* of crime, the idea that too many Americans had come to tolerate crime. When judged on this basis, it's difficult to say it wasn't a success. Once the FBI became involved, kidnapping rates fell immediately and precipitously. Hoover's emphasis on indicting those who harbored criminals gradually eliminated safe havens such as St. Paul and Hot Springs. (The FBI helped clean up Hot Springs itself; the detective Dutch Akers and several other corrupt city officials served jail terms after trials in 1938.)

The War on Crime's legacy was deep and enduring. In the short term, it served as powerful evidence of the effectiveness of the Roosevelt administration's New Deal policies, boosting faith in the very idea of an activist central government. On a broader scale, it reassured a demoralized populace that American values could overcome anything, even the Depression. Despite the crowds of theatergoers who applauded them in life, in death John Dillinger and his peers were seen as symbols of all that was wrong in America. Coming as the worst of the Depression was passing, their defeat was the Depression's symbolic defeat; overnight their pedestals were reoccupied by clean, upstanding symbols of moral rectitude, the first being Melvin Purvis.

"The country seized on Melvin Purvis," the historian Richard Gid Powers has noted, "with his squeaky voice and diminutive build as a kind of Frank Capra hero, proof that ordinary citizens, provided they stuck together, could lick anything and anybody, even John Dillinger, the age's chosen symbol of social disintegration."

In short order Purvis was replaced in the pantheon of American heroism by the Bureau itself. Indeed, the most important legacy of the War on Crime is the modern FBI. Everything the Bureau has achieved since, every crime it has solved, every abuse its overzealous agents committed, sprang from the powers it accrued during the War on Crime. The manhunts for Dillinger and his peers introduced America to an idea that we take for granted today: that the federal government bears the ultimate responsibility for the nation's law and order.

The War on Crime not only enshrined Hoover's FBI as the bearer of this responsibility, it made Americans comfortable with its existence. It created a public trust so enduring that the Bureau's later abuses were only belatedly questioned. As Claire Bond Potter notes, "[T]he War on Crime produced lasting changes in the ways Americans would come to understand crime as a national problem, police power as socially positive, and crime control as a federal responsibility."[1]

But while the FBI's "socially positive" role was on public display during 1933 and 1934, so too can the seeds of the FBI's later abuses be seen: the beating of suspects; the "kidnapping" of Verne Miller's girlfriend, Vi Mathias; the conviction of Adam Richetti on perjured FBI testimony; and the arrest and trial of Roger Touhy for the Hamm kidnapping. The War on Crime bestowed upon Hoover's FBI something close to absolute power, and the day eventually came when Hoover's FBI was corrupted absolutely by it. The Bureau wrestles with its legacy to this day.

Few of the FBI agents who fought the War on Crime ever received any public credit for their work. A number enjoyed long careers in the Bureau before retiring in the 1960s and 1970s. Others left the Bureau as soon as they could, bolting in 1935 and 1936 to join hometown law firms or to become corporate executives. The last surviving member of the Dillinger Squad, the rookie agent Tom McDade, died in 1996.

Frank Smith, who survived the Kansas City Massacre, resigned from the FBI in 1939 to become Oklahoma City's police chief. He died in 1953. Reed Vetterli, the Kansas City SAC, became Salt Lake City's police chief. He died in 1949. Despite his statements to the contrary in FBI files, the massacre's third survivor, Joe Lackey, insisted until his death that he was able to identify Richetti, Floyd, and Miller.

Gus Jones, who led the Urschel investigation, retired from the FBI in 1940. He died in 1963. Bill Rorer, the agent who arrested Machine Gun Kelly and exchanged gunfire with Dillinger at Little Bohemia, left the FBI in 1937. He was CEO of a Georgia dairy until his death in 1967. The agent whose bullets felled Dillinger, Charles Winstead, retired from the FBI in 1943. He died at the age of eighty-two in 1973. His partner, Clarence Hurt, retired in 1955 and was a sheriff in his native Oklahoma for several years. He died in 1975. Jerry Campbell, the FBI marksman who captured Dock Barker, died in Palo Alto in 1991.

Hugh Clegg, the assistant director who nominally headed the agents at Little Bohemia, founded the FBI Academy in 1935. After his retirement, he served as a special assistant to the chancellor at the University of Mississippi, where he was a pivotal figure in the school's acceptance of its first black student, James Meredith. Likewise, Earl Connelley remained a top FBI administrator for two decades after the War on Crime. He retired in 1956 and died a year later. Pop Nathan, often called "the grand old man of the FBI," retired from the FBI in 1945. He died in 1963.

After working as a public spokesman for several companies during the 1930s, Melvin Purvis faded from public view. He served as a colonel in World War II, then returned to South Carolina, where for several years he ran a radio station. Hoover never forgave Purvis for his hubris in the wake of the Dillinger and Floyd cases. He repeatedly frustrated Purvis's attempts to return to the public eye, blocking his chance for a federal judgeship in 1952. Hoover, in fact, did everything possible to destroy his onetime protégé's legacy; Purvis's name did not appear once in the Bureau's 1956 authorized history, *The FBI Story*.

On February 29, 1960, Purvis was found dead in his study, a single bullet wound to the head. The gun in his hand had been given him by fellow agents upon his retirement. Some called it suicide, others an accident. Hoover made no public comment and sent no note of condolence. "We are honored that you ignored Melvin's death," his widow wrote Hoover. "Your jealousy hurt him very much but until the end I think he loved you." At the time of his death, Melvin Purvis was fifty-six.

For the rest of his life Hoover remained obsessed with the War on Crime era. As the FBI sank into controversies over its handling of civil rights and other cases, his fascination with Dillinger and his peers only grew. "Hoover had a thing about Dillinger," the FBI assistant director William Sullivan once said. "If he were alive today and you went to see him, he'd tell you about Dillinger. The older he got the more he talked about John Dillinger, Ma Barker, and all those old cases of the thirties. He would talk on and on about this stuff."[2] One senses in Hoover's reveries a longing for the clear-cut distinctions of good versus evil the War on Crime afforded the FBI. In a way, Dillinger became Hoover's "Rosebud."

J. Edgar Hoover died in his sleep on May 1, 1972.

Of those the FBI captured, many became the earliest inmates at Alcatraz, which opened in January 1935. When Alvin Karpis arrived as its 325th inmate on August 7, 1936, he quipped that it was like Old Home Week. On his first day on The Rock, Karpis, as Prisoner AZ-325, renewed acquaintances with Machine Gun Kelly (AZ-117), Kelly's partner Albert Bates (AZ-137), and their old mentor Harvey Bailey (AZ-139). In the cafeteria he saw Dock Barker (AZ-268), Harry Sawyer (AZ-299), Volney Davis (AZ-271), and Elmer Farmer (AZ-299). He later came to know Dick Galatas, Deafy Farmer, John Chase, and many others.

Those who avoided Alcatraz, and those who chased them, met a multitude of fates. The man who betrayed Bonnie and Clyde, Henry Methvin, was run over and killed by a train, apparently while sleeping, in 1948. Frank Hamer died in 1955. W. D. Jones lived long enough to watch the 1967 movie *Bonnie and Clyde* and wrote an article in *Playboy* about the gang. Jones was killed during a fight in Houston in 1974. Clyde Barrow's last sibling, Marie Barrow Scoma, died in 1999.

The Urschel mansion still stands in Oklahoma City; a historical society plaque is the only reminder of that warm night in July 1933 when Kelly paid his only visit. Ed Weatherford, the Texas detective who brought Kelly to the FBI's attention, never received credit outside Fort Worth for his work on the case; he died in 1949. Kathryn Kelly's father, Boss Shannon, was paroled from prison in 1944; he died in 1956. Albert Bates died of a heart attack at Alcatraz in 1948. Kelly died, also of a heart attack, at Leavenworth six years later.

Kathryn Kelly outlived her husband. In 1958, after years of begging Hoover for her release, she persuaded an Oklahoma judge to grant her a new trial. The Bureau, caught off guard, scrambled to reassemble its twenty-five-year-old case. It was all but impossible. Frank Blake, the Dallas SAC, had retired in 1942 after a heart attack and died six years later. Ralph Colvin, the Oklahoma City SAC, died in Tulsa in 1947. The Urschels' bridge partner, Walter Jarrett, died in Midland, Texas, in 1947. The Bureau spent months trying to locate the Luther Arnold family, the sharecroppers who figured prominently in the Kellys' capture. At one point agents pursued rumors that twelve-year-old Geralene Arnold had changed her name and become a famous movie actress. The Arnolds were never found. When the FBI was unable to provide evidence to reconvict her, Kathryn was freed. She worked in an Oklahoma hospital for many years before her death in 1985.

The bit players of the Dillinger case died in obscurity. Harold Cassidy, the doctor who assisted in Dillinger's surgery, committed suicide in Chicago in 1946. The FBI paid reward money to Ana Sage, the "Woman in Red," but it couldn't prevent her deportation; she died of liver failure in Romania in April 1947. Patricia Cherrington died two years later, apparently of natural causes, her body discovered in a Chicago flophouse. Louis Piquett became a bartender after his release from prison. He died of a heart attack in Chicago in 1951. Pete Pierpont and Charles Makley attempted to escape from Ohio's death row in September 1934, using fake guns carved from soap. Makley was killed; Pierpont was later executed. The last surviving member of the Dillinger Gang, Russell Clark, was released from prison in August 1968, having served thirty-four years. He had inoperable cancer and died four months later.

Billie Frechette married a Wisconsin man named Arthur Tic, bore him children, and died in January 1969. Dillinger's last girlfriend, Polly Hamilton, lived quietly in Chicago for years as a salesman's wife. She died a month after Frechette. Nine months later, in October 1969, Martin Zarkovich died. Whatever secrets he harbored about the East Chicago Police Department's ties to Dillinger went with him to the grave. John Chase was paroled from Leavenworth in 1966. He became a janitor in Palo Alto and died there in 1973. Baby Face Nelson's widow, Helen Gillis, lived out her years working in a Chicago factory and raising the couple's children. She died in 1987. The fates of Fatso Negri and Chase's girlfriend, Sally Backman, are unknown.

Friends say William Hamm was never the same after his kidnapping by the Barker Gang. Though he continued as chairman of Hamm Brewing until his retirement in 1965, he tended to brood, and he surrounded himself with bodyguards. He died in 1970. Roger Touhy, the gangster who was acquitted in the Hamm case, was wrongfully convicted of the kidnapping of the syndicate con man Jake Factor. He served more than twenty years in prison before his release in November 1959. Touhy was shot and killed on the front porch of his sister's home less than a month later, presumably by old enemies in the syndicate.

Edward Bremer died of a heart attack following a swim at his Florida home in 1965. His father, Adolph, had met the same fate in a Seattle hotel in 1939. Tom Brown, the corrupt detective who conspired with the Barkers, was never prosecuted. He was fired after a civil inquiry and died in 1959 in Ely, Minnesota, where he ran a liquor store.

Dock Barker was shot and killed attempting to escape from Alcatraz in January 1939. Ma Barker's last living son, Lloyd, who never joined the Barker Gang, was released from Leavenworth in 1947 and was shot to death two years later by his wife at their Denver home. The Barker Gang's Bill Weaver was felled by a heart attack in Alcatraz in June 1944. Charles Fitzgerald died seven months later, at Leavenworth. Harry Sawyer was released from prison in February 1955 after doctors diagnosed him with inoperable cancer. He died four months later.

Harry Campbell was still in a federal prison hospital in Missouri in 1958; his fate is unknown. Volney Davis was paroled from Alcatraz in the 1950s; according to one source, he died in Oregon in 1978. Wrongfully convicted of taking part in the Urschel kidnapping, Harvey Bailey was finally released from federal custody in 1961 but was immediately rearrested for an old Kansas bank robbery. Released for good in 1965, he married Deafy Farmer's widow and settled down to a quiet life of carpentry in Joplin. He died in 1979 at the age of ninety-one.

The Barker Gang's girlfriends and wives faded from public view. Paula Harmon was last seen living with her parents in Port Arthur, Texas, in the late 1930s. Wynona Burdette disappeared, as did Delores Delaney and Harry Sawyer's wife, Gladys. Mildred Kuhlmann, the Toledo girl whose dalliance with Dock Barker led to the demise of the gang, returned to Ohio, where she married a Sandusky man named Joseph Auerbach; the couple operated a lounge for years. The Auerbachs had two children; today their daughter is married to one of New York's most prominent criminal-defense attorneys. According to family members, Mildred Kuhlmann Auerbach never spoke of the role she played in the FBI's war against the Barkers. She died at the age of eighty-five in a Sandusky nursing home on December 10, 1993.[3]

Then there was Alvin Karpis. After thirty-three years behind bars, Karpis was paroled from the federal prison at McNeil Island, Washington, in January 1969 and deported to Canada. He authored two ghostwritten books, including an autobiography, before moving to Spain in the early 1970s. He died in Torremolinos, Spain, apparently from an accidental overdose of sleeping pills, on August 26, 1979.

So much has changed in seventy years, and so little. Many of the War on Crime's battle sites remain as they did then, out-of-the-way spots, now dusty and cobwebbed, of interest only to the middle-aged crime buffs who come with their cameras and trivia questions. In northern Wisconsin Little Bohemia still sits on the shores of Star Lake. It's bigger now, with a new bar and lacquered wooden tables in the dining room, the kind of sturdy place where tourists can grab a cheeseburger before an afternoon swim. The foyer walls are lined with cuttings about that night in 1934, but the simplest questions draw friendly shrugs from the bartenders. On a bright August afternoon in 2002 Emil Wanatka's son was there, visiting from his Florida retirement; the poor man couldn't get away fast enough when someone asked what it was like playing catch with Baby Face Nelson.

The Barker deathhouse in Oklawaha, Florida, still sits amid silent oaks dripping with Spanish moss on the shores of Lake Weir. Abandoned for years now, it's filled with an absentee owner's garbage, empty boxes, and a child's yellowing hobby horse; close your eyes and you can almost see Earl Connelley scrambling across the grass to escape Freddie Barker's bullets. There's a historical marker beside the field where Pretty Boy Floyd died in far eastern Ohio. Ellen Conkle's home was torn down years ago, and the area is being reclaimed by the surrounding woods. On a cold December day the wind blows leaves across the yard where Purvis shouted for his men to "Fire!" There's not another farm in sight. It's an eerie, barren place.

A concrete marker was erected on the country road not far from where Bonnie and Clyde were killed in northwest Louisiana. It's a sad, forgotten spot, hard to find, littered with green-glass shards of broken beer bottles and used condoms. The Biograph is still there, despite periodic attempts to tear it down; there's no marker where Dillinger fell, just a cracked stretch of concrete, pockmarked with black splotches of ancient bubble gum. In the summer of 2003 an office building was going up in the rear parking lot where Chicago detectives accosted the Dillinger Squad that night.

People still live in Dillinger's flat on Lexington Avenue in St. Paul, in the Joplin apartment where Bonnie and Clyde killed two policemen, in the Dillinger farmhouse outside Mooresville, and in the small frame house where Baby Face Nelson died. Some occupants know their home's history; others, like the family living in the Italianate home Alvin Karpis rented at the Indiana lakeshore, are startled to learn that a murderer once laid his head in their master bedroom.

Jimmy Probasco's place is gone. So is Louis Cernocky's; the ladies at the local historical society look skeptical when told one of the area's leading citizens was a welcoming host for John Dillinger. The Green Lantern is gone, too; not even photographs remain. So is the house in suburban Chicago where the Barkers held William Hamm and Edward Bremer. The Crown Point jail sits abandoned. There's a faded pink marker on the building where Frank Nash was snatched off Central Avenue in Hot Springs. On a blustery January day, a man and his teenage son linger a second to read it, then shrug, then walk on.

They don't know the stories. So many people don't. More than two dozen sons and daughters of the Dillinger Squad's men were interviewed for this book; only a handful fully understood what their fathers had lived through. By and large, relatives of the outlaws and their "molls" knew even less or didn't care to know more. The dark side of their heritage has split more than one of these families. The sons of Frank Nash's widow do not speak to this day. One beseeched the author to tell him more about his mother. His half-brother hung up the phone.

You can still find the public enemies, if you know where to look. Their graves lie, mostly unnoticed, in remote country cemeteries and along the busy avenues of twenty-first-century Middle America. In the Crown Hill Memorial Park in Dallas, Bonnie Parker is buried beside a budding hedge, a Bally Total Fitness in view to her left, an H&R Block and a Hollywood Video to her right. Three bundles of artificial flowers wreath her headstone and its jarring inscription: AS THE FLOWERS ARE ALL MADE SWEETER BY SUNSHINE AND THE DEW, SO THIS OLD WORLD IS MADE BRIGHTER BY THE LIKES OF FOLKS LIKE YOU. Clyde lies across town in a padlocked, weed-strewn graveyard in west Dallas. He is buried in a corner with his brother Buck, next to their parents, about thirty feet from the white-concrete side wall of Many's Transmission Service. The headstone's inscription reads, GONE BUT NOT FORGOTTEN.

That's more than one can say about Machine Gun Kelly and the Barker family. An hour northwest of Dallas, in the tidy country cemetery at Cottondale, Texas, Kelly molders in a pauper's grave. The only marker is a six-by-eight-inch brick with his name misspelled: GEORGE B. KELLEY, 1954. The

Barkers couldn't afford that much. Their graves lie in a row in a windswept graveyard outside the town of Welch in far northeastern Oklahoma. For decades several of their resting places were unmarked. Recently someone adorned them with tiny steel markers inscribed with Biblical verse. LET US NOT FORGET, Fred's reads. HE WHO GAVE US LIFE, UNDERSTANDS ALL THE REASONS.

Two hours south, Pretty Boy Floyd is buried in the Akins Cemetery beside his parents, in a quiet field dotted with Floyd family tombstones; there is a comforting, familial quality here, as if Floyd were welcomed back into the bosom of his kin. By contrast, Baby Face Nelson's grave feels cold and functional. Buried beside an access road at the St. Joseph's Cemetery in the River Grove section of Chicago, Nelson lies between his wife, Helen, and his mother, beneath a string of five identical blue-gray markers. The Gillis family tombstones have the look and feel of discarded paving stones; standing among the graves, one is distracted by the distant roar of jetliners at O'Hare International Airport a few miles north. LESTER J. GILLIS, Nelson's marker reads. DIED NOVEMBER 27 1934. AGE 26 YEARS.

Fittingly, only Dillinger's grave retains a dash of flair. He is buried in a meadow of thick grass in Indianapolis's vast Crown Hill Cemetery. His tombstone, a four-foot obelisk that looms over neighboring graves, has a single word, DILLINGER, flanked on both sides by an ivylike decorative flourish. Tourists come to see it all the time. In 1991 the children of a woman named Maude A. Grubb asked the cemetery to bury her near Dillinger. She lies a hundred feet away, the words JOHN D. carved in a corner of her headstone. "They said she always had a thing about Dillinger," a cemetery official says.

It's a peaceful place, in the way cemeteries are. Squatting in the damp grass, surrounded by the graves of grocers, lawyers, and farmers, you hear no echoes of machine-gun fire, no ghostly screams of dying men, no reminder at all of Dillinger's fourteen months of fame. Like his peers, Dillinger was not Indiana Jones or Luke Skywalker. He was a man, five-feet-seven, 145 pounds. It's startling to realize he's actually still there, just an arm's length beneath the grass. You can sit beside Dillinger's grave with the morbid knowledge that, given a shovel and a few hours, you could literally touch the man's body. You won't do that, of course. Instead you run your hand over his tombstone. It is nothing more and nothing less than polished granite—smooth, hard, cold. Real.

BIBLIOGRAPHICAL ESSAY

The primary source materials for this book are the FBI's files on the War on Crime's major cases, which have been released in bits and pieces since the mid-1980s. The files themselves line a series of shelves in a basement reading room at FBI headquarters in Washington. You can leaf through them there or, if you're hardheaded (like me), you can buy them outright, several hundred thousand pages of internal reports, telegrams, correspondence and witness statements, at a cost of ten cents per page. My copies fill a half-dozen file cabinets. I've cited a sampling of the documents I used for this book in the Notes. (The codes in the Notes refer to the FBI cases: "BKF" is the Bremer kidnapping file; "UF" is the Urschel kidnapping; "Jodil" is the John Dillinger file; and so on.)

The main areas where I've relied on published sources are the background sections on the FBI and the criminal gangs. There are several good biographies of J. Edgar Hoover. Probably the best remains Curt Gentry's *J. Edgar Hoover: The Man and the Secrets.* Also helpful were Fred J. Cook's *The FBI Nobody Knows;* Ralph de Toledano's *J. Edgar Hoover, the Man in His Time; The Bureau: My Thirty Years in Hoover's FBI,* by William Sullivan with Bill Brown; the salacious but well-researched *Official and Confidential: The Secret Life of J. Edgar Hoover,* by Anthony Summers; *The FBI Story: A Report to the People,* by Don Whitehead; and two books by Richard Gid Powers, *G-Men: Hoover's FBI in American Popular Culture* and *Secrecy and*

Power: The Life of J. Edgar Hoover. An outstanding analysis of the War on Crime's sociological context can be found in Claire Bond Potter's *War on Crime: Bandits, G-Men, and the Politics of Mass Culture.* Also worth reading is David E. Ruth's *Inventing the Public Enemy: The Gangster in American Culture, 1918–1934.*

Many books were helpful in understanding Depression-era America. Among the best were *The '30s: A Time to Remember,* a collection of articles edited by Don Congdon; and two books by T. H. Watkins, *The Great Depression: America in the 1930s* and *The Hungry Years: A Narrative History of the Great Depression in America.*

For background on Pretty Boy Floyd's early career, I relied on FBI files, newspapers in Tulsa and Oklahoma City, and Michael Wallis's outstanding *The Life and Times of Charles Arthur Floyd.* Wallis enjoyed extensive access to Floyd's family, and it shows. Curiously, he made no use of the FBI's Kansas City Massacre file, which was released during the 1980s to a dogged Kansas City newspaper-reporter-turned-professor, Robert Unger. A book that does is Jeffrey King's *The Life and Death of Pretty Boy Floyd,* which suffers from a lack of firsthand sources and feels colorless by comparison. For anyone interested in the Kansas City Massacre, I heartily recommend Unger's *The Union Station Massacre: The Original Sin of Hoover's FBI.*

The story of Bonnie and Clyde has been told in more than a dozen books. One of the best remains the first, *Fugitives: The Story of Clyde Barrow and Bonnie Parker,* by Emma Parker and Nell Barrow Cowan. I also recommend *Running with Bonnie and Clyde: The Ten Fast Years of Ralph Fults,* by John Neal Phillips. Phillips did a good deal of original research for his book, including interviews with Blanche Barrow.

Background on Melvin Purvis can be found in Purvis's FBI file, which is available via Freedom of Information Request. Purvis told a sanitized version of his life story in the book he published after leaving the FBI, *American Agent.* For personal detail, I am deeply indebted to Purvis's son Alston, who is writing a biography of his father, and to Purvis's former secretary, Doris Lockerman. The story of how Purvis was hoodwinked into arresting Roger Touhy was pieced together from FBI files, Touhy's 1954 appeal at the Federal Archives in Chicago, and Touhy's own book, *The Stolen Years.*

Details of Machine Gun Kelly's early life can be found in multiple articles that appeared in various Memphis newspapers, and in an odd little book his son Bruce Barnes published in 1991, *Machine Gun Kelly: To Right a Wrong.* While accepting a number of canards his father passed on, Barnes does an admirable job of filling in gaps in Kelly's life story. The Urschel ransom negotiations are chronicled in FBI files and in a florid 1934 book written by E. E. Kirkpatrick, *Crimes' Paradise: The Authentic Inside Story of the Urschel Kidnapping.*

I found background on Baby Face Nelson's early career in a series of 1930 and 1931 *Chicago Tribune* articles pointed out by that indefatigable researcher, Tom Smusyn. The first biography of Nelson, *Baby Face Nelson: Portrait of a Public Enemy,* written by Steven Nickel and William J. Helmer, was issued during my research. I found this a disquieting book, laden with all manner of unsourced information, including a story of Nelson meeting with Dillinger in the summer of 1933. After finding no one in the field who could substantiate these stories, I ignored them.

Conversations within the Barker Gang are derived almost exclusively from the Karpis transcripts, more than a thousand pages of unpublished interviews Karpis gave to his biographer, Bill Trent, in 1969 and 1970. Background on John Dillinger's upbringing and early career can be found in John Toland's *Dillinger Days,* as well as in contemporary newspaper and magazine articles and in *Dillinger: A Short and Violent Life,* by Robert Cromie and Joseph Pinkston. For the portrait of Alvin Karpis's last years in Spain, I am grateful to Robert Livesey, who spent many hours there with Karpis compiling their book, *On The Rock: Twenty-five Years in Alcatraz.*

Material in the latter half of this book is drawn almost exclusively from FBI files. A prominent exception is material drawn from *Dillinger: The Untold Story,* by Russell Girardin, with Bill Helmer. I strongly recommend this book. Most of the conversations Dillinger had with Louis Piquett and Art O'Leary were drawn from Girardin's long-lost manuscript.

I reserve the final mentions for my two favorite books on Depression-era outlaws. I kept both on my desk at all times. One is Paul Maccabee's *John Dillinger Slept Here: A Crook's Tour of Crime and Corruption in St. Paul, 1920–1936.* This is local history at its very best, and a must-read for anyone interested in the War on Crime period. The other is probably the most comprehensive reference available, *Public Enemies: America's Criminal Past, 1919–1940,* by Bill Helmer and Rick Mattix. These two men probably know more about Depression-era outlaws than anyone alive, and they have poured their passion into this fine book.

NOTES

1: A PRELUDE TO WAR

1. Cited in *The Crisis of the Old Order,* by Arthur Schlesinger, Houghton Mifflin, 1957.
2. Cited in *J. Edgar Hoover: The Man and the Secrets,* by Curt Gentry, W. W. Norton, 1991.
3. Clegg quoted in *The Mississippi Oral History Program,* volume XCIX, 1977.
4. Memo, Nathan to Hoover, June 24, 1932. 67-822-148.
5. Moley cited in Gentry, pp. 159–60.
6. *War on Crime: Bandits, G-Men and the Politics of Mass Culture,* Claire Bond Potter, Rutgers University Press, 1998, p. 68.
7. Potter, p. 62.

2: A MASSACRE BY PERSONS UNKNOWN

1. "The Fugitives (renamed *The True Story of Bonnie and Clyde*), Signet Paperback Edition, 1968, pp. 52–54.
2. Ibid, p. 64.
3. Karpis, p. 84.

3: THE COLLEGE BOYS TAKE THE FIELD

Epigraphs taken from *The Union Station Massacre,* Robert Unger, Andrews McMeel Publishing, 1997, p. 13.

1. Harvey memo, Feb. 15, 1935, KCM #3570.
2. Miller's visit to the Davis apartment is confirmed in FBI records. The Bureau's source was Edna Murray. The only detailed version of events is one Murray wrote in a four-part series of articles in *Startling Detective Adventures* magazine beginning in August 1936.
3. This is courtesy of the memory of former agent James J. Metcalfe, who told the story to his daughter Krista Metcalfe.

4. Unger, *Union Station Massacre*, p. 13.
5. *Missouri State Trooper Magazine,* Capt. E. M. Raub, August 24, 2000.
6. Allanna Nash article, July 18, 1976.
7. *Muncie Sunday Star,* July 16, 1933; *Muncie Evening Press,* July 15, 1933.
8. *Muncie Evening Press,* July 17, 1933.
9. *Muncie Evening Press,* July 17 and 18, 1933; *Muncie Morning Star,* July 18 and 19, 1933.
10. *Official and Confidential: The Secret Life of J.Edgar Hoover,* Anthony Summers, G. P. Putnam's Sons, 1993, pp. 67–72.
11. *Chicago Tribune,* July 25, 1933.
12. Hoover to Purvis, July 26, 1933, Hamm kidnap file #67.
13. USA ex rel. *Roger Touhy v. Joseph E. Ragen,* U.S. District Court, No. Dist. of Illinois. Eastern Division No. 48 C 448, Opinion of Court.
14. There are many versions of the scene on the Urschels' sunporch that evening. None of them vary in any substantive way. Probably the most detailed, on which this account is based, was written by Harrison Moreland in *True Detective Mysteries,* March 1934. Though none of his material is attributed, Moreland's facts mirror those in FBI files, and it's clear he interviewed many, if not all, of the principal players.
15. This glimpse of Bates and Kelly is taken from an odd, privately published 1991 book, *Machine Gun Kelly: To Right a Wrong,* Tipper Publications. The book was written by Kelly's son, Bruce Barnes, a California lighting designer who as a young man was able to interview his infamous father about his crimes. Barnes's book deals mostly with Kelly's precriminal life, when he was married to his first wife, Barnes's mother. Of the stories Kelly tells of his crimes, a number are demonstrably false. But many others, including this one, are surprisingly close to versions found in FBI files.
16. Ellis, *A Man Named Jones*, p. 84.

4: THE BAYING OF THE HOUNDS

1. Hoover, p. 143.
2. Blake to Vetterli, July 7, 1933, KCM #220.
3. Charles Winstead, untitled autobiographical essay, p. 22. Winstead's essay, written shortly before his death in 1972, is on file at the Red River Historical Museum in Sherman, Texas.
4. Detective Weatherford's role is described in Dallas report, Aug. 18, 1933, UKM #293.
5. *Fugitives,* p. 137.
6. Phillips, p. 152.
7. Ibid.
8. Dexter (Ia.) *Sentinel,* Oct. 5, 1967.
9. Dallas report, Aug. 7, 1933, UKF #99.
10. Kirkpatrick tells his story in *Crimes Paradise,* Naylor Press, San Antonio, Tex., 1934.
11. No explanation for the incident is contained in FBI files. The flooded-engine story is told by Lew Louderback in *The Bad Ones,* Fawcett Publications, Greenwich, Conn., 1968.
12. Kirkpatrick, p. 86.
13. Letter, N.Y. office to Oklahoma City office, July 31, 1933, KCM #413.
14. The Mathias investigation is described in an August 5, 1933, New York office report, KCM #418.

15. This version of Charles Urschel's debriefing I found in a thin volume not cited in bibliographies of Depression-era criminal literature. The book, a biography of Jones, is *A Man Named Jones,* by George Ellis.
16. Ellis, p. 113.
17. Colvin to Hoover, Aug. 11, 1933, UKF #201.
18. Jones and Bailey told consistent versions of their confrontation. Ellis, p. 136. Haley, p. 134. Fitzpatrick, p. 130.
19. *Serb World USA,* May/June 1992, p. 48.
20. Both Toland and Cromie assert Dillinger vaulted the railing at Montpelier, as he had at Dalesville. Contemporary newspaper accounts do not mention such a leap. Bluffton *Evening News-Banner,* Aug. 4, 1933; Fort Wayne *News-Sentinal,* Fort Wayne *Journal Gazette,* Hartford City *Times-Gazette,* Aug. 5, 1933.

5: THE KID JIMMY

1. I am deeply indebted to a Chicago amateur historian, Tom Smysyn, who discovered these articles during the early 1990s, for bringing them to my attention.
2. *Chicago Tribune,* January 7, 1930.
3. *Chicago Tribune,* January 23, 1930.
4. *Chicago Tribune,* April 1, 1930; *Chicago Herald & Examiner,* April 1, 1930.
5. *Chicago Herald,* October 8, 1930.
6. *Chicago Tribune,* February 15, 1931. The article contains a lengthy list of the gang's confirmed crimes.
7. *Chicago Tribune, Joliet Evening Herald,* February 18, 1932.
8. The story of Bentz's tutelage of Nelson is told in an article Bentz, then in prison, wrote in 1951 for *Argosy* magazine. The salient facts are confirmed in FBI reports.
9. The South St. Paul robbery is one of the Barker-Karpis Gang's more confusing to unravel. Fitzgerald would later claim that Bryan Bolton and George Ziegler took part; according to Karpis, they didn't. Karpis says the gang's fifth man that day was Bill Weaver, and says it was Weaver who first shot Officer Yeaman, who was then further wounded by fire from Fred Barker's Thompson gun. All the witnesses but one indicate Fred Barker emerged from the car along with Fitzgerald and Dock Barker. The owner of the bar where Weaver waited would later claim Barker waited with him.
10. Dallas report, UKF #508.
11. The Arnolds' story is told in detail in an Oklahoma City report, UKF #732.
12. Chicago report, Nov. 13, 1933, UKF #994.
13. Gus Jones, Oklahoma City report, Oct. 3, 1933, UKF #732.
14. Colvin report, UKF #1110.
15. Durham's story told in Dallas report, Sept. 25, 1933, UKF #598.
16. Details of the Kellys' Chicago trip are told by Geralene Arnold in a Chicago report, Nov. 13, 1933, UKF #994.
17. Letter, Purvis to Hoover, Dec. 18, 1933, UKF, #1039.
18. Memo to D. O. Smith, Oct. 24, 1933, UKF, #956.
19. Dayton *Daily News,* Sept. 22, 1933, Dayton *Herald,* Sept. 23, 1933. Toland, p. 108.
20. Karpis transcripts, tape 15.
21. *Chicago Daily Times,* Sept. 25, 1933.

22. Statements from Cass Coleman and Geralene Arnold, UKF #918.
23. The story of Rorer's morning is told in detail in a Birmingham report, Oct. 6, 1933, UKF #778.
24. *Chicago American,* Sept. 26, 1933.

6: THE STREETS OF CHICAGO

1. Toland, pp. 6–8.
2. *Chicago Reader,* July 20, 1984.
3. Toland, p. 127.
4. *Auburn* (Ind.) *Evening Star,* Oct. 16, 1934.
5. *Indianapolis Times,* Oct. 21, 1933.
6. *Greencastle Banner,* Oct. 24, 1933; *Indianapolis News,* Oct. 22, 1983.
7. Karpis transcripts, tape #15.
8. Letter, Purvis to Kansas City office, Aug. 29, 1933.
9. FBI statements on Miller's escape in Kansas City Massacre files.
10. Jodil #4, Oct. 23, 1933.
11. Hoover, memo to file, Oct. 24, 1933, Jodil #19.
12. *Indianapolis News,* June 15, 1955.
13. *Chicago Herald and Examiner,* Aug. 27, 1934.
14. Mary Kinder, "Four Months with the Dillinger Gang," *Chicago Herald and Examiner,* July 30, 1934.
15. "My Adventures with The Dillinger Gang," *Chicago Herald and Examiner,* September 1934.
16. Toland, p. 147.
17. Ibid.
18. Cromie, p. 89.
19. *Chicago Tribune,* Nov. 16, 1933.

7: AMBUSHES

1. Racine *Journal,* Nov. 21, 1933.
2. Cromie, pp. 111–12.
3. Toland, p. 149.
4. Memo, Hughes to Hoover, Nov. 9, 1933, Hamm kidnap file, #214.
5. Memo to file, Hoover, Oct. 21, 1933, Hamm kidnap file, #182.
6. F. X. Fay to Kansas City SAC, Nov. 29, 1933, KCM #926.
7. KCM #904.
8. Conroy to Hoover, December 1, 1933, KCM #906.
9. Maccabee, p. 229.
10. "Daring Machine Gun Mob Robs First National Here," *Brainerd Daily Dispatch,* Oct. 23, 1933; "It was no gangster movie," *Brainerd Daily Dispatch,* December 4, 1988.
11. San Antonio report, June 5, 1934, Jodil #1829. *San Antonio Light* articles, Dec. 11–15, 1933. *A Man Named Jones,* p. 157.

8: "AN ATTACK ON ALL WE HOLD DEAR"

1. Cherrington statement, Jodil #2617.
2. Toland, p. 175.
3. Gary *Post-Tribune,* January 16, 1934.

4. The *Times,* Hammond, Indiana, July 22, 1984. (Interview with Hobart Wilgus's widow.)
5. Gary *Post-Tribune,* January 16, 1934.
6. BKF #66.
7. *Chicago Tribune,* January 26–29, 1934.

9: A STAR IS BORN

1. Toland, p. 195.
2. BKF #667.
3. Girardin, pp. 72–73.
4. *Chicago American,* Feb. 9, 1934.
5. Girardin, p. 74.
6. BKF #295.
7. Girardin, pp. 77–78.
8. Simmons, pp. 166–67.
9. Springfield *Leader,* Feb. 13, 1934.
10. Hamilton, *Public Enemy Number 1,* p. 33.
11. Phillips, pp. 175–76.
12. *Fugitives,* pp. 158–59.
13. Simmons, p. 127.
14. Winstead, unpublished manuscript, p. 24.

10: DILLINGER AND NELSON

1. This section, including dialogue, was taken from statements given to the FBI by all the participants, including Cahoon, Blunk, and Warden Baker. The statements are located in a series of Chicago reports from March to May 1935, Jodil #5583, #5692, #5711.
2. This version of events that Saturday is taken from FBI files and the Girardin manuscript. The dialogue is from Girardin.
3. Undated St. Paul and Minneapolis newspaper articles. Memo, Rosen to Tamm, March 14, 1936, Jodil #6648. Undated letter from Kidder relative to Helen Gandy, Jodil #6789.
4. *Sioux Falls Daily Argus-Leader,* March 6–7, 1934; South Dakota Hall of Fame magazine, vol. XXI, no. 2, Summer, 1995; Toland, pp. 220–24.
5. Clegg to Hoover, March 3, 1934, Jodil #83.
6. Hoover to Purvis, March 6, 1934, Jodil #93.
7. Cowley to Hoover, March 7, 1934, Jodil #128.
8. Purvis to Hoover, March 31, 1934, Jodil #226.
9. Mason City *Globe Gazette,* March 14, 1934.
10. Mason City *Globe Gazette,* August 21, 1973.
11. Mason City *Globe Gazette,* Feb. 5, 1982.
12. Mason City *Globe Gazette,* Dec. 24, 1942.
13. Toland, p. 237.
14. *New Republic,* June 6, 1934.
15. Mason City *Globe Gazette,* June 26, 1964.
16. Toland, p. 235.
17. Ibid, p. 237.
18. Mortensen statement, April 20, 1934, Jodil #754.

19. Cherrington statement, Jodil #2617.
20. Girardin, p. 121.
21. Ibid.
22. Letter quoted in Alanna Nash article, *Satellite Orbit* magazine, November 1984.
23. Hoover to Purvis, March 27, 1934, Jodil #204.

11: CRESCENDO

1. Testimony of Det. Henry Cummings, *U.S. v. Frechette.*
2. Frechette told her story in *Startling Detective Adventures,* September 1934.
3. Maccabee, p. 221.
4. Phillips, p. 182.
5. Hoover, memo to file, April 1, 1934, Jodil #269.
6. Notesteen's statement, which quotes Inspector Rorer, is included in Hugh Clegg's April 9, 1934, report to Hoover, Jodil #467.
7. Cowley, memo summarizing conversation with Clegg, April 19, 1934, Jodil #1574.
8. Hinton, p. 139.
9. *Methvin vs. Oklahoma,* p. 73.
10. Hubert Dillinger statement, April 11, 1934, Jodil #1090.
11. Ibid.
12. Cowley to Hoover, April 7, 1934, Jodil #367.
13. Girardin, p. 139.
14. Chicago summary report, April 18, 1934, Jodil #630. Purvis knew he had botched the arrest. It is the one major arrest he made that is not described in *American Agent.*
15. Girardin, p. 141.

12: DEATH IN THE NORTH WOODS

1. Associated and United Press dispatches, April 15, 1934.
2. Girardin, p. 143.
3. Ibid., p. 143.
4. Pat Cherrington statement, Chicago report, July 16, 1934, Jodil #2617x.
5. Ibid.
6. St. Paul report, July 16, 1934, Jodil #2655.
7. St. Paul report, May 14, 1934, Jodil #1460.
8. The LaPorte family's history is told in loving detail in a book written by one of their descendants, Ruth Dickerson Gardner, *Lunch at Boney's Mound.*
9. Wanatka statement, Jodil #935.
10. Ibid.
11. Cromie and Pinkston, p. 211.
12. Wanatka told this story often in later years. The details never varied. This version is taken from an interview with the Wisconsin historian Robert Gard.
13. Cromie and Pinkston, p. 208.
14. Ibid., p. 210.
15. Cherrington statement, Jodil #2617.
16. Nan Wanatka's original note is included in FBI files.
17. Toland, p. 270.

18. Ibid., pp. 270–71.
19. Hoover, memo to file, April 24, 1934, Jodil #1561.
20. One of the great pleasures of perusing the FBI files is reading the statements and reports of those at Little Bohemia. Clegg, Purvis, and Rorer each made multiple reports on the evening's events. Every other agent on the ground that night also made a report; some are long and detailed, others are a single paragraph.
21. Statement of Agent Virgil Peterson, May 9, 1934, Jodil #1409.
22. Pat Cherrington statement included in Chicago report, July 16, 1934, Jodil #2617.
23. Toland, p. 278. Mitchell statements, Jodil #934.
24. Lange statements in Chicago report, Jodil #934.

13: "AND IT'S DEATH FOR BONNIE AND CLYDE"

1. Washington *Times,* April 24, 1934.
2. Chicago *American,* April 27, 1934.
3. Hoover memo to file, April 25, 1934, Jodil #1044.
4. Hoover to Stanley, April 25, 1934, Jodil #882.
5. Statement of James Wilson, including in Chicago report, Sept. 29, 1934, Brekid #2918.
6. Memo summarizing Volney Davis FBI interview, August 26, 1935, Jodil #6344.
7. Chicago report, Sept. 9, 1935, Jodil #6381.
8. Edna Murray, "I Was a Karpis-Barker Gang Moll," *Startling Detective Adventures,* October 1936.
9. Ibid.
10. Murray, *Startling Detective Adventures.*
11. Chicago report, May 17, 1934, Jodil #1478.
12. The aborted raid is described in a Cincinnati report, May 2, 1934, Jodil #1118, and in a May 3, 1934, letter to Hoover from Connelley, Jodil #1787.
13. "Local woman recalls Dillinger hold-up," Fostoria *Review Times,* April 10, 1990.
14. "When the Dillinger gang visited Fostoria," Fostoria *Review Times,* January 15, 1981.
15. Hoover to Nathan, May 10, 1934, Jodil 1–8x.
16. Nathan to Hoover, June 1, 1934, Jodil #2505.
17. Purvis, pp. 285–86.
18. *Time,* April 23, 1934.
19. Indianapolis *News,* April 4, 1934.
20. Each of the agents at the Russ home was obliged to file memos on the stakeout in 1936 after Mrs. Russ complained of damage to her home.
21. Girardin, pp. 159–60.
22. "The Day They Shot Bonnie and Clyde," by Carroll Rich, p. 37, included in *Hunters and Healers,* University of North Texas Press, Denton, Texas, 1971.
23. Ibid., p. 37.
24. Winstead, p. 27.
25. *Methvin v. Oklahoma,* p. 135.
26. Much of the confusion surrounding the chronology of events lies in the timing of Methvin's "escape." Various accounts have placed it anywhere from Saturday evening, May 19 (Milner, Treherne, Hinton) to Monday evening, May 21 (Phillips). In his 1936 testimony in an

Oklahoma court, where he stood trial for the murder of Constable Cal Campbell, Methvin makes clear it happened on Tuesday morning, May 22.

27. Hinton, p. 159.
28. Phillips, p. 197. Ringgold *Record,* April 26, 1968.
29. Hinton, pp. 169–70.

14: NEW FACES

1. Girardin, pp. 162–63.
2. Memo, Cowley to Hoover, May 25, 1934, Jodil #1635.
3. Girardin, p. 170.
4. Ibid.
5. Clegg report, March 11, 1932, included in Hollis personnel file.
6. Ron Owens, *Oklahoma Justice,* Turner Publishing, 1995, p. 121.
7. Purvis to Hoover, June 1, 1934, Jodil #1810. Hoover to Cowley, May 28, 1934, Jodil #1685.
8. Hoover to Purvis, May 29, 1934, Jodil #1832.
9. Cowley to Hoover, May 29, 1934, Jodil #1707.
10. Purvis to Hoover, June 2, 1934, Jodil #1762.
11. Purvis to Hoover, June 1, 1934, Jodil #1810.
12. Hoover, memo to file, June 4, 1934, Jodil #1877.
13. Today Samuel Cowley, Jr., is a retiree living in Salt Lake City. Mr. Cowley was very helpful in sharing his mother's memories of his father.
14. Hoover memo, Jodil #1877.
15. Hoover, memo to file, June 4, 1934, Jodil #1819.
16. Memo, Hoover to Tamm, June 8, 1934, Jodil #1875.
17. Hoover, memo to file, June 5, 1934, Jodil #1806.
18. Girardin, p. 176.
19. Ibid., p. 182.
20. *New York Times,* June 29, 1834.
21. Girardin, p. 183.
22. Tamm to Hoover, June 9, 1934, Jodil #1899.
23. Omaha report, June 15, 1934, Jodil #2043; "How Iowa Rubbed Out Dillinger's Ace Gunman," *Startling Detective Adventures,* undated.
24. Girardin, p. 184.
25. Girardin, p. 195.
26. Girardin, pp. 202–3.
27. Girardin, pp. 197–98.
28. Girardin, pp. 189–90.
29. Memo for Hoover, June 29, 1934, Jodil #2454.
30. Fatso Negri debriefing in Portland, Oregon, report, Dec. 31, 1934, Jodil #5067.
31. *Michiana* magazine, June 17, 1984; South Bend *Tribune,* June 30–July 1, 1934, January 18, 1970.

15: THE WOMAN IN ORANGE

1. Girardin, pp. 203–4.
2. Hammond *Times,* Jan. 22, 1995.
3. Chicago *Tribune,* July 16–17, 1934, Chicago *Daily Times,* July 16, 1934.

4. Chicago report, Aug. 4, 1934, Jodil #3218.
5. Chicago report, July 31, 1934, Jodil #3241.
6. Girardin, pp. 210–11.
7. Ibid., pp. 211–12.
8. Ana Sage statement, Aug. 1, 1934, Jodil #3233.
9. The Harris letter was discovered in Sage's apartment during a search by Chicago police. It is described in detail in the *Chicago Daily Times,* July 25, 1934.
10. Negri debrief, Dec. 31, 1934.
11. Tamm to Cowley, July 23, 1934, Jodil #3182.
12. Every FBI agent involved that night subsequently filed memos detailing their activities. Most are brief, giving few details. Only a handful describe the scene on the nineteenth floor. The time of the assembly, 7:15, is given in Agent Bob Gillespie's memo.
13. Purvis vividly describes his feelings that night in *American Agent.*
14. Unpublished manuscript, John E. Welles, 1959.
15. *Chicago Tribune,* July 23, 1934.
16. Ibid.
17. *Chicago Tribune,* July 26, 1934.
18. *Chicago Daily Times,* July 23, 1934.
19. Hoover to Purvis, July 23, 1934. Purvis personnel file, #270.
20. *Chicago Tribune,* July 25, 1934.
21. Sage gave a detailed version of her days after Dillinger's death in a 1935 immigration hearing.
22. Hoover to Tamm, July 25, 1934, Jodil #1–17.
23. Hoover, memo to file, July 26, 1934, Jodil #3233.
24. Hoover to Tamm, July 27, 1934, Jodil #2966.
25. Agents Connor and Murphy to Cowley, Aug. 2, 1934, Jodil #3233.
26. Connelley to Cowley, Aug. 15, 1934.
27. *Chicago Tribune,* July 30, 1934.

16: THE SCRAMBLE

1. San Francisco report, Feb. 20, 1935, Jodil #5492.
2. Chicago report, Feb. 1, 1935, Jodil #5333.
3. Salt Lake City report, March 7, 1935, Jodil #5607.
4. San Francisco report, Aug. 18, 1934, Jodil #3596.
5. Benedict statement, San Francisco report, Jodil #4331, p. 45.
6. Negri statement, Chicago report, Jodil #5070, p. 32.
7. Negri article, July 1941. Negri used the pseudonym "Flo" for Backman.
8. Brantley to Floyd, May 18, 1934, KCM #1659.
9. Hoover to Cowley, May 18, 1934, KCM #1662.
10. Hoover to Cowley, May 31, 1934, KCM #1701.
11. Brantley to Hoover, June 15, 1934, KCM #1781.
12. Hoover to Tamm, June 23, 1934, KCM #1838.
13. Hoover to Nathan and Tamm, June 28, 1934, KCM #1868.
14. Kansas City report, Sept. 5, 1934.
15. Ibid.
16. Hoover to Cowley, Sept. 5, 1934, BKF #2791.

17. Cleveland report, August 25, 1936, BKF #12720.
18. *Cleveland Press,* Sept. 6, 1934.
19. BKF #2978.
20. BKF #2978, #2918.

17: A FIELD IN OHIO AND A HIGHWAY IN ILLINOIS

1. Newby to Tamm, Sept. 17, 1934, KCM #2517.
2. Hoover to Tamm, Sept. 23, 1934, KCM #2584.
3. Hoover to Tamm, Sept. 24, 1934, KCM #2585.
4. New Orleans report, Sept. 27, 1934, KCM #2574.
5. Galatas statement included in New Orleans report, KCM #2574.
6. Tamm to Hoover, Sept. 24, 1934, KCM, #2596.
7. Tamm to Hoover, Sept. 24, 1934, KCM #2659.
8. Tamm to Hoover, Sept. 25, 1934, KCM #2617.
9. Harvey to Hoover, Sept. 26, 1934, KCM #2568.
10. *Chicago Tribune,* Oct. 16, 1935.
11. Chase statement, Jodil #5488, p. 9.
12. Negri statement, Jodil #5271. Quotes taken from Negri article, *True Detective* magazine, July 1941.
13. Tamm, memo to file, October 12, 1934, Jodil #4207.
14. Hoover to Purvis, Sept. 13, 1934. Purvis personnel file, #291.
15. Hoover to Tamm, 7:35 P.M., Oct. 21, 1934, KCM #2854.
16. Hoover to Tamm, 1:00 P.M., Oct. 22, 1934, KCM #2701.
17. Hoover to Tamm, 5:45 P.M., Oct. 22, 1934, KCM #2903.
18. Newby memo, Oct. 24, 1934, KCM #2946.
19. Negri article, July 1941.
20. Chase statement, Jodil #5488.
21. Doris Lockerman article, *Chicago Tribune,* Oct. 17, 1935.
22. Tamm to Hoover, Jodil #4601.
23. Chicago report, Jodil #5813.
24. Hoover memo to file, Nov. 27, 1934, Jodil #4610.
25. Hoover memo to file, Nov. 27, 1934, Jodil #4611.
26. *Chicago American,* November 28, 1934.
27. Hoover memo to file, Nov. 28, 1934, Jodil #4665.
28. Chicago *American,* December 5, 1934.

18: THE LAST MAN STANDING

1. Tolson to Hoover, Dec. 4, 1934, BKF #3546.
2. Years later, Karpis clearly remembered this episode and the name "Kingman" (Karpis transcripts, tape 20, page 135). Both his instincts and his memory proved excellent. A confidential report on Kingman's trip to Havana is included in FBI files, BKF #3621.
3. Karpis transcripts, tape 20, p. 149.
4. Statements from all agents involved at BKF #4198.
5. BKF #3807.
6. BKF #3743.

7. BKF #3771.

8. "Barker's Cook Remembers Day," The Belleview (Fla.) *Leader,* Jan. 16, 1980; Ocala *Evening Star,* Jan. 16, 17, 1935; Toronto *Star,* Oct. 11, 1986.

9. New York *Evening Journal* magazine, March 3, 1935.

19: PAS DE DEUX

1. Cleveland report, Sept. 5, 1936, BKF #12794.

2. Richard Gid Powers, *G-Men: Hoover's FBI in American Popular Culture,* Southern Illinois University Press, 1983.

3. *Harper's,* November 1934.

4. Tamm to Hoover, Aug. 1, 1935, BKF #6886.

5. Little Rock report, Oct. 17, 1935, BKF #7721.

6. Tamm to Hoover, Feb. 4, 1936, BKF #9460.

7. Connelley to Brantley, Feb. 17, 1936, BKF #9581.

8. Nathan to Hoover, March 28, 1936, BKF #10245.

9. P. E. Foxworth to Hoover, March 28, 1936, BKF #10244.

10. Connelley to Hoover, March 30, 1936, BKF #10255.

11. Gentry, p. 182.

12. Ibid., pp. 184–87.

13. Tamm to Hoover, April 26, 1936, BKF #11004.

14. Fletcher to Connelley, April 25, 1936, BKF #11011.

15. Tolson to Hoover, April 27, 1936, BKF #11006X.

16. Cincinnati report, May 18, 1936, BKF #1165.

17. Hoover gave his version of events in a phone call to headquarters the next morning. T. D. Quinn, memo to file, May 2, 1936, BKF #11099.

18. New York *Evening Journal,* May 2, 1936.

19. *Chicago American,* May 2, 1936.

20. Karpis, p. 230.

21. Ibid., p. 236. This anecdote is confirmed by a contemporary news account.

EPILOGUE

1. Potter, p. 4.

2. Cited in Powers, p. 114.

3. Sandusky *Register,* December 11, 1993.

SELECTED BIBLIOGRAPHY

Alix, Ernest Kahlar. *Ransom Kidnapping in America, 1874–1974: The Creation of a Capital Crime.* Carbondale, Ill.: Southern Illinois University, 1978.

Barnes, Bruce. *Machine Gun Kelly: To Right a Wrong.* Perris, Calif.: Tipper, 1991. (Biography by Kelly's son. Excellent material on Kelly's early years. Less reliable on his crimes.)

Callahan, Clyde C., and Byron B. Jones. *Heritage of an Outlaw—the Story of Frank Nash.* Hobart, Okla.: Schoonmaker, 1979.

Clayton, Merle. *Union Station Massacre.* New York: Bobbs-Merrill, 1975. (Unreliable, but useful for Agent Joe Lackey's recitation of events leading to the massacre.)

Congdon, Don. *The '30s: A Time to Remember.* New York: Simon & Schuster, 1962.

Cook, Fred J. *The FBI Nobody Knows.* New York: Macmillan, 1964.

Cooper, Courtney Ryley. *Ten Thousand Public Enemies.* Boston: Little, Brown, 1935.

———. *Here's to Crime.* Boston: Little Brown, 1937.

Corey, Herbert. *Farewell, Mr. Gangster!* New York: D. Appleton-Century, 1936.

Cromie, Robert, and Joseph Pinkston. *Dillinger: A Short and Violent Life.* New York: McGraw Hill, 1962. (First detailed biography of Dillinger, overshadowed by Toland's *Dillinger Days.* Largely derived from newspaper clippings.)

de Toledano, Ralph. *J. Edgar Hoover, the Man in His Time.* New Rochelle, N.Y.: Arlington House, 1973.

Edge, L. L. *Run the Cat Roads.* New York: Dembner Books, 1981.

Ellis, George. *A Man Named Jones.* New York: Signet Books, 1963.

Fried, Albert. *The Rise and Fall of the Jewish Gangster in America.* Revised ed. New York: Columbia University Press, 1993.

Friedman, Lawrence M. *Crime and Punishment in American History.* New York: Basic Books, 1993.

Gardner, Ruth Dickerson. *Lunch at Boney's Mound: A Portrait of Family and Friends.* Privately published, 1997. (Lovingly produced family portrait of the LaPorte–Wanetka families.)

Gentry, Curt. *J. Edgar Hoover: The Man and the Secrets.* New York: W. W. Norton, 1991. (Superb Hoover biography.)

Girardin, Russell G., with William Helmer. *Dillinger: The Untold Story.* Bloomington, Ind.: Indiana University, 1994. (Girardin's manuscript, augmented by Helmer's excellent footnotes, sheds much new light on Dillinger's final weeks.)

Haley, J. Evetts. *Robbing Banks Was My Business.* Canyon, Tex.: Palo Duro Press, 1973. (Harvey Bailey's biography. Though Bailey's memory is spotty in places, Haley's book is one of only two in which Depression-era outlaws tell their side of the story.)

Hamilton, Floyd. *Public Enemy No. 1.* Dallas, Tex.: Acclaimed Books/International Prison Ministry, 1978.

Helmer, William, with Rick Mattix. *Public Enemies: America's Criminal Past, 1919–1940.* (An invaluable almanac-style overview of the War on Crime and the 1920s by two leading amateur historians.)

Hinton, Ted, with Larry Grove. *Ambush: The Real Story of Bonnie and Clyde.* Bryan, Tex.: Shoal Creek, 1979.

Hoover, J. Edgar. *Persons in Hiding.* Boston: Little, Brown, 1938.

Illman, Harry R. *Unholy Toledo: The True Story of Detroit's Purple-Licavoli Gang's Take-Over of an Ohio City.* San Francisco: Polemic Press, 1985.

Jenkins, John H., and H. Gordon Frost. *I'm Frank Hamer: The Life of a Texas Peace Officer.* Austin, Tex.: Pemberton Press, 1968.

Karpis, Alvin, with Bill Trent. *The Alvin Karpis Story.* New York: Coward-McCann & Geoghegan, 1971.

Karpis, Alvin, with Robert Livesey. *On the Rock.* Don Mills, Ontario: Musson/General, 1980.

King, Jeffrey S. *The Life and Death of Pretty Boy Floyd.* Kent, Ohio: Kent State University Press, 1998.

Kirchner, L. R. *Triple Cross Fire!: J. Edgar Hoover & the Kansas City Union Station Massacre.* Kansas City, Mo.: Janlar Books, 1993. (Avoid.)

———. *Robbing Banks: An American History, 1831–1999.* Rockville Centre, N.Y.: Sarpedon, 2000.

Kirkpatrick, E. E. *Crimes' Paradise: The Authentic Inside Story of the Urschel Kidnapping.* San Antonio, Tex.: Naylor, 1934.

Kobler, John. *Capone: The Life and World of Al Capone.* New York: DaCapo Press, 1992.

Larsen, Lawrence H., and Nancy J. Hulston. *Pendergast!* Columbia, Mo.: University of Missouri Press, 2000.

Louderback, Lew. *The Bad Ones: Gangsters of the '30s and Their Molls.* Greenwich, Conn.: Fawcett, 1968.

Maccabee, Paul. *John Dillinger Slept Here: A Crook's Tour of Crime and Corruption in St. Paul, 1920–1936.* St. Paul, Minn.: Minnesota Historical Press, 1995. (One of the very best books on St. Paul's role in the War on Crime, and a personal favorite.)

Milner, E. R. *The Lives and Times of Bonnie and Clyde.* Carbondale, Ill.: Southern Illinois University Press, 1996.

Newton, Willis, and Joe Newton, with Claude Stanush and David Middleton. *The Newton Boys: Portrait of an Outlaw Gang.* Austin, Tex.: State House, 1994.

Nickel, Steven, and William J. Helmer. *Baby Face Nelson: Portrait of a Public Enemy.* Nashville: Cumberland House, 2002.

Owens, Ron. *Oklahoma Justice: The Oklahoma City Police: A Century of Gunfighters, Gangsters and Terrorists.* Paducah, Ky.: Turner Publishing, 1995.

Parker, Emma, and Nell Barrow Cowan, with Jan Fortune. *Fugitives: The Story of Clyde Barrow and Bonnie Parker.* Dallas, Tex.: Ranger Press, 1934. Reprinted by Signet, 1968. (Still one of the two best books on Bonnie and Clyde, told by Clyde's sister and Bonnie's mother.)

Peterson, Virgil W. *Barbarians in Our Midst.* Boston: Little, Brown, 1952.

Phillips, John Neal. *Running with Bonnie and Clyde: The Ten Fast Years of Ralph Fults.* Norman, Okla.: University of Oklahoma Press, 1996. (Excellent book, much of it told by Clyde's onetime partner Ralph Fults.)

Potter, Claire Bond. *War on Crime: Bandits, G-Men, and the Politics of Mass Culture.* New Brunswick, N.J.: Rutgers University Press, 1998. (Outstanding academic analysis of the War on Crime period.)

Poulsen, Ellen. *Don't Call Us Molls: Women of the John Dillinger Gang.* Little Neck, N.Y.: Clinton Cook Publishing, 2002.

Powers, Richard Gid. *G-Men: Hoover's FBI in American Popular Culture.* Carbondale, Ill.: Southern Illinois University Press, 1983.

———. *Secrecy and Power: The Life of J. Edgar Hoover.* New York: Free Press, 1987.

Purvis, Melvin. *American Agent.* Garden City, N.Y.: Doubleday, Doran, 1936.

Quimby, Myron. *The Devil's Emissaries.* New York: A. S. Barnes, 1969.

Reddig, William M. *Tom's Town: Kansas City and the Pendergast Legend.* Philadelphia: J. P. Lippincott, 1947.

Ruth, David E. *Inventing the Public Enemy: The Gangster in American Culture, 1918–1934.* Chicago: University of Chicago Press, 1996.

Sanborn, Debra. *The Barrow Gang's Visit to Dexter.* Dexter, Iowa: Bob Weesner, 1976.

Simmons, Lee. *Assignment Huntsville: Memoirs of a Texas Prison Officer.* Austin, Tex.: University of Texas, 1957.

Steele, Phillip W., with Marie Barrow Scoma. *The Family Story of Bonnie and Clyde.* Gretna, La.: Pelican, 2000.

Sullivan, William, with Bill Brown. *The Bureau: My Thirty Years in Hoover's FBI.* New York: W. W. Norton, 1979.

Summers, Anthony. *Official and Confidential: The Secret Life of J. Edgar Hoover.* New York: G. P. Putnam's Son, 1993.

Swierczynski, Duane. *This Here's a Stick-Up: The Big Bad Book of American Bank Robbery.* Indianapolis, Ind.: Alpha Books, 2002.

Toland, John. *Dillinger Days.* New York: Random House, 1963.

Touhy, Roger, with Ray Brennan. *The Stolen Years.* Cleveland, Ohio: Pennington, 1959.

Treherne, John. *The Strange History of Bonnie and Clyde.* New York: Stein & Day, 1984.

Unger, Robert. *The Union Station Massacre: The Original Sin of Hoover's FBI.* Kansas City, Mo.: Andrews McMeel Publishing, 1997. (Definitive.)

Wallis, Michael. *The Life and Times of Charles Arthur Floyd.* New York: St. Martin's, 1992. (Excellent biography, with full cooperation of Floyd family.)

Watkins, T. H. *The Great Depression: America in the 1930s.* Boston: Little, Brown, 1993.

————. *The Hungry Years: A Narrative History of the Great Depression in America.* New York: Henry Holt, 1999.

Webb, Walter Prescott. *The Texas Rangers: A Century of Frontier Defense.* Boston: Houghton Mifflin, 1935.

Whitehead, Don. *The FBI Story: A Report to the People.* New York: Random House, 1956.

Winter, Robert. *Mean Men: The Sons of Ma Barker.* Danbury, Conn.: Rutledge Books, 2000. (Unusual if well-researched book on the Barker family in the pre–War on Crime period.)

ACKNOWLEDGMENTS

For forty years much of the new material uncovered on the War on Crime period has been un-earthed by a dedicated band of amateur historians, many of whom provided tremendous help to me during my four years of research. Probably no one person has amassed more information on Depression-era outlaws than Rick Mattix of Bussey, Iowa, who opened his files to me and was always there to answer a thorny question. Thomas Smusyn, who knows more about John Dillinger than any man alive, was an expert guide through Dillinger's old Chicago haunts.

I am deeply indebted to Paul Maccabee, whose history of the St. Paul underworld, *John Dillinger Slept Here,* is one of the finest books produced on the War on Crime period; to Robert Unger, who knows more about the Kansas City Massacre than anyone; to Bill Helmer, the dean of Dillinger historians; to Bob Bates in Oregon; to Curt Gentry, whose J. Edgar Hoover biography remains the finest in or out of print; and to Richard Jones in Oklahoma City, who allowed me to borrow from his great trove of 1930s-era detective magazines.

Dawn Trent, the widow of Bill Trent, Alvin Karpis's ghostwriter, kindly lent me thousands of pages of interview transcripts that her husband made with Karpis in the late 1960s; these transcripts are a source of much new information on the period. A former FBI archivist, Susan Rosenthal, pro-vided files on former FBI agents. Thanks as well to historians Glenn Jordan in Monroe, Louisiana; Arch McKinney in East Chicago; Robert Beresford in Wellesville, Ohio; Clyde Woolridge in McAlester, Oklahoma; and Orville Albritton and Bobbie McClain in Hot Springs, Arkansas.

A huge thank-you to the staff at *The Grapevine* in Quantico, Virginia, who allowed me to spend three days wading through back issues, and to the wonderful archivists at FBI headquar-ters in Washington. Thanks, too, to the children and extended families of the many FBI men and prosecutors who fought the War on Crime, including Alston Purvis, Melvin Purvis's son; Samuel Cowley, Jr.; Doris Lockerman; Jared McDade in Ossining, New York; John Davis Rorer; Kristina Metcalfe, daughter of James Metcalfe; Werner Hanni, Jr.; Frazier Reams, Jr.; and the families of John Welles, Jay Newman, John Madala, and Hugh Clegg.

Thanks to the staff at the Chicago Public Library; the Chicago Historical Society; the Minnesota Historical Society in St. Paul; the Oklahoma Historical Society; the Missouri Historical Society; the J. Evetts Haley Museum in Midland, Texas; the Red River Historical Museum in Sherman, Texas; and the Hot Springs Historical Society in Hot Springs, Arkansas; the federal archives in College Park, Maryland, and Chicago, and Kansas City; as well as the Ohio public libraries in Cleveland, Akron, Toledo, Bluffton, Lima, and Dayton; the Indiana public libraries in Muncie, Fort Wayne, Indianapolis, Crown Point, East Chicago, Gary, Peru, Hammond, and Terre Haute; the Texas public libraries in Dallas, Fort Worth, Coleman, Waco, Austin, Houston, San Marcos, and San Antonio; the Iowa public libraries in Des Moines and Mason City; the Missouri public libraries in Kansas City, Joplin, and Springfield; the New Jersey public libraries in Summit, Maplewood, Newark, and Atlantic City; the Florida public libraries in Miami, Fort Lauderdale, Ocala, Orlando, and Daytona Beach; the Arkansas public libraries in Little Rock and Hot Springs; the public library in Memphis; the Georgia public library in Albany; and the Wisconsin public libraries in Lake Geneva and Elkhorn.

I could not have attempted this book were it not for the patience of *Vanity Fair*'s editor, Graydon Carter, who looked the other way when I should have been writing stories for him. Anna Bakolas was a terrific researcher in the early months of this project. Marla Burrough, Doug Stumpf, Steve Swartz, and Jordan Glatt gave invaluable reviews of the manuscript. Andrew Wylie and Jeffrey Posternak at the Wylie Agency remain the best literary agents in the business. This project began as a television miniseries for the Home Box Office network; only after research began did I realize I loved it all too much not to write a book. Thanks to Brian Siberell for guiding me through Hollywood.

At Penguin Press, Scott Moyers always believed in this project and gave terrific advice in winnowing the final manuscript. His trusty assistant, Sophie Fels, kept the trains running on time. Melissa Goldstein ransacked archives across the country to gather the photographs. Thanks as well to my parents, Mac and Mary Burrough, in Temple, Texas, who are never too busy to listen. And as always, my greatest thanks goes to my family, Marla, Griffin, and Dane, who never complain about all the long hours Daddy spends alone in his office.

INDEX

Tewksbury, Merle, 95
Thomas, Grace, 511
Thomas, Lowell, 489
Thompson, Edwin R., 104
Thompson, Mary Walker, 102–3
Thompson, Tommy, 290*n*
Thompson, William "Big Bill," 102
Tic, Arthur, 548
Time, 7, 70, 344
Toland, John, 32, 64*n,* 136, 242*n,* 308, 361
Tollett, Raymond, 538
Tolson, Clyde, 54, 537, 538, 541
Touhy, Roger, 66–68, 101*n,* 104, 113, 114, 169, 434*n,* 470, 545, 548–49
Trainor, Walter, 428–29
Travelers Insurance Company, 16
Trent, Bill, 521
True Detective, 200
True Detective Adventures, 244*n*
Truman, Harry, 48
Tyler, Ethel, 472*n*

Underhill, Wilber, 55, 60, 171, 308
    arrest of, 178–80
Unger, Robert, 521*n*
Union Station Massacre, The (Unger), 521*n*
Untouchables (television show), xii
Urschel, Berenice, 68–70, 71–72, 80, 81, 83–84
Urschel, Charles F., 68, 75, 80, 83–84, 85, 87–88, 90–91, 93, 123, 543
Urschel kidnapping, 68–70, 75, 146, 434*n,* 543, 549
    debriefing of Urschel in, 87–88
    FBI and, 72, 75, 81, 83, 84, 87–93, 119, 122
    hunt for Kelly in, 92–93
    Kelly and, 69, 72–74, 75, 80–83
    ransom negotiations in, 80–81
    ransom paid in, 82–83

Shannon raid and, 89–92
Urschel released in, 83–84
Utah, U.S.S., 137

Vande Houton, Albert, 100–101
Vande Houton, George, 100–101
Van Meter, Homer, xvii, 106*n,* 107, 178, 221, 231–32, 257–58, 267, 275, 290, 292–93, 295, 300, 326–27, 330*n,* 333, 334, 335, 336, 337, 338–40, 342, 346, 362, 363, 364, 366, 378, 379, 380, 381, 382, 388, 393–94, 396, 397, 410, 412, 415, 421, 434, 533
    background of, 138
    cosmetic surgery of, 375
    death of, 422–23, 435
    in First National Bank robberies, 175–76, 250–54, 255
    gunshot wound of, 386–87
    in Little Bohemia episode, 301, 303–5, 314–17
    in Merchants Bank robbery, 383–87
    Nelson's confrontation with, 383–84
    in St. Paul shoot-out, 270–71
    in Security National Bank robbery, 245
Vetterli, Reed, 48, 49, 52, 53–55, 146, 520, 545
Vidler, William, 328, 331–32
Viosca, Rene, 448
Von Beulow, Count, 102
Voss, Henry, 300, 304–7, 315, 320
Voss, Ruth LaPorte, 300, 302, 305–6, 307

Wagner, Howard, 384–85
Wakelin, Joe, 533*n,* 537
Walker, P. E., 377
Wallis, Michael, 521
Walsh, Thomas, 9, 14
Walters, Tom, 251–52
Wanatka, Emil, 301–3, 305–6, 313, 318–19, 321, 329, 550

ONE OF *THE WASHINGTON POST'S* TEN
BEST BOOKS OF THE YEAR

A BEST BOOK OF 2018 SELECTION BY *PEOPLE*,
NPR, *ESQUIRE*, *ELLE*, *WIRED*, AND REFINERY29

"[A] rousing look at the political uses of this supposedly unfeminine emotion.... Written with energy and conviction . . . galvanizing reading." —*THE NEW YORK TIMES BOOK REVIEW*

"Urgent, enlightened . . . well timed for this moment even as they transcend it, the kind of accounts often reviewed and discussed by women but that should certainly be read by men.... Realistic and compelling . . . Traister eloquently highlights the challenge of blaming not just forces and systems, but individuals." —*THE WASHINGTON POST*

"Traister specializes in writing about feminism and politics, and she knows the turf.... Traister is especially astute in emphasizing the ways in which black women laid the cornerstones for women's activism in this country.... Feminism forces certain complexities into the stream of our daily lives, and Traister has a great gift for articulating them." —*TIME*

"While the anger of men is seen as 'stirring' and 'downright American,' women's is 'the screech of nails on our national chalkboard,' asserts journalist Traister in this invigorating look at the achievements of angry women from Carrie Nation to Beyoncé to the Parkland high school students. Through this lens she revisits the 2016 election, [the] #blacklivesmatter and #metoo movement[s] (including her own Harvey Weinstein story), and cites a study showing you can tolerate pain longer—*damn!*—if you curse. Perfectly timed and inspiring." —*PEOPLE* (BOOK OF THE WEEK)

"Cathartic . . . A celebration of a catalytic force that burns ever brighter today." —*O, THE OPRAH MAGAZINE*

"A deeply researched treatise on female anger—its sources, its challenges, and its propulsive political power." —*ESQUIRE*

"A gripping call to action that portends greater liberty and justness for all." —*KIRKUS REVIEWS* (STARRED REVIEW)

"[A] rousing look at the political uses of this supposedly unfeminine emotion . . . written with energy and conviction . . . galvanizing reading."
—THE NEW YORK TIMES BOOK REVIEW

"Urgent, enlighten[ed] . . . well timed for this moment even as they transcend it, the kind of accounts often reviewed and discussed by women but that should certainly be read by men. . . . Realistic and compelling . . . Traister eloquently highlights the challenge of blaming not just forces and systems, but individuals."
—THE WASHINGTON POST

"While the anger of men is seen as 'stirring' and 'downright American,' women's is 'the screech of nails on our national chalkboard,' asserts journalist Traister in this invigorating look at the achievements of angry women, from Carrie Nation to Beyoncé to the Parkland High School students. Through this lens she revisits the 2016 election, #blacklivesmatter and the #metoo movement[s] (including her own Harvey Weinstein story), and cites a study showing you can tolerate pain longer—damn!—if you curse. Perfectly timed and inspiring."
—PEOPLE (BOOK OF THE WEEK)

"Traister specializes in writing about feminism and politics, and she knows the turf . . . especially astute in emphasizing the ways in which black women laid the cornerstones for women's activism in this country. . . . Feminism forces certain complexities into the stream of our daily lives, and Traister has a great gift for articulating them."
—TIME MAGAZINE

"Cathartic . . . A celebration of a catalytic force that burns ever brighter today."
—O, THE OPRAH MAGAZINE

"From suffragettes to #metoo, Traister's book is a hopeful, maddening compendium of righteous feminine anger, and the good it can do when wielded efficiently—and collectively."
—VANITY FAIR

"An admirably rousing narrative."

—*THE ATLANTIC*

"A resounding polemic against political, cultural, and personal injustices in America. . . . With articulate vitriol backed by in-depth research, Traister validates American women's anger. . . . Traister has meticulously culled smart, timely, surprising quotations from women as well as men. The combined strength of these many individual voices and stories gives the book tremendous gravity. . . . A gripping call to action that portends greater liberty and justness for all."

—*KIRKUS REVIEWS* (STARRED REVIEW)

"A trenchant analysis . . . Traister argues forcefully that women are an 'oppressed majority in the United States,' kept subjugated partly by racial divisions among the group. Traister closes with a reminder to women not to lose sight of their anger—even when things improve slightly and 'the urgency will fade . . . if you yourself are not experiencing' injustice or look away from it."

—*PUBLISHERS WEEKLY* (STARRED REVIEW)

"Timely and absorbing, Traister's fiery tome is bound to attract attention and discussion. Traister takes a deep dive into the current political climate to explore the contemporary and historical relationship women have with anger and the ramifications of expressing and suppressing feminine rage. Traister uses . . . startlingly obvious double standard[s] to explore how attaching negative connotations to women's anger has always been used to silence and dismiss them."

—*BOOKLIST* (STARRED REVIEW)

"*Good and Mad* is Rebecca Traister's ode to women's rage—an extensively researched history and analysis of its political power. It is a thoughtful, granular examination: Traister considers how perception (and tolerance) of women's anger shifts based on which women hold it (*cough* white women *cough*) and who they direct it toward; she points to the ways in which women are shamed for or gaslit out of their righteous emotion. And she proves, vigorously, why it's so important for women to own and harness their rage—how any successful revolution depends on it."

—*BUZZFEED*

"Women are angry, and Rebecca Traister is just the person to chart the topography of their rage, its causes, and its effects. . . . A galvanizing, timely study of righteous rage."

—*ELLE*

"With Traister's incisive prose and a topic that couldn't be more timely, this book is sure to be a fiery read."

—*HUFFINGTON POST*

"A deeply researched treatise on female anger—its sources, its challenges, and its propulsive political power."

—*ESQUIRE*

"Brilliant and bracing."

—*THE NATION*

"[Traister] writes with convincing clarity . . . a feel-good book."

—*JEZEBEL*

"A bracing, elucidating look at how transformative it can be for women to harness our rage, and how important it is to use that anger, that energy, for revolution."

—*NYLON*

"Brilliant and impassioned, and yes, angry."

—*MINNEAPOLIS STAR TRIBUNE*

"*Good and Mad* comes out at just the right time . . . the [Kavanaugh] hearing and its aftermath just proved the point Traister was making all along."

—*MOTHER JONES*

"Traister's reported manifesto on feminism after Trump . . . offers a forceful . . . inventory of the ways in which women's anger in the public sphere is exaggerated, pathologized, and used to discredit them in a manner unimaginable for men."

—*BOOKFORUM*

"An exploration of the transformative power of female anger and its ability to transcend into a political movement . . . Read this."

—*PUREWOW*

"One of our country's wisest writers on gender and politics."

—*PORTLAND MONTHLY*

"Every fifty years since the French Revolution there's been an uprising on behalf of women's rights—we're in the middle of one right now—and each time around a fresh chorus of voices is heard, making the same righteous bid for social and political equality, only with more force and more eloquence than the time before. Among today's strongest voices is the one that belongs to Rebecca Traister. Deeply felt and richly researched, her new book, *Good and Mad*, is one of the best accounts I have read of the cumulative anger women feel, coming up against their centuries-old subordination. Read it!"

—VIVIAN GORNICK

"Rebecca Traister has me convinced in this deftly and powerfully argued book that there will be no twenty-first-century revolution until women once again own the power of their rage. Righteous fury leaps off every page of this book, with example after example, from the present and the past, coaxing, chiding, and indeed reminding us that the political uses of women's anger have been good for America. As I read, my blood started pumping, my fist tightened, and my spirit said, "Hell yeah! We aren't going down without a fight." Women's anger rightly placed and soundly focused can be good for America, once again. In fact, it is essential. Tell the truth: We're all sick and tired of being sick and tired. It's high time we got good and mad."

—DR. BRITTNEY COOPER, author of *Eloquent Rage*

ALSO BY REBECCA TRAISTER

All the Single Ladies:
Unmarried Women and the Rise of an Independent Nation

Big Girls Don't Cry:
The Election That Changed Everything for American Women

GOOD

AND

MAD

THE REVOLUTIONARY POWER OF
WOMEN'S ANGER

REBECCA TRAISTER

SIMON & SCHUSTER PAPERBACKS

NEW YORK LONDON TORONTO SYDNEY NEW DELHI

Simon & Schuster Paperbacks
An Imprint of Simon & Schuster, Inc.
1230 Avenue of the Americas
New York, NY 10020

First Simon & Schuster trade paperback edition September 2019

SIMON & SCHUSTER PAPERBACKS and colophon are
registered trademarks of Simon & Schuster, Inc.

For information about special discounts for bulk purchases,
please contact Simon & Schuster Special Sales at
1-866-506-1949 or business@simonandschuster.com.

The Simon & Schuster Speakers Bureau can bring authors to your live event.
For more information or to book an event, contact the
Simon & Schuster Speakers Bureau at 1-866-248-3049
or visit our website at www.simonspeakers.com.

Interior design by Ruth Lee-Mui

Manufactured in the United States of America

1   3   5   7   9   10   8   6   4   2

The Library of Congress has cataloged the hardcover edition as follows:

Names: Traister, Rebecca, author.
Title: Good and mad : the revolutionary power of women's anger / Rebecca Traister.
Description: New York : Simon & Schuster, 2018.
Identifiers: LCCN 2018035975| ISBN 9781501181795 (hardback) |
ISBN 9781501181818 (trade paperback) | ISBN 9781501181801 (ebook)
Subjects: LCSH: Feminism—United States—History—21st century. |
Women—United States—Political activity—History—21st century. |
Anger—Social aspects. | BISAC: HISTORY / United States / 21st Century. |
HISTORY / Social History. | SOCIAL SCIENCE / Women's Studies.
Classification: LCC HQ1421 .T73 2018 | DDC 305.420973/0905—dc23
LC record available at https://urldefense.proofpoint.com/v2/url?u=https-3A__lccn.loc.gov_2
018035975&d=DwIFAg&c=jGUuvAdBXp_VqQ6t0yah2g&r=BLtwNjxI6xU1TowZZXPw62r
xL1h5Yh02Ol72-V1YNSunoH38hlyco6RBfK8BXD8O&m=1-8SAAVvrYO8O4-9Tmy6PNfP
kpxpFrLQsX5Rwr9hOco&s=6XpyD8_k5d6Qx1HbP7lppOO_vBz4qSPeoTSo_v3ugIg&e=

ISBN 978-1-5011-8179-5
ISBN 978-1-5011-8181-8
ISBN 978-1-5011-8180-1 (ebook)

For Bella and Rosie

Do not put such unlimited power into the hands of the husbands. Remember, all men would be tyrants if they could. If particular care and attention is not paid to the ladies, we are determined to foment a rebellion, and will not hold ourselves bound by any laws in which we have no voice or representation.

—ABIGAIL ADAMS

The Feminine
Is not
Dead
Nor is she
Sleeping

Angry, yes,
Seething, yes.

Biding her time;

Yes.
Yes.

—ALICE WALKER

Contents

GOOD
AND
MAD

INTRODUCTION

When I was hosting my CNBC show, it was ten years ago [2008] during the crisis. I was counseling people daily who'd lost every penny. It was heartbreaking and intense. I had on the head of the SEC at the time and asked him some pointed questions about his department's lack of oversight. I got pulled into the executive producer's office after we wrapped—was forced to sit and watch the segment, then lectured about how I looked "angry." All I did was not smile. My jaw was tight. My eyes, maybe burning a bit. My response: "I was and am angry." Soon after, another host has a meltdown on the floor of the stock exchange, screaming in anger, *male*, and he's lauded as starting the Tea Party. I mean . . . *Fuck it!*

—Carmen Rita Wong

"Get your fucking hands off me, goddamn it!" bellowed Florynce Kennedy, enormous peace sign earrings flying, her head wrapped in a red turban. "Don't touch me, you motherfucker!"

It was an electrifying interaction in the midst of the 1972 Democratic National Convention in Miami. Kennedy, the black feminist and lawyer, was aiming all her ire at a bunch of white network news guys, including CBS's Mike Wallace and Dan Rather, who were taking a break on the mostly empty convention floor; for the most part, the men were showing little interest in Kennedy's fury. But one was trying to calm her and persuade her to back away by putting his hands on her. "The next son of a bitch that touches a woman is gonna get kicked in the balls," she vowed.

In 1972, Shirley Chisholm—the first black woman ever elected to Congress—had run for the presidency and made it all the way to the convention. The party's national gathering had been a wild one, thanks in no small part to the participation of the National Women's Political Caucus, which had been founded the previous year by Chisholm, Kennedy, and other feminists and civil rights leaders including Gloria Steinem, Betty Friedan, and Dorothy Height.[1] In Miami, they'd convened and argued: over Chisholm's candidacy; over the eventual nominee, George McGovern; over the Equal Rights Amendment; and over a controversial abortion plank proposed for the party's platform.[2] And as it was all unfolding, they'd gotten almost no television coverage.

This was what had led Kennedy and a group of other women that included Sandra Hochman—a white feminist poet, who had been given

$15,000 by independent film producers to make a documentary about feminists at the convention—to storm the TV crews and reporters gathered on the convention's floor during a down moment.

The powerful newsmen had sat, silent and amused, some not looking up from their newspapers, as the scrum of women had berated them. The women's fury had only built in response to the men's inattention to it, bubbling over at the couple of guys who'd tried to hush them.

Hochman's camera crew had recorded it all for her documentary, which would be called *Year of the Woman*. The film captured so much of the gendered derision and dismissal that was provoking those women to scream their heads off: footage of the news crews who wouldn't cover Chisholm, instead falling all over Liz Renay, a beautiful stripper and actress; a Democratic power broker telling Hochman that there *were* women working on George McGovern's campaign, "so far mostly in the childcare centers and things like that"; McGovern's dashing young campaign manager, Gary Hart, then two years away from his own bid for the Senate, telling Hochman that his boss wouldn't pick a female vice presidential candidate because there was no "satisfactory woman candidate . . . qualified to be president of the United States." (Chisholm, then in her second congressional term, had already worked to expand the food stamp program as well as the Special Supplemental Nutrition Program for Women, Infants, and Children; she had pushed a $10 billion subsidized childcare bill, a version of which would be introduced by Walter Mondale and passed by Congress before Richard Nixon vetoed it. For his running mate, McGovern would wind up selecting Thomas Eagleton, a senator from Missouri who had not disclosed his previous history of depression treatments and had to resign from the ticket eighteen days after having been chosen.)

Hochman's movie played for five nights in New York City's Greenwich Village to sold-out crowds in 1973, and then, except for a handful of screenings, mostly disappeared from public view for forty-two years. In 2004, the *Washington Post* described *Year of the Woman* as having been "too radical, too weird, and too far ahead of its time for any distributor to touch."[3] When, in 2015, I was assigned to write about it as a feminist journalist heading into the 2016 presidential election, I immediately understood what had made it so charged and dangerous, what had made it *too much*: it was a celluloid time capsule, its wholly unfiltered view of women's outrage, acute and strange to contemporary ears and eyes, trapped in amber.

"We are people that have been left out!" Hochman shouts in the film, and it's hard to disagree with her frustration, although it's also hard not to notice that she is wearing a papier-mâché crocodile mask while screaming. "People don't take women seriously. They make them into freaks. So I say, as a poet, be a freak." The whole documentary is filled with women activists acting, from a 2015 vantage point, like freaks: wearing sparkly eyeglass frames, snorkeling masks, and Mickey Mouse ears. They sing an anthem to the tune of the "Battle Hymn of the Republic," appropriated by the feminist songwriter Meredith Tax, via the Black Panthers.[4]

> *Mine eyes have seen the glory of the flame of women's rage*
> *Kept smoldering for centuries, now burning in this age*
> *We no longer will be prisoners in that same old gilded cage*
> *That's why we're marching on . . .*
> *You think that you can buy us off with crummy wedding rings*
> *You never give us half the profit that our labor brings*
> *Our anger eats into us, we'll no longer bend to kings,*
> *That's why we're marching on . . .*

This view—of anger burning raw and hot, profane and freakish; of the men who controlled the national popular narrative about women, politics, and power; who tried to get Flo Kennedy to stop yelling by putting their *fucking hands* on her—brought a jolting realization when I first saw it three years ago: that the freakishness was, as Hochman noted, a by-product of un-adulterated fury. A desperate *rage* at being manhandled, ignored, sidelined, and not taken seriously was driving this group of revolutionaries—some of them leading public figures in the still-coalescing second-wave feminist movement—to behave outlandishly. Their frustration at the seeming im-possibility of their project was being disgorged, superseding common sense about decorum and polite discourse. They would do *anything* to get people to really hear how livid they were, lizard cosplay its own furious reflection of the amusement and contempt with which these powerful men regarded them.

Back in that summer of 2015, when I watched these giddy scenes of

cascading female wrath, wrath aimed at men—who demeaned and diminished and degraded women, who ignored them and touched them
against their will, who bullied and insulted them and refused to take them
seriously—they felt retro, like a relic of an angry second-wave past. Here we
were, in the second term of our first black president, on the verge of actually
running a woman for the presidency who was by all estimations the favorite, a woman whose future as president of the United States of America, we
were repeatedly assured, was so inevitable that its history-making character
was barely discernible. It felt a world away from the era in which cameras
wouldn't even cover Shirley Chisholm's convention speech.

While I understood, and made my living writing about, the persistent—
and in many ways expanding—inequities faced by all kinds of Americans,
especially those who were not white men, the outward signs of progress
were so visible, so indisputable, that it was hard to conceive of being so bel-
ligerent. Privately, I yearned for such open, unapologetic confrontation of
the men, and the male-designed systems, that until now had kept women
from ever becoming president—or from holding any comparable share of
political, social, or economic power—but I understood that they would
feel anachronistic, theatric, and unnecessary in an age in which there were
more women in colleges and graduate schools than men and our next
president was probably going to be a woman.

Yet just two and half years later, while taking the subway home from
the second annual Women's March, protests conceived in response to the
inauguration of President Donald Trump, I scrolled through images on my
social media feeds and saw another cascade of wrath. There were pictures
of the marchers, middle fingers raised in vivid loathing at buildings owned
by the president, who was of course *not* a woman, but rather a white supremacist, admitted sexual harasser, and businessman who'd capitalized
on the fury of white America and male America to defeat a woman and
replace the black man who'd previously held the job.

Some of the women I'd stood near at this 2018 march had held an effigy
of Trump's testicles in the air, decorated with a poof of orange hair. Others
had depicted him as a pile of excrement. I looked at homemade signs from
across the nation, where protests had, for the second year in a row, taken
place not just in New York and Los Angeles and Washington, but in Bangor,

Anchorage, Austin, and Shreveport: "Fuck you, you fucking fuck," read one of my favorites. "Feminazis against Actual Nazis," "Fuck the Patriarchy," and "Angry Women Will Change the World" were other examples. One woman had cut out a hole for her head and written around it, "Resisting Bitch Face."

Many others held aloft signs that read "#metoo"—in one case: "me *fucking* too"—the phrase a reference to activist Tarana Burke's campaign against pervasive sexual violence inflicted on women and girls, now describing the reckoning with workplace sexual assault and harassment that had burned through the media in preceding months, a conflagration in which many powerful men had been relieved of their jobs. The #metoo movement had felt almost like a forty-five-year-late return on Flo Kennedy's promise that "The next son of a bitch that touches a woman is gonna get kicked in the balls."

And then, on the Instagram feed of a friend in San Francisco, I saw her, like something out of a 1972 fever dream: a woman riding BART, wearing enormous lizard slippers strapped above her sandals and socks, a soft, sparkly, green reptilian boob-bib across her front, and a sharp-toothed lizard's mask over her head. She was carrying a sign.

"Goddess-zilla got woke. Watch out."

This is not an emotional exploration of women's anger. There are already long, fascinating volumes about the psychology and resonance of anger within our personal relationships, with more writers out there wrestling with the internal dimensions of the rage women are feeling and expressing anew. Some posit that women are inherently angry, others that women need to harness more of their fury. There are self-help books and also critical examinations of the ways in which women's anger at their subjugation plays out within their families, partnerships, friendships, and at work. This is not that book, though it will certainly touch on how personal rage and frustration have felt to many women, and the ways that they are echoed in political discourse, keeping in mind that for women, the personal is indeed always political.

But more broadly: this is about the specific nexus of women's anger and American *politics*, about how the particular dissatisfactions and resentments of America's women have often ignited movements for social change and progress. It is an exploration of how an impulse that many women have taken pains to hide or disguise or distance themselves from—the impulse to be really mad—has been crucial in determining their political power and social standing, how women's rage has played parts in revolutionary social movements, and how it has shaped how women leaders and political candidates have been received.

In the United States, we have never been taught how noncompliant, insistent, furious women have shaped our history and our present, our activism and our art. We should be.

These stories exist in other cultures. *Lysistrata* is an ancient yarn about women so angry at their husbands' propensity for combat that they withhold sex until the fighting stops (a particularly self-defeating approach to female satisfaction, but one that emphasized women's power with its assurance that "no man is ever going to get satisfaction if the woman doesn't choose that he should"). The Greeks also tell the tale of Thaïs, a courtesan and companion of Alexander the Great, who urged her lover to burn down the temple of Persepolis as revenge for Persian king Xerxes's destruction of the Temple of Athena during his attack on Athens one hundred and fifty years earlier. In real life, it was Parisian women, furious and starving, who rioted over the high price of bread, leading a march to Versailles in October of 1789 that would help kick off the French Revolution and ultimately dethrone King Louis the XVI. In 2003 in Liberia, after fourteen years of civil war, a group of the nation's women—Muslim and Christian, indigenous and Americo-Liberian—joined together, their anger at the ravages of war put to work in a call for its end. "In the past we were silent, but after being killed, raped, dehumanized, and infected with diseases . . . war has taught us that the future lies in saying NO to violence and YES to peace!"[5] the Liberian activist Leymah Gbowee declared to a crowd of raging women at the start of their crusade. It took two years of protest, but in 2005, the women's mass action ended with the election of the nation's first female president, Ellen Johnson Sirleaf.

While we in the United States may not have been told the stories, our nation, too, has been transformed by women's anger—in response not just to sexism, but also to racism, homophobia, capitalist excess, to the many inequities to which women and those around them have been exposed. In *A Place of Rage*, a 1991 documentary about black women activists and artists, the poet June Jordan, whose writing was a tender chronicle of rage at having her liberties restricted "because I am the wrong sex, the wrong age, the wrong skin," recalled the event that brought her to her political and ideological sensibilities. In her childhood in Bedford-Stuyvesant in Brooklyn, a young man in her neighborhood was beaten on his roof by the police in a case of mistaken identity. "To see this boy I idolized, who belonged to us, in the sense of our block . . . disfigured by these strangers who came in with all this force and license to use that force was really terrifying. And also it hardened me early on in a kind of place of rage."

It's crucial to remember that women's anger has been received—and often vilified or marginalized—in ways that have reflected the very same biases that provoked it: black women's fury is treated differently from white women's rage; poor women's frustrations are heard differently from the ire of the wealthy. Yet despite the varied and unjust ways America has dismissed or derided the rages of women, those rages have often borne substantive change, alterations to the nation's rules and practices, its very fabric.

This book is about women so angry at slavery and lynching that they risked their lives and reputations and pioneered new forms of public expression for women, including speeches in front of mixed-gender and mixed-race audiences; about women so furious at their lack of a franchise that they walked 150 miles from New York City to Albany to petition for the vote, went on hunger strikes, and picketed outside the White House. Women so angry that they stayed angry for the decades—their lifetimes—it took to get the right to vote, first via the Nineteenth Amendment and then the Voting Rights Act, their rage leading them to acts of civil disobedience—marches and sit-ins and voting when it was not legal to do so—for which they would be jailed, beaten. Women who took conversations that had historically been whispered and chose instead to broadcast them via open-air rallies and in the pages of newspapers and in lawsuits and in front of political conventions and judiciary committees.

Anger has often been the sparking impetus for long-lasting, legal, or institutional reform in the United States. It is, in fact, the founding, canonical narrative of the nation's revolutionary rupture from England. Yet somehow the rage has rarely been acknowledged as righteous and patriotic when it has originated with women, though women have often taken pains to mimic or reference the language and sentiments of America's founding while making their own angry demands for liberty, independence, and equality. So this is a book about the impulse that led an enslaved Massachusetts woman known as Mumbet, and later as Elizabeth Freeman, to hear the revolutionary rhetoric in the home in which she labored, and—in angry response to abuses she suffered at the hands of her owners, including being hit with hot kitchen implements—to apply ideas of liberty to her own circumstances and petition for her freedom; her case was instrumental to Massachusetts's abolition of slavery in 1783.

It's about how young girls laboring in the Lowell mills in the 1830s saw in their own situation a similar reflection of the insurgent rhetoric of the American Revolution, declaring that "as our fathers resisted unto blood the lordly avarice of the British ministry, so we, their daughters, never will wear the yoke which has been prepared for us," as they staged the walkouts that were one of the first iterations of what would become the American labor movement.[6] And how seventy years later, a twenty-three-year-old labor organizer named Clara Lemlich, who'd already been beaten for her participation in earlier strikes, grew impatient with all the talk from men at a meeting at Cooper Union in 1909, and stood up to call for a general strike that became the great uprising of twenty thousand shirtwaist workers, and resulted in new labor agreements with all but a few shirtwaist factories in New York. Triangle, one of the shirtwaist shops that did not give in to the strikers, burned two years later, killing 146 people inside, the vast majority women. That deadly fire would provoke the wrath of other activists, women who would in turn be driven to remake America's workplace safety regulations.

This book also aims to show how this anger—so instrumental to the nation's growth and progress—has never been celebrated, rarely even been noted in mainstream culture; how women are not lauded for their fury, and too often have had their righteous passions simply erased from the record. We aren't taught that Rosa Parks, the perfectly demure woman whose refusal to give up her seat kicked off the Montgomery Bus Boycott in 1955, was a fervent antirape activist who had once told a would-be attacker that she'd rather die than be raped by him and who, at ten years old, threatened by a white boy, picked up a piece of brick and drew it back to strike him if he approached. "I was angry," she'd later say of that youthful act of resistance. "He went his way without further comment."[7]

We are never forced to consider that rage—and not just stoicism, sadness, or strength—were behind the actions of the few women's heroes we're ever taught about in school, from Harriet Tubman to Susan B. Anthony. Instead, we are regularly fed and we regularly ingest cultural messages that suggest that women's rage is irrational, dangerous, or laughable.

This book is about how anger works for men in ways that it does not for women, how men like both Donald Trump and Bernie Sanders can wage yelling campaigns and be credited with understanding—and compellingly channeling—the rage felt by their supporters while their female opponents can be jeered and mocked as shrill for speaking too loudly or forcefully into a microphone. This is about women, some of whom have been angry for a long time, but didn't have an outlet for it, didn't realize how many of their neighbors, their coworkers, their friends and mothers and sisters, felt the same, until someone yelled, loud and fierce and ugly, and everyone heard her. It's about women who found themselves at the Women's March holding signs, and experienced a kind of awakening there—one third of those women had never been to a political protest before—and wondered for the first time how on earth they'd been lulled to sleep in the first place.[8]

Which means that this is also a story about women's anger at one another: at the kinds of privileges and incentives certain women—white women—have been offered in exchange for shutting off or turning down their anger, and about the price other women—nonwhite and especially black women—have paid, always having *had* reasons to be angry and having rarely been offered reprieve or reward for the act of suppressing it.

In her book *Anger and Forgiveness*, the philosopher Martha Nussbaum argues that anger in both personal and political contexts is an inherently vengeful impulse, and is therefore punitive and counterproductive. But not all political anger is about a drive to get even; it's not necessarily about seeing a president and his cronies rot in the jails they put so many struggling Americans in; it's not just about those who want to lock *him* up. It can also stem from a straightforward objection to injustice, a desire to free those who've been unjustly constrained or harmed. For women, who have long had their anger censured, vilified, ridiculed, tsked as incivility, the pressure to *not be angry,* to bottle up their resentments, or conversely, the pushback they've encountered when they've chosen to express themselves, has often been the vengeful, punitive act to begin with.

As another philosopher, Myisha Cherry, has recently argued, "I want to convince you that there are types of anger that are not bad." In particular, she is interested in anger at injustice, regarding it as a wholly appropriate response to inequity. "Here are some of the features of the anger at injustice: it recognizes wrongdoing. This recognition is not mistaken; this person is not delusional or making this up in their head. It is not selfish. So when someone is angry at injustice they're not just concerned with themselves but also other people . . . this anger does not violate other people's rights and most importantly, it desires change."[9]

As Cherry makes clear, political anger—which can stem from personal fury and be felt individually, but which is distinct from a personalized and punitive anger—can be, and in many cases has been, far more expansive and optimistic in its goals than the anger Nussbaum describes; it can be a communicative tool, a call to action, engagement, and collaboration between ideological compatriots, who, without first having made their ire loud and public, would not have known that they had the numbers to form an army, or to see past differences and toward powerful cooperation.

This is a book that seeks to identify the warmth and righteousness of women's rage, but not simply to cheer it. Because it does have limits, perils; of course it can corrode. Anger at injustice and inequality is in many ways exactly like fuel. A necessary accelerant, it can drive—on some level *must* drive—noble and difficult crusades. But it is also combustible, explosive; its power can be unpredictable and can burn.

In an era of renewed rage, an age of women who are mad as hell, this is a volume that examines how this emotion has functioned in our past— what it has brought us and what damage it has wrought—at the same time that it questions where it will take this nation next. On some real level, it is bananas that women's rage has never been given its proper due, its historical credit, that too few historians and journalists have noticed the catalytic role that furious women—speaking alone or working together against tyranny or oppression or injustice—have played in shaping and reshaping this country, in moving it closer to where it must be if it is to fulfill its patriotic, and yet unmet, promise of equality.

But it also posits that there is a lesson in how hard the powerful—very often the white and the male—have worked to shut up angry women, to divert attention from them. In 1964, the civil rights activist Fannie Lou Hamer began to give her testimony before the Democratic National Convention's credentials committee about how she had been arrested and then badly beaten by police after attempting to register voters in Mississippi. The president, Lyndon B. Johnson, concerned that Hamer's speech would alienate white voters, held an impromptu press conference about the nine-month anniversary of John F. Kennedy's death, forcing the news networks to turn away from Hamer's words and instead broadcast his own. Johnson knew that Hamer's anger would be meaningful and sought to draw America's attention away from it.[10]

On some level, if not intellectual than animal, there has *always* been an understanding of the power of women's anger: that as an oppressed majority in the United States, women have long had within them the potential to rise up in fury, to take over a country in which they've never really been offered their fair or representative stake. Perhaps the reason that women's anger is so broadly denigrated—treated as so ugly, so alienating, and so irrational—is because we have known all along that with it came the explosive power to upturn the very systems that have sought to contain it.

What becomes clear, when we look to the past with an eye to the future, is that the discouragement of women's anger—via silencing, erasure, and repression—stems from the correct understanding of those in power that in the fury of women lies the power to change the world.

I am a white woman who has been angry in my life and my work, occasionally on my own behalf but more often about politics, about inequity, and the grotesque *unfairness* of the world, this country, how it was built and who it still excludes and systematically diminishes. Some of that rage has become the driving force of my professional life. For fifteen years I have written, as a journalist, about women in media and politics and entertainment from a feminist perspective; that work itself has been rooted in anger, and in turn often strengthened by critics who got mad at me, and forced me to reconsider my perspective and think differently and more rigorously about race and class and sexuality and identity and opportunity. I value my own rage and the rage of others, especially of women.

But I also live in the world. I have, for years, made the rage that guided my work appear palatable. I'd absorbed the message that open anger was needlessly overdramatic and unattractive—that it would be too *much*, really—and I had worked to accommodate these assumptions, tempering my fury in my writing. As thoughtful as I tried to be about contemporary gendered, racial, and economic inequality, I'd nevertheless, on some level, swallowed the myth that circumstances were no longer so severe that they called for, or could be effectively addressed by, livid public display. I had soaked in the admonition—implicit from the moment I was first taught about a version of Martin Luther King, Jr. that was never angry, that I first understood that to be called a Dworkinist (as I was by some commenters on my stories who compared me to the radical feminist Andrea Dworkin) was a bad thing—that women who talked too loudly and too aggressively were considered immensely unappealing, sexually and intellectually, by the men whose opinions still shaped the world. That to be openly angry was a bad idea. That even when things were bad, a nonconfrontational approach was preferable, for strategic, aesthetic, and moral reasons.

So I was funny! And playful, cheeky, ironic, knowing! I worked to make it clear that I am a fun person who enjoys friends and beer and laughter. I took great care to be nice and respectful to opposing viewpoints. To full-throatedly express my ire would have been alienating, tactically unsound. I have watched as my peers have made similar choices. When feminism came roaring back to life, those of us who were engaging its new idioms and locutions were careful to distance ourselves from the angry ghosts we'd been assured haunted feminism's past. It is ironic that the generation that I, in some unconscious way, worked to distance myself from is now the generation that thrills me in its bonkers rage: the women who yelled at men and gave every direct indication that they had had it with their bullshit. Yet when I was younger, it was important that I made every effort to differentiate my wise-but-cool, sharp-but-easygoing critique from that past radicalism.

But all the good humor and in-jokes can't cover for the reality of wrath, the thing that makes you want to hit a wall or smash a glass or throw something, the electric impulse that occasionally streaks across our brains, making reason fuzz out, and our insides light up like firecrackers, in a way that does not permit hearty laughs over cold beers. Many of us who may have covered our fury in humor have occasionally found ourselves exploding.

In 2014, I was writing a semiregular column for the *New Republic*. One day, I was tired. I was pregnant. I was mad at my workplace for a variety of reasons having to do with my pregnancy and my economic status in relation to my gender. I read some things in other publications that pissed me off: a patronizing story by a man congratulating women over forty on suddenly being "hot"; a piece about the constant appraisals of Hillary Clinton's facial expressions; a story about teenaged boys speculating over a young woman's HIV status; the tale of a sixteen-year-old Houston girl who'd been drugged and assaulted and then had photos of her naked, limp body posted on social media; a *New York Times* investigation of a college's botched handling of a sexual assault case. This was the summer when a woman had been jailed and separated from her child for using meth while pregnant, and a mother had been arrested for letting her nine-year-old play alone while she worked her McDonald's shift; the Supreme Court had decided that corporations could elect not to cover birth control for their employees based on religious belief, and also that abortion clinic protesters were free to get close-up into the faces of women seeking reproductive health care and offer their jeering judgment.

The column I wrote, quickly, was its own meta-reflection on my willingness to get mad in public: in it, I expressed my yearning for a world in which women's worth was no longer measurable on scales fashioned by men, be they cultural, legal, legislative . . . or expressive. For a moment, I felt completely done with—temporarily unable to tolerate—the male-determined metrics of female acceptability, and in my exhausted ire, I did something that I had previously understood to be unacceptable: I wrote out of acidic and untempered anger, drawing on a remembered moment recalled in the comedian Tina Fey's memoir, in which she'd described how fellow comedian Amy Poehler had once unexpectedly wheeled around on a male colleague who'd told her that her vulgar jokes weren't cute and said "I don't fucking care if you like it." Perhaps for the first time in my writing life, I myself did not fucking care if readers liked that I was mad.

I didn't know, then, about what Rosa Parks had reportedly told her terrified grandmother after explaining why she'd raised that brick at the boy who'd been threatening her: "I would rather be lynched than live to be mistreated and not be allowed to say 'I don't like it.'" I had no idea how old and deep and urgent was women's impulse to sometimes just let their fury out without a care to how it would be evaluated, even if that expression of rage put them at risk: in young Rosa Parks's case, at the risk of death; in my case, at the risk of being mocked on the internet.

To my surprise, that column quickly became the most popular I'd ever written; it went viral; someone made T-shirts reading "I don't care if you like it"; my friend from an evangelical midwestern community told me that her religious childhood friends were posting it on their Facebook pages. There had been something in my eruption that had worked, communicatively.

It's not a formula I have ever tried to replicate; explosive fury cannot be faked. But I have permitted myself more often in the years since to write out of anger when I felt it and to express it in speeches and on television. Sometimes—once, memorably, at the height of #metoo—an editor has advised me not to publish, and I have heeded the advice, because I am all too sensitive to the ways in which anger can backfire strategically. But then, during the fall of 2016, after the presidential debate to which Donald Trump had brought women who had accused Hillary Clinton's husband of sexual misconduct, I went onto a cable news show, shaking and red-faced with rage at the degradation directed toward the first female candidate for the presidency. That clip, too, went briefly viral, and I got hundreds of messages from people telling me how much it had meant to them to hear someone say out loud what they'd been longing to yell.

What I have glimpsed, in the moments when I have let myself give voice to the deep, rich, curdled fury that for years I tried to pretty up and make easier on everyone's stomach, is that for all the care we take to bottle it up, rage can be a powerful tonic. It is a communicative tool, which speakers and writers and activists not only find freeing, but which acts as a balm to listeners and readers struggling with their own subsumed vexations.

We must come to recognize—those of us who feel anger, who have in our lives taken pains to disguise it, who worry about its ill effects, who rear back from it and try to tamp it down in ourselves for fear that letting it out will hurt our goals—that anger is often an exuberant expression. It is the force that injects energy, intensity, and urgency into battles that must be intense and urgent if they are to be won. More broadly, we must come to recognize our own rage as valid, as rational, and not as what we're told it is: ugly, hysterical, marginal, laughable.

I first decided to write this book as a means to channel and make sense of my own rage: how I've suppressed it or cloaked it in more officially attractive stuff. After the 2016 election, and two years of having been assured every day by the political press, by popular culture, by my friends and by those on the right and the left that there was no reason for women to be angry—that sexism would not be a factor in the candidacy of Hillary Clinton, that she was in fact the candidate with the disproportionate share of power; that the impulses guiding the support of Donald Trump were not sexism, racism, or xenophobia but rather economic anxiety; that it was the anger of *his* supporters that we needed to be paying attention to and that *in fact*, it was the overheated expressions of feminism and civil rights activism that had provoked white America into this Trumpian frenzy to begin with—I felt as though I might lose my mind with the rage I'd not been able to give full voice to.

I had to look into women's rage in America: how it has been suppressed, discouraged, discounted, when I felt very surely that it was central to our growth and history as a nation. When I began to tell people I was writing about women's anger and social change, I began to understand the depth and breadth and desperation of other women's desire to talk about their fury. Women told me they *needed* to read, and to write themselves, and to talk about their anger, even if it was in an email to me or in a tweet or conversation with their friends. They couldn't hold it in anymore, to keep it bottled up one more second would make them explode. What did they hope to gain from letting it out? I asked many of them. Validation was the answer I got, over and over again.

Here's the validation that I hope it can offer: that those who are furious right now are not alone, are not crazy, are not unattractive. That in fact, female rage in America has a long and righteous history, one that we have, very pointedly, never been taught.

But also, crucially: the women who are *suddenly* angry, newly angry, and are discombobulated by the intensity of their rage, are not the first to have felt this way. They did not invent rage at injustice, and in addition to realizing that they are in good company, they will find excellent models for activism and expression in the women around them who have never *not* been angry, and who have done so much work already to change things in America for the better.

We've got to think about these things—history and future—because we are in the midst of a potentially revolutionary moment: not one in which all wrongs will be righted or errors fixed. But one with the potential for a big alteration in who has power in this country. Progress in America takes a punishingly long time; but it also happens in fits and bursts, sometimes in reaction to terrible, deadening, deeply damaging setbacks. We are in one of those moments now, and we need to pay attention, to be aware of what is possible if we think hard about what we're angry about, and what needs to change. Because change *can* happen quickly.

At the height of the #metoo-inspired movement around sexual harassment in early 2018, I sat at a family holiday table listening to my mother and my aunt tell stories of their early days in academia, in the 1960s and early 1970s. Sisters from a farm in northern Maine, both women went on to get PhDs from the same graduate school and go into the same field. My mother, just five years older than my aunt, recalled going on the job market after earning her degree and seeing interview postings that read "We will not be hiring a woman for this position." At one interview, she was told as she walked in the door, "We're not considering women, but I thought it was unfair that they didn't get practice interviewing, so you can have a trial run." At another, she was told, "You're very good, but we already have one of you in the department." By the time her sister came along, just five years later, these hiring practices were not only frowned upon, they were illegal.

They were illegal in part because in those years women, mad at how they were discriminated against and harassed, had expressed their fury, had brought lawsuits. Some had become lawyers themselves, and some of these, including Eleanor Holmes Norton and Ruth Bader Ginsburg, went to work advocating for women. A willingness to be mad as hell changed the legal system and provoked legislative changes and protections, including the Civil Rights Act, altering the professional landscape for my aunt, in ways that would have been inconceivable to even her older sister.

That same week in 2018, again talking about the frankly terrifying intensity of the #metoo movement, my friend Esther Kaplan, an editor of the Investigative Fund at The Nation Institute, told me that the furor had made her think back to the era of feminist consciousness raising, of how women in the 1970s had gathered together in suburban homes and city apartments, had talked about liberation and equality and sexuality. They had learned to look at their own bodies and lives in new ways, to recognize the ways in which their domestic arrangements subjugated them, to question what they'd always been taught was the way things were.

"Those women *left their husbands*," Esther marveled to me, noting with wonder that "social movements have the potential to radically change us, not just radically change the world." What she was pointing out was that this contemporary wave of women's rage in the early twenty-first century—over sexual assault and harassment and workplace discrimination and political power imbalances—*also* entailed a wholesale reevaluation of women's pasts, a remaking of their perspectives, on themselves and on gendered power and its abuses. And of course it was happening at unprecedented speed, thanks to the internet. "This kind of thing can be culturally explosive, radical, out of control." She meant this, and I understood it, positively. But for some, the eruptive velocity is too much.

She's right, the fury can upend institutions, cut through our bedrock assumptions, and remake the geography of possibility. Not only did the consciousness raising of the 1970s result in a massive spike in the divorce rate, it also created a next generation that wanted to avoid the pitfalls of broken marriages that their parents had experienced, a population of women who expected more from the institution and so delayed marriage, or didn't marry at all, and instead expanded the possibilities for women to enjoy economic, social, and sexual independence. Those women's lives were remapped. Generations of women moved forward at new speed, their dependency not just on marriage but on men wholly revised. The anger of the second wavers, anger that has been used to caricature them as retrospectively unappealing, had blown off the doors for their daughters and their granddaughters.

The black feminist Audre Lorde famously argued in her germinal essay "The Uses of Anger," which is about women responding to racism, including the racism of other women, that "every woman has a well-stocked arsenal of anger potentially useful against those oppressions, personal and institutional, which brought that anger into being. Focused with precision it can become a powerful source of energy, serving progress and change." Lorde was very firm that she did not mean temporary, cosmetic change, not simply "the ability to smile or feel good." Rather, she argued, well-aimed anger from women can lead to "a basic and radical alteration in those assumptions underlining our lives."

On February 14, 2018, a gunman who had stalked an ex-girlfriend shot and killed seventeen people at Marjory Stoneman Douglas High School in Parkland, Florida. That afternoon, in response to a tweet from Donald Trump, offering "prayers and condolences" to the families of victims, one of the survivors of the shooting, sixteen-year-old Sarah Chadwick, tweeted "I don't want your condolences you fucking piece of shit, my friends and teachers were shot. Do something instead of sending prayers. Prayers won't fix this. But gun control will prevent it from happening again." Chadwick's livid message was retweeted 144,000 times before it was made unavailable; the rage it expressed would help to set the furious tone for what would become the Parkland students' righteous crusade to alter the gun laws in the United States.

The day after her tweet, Chadwick returned to Twitter under a different handle, and again addressed the president, making clear that while she had been chastised for her profanity, she had no intention of backing away from the rage that had undergirded it, the rage that would continue to drive her and her classmates toward changing the nation. "I apologize for the profanity and harsh comment I made," she wrote. "I'm a grieving sixteen-year-old girl who lost friends, teachers, and peers yesterday. I was and am still angry. I am apologizing for my comment but not for my anger."

We cannot afford to dismiss or fetishize or marginalize or rear back from women's anger any longer if we want this moment to be transformative. We have to look at it straight, stop hemming and hawing around it or trying to disavow it or worrying that it might offend and discomfit. It must be and always has been at the heart of social progress.

PART I

ERUPTION

I remember the first time I got angry. I was about ten. We were at McDonald's with our family friends, who were African American. I'm really light-skinned, my mom has light skin, so a lot of people don't always recognize that we are Mexicans. But our friends were very dark-skinned. The woman who was at the counter—who in retrospect was almost certainly herself a Mexican immigrant—let us play in the ball pit but didn't let our friends play. My mom fucking flipped her shit. She screamed like a banshee at this woman in the McDonald's. My mom said "I will never come back. I will tell all my friends never to come here. Give me the number of *your* manager; is there a regional manager? I'm going to call corporate headquarters." She just blew a gasket. Then she took us all out for ice cream and we all got gigantic sundaes that we had no business eating. I remember watching her and thinking: She's doing the right thing.

—Jessica Morales

CHAPTER ONE

SLEEPING GIANT

The contemporary reemergence of women's rage as a mass impulse comes after decades of feminist deep freeze. The years following the great social movements of the twentieth century—the women's movement, the civil rights movement, the gay rights movement—were shaped by deeply reactionary politics. When Phyllis Schlafly led an antifeminist crusade to stop the ratification of the Equal Rights Amendment—the twenty-four-word constitutional amendment that would have guaranteed equal rights regardless of gender—finally succeeding in 1982, it was a sign that the second-wave feminist movement of the 1970s, and the righteous fury that had ignited it, had been sidelined.

More broadly, the Reagan era, in which increasingly hard-right reactionary politics had joined with a religious "moral majority," gave rise to a cultural backlash to all sorts of social progress. Under sharp attack were the benefits, rights, and protections that afforded poor women any stability, as well as the parts of the women's movement that had produced legal, professional, and educational gains for middle-class women, better enabling them to live independently, outside of marriage, the patriarchal institution that had historically contained them and on which they had long depended.

The right wing of the 1980s was driven to restrict abortion access and deregulate Wall Street while simultaneously destroying the social safety net, which Ronald Reagan had made sure was embodied by the specter of the black welfare queen. A 1986 *Newsweek* cover story, meanwhile, blared the news that a single woman at forty was more likely to get killed by a terrorist than get married. That later-debunked study was a key point of Susan Faludi's chronicle of the era, *Backlash*, in which she tracked the varied, suffocating ways in which women's anger was muffled throughout the Reagan years: how feminist activism was blamed for the purported "man shortage"; the day-care that enabled women to work outside the home vilified as dangerous for children.

Popular culture showed liberated white career women as oversexed monsters, as in *Fatal Attraction*, or as cold, shoulder-padded harpies who had to be saved via hetero-union or punished via romantic rejection (see Diane Keaton in *Baby Boom*, Sigourney Weaver in *Working Girl*). There was far too little space afforded to black heroines, and even some of the most nuanced were often crafted to serve male creators' investments in how women's liberation might serve their messages: Spike Lee's view of the sexually voracious Nola Darling in the 1986 film *She's Gotta Have It* and Bill Cosby's Clair Huxtable, the successful matriarch who, given the context of Cosby's own racial politics, served as a repudiation of black women who were *not* wealthy hetero-married mothers with law degrees.

Who wanted to be a feminist? No one. And the anxiety about the term wasn't about any of the *good* reasons to be skeptical of feminism—like the movement's racial exclusions and elisions—but because the term itself, the idea of public and politicized challenge to male dominance, had been successfully coded as unattractively old, as crazy, as ugly. Susan Sarandon, the rare celebrity who actually maintained her publicly left politics through the 1980s and 90s, once explained why even she of the unrelenting commitment to disruptive political speech preferred the misnomer "humanist" to calling herself a "feminist": "it's less alienating to people who think of feminism as being a load of strident bitches."[1]

To be sure, there were eruptions of fury, coming from people—often from women—who were waging battles against inequities. In 1991, the law professor Anita Hill testified in front of an all-white, all-male Senate

Judiciary Committee that Clarence Thomas, her former boss at the Equal Employment Opportunity Commission, then a nominee for the Supreme Court, had sexually harassed her. Many women were taken aback by the way the committee insulted, dismissed, and ultimately disbelieved Hill, confirming Thomas to the court, where he sits today.

"It was so stark, watching these men grill this woman in these big chairs and looking down at her," Patty Murray, senator from Washington state, has recalled. Murray and a lot of other women were so outraged by the treatment of Hill that an unprecedented number of them ran for office in 1992. Four, including Murray, won Senate seats; one of them, Carol Moseley Braun, became the first-ever African-American woman elected to the Senate. Twenty-four women were elected to the House of Representatives for the first time, more than had been elected in any other previous decade.

These years sometimes included violent rage in response to racism: in 1992, after four white cops were acquitted by a mostly white jury in the brutal beating of African-American taxi driver Rodney King in Los Angeles, the city erupted in fury. Angry protesters looted stores and set fires; sixty-three people died. At the time, the news media and local politicians were quick to describe the events as riots, throwing around the term "thugs."

But one Los Angeles Democratic representative saw something else in the riots: "There are those who would like for me . . . to tell people to go inside, to be peaceful, that they have to accept the verdict. I accept the responsibility of asking people not to endanger their lives. I am not asking people not to be angry," said first-term congresswoman Maxine Waters, who represented a big part of the South Central Los Angeles neighborhood where much of the unrest was unfolding. "I am angry and I have a right to that anger and the people out there have a right to that anger."[2]

Waters spent days tending to her constituents, bringing food, water, and diapers to Angelenos living without gas or electricity; she also pushed to charge the police officers civilly, and objected to Mayor Tom Bradley's use of the word "riot" to describe events. Instead, she saw the politically rational frame for the resentments being expressed, calling it "an insurrection."[3]

Eventually, Los Angeles Police Chief Daryl Gates was fired, and two of the police officers were convicted for violating Rodney King's civil rights.[4]

There were other moments of political protest: those against the World Trade Organization in Seattle in 1999 and marches against the invasion of Iraq in 2003, for example. But much of the spirit of mass, brash, sustained political fury that had animated the 1960s and 1970s was muffled in the 1980s and stayed that way for decades.

The journalist Mychal Denzel Smith has written of how this suppression worked itself out around expressions of black rage in the years in which he'd grown up, noting that during most of the 1990s, "there was no longer a Reagan or a Bush to serve as an identifiable enemy," and that a pop commitment to "multiculturalism" permitted the illusion that racial progress had been achieved, so rage as a mass impulse had subsided.[5]

There had been a brief revival during the second Bush administration, Smith argued, recalling how, in the wake of the derelict response to Hurricane Katrina, rapper Kanye West had yelled that George W. Bush "doesn't care about black people." But that surge of fury had been quieted by the presidential campaign of Barack Obama. Obama's historic drive had relied in part on his ability to reassure white voters that he was not an angry black man, that he was cut from a different cloth than some of his more bellicose black predecessors, including Jesse Jackson and Al Sharpton, and did not in his demeanor threaten white supremacy. But Obama's reputation for cordiality was gravely imperiled by the appearance of old-style black rage, when Reverend Jeremiah Wright, the man who had married the Obamas, became a campaign story, along with his much-played sermon, during which he'd exhorted, "God *damn* America!" The specter of Wright's version of confrontational blackness was enough to remind America of Obama's outsider status, and thus Obama was forced to quash it, becoming, in Smith's words, "the first viable black presidential candidate to throw water on the flames of black rage." The anger expressed by Wright, Obama would say in his famous speech on race, "is not always productive; indeed, all too often it distracts attention from solving real problems."

But partway through the Obama administration, some political fury had begun to bubble over and break through this veneer of calm, in part driven by, or in ways that meaningfully sidelined, the angry voices of women.

ANGER RIGHT AND LEFT

Perhaps the most politically effective strike came from the right, with the Tea Party protests that began in 2009, soon after President Barack Obama took office. In response to Obama's plan to bail out some homeowners who'd been caught in the housing crisis, cable news reporter Rick Santelli angrily called on television for the "Tea Party" to object. The reference, of course, was to the 1773 revolutionary protest of colonists who threw tea in Boston Harbor to register their objection to being taxed by Britain, which was using tariffs not to support the colonies but to stabilize its own floundering economy, and had imposed them on colonists who had no representation in British Parliament.[6]

The contemporary version was portrayed as a leaderless grassroots movement, though almost from its start, right-wing mega donors the Koch brothers had been funding its protests and its candidates. In theory, the agitation was in response to the far right's view that Barack Obama's administration was misusing taxpayer money, but the Tea Party was also driven by a wave of revanchist rage and racial resentment toward Barack Obama; no amount of nonconfrontational rhetoric could convince overwhelmingly white Tea Partiers he wasn't a threat to their status and supremacy.

Though the public face of the Tea Party protesters was that of furious white men—often dressed in colonial-era tricorn hats in their early gatherings—some polls indicated that the majority of the faction's supporters were women. Its most audible early female voice belonged to former vice-presidential candidate Sarah Palin, who in one address to activists called the movement "another revolution." In 2010, a number of Tea Party–affiliated female candidates ran; Palin, who'd cast herself as a pit-bullish hockey mom, dubbed them "Mama Grizzlies." And while the movement's theatrics—funny hats and grizzly bears—were reminiscent of some of the performative exertions of the Second Wave, its mission was the precise opposite, more of a callback to the Schlafly-led antifeminist crusades of the 1970s and 80s.

Somehow, as with Schlafly, these women voicing their anger and throwing around their political weight weren't caricatured as ugly hysterics; instead they were permitted to cast themselves as patriotic moms on steroids, some bizarro-world embodiment of female empowerment, despite the fact (or, more precisely, *because* of the fact) that what they were advocating was a return to traditionalist roles for women and reduced government investment in nonwhite people. Once they landed in the United States Congress, their obsessive mission was to vote to take away the federal funding received by family planning programs, to outlaw abortion, to punish Planned Parenthood, and to reduce government safety net programs such as food stamps and what remained of welfare.

"Conservative women have found their voices and are using them, actively and loudly," Tea Partier Rebecca Wales told *Politico* in 2010. Another Tea Partier, Darla Dawald, put it this way: "You know the old saying 'If Mama ain't happy, ain't nobody happy'? When legislation messes with Mama's kids and it affects her family, then Mama comes out fighting—and I don't mean in a violent way, of course."[7]

As more moderate Republicans got knocked out of their seats by Tea Party candidates, and those who remained moved further right, an angry protest in New York was drawing crowds of agitators from the other side. In the fall of 2011, in Zuccotti Park in downtown Manhattan, young people gathered to voice their fury at economic inequality, the widening gap between rich and poor, the rampant deregulation of and tax breaks for corporate America and Wall Street, and the steady gutting of social welfare programs.

Occupy Wall Street's impact on the American left was crucial and long-lasting; the movement helped to popularize the view of economic inequality that set the 99 percent against the nation's richest 1 percent. It was both a symptom and a fomenter of increased interest in socialist economic policy. That interest would help push the Democratic Party—which had for decades run screaming from the notion of even "liberalism"—further left, boosting the profiles and fortunes of politicians including Elizabeth Warren, who was elected Senator for Massachusetts in 2012, and Bernie Sanders, an independent who'd served in Congress for twenty-six years and would mount an electrifying campaign for the presidency in 2016.

Many different types of people participated in Occupy—estimates varied, but reportedly around 40 percent of the protesters were women, and 37 percent identified as nonwhite, making it *far* closer to representative of the United States than, say, Congress.[8-10] Yet despite the fact that its structure was consciously collaborative and nonhierarchical, it was nevertheless a movement dominated publicly by the voices and ideas of white men. There were enough allegations of rape, groping, and sexual assault at Zuccotti Park that after several weeks, women-only tents were set up. Kanene Holder, an artist, activist, and black woman who served as one of Occupy's spokespeople, told the *Guardian* that even within this progressive space, "white males are used to speaking and running things. . . . You can't expect them to abdicate the power they have just because they are in this movement." Eventually, Occupy had to adopt special sessions in which women were encouraged to speak uninterrupted.[11]

More than that, some of the righteously radical men who dominated Occupy were reportedly inhospitable to internal feminist critique. As one activist, Ren Jender, wrote after a proposal to better address sexual assault allegations was met with defensive anger from some of these radically progressive men, "I wasn't angry with only the people who . . . said stupid, misogynistic shit . . . I was angry with the greater number of people who hadn't confronted the misogyny."[12] Occupy was a reminder to many who agreed with its principles that the left was no more free of gender hierarchies and power abuses than the rest of the country.

Then, in 2013, in the wake of the acquittal of George Zimmerman in the murder of seventeen-year-old Trayvon Martin, the longtime progressive activist Alicia Garza wrote a note on Facebook, which concluded with the sentences, "Black people, I love you. I love us. We matter. Our lives matter." The artist and activist Patrisse Khan-Cullors appended a hashtag to it, #BlackLivesMatter; the writer and community organizer Opal Tometi helped to push the message out over social media.

A movement—born of grief, horror, and unleashed fury at the persistent killing of African Americans by the state, by the police—was born. And while it, like Occupy and the Tea Party, was purposefully nonhierarchical in its internal structure, it had been founded by women, and many of the most prominent voices of the movement belonged to women, including

Brittany Packnett, Johnetta Elzie, Nekima Levy-Pounds, and Elle Hearns. Khan-Cullors later wrote of how black liberation movements of the past had been led largely by straight men, "leaving women, who are often queer or transgender, either out of the movement or in the background to move the work forward with little or no recognition. As younger organizers, we recognized a need to center the leadership of women."[13]

Black Lives Matter increased national awareness of common racist policing practices that had remained largely invisible, especially to white eyes, but which millions of Americans now understand to be a systemic reality. The movement, which spread across the country and the world, staged days of protest in Ferguson, Missouri, after the police killing of Michael Brown; activists pioneered a new age of public demonstration, staging "die-ins," in which protesters laid on the ground in recognition of African Americans gunned down in the streets. In 2015, in the wake of the mass killing of black churchgoers by a white man in Charleston, activist Bree Newsome scaled the flagpole at the South Carolina State House, removing the Confederate flag that had long hung there, an act that provoked a wave of removal of statues of Confederate leaders throughout the South.

So in the years leading up to the 2016 election, there was a building, public rage—rage that had an impact on politics, on civic structures, on public spaces. More than that, there were women finding contemporary ways to broadcast their powerful, desperately felt anger to the nation. And, at least on the left, they were doing it in a way that specifically challenged patriarchal, male-dominated histories of movement-building.

But in mainstream feminism, there was a different spirit. Hot fury—expressed through public acts of protest, mass movements to the streets, or defiant profanity bellowed loudly at the powerful—was simply not the main mode of feminist expression. And it's not that feminism itself was in remission.

FEMINIST COOL

What used to be called "the women's movement" had found energetic new life in the media in the first decades of the twenty-first century. After years of backlash, feminist journalists and bloggers had revived a conversation about gender, and many of us who participated in that conversation were angry—angry about sexism, and racism, and economic inequality, and how all of these injustices were woven together. But, perhaps anxious to differentiate ourselves from our spitting-mad forebears, many contemporary feminists (including me) had worked to make the expression of our frustrations sound agreeable, relatable, and inviting to others, including to the very men who might have a hand in oppressing us.

The popular feminist site Feministing used the ironic image of a sexy mudflap girl flipping the bird as its mascot; young feminists traded in jokey signifiers of man-hating: mugs and T-shirts reading "I bathe in male tears" and "misandry." The hashtag #banmen conveyed frustration with bad men in a way that strenuously mocked the absurd notion that feminists hated *all* men. And while plenty of men's rights activists did not see these sentiments as funny or ironic, the exaggerations radiated reassurance: that a truly abrasive challenge to patriarchy wasn't a real political threat, rather the stuff of screen-printed punch lines.

There *was* a heated movement to combat sexual assault on campus, and, in 2011 and 2012, a string of vibrant street protests, dubbed Slutwalks, in which women furiously objected to the victim-blaming to which they were so often subjected. The Slutwalks were, perhaps, the first sign that a more raw grade of feminist fury was about to erupt. But they too trafficked in a kind of winking, eroticized irony: the re-embrace of a degrading but sexualized word, the "I [heart] sluts" buttons, the marchers dressed in short skirts and garters; it was all in line with another aspect of revived feminism: its exuberant positivity about sex.

"Sex positivity" was a theory that had sprung up in response to anti-porn activists during ideological wars waged by another generation; it endorsed the idea that any kind of sexual behavior, from celibacy to kink, might bring women pleasure, and not on terms laid out by a misogynistic culture. In the hands of a new generation, however, it had become a kind of shorthand for boosterism, as opposed to a censor, of sex: all sex, as long as it was consensual. And it could sometimes feel as though the eagerness to express a feminist sexual appetite was a strategic attempt to obscure or distract from more unpleasant challenges to male power. So while plenty of writers weighed in powerfully on gendered and racial injustice, many were also penning essays defending a feminist prerogative to wear makeup and sky-high heels and scanty outfits. And that was fine; it just also sent a direct message: that when it came to clashing with male sexual expectation, this wave of feminism wasn't so spiky, wasn't so aggressively rigid and confrontational. New, mainstream feminism was funny, hip, enthusiastic about sex . . . and kind of cool.

And, not for nothing, it worked! In the years leading up to 2016 feminism was becoming a bit trendy. There were all-women reboots of *Ghostbusters* and female Jedis and powerful female leads all over television—tough and complicated women created by Shonda Rhimes, feminist heroines like *The Good Wife*'s Alicia, and the stoned, raunchy heroines of *Broad City*—whose stories exposed the limitations still put on women by the patriarchy. But a lot of the critique was at a remove—analytical and observed, not vulgar, not *animal*. Not angry.

In 2013 Facebook mogul Sheryl Sandberg published *Lean In*, a book looking at the disadvantages still faced by women in the workplace; it focused largely on individual behavioral strategies to get around inequities, earning sharp, fair criticism for not focusing more on systemic overhaul. This incomplete but unapologetic expression of feminist complaint, from someone who had risen within the system, became a massive bestseller.

The next year, Beyoncé performed at the MTV Video Music Awards, backed up by a recording of Chimamanda Ngozi Adichie's TED Talk "We Should All Be Feminists": "We teach girls to shrink themselves, to make themselves smaller. We say to girls 'You can have ambition, but not too much. You should aim to be successful, but not too successful. Otherwise, you will threaten the man.'" Then up came a giant bright sign, "FEMINIST," and Beyoncé, glittering like a disco ball, stood in front of it.

It was pop culture, packaged and polished to a high gloss. But it was also a feminist assertion—all too prescient, as it would turn out—delivered by a woman of color, citing another woman of color, a crucial but powerful correction to the ways in which media had historically (and falsely) presented the project of women's liberation as having been led by white women. Here was a woman who had amassed enough power—had become, arguably, the most powerful person in pop music—to create her own narrative: she was not left at the margins to yell at media about what they were getting wrong or ignoring. Beyoncé had certainly made compromises with power structures; bell hooks had described her as "this super rich, very powerful black female" who had worked "in the service of imperialist, white supremacist capitalist patriarchy."[14] But she also seemed to have delivered on the promise of what a new, less furious, less confrontational approach to feminism could achieve: broad, attractive appeal.

And that was it, wasn't it? The loud angry battles waged by earlier generations of women had produced some dramatic results. An admittedly small number of women who had gained unprecedented power—within colleges and graduate schools, in business, in entertainment, in media, in politics—had begun to enjoy opportunity and power that had historically been denied. And if those women wanted to move forward, they couldn't afford to behave in the confrontational, angry ways that had marked a past approach to a fight for something closer to actual equality. Because that challenge, that fury, would designate them as outsiders, as marginal. To have climbed within the system was to agree not to tear it down, not to remind America too aggressively of its gender and racial inequities or distract from the cheery view of progress and empowerment.

Anyone who wants power within a white male power structure has been asked to quell anything that sounds like wrath, to reassure that they come in cooperative peace and are not looking to mete out repercussion against those who have oppressed or subjugated them. Women signaling fury—by cursing, organizing, marching, yelling, threatening retribution— would have been marked as unstable forces, exactly what couldn't happen going into a 2016 election in which there seemed for the first time in American history to be a chance that the country would elect a woman and protect the legacy of the nation's first black president.

As Hillary Clinton geared up to run for the presidency, the stakes were far too high for the kind of anger that had been so openly and defiantly expressed by the activists—in suffrage, abolition, civil rights, feminism— whose achievements had, ironically, made her candidacy possible. Female power was visible at the Video Music Awards, it was the COO of Facebook. It was in the *Ghostbusters* reboot and a slick, funny feminist media, and the inevitable presidential candidate. What was there to complain about?

Any hint of truly angry, truly challenging feminist resentment behind a political movement would get written off as performed. Senate Majority Leader Mitch McConnell had already called it playing "the gender card," like it was a move in a game, a put-on. Authentic expressions of resistance—marches, hunger strikes, demonstrations, sit-ins—had been useful for getting attention, banging down doors, forcing women's way in. But the public antics and outpourings of vivid fury at an unequal system that had been useful in eras when women were so far from the inside would work against those who'd *gotten* inside, making them look and sound like outsiders once more.

CHAPTER TWO

THE GRAND ILLUSION

Of course women weren't *really* inside. And you could tell because the ones who looked to be had actually walked into the most ingenious trap of all: the one in which their insider status, the illusion of their assured claim to political power, gained after centuries of exclusion, would be the very thing that worked to disqualify them.

The fact is that when Hillary Clinton began her second campaign for the presidency, not only had we not elected a single woman president in 226 years of presidential history, we had not elected a single woman *vice* president. Despite the more than two hundred women who had thrown their hats in, the country had never managed to make a woman a major party *nominee* for the presidency. Congress was still only 19 percent female and had only ever elected one black woman to the Senate. And all of these representational gaps existed in a country in which women's bodies were ever more heavily legislated and their wages and economic stability were under new attacks from the right.

Yet the climate was one in which furious displays of anger on behalf of women's equality had been ceded and replaced by some milder forms of agitation coming from the few who *had* worked their way to power, permitting the propagation of the myth that centuries of gendered and racial discrimination were over, that things were pretty much even, that those who had been barred from power historically now possessed an equal share of it.

That myth—the fantasy that racism and sexism were stages through which the country had successfully passed, leaving new kinds of people, like President Barack Obama and "inevitable" next president Hillary Clinton, in charge—had unleashed another kind of anger. The rage that was alight, and openly, eagerly expressed in the years before the 2016 election was the rage of those *already* on the inside: the greedy anger of the kind of Americans who had been, over centuries, afforded the disproportionate share of political, economic, social, and sexual power, and who were explosively furious at the perception that others were grabbing shares away from them.

The political profile of Donald Trump was built on his racist birther campaign, his public claims that Barack Obama's presidency had always been illegitimate. His campaign kicked off with his statements about Mexicans as rapists, promises to build walls and make laws to keep foreign interlopers out. He had once taken out a full-page ad calling for the death penalty for the so-called Central Park Five—the group of young black men arrested for the rape of a white woman jogger and later exonerated. Trump's scorn for women was on prominent display from the start: he called them pigs, dogs, evaluated them on scales of one to ten, had run beauty pageants, been accused by his first wife of rape, and bragged to Howard Stern of never having changed a diaper. He had told a magazine that you have to "treat [women] like shit."

Because of the national illusion that we as a country were too culturally advanced for this kind of retrograde white patriarchal expression, we were regularly assured by political experts that Trump's candidacy would never get off the ground, that these kinds of locutions of racist and sexist resentment and dismissal would make him ineligible for the presidency.

But not only did Trump seem to surge ahead in *spite* of his hatred and dismissal of nonwhite non-men, his supporters seemed to love him *because* of it. Even those who claimed he'd never be president credited him with reaching voters in a visceral way, as having a gift for channeling the rage of a white America which felt it had been left behind, had its privileges stolen by female, nonwhite interlopers—the kinds of people who'd never occupied the White House or held representative numbers of seats in legislative bodies, people who were paid less, taxed more for health care, and denied full control of their reproductive lives, but who had given such a convincing impression of having taken up more than an equal share of space that they were the objects of the resentful ire being channeled by the orange-tinted and toupéed businessman from Queens. The guy who just kept winning primaries.

His rallies were raucous and furious events, stadium-sized yell-ins, with supporters offering "Sieg Heil" salutes and wearing white nationalist insignia. Trump himself encouraged angry violence in his crowds, at one point telling a crowd, as a protester was removed, "I love the old days; you know what they used to do to guys like that when they were in a place like this? They'd be carried out in a stretcher . . . I'd like to punch him in the face." But as he waxed nostalgic for the good old days of quelling protest through brutality, Trump's supporters acted like furious protesters themselves, screaming insults and profanity at anyone they imagined to be challenging their authority: "Build a wall!" "Fuck political correctness!" "Fuck Islam!" In one video report, the *New York Times* recorded Trump supporters responding to the candidate's mention of then-president Obama with "Fuck that n—!"

And then there was the fury with which Trump supporters treated Hillary Clinton: effigies of the candidate in prison garb and coffins were carried at Fourth of July parades in the summer of 2016; Trump's crowds were energized by their hatred for her: "Hillary is a whore!" "Trump that bitch!" "Tramp!" "Bitch!" "Kill her!" "Hang the Bitch!"[15] And always, always the drum beat: "Lock! Her! Up!" And it wasn't just the anonymous crowds. Retired Army Lieutenant General Michael Flynn led the crowd in a chorus of "Lock her up" at the Republican National Convention; at the same gathering, New Jersey Governor Chris Christie, who would soon fall under criminal investigation himself, led a mock trial of Clinton, rousing the crowd on the floor to a writhing, frenzied scream of "Guilty!" that recalled seventeenth-century Salem, as if Clinton were a witch about to be sentenced to death. A month later, at a North Carolina rally, Trump told his supporters that

Clinton wanted to take away their guns, telling them, "If she gets to pick her judges, [there's] nothing you can do, folks. Although the second amendment people, maybe there is, I don't know." Trump's deranged syntax didn't effectively cover up the fact that he was hinting at Clinton's assassination. More direct was his advisor on veteran's affairs, a state representative from New Hampshire named Al Baldasaro, who said in a radio interview that Clinton "should be put in the firing line and shot for treason."[16]

The vitriolic hatred of Clinton was sometimes only slightly less muted on the left, in part because of the sticky truth of her position: she *did* have power, she was one of the exceptional women to have risen within a white patriarchal capitalist system that hadn't been built for her, and she'd risen in part by participating in it.

Other women who'd attempted runs for the presidency, from Shirley Chisholm in 1972 to Patricia Schroeder in 1987, had been stopped by their outsider status or their inability to fund-raise or garner enough serious support from the powerful men who ran their party. Clinton had been hell-bent on overcoming these hurdles, but in doing so, had offered her opponents on the left the ammunition to undercut the historic nature of her candidacy. She'd played far too nicely with Wall Street, voted for the invasion of Iraq, and worked too eagerly with Republicans on centrist policy during her time as a senator. She'd supported her husband's neoliberal policies as first lady, including the 1994 crime bill, 1996's disastrous and despicable welfare reform legislation, and the 1996 Immigration Reform and Immigrant Responsibility Act, all of which had done disproportionate harm to poor and nonwhite communities.

The very fact that she had carefully established close relationships with big donors and garnered the support of bigwigs made her part of a political elite and vulnerable to the anti-establishment rhetoric of the men she'd wind up running against; it kept her from being understood or celebrated as the outsider that, as a member of a gender that had been historically denied access to executive power, she was. In figuring out how a woman might *win* within a system that had not been designed with her in mind, Clinton had set herself up to lose.

Clinton's affiliation with the power structure created a terrific incentive for many on the left to support her primary opponent, the genuinely left-wing Democratic Socialist senator from Vermont, Bernie Sanders, a man who had long retained his independence from the Democratic Party. The Sanders campaign turned into its own kind of buoyant social movement, one that had a salutary effect on Clinton's campaign: it pushed her leftward.

But some of the left's loathing for her, and for her supporters, could often seem as though it were about more than simple policy differences or distrust of the establishment. It could be deeply gendered, and it occasionally reeked of condescension and belittlement, as when Sanders's campaign manager, Jeff Weaver, sneered to a political reporter regarding Clinton, "We're willing to consider her for vice president. . . . We'll even interview her." Some progressives—echoing the attitudes of some of the Occupiers who had been the forerunners of the Bernie core—remained inhospitable to feminist arguments on behalf of Clinton, even to the basic claim that it mattered, democratically and representatively, that there'd never been a woman in the White House, much less a liberal woman running on the abolishment of the Hyde Amendment (which barred the use of federal insurance money to pay for abortion, making abortion inaccessible to poor women) and increasing funding for childcare and paid leave programs. "Ppl voting for Hillary for this reason are like southern GOP neighbors wanting GOP for culturally affirming reasons," tweeted the leftist writer Zaid Jilani during the primary, while *Salon*'s Daniel Denvir claimed that Clinton was "getting a free pass as a feminist," waving off "the notion that Hillary Clinton is a feminist choice because she is a qualified woman" as "really very caricatured identity politics."[17]

The frustration that some Sanders supporters felt, as enthusiasm for him grew but Clinton kept winning anyway, prompted some of them to borrow from the vilifying imagery and delegitimizing accusations being lodged on the right, including the propagation of the story that Clinton had rigged the primary. At the Democratic National Convention, *progressive* protesters held up signs saying "Hillary for Prison" and chanted "Lock her up!" while Green Party candidate Jill Stein stoked the rage, promising to urge Sanders to withdraw his endorsement of Hillary, "based on the outright, purposeful sabotage of your campaign by the DNC and by Hillary Clinton."[18]

Of course, lots of Hillary's most vociferous and vivid critics on the left were feminist women, women who described how Hillary's fervid supporters attacked *them* in sexist and degrading terms, calling them gender traitors, diagnosing them as victims of internalized misogyny. As one feminist Sanders supporter, Sarah Jones, wrote "No one's liberated by portraying left-wing women as oppressed automatons incapable of independently formulating political thought."

One of those who was attacked from both sides was Kathleen Geier, who, during the primary, described to the journalist Michelle Goldberg how some of her fellow Berners used a "sanctimonious, lecturing, hectoring tone" when discussing Clinton and feminism. "They're trying to delegitimize any critique of sexist Hillary coverage . . . my politics are with that side, but this ancient left-wing misogyny has risen its ugly head."[19]

While the gender dynamics here were far more nuanced and complex than those on the right, there was no question that there were weird misogynist resentments at play. After Clinton finally beat Sanders and earned the nomination in June of 2016, two of the progressive politicians who had purposefully withheld endorsements came out for Hillary: Russ Feingold and Elizabeth Warren. But it was Warren who was subject to the brunt of the ire from Sanders's supporters; her Facebook page was flooded with messages calling her a hypocrite and "another pseudo progressive we must vote out of office"; graffiti spray-painted on a bridge in Northampton, Massachusetts, read "#JudasWarrenSellout."

On both the right and the left, the kind of foul-mouthed, performative anger that I had gawked at coming from women trying to storm the political gates in earlier eras was in 2016 being directed *at* the woman who had come closer to knocking those gates down than any other before her.

CHAPTER THREE

WE'RE NOT CHEERFUL ANYMORE

"I tried to change. Closed my mouth more, tried to be softer, prettier, less awake."

There was Beyoncé, riffing on a poem by Warsan Shire called "For Women Who Are Difficult to Love"—about a female subject who is with a man who finds her intensity frightening—in her visual album, *Lemonade*, released in April of 2016, the week before Donald Trump would officially become the Republican candidate for president.[20]

In the video, Beyoncé strides jauntily through city streets in a big yellow dress, swinging a baseball bat with which she smashes car windows and takes the tops off fire hydrants, releasing furious geysers of water and causing flames to erupt behind her. In the video, women look on with surprised delight while men stare at her, wary. At the time, the narrative arc, words, and visuals of *Lemonade*, understood to be Beyoncé's ferocious response to her husband Jay-Z's infidelities, appeared wholly unconnected to politics.

But the shift between the public performance of polished empowerment feminism offered by the pop star just two years earlier, and the unleashed rage at men's bad behavior (and at the women who enable it, including Beyoncé's "Becky," the slang term connoting white women) also marked a certain kind of turning point. Even in Beyoncé's universe—still glossy and gorgeous, still with men near the center—cheerful feminism was gone; in its place a slick wrath, a punitive and righteous rage, presented as having been pent up, like floods and flames, now pouring forth onto the streets. By the spring of 2016, Beyoncé was mad, and at least some of her anger was about men—the husbands and fathers of her lyrics—and how they treated women.

Her rage would turn out to be a harbinger in the months to come, as the reality that Donald Trump was going to be the Republican nominee for president set in and revelations of his vile behavior toward women became better known. Trump found women's bodies and their functions grotesque, called Clinton's trip to the bathroom during a debate "disgusting," made a comment about debate moderator Megyn Kelly having "blood coming out of her wherever," and had once told a lawyer who'd had to take a break to pump breast milk during a meeting, "you're disgusting." It was perfectly clear that when he promised to "Make America Great Again," part of what Donald Trump was promising was a return to a retro version of white masculinity, and all of the misogynist subjugation and objectification it comprised.

That he was the candidate felt absurd, anachronistic in the era we were assured was postfeminist. Yet a postelection study done by Harvard Kennedy School's Shorenstein Center, looked at the nation's leading newspapers and news networks and found that the press covered Donald Trump and Hillary Clinton equivalently, as if they and their faults were legitimately comparable. The ratio of negative to positive coverage of their fitness for office was the same: 87 percent of the stories about each of them were negative, thirteen percent were positive.[21]

This relative parity in coverage, the both-sides-ism that defined media coverage of the race, was a reflection of the lie at the center of everything. Because the reality was that Trump's racist and sexist attitudes were *not* in fact out of line with contemporary assumptions; they were not disqualifying. They were measured on the same scale that weighed Clinton's real but politically ordinary flaws, because on some level, his biases were still considered legitimate. The idea that the nation had moved beyond retro, macho white attitudes about who could lay claim to political power had always been a fable, one that had worked to quash the dissent and discourage the disruptive fury that might have otherwise had more power to beat back Trump before his rise.

When, a month before the election, it was revealed that Donald Trump had been caught on tape joking about women with Billy Bush—a *Today* show host and member of a family that had produced two American presidents, the cousin of another man who'd run for president against Donald Trump—about how "when you're a star, they let you do it. You can do anything . . . grab 'em by the pussy. You can do anything," people got mad. Women got mad. The night that the *Access Hollywood* tape was made public, a Canadian author, Kelly Oxford, tweeted, "Women: tweet me your first assaults. They aren't just stats. I'll go first: Old man on city bus grabs my 'pussy' and smiles at me, I'm 12." In response came more than twenty million tweets and visits to her Twitter page, many posting under the hashtag #notokay to signify stories of unwanted sexual contact, many women recalling incidents from when they were children or teens.[22]

The next week, women began to come forward with stories about how Trump himself had kissed or groped them against their will: a former *People* reporter, Natasha Stoynoff, wrote about how years before, while she'd been reporting a story on Trump and his third wife, Melania, he'd taken her into a room alone and "within seconds . . . was pushing me against the wall and forcing his tongue down my throat."[23] Stoynoff recalled her surprise at the incident, how when she got back to the hotel room, her "shock began to wear off and was replaced by anger. I kept thinking, 'Why didn't I slug him? Why couldn't I say anything?'" Another woman, seventy-four-year-old Jessica Leeds, recalled to the *New York Times* how, on a flight three decades earlier, she had been seated next to Trump, and he had groped her, touching her breasts. "He was like an octopus," Leeds told the *Times*. "His hands were everywhere."[24] She had changed airplane seats and not reported the incident, she said, because she was groped so frequently back then. "We accepted it for years," she told the paper. "We were taught it was our fault." But hearing Trump deny on television, in response to the *Access Hollywood* tape, that he had ever grabbed a woman against her will, Leeds said, "I wanted to punch the screen."[25]

Michelle Obama—the nation's first lady, who had been caricatured during her husband's 2008 campaign as an angry black woman and had worked relentlessly to battle that perception—roared to furious life, making a remarkable speech, in which she called out the "hurtful, hateful language about women" that Trump had been deploying on the campaign trail and described how the flood of stories from women about abuse and harassment had "shaken me to my core in a way that I couldn't have predicted." It was a critical speech, in part because it had been Obama who that summer had issued the left its directive during the Democratic Convention, after a week of unreconstructed racism and sexism at the Republican Convention in Cleveland. "When they go low, we go high," she had admonished, advising her side to behave with the assuredness that morality would surely win the day.

Now Obama was mad. And crucially, while so much of the angry reaction to Trump's abhorrent trespasses had come on behalf of *white* women, she was ensuring that the white experience of coercion and harassment was not the only one that would be heard in a country in which black women are even less likely to be believed as victims of assault, and far less likely to be treated with respect. Obama called out the press for its inattention to women's anger, chiding those who were "treating this as just another day's headline, as if our outrage is overblown or unwarranted."

Powerfully, Michelle Obama argued that there was something to *do* with this outrage, urging all the women out there who were livid to take action. "While our mothers and grandmothers were often powerless to change their circumstances, today, we as women have all the power we need to determine the outcome of this election. We have knowledge. We have a voice. We have a vote."

Many women took Obama's words to heart. We were furious; I heard from friends who were rounding on their street harassers for the first time, yelling back at them. Men, including a former senator, told me of how shaken they were to hear from their wives and friends and mothers and coworkers about the ubiquity of sexual assault and harassment, how they had had their hair blown back by the anger they hadn't even known had been pent up. Women took some of Trump's sexist words and worked to reappropriate them—turning the phrase "nasty woman," which he'd called

Clinton in a debate, into a T-shirt slogan, and printing up all manner of Etsy merchandise promising that soon "pussy" would "grab back." Millions of women, and some men, rushed to join the Clinton-supporting internet group Pantsuit Nation. But in a season in which Clinton supporters were still being lectured by many in their lives on the right *and* the left, the group was private, visible only to its members on Facebook.

There was a creeping fear that this explosion was too little, and perhaps too late. The week before the election, I traveled to Boston to speak to a group of women, most of them lifelong feminists. One former National Organization for Women (NOW) chapter president in her fifties expressed her anxiety to me: why were these groups secret? She recalled how furious her friends had been over the treatment of Anita Hill in 1991, how in her memory, women had left their office buildings and stormed outside en masse to show that they had indeed had enough. How their public show of anger—the current of outrage and desperation to express it—had eventually led to women's electoral run on Washington the next year. Why weren't women taking to the streets? she asked me with concern. I didn't know, I replied, but I hoped that perhaps it was because they knew that they didn't have to; as Michelle Obama had noted, now—as had not been possible in 1992, as had never been possible before—they knew they could walk out the door on an upcoming Tuesday and vote for a woman for president.

The weekend before the 2016 presidential election, an old family friend and political science professor joked to me, "I'll see you in our female-led future." I looked at him, pretending to hold my breath with fear. "Be kind to me in the reeducation camps," he said with a smile. This was an optimistic joke. So many were optimistic.

But the optimism was part of the trick: the reaffirmation of the myth of Clinton's power. On an episode of *Saturday Night Live* that followed the release of the "pussy tape," comedians portraying debate moderators Anderson Cooper and Martha Raddatz introduced the candidates as "Republican nominee Donald Trump and . . . can we say this yet. . . ? Probably fine. . . . *President* Hillary Clinton."

This surety, that Clinton had already won the presidency, was what prompted so many white people on the right, including white women, to vote against the creeping ascendency of women, especially against *the* woman who'd been so effectively vilified on both the left and the right. It was *also* what disabused women on the left of the purportedly overdramatic notion that the country was still powered by enough misogyny and racism that it would elect an openly hateful bigot, or that they needed to truly stir themselves on Clinton's account in order to combat those biases and beat Trump. In treating her as though she had already beat him, and not like the single tool on the table with which the nation might stop this monstrous racist patriarch, we talked ourselves out of the outrage we should have been mustering. We didn't have to be angry on *behalf* of Hillary Clinton, this seductive song went. If anything, we should be angry *at* her, for not having done enough for us with the power we imagined she had.

After the election, Senator Claire McCaskill of Missouri would tell TV audiences about what she'd heard from women in her state immediately after the election: "I just assumed he wouldn't win," her constituents said in retrospect. "I could have done more. I should have done more."[26] Americans who might have exerted more energy to oppose Trump or support Clinton—especially white women—were goaded into *in*action by the assurance that sexism and racism were things of the past, and that to work themselves up about either would look silly, would be unnecessary exertions on behalf of an imperfect candidate. And of course, many other Americans—including white women—were moved to support Trump for essentially the same reason: what they heard as the *threat* that white patriarchy had lost its grip.

Which is why Donald Trump kept doubling down on the thing that made him purportedly unelectable, alleging that his opponent didn't have the "stamina" to be president, inviting women who had previously accused her husband of sexual misconduct to a debate—*not* in an effort to jumpstart the overdue feminist reassessment of Bill Clinton's sexual improprieties, but rather to humiliate and destabilize Hillary. Trump's primary defense against accusations of assault and harassment was that the women weren't attractive enough to hit on—"Believe me, she would not be my first choice," Trump had said of Jessica Leeds[27]—and he took care to note, after watching Clinton walk in front of him at a debate: "I wasn't impressed."

Clinton's left critics would often comment that she'd lucked out in her draw of opponents, that she'd won—and then blown—a once-in-a-lifetime opportunity to run against such a cartoonishly awful man. What this view failed to acknowledge was that it was the opposite of both luck and accident that this man had been summoned, elected by his party to face down the first woman who was running to be president, the woman we'd been assured *would* be president. To fight her, and her predecessor—another history-making challenge to white masculinity—the Republican Party had chosen a figure who embodied every one of the strains of denigration and disrespect that had historically worked to bar women and nonwhite men from the presidency and to deny them equal access to political power.

It worked. He won.

CHAPTER FOUR

THE WINTER OF OUR DISCONTENT

The election of Donald Trump over Hillary Clinton for the presidency of the United States in 2016 may have felt like a stinging, agonizing shock to many of us who lived through it. But in the context of American history, it should have been wholly unsurprising. In the wake of a challenge to white supremacy, in the form of two Obama administrations, racism won. Over the threat of a potential female leader, brutal masculinity won.

For older women, the metaphor was quotidian, familiar, the stuff of 80s shoulder-padded boardroom movies like *9 to 5*: the sexist, egotistical, lying hypocritical bigot who gets the big job over the woman, even when he's less qualified, even when he's been reported to human resources. This was not extraordinary; this was just another Tuesday in America.

We'd allowed ourselves to be taken in by the lie, by the illusion that we had come farther than we had, and in so doing we'd forfeited our right to be furious. We'd permitted those who *had* expressed anger or passion on behalf of Clinton to become the punch lines, and not the prognosticators.

In the months that followed, after the Women's Marches that would take place in January, many people asked where this raucous fury had been *before* November 9. But the truth was that had it been expressed, it would have been laughed off as silly and faddish, performed and unserious. Rage about sexism would have been its own meta threat to a male-dominated political discourse convinced that sexism was a long-eradicated American ghost, that it would have no damaging impact on a woman as powerful as Clinton.

Even in her loss, instead of bracing acknowledgment of the unabated power of racism and sexism and the structural disadvantages faced by non-white non-men in a country that had just elected an openly racist and misogynistic president, there came an outpouring of concern from some on the left who promptly blamed progressives for having been *too* focused on racial and gender disparities. "American liberalism has slipped into a kind of moral panic about racial, gender and sexual identity that has distorted liberalism's message and prevented it from becoming a unifying force capable of governing," wrote Columbia professor Mark Lilla in the *New York Times*.[28]

But in the wake of that loss, there was no longer a tool at hand—no candidate who could beat this man and his administration of white men and racists, men who would be revealed as wife-beaters and harassers and corrupt grifters. It would be years before an election would provide an opportunity to replace or control him, and now the anger poured out like the water in the Beyoncé video, women amassing—not always as smoothly or peaceably as we might wish—and getting into some rough sort of formation.

The night after the election, Teresa Shook, a retired lawyer and grandmother in Hawaii, feeling shattered, made a Facebook page proposing a march on Washington set for the day after Trump's inauguration. By the time she woke up the next morning she had ten thousand replies; in the same days, New York fashion designer Bob Bland—who had made those "Nasty Woman" T-shirts—had had the same idea. It wasn't a fluid organizational process; the white women who'd thought of it first called the event the Million Women March, without being aware that they were appropriating the name of a 1997 demonstration staged by African-American women in Philadelphia. This only heightened the racial resentments that had sprung up with the news that that while *94 percent* of black women had voted for Hillary Clinton, the majority of white women had voted for Donald Trump: *now* white women organizers were going to stage an angry protest, co-opting the name of an event that had been led by black women twenty years earlier?

But within a couple of weeks, organizers from other movements had taken over the event. Tamika Mallory, a gun control advocate; Carmen Perez, who had worked on behalf of criminal justice reform; and Linda Sarsour, a Muslim-rights activist who'd been active on Bernie Sanders's campaign, all joined Bob Bland to organize the millions who would show up not just in Washington, but in cities around the country and the world—including in Antarctica. The Women's March on January 21, 2017 was the biggest one-day political protest in this country's history, and it was staged by angry women.[29]

At one of the only other comparable protests of a presidential inauguration, held at the height of the New Left, to protest the swearing-in of Richard Nixon in 1969, women in the movement had fought for space for two speakers, Marilyn Salzman Webb and Shulamith Firestone. As soon as Webb had begun to speak about abortion, childcare, and how men on the left treated women, the booing from the male crowd had drowned her out; Webb has recalled that "people were yelling 'Take her off the stage and fuck her!' and 'Fuck her down a dark alley!'" She left the stage crying, and decades later she told the historian Annelise Orleck that that was when she knew that women "couldn't build a coalition with the left; women's liberation was going to be its own movement."[30] Firestone, who'd also been unable to give her speech in the face of booing from her ideological brethren, wrote more bluntly after the event: "Fuck off Left! We're starting our own movement."[31]

Forty-eight years later, decades during which the women's movement had exploded and then receded again, and wrestled with its own internal biases and inequities, here was an inauguration protest that spanned all fifty states, led by a young, multiracial coalition of women hoping to lead a new iteration of the movement into the future. It was groundbreaking that these women weren't asking for speaking slots at a left event; they *were* the left, and they were (imperfectly but insistently) situating leftist progressive priorities—including civil rights, reproductive justice, disability rights, immigrant rights, workers' rights, economic equality, and environmental justice—all within a feminist framework.

As the longtime activist Angela Davis said during her speech from the dais in Washington, DC, the event offered "the promise of *feminism* against the pernicious powers of state violence—an inclusive and intersectional feminism that calls upon all of us to join the resistance to racism, to Islamophobia, to antisemitism, to misogyny, to capitalist exploitation."[32]

And when, the morning after the march, ABC anchor George Stephanopoulos had seventeen minutes to interview Trump spokeswoman Kellyanne Conway on his Sunday morning news show, it was Conway herself who brought up the demonstration against her boss, mentioning it twice before she drew a direct question from Stephanopoulos, who asked, thirteen minutes deep: "What did the president think of that march?"[33]

Conway's response was to criticize the "profanity-laced, threatening, vulgar comments" of the celebrities onstage, citing in particular the pop star Madonna, who had said that she dreamt of "blowing up the White House." (In fact, she had said, "Yes, I'm angry. Yes, I am outraged. Yes, I have thought an awful lot about blowing up the White House. But I know that this won't change anything.") Stephanopoulos—who'd talked with Conway at length about the new president's provably false claims that his inauguration crowds had been bigger than Obama's—did not follow up with any questions about the relative size of the Women's March, or about the impact such unprecedented mass resistance might have on the incoming administration. In the next segment, Senate Minority Leader Chuck Schumer told Stephanopoulos that he'd participated in the Women's March in his home state of New York, and Stephanopoulos responded with only one question, in reference to Madonna's profane rage: "Were you comfortable with everything you heard?"[34]

It was such a neat trick, a way to reduce all the strains of righteous anger that had been on display the previous day to a sound bite that could be swiftly rejected as inappropriate. A way to crumple the mass display of resistance into a ball of paper and toss it into the media trash can of public impropriety; Stephanopoulos's hanky-waving was especially irrational after two years of a presidential candidate who encouraged violence, led public calls for incarceration of his opponent, and whose supporters spoke of killing her for treason. Yet Trump was rarely censured by the Beltway press for having made anyone feel uncomfortable.

It was telling that it was *Conway*—the enabler of the president against whom so much of the ire was directed and one of the very few women in his inner circle—who seemed attuned enough to the potential power of what she'd seen on the streets the day before to bring it up with more interest than her interrogator. It was as though a massive political eruption of women had happened, and the male-dominated political media *hadn't even seen it.*

But the shrugging incuriosity displayed by some in the press was better, by some measure, than the shrugging condescension with which other political commentators treated the march. David Axelrod, one of Barack Obama's former advisors, tweeted on January 21, 2017, "This outpouring today is extraordinary and inspiring. But if all this energy isn't channeled into sustained pol action, it will mean little." Micah White, one of the architects of Occupy Wall Street, worried in the *Guardian* that "Without a clear path from march to power, the protest is destined to be an ineffective feelgood spectacle adorned with pink pussy hats."[35] It was enough to recall Madonna's speech itself, in which she had bellowed, "To our detractors that insist that this march will never add up to anything? Fuck you. Fuck you!"

To anyone who actually attended the event, the proposition that it was some casually undertaken dilettante party about hats was nuts. The day before the march I'd been part of a panel about women's resistance at a Washington, DC, bookstore where so many people showed up that they had to bar the door. Inside, the conversation had been urgent, tactical: about promising candidates and which organizations were doing voter registration and fighting gerrymandering. As soon as the march had concluded, its organizers had staged a gathering called "Where do we go from here?" EMILY's List, the political action committee dedicated to electing pro-choice Democratic women to office, partnering with other organizations designed to get Latinx, gay, lesbian, African-American, Asian-American, and female progressive candidates elected, held a massive candidate training in Washington, DC; its press release read, "This fight may start in the streets, but it's going to end at the ballot box. Let's bring our army to both."[36]

The same day, Planned Parenthood held a political action training session for two thousand people, zeroing in on how to organize around protecting and expanding health care under the incoming administration. Marchers told reporters that they were thinking of running for office, and if they were not thinking of running for office themselves, they were looking at their local- and state-level candidates with an eye toward volunteering, organizing, and donating; they described their new awareness of how many Republicans across the country had been running unopposed and of the need to recruit candidates to challenge incumbents. Marchers spoke of sending postcards and making phone calls to representatives, of lobbying for increased funding to women's health organizations.[37] Women were in it for the long haul. "Immediate outrage and sustained outrage are two different things," a protestor named Sarah Jaffe told *Politico*. "I'm gearing up to be mad as hell for a long time."[38]

But it seemed that there was nothing that women could say, or post on a sign, or yell, or express through organizing or training sessions or strategic planning that would persuade some people that what they were promising, in the context of American history, was revolution. Speaking on *Morning Joe* to Missouri Senator Claire McCaskill, who, in discussion with Mika Brzezinski, had just detailed the marchers' stated commitment to equal pay, women's health care, defending Obamacare, environmental activism, and their plans to run for office and get involved in campaigns as volunteers leading to the midterms, MSNBC analyst Mark Halperin—a man who had spent previous years reporting on the Tea Party's "huge impact on America"—asked her with suppurating condescension, "Senator, [can I] just ask you to be a notch more specific" about how the marchers might "impact what's going on in Washington [this week], not running for [the] school board down the road?"[39]

What happened within the next week was that Donald Trump issued his first version of the travel ban that barred people from several predominantly Muslim nations from entering the country, and it was women who stepped up to oppose him. People rushed to airports; New York congresswoman Nydia Velázquez was one of the first at JFK in New York, demanding the release of immigrants being held there after Trump's executive order barred even those with valid visas and green cards from entry. Lawyers arrived to help those who'd been detained by the ban, and one journalist, Matt Ford, noted the "striking" gender disparity among attorneys who'd sprinted to fight the ban.[40] At Dulles Airport, he tweeted, "Probably 70 percent of lawyers volunteering . . . are young women." In a later story, Ford noted how many of those attorneys were also people of color, an observation that corresponded to the fact that women and people of color are overrepresented in public interest law jobs, and that it was the public interest lawyers who were hurrying to airports.

It was four women judges, and one man, who initially issued stays on Trump's travel ban. These were the fruits of the last furious women's movements, the First and Second Waves, which had opened doors to colleges and law schools, producing a generation of women with law degrees, women who had ascended to the federal bench, and were therefore in the position to block a president's unconstitutional order.

At the rallies objecting to the ban, politicians including Velázquez, New York City Public Advocate Letitia James, Representatives Pramila Jayapal and Nanette Barragán, Senators Elizabeth Warren and Kirsten Gillibrand—the only senator to vote "no" on all but one of Donald Trump's cabinet appointments—joined the leaders of the Women's March, Linda Sarsour and Tamika Mallory, as impassioned speakers. Many of these women had also spoken at the marches the weekend before, conveying that in this moment, those on the inside of the political structure—the senators and elected officials—were *not* going to distance themselves from the angry rabble of activists at the gates. "It is clear that the resistance to Trump's radical agenda will be led by courageous women fighting for our future," tweeted Kamala Harris, the newly sworn-in senator from California, and only the second black woman elected to the body in its history.

In Congress the following Monday, it was Harris and Washington state's Patty Murray who led their caucus in objection to the travel ban, penning a livid letter that expressed their "outrage" at the executive order "and its haphazard implementation," which "run counter to our American values and the Constitution." The letter went on to call Trump's order "unconscionable and unconstitutional."[41] That day, Acting Attorney General Sally Yates sent a letter to Justice Department lawyers, noting that she was unconvinced that Trump's order was lawful, and that "Consequently, for as long as I am the Acting Attorney General, the Department of Justice will not present arguments in defense of the Executive Order unless and until

I become convinced that it is appropriate to do so." Yates was fired before midnight, and Trump called her, in a statement, "weak on borders and very weak on illegal immigration."

But of course, what those first days of Trump's administration showed was that women were the opposite of weak in their opposition to the Trump administration; and every attempt to cut them down was taken up as an opportunity for replenishing their fury.

In the week following, Massachusetts Senator Elizabeth Warren voiced her opposition to Trump's appointment of Jefferson Beauregard Sessions III as attorney general by calling on the words of another woman, the late Coretta Scott King. During Sessions's confirmation hearings, Warren began to read the statement that King had sent to the Senate Judiciary Committee, objecting to the 1986 nomination of Sessions to be a federal district court judge. King had detailed Sessions's history of working against voting rights for African Americans, arguing that Sessions "lacks the temperament, fairness, and judgment to be a federal judge."

But when Warren stood on the Senate floor to read the letter, Republican Senate Majority Leader Mitch McConnell ordered her to stop, forcing her to leave the floor. McConnell surely made this move as his own symbolic message to his base: that he was willing and able to shut down a mouthy woman and aggressive challenger to Republican policies. He would later offer this view of his choice, using the interaction—perhaps consciously, to serve his own purposes—as a metaphor for the suppression of female dissent: "She was warned," McConnell said of Warren's attempt to read King's letter. "She was given an explanation. Nevertheless, she persisted."

Whether or not McConnell's base warmed to his performative dickishness, women around the country immediately took to his words with even more fervor than they'd displayed for nasty women or pussies grabbing back; across social media and Etsy shops, "Nevertheless, she persisted" became a phrase appended to images of tough women, from Harriet Tubman to Malala Yousafzai. One woman in Minneapolis persuaded more than a hundred of her friends and strangers to get "She persisted" tattoos, arranging—as if to show the blowhards sure it was *all* about aesthetics that there was more to it than that—that $55 of the $75 cost of the ink would go to an organization that supported pro-choice women running for office.[42]

As Warren herself said on cable television, eager to capitalize on the optics with her own base, whose potential power she clearly saw: "They can shut me up, but they can't change the truth."[43]

As had happened in the wake of Trump's election, the perceived vanquishing of one threatening woman was provoking a million more—many of them a million times angrier than they'd ever been before—to raise their own voices.

By June, protesters had so powerfully clogged the phone lines and registered their names in the logs of congressional staffers that progress on undoing the accomplishments of the Obama era had been effectively delayed. They camped out outside the offices of Senate Majority Leader Mitch McConnell, some arriving in their wheelchairs, to protest threats to overturn the Affordable Care Act. One poll revealed that 86 percent of those taking daily action to contact their representatives were women, the majority of them over the age of forty-five. Most of them had been to the women's marches.[44]

Protest took both quotidian—calls and letters—and more theatrical forms: In March, women protested an abortion bill in Texas dressed in the red dresses from the television adaptation of *The Handmaid's Tale*, Margaret Atwood's dystopian novel of authoritarian misogyny run amok.[45] In August, protesters in Boston gathered in the wake of the Nazi march on Charlottesville, Virginia, to counter another march of white supremacists; among the counterprotesters was a group of women dressed in black witches' hats, their faces shrouded by black fabric, carrying signs that read things like "Hex White Supremacy." They were members of W.I.T.C.H. Boston, "an intersectional coven" convened in the spirit of the original second-wave radical group W.I.T.C.H., whose members had dressed as witches and "hexed" Wall Street bankers in the 1960s, and which had originally stood for Women's International Terrorist Conspiracy From Hell or Women Inspired to Tell their Collective History, depending on which witch you asked.[46]

To many commentators, it surely appeared that it was all about Donald Trump. But in fact the fury was in response to many of the varied inequities, injustices, and abuses that Donald Trump's ascendance had made so visible. Patrisse Khan-Cullors would say in 2018, "The fight against 45 is not just against him. It's a bigger fight against white supremacy. It's a bigger fight against patriarchy. It's a fight against classism."[47]

In the fall, Carmen Yulín Cruz, the mayor of San Juan, Puerto Rico, furious at the way the U.S. government was leaving the territory without power in the wake of a disastrous hurricane, responded to Acting Homeland Security Secretary Elaine Duke's remark about hurricane response being a "good news story" by saying, "Dammit, this is not a good news story. This is a people-are-dying story." In turn, Donald Trump called her "nasty."

"I don't give a shit," Cruz told reporters when asked about the president's criticism. "I am done being polite, I am done being politically correct, I am mad as hell." A few months later, Kirsten Gillibrand would invite Cruz to be her guest at Trump's first State of the Union address.[48]

Gillibrand, too, stopped being polite, telling me during a spring 2017 interview that officials are in Washington "to help people, and if we're not helping people we should go the fuck home." In winter of 2018, Illinois Senator Tammy Duckworth, a veteran and an amputee, laid into Donald Trump in a blistering floor speech in the Senate, asserting that "I will not be lectured about what our military needs by a five-deferment draft dodger," and later called the president "Cadet Bone Spurs" in reference to his stated medical reason for evading the military draft of his youth. In January 2018, Hawaii Senator Mazie Hirono began to ask every nominee for the federal judiciary whether they'd been accused of sexual misconduct; when questioned on what she'd say to those who argued that this was a partisan strategy, Hirono responded in the summer of 2018, "Fuck them." And Maxine Waters, still a congresswoman from California, and still staunch in her regard for fury as a rational response to injustice, made a cottage industry of tearing into Trump. "I don't honor him, I don't respect him, and I don't want to be involved with him," Waters said early in the administration, later calling him a "disgusting, poor excuse of a man."

Here it was, an anger that was so intense it blazed its way via stupid hats and foul-mouthed tirades, even from the most official and respectable sources—anything to let people know this: Women. Were. Furious. After the election, everything that had been restrained and secret and muffled could no longer be contained beneath a veneer of "going high," or venting only to the like-minded. "Of all the feelings that have surfaced since January—sadness, depression, hopelessness, rare bits of joy," wrote the feminist journalist Samhita Mukhopadhyay at the end of 2017, "the one that has sustained, motivated and sometimes felt like it was destroying me has been anger."[49]

The anger had spilled out into speech and into streets and into organizing, scrambling the daily schedules of women whose lives had been kick-started by writing postcards and calling their representatives, going to organizing meetings and town halls and making signs on oaktag with smelly markers and spending Saturdays at rallies and learning for the first time about intersectionality (and, too rarely, about those who'd been making the calls and drawing the signs *before* the anger reached their doors). The British feminist Laurie Penny tweeted in July 2017, "Most of the interesting women you know are far, far angrier than you'd imagine."[50]

Women signed up to run for office, in numbers higher than the country had ever seen: EMILY's List put the number at over forty thousand in the year and a half after the election. Many of them spoke openly of how it was their fury at Trump, about the fact that he'd won and what it had shown them about the biases and inequities that still existed, contrary to everything they'd been told, that had motivated them to throw their hats in the ring.

Patricia Russo, the head of the Women's Campaign School at Yale, which had been training women to run for office since the 1990s, spoke of the numbers of women who called her, starting in November and then increasing exponentially after the first Women's March, telling her, "I'm mad, I marched, I want to run." So great a motivating force was the anger that Russo worried to me in the late summer of 2017 that it might inevitably fade, dry up, that soon, all these activated women would wilt with the discomfort and the exhaustion and sorrow of all their rage.

A TIME FOR RAGE

And then, in October 2017, the *New York Times*, followed swiftly by the *New Yorker*, published long, frightening, heavily reported stories about the movie producer Harvey Weinstein and his long history of violent sexual harassment and assault, and about how his abusive, misogynistic behavior had done so much damage to the careers of the women he'd harassed, and how it had been systematically covered up for decades. It was—while grotesque and a long time coming—not *so* different from other stories—about Roger Ailes or Bill O'Reilly or Bill Cosby or Donald Trump himself—that had been published in recent years, stories that had attracted increasing interest, that had been taken, slowly, more seriously, but which had not changed the world or workplaces, or how they continued to function.

But American women were a tinderbox and the Weinstein story was an extremely hot match. Of the reverberations in Hollywood, the *New York Times*' Manohla Dargis wrote, "The movies can break your heart, but this isn't the time only for tears. It is also the time for rage."[51]

Suddenly, the media, not to mention the women making it and consuming it, were newly aflame. Many took to using the hashtag #metoo, which had been pioneered in 2006 by Tarana Burke as a movement to address sexual violence, and using it to tell their stories of harassment and abuse. Women and men broadened the conversation beyond sexual violence, using "#metoo" as a catchall that also encompassed tales of denigration and diminution in the professional sphere. Long bottled-up stories poured forth. Powerful, wealthy men—film directors, high-profile professors, morning show anchors who made millions, senators and congressmen and hotel magnates and radio hosts and editors—were losing their jobs, the institutions that had promoted and protected them for decades suddenly jettisoning them. One year after Donald Trump had faced no repercussion for having admitted to grabbing women nonconsensually, women appeared hell-bent on ensuring that other men *would* be forced— at long last—to accept some consequence.

Women were telling stories they'd never told aloud before, to reporters and to one another. And where moments like this had lasted, in the past, for a few days or weeks, what was most startling, given the seizing, rapid-fire pace of the news cycle under Donald Trump, was that this movement just kept going . . . for weeks, then months, expanding to include debate and acknowledgment of assault, bad sex, domestic violence. Hollywood's interest went beyond dress adornments and lip service; activists were brought onto red carpets; a fund was established to legally support women in less stable industries; Anita Hill signed up to head an entertainment industry commission on how to move forward.

It was a conflagration, an eruption of so much that had been held back, hidden from view, for decades, for centuries. Ijeoma Oluo wrote in *Elle* in January 2018: "To the men scratching their heads in concern and confusion: The rage you see right now, the rage bringing down previously invulnerable men today, barely scratches the surface. You think we might be angry? You have no idea how angry we are."[52] The same magazine would publish a survey in March, finding that 57 percent of women were angrier in 2018 than they had been in 2017, and that a whopping 83 percent of Democratic women were getting furious, particularly at the news, at least once a day.[53]

Those who were anxious about the velocity and intensity of #metoo spoke of dangerous category collapse, about how anger in response to rape and assault was mingling with anger about workplace sexual harassment, which in turn melded into anger about plain old bad sex. They weren't wrong, exactly. There was a blurring, there was confusion, in part because what was coming into view was the tie that bound all of these behaviors: sexism, plain and simple. Sexism and the systemic damage that it did; sexism as it mingled with class and race to create unequal opportunities and outcomes. Sexism made suddenly, enragingly clear to lots of people for whom it had long been obscured.

"The antipatriarchy movement," warned presidential advisor Steve Bannon, was building, and aiming to "undo ten thousand years of recorded history . . . You watch. The time has come. Women are gonna take charge of society. And they couldn't juxtapose a better villain than Trump. He is the patriarch. This is a [defining] moment in the culture. It'll never be the same going forward." Bannon, a living embodiment of sexist, racist, white patriarchal impulse, seemed to see the fury that was amassing, and understand its potential power. [54]

"Grab the broom of anger and drive off the beast of fear," wrote Zora Neale Hurston, and I thought hard about that formulation through the fall of 2017, as the fear that Patricia Russo had expressed to me—that the anger was going to fade—itself began to dim. The anger that had propelled women into the streets in January and to the phones and protests and onto ballots through the spring was still burning, alighting on new subjects, picking further fights. Anger was the broom that swept America's newly infuriated women into a new year, 2018, the year in which electoral opportunity provided a new channel for their furious drive.

A REPRESSED MAJORITY

"Female rage is the essential fuel of #metoo," wrote Caitlin Flanagan in the *Atlantic*. "Unchecked it is the potent force that will destroy it."[55] That anger was hot, bubbling, wholly out of control.

Yes, it is out of control. It is a loud and livid objection to the kinds of control that have long been in place in a nation built by white men who, when they angrily broke free of imperialist control themselves, promptly encoded protections of liberty and independence only for themselves, building their new nation on slavery and the oppression of women, on the legal and civic subjugation of that nation's majority.

Social movements are necessarily about challenging social controls. This is what social change is built on, and what America's politics themselves are built on, that political act that Maxine Waters could see twenty-five years earlier when others simply saw "riots" and "thugs": *insurrection.*

Insurrections don't always work; in fact, they don't *often* work, in part—as Flanagan suggested—because the rage that fuels them has the power to burn them up. Which is just part of what makes them scary; the other thing that makes them scary is that they are designed to destabilize power structures, often the ones that have been abusive, but are nonetheless the only ones we've got.

As America approaches its two hundred and fiftieth year since revolution was declared, still just one hundred and fifty years since abolition, a century since some women won the right to vote, and fifty years since African Americans in the Jim Crow South were fully enfranchised—all events that occurred in the wake of *uprisings* of Americans furious at the injustices they faced—women in America are coalescing in anger again. It is messy; it is riven by division—racial and generational and political.

It is not civil, it is often profane; calls for civility are designed to protect the powerful by casting them as victims. It is a mass fury: occasionally so frenzied that it makes people nervous. Were it any other way, nothing would ever change.

This is the revolutionary mission, what the idealized vision of what this country might be was born of: the righteous fury of the unrepresented. We are taught it—*give me liberty or give me death, live free or die, don't tread on me*—as patriotic catechism, but only when it has been expressed by white men has it sounded or been transmitted to us as admirable, reasonable, as the crucial catalytic ingredient to political change. That's because white men were always and have remained the rational norm, the intellectual ideal, their dissatisfactions easily understood as being grounded in reason, not in the unstable emotional muck of femininity.

Those founders, so determined that no one would tread on them, were furiously codifying liberty for themselves, built on the oppression of others—enslaved people, women. Those who were oppressed made the opportunities for the oppressors greater, just as the colonies had enriched the British Empire. What our founders established was not a true representative democracy, but rather one in which a minority ruled, based on a myth of wide and just representation, and in which that minority benefitted from the labor of and reduced competition from a subjugated majority. In order to maintain minority rule, the majority's resistance must be repressed, its anger discouraged.

What happened in the second decade of the twenty-first century is that women began to rage publicly in ways that made them audible to one another; we began to hear one another and understand that we were not as isolated in our rage as we had been led to believe. Whether it was about police violence, or the election of a megalomaniac, or the defeat of Hillary Clinton, or about gun violence, or about low wages, or about abortion, women began yelling, and the effect was—is—seismic.

"People are starting to get angrier and remember our history, remember our roots," Jenny Craig, a teacher in West Virginia, striking for higher wages, told *New York Times* columnist Michelle Goldberg of the drive to stage a successful walkout in a state where striking is illegal.[56]

The teacher strikes, which spread from West Virginia to Arizona and

Oklahoma, were taking place in the same weeks of 2018, one year into a Trump presidency, when a group of high school students, the young women and men who'd survived the mass shooting in Parkland, Florida, began their own campaign to end gun violence. The most incandescently furious of the group was perhaps the Cuban-American teenager Emma González, who wiped away her tears and bellowed into a microphone, "The people in the government who were voted into power are lying to us. . . . Politicians who sit in their gilded House and Senate seats funded by the NRA telling us nothing could have been done to prevent this; *we call B.S.*"[57]

In her public oratory, González recalled no one so much as Rose Schneiderman, the twenty-eight-year-old labor organizer who, one week after the 1911 Triangle Shirtwaist Factory fire killed 146 workers, almost all of them women, stood at a memorial service for the dead at the Metropolitan Opera House and angrily declared:

"This is not the first time girls have been burned alive in the city. Every week I must learn of the untimely death of one of my sister workers. Every year thousands of us are maimed. The life of men and women is so cheap and property is so sacred . . . But every time the workers come out in the only way they know, to protest against conditions which are unbearable, the strong hand of the law is allowed to press down heavily upon us. Public officials have only words of warning to us—warning that we must be intensely peaceable . . . I can't talk fellowship to you who are gathered here. Too much blood has been spilled. I know from my experience it is up to the working people to save themselves. The only way they can save themselves is by a strong working-class movement."[58]

Many in the press, and likely in government, scoffed at González's speech in a country in which the National Rifle Association's power has held such immutable sway, a nation in which, in the years since the killing of twenty-six at Sandy Hook Elementary school, gun restrictions have only been made looser by state legislatures around the country. But those same assured and cynical pundits might remember that Schneiderman—alongside Frances Perkins, who witnessed the Triangle fire and was so enraged by it that she changed the course of her career to address labor issues—wound up drafting some of the very workplace safety requirements that are still in place today.

We must train ourselves to even be able to see and hear anger from women and understand it not only as rational, but as politically weighty. It is, in fact, an anger on behalf of the nation's suppressed majority and therefore especially frightening and combustible because of the threat it poses to the minority. We are primed to hear the anger of men as stirring, downright American, as our national lullaby, and primed to hear the sound of women demanding freedom as the screech of nails on our national chalkboard. That's because women's freedom would in fact circumscribe white male dominion.

There will be, already is, a desire to treat this iteration of women's uprising as hysteria, a mob, a witch hunt, a passing phase, a childish tantrum, something irrational, something niche, something that can be averted or neutralized as soon as everyone just calms down. There will be assertions that the anger is not authentic but performed. There will be tremendous pressure to not take it seriously, to not listen too carefully to what the loud shrill voices are saying, insistence that women giving voice to their rage are sure to lose, or are simply working to provoke further discrimination and disregard. Women's anger will be—as it has long been—cast as ugly, unappealing, dangerous, something to be shut down or jeered. Nothing, we have long been assured, is more unattractive in a woman than anger, and those messages will be especially damaging—as they have always been—to nonwhite women. But these are all strategies that have long been used to get people, including women themselves, to look away from, disregard, and suppress one of the great drivers of social upheaval and political change in this country: their own fury.

PART II
MEDUSAS

My mother, when she was about to deliver me in El Paso, Texas, needed a cesarean section and they wouldn't admit her because she was black. It was a Catholic hospital. My grandmother, who was half Irish—because my great-grandmother, who was a domestic worker, had been raped by her white employer—looked white, so she had to convince the people in the admitting office that my mother was her daughter. They finally let her in and they left my mother on a gurney in the hall, unattended, and she was delirious. She *needed* a C-section. Finally a doctor noticed her, drove her into the operating room, and it was too late for a C-section. She almost died; they had to pull me out using forceps and I barely made it. She almost didn't live and I almost didn't get here. So you think I'm not mad? Please. I don't like talking about this stuff a lot. But I guess anger has been just a part of my life since the day I was born. It's part of what's motivated me to deal with racism, sexism, lack of access to health care for women—for my whole life—*that's* why I fight.

—Congresswoman Barbara Lee

HOLD YOUR TEMPER/ HOLD YOUR TONGUE

Congresswoman Barbara Lee was mad.

It was the summer of 2017, and the very liberal Democrat representing Oakland, California, had recently produced one of the only true—and surprising—bipartisan victories of the long, miserable congressional term, one she'd been working toward for over a decade.

Lee, the *only* member of Congress to have voted against the Authorization for the Use of Military Force (AUMF) in 2001, three days after the September 11 terrorist attacks, had been campaigning practically ever since to have that authorization—which had granted the president the ability to go to war without congressional approval and had been used to justify at least thirty-seven military interventions in fourteen nations—repealed. Lee had, in June, finally rallied Republican support for the AUMF repeal, with a window of eight months to revise and replace it. Over the objections of House Speaker Paul Ryan, Lee's amendment to a Defense Department spending bill had passed by a voice vote out of the Appropriations Committee with support from both Democrats and Republicans.[1] *Politico* had called the Appropriations vote "the rarest of congressional spectacles: an earnest debate in which minds were changed, followed by a vote no one could have predicted." In other words, in a very dark year, the vote to repeal the AUMF had been a singular example of functional democracy; when it passed the Appropriations Committee with overwhelming support, other lawmakers in the chamber had actually applauded.[2]

And then, three weeks later, Paul Ryan stripped Lee's amendment from the defense bill before it could come to a full House vote. The repeal was removed in the middle of the night, with no vote and no explanation.

"It evaporated," Lee said to me a few weeks after her repeal had been vaporized. "It's like they whited it out and rewrote something in. This is sleazy. This is sleaze all the way."

A shocked Lee appeared before the Rules Committee, where she calmly described her objections to the process by which the repeal had been stripped to the committee chairman, Texas Republican Pete Sessions, who responded to her politely stated points with cheerful condescension. "I was so mad at Pete Sessions," Lee recalled. "But I tried to control my anger."

Lee recalls her inner calibrations, during the back-and-forth with Sessions: "I've got to not let them think that I'm not responsible, and that I don't know what I'm talking about. I've got to be logical and coherent, I can't let my emotions come out because otherwise they'll say 'There is this angry black woman again. She's always angry about something; here she goes again.'"

Lee remained measured. She repeatedly expressed her disbelief and dismay at how and why the amendment had been removed at the discretion of a couple of individual lawmakers, despite its having passed the Appropriations Committee with broad support from both parties. She remained stone-faced as Sessions, a white man from Texas who's served in the House for about the same amount of time that she has, explained to her that this was just how things worked.

At the very end of the interaction, Lee finally allowed some of her frustrations to show, telling Sessions, "I am very shocked at this process and how this went down, and I hope that in the future . . . in the spirit of bipartisanship and regular order and our democratic processes that this not be done very often, because this is really *raw*." She quoted him numbers, noting that it had only happened two other times in the past year; he put his head in his hands, in a show of exhaustion. Lee pressed on: "I just hope people understand that democracy is very important and the Democratic process is important and members should not be undermined by three or four or five individuals if they have worked together, and put something together and gotten it in a bill, bipartisan, and then it's ripped out . . . It is perplexing that this could happen in the middle of the night."[3]

Her colleagues watching from her California district, she said, had cheered at the insistence with which she'd kept pointing out the injustice that had just been enacted. "They said, 'You kept coming back at him, wearing him down.' So it may have worked, because if I had gone off like he expected me to go off, then I may not have been able to wear him down." Lee's appearance was, indeed, a study in strategic containment, just as she knew it must be. While she was confronting a male colleague—and describing other male colleagues, who had tricked, attempted to deceive, and were now condescending to her—she was, above all, courteous.

Those in her own party noticed, and, as she would tell me later, congratulated her for it. "Everyone told me how gracious I was, and how they could tell I was really getting ready to go off on him, but I was restrained. They could see my anger, but they were so proud of me because I handled it right," she said.

Their response, Lee said, enraged her even more than the committee's dirty play had.

"They expected me to be the angry black woman, okay? They were applauding me for not being the angry black woman, and I wanted to cuss them out. Because that was the implication: *you were so cool, you were so restrained, you handled it so well, and toward the end you were a little emotional but you were great.* And I'm [thinking] 'Doggonit, you guys don't even know what you are saying!'"

What they were saying was that it hadn't even occurred to them how limited Lee—an esteemed colleague who had every reason to be livid that the amendment she'd been trying to pass for fifteen years had been improperly removed by her political opponents—had been in her ability to fight against those who wronged her professionally. They were suggesting to her, by congratulating her on not having shown her anger, that anger would have been the improper recourse, when in fact it would have been a wholly reasonable response to improper professional behavior by her colleagues. They were telegraphing to her that they had never considered the kinds of racial and gendered pressures put on women, and especially on black women, to bottle up their resentments and their frustrations, no matter how justified they might be.

The fact that Lee had understood that she *couldn't* get openly mad, that she had known that an expression of wholly valid, justified, rational rage would have worked to weaken her position, is a symptom of the same kinds of skewed power dynamics that permit white men to hold so much sway in government—to be the chairmen and the speakers in numbers so much greater than any other demographic.

The result of the hosannas for not having expressed her anger, Lee said, was that she just got angrier—at her colleagues, her opponents, and because the AUMF *still* wasn't repealed. "I was totally hurt and, yes, livid." But, Lee said, she will try again. "And again and again and again until it is done. I am not going to let anyone stop me."

Barbara Lee was born in Texas, to a mother who was always upfront about her anger. "She didn't take any prisoners. She was really upfront about inappropriate speech and behavior. She didn't mince her words; she wouldn't take any mess," said Lee. Lee recalled a story her mother had relayed about how as a college student, she and a friend had wanted to join Alpha Kappa Alpha, the nation's first black sorority. Back then, AKA admitted only light-skinned women; that wasn't a problem for Lee's mother, the granddaughter of a domestic worker who'd been raped and had children by her Irish employer. "So my grandmother looked like she was white, and my mother was very fair with green eyes," said Lee. But the sorority turned down her mother's best friend Juanita, whose skin was darker. "My mother got furious," said Lee. "She said 'To hell with this; I'm not joining,'" and called on the civil rights activist and educator Mary McLeod Bethune to come down to Texas Southern University and help students organize in protest. "That's how my mother was," Lee said. "She was constantly pushing."

When Lee herself was a high school student in San Fernando, California, she wanted to be a cheerleader, but the school had never had a black cheerleader, in part because of the way the selection process was conducted, privately. "I was mad," recalled Lee of her teenage self, "because I knew all these white girls had had the opportunity to be cheerleaders, and

I knew I couldn't. So I went to the NAACP out of anger and asked them if they could help me and they said yeah." Lee and her classmates staged protests to change the rules, ensuring that girls could try out in front of the student body. Lee became the first black cheerleader at San Fernando High, and was soon joined on the squad by an Asian American student. "That was anger," she said. "I was *really* angry. I voiced my anger. But I was strategic, and I got what I wanted, not just for me but for everybody else, for all these girls of color who wanted to be cheerleaders."

In her early twenties, Lee was a student at Mills College in California; she was by then a single mother of two sons, on welfare and Medicaid. "I was angry at the system of oppression and racism because I saw it, I lived it every day, and who wouldn't be angry? I was being dissed by social workers and jerked around by guys and all that stuff." She became the head of the campus Black Student Union, and started doing community work with the Black Panther Party. "I wanted to make whatever intervention I could to make things better for other people." But her interventions did not include electoral politics; she had no interest in working within the American political system. "I mean, I was saying it was rigged back then," Lee said of electoral politics. Lee's lack of belief in the system was imperiling her grades; as a government major, she was required to do field work for a campaign, but she was not even registered to vote in early 1972.

That's when Shirley Chisholm came to speak at Mills College. Chisholm, in the midst of her presidential campaign, spoke to students in fluent Spanish; she talked about health care, poverty, women's rights, racial justice, and immigrants' rights. Lee couldn't believe it. She approached Chisholm afterward and suggested that she'd like to work on her campaign in the California primary, confessing that she'd previously not had anything to do with electoral politics. Chisholm, Lee recalled, "Shook her finger at me. 'Little girl!'—I was twenty-five! I had two little kids, they were probably with me!—But anyway, she said 'Little girl! If you really believe in what you stand for, then you'll register to vote, get involved with politics, and try to make change. Because we need you.'"

Lee wound up organizing Chisholm's Northern California campaign with other Bay Area college students, attending the Democratic National Convention in Miami as a Chisholm delegate. After Chisholm's campaign, and a stint working for Black Panther cofounder Bobby Seale's 1973 mayoral race, Lee worked for a decade for Congressman Ron Dellums, who had been one of Chisholm's supporters in the Congressional Black Caucus; she was then elected to the California State Assembly and the California State Senate. Lee would eventually win Dellums's seat after his retirement from Congress. She has served Oakland as a congresswoman for twenty years.

And in that capacity, she told me, "I've learned how to . . . I won't even say *finesse* it, but how to handle life without going ballistic every time I feel like I'm treated unjustly, or other people are treated unjustly."

For women in public life, especially those engaged in a fight for more equal opportunities for more kinds of people, the message has long been clear: their anger and desire to challenge the system—ironically, perhaps the thing that motivated their engagement in social change and political life to begin with—will be used against them.

BRING IN THE BRANK

The furious female is, we are told to this day, in innumerable ways, both subtle and stark, a perversion of both nature and our social norms. She is ugly, emotional, out of control, sick, unhappy, unpleasant to be around, unpersuasive, irrational, crazy, infantile. Above all, she must not be heard.

The brank—also known as a scold's bridle, or a witch's bridle—was a sixteenth-century torture device used to muzzle a defiant or cranky woman, her head and jaw clamped into a metal cage. Some of the bridles, which were made of iron, included tongue depressors that would be inserted into the woman's mouth; some of those had spikes on the bottom to pierce the tongues of the insubordinate. The Tower of London features an internally spiked metal neck collar dating from 1588, labeled a "collar for torture," but described in guidebooks as a device to be "put around the necks of scolding or wayward wives."[4]

We may not be literally collared anymore, but the men who tell us to smile on the street so we'll be prettier (reminding us simultaneously to stifle negative thoughts *and* that our purpose is to decorate their world) are echoed around us on national stages. During the 2016 primaries, MSNBC host Joe Scarborough chided Hillary Clinton, after a winning night, "Smile. You just had a big night."[5] In 2018, White House press secretary Sarah Huckabee Sanders said during a CNN appearance, about Nancy Pelosi's grim visage during Donald Trump's first State of the Union address, "I think she should smile a lot more often; I think the country would be better for it. She seems to embody . . . bitterness."[6]

The notion of bitterness, a word and descriptor that suggests cramped, uptight sourness—something that no one wants to express—crops up all the time around angry women. But bitterness tends to be an aspersion cast only at those with most to be bitter about, something that James Baldwin described decades ago with regard to black anger. "People finally say to you, in an attempt to dismiss the social reality, 'But you're so bitter.' Well, I may or may not be bitter, but if I were, I would have good reasons for it, chief among them that American blindness, or cowardice, which allows us to pretend that life presents no reasons for . . . being bitter."[7]

The old view of disruptive women as Medusa—who was punished by Minerva after having been raped in Minerva's temple, cursed with a head full of snakes and the ability to turn men into stone just by looking at them, and who was finally effectively disarmed, via beheading, by Perseus—was not lost on Susan B. Anthony, who observed in 1893 to the *Chicago Tribune* that women were asked to echo the sentiments of the men who ran the major newspapers, "and if they do not do that, their heads are cut off."[7] In the same period, one preacher described the figure of the woman reformer, jostling into male spaces with her arguments for enfranchisement and temperance, as "a monstrosity of nature, a subverter of society . . . the head of Medusa, a bird of ill omen, a hideous specter, a travesty of all that is sacred and divine."[8] As the British historian Mary Beard has chronicled, critics have often used the same frame for Hillary Clinton, producing endless memes of snakes emerging from her scalp[9]; one Breitbart writer claimed that statues of the candidate hadn't been erected since "anyone who saw them would turn instantly to stone."[10]

But the labeling of the powerful political woman as monstrous doesn't stop at Medusa; it's in the endless barrage of Republican campaign mailers featuring Pelosi as cackling witch or ghoulish villain. As the journalist

Peter Beinart reported in 2018, "within days of Pelosi's ascension to House minority leader, in 2003 . . . the Republican Party featured her visage—'garish and twisted,' in the words of a magazine article at the time—in an ad against a Democrat running for Congress in Louisiana." Pelosi is always shown with her mouth open, unrestrained by any brank or bridle. The impulse to depict the most powerful woman in Congress as threatening or unstable, and to direct her ideological foes to do what they can to shut her mouth, almost certainly can be traced directly to fear of her efficacy. She has been one of the most successful legislative strategists of the modern era, shepherding her often fractious caucus through the passage of health-care reform and stimulus spending during the Obama administration. All this in contrast to the Republican men who've occupied the same spot and exhibited only the most flaccid leadership abilities: from Paul Ryan to John Boehner to Dennis Hastert.

Powerful women—especially those whose talents are inarguably more impressive than that of their male peers—are often perceived as monstrous or perverse, unwell or unwholesome in their challenge to male authority. "Madness," a term used to designate mental illness, is also a description of anger, and for women, the two seem to be understood as related.

THE MADWOMAN IN THE STATE HOUSE

The aspersion that a woman who is angry is also *unstable* is cast every day in popular political discourse, so often we probably don't understand how completely we absorb the connection. In 2017, Senator Kirsten Gillibrand aggressively questioned Marine Corps Commandant Robert Neller about a failure of the military to address a pervasive pattern of sexual harassment in its ranks. That night, Fox News anchor Tucker Carlson went on national television and announced, "Senator Kirsten Gillibrand of New York came positively unglued," describing her as "barking" at the commandant.

When Maxine Waters refused to yield in her questioning of Treasury Secretary Steven Mnuchin, announcing that she was "reclaiming [her] time," the website RealClearPolitics described it as a "meltdown"[11]; at right-wing sites TheBlaze and Breitbart, Waters is regularly described as "unhinged."[12] Trump-supporting black pastor Darrell Scott has referred to Waters as a "crazy aunt . . . rambling and babbling incessantly over every little thing."[13]

The idea that women's anger is fundamentally illegitimate, because they have nothing *real*, no big things to be rationally angry about, is part of what undergirds the claim that furious women are mentally ill. But it can also cause women to *feel* crazy. "Our anger gets dismissed and devalued and gaslighted," Black Lives Matter cofounder Alicia Garza told me, speaking specifically about black women. "We are angry because people are telling us what is happening to us right in front of our faces is not in fact happening, and that is crazy to me."

Whether angry women are driven crazy, or whether their anger is confused for mental illness, the claim about them in a society that treats mental illness as a delegitimizing aberration becomes the same: they are received as emotionally precarious, irrational, untrustworthy, marginal, and unattractive.

Do a Google image search on any of the powerful women in politics or public life, especially those who threaten white male power—by pressing for reforms in the military, the criminal justice system, the banking industry, or by running to beat powerful men—and you'll turn up scores of photos of Waters and Pelosi and Senators Kamala Harris and Elizabeth Warren with their mouths open, unrestrained: mid-yell, spittle-flecked, the very act of making a loud noise a sign of their ugly and unnatural personalities. The best way to discredit these women, to make them look unattractive, is to capture an image of them screaming; the act of a woman opening her mouth with volume and assured force, often in complaint, is coded in our minds as ugly.

"I struggle to think of women who lost their tempers in public and didn't face ridicule, temporary ruin, or both," wrote the feminist essayist Lindy West in 2017, citing public outcry against and condemnation of singers Sinead O'Connor, the Dixie Chicks, and Solange Knowles, as well as Juli Briskman, a government contractor who was fired after she was photographed giving Trump's presidential motorcade the finger.[14] When Caitlin Marriott, a twenty-one-year-old congressional intern, shouted, "Mr. President . . . fuck you!" at Donald Trump as he entered the Capitol in the summer of 2018, she was suspended for a week and had her credentials removed, though notably her boss, New Hampshire senator Maggie Hassan, told the press that Marriott's behavior "shouldn't be equated with the president's destructive and divisive actions, like ripping health care away from people . . . like separating children from their parents. . . . And this young woman immediately accepted responsibility for her actions and is facing consequences for them. The president is doing neither."[15]

Perhaps the negativity around the yelling woman goes back to the disproportionate labor they perform as caretakers of the young, women's raised voices an unhappy reminder of reprimands, tones that make men feel like children again, under the punitive thumbs of their mothers, grandmothers, older sisters, nannies, and teachers who nurtured and educated them. "We're raised by women," said Gloria Steinem, "so we experience female power when we're younger. And men, especially, when they see a powerful woman as an adult, feel regressed to childhood and strike out at her."[16]

But the way in which adult female censure may return us to a youthful, domestic sphere—the only one in which women have been granted a kind of unchallenged power—speaks to the thing that women's full-throated challenge does: it turns things upside down, reminds us of a time and place where women had authority, but when it's happening in politics, or in workplaces, or in activism, or elsewhere in the public sphere, it's an aberration, contextually inappropriate. In this way, women's angry voices, raised in challenge to power structures, vibrate with the threat of insurgency.

When Senator Kamala Harris, a former prosecutor, aggressively questioned Attorney General Jeff Sessions in 2017, Harris was instructed to stop interrupting Sessions by his friend, Arizona Senator John McCain. During that exchange, Sessions said aloud that Senator Harris's interrogation was making him "nervous." After the contentious exchange, former Trump advisor Jason Miller described the Attorney General as having had "vinegar and fire in his belly"; by contrast, in his view, Harris displayed "hysteria" in her interrogation of Sessions.

This coding doesn't just come from men: an angry woman can make other *women* very nervous too. After one furious postelection rant from Elizabeth Warren, MSNBC anchor Mika Brzezinski warned viewers, "there's an anger there that was shrill . . . unmeasured and almost un-hinged." Even in the *New York Times*, Warren—whose great gift is her ability to tell clear stories about the American economy that convey the frustrations and resentments of Americans who've been cheated or left behind as financial institutions have gotten more powerful—has been la-beled a "scold," a word that seems well paired with another descriptor the paper has applied to her: "imperious."

What these women seem to represent is a kind of disarray. And here there is a deep historical reverberation: In early twentieth-century propa-ganda film strips about suffragists, women demanding enfranchisement are shown leaving their babies at home with their incapable husbands.[17] Nature has been thrown awry; the women's fury at their exclusion from civic participation has provoked disorder in the home. Women's ire in any political context remains coded as chaotic, while men's is comprehensible, understood as rational and often admirable.

This is probably why, as I was reporting for this book, nearly every woman I spoke to—especially in the months immediately following the inauguration of Donald Trump—described her anger as a thing of the past. "I *was* angry," an interviewee would say, "but I'm not angry anymore; I've taken my anger and turned it into action." Anger had to have been felt in the past tense in order to be something that many women I spoke to could describe to me with authority or confidence, let alone enthusiasm. About ten minutes into every interview I did in which a woman had as-sured me that she'd cast off her anger, I'd find her cursing and raising her voice, yelling about how livid she was: at Donald Trump, or her father, or her friends, or more broadly, at the nation and its injustices. These women were angry; *of course* they were angry. But they were conditioned to deny it from the start.

RECOGNIZING FURY

Gloria Steinem described to me the lifelong process of learning to feel, rec-ognize, acknowledge, and express anger in real time. Steinem was raised in Toledo, Ohio, in a family in which her mother had given up a career as a journalist to raise children, and then suffered a mental illness that left her daughters as her caretakers. But Steinem was resistant to anger. "Coming from the Midwest, we have to be on LSD to know when we're angry," she said. For a while, she said, she "transplanted [her] anger, which is not uncommon for women to do, into other things." She could be angry at anyone who treated an animal badly, or another person, but not angry on her own behalf.

When she was in her thirties and a working journalist herself, established as a glamorous denizen of the early 1970s New York media scene, Steinem made waves by posing as a Bunny at the New York Playboy Club and then writing about the experience; she'd also covered the antiwar and black power movements, and she'd been sent to cover a hearing on abortion. As Steinem recalled, "I'm sure that [anger is] what I felt at the first abortion hearing, the moment when I suddenly realized that *yes*, I had had an abortion, and so had one in three other women [but that it was illegal]. I'm sure what I felt was anger: *How is this okay? This is completely irrational!* I was fueled by anger." That fuel propelled her into the women's movement. Still, she said, for many years, "I could finally tell people on a Thursday that I'd been angry on Monday. I couldn't tell them in real time." Still, she said, with half a century as a feminist organizer and women's leader under her belt, as a woman who understands that "anger is great fuel for political activism; it's wonderful and I value it, I treasure it"—still, she said, to this day, she can express anger in real time "only occasionally."

If it is so difficult for Gloria Fucking Steinem to confidently let loose with fury, is it any wonder that in many places when I speak to students, young women ask me how *they* might express their own ire? They are scared, they tell me—in high schools, and on college campuses—to be publicly open about their rage, because they are afraid it will be alienating to their friends, to their peers, to men. They fear it will make them sound deranged or aggressive. They're not deranged and they're not aggressive; they're just angry. But how can they say that they're mad without drawing condemnation and raised eyebrows? How can they be confident and unapologetic in their rage? Won't they scare people off? They ask me what my secret is: How did I figure out how to get up on the stages at their schools and speak angrily?

What can I tell them? That when I was thirty-two and visiting a beach community with a friend, I told a glamorous older woman to whom I'd been introduced that I wrote about feminism, and that she looked me up and down and asked coolly, "How do men feel about your work?" as if this were the most crucial question about its consequence. When I told her that the man I was dating seemed interested in it, she raised an eyebrow and, disconcertingly, ran a finger along my leg, perhaps checking to see if it was hairless. "We'll see how that lasts." I don't want to recall to them that when I first started to write about politics and culture from a feminist perspective—and nearly always with careful humor and lightness intended to obscure my fury—about half of the responses I received were from readers anxious to tell me how furious I sounded, as if the assertion that I was angry was its own self-contained insult. Others suggested that the rage they presumed I must be feeling originated with the fact that I was ugly and that no man wanted me, while others were sure that if I could only land a man, he might be able to help me. Perhaps I should not mention to them that I was once told that a male friend—a good friend, a man I trust and care about—had said privately to another man, who had in turn told me, "Rebecca is so warm and so funny, you'd never connect the person she is with the angry stuff she writes."

But! I long to say to that friend, though he has no idea that his remarks were reported to me: the warm and funny me is the *same* as the writer who's furious about inequality; the woman who has been both happily single and happily partnered, who is in love with a man who loves her, who has fun and feels joy and cares about her work and her friends and who vacations and drinks and eats and cooks and has kids she adores: she's also very angry.

But perhaps the belief that anger is somehow at odds with the otherwise affable feminine personality has to do with the fact that women have been so well conditioned to tamp down the rage, to disguise it or compartmentalize it, that the revelation that it's bubbling underneath feels surprising and discombobulating—even worrying—to others.

IT'S BAD FOR YOU

There is a persistent conviction that to be angry is *bad* for women. In early 2018, my dentist estimated to me that three-quarters of the women who'd come to see him since Trump's election were livid, information I quickly understood as a hopeful sign. But he shook his head sadly. "It's bad for them," he said. "They grind their teeth."

My dentist was not alone in his concern; plenty of activist, feminist women have shared his worries about rage's detrimental health effects. In the same days of 2018 that flood waters were covering Houston and Donald Trump was once again threatening to repeal DACA and had pardoned racist sheriff Joe Arpaio and rolled back Obama administration provisions that forced companies to turn over their pay statistics, I received in my inbox a newsletter from goop, Gwyneth Paltrow's health and wellness brand, advising me on how to manage my anger. Though the newsletter assured me that according to psychotherapists, anger is "essential to our development" and acts as "a fuel that propels you through different life stages," the Q and A with the experts told a different story, warning goop's overwhelmingly female readership that feeling anger was an easy way out in personal relationships ("We'd rather get angry than admit our deep feelings of vulnerability") and also admonished that in politics, "So many politicians . . . are blinded by their own rage, leading to more mistakes. The mark of a true leader is that they can . . . make a mistake or people can disagree with them and they aren't taken over by anger. They may feel angry, but they don't act it out."[18]

So stigmatized is anger—viewed as somehow unclean, unhealthy—that even women whose politics have in part been driven by rage at injustice often renounce it and warn against its ill effects. The civil rights activist Septima Poinsette Clark, daughter of a formerly enslaved man, who grew up with reduced educational and economic opportunity and became a prolific educator and the founder of "citizenship schools" to increase black adult literacy and provide African Americans with tools they needed—and were often denied—to increase their chances at civic participation, famously said, "I never felt that getting angry would do you any good other than hurt your own digestion, keep you from eating, which I liked to do."

But women tamp it all down so effectively that I didn't realize until recently—as the rage began to overflow—how many other women, speaking about feminism around the country, get the same kinds of questions asked of them by young women as I do. The writer Roxane Gay has described how "at many events where I am speaking about feminism, young women ask how they can comport themselves so they aren't perceived as angry while they practice their feminism. They ask this question as if anger is an unreasonable emotion when considering the inequalities, challenges, violence, and oppression women the world over face."

Women yearn for permission, and simultaneously hunger for someone to express any curiosity at all about what they might be feeling.

"We get told all the time that our anger is disruptive, that it is a distraction, that it is not helpful, and that in fact it is divisive and moving us backwards," said Alicia Garza. "Yet nobody ever seems to question: *why are you so fucking mad?*"

"You are the first person who's ever asked me explicitly about anger," said Aditi Juneja, a twenty-seven-year-old lawyer and activist who co-created an activism guide called *The Resistance Manual* in the wake of the 2016 election. "People ask me about self-care, about inclusion; no one ever asks me if I'm pissed off." But Juneja said she knows why. "If you ask women if they're angry, everyone will say no."

Juneja said she'd been thinking a lot about "who's even allowed to be pissed off and how they're allowed to express it" since the election. She said that she stopped watching Trump speeches or news about him almost a month before he was elected, because the experience of watching him, yet not seeing any of the rage he inspired in her reflected in the news media's coverage of him, was leaving her crippled by vertiginous self-doubt. "I felt like I was hearing him say things that didn't make sense or that contradicted what he'd just said, but no one else was hearing this." The political media was covering him and the things he said as legitimate. "And I was questioning myself."

At some point in 2017, Juneja mentioned to her father that she'd stopped watching coverage of Trump because it had made her feel so confused and her father replied, "Well, I wasn't confused; I knew exactly who he was." Juneja said that she looked at her father with perplexity before realizing: "Oh, congratulations, no one has socialized you to wonder if maybe *you're* the one who's wrong. No one ever told you that the way you feel about the world is not valid."

There's perhaps no neater example of how rage is an emotion that is permitted and encouraged in (some) men—and can be used to their advantage—while for women it is forbidden, invalidated, and treated as a path to self-defeat, than the 2016 presidential election.

CHAPTER TWO

THE CIRCLE OF ENTRAPMENT: THE HEAVY PRICE OF RAGE

Back in 2008, when Hillary Clinton first ran for president, there was plenty of commentary about her voice and her aggressive, ambitious demeanor, which often got confused with each other. Her tone was understood on many levels to sound inherently villainous: whether it was when she laughed—routinely referred to in the press as her "cackle"—or when she spoke loudly, it was heard to match what was largely believed to be her unnerving ambition. Back then, *Washington Post* reporter Joel Achenbach fantasized about the good old days of the brank's bridle, writing that Clinton "needs a radio-controlled shock collar so that aides can zap her when she starts to get screechy."[19]

In 2008, the reaction to Clinton was in part about the sheer novelty of hearing a woman's voice register on a presidential campaign trail, and her volume and pitch stood out especially against that of her opponent Barack Obama, who, for reasons relating to his own historic identity and firstness, could not afford to raise *his* voice in anger, and whose calm tone and oratorical gifts proved a stark contrast to Clinton's. During Obama's administration, Clinton would continue to be caricatured as threatening and angry, with the *Washington Post*'s Dana Milbank and Chris Cillizza joking that if she'd ever attended a beer summit with the president, she'd be served "Mad Bitch" brew.[20]

The 2016 election was a different ball game. From the start, the theme of the presidential race *was* anger: Bernie Sanders was angry. Donald Trump was angry. And they talked about it directly. In 2016, after Republican South Carolina governor Nikki Haley advised voters not to listen to "the angriest voices," including Donald Trump's, on immigration, Trump told CNN, "She's right. I am angry. . . . As far as I'm concerned, anger is okay. Anger and energy is what this country needs."[21] Ten days later, Sanders took a similar approach, responding to Bill Clinton's description of him as angry. "You know what? It's true. I am angry. And the American people are angry." Four days later, Clinton herself got into the act. "A lot of people are not only worried and frustrated," she said. "They're angry. . . . I'm angry too."

But somehow Clinton couldn't persuade people that she was furious in the same way, perhaps in part because she couldn't quite get the tone of her voice right. A *Washington Post* write-up that included coverage of that speech opened with a description of how Clinton's voice "thundered through a bowling alley . . . then turned soft and thoughtful." The rest of the piece included two descriptions of Clinton as "shouting" and ended with a quote from one of Clinton's supporters who opined, "Bernie Sanders has an ability to connect in a charismatic way. It's that magnetism that she's not inherently able to transmit."

How could a candidate whose assertive expressions of anger were understood only as performative, imitative, and inauthentic *also* be heard by so many people, at the very same time, as constantly yelling at them?

After her first debate with Sanders, the *New York Times* evaluated the Vermont senator—whose everyday communication style involves finger-pointing, raised tones, and vigorous head-shaking—as having "kept his cool," while claiming that Clinton "appear[ed] tense and even angry at times"[22] and wondered if her "ferocity" wasn't "risky, given that many voters . . . already have an unfavorable opinion of her." Watergate journalist Bob Woodward opined that Clinton's challenges originated with her "style and delivery . . . she shouts. There is something unrelaxed about the way she's communicating." On his radio show, after playing a clip of Clinton talking loudly—yes, angrily!—about standing up to the gun lobby, Sean Hannity asked, "What is likable about that? . . . Angry, bitter, screaming?"

And it wasn't just the right-wing or mainstrean press. It was the left as well. "Is she a presidential candidate or is she trying to star in the *Scream* reboot?" asked John Iadarola of the left-wing news network *The Young Turks*, arguing that what "needs to be borne in mind . . . is something can be historically true, a form of discrimination or stereotyping like women are shrill and they're nags and men have said that historically way too much . . . but that doesn't mean it's impossible for a woman . . . to speak loudly when she doesn't need to."[23] In other words, just because it's sexist doesn't mean it's not true.

It was a perfect, and perfectly maddening, circle of entrapment: a candidate who yelled too much, but who didn't express anger enough, and when she tried to express anger better, was presumed to be faking it.

"She was exactly the wrong candidate for this angry, populist moment," wrote liberal journalist Thomas Frank in his election postmortem, noting that Clinton was "an insider when the country was screaming for an outsider." Frank could see the anger of people who were screaming, and understood the moment as a furious one. Yet what Frank saw in *Clinton*, working to her detriment, was a "shrill self-righteousness, shouted from a position of high social status, that turns people away."[24] Given that her opponents were also multiple-home-owning powerful white people, one an almost three-decade veteran of Congress and one a billionaire real estate tycoon, it's hard to imagine that it was the high social status and not something qualitatively different about her shouting that struck Frank as the *really* shrill turn-off.

The irony was that while there was plenty of reasonable debate about Clinton's friendliness with banks and history of centrist compromise, her economic agenda was directly targeted at many of the populations that were angriest, *including* coal miners and those white working-class communities in the throes of the opioid epidemic. Clinton had policies on subsidized childcare and creating more economic stability for caregivers, on addressing racial and economic inequality around reproductive autonomy via abolishment of the Hyde Amendment. But she was widely understood to be bad at talking about these issues in a persuasive way, and part of that badness surely did stem from her own oratorical shortcomings. But those shortcomings might well have been exacerbated by all the ways that Clinton—and lots of public-speaking women who came before her—had been discouraged from talking loudly or too aggressively, leaving her nervous and hesitant about getting too passionate, too enflamed, too screechy or shrill or emotional or any of the other ways America hears women's voices raised in feeling. She had to walk a very thin communicative tightrope, often sounding boring and robotic, wholly unable to viscerally convey her interest in the frustrations of voters.

That the forceful expression of fury might not just be okay from (white) men but might in fact actually work to their benefit, while at the same time working *against* their female peers and competitors, is backed up by some emerging research.

The psychology professor Lisa Feldman Barrett has described in the *New York Times* a study in which her research team showed people photographs of men and women making facial expressions. They found that their subjects were more likely to assume that whatever was causing a woman's emotion was something internal, whereas whatever was provoking a man's response was something external, or as she put it, "She's a bitch, but he's just having a bad day."[25]

It's a problem that John Neffinger, a political advisor who's been coaching candidates for years, and who wrote a series of memos to Clinton during the race, trying to help her balance the ways in which she expressed herself, has been wrestling with. He and fellow researchers have reviewed studies on two general criteria in how the public evaluates candidates: strength and warmth. Going in, he explained, male candidates are presumed to have strength—a category imaginatively tied to skill, authority, capability, and economic power—and female candidates are intrinsically assumed to possess warmth—which in political terms is meant to convey affinity, fun, friendliness, and also the sense that a candidate really cares about the people they want to represent.

"When somebody manages to project a lot of strength and a lot of warmth, we say they're charismatic and magnetic, we want to be *with* that person, we want to *be* that person," said Neffinger. Those who read as having more strength than warmth are viewed as "fearsome" and those with more warmth than strength as "adorable." The question of how these qualities are valued in politicians is as old as Machiavelli's argument that it is better to be feared than loved, though best to be both. According to Neffinger, "It's really hard to find candidates who combine the two." Male candidates *can* theoretically squeak by as fearsome, especially in times of national crisis, when authoritarian male figures are generously viewed as protectors: think Rudy Giuliani after 9/11, or famously ill-tempered John McCain, revered as a war hero. They can't be wholly adorable, precisely because that means they've been feminized and are therefore taken less seriously.

For women, both poles are toxic: to be fearsome is to be vilified and unpalatable, unnatural and monstrous. To be adorable is to be unserious and incompetent. The strategic problem for women is that the work to balance both poles is delicate and precarious: As it turns out, for men, a little warmth goes a long way. For women, a little strength goes way too far.

Bernie Sanders, a disheveled grump whose style was to yell righteously but repetitively at his audiences about inequality, was able to exude charm simply by smiling at a small bird that landed on his podium during a speech. But when a woman, said Neffinger, "asserts herself in some fashion having to do with strength, she quickly slides out of the warmth category. She becomes perceived as a threat to the social order. Guys can be a little nice, without throwing out their strength. But women cannot add a little strength without losing warmth."

Those were the dynamics facing Hillary Clinton as she competed against two men who were trading on their strength—their anger—as a major selling point to the American public. To compete with them in this vein would be to invite further, compounding anxiety about the ways in which she was already upsetting the order of things simply by running against these men for the highest office in the land. And no one on her team was naive about what kind of impact these conditions had on her range of expression.

As her lead speechwriter Dan Schwerin told me in 2017, "There's a reason why male candidates can shout and are called passionate, and if a woman candidate raises her voice to whip up a crowd, she's screeching and yelling." Because his boss understood this, Schwerin said, "she's controlled, she doesn't rant and rave, she's careful. And then that's read as inauthentic; it means that she doesn't understand how upset people are, or the pain people are in, because she's not angry the way those guys are angry. So she must be okay with the status quo because she's not angry."

Clinton herself addressed her frustration with this seemingly unsolvable equation in her campaign memoir *What Happened*, barely able to contain her simmering disdain for the impossibility of the dynamics facing her as a candidate. "I've tried to adjust," she wrote. "After hearing repeatedly that some people didn't like my voice, I enlisted the help of a linguistic expert," who told her to focus on deep breathing and positivity. Clinton is drily smoldering as she explains how she was pushed to such *un*natural lengths to maintain the illusion of a naturally cheery femininity: "That way, when the crowd got energized and started shouting—as crowds at rallies tend to do—I could resist doing the normal thing, which is to shout back." Clinton told the linguistic expert that she'd try her best to comply. "But out of curiosity, can you give me an example of a woman in public life who has pulled this off successfully—who has met the energy of a crowd while keeping her voice soft and low?"

The linguistic expert could not.

MICHELLE OBAMA, THE "ANGRY BLACK WOMAN"

If Hillary Clinton had a hard time figuring out how to express complex emotions, including frustration, without being understood as threatening, her path was a walk in the park compared to that of Michelle Obama.

Michelle Robinson had grown up on Chicago's South Side, the daughter of a stay-at-home mother and a city employee. She graduated from Princeton and Harvard Law School, and met her future husband Barack Obama when she was assigned to professionally mentor him at the white-shoe Chicago law firm Sidley Austin. During the years in which the couple lived in Chicago, when Barack worked as a community organizer and law professor, and Michelle left the fancy firm to work for the city, and then for the University of Chicago, she was considered the star of the couple: the gregarious, charismatic, funny, dynamic one. Having grown up around Chicago's corrupt political machine, she was distrustful of politics and didn't want anything to do with them. But her husband did.

Then Barack Obama became the brightest star to streak across the American political landscape in a generation, and his wife fell under national scrutiny. Her impassioned speeches, her emotive candor, her clear and informed view of American history, including her grim take on politics and her sharp sense of humor, all began, perplexingly, to work against her.

As her husband became a sensation in the Senate, she was caught by a reporter rolling her eyes and commenting, "Maybe one day he will do something to warrant all this attention"; by the time he hit the presidential campaign trail two years later, she was still affectionately complaining about his failures to make the bed or put his socks in the laundry basket; she called him "snore-y and stinky" when he woke up in the morning, and described him, memorably, as "a gifted man, but in the end, he's just a man." This quickly earned her the attention of the *New York Times* columnist Maureen Dowd, who worried that people heard Michelle as "emasculating" for "casting her husband . . . as an undisciplined child." Again, the critical voice of a woman was cast as maternal reproach.

This was the gentlest treatment Michelle Obama was to receive in the press during that presidential campaign.

After her husband began to win primaries and it seemed possible that he might win the Democratic nomination, Michelle gave a speech in which she said, "People in this country are ready for change and hungry for a different kind of politics. . . . For the first time in my adult life I am proud of my country because it feels like hope is finally making a comeback."

It was a positive, warm, forward-looking statement. But coming from the mouth of Michelle Obama, it was heard in some quarters as a resounding and unpatriotic affront. Conservative columnist Bill Kristol chided her for not having been grateful for America winning the Cold War, while at the *National Review*, Jim Geraghty wrote, "America hasn't been good to her? What, opportunities to go to Princeton, Harvard Law, working for top-shelf law firms and hospitals . . . that's not enough?" as if any sentiment short of fawning appreciation for the country in which she had worked hard and excelled was unthinkable.

The very act of mild critique—of a nation in which her great-great-great-grandmother had been enslaved, in which her husband was the first black man ever to come close to being nominated for the presidency, in which she was being asked to sacrifice her job and independent identity to try to move into the White House, a building constructed by slave labor—was enough to confirm a popular vision of Michelle as a worryingly angry black woman.

She appeared on the cover of the *National Review:* mouth open (of course), her eyes cutting menacingly toward the viewer, under the headline "Mrs. Grievance." The conservative columnist Michelle Malkin began referring to her as "Barack's Bitter Half." The black conservative columnist Mychal Massie wrote that Michelle "portrays herself as just another angry black harridan who spits in the face of the nation that made her rich, famous, and prestigious."

As the novelist Chimamanda Ngozi Adichie would write of Michelle, "Because she said what she thought, and because she smiled only when she felt like smiling, and not constantly and vacuously, America's cheapest caricature was cast on her: the Angry Black Woman. Women, in general, are not permitted anger—but for black American women, there is an added expectation of interminable gratitude, the closer to groveling the better, as though their citizenship is a phenomenon that they cannot take for granted."

Medusa-Michelle memes proliferated on the internet. The already incorrect description of Michelle as angry transformed into her being militant. Juan Williams, then an NPR commentator, called Michelle Obama "Stokely Carmichael in a designer dress," connecting her to the civil rights leader who had in the 1960s transitioned from nonviolent organizing to the more militant approach he described as "black power." In *Slate*, the former left journalist turned neo-con Christopher Hitchens published a breathtakingly dishonest attempt to connect Michelle's undergraduate thesis at Princeton—which had been about the experience of being black at Princeton—to the black power movement, claiming inaccurately that twenty-one-year-old Michelle said she had been "much influenced" by

Carmichael, who in turn Hitchens connected to Nation of Islam leader Louis Farrakhan. Fox News went further, asking if the fist bump, or dap, that Michelle had shared with her husband on the night he'd clinched the Democratic nomination was in fact a "terrorist fist jab." A *New Yorker* cover parodied the panic over Michelle's perceived militancy—and memorialized the view of her angry black femininity—with a Barry Blitt cartoon portraying her in a 70s-style Afro, carrying a machine gun. The illustration was called *The Politics of Fear*.

By the time her husband was accepting the nomination in Denver, Michelle's public persona had been remade: she talked about clothes and pantyhose, not about politics or the nation, and not with any critical inflection about her spouse. At the convention, she was framed (accurately!) as a devoted wife and mother, a little girl who'd loved the Brady Bunch, but as nothing else. In her own speech, she carefully expressed her love of country and gratitude for the chances it had afforded her. Michelle had been effectively muzzled, any querulousness tamped down. She'd never actually expressed true anger on the trail, but the very act of having opened her mouth in a free and frank way had so quickly been heard as rancor that her opinions and her open mouth, and anything that could be heard as frustration or complaint, had had to go.

Before she left the White House, in an interview with Oprah Winfrey, Michelle would say of that period, of being cast as "that angry black woman," "Dag, you don't even *know* me, you know? . . . Where'd that come from?"[26] More than a year later, Michelle—speaking at a gathering of black women in Florida—would speak even more frankly to former White House advisor Valerie Jarrett of this process, explaining that early on, "I looked at one of my speeches and I saw that what was animation and passion to me, could easily be turned into sound bites of anger and aggression." At that point, she said, "I was like, *oh, this is a game*. It's a game. And what was I thinking? I thought this was real, but it was a game too. And I wasn't playing the game, I was just being passionate because I thought that's what people wanted . . . But they don't know what they really want. So I had to learn how to deliver"—and here, she pasted a big smile on her face, and offered a shake of her hair—"a *message*."[27]

Writing at the start of her 1940 memoir, the civil rights and suffrage activist Mary Church Terrell described her story as one about "A colored woman living in a white world. It cannot possibly be like a story written by a white woman. A white woman has only one handicap to overcome—that of sex. I have two—both sex and race. I belong to the only group in this country which has two such huge obstacles to surmount. Colored men have only one—that of race." Terrell's is what the Rutgers women and gender studies professor Brittney Cooper has called "one of the earliest articulations of the political stakes of intersectionality," a term that would be coined by Kimberlé Williams Crenshaw nearly five decades later to describe the interlocking sets of biases faced by women of color in America. This was more than simply a doubling of bias; for the racism faced by nonwhite women is amplified and altered by sexism, and the sexism they encounter is perverted and exacerbated by racial bias.

In practice, these dynamics have long meant that black women's expressions of frustration, resistance, or even mild critique have been refracted through an American lens that has enlarged them, rendering them as some defining feature of black femininity. One crucial result of the national mythos around black women's anger, said the writer Joelle Owusu in 2018, is that as a black woman, she is regularly "perceived as the aggressor in every situation . . . Even when you are being polite and respectful during an altercation, someone will always make a remark about a black woman's 'attitude' or 'aggression.' "[28]

The problematizing of anger in black women takes many forms. There's a reflexive defensiveness against it from white women and from men, a resistance to actually reckoning with the roots of black female dissatisfaction—whether that dissatisfaction is expressed gently or furiously or perhaps merely inferred—that gets conveyed via irrational allegations of spoilt ingratitude, negativity, or instability.

"We are told we are irrational, crazy, out-of-touch, entitled, disruptive, and not team players," writes Cooper in her exploration of black feminist anger, *Eloquent Rage*. "Angry Black women are looked upon as entities to be contained, as inconvenient citizens who keep on talking about their rights while refusing to do their duty and smile at everyone."

THE RIGHTEOUS FURY OF MAXINE WATERS

In October of 2017, Maxine Waters, speaking at an event to benefit the Ali Forney Center, which supports LGBTQ homeless youth, made remarks about how moved she'd been, hearing the story of the black, homeless, trans youth advocate after whom the center had been named, noting that "with this kind of inspiration, I will go and take Trump out tonight."

Waters, a leading and vocal proponent of impeachment, was quite clearly not referring to any sort of violent action, but in the following days, conservatives pounced on her sound bite. One right-wing pundit, Lawrence Jones, said on *Fox and Friends* that, "When you incite violence, that should be investigated," expressing his concern that Waters's remark would "[send] people out to assassinate Republicans" and when challenged, reiterated that "She could have said impeachment if she wanted impeachment; she talked about essentially assassinating the president."[29] Omar Navarro, Waters's political opponent in California, tweeted, "I'm calling for the arrest of Maxine Waters."[30]

The deranged attempt to cast Waters's remarks as a murder threat didn't remain on the Fox News fringes of political coverage; it was repeated in the mainstream press, with CNN anchor Chris Cuomo asking Waters on air about her comments in ways that cast her as militaristic from the start. Cuomo observed that the conflict between the president and his critics "has become an ugly war of words" with Waters "a named combatant in this battle." Playing the clip of Waters's speech, Cuomo said, "those words have been interpreted as an attempt on the president's life." Waters called his assessment "absolutely ridiculous," noting that "nobody believes that a seventy-nine-year-old grandmother who is a congresswoman and who has been in Congress and politics for all these years [was] talking about doing any harm."[31]

But of course people *did* believe that, or were willing to, in part because rational political challenge to white male presidential authority, coming from a black woman, was such a disruption of the power structure. Cuomo's interrogation of Waters made clear that her words had violated natural assumptions about which kinds of people were permitted to deploy aggressive language, and toward whom, when he asked her if she believed that she should "have a more high level of decency in how you discuss those that you want to criticize, especially when it's the president of the United States?"

Waters understood the resonance of his analysis perfectly. "I think I have been extremely responsible in laying out the case in which this president should be impeached," she said, but "people are not accustomed to a woman, in particular an African-American woman, taking this kind of leadership. How dare *me* challenge the president of the United States?"[32]

A cult of adoration sprang up around Waters during 2017 and 2018, and millions publicly appreciated her willingness to speak in lengthy and righteously aggressive tirades about Donald Trump, to snap back and stand up for herself. Memes of Waters staring censoriously over her glasses spread across social media. A clip of Waters, insisting during her questioning of Treasury Secretary Steve Mnuchin that she was "reclaiming [her] time," became a viral GIF and was remixed as a gospel song. The performer of that remix was a surprise guest during Waters's interview on the daytime talk show *The View*, provoking a dizzying moment during which the show's four white and one black cohosts, along with a predominantly white studio audience, danced along to a man singing words Maxine Waters had said during a tense congressional hearing.[33]

It was kind of great, but also kind of weird, the popular celebration of the woman who became known in some quarters as "Auntie Maxine," in reference to a black familial figure who expresses her regard and affection in part by taking no shit and doling out real talk. Waters was celebrated as "righteous, furious, uncowed" in a Buzzfeed piece in which Campaign Zero cofounder and Black Lives Matter activist Brittany Packnett described Waters as "the Auntie Boss: As real as your auntie and as powerful as only a black woman could be." The mass feting of Waters, a black woman who was quoted back in 1989 saying "I have a right to my anger, and I don't want anybody telling me I shouldn't be, that it's not nice to be, and that something's wrong with me because I get angry," was surely a balm in a nation that has rarely acknowledged black female rage as beautiful, patriotic, or inspirational.

Yet Waters wasn't just signaling righteous fury, she was also incurring the costs of that fury, costs that many of those deploying her side-eye GIFs and memes had never incurred through all the many years in which Waters had stood against the tide and been vilified for it.

It's true that Waters had been the subject of a long-running ethics investigation on charges that she helped a bank in which her husband held stock (she was cleared of wrongdoing and one of her top aides was reprimanded). But before and after that investigation, she was treated as a sideshow, and with often virulent racism by her political detractors. In 2012, after she'd torn into Republican leaders Eric Cantor and John Boehner, calling them "demons," Fox News anchor Eric Bolling advised her, "Congresswoman, you saw what happened to Whitney Houston. . . . Step away from the crack pipe." In 2017, Bill O'Reilly responded to a clip of one of Waters's speeches excoriating Trump by claiming that he hadn't heard a word of it, having been too distracted by her "James Brown wig."[34]

But it's not just her political opponents who have fallen in line with the vilification of black female anger. In the summer of 2018, as fury on the left built, partly in response to the Trump administration's zero tolerance policy regarding refugee seekers at the Mexican border, their separation of at least three thousand young children from their parents, and the expansion of family internment camps meant to house asylum seekers indefinitely, angry protesters began interrupting the meals and movie nights of Trump administration officials; one restaurant owner in Virginia refused to serve Trump press secretary Sarah Huckabee Sanders. Maxine Waters was one of the only Democratic politicians to meet this rising tide of politically meaningful and valid rage with respect, acknowledgment, and encouragement.

In a speech in California, she urged those who were furious to "show up wherever we have to show up," suggesting that "if you see anybody from that Cabinet in a restaurant, in a department store, at a gasoline station, you get out and you create a crowd and you push back on them and you tell them they're not welcome anymore, anywhere." Waters was not advocating violence; she was calling for assembly and pushback. It was in line with her history as a representative of disempowered populations; she was hearing and channeling the exertions of the furiously oppressed against the oppressors.

But when Waters applied her view of the role of insurrectionist protest in 2018, members of her *own party* stepped in to censure her. Senate Minority Leader Chuck Schumer advised that "no one should call for the harassment of political opponents," chastising Waters's suggestion as "not American." (It was of course deeply American, a tradition stretching back to the Revolution.) Nancy Pelosi also chimed in, claiming, "Trump's daily lack of civility has provoked responses that are predictable but unacceptable." Horrifyingly, neither Democratic leader bothered to defend Waters against the implicit threat sent in a tweet by the president, where he called Waters "an extraordinarily low IQ person" and falsely accused her of advocating "harm to [his] supporters," concluding with the grim warning, "Be careful what you wish for Max!"

To publicly rebuke a black woman's support for political protest but not the powerful white patriarch's thinly veiled call to violence against her was to play on the very same impulses that Trump and the white patriarchal party that supported him played on: racist and sexist anxiety about noncompliant women and nonwhites, and the drive to punish them. That her own colleagues would cast Waters as too much, as too combative and fearsome, while letting the threat made against her by the most powerful of white men go unremarked upon, was a goddamn travesty. Especially given the decades of work Waters had done to recognize and address the potentially consequential fury of underrepresented and disempowered populations on behalf of whom her party is supposed to advocate, and the way in which her exertions are a service to those yearning to have their fury heard and seen and acknowledged as valid.

Alicia Garza recalled to me how Waters had gained early prominence "fighting to make visible" the case of Eula Love, a poor black woman shot and killed by police in her district after a dispute over a gas bill in 1979.[35] Describing the news coverage of the event, Garza said, "Maxine was certainly angry. And she was portrayed as absolutely batshit crazy. She was portrayed as not credible. And she kept going."

These days, Garza said, "everybody is all 'Auntie Maxine, you go girl!' But this has been her *career*. She has always used anger in the service of a higher purpose." Garza pointed out how black women's anger can get fetishized, yet never really taken to heart. "So we can love Maxine reclaiming her time, but do we love what she is saying about the conditions that black people are living in? We get to ignore that in a way by taking on this trope of the angry black woman as someone who is performing for us, as opposed to taking on the substance of what she's talking about."

It also matters that enthusiasm for Waters has ballooned in a period when her party wields no power: Republicans haven't had as big a majority in the House since the 1920s. Waters may talk directly about the desire to impeach a president—a desire she's channeling for millions of Americans—but she has no power to do so. It's far easier to admire the spitting fury of a woman when she poses absolutely no political threat, a phenomenon that is also observably true about the adoring memes around nonblack women including Ruth Bader Ginsburg and Hillary Clinton When She's Not a Candidate, but that sheds light onto how the sometimes appreciative treatment of certain Angry Black Women in fact reflects their relative powerlessness.

Ginsburg, whose fiery dissents have become the stuff of internet legend, and who has become known on the internet as the Notorious RBG, is in the minority of the Supreme Court. The pleasures of celebrating her toughness stem in part from her actual physical stature: she is a short, thin, octogenarian who has twice had cancer; the whole punch line of admiration for her is in part rooted in the improbability of her threat; she's like a little doll of female anger who we can all cheer for, even as she is outvoted again and again and again. It's extremely difficult to imagine the same kind of tattoo-inspiring admiration for her angry opinions if those opinions were actually reshaping the law.

As for Clinton, she was perhaps never more lauded for her aggressiveness than in the years after having lost the Democratic primary to Barack Obama when she went on to work for him as his secretary of state. In those years, she was the subject of social media love; a Tumblr called "Texts from Hillary" was built around an image of her looking like a badass in sunglasses, sending savage messages to other powerful people. But this was in an era when she was widely celebrated for having been a team player, subsidiary to her former political rival. As soon as she again became a candidate for president, the fact of her individual power and the threat it posed to her male competitors was recalled, and the mass affection for that tough and righteously censorious version of Hillary was extinguished almost instantly.

These provisos on a celebration of female fortitude—that they take place almost exclusively around women who do not pose an imminent threat to power—must be acknowledged when considering the ways in which black women's anger can get fetishized and celebrated. In some ways, the cultural caricature of neck-snapping, side-eye-casting black female censure becomes easily embraceable precisely *because* it is disconnected from real political, economic, or social power, because its relationship to the threat of actual disruption of white male authority can be understood as inherently comical. Black women's relative distance, from both white supremacy and patriarchal advantage, makes it easier, in some ways, to applaud their toughness, precisely because it is so far removed from being a true threat to white male domination.

And when it *does* threaten a white man? John Neffinger pointed to the treatment of Kamala Harris, whose sharp prosecutorial interrogations knocked Attorney General Jeff Sessions off his game in 2017, bringing the punitive force of white patriarchy on her head. "When Kamala took Jeff Sessions apart," he said, "it immediately became a Republican talking point, and they pushed the narrative that she was hysterical. Now, you watch that interaction and my god, she's the furthest thing from hysterical. But they knew that to discredit her, that's where they had to go, that that's how you undermine a cool customer and threateningly competent woman like Kamala Harris. You cast her as an Angry Black Woman."

As with Waters, some on Harris's side quickly took up the video as a meme, cheering her as a you-go-girl rebuke to Sessions's assumptions of white male authority. But the popularity of the Angry Black Women cartoon also leaves these women doing a lot of the work of expressing anger that white women feel, but are discouraged, in different ways, from expressing themselves. This is crucial to an online social media phenomenon that has been dubbed "digital blackface," a practice whereby white and other nonblack users turn to GIFs of black people expressing the emotions they wish to convey.

For example, among the most popular means of conveying women's cutting feminist rage at men in digital shorthand is to post a GIF of the actress Angela Bassett taken from a scene in the 1995 film *Waiting to Exhale*, a scene in which Bassett's character, angry at her husband for leaving her for a white mistress, puts all his clothes and belongings in a car and sets it on fire. When people on the internet are anxious to express suspicion or the feeling of seeing through some bullshit, it's to the side-eye of black women—from actress Viola Davis to pop star Rihanna to civil rights hero Dorothy Height staring at Dr. Martin Luther King, Jr., during his 1963 "I Have a Dream" speech—that they often turn to do the work of expressing their anger for them.

"We're your sass, your nonchalance, your fury, your delight, your annoyance . . . " the writer Lauren Michele Jackson told journalist Amanda Hess, who argued that "on the internet, white people outsource their emotional labor to black people."[36] When so much social opprobrium is directed at women for expressing anger toward the white men to whom white women are likely to be more proximate, many white women rely on black women, expected to be angry as a default setting, to perform the emotion in their stead.

These are the dynamics that the black feminist Audre Lorde details in her famous 1981 address to the National Women's Studies Association, "The Uses of Anger," when she describes reading from her work, "A Poem for Women in Rage" and having a white woman approach her to ask, "Are you going to do anything with how we can deal directly with *our* anger? I feel it's so important." Lorde asks her how she uses her rage, and then has to turn away "from the blank look in her eyes." "I do not exist," Lorde writes, "to feel her anger for her."[37]

These relationships have long been in play politically. For generations, black women have been asked to do the work of opposing the rise of the right wing—as the most reliable Democratic voting bloc, as some of the most vocally furious women in Congress, as the backbone of organizing, activism, and political and civic engagement in the nation—even as the Democratic Party has invested little in them as candidates, and too little in policy that would better support and protect them. Meanwhile, during the Trump administration, the political media has regularly passed them over for serious political analysis, while filling newspapers with endless deep ethnographic dives into the lives and motivations of white working-class Trump supporters.

In a crucial 2017 special election for the Alabama senate seat, 98 percent—*98 percent*—of black women voters voted for Democrat Doug Jones over the openly racist accused sexual predator Roy Moore; almost 50 percent more black women than black men voted in that election; and 63 percent of white women voted for Moore. After Alabama, there were all kinds of social media messages and op-eds "thanking" black women for "saving America," a message that implicitly suggested that black women were themselves inherently adjacent to, or marginal within, America, even in the very moment at which their centrality to deciding its representation was purportedly being acknowledged. The credit that black women received in the wake of the Alabama election, wrote political consultant Angela Peoples in the *New York Times*, is "one small step in the right direction. But we don't need thanks—we need you to get out of the way and follow our lead."[38]

MEN AND ANGELS GIVE ME PATIENCE

In the face of all of this multifaceted judgment of their fury, how are women in public and political spheres supposed to strategize around the anger that they sometimes—often—feel?

"Men and angels give me patience," Elizabeth Cady Stanton wrote to Susan B. Anthony in 1852, frustrated about the impositions of motherhood and wifely duty on her ability to express her political anger through writing and speaking. "I am at the boiling point! If I do not find some day the use of my tongue on this question I shall die of an intellectual repression, a woman's rights convulsion."[39]

In 2017 came a million schemes for how to get women to express their anger in some appropriate way, something that might release them from it, but that still fell within the purview of acceptability. Magazines recommended exercise classes to women for whom "Scream ALL the expletives" was the first thing written on [their] to-do list today[40]; Mama Gena, head of "The School of Womanly Arts," urged her devotees to "FEEL loudly . . . RAGE like an angry lioness . . . HOWL like a bitch in heat . . . cry MORE . . . SCREAM your head off."[41]

For A Bad Time, Call, "a podcast dedicated to women's anger," launched, encouraging nonmale-identifying people to phone into a recorded line and vent their frustrations. The litanies were then stitched together into audible quilts of female ire: "I am just really, really tired of grown-ass men who have their own jobs and their own lives telling me what I should be doing with mine/I'm just so tired of women being made to feel like we're not enough in anything we do/I'm just so pissed off about having to be pissed off. It's almost the new normal to be pissed off literally all the time because bad shit is constantly happening to women." At the end of the podcast, one of the hosts reassures listeners and callers alike: "Your anger is real. Your rage is valid. And we want to hear it."

In the fall of 2016, I appeared on *Real Time with Bill Maher*. It was days after the second presidential debate, to which Donald Trump had invited the women who'd accused his opponent's husband of sexual misconduct, at which he'd loomed over Clinton, practically pawing the ground with undisguised loathing and resentment toward her. Clinton had gripped her microphone with white-knuckled control, had not confronted him nor acknowledged the bizarre malevolence of his approach; she had kept her voice steady and her manner professional. Maher was frustrated by this, suggesting to me during his panel discussion that she should "say it to his face; he's right there, say 'You're full of shit, you asshole!'"

Maher likely hadn't done the math on how risky it would have been for Clinton to have turned on Trump in anger—the ease with which any ire directed toward him would have been reframed as her having played the woman card for strategic effect, how promptly she'd have been understood as having cast herself as a victim of bullying in order to earn cheap sympathy, how she might have come off as castrating, unhinged; the satisfaction that might have been gained by her critics in having seen evidence that her opponent had gotten under her skin.

But the person who *had* done that math—in real time—was Hillary Clinton, who months later would describe that debate to me as one of the most difficult moments of the campaign, shivering with the visceral recollection of how Trump's demeanor had been "so personally invasive . . . following me, eyeing me." She said that she *did* consider, as a presidential debate was going on, whether she should turn on him and shout "Get away from me!" But she had figured that that would be playing into his hands: "He will gain points and I will lose points," she recalled thinking (she had thought right; she was widely acknowledged to have kicked the ever living shit out of Trump in that debate, even without actually kicking him). Acknowledging how tight her grip on her microphone was during the debate, Clinton told me it was an extension of the internal control she was mustering. "Think of all the times where you are either mentally or physically gripping yourself," she said. "[Willing yourself] not to respond, not to lash out, not to display the anger that you feel, because you know it will redound to your detriment. So you swallow it."

You swallow it. It's a choice made by millions of women throughout time: the decision that the best strategic approach is to take the anger you feel and stuff it way down deep. Because to let it out is going to do more damage to you than it's going to damage the person or forces you're angry at. As a woman in public life, "you can't be angry for yourself," said Clinton. "You just can't. You can be indignant, you can be annoyed, you can be frustrated, but you can't be angry."

When Barbara Lee described to me the efforts she has made, in multiple circumstances, to contain and channel her fury in ways that are productive and will not backfire on her, I asked her whether she guessed that men had any idea how much internal strategizing went on inside women's heads. She sighed. "No, they're not aware of anything, if you ask me," she said with a smile. "They can't see women differently from the way they think women are." Which is often contained, their simmering unease covered over by politesse. But, Lee maintained, the fact that men have no idea how mad women are beneath the surface "works to our advantage, because that's how we win."

Perhaps it is how we win the debates, but so far, it is not how we win the elections. And it can be maddening—in both the enraging and the crazy-making sense of the term—to come to grips with the fact that many men have no idea how rocky the terrain of anger is for women.

CHAPTER THREE

DRESS UP YOUR ANGER

Understood plainly by many women to be an impediment to effective communication, anger is often dressed up in other guises to make it more attractive, more legitimate. These are some of them.

GOD'S GO-AHEAD

Among the most popular strategies used to justify women's rage in public spheres is to attribute it to someone else, emphasizing that whatever anger you're feeling is actually channeled from a more authoritative source. Like, for instance, God.

This was a point made to me about women in politics by Senator Kirsten Gillibrand, who said in 2018 that "women have to be angry on behalf of someone else in order to be taken seriously. So if you're Harriet Tubman, or Joan of Arc, you have God bringing you this passion." Gillibrand nudged me toward the eccentric case of Victoria Woodhull, the first woman ever to run for president of the United States. Woodhull, a Wall Street broker, clairvoyant, and a free love advocate, made outrageously bold assertions, once declaring, "We mean treason; we mean secession . . . We are plotting revolution; we will [overthrow] this bogus Republic and plant a government of righteousness in its stead." But she also believed herself to be a medium speaking on behalf of the long-dead Greek orator Demosthenes, or channeling Napoleon and Josephine.

In this, Woodhull was not so different from some of her more officially respectable suffragist peers, some of whom took advantage of the period's fever for spiritualism to give a valence of beyond-the-grave authority to their disruptive ideas. The table in Seneca Falls at which Elizabeth Cady Stanton would write the Declaration of Sentiments was one that had previously been used for séances.[42] And the nineteenth-century reformer and suffragist Frances Willard described how, in the midst of her travels on behalf of the temperance movement, she sat down to pray one Sunday morning in 1876: "Upon my knees alone . . . there was borne in upon my mind, as I believe from loftier regions, the declaration: 'You are to speak for a woman's ballot as a weapon of protection to her home and tempted loved ones from the tyranny of drink.'"[43]

In addition to getting God's go-ahead to push for voting rights as a means to curb drinking, as the historian Carolyn DeSwarte Gifford has noted, Willard "also received 'a complete line of argument and illustration' for her first speech on home protection, which she delivered later in the year at the Woman's Congress in Philadelphia." Indeed, Gifford writes, those women advocating for temperance via the vote—largely, it should be noted, as a means to protect women from physical abuse at the hands of drunken husbands—"had to be able to justify their political and suffrage activity religiously. It was absolutely essential for them to believe that their behavior sprang from an experience that convinced them that God wanted them, indeed called them, to vote."[44]

Willard's more radical peer in the temperance movement, Carrie Nation, would also cite God as working through her, not only to rage against the evils of alcohol, but also to physically destroy drinking establishments. As Nation would later recall, she was visited one day in 1900 "by a voice which seemed to me speaking in my heart, these words, 'GO TO KIOWA,' and my hands were lifted and thrown down." The interpretation of this message from the divine, Nation felt, "was very plain, it was this: 'take something in your hands and throw at these places in Kiowa [Kansas] and smash them.'" It was plainly God's direction, Nation maintained, that she gather up large rocks and use them to destroy saloons in Kansas, until her husband joked to her that she should use hatchets instead, which she described as "the most sensible thing you have said since I married you." They divorced the next year. Nation, who took the hatchet suggestion to heart, and became famous for chopping up bars all over the west, would go on to describe herself as "a bulldog running along at the feet of Jesus, barking at what He doesn't like."

JUST A MOTHER AND A WIFE

Close behind calling on the divine as a justification for rage—at least rage that has taken the form of social, political, or economic challenge—has been the practice of invoking maternal morality, mothering instincts, and wifely responsibility as the motivator for political agitation.

Mary Harris Jones was a dressmaker and a teacher who became a labor organizer and an early member of the Industrial Workers of the World after her family died of yellow fever and her dress shop burned in the Great Chicago Fire of 1871. Jones opposed women's suffrage, believing it was a diversion of the upper classes, and arguing that "you don't need the vote to raise hell." She herself raised a lot of hell, and is responsible for the labor movement's famous call to action, "Pray for the dead and fight like hell for the living"; she also dressed in the clothes of an old woman, referred to the miners and other workers on whose behalf she fiercely battled "her boys," and in her fifties became known as "Mother." A US senator once condemned Mother Jones as the "grandmother of all agitators," to which she replied, "I hope to live long enough to be the great-grandmother of all agitators."

Twenty-five years her junior was Ella Reeve Bloor, a trade union organizer and socialist agitator who was a founding member of the American Communist Labor Party. Bloor helped Upton Sinclair gather data for his exploration of urban poverty *The Jungle*; she was a great proponent of women's rights and suffrage; she helped to organize farm workers in Iowa in the 1930s—including an action in which dairy farmers protested low wages by dumping milk off delivery trucks. She was arrested thirty-six times and dubbed by *Life* magazine "the grand old woman of the U.S. Communist Party."[45] And she was known as "Mother Bloor." The historian Mary Triece has described both Mothers Jones and Bloor, while different in their particular politics, as having "enacted a persona of militant motherhood that proved successful in organizing entire families in struggles against corrupt bosses and company-owned towns across the country."[46]

In 1930, Fannie Peck was fed up with the limited professional opportunities available to the swelling population of African Americans who'd moved into northern cities as part of the Great Migration. She gathered a group of fifty women in the basement of the Bethel AME Church in Detroit, and together they strategized the boycotting of businesses that did not hire black employees or that charged exorbitant prices, particularly targeting the meatpacking industry; some accounts claimed that the group burned down a huge packinghouse. By 1935, there were more than ten thousand women members of what Peck had dubbed "Housewives Leagues" in cities across the country, and thousands of members marched through Chicago, shutting down the whole meatpacking industry. The historian Stephen Tuck has argued that Peck "was a canny strategist" in that—despite being a successful mass organizer—she adopted "the non-threatening posture of a group of housewives."[47]

You can see the evidence of exactly this sort of nonthreatening posture—or perhaps the way it is taken on, cannily, in response to the diminution and underestimation of motherhood—in the 1992 Senate campaign of Patty Murray from Washington. In 1980, Murray was a stay-at-home mom of two who became enraged after her state cut preschool funding. She put her kids in the car and drove to the state capitol to register her fury. "I was going around the hall and finding who I could talk to," Murray recalled to Jay Newton-Small, "and one state legislator said, 'That's a nice story, but you're just a mom in tennis shoes.'" Murray, further enflamed, went home and called the other moms in tennis shoes. "And they called the moms they knew—all were mad—and we were back at the state legislature." The women staged an uprising, ultimately succeeding in having the education cuts reversed, and Murray embarked on a career in electoral politics, further motivated by her fury over the treatment of Anita Hill in 1991 to run for the Senate in 1992. She was among the historic group of four women to win seats that year; her campaign's tag line was "Just a mom in tennis shoes."

Murray's self-minimizing reputation has worked to continue to disguise the anger that first prompted her entry into electoral politics. "[Patty's] not emotional," Republican House Speaker Paul Ryan once said of Murray. "Some of these folks walk out of the room, and they huff and they puff. She's not like that."

During the eighty-year suffrage battle, a concerted effort was made by feminists in the press to rehabilitate the image of legendarily prickly Susan B. Anthony as a kind of familial goddess, despite the fact that she had very intentionally chosen not to marry or bear children, and had shown nothing but disdain for the institution of marriage entered into by her colleagues, including Ida B. Wells, whom she endlessly belittled for having wed. But just a few years before Anthony's 1906 death, as the movement to enfranchise women ground on, *Pearson's Magazine* published a profile called "Miss Anthony At Home" in which the writer Ida Husted Harper marveled, "What a housekeeper is Susan B. Anthony, domestic in every fiber of her body!" Harper referred to the aged suffragist and labor leader as "Aunt Susan," and enthused, "like a lovely grandmother . . . [she] never has suggested ways for repairing the damages of society with one-half the skill she employed in teaching her nieces her wonderful method of darning rents in garments and household linens." As historian Sara Hunter Graham writes of the process of taming Anthony's reputation through domesticating and maternalizing her, it "helped to replace the stereotypical image of a masculinized fanatic with a nonthreatening feminine heroine imbued with domestic virtues."[48]

And damned if it didn't work. When Anthony died, the press would report warmly on mourners at her grave; the progressive organizer and politician Eugene V. Debs described her as "a moral heroine, an apostle of progress, a herald of the coming day." Graham argues that the remaking of Anthony meant that in this stage—the final haul—of the suffrage movement, "gone was the taint of extremism that suffragists believed had haunted the movement for decades; the parlor meeting had adopted 'Aunt Susan' as its patron saint, and suffragism had come of age."

But while the maternalizing of female political participation permits it to exist without grave social penalty, it can simultaneously obscure the anger that so often drives that participation—and insurrection.

Perhaps the most viscerally catalytic moment in the nascent civil rights movement was the murder of Emmett Till, a fourteen-year-old African-American child from Chicago, who was beaten to death and left in a river after having been accused of making a pass at a white woman while visiting an uncle in Mississippi in 1955. After his body was finally found, authorities tried to bury him in Mississippi without allowing his mother, Mamie, who was back in Chicago, to even look at him. "I don't know what authority [they] had to bury my son but [they] took that authority," Mamie Till recalled in a 2005 documentary. She insisted on having the casket delivered back to Chicago. Once there, the Chicago funeral director told her he had been prohibited from opening the box containing her son's body. Till recalled saying to the funeral director "Do you have a hammer? . . . [Because] if you can't open the box, I can, and I'm going in the box."

The box was opened, and interviewed fifty years after the fact, Mamie Till was still driven to describe in detail what she saw as she gazed at her son's dead body: "I saw his tongue had been choked out and was lying down on his chin. I saw that his eye was out and was lying about midway to his cheek. I looked at this eye and it was gone. I looked at the bridge of his nose and it looked like someone had taken a meat chopper and chopped it. And I looked at his teeth because I took so much pride in his teeth . . . and I only saw two . . . They'd been just knocked out, and I was looking at his ears . . . and I didn't see the ear . . . . That's when I discovered a hole about here and I could see daylight on the other side . . . And I also discovered that they had taken an axe and they had gone straight down across his head and his face and the back of his head were separate."

Mamie Till recalled looking at the funeral director and saying "Oh yes, we're gonna open the casket." When he looked back and asked if he should try to fix Emmett's features, she replied, "No, let the people see what I've seen."[49]

The people saw. More than fifty thousand of them saw Emmett's body—identifiable only because of a ring he wore—in person. They saw because Mamie Till, grieving the brutal murder of her child, insisted on having an open-casket funeral to which the public was invited. They saw because Mamie Till wanted the photos of his bloated, mutilated face to be published nationally in *Jet* magazine.

Mamie Till is credited as a transformative figure, but is most often pictured as a grieving mother being held up at her son's coffin, weeping at his gravesite, supported and barely able to stand, her mouth open not in fury but in keening loss. What we are never trained to consider is that alongside her sorrow and suffering was a burning rage. Lamentation and sadness do not drive a woman to fight for her son's body, to vow to smash open his casket, to commit the crimes done to his body and face to eternal memory, to *make damn sure* that the world has to look at the same image of racist brutality that has been visited on your family and your life.

Anger does that. In the case of Mamie Till, anger lit a match under a burgeoning social struggle that would help to partially remake the United States and lessen (though not in any way obliterate) many of the legal and political obstacles to racial parity.

And we never think—have never been asked to think—of *her anger* as that righteous spark.

SIMPLE ERASURE

Of course, there is also the reality that when women do explode with rage, even if the effect is to catalyze a social movement, their anger will never be recorded, never noted, never recalled or understood as nation-reshaping. The fact that we can often only register the fury of white men as heroic is so established that it would verge on the comical if it weren't so deeply tragic.

Lots of people were gathered inside a bar in lower Manhattan in the early morning hours of June 28, 1969. In the years since, there have been angry disputes over who was inside, who was outside, who said what or threw what and at what time. But what is established is that the Stonewall Inn, a dingy establishment that lacked running water, was the rare gay bar in New York City that permitted dancing, and that it had become a mecca not only for gay white men, but also for drag queens, transvestites, some lesbians, sex workers, and homeless youth. It was a bar for the particularly marginalized, in a city and an era that already marginalized homosexuality in any form. Police raids on gay establishments were a regular occurrence, and cops often forced cross-dressing patrons to go to the bathrooms and reveal their genitalia to them; at the time, impersonating a member of another gender was illegal in New York City, dressing in less than three pieces of gender-appropriate clothing was considered grounds for arrest.

Historians and participants may still disagree about exactly what happened in 1969, but in most recollections of the night, transvestites, drag queens—people who would now be called trans—as well as a handful of lesbians were probably at the center of events. Marsha P. Johnson, an African-American trans drag performer, was celebrating at the bar. A butch lesbian named Stormé DeLarverie was there; Sylvia Rivera, a trans gay rights activist, was outside on the street.

When the cops raided the Stonewall Inn that night, patrons were not in the mood to comply. Because they resisted, the raid took a long time, and onlookers and friends began to gather in large numbers outside. By some accounts, Johnson was among the first to resist inside the bar, throwing a shot glass and shouting "I got my civil rights"; many agree that it was De-Larverie who pushed back hard at cops, cursing and angrily complaining about her handcuffs being too tight as she was led out of the bar. When cops put her in a police car, DeLarverie is reported to have shouted at the staring, sympathetic crowd, "Why don't you guys do something?" It's at this point that Rivera, perhaps, threw a bottle at police, and others threw pennies, and the crowd outside rushed toward the paddy wagon containing those who'd already been arrested. Soon bricks, bottles, and glasses were flying and the crowd outside had launched an attack on the officers still in the bar, throwing rocks through its windows, pulling a parking meter from the street and using it as a battering ram. As Rivera would recall later in life, the resistant fury that overtook the crowd and patrons of Stonewall felt like this: "You've been treating us like shit all these years? Uh-huh. Now it's our turn!" She would also recall it as "one of the greatest moments in my life."[50]

The so-called Stonewall Riots would last for days and mark the start of the gay liberation movement. Johnson and Rivera would go on to found and be active in the Gay Liberation Front, and together found STAR, the Street Transvestite Action Revolutionaries, dedicated to supporting homeless drag queens and trans people of color. DeLarverie was described in her *New York Times* obituary as, in her post-Stonewall years, having walked the streets of lower Manhattan, "like a gay superhero . . . She was not to be messed with by any stretch of the imagination."[51]

DeLarverie would also later insist that the events of those nights be spoken about with care, and is reported to have framed them consciously as righteous political action. "It was a rebellion, it was an uprising, it was a civil rights disobedience," she reportedly told a symposium of Stonewall veterans. "It wasn't no damn riot."[52]

But the angry women and gender nonconformists who were likely at the heart of that rebellion were very often erased from its retelling, and from the popular view of the gay rights movement, a movement so often embodied by the wealthy straight white men who were its most public figures. When, in 2015, Hollywood released its big film about the movement, *Stonewall*, focusing on the events at the Stonewall Inn, it did not star trans women, drag queens, lesbians, or nonwhite gender nonconformists as its heroes. Rather it was a fictionalized story of a young white cisgender man from the Midwest, the figure who could most comfortably be cast as the first to hurl a brick through a window and yell, "Gay power!"

CHOOSING TO HOLD OUR TONGUES

During the flood of #metoo stories about sexual harassment and gendered inequity, flowing particularly out of Hollywood, a reporter asked the actress Uma Thurman about her feelings on the movement. "I've learned that when I've spoken in anger," Thurman replied, "I usually regret the way I express myself. So I've been waiting to feel less angry. And when I'm ready, I'll say what I have to say."[53]

Thurman's forbearance drove feminist Lindy West wild with frustration. "Not only are women expected to weather sexual violence, intimate partner violence, workplace discrimination, institutional subordination, the expectation of free domestic labor, the blame for our own victimization, and all the subtler, invisible cuts that undermine us daily," wrote West. "We are not even allowed to be angry about it."

Sometimes, there is a strategy behind the suppression of rage; in Thurman's case, she was waiting to tell her story in full, as she later did to *New York Times* journalist Maureen Dowd.

Cecile Richards, the longtime president of Planned Parenthood, described in her memoir, *Make Trouble*, how, as she was entering the House of Representatives in 2015 to be grilled for five hours by Republicans over a set of doctored videos that inaccurately claimed to show members of her organization selling baby parts, a friend had texted her to stay strong, reminding her "to carry the rage of women through the centuries with you this morning!" The message bolstered Richards, yet her tactic while being interrogated by her ideological foes was to *contain* all that rage. Her refusal to show her ire, she said, worked to drive her inquisitors bonkers, which in turn put their spluttering, punitive frustration on display in front of a television audience.

When, in public conversation with Richards, I pointed out to her that this strategy perfectly mirrored that of nonviolent civil rights organizing in the Gandhian tradition—the idea that peaceful protest on the part of the oppressed would provoke aggressive and discrediting rage on the part of the oppressors, hopefully in full view of television cameras—she said that she hadn't considered it a strategy going into the hearings. "It was just my instinct," she said. Remaining cool, keeping that anger simmering, and watching her interrogators explode in response was part of an unconscious plan.

It can be effective, but is also part of the dynamic that leads us to ignore—to never even see—the catalytic power of women's rage, simply because if it is kept beneath the surface, even strategically, we never have to acknowledge its existence. It was the teachings of nonviolent protest techniques that led Rosa Parks—in the same year that Mamie Till forced the world to see what lynching looked like—to not give up her seat on a Montgomery bus in 1955.

Parks is widely remembered and celebrated as a civil rights heroine, but she is also memorialized as stoic, pitied for having been exhausted, appreciated for her very refusal to show anger.

In fact, Parks was a lifelong furious fighter against sexual and racial violence, a defender of black men wrongly accused of sexual misconduct by white women, and an elected NAACP secretary who investigated the rape claims of black women against white men, including the brutal 1944 gang rape of the sharecropper Recy Taylor in Abbeville, Alabama. In her later life, Parks became interested in the black power movement, and expressed admiration for Malcolm X. Much of Parks's antirape activism wasn't unearthed for the general public until Danielle McGuire's 2010 book *At the Dark End of the Street*, and the intensity of her political investments was obscured beneath the sanitized, rage-free caricature of her propagated by the press and by the leaders of the very movement she helped to kick-start. But women within the civil rights movement, including activists Pauli Murray and Anna Arnold Hedgeman, were angry at movement leaders who minimized Parks's role as an active, dynamic, driven political agitator, and many have strained since to offer a fuller and more complete picture of her.

"Dr. Martin Luther King, [Jr.] is the name most people associate with the Montgomery bus boycott," observed Angela Davis in *A Place of Rage*. "Of course Rosa Parks's name is known because she refused to sit in the back of the bus, but most often she is portrayed as someone who was not politically involved, who simply one day got tired of sitting in the back of the bus and refused to move. . . . Well of course she probably did get tired of sitting in the back of the bus. But that wasn't the reason why she refused to move to the back of the bus. That was a political act on her part."

And of course, keeping anger tempered and controlled isn't always a positive, strategic approach; sometimes it's about flat-out repression, the stuffing down of rage, the terror of revealing or even permitting ourselves to *feel* anger, precipitated by a culture that tells us it is bad for us physically and mentally, that it perverts and distorts us, rendering us ugly and marginal.

In her memoir of the election, Hillary Clinton describes the anxiety she felt about her own rage, explaining that she prayed "to stay hopeful and openhearted rather than becoming cynical and bitter . . . so that the rest of my life wouldn't be spent like Miss Havisham . . . rattling around my house obsessing over what might have been." Many of us recognize this impulse; none of us *wants* to be driven by unwaning anger for the rest of our lives; but Clinton wrote this less than a year after her loss; she had every rational reason in the world to feel rage, and yet she was so terrified that it would poison and dement her that she asked God to help her stop it up.

June Jordan speculated in *A Place of Rage* that "one of the reasons why you see such an affliction of drugs on black communities and low-income communities throughout the United States today is because rage has lost its respectability since the 1960s. The thing that you had in the civil rights revolution was an absolute upfront embrace of rage . . . when you don't rage against the evils and the enemies against you what you do is you turn in against yourself and you begin to despair and give up . . . and that leads to this kind of plague proportion of drugs."

Others, from Sigmund Freud to Gloria Steinem and the fictional therapist Jennifer Melfi from *The Sopranos*, have warned that anger turned inward leads to depression, perhaps making it no coincidence that one of the most common ways for women to express their anger is through tears.

THE TEARS OF WRATH

Maybe we cry when we're furious in part because we feel a kind of grief at all the things we want to say or yell that we know we can't. Maybe we're just sad about the very same things that we're angry about.

The writer Meghan O'Rourke, who has studied grief in the wake of her mother's death from cancer, wrote of friends who suggested that they needed to sit Shiva in the week after the 2016 election, noting that "we are experiencing not just the pain of political defeat but the grief of mourning something that feels irrevocably lost." What we were grieving, O'Rourke argued, was "for the nation we could have been, a nation some of us feel we *are*: a nation that elected a female president and rejected the rhetoric of nativism and fear that Donald Trump so casually embraced."[54]

But maybe it's also the instinct that it will go better for us tactically—especially if we are white—if we emote through tears, which are associated with women's vulnerability, rather than through rage, which is associated with our threat. Crying affirms us as female, and if you're a woman (again, especially a white woman), comporting yourself in traditionally female ways is rewarded, while lashing out is punished. There have been studies showing that when women who accuse men of domestic violence get angry while testifying, judges are likely to go easier on the accused; but if they show grief while on the stand, and thus comport with a view of vulnerable and nonabrasive femininity, the sentence is likely to be heavier.[55]

As the writer Leslie Jamison wrote about the pride she used to take in claiming she was "sad" rather than "angry": "Sadness seemed more refined and also more selfless—as if you were holding the pain inside yourself, rather than making someone else deal with its blunt-force trauma."[56]

A 2000 review of studies compiled by psychology professor Ann Kring found that while men and women self-report instances of anger at similar rates, women report feeling more shame about them. Kring also found men more likely to express anger through physical or verbal assault, while women, in Jamison's words, "are more likely to cry when they get angry, as if their bodies are forcibly returning them to the appearance of the emotion—sadness—with which they are most commonly associated."[57]

Whatever the connection, there's been a lot of crying in politics, and very little of it has stemmed from women feeling sad.

Back in 1876, when five suffragists, including Susan B. Anthony, disrupted an official celebration of the nation's centennial, they handed out their own declaration of women's rights and read a speech about the injustice of women's disenfranchisement, one that began by framing their political resistance as having been undertaken in grief: "While the Nation is buoyant with patriotism, and all hearts are attuned to praise, it is with sorrow we come to strike the one discordant note."[58]

And Congresswoman Barbara Lee recalled to me a century later how Congresswoman Shirley Chisholm, "cried behind closed doors when she was hurt. You know how pain leads to anger." In public, Lee recalled, Chisholm would be "so cool, her voice and demeanor tough and strong and *boom, boom, boom*. But get her behind closed doors? She'd let her guard down and acknowledge her pain." Lee recalled Chisholm's propensity for tears as a product of her being "very sensitive, very hurt, and very angry."

"Remember," Lee told me, "she was the only black woman with all these men, white and black. You come into an environment that is really the deck stacked against you: you're black and you're a woman. I remember she'd say, 'Barbara, these rules weren't made for you or me.'" Lee remembered Chisholm as equally sensitive to the slights of the Congressional Black Caucus and her white colleagues in the women's movement. "Shirley was very clear that the white feminist movement did not understand the nature of racism and what black women and black people have to deal with. And she was equally angry at a lot of the African-American leadership, because she didn't think they understood how women were being treated." And so, while Lee emphasized that Chisholm "never let anyone break her down in public," in private, she cried.

And she was never the only one. In 1972, at the convention to which Chisholm brought her delegates, at which Flo Kennedy and her group of agitators screamed at newscasters to keep their hands off, George Mc-Govern had persuaded many feminists to support him (over Chisholm and others). But McGovern would double-cross them, instructing his delegates not to support a plank that would legalize abortion and violating an explicit promise to the women by permitting an antiabortion activist to speak from the floor. The journalist (and later screenwriter) Nora Ephron covered the messy convention for *Esquire*: At four o'clock in the morning, Ephron wrote, Gloria Steinem "in tears, was confronting McGovern campaign manager Gary Hart: 'You promised us you would not take the low road, you bastards.'"

The next day, Ephron trailed Steinem out of a hotel where she'd gone to confront McGovern directly, but hadn't succeeded. "If you're a woman, all they can think about your relationship with a politician is that you're either sleeping with him or advising him about clothes," Steinem seethed to Ephron, walking away from the hotel and starting to cry again. "It's just that they won't take us seriously," Steinem told Ephron through tears. "And I'm just tired of being screwed, and being screwed by my friends. By George McGovern, whom I raised half the money for in his first campaign, wrote his speeches . . . he just doesn't understand. We went to see him at one point about abortion, and the question of welfare came up. 'Why are you concerned about welfare?' he said. He didn't understand it was a woman's issue. They won't take us seriously. We're just walking wombs. And the television coverage . . . saying that now that the women are here, next thing there'll be a caucus of left-handed Lithuanians."[59]

Steinem's tirade, as recorded forever by Ephron, is righteous diatribe, months and years of fury spilling over, and she can't get it out without weeping.

"We cry when we get angry," Steinem said to me forty-five years later, recalling the conversation, and still shaking her head with some apparent regret that she wept, and that Ephron had caught her at it. "I don't think that's uncommon, do you? That women cry when we get angry?" That Steinem would look for reassurance on this point is stunning in itself: of course women cry when they get angry. But she continued, "I was greatly helped by a woman who was an executive someplace, who said she also cried when she got angry, but developed a technique which meant that when she got angry and started to cry, she'd say to the person she was talking to, 'You may think I am sad because I am crying. No. I am angry.' And then she just kept going. And I thought that was brilliant."

The unpleasant revelation accompanying the realization that tears are one of the most frequent outlets for our wrath is that they are permitted in part because they are fundamentally misunderstood. One of my sharpest memories from an early job, in a male-dominated office, where I too once found myself weeping with inexpressible rage, was being grabbed by the scruff of my neck by an older woman—a chilly, hard-ass manager of whom I'd always been slightly terrified—who dragged me into a stairwell. "Never let them see you crying," she told me. "They don't know you're furious. They think you're sad and will be pleased because they got to you."

Congresswoman Patricia Schroeder from Colorado was working as the chair of Gary Hart's presidential campaign in 1987 when the married Hart was caught in an extramarital affair aboard a boat called *Monkey Business*. Schroeder, angry with Hart and deeply frustrated by the situation, thought, "Well, I've been going out and doing appearances for him, engaging in some debates." She decided that with her candidate out of the race, there was no reason that she shouldn't explore the idea of running for president herself.

"It was not a well-thought-out decision," she said to me with a laugh thirty years later. "There were already seven other candidates in the race and the last thing they needed was another one. Somebody called it *Snow White and the Seven Dwarves*." She understood that because she was a late entry, she was behind on fund-raising, and vowed that she wouldn't enter the race unless she raised two million dollars, but it was an arduous battle. Studying the fund-raising documentation, she'd find that some of her supporters who gave a thousand dollars to men would then give her only $250. "I'd read this and think: do they think I get a discount?" Schroeder recalled that as the fall of 1987 came into view, a *Time* magazine poll had ranked her third in the Democratic field, "but when you looked at the polls, and how many people said they'd never vote for a woman, and then realized that a lot of people lied when they said yes, they would, I figured *no way this is going to happen; I'm gonna be third forever and third won't get me there.*"

She decided to announce that she would not launch a formal campaign. And when she made her speech, she was so overcome by a series of emotions—gratitude for the people who'd supported and fought for her throughout a long hot summer, frustration with the system that made it so difficult to raise money and to target voters rather than delegates, and anger at the sexism—that she got choked up."[60]

"You would have thought I'd had a nervous breakdown," recalled Schroeder of how the press reacted to her. "You'd have thought Kleenex was my corporate sponsor. I remember thinking, *What are they gonna put on my tombstone? 'She cried'?*" For a while Schroeder kept what she called "a crying file," a little list of all the male politicians who'd wept publicly that year. "Reagan would tear up every time he saw a flag," she remembered. Her file included records; New Hampshire governor John Sununu, who cried as he was stepping down as governor of New Hampshire, and George H. W. Bush, who was a steady weeper. But the reaction to tears from those men was wholly different from what Schroeder got in response to her congestion.

Saturday Night Live mocked Schroeder in a skit in which Nora Dunn, as Schroeder, repeatedly burst into tears while moderating a debate. Later, the *New York Times* would describe her as having dissolved "in a flood of tears."[61] An editorial in one Vermont paper read, "What a devastating indictment of this girl's character." One *Washington Post* columnist wrote about how older women like Schroeder were setting the cause of young women back a century, calling it "crazy, reckless, for one of Congress's few women . . . to give ammunition to those who saw women as sugary little girls rather than serious people to be taken seriously."

Schroeder found this last argument the most galling. Recalling a man who *had* suffered politically after he wept in public, Edmund Muskie, whose tears effectively ended his bid for the presidency back in that crucial year, 1972, she still wondered, thirty years later, "Why don't I remember anyone saying that he set *men* back?"

There is another dimension to the choice that many women make to cry: the fact that this emblem of helpless suffering provokes a sympathetic and protective response, mostly when the tears are being shed by white women. The protection those tears are understood to invite has often been used as the justification for racial violence. "White women's tears" have derailed important conversations about race, provoking sympathy for and connection with *some* kinds of women, but not others. "Not all tears matter," observed the writer Shay Stewart-Bouley in 2018. "Rarely do the tears of a nonwhite woman carry any value. . . . The damsel in distress is never black."[62]

When I described to Alicia Garza some of the stories I'd been hearing during my reporting for this book, she said that they make *her* feel sad. "What is underneath my anger is a deep sadness," she said. "It actually breaks my heart to hear that a woman as visionary as Shirley Chisholm used to cry. It breaks my heart to hear that a woman as courageous as Barbara Lee has to keep her voice from shaking. It bothers me to no end that Maxine Waters gets portrayed as a crazy person, with no shade to people that are crazy, but she's not. And I know that feeling, and I often feel like *I'm* crazy. I often feel like there's something wrong with me and if I wasn't really intentional about building a community of people around me that get me one hundred percent, I would probably not be in this movement. And that makes me sad."

A SPOONFUL OF HUMOR MAKES
THE MEDICINE GO DOWN

The close cousin of sadness is laughter, and another common—and widely misunderstood—means of expressing socially acceptable wrath has come through comedy.

Pat Schroeder used to channel her congressional frustrations into witty, sharp-tongued retorts that didn't always fall merrily on the ears of her colleagues. Some of her witticisms became famous, like her dubbing Ronald Reagan "the Teflon president." After the millionth time she was asked whether she would run for president "as a woman," she began to snap back "What choice do I have?" As a member of the Committee on Armed Services, Schroeder once cracked to Pentagon officials that if they were women they'd always be pregnant because they never said "no." A *New York Times* story noting that Shroeder had been sworn into Congress with diapers in her purse also included reference to her most famous comeback, her response to being asked how she could be both a mother and a congresswoman: "I have a brain and a uterus, and I use both."[63]

"That was obviously sharp and I shouldn't have said it," Schroeder said to me in 2017, and has long noted—including in that same *Times* story—that "I don't think anyone likes a smart aleck."[64] To me, she said retrospectively, that a lot of her sharp humor was understood as aggression. She remembered being referred to by colleagues as "the wicked witch—or bitch—of the West." Schroeder recalled the unfairness of it all, noting that often her barbs came in her own defense against sexist diminishment. "If a guy says something in his own defense," she said, "he's standing his ground. If you say it, you're just being petty or being thin-skinned. Women are just supposed to put up with it, suck it up, and move on."

The irony is that Schroeder was consciously using her wit and her cheery feminized persona—she famously drew smiling faces in the "P" in her signature and giggled a lot—to ease anxieties about her political ambitions, her willingness to censure her opponents, and her often-confrontational style. When she was the most senior woman in Congress in 1990, the *New York Times* described Schroeder's "shrewd, even lethal political savvy," noting that "over the years she has helped bump not one, but two, chairmen off the House Armed Services Committee." But she often cited advice from her father: "Never frown at your enemies. Smile—it scares the hell out of them."

Among the commands the antifeminist crusader Phyllis Schlafly issued her foot soldiers during her campaign against ratification of the Equal Rights Amendment in the 1970s was that they should always, always smile; one of Schlafly's best-known books was titled *The Power of the Positive Woman*.[65] But grinning positivity may disguise ambitious intent only in women fighting on the side of white patriarchy. After all, Schlafly defeated the ERA, and was rarely pressed too hard on the disingenuousness of her message: as a powerful political woman who traveled the country, she was regularly telling other women that their calling was to stay at home. Meanwhile, despite all the smiley faces drawn by the left-leaning feminist Schroeder, her critics still saw in *her*, according to the *Times*, "a 'hard' look, a grin that is really a grimace, a nasal-voiced delivery through clenched jaws and eyes that disappear behind a squint.... The reality is that Schroeder is a driven politician who smiles too hard" and whose penchant for one-liners "belies and often undercuts [her] seriousness."[66]

But even if it doesn't always work to fully obscure ambition and aggression, humor can certainly make it go down a little easier. Despite a reputation for humorlessness—earned, ironically enough, by objections to dirty jokes and the injunction *against* telling all women to smile as if they were decorative objects—many of the second-wave feminists were in fact pretty hilarious. Chief among them, Flo Kennedy.

"The classic Flo line," recalled Steinem, her regular speaking partner, "was when some guy in the back got up and asked us 'Are you lesbians?' and she responded 'Are you my alternative?'" Kennedy, said Steinem, "could always say something that made people laugh. But it always had a point. I mean, she was not letting anybody off the hook by making people laugh."

Sometimes humor is the best way to stick the shiv in, to express the vivid fury that, for any number of reasons, can't emerge straight, but can be more plausibly laid out as parody of what a marginalized angry person would say were her anger permitted space and respect.

During the Obama presidency, comedians Jordan Peele and Keegan-Michael Key had come up with a character named Luther, who served as the "anger translator" for the preternaturally even-tempered commander in chief—the black president who could never be mad. During the 2016 campaign, the best retailing of Hillary's imagined anger came on the internet, on the website Medium, via a pair of pieces filed under the byline @shitHRCcantsay, absolutely ripping apart the way that Clinton had been treated: "I've been preparing my whole fucking life for this job. So stop making me dab on Ellen and just give me a fucking chance already," read one. The fantasy Hillary of this parody was all the things women are not supposed to be and therefore what the real Hillary could *never* be: self-confident, braggadocious, condescending, and livid at the petty stupidity she had to wade through in order to comport with America's standards of femininity. And it provided such relief to read.[67]

The release was even more necessary when the parody account produced a post, five days after Clinton's loss, cutting through the pitiless finger-pointing at Clinton's sole culpability. In the parody, Clinton turned the blame on everyone *but* herself with a defensive self-righteousness that was as satisfying in parody form as it would have been disqualifying in real life, precisely *because* it was a torrent of vivid wrath that no actual woman could ever unleash on the public and survive:

I'd like to extend a hearty fuck you to the national news media. This is for spending more time talking about my emails than all policy issues combined. . . . This is for constantly saying I "am flawed" or "have flaws" . . . motherfucker, name one!!! My fucking charity that gives HIV meds to poor people? Are you for real with this shit? And the Monday morning quarterbacks right now? You're gonna criticize my campaign?? Bitch, I won the popular vote and I was running against America! Last toast: undecided voters . . . honey, if you were undecided after the Mexican rapist speech it means one thing: You needed me to be perfect. . . . You know, back in 1965, I ran for class president of my high school and lost to a boy who told me, "You are really stupid if you think a girl can be elected president." Well, I put in fifty years of tireless, grueling work, and now, at long last, that little boy has been vindicated.[68]

Comedy gives cover to the unspeakable, and for women, that can be the anger that needs to boil over sometimes—not just in righteousness but also in ugliness and self-pity. Why the hell shouldn't Hillary's supporters, the ones who'd actually been committed to her winning the presidency— and who'd been the object of angry tirades from all sides—get to engage in some mean, vulgar, angry release of their own?

Plenty of women who went into the business of comedy understood it to be an outlet for their fury, or perhaps that their anger was the predicate for their profession. "The minute you're not angry about things, the minute you're not upset about things, what are you talking about?" Joan Rivers asked in the 2010 documentary *A Piece of Work*. "I'm furious about everything. . . . But if I didn't have the anger . . . I wouldn't be a comedian. Anger fuels the comedy."

Phoebe Robinson, a comedian from an entirely different generation, has written in her memoir, *You Can't Touch My Hair*, of the way that comedy helped her to channel her pain and temper the public's view of her dissatisfactions. "If I expressed my hurt in a clever, joking manner, no one can take offense then, right?" Robinson, half of the comedy podcast partnership *2 Dope Queens*, wrote, "No one can call you an angry black woman if we're all laughing, right?"[69]

Humor can be such a good way to hide anger at racist, sexist degradation and to challenge white male authority sideways—without risking as much direct blowback—that it perhaps shouldn't be a surprise that the comedian Tina Fey wrote jokes about Harvey Weinstein's sexual predation— lines about being pinned under Weinstein, and turning down sex with him—that aired on her show *30 Rock* in 2012, years before his behavior could be reported straight. In 2013, during the Oscars, the white male comedian Seth MacFarlane also made a Weinstein joke—about the lead actress nominees no longer having to pretend to be attracted to the producer. After 2017 reporting revealed the extent of Weinstein's predation, MacFarlane explained that a friend of his, an actress who'd been harassed by Weinstein, had confided in him, prompting his joke. "Make no mistake," he said at the time, his one-liner had come "from a place of loathing and anger."[70]

After years of stories about women who claimed to have been sexually assaulted by the comedian Bill Cosby prompted no repercussions, the comedian Hannibal Buress, angry at how Cosby lectured African Americans to "pull their pants up," began retorting during his stand-up act, "Yeah, but you rape women, Bill Cosby. So turn the crazy down a couple notches." It was only after Buress's joke got picked up by the media that the multiple allegations against Cosby finally began to take hold.

Comedy doesn't just offer an affable disguise for fury. It can also absorb and defuse it. When her TBS show launched, comedian Samantha Bee set up a special "rape-threat line" in response to the kind of online abuse that she took as a female comedian. Callers heard this message: "No one is here to take your call, but your offer of nonconsensual sex is important to us, so please select from the following menu: to tell me I'm a dumb bitch that needs to be raped, press 1; to tell me you're going to violate every hole in my idiot libtard body, press 2 . . . "

"It's not a joke for everyone," Bee told me drily in 2016. "This is as dark as satire can probably be. It's also about the condition of being a woman in this business."

Bee's weekly show would turn out to be one of the major outlets for angry feminist humor throughout the election and the years that followed, her opening monologues often simply extended rants, the laughs stemming not even always from *jokes* but from the giddy pleasure of hearing bad people correctly excoriated. The raw venting of spleen became its own humor, the punch line being that this was the most rational response, but one that couldn't be voiced—or wouldn't be taken seriously—outside the confines of a comedic monologue.

During the 2018 week that Paul Ryan announced his retirement from the House of Representatives, my husband and I had sat slack-jawed in front of very serious cable news programs, on which many experts told us gravely that Ryan—the Wisconsin congressman who'd been serving as Republican House Speaker since 2015, and who had spent years on the leading edge of the virulent strain of conservatism that had landed us with President Trump—was in fact just a well-meaning tax geek, his resignation a signal that Ryan's brand of responsible, moderate conservatism was out of favor in Trump's administration. We had been incandescent with anger: this retroactive beatification of Ryan, a man who'd been fantasizing about stripping poor people of health-care benefits through Medicaid since he'd been standing around a keg in college, a guy who'd stayed in the administration long enough to push through a tax break for the very rich, a legislator who'd spent his whole career maintaining his total opposition to abortion rights, even in cases of rape and incest . . . it was irrational, untrue, divorced from reality. But on the straight news, the idea that Ryan was a man fueled by personal moral convictions was everywhere.

Days later, we settled in to watch *Full Frontal with Samantha Bee* and found Bee, fuming. "Paul Ryan is a bad person," she said in her opening monologue. "He's not a statesman, he's a wing-nut." Predicting that Ryan would someday run for president, Bee continued, "He's counting on us forgetting how fuckin' horrible he is, but we will not forget. Paul Ryan, your legacy is making poor people pay for rich people's massive tax cuts, fighting to take health care away from millions, trying to gut social programs, defending the Muslim ban, enabling a constitutional crisis and somehow convincing everyone that torching Democratic norms and the social safety net is *moderate.*" My husband and I cheered. There was practically no pretense that there was even a joke here. It was just the furious truth, laid bare so unapologetically that it elicits a laugh.

Not everyone sees Bee's approach to angry expression as useful. After Bee dedicated an October 2016 monologue to the *Access Hollywood* tape—during which she called Trump and Billy Bush "two leering dildos" and claimed that "every woman I know has had some entitled testosterone monster grab her like a human bowling ball"—the *Atlantic* writer Megan Garber worried that Bee's response to Trump's predatory incivility had offered "anger that didn't attempt to temper itself under the guise of 'satire.' Anger that seethed . . . anger that trusted in itself as its own end." Garber felt that while Bee's "anger at Trump may be . . . righteous, it's an open question how productive it is . . . Anger is one way of making sense of things. Very rarely, however, is it a terribly good one."[71]

Garber's anxiety about Bee's profane ire may have stemmed from the understanding that when comedy actually challenges power too sharply, power will condemn the comedy. That dynamic couldn't have been made clearer than it was during the 2018 White House Correspondents' Dinner, at which the comedian Michelle Wolf performed a venomously funny skewering of the Trump administration and the press corps that had gathered for its annual self-celebration. Wolf's foul-mouthed excoriation of the press employed a comedic distancing device, getting the audience to chime in on a riff about Donald Trump's lack of wealth, with a chorus of *How broke is he?* and answering with a bunch of anodyne one-liners before going in for the kill with the final punch line that was not a joke at all: *How broke is he?* "He had to borrow money from the Russians, and now he's compromised and susceptible to blackmail and possibly responsible for the collapse of the republic . . . Yay. It's a fun game."[72] Wolf went hard after Trump's press secretary, Sarah Huckabee Sanders, comparing her to Aunt Lydia from *The Handmaid's Tale*, a reference to a woman who works to uphold a violent patriarchal political regime, suggesting that Sanders "burns facts" in order to get a good eye-makeup effect, and wondered how to refer to her, asking, "What's Uncle Tom, but for white women who disappoint other white women? Oh, I know: Aunt Coulter."

It was brutal, and Wolf was no more sparing toward the press, riffing, "I think what no one in this room wants to admit is that Trump has helped all of you. . . . He's helped you sell your papers and your books and your TV. You helped create this monster, and now you're profiting off him. And if you're gonna profit off Trump, you should at least give him some money because he doesn't have any."

Wolf's ire was direct and unmistakable; she concluded the speech—in a room that had turned cold—with a double-angry sign-off, reminding guests at the high-end, civilized, bipartisan party of grittier realities, experienced by Dreamers and by residents of the Michigan city where a government choice to save money had led to toxic levels of lead in the drinking water: "All right, like an immigrant who was brought here by his parents and didn't do anything wrong, I gotta get the fuck out of here. Good night. Flint still doesn't have clean water!"

As Masha Gessen wrote for the *New Yorker*, the monologue "burst the bubbles of civility and performance, and of the separation of media and comedy. It plunged the attendees into the reality that is, in the Trump era, the stuff of comedy. Through her obscene humor, Wolf exposed the obscenity of the fictions—and the fundamental unfunniness of it all."[73]

Right-wingers predictably hit back, but so did members of the political press corps. *Morning Joe's* Mika Brzezinski tweeted in defense of Sanders, "Watching a wife and mother be humiliated on national television for her looks is deplorable,"[74] while the *New York Times'* Maggie Haberman tweeted that the fact that Sanders "sat and absorbed intense criticism of her physical appearance"—despite the fact that Wolf had not in fact criticized her appearance—"her job performance and so forth, instead of walking out, on national television, was impressive."[75] CNN's Chris Cillizza also marveled at Sanders's ability to withstand the attack, arguing that "being funny is one thing. Bullying people because you can is another. And Wolf's treatment of Sanders was bullying . . . [bullying is] wrong. Always." Recall that Cillizza was the reporter who in 2009 made a joke about Hillary Clinton being a "mad bitch" and has published a list of his favorite Donald Trump insults—including near the top his racist references to Elizabeth Warren as "Pocahontas"—referring to the then-candidate Trump as "the Michael Jordan of name-calling."

Through unflinchingly angry comedy, Wolf had framed the argument she was making about the press and Trump henchwoman's complicity in the rise of an abusive, cruel, and authoritarian political regime as a neat trap. The objects of her monologue reacted to it in a way that proved her point, about their drive to protect and cover for power, very precisely.

FUCK IT

Getting an equally mixed reaction from the public is women's use of profanity as a cathartic and communicative tool to express their ire. I had been startled—though pleased; I love profanity—when, during the 2016 Democratic National Convention, I'd been interviewing Congresswoman Gwen Moore from Milwaukee; she'd been describing the economic obstacles she'd faced all her life as a single black mother, and offered what she called a "one-finger salute" to anyone planning to vote third party in November. She'd then looked at me steadily and confessed, "I'm scared shitless." I'd rarely heard elected officials, especially *female* elected officials, curse on the record to a reporter, but it was refreshingly direct. After all, I knew *exactly* what she meant.

By 2017, plenty of other women in Washington were cursing. Both Kamala Harris and Kirsten Gillibrand, U.S. senators, had turned to public vulgarity in their attempts to convey the intensity of their antipathy to the Trump administration and the party that had enabled it and was standing by it.

While discussing the GOP's plan to repeal and replace Obamacare at an event in San Francisco, Harris had mocked a congressman who'd said, "Nobody dies because they don't have access to health care." "What the fuck is that?" Harris asked onstage. Some months later, profiled in the *New York Times*, Harris was only slightly more careful. "I was told one should not say"—here the reporter left a blank, but enough description to let readers know the word was "motherfucker"—"in these kinds of interviews . . . So I'm not going to say it."[76] After Gillibrand was freely profane in conversation with me during the same health-care fights of 2017, noting at one point that as senators, "if we're not helping people, we should go the fuck home," I got plenty of responses from readers who felt that her use of expletives was imitative of the president. She had in fact used profanity throughout her 2014 memoir, and acknowledged within it her particular weakness for bad words, but the Trump era was permitting her to deploy them from the stump, and she didn't stop. In July of 2017, Gillibrand asked a crowd, "Has [Trump] kept his promises?" and then responded, "No, fuck no!" In response, she was, naturally, labeled "unhinged" in right-wing publications.

It turns out that the women immersed in the legislative hell of the Trump administration might have been turning to obscenities as an analgesic. The psychology professor Richard Stephens told the *New York Times* of a study he'd done, in which he'd asked subjects to submerge their hands in ice water for as long as they could, repeating a word that was either a profanity or a neutral term. Those who swore were able to keep their hands in the ice water for fifty percent longer and reported that the pain had felt less intense. Cursing, the *Times* summed up, can "offer catharsis . . . [and] might help you tolerate the pain better." Other studies are underway, trying to determine if, in addition to numbing our discomfort, cursing might also increase our strength, a possibility that would inform and complicate an understanding of why so many protesters—feeling impotent in the face of a Trump administration—might choose to decorate their marching signs with expletives.

Like anger itself, cursing has been discouraged in women, as it is considered unladylike and masculinizing. But in fact it's useful precisely because it is an outlet for all that pent-up anger. "Cursing is coping, or venting, and it helps us deal with stress," the professor Timothy Jay told the *New York Times*. Profanity, he said, permits us to "express our emotions, especially anger and frustration, towards others symbolically," rather than physically or violently.[77]

Unlike direct voicing of anger or displeasure from women, foul language has more readily become a calling card of coolness, good humor, a sign of integration with the men. It can be funny, humanizing. And also, in moments of true explosive rage, it can be instinctive, almost animal.

The former NPR ombudsman Alicia Shepard has recalled a meeting of a trade group at which she asked for clarification from the executive director, an older white man. When he replied "It's on the website, dear," she reflexively responded, "Don't call me dear, fuckface." "I don't even know where I got the word 'fuckface,'" Shepard told the media organization Poynter in 2017. "It was years of being called sweetie and dear . . . that came bubbling to the surface and caused an outburst."[78]

"There are some people who are really offended by profanity," Gloria Steinem told me. "But I find the art is to put the "fuck" in the middle of the word, not to say it by itself." Steinem said she learned this trick from the musical *Hair*, in which a song lyric to "Abie Baby," about Abraham Lincoln, refers to the sixteenth president as "the Emanci-mother-fucking-pator of the Slaves." Steinem loved it, and uses oaths to break up, draw emphasis to, and otherwise play with the words she's using. "So I say fan-fucking-tastic or fan-fucking-ridiculous or something."

But there's also perhaps a lesson in how curse words came to carry such outsized weight. According to the researchers cited in the *New York Times*, "profane words are powerful only because we make them powerful. Without their being censored [so-called bad words] would just be average terms."[79] It is the suppression and censure of profanity that gives it its potency, something that those who remain invested in repressing women's fury might do well to remember.

GETTING VOLCANIC

When every other method—suppression, almighty justification, tears, jokes, and four-letter words—has failed, some women in politics have simply decided to throw their cards in the air and get openly mad. Without apology or pause. When, in 2014, Congress failed to pass the Paycheck Fairness Act, which would have added protections to the Equal Pay Act and better ensured equal pay for women, especially women of color, Maryland senator Barbara Mikulski gave a speech on the Senate floor.

"I'll tell you what I'm tired of hearing: that somehow or another we're too emotional when we talk," Mikulski thundered. "Well, I am emotional . . . It brings tears to my eyes, to know how women every single day are working so hard and are getting paid less. It makes me emotional to hear that. Then when I hear all of these phony reasons, some are mean and some are meaningless, I do get emotional. I get angry. I get outraged. I get volcanic."

There are plenty of instances in which the expression of their fury—raw and remorseless—has been effective rhetorically, even if, as in Mikulski's case, it did not produce a desired legislative or legal or political or repercussive effect.

People often consider Gloria Steinem—white, cisgender, traditionally feminine and foxy—as the great communicator of feminist rage. During her decades in the spotlight, the media regularly, and hungrily, positioned her as perhaps the *only* feminist that America was interested in hearing from. But on the road, she said, where she spoke regularly with Flo Kennedy—the unapologetic purveyor of frank fury—"I always had to speak first because if I went after Flo, it was such an anticlimax. There was no question, I had to go first."

There is perhaps no better example of undisguised anger working as a rhetorical super-power than Flo Kennedy. Kennedy's life was a study in unapologetic and furious resistance to injustice. As a young woman in Kansas City, Missouri, she had participated in a boycott of a nearby Coca-Cola bottling company that did not hire African-American truck drivers. When she was denied entry to Columbia law school—not because she was black but because she was a woman, administrators told her—she threatened a discrimination suit and was admitted, as one of eight women, and the only African American, in her class. As a lawyer, she represented members of the Black Panther Party on charges of conspiracy to commit bombings, sued the Catholic Church, and in 1969 organized feminist legal objection to New York State's abortion ban, which was overturned in 1970. In 1973, when students at Harvard were agitating to get the gender ratio at the school to 50–50, Kennedy waded in, calling Harvard Yard "the ass-hole of the world" and orchestrating a legendary "pee-in" protest there, in response to the school's paucity of women's bathrooms.[80] Kennedy was in the cast of the 1983 feminist movie *Born in Flames*, about revolutionary women who band together in a renegade women's army to battle gender and racial oppression.

She was described by *People* magazine as having "the biggest, loudest, and, indisputably, the rudest mouth on the battleground where feminist activists and radical politics join in mostly common cause."

When they were on the speaking circuit as partners, Steinem recalled being admonished by Kennedy for being too schoolmarmish, too afraid to yell and get viscerally emotional, and instead relying too heavily on annotated backup in her speeches. "In the beginning I remember her taking me aside, because I was into facts and figures—I felt I had to prove that we were discriminated against. And Flo hauled me off and said, 'Honey, when you are lying in a ditch with a truck on your ankle, you do not send someone to the library to find out how much the truck weighs. You get it off!'"

But even if Kennedy was rhetorically indefatigable in her anger, her dynamism wasn't always embraced by those in the movement. Steinem

recalled inviting Kennedy to speak in Washington at a big women's organizing meeting. "Tons of people were coming from all over, in complete disorganization, and I invited Flo," Steinem recalled. "I remember
Betty Friedan calling me up, furious, saying, 'You cannot invite her, you
cannot have her there. She will mau-mau us'" (a racist term taken from
the Kenyan rebellion, meant to indicate hostile attack). Steinem ignored
Friedan. Kennedy came and spoke at the meeting, "and of course it was
fine." More than fine. Along with Kennedy's rage burned an "incredible
generosity" and good humor, Steinem recalled. In all the hand-wringing
over the perils of feeling too much rage, or the idea that to be angry is to
be prickly, inhospitable, aggressive, what's often missed is that the exhala-
tion of anger can accompany, and perhaps prompt, joy, goodwill, warmth,
and kindness.

"Flo was very accepting of the idea that people are activists in a lot
of different ways and that's okay," Steinem remembered. But Kennedy's
willingness to unleash anger—the impulse that is so derided in some
women—was also a habit that inspired (if occasionally terrified) so many
others.

"A big reason it's very important for women in public life to be able to
express anger on behalf of all of us who feel it [is] so that we can have a
champion," said Steinem, recalling another friend and contemporary, the
throaty, tough-talking fireplug of a congresswoman Bella Abzug. At the
1977 Women's Conference in Houston, at which Maxine Waters, then a
thirty-nine-year-old state assemblywoman, was waiting to talk to Abzug,
Steinem recalled, "Bella was yelling at me, screaming at me something like
'You've ruined everything!'" Steinem remembered noticing Waters watching her altercation with Abzug. "I could see that Maxine was appalled. So
I took Maxine aside and said, 'This is just the way we talk to each other in
New York. Don't worry about it.'"

But however startling her asperity, Steinem continued, "Bella could be
our champion. I mean, she pushed some people away, but the people *loved*
her for getting angry. Flo too. Flo could be our champion."

Kennedy's close friend, the former New York Supreme Court judge
Emily Jane Goodman, said at the time of Kennedy's death in 2000 that
Kennedy "showed a whole generation of us the right way to live our lives."

The exuberance of Kennedy's rage was contagious. Here was a model of righteous female fury that people wanted to be near. As Kennedy wrote in her memoir, "I'm just a loudmouthed, middle-aged colored lady with a fused spine and three feet of intestines missing, and a lot of people think I'm crazy. Maybe you do too, but I never stop to wonder why I'm not like other people. The mystery to me is why more people aren't like me."

CHAPTER FOUR

HOW MINORITY RULES

Among the trickiest and most central dynamics between angry women is the degree to which they have often been angry at one another, and often for very good reasons, chief among them, the racial, economic, and sexual inequities that have contributed to making solidarity between women so elusive, so difficult, and often so painful.

In January 2017, twelve days before millions of women would gather in Washington, DC, and in cities around the world in furious mass protest, the *New York Times* ran a front-page story about the anticipated demonstration. It was headlined "Women's March Opens a Raw Dialogue on Race" and detailed the internal conflicts between women planning to march—or not march—later in the month.

"Many thousands of women are expected to converge on the nation's capital," read the first paragraph. "Jennifer Willis no longer plans to be one of them." Willis, the story explained, was a fifty-year-old wedding minister from South Carolina who had planned to take her daughters to Washington but would no longer be doing so because "she read a post on the Facebook page for the march that made her feel unwelcome because she is white."

The 1,600-word piece went on to examine the racial anxieties cropping up around the march, whose aims were not simply about addressing gendered inequality, but criminal justice reform, the Middle East conflict, the mistreatment of native populations, environmental racism, and a broader approach to reproductive justice beyond just abortion rights. It was a thrilling, if risky, pushing forward of a conversation, using the moment of mass dissatisfaction as an opportunity to expand the scope of a feminist conversation and call it to account for its previous inequities and omissions.

The *Times* coverage—written by the Pulitzer Prize–winning journalist Farah Stockman, who quoted organizer Linda Sarsour as explaining that the contentiousness was by design, that "this was an opportunity to take the conversation to the deep places"—nonetheless zeroed in, via its headline and choice of emphasis, on what it framed as the fragility of the imagined coalition. It described the white South Carolina woman it began with as having been "stung by the tone" of a post by a black activist from Brooklyn, who'd urged "white allies" to do less talking and more listening and reminded white women who were newly awakened to political rage that many other women—women of color—had never had the luxury of *not* being mad. It was this post that had caused Jennifer Willis to cancel her trip, telling the *Times*, "We're supposed to be allies in equal pay, marriage, adoption. Why is it now about [how] 'white women don't understand black women'?"

The *Times* story wondered whether "debates over race . . . reflect deeper questions about the future of progressivism in the age of Trump. Should the march highlight what divides women, or what unites them?"

The irony was that the story itself was making that choice: electing to headline divisions between activists, rather than the possibilities that hundreds of thousands of women and men might move past those divisions and come together in what would turn out to be the biggest single-day protest in America's history.

The next year, in 2018, as women geared up for a reunion protest—one that would turn out to be bigger, in some American cities, than it had been the year before—the *Times* again ran a front-page story in anticipation. "One Year After Women's March, More Activism but Less Unity."

To point out that an undue amount of attention is regularly paid to the internal conflicts within feminism is not to diminish the seriousness and centrality of those conflicts: they are real, and understanding whence they stem is crucial to understanding the very mechanisms of bias, oppression, and inequality that the women's movement theoretically aims to dismantle.

DISPUTE IS THE MIDDLE NAME OF ACTIVISM

In the popular imagination, feminism has since its inception been on the verge of collapse, thanks to the intensity of its very real internal conflicts: divisions over race, class, sexuality, and generational difference, not to mention the flare-ups of personal jealousies and combative power plays. These rifts have often been serious and damaging. But they have not set the women's movement apart from any other social justice movement, from the civil rights or Black Power or immigration or gay rights or the New Left or socialist movements, all of which have at times been riven by generational, racial, gendered, and class divides, by homophobia, strategic differences, and personal feuds. To some degree, this is the nature of mass activism.

The natural fractiousness of any large political movement or campaign is so universal that it was one of the key elements of America's revolutionary rhetoric. The nation's first political cartoon, attributed to Benjamin Franklin, is of the colonies represented as a segmented snake; it accompanied his editorial about the importance of bringing together the "disunited state" into a unified force; the cartoon exhorted colonists to "Join, or Die." There is also a famous revolutionary-era story about a snowball fight that broke out between militia members from different colonies—men from rural and urban areas, men who dressed differently from one another, some of whom were black, some southern, some northern—as they were amassing an army against the British in Harvard Yard. The snowball fight turned so violent that General George Washington had had to step in and break it up. I was taught this story young, as one that exemplified the best of the United States in its revolutionary moment of birth: an ability to bring diverse people together toward a greater civic, political, and national goal.

As Linda Sarsour told me in 2017 about the reports of internal dissent in the lead-up to the women's march, "The idea that we were supposed to immediately and seamlessly bring strangers together in a kumbaya march team, when we're from different backgrounds, have different experiences, religious backgrounds, are from inner cities and suburbs, is crazy." She was exactly right; that expectation looks positively foolish in light of the nation's own founding history, which we're taught as an example of overcoming differences to form a united and victorious revolutionary front.

Yet very few movements—from the amassing of America's first rebel forces through its civil rights campaigns—have had their squabbles regularly presented as the most notable thing about them, often in advance of, or in place of, acknowledgment of their unifying aims and their improbable achievements. The highlighting of dissent over accomplishment is a way to undermine a movement, and it has everything to do with the structural reality of the lengthy campaign for gender equality.

The women's movement is a movement not of an oppressed minority, but of a subjugated majority. Majorities, by the very nature of their scale, are bound to include groups with varying—and warring—priorities and goals. By dint of size, a majority has the power over a minority—unless its foundations are eroded. The cheapest way to weaken and undermine a mass movement is to use its differences to divide it, and thus maintain power over it.

But there have been periods in which alliances have formed among women, and between divergent groups, on behalf of marginalized Americans who can see their struggles as interlocked. In the 1830s, for example, seeds of what would later become nation-shaping movements to diminish the grip of white male capitalist power began to germinate together.

Young girls who worked in the Lowell Mills in New England staged their first walkouts, the antecedent for what would become the labor movement; at the same time they were forming one of the country's first women's anti-slavery societies, a recognition of the ways in which oppressions and injustices were linked.[81] In 1833, the American Anti-Slavery Society was founded by William Lloyd Garrison, with Frederick Douglass as an active member; in 1835, Garrison would publish a letter written by Angelina Grimké, the daughter of a southern plantation owner, in his abolitionist newspaper, *The*

Liberator. Grimké and her sister Sarah would go on to be leading abolitionists, sympathetic also to the fight for women's rights, and among the first women in America, along with Maria Stewart, to give speeches to mixed audiences of men and women. It was in the early 1830s that Stewart, the daughter of free blacks from Connecticut, became the first American woman to address mixed-race audiences, and the first black woman to give public lectures on both abolition and women's rights. In 1837, black and white American women came together for the first of three conferences on ending slavery. The second of those three conventions, held in Philadelphia, posed such a threat that the hall in which it was to be held was burned to the ground. At the World Anti-Slavery Convention in London in 1840, women attendees—including Elizabeth Cady Stanton and Lucretia Mott—were barred from speaking, but many met one another for the first time, and together started to put down the roots of the suffrage movement.

In 1848, Frederick Douglass attended the convention at Seneca Falls at which Stanton would draft the Declaration of Sentiments. Of Stanton, Douglass would later say, "She saw more clearly than most of us that the vital point to be made prominent, and the one that included all others, was the ballot, and she bravely said the word." Douglass would also later claim that "There are few facts in my humble history to which I look back with more satisfaction than to the fact . . . that I was sufficiently enlightened at that early day, and when only a few years from slavery, to support [her] resolution for woman suffrage."

It seemed there was a possibility that the young nation's majority, people on whose subjugation and labor the country's economy and political power were being built, might come together, coalescing around what they understood to be their linked conditions, ready to do battle against the white patriarchal minority power that oppressed them. The fight would be for abolition, for women's suffrage, for reform of exploitative capitalism.

THE BALLOT BOX DIVIDE

But a minority power has ways of preserving itself against attack by an allied majority, and in the wake of the Civil War and emancipation of the slaves, when the vote was granted by the American government to black men, but not to women of any color, this extension of patriarchal power managed to sever the cooperative forces. Some of those who were most committed to both abolition and slavery sided with the granting of black men the vote over women; Frederick Douglass believed black men to be in greater need, due to the violent treatment they faced, and because white women already enjoyed proximal political power via their white husbands.

But other activists saw the move to grant citizenship and the vote to black men as a way to *strengthen* systemic sexism by defining citizenship for the first time—as masculine. "The sons of pilgrims" in Congress, Stanton wrote, were simply "trying to get the irrepressible 'male citizen' into our immortal constitution."[82] And the formerly enslaved abolitionist and suffragist Sojourner Truth is reported to have said, "There is a great stir about colored men getting their rights, but not a word about the colored women. And if colored men get their rights, and colored women not theirs, the colored men will be masters over the women, and it will be just as bad as it was before."

Some white suffragists, including Stanton and Susan B. Anthony, livid at having put aside their emphasis on women's enfranchisement to focus on abolition through the Civil War, and angry at their abolitionist allies for what they understood as political abandonment—were so mad at having to stand back as their allies moved a step forward, that they struck out fiercely, revealing their own deep racism.

Stanton began giving speeches in which she spoke freely of her disdain for the black men she was affronted would now be able to cast votes while white women like herself would not. After years of working toward woman suffrage and abolition, she wrote in 1865, "It becomes a serious question whether we [white women] had better stand aside and see 'Sambo' walk into the kingdom first." Activist forces were further splintered by the strategic pitting of women's suffrage against black male suffrage, including on state ballot referenda, such as one in Kansas in 1867, and via racist arguments that enfranchising white women, who, it was presumed (not incorrectly) would vote like their white husbands, would negate the new power of black voters, and thus keep power in white hands.

Overriding the pleas of her fellow suffragists, Susan B. Anthony accepted the offer of George Francis Train, a so-called Copperhead Democrat who had opposed abolition, to fund a women's suffrage publication called *The Revolution*. Anthony and Stanton toured Kansas with Train, denouncing the Republican Party (which was on the side of black male suffrage) and standing by his side as he made, in the words of historian Andrea Moore Kerr, "demagogic pronouncements about the dangers of black suffrage."[83]

Train was using the competing factions as grist for his own racist political platform, pitting the prospects of white women against those of African Americans, both rhetorically—arguing that if African Americans were permitted citizenship and the franchise "we shall see some white woman in a case of Negro rape being tried by twelve Negro jurymen"—and strategically, by offering Anthony the support and economic resources she was desperate for but not getting from her former allies. As Anthony explained at the time about her association with Train: "All there is about him is that he has made it possible for us to establish a paper. If the Devil himself had come up and said ladies I will help you establish a paper I should have said 'Amen!'" In this paper, Anthony and Stanton pushed an ever more racist line of argument, Kerr writes, "making frequent references to the 'barbarism,' 'brute force,' and 'tyranny' of black men."[84]

In 1869, during the months after the Fifteenth Amendment had been passed by Congress and activists were working to get it ratified by the states, there was an ugly showdown at the annual gathering of the American Equal Rights Association. Though Train had by then backed away from *The Revolution*, Anthony and Stanton were still agitating against ratification, while their fellow suffragist and staunch supporter of the Fifteenth Amendment, Lucy Stone, was trying to herd the rest of the suffragist and abolitionist allies into line in support of the Amendment—and of an imagined *Sixteenth* Amendment that would bring women the vote.

"It is still true today over almost this entire country that no black man or woman finds the same sort of recognition either in public or in private that the white man or woman finds," Stone had said in a speech, as she worked desperately to allay fears that all of the suffrage movement was opposed to African-American men getting the vote. Stone correctly feared that if Stanton and Anthony's racist arguments against the Fifteenth

Amendment worked to doom its ratification, it would be suffragists who'd be blamed. "It is not true that our movement is opposed to the Negro," Stone would write anxiously to fellow suffragists. "But it will be very easy to make it so, to the mutual harm of both causes. . . . I feel dreadfully hurt by this new load we have to carry, and there is no need of it."[85]

The Fifteenth Amendment would, of course, be ratified. And the fantasized Sixteenth Amendment, which Stone had imagined would give women the vote, would not come to fruition . . . at least not for another fifty years, until it was, in fact, the Nineteenth Amendment. The racial tensions that had riven the women's movement did not lessen, and suffragists would split into two separate organizations: one headed by Anthony and Stanton, another by Stone. The groups would not be reconciled for another twenty years, and the split would delay the progress of the suffrage movement by decades.

Even the eventual passage and ratification of the Nineteenth Amendment in 1920—widely understood as the moment at which "American women" got the right to vote—represented forward motion principally for *white* women, since black women in the Jim Crow South remained stopped at the polls by taxes, literacy tests, and the threat of lynching. The long-fought victory for women was in fact a victory only for *some* women, creating resentments that lasted well beyond the additional forty-five years it took to pass the Voting Rights Act of 1965.

To campaign on behalf of just over half the population is by definition an unwieldy enterprise, one that tries to represent fundamentally conflicting interests, divergent perspectives, and people from varied backgrounds who have lots of good reasons to distrust, resent, and disagree with one another. The immensity and diversity of the women's movement has always been used against it by those who fear its potential power. As Gloria Steinem told me two days before the first Women's March, "Because it's a majority movement, it is subject to the same divide-and-conquer tactics that colonial powers used on countries—turning races, classes, and generations against each other" and using as its particular cudgel "the myth that women can't get along and are our own worst enemies."

And so, in moments at which it seemed that women might in fact come together in massive and meaningful numbers to voice their anger—as they did in 2017 and again in 2018, from Hawaii to Houston, and from Poland to Antarctica—it was wholly unsurprising that the frame offered to the public for this unsettling and potentially disruptive event would be one of internal tension, rather than of the will to overcome it and gather together in temporary but furious solidarity.

But importantly, the *magnification* of internecine resentments to diminish the power of insurgent movements isn't the only tool available to the powerful against the marginal: the powerful minorities also have the power to *create* the inequities that provoke those resentments to begin with.

White patriarchal minority rule was established by America's founders when they encoded slavery into our founding documents and built our electoral apparatus around its protection. It was strengthened when they granted white men the franchise and violently guarded that exclusivity for almost a century, ensuring that it was only they who created and controlled the courts, the businesses, the economic systems, who wrote the legislation and created the customs and set the norms on which the country was built. The mechanisms of white male minority rule have been varied: from the denial of equal pay protections to the criminalization of reproductive autonomy and the denial of full health-care options to women, and especially to poor and nonwhite women. From racist housing policy to social safety nets and government-subsidized benefits that have accrued predominantly or exclusively to white Americans, from the enforcement of marital law that left women unable to exert financial or legal independence to the failures of protection against rape, lynching, assault, harassment, and discrimination.

White men have had a nearly exclusive grip on political, economic, social, and sexual power in the United States, despite being only around a third of its population. The way that a minority power protects itself from the potential uprising of a majority is to discourage unification of that majority. And the best way to discourage unification is to split the majority against itself, by offering benefits and protections of power to some, while denying them to others.

WHAT'S THE MATTER WITH WHITE WOMEN

And so, some American women have been offered the advantages of white supremacy, advantages that turn on other women's disadvantages. But even white women's privileges to some degree have turned on all women's patriarchal subjugation, and the dependency dynamics that patriarchy creates: Women were historically legally barred from property ownership, educational and professional opportunity, the chance to build their own credit or the ability to control their own reproduction; some of these challenges remain, as does wage inequality that means, simply, that women earn less money than men; these conditions have rendered them dependent on men. And women's dependence on men has in turn made it in many women's interests to support policies and parties that protect the economic and political status of the men on whom they depend.

This dynamic applies most specifically to white women, who—as wives, daughters, mothers, sisters, neighbors, employees, colleagues, and friends of white men—have been offered a kind of proximal power: greater access, via their relation to powerful white men, to wealth, jobs, educational opportunities, housing, and health-care options. For white women, this dependency on white men incentivizes a dedication to and protection of white male power, because these women's advantages are linked so closely to white men having the power to in turn dole out to them.

But the particular form of their subjugation and ensuing dependency also works to divide them from nonwhite women, to whom none of the advantages or protections of this economic or social or political supremacy accrue, and discourages potential alliances between white and nonwhite women who might otherwise rise up together to challenge white male power. This is what Hillary Clinton was trying to describe, in the months after the election, when she, often ham-handedly, spoke of the women, "principally . . . white women," who faced "tremendous pressure from fathers and husbands and boyfriends and male employers not to vote 'for the girl.' "[86]

Many of Clinton's critics, on the right and the left, seized on this analysis as a fundamentally antifeminist one, in which Clinton was ascribing to women a lily-livered lack of intellectual and political self-direction.

But her error was in using the language of individualized relationships and choices (which, not for nothing, probably applied in some cases) when what she was in fact aiming to describe were the architectural, systemic incentives that work to secure white women's fealty to and investment in the protection of white male power. She was describing how white patriarchy persists in part by making white women dependent on white men, and then ensuring that those women enjoy benefits in exchange for their support of those men's continued dominance, at the purposeful expense of identification with, connection to, and support of other women—whether those other women are political candidates or simply other marginalized people who would benefit from the diminishment of white male control.

This partially explains the huge partisan divide between married and never-married women, especially white women. Those white women who are or have been most directly connected by marriage to white men are far more likely to vote Republican than their never-married peers. According to a paper published by political scientists Dara Strolovitch, Janelle S. Wong, and Andrew Proctor, who reviewed the 2016 Cooperative Congressional Election study numbers on voting patterns, a majority 59 percent of never-married white women voted for Hillary Clinton, compared to the almost reverse majority of married white women, 57 percent, who voted for Donald Trump. Sixty percent of white widows voted for Trump; 56 percent of white women who were separated from husbands voted for Trump; and 49 percent of white divorced women voted for him. In other words, the study concluded, "The more distant" white women are "from the benefits of and investments in traditional heterosexual marriage, the less likely they are to support Republican presidential candidates," i.e., candidates of the party more likely to support traditional white heteropatriarchy.

It has long been true that some of the most energetic opponents of women's political advancement have been . . . women. Back in the nineteenth century, anti-suffrage campaigns were led by women, and of course the campaign that defeated the ERA in 1982 was led by a woman, Phyllis Schlafly. This dynamic repeated itself in focus groups leading up to the 2016 election.

Jessica Morales, a left-wing activist who worked for the Clinton campaign, remembered those groups. "In every focus group for two years basically, always white women, some college-educated, but most not, would say things [to us] like, 'I'm not sure if my husband likes her. He's gotta like her for me to vote for her.' 'It doesn't really matter to me that she's the first woman president.' 'Is it really that historic?' A thing that people don't realize is that we knew that non-college-educated white women were the problem." Morales believed that these women were the crux. "It's them basically deciding to be on our side and not be Phyllis Schlafly. And the answer is that of course we lost because these women have never chosen our side, ever. Never, ever, ever."

YOU, TOO, CAN BE A PATRIARCH

But racial advantages are not the only thing the white patriarchy is willing to dole out to divide people. There is also patriarchy itself, the benefits of which have been offered up to men of all races. Though nonwhite voters overwhelmingly chose Clinton over Trump, in all racial categories, more men than women voted for Trump. Only 4 percent of black women voted for Donald Trump, but 13 percent of black men did. According to forecaster Harry Enten, that number inched slightly higher, to 15 percent, for black men who made over $100,000 a year.[87] Black men may enjoy, and work to perpetuate, advantages that accrue to their gender, even as they are oppressed because of their race.

The student activist and civil rights leader Diane Nash has recalled how when she was working to found the Student Nonviolent Coordinating Committee, "there was a huge problem of good old boys getting together, and I was the only female in the group that was setting up SNCC originally. . . . Later on, in the Southern Christian Leadership Conference, black ministers dominated it. There was a great deal of misogyny there . . . it was expected that leadership would be male."[88]

Civil rights leaders including Nash, Rosa Parks, Gloria Richardson, Dorothy Height, and Anna Arnold Hedgeman, who'd been charged with drawing thirty thousand white Protestants to attend the 1963 March on

Washington, bristled during some of Martin Luther King, Jr's speech that day, frustrated that they'd been discouraged from giving speeches themselves, that they'd been instructed to march with the male leaders' wives, behind the men. Height would later recall, "I've never seen a more immovable force. We could not get women's participation taken seriously." What she learned, she'd go on to say, was that if black women "did not demand our rights, we were not going to get them." And Hedgeman would later admonish, crisply, "The male would be better advised to spend less time mourning the loss of his superiority and more time working in partnership with women."

As Brittney Cooper has regularly observed, it's the fact that black women have been offered neither patriarchal nor racial advantage in exchange for support that has enabled their steady and unremitting leadership of the resistance to white patriarchal power in America. "White women and black men both want what white men have—white women want to have corporate power and black men want to be patriarchs. Black women a) know we're never going to get that and b) don't want that. We don't want to wield corporate power and we don't want to oppress people. That's why I look to black women as the political future."

Black women have long been the backbone of our political and progressive past: the strategists and protesters and organizers and volunteers, the women who've gotten out the vote and licked the envelopes, pioneered the thinking that led to the revolutions. Yet they've been only barely represented in leadership of the political parties they've bolstered, their policy priorities have often gone unaddressed and unrecognized; their participation has long been taken for granted. And when white women have caught up to where black women have been for a long time, the work of the black women has often been appropriated, ignored, and uncredited by those with greater economic, cultural, and racial advantage.

In the 1930s, the black Philadelphia lawyer Sadie Alexander wrote extensively about how women's work outside the home had salutary benefits for black women and their families. But it wasn't until 1963, when Betty Friedan published *The Feminine Mystique*, that the argument was understood as revolutionary. Of course, the suburban white women woken by Friedan desperately *needed* to be woken; Friedan's address of their isolation and suffocation within the homes of the white men in whom the government had invested so much power and authority would become politically revolutionary precisely because of the mass power of that anesthetized population. Yet her book made no acknowledgment of black women or their very relevant circumstances: that racism and its economic disadvantages meant that the majority of black women in America had *always* had to work for wages, had never en masse experienced "the problem that has no name." The asphyxiating ennui of stay-at-home subservience mostly plagued a generation of white women who'd been nudged out of the colleges and off the factory floors into which they'd only recently won entry, and into early married middle-class homes via the very same mechanisms—housing loans and the GI Bill and new highways—that had cut black families off from the resources that might boost them into a middle class. *The Feminine Mystique* was aimed squarely and exclusively at white women. Yet Friedan was long hailed as "the mother of the movement."

But when black women push back against the white women who come in and take up a disproportionate amount of space, when their own complaints about race complicate a white women's movement, it is too often black women who are framed as the ones being divisive. This dynamic was reflected in the coverage of the Women's March conflicts, in which black women letting white women know that they had not invented political resistance to white patriarchy were viewed as somehow inhospitable.

Part of the problem stems from understanding whiteness as simply normative, central—any challenge to it is disruptive in the same way that challenges to patriarchy are disruptive, insofar as they discomfit the more powerful group. But that echo is lost on too many white women, who have a hard time absorbing the ways that even as they have been marginalized by men, so they themselves have often marginalized nonwhite women.

Alicia Garza described her experience of reading Hillary Clinton's righteously angry memoir about the 2016 election and being "befuddled" by it. "Yes, women's anger is not considered to be valid or legitimate," said Garza. "So in one way she has every fucking right to be mad as shit about the way in which the patriarchy has impacted her aspirations and goals, and even though I disagree with her on a lot of things, she deserves to be seen in her humanity and in her dignity." But, she went on, "I am livid when I read these excerpts. Because, yes, you get to be in all of your anger. But what I felt very viscerally from her anger was that it wasn't just [directed] at the men who kept her down, it was also very much [directed] at the people"—including Black Lives Matter activists and criminal justice reformers—"who challenged her around things she absolutely should have been challenged around."

Saira Rao, a lawyer and editor who lives in Colorado and became so angry in the wake of 2016 that she decided to run for office against her incumbent Democratic congresswoman, Diana DeGette, said that anytime she brings up race or white privilege among her friends, "this particular group of white women fly off the handle." She said she has had a friend, "a white woman, a liberal feminist, tell me 'the problem with you is it's always about race.'" Rao said, "I think the reason white women are the way they are is because the system is working for them and because they're comfortable in their Lululemon and comfortable putting aside their law degrees. So they want us to shut the fuck up because the system is working for them."

These are the dynamics that Audre Lorde works to describe in "The Uses of Anger," when she recalls "the most vocal white woman" responding to a week-long forum on black and white women, "'I think I've gotten a lot. I feel black women really understand me a lot better now; they have a better idea of where I'm coming from.'" This, Lorde points out, is an example of the assumption that "understanding her"—the white woman— "lay at the core of the racist problem."

Women of color, and specifically black women, are the demographic most likely to see their struggles as intertwined both with other women's and with black men's, and to work alongside white women and black men—often pioneering the thinking and doing the labor of organization— central to movements for liberation and equality. Which makes it a terrific injustice that the movements to liberate women and African Americans have so often been understood as having been led by white women and black men. They are understood this way because white supremacy and patriarchy permit white women and black men greater access to money, and more proximity to the media that covers social movements and the politicians who respond to them, than black women have.

So it should be no wonder that when white women decided to

participate in a protest against Donald Trump, after an election in which white women's willingness to protect white male power by electing an openly racist and misogynistic incompetent with authoritarian tendencies had been laid bare, black women would be anxious to explain that the white women newly awakened to rage were just that: newly awakened, and might have something to learn.

The post-2016 moment offers a chance for white women to be awakened to the many reasons that they should be angry. But crucially—*urgently*—the opportunity is not simply to be angry on their own behalf, but also at the injustices faced by other women, women who experience those injustices in part thanks to the very mechanisms that protect and enrich those white women. And in order for a new white wokeness to be integrated effectively into a contemporary movement, it must not take it over; there must be acknowledgment that white women are late to the party.

WHAT'S WRONG WITH MESSY?

"I have started to tell people when I do talks that there has been no movement ever in history that hasn't been messy or that hasn't had issues internally," said Alicia Garza. "That is a characteristic of human behavior and human relationships. The question for us is: are we prepared to try and be the first movement in history that learns how to work through that anger? To not get rid of it, not suppress it, but learn how to get through it together for the sake of what is on the other side? And I think that is what our core challenge is in this moment."

"Contentious dialogue is by design," Linda Sarsour told me before the Women's March. "As women of color who came into this effort, we came in not only to mobilize and organize, but also to educate, to argue that we can't talk about women's rights, about reproductive rights, about equal pay, without also talking about race and class." Organizers, Sarsour said, "are actually okay with people being offended. We are hoping the conversation continues and that we can move into a different place and focus on the way we're coming together *nonetheless.*"

There is indeed an argument that the women's movement has survived over centuries not in spite of but *because of* its cacophony: because those who have pushed the movement from the inside, forcing it to grow and change and be better—even when they haven't always agreed on what better meant—have helped it to meet the shifting forms and expressions of inequity from era to era.

And whatever the tensions in advance of the Women's March, it *did* turn out to be the largest single-day demonstration in United States history. Millions of women, many of them white, many of them new to activism, drove and walked and took trains and planes to come together under banners and alongside women who'd long been fighting for black lives and indigenous rights and better health care and fairer wages and not just for reproductive rights but for reproductive justice that takes into account racial and economic inequities. An iconic photo from that march showed a sign reading "I'll see you nice white ladies at the next #BlackLivesMatter march, right?" A lot of white women have seen that sign, and at least some of them have been reckoning with its troubling, and accurate, premise.

In the summer of 2017, after white supremacists marched in Boston as a follow-up to their torchlight brigade in Charlottesville, a massive counterprotest was held—in Boston, a city with a deep, old strain of racist white supremacy. That march was dominated by a fair number of those nice white ladies. When the Women's March held its 2017 convention in Detroit, the session called "Confronting White Womanhood," billed as being "designed for white women committed to being part of an intersectional feminist movement to unpack the ways white women uphold and benefit from white supremacy," had a line out the door. It was so oversubscribed that they had to hold it twice, and on the second day, they had to move it to a space that could hold five hundred.[89]

In 2018, it was a white actress, Ashley Judd, who first used the word "intersectionality"—in reference to Kimberlé Crenshaw's theory of intersecting forms of bias and how they shape the differing experiences and perspectives of oppression—on an Oscar stage. In the summer of 2018, when six hundred women took over the central lobby of the Senate's Hart office building, wrapping themselves in foil blankets and sitting on the floor, arms locked protesting immigration policy, the majority of them looked to be white; most of them were arrested. The next week, after Nancy Pelosi rebuked Maxine Waters for encouraging angry protest and failed to defend her against the implicit threat made against her by Donald Trump, some white women wrote an open letter. "When you attack a Black woman for speaking out about injustice, and when you call for 'civility' in the face of blatant racism," it read in part, "you invoke a long history of white supremacist power . . . To our great discredit, white women continue to act far too often in ways that support white supremacy, even when it is to our detriment . . . when you chide Representative Waters for bravely and passionately speaking up for the most marginalized, you're on the wrong side of history." Within a week, more than six thousand women had signed the letter.

It seems possible that we are witnessing a large-scale civic and social education. That in the wake of Trump's election millions of previously somnambulant Americans have been provoked, in their shock and panic, to evolution. Some of them decided to learn: about local and state elections, about the way that government works, about policy, and about what it means that racism, sexism, and economic inequality are *systemic*; some began to see how these issues are linked in ways that go beyond academic jargon.

Kat Calvin, whose organization, Spread the Vote, aims to help voters get their voter IDs in states with restrictive laws, has noted with surprise that while black women turn out in higher numbers to vote, "the women who make up resistance volunteers and run resistance organizations are actually an incredibly diverse mix. It's been amazing to see. I'm a black woman who runs a resistance organization and I'm pretty shocked every day." A majority of her organization's volunteers, Calvin said, "are white women who are going to homeless shelters every week, driving people they have never met and wouldn't normally speak to all over town, and [they] are really putting their hearts into it. It's kind of amazing."[90]

"Look, grandmothers were knitting something called a pussy hat," marveled Jessica Morales of the Women's March. "And they cherish it like it's a keepsake. And when you went on social media there was the Native Women's Caucus, who looked dope as hell, and they were singing next to the domestic workers, who had their red shirts on, and English is their second language and they all make about $11,000 a year, and they're standing next to this rich-ass lady who has a sign about her vagina. And you think, you know: *America*!"

"There was something about the Women's March that shook me to my core," says Alicia Garza. "Because this regime change is unlike anything we've ever seen in my lifetime. Not even in the lifetime of my parents. And that to me seemed more important than anything else." Garza acknowledged that many of her peers feel differently, that their communities' suffering has been steady and is not materially worse now. But she feels the key difference is that the democracy is dismantling *itself*. "So the notion that we shouldn't try to figure out how to build a movement that is bigger than the people who already agree with us seems like a death warrant," she said.

But, she hastened to add, "That does *not* mean that you don't continue to hold people accountable. It is not my job to make white women less racist; that is the job of other white women. And I will absolutely hold white women accountable every step of the way. But at the same time, when somebody says 'I want to learn,' I want to figure it out."

As Morales says, "I like to play chess, not checkers. The checkers part of me is like, 'Look at all these white ladies. . . . Where were you?' But honestly, I don't want to be a part of a movement that demands that you flagellate yourself to prove you're real." And so, she said, she's trying to cultivate a different approach: "Welcome. We really need you, because even if every person of color woke the fuck up and was like *La raza!* that's only 38 percent of America. And y'all control the banks, the businesses, you're the head of all the entertainment companies. So let's go, we need you."

This isn't, of course, satisfactory or reparatory. Asking nonwhite activists to grade newly hatched white protesters on a forgiving curve is itself unfair. But it's also part of the project if we want to move forward, and in fact leverage that proximal power enjoyed by white women—who can draw media attention, who have more access to political power, without whom we lose elections to disastrous effect—and use that power as a cudgel against the minority of white men who have had everyone in their grip.

Garza said that she's been thinking a lot about Lorde's "Uses of Anger." "Lorde projects a vision," she said. "What if we could be in anger with accountability? Yeah girl, you get to be mad as shit that all of those things happened, but also where are the places in which you were liable for the anger of others? It's a both approach and not an either-or."

"For black women and white women to face one another's angers without denial or immobility or silence or guilt is in itself a heretical and generative idea," wrote Lorde, arguing that the honest expression of anger between women of different races is necessary if coalition building is ever going to happen. "It implies peers meeting upon a common basis to examine difference[s], and to alter those distortions which history has created around our difference. For it is those distortions which separate us. And we must ask ourselves: Who profits from all this?" The angers between women, Lorde argued, "can transform difference[s] through insight into power. For anger between peers births change, not destruction, and the discomfort and sense of loss it often causes is not fatal, but a sign of growth."

Garza's still wrestling with it. "For me, my anger at white women for excluding women of color, and black women specifically, for generations is still very palpable. That hasn't changed. What has changed is that I understand that the coalition that is going to save us has to be much bigger than what it is. I want people to get free. I'm mad as hell about a whole bunch of things, every single day I'm mad inside, seething right beneath the surface. But I want to be free more than I want to be mad. And I want to work with people who *also* want to be free more than they want to be mad, because maybe we will actually get to something that makes sense."

EPITAPH

On the day that Frederick Douglass died in 1895, he had spent the morning with Susan B. Anthony at a meeting of suffragists. In fact, he'd had such a good time that he had been in the midst of telling his wife about the meeting when he'd fallen to his knees, hands clasped, and his wife had simply believed that his pose was one of narrative enthusiasm, not realizing that he was in fact dying.

"It is a singular fact," the *New York Times* reported in Douglass's obituary, "that the very last hours of his life were given in attention to one of the principles to which he has devoted his energies since his escape from slavery. . . . Mr. Douglass was a regularly enrolled member of the National Woman Suffrage Association, and had always attended its conventions." The obituary noted that his companion at the suffrage meeting that day was "Miss Anthony, his lifelong friend," and that when "Miss Susan B. Anthony heard of Mr. Douglass's death, at the evening session of the council, she was very much affected. Miss Anthony has a wonderful control over her feelings, but tonight, she could not conceal her emotion."[91]

The racism that had riven the women's movement had by no means abated, nor would it anytime soon; twenty years later, one of the next generation's white suffrage leaders, Alice Paul, would try unsuccessfully to force her elder, the black suffragist and anti-lynching leader Ida B. Wells, not to walk with her state's delegation in the enormous 1913 suffrage march on Washington, DC, but instead to march with the rest of the black women suffragists where they'd been told to position themselves: behind all the white women. And the year that he died Anthony had asked Douglass not to appear at a suffrage convention in the South, because she was trying to strategically win white women to the cause. But neither did women of any race have the vote, nearly six decades after the first meetings of the black and white women joining to push for abolition, more than forty years after Douglass had joined Stanton at Seneca Falls.

Frederick Douglass was seventy-eight at his death; Susan B. Anthony would die eleven years later at eighty-six. Elizabeth Cady Stanton, who had turned to such baldly racist rhetoric in her anger at the inclusion of black men in the franchise before she herself had won the vote, was seventy-nine at the time of Douglass's death and would live another seven years. Near the end of his life, Douglass would observe of their linked battles, "We should all see the folly and madness of attempting to accomplish with a part what could only be done with the united strength of the whole."[92]

None of the three, of course, would live to see the passage and ratification of the Ninteenth Amendment, much less conceive of the Voting Rights Act. In fact, only *one* woman who attended the Seneca Falls convention would survive long enough to cast a ballot after the ratification of the Nineteenth Amendment. These struggles, and the internal dissent they engender, have the power to last longer than any of us, even those who have given lifetimes to the fights, both external and internal. But every once in a while, in the long, conjoined fight for liberation and equality, there is a rare opportunity to unite—if never in perfect alignment—the whole.

PART III

SEASON OF
THE WITCH

I've been thinking a lot about the ways that women are required to perform our emotions during this moment, and in particular how much thought and effort we put into mitigating the risk of being seen as angry. These performances have belied the reality that if you consider yourself fully human as a woman, and fully endowed with dignity, then anger is a very reasonable response to sexual harassment, assault, or other gendered violence. This is another thing I've been thinking about: How anger has both limited me and led me astray, and also been a wonderful motivator. Anger leads me to seek answers, to seek change.

—Moira Donegan, via Twitter

CHAPTER ONE

GETTING AWAY WITH IT

HARVEY

For several months, in the late summer and early fall of 1789, after the storming of the Bastille and the food shortages that had come in its wake, some of the men agitating for political change in France had spoken of staging a protest at the royal palace at Versailles. There had been talk of a mass demonstration of starving Parisians outside the opulent home of King Louis the XVI and his family; it had not yet come to fruition.

But on the morning of October 5, a Parisian woman, driven to a seething fury by the scarcity and high price of bread at the city's markets, began to bang a marching drum. Other women quickly joined her and began to walk through the Paris streets. As the crowd of women grew, some of them brought along their knives; some forced a church to begin tolling its bells to draw attention to their growing protest. They gathered outside the Hôtel de Ville, Paris's city hall, demanding both food and weapons.

From there, the mob, by then reaching perhaps ten thousand, headed to Versailles, dragging cannons they had seized. After an overnight standoff, the crowd would grow to more than fifty thousand and return to Paris the next afternoon, the king and his family with them.

Two hundred and twenty-eight years later, on October 5, 2017—also nearly a year to the day of the release of the *Access Hollywood* tape that had not succeeded in delegitimizing the man who was now our sitting president—the *New York Times* published a story by Jodi Kantor and Megan Twohey headlined "Harvey Weinstein Paid off Sexual Harassment Accusers for Decades." It chronicled multiple allegations of sexual predation and harassment made by women—including some famous actresses—against Weinstein, a powerful movie producer.

It was a story that I had been waiting, hoping, and, to the degree that I'd been able, agitating to read for almost twenty years. Frankly, I had never believed that I would ever see it in print.

One of my earliest jobs out of college had been back in 1999 when I was an editorial assistant at a magazine that Harvey Weinstein's company Miramax had financed. As a young secretary at the magazine, adjacent to his then company, I knew of his brutal bullying of employees, had begun to hear hushed rumors of hotel rooms, nudity, and then of whispered payoffs; I'd also heard plenty of gossip about which actresses in which movies— the beneficiaries of which book deals or writing contracts—had slept with Harvey in order to get them. Back then it had been gossip, and also unthinkable that anyone would have or could have gotten *angry* about it, to any effect at all. Harvey was the key to the resurgence of New York's film culture; he opened doors to stardom, to Oscars, to edgy writers and directors; he even financed feminist movies directed by Jane Campion.

My next job, which I'd begun in my midtwenties, had been as a reporter at a weekly New York newspaper, where part of my beat was covering the film business in the city. In the weeks before the 2000 presidential election, I had been working on my first deeply reported story, about *O*, a star-studded but violent reimagining of *Othello* that Miramax's Dimension Films division had been refusing to release, perhaps out of deference to the cringy clean-media message of the Al Gore–Joe Lieberman campaign, which Weinstein was publicly supporting; already there was talk of Weinstein's ambitions in Democratic politics.

Since Weinstein had failed to respond to my calls for comment, I had been sent by my editor, on Election Eve 2000, to cover a book party he was hosting, along with a more senior male colleague whom I happened to be dating at the time. I asked Weinstein to comment for my story; he didn't like my question. There was an altercation; he began shouting at me, pushing me hard with his finger against my shoulder; he called me a "cunt" and a "bitch" and declared that he was glad he was the "fucking sheriff of this fucking lawless piece-of-shit town." When my colleague intervened, first trying to calm Weinstein and then trying to extract an apology from him, Weinstein went nuclear, pushing my colleague down a set of steps, knocking him over with such force that his tape recorder hit a female party guest in the head, knocking her out. Then, screaming to the crowd about how my colleague had "hit a woman," Weinstein had dragged him onto Sixth Avenue in Manhattan and put him in a headlock.

Such was the power of Harvey Weinstein in 2000—when you're a star, you can do anything—that despite the dozens of camera flashes that had gone off on that sidewalk that night, capturing the sight of a famous and physically gargantuan film executive trying to pound in the head of a young newspaper reporter, I never once saw a photo. None were published. Harvey was famous for having the power to spin—to suppress—anything.

The next day, Election Day, the *New York Post* reported on the event and cast it as "a couple of pushy reporters" who had "pushed [Weinstein] to the breaking point." The *New York Times* reported that Harvey and my colleague had "had words" and that I had started the whole thing by "question[ing] Mr. Weinstein about an article that had nothing to do with . . . the party"; Weinstein, according to a Miramax official quoted by the *Times*, had "realized it really wasn't appropriate and was upset."

Here it was: power at work. Weinstein's physical aggression, the act of beating up a journalist, transformed into an exchange of "words," while the actual *words* in question—my questions of a powerful man, questions lodged as part of my *job*, my work as a reporter—were described in the newspaper of record as "inappropriate" and "upsetting." Though he had done the physical pushing, we—the less powerful human beings he had pushed—could be comfortably described in the press he controlled as "pushy."

In the months and years that had followed my own run-in with

Weinstein, I began to hear from other reporters who'd gotten wind of other kinds of power abuses: the whispered dalliances I'd heard about in my earlier job were rumored to be worse than what I'd understood—did I know anything? Could I, as someone who'd been a firsthand witness to his verbal and physical aggressions, help them track down evidence of his sexual misbehaviors? I talked to every reporter who ever came to me for help with these attempted stories—and there were many, some of them legendary investigative journalists; I shared what I had heard, the rumors and gossip; I collected numbers and shared email addresses of anyone I thought could help them tell a full story about Harvey.

But mostly from these other journalists, I learned more than I offered. I heard about the stories *they'd* heard, yes—about the ubiquity of his behavior, about an ever clearer view of this man as a monster, perhaps a rapist. But far more than that, I learned about what felt like the complete, Sisyphean impossibility of ever bringing this information to light. Because all of these journalists, some working for *years* to report the story of Harvey Weinstein, traveling the globe to track down leads, fearing weirdly (as I had, after my incident with him) that their phones were tapped and that they were being followed (it seems it was all true): they never got the story.

The danger and impossibility of challenging a powerful man was made all too clear. I remembered what it was like to have the full force of this mountainous man screaming vulgarities at me, his spit hitting my face; of watching him haul my friend into the street and try to hurt him. Among the reasons that I never really entertained the idea of reporting the story myself was that I had been shown *so clearly* that I could not have won against that kind of power—both physical strength and the ability to manipulate the power of systems and institutions to cover up its abuses.

There was the suffocating force of cultural expectation itself, long since calibrated around patriarchal abuses, making it hard for any woman to trust that anyone would believe she had been wronged. We *knew* that rape and even sexual harassment were wrong, of course: this was years after Anita Hill. But the normalized notion of a casting couch, the nostalgic view of legendarily brutal studio bosses like Louis B. Mayer and of desperately ambitious actresses willing to do anything for a part: these had been worked into our romantic, imaginative DNA, and that romance, the easy way we integrated the exchanges made between men who had power and women who needed a piece of it as just part of how things worked, provided insulation to those men.

Then, there were less sentimentalized protections in place: Weinstein had employees sign elaborate nondisclosure agreements; he gave consulting jobs and book contracts to journalists who might otherwise expose his behavior; he gave money to powerful people in politics, building enough goodwill with them to provide a layer of protection, a kind of deafness to the ugly rumors that might circulate among *less* powerful people. For decades, the reporters who *did* try to tell the story butted up against a wall of sheer power that was leveraged against those who'd otherwise want to challenge him: the ambitious actors, vulnerable assistants, all the executives and subordinates whose careers, salaries, and reputations were in Harvey's hands.

And then all of a sudden, the power was imbalanced. The revelation of Weinstein's abuse—sexual submission fetishized, yes, but also simply submission and humiliation, the transformation of power into a weapon of degradation via massages and masturbation and daily diminution—was laid bare.

After the *Times* piece came one from Ronan Farrow at the *New Yorker*, reporting on long-suspected allegations that Weinstein was not simply a harasser but a rapist. Then came more. And more. And more. Women, and a few men, poured into magazines and newspapers and onto television to tell their own stories, about Harvey and about so many others: actor Kevin Spacey and television journalist Charlie Rose and magazine editor Leon Wieseltier and political pundit Mark Halperin and morning show host Matt Lauer and chef Mario Batali and comedian Louis C.K. and restaurateur John Besh and professors and Ford factory plant managers and progressive activists and fast food managers and senators and congressmen. The stories were told by farmworkers and flight attendants and hotel workers and union organizers and police officers and by women in Silicon Valley and Sweden and China and France.

The rage had been building, had leaked out earlier in the mini-uprisings, the insistence that other men whose behaviors had been open secrets—from comedian Bill Cosby to Fox News machers Bill O'Reilly and Roger Ailes—be finally made to pay a price for their behavior toward women. But something had shifted. Perhaps it was the election of Donald Trump, the fact that he stood in as the ultimate, inflated embodiment of white patriarchal power abuse who had faced no repercussion for his behavior, or maybe it was having seen women gather as armies to bring down Cosby and Ailes and to protest Trump's inauguration and the Muslim ban and efforts to repeal health care. Then again perhaps it was simply the impossibility of containing the fury any longer, after we'd had this view of its injustice, its breadth and depth.

The reporters and the storytellers had finally banged the marching drum, bringing thousands onto the streets and ringing the bells, in 2017, insistent on making a historic charge and extracting the kings from their grotesquely guarded palaces.

THE RECKONING

The anger window was open. For decades, for centuries, it had been closed. Something bad happened to you, you shoved it down, you maybe told someone but probably didn't get much satisfaction—emotional or practical—from the confession. Maybe you even got blowback. No one really cared, and certainly no one was going to do anything about it.

But in the four months that followed the reporting on one movie mogul's sexual predation, a Harvey-sized hole was blown in the American news cycle, and there was suddenly space and air for women to talk—to yell and scream and rage.

Fixing on a hashtag—#metoo—that had been pioneered by the activist Tarana Burke in 2006 as a movement designed to reveal the ubiquity of sexual violence done to women and girls, but was taken up more broadly as an internet campaign in the fall of 2017, women spilled so much that had been bottled up for so long: they told stories of bosses and colleagues and teachers and mentors who had grabbed them or coerced them or insulted them or belittled them. There was a huge range of tales—everything from violent assaults to unwanted kisses to quid-pro-quo offers of professional advancement in exchange for sex, to more minor offenses, like groped butts and grazed boobs, unwanted come-ons and lewd late-night messaging from colleagues.

What united the stories was the way that they made the storytellers feel, what the events had led them to understand: that in public spheres, they had been regarded, treated, evaluated differently; that they had been used or degraded, had not been taken seriously professionally by powerful men. Many of the women who told their stories (there were men who told theirs too, but the majority were women) felt that the treatment they'd experienced had damaged their careers, dulled their prospects, muffled their ambitions, and kept them from the kinds of achievements in the public sphere that the powerful men of whom they complained had reached.

Some of those who spoke did so to friends or family members or to other colleagues, many for the first time. Some women lodged complaints, years later, with HR departments. Some spoke to reporters, providing corroborating evidence, contemporaneous witnesses, photographs and diaries for documentation; they showed their nondisclosure agreements and settled lawsuit filings; they produced the friends and husbands they'd told at the time, though many, many of them had told *no one*.

Then there were others who simply took the things that had always been private, quiet—the whispers, nudges, and meaningful stares that had served as warnings—and made them public and loud, with no mediation; they wrote their stories on social media, in tweets and Facebook posts that could be sent around the world in seconds. Some women in the media compiled a shared document, anonymously detailing their encounters with "shitty men" in their industry, men they named. It was dangerous and irresponsible and a sign of exactly how desperate, how utterly, profoundly furious they were, and how out of fucks they were about letting the world know.

There were other bizarre and creative acts of revolt: when the feminist writer Nicole Cliffe got wind of the fact that the antifeminist polemicist Katie Roiphe was planning to leak the name of the original compiler of the Shitty Media Men list in *Harper's Magazine*, she announced that she would match the fees writers would have otherwise been paid for publishing their pieces in that issue, in exchange for pulling them from the magazine in protest. Cliffe was open about the fact that she did not ask her husband before promising funds from their joint account—a move that recalled the second-wave feminist Alix Kates Shulman, who'd remembered writing a check from her joint checking account, her first without asking her husband's permission, in order to pay for members of the New York Radical Women's collective to get inside the 1968 Miss America pageant and drop a banner reading "Women's Liberation" at the moment the new winner was crowned.[1]

I wasn't sure I liked the Cliffe approach, or the Shitty Media Men list; they were destabilizing to my profession, to the norms of professional and ethical behavior I'd been raised to respect, and—I feared—to feminism itself. They seemed too much, too risky, too intense. I felt like I was in some space movie, on a ship getting rocked by fire as it moved forward at a speed I'd never traveled before. Would it hold? Would we survive? I think it was the first time that I had experienced anything like radicalism in my own sphere, and it felt unsafe. Exhilarating. Terrifying. Uncomfortable. Necessary and long overdue and as if it were either going to burn us all up or save us.

It was definitely not feminism as I'd known it in its contemporary rebirth—packaged into think pieces or nonprofits or Eve Ensler plays or Beyoncé VMA performances. That stuff had certainly had its place and had done its crucial job, pulling feminism out of the suffocating murk of backlash. But this was different. This was 70s-style, organic, mass radical rage, exploding in unpredictable directions. It was loud, thanks to the human megaphone that is social media and the "whisper networks" that were now less about speaking sotto voce than about frantically typed texts and all-caps group chats.

Extremely powerful men lost their jobs—Harvey Weinstein lost his company; Charlie Rose was fired; Mario Batali was exiled from his restaurant empire; Matt Lauer was dismissed from the *Today* show; Senator Al Franken was asked to resign by his colleagues, many of them female. The list of men kept growing until there were too many too count, too many pieces to read. Never before, in my memory, had so many white male authority figures been censured, dismissed.

It was feral in its intensity, and even for those of us who were completely persuaded of how urgent and correct the process of reckoning was, it was not fun. Because the stories were so awful, many of them the sickening, chilling stuff of nightmares. But also because the conditions that had created this perfect storm of female rage—the pervasiveness of harassment and abuse; the election of a multiply accused predator who now controlled the courts and the agencies that were supposed to protect us from criminal and discriminatory acts—were so undeniably grim.

It was also harrowing because it was confusing, because the wrath might have been fierce, but it was not uncomplicated. In the shock of the house lights having been suddenly brought up—of being forced to stare at the ugly scaffolding on which so many of our professional lives had been built—we had scant chance to parse what exactly was enflaming us and who. It was the tormentors, obviously, but it was also our friends, our mentors, *ourselves*.

GETTING MAD AT MEN

Among the greatest challenges faced by the women's movement in all its iterations has been the structural difficulty of persuading women to express sustained, public anger toward their most direct oppressors: men.

This difficulty exists for many reasons, and takes us back to the fact that women, unlike many racial, ethnic, or religious groups in the United States, are not an oppressed minority, but rather a majority population, integral to homes, families, personal and professional networks in every geographic, religious, racial, and ethnic category. Here's what that means, practically: every man has a woman in his life, and every woman has a man in hers.

The intransigent bitch about sexism and misogyny is that even when women recognize, truly *feel* the weight of the numerous and varied ways in which they have been subjugated and offered less based on their gender, we must confront the fact that the bad guys are, in many cases, also our good guys: the men in our beds, our hearts, our families. They are our brothers and fathers and uncles and friends and lovers and husbands and roommates and sons.

We love them.

We also often *need* them: to be our colleagues and family members and boyfriends and buddies, to help us raise our kids, to bring home paychecks on which we subsist. Because they have so much more professional and economic power, men are very often our bosses, our mentors, the guys who gave us our breaks and who we continue to rely on to give us promotions, raises, assignments. Because white men have had such disproportionate political power, it is often they on whom women—feminists, left activists—rely on a larger scale: as representatives, advocates, party leaders; to challenge them is to potentially imperil a whole political party, and with it, crucial protections, advocacy, an ideological agenda itself.

Of course it is precisely this reality—once again, this *dependence*—that has permitted powerful men to mistreat and discriminate against those with less power. It is also what has often kept women paralyzed—by fear, risk, love, loyalty—and reluctant to push back angrily against their own ill treatment, or in response to the ill-treatment of other women.

The potential for damage to relationships on which women depend is *real*; consequences may be both emotional and material. Women's challenge to male authority or power abuse can send a family into disarray, end a marriage, provoke a firing, either of a woman *or* of a man on whom other women—colleagues and family members—rely economically. Fear of these repercussions (alongside a long-ingrained and realistic fear of simple futility) are very often fierce enough to inoculate women against expressing, and perhaps in many cases even feeling, the outrage at men that they might otherwise make known.

It is so much more peaceful to not get mad, to not even *think* about the gross injustices that pepper our daily interactions with men: double standards, intellectual disregard, objectification, sexual harassment, pay inequity, differential domestic expectations and burdens, unequal representation, the banality of daily diminution. Often it is simply easier not to consider any of this, much less try to fight back against it, especially when fighting back means fighting men you'd prefer to keep thinking well of.

"Once you know something, you cannot unknow it," wrote Judith Levine of what it means to have felt feminist anger toward men in her 1992 book *My Enemy, My Love.* "You can't sign up for consciousness-razing groups . . . but neither does the new knowledge erase the feelings that preceded it. . . . [W]hat do you do if you also love the hated person, need him emotionally, or depend on him materially, if you feel compelled to placate him or fearful to disturb him? A powerful unspoken theme of post–World War II feminism—and women's lives since feminism—is the struggle with . . . the fury of recognized oppression."

During the onslaught of #metoo-inspired allegations, a few of the many women who were both supportive of the movement and close to the public men accused of harassment gave eloquent voice to the paradoxical pains they felt.

CBS This Morning host Gayle King said of her former coanchor Charlie Rose, a man who was accused, all told, by more than thirty women of harassment, of exposing and forcing himself on younger colleagues, "I've enjoyed a friendship and a partnership with Charlie for the past five years. I have held him in such high regard and I am really struggling, because what do you say when someone that you deeply care about has done something that is so horrible? I can't stop thinking about the anguish of those women: what happened to their dignity, what happened to their bodies, what happened, maybe, to their careers."[2]

The comedian Sarah Silverman spoke about *her* close friend and fellow comedian Louis C.K., accused by other female comedians of masturbating in front of them without their consent and then relying on a system of enablers to punish them professionally for telling the story. The process of exposing the culture of pervasive harassment, Silverman said, was like "cutting out tumors: it's messy and it's complicated and it is gonna hurt but it's necessary and we'll all be healthier for it." But, she went on, "It sucks. And some of our heroes will be taken down and we'll discover bad things about people we like. Or in some cases people we love." Describing her long friendship with C.K., she said, "I love Louis, but Louis did these things. Both of those statements are true. So, I just keep asking myself: can you love someone who did bad things? I hope it's okay if I am at once very angry for the women he wronged and the culture that enabled it, and also sad, because he's my friend."[3]

It was a dynamic that was not simply painful for female accusers and friends of the accused, but an obvious weak spot that those who were *not* supportive of the #metoo movement were eager to exploit, in an effort to defend against the female anger and put a stop to the campaign. "When we start conflating and putting all these things all in one bucket," warned the conservative Fox News personality Greg Gutfield of the breadth of complaints, "we're going to start hurting your fathers, your brothers, your sons, your grandfathers." The retired NBC anchor Tom Brokaw, defending himself against the claim of a former younger colleague that he had come to her hotel room and tried to forcibly kiss her in the 1990s, pounded out a middle-of-the-night, bathetic letter of self-defense in which he proclaimed, "I am proud of who I am as a husband, father, grandfather, journalist, and citizen."

In May Samantha Bee would joke darkly about the dynamic of emotional captivity to the men close to us, in both its personal and political forms, in a furious tirade against New York's freshly resigned attorney general Eric Schneiderman. Schneiderman had not only been a guest on Bee's show, but a prosecutor whom she'd previously hailed as a feminist superhero, a man on whom feminist women were depending, and who had just been revealed as an allegedly violent abuser of his girlfriends.

"The good legal work that you did for women does not absolve you," she bellowed, during a nuclear-grade opening monologue. "It will not give me one second's pause about tearing you a new asshole on television. I give *zero fucks*. I would do an act entitled 'My Dad Is a Monster' if I had to. . . . Eric Schneiderman, you are trash and we do not *need* you."

Bee's rage resonated in 2018, in part because it reflected the liberating and livid surprise of having gotten to this point. It takes years, it takes emergency circumstances, it takes the electric shock of having so much injustice laid bare, to goad mass numbers of women into actually turning on the men in their lives—their elected officials or their dads or their partners or their bosses—and telling them what Bee told Eric Schneiderman over and over again in that seven-minute monologue: Fuck you, fuck you, fuck you.

It may have felt cathartic in its pop culture iteration, coming from a comedian in charge of her own show. But the catharsis stemmed in part from the fact that letting loose any comparable anger within workplaces or families might come at steep costs for women who did *not* have their own shows.

"I saw the people who spoke up evaporate," said public radio producer Kristen Meinzer, who publicly accused radio host John Hockenberry of sexual harassment, during a conversation with other #metoo storytellers.

"I couldn't lose my job." She went on to note that "so much of how we're taught to live in this world as women is to keep the peace, to smile, to try and giggle it off, to say, 'Oh, that's fine' when it doesn't feel fine . . . How do you preserve your own job, how do you preserve your own space, and how do you preserve your physical safety as a woman? A lot of that is: we have to be nice."[4]

NOT NICE LADIES

There is, of course, a long history of women who, in moments of political or personal crisis, make the revolutionary decision to *not* be nice, though the personal and political implications of this choice have rarely been obscure.

"Do not put such unlimited power into the hands of the husbands," Abigail Adams warned her own husband presciently in the spring of 1776. "Remember all men would be tyrants if they could. If particular care and attention is not paid to the ladies, we are determined to foment a rebellion."

Seventy-two years later, in 1848, two hundred women and forty-odd men convened in Seneca Falls, New York, to draft the Declaration of Sentiments, a document modeled on the colonists' Declaration of Independence, which Adams's husband John had signed. The Declaration of Sentiments was also a statement of independence—women's direct rebuke of male power and a seeming return on Abigail's promise of rebellion: "The history of mankind is a history of repeated injuries and usurpations on the part of man toward woman," the Declaration read in part, claiming that the object of these injuries and usurpations had been "the establishment of an absolute tyranny over her."

And then they described that tyranny:

He has never permitted her to exercise her inalienable right to the elective franchise.

He has compelled her to submit to laws, in the formation of which she had no voice . . .

He has made her, if married, in the eye of the law, civilly dead.

He has taken from her all right in property, even to the wages she earns.

. . . In the covenant of marriage, she is compelled to promise obedience to her husband, he becoming, to all intents and purposes, her master—the law giving him power to deprive her of her liberty, and to administer chastisement . . .

He has so framed the laws of divorce . . . as to be wholly regardless of the happiness of women—the law, in all cases, going upon the false supposition of the supremacy of man, and giving all power into his hands.

He has monopolized nearly all the profitable employments, and from those she is permitted to follow, she receives but a scanty remuneration.

He closes against her all the avenues to wealth and distinction, which he considers most honorable to himself. As a teacher of theology, medicine, or law, she is not known.

He has denied her the facilities for obtaining a thorough education—all colleges being closed against her.

He allows her in Church as well as State, but a subordinate position . . .

He has endeavored, in every way that he could to destroy her confidence in her own powers, to lessen her self-respect, and to make her willing to lead a dependent and abject life.

It was a deeply subversive document. By making it a play on the Declaration of Independence, the suffragists were employing the language and logic of righteous rage that America revered—the rage of the founders, white men who were furious about limitations set on their liberty—and using that blueprint to express ire on behalf of a population on whose liberties those founders had, in their moment of righteousness, set about limiting.

It happens also, in its call for *in*dependence, to be an outline of the building blocks of dependency, the very things that codified and enforced the imbalance of gendered power that got us straight to the present moment, one hundred and seventy years hence.

The women who wrote it knew that it wasn't going to be warmly received. "We anticipate no small amount of misconception, misrepresentation, and ridicule."

They anticipated correctly. As the historian Marjorie Spruill has noted, "Outraged newspaper editors denounced the convention as shocking, unwomanly, monstrous, and unnatural, or ridiculed them as Amazons or love-starved spinsters."[5] The *New York Herald* publisher James Gordon Bennett, Sr., a rabid opponent of both abolition and suffrage, called the activists a "motley gathering of fanatical mongrels, of old grannies, male and female, of fugitive slaves and fugitive lunatics." He predicted that "full consummation of their diabolical projects would reduce society to the most beastly and promiscuous confusion." More plaintively, one unsigned article in the *Daily Oneida Whig* of Utica, New York, wondered, "Was there ever such a dreadful revolt? This bolt is the most shocking and unnatural incident ever recorded in the history of womanity. If our ladies will insist on voting and legislating, where, gentlemen, will be our dinners?"[6]

This same question would again reverberate in the wake of the uprising of feminists of the Second Wave, more than a century after Seneca Falls. That mass feminist movement, kicked off by Friedan's *The Feminine Mystique*, and then taken up by activists more radical and diverse in their priorities, coincided with the sexual revolution, and enacted material and legal changes in opportunities for women that would permit them to remap their lives in relation to men. Activists of the Second Wave demanded more educational and professional access for women, better legal protections against rape, harassment, and workplace discrimination. Feminists fought for the legalization of birth control and abortion and for laws that made it easier for them to leave bad marriages; they fought *about* pornography, and worked to acknowledge women's sexual appetites and establish their right to sexual autonomy and self-determination.

In many ways, the Second Wave was tackling the same laundry list of inequities laid out in the Declaration of Sentiments. In part this was because while the Declaration had been broad in its demands, and women of the late nineteenth and early twentieth centuries had succeeded in expanding educational and professional opportunities and altering some property laws, the major material win, more than seventy years after the Declaration's composition, had been the Nineteenth Amendment. So much was still left to be done.

Activists of the 1960s and 1970s, whose revolutionary movement lasted less than twenty years, made many changes in a short amount of time, challenging their own circumstances and assumptions so swiftly and dramatically that they altered the power dynamics within their own marriages and made their husbands uncomfortable and confused, suddenly rebuked for behaviors and attitudes which had never before been presented as problematic. Many men felt that they had entered marriages with a shared set of expectations but that the personal-is-political upheaval of the Second Wave had very suddenly rendered those expectations invalid. The men were not wrong: the rules had changed midgame; their dinners were no longer, necessarily, on the table.

Cecile Richards, the former president of Planned Parenthood, has written of how her progressive dad, a lawyer who'd fought on behalf of labor unions and for voting and civil rights, was undone by the subversions of the women's movement. Cecile's equally progressive mother, Ann, had experienced a change during the 1970s, campaigning on behalf of the Equal Rights Amendment. Her father, Richards wrote, was confused. "He had a wife who raised the kids, took care of every single dog and cat we brought home, threw dinner parties, and grew organic vegetables," wrote Richards. "Dad had grown up—and was living in a household where women threw themselves into volunteer work and didn't have careers. I realize now that for him (and so many other men of his generation) the prospect of total upheaval of the domestic scene must have seemed pretty frightening. Suddenly the tumult around women's roles and aspirations wasn't happening just on television; it was happening in our own home." The Richards' marriage, like so many of the era, ended in divorce.[7] And Ann went on to become governor of Texas.

It was surely not entirely fun to live through the era of quickly disintegrating marriages, though let's pause to acknowledge that it was *also* not fun to live through eras in which divorce was hard to obtain, and marriages, even abusive and unhappy ones, were not easy for women to extract themselves from. But the swiftness of the feminist rupture of early-married hetero expectation meant that the divorce wave was fast and big and produced many acrimonious splits; lots of kids suffered for it, lots of women and lots of men suffered through it. The chaos provoked by the divorce boom fueled an extremely potent antifeminist line: that feminists, in their political aims, were enemies of family, men, and marriage.

"If there's one thing feminists love, it's divorce," Phyllis Schlafly loved to croon, practically until her death.[8] What she did not acknowledge, of course, was that what feminists loved was equality of the sexes, and that the divorces that happened during the course of and in the wake of the Second Wave were often provoked by women's refusal to remain legally bound to men who did not want to have equal partnerships. Or by the realization that if they could attain economic security on their own, they did not *need* to stay in marriages that didn't make them happy, or in which they were treated badly.

As the historian Stephanie Coontz, who has written about the history of marriage, has pointed out, "Feminism didn't make good marriages go bad."[9] But it did challenge men to be better, and offered women the opportunity to plan their lives around ambitions and desires not directly tied to husbands. These opportunities for escape and for alternate paths were, in fact, uncannily similar to what Elizabeth Cady Stanton had been clamoring for in the Declaration of Sentiments, what marriage reformers had been speaking about for more than a century.

Any time that men's power is questioned or tempered or rebuked or challenged, it seems, they are made to feel uncomfortable, and it often feels that any form of male discomfort is untenable.

The doctor Larry Nassar, accused of molestation by more than one hundred young gymnasts, complained about having to listen to multiple women's testimony against him, and about his fear that he might pass out on account of this ill-ease, during his 2018 trial; Senator Jeff Sessions squeaked about the way that Kamala Harris's intense questioning of him was making him "nervous" during a Senate hearing on Russian interference in the Trump campaign.[10] Recall that when Chuck Schumer was interviewed about his reaction to the Women's March by George Stephanopoulos, the host's question to the senator had been "Were you comfortable with everything you heard?" as if Schumer's sense of ease were the pressing concern.

More punishing is the increasingly common intimation that the discomfort women cause men by rejecting or challenging them is the thing that explains why some of those men enact violence against women. In the wake of the mass shooting at Marjory Stoneman Douglas High School by a former student, one survivor, Isabelle Robinson, wrote in the *New York*

Times of the "disturbing number of comments I've read that go something like this: 'Maybe if [the shooter's] classmates and peers had been a little nicer to him, the shooting . . . would never have occurred.'"

Many powerful men, and the women who seek to retain warm association with them, strain to ease their discomfort. Part of that is understanding—seeing—whatever disruption has upset men as destructive, problematic, and unnatural, rather than as corrective or overdue.

"The public censure of women as if we are rabid because we speak without apology about the world in which we live is a strategy of threat that usually works," wrote Andrea Dworkin in the preface to *Intercourse*, her incendiary 1987 volume on the politics and power inequities of sex. "Men often react to women's words—speaking and writing—as if they were acts of violence; sometimes men react to women's words with violence. So we lower our voices. Women whisper. Women apologize. Women shut up. Women trivialize what we know. Women shrink. Women pull back."

Andrea Dworkin did not pull back, did not shrink herself or her words to be better in tune with male preference. She was a radical, lyrical, furious feminist writer whose thinking and prose were so provocative and so fiery that reading her work, even now, can burn.

Molested as a child, beaten by her first husband, Dworkin worked briefly as a prostitute in the Netherlands before coming to feminism after having been active in other social movements including the struggles against the Vietnam War and South African apartheid. As a feminist activist, she and the radical feminist lawyer Catharine MacKinnon—a kind of twentieth-century answer to Elizabeth Cady Stanton and Susan B. Anthony, with Dworkin as the scribe and MacKinnon as the action-oriented doer—stepped on a First Amendment third rail by proposing legislation to ban pornography.

Dworkin and MacKinnon were not alone in their fight against the pornography industry; Gloria Steinem, Audre Lorde, and others also argued for setting limits and exposing its misogynistic abuses. But Dworkin and MacKinnon went furthest, in 1983 writing a series of local ordinances, known as the antipornography civil rights ordinances, which sought to ban porn by treating it as a violation of women's civil rights. Their mission, which launched first in Minneapolis, and was later taken up, with varying degrees of success and failure, in Indianapolis, Cambridge, and Bellingham, Washington, set off an internal battle within feminism—again an echo of Stanton and Anthony—between self-described "prosex feminists" and the antiporn (though as they might clarify, not anti*sex*) work done by Dworkin and MacKinnon. The prosex feminists won, conclusively.

Perhaps most famously, Dworkin wrote, in *Intercourse*, that "violation is a synonym for intercourse," which was widely read and understood as an argument that *all sex is rape*. She would maintain staunchly for years after that this was a misreading of her sentiment, that what she believed was that "sex must not put women in a subordinate position. It must be reciprocal and not an act of aggression from a man looking only to satisfy himself." But the cruder reading of her words was the one that stuck, largely because it did the job of discrediting her as a deranged fringe heretic, as somehow broken in her noncomportment with male-established aesthetic standards for femininity (Dworkin was obese throughout her life and often wore overalls). Her presumed dysfunction could be smeared into an understanding of her brazen anger at sexist power structures, and would thereby work to invalidate that anger.

"People didn't just disagree with Dworkin. They *hated* her," wrote one of her most elegiac later critics, the journalist Ariel Levy, a description that could be applied to lots of public, challenging women in America, including many who have shared almost none of Dworkin's radical politics, perhaps suggesting that it's not the specifics of the ideology but rather the threat to male comfort and supremacy that provokes the loathing. "To her detractors," Levy continued, "she was the horror of women's lib personified, the angriest woman in America."

The more pernicious and consequential threat of the censure Dworkin's ire provoked was the way that her unapologetic fury could be blamed for turning *other* women off and away from feminism. After her death in 2005, one writer for the *Guardian* suggested, horribly, that "Dworkin's true legacy has been that far too many young women today would rather be bitten by a rabid dog than be considered a feminist."[11] This was a terribly twisted knife: the suggestion that the legacy of willingness to express rage would be a generation of women less willing to voice their own fury, more willing to remain complacent.

Yet Dworkin's reputation was its own meta-testament to how right she was about so many things, even as she was wrong about other things, from pornography to sex work. Her medium was part of her message, and it explains why Gloria Steinem once called Dworkin feminism's "Old Testament prophet, raging in the hills, telling the truth."

She knew what she was doing; "I'm a radical feminist," she once said. "Not the fun kind." In a *New York Times* review of Dworkin's 1988 volume *Letters from a War Zone*, the reviewer, a woman named Lore Dickstein, wrote that "much of what Andrea Dworkin has to say is important . . . but how she says it tends to undermine her argument. . . . It rings in the ears, pummels the mind; one begs for release from this relentless harangue. But then, this is precisely Ms. Dworkin's point, her message as well as her method; to hound and harass, to respond to indifference or even civility with a shrill pitch of outrage."[12]

One of the hardest parts about writing this book, and about living through the #metoo movement, was realizing the sorrow I felt that Dworkin was not here to see what was happening. *Not* because I felt she would be wholly satisfied by #metoo; though I do hope she would be cheered that it was taking place. Far more than that, I was sad because during her career, as Levy has pointed out, Dworkin was unafraid to say that she longed to be read, to be *heard*, to be understood. And the tenor of the feminist conversation, as it bubbled over in the years after the 2016 election, was in moments so in the spirit of what she wrote that I have discovered, in returning to her work, sentiments that left her ostracized from popular political debate in her time, but which today—this week, this afternoon—might feel wholly appropriate in their tenor and pitch, even earn a bunch of fire emojis on Twitter.

"Feminism is dying here," wrote Andrea Dworkin, "because so many women who say they are feminists are collaborators or cowards." And "Men are shits and take pride in it." And, of the western canon of white male novelists and their sexism, "I love the literature these men created; but I will not live my life as if they are real and I am not," a sentiment I tweeted as I composed this chapter, and which quickly earned three hundred "likes."

The relentless, pounding march of #metoo—an angry surge that I expected to last only a few days or weeks but which stretched months, and then, even after briefly abating, came roaring back in the form of new relentlessly reported exposures of systemic power abuse, lawsuits, committees to push forward new legal protections for women who've been harassed—told me that contemporary women were in no mood to play nice, even when it would have been so much simpler, so much easier, to just let it stop, make all the risk and discomfort go away.

They reminded me of the bulldozing insistence of Dworkin, her determination not to give in to the easier path. Her work, she wrote, "does not say forgive me and love me. It does not say, I forgive you, I love you. . . . No. I say no."

CHAPTER TWO

TRUST NO ONE

During the three fall months at which #metoo was at its peak, I received somewhere between five and twenty emails every day from women wanting to tell me their experiences: of being groped or leered at or rubbed up against in their workplaces. They told me about all kinds of men—actors and midlevel managers; judges and philanthropists; store owners and social-justice advocates; my own colleagues, past and present—who'd hurt them or someone they knew. It had happened yesterday or two years ago or twenty.

"It's a 'seeing the matrix' moment," one woman told me in the midst of it all. "It's an absolutely bizarre thing to go through, and it's fucking exhausting and horrible, and I hate it. And I'm glad. I'm so glad we're doing it. And I'm in hell."

That period forced many of us to do that daily labor of sorting through our own anger—at the men we liked, loved, worked with, and needed—examining the many angles from which our rage emanated, taking a hard look at how our lives and careers had been shaped by the systemic abuses of patriarchal power that any of us in the system had had to work around. And, at the same time, god damn it, managing the discomfort and injuries of the men who'd just recently been informed that women had reason to be angry at them.

I was challenged, in my exchanges with men—my own friends and colleagues, self-aware enough to be uneasy, to know they were probably on a list somewhere or imagine that they might be. They'd text and call, not quite saying why, but leaving no doubt: They had once cheated with a colleague; had once made a pass they suspected was wrong; they weren't sure if they got consent that one time. Were they condemned? What was the nature and severity of their crime? The anxiety of this—how to speak to guys seeking feminist absolution, the reassurance that I wasn't mad at them, but whom I suspected to be compromised—was real.

Some of my friends had no patience for men's sudden penchant for introspection, but I was always a sucker; I felt for them. When they reached out, my animal impulse was usually to comfort, to forgive. Yet reason—and a Dworkinian determination not to placate, not now—drove me also to be direct, colder than usual: Yes, this is a problem. In fact, it's your problem. Seek to address it.

Then there were the men who were looking at the world with fresh eyes, wholly shocked by the unseemly parade of sexual molesters and manipulators. These men had begun to understand my journalistic beat for the first time: They hadn't known it was *this* bad. They hadn't seen how systemic, architectural, it was—how they were part of it, had benefitted from it, even if they hadn't pawed anyone, hadn't raped anyone. That faction included my husband, a criminal defense attorney who was certainly not ignorant of the pervasiveness of sexual assault, yet read the endless stream of reports with a furrowed brow. "Who does this?" he asked me. "Who *does* this?" Then one night, with genuine feeling: "How can you even want to have sex with me at this point?"

Months after I originally published this anecdote about my mate, Katie Roiphe would cite it, pairing it with anger I'd expressed elsewhere, to surmise that, given my fury and disgust, it was "not entirely surprising" that my husband would question my desire for him. It was a nonsensical elision—designed to cast me as castrating and my husband as a victim of wrathful feminist frigidity, rather than as my boon companion in fury and disgust.

In part Roiphe was simply reaching for the quickest, oldest, and most reliable weapon to turn on feminists: the aspersion that we don't want sex or men. But on some deeper level, she was flailing against a scarier possibility: that the exertions of #metoo were moving not only masses of women, but some men to empathize with women in very real ways, to consider the world through a female lens, destabilizing their own centrality and the argument that feminism is men's natural enemy—and in doing so, threatening generations of antifeminists who'd made careers out of soothing the lacerations men had incurred under feminist siege.

As cheered as I was by the nervous self-reflection of some of my male compatriots, I was simultaneously frustrated by those who claimed they couldn't differentiate between harmless flirtation and harassment, because I believed that most women could. The rational part of me was glad that these guys were doing this accounting, examining the instances in which they wielded power. Maybe some simply hadn't understood the ways they were putting the objects of their attention at a disadvantage, but like Sarah Silverman and Gayle King and Judith Levine and Samantha Bee and every woman who has known and loved and relied on and trusted a man, I had to acknowledge that some of them, even my friends, surely had. One day, my friends and I learned that a man who'd been bemoaning the prevalence of harassment had also stuck his hand up a colleague's skirt when he was her boss. "It feels like Allison Williams with the keys in *Get Out*," said my friend, the feminist journalist Irin Carmon, in reference to the recent horror movie about systemic racism. "Trust no one."

One of the revelations of #metoo—and the anger that it provoked in me, and in my friends—was the degree to which powerful men may have been behaving horribly for their entire careers, while it was women's reactions to that behavior that were regularly judged. Women were the cops, the ones held responsible for patrolling and controlling and adequately punishing and generously forgiving men's trespasses. And God help them if they chose wrong.

"Why do women think they have to support these guys?" Pat Schroeder wondered to me, recalling her fury at former Democratic presidential candidate Gary Hart, whose campaign she managed, until it was derailed when he was caught cheating on his wife and lying about it. "I couldn't have gotten out of the Hart campaign fast enough," she said, but Hart's wife stayed with him. And the worst part, she said, was that both Hart and his wife got angry at her for not sticking by him. "So I guess I was supposed to suck it up and come out and defend him," said Schroeder. "But I just can't believe that men are that weak. I'm really sorry, but if men are that weak and we have to defend them all the time, then why do *they* have all the power?"

Of course, the fact that they have all the power is precisely what permits them to turn every instance of their misbehavior into a referendum on whether the women around them are reacting appropriately. It's another way that women are asked to foot the bill for men's bad acts, another pattern that was being exposed and provoking a whole other level of anger in women who were seeing, some for the first time, what a crap position they'd been in, and how impossible it was to wiggle out—even now.

The degree to which the interest, after each revelation of male power abuse, turns to the women in his life—or even in his vague professional circle, past or present—could not have been made clearer than in electoral politics during the fall of 2017, when every time allegations were lobbed at a male politician, the headlines quickly turned to how his female colleagues were reacting.

After the much beloved liberal senator and former *Saturday Night Live* comedian Al Franken was accused by a woman of having kissed her against her will and groped her while she was sleeping on a USO tour, Franken apologized and asked for an ethics committee investigation into his behavior. His female peers in the Senate—especially those who had been openly supportive of the #metoo movement—were promptly asked what they thought and all agreed to wait for the ethics committee findings. But then more women began to come forward with stories about Franken: about ass-grabbing, boob-touching, and openmouthed kissing. These tales ate up daily headlines, particularly galling in the lead-up to a crucial senate election in Alabama, where Doug Jones, a Democrat, was looking to flip a seat by beating Roy Moore, a Republican who'd been accused by multiple women of having assaulted them when they were teenagers.

After his first statement, Franken did not respond at length to further allegations, but his female colleagues were regularly asked why—given their party's stated lack of tolerance for harassment and assault—they weren't calling on their own colleague to resign. The reluctance of the party to condemn Franken was giving cover to Republicans who wanted to go back to supporting the accused molester in Alabama. Franken's behavior, dubious and disappointing, but not violent, was redounding negatively to his party, eating up the time and energies of his colleagues, and in many ways echoing patterns of twenty years earlier, when then-president Bill Clinton had been revealed to have been having an affair with White House intern Monica Lewinsky. There had already been much talk in 2017 of the hypocrisy of the many feminists who had supported Clinton and not been kind to Lewinsky during the 1990s, including Gloria Steinem and Susan Faludi.

They had defended him in part because they had been forced to depend on him after twelve years of Reagan and Bush administrations; he was the leader of the party that was invested in women's rights, the president who had appointed Ruth Bader Ginsburg to the Supreme Court, who had signed the Family and Medical Leave Act, who was married to a feminist many of them had then admired tremendously. But the choice not to condemn Clinton for his abuse of professional and sexual power had in fact worked to halt feminist momentum in the years after the Anita Hill accusations against Clarence Thomas had brought the term "sexual harassment" into the national lexicon.

This history meant that every contemporary feminist who wanted to make a point about #metoo—even those of us who had been in high school or college during the Clinton administration—had to answer for Clinton's behavior: Did we condemn it? Yes we did. But we were also called on to evaluate the feminists who had come before us and defended Clinton: Had this been a strategic and moral error? Yes it had been. Any of us who had supported Hillary Clinton in 2016 were additionally asked whether the feminist argument for her was compromised by her own complicity in defending her husband and denigrating Lewinsky to a friend in a conversation that would later be reported.

The answer to that last one—for me, anyway—was perhaps especially fraught, but at some point it was hard not to notice that there seemed to be an extremely wide circle of censure in which everyone—from old feminists to young feminists to Hillary Clinton to anyone who had ever said a good word about either Hillary Clinton or about feminism—was being asked to answer for Bill Clinton's shitty behavior . . . everyone that is, *except for Bill Clinton.*

Among those who had been caught up in this ricocheting trap of tenuous and retroactive culpability was New York Senator Kirsten Gillibrand, who had, as a legislator, concentrated on issues of sexual harassment and assault in the military and on college campuses, and was therefore asked regularly to answer for bad men, her associations with whom might prove her lack of actual commitment to the issues she advocated for.

During #metoo, Gillibrand was asked by the *New York Times* if she believed that Bill Clinton—whose wife Gillibrand had long cited as a mentor, and whose Senate seat she now held—should have resigned the presidency, and she said "Yes, I think that is the appropriate response." The fury she faced in response was intense. "Over 20 yrs you took the Clintons' endorsements, money, and seat. Hypocrite," wrote the Clintons' longtime aide Philippe Reines on Twitter, while Democratic strategist Hank Sheinkopf called Gillibrand "traitorous" and a "disloyal" "political opportunist."

A week later, Democratic House minority leader Nancy Pelosi was being interviewed on *Meet the Press*, and spoke positively about #metoo as "transformative" and "wholesome." But when she was asked about allegations against one of her caucus members, longtime Michigan congressman John Conyers—that he had harassed former members of his staff and reached at least one cash-settlement with an accuser—Pelosi didn't condemn her colleague. Instead she praised him as an "icon." The resulting condemnation of Pelosi was harsh—and correct. Democratic strategist Lis Smith observed that, "we have no moral high ground against the likes of Roy Moore if we sit by in silence when Al Franken and John Conyers get to sit in their seats. . . . We can't be the party that says we stand up for women only when it's politically convenient. We have to apply the same standards to ourselves." And in its coverage of Pelosi's remarks, *NBC News* noted that they "raised questions about the credibility of the party's messaging and the degree to which its elected leaders are willing to put the protection of women ahead of political considerations."[13]

So one woman who had condemned a Democrat accused of harassment had been vilified as a traitor and another who'd defended one had been called a hypocrite. And each day brought Democrats closer to an election that might bring an accused assaulter of teenaged girls—not to mention another Republican—to the Senate.

On December 6, Al Franken's seventh accuser came forward. Hours before an eighth accuser would follow, Gillibrand released a statement saying that she believed that "while Senator Franken is entitled to have the Ethics Committee conclude its review, I believe it would be better for our country if he sent a clear message that any kind of mistreatment of women in our society isn't acceptable by stepping aside to let someone else serve." Within minutes, other women senators, including Washington's Patty Murray, California's Kamala Harris, Missouri's Claire McCaskill, and Hawaii's Mazie Hirono issued similar statements.

Some of the Senate's Democratic men would soon join the women, but it was unquestionably the women who had led the charge. One senate aide would eventually tell me that the Democratic women had been speaking angrily with one another—sometimes, truly, in the women's bathrooms in the Senate buildings—about their frustration at the situation, and the bad position it had put them in, for days.

Perhaps most difficult to absorb about the Franken decision was that it wasn't, in the end, about him. It was about the party, the caucus, the Alabama election, the women who'd come forward, the future of being able to advocate for harassment and assault protections. The maddening dynamic faced by Franken's colleagues, many of whom genuinely liked and respected him, was that they had a set of choices—to stand by and support him, or to ask for him to step aside—each of which left *them* imperiled. The women of the Senate chose to do what women had been unable to, or had chosen not to do, during the Clinton mess—they openly rebuked a powerful and widely beloved man, thus courting tremendous blowback.

But those senators surely understood that if they had *not* spoken out against Franken, they would have been tarred as self-interested hypocrites, only invested in zero-tolerance for sexual assault if allegations were made against someone in an opposing party. They would have hobbled the whole #metoo movement, since their failure to condemn one of their own would have given its critics fuel to say it was partisan-motivated, and not rooted in true objection to gendered power abuse. They certainly *also* understood that in speaking out against Franken, they would be viewed as self-interested executioners.

That they chose the latter path—that it was even an option, that they had the numbers, the strength, the confidence—spoke volumes about the unprecedented shifts in possibility this moment seemed to be heralding, and about the cumulative impact of increased women's participation in electoral politics: there were twenty-one women in the Senate, compared to the nine who'd been serving at the time of Bill Clinton's scandal.

Immediately after the call for Franken to resign, the *New York Times* Metro section's Twitter account asked of Gillibrand: "Is courage or opportunism at play?" A 2018 op-ed in the *Daily Beast* asked the same, wondering "whether she is too transparently opportunistic to be a viable presidential candidate." The charge that a woman who crosses a well-liked and powerful man is being opportunistic was illogical in part because there have rarely been plush opportunities on offer to women who transgress in this manner; a woman who *supports* a powerful man in the face of criticism is surely also being opportunistic, perhaps even more so.

But it also was kind of funny: opportunism is grabbing a woman's ass if she's near you at a party, or kissing her onstage because you have the *opportunity* to do so with impunity; it's taking advantage of a sleeping woman to make a funny joke about grabbing her tits because you're a comedian who came of professional age in the 80s when there was not only no price to be paid for objectifying women, but laughs and stature to be gained by it. Opportunism is converting a career as a comedian into a run for the Senate. But none of that is discernible as opportunistic because it is simply assumed that that's how white male power works, how it's *supposed* to work: it takes advantage of the opportunities at hand.

Most women I knew did not *want* the "opportunity" to patrol the borders of patriarchal overreach; we felt torn about both the vague prospect and the observed reality of these men losing their jobs. We thought of their feelings and their families, fretted that the disclosure of their misdeeds might cost them future employment, or even provoke them to harm themselves. But this was something else we were being compelled to notice: the ways in which we were still conditioned to worry for the men, but somehow not to afford the same compassion for women—their families, their feelings, their future prospects—even in a reckoning that was supposed to be about us, not them.

As the *n+1* editor Dayna Tortorici wrote in 2017, "I imagine that some people feel good about bringing perpetrators to justice, such as it is under the system we have. But I imagine just as many do not want to be responsible for their offender's punishment. They might say: Please don't make it my decision whether you lose your job, are shunned by your peers, or get sent to prison. Prison, unemployment, and social exile are not what I want for men. I'm not here to be the police. I don't want to be responsible for you."[14]

And this was just some of what we were mad about.

CATEGORY ERROR

Women, of course, were doing our own accounting, attempting to classify moments from our pasts to gauge how they fit into the larger picture. *Sure, he DM-ed me late at night asking me what my sexual fantasies were, but he didn't masturbate against my leg and then threaten to kill me; he didn't hire ex–Mossad agents to dig up dirt about my sex life; he didn't rape me.*

We *knew* there were differences. We were not dumb. We knew, when we looked at documents like the Shitty Media Men list and read social media accounts of everything from uncomfortable dates to physical assault, when we heard friends sift through their own churning memories, that there were legal distinctions between behaviors, as well as moral ones. There were the cheating dogs who propositioned us, the artless boy-men who made fumbling passes over work lunches, the bosses who touched us against our will, the men who retaliated professionally if we dared to reject them. These were different behaviors, with different costs, deserving of different reactions and repercussions.

Yet the rage that many of us were feeling didn't necessarily correspond with the severity of the trespass: Lots of us were, in those tumultuous months, as incensed about the guy who looked down our shirt at a company retreat as we were about Weinstein, even if we could acknowledge that there was something fundamentally nuts about that, a weird overreaction.

But even this feeling was rooted in the expectation, warped by generations of normalized patriarchal power, that we had nothing to be angry about to begin with. We had, all of us, spent decades being pressured to *under*react, our objections to the small stuff (and also to the big stuff) bantered away, ignored, or attributed to our own inability to cut it in the real world. Resentments had accreted, matured into rage.

"I stuffed all my harassment memories in an emotional trash compactor because there are just so many," said my friend, the writer and podcaster Aminatou Sow. "Now the trash compactor is broken, and everything is coming up." Sow said that among the things she'd recalled in the fall were an old boss "who definitely jerked off in the office and would make sure to let me see the porn on his computer. He has a bigger job now. And the man who pinned me to the wall in the copy room and told me I should be grateful he's paying attention to me because I'm a fat pig. I reported both those incidents, by the way, and nothing happened."

Part of it was that while there were infinite gradations and varieties and severity of sexual and physical trespass, what they all had in common were their reflection of women's smaller share of professional, public worth.

Some, including the journalist Masha Gessen, writing for the *New Yorker*, worried that as we tried to parse how butt-groping and unsolicited kissing could exist on the same scale as violent rape, we risked transforming the moment of reckoning into a full-blown sex panic, and in doing so, reverting to ideas about women as inherently vulnerable, sexually infantilized. If all sexual contact, this fear went, was being categorized in this storm as dangerous for women, we were reverting back to Victorian ideas about women as victims, without sexual appetites and agency of their own.

But what Gessen saw as potential category collapse was in fact a crucial category *error*. Because the thing that united the varied revelations wasn't sexual harm, but *professional* harm and power abuse. Tarana Burke's original Me Too campaign had been about sexual assault and violence. But in the fall of 2018, the conversation being held under the umbrella of the hashtag #metoo was addressing a broader range of power abuses, chief among them, sexual harassment. Yes, sexual and professional damage were certainly related, and in some cases were combined. But the reason that they were sharing conversational and journalistic space during this reckoning was because sexual harassment is understood as a crime not because it is a sexual violation, but because it is a form of discrimination.

The term "sexual harassment" had been used for the first time in public in 1975 by feminist author Lin Farley, when she testified at a hearing on women in the workplace before the New York City Commission on Human Rights.

Farley, who was teaching a class on women and work at Cornell University, had helped to coin the term after hearing about Carmita Wood. Wood was an administrative assistant at the nuclear studies lab at Cornell University, the first woman to have held that job. After years of dealing with a boss who rubbed up against her, groped her, kissed her against her will, appeared to stimulate himself in front of her, and publicly put his hands under her shirt at a company Christmas party, and after having been denied transfer to another department by the university, Wood resigned her job. When she applied for unemployment benefits, the New York State Department of Labor rejected her claim; she appealed the decision, and presented testimony, which was corroborated by two of her former coworkers, but her claim was again rejected.[15]

Unsure of where else to turn, Wood had approached the office of the human affairs program at Cornell, where she encountered Farley and a group of other women. Compelled by her case, they held meetings to come up with a word that described the degrading, diminishing professional treatment Wood had endured, treatment that was all too common, yet so integrated into the life of women in the professional sphere that no descriptor had ever before been necessary. "It was something that we all talked about but because we didn't have a name," Farley has said, "we didn't know we were all talking about the same thing."[16] Farley and her colleagues searched for something all-encompassing, and eventually settled on "sexual harassment."[17]

In April of 1975, Wood published an op-ed in the *Ithaca Journal*, in which she wrote, "Women must be judged on their ability to perform their jobs—not on whether we maintain a sexual rapport with our bosses." Along with the women from Cornell's human affairs program, and the lawyer Eleanor Holmes Norton, then the chair on the New York City Commission on Human Rights, Wood formed a group called Working Women United, and they sent out a letter to hundreds of lawyers.[18] It crossed the desk of Catharine MacKinnon, who then began what would become a multiyear legal battle to assert that sexual harassment violates prohibitions against professional discrimination, which had been laid out in the Civil Rights Act with regard to race.

In 1977, an appeals court upheld decisions defining sexual harassment as sex discrimination, barred by Title VII of the Civil Rights Act. In 1979, as harassment cases worked their way up through the American legal system, MacKinnon argued that there was a link between sexual harassment and professional discrimination, citing among other things the siloing of women into lower-paying professions that demand their sexualization. "Sexual harassment perpetuates the interlocked structure by which women have been kept sexually in thrall to men and at the bottom of the labor market," MacKinnon wrote. "Two forces of American society converge: men's control over women's sexuality and capital's control over employees' work lives."

In 1986, the Supreme Court ruled in favor of Mechelle Vinson, an assistant bank manager who described being assaulted and raped by her boss in the bank's vaults and basements more than forty times. Justice William Rehnquist wrote in the unanimous decision, "Without question, when a supervisor sexually harasses a subordinate because of the subordinate's sex, the supervisor discriminates on the basis of sex." In other words, sexual harassment *might* entail behaviors that on their own would be criminal—assault or rape—but the legal definition of its harm is about the systemic disadvantaging of a gender in the public and professional sphere.

Those structural disadvantages did not begin or end with the actual physical incursions—the grabbing, kissing, or assault. In fact, the gender inequity that created the need for civil rights protections is what permitted so many of these trespasses to occur so frequently, and for so long. Gender inequity explained why women were *vulnerable* to harassment before they are even harassed—it left them with less stature, authority, and economic security, making it harder for them to resist or object to ill-treatment. It explained why it was difficult for them to come forward with stories after they had been harassed, why they were often ignored or punished when they did. It clarified why so many women worked with or maintained relationships with harassers and why their reactions to those harassers became key to how they themselves would be treated, professionally—because when men, and specifically white men, have a disproportionate share of public, professional, and political power, women must act around and in reaction to them; they rely on men's approval for work, security, and any share of power they might aspire to. Gender inequity is cyclical, all-encompassing.

Many of the women who told their stories during #metoo explained that they did not do so before because they feared for their jobs. When women *had* complained, many had been told that putting up with these behaviors was just part of working for the powerful men in question. "That's just Charlie being Charlie" and "That's just Harvey being Harvey" were verbatim quotes cited in reported stories about the predatory behavior of Charlie Rose and Harvey Weinstein, offered as explanation for why those men had exposed themselves, attempted to coerce, berated, and pressed their penises onto younger female colleagues.[19] For years—forever—simply *being* the powerful man was plausible exculpation for monstrous behavior toward women.

Remaining in the good graces of these men—men who were just being themselves—because they were the bosses, the hosts, the rainmakers, the legislators, was the only way for those they'd aggressed against to preserve employment, and not just their own: Whole offices, often populated by female underlings, were dependent on the steady power of the male bosses. When a prominent alleged abuser lost his job, he wasn't the only one whose salary stopped; it often meant that his employees, many of them women, also lost their paychecks, which of course were smaller to begin with. When men held the most politically powerful posts, people who were less powerful depended on them for advocacy and representation. Complaints that imperiled these leaders immediately imperiled entire political parties, and ideological agendas on both the left and the right.

And that means that damage done by sexual and professional

impropriety extended well beyond a harasser's colleagues, well beyond the actual object of harassment, sometimes to people the harasser didn't even know.

Consider the damage done to feminism, to his wife, and by extension to the Democratic Party, by Bill Clinton's behavior. Consider the ways in which Franken's alleged groping imperiled his party's interests in Alabama, and was detrimental to his female colleagues' ability to do their work and not get labeled hypocrites, and how in calling him out, they lost stature with many of his loyal fans. Consider Ted Kennedy, the legendary liberal of the U.S. Senate. Kennedy sat on the all-male, all-white Senate Judiciary Committee that treated Anita Hill with such derision when she testified about the sexual harassment she'd experienced while working for Clarence Thomas. And Kennedy, on whom his party relied to do right, had to keep his mouth shut, both because of his own history of ill treatment of women—most notably the death of Mary Jo Kopechne, whom in 1969 he'd driven into a Martha's Vineyard pond and left to drown, after escaping himself—but also because at the same time that Anita Hill was testifying, Kennedy's nephew was about to be tried for rape in Florida. Kennedy's behavior—and his nephew's alleged behavior—had left him paralyzed, which in turn smoothed the confirmation of Clarence Thomas, a justice who would vote to dismantle injunctions against sexual harassment, as well as to make it easier to strip voting rights and make reproductive health care inaccessible.

But to get angry and challenge the authority of these men meant jeopardizing not just an individual job in an individual office; rather it risked far broader harm within whole professions where men hold sway. Lauren Greene, an ambitious congressional staffer who had accused her former boss, Republican congressman Blake Farenthold, of sexual harassment after he reportedly told another aide of his wet dreams about Greene and commented on her nipples, told reporters that her challenge to her boss had left her blackballed from politics, the profession she wanted to succeed in, and that in the fall of 2017, she was working part-time as an assistant to a home builder in North Carolina and babysitting on the side to make extra money.

These were the economics of sexual harassment, but also, simply, of sexism. The movement inspired by #metoo in 2017 and 2018 involved a recognition of and revolt against *sexism*, often in combination with white supremacy.

One of the reasons that a story about WNYC's radio host John Hockenberry had been particularly arresting was because it made clear that there was a web of ill treatment, a connection between his comparatively mild but still discomfiting come-ons to colleagues, and his ugly (but nonsexualized) treatment of his cohosts. To one of them, Farai Chideya, he reportedly said, "You shouldn't stay here just as a 'diversity hire.'" Another, Celeste Headlee, complained of how he'd interrupt and sabotage her on air. This man literally broadcast, on air, his disdain for the women—notably women of color—who were his professional peers. Headlee said she was told that her poor performance was to blame for Hockenberry's bullying behavior; she, like the two women who preceded her, eventually lost her post as cohost, while Hockenberry retained his position. All of that was public record. But none of it would have made it to print had there not *also* been an accusation of sexual impropriety.

How to make clear that the trauma of the smaller trespasses was not necessarily even *about* the sexualized act in question? It was also about the cruel reminder that these were still the terms on which we were valued, by our colleagues, our bosses, and sometimes our competitors. It's not that we were horrified—as some of the "sex panic" critics feared—like Victorian damsels; it's that we were horrified like women in 2017 who had briefly believed they were equal to their male peers but had just been reminded that they were not, like women who had suddenly had their comparative powerlessness, their essential inequality, revealed to them. "I was hunting for a job," said one of the women who accused Charlie Rose of assault. "And he was hunting for me."

A woman who was harassed, or who worked in a workplace where other women were, might feel vividly the full weight of the system that was not set up with her in mind, might see with clarity how much more difficult her professional path would be at every turn, how success might not be on her terms, but on terms set by powerful men. She might wonder if having laughed at her boss's degrading joke in a meeting had been the thing that earned her a reputation of willing to play along, had sped her success, or if *not* having laughed had earned her a reputation for humorlessness that had resulted in her not being invited to the next meeting, or on the next trip. After having accepted or rejected a boss's unwanted proposition, she might have felt shame, or embarrassment that wormed its way into her head, affected her confidence. She might have had her ambition sapped, might have removed herself from the profession in which she had hoped to succeed.

Heather McLaughlin, a sociology professor at Oklahoma State University, described in an interview with the radio show *Marketplace* her study showing that about half of women in their late twenties who've experienced harassment start looking for a new job within two years of the incident. For those who've endured more serious harassment, the figure is around 80 percent—and many opt to leave their chosen professions altogether: to start over, often in less male-dominated fields, which of course tend to be lower-paying. Ina Howard-Parker, a former book publicist who told me she was harassed at several progressive publishing houses, did just that. "I ended up deciding I'd rather work at Trader Joe's, where at least there's an HR department and rules of engagement at work." She now renovates houses in rural Pennsylvania.

Another reason that handsy colleagues existed on the same plane as violent predators was that the harm done to women simply didn't end with the original offense. It was also in how we were evaluated, punished, or promoted based on our reactions to it. Did we smile or remain stone-faced, reciprocate or retreat, ignore or complain? What became of us might hang on what we chose.

What became infuriatingly evident, through all of it, was how much time and energy women had been forced to spend maneuvering around the harasser, time and energy that might otherwise have been spent in service of their own ideas, work, advancement. This was a longtime cost for so many women who had dedicated percentages of their careers to fighting the many biases that kept their opportunities reduced and one of the true tolls of anger at injustice: the amount of time it takes away from the work we might otherwise be doing. "The very serious function of racism is distraction," Toni Morrison once said. "It keeps you from doing your work. It keeps you explaining, over and over again, your reason for being."[20]

Jennifer Scanlon, biographer of the civil rights organizer Anna Arnold Hedgeman, has written of how Hedgeman, a woman "raised to seek excellence and showcase her talents," had often wondered "what her life would have been like had she not felt the need to fight relentlessly for racial justice." Hedgeman herself recalled an exchange with a white woman, who'd been "taken aback when I told her that I had been forced to spend my whole life discussing the implications of color and that this was to me a waste of time and of whatever talent I had."

That sentiment was echoed in a story about one Harvard government professor's quest to hold the powerful head of her department accountable for the harassment and discrimination she experienced at his hands. According to the *Chronicle of Higher Education*, Terry Karl, who eventually left Harvard, despite the fact that her boss and alleged harasser, Jorge Domínguez, got to stay, "still resents the time she spent fighting this battle rather than focusing on her research and her students. She's still upset that it was her career that got derailed" and that "she had wasted precious time filing grievances rather than finishing her book."[21]

WEBS OF MALE POWER

Of course it's not a waste to fight for justice, to work to right wrongs; but it is an extra tax on those already working from power deficits. It's time and energy expended by people who could otherwise be advancing their own careers, doing their work, making their art, gaining economic security or perches in the public sphere—the very things that men seem to be able to do, sometimes for decades, even if they themselves are the ones who have been alleged to have committed trespasses against these women.

Because networks—sometimes, literal television *networks*—of male power had worked to build, protect, and further reinforce male power. Fox News chief Roger Ailes had protected Bill O'Reilly, keeping him in a multimillion-dollar berth for years after public claims of harassment had surfaced; O'Reilly in turn had defended Ailes when Ailes was accused of serial harassment of the women at his network. And their network had defended Donald Trump, whose roles as birther and politician were built in part by the Fox News team—and he had defended both O'Reilly and Ailes—all against charges of sexual harassment of women.[22]

That both Ailes and O'Reilly had finally lost their jobs, and that Ailes himself was now dead, offered little relief from the compounding injustices. After all, the party and candidate Fox had labored to create and sell to America were now in power, installing judges and heads of agencies who would further reinforce the stultifying dominance of white men.

The female accusers of all these men had received no such support, no such defense; instead they had been called liars from public, political, and media pulpits, had been chased out of the news business, hushed up with settlement money and nondisclosure agreements, insulted by the man who had become the president as being too ugly to grope. All while the men accused of harassing them had continued to draw paychecks and shape how our national narratives—including those about gender and power—were told.

Matt Lauer, accused of sexual misconduct by multiple subordinates at the *Today* show, had given Donald Trump an absolutely free pass at a 2016 presidential forum on foreign policy, failing to ask even a simple follow-up question about Trump's demonstrably false claim that he'd always opposed the 2003 invasion of Iraq. In the same forum, Lauer had grilled Hillary Clinton at length about her email server, interrupted her repeatedly, and then—after finally having asked her a question about policy—urged her to hurry up because her time was almost up.

In his years as cohost of the *Today* show, NBC's prize pig had amassed a long history of having been callous and dismissive to women on air, including his former cohost Ann Curry, whom he was rumored to have pushed from her perch. In 2014, Lauer had asked Mary Barra, the first female CEO of General Motors, whether she might have been hired for her job in part because the company was in trouble "and as a woman and a mom you could present a softer face and softer image for this company," and wondered, since she was a mother of two, "given the pressures of this job at General Motors, can you do both well?"

Lauer wasn't the only one whose alleged ill treatment of specific women seemed to correspond with public disregard for other women and their claims to equality. Amazon Studios president Roy Price, a man who had canceled the proto-feminist show *Good Girls Revolt* and passed on *The Handmaid's Tale* and *Big Little Lies*, resigned after being accused of making aggressively lewd comments toward a female producer. These kinds of decisions were certainly on a different scale than those that helped determine the outcome of a presidential election, but they nonetheless mattered: entertainment executives help to determine whose stories, what kinds of stories about women and power, audiences receive.

Leon Wieseltier, the former literary editor of the *New Republic,* had been a feared force within his highbrow institution, and he'd shaped the worldview of generations of journalists at what used to be called, only half-jokingly, the "in-flight magazine of Air Force One." Wieseltier also kissed women subordinates against their will and commented on the bodies and clothing of his young female colleagues, and spent portions of editorial meetings criticizing women—including Hillary Clinton and the writer Nora Ephron—whom he thought were stupid yet had somehow managed to get far in life. It seemed a rich irony, perhaps lost on Wieseltier, that the history of America had been one of wholly mediocre white men wielding unearned influence, often building their power by stoking resentments against nonwhite non-men via belittlement and vilification. Wieseltier's magazine had done just this on an editorial level, famously endorsing Bill Clinton's welfare reform, economic policy that had redounded terribly on America's least powerful populations, by deploying a cover image of a black mother smoking a cigarette.

In 2008, MSNBC anchor Chris Matthews said on television that Hillary Clinton had only become a senator and a candidate for the presidency "because her husband messed around . . . she didn't get there on her merits." In 2018, a tape turned up of Matthews asking, on a hot microphone before interviewing Clinton during the 2016 campaign, for a glass of water and then joking, "Where's that Bill Cosby pill I brought with me?" in reference to the prescription medication Cosby is alleged to have administered to dozens of women before raping them. In 2017, it was also revealed that Matthews had been accused in 1999 of sexual harassment by a former assistant producer on his show.

Joel Achenbach, the *Washington Post* reporter who in 2008 had suggested that Clinton needed a bark collar, was temporarily suspended by the *Post* in 2018 for what was described as "inappropriate workplace conduct." Mark Halperin, an NBC commentator and author of the soapy political bestseller *Game Change*, had presented a view of Hillary Clinton as a grasping and scandal-plagued candidate, while his coverage of Trump in 2016—an *actual* scandal-plagued candidate—had, by contrast, been notably soft, even admiring: Halperin once argued that the sexual harassment claims leveled at Trump would only help burnish the candidate's brutish brand.[23] In 2017, Halperin was accused by multiple women of having hit on them against their will when they worked for him, or as junior to him, at ABC News. One woman described how he had pressed his penis into her shoulder while she sat in a chair at the office.

The same power that had afforded Halperin the ability to press himself into younger colleagues—colleagues who had shared stories with one another but had never felt they had enough power to file a formal complaint at ABC, where he had held so much sway—also meant that he'd gotten to shape the nation's view of Hillary Clinton, whose political story had *already* been shaped by other men who had abused their power, including her husband and her 2016 opponent Donald Trump, not to mention Anthony Weiner, former New York legislator and husband of her colleague Huma Abedin, who in 2017 pled guilty after having exchanged sexts with a minor.

In hearing these tales of sexual harassment, we were getting a view of the architecture of sexism that had been holding everything up. We could see that the men who had had the power to abuse women's bodies and psyches throughout their careers were in many cases also the ones in charge of our political and cultural stories. And perhaps most chillingly, that part of the reason they had gotten so far was not simply that they had cleared the field of competition by harassing or demeaning women around them, but because they had capitalized on a broad cultural desire to see women belittled, humiliated, diminished.

The reality was that in many, many instances, men had not succeeded in *spite* of their noxious behavior or disregard for women; they have often succeeded *because* of it. They'd been patted on the back and winked along—their retro-machismo hailed as funny or edgy—at the same places that were now dramatically jettisoning them.

"The incredible hypocrisy of the boards, employers, institutions, publicists, brothers, friends who have been protecting powerful men/harassers/rapists for years and are now suddenly dropping them," said one of my colleagues at *New York* magazine, at once both livid and depressed. "What changed? Certainly not their beliefs about the behavior, right? Only their self-interest. On the one hand, I'm so happy they're finally being called out and facing consequences, but there's something so craven and superficially moralizing about the piling on by the same people who were the snickerers and protectors."

Because while it surely felt cathartic to see it all laid bare, even briefly, the view did not undo the damage. We could not go back in time and have the story of Hillary Clinton be written by people who had not also pressed their erections into the shoulders of young women who'd worked for them. We could not retroactively resituate the women who'd left jobs and whole careers because the navigation of the risks, of the daily abuses, drove them out. We would not see the movies or the art that those women would have made, could not live by the laws that they might have enacted, could not read the news as they might have reported it, had they ever truly had a fair shake at getting to tell it their way. The tsunami of #metoo stories hadn't just revealed the way that men had grabbed and rubbed and punished and shamed women; it had also shown us that they had done it all while building the very world in which we still were forced to live.

CHAPTER THREE

COLLATERAL DAMAGE

When I thought about my own history of having been harassed, I first recalled the restaurant manager who instructed me to keep my blouse unbuttoned as I served pizzas with fried eggs on top in high school, about the manager at Bruegger's Bagels who'd rub his dick against my ass as he passed me setting out the cream cheeses in the morning. I've never had a job in which there wasn't a resident harasser, but in my postcollege life, I believed I'd stayed out of his crosshairs.

Perhaps, in the story I'd told myself, it was because I was never wowed by powerful men, sensing on some visceral level that they were mostly full of shit. I had gravitated toward female mentors instead. But even given my wariness of Important Men, as a young woman I had had trouble *truly* believing that members of the opposite sex could be as cartoonishly grotesque as they sometimes were, even as I aged and acquired evidence.

I once heard that a choking person reflexively leaves the room, embarrassed for others to see her gasping for breath. I have no idea if that's true, but it's how I've dealt with harassment by men outside the workplace. Once on the subway, the man next to me wound his hand under my thigh and between my legs, and I sat there debating whether or not to stand up or scream because *I didn't want to embarrass him on a full train*. That's why, when an important writer took me to coffee, offering to help me find a new job, and asked if I'd ever fantasized about fucking a married man, I simply laughed maniacally, as if he'd just made a *joke* about a sixty-five-year-old man who suggests to a twenty-five-year-old woman that she fuck him during a coffee that was supposed to be about professional mentorship.

Once, when I was running down a sidewalk to hail a taxi in the pouring rain, an older, expensively dressed white guy had cut me off and jumped in; as he'd closed the door and just before it drove off, he looked at me through the window of the cab, put two fingers to his mouth and waggled his tongue, the gesture meant to suggest cunnilingus, grinning meanly at me as he sped off. I'd just stood there, and then spent the next ten minutes—or maybe it was ten years—imagining all the better ways I could have responded, wishing that I'd given him the finger, or better yet, laughed at him. I thought of that anonymous man frequently during the fall of 2017. Bizarrely, the most gleefully punitive thoughts I entertained were toward him; I actively imagined him having been professionally humiliated and disgraced.

I thought about him again at a party at which a former colleague, *Slate*'s book critic Laura Miller, speaking of #metoo, recalled to me how badly men had reacted to the 1991 film *Thelma & Louise*, a gorgeous, flawed paean to women's fury. She remembered them being particularly upset by the scene in which the two heroines-turned-renegades blow up the oil tanker of a truck driver who'd waggled his tongue at them just as my dapper nemesis had at me. The scene was a perfect illustration of the fluid combustibility of women's rage, in the context of the film and the #metoo moment: about how women's fury at having experienced violent rape became murderous but also capacious, spilling over to crap husbands, lecherous truck drivers, all the men who'd ever treated them as objects. I'd been a teenager when I'd seen the film in theaters, but Laura had been an adult, and she recalled to me the scene of their blowing up the truck as one of the most exhilarating and cathartic moments she'd experienced in a movie theater, and how utterly terrified the men she'd known had been by it.

"But my feeling," she told me, smiling and shrugging, "was just, 'hey, don't go like this'"—and here she imitated the tongue-waggling—"to women, and you won't have to worry about us blowing up your oil tanker. It's really simple!"

At one of my early and formative workplaces, there had been a textbook harasser: a high-on-the-food-chain, late-night direct-messager who propositioned and sometimes slept with female subordinates, who could be vindictive if turned down, and who'd undertake elaborate, misogynistic pranks, including sending provocative emails under another staffer's name. One of the preyed-upon women was older than I: talented, glamorous, and definitely not game. She recalled to me in 2017 how she had initially believed that she could ride it out, but instead had been undone by her bewilderment and humiliation at having being played for a fool, for a *girl*. She'd quit after about a year at the company.

I remembered having watched her treatment, appalled, almost disbelieving that something this outrageous could happen. Yet I also remembered not wanting to get too close to her, as if her status as quarry might be catching. I remembered hearing company honchos say that they were well aware that they had a "walking lawsuit" in our midst. Even then, it struck me that the concern was for the potential tarring of the institution, not for the women who were suffering within it.

That harasser didn't sexually pursue me, but he did endeavor to undermine me. When I began dating a slightly older colleague, my direct supervisor (a married man on whom I had a fierce and never-requited crush, in part because it was safe; he had been a model mentor) pulled me aside to let me know that other people at the office—i.e., the Harasser—had been spreading rumors about how my work ideas were being fed to me by my boyfriend, trying to intimate that I was attempting to sleep my way to the top.

Just a few years ago, I was at another job. A new boss had been installed and wanted to hire the Harasser from my old workplace; I told him I would not work in the same office as that man. I was on maternity leave; he promised that the hire was only temporary, that the Harasser would be gone by the time I returned. And he was. But soon after I got back, the office's youngest women began recounting to me that in the few months the

Harasser had been in place, he'd creeped them out and sent them off-color, middle-of-the-night DMs. I had made a stand on my own behalf—I would not work with that man!—and yet had failed to consider or protect my less powerful associates.

So, no, I had never been serially sexually harassed. But the stink got on me anyway. I was implicated. We all are, our professional contributions weighed on scales of fuckability and willingness to go along, to be good sports, to not be humorless scolds or office gorgons; our achievements chalked up to male affiliation—the boyfriend who supposedly supplies you with ideas or the manager who was presumed to have taken you under his wing because he wanted to get inside your pants. We can rebuff the harasser; we can elect not to fuck the boss; we can be lucky enough to escape being targeted or directly punished. But in a world where men hold inordinate power, we were still in bed with the guy.

When I wrote about my own experiences, I struggled internally about whether to name the Harasser at my former job. I decided not to, largely because I understood something about how things had turned out. In a rare outcome, I—along with some of the women he pestered—had, in that moment, more power than he did. As Caitlin Flanagan would put it, in a piece that expressed anxiety about the perceived excesses and risks of #metoo, the women who were naming names were "temporarily powerful." She was right, we were. He was, as far as I knew, not in charge of any young women. And so I decided, in consultation with former colleagues, not to identify him.

But here was a crucial reason that he'd behaved so brazenly and badly for so long: He did not consider that the women he had tortured, much less the young woman who'd been mutely and nervously watching his performance and trying to steer clear of him, might one day have greater power than he did, however temporary it might be. He hadn't considered this because in a basic way, he had not thought of us as his equals.

That made me angry too.

COOL GIRLS OF THE SUNKEN PLACE

My own reckoning got me close to one of the most complicated mind-fucks of them all: the recognition of how women, all of us, really, had participated in, were ourselves implicated in, this system.

After Leon Wieseltier lost his post at a new magazine after the exposure of his decades as a harasser, I heard from many friends and former colleagues who were pained about the situation. "He was, really, my champion," one woman told me. "All these things about him are true, but it is simultaneously true that if you were on his good side, you felt special—protected, cared for, like he believed in you and wanted you to succeed." In a profession where far too few women find that kind of support from powerful men, Wieseltier's mentorship had felt like a prize.

But many of even his most conflicted former admirers admitted that the stories about him—reportedly thanking women for wearing short skirts, kissing colleagues against their will, threatening to tell the rest of the company he was fucking a subordinate if she displeased him—had convinced them that sacking Wieseltier was the correct choice. They were sad for him, for his family, but acknowledged to me that he should not be in charge of women. It had left some of them reexamining how they had excused his conduct, worked around it. "I got so much from him intellectually and emotionally, but I wonder if part of it was because I was game," said one woman, "and what's the cost of that?"

Not all women who had played along with their bosses expressed shame or guilt; some spoke of it with pride. "Men have their fraternities and golf games to get ahead. Why shouldn't I have used the advantage of my sexuality to my benefit? God, what else was I supposed to do?" said one woman in her early fifties.

And then there were the many women who said nothing at all, or if they did speak, spoke up on behalf of the men who were being called out, criticized, or accused. In the *New York Times*, the writer Daphne Merkin described how her "feminist friends" of all ages had been whispering about women angry at harassment, "Grow up, this is real life" and "What ever happened to flirting?" Merkin argued that "stripping sex of eros isn't the solution"—again, mistaking the moment as being about objecting to erotic fun, not inequality.

Several of these women seemed to view their critiques of the #metoo movement as transgressive and dangerous; in her dissenting piece, Katie Roiphe claimed to be channeling the terrified whispers of friends afraid that they'd be the victims of violent feminist retribution should they dare to bring nuance to the conversation. Merkin framed the #metoo movement as reliant on a kind of "political correctness" that stifled dissent.

In Merkin's and Roiphe's view, they were the brave outsiders, heretics storming the feminist battlements. They were wrong on a couple of levels, including in their claim the #metoo conversation had been one-dimensional and unnuanced: all of it, including pieces by the most radical feminist critics of harassment, including Shitty Media Men list creator Moira Donegan, had been full of contradiction, self-doubt, ambivalence, anxiety, and worry. #metoo had produced some of the richest and most complex feminist writing I'd ever read. It was also simply a lie that the voices of dissent had been muffled: these women, along with plenty of other #metoo critics (some of whom were *also* #metoo proponents! Because the conversation was varied and self-interrogating!), had been published in major magazines and newspapers, given the same real estate the #metoo reporters and opinion writers had been given.

But more crucially, the ideas that Roiphe and Merkin were presenting as transgressive and edgy objection were anything but. What they were serving up, in the guise of concerned feminist critique, was in fact a giant helping of white patriarchal justification. They were simply giving voice to the same arguments and defenses that had quelled broad objection to a culture of harassment and denigration up until that moment. And in doing so, as women, they were performing a valuable service on behalf of the system in which they had risen, and specifically on behalf of the powerful men whose power they were protecting.

These women could say things that would, and did, sound defensive coming from men: that the anger of the #metoo-ers was hysterical and vicious, that men's incursions on women's bodies were natural and normal; they could be the women who assured men that they *liked* being treated as men wanted to treat them. They did men's work of confusing groping for eros, and workplace coercion for flirtation.

Women who are willing to defend white patriarchy and its abuses—usually women with proximity to powerful men and the chance to gain from it, and who are therefore themselves often white—have historically found reward from those powerful men, in the form of sexual or romantic attention, marital alliances, as well as jobs and stature, in exchange for their defense of the very power structure from which they benefit.

Part of the defense they've offered has long been the reassurance that whatever *other* women are angry at the powerful men about isn't quite real, or justified, or rational. Part of it is modeling cheerful and affectionate allegiance to those men, appreciation for their behaviors as natural and even exciting in their unreconstructed adherence to old masculine norms.

Perhaps the most popular iteration of the woman who makes herself more valuable to patriarchy by adhering to its every expectation for femininity, and distancing herself from other kinds of women who challenge it, is the figure of the "cool girl." The Cool Girl is a type of woman, imagined nearly uniformly as young and white, who raises no querulous objection to—and indeed embraces—masculine norms, conforming to a kind of ideal femininity imagined by men to best suit and support male dominance. The best-known literary description of the Cool Girl is from *Gone Girl*, Gillian Flynn's novel about women's rage turned psychopathic. In it, Flynn's narrator describes how being called a Cool Girl is "the defining compliment" from men, and entails being a "hot, brilliant, funny woman who adores football, poker, dirty jokes, and burping." Crucially, she continues, "Cool Girls never get angry . . . and let their men do whatever they want. Go ahead, shit on me, I don't mind, I'm the Cool Girl."

But where the Cool Girl has been presumed to be in it for personal—often sexual or romantic—affirmation from men, there was another version of this figure who emerged during #metoo: the women, many of them older and professionally powerful themselves, who spoke out in defense of the men who were being accused of assault. In France, a group of women, including the actress Catherine Deneuve, wrote a petition defending men's "right to bother" from the incursions of #metoo and its French sister, #balancetonporc (expose your pig). Deneuve's petition explicitly distanced herself from the kind of woman who would object to sexual harassment: "As women we do not recognize ourselves in this feminism, which beyond denouncing the abuse of power, takes on a hatred of men and sexuality."

Less aggressively antifeminist, but still troubling, was the public performance of support for retired NBC anchor Tom Brokaw after a former NBC reporter, Linda Vester, told reporters that Brokaw had come to her hotel room and tried to kiss her against her will in the 1990s. Vester had corroborated her tale with contemporaneous diary accounts and the word of a friend who said she'd spoken to her on the night of the alleged encounter. Her story was in fact just a small part of a far larger *Washington Post* piece about a male-dominated culture at the news network that had been home to Matt Lauer and Mark Halperin; yet no one was calling for Brokaw to be fired. But the day after the story broke, a letter circulated, signed by sixty-four women, many of them prominent NBC figures including Andrea Mitchell, Mika Brzezinski, and Rachel Maddow, assuring the world that "Tom has treated each of us with fairness and respect. He has given each of us opportunities for advancement and championed our successes throughout our careers."

The letter was mysterious in a couple of ways: the spate of #metoo stories should have put to rest the idea that man's good treatment of some women assures that he has treated all women well. Many of the same men who'd been great mentors to women had also harassed or assaulted women. And while their letter didn't directly defend Brokaw against Vester's claim, it certainly acted as a suppressant to any *more* women who might want to come forward with their own stories about Brokaw to corroborate Vester's: Why risk crossing a man that these powerful, admirable women—*Rachel Maddow?!?*—had taken such pains to stand alongside in solidarity?

But the letter was clarifying in certain ways. It made explicit what had been implicit in much of the internal feminist criticism of #metoo: that some of the accused men's staunchest female defenders were defending in part their own ascension within the system that had permitted the men to be abusive. The appreciation of the man in question hinged on women's experiences of having been personally offered opportunities for advancement by him; they owed him. Never mind that this same power—the chance that he might champion her, and that his ability to offer women at the network opportunities for advancement—was exactly what Vester understood, what she said kept her from barring him from her hotel room, or crossing him earlier in her career by telling people what had happened there or filing a complaint.

My friends and I, including Irin Carmon, who had made the "trust no one" reference to *Get Out*, began to describe female defenders of powerful men as Women of the Sunken Place, a reference via that same film to their inability to resist the powerful pull of white patriarchy. It was just a dumb joke, memed in other contexts on social media, but I thought about it a lot. Lots of people talked about Weinstein and some of the other guys as monsters, but the real horror-movie terror wasn't about individual Freddies or Jasons. It was the revelation of systemic menace: that everyone around you was in on the threat.

Plenty of people, including me, initially understood the divides between some feminists on the usefulness and righteousness of #metoo as breaking along generational lines—between the angry young women and a more sanguine older generation. On one side of this divide, I thought for a while, were women who had come of age before Anita Hill's testimony against Clarence Thomas, who had perhaps been raised to assume they'd encounter harassment and had resolved to tough it out, whose own desires and turn-ons had been shaped by assumptions about power and sex, masculinity and femininity, and were very different from what younger women wanted and assumed them to be. To this contingent, younger women's complaints could sound hand-wringingly excessive: What did those girls expect? Wasn't part of the *thrill* of a heterosexual encounter tied to domination and power differentials?

But here was a sharp irony: as a feminist journalist, I'd for years been interrogated by older women about what was wrong with young women: *Why weren't they angry?* Why didn't they identify with feminism? Why were they complacent? Why didn't they want to go further toward chang-ing the world?

Well, now those young women had gotten angry. And some older women were rearing back in horror at the force of their rage, and at the fact that a lot of that rage involved interrogating the whole system within which their feminist elders had risen. This moment was asking not just men but the pioneering women who'd succeeded alongside them to reckon with what had *not* been changed by feminism, how much gendered inequity older feminists had decided to live with, to participate in.

In other words, what the feminists who'd long yearned for a wave of youthful fury had not expected was that some of that fury might be directed toward them, or at least toward the men who had become their friends, lovers, husbands, and colleagues; that a fresh generation of enraged activ-ists would be looking straight at them, their feminist foremothers—the generation from which younger women had run for decades, imagining them to have been wicked old man-hating hysterics—and pretty much ac-cusing them of not having been angry *enough*.

But the generational explanation for division over harassment wasn't quite right: for one thing, there were plenty of older women cheering the movement on with joy and satisfaction, and plenty of young women who were wary and put off by its intensity. Polling would confirm that there w*asn't* much of a difference of opinion on #metoo dependent on age.

What was true was that the skeptical intrafeminist voices that had been in a position to get blared by cable TV networks and in newspapers and magazines, the women who were prominent enough to serve as use-ful critics of the movement, were women who had achieved a certain notoriety, accrued a degree of power themselves, had benefitted from the system they were now prepared to defend against #metoo's wrathful censure. That system had been run by the men whose honor they were now upholding; their defenses were inherently defenses of the institu-tions in which they themselves had flourished. And some number of those women were older, simply because by definition the most success-ful had been at it longer.

And to be fair, for many of those women, women who'd spent years breaking ground in their industry, there'd been plenty of evidence that there were certain behaviors, certain realities of male-dominated culture and institutions, about which they simply had not ever been *allowed* to be angry.

I'd felt that, as a young woman, wide-eyed at the realization that this kind of thing—coercion, harassment, assault—happened to lots of people, regularly, and that no one else around me in the adult world seemed to treat it like it was worth objecting to, making a big deal about. In the *New York Times*, film critic Manohla Dargis had written about how, since reading about the women who claimed that Harvey Weinstein had raped them, she'd been thinking about her own experiences, including a time that a film director had lurched at her during an interview and she'd simply kept talking, calmly. "In the moment . . . he was just another man trying to wield power over a woman. It wasn't traumatic—it was *ordinary*." Dargis continued, observing that it is "the perverse, insistent, matter-of-factness of male sexual predation and assault—of men's power over women" and "this banality of abuse" that she understood, now "haunts the movie industry," the revelation of which had given way to her realization that now was the "time for rage."[24]

Irin Carmon, who reported two *Washington Post* pieces about Charlie Rose's harassment of more than thirty young female employees, said that she had been thinking a lot about how when she'd arrived at Harvard as a young feminist undergraduate, she had been aghast at the elite all-male final clubs there. She had refused to attend events at the clubs for her first two years of college. But with time, after years of watching those around her behave as though the existence and exclusions of the clubs were normal, *ordinary*, just part of college life, she had surmised that she was the crazy one and acquiesced to their presence, eventually giving in and going to parties there.

When, in the years after her graduation, students began protesting the clubs in earnest, leading Harvard's then president, Drew Faust, to announce a plan to impose penalties on those who joined them in 2017, Irin's reaction had been to think, "Wow, I didn't know I'd been allowed to be angry about that."

Irin's perplexity, as a teenager, about why more women weren't angry about things that it seemed they had every right and reason to be angry about, is discernible in a question she asked as a freshman journalist at the *Harvard Crimson*, while interviewing visiting speaker Andrea Dworkin three years before Dworkin's death.

"How do you save people who don't think very much is wrong?" Irin had inquired of Dworkin.

Dworkin's response had been prophetic. "That's where first-person testimony of women has been so important," she'd said. "Because the mainstream will say 'Oh, that doesn't happen,' and then a group of women will say, 'Well, it happened to me.'"[25]

Yeah. Me too.

That is what the movement had done. It had offered women the chance to hear from others that it had happened to them too, and that they too were angry, and that they too could say it aloud.

Kristen Meinzer, the radio producer who'd leveled allegations at WNYC's John Hockenberry, said in a conversation conducted by the *Cut*, that she felt "fortunate" for the women who'd first broken their silence on Weinstein, who'd helped create a world "where we're allowed to be angry finally." She went on, "I feel that for the longest time, we weren't allowed to be furious. And my god, shouldn't we *all* be enraged? And I don't just mean the women in this room. But shouldn't everybody be?"

Yes, everyone should be. But it wasn't that simple. It had mattered that the women whose experiences had finally stirred a nation to feminist fury, the women who had given other women—white women—*permission* to finally recognize and express their anger had themselves been wealthy, white, famous, beautiful actresses who'd first gone on the record against Weinstein. It mattered, structurally, that they had had the social, professional, and economic ability to risk crossing their powerful tormentor; that they had had access to the media and platforms and that their power—derived from a combination of their beauty, fame, and in most cases, whiteness—ensured that they had a hold on public sympathy.

The fact that *they* of all people had figured out that they were allowed to be angry and had voiced that anger had been critical in helping other women recognize their own fury. For years, women—and again, especially white women, *especially* economically privileged white women—had been assured that there was no reason for them to be legitimately furious about anything having to do with gender inequity: not about social clubs, not about sexual harassment, not about lack of representation in politics.

But as with Hillary Clinton's defeat at the hands of Donald Trump, there was something about the recognition that even these powerful women—women who had "won" at white patriarchy—still sustained harm, that laid bare the truth of it. If *they* had been discriminated against, had been assaulted, had lost jobs because of the bad behavior of men more powerful than they, if *they* had something to be pissed about, then perhaps other women—toiling in cubicles and restaurants and on factory floors, working multiple jobs without equal pay or a humane minimum wage or paid leave or affordable health care—weren't in fact delusional in their suspicions that they had something to be mad about too.

These sleek, beautiful movie stars and the powerful establishment presidential candidate had given ordinary women the permission to explode with the rage they'd been pressured to keep inside for so long. From some angles, the original Harvey accusers were benevolent emissaries, sent to set loose the rage of the masses.

Except, of course, the fact that it took these privileged white women's stories to get anyone to take sexual power abuse seriously also made them emblematic of the stark, maddening inequalities in place when it came to which kinds of women's stories were of interest, and which kinds of women were readily believed.

"You're a farmworker? A lady who cleans offices? You're a prostitute or an immigrant? You're not going to tell your story," said one Democratic lawmaker to me in exasperation in the fall of 2017. Lin Farley, the woman who'd coined the term "sexual harassment" to begin with, had agreed. "If it's Angelina Jolie, it makes headlines," she told the *Washington Post*. "If it's a woman on the assembly line at Grayson Heat Control, she doesn't make headlines and it goes unnoticed and unseen."[26]

These omissions were particularly galling given that it had been black women's willingness to get mad and press for change that had created sexual harassment law to begin with, starting with the cases brought by Mechelle Vinson and Paulette Barnes and Diane Williams. These women had been first to engage a legal fight in part because they had applied the logic of race-based discrimination law to sex discrimination. "Racism may well provide the clarity to see that sexual harassment is neither a flattering gesture nor a misguided social overture but an act of intentional discrimination that is insulting, threatening, and debilitating," Kimberlé Crenshaw has written.[27]

It had been Anita Hill who had made the term sexual harassment a familiar one, and other black women—Angela Wright, Rose Jourdain, Sukari Hardnett—who had been willing to corroborate her story, not that the Senate Judiciary Committee ever asked. It had been Tarana Burke, a lifelong advocate for the rights and health of women of color, who had first coined the term "me too" *precisely because* she wanted to let women, "particularly young women of color, know that they are not alone."[28]

And yet, the earliest iterations of the contemporary #metoo wave were about exposing abusers of predominantly white women, men in white-dominated industries—movies, television, art, restaurants, politics—while too little attention was paid to factory workers, tipped employees, women in the service industries, and low-wage employees, among the most economically precarious, therefore the most vulnerable to harassment, and also far more likely to be nonwhite.

CHAPTER FOUR

SYMPATHY FOR THE DEVILS

It was Woody Allen who first called it "a witch hunt," publicly at least, in a particularly ill-thought-out interview given ten days after the Weinstein allegations came to light. Professing his sadness for the women who'd accused Weinstein, the producer of several of his films, Allen had warned, "You also don't want it to lead to a witch-hunt atmosphere, a Salem atmosphere, where every guy in an office who winks at a woman is suddenly having to call a lawyer to defend himself."

The analogy was inane for several reasons, primarily that the atmosphere in Salem, Massachusetts, between 1692 and 1693, during which twenty people, fourteen of them women, were executed and four others died in prison after having been accused of witchcraft, was probably not at all like the atmosphere in the office where the guy winked at a girl that one time and then had to call his lawyer.

But even putting aside these niggling details, the many, many critics who would follow Allen's lead by describing the #metoo movement as a "witch hunt"—and this august group included the actor Liam Neeson, the Austrian film director Michael Haneke, one of Bill Cosby's defense attorneys in his trial for raping women, and Missouri Governor Eric Greitens, himself under investigation for allegedly having tied up, assaulted, and then threatened to blackmail a woman in his basement, which led to his resignation in 2018—failed to grok some of the key differences between witch trials and stories of sexual assault.[29]

Witch hunts entailed agents of the state prosecuting and trying civilian women and some men for—and this part is important—*a crime that was not real.* Those same powerful agents of the state, magistrates and governors, would then sentence those civilians, often to long-term imprisonment or death, based on fantasized evidence of meetings with the devil in the dark woods.

The movement spurred by #metoo, by contrast, involved civilian women, and some men, telling reporters the stories of how men more powerful than they had discriminated against them, assaulted them, coerced them, touched them, and damaged their careers. In the cases in which those accused faced repercussion, the sentence—often a firing or a forced resignation—was decided not by the state, or by the accusers themselves, but by individual employers and institutions, many looking to cover their own asses and obscure their own complicity. As of this writing, none of the men accused, even of violent rape, had yet been summarily executed or imprisoned; only Weinstein had been indicted, though it remained unclear whether he would ever go to jail. None had ever been asked to return the hefty salaries or advances they'd earned while they'd been allegedly groping their colleagues; some were still being paid out the terms of their thick contracts, and others had already returned to work.

It was not a witch hunt.

But it was an instance in which some men had lost their jobs or sustained reputational damage, and apparently that felt to many men as if they were being massacred. Their hyperbolic language offered a hint of how instinctively men *understood* the potentially revolutionary power of women's anger, and provided clues about what had prompted them to work to suppress it via so many strategies for so many years. Because apparently, when women raised their voices with rage—or even critique—of these men's behavior, these men got *terrified.*

"I was ambushed and then perp walked," Tom Brokaw had written in his letter to colleagues after Linda Vester had told a story about him trying to kiss her against her will, "taken to the guillotine and stripped of any honor and achievement I had earned in more than a half century of journalism and citizenship." (There had been no guillotine or perp walk or stripping of honor, at least not until this stupid letter.)

MSNBC commentator Mike Barnicle had mourned publicly for the injury done to his friend and former colleague Mark Halperin: "He deserves to have what he did deplored," Barnicle declared on television. "But does he deserve to die? How many times can you kill a guy?" (Halperin was not dead.)

When people were mean to Matt Damon on the internet for being patronizing and reductive about what he perceived as #metoo's shortcomings, the British director Terry Gilliam described the actor as having been "beaten to death" (he was fine) in the same interview in which Gilliam shrugged off the experiences of the women who'd been raped by Weinstein by suggesting that they'd known what they were getting into.

The view of a man's lost job as a death had become so much a part of our mind-set, that while reading an ordinary news report the day after the resignation of Eric Schneiderman from the post of New York attorney general after accusations that he'd beaten and demeaned multiple girlfriends, I noticed that the *New York Times* casually referred to his "abrupt demise."[30] (He was still alive.)

Of Charlie Rose, a wholly mediocre journalist who'd been elevated in part by an industry built on the sidelining of women, the business magnate Barry Diller told Maureen Dowd, "You get accused, you're obliterated. Charlie Rose ceases to exist." Rose had certainly not ceased to exist. In fact, just days before Dowd's interview with Diller had run, Rose had butt-tweeted the letter "H" and received a torrent of supportive replies from men and women, asking how he was holding up, telling him that they missed him, that they wanted him back, that they were worried for him. Rose would soon be profiled by the *Hollywood Reporter*, the headline describing him as "brilliant," "broken," and "lonely."[31]

The fact that lots of people could extend such sympathy for Rose, a man who'd been reported to have trapped young assistants at his fancy waterside mansion and forced himself on them, to have exposed himself to multiple female employees, to have called subordinates in the middle of the night to tell them his fantasies about them—yet extend none of the same sympathy toward the women he'd chased out of his business—affirmed a bunch of things. First, that the world is stacked in favor of men, yes, in a way that is so widely understood as to be boring, invisible, just life.

But more deeply, it was a reminder of how easily we can see in men—even in the bad ones—talent. Brilliance. Complexity. Humanity. We manage to look past their flaws and sexual violations to what value they bring to the world. It is the direct opposite, in many ways, of how we view women, whose successes can still be blithely attributed to the fact that the boss wanted to fuck them.

During the spring of 2018, there was a spate of stories about disgraced men who were working to stage comebacks: a rumor floated that Rose would host a show on which he interviewed other accused men. There were tentative "comeback" feelers put out by *Today* host Matt Lauer, and chef Mario Batali. One of Batali's accusers described reading a piece on what the chef would do next. " 'He gets to choose: Will he go back into business? Will he go to Rwanda? Or does he just want to retire in Italy? Those are his choices,' " she said through gritted teeth. Another woman, a Weinstein accuser, added, "Most of us never got a first chance to have the careers we dreamed of."[32]

And still more: when white men have had such a disproportionate share of public, political, and social power, when they have been allowed and encouraged to be the leaders, the celebrities, the bosses, the voices that explain the news to us and make our movies and tell our stories, they have a disproportionate grip on our sympathies, imagination, and affection. Other kinds of people, people we don't hear and see as often, who are not sent to us to comfort and explain and reassure and lead, people with less access to the kind of fame that breeds familiarity and a sense of humanity, are simply not valued, or even acknowledged, in the same way.

We just don't consider, don't even see, the loss of all the women who—driven out, banished, self-exiled, or marginalized—might have been *more* talented or brilliant or comforting to us, on our airwaves or in our governing bodies, but whom we have never even gotten the chance to know.

The writer Rebecca Solnit has noted that this dynamic was also in play when the *New York Times* called Robert Lewis Dear, who shot and killed three people in a Colorado Springs Planned Parenthood facility in 2015, "a gentle loner," what led the Associated Press to describe a 2018 Maryland school shooter as a "lovesick teen," and the *New York Times* Twitter account to describe an Austin, Texas, mail bomber who'd set out to kill and terrorize black people a "quiet, 'nerdy' young man who came from 'a tight-knit, godly family.'" It's what led police to buy a hamburger for Dylann Roof—who'd just killed nine people in their church—because he felt hungry.

It's not that the compassion for these criminals is wrong; it is morally correct. But it is not applied to those who are not white men, who are routinely and easily described in the press as "terrorists" if they are Muslims, and who, if they are black, are lucky to be arrested alive.

It's a disproportionate dynamic that the philosophy professor Kate Manne has written about extensively, calling it "himpathy," connecting this impulse to the way in which we've been directed to feel for the white working-class male voters so fetishized by a political media since 2016. "We need to look . . . not just at the domineering 'successful' misogynists," Manne said in an interview at *Slate*, "but [at] this disappointed, aggrieved, down-on-his-luck, ripe-for-empathy kind of proverbial working-class white guy . . . who gets a heck of a free pass for all sorts of terrible behavior because he's disappointed and feels in various ways like he's been shortchanged."[33]

In other words, the dynamics of understanding white male aggrievement as paramount to our national interests, and as a justification for racism and misogyny—via, say, the election of a man who promises to ban Muslims, deport Mexicans, and who brags of grabbing women against their will—are related to the dynamics that lead us to reflexively worry about the men who drove women out of careers by waving their penises at them till they fled, and by our comparative inability to imagine, let alone prioritize, the humanity of Muslims, Mexicans, or women.

The ability to narratively flip the dynamics of aggression and abuse—to view the less powerful as a menace to the aggressors—has been key to how white patriarchal structures have persisted. It's how police can

systematically kill black people, but when black people protest those killings with Black Lives Matter marches, those protesters can be called "terrorists" on the news, or a "hate group," by the Republican pundit Meghan
McCain. It's why, when Baltimore resident Freddie Gray was hauled into a
van by police in Baltimore in 2015 and taken on a rough ride that resulted
in his death, multiple news reports asserted that the "violence started"
when protesters threw rocks in protest of his killing, and not when he was
murdered.

The violence done by the more powerful entity—the police and the
state—to the less powerful entity is often so normalized, so banal, so expected as to not even be discernible, not even visible. But angry resistance
to that violence, coming from the less powerful and directed at the more
powerful, is automatically understood as disruptive, dangerous, electric.
The upset of power dynamics creates chaos.

Women's anger, publicly and loudly expressed, is all of that: unnatural,
chaotic, upsetting to how power is supposed to work. Women's determination to voice that fury toward men in 2017 and 2018 had led those men to
feel some fraction of the anxiety that nonwhite non-men feel daily.

That these men experience any anxiety or discomfort is intolerable
enough that in 2018, a Canadian clinical psychologist named Jordan Peterson became a mega-bestselling author of a kind of men's manifesto, called
12 Rules for Life: An Antidote to Chaos. "Order is where the people around
you act according to well-understood social norms. . . . Chaos, by contrast,
is where—or when—something unexpected happens." And just in case it
wasn't clear, Peterson sexes both sides of the paradigm; according to Taoist symbolism, he claims, "Order is the white, masculine serpent; Chaos,
its black, feminine counterpart." Chaos is the thing that Peterson and his
devout readers were searching for an antidote to in their struggle to reim-
pose . . . order.

These structural assumptions are why calls for civility almost always
redound positively to the oppressors, because incivility against the oppressed is not only so normalized, it is also so comforting that it can
barely be detected as oppression; while even the most trivial challenge
from the less powerful sets off alarms. Donald Trump can call women

pigs and cows and dogs and call Mexicans rapists and promise to build walls and encourage racist violence and still be elected president. But a female comedian makes a joke about the dissembling of a White House press secretary and gets instantly reprimanded for having "grossly insulted" her by Andrea Mitchell, who also signed the NBC letter in support of Tom Brokaw.

During the period in which newspapers were initially reporting on how asylum-seeking immigrants were having their young children ripped from them, presidential daughter and advisor Ivanka Trump tweeted a photograph of herself beatifically embracing her small son. When Samantha Bee performed a fierce excoriation of Trump's incivility in both supporting her father's administration, and posting such a cruel celebration of her own intact family, she called her a "feckless cunt." It was this epithet, one that Donald Trump had himself used as an insult against women on multiple past occasions, that sent the media into a spiral of shocked alarm and prompted Trump himself to recommend, via Twitter, that Bee's network, TBS, fire her. But neither Trump's past use of the word to demean women, nor his possible violation of the First Amendment, provoked as much horror as the feminist comedian's deployment of a slur that she had used before on her show often in reference to herself.

Typically only the incivility of the less powerful toward the more powerful can be widely understood as such, and thus be subject to such intense censure. Which is what made #metoo so fraught and revolutionary. It was a period during which some of the most powerful faced repercussion.

The experience of having patriarchal control compromised felt, perhaps ironically, like a violation, a diminishment, a threat to professional standing—all the things that sexual harassment feels like to those who've experienced it.

Frequently, in those months, I was asked about how to address men's confusion and again, their discomfort: How were they supposed to flirt? What if their respectful and professional gestures of affiliation had been misunderstood? Mothers told me of sons worried about being misinterpreted, that expression of their affections might be heard as coercion, their words or intentions read incorrectly, that they would face unjust consequences that would damage their prospects.

The amazing thing was the lack of acknowledgment that these anxieties are the normal state for just about everyone who is not a white man: that black mothers reasonably worry every day that a toy or a phone or a pack of Skittles might be seen as a gun, that their children's very presence—sleeping in a dorm room, sitting at a Starbucks, barbecuing by a river, selling lemonade on the street—might be understood as a threat, and that the repercussions might extend far beyond a dismissal from a high-paying job or expulsion from a high-profile university, and instead might result in arrest, imprisonment, or execution at the hands of police or a concerned neighbor. Women enter young adulthood constantly aware that their inebriation might be taken for consent, or their consent for sluttiness, or that an understanding of them as having been either drunk or slutty might one day undercut any claim they might make about having been violently aggressed upon. Women enter the workforce understanding from the start the need to work around and accommodate the leering advances and bad jokes of their colleagues, aware that the wrong response might change the course of their professional lives.

We had been told that our failures to extend sympathy to the white working class—their well-being diminished by unemployment and drug addictions—had cost us an election; now we were being told that a failure to feel for the men whose lives were being ruined by harassment charges would provoke an angry antifeminist backlash. But with these calls came no acknowledgment of sympathies that we have *never* before been asked to extend: to black men who have *always* lived with higher rates of unemployment and who have faced systemically higher prison sentences and social disapprobation for their drug use; to the women whose careers and lives had been ruined by ubiquitous and often violent harassment. Now the call was to consider the underlying pain of those facing repercussions.

Rose McGowan, one of Weinstein's earliest and most vociferous accusers, recalled being asked "in a soft NPR voice, 'What if what you're saying makes men uncomfortable?' Good. I've been uncomfortable my whole life. Welcome to our world of discomfort."[34]

Suddenly, men were living with the fear of consequences, and it turned out that it was not fun. And they very badly wanted it to stop. One of the lessons many men would take from #metoo was not about the threat they had posed to women, but about the threat that women pose to them.

BACKLASH

Everyone, including me, was waiting for the backlash from practically the first moment that #metoo kicked off. And then, with every dissenting piece, came the tremor of a question: Was this it? The backlash?

Enough of us knew enough about our history to know that it was on its way. Any minute, coming to swallow us up and feed us to Phyllis Schlafly's ghost for dinner before we knew what hit us. And there *was* plenty of backlash. Lots of it contained in predictions about the instability of the moment, the self-inflicting dangers of mass fury and chaotic social upheaval. "This kind of mania will always at some point exhaust itself," wrote the conservative columnist Andrew Sullivan calmly, even as he himself was being driven to irritated paroxysm by the #metoo crusade.

"You may . . . have noticed that we're starting to lose the crowd," wrote Caitlin Flanagan, simultaneously a #metoo supporter and one of its sharper critics. "This gets called 'backlash,' which makes it seem [to be] a product of sexism, but to a significant extent it's also a product of the rage itself, and the irrational, score-settling things it can make people do." Flanagan was very worried about the intensity of women's rage. "How many women have alienated the very people they need to make this movement successful because they are so blinded by rage that they can only speak in radical and alienating terms?"[35]

Laurie Penny wrote, "This was always how the counternarrative was going to unfold: It was always going to become a meltdown about castrating feminist hellcats whipping up their followers into a Cybelian frenzy . . . We know what happens when women get out of control, don't we?"[36]

Yes. That's when we change the world.

It seemed that a good deal of the pushback to the frenzy of #metoo was either blind to—or perhaps all too aware of—the fact that the destabilizing disorder of the period was a sign that it was at least potentially a *part* of an actual revolution.

Chaos was what former senator Barbara Mikulski had remembered in 1991 when the women of the House had banged on the door and insisted that Senate leader George Mitchell talk to them about letting Anita Hill testify against Clarence Thomas. "There was a sense that the whole process, if not spinning out of control, was getting very chaotic," Mikulski remembered of that day,[37] in an oral history in which Hill recalled that Senator Mitchell's approach had been "'Let's keep things under control, under his control.'" The women's insistence they get to talk, that they got to insist that Hill get to tell her story, was the moment that George Mitchell lost control.

Yes, things were out of control. That was the point. Because *control* was when no one was able to report the story of Harvey Weinstein raping women; *control* was Donald Trump getting elected president, thanks to voter suppression and the electoral college systems designed to suppress, and thus better control, nonwhite populations. *Control* was the unchallenged reigns of Bill O'Reilly and Roger Ailes and Bill Cosby. *Control* was women being too terrified to defy Eric Schneiderman by telling of how he hit them; *control* was ensuring that no one cared about the abuses sustained by Ford factory employees or flight attendants; *control* was all male presidents and vice presidents; *control* was only two black women senators and no black women governors in the history of the country; *control* was marital rape being legal to the seventies; *control* was slavery and locking women in unsafe shirtwaist factories. *Control* was Jordan Peterson's Taoist white serpent, thrust at us against our will.

And women, ordinary women, understood this. The pollster Tresa Undem, carefully tracking Americans' attitudes about gender, told me in 2017 that her polling had shown a huge majority of voters—86 percent—who connected the notions of harassment and assault to a "desire for power and control over women." Undem told me that she'd also seen a very sudden and striking shift after years of polling on reproductive rights:

for the first time, she had begun to hear voters use the words "control" and "controlling women" when discussing efforts to restrict women's access to abortion and to contraception.

To some extent, women who wanted liberty and equality knew they had to create some chaos. And yes, it was moving with such velocity and intensity that it was terrifying in its unpredictability. But it had to be radical and wrathful and energetic to get people to pay attention and to actually alter the power dynamics. Rules had to be changed, as they had been in the Second Wave, when marriages entered into on unequal terms were no longer acceptable and the fact that some of them ended was a sudden shock to the system and some men felt they had been unfairly victimized by swiftly changing expectations. Now butt-groping and salacious come-ons and harassment were no longer going to be acceptable and some men were going to lose their jobs and some of them would no doubt feel that they had been unfairly victimized.

But this was what it meant to say that we wanted the world to be different: not in some hazy future after all the old not-different men had retired from their perches and died peacefully in their sleep. We wanted it to be different now, and that meant dethroning some of them early. Things had to get out of control.

"The law cannot do it for us," Shirley Chisholm had said. "We must do it for ourselves. Women in this country must become revolutionaries."

Women knew they'd be punished. In every conversation was the threat: men won't mentor you anymore; they won't have lunches with you; they won't hire you. But these threats—while surely correct—didn't seem to stop the steady march of #metoo.

In part that was because many of us understood that part of the problem here was that the men who weren't going to invite women to lunches anymore were the same men who would have harassed us over them anyway. The idea that we could have protected ourselves from these men's subjugation of women by being nice to them was *also* part of the control they tried to exert over us.

We also understood that the backlash to female empowerment wasn't on its way; it was already here. It was Donald Trump. "The backlash is here," said Tarana Burke at a conference in 2018. "We have millions of women pouring their hearts out, and you think it's about taking down individual powerful men? This is about the system that held them up."[38]

That system was working away, even as men were balking at being taken to the guillotine, to further disempower women, socially, professionally, politically, and economically. As Susan Faludi observed in the *New York Times*, Trump had "signed into law a tax bill that throws a bomb at women . . . [it] systematically guts benefits that support women who need support the most: It means an end to personal and dependent exemptions (a disaster for minimum-wage workers, nearly two-thirds of whom are women). An expiration date for childcare tax credits and a denial of such credits for immigrant children without Social Security cards. An end to the Affordable Care Act's individual mandate. And, barely avoided, thanks to Democrats' objections: an enshrinement of 'fetal personhood' in the form of college savings accounts for unborn children, a sly grenade lobbed at legal abortion."[39]

The agencies that were supposed to protect women from harassment and discrimination were being headed by people who didn't believe harassment and discrimination existed. The administration had asked to stop getting reports on pay inequality, and had rolled back protections that prevented car dealerships from discriminating against minority buyers; a domestic gag rule had been proposed, withholding federal funds from Title X health clinics that provided pregnant patients referrals to abortion providers; Donald Trump was separating immigrant children from their families and housing them in warehouses; and Jeff Sessions was declaring that domestic abuse no longer qualified women for asylum in the United States. Trump was promising to fill the retiring justice Anthony Kennedy's Supreme Court seat with a judge likely to overturn Roe vs. Wade. The highest court in the land, shaped by Donald Trump, was likely to outlaw abortion, curtail contraceptive access, roll back affirmative action, further erode voting and collective bargaining rights, and strengthen anti-immigration policy.

Being scared of the coming backlash was nothing compared to the one we were in the midst of, which was itself the reaction to the disorder represented by a black president and a would-be female president, to the increased educational and professional and entertainment space taken up by women and people of color. This was the backlash to *Ghostbusters* and *Mad Max* and lady Jedis and Beyoncé. Backlash was Elliot Rodger, who had killed six people in 2014 because women had refused to have sex with him, and become a patron saint to other so-called incels (involuntarily celibate men), including Alek Minassian, who in 2018 drove a car onto a Toronto sidewalk and killed ten people.

So it wasn't as if threats that our bosses were going to stop having lunch with us were quite enough, at this juncture, to slow down the anger of women. Many of them were less anxious about going too far than about not going far enough.

"What bothers me is that this moment, as good as it is, prompts the question: What are women getting out of it?" Kristen Gwynne, a woman who had worked for multiple harassers, told me. "I lost time. It affected my self-esteem and my ability to produce work. So even if the people who did target me were punished, I still feel like I deserve some sort of compensation. I don't want them to release a public apology—I want them to send me a check. I wish we could storm the offices of these men, kick them out, and change the locks. We should demand something different of men that's not just them going to rehab. Put women in power."

That was what many women wanted: a remaking of the structure, of the systems and the institutions. And given what was happening on election nights in 2017 and 2018, it wasn't such an outlandish request. Because all around us, in special elections and in primaries, women were running for office. And winning. Perhaps #metoo wasn't going to be about retribution, rather it might be about *replacement*.

On election night in the fall of 2017, Virginia seated a record number of women in its general assembly, including its first Asian-American woman, its first two Latina women, and its first transgender woman, Danica Roem, who had run against the Virginia delegate who had written the state's transphobic bathroom bill. In New Jersey, Ashley Bennett had run against a Republican city county freeholder because he'd openly mocked women who'd attended the women's march—via a meme asking whether the protest would end in time for them to cook him dinner—and beaten him.

Watching the returns, I got a text from an old friend, a woman who'd worked on the Clinton campaign and who'd been there next to me, shell-shocked, on that night that Clinton had lost. She told me she'd been crying while watching the Virginia results come in.

"Maybe *we're* the backlash," she wrote.

PART IV
THE FURIES

After the election, first I felt totally numb, just deflated. But soon I felt angry. And I was out on the street in New York when the election happened and I went to meet a friend for lunch, and I was walking down the street and there were just all these big white guys in suits in New York City and I was just mad at every single one of them. I have no idea what their political affiliations were, who they voted for, but I just felt betrayed by every single one of those people. And I remember thinking, *I'm in New York City, I'm in this place that is supposed to be so liberal and I know that some of you voted for this guy* and that made me so, so mad. Anyway, I walked down the street stiff-shouldered and I didn't move out of the way for any of those people, and that meant that I got knocked in the shoulder a bunch of times because usually you're playing that kind of dodging game down the street and I was just like, *No, today I am not moving for you because I am pissed and I own this street as much as you do, so I'm gonna walk down it with even more of a straight back and a straight line than I have before.* I've sort of kept that up, I have to say. Because it feels pretty good when you realize how much you dodge out of other people's way when you walk down the street and it's a little victory to get someone else to move for you.

—Cortney Tunis

CHAPTER ONE

THE EXHILARATION OF ACTIVISM

I'm turning my anger into action.
I'm trying to convert my anger into inspiration.
I've taken my anger and channeled it into activism.
My anger has hardened into determination.

Throughout conversations about this book, with women candidates and activists and feminists and #metoo accusers and friends and colleagues and strangers, this was something I heard again and again: the desire to take anger and transform it into something else, something that was *not* anger.

"There's something about feeling sadness, and nurturing sadness, that makes you want to be alone in a quiet room," said Cortney Tunis, one of the administrators for Pantsuit Nation, the formerly private Facebook group of Hillary Clinton supporters that had mushroomed in the days before the election, and later became the springboard for some women to engage in postelection organizing. Tunis was mulling the differences between the anger and the grief that so many of the women in Pantsuit Nation felt after the election. "But there's something about anger that makes people want to—metaphorically—break a window. Really what that means is they are showing up at a town hall and telling their story about how the immigration ban is bullshit."

In other words, anger should not *need* to be transformed in order to count as worthy; anger on its own can have progressive value. As Amanda Litman, a young Clinton campaign staffer who after the election launched an organization called Run for Something, which recruits and supports millennials running for office, has written, "Instead of resisting [anger] or avoiding it, let your fury push you to action. Embrace your anger and put it to work."[1]

I often found that by the time women were talking, or acting, out of political or feminist rage, the anger itself had already been a productive or catalytic force. Their fury was already a tool they used in speaking to me and to one another. It had offered them a lens through which to see and understand the world and its inequities anew; its expression had already been a mode of introduction and connection to other angry women; it had already spurred the making of art or telling of a story or the filing of a lawsuit or an HR complaint; it had already prompted a vote or volunteering for a campaign or attendance at a protest or a run for office or a desire to become civically engaged and educated.

It's the choices to work together, to talk about shared dissatisfactions and frustrations, to begin to organize or strategize or learn more about the forces that have provoked our rage and how to dismantle them, that are the stuff of rebellion. They're the makings of insurgency, of the kinds of political upheavals that can change, and have in the past changed, the nation and its power structures.

The ability to feel the anger and convey it to others is itself the transformative experience for many women. Women's anger spurs creativity and drives innovation in politics and social change, and it always has.

In the nineteenth century, women who previously had been kept largely isolated in their domestic spheres, bound by the gendered responsibilities of wifeliness and motherhood in the agrarian economy of the early Republic, began to come together thanks both to the religious revivals of the time and the industrialization that brought many of them into factories as workers and into schools as students and teachers. Once they gained access to one another, the ability to communicate their anger—over the enslavement of African Americans, over their lack of a franchise, over the dangerous working conditions many of them faced, over the drunken domestic abuse many women suffered at home—quickly produced agitation that would become the abolition, suffrage, labor, and temperance movements.

Sometimes the mere public expression of women's anger was its own innovation. Female suffragists of the nineteenth century, including Maria Stewart and the Grimké sisters, were among the first women to lecture in public spaces to audiences of mixed genders and races. Their speeches themselves provided a radical new model for women's participation in civic and political life. Suffragists' open-air rallies and parades in support of the vote upended expectations for female behavior and decorum.

In the early twentieth century, young suffragist reformers Alice Paul and Lucy Burns studied new modes of resistance abroad with militant British feminists, and returned to the United States prepared with new strategies, including hunger striking, chaining themselves to the White House fence, and burning President Woodrow Wilson's speeches. Suffragist Carrie Chapman Catt took another tactic: supporting Woodrow Wilson's entrance into World War I, enraging her pacifist sisters, but perhaps greasing the wheels for Wilson's signing off on the Nineteenth Amendment in 1920.

Suffragists made pragmatic inroads in other ways as well. The Polish-born Jewish suffragist and abolitionist Ernestine Rose, angry that her inheritance had been forfeited when she refused to marry the man her father had betrothed her to against her will, dedicated herself in part to a legal campaign to reform women's property laws in the United States. She lobbied through the 1850s alongside Stanton and Anthony for a set of reforms called married women's property acts, which would eventually pass in New York and be adopted by other states, and permit wives to retain more rights to inheritances and property than ever before.

The politicized female educators of the late nineteenth and early twentieth centuries, frustrated by the reduced educational opportunities for women and African Americans, would open, run, and teach at many of the land-grant, women's, and historically black colleges that would educate future generations; they pioneered new fields—such as teaching and nursing—and later unionized and strategized alongside male-dominated unions to become politically powerful. The civic education schools started by Septima Clark in the Jim Crow South would become a training ground for many civil rights activists.

Female activists of the civil rights movement not only organized marches and sit-ins, they pamphleted and mimeographed and strategized; their thinking was fundamental to the legal strategies that enshrined racial and gender equality. The civil rights lawyer Pauli Murray's writing on race, gender, and discrimination was so original and crucial that it would be cited both by Supreme Court Justice Thurgood Marshall as the "bible for civil rights lawyers" and by Ruth Bader Ginsburg, who credited Murray as one of the "brave women" whose intellectual efforts had been the basis for the sex discrimination protections Ginsburg was fighting for as a lawyer arguing in front of the Supreme Court.

Anger has driven women to develop a million approaches to changing the world.

It's prompted some to put the sources of their pain and suffering on display: from Mamie Till's determination to show the world her son's battered dead body to the editors of *Ms.* magazine, who in 1973 published a photo of Geraldine Santoro, a Connecticut woman who'd bled to death after an illegal abortion, to Diamond Reynolds, who in 2016 live-streamed the murder of her boyfriend, Philando Castile, by policemen, as her four-year-old daughter watched in terror from the back seat.

Anger has prompted women to make radical art—from novels of sexual liberation, like Erica Jong's *Fear of Flying*, to poetic theater, like Ntozake Shange's *For Colored Girls Who Have Considered Suicide/When the Rainbow Is Enuf*—and to create better medical and sexual education materials, like *Our Bodies, Ourselves*, which taught generations of women around the world about their anatomy, about sexual pleasure, and about their reproductive options. Anger has led academics to recover and reclaim women's share of the academy, creating new fields of women's and gender studies and remaking university curricula.

Women's anger has led to entirely new forms of civil disobedience: In 1965, a University of Chicago student named Heather Booth helped a friend's sister get an illegal abortion. When other women began to call for help, she and a cohort of young feminists began to develop an elaborate system of phone numbers, code words, and houses that would be known as the Jane Collective; they would assist more than eleven thousand women in getting safe abortions between 1969 and 1973.

The 2016 presidential victory of an unqualified and monstrously abusive white patriarch over a qualified female competitor provoked rage in direct response to that loss, rage that quickly prompted political reaction and certain kinds of creative new activism.

Everywhere you turned in 2017 and 2018, new ideas arose, fueled by women's fury, including the TIME'S UP movement and its Legal Defense Fund, established by the women of Hollywood as an attempt to redistribute economic resources to afford women in other industries more stability to come forward with harassment claims.

The media's slow but steady acknowledgment of the role of black women's catalytic, foundational, leading roles in progressive and feminist politics has spurred boosts in attention to organizations like Higher Heights and Jessica Byrd's Three Point Strategies, which aim to center issues of racial justice and transform them into electoral victories for black women running for mayor, for House seats, for the Senate and governors' mansions.

Newly minted activists created new kinds of organizations: Kat Calvin quit her job in Los Angeles and founded Spread the Vote, in which volunteers do the arduous work of helping prospective voters get the materials they need to obtain IDs in states with restrictive voter ID laws; Rita Bosworth, Gabrielle Goldstein, Lala Wu, Candis Mitchell, and Lyzz Schwegler came up with the Sister District Project, which matches energetic volunteers in deep blue America with "sister" races in red districts that need more fund-raising and volunteer help.

In special elections and primary campaigns, newly angry women brought skills they'd learned in the PTA to canvassing and organizing. After an early primary in Georgia, a pharmaceutical research employee and mother of three young children named Jessica Zeigler, frustrated by low turnout of millennial voters, began implementing a plan to reach older high school students and recent graduates who were eligible to vote in the district, but who might live with conservative parents unfriendly to

Democratic door-knockers, by setting up a text-banking system via seniors and recent graduates of all the local high schools. By the time the post-primary run-offs happened, 1,800 additional voters between the ages of eighteen and twenty-three had been registered in her district.

A Missouri copywriter and former lawyer named Michele Hornish, furious and wanting to do something, began a website called Small Deeds Done, which offers weekly small tasks that other angry women can undertake, from writing postcards and calling representatives, to learning about the history of civil rights, labor, and feminist activism. With a partner, Hornish also developed a new fund-raising structure via a website called It Starts Today, through which people can make monthly small donations that get evenly distributed between the whole slate of Missouri's Democratic candidates, circumventing the larger party establishment that tends to divert funds only to districts it deems "winnable."

And in 2018, Liuba Grechen Shirley, who entered politics after the 2016 election to challenge her local Long Island congressman Pete King, furious after he supported Trump's Muslim ban, successfully petitioned the Federal Election Commission to be able to use campaign funds to pay for childcare, a potentially game-changing structural shift for women candidates who happen to be mothers. "I was enraged," she said of her entrance into politics, and her realization, as she was mounting a campaign while trying to juggle and pay for care of two young children, about "why there are so many millionaires in office."

Around the world, women have come up with innovative forms of protest and expression, from the black actresses who protested "Noire n'est pas mon metier" on the red carpet at the 2018 Cannes Film Festival to Frances McDormand, who used her 2018 Oscar acceptance speech to introduce the world to the term "inclusion rider," a clause by which those with power in Hollywood—the actors and directors—might leverage their heft to guarantee racial and gender diversity by demanding it in their contracts. At the spring March for Our Lives, the young, furious activist Emma González dared to make everyone terribly uncomfortable by holding them in silence, without explanation or apology, until the six and a half minutes it had taken for a student to kill seventeen of his former classmates had ticked out.

Hashtag campaigns, die-ins, senators demanding reform to Congress's *own* rules about sexual harassment; these are all strategies and ideas being pushed by women who are upset, who are mad, who are angry about the conditions as they have been.

Meanwhile, angry art of the new era—from Naomi Alderman's best-selling novel *The Power*; to *Dietland*, a television show about a women's magazine . . . and a feminist terrorist group that throws men out of planes; to Hannah Gadsby's cult stage show *Nanette* and the exhibition of Adrian Piper's art at MoMA and the feminist street art of Tatyana Fazlalizadeh—captures the furious female energy of contemporary America.

Some of the ideas are very old, some are brand-new; some will transform the world, others will fail. But the anger is moving women and their thinking on inequality forward, in ways that are both legal and tangible, and also imaginative and ideological. And sometimes the anger is working its magic simply by existing, persisting, unrelenting and unapologetic.

As Catharine MacKinnon herself declared in 2018 about the innovations of the #metoo movement, it "is accomplishing what sexual harassment law to date has not . . . This mass mobilization against sexual abuse . . . is eroding the two biggest barriers to ending sexual harassment in law and in life: the disbelief and trivializing dehumanization of its victims."

In MacKinnon's view, it was the surging movement itself, and the emotions—the rejection, the unwillingness to look away any longer; in short, the anger it had drawn forth—that was shifting what the law had not been able to: the culture, our shared assumptions. "Revulsion against harassing behavior . . . could change workplaces and schools. It could restrain repeat predators as well as the occasional and casual exploiters that the law so far has not . . . this uprising of the formerly disregarded . . . has made untenable the assumption that the one who reports sexual abuse is a lying slut, and that is changing everything already."[2]

LET'S GET ELECTED

And then there have been the women pushing for more power in electoral politics, traveling a path long forged by furious women.

Shirley Chisholm didn't win the Democratic nomination in 1972, but she knew that she was creating a precedent that might bear fruit deep into the future. Writing in 1973, Chisholm averred, "What I hope most is that now there will be others who will feel themselves as capable of running for high political office as any wealthy, good-looking white male."

Chisholm had been the first black woman elected to the House of Representatives. Twenty years after her presidential bid, Carol Moseley Braun would become the first to be elected to the Senate. "I was absolutely offended," Moseley Braun recalled to me in 2017, of how she had felt, in 1991, when Clarence Thomas was nominated to the Supreme Court. "No, that's too light a word. I was appalled. I was apoplectic about it." Moseley Braun, who'd served in the Illinois state legislature and in the U.S. Attorney's office, decided to run for the Senate in 1992.

"It was such a complete repudiation of Thurgood Marshall's legacy," she said. "Marshall had been so important to the liberation of black people, and this was turning the table over on everything the Warren court did. I had had a lifetime of possibilities because of the Warren Court; my husband was not black, and our marriage would have been illegal but for the Warren Court; I had marched with Dr. King. The Clarence Thomas nomination was a repudiation of everything I had fought for or worked for and it would not stand was my attitude."

Moseley Braun was especially livid at the Illinois senator, Democrat Alan Dixon, who was planning to vote to confirm Thomas. She went to meet with him about it. "He was so obtuse about the whole thing, that the conversation lit a fire in my belly. Then came the Hill hearings and then women said, 'Okay. Enough of this.'" The hearings, and the view of the "tired, old white men on this committee," she said, "became the wind under the wings of my candidacy."

Moseley Braun challenged Dixon in a primary and beat him, becoming the first candidate to successfully topple a sitting senator in a primary in more than a decade.[3] One of her campaign slogans was the unapologetically frank, "We don't need another arrogant rich guy in the Senate."[4] It worked. When she won her seat, she not only became the first black woman ever elected to the United States Senate, but only the second African-American senator elected since Reconstruction. In the Senate, Moseley Braun became the first woman to ever sit on the Finance Committee, and she and Dianne Feinstein became the second and third women in history to ever join the Judiciary Committee, that group whose pale homogeneity had prompted their attack on Washington. "There was great anger," Moseley Braun said of the time. "There were people really, really mad and rightly so."

Between 1931, when Hattie Wyatt Caraway of Arkansas had been appointed to fill her husband's seat as senator, and 1992, only six women had ever served in the United States Senate for more than about a year. In 1992, four women were elected to the Senate, tripling the number of women in that chamber; since then, thirty women have been sent to Washington as senators, including six by appointment. Of the roughly 290 women who have ever held a seat in the U.S. House of Representatives, nearly 60 percent of them have been elected since 1992, when twenty-four won seats at the same time; this was the same number of congresswomen as had been elected in the entire previous decade.

In 2018, all previous records were being broken. By the spring, 309 women had announced that they were running for seats in the House of Representatives, a number higher than any other time in American history and nearly twice the number that had run just two years before. More broadly, according to the Black Women in Politics database, forty-seven black women were running for federal seats in total, at least twenty-four of them nonincumbent black women running for the House of Representatives, then home to only twenty black women.

Kelly Dittmar at Rutgers University Center for American Women and Politics has cautioned that that historic number still only represented 22 percent of the total number of House candidates, and that many of the women running will be up against incumbents in general elections. More women running does not always translate to more women winning. Everything is still changing. There is no predicting.

And yet.

The rise felt meaningful, and 2018 saw wave after wave of long-shot primary wins by underestimated women, many of them nonwhite, sometimes against entire fields of men.

"Women have been the leaders of the Resistance," Lauren Underwood, a young black candidate who beat six white male opponents in the Illinois House race, said the week before her primary, in a podcast interview in which she expressed what she understood to be so many of her fellow female candidates' frustration with the fact that current members of Congress, so many without the life experience of women, would not even convene to vote on policy issues like paid leave or equal pay. "Part of the reason that we're seeing women running is we know that our voices are needed to see the change we're looking for," she said, "because we can't count on someone else to be the advocate."[5]

Everywhere you turned, there were women running for office for the first time: military wife Tatiana Matta beat out other Democrats to challenge House Republican Majority Leader Kevin McCarthy in California; Nebraska's Kara Eastman, a president of a nonprofit organization, staged a surprise win in a Democratic House primary over former congressman Brad Ashford.

The challenge wasn't just crossing partisan lines, either. Angry liberal women were challenging the men, and some of the other women, in their own parties. The actress Cynthia Nixon mounted a primary campaign against New York governor Andrew Cuomo, while Alexandria Ocasio-Cortez, a twenty-eight-year-old former organizer for Bernie Sanders running on a Democratic Socialist platform, staged a shocking upset of ten-term incumbent New York City congressman Joe Crowley.

While the vision of women storming the ramparts of government was radical from one vantage point, it was as American as the idea of representative democracy laid out by our forefathers. "Representative citizens coming from all parts of the nation, cobblers and farmers—that was what was intended by the founders," said Marie Newman, a former small-business owner and antibullying advocate who challenged longtime antichoice Illinois incumbent Democrat and machine politician Dan Lipinski in a 2018 primary and came within three percentage points and less than three thousand votes of beating him. "You come to the House for a while and bring your ideas and then you probably go back to your life."

What Newman and her fellow female candidates were challenging were often the structural realities of patriarchal power in its purest form: her opponent had been in office himself for thirteen years, and his father had held the same seat for twenty years before that. "It's a family that has reigned supreme, like a monarchy, for over thirty years," she said during her race, her frustration with the bonkers unfairness of it unhidden. "He's an old white man who doesn't understand what his district wants, and it doesn't matter what party you're in. We are more than half the population, but only twenty percent of Congress."

And while Marie Newman may not have won her primary, the closeness of the race, against such an entrenched example of inherited white male power, offered some hope that it could be done.

In the wake of Trump's defeat of Clinton, a gang of women were eyeing the aging cast of men who'd been hogging America's political power . . . forever, and imagining that they might replace them. Replacement. It was a particularly charged concept, exactly the threat that seemed to have been motivating so many Trump Republicans and the voters who supported them. "You will not replace us" had been the chant of white supremacists marching in Charlottesville in the summer of 2017, and the fear that white male power might be redistributed had been the symbolic motivator behind the rhetoric of so much of the Trump campaign, as well as the Republican Party's efforts to disenfranchise precisely the voters—nonwhite voters, nonwealthy voters—most likely to vote them out.

CHAPTER TWO

RESTORATIVE JUSTICE

The fantasy of restorative justice was particularly resonant in the midst of the cascade of #metoo revelations of sexual abuses by those who've had too much power, in too many industries, for too long. "Let's make a full-blown trend out of replacing predatory men with women who were long overdue to hold their jobs in the first place," one writer had crowed in *Vogue*. "It's really the least the patriarchy can do."

The idea of replacing the bad men, the ones who'd been removed from power by #metoo, with women—many of them nonwhite women—was not just imaginatively attractive; it was happening, at least in some industries. Alex Wagner stepped in for Mark Halperin on *The Circus*; Hoda Kotb replaced Matt Lauer on *Today,* and Kitty Block took over the Humane Society of the United States after former head Wayne Pacelle stepped away after charges of sexual misconduct. One day in June 2018, I turned on the television and saw Christiane Amanpour, the woman hired to host Charlie Rose's PBS show, interviewing Barbara Underwood, the woman who replaced Eric Schneiderman as New York's attorney general, about the lawsuit she'd just filed against the Trump Foundation.

Of course, in most fields, altering power ratios is neither swift nor easy.

Even when men are pushed from lofty perches, those waiting to take their places, the ones who've accrued seniority, expertise, and connections, still tend to be mostly men. Women who've been driven out or self-exiled from their chosen professions often cannot simply reenter them—not as partners or managers or even midlevel employees.

This is one of the relative virtues of politics: It can be swiftly responsive to change. You can, in theory, run for local or state or even federal office, even if you've never been so much as a student council secretary. If you're a preschool teacher or a law professor or a sanitation worker, there will be substantial obstacles—yes, weaker networks, fund-raising disadvantages, party machinery, institutional obstruction, and identity bias—to push past. Yes. But you can run. And if you win, whether the office is small or large, you might be able to shake things up. Ocasio-Cortez, brilliant and charging into Congress with a righteously leftist agenda, had until recently worked as a bartender.

The people who control state and local legislatures often determine who in their communities gets to vote easily, who has access to health care or to legal sanctuary; local governing bodies around the country have in recent years passed legislation for paid leave and paid sick days and higher minimum wages. No, not all women candidates want to determine those policies in ways that benefit nonwhite men, and numbers of Republican women running for office in 2018 were up too. But the vast majority of the female candidates storming the polls in 2018 were Democrats.

More broadly, the idea of replacing men with women would be a way to alter one of the most deeply entrenched structural realities of how the nation has been built, who makes its rules, and who enforces them. It would be a seismic shift toward representational democracy.

In the wake of #metoo, and the view it offered of the corroded and corrupted layer of male power, women had already stepped into political space left by men. Tina Smith took Al Franken's Senate seat; not only was Solicitor General Barbara Underwood named to fill Schneiderman's job, within a few weeks of his resignation, at least two other women had announced that they would run for his seat in the fall. In Pennsylvania, a woman named Mary Gay Scanlon won the primary to fill the seat of Patrick Meehan, who resigned after harassment allegations,[6] and two women ran for the seat vacated by John Conyers in Detroit. Debbie Lesko, a Republican woman, defeated Hiral Tipirneni, the Democratic woman who ran against her, for the seat left open by Trent Franks, a congressman who repeatedly asked a female staffer to be a surrogate mother for his child.

In May 2018, Rachel Crooks, one of the women who'd accused Donald Trump of sexual misconduct before the election, claiming that when she'd been a twenty-two-year-old receptionist at Trump Tower, he'd kissed her against her will, won a Democratic House primary. When Trump had denied her claim on Twitter, Crooks had shot back, daring him to find security footage of the day and stating that "It's liars like you in politics that have prompted me to run for office myself."[7]

It felt like an avenue toward something like the unimaginable: reparations for all the power that had been denied to women for so many centuries. "What if women hadn't been taken out of the pool like this?" asked Erin Vilardi, the head of VoteRunLead, which trains and supports women running for state and local office. "Imagine having had our first woman president run and win in the 1980s! We're still not allowed to be mad about this. These guys need to *resign*. They *all* need to resign. If you are not willing to work *for* gender equality, you must step aside. We need all those open seats because research shows that women are more likely to win open seats. If you've groped or harassed, step aside right now. Pick a young woman as your successor."

The video game developer Brianna Wu, who'd been a target of the coordinated misogynistic mass attack called "Gamergate" in 2014, told me in 2018 of her "unmitigated anger at the way that women had been treated" in her field, from groping to not being taken seriously by the men who dominated gaming. After becoming a target of harassment and threats during Gamergate, Wu wrote to male peers asking them for help; she said she received none; the FBI closed its investigation into the dozens of threats she had received, provoking in her an "unbelievable fury" that she said was the catalyst for her to run for Congress, challenging a moderate congressman in Massachusetts in the state's primary.

"It turns out those were angry tears everybody cried on November 8, and nobody knew they were angry tears until later," said Vilardi, who also noted that until recently, women have had no road map for what to do with their resentments and furies. "Women are not allowed to scream from podiums, not allowed to slam doors in workplaces," she said, acknowledging that this expressive limit is part of what's earned women the reputation as more benevolent bosses. "But that's bullshit," she went on. "Because if you look at all those studies about how women are better bosses, they're better at everything *except* in areas of decisiveness, and that's because we don't get to *have* that split-second, I'm-the-goddamn-boss-that's-why gut reaction. We have zero role modeling in channeling our anger into decisiveness or 'That's just the way he is" stuff people said about Harvey Weinstein. We don't get *any* of those passes."

Brianna Wu told me that her battle, as a candidate, was also in learning to communicate her anger, which she longs to simply lay out for audiences, point by point, but which she refrains from doing. "If you say things like that to men, they shut down; they think you're being a bitch. Anger terrifies men." Wu said that she has one particularly visceral memory from her campaign, at a town hall at which an elderly woman asked her about women's health-care access "because she was angry about it." As soon as Wu began to answer her question, "the three men sitting beside that woman, the instant I started talking, pulled out their phones on cue and started surfing." Wu said she recalled standing in the midst of the town hall, "this fury boiling up in me. But because I was in front of a whole crowd, it was so hard to stay professional."

Despite the efforts to suppress or disguise anger, Amanda Litman, the cofounder of Run for Something, said that she believed that angry candidates make the *best* candidates, because their passion propels them out the door every day to do the work of knocking on doors and making calls, producing the most crucial result: getting out the vote.

Litman's theory was that the anger of the women in the Virginia elections had had a reverse coattails effect: the first-time women candidates had done such a stellar, driven job of canvassing and pavement-pounding that they had produced a higher turnout and helped Democrat Ralph Northam defeat Republican Ed Gillespie for governor. "Getting those candidates out there knocking [on] doors, speaking from a place of fury and commitment to change, gets more voters up, drives up turnout," said Litman.

"When we started," said Patricia Russo, the head of the Women's

Campaign School at Yale, which had begun training women candidates in 1994, in the wake of the Year of the Woman, "the median age for women attending our school was midforties. Now the median age is around thirty." That shift reflected new attitudes about when women were "allowed" to enter politics. They didn't have to wait until their kids were grown anymore, and there was a better chance that they'll be taken seriously in their thirties or even twenties—being young and single was no longer a deal-killer, nor was being the mother of little children. Also different now, Russo said, is that the majority of those who enroll in the school are women of color.

Other groups had also gotten into the candidate-training-and-support business over the past two decades, and registered exponential growth in the wake of 2016. For Higher Heights—founded in 2011 to harness the power of black women as voters, organizers, and candidates—a slow rise in engagement in the months after Trump's win became an enormous spike with the fall 2017 elections in Virginia, New Jersey, and Alabama, when the role of black women *voters* as responsible for Democratic wins had been heralded by the political media. "Black women were really acknowledged as political drivers of change, as first-time candidates and as the voters who made the difference," said cofounder Kimberly Peeler-Allen. Peeler-Allen recalled attending a candidate training in Minneapolis in the fall of 2017, at which she'd been told to expect forty or fifty black women. When she walked in she'd been greeted by seventy. "Nearly sixty percent of the women who were there were women of color," she recalled. "It was mind-blowing!"

VoteRunLead's Erin Vilardi said that in a typical year, two-thirds of the organization's resources were devoted to persuading women to run, with a goal of tapping two thousand nationwide. In 2017, 3,200 women were trained by VoteRunLead and over ten thousand had contacted the group completely unsolicited. EMILY's List, meanwhile, had nearly tripled the size of its state and local team and doubled its digital staff to handle the forty thousand inquiries they'd received about jumping into the electoral fray post-Trump.

"I think there's a disgust," Vilardi said, "when women find themselves running against a guy who hasn't changed the photo on his website since the 1990s—these men have been in office for so long." Then there was another kind of disgust, increasingly articulated by at least some of the rookie politicians she'd met: "There's disgust very much about the abuse that men in power have systematically been engaging in unchecked, and disgust with the people who continue to keep those men in power."

The anger that was bubbling to the surface over so many injustices—incursions on reproductive autonomy, the shootings of African Americans by police officers, the stranglehold of the NRA over American politics and thus the inability to enact gun control legislation, the gerrymandering and voter suppression efforts that left nonwhite voters with so much less electoral power, the pervasiveness of sexual harassment and assault, the paucity of women and nonwhite officials in representative government—was propelling women to run. The idea that the election of more women, especially more nonwhite women, was structurally, architecturally corrective, was clear.

But persuading the kinds of organizations and institutions that had long held up the party system in the United States that this was an opportunity for a major overhaul was difficult. Marie Newman, the challenger to anti-choice, anti-immigration incumbent Dan Lipinski, had a hard time getting party machinery to support her, even against a politician who often voted against his party. While she garnered early support from Senator Kirsten Gillibrand, the National Abortion Rights Action League (NARAL), and Gloria Steinem, it took Planned Parenthood and EMILY's List a long time to start diverting money toward her. Newman's eventual primary loss to Lipinski was so close that it seemed possible that an earlier willingness to take a chance on her candidacy could have meant a different result.

"This is a moment to take significant risks, and we're hedging our bets," Vilardi said to me at one point, in reference to the foot-dragging in Newman's race, and also to the Democratic Congressional Campaign Committee and state parties, all cogs in a political machine that tended to be slow about directing money toward new kinds of candidates in crowded primaries. "Not throwing every dollar behind the exciting new women candidates, especially women of color," Vilardi says, "is missing the political moment if I ever did see it."

The throng of disgusted women, most of them brand-new to politics, did require the investment of time and resources. And many of the mechanisms in place to train women candidates were quickly at capacity, thanks to the rush of women who knew mostly that they were furious, but did not know much beyond that.

Across the nation, on practically every weekend in late 2017 and early 2018, women who hoped to one day lead their communities and perhaps their country were getting crash courses in civic participation. On a Saturday in late October 2017, as EMILY's List's president Stephanie Schriock was addressing potential candidates at the Detroit Women's Convention, the group's executive director, Emily Cain, was doing the same for a hundred women in Manhattan. "If you wake up in the morning caring about something," Cain told the potential future leaders of America crowding the wood-paneled room, notepads out, "you are qualified to run for office." The message echoed one delivered by Higher Heights cofounder Peeler-Allen to the black women she advises, many of whom lack confidence: "Each one of you is beyond prepared to run for public office. You need to channel your inner mediocre white boy and use that to run."

If that seemed a depressingly low bar for entry, consider that one of the grim gifts of the Trump administration was the recognition of how low the bar could go for political plausibility. As Jennifer Carroll Foy, a public defender who won a Virginia House seat while pregnant with twins, replacing a Republican white man, said in a short documentary about her candidacy, "If *he* can do it, I know that I can do it."[8]

The whole training curriculum of VoteRunLead was overhauled in 2017 and could now be summed up with its call to action: "Run As You Are." Vilardi mentioned Eve Hurwitz, a Navy reservist and small-business owner running for state senator in Maryland. She'd long colored her hair a vivid shade of purple, but, said Vilardi, "Everybody told her that you can't run with purple hair, so she lost it, but other people said, 'How are you not going to run with purple hair? That's who you are!' So she dyed it back." Similarly, Peeler-Allen recalled reassuring a recent candidate who was fretting about whether she had to code-switch—alter her speaking style and mannerisms—to speak before different audiences. "Be genuine in what you're saying," Peeler-Allen said she advised. "As long as people feel you have their best interests at heart, it won't matter whether you twang or drawl or drop a consonant here or there."

Which is not to say that the political waters would suddenly part, allowing women to walk serenely into office. "You can know you're the best person for the job, and come out of a tearjerker of a training session, having just been inspired by the first Somali refugee to gain elected office," Vilardi said. "But the world is still gonna come at you and tell you that Jim Smith, Jr. has been waiting for ten years and is next in line for that seat you want to run for."

For all the obstacles first-time female candidates face, Vilardi noticed a refreshingly new mind-set post 2016. "The 'Am I qualified?' stuff we used to hear, when women would talk themselves out of running for office— what is the time management going to be, wondering how they'll talk to their husband or partner or boss about this, worrying that they can't make this work with their job, or that legislatures pay crap—now all of that is being negotiated in a positive way." Instead of talking themselves out of it, they're talking themselves into it. "It's like lightbulbs are going off everywhere," Vilardi said. "Prior to the 2016 election, two-thirds of VoteRun-Lead women would tell us they wanted a five-year plan. Now sixty percent want to run by 2020."

Part of it was a feeling of urgency in response to what had recently been exposed, after years of the myth that it was in abeyance: sexism. When Tresa Undem conducted a poll in December 2016 asking if the Trump campaign and election had made voters "think more about sexism in our society," 40 percent of respondents said yes. In November 2017, when she asked whether the news about sexual harassment and assault made people think more about societal sexism, 73 percent said that it did. In December 2016, 52 percent of those surveyed by Undem said that the country would be better off with more women in office; in November 2017, 69 percent gave that answer. And in 2016, 65 percent of people Undem had polled had felt that men held more positions of power in society than women; in 2017, that number had risen to 87 percent.[9] "As pollsters, we don't see shifts in attitudes this big," Undem said, also noting that women were using the word "misogyny," a word she'd rarely, if ever, heard in previous years.

The sight of so many women rushing to occupy elected office is almost sure to draw out antagonists. All reassurances to the contrary, this is a zero-sum game: If women gain greater political power, white men lose some of theirs. After a 2018 Indiana primary propelled multiple women to wins, a law professor named Kenneth Dau-Schmidt wrote to his local paper, describing how "disturbed" he was by the results. "The fact that all women candidates won, even against accomplished male incumbents," he wrote, "was troubling." It was clear to Dau-Schmidt that "hundreds of Democratic women are voting just for female candidates based on their gender." It had apparently never occurred to him that the history of electoral politics in America was one of voters pulling levers for candidates based on their gender, but he was certainly not alone in his irritation, and his response felt particularly resonant as we lived through the potent and damaging backlash to the election of Barack Obama and the symbolic threat of Hillary Clinton, the real and presumptive victories that had landed us with the Tea Party and eventually the Trump presidency.

Andrea Steele of Emerge America, which trains Democratic women candidates in twenty-four states, worked on Carol Moseley Braun's campaign in 1992 and remembered the drop-off in women candidates that happened *after* 1992. "We thought everything was going to change," she said, recalling the deep disappointment when it didn't. "The difference between then and now is we have infrastructure. EMILY's List is stronger, Emerge is growing its support structure, there are state organizations helping to fund candidates. And a big part of what we've seen over the years is that when women get into politics, they start bringing other women in."

CHAPTER THREE

MY SISTERS ARE HERE

Of course, change, even political change, won't come simply from the women who are running for office; it will also come from the women who are engaging in their campaigns, volunteering, paying attention, educating themselves, becoming activists for the first time in their lives. And in the years since Donald Trump became president, those women are legion. A 2017 Pew survey found that nearly six in ten women said they were paying increased attention to politics since the 2016 election, a greater share than men.

The self-styled "Resistance" that grew up in response to the Donald Trump administration was made of, built on, the efforts of women. Women were running the local chapters of Indivisible, one of the biggest organizations to rise in opposition to Trump and Republicans, at a rate of two to one, according to one of Indivisible's founders; more than three quarters of Indivisible's email subscribers were women.[10] Journalist Charlotte Alter reported that Planned Parenthood said its volunteers, the majority of them women, had made more than 200,000 phone calls to members of Congress and organized more than 2,200 events across the country opposing the repeal of the Affordable Care Act, as well as having delivered more than a million petitions to members of Congress, asking them not to defund women's reproductive health care. One 2017 survey found that 86 percent of the people using an anti-Trump text-messaging service were women. In a survey of twenty-eight thousand people who'd contacted Congress in 2017 to protest the administration, Democratic pollster Celinda Lake found the same percentage were women.

Yes, progressive politics had long relied on the labor of women, many of them women of color, the hard-working base of state and local political organizing. But what happened after Clinton's loss, and grew through the #metoo movement, and the fury over mass shootings, was the activation of another population, long dormant: suburban white women.

I'd met and spoken to some of them, traveling to Georgia in June of 2017, in the lead-up to the special election campaign of Jon Ossoff, and landing among them was like walking onto the set of *Thelma & Louise*, encountering women who had just been rousted from political somnambulence and were certain that they would never be the same. "Something's crossed over in me," says one of the heroines in that old cinematic testament to the alchemical changes brought on by wrath, "I can't go back." And then, in another scene, "I feel *awake*. I don't remember feeling this awake. Everything looks different."

"If I'm not knocking on doors, I'm making calls; if I'm not making calls, I'm writing postcards; if I'm not writing postcards, I'm replacing my lawn sign," I heard one woman saying at a suburban restaurant outside Atlanta. She and her peers were using a language of awakening and liberation that was redolent of past insurgencies.

"I am no longer in the closet," Ann White, a sixty-four-year-old former speech pathologist told me. "I am out, I am out blue. Everybody knows now that I'm a Democrat, that I'm liberal. And they're kind of tired of it, but that's okay. I'm not done. I'm just getting started." White, like so many previously complacent white women, had simply believed that Hillary Clinton would beat Donald Trump. When she hadn't, White said, she had felt herself transforming. "The profanity filter on my mouth totally went away," she said, recalling cursing like a sailor on the phone with a friend, shocking her teenaged children, who'd "never heard me say the F-word before." She attended the Women's March in Atlanta in January, and said that "it was the very first time since the election that I felt empowered." She'd also realized, for the first time, that "there's a whole lot of people like me who are not going to take this lying down!"

White joined a group called Liberal Moms of Roswell and Cobb Counties. "My favorite slogan," she told me, trying not to cry, "is 'You Are Not Alone.' I found my people."

This is one of anger's most important roles: it is a mode of connection, a way for women to find each other and realize that their struggles and their frustrations are shared, that they are not alone, not crazy. If they are quiet, they will remain isolated. But if they howl in rage, someone else who shares their fury might hear them, might start howling along. This is, of course, partly why those who oppress women work to stifle their anger.

Woman after woman spoke to me of how the loud eruption of their rage had brought them into a community they'd never known existed. "I never even put a sign in my yard because I wasn't sure how it would be received if it wasn't a Republican sign," said Cherish Burnham, forty-four, of her life as a Democrat growing up in a red suburb. On the morning of November 9, consumed by hopelessness, she'd gone to volunteer at her sons' elementary school science class and seen two other mothers who also looked stricken. After tentative inquiries, the trio realized they were all upset about the same thing; they stood outside the school in conversation for an hour.

Them too.

The expression of primal, agonizing anger that followed Trump's election meant that for the first time, some women—even those who'd been living in proximity to one another for years—could hear one another for the first time.

"Every time I see an Ossoff sign I feel like I have an ally," said Tamara Brooking, a fifty-one-year-old research assistant to a novelist. A lifelong Democrat who voted for Bernie Sanders before she voted for Clinton, Brooking said that after the election, "I was fucking furious. I was insanely mad." Now that she's become active in Democratic organizing, she said, "I'm feeling like I'm working toward something. After the anger and depression faded, the motivation kicked in."

Many women had put magnets with the logo of their activist group on their cars; if they spotted a magnet on the parked car, they turned it 180 degrees as a kind of greeting and signal of communion. "It's to let each other know, 'my sisters are here,'" said Jennifer Mosbacher, forty-four, reaching for the language of sisterhood evocative of the 1970s, or more activist spheres. "It's this feeling of camaraderie in an area where you have often felt very isolated and disenfranchised. But now you can go to your neighborhood grocery store and get flipped, and you're like, 'Cool, someone else is here.'"

Women spoke with the youthful fervor of having found new friends and new love—of politics and one another. Several described how they'd not been sleeping, staying up all night scrolling through Facebook and message boards, reading political posts and messaging one another.

Their ardor echoed the recollections of the feminist writer Vivian Gornick in a 1990 essay, in which she recalled the period of second-wave feminism in which "Every week, there was a gathering of some sort at which the talk was an exhilaration. There wasn't a woman in the room whose conversation did not engage. . . . We saw our inner lives being permanently marked by the words we spoke. We were changing before each other's eyes, taking our own ideas seriously, becoming other than we had been."[11]

The language I heard in Georgia was audible in interviews with women all over the country. The *Washington Post* reported on Kim Drew Wright, a forty-six-year-old writer and mother of three who, the week after the 2016 election, had invited local members of Pantsuit Nation to join her for a drink at a local bar; ninety people had come. She'd become a leader of liberal women in her conservative suburb, and helped to drive Democrats to victory in the fall 2017 elections in Virginia. "I wouldn't have done this every day for the past year if I hadn't gotten so angry about Trump," Wright told the *Post*. "Once you wake up and see how important local elections are, it's hard to go back to the shadows and stick your head in the sand."[12] To another outlet, Wright explained, "On election night, a switch got flipped in me. I'm starting to call it my 'I'll be damned' switch. I'll be damned if I'm going to be quiet anymore."

The sheer amount of time these women were devoting to political organizing was staggering, especially given that most of them worked full-time and had children. "My business [and] my family have suffered from the work we're doing," Mosbacher told me. "Our fridge is barren; my daughter is like 'Are we going out *again*?'"

"I tell people that I am fresh out of fucks," Tamara Brooking told me. "I'm done. I'm done pretending that your hateful rhetoric is okay. I'm done pretending that people like us must be quiet to make you feel comfortable."

There's that willingness to discomfit again; it turns everything upside down, disturbs the equilibrium of households and partnerships that had been built around earlier states of complacency and quiet. And in this too, there were other kinds of reminders of the Second Wave, the kinds of intimate upheavals it had provoked.

The writer and professor Amy Butcher would describe the tolls of some of this in her essay "MIA: The Liberal Men We Love," which she published in the weeks after the second Women's March. "*I'm frustrated and embarrassed*, my boyfriend of three years said to me, *with how worked up you are*. He didn't find palatable my rage, the anger I felt for Trump, for the men and women who voted for him, was . . . embarrassed that I led ninety students from my small Ohio university through the streets of Washington with half a million Americans . . . when I returned, delirious for sleep but feeling righted, in some small way satiated, he stood there in the hall and told me he was overwhelmed. *All of you women with your labia hats*, he said. *All of you with your clitoris signs*."[13] Butcher and her boyfriend broke up.

And still she wrote, she wished that the men who were put off by this surging fury could know what it was like to feel communion with the other women, the angry women on the road back with her from the Washington march. "I woke that night to a thousand taillights—many cars but far more buses, thousands of stories packed onto wheels—as we traced the edges of America, making our way home . . . as we climbed the smudged dusk of West Virginia—the heart of America, indeed, the heart of Trump Country—it seemed, if only for that evening, as if the porch lights had been left on for us . . . and how amazing it was, truly, to watch our steady stream of red lights blink and brake as we led one another home."

The connection women were feeling in shared fury was its own home, its own reward, its own community, and for some the pushback to their activism, the losses it incurred—money, domestic comforts, relationships built in other circumstances, based on earlier expectations for comportment—were not worth retreating for.

"I know five people who are getting divorced over it," Dawn Penich-

Thacker told me in the spring of 2018. "Because it has fundamentally changed how they see themselves as women." Penich-Thacker was a thirty-eight-year-old college professor and former Army public affairs officer in Tempe, Arizona. She became energized in the wake of the Trump election to become more civically involved, led a petition to reverse a universal voucher program in Arizona, and assisted in the teachers' strike there in 2018.

She had been a Democratic voter, but not much of an activist, and had joined Pantsuit Nation in the run-up to the election. After Clinton's defeat, local members of Pantsuit Nation discussed taking the group offline and turning it into a live and in-person activist organization; they formed Stronger Together Arizona. In December of 2016, "we called a statewide meeting and eight hundred people showed up, mostly women," Penich-Thacker recalled. "It was a surprise to the organizers; the museum we'd booked couldn't even accommodate that many people." During the meeting, attendees divided up according to policy interests and Penich-Thacker headed over to a group discussing education. She began making trips to the capitol to protest planned changes in state funding for schools. When the state legislature passed a bill to privatize education, a mission to expand vouchers spearheaded by Trump's Education Secretary Betsy DeVos, Penich-Thacker and five other women, all mothers of varying ages, who had seen one another over and over again, gathered together and asked what they could do next. They realized the state permitted a right to referendum; if they collected enough signatures they could block a law.

"We had the blessing of ignorance," said Penich-Thacker, noting that they had no idea how unlikely it would be that they could collect more than seventy-five thousand signatures in ninety days. "We literally did not have a penny, and we were six people. But we knew all these other pissed off people, the lion's share of them women, ninety percent through Stronger Together, Facebook, and Indivisible." They collected more than one hundred ten thousand signatures and successfully blocked the law. Sued by organizations with ties to DeVos and the Koch brothers, the group soldiered on, winning their court cases. "We kept education in the headlines and our network kept growing and growing," she said. "We have about five thousand volunteers now." When teachers went on strike in West Virginia and Oklahoma, the grassroots group that moved to strike in Arizona had been involved with Penich-Thacker's volunteers, circulating the original petitions. In May, Arizona teachers won a 19 percent pay raise.

"I would be lying if I said I see an end to this," Penich-Thacker told me she had said to her husband the night before our conversation. "It's not going to be over in November. It's not going to be over next year, because you don't change things overnight." When she and her five original coconspirators started working together, she said, she believed that it was just to fight and roll back the one bad law. "But it's now clear to all of us for various reasons that there's way more work to do than stopping one law." She paused. "But also, I think that in many ways, we actually love this. It has consumed our lives."

The marital, romantic, domestic tolls were real, she said. But her relationships with her fellow activists, she said, "are the deepest friendships I've ever had. These women in this movement are my battle buddies. I can't imagine leaving this behind, even if it ravaged my life." Penich-Thacker said that part of the intensity of the bond is living through the aftershocks of such personal transformation. "There is the bond over the shared political vision, the bond over doing *work* together: we set out to do something, we accomplished it, we feel good. But also the spiritual and emotional bond of saying 'My partner is basically done,' or 'I'm struggling at work.' We have each other to talk through that."

"That is a moment of joy," Gornick wrote in 1990, looking back at the 1970s, "when a sufficiently large number of people are galvanized by a social explanation of how their lives have taken shape, and are gathered together in the same place at the same time, speaking the same language, making the same analysis, meeting again and again in restaurants, lecture halls and apartments. . . . It is the joy of revolutionary politics, and it was ours. To be a feminist in New York City in the early 70s—bliss was it in that dawn to be alive. Not an I-love-you in the world could touch it. There was no other place to be, except with each other. We lived then, all of us, inside the loose embrace of feminism. It was as though we'd been released from a collective lifetime of silence."[14]

When women awaken in their thirties, Penich-Thacker told me, "I think some men are like, 'This isn't who you were when I met you.' Well, it's who I am now and for any future I can foresee."

"I believe this is the beginning of a new wave of feminism," Mosbacher told me. "And I hope by the time my nine-year-old daughter is in college, she'll be reading books about this movement and how it changed the tide in this country."

So many of the newly hatched activists, describing their previous ennui and isolation, and their subsequent rebirth in sisterhood, could indeed sound like the quivering start of a women's movement, and bring to mind the first paragraph of Betty Friedan's *The Feminine Mystique*, about the "strange stirring," and "sense of dissatisfaction [and] yearning" that "each suburban wife struggled with ... alone."

Stacey Abrams, then Georgia's House Minority Leader, who in 2018 would win a primary to become the nation's first black female gubernatorial nominee, told me that women "understand that this has to be the beginning of something. . . . Because they've seen, for the first time, the real consequences of inaction. So you have women who are waking up and seeing that they don't have the luxury of going back to sleep."

She acknowledged that "among African-American women there's been a long consistency of action, which has moved our communities closer and closer to political power over time. What you're seeing in the suburbs now is a version of that."

For some, these repetitions of history were intolerable.

Aditi Juneja said that she had been working with newly active white women throughout the summer of 2017, and "so many of them don't realize they're not the first people to be activists and organizers." When she speaks to them, she said, "I try to make an effort to say, 'Well, Black Lives Matter dealt with this; Dreamers dealt with this.' I try to reference these other people-of-color-led organizations, to let them know that they are not the first women to do this."

Juneja had noticed that the white activists were very focused on rules. "They ask questions I've not ever heard from women-of-color organizations, like 'Do we need permits to canvas?' They are very hierarchy-oriented, very rules-oriented in a way I have not seen when organizing with people of color." She suggested that one of the reasons the town-hall format had caught on in 2017 was that "white people, even white women, have faith that if they voice their opinions to their representatives, that they will be heard, that they will have influence, that they have a political voice to which officials will be responsive." Black and brown people, Juneja said, know that they have representatives, and know how government works. "But there is no faith that politicians will see that there is any cost to disappointing black and brown people. But these women believe that you work through making calls and going to town halls because you assume that they will *care* what you have to say."

There were other forms of structural bias underpinning some of the activism, including the fact that the vast majority of women giving up their lives to work for campaigns and around policy issues—often offering some of the most innovative ideas and fresh thinking about how to reach members of their own communities, all while balancing kids and full-time jobs—were doing so on a volunteer basis, while so many of the highly paid party consultants were men.

Jessica Morales noticed that the resistance groups that sprang up at the end of 2016 and throughout 2017, many of them led or organized by women, were operating at strategic odds with the better-remunerated "thought-leaders," who, she said, "somehow kept coming back to: You know what we should do? Focus on white men." To those activists who pushed back at this, Morales said, the message was clear: "'You don't understand the math; you're not being technical; you're so emotional about this election.'" To that, Morales herself said, "Literally go fuck yourselves."

Morales believed that political professionals were dismissing the impact of resistance groups in part because they're so often led by and comprised of women. "They're just not seeing, not understanding, the impact of these organizations," she said. "But there simply have not been organizations before this that could drive millions of calls in one day, just like that. And that's what's been happening."

But the repetition of unequal history, hierarchical patterns, and internal marginalization cannot be the end of the story if angry women are to move forward. And so, the task for activists and candidates and participants in the political struggles of the Trump era is to find the places where there can be long-awaited growth.

"The question we have now in this resistance movement," said Juneja, "is: Are white women going to use their power to defend their own interests or are they going to use it to transform systems so that we all have more power? If this movement is going to be sustainable, once you stand shoulder-to-shoulder with someone who's not quite like you, can you see how connected your fights are? Do you realize: I have to show up for them? Because our liberation is intertwined. And that's not a meme that I retweeted. That's actually really a thing."

That struggles were connected was not a new idea: it's how the suffrage and abolition movements kicked off together; how suffrage bled into labor and settlement house movements, how civil rights and the New Left informed—in part through their sexist shortcomings and in part through their approach to structural inequality and liberation—the women who would drive the Second Wave.

The idea that anger at injustice is contagious, transferable to other contexts, has long been a principle of progress. As the education reporter Dana Goldstein wrote in the *New York Times*, in reference to the 2018 wave of teachers' strikes, "the politics of teacher strikes shift over time, but in every generation, their leaders have forged ties to broader social movements." Nineteenth-century Chicago Teachers Federation leader Margaret Haley, Goldstein noted, had been "inspired by Susan B. Anthony and other suffragists," while "many of the union leaders who led the nation's most famous . . . teacher strike, in New York City in 1968, were first active in the civil rights movement." The seven-day Chicago teachers' strike, Goldstein wrote, had come in the wake of Occupy Wall Street. And in 2018, West Virginia teachers had told her that they'd "come to activism through the 2017 Women's March, the #metoo movement or Black Lives Matter," a sentiment echoed by one West Virginia striker who told *Times* journalist Michelle Goldberg that the Women's March, "as well as the explosion of local political organizing that followed it" had been a "catalyst" for her and other strikers.

Jessica Morales hoped that connections can be forged by those who've never made them before. She told a story of a woman who contacted her by direct message on Twitter, as she was trying to organize protesters on social media to stand against Trump's travel ban. "She was this nice teacher in St. Louis who wrote me and said 'I've never started a protest but I am willing to go to the airport and I can leave right now. I really want to do this; I feel passionate about this, but I don't know how to protest.'"

Morales sent her a list of things to do: "get in your car; get friends, fit as many as you can; if you can, make signs; when you get there sing some songs and do some chants, here are examples; don't leave; they are going to tell you that you have to leave, but don't; make a Facebook event and I'll promote it and that's a protest." The woman made the Facebook event. And hundreds of people went to the airport in St. Louis, as they did to airports all around the country, by the tens or perhaps hundreds of thousands.

"I don't think that woman probably knew a lot of immigrants," said Morales, months later. "But it goes to show what we are learning, which is that morally, she knew that this was the wrong thing. And that is really good. We can move forward with that."

By 2018, the rising generation of activists seemed to be absorbing these messages faster than their foremothers and forefathers ever had.

The March for Our Lives, held in March 2018 and organized by the high school students of Parkland, Florida, in the wake of the mass shooting at their school, was a model of interconnected anger. Officially a protest against gun violence and the NRA's grip on American politics, its speakers seemed to see it as all part of one piece: "We need to arm our teachers with . . . the money they need to support their families and to support themselves,'" said one speaker, while eleven-year-old Naomi Wadler named the too-often forgotten names of African-American girls, "whose stories don't make the front page of every newspaper."

The protest felt effortlessly integrated in its concerns. Signs about gun violence acknowledged how deeply white patriarchy was embedded in the crisis of mass shootings, and read things like "White Men Are Terrifying (Statistically)" and "Your Guns Have More Rights Than My Vagina" and "We Live in a Country Where Guns Matter More Than Black Women's Lives." Common rapped, "I stand for peace, love, and women's rights." One young woman, nervous about speaking in front of millions, simply leaned over in the middle of her speech and vomited, while speakers wept, and their noses ran; it was astounding, moving to see the viscera of women's passions on display, without apology or shame—its own testament to urgency and fury and the will to change.

That march recalled the explosive drive behind a 1917 statement written by Lavinia Dock, a suffragist, called "The Young Are At the Gates," a phrase that would become the National Women's Party banner in the suffrage fight.

"What is the potent spirit of youth?" Dock asked. "Is it not the spirit of revolt, of rebellion against senseless and useless and deadening things? Most of all, against injustice, which is of all stupid things the stupidest? Such thoughts come to one in looking over the field of the Suffrage campaign and watching the pickets at the White House and at the Capitol, where sit the men who complacently enjoy the rights they deny to the women at their gates . . . A fatal error—a losing fight. The old stiff minds must give way. The old selfish minds must go. Obstructive reactionaries must move on. The young are at the gates!"

In 2018, it was both the literally and the more metaphorically young—those whose willingness to give voice to rage was nascent—who were at the gates, challenging the men who complacently enjoy the rights they deny others.

As Ann White, the suburban Georgia sixty-four-year-old woman who'd been newly woken from her carapace of political apathy, told me, she was feeling the responsibility of taking a stand, not on her own behalf, but "for people of color, for those who cannot afford health insurance, who are lesbian, gay, and transgender, for immigrants. I'm a white older woman. There's a lot of old white people that are on [the Republican] side right now. Well I'm an old white person and I can be vocal too."

On the day of Trump's first State of the Union address, Jessica Morales wrote to me, excited about a response event being put on by the National Domestic Workers Alliance, at which leaders including head of the Domestic Workers Alliance Ai-Jen Poo, Black Lives Matter's Alicia Garza, Planned Parenthood's Cecile Richards, Congresswomen Barbara Lee and Pramila Jayapal, Tarana Burke, and Mónica Ramirez of the National Farmworker Women's Alliance, who'd stood in solidarity with the #metoo actresses, were coming together to respond to the president's speech.

"It's so powerful and kind of reminds me that the other side of the anger is the hope," Morales wrote to me. "We wouldn't be angry if we didn't still believe that it could be better."

And if it gets better in part because of women's ability and willingness and need to feel their anger and to let it out into the world, then what we would be living through right now would not be a trend or a fad or a witch hunt, but an insurrection—a righteous revolution, led by angry women.

CONCLUSION

Men literally have no idea how to even legitimately recognize or name our anger—largely because we don't either. This is new territory for everybody. Women's rage has been so sublimated for so long that there's simply no frame for what happens when it finally comes to the surface.

—Sara Robinson

I first met the activist Amanda Litman, fifteen years my junior, when she was an undergraduate, studying with a beloved college professor of mine, writing a thesis on women in politics and looking to me, who had written a book on the 2008 presidential election, for guidance. It was with tremendous pleasure, in the months before I began this book, that I found myself reading her words—printed in *Women's Health* magazine—and realized that she was offering guidance to me.

In an essay about how devastated she had been by the 2016 election, as a dedicated member of Hillary Clinton's campaign staff, she described how she had moved forward, founding Run for Something, one of the most successful new political organizations in the country.

"My anger is my cup of coffee in the morning," she wrote. "It gets me out of bed and keeps me focused. . . . Simply doing the damn thing has soothed me and brought me back to myself. Every memo I write, every donor I meet with, every reporter I speak to, each conversation I have, is guided by strategy but fueled by the fury I feel at my country, at dangerous men, at my party, and at the very system of democracy I love that painfully let me down."

When I first read these words, I was already thinking about this book, which I had decided to write in the months after the election, but had intended to report slowly, imagining that it would chronicle the steady evolution of women's rage in the age of Trump. But by the fall of 2017, as the wildfire of female fury was spreading, it had become clear that I needed to work swiftly, to capture this rebellion before its sharp, spiky contours got retroactively smoothed and flattened by time. And so I wrote these pages over the course of four months.

I mention this because as I was finishing them, I realized that those four months—while enormously stressful, professionally—had comprised one of the physically healthiest periods of my adulthood. Yes, I was sickened and terrified by the world around me, the ravages of the Trump administration, the dangers to the democracy and the harm being done to the people in it. Yes. Of course I was.

But while I was pouring some of that fear—and all of my anger—into this project, I realized that I had begun to sleep well and deeply at night; I had wanted to exercise more than I ever had before. My appetite was healthy; I was communicating well with the people I loved; I was having great sex. It certainly wasn't about the good effects of book-writing; I had, after all, done this twice before, under far less punishing deadlines, and had not found either process salutary—quite the opposite. But as Litman had described of her own experience, there had been something about spending my days and nights immersed in anger—mine and the anger of others—that had been undeniably good for me.

It seemed to fly in the face of everything I had ever been taught about fury's ill-effects on the human body, things I had believed to be true on some level even as I had begun this book's introduction, four months earlier. Yes, I wanted to reclaim and excavate the value in women's anger, I had written in an early February draft, but I also understood the emotion to have other, damaging dimensions, the ones that had been affirmed to me so often by culture, by my sources, that I had absorbed as truth. What I wrote when I started this book was that while anger might be politically useful, catalytic, thrilling, and communicatively indispensable, I knew that too much of it was *also* bad for you . . . poisonous, internally corrosive.

By June, I no longer believed that it was deleterious. In fact, I returned again and again to a proclamation made by Elizabeth Cady Stanton, nearly two centuries earlier, that "if women would indulge more freely in vituperation, they would enjoy ten times the health they do. It seems to me they are suffering from repression."

My fitness had not been buoyed simply by my ability to loose my ire;

it had also been the chance to take seriously *other* women's rage, the fact that I'd been forced—encouraged—to really examine those emotions that we spend so much of our lives being told to avoid or look away from or laugh at. Writing this book had permitted me to stare straight at them, to think hard about them and consider the credit they deserve for shaping the nation.

I confess that I am now suspicious of nearly every attempt to code anger as unhealthy, no matter how well meaning or persuasive the source. I believe that Stanton was correct: what is bad for women, when it comes to anger, are the messages that cause us to bottle it up, let it fester, keep it silent, feel shame and isolation for ever having felt it or rechannel it in inappropriate directions. What is good for us is opening our mouths and letting it out, permitting ourselves to feel it and say it and think it and act on it and integrate it into our lives, just as we integrate joy and sadness and worry and optimism.

I had been given a gift: the opportunity—the incentive—to explore the dimensions and be curious about and respectful of my own anger, as well as the rage of other women. It felt *great. I* felt great. In getting to voice and appreciate fury, I had found relief, release, inspiration, and exhilaration.

But I was also aware that my experience was unusual, that it could not be converted into advice that might apply to others. So while sure, I urge those who can comfortably do so to scream, yell, curse, write it out, phone a friend, and not keep themselves from *feeling* their own anger, you will find here no exhortation to lean into your own rage as I have into mine.

I was not paying any price for expressing my ire, in fact I was *being paid* for it; it was my work, my job to take women's anger seriously. My editors, bosses, friends were taking this project, and therefore the fury it was unpacking, seriously. It was glorious. But it was not replicable.

To suggest to other women that they should simply let it out, channel their fury and scream it to the world, would be to repeat a long history of well-intentioned, idealistic, but ultimately impractical approaches to feminist strategy: the urging of individual women to work around or within the systems that have not been built to accommodate or even acknowledge them. I can't tell women to express their anger as

I have and not acknowledge that in the real world, this rage might get them fired, denied raises and promotions, incur punishments and violence. We live in a world in which a black woman, angry at being pulled over for no reason, risks arrest, and a woman angry at being unjustly arrested risks death; in which young women are shot, or run down by cars, because they—or because another woman—have rejected the advances of a man.

Having had the rare and privileged experience of having had my anger taken seriously, valued on its merits, I no longer believe that it is *anger* that is hurting us, but rather the system that penalizes us for expressing it, that doesn't respect or hear it, that isn't curious about it, that mocks or ignores it. *That's* what's making us sick; *that's* what's making us feel crazy, alone; *that's* why we're grinding our teeth at night.

And so it is not women (or not *only* women) who must change our behaviors; it's the system built to suppress our ire, and thus our power, by design. We can change it by protesting and marching and calling and sending postcards; by donating money and knocking on doors for candidates and running for office, and making demands of our government and in our workplaces, on behalf of ourselves and, crucially, alongside and on behalf of those with more reason to be furious and less ability to leverage that fury than we have.

But more immediately, we can change it by doing what the world does *not* do: by acknowledging, paying attention to, respecting, and not shying away from *other* women's anger. Seek it out, notice it, ask women what makes them angry and then listen to them when they tell you. If part of what they're angry at is you, take it in, acknowledge how their frustrations might mirror your own, even if they are refracted at you.

Consider that the white men in the Rust Belt are rarely told that *their* anger is bad for them. Rather, and correctly, we understand that what's bad for them are the conditions that have provoked their frustration: the loss of jobs and stature, the shortage of affordable health care, day-care, the scourge of drugs. We understand their anger to be politically instructive, to point us toward problems that must be addressed. What we all—in the media, and in politics, and in our personal lives—can endeavor to do is to treat the anger of women as we treat the anger of white men. That also means considering its potential: understanding that the fury of contemporary women at inequity, at sexism and racism and lack of representation, is made of the very same stuff that Thomas Paine's anger was, and that the demands it prompts might be just as transformative. Rage birthed this nation—along with its attendant, baked-in inequities, the very strictures against which members of its majority population are now furiously straining.

Consider what Catharine MacKinnon wrote in February of 2018, arguing that #metoo has made a kind of progress that decades of legal reforms had not: "It is . . . this uprising of the formerly disregarded . . . that is changing everything already . . . [T]oday's movement that is shifting gender hierarchy's tectonic plates."

Of course we must not underestimate the pushback to any shift that can be reasonably described as tectonic. The desire to push disruptive social fury back down underground is strong. The rage must be stronger still, to resist the pull of apathy, the censure of the powerful.

Martin Luther King, Jr. understood that as well as anyone, and it's what made him insist, in his most famous speech, that "this sweltering summer of the Negro's legitimate discontent will not pass until there is an invigorating autumn of freedom and equality. Nineteen-sixty-three is not an end, but a beginning. And those who hope that the Negro needed to blow off steam and will now be content will have a rude awakening if the nation returns to business as usual. . . .The whirlwinds of revolt will continue to shake the foundations of our nation until the bright day of justice emerges."

What King commanded we too must command: that this not get written off as a summer storm, an aberration or fad or period of hysteria until our demands have been met. We must insist on our discontent, not permit it to be muffled or put behind us swiftly. We must emerge on its other side with substantive victories: changes in law, policy, representation, power, a remaking not only of rules to better support equality—via criminal justice and environmental reform, the expansion of reproductive justice, of workers' rights and strengthening of a social safety net—but a reformation of the very attitudes that have permitted inequality to be codified again and again.

Repeatedly, during 2017 and 2018, I was asked—of the Women's March, of #metoo, of women's drive toward elected office: "Is this a moment or a movement?" In part, the questioners craved reassurance that this hard work, these difficult feelings, this fear and pain and risk, was in service of something big, long-term, and important.

But the question, and the binary on which it relies, doesn't track. Because movements are made up of moments, strung out over months, years, decades. They become discernible as movements—are made to look smooth, contiguous, coherent—only after they have made a substantive difference. It was nine years between Emmett Till's murder and the passing of the Civil Rights Act. It was more than eighty years between the first 1830s meeting of abolitionists and suffragists and the passage of the Nineteenth Amendment, more than 130 years before the passage of the Voting Rights Act. That law was recently gutted by the Supreme Court, a body that in 2018 also defended states' rights to purge voter rolls, disproportionately targeting minority voters. Which means that the movement for full democratic enfranchisement in the United States is ongoing, two centuries hence. It's easy to feel defeated by this, but more worthwhile to instead feel inspired: to know that in resisting and dissenting today, we are playing our parts in a story with long, righteous, proud roots.

No deus ex machina is going to appear to announce to those agitating for revolutionary change in the United States and around the world that the project we have embarked upon is a movement; no one can promise that our work now will remap our landscape and remake our future. That burden is on those of us who want desperately for it to do so. *We* determine whether or not we change the world.

The task—*especially* for the newly awakened, the newly angry, *especially* for the white women, for whom incentives to renounce their rage will be highest in coming years—is to keep going, to not turn back, to not give in to the easier path, the one where we weren't angry all the time, where we accepted the comforts of racial and economic advantage that will always be on offer to those who don't challenge power. Our job is to stay angry . . . perhaps for a very long time.

"It is probably going to be years," Emma González told reporters in 2018 about her battle against the gun lobby. "And at this point, I don't know that I mind. Nothing that's worth it is easy . . . We could very well die trying to do this. But we could very well die *not* trying to do this too. So why not die for something rather than nothing?"

González seems to know in youth what it took some activists ages to figure out: what's ahead of her. Vivian Gornick has written of her initial delight, as a woman in the 1970s, discovering the writing of the first wave feminists who had preceded her by a century: "We were . . . reincarnating as the feminists of previous generations," she wrote. "I remember reading Elizabeth Cady Stanton and feeling amazed that a hundred years ago she had said exactly what I was now saying. Amazed, and gratified. Not sobered. That would come later."

What should have been sobering, of course—what was sobering to me, in the summer of 2018, reading Andrea Dworkin and Flo Kennedy and Audre Lorde and Gornick herself—is that if women have been here before, yet we had to get here again, the process of change was going to be slow, hard, and often circular.

As Gornick recalls of how she thought in the 1970s, "Any minute now the whole country would be converted to the rightness of our cause. After all, it wasn't as if it hadn't all been said before. Now, surely, it was being said fully, freely, and for the last time. Women and men alike would set quickly about correcting the painful imbalance and then, existentially speaking, let the chips fall where they may." But as the years wore on, she began to hear in the glibness of her own assured analysis—of "how frightened we all are to look clearly at the meaning of sexism, how difficult it is to reverse the emotional habits of centuries, what anxieties the effort induces"—a stark and defining truth. She had been correct in her assessment of the challenges. "I began to see it was going to take longer than any of us had expected. Much longer."

That it will take a long time shouldn't scare us. It should fortify us. It *must* fortify us, as it seems to fortify Emma González. And we should remember that with each imperfect, and eventually stalled, stage of major social change has come some real progress: expanded enfranchisement, increases in liberty for more kinds of people, greater bodily autonomy. And yes, after each step has come the siren song of not-anger—of complicity and satisfaction and fealty to the traditional structures that soothed the burns left by the revolt. But it's nowhere near time for that yet.

We need to work to ensure that this moment will have spurred real change, to know that the changes we make will reverberate far into the future. Consider Shirley Chisholm, who cried when she was mad, and who didn't win. She lost. And yet. She pulled Barbara Lee into politics. Barbara Lee, who was the only person in Congress to vote against the AUMF, which she has been trying to repeal ever since; a fight she has also lost. Barbara Lee, who pioneered a bill in 2015 that would overturn the Hyde Amendment—a major step forward for poor women on an issue that no one had dared to touch since the 1970s. Lee's bill went nowhere. But enthusiasm for her efforts would help opposition to Hyde to find its way into the presidential agenda of Hillary Clinton. Who lost. And whose loss helped spur the entry of perhaps tens of thousands of women into electoral politics and provoked this country to take women's experiences of sexual harassment seriously for the first time. Some of those women will lose, too. But that will not be the end of the story either.

At all the marches, all the rallies, you'll see one sign over and over again. It is a Mexican proverb, apparently taken from the Greek: "They thought they could bury us; they didn't know we were seeds." Women's anger has been buried, over and over again. But it has seeded the ground; we are the green shoots of furies covered up long ago.

If you happen to be reading this in the future, having stumbled across it in an attempt to find out if you're allowed to be angry about whatever you're angry about, let me say: yes. Yes you are allowed. You are in fact compelled.

And if you're reading this now, in its moment, with me; if you've gotten to this page because you've been feeling rage at the unfairness and injustice and at the flaws of this country and because your anger is making you want to change your life in order to change the world, then I have something incredibly important to say: Don't forget how this feels.

Tell a friend, write it down, explain it to your children now, so they will remember. And don't let anyone persuade you it wasn't right, or it was weird, or it was some quirky stage in your life when you went all political— *remember that, honey, that year you went crazy*? No. No. Don't let it ever become that. Because people will try.

The future will come, we hope. If we survive this, if we make it better— even just a little bit better, but I hope a lot better—the urgency will fade, perhaps the ire will subside, the relief will take you, briefly. And that's good, that's okay.

But then the world will come and tell you that you shouldn't get mad again, because you were kind of nuts and you never cooked dinner and you yelled at the TV and weren't so pretty and life will be easier when you get fun again. And it will be awfully tempting to put away the pictures of yourself in your pussy hat, to stuff your protest signs in the attic, and to slink back, away from the raw bite of fury, to ease back into whatever new reality is made after whatever advances we achieve now.

But I say to all the women reading this now, and to my future self: What you're angry about now—injustice—will still exist, even if you yourself are not experiencing it, or are tempted to stop thinking about *how* you experience it, and how you contribute to it. Others are still experiencing it, still mad; some of them are mad at you. Don't forget them; don't write off their anger. Stay mad for them. Stay mad *with* them. They're right to be mad and you're right to be mad alongside them.

Being mad is correct; being mad is American; being mad can be joyful and productive and connective. Don't *ever* let them talk you out of being mad again.

Acknowledgments

Many thanks to everyone at Simon & Schuster, especially to my exceptional editor, Marysue Rucci. She, along with Jonathan Karp, Carolyn Reidy, Zachary Knoll, Sarah Reidy, Christine Pride, and Cary Goldstein have given my work a supportive and enthusiastic home, for which I'm so grateful. My agent, Linda Loewenthal, has long guided me, and this time brought me to Jane Isay, whose sharp and joyous editorial eye I could not have done without. Further gratitude to Meredith Tax, Alice Walker, and to the Women's Film Archive for permissions and access.

My colleagues at *New York* magazine helped shape many of the ideas in this volume, especially Noreen Malone, Laurie Abraham, Stella Bugbee, Jared Hohlt, Adam Moss, Pam Wasserstein, and Lauren Kern; Ann Clarke's support and humor buoyed this project. I am grateful for the thorough, speedy fact-checking of my colleague Jordan Larson, and the research assistance of Aubri Juhasz. Thanks to Bonnie Siegler for the cover and to Amy Bass for checking my history (fast!). For sustaining insight throughout these terrible years, thanks to Brittney Cooper, Katha Pollitt, Michelle Goldberg, Liz Meriwether, Rebecca Solnit, Lisa Miller, Emily Nussbaum, Bene Cipolla, Edward McPherson, Tom McGeveran, Dahlia Lithwick, Lizzie Skurnick, Jen Deaderick, Amy Goldwasser, Melissa Harris-Perry, Greg Veis, Jamelle Bouie, Joan Walsh, Geraldine Sealey, Lori Leibovich, Zoe Heller, Ta-Nehisi Coates, Chris Hayes, Jean Howard, Jim Baker, Pheroze Wadia, and Aaron and Karel Traister.

I thank especially Heather McPherson, Sara Culley, Kate Shaw, and

Krista Williams, all of whom read portions of this book as it was being written. I'm beholden to the furious, hilarious women whose voices are in my head every single day: Irin Carmon, Anna Holmes, and Aminatou Sow; I'd be a different thinker without them. And I'd be no thinker at all without Marion Belle, whose humor, political enthusiasms, and hard work brighten my days and make my work possible. I am lucky, too, to have Zoe Reich and Paul Margarites, Peter Koechly and Krista Williams, all of whom have offered friendship, ideas, and logistical help. It is inconceivable to me that this book was written and will be published in a world without my lifelong comrade, Michael Friedman, in it. The echo of his voice—and his prescience about this period—are contained in this volume.

My parents housed and fed and urged me to go outside while I wrote; my debt to them, like my love for them, is incalculable. To my daughters: I adore you, am proud of you, and am grateful for your patience and good humor, as well as for your impatience and ill humors. This book is dedicated to you in part because I want you to know that it is okay to be mad; it is *important* to be mad. My husband, Darius Wadia, is a finer partner, better friend, and kinder man than I ever expected to find in this world; he worked to make this book real every bit as hard as I did, all while doing his own difficult and important work, of which I am so proud. I am lucky to navigate this world alongside him.

Notes

INTRODUCTION

1. See the National Women's Political Caucus website at: http://www.nwpc.org/about/nwpc-foundation/.
2. Nan Robertson, "Democrats Feel Impact of Women's New Power," *New York Times*, July 15, 1972, http://www.nytimes.com/1972/07/15/archives/democrats-feel-impact-of-womens-new-power-womens-power-has-an.html.
3. Douglas Rogers, "Lights, Camera, Sexism!," *Washington Post*, July 4, 2004, http://www.washingtonpost.com/wp-dyn/articles/A16333-2004Jun29.html.
4. John Stauffer and Benjamin Soskis, *The Battle Hymn of the Republic: A Biography of the Song That Marches On*, (New York: Oxford University Press, 2013), p. 22. The folk musician Len Chandler rewrote the lyrics to the "Battle Hymn of the Republic" as "Move on Over" in 1965, at a commemoration of the Harpers Ferry uprising; its chorus was adopted as a slogan by the Black Panther Party.
5. Leymah Gbowee, "Leymah Gbowee in Her Own Words," PBS.org, September 13, 2011, http://www.pbs.org/wnet/women-war-and-peace/features/the-president-will-see-you-now/.
6. Alice Kessler-Harris, *Out to Work: The History of Wage-Earning Women in the United States* (New York: Oxford University Press, 2003), p. 41.
7. "Rosa Parks Essay Reveals Rape Attempt," *Huffington Post*, July 29, 2011, https://www.huffingtonpost.com/2011/07/29/rosa-parks-essay-rape_n_912997.html.
8. Sarah Kaplan, "A Scientist Who Studies Protests Says 'The Resistance' Isn't Slowing Down," *Washington Post*, May 3, 2017, https://www.washingtonpost.com/news/speaking-of-science/wp/2017/05/03/a-scientist-who-studies-

protest-says-the-resistance-isnt-slowing-down/?utm_term=.758284a8c17d. First brought to my attention in a tweet by Zeynep Tufekci, from a panel she was on with Dana Fisher at the 2017 American Sociological Association Annual Meeting.

9. Myisha Cherry, "Anger Is Not a Bad Word," TEDxUofIChicago, June 2, 2015, http://www.myishacherry.org/2015/06/02/my-tedx-talk-anger-is-not-a-bad-word/.

10. Kathy Spillar, "Not Backing Down," *Ms. Magazine,* August 31, 2017, http://msmagazine.com/blog/2017/08/31/not-backing-down/.

PART I

1. Susan Sarandon with Elizabeth Day, "Susan Sarandon: Feminism Is a Bit of an Old-fashioned Word," *The Guardian,* June 29, 2013, https://www.the-guardian.com/theobserver/2013/jun/30/susan-sarandon-q-and-a.

2. For a good discussion of the impact of Waters's riot statements, listen to Janet Mock's podcast, https://janetmock.com/podcast/.

3. Evans Rowl and Robert Novak, "No Insurrection in Los Angeles," *Washington Post,* May 4, 1992, https://www.washingtonpost.com/archive/opinions/1992/05/04/no-insurrection-in-los-angeles/1ff2c017-9674-4bc8-8667-51e7325f43ce/?noredirect=on&utm_term=.30f1bab1d799.

4. Taryn Finley, "Maxine Waters: '92 L.A. Rebellion Was a 'Defining Moment' for Black Resistance," *Huffington Post,* April 27, 2017, https://www.huffingtonpost.com/entry/maxine-waters-la-rebellion-was-a-defining-moment-for-black-resistance_us_58fe2861e4b00fa7de165e18.

5. Mychal Denzel Smith, "The Rebirth of Black Rage," *The Nation,* August 13, 2015, https://www.thenation.com/article/the-rebirth-of-black-rage/.

6. "Tea Act," History.com, https://www.history.com/topics/american-revolution/tea-act.

7. Kenneth P. Vogel, "Face of the Tea Party Is Female," *Politico,* March 26, 2010, https://www.politico.com/story/2010/03/face-of-the-tea-party-is-female-035094.

8. "New Demographic Profiles of Occupy Wall Street vs. Tea Party Movements," prri.com, December 1, 2011, https://www.prri.org/spotlight/new-demographic-profiles-of-occupy-wall-street-vs-tea-party-movements/.

9. Tina Dupuy, "The Occupy Movement's Woman Problem," *Atlantic,* November 21, 2011, https://www.theatlantic.com/politics/archive/2011/11/the-occupy-movements-woman-problem/248831/.

10. Quinn Norton, "A Eulogy for #Occupy," wired.com, December 12, 2012, https://www.wired.com/2012/12/a-eulogy-for-occupy/.

11. Karen McVeigh, "Occupy Wall Street's Women Struggle to Make Their

Voices Heard," *The Guardian*, November 30, 2011, https://www.theguardian
.com/world/2011/nov/30/occupy-wall-street-women-voices.

12. Ren Jender, "When the Stupidity about Rape Wouldn't Stop, I Quit the Movement I Loved," xojane.com, January 14, 2013.

13. Patrisse Khan-Cullors, "We Didn't Start a Movement. We started a Network," Medium.com, February 22, 2016, https://medium.com/@patrissemariecullorsbrignac/we-didn-t-start-a-movement-we-started-a-network-90f9b5717668.

14. Cavan Sieczkowski, "Feminist Activist Says Beyoncé is Partly 'Anti-Feminist' and 'Terrorist,' *Huffington Post*, May 9, 2014, https://www.huffingtonpost.com/2014/05/09/beyonce-anti-feminist_n_5295891.html.

15. Barbara Marcolini, "Trump Voters, One Year Later," *New York Times*, video, n.d., https://www.nytimes.com/video/us/politics/100000005538314/trump-voters-one-year-later.html.

16. Laura Barrón-López, "Donald Trump Adviser Says Hillary Clinton Should Be Shot by Firing Squad," *Huffington Post*, July 20, 2016, https://www.huffingtonpost.com/entry/al-baldasaro-donald-trump-hillary-clinton_us_578fa150e4b07c722ebd2fd1.

17. Daniel Denvir, "The Betrayal That Should Haunt Hillary Clinton: How She Sold Out Working Women and Then Never Apologized," *Salon*, https://www.salon.com/2015/11/02/the_betrayal_that_should_haunt_hillary_clinton_how_she_sold_out_working_women_then_never_apologized/.

18. Rebecca Traister, "The Left Is Borrowing Hillary Clinton Hate from the Republican National Convention—with Dangerous Consequences," *New York Times*, July 25, 2016, http://nymag.com/daily/intelligencer/2016/07/left-is-borrowing-hillary-hate-from-the-rnc.html.

19. Michelle Goldberg, "Men Explain Hillary to Me," *Slate*, November 6, 2015, http://www.slate.com/articles/double_x/doublex/2015/11/hillary_clinton_bernie_sanders_sexist_coverage_some_men_want_to_mansplain.html.

20. Alexis Okeowo, "The Writing Life of Warsan Shire, a Young, Prolific Poet," *New Yorker*, October 21, 2015, https://www.newyorker.com/culture/cultural-comment/the-writing-life-of-a-young-prolific-poet-warsan-shire. For the complete poem, "For Women Who Are 'Difficult' to Love," see https://genius.com/Warsan-shire-for-women-who-are-difficult-to-love-annotated.

21. Thomas E. Patterson, "News Coverage of the 2016 General Election: How the Press Failed the Voters," Shorenstein Center, December 7, 2016, https://shorensteincenter.org/news-coverage-2016-general-election/?platform=hootsuite.

22. Jonathan Mahler, "For Many Women, Trump's 'Locker Room Talk' Brings

Memories of Abuse," *New York Times*, October 10, 2016, https://www
.nytimes.com/2016/10/11/us/politics/sexual-assault-survivor-reaction.html
?action=click&contentCollection=Politics&module=RelatedCoverage&regi
on=Marginalia&pgtype=article.

23. Natasha Stoynoff, "Physically Attacked by Donald Trump—a *People* Writer's Own Harrowing Story," *People*, October 12, 2016, http://people.com
/politics/donald-trump-attacked-people-writer/.

24. Megan Twohey and Michael Barbaro, "Two Women Say Donald Trump
Touched Them Inappropriately," *New York Times*, October 12, 2016,
https://www.nytimes.com/2016/10/13/us/politics/donald-trump-women
.html.

25. Ibid.

26. NTK Staff, "Claire McCaskill Lacks Specifics on Goals of the Women's
March," *NTK Network*, January 23, 2017: https://ntknetwork.com/claire-
mccaskill-lacks-specifics-on-goals-of-the-womens-march/.

27. Margaret Hartmann, "What Happened to the 19 Women Who Accused Trump
of Sexual Misconduct," *New York* magazine, December 12, 2017, http://nymag
.com/daily/intelligencer/2017/12/what-happened-to-trumps-16-sexual-
misconduct-accusers.html.

28. Mark Lilla, "The End of Identity Liberalism," *New York Times*, November
18, 2016, https://www.nytimes.com/2016/11/20/opinion/sunday/the-end-
of-identity-liberalism.html.

29. Eliza Newlin Carney, "Who's Behind the Women's March," *American Prospect*, January 19, 2017, http://prospect.org/article/who%E2%80%99s-behind-
women%E2%80%99s-march. See also: Nina Agrawal, "How the Women's
March Came into Being," *Los Angeles Times*, January 21, 2017, http://www
.latimes.com/nation/la-na-pol-womens-march-live-how-the-women-s
-march-came-into-1484865755-htmlstory.html.

30. Annelise Orleck, *Rethinking American Women's Activism* (New York: Routledge, 2015), pp. 112–13.

31. Lawrence O'Donnell, "Something Is Happening: Women's March Makes
History," MSNBC.com, "The Last Word," video, January 23, 2017, https://
www.msnbc.com/the-last-word/watch/-something-is-happening-women-s
-march-makes-history-861237315678.

32. Annelise Orleck, *Rethinking American Women's Activism* (New York: Routledge, 2015), pp. 112–13.

33. ABC News, "Kellyanne Conway Interview: 'Didn't See the Point' to Women's
March on Washington," YouTube Video, 17:15, January 22, 2017, https://
www.youtube.com/watch?v=H8tErpLLFbE.

34. ABC News, "Chuck Schumer on Women's Marching 'Part of the Grand

American Tradition,' " YouTube Video, 7:33, January 22, 2017, https://www.youtube.com/watch?v=tTLcREwdNp0.

35. Micah White, "Without a Path from Protest to Power, the Women's March Will End Up Like Occupy," *The Guardian*, January 19, 2017, https://www.theguardian.com/world/2017/jan/19/womens-march-washington-occupy-protest.

36. "Don't Just March, Run!" EMILY's List, https://emilyslist.org/pages/entry/getting-ready-to-run.

37. Edward-Isaac Dovere and Elana Schor, "Will the Women's March Be Another Occupy, or a Democratic Tea Party?" *Politico*, January 21, 2017, https://www.politico.com/story/2017/01/womens-march-organizing-strategy-233973.

38. Ibid.

39. "McCaskill on Women's March: I Hope Trump Pays Attention," *Morning Joe*, January 23, 2017, https://www.msnbc.com/morning-joe/watch/mccaskill-on-women-s-march-i-hope-trump-pays-attention-860604483733.

40. Matt Ford (@fordm), "Leaving Dulles now to file from home. Gender disparity was striking: Probably 70 percent of lawyers volunteering there are young women," Twitter, January 29 2017, 6:53 pm, https://twitter.com/fordm/status/825899790785454083.

41. Patty Murray, Kamala D. Harris, et al., "Letter to President Donald J. Trump," United States Senate, January 30, 2017, https://www.harris.senate.gov/imo/media/doc/013017%20Harris-Murray%20Letter.pdf.

42. Nora Mcinerny Purmort, "How I Accidentally Convinced 100 Strangers to Get Matching Tattoos," *Cosmopolitan*, March 1, 2017, http://www.cosmopolitan.com/politics/a9078317/how-i-convinced-100-women-to-get-matching-tattoos/.

43. Megan Garber, " 'Nevertheless, She Persisted' and the Age of the Weaponized Meme," *Atlantic*, February 8, 2017, https://www.theatlantic.com/entertainment/archive/2017/02/nevertheless-she-persisted-and-the-age-of-the-weaponized-meme/516012/.

44. Sady Doyle, "New Survey Says Women Are Leading the Resistance, Because of Course They Are," Talk Poverty, April 11, 2017, https://talkpoverty.org/2017/04/11/new-survey-says-women-leading-resistance-course/.

45. Catherine Pearson, "Women Wore 'Handmaid's Tale' Robes to the Texas Senate," *Huffington Post*, March 20, 2017, https://www.huffingtonpost.com/entry/women-wore-handmaids-tale-robes-to-texas-senate_us_58d034bee4b0ec9d29de74f5.

46. Ruptly, "Torched Confederate Flag & Witch Costumes: Activists Protest Against 'Free Speech' Rally in Boston, YouTube Video, 2:10, August 19, 2017, https://www.youtube.com/watch?v=gg5Mkiv_djA.

47. Timothy Bella, "Patrisse Khan-Cullors on 5 Years of Black Lives Matter," *New York* magazine, January 18, 2018, http://nymag.com/daily/intelligencer/2018/01/patrisse-khan-cullors-on-5-years-of-black-lives-matter.html.

48. Kirsten Gillibrand (@SenGillibrand), "It is an honor to announce that Mayor@ Carmen YulinCruz of San Juan, Puerto Rico will join me at the #SOTU. Throughout the crisis in Puerto Rico, Mayor Cruz has shown extraordinary leadership and fearless advocacy for her city," Twitter, January 29, 2018, 6:21 am, https://twitter.com/SenGillibrand/status/957982123377545216.

49. Samhita Mukhopadhyay, "2017: The Year Women's Anger Was Unleashed," Mic, December 22, 2017, https://mic.com/articles/187016/2017-the-year-womens-anger-was-unleashed#.XymO8o0op.

50. Laurie Penny (@PennyRed), "Most of the interesting women you know are far, far angrier than you'd imagine," Twitter, July 18, 2017, 2:27 am, https://twitter.com/pennyred/status/887423515892342786?lang=en.

51. Manohla Dargis, "Harvey Weinstein Is Gone. But Hollywood Still Has a Problem," *New York Times*, October 11, 2017, https://mobile.nytimes.com/2017/10/11/movies/harvey-weinstein-hollywood.html?hp&action=click&pgtype=Homepage&clickSource=story-heading&module=first-column-region&region=top-news&WT.nav=top-news&_r=0&referer=https://t.co/Jl3eXTRHqT?amp=1.

52. Oluo Ijeoma, "Does This Year Make Me Look Angry?" *Elle*, January 11, 2018, https://www.elle.com/culture/career-politics/a15063942/ijeoma-oluo-women-and-rage-2018/.

53. Melissa Harris-Perry, "Women Are Angrier Than Ever Before—and They're Doing Something About It," *Elle*, March 9, 2018, https://www.elle.com/culture/career-politics/a19297903/elle-survey-womens-anger-melissa-harris-perry/.

54. Amanda Arnold, "Steve Bannon Is Really Worried About the 'Anti-Patriarchy' Movement," *The Cut*, February 10, 2018, https://www.thecut.com/2018/02/steve-bannon-is-worried-about-the-anti-patriarchy-movement.html.

55. Caitlin Flanagan, "The Conversation #MeToo Needs to Have," *Atlantic*, January 29, 2018, https://www.theatlantic.com/politics/archive/2018/01/the-right-conversation-for-metoo/551732/.

56. Michelle Goldberg, "The Teachers Revolt in West Virginia," *New York Times*, March 5, 2018, https://www.nytimes.com/2018/03/05/opinion/west-virginia-teachers-strike.html?action=click&contentCollection=opinion%C2%AEion=rank&module=package&version=highlights&contentPlacement=3&pgtype=sectionfront.

57. "Florida Student Emma González to Lawmakers and Gun Advocates: 'We Call BS,'" CNN.com, February 17, 2018, https://www.cnn.com/2018/02/17/us/florida-student-emma-gonzalez-speech/index.html.

58. Leon Stein, ed., *Out of the Sweatshop: The Struggle for Industrial Democracy* (New York: Quadrangle/New York Times Book Company, 1977), pp. 196–97.

PART II

1. John Nichols, "16 Years Ago, Barbara Lee's Warning Against the AUMF Was Ignored. Nevertheless, She Persisted," *The Nation*, June 30, 2017, https://www.thenation.com/article/16-years-ago-barbara-lees-warning-against-the-aumf-was-ignored-nevertheless-she-persisted/.
2. Austin Wright, "How Barbara Lee Became an Army of One," *Politico*, July 30, 2017, https://www.politico.com/magazine/story/2017/07/30/how-barbara-lee-became-an-army-of-one-215434.
3. Rep. Barbara Lee, "Rep. Lee Testifies on AUMF Sunset Amdt in Rules Committee," YouTube Video, 51:56, July 25, 2017, https://www.youtube.com/watch?v=BS51Lr0ibLc.
4. Thomas Carnan, *An Historic Description of the Tower of London and Its Curiosities*, (London: Londres, 1787, via Google Books), p. 47. This so-called "Collar of Torment" was on exhibit at the Tower of London in fall of 2017. It is described in colorful terms as an item that was once "used formerly to be put about the women's necks that made cuckolds of their husbands or scolded at them when they came late; but that custom is left off now-a-days, to prevent quarrelling for collars, there not being enough smiths to make them."
5. Jennifer Hansler, "A Brief History of Female Politicians Being Told to Smile," CNN.com, January 31, 2018, https://www.cnn.com/2018/01/31/politics/women-politicians-told-to-smile/index.html. See also: Joe Scarborough (@JoeNBC), "Smile. You Just had a big night. #PrimaryDay," Twitter, March 15, 2016, 6:10 pm, https://twitter.com/JoeNBC/status/709909770619248640.
6. Hansler, "Brief History of Female Politicians." See also: Chris Cillizza (@CillizzaCNN), "I think Nancy Pelosi looks like that all the time. I think she should smile a lot more often. I think the country would be better for it. She seems to embody the bitterness that belongs in the Democratic party," Twitter, January 31, 2018, 5:43 am, https://twitter.com/CillizzaCNN/status/958697219401682944.
7. Rodger Streitmatter, *Mightier Than the Sword: How the New Media Have Shaped American History* (New York: Routledge, 2018). See also: Elizabeth Johnston, "The Original 'Nasty Woman,'" *Atlantic*, November 6, 2016, https://www.theatlantic.com/entertainment/archive/2016/11/the-original-nasty-woman-of-classical-myth/506591/. And Mary Beard, *Women and Power: A Manifesto* (New York: Liveright, 2017).
8. Marjorie Spruill Wheeler, ed., *One Woman, One Vote* (Troutdale, OR: NewSage Press, 1995), p. 121.

9. Mary Beard, *Women & Power: A Manifesto* (New York: Liveright, 2017).

10. Joel B. Pollack, "The Naked Hillary Clinton Statues You've Never Seen—and Lived to Tell," Breitbart.com, August 21, 2016, http://www.breitbart.com/california/2016/08/21/naked-hillary-clinton-statues-youve-never-seen/. See also: Elizabeth Johnston, "The Original 'Nasty Woman,'" *Atlantic*, November 6, 2016, https://www.theatlantic.com/entertainment/archive/2016/11/the-original-nasty-woman-of-classical-myth/506591/.

11. Ian Schwartz, "Mnuchin vs, Waters: 'You Acknowledged I Shouldn't Interrupt'; Waters: 'I'm Reclaiming My Time!'" RealClear Politics, July 27, 2017, https://www.realclearpolitics.com/video/2017/07/27/mnuchin_vs_maxine_waters_you_acknowledged_i_shouldnt_interrupt_waters_im_reclaiming_my_time.html.

12. Sarah Taylor, "This Is Exactly Why Maxine Waters' Televised, Unhinged Threats Against Trump Need to Stop," TheBlaze.com, August 23, 2017, https://www.theblaze.com/news/2017/08/23/this-is-exactly-why-maxine-waters-televised-unhinged-threats-against-trump-need-to-stop. See also: Tony Lee, "Maxine Waters Unhinged: I'm Going to Take Ben Carson's A** Apart,'" Breitbart.com, July 3, 2017, http://www.breitbart.com/big-government/2017/07/03/maxine-waters-unhinged-im-going-take-ben-carsons-apart/.

13. "Trump-Loving Pastor Darrell Scott Comes for Maxine Waters, Calls Her a 'Crazy Aunt,'" TheGrio.com, February 2, 2018, https://thegrio.com/2018/02/02/pastor-darrell-scott-maxine-waters/.

14. Lindy West, "Brave Enough to Be Angry," *New York Times*, November 8, 2017, https://www.nytimes.com/2017/11/08/opinion/anger-women-weinstein-assault.html?smid=tw-nytimes&smtyp=cur&_r=0.

15. Andy B. Wang and Sean Sullivan, "Congressional Intern Suspended After Yelling Obscenity at President Trump in the Capitol," *Washington Post*, June 26, 2018, https://www.washingtonpost.com/news/powerpost/wp/2018/06/26/congressional-intern-suspended-after-yelling-obscenity-at-president-trump-at-the-capitol/?utm_term=.e6872a3b4676.

16. Author interview with Gloria Steinem.

17. Joanna Scutts, *Hotbed*, New York Historical Society, November 3, 2017–March 25, 2018.

18. Barry Michels and Phil Stutz, "The Root of Anger—and Using Its Force for Good," goop.com, n.d., http://goop.com/roots-anger-using-force-good/?utm_campaign=socialflow&utm_source=twitter.com&utm_medium=social-jp.

19. Matthew Biedlingmaier, "*Wash. Post*'s Achenbach: Hillary Clinton 'needs a radio-controlled shock collar so that aides can zap her when she starts to get screechy,'" *Media Matters*, January 8, 2008, https://

urldefense.proofpoint.com/v2/url?u=https-3A__www.mediamatters.org
_research_2008_01_08_wash-2Dposts-2Dachenbach-2Dhillary-2Dclinton-
2Dneeds-2Da-2Dra_142081&d=DwMFaQ&c=jGUuvAdBXp_VqQ6t0yah2g&r=BL
twNjxI6xU1TowZZXPw62rxL1h5Yh02Ol72-V1YNSunoH38hlyco6RBfK8BXD8O
&m=sL2dj6nPNRrhSTnketBXS3yIKp1p_iNSqJEEq9TW4t8&s=APPmAsKAR38o3-
gywLe-D5Cj0xCoFcoXx1XQq_L2Odg&e=.

20. Amanda Terkel, "Millbank Jokes That Hillary Clinton Should Drink
'Mad Bitch' Beer," ThinkProgress.org, July 31, 2009, https://thinkprogress
.org/milbank-jokes-that-hillary-clinton-should-drink-mad-bitch-beer-
fa187583bd18/.

21. MoxNews.com, "Donald Trump 'I AM ANGRY,'" YouTube Video, 14:55,
January 13, 2016, https://www.youtube.com/watch?v=v2dNzmaekmU.

22. Jonathan Martin and Patrick Healy, "In Democratic Debate, Candidates
Clash on Money's Role," *New York Times*, February 5, 2016, https://www
.nytimes.com/2016/02/05/us/politics/democratic-debate.html.

23. The Young Turks, "Hillary Having Problems Controlling THE VOLUME OF
HER VOICE," YouTube Video, 2:54, February 4, 2016, https://www.youtube
.com/watch?v=a5sXLoXxvBM.

24. Thomas Frank, "Donald Trump Is Moving to the White House, and Lib-
erals Put Him There," *The Guardian*, November 9, 2016, https://www.the
guardian.com/commentisfree/2016/nov/09/donald-trump-white-house-
hillary-clinton-liberals.

25. Lisa Feldman Barrett, "Hillary Clinton's 'Angry Face,'" *New York Times*, September 23, 2016, https://www.nytimes.com/2016/09/25/opinion/sunday/
hillary-clintons-angry-face.html.

26. "Michelle Obama: 'Angry Black Woman' Label Hurt," CNN.com, video,
December 19, 2016, https://www.cnn.com/videos/politics/2016/12/19
/michelle-obama-angry-black-woman-nr-sot.cnn.

27. I transcribed this interview immediately after video of the conversation ran
alongside a story by Robin Givhan, reporting on the conversation. After a
dispute about whether or not the conversation was on the record, the network, BET, which had supplied the video, pulled it from Givhan's story:
Robin Givhan, "Michelle Obama Wanted to Gain the Public's Trust. So
She Started With a Garden," *The Washintgon Post*, March 21, 2018, https://
www.washingtonpost.com/news/arts-and-entertainment/wp/2018/03/21/
michelle-obama-wanted-to-gain-the-publics-trust-so-she-started-with-a-
garden/. See also: Danielle C. Belton, "They Said It Was Private. She Said It
Was On-the-Record. The Reality? It's Complicated," *The Root*, March 23, 2018,
https://www.theroot.com/they-said-it-was-private-she-said-it-was-on-the
-record-1824024113.

28. Katy Guest, "Women! Reclaim Your Rage," Unbound.com, January 15, 2018, https://unbound.com/boundless/2018/01/15/women-reclaim-your-rage/.

29. Jason Le Miere, "Maxine Waters's 'Take Trump Out' Remark Was About 'Assassination,' Not 'Impeachment,' Says Fox News Guest," *Newsweek*, October 23, 2017, http://www.newsweek.com/maxine-waters-trump-assassination-impeachment-690761.

30. Mark Swanson, "GOP Challenger Calls for Rep. Waters' Arrest After Trump Remarks," Newsmax, October 23, 2017, https://www.newsmax.com/politics/maxine-waters-omar-navarro-donald-trump-take-him-out/2017/10/23/id/821549/.

31. Ian Schwartz, "Maxine Waters: Trump Supporters 'Not Accustomed' to a Black Woman 'Taking Leadership' to Impeach Him," RealClear Politics, October 24, 2017, https://www.realclearpolitics.com/video/2017/10/24/maxine_waters_trump_supporters_not_accustomed_to_a_black_woman_taking_leadership_to_impeach_him.html.

32. Ibid.

33. " 'Reclaiming My Time': Rep. Maxine Waters Interrupts Mnuchin's Roundabout Answer," *Washington Post*, video, August 1, 2017, https://www.washingtonpost.com/video/national/maxine-waters-reclaiming-my-time/2017/08/01/30fae7f4-76d4-11e7-8c17-533c52b2f014_video.html?utm_term=.e2dd5dd34636. See also IdolxNews, "Maxine Waters 'Reclaiming My Time' Performed Live—The View," YouTube Video, 1:54, August 4, 2017, https://www.youtube.com/watch?v=lRuRdEaatio.

34. Joe Concha, "O'Reilly Mocks Dem Maxine Waters for Wearing 'James Brown Wig,' " The Hill.com, March 28, 2017, http://thehill.com/home-news/media/326107-oreilly-mocks-maxine-waters-for-wearing-james-brown-wig.

35. Jamilah King, "Maxine Waters' Battle Against Powerful White Men Began When Eula Love Was Killed in 1979," Mic, April 26, 2017, https://mic.com/articles/174565/maxine-waters-battle-against-powerful-white-men-began-when-eula-love-was-killed-in-1979#.seD4bEkf9.

36. "Internetting with Amanda Hess: Episode 5: The White Internet's Love Affair with Digital Blackface," *New York Times*, November 28, 2017, https://www.nytimes.com/interactive/2017/11/28/arts/internetting-with-amanda-hess.html.

37. Audre Lorde, "The Uses of Anger: Women Responding to Racism," keynote presentation, National Women's Studies Association Conference, Storrs, Connecticut, June 1981, BlackPast.org, http://www.blackpast.org/1981-audre-lorde-uses-anger-women-responding-racism.

38. Angela Peoples, "Don't Just Thank Black Women. Follow Us," *New York*

Times, December 16, 2017, https://www.nytimes.com/2017/12/16/opinion/sunday/black-women-leadership.html.

39. Lori D. Ginzberg, *Elizabeth Cady Stanton: A Life*, (New York, NY: Farrar, Straus and Giroux, 2009); p. 91.

40. Adjua Fisher, "4 Philly Fitness Classes Where You Can Fully Express Your Rage," *Philadelphia*, November 9, 2016, https://www.phillymag.com/be-well-philly/2016/11/09/boxing-classes-philadelphia/.

41. Regena Thomashauer, "Get Right with Your Darkness," MamaGenas.com, March 2, 2017, http://www.mamagenas.com/get-right-with-your-darkness/.

42. Richard Brookhiser, "The Happy Medium," review of *Other Powers: The Age of Suffrage, Spiritualism, and the Scandalous Victoria Woodhull* and *Notorious Victoria: The Life of Victoria Woodhull, Uncensored, New York Times Books*, March 29, 1998, https://archive.nytimes.com/www.nytimes.com/books/98/03/29/reviews/980329.29brookht.html?scp=9&sq=Napoleon%2520and%2520Josephine:%2520A%2520Love%2520Story&st=Search.

43. Marjorie Spruill Wheeler, ed., *One Woman, One Vote* (Troutdale, OR: New-Sage Press, 1995), p. 127.

44. Ibid., p. 126.

45. "Mother Bloor: U.S. Communist Heroine," *Life*, July 26, 1937, https://books.google.ca/books?id=pEUEAAAAMBAJ&pg=PA27&lpg=PA27&dq=grand+old+woman+of+the+U.S.+communist+party&source=bl&ots=5SP8GXcvZf&sig=2lwUS5XCddb5z-6VAGT95wMGZ9I&hl=en&sa=X&ved=0ahUKEwiu6ofQrNLMAhXi44MKHYUtBrgQ6AEIIDAC#v=onepage&q=grand%20old&f=false.

46. Mary Triece, *On the Picket Line: Strategies of Working-Class Women During the Depression* (Champaign: University of Illinois Press, 2007), p. 19.

47. Stephen Tuck, *We Ain't What We Ought To Be: The Black Freedom Struggle from Emancipation to Obama* (New York: Belknap Press, 2011), p. 189.

48. Marjorie Spruill Wheeler, ed., *One Woman, One Vote* (Troutdale, OR: New-Sage Press, 1995), p. 175.

49. Mamie Till Mobley, "The Untold Story of EMMETT LUIS TILL (Documentary 2005) by Keith Beauchamp," YouTube Video, 1:08:18, November 19, 2012, https://www.youtube.com/watch?v=bvijYSJtkQk.

50. David Deitcher (ed.), *The Question of Equality: Lesbian and Gay Politics in America Since Stonewall*, (New York, NY: Scribner, 1996), p 67.

51. Manny Fernandez, "A Stonewall Veteran, 89, Misses the Parade," *New York Times*, June 27, 2010, https://www.nytimes.com/2010/06/28/nyregion/28storme.html?_r=1.

52. Alexandria Piette, "In Remembrance of the Stonewall Riots," *Women's Republic*, June 8, 2017, http://www.womensrepublic.net/in-remembrance-of-the-stonewall-riots-the-lasting-impact-on-the-lgbtq-community/.

53. Megan Garber, "All the Angry Ladies," *Atlantic*, November 6, 2017, https://www
.theatlantic.com/entertainment/archive/2017/11/all-the-angry-ladies/545042/.

54. Meghan O'Rourke, "Mourning Trump and the America We Could Have
Been," *New Yorker*, November 10, 2016, https://www.newyorker.com/
culture/culture-desk/mourning-trump-and-the-america-we-could-have-
been?irgwc=1&source=affiliate_impactpmx_12f6tote_desktop_Skim
bit%20Ltd.&mbid=affiliate_impactpmx_12f6tote_desktop_Skimbit%20Ltd.

55. Lisa Feldman Barrett, "Hillary Clinton's 'Angry' Face," *New York Times*, September 23, 2016, https://www.nytimes.com/2016/09/25/opinion/sunday/hill
ary-clintons-angry-face.html. See also: Mary Lay Schuster and Amy D. Propen,
*Victim Advocacy in the Courtroom: Persuasive Practices in Domestic Violence
and Child Protection Cases* (Boston: Northeastern University Press, 2011).

56. Leslie Jamison, "I Used to Insist I Didn't Get Angry. Not Anymore," *New York
Times Magazine*, January 17, 2018, https://www.nytimes.com/2018/01/17/
magazine/i-used-to-insist-i-didnt-get-angry-not-anymore.html.

57. Ibid.

58. National Woman Suffrage Association, "Declaration of Rights of Women of
the United States," in *Selected Papers of Elizabeth Cady Stanton and Susan B.
Anthony, vol. 3, National Protection for National Citizens, 1873 to 1880*, ed.
Ann D. Gordon (New Brunswick, NJ: Rutgers University Press, 2003).

59. Nora Ephron, "Miami," *Huffington Post*, n.d., https://highline.huffington
post.com/articles/en/lets-go-full-crocodile-ladies/essay/.

60. Warren Weaver, Jr., "Schroeder, Assailing 'the System,' Decides Not to Run
for President," *New York Times*, September 29, 1987, https://www.nytimes
.com/1987/09/29/us/schroeder-assailing-the-system-decides-not-to-run-
for-president.html.

61. Susan Ferraro, "The Prime of Pat Schroeder," *New York Times*, July 1,
1990, https://www.nytimes.com/1990/07/01/magazine/the-prime-of-pat-
schroeder.html.

62. Robin DiAngelo, "White Fragility," *The International Journal of Critical Ped-
agogy*, Vol. 3, No. 3, 2011, http://libjournal.uncg.edu/ijcp/article/view/249.

63. Susan Ferraro, "The Prime of Pat Schroeder," *New York Times*, July 1,
1990, https://www.nytimes.com/1990/07/01/magazine/the-prime-of-pat-
schroeder.html.

64. Ibid.

65. PBS, "Makers: The Women Who Make America," Season 1, Stop the ERA
video: https://www.pbs.org/video/makers-women-who-make-america-stop-era/.

66. Susan Ferraro, "The Prime of Pat Schroeder," *New York Times*, July 1,
1990, https://www.nytimes.com/1990/07/01/magazine/the-prime-of-pat-
schroeder.html.

67. "Hillary Clinton" (parody); "Let Me Remind You Fuckers Who I Am," *Medium*, July 25, 2016, https://medium.com/@shitHRCcantsay/let-me-remind -you-fuckers-who-i-am-e6e8b297fe47.

68. "Hillary Clinton" (parody); "Are you Fucking Kidding Me," November 13, 2016, https://medium.com/@shitHRCcantsay/are-you-fucking-kidding-me -86bdc2c638d6.

69. Robinson, Phoebe, *You Can't Touch My Hair (And Other Things I Still Have to Explain*, (New York: New York, Plume, 2016).

70. Nellie Andreeva, "Seth MacFarlane Opens Up About His 2013 Harvey Weinstein Oscars Joke, Condemns 'Abhorrent' Abuse of Power," Deadline, October 11, 2017, https://deadline.com/2017/10/seth-macfarlane-harvey- weinstein-oscar-joke-explained-1202186425/.

71. Megan Garber, "The Anger of Samantha Bee," *Atlantic*, October 11, 2016, https://www.theatlantic.com/entertainment/archive/2016/10/the-angers-of- samantha-bee/503612/

72. Callum Borchers, "Michelle Wolf's Caustic Comedy Routine at the White House Correspondents' Dinner, Annotated," *Washington Post*, April 29, 2018, https://www.washingtonpost.com/news/the-fix/wp/2018/04/29/michelle- wolfs-caustic-comedy-routine-at-the-white-house-correspondents-dinner- annotated/?utm_term=.2beb058203b6.

73. Masha Gessen, "Michelle Wolf Blasted Open the Fictions of Journalism in the Age of Trump," *New Yorker*, April 30, 2018, https://www.newyorker.com/ news/our-columnists/how-michelle-wolf-blasted-open-the-fictions-of- journalism-in-the-age-of-trump.

74. Mika Brzezinski (@morningmika), "Watching a wife and mother be humiliated on national television for looks is deplorable. I have experienced insults about my appearance from the president. All women have a duty to unite when these attacks happen and the WHCA owes Sarah an apology," Twitter, April 29, 2018, 6:37 am, https://twitter.com/morningmika/ status/990585968825597954.

75. Maggie Haberman (@maggieNYT), "That @PressSec sat and absorbed intense criticism of her physical appearance, her job performance, and so forth, instead of walking out, on national television, was impressive," Twitter, April 28, 2018, 8:14 pm, https://twitter.com/maggieNYT/status /990428993542414336.

76. "Can you Guess Kamala Harris' Favorite Curse Word?", *The Week*, July 6, 2017, http://theweek.com/speedreads/710360/guess-kamala-harris-favor- ite-curse-word.

77. Kristin Wong, "The Case for Cursing," *New York Times*, July 27, 2017, https:// www.nytimes.com/2017/07/27/smarter-living/the-case-for-cursing.html.

78. Katie Hawkins-Gaar, "The Cohort: Don't Call Me 'Dear,' f**kface, and Other Ways to Approach Anger at Work," *Poynter*, August 31, 2017, https://www.poynter.org/news/cohort-dont-call-me-dear-fkface-and-other-ways-approach-anger-work.

79. Kristin Wong, "The Case for Cursing," *New York Times*, July 27, 2017, https://www.nytimes.com/2017/07/27/smarter-living/the-case-for-cursing.html.

80. Eric Grundhauser, "The Great Harvard Pee-In of 1973," Atlas Obscura, December 23, 2016, https://www.atlasobscura.com/articles/the-great-harvard-peein-of-1973.

81. Alice Kessler-Harris, *Out to Work: A History of Wage-Earning Women in the United States* (New York: Oxford University Press, 2003), p. 41.

82. Leigh Fought, *Women in the World of Frederick Douglass* (New York: Oxford University Press, 2017) p. 195.

83. Marjorie Spruill Wheeler, ed., *One Woman, One Vote* (Troutdale, OR: NewSage Press, 1995), p. 38.

84. Ibid.

85. Ibid.

86. "Transcript: Hillary Clinton's Full Interview with NPR's Rachel Martin," NPR.com, September 12, 2017, https://www.npr.org/2017/09/12/549430064/transcript-hillary-clinton-s-full-interview-with-npr-s-rachel-martin.

87. Harry Enten (@ForecasterEnten), "I cannot believe I did this. . . but! Per the 2016 CCES (again I can't believe I'm doing this), only 8% of black voters went for Trump. But among black men earing at least 100k a year, it was 15%. So Kanye isn't completely alone," Twitter, April 25, 2018, 1:18 pm, https://twitter.com/ForecasterEnten/status/989237343948328960.

88. Travis Deshong, "Diane Nash: An Activist's Lessons for a New Generation," *Yale Daily News*, January 27, 2017, https://yaledailynews.com/blog/2017/01/27/diane-nash-an-activists-lessons-for-a-new-generation/.

89. The Women's Convention, Women's Convention Schedule: http://www.womensconvention.com/schedule.html.

90. Kat Calvin (@KatCalvinLA), "This is actually true. A majority of our STV vols are white women who are going to homeless shelters every week, driving people they have never met and wouldn't normally speak to all over town, and are really putting their hearts into it. It's kind of amazing," Twitter, December 13, 2017, 8:31 am, https://twitter.com/KatCalvinLA/status/940982502126006272.

91. "Death of Fred Douglass," *New York Times*, February 21, 1895, https://archive.nytimes.com/www.nytimes.com/learning/general/onthisday/bday/0207.html.

92. Ta-Nehisi Coates, "Frederick Douglass 'A Woman's Rights Man,' " *Atlantic*, September 30, 2011, https://www.theatlantic.com/personal/archive/2011/09/ frederick-douglass-a-womens-rights-man/245977/.

PART III

1. Joy Press, "The Life and Death of a Radical Sisterhood," The Cut, November 15, 2017, https://www.thecut.com/2017/11/an-oral-history-of-feminist-group-new-york-radical-women.html. See also: Roxane Gay, "Fifty Years Ago, Protesters Took on the Miss America Pageant and Electrified the Feminist Movement," *Smithsonian*, January 2018, https://www.smithsonianmag .com/history/fifty-years-ago-protestors-took-on-miss-america-pageant-electrified-feminist-movement-180967504/.

2. CBS This Morning, "Gayle King and Norah O'Donnell respond to Charlie Rose allegations," YouTube Video, 3:18, November 21, 2017, https://www .youtube.com/watch?v=-SIp6xSP7ds.

3. Bryn Elise Sandberg, "Sarah Silverman Addresses Louis C.K.'s Sexual Misconduct: 'It's a Real Mind—,'" *Hollywood Reporter*, November 16, 2017, https://www.hollywoodreporter.com/live-feed/sarah-silverman-addresses-louis-cks-sexual-misconduct-a-real-mindf-1059117.

4. "To Tell the Truth," The Cut, video, December 20, 2017, https://www.thecut .com/2017/12/rose-mcgowan-harvey-weinstein-sexual-assault-and-harass ment.html?utm_source=nym_press.

5. Marjorie Spruill Wheeler, ed., *One Woman, One Vote* (Troutdale, OR: New-Sage Press, 1995), p. 38.

6. E. W. Capron, "Women's Rights Convention," *National Reformer*, August 3, 1848, http://facstaff.elon.edu/dcopeland/fourth%20hour/seneca%20falls.pdf.

7. Cecile Richards, *Make Trouble*: *Standing Up, Speaking Out, and Finding the Courage to Lead* (New York: Simon & Schuster, 2018).

8. Beverly Willett, " 'Feminists Love Divorce!' " *Huffington Post*, May 25, 2011, https://www.huffingtonpost.com/beverly-willett/feminists-love-divorce_b_ 825208.html.

9. Jill Brooke, "Did Feminism Cause Divorce?" *Huffington Post*, May 25, 2011, https://www.huffingtonpost.com/jill-brooke/did-feminism-cause-many-d_b_836327.html.

10. Tracy Connor, "Larry Nassar Complains It's Too Hard to Listen to Victim Stories," NBCNews.com, January 18, 2018, https://www.nbcnews.com/news/us-news/larry-nassar-complains-it-s-too-hard-listen-victim-stories-n838731.

11. Havana Marking, "The Real Legacy of Andrea Dworkin," *The Guardian*, April 15, 2005, https://www.theguardian.com/world/2005/apr/15/gender .politicsphilosophyandsociety.

12. Lore Dickstein, "Street Fighting Feminist," *New York Times*, October 29, 1989, https://www.nytimes.com/1989/10/29/books/street-fighting-feminist .html.

13. Jonathan Allen, "Pelosi Stumbles on Alleged Harassment in Her Own Ranks," NBCNews.com, November 27, 2017, https://www.nbcnews.com/politics/ congress/pelosi-stumbles-alleged-harassment-her-own-ranks-n824041.

14. Dayna Tortorici, "In the Maze," *n+1*, Winter 2018.

15. Jessica Campbell, "The First Brave Woman Who Alleged 'Sexual Harassment,'" Legacy.com, February 5, 2016, http://www.legacy.com/news/culture- and-trends/article/the-first-brave-woman-who-alleged-sexual-harassment.

16. Kyle Svenson, "Who Came Up with the Term 'Sexual Harassment,'" *Washington Post*, November 22, 2017, https://www.washingtonpost.com/ news/morning-mix/wp/2017/11/22/who-came-up-with-the-term-sexual- harassment/?utm_term=.d49729fcce2a.

17. Ibid.

18. Susan Brownmiller and Dolores Alexander, "From Carmita Wood to Anita Hill," *Ms.*, January/February 1992, http://www.nfwfwf.org/wp-content/ uploads/2018/02/BROWNMILLER-ALEXANDER-MS-MAG-1992.pdf.

19. Megan Twohey, Jodi Kantor, Susan Dominus, Jim Rutenberg, and Steve Eder, "Weinstein's Complicity Machine," *New York Times*, December 5, 2017, https://www.nytimes.com/interactive/2017/12/05/us/harvey-weinstein- complicity.html. See also: Irin Carmon and Amy Brittain, "Eight Women Say Charlie Rose Sexually Harassed Them—with Nudity, Groping and Lewd Calls," *Washington Post*, November 20, 2017, https://www.washingtonpost .com/investigations/eight-women-say-charlie-rose-sexually-harassed- them—with-nudity-groping-and-lewd-calls/2017/11/20/9b168de8- caec-11e7-8321-481fd63f174d_story.html.

20. Toni Morrison, "A Humanist View" as part of Black Studies Center public dialogue, Pt. 2, May 30, 1975.

21. Tom Bartlett and Nell Gluckman, "She Left Harvard. He Got to Stay," *Chronicle of Higher Education*, February 27, 2018, https://www.chronicle.com/ interactives/harvard-harassment.

22. Gabriel Sherman, *The Loudest Voice in the Room* (New York: Random House, 2014).

23. Ella Nilsen, "Mark Halperin Once Downplayed Sexual Harassment Claims Against Trump. Now He's Facing His Own," *Vox*, October 27, 2017, https://www .vox.com/2017/10/27/16559880/mark-halperin-trump-sexual-harassment.

24. Manohla Dargis, "Harvey Weinstein Is Gone. But Hollywood Still Has a Problem," *New York Times*, October 11, 2017, https://mobile.nytimes .com/2017/10/11/movies/harvey-weinstein-hollywood.html?hp&action

=click&pgtype=Homepage&clickSource=story-heading&module=first-column-region&region=top-news&WT.nav=top-news&_r=0&referer=https://t.co/Jl3eXTRHqT?amp=1.

25. Irin Carmon, "Porn Free: Talking to Andrea Dworkin," *Harvard Crimson*, March 22, 2002, https://www.thecrimson.com/article/2002/3/22/porn-free-talking-to-andrea-dworkin/?utm_source=thecrimson&utm_medium=web_primary&utm_campaign=recommend_sidebar.

26. Kyle Swenson, "Who Came Up with the Term 'Sexual Harassment,'" *Washington Post*, November 22, 2017, https://www.washingtonpost.com/news/morning-mix/wp/2017/11/22/who-came-up-with-the-term-sexual-harassment/?utm_term=.d49729fcce2a.

27. Raina Lipsitz, "Sexual Harassment Law Was Shaped by the Battles of Black Women," *The Nation*, October 20, 2017, https://www.thenation.com/article/sexual-harassment-law-was-shaped-by-the-battles-of-black-women/.

28. Cristela Guerra, "Where Did 'Me Too' Come From? Activist Tarana Burke, Long Before Hashtags," *Boston Globe*, October 17, 2017, https://www.bostonglobe.com/lifestyle/2017/10/17/alyssa-milano-credits-activist-tarana-burke-with-founding-metoo-movement-years-ago/o2Jv29v6ljObkKPTPB9KGP/story.html.

29. Jason Hancock and Bryan Lowry, "Missouri Gov. Eric Greitens Says He's Target of 'Political Witch Hunt,' Vows to Fight," *Kansas City Star*, April 27, 2018, http://www.kansascity.com/news/politics-government/article208615764.html.

30. Alan Feuer, "Lawyers for Two Schneiderman Accusers Brought Their Claims to Michael Cohen," *New York Times*, May 11, 2018, https://www.nytimes.com/2018/05/11/nyregion/eric-schneiderman-michael-cohen.html.

31. James Oliver Cury, "Charlie Rose's Life Now: 'Broken,' 'Brilliant' and 'Lonely,'" *The Hollywood Reporter*, April 12, 2018, https://www.hollywoodreporter.com/features/what-happened-charlie-rose-we-asked-his-friends-associates-1101333.

32. Anna Graham Hunter, "How #MeToo Accusers Cope After Going Public: 'My Hatred Has Deepened,'" *The Hollywood Reporter*, May 9, 2018, https://www.hollywoodreporter.com/news/how-metoo-accusers-cope-going-public-my-hatred-has-deepened-1109891.

33. Isaac Chotiner, "Punishment Is Not Enough," *Slate*, December 11, 2017, http://www.slate.com/articles/news_and_politics/interrogation/2017/12/the_limitations_of_punishment_in_the_metoo_moment.html.

34. "To Tell the Truth," The Cut, video, December 20, 2017, https://www.thecut.com/2017/12/rose-mcgowan-harvey-weinstein-sexual-assault-and-harassment.html?utm_source=nym_press.

35. Caitlin Flanagan, "The Conversation #MeToo Needs to Have," *Atlantic*, January 29, 2018, https://www.theatlantic.com/politics/archive/2018/01/the-right-conversation-for-metoo/551732/.

36. Laurie Penny, "We're Not Done Here," Longreads, January 2018, https://longreads.com/author/pennyred/.

37. Annys Shin and Libby Casey, "Anita Hill and Her 1991 Congressional Defenders to Joe Biden: You Were Part of the Problem," *Washington Post*, November 22, 2017, https://www.washingtonpost.com/lifestyle/magazine/anita-hill-and-her-1991-congressional-defenders-to-joe-biden-you-were-part-of-the-problem/2017/11/21/2303ba8a-ce69-11e7-a1a3-0d1e45a6de3d_story.html.

38. Sarah Kendzior, https://twitter.com/sarahkendzir/status/996395282828091392.

39. Susan Faludi, "The Patriarchs Are Falling. The Patriarcharchy Is Stronger Than Ever," *New York Times*, December 28, 2017, https://www.nytimes.com/2017/12/28/opinion/sunday/patriarchy-feminism-metoo.html.

PART IV

1. Amanda Litman, "I Wake Up and Go To Sleep Angry—And That's a Good Thing," *Women's Health*, October 17, 2017, https://www.womenshealthmag.com/life/a19948724/amanda-litman-run-for-something/.

2. Catharine MacKinnon, "Me Too Has Done What the Law Cannot," *New York Times*, February 4, 2018, https://www.nytimes.com/2018/02/04/opinion/metoo-law-legal-system.html.

3. "The Last 25 Senate Incumbents Defeated in Primaries (1962–Present)," NPR.com, April 28, 2010, https://www.npr.org/sections/politicaljunkie/2010/04/24/126248204/senate-incumbents-defeated-in-primaries.

4. Carol Moseley Braun, History, Art & Archives, U.S. House of Representatives, n.d., http://history.house.gov/People/Listing/M/MOSELEY-BRAUN,-Carol-(M001025)/.

5. Lauren Underwood with Andrea Cambron, WERA-FM, March 21, 2018, https://urldefense.proofpoint.com/v2/url?u=https-3A__enlightenmeonwera.com_2018_03_21_3-2D21-2D18-2Dspotlight-2Dlauren-2Dunderwood_&d=DwMFaQ&c=jGUuvAdBXp_VqQ6t0yah2g&r=BLtwNjxI6xU1Tow ZZXPw62rxL1h5Yh02Ol72-V1YNSunoH38hlyco6RBfK8BXD8O&m=09_aBCGDqXOZ9T8KMIoXJ04S8XPdJs7scFA3SmWWjFU&s=9mru0fRfF--KXqrUJB0egkxipvH6SUIi3wTB9SsDehw&e=.

6. Dan Mangan, "Rep. Patrick Meehan of Pennsylvania Resigns After Sexual Harassment Case Forced End of Re-election Bid," CNBC.com, April 27, 2018, https://www.cnbc.com/2018/04/27/rep-patrick-meehan-of-pennsylvania-resigns-after-sexual-harassment-claim.html.

7. Natasha Bach, "This Woman Said Being Sexually Harassed by Trump Inspired Her to Enter Politics. Now She's Won Her First Election," *Fortune*, May 9, 2018, http://fortune.com/2018/05/09/rachel-crooks-trump-accuser-wins-ohio-primary/.

8. "She's the Ticket," Episode 104: Jennifer Carroll Foy, Topic, https://www.topic.com/she-s-the-ticket/she-s-the-ticket-episode-104.

9. Amanda Marcotte, "#MeToo Is Working: Now Data Shows Attitudes on Harassment Are Changing," *Salon*, December 7, 2017, https://www.salon.com/2017/12/07/metoo-is-working-new-data-shows-attitudes-on-harassment-are-changing/.

10. Ezra Levin (@ezralevin), "This piece by @CharlotteAlter is right on the money. Women are running indivisible groups at a 2-1 margin or more," Twitter, July 29, 2017, 5:33 pm, https://twitter.com/ezralevin/status/891456596647268352.

11. Vivian Gornick, "Who Says We Haven't Made a Revolution?; A Feminist Takes Stock," *New York Times*, April 15, 1990, https://www.nytimes.com/1990/04/15/magazine/who-says-we-haven-t-made-a-revolution-a-feminist-takes-stock.html.

12. Paul Schwartzman, "Why a Historically Conservative County in Virginia Is Making National Republicans Nervous," *Washington Post*, November 25, 2017, https://www.washingtonpost.com/local/virginia-politics/why-a-historically-conservative-county-in-virginia-is-making-national-republicans-nervous/2017/11/25/654a90f4-cbbb-11e7-8321-481fd63f174d_story.html?utm_term=.1b85f835d3da.

13. Amy Butcher, "MIA: The Liberal Men We Love," Literary Hub, February 27, 2018, https://lithub.com/mia-the-liberal-men-we-love/.

14. Vivian Gornick, "Who Says We Haven't Made a Revolution?; A Feminist Takes Stock," *New York Times*, April 15, 1990, https://www.nytimes.com/1990/04/15/magazine/who-says-we-haven-t-made-a-revolution-a-feminist-takes-stock.html.

Index